THE SOUTH IN
AMERICAN LITERATURE
1607–1900

THE SOUTH
IN AMERICAN LITERATURE
1607-1900

JAY B. HUBBELL

*Professor of American Literature in Duke University & Chairman
of the Editorial Board of American Literature*

1954

DUKE UNIVERSITY PRESS

To My Son

JAY B. HUBBELL, JR.

Foreword

> No one can make a sectional list of the men and women who have achieved distinction in [American] literature, and fail to see that, whether in prose or poetry, fiction or essay, there is a special sectional quality in each, a reflection of the region's common interests and soul. Our American literature is not a single thing. It is a choral song of many sections.
> FREDERICK J. TURNER, *The Significance of Sections in American History* (1932), p. 329.

THE LITERATURE of the South has long occupied a somewhat anomalous place in our literary histories. For many years those Southerners who wrote about it were less concerned with appraising its literary values than with using it to refute the Abolitionist notion that the South was a semibarbarous region with no claim to cultural importance. In books and articles which prejudiced many scholars against any sectional approach to the study of our literature they not only overrated Southern writers, but they also charged Northern critics and literary historians with deliberately neglecting them. Neglect there undoubtedly was forty years ago, but it was seldom intentional. The earlier Northern literary historians, it is true, were definitely influenced by the Abolitionist conception which they had unconsciously absorbed; and some of them may be said to have mistaken the literature of New England and New York for the literature of the United States.

In the twentieth century the chief reason why some Northern historians have treated the Southern writers inadequately has been the difficulty of finding materials. And these, until about 1920, Southern scholars had done little to provide. The literature itself was in many instances to be found only in rare books, magazines, and pamphlets; and good biographical and critical studies of most of the writers were nonexistent. It was far easier to discuss intelligently the writings of Cotton Mather or Jonathan Edwards than it was the work of Henry Timrod or William J. Grayson, whose name is not, strangely enough, included in the *Dictionary of American Biography*. Even today it is more difficult to find adequate materials for many a Southern writer than it is for a New York or New England writer of equal importance.

The outcome of the Civil War confirmed the North in its opinion that the literature of the Old South was un-American and essentially valueless since it came out of the discredited slavery regime. Even the better writers of the New South—though they protested vigorously against the Abolitionist conception of a semibarbarous South—reluctantly conceded that the ante-bellum Southern literature was of little intrinsic value. Not until the twentieth century did the literary historians question the accepted opinion. Then a new generation of scholars, intent upon reinterpreting our national literary achievement, made discoveries which led them to assign a new importance to William Byrd, John Pendleton Kennedy, Thomas Holley Chivers, and the Southern humorists. In the second volume of his *Main Currents in American Thought*, published in 1927, Vernon L. Parrington brought to life some half-forgotten figures, notably William Alexander Caruthers, Beverley Tucker, and Hugh Swinton Legaré. Since 1927 important books and many articles have been written by scholars in Northern and Southern universities and colleges. Many of these, I gratefully remember, are the work of my friends and in not a few instances of my former students. Without their substantial contributions to scholarship to build upon, I should never have undertaken to write a history of Southern literature.

In preparing this survey of the field—the first since Montrose J. Moses published *The Literature of the South* in 1910—one of my chief aims, as I have suggested in my title, has been to integrate the literature of the Southern states with that of the rest of the nation. Earlier Southern historians treated it too often as a thing apart; but as my old teacher, William Peterfield Trent, wrote in 1905, "The history of the South and its literature cannot profitably be divorced from the history and literature of the entire country. . . ." To the creative writer the South has long furnished exceptionally rich materials, and these have attracted Northern and European as well as Southern writers—so many, indeed, that the literature which deals with the South since 1830 represents not one but two diverse and changing literary traditions.

The South has more than once been in and out of the main stream of national development. During the American Revolution and for many years afterwards the South was in the lead; and Washington, Jefferson, Madison, and other Southerners played a large part not only in building the framework of the nation but also in creating a notable political literature. That was a time of good feeling between Northern and Southern writers. All our early presidents came from either Virginia or Massachusetts, and in those years Northern and Southern travelers found much to admire when they visited in Virginia or Massachusetts.

In the fourth decade of the nineteenth century this situation changed for the worse. The South, beginning now to defend slavery on principle, had finally turned its back upon the liberalism of Washington, Jefferson, and Madison. By this time New England, which had not felt the full force of Revolutionary liberalism, was sprouting all kinds of isms repugnant to the conservative South. The rapidly developing industrial North saw the slave-holding South in the ominous shape of an economic, political, and moral problem. The South was felt to be resisting the progress of industrialization and democracy, and so at all costs it must be made to fit into the "national" or "American" pattern. The South, on the other hand, felt that it was being exploited by Northern merchants and manufacturers and that its civilization was being attacked by fanatical reformers and unscrupulous politicians who knew nothing about Southern life. And so the South fought against what it regarded as the all-devouring state and ultimately left the Union to protect what it believed to be the rights of the states.

In the 1830's Southerners, who had been generally content to get their literature from England and the Northern states, were increasingly disturbed by the hostility to their section of the newer literature of the North, especially New England. They then began slowly and half consciously building up a rival literary tradition and creating a regional literature, which was often designed as a defense against Northern misrepresentation of Southern life.

The victorious North, after it had won the war and freed the slaves, repudiated the literature of the Old South on the dubious theory that no slaveholding people could possibly produce a literature of any intrinsic importance. The South, now chastened by defeat, accepted in good faith the end of slavery and secession and sought once again to find its place within the framework of the reunited nation. After the end of Reconstruction in 1877 a new era of intersectional good feeling developed. Constance Fenimore Woolson and other Northern writers rediscovered the charm of Southern life. A new generation of Southern writers created a notable body of local-color fiction, which was in part designed to correct the distorted picture of Southern life found in the writings of Harriet Beecher Stowe. Very slowly the South came to realize the tragic mistake it had made in abandoning the liberalism of Thomas Jefferson.

The New South, however, was less "new" than is generally supposed. It was thoroughly loyal to the Union, but it cherished the memory of the Lost Cause and it was still critical of the aims and methods of Northern

merchants, manufacturers, and politicians. It was now politically a Solid
South and it was intolerant on the race question. In the 1880's George W.
Cable of Louisiana alienated his Southern readers when he went over to
the extreme Northern view of the Negro problem. In the eyes of the South
he had refused to abide by the terms of the Compromise of 1877, by which
the North had agreed to leave the problem of the emancipated Negroes in
Southern hands.

Twentieth-century Southern writers, however, represent a region which in
the literary sense is certainly no longer a Solid South. There are living Southern writers of fiction, like Erskine Caldwell and Lillian Smith, who write
not in the tradition ,of Simms, Harris, Page, and the Southern Agrarians
but in that of Lowell, Whittier, Mrs. Stowe, and that "Southern Yankee,"
George W. Cable.

The literature of the South, as I have said, cannot be understood and
appraised if one neglects its many and complicated relations with the literature of the rest of the nation. I have accordingly discussed Southern life as
it is represented not only by writers who lived below the Mason-Dixon Line
but also as it appears in the writings of Irving, Cooper, Lowell, Emerson,
Mrs. Stowe, John W. De Forest, and various others. In my discussion of
Southern writers I have pointed out the importance of their relations with
Northern writers, editors, and publishers, who helped them to put their
materials into acceptable form.

It should be continually borne in mind that for more than a century the
Southern writer has always had to remember that if he wanted a market
for his writings, he must reckon with literary fashion and the unpredictability
of the changing Northern attitude toward the region in which he lives.
The Northern writer who lived in the South sometimes found readers in
his own section unwilling to accept his picture of Southern life. Albion W.
Tourgée, who had lived in North Carolina in the Reconstruction period,
was so irritated by Northern criticism of his novels that he wrote in the
Preface to A Royal Gentleman in 1881: "The trouble is that the Northern
man has made up a South for himself, and without the least hesitation,
criticises any departure from the original of his own imagination as untrue
to life." This situation goes far toward explaining the limitations of fiction
as a full and accurate picture of Southern life; and it helps to explain why so
many Northern visitors to the South fail to find what they have been led to
expect to see. Southern mansions and poor-white cabins are not to be found
at every bend in the road.

It is a singular fact that from the beginning down to the present time
few Southern writers have been appreciably influenced by the classic writers
of New England. Their models from the time of William Byrd to that of

James Branch Cabell have been English writers. Much the same statement could be made, I suspect, of most Western writers from the time of Bret Harte to that of Sinclair Lewis and Theodore Dreiser. Our American literary tradition, it seems to me, owes less to the great New Englanders than is generally supposed in academic circles. Until after the Civil War what we had was not so much a genuinely national literature—though there were strong national elements—as an aggregation of sectional literatures. With the emergence of the New West and the New South and the rise of New York as the chief publishing center, our literature became national in a sense not true of any earlier period. New England of course played its part in this development; but with the exception of Emily Dickinson the more important authors writing in New England in the Indian Summer period—Howells, Mark Twain, and (until he became an expatriate) Henry James—were not natives of that region. Emerson, Hawthorne, and Thoreau are among our greatest writers, but I think our later literature owes comparatively little to them. We can no longer think of the American literary tradition as primarily the creation of these men and their New England contemporaries.

I have tried to suggest the pattern of literary culture in the Southern states, and I have given considerable space to pointing out the books which Southerners read. The South before 1861 was, comparatively speaking, a more important book market than it is today. In those years the percentage of the college-bred was higher in the South than it was anywhere in the North, and at the beginning of the nineteenth century the center of population in the United States was not far from Baltimore, Maryland. Southern readers helped to make the reputations and increase the earnings of Irving, Cooper, Longfellow, Melville, and many another Northern writer, including some who, like Emerson and Whittier, were felt to be hostile. Yet even in recent years there have appeared special studies which pay little or no attention to the Southern half of the nation. The so-called "standard" studies of Deism in America, for example, play up Jefferson, who was a Unitarian rather than a Deist, and they ignore the rest of the South, which in those years held approximately half the population of the United States. Similarly, the South is almost ignored in well-known studies of the American reputations of Byron, Wordsworth, and Voltaire. Whether the authors of those books assumed that Southerners read the same books as were being read in the North or read no books at all, I do not know. The result is much the same: studies which ought to have a certain finality will eventually have to be done over, and the generalizations made by some of our literary historians will have to be revised.

I have given more space to biographical details than would be desirable in a literary history of New York or New England. The historian can assume on the part of his readers some knowledge of the life of Irving or Lowell; he cannot when he is writing about William Wirt or Hugh Swinton Legaré. I have therefore given more space to narrative and exposition than to criticism. I have quoted frequently from the writings of the authors whom I have discussed—not as a labor-saving device, which it certainly is not—but because for those who have read nothing, say, from George Tucker or Joseph Glover Baldwin a discussion which does not illustrate his individual way of writing has little value. When possible I have permitted the writer to explain his literary aims in his own words. I have tried to give my readers the feeling that the writers of the South were once very much alive. Whatever one may think of the literature of the South, the men and women who created it were for the most part interesting and admirable Americans.

I have demonstrated, I think, that there was more and rather better writing in the Old South than is generally supposed, but I make no claim to having discovered a neglected Southern literary genius. If I seem to write with undue enthusiasm about certain little-known authors, I have also reminded my readers that while the nineteenth-century South had many intelligent men and women who put pen to paper, some of whom are not even mentioned in my pages, it produced only two writers of the very first rank, Edgar Allan Poe and Mark Twain. These two writers have been so often described as "Southern only by courtesy" (as Barrett Wendell remarked of Poe) that I have been at some pains to point out the influence of their Southern upbringing and their relations with their Southern contemporaries.

I have tried as well as I could to let the various writers, Northern and Southern, speak for themselves; and I am anxious that no casual reader shall confuse my own opinions with such sweeping pronouncements as Simms's "Charleston is worth all New England," or Emerson's "I do not see how a barbarous community and a civilized community can constitute one state." The best living Northern and Southern historians are now so nearly one in their interpretation of the place of the South in American history that it is often difficult, by internal evidence, to distinguish the Northern historian from the Southerner. That unfortunately is not quite the case in American literary history. And yet, it seems to me, today, three quarters of a century after the end of Reconstruction, it should be possible for a scholar who is a native of the South but who has lived and taught in the North and the West to view the writers of the South from a national point of view.

So far as character and intelligence are concerned, the differences among

Americans have little to do with their sectional origin. It does not follow, however, that all sections have contributed equally to American literature. No other section since 1830 has in any period contributed more in proportion to its population than New England. If circumstances had been more propitious, the literary achievement of the Southern states would have been greater. As it is, the literature of the South is nothing that any one need apologize for. It is hardly the best index to Southern achievements, but it is an important part of the literature of the American people.

When I began this study nearly twenty years ago after some research and much miscellaneous reading in the field, I did not foresee that a Second World War and various other circumstances would necessitate my frequently laying it aside; nor did I realize in the beginning the immense amount of spade work which I should have to do in the work of writers who have been little studied. At one time I decided to end the story with the Civil War. I felt that the literature of the New South had not lacked recognition and stood less in need of reinterpretation than that of earlier periods. And yet, I finally concluded, it was important to point out the large and little-recognized debt which the literary New South owes to the Old. My treatment of the New South, however, covers in detail only seven writers: Paul Hamilton Hayne, Sidney Lanier, Richard Malcolm Johnston, Joel Chandler Harris, Thomas Nelson Page, George W. Cable, and Mark Twain. For lack of space as well as time I have regretfully omitted other important writers, particularly Irwin Russell, Sherwood Bonner, Walter Hines Page, Mary Noailles Murfree, Kate Chopin, Lafcadio Hearn, Grace King, and John Banister Tabb. In a final section, which deals with the twentieth century, I have discussed all too briefly O. Henry, Ellen Glasgow, James Branch Cabell, and one or two others; and I have pointed out some of the historical factors which still have a large influence upon both Northern and Southern writing about the states that lie south of the Potomac and the Ohio. I have not given as much space to the orators, scientists, historians, and playwrights as some readers would have liked; and I have not discussed the French literature of Louisiana, which fortunately has found its own historians. I have not included the Negro writers, who, as it happens, belong mainly to the Northern states and whose most important work falls outside the period covered in this book. For that period Vernon Loggins has told the story well in *The Negro Author.*

With the many students of American literature in mind, I have included a much fuller bibliography than is found in other discussions of Southern literature. In the interest of economy and readability, however, I have reduced the number of footnotes to the indispensable minimum. In my frequent quotations, especially from periodicals, I have tried to include in my text sufficient information for the scholar to find each quoted passage in the context in which it first appeared. Only rarely have I used the conventional [sic] to call attention to a misspelled word. The reader will not, I hope, blame the author or the publisher for Thomas Jefferson's habitual misspelling of *its* as *it's* or William Gilmore Simms's *recieved* for *received*.

I have incurred many obligations in the preparation of this book. I am indebted to some of my Duke University colleagues for helpful suggestions: Clarence Gohdes, Benjamin Boyce, Charles E. Ward, C. Richard Sanders, the late C. S. Sydnor, Lewis Leary, now of Columbia University, and J. C. Robert, now President of Coker College. I owe a still greater debt to my colleague, Arlin Turner, to Stanley T. Williams of Yale University, and to Ashbel G. Brice, Director of the Duke University Press, all of whom have read the book in manuscript and made suggestions for its improvement. I wish to acknowledge the help given me some years ago by my assistants under the National Youth Administration: Elizabeth Chitwood, James B. Haman, Milledge B. Seigler, and Ralph E. Purcell. I am more deeply indebted to my research assistant of 1951–1952, James Brady Reece, now of William and Mary College, who checked my bibliography, quotations, and footnotes. I am very greatly indebted to my son, Jay B. Hubbell, Jr., for helpful criticism, especially of my historical chapters. My secretary, Mrs. Lucretia Duke, made for the printer an exceptionally accurate and clean copy of my manuscript, and Mr. Truman Frederick Keefer, my research assistant of 1953–1954, has helped me with the proofreading. I owe a large debt to many of the one hundred and more graduate students who have written master's or doctor's theses under my direction. My bibliography indicates my indebtedness to the many scholars who have studied one or another aspect of the literature of the South. I wish also to express my appreciation of the highly efficient work of the proofreaders of the Vail-Ballou Press.

The Duke University Research Council has supplied funds which made it possible for me to secure rare materials and to visit other libraries, and it has also contributed a subsidy which has made it possible to publish the book in its present form. I have received courteous and efficient assistance from the staffs of many libraries, especially the Library of Congress, the Huntington Library, the New York Public Library, the Library of the Virginia Historical Society, the Virginia State Library, the North Carolina State Library, the North Carolina Department of Archives and History; from the libraries of Columbia University, Yale University, and New York University; from the libraries of the Universities of Virginia, North Carolina, South Carolina, Pennsylvania, and California at Los Angeles; and from the Charleston Library Society. My greatest debt of this kind is to Dr. Benjamin E. Powell and other members of the staff of the Duke University Library, which has by purchase, interlibrary loan, or microfilm made available to me rare materials which otherwise I might not have seen.

JAY B. HUBBELL

Duke University
Durham, North Carolina
February 26, 1954

CONTENTS

I. The Colonial Period, 1607–1765

II. The American Revolution, 1765–1789

III. *The Era of Good Feeling, 1789–1830*

IV. *The Road to Disunion, 1830–1865*

V. *The New South, 1865–1900*

VI. *Epilogue: The Twentieth Century*

Bibliography

I

THE COLONIAL PERIOD

1607-1765

VIRGINIA

1

The Historical Background

The public-spirited British merchants and noblemen of the Virginia Company wished to establish a colony which would ultimately return a fair profit on their investment, but they also wished to furnish an outlet for the surplus population, to supply England with raw materials difficult to obtain elsewhere, and to convert the Indians to the Christian religion. The venture proved troublesome and expensive. The malarial mosquitoes and hostile Indians almost wiped out the colony before it could be firmly established. By the time the future of the colony seemed secure, the Virginia farmers had staked everything upon tobacco. Such enterprises as mining, manufacturing, and silk-raising came to nothing; the tobacco plantation remained. Disappointed, the promoters finally made the best of the situation, and ultimately the British merchants sold tobacco at a profit to all Europe.

In the economic and social development of the colony tobacco was a determining factor. Living in a village was impracticable for the Virginia farmer. The tobacco plant rapidly exhausts the soil, and the land-hungry farmer's need for more new-ground land was perennial. The rivers of Tidewater Virginia, which John Fiske likened to a "sylvan Venice," made it possible for the planter to ship his hogsheads of tobacco from his own wharf and to deal directly with his British agent. Eastern Virginia resembled a rural England—if one can imagine an England without its towns and villages—modified by the presence of tobacco, indentured servants, and Negro slaves. The dominant occupation was that of the farmer. Except for the none too numerous clergymen, merchants, and lawyers, there were few representatives of the professional classes. The plantation economy destined Virginia and the other Southern colonies to a somewhat wasteful agricultural system, to dependence on the outside world for a market, to provincialism, and to comparative unproductiveness in literature and the fine arts. It was also the foundation for a most attractive social life; and in the Revolutionary statesmen of Virginia it produced the most remarkable group of men in American history.

The first Negro slaves were brought in by a Dutch ship as early as 1620—a year after the colony was given its General Assembly—but slaves were not numerous until near the end of the century. Before 1700 labor was supplied chiefly by indentured servants or by workmen able to pay for their passage across the Atlantic. Most of those able to pay their way eventually bought or took up land and became farmers. The poorer immigrants bound themselves by indentures for four or five years to repay the merchant or planter who·advanced the passage money (about six pounds). Under this arrangement laborers came to Virginia, as to all the other colonies, and there was no serious stigma attached to the status of the "redemptioner." Properly speaking, he was not a slave. When his term was out, the freedman was supplied with food, clothing, and tools for one year. He had an opportunity to take up land and set up as a farmer.

Among the indentured servants, however, there were some convicts, the number of whom is difficult to estimate. Some of them were political prisoners sent over during the wars of the seventeenth century. Sometimes unscrupulous sea captains or their associates kidnaped boys and men and sold them in the colonies. Historians do not now believe that the proportion of actual criminals was ever large. They point out that under the British criminal code over three hundred offenses were punishable by branding, transportation, or death.

As Governor Francis Nicholson's Rent Roll shows, the great majority of Virginia landholders—as late as 1704—were small farmers. There was also a small but influential class of large planters, who in the cultural and political history of the colony hold a conspicuous place. The seventeenth century witnessed the founding of most of the great Virginia families: the Beverleys, Blands, Burwells, Byrds, Carters, Carys, Harrisons, Lees, Ludwells, Masons, Pages, Randolphs, Washingtons, and a few others. In his edition of the *Writings* of William Byrd, John Spencer Bassett wrote: "The aristocratic form of Virginia society was fixed soon after the Restoration of the Stuarts. It proceeded from economic, social, and political causes. On its economic side it was supported by land and servitude; on its social side it was sustained by the ideals, and somewhat by the blood, of the English country gentlemen; on its political side it was fostered by a system of appointments to office which left the least room for a democracy. In the century which preceded the Revolution it was in its greatest vigor." [1]

The large-scale planters were in the main of good birth, but they are hardly to be described as scions of the British aristocracy. Among them were sons of sea captains, army officers, and country gentlemen who came with enough capital to buy land. The largest number seems to have sprung from the merchant class. In England the acquisition of land was the chief ambition of those who aimed at social or political power or prestige. In the Southern states likewise until after the Civil War the man who made money in whatever profession or trade felt that he must own a plantation. If well-to-do, the English merchant, lawyer, or country gentleman bought estates for his younger sons in the mother country; if he was not wealthy, he could buy them far more cheaply in Virginia. [2] The late Lyon G. Tyler once said that when he began his study of colonial records, he discovered to his surprise that many of the early planters were "tradesmen and storekeepers who had taken up the raising of tobacco, corn and other farm produce as incidental to the main purpose of merchandising. Thus," he continues, "every prominent Virginian in these early days called himself 'merchant,' and had his storehouse from which he provided for his neighbors, his servants and dependents. . . ." Such men, as one might expect, were interested more in quick financial profits than in farming as a way of life. The Germans who settled in the Shenandoah Valley were more careful to preserve the natural resources of their region.

Most of the Cavaliers who came to Virginia during the protectorate of Oliver Cromwell were not noblemen, as Southerners in the nineteenth century came to believe, but a considerable number of them belonged either to the gentry or the upper middle class. In the seventeenth century the term "Cavalier" indicated political affiliation and not social status. Of the influence of the Cavalier planters, Bassett writes: "They were not numerous, as compared with the older population, but they had an influence out of proportion to their numbers. They gave manners a warmer tone; they emphasized the ideal of country life; they gave Virginians their passion for

[1] *The Writings of "Colonel William Byrd of Westover in Virginia Esqr"* (1901), p. ix. In this passage Bassett anticipated the whole thesis which T. J. Wertenbaker set out to prove in his *Patrician and Plebeian in Virginia* (1916); see p. 1. Wertenbaker has high praise for Bassett's Introduction in his Bibliography but expresses no specific obligation.

[2] Even after the American Civil War Englishmen were buying farms in Virginia. Edward King wrote in *The Great South* (1875), p. 554: "Among the immigrants there were many Englishmen of education and refinement, country gentlemen's sons who had made up their minds to try farming in the new country, or to purchase coal or iron tracts for speculation." See also p. 657.

handsome houses and fast horses; and they gave public life something more than it had before of the English notion that offices should be held for the benefit of the gentry." [3] The social and political order which the planters established was modeled on the English system. Class distinctions were not forgotten in Virginia. Adam Thoroughgood, the only large-scale planter who had come over as an indentured servant—just why is not clear—was brother to a baronet.

There was in Tidewater Virginia little of the democratic spirit and approximate equality which characterized the frontier in western Virginia and North Carolina. The large-scale planters wished to establish country estates worked by white laborers, and they turned to Negro slaves only because white workmen could not be procured in large numbers. It was ability as well as wealth that enabled the planters to dominate the political life of Virginia. Few of them marched in the "rag, tag, and bobtail" army of the well-born Nathaniel Bacon, who attempted by force to reform the government of the colony. Jealous of their prerogatives, the planters were as little inclined to pure democracy as John Winthrop or Increase Mather, and they contested strenuously with royal governors for what they regarded as their political rights. When the Revolutionary crisis developed, the descendants of these men were fully prepared for the notable role they had to play.

The eighteenth and not the seventeenth century was the golden age of the Virginia planters. The importation of Negro slaves in larger numbers, coinciding with a decline in the number of identured servants, tended to lessen the opportunities of the poorer farmers and to increase those of men who had more land and more money. As the plantation system gradually spread over the Tidewater, many of the smaller farmers and freedmen removed to the up-country west of the fall line or to North Carolina, which was for a time a kind of Virginia frontier.

West of the fall line, which runs through Petersburg, Richmond, Fredericksburg, and Washington, a different kind of society was developing. In what Frederick J. Turner called "The Old West" we find that new and un-English type, the frontiersman, destined to play a notable part in the winning of the great West. Much of western Virginia was first settled by the Scotch-Irish and the Germans, who in the early eighteenth century poured into the Valley of Virginia. In the west the nights were too cool for the tobacco then being grown, and the slave plantation found scant foot-

---

[3] Bassett, *op. cit.*, p. xi. I have discussed the Cavalier legend more fully in a later chapter. See pp. 332–334. See also my article, "Cavalier and Indentured Servant in Virginia Fiction," *S.A.Q.*, XXVI, 22–39 (Jan., 1927).

For abbreviations used in the footnotes and the bibliography, see p. 882.

hold there. The westerners held notions of society, government, and religion markedly at variance with those of the Anglican planters of the lowlands. In the Revolutionary period these men became insistent in their demand for a larger share in the government of Virginia. Under the leadership of Jefferson, who was born west of the fall line, they finally disestablished the Anglican Church and abolished the laws of primogeniture and entail, by which the great planter estates had been held intact from generation to generation.

In noting the contrast between eastern and western Virginia, I have oversimplified the complex social arrangement of the colony. A truer picture of colonial society as it was in the middle of the eighteenth century is given in a letter which Jefferson in 1815 wrote to William Wirt, who was at that time writing his life of Patrick Henry:

To state the differences between the classes of society and the lines of demarkation which separated them, would be difficult. The law, you know, admitted none except as to the twelve counsellors [members of the Governor's Council]. Yet in a country insulated from the European world, insulated from its sister colonies, with whom there was scarcely any intercourse, little visited by foreigners, and having little matter to act upon within itself, certain families had risen to splendor by wealth and the preservation of it from generation to generation under the law entails; some had produced a series of men of talents; families in general had remained stationary on the grounds of their forefathers. . . . In such a state of things, scarcely admitting any change of station, society would settle itself down into several strata, separated by no marked lines, but shading off imperceptibly from top to bottom, nothing disturbing the order of their repose. There were then aristocrats [the great planters], half-breeds [yeomen who had married into aristocratic families], pretenders [men of wealth not belonging to established families], a solid independent yeomanry, looking askance at those above, yet not venturing to jostle them, and last and lowest, a seculum of beings called overseers, the most abject, degraded and unprincipled race. . . .

To the five classes listed by Jefferson should be added the tradespeople, mainly Scotch, a small number of indentured servants, an uncertain number of poor-whites, and the numerous Negro slaves.

The well-to-do Virginia planter might or might not come of gentle blood; but his ambition was, so far as was possible in the new land, to emulate the virtues and copy the way of life of the English country gentleman. His ideal had for him far different connotations from those which the word *gentleman* suggests to Americans today, for the vitality of the ideal pretty well disappeared after the destruction of the Southern plantation system in the Civil War. It reached its peak in the Virginia statesmen of the Revolution, but Robert Beverley and William Byrd were earlier exemplars of the type.

The Virginia gentlemen—and this is true of those in other Southern colonies —were perhaps less polished than their English contemporaries; but they were harder workers and they attached less importance to birth. While the English gentleman, his character formed in the "public schools," relatively declined, tending to become a figurehead or the vulgar drinking ruffian so vividly described by Thackeray, the Virginia gentleman held on to the older ideal exemplified in Sir Philip Sidney and Sir Walter Raleigh. In the eighteenth-century South the gentleman—whether or not he actually lived up to the code—never questioned the virtues which that code demanded of him: truth, honor, justice, liberality, courtesy, decorum, hospitality, and the spirit of public service. The Virginia gentleman shared in the Renaissance ideal of the well-rounded man; and even if his chief passion was fox hunting, he knew that literary culture was a desirable thing. And to strengthen the ideal in himself and his sons, he read Henry Peacham's *The Compleat Gentleman* and other books in the Renaissance tradition most notably expressed in Castiglione's *The Book of the Courtier.*

2

Education

WHEN GOVERNOR BERKELEY in 1671 thanked God that there were "no free schools" in Virginia, he ignored the fact that there were in the colony endowed free schools which gave classical training of the sort required for admission to the English universities. There were of course nowhere in the colonies free public schools like those of our time. In the extant Virginia court records there are many indications that the colonists were sufficiently interested in education to make some provision for it. The greatest handicap was the distance between plantations which made it difficult and often impossible to build a schoolhouse on a site to which pupils could walk without hardship. Education in Virginia, as in other colonies, was largely a private affair. The teachers employed in the old-field schools or in the planters' schoolrooms were in many cases clergymen eking out their slender stipends. Sometimes, after the Roman fashion, the planter employed an educated indentured servant. Whatever the educational deficiencies of the masses, the planters who governed the Southern colonies were educated men.

More than a decade before the founding of Harvard College in 1636, plans were made for a college in Virginia, but it was not until the reign of William and Mary that the institution which bears their names actually came into being. The man chiefly responsible for its founding was the vigorous Scotch minister James Blair, who was Commissary for the Bishop of London; that is, head of the Anglican Church in Virginia. When he visited England in the interest of the proposed college, Blair fortunately obtained from the King a more favorable reception than he got from Attorney-General Seymour, who, when Blair reminded him that there were souls to be saved in Virginia, broke out: "Souls! Damn their souls! Make tobacco."

Rated by modern standards, William and Mary may seem only a glorified preparatory school. When, however, one remembers the quality of the men whom it turned out—Jefferson, Marshall, Monroe, for example—one looks for a standard different from that employed by school-accrediting associations of the present time. William and Mary was fortunate in its situation in the little colonial capital. "Never before or since in this country," writes Herbert B. Adams in his historical sketch of the College, "was there such a constant object lesson for the students in the art of government and in the constitution of society. The College of William and Mary, almost from its original planting, was a unique seminary of history and politics—of history in the making, of politics in the praxis. . . . The young Virginians did not study text-books of historical and political science. They observed the real things." [4] In his autobiography Jefferson testified to his great debt to three men with whom he was intimately associated in Williamsburg: Dr. William Small, Scotch mathematician and philosopher; George Wythe, who trained Marshall as well as Jefferson in the law; and Governor Francis Fauquier, whom Jefferson regarded as the ablest of Virginia's royal governors. With the state universities of Virginia and South Carolina also in mind, Adams writes: "Indeed the conspicuous merit of Southern leaders in politics was due to their superior political education, which early ranged over topics that were not prominent in northern colleges until after the [Civil] War, notably history, political economy, and the science of government and administration."

"To call the names of notable Virginians in the Revolution," writes Gaillard Hunt, "is almost to call a roll of the graduates of William and Mary." When the youthful planter came to Williamsburg, he found something like an *entente cordiale* among college, church, and state. The government was largely in the hands of Anglican planters. The President of the College was the head of the Church in Virginia. The College had its own representative

---

[4] *The College of William and Mary* . . . (1887), p. 28. See also S. E. Morison, "American Colonial Colleges," *Rice Inst. Pamphlet*, XXIII, 246–282 (Oct., 1936) and C. F. Thwing, *A History of Higher Education in America* (1906), which notes that while Harvard represented the English tradition, William and Mary was deeply influenced by the University of Edinburgh (p. 56).

in the House of Burgesses; and before the building of the Capitol, the House met in the College halls.

3
Books and Reading

THE STATE OF literary culture in the South, in the Colonial or any later period, is not to be judged by the presence or absence of facilities for printing. A truer test of the literary culture of any region is the presence or absence of books. In the homes of well-to-do Virginians there was no dearth of books. In spite of widespread destruction by fire, war, deterioration, and neglect, many inventories of planters' libraries have survived and been published in the Virginia historical magazines. For the last quarter of the seventeenth century, Philip Alexander Bruce found evidence of the existence of something like a thousand private libraries averaging perhaps twenty volumes each. Since books were comparatively expensive, it is safe to assume that the planter bought no book which he or his family did not intend to read.

As one glances over the lists of books which found their way into seventeenth-century plantation libraries, one is immediately struck by the extraordinarily large proportion of books concerned with religion and morals. If the planter owned only one book, that book was of course the Bible. Among his favorites were *The Book of Common Prayer*, *The Whole Duty of Man*, Lewis Bayly's *The Practice of Piety*, and Sir Thomas Browne's classic *Religio Medici*, valued more for its piety than for its literary qualities. The Puritans had no monopoly, in the Old World or the New, of either piety or interest in religious books; and the intellectual interests of Virginians and New Englanders in the seventeenth century were not nearly so unlike as their descendants have often imagined.[5] Although there were few Puritans in Virginia, the planters read the works of Richard Baxter and other Puritan divines. When we come to the eighteenth century, we shall find in Virginia as in New England that secular interests of many kinds predominate although there is still no scarcity of religious books.

The number of books of a utilitarian character was large. Men bought books because they expected to use them, not to furnish an "escape" from the monotony of farm life. Medical treatises and handbooks were common,

[5] In "The Colonial Library and the Development of Sectional Differences in the American Colonies," *Library Quart.*, VIII, 373–390 (July, 1938) T. E. Keys upheld the very dubious thesis that "the striking differences revealed in the libraries of the North and the South . . . show the beginnings of the disastrous sectional cleavage which continued for the next hundred years" (p. 373).

and so were books dealing with agriculture and gardening. Virginians often bought the formless dictionaries of arts and sciences of the time. Law books are often found, and the well-known litigiousness of the planters of later times must have had its parallel in earlier years. There were also treatises on political science and occasional works of travel, history, and biography. John Locke's treatises on education and government and his *Essay concerning Human Understanding* were widely read. The English liberalism of the Revolution of 1688, of which Locke was the best spokesman, had a more lasting influence in America than in England, and Locke continued to be America's favorite philosopher well down into the nineteenth century.

The Virginia planter might read for pleasure the literature written in his own language, but he felt that a knowledge of the Greek and Latin classics was an essential part of the education of a gentleman. The Humanistic tradition of the Renaissance, though now on the wane, was still a powerful influence. No Thorstein Veblen had yet arisen to tell the planter that one mark of the idle aristocrat was his concern with dead languages. The study of the classics had an important influence upon the thinking of the Virginia statesmen of the eighteenth century. It gave them a sense of the past and a feeling of the continuity of civilization. It acquainted them with some of the best thinking ever done by men, and it gave them sound models for reasoning and for speaking and writing. In the South the influence of the classics—though frequently overrated—continued a vital force down to the time of the Civil War. In the earlier period among the works more commonly found are those of Xenophon and Homer, Ovid, Cicero, Vergil, Caesar, Horace, and Sallust. The frequent occurrence of some of these is due of course to their use as textbooks. Some of the classics are found in translation, and Greek texts are often accompanied by Latin translations. Montaigne's *Essays* are not uncommon, and certain French classics taught in schools are found; but the vogue of French literature did not reach its peak until about the middle of the eighteenth century.

The Virginia gentleman felt it his duty to read the Greek and Latin classics, but he read English literature for pleasure or utility. He had not been told by schoolmasters and literary historians that he must read Chaucer, Spenser, Shakespeare, Milton, Dryden, Addison, and Pope. He read what he liked, or what his friends were reading, or what his English agent told him was being read in London. Naturally, he was often more impressed by lesser writers than by those who are now calendared as the truly great. Nevertheless, the works of Shakespeare and Milton were not uncommon in plantation libraries, and in the early eighteenth century Pope and Swift were as popular as in England. The religious poets of the seventeenth century

were more common than the works of the lighter Cavalier poets. Although
the novel and the drama are fairly well represented, the masterpieces of
Bunyan and Defoe for some reason do not often appear. A not untypical
private library, that of Daniel Parke Custis, the first husband of Martha
Washington, contained about four hundred and sixty volumes.[6] Among
them were the poems of Milton, Vaughan, Herbert, Cowley, Waller, and
Dryden; Butler's *Hudibras*; Browne's *Religio Medici*; several volumes of the
Tatler and the *Spectator*; the plays of Shakespeare, Lee, and Steele; and
several novels, among which were *Robinson Crusoe*, *Gulliver's Travels*, and
Smollett's *Peregrine Pickle*.

In Colonial times women were not usually expected to read much except
in books prepared especially for them. There were exceptions, however, like
Eliza Lucas Pinckney of South Carolina, who wrote: "I love a garden and a
book. . . ." She found pleasure in Plutarch, Vergil, and Locke as well as in
Pope and Richardson. She even read law books. Two widely read books in
Colonial times were E. Smith's *The Compleat Housewife; or Accomplished
Gentlewoman's Companion* and Hannah Glasse's *The Art of Cookery Made
Plain and Easy*. Well known also were *The Ladies Calling*, which incul-
cated the virtues of modesty, meekness, compassion, affability, and piety,
and *The Ladies Library*, a compilation which purported to be "written by a
Lady and published by Sir Richard Steele." And of course there was Dr.
James Fordyce's *Sermons to Young Women*, which Lydia Languish in Sheridan's *The Rivals* leaves on the table, open at *Sobriety*—even though the hair-
dresser has torn away as far as *Proper Pride*. In the eighteenth century women
in England—and doubtless in America also—were coming to form a larger
proportion of the readers and writers of books, particularly fiction. Novels
were becoming increasingly popular, and in the South the moral objection
was less rigid than in New England. In the latter half of the eighteenth century novels of sentiment and seduction were becoming so numerous as to
constitute a public nuisance; and many of those written in America seem to
have been aimed particularly at women readers in a country where, one
would think, there was less danger of seduction than anywhere else in the
world.

4

The Theater

As EARLY AS 1716 there was a playhouse in Williamsburg, but the first
record of a play given in English in this country tells of the performance in

[6] *Va. Mag.*, XVII, 404–412 (Oct., 1909).

1665 on the Eastern Shore of Virginia of *Ye Bare and ye Cubb*. Court records show that three citizens of Accomac County—Cornelius Watkinson, Philip Howard, and William Darby—were required to repeat their performance before the court, which found them "not guilty of fault" and required the complainant, Edward Martin, to pay the costs. In 1702 the students at William and Mary recited before Governor Berkeley, himself a playwright, a "pastoral colloquy." On September 10, 1736, the *Virginia Gazette* announced several performances: "The Young Gentlemen of the College" were to give Addison's *Cato*, a favorite of George Washington, while "the young Gentlemen and Ladies of this Country" were to perform Mrs. Centlivre's *The Busybody* and George Farquhar's *The Beaux' Stratagem* and *The Recruiting Officer*. An important event in American theatrical history was the coming from London in 1752 of Lewis Hallam's company of professional actors, who opened in Williamsburg on September 15 with a performance of *The Merchant of Venice*. After eleven months in Virginia, the company went on to New York and Philadelphia.[7] There were significant early dramatic performances in Annapolis and in Charleston, but in the main the theatrical history of the United States concerns the larger cities of the North.

5

Deists and Dissenters

In THE EIGHTEENTH century two antipathetic movements flourished and finally came to battle: Deism and evangelical religion. In the end the latter won a complete victory in the South and a less decisive one in the North, where Deism merged into Unitarianism and other liberal movements.

Except for some discussion of Jefferson, the South has been almost ignored by those who have written the history of Deism in the United States.[8] Deism, an upper-class religion but not a church, had many adherents among educated Southern planters. Among the Virginia statesmen Jefferson, Washington, Madison, Mason, Edmund and John Randolph, and others had leanings in that direction; but none of them was a militant Deist, like Ethan Allen or Thomas Paine. The College of William and Mary came to be re-

[7] The Hallam company figures prominently in John Esten Cooke's *The Virginia Comedians* (1854).

[8] Herbert M. Morais, *Deism in Eighteenth Century America* (1934); G. Adolf Koch, *Republican Religion: The American Revolution and the Cult of Reason* (1933); and Woodbridge Riley, *American Philosophy: The Early Schools* (1907), pp. 266–295.

garded as a hotbed of infidelity. Jefferson's Williamsburg friends—Governor Fauquier, Dr. Small, and George Wythe—were all Deists.

Deism, a phase of the Age of Enlightenment, is not easy to define with exactness, but its general nature is clear enough. After the downfall of the Puritan regime in 1660, Englishmen and Americans lost much of that intimate sense of the spiritual world which had marked both Anglican and Puritan. The science of Newton and the philosophy of Locke glorified reason rather than intuition. The influence of Newtonian science, like that of Darwin or Einstein in later centuries, was a subtle and pervasive one. Few men mastered Newton's mathematics, even if they were able to read his *Principia* in Latin. His discoveries, added to those of Copernicus and Galileo, revealed a universe of unimaginable magnitude, governed by universal law, in which the earth and its inhabitants played only an insignificant part. It became increasingly difficult for the enlightened man to believe in the, Puritan doctrine of a Special Providence. God, now seen as the Great First Cause working only through universal and unalterable scientific laws, began to seem almost as remote from the little earth as the gods of Lucretius. Nature had come to intervene between man and God, and God was to be best studied in Nature. Reason supplied the method, and the Deists glorified both Reason and Nature. Under these circumstances the Bible lost much of its authority, and Jesus became for many simply one of the great ethical teachers of the world. Not an essential part of Deism but often found with it was the complacent kind of optimism suggested by Pope's line: "One truth is clear, Whatever is, is right."

In the Southern colonies the Anglican clergy had little missionary zeal, and they left it to the Presbyterians, Baptists, and Methodists to carry the gospel to the people of the back country. The evangelical clergymen regarded the Deists as little better than atheists, while the Deists scorned the dissenters as vulgar fanatics who gave free rein to their undisciplined emotions. "Enthusiasm"—a word which in its earlier usage suggested vulgarity and unrestraint—was a quality of the dissenters which educated eighteenth-century gentlemen did not admire. John Randolph of Roanoke, who gave up Deism in 1817, wrote of his own early life and education: ". . . me, who have been bred in the school of Hobbes and Bayle, and Shaftesbury and Bolingbroke, and Hume and Voltaire and Gibbon; who have cultivated the skeptical philosophy from my own vain-glorious boyhood—I might almost say childhood—and who have felt all that unutterable disgust which hypocrisy, and cant, and fanaticism never fail to excite in men of education and refinement, superadded to our natural repugnance to Christianity."

From the time of the Great Awakening under the influence of Jonathan Edwards, George Whitefield, and the Wesley brothers, all of whom preached in the American colonies, the evangelical movement gained rapidly at the expense of the Established Church. During the Revolution the Anglican Church lost still further ground because too often its clergymen proved to be Tories. The dissenters collaborated with Madison and Jefferson to disestablish the Anglican Church, but they disliked the unorthodoxy of these statesmen. In the early nineteenth century the evangelical denominations won an almost complete victory which the unsympathetic Woodbridge Riley has compared to the triumphant advance of "a kind of intellectual glacier . . . which moved slowly southward and ground out all opposition."

6

Characteristics of Colonial Writing

THE WRITING DONE in Virginia in the early seventeenth century is of a different character from that which one expects from English men of letters. It comes from men with whom writing was a secondary activity, who had visited or lived in Virginia and who recorded not what they imagined but what they saw and experienced. What we find is not plays and poems but narratives of voyages or exploration, proclamations and addresses, laws, and official and private letters. Fortunately, much that was written survives in dingy pamphlets and in the published records of the Virginia Company or in various historical journals. Since some of these materials were written by men who were in the colony for only a few years, they may be said to belong more properly to the literature of England than to that of America. Yet English literature in these years is so rich that its literary historians seldom even mention John Smith or William Strachey, who rank as "major" writers in our scanty seventeenth-century literature. More than any of his contemporaries, Captain John Smith, though he was in Virginia only two years, deserves a place in a work on American literature. His writings have for more than two centuries constituted an important source for historians and an inspiration to poets, novelists, and dramatists. He himself is the first on the beadroll of our national heroes.

Virginian writing of the early seventeenth century indicates a comparatively high cultural level among the governing classes to which the writers belonged. Howard Mumford Jones, who has devoted an excellent monograph to it, finds it "richer and more varied than much 'literary' history has hitherto allowed." [9] It is a secular literature unconcerned with the theological questions which troubled New England divines, and it shows a keen interest in the strange new land and its flora, fauna, and primitive inhabitants. What these men wrote was set down for an Old World audience, and their literary ideals came from the meridian of London. The later writings of the colonists often seem somewhat old-fashioned—evidence of a cultural "lag" characteristic of colonial writing everywhere.

Among writers who must be mentioned—there is not space for discussion —are George Percy, a descendant of the Hotspur of Shakespeare's 1 *Henry IV* and author of *Observations* printed in abridged form by Purchas in *Hakluytus Posthumus* (1625); John Pory, who put into excellent form the proceedings of the House of Burgesses; Alexander Whitaker's *Good Newes from Virginia* (1613); Ralph Hamor's A *True Discourse of the Present Estate of Virginia* (1615); and *The Discoveries of John Lederer* (1672).

In such a society as that of the Virginia tobacco farmers there was less room for authorship than one might infer from the cultural level of the large-scale planters. In no country and in no age have country gentlemen distinguished themselves as writers—except perhaps on political questions or sports—and seldom have they been eager patrons of living authors. In Virginia men regarded themselves as Englishmen and were content with what in the way of belles-lettres they could import from London. There was, however, a considerable amount of writing not intended for publication: diaries and journals, letters, and a mass of official letters, reports, and documents, of which many are preserved in the Public Records Office in London. There was a fair amount of verse, but native fiction and drama were almost nonexistent.

Louis B. Wright notes in *The First Gentlemen of Virginia* that among the educated planters there was an inherited feeling that writing for publication was not the proper thing for a gentleman: ". . . men like Richard Lee and his kind maintained a spiritual and intellectual reticence. They would no more have dissected their emotions or ostentatiously displayed their erudition in the manner of Cotton Mather than they would have appeared at a social gathering stripped of their shirts." What we know of William Byrd, James Iredell, and St. George Tucker suggests that in the Southern colonies a considerable amount of literary material was circulated in manuscript and was either never printed or was published by accident or long after the writer's death.

[9] *The Literature of Virginia in the Seventeenth Century* (Boston: American Academy of Arts and Sciences, 1946), p. 46.

American literature had it beginnings as a very minor branch of the great stream of English literature, and not until the time of the Revolution was there in this country any appreciable demand for a national literature. For the most part, men were content with what books they could import from the Old World. When an American took his pen in hand, he had no thought of contributing to a literature separate from that of the mother country. As time passed, however, men discovered that English books did not express the American point of view and often misrepresented things American. The motive behind much Colonial writing, particularly in the South, was a desire to correct British misconceptions of American life.

7
Captain John Smith

THE EARLY LIFE of Captain John Smith (1580?–1631) recalls the wandering knights of the age of chivalry who set forth in search of adventures trusting in their personal prowess and resourcefulness. This yeoman's son was born at Willoughby in Lincolnshire and educated at the free schools in the neighboring towns of Alford and Louth. Left an orphan at fifteen, he was apprenticed to a merchant but ran away and began a life of adventure. Until he was thirty, he was chiefly a soldier of fortune, and he experienced adventures which he says were used as the basis of a play. The story of these adventures is told in his last and least credible work, *The True Travels, Adventures, and Observations of Captain John Smith* (1630). While fighting against the Turks under the Transylvanian Prince Sigismund Bathor, he says, he killed three Turkish champions in single combat and as a reward received from the Prince the title of Captain, a coat of arms, and an annual pension of three thousand ducats. He was captured several times but always managed to escape either through his own courage and ingenuity or through the help of some lady who took pity on him. This bachelor adventurer evidently had a way with the ladies.

The Virginia Company sent Smith to Virginia in the first expedition of 1606–1607 as a member of the Council. He quarreled with a number of his companions; but he proved himself, if not a good colonizer or administrator, at least an excellent soldier, a good explorer and map-maker, and the ablest man in the colony to deal with the Indians. He probably saved the colony from starvation, but in his writings he left a distorted account of men to whom the Jamestown colony owed much if not so much as to himself. He left the colony after two years and never returned. He undertook, however, other voyages of exploration and he was always a propagandist for building up an English empire in America. He was not a "little Englander," as Shakespeare seems to have been. He offered to guide the Pilgrim Fathers to the New World. They declined, he says, on the ground of expense, but they made use of his *Description of New England* (1616). The Plymouth Colony, as S. E. Morison suggests, owed nearly as much to Smith as did Virginia, but New England has wellnigh forgotten his services to that region.

Most of Smith's writing was done after he had ceased to be employed as explorer. While in Virginia, however, he had written a pamphlet, published in London in 1608, *A True Relation of Occurrences and Accidents in Virginia,* from which all mention of his rescue by Pocahontas was omitted for reasons over which historians have long been in disagreement. In 1612 he published *A Map of Virginia, with a Description of Its Commodities, People, Government, and Religion,* which gives an excellent account of the culture of the Indians. In 1616 came *A Description of New England* and in 1620 *New Englands Trials.* His longest and most important work, *The Generall Historie of Virginia, New England, and the Summer Isles* (1624), includes much of his earlier work, sometimes in revised form, and also materials from other hands. The book is perhaps as accurate as the work of most Elizabethan historians. Smith, however, was a partisan of James I, who had recently revoked the charter of the Virginia Company. He had little use for Sir Edwin Sandys, brother of the poet, and the other liberals who in 1619 had given the colony a large degree of self-government.

Smith's volumes include congratulatory verses from about thirty Elizabethan poets and also a poem of some merit entitled "The Sea Marke," which is presumably Smith's own composition. There are also poems by George Wither, John Davies of Hereford, and John Donne. Donne, who in 1609 hoped to become Secretary of the Virginia colony, contributed a poem, still uncollected, "To His Friend Captaine John Smith, and His Worke," which begins:

> This Gentleman whose Volume heere is stoard
> With strange discoveries of GODS strangest Creatures,
> Gives us full view, how he hath Sayl'd, and Oar'd,
> And Marcht, full many myles. . . .

Smith, though a very uneven writer, is ordinarily a good raconteur. Sometimes his instinct for orderly narrative fails him, but he has an eye for effect and he occasionally hits off a striking phrase. More than once he deprecatingly notes that he has imitated Julius Caesar in laying aside the sword for the pen. His taste is for highly embroidered Euphuistic diction. A good specimen is the following from The Epistle Dedicatory to the Duchess of Richmond and Lenox: "I confesse, my hand, though able to weild a weapon among the Barbarous, yet well may tremble in handling a Pen among so many *Judicious*: especially when I am so bold as to call so piercing, and so glorious an *Eye*, as your *Grace*, to view these poore ragged lines."

Smith's reliability as a historian has long been called in question, but so far as we know no one doubted it until after his death. In 1660 Thomas Fuller remarked of Smith's adventures in the Balkans that "they are cheaper credited than confuted" since they took place far from England. On Smith's Virginia exploits Fuller commented: ". . . such his perils, preservations, dangers, deliverances, they seem to most men above belief, to some beyond truth." Two centuries later a Massachusetts scholar, Charles Deane, expressed his doubts as to the truth of Smith's account of the rescue by Pocahontas. On the eve of the Civil War Virginians naturally resented the New Englander's attack and rallied to Smith's defense. One of his champions, Governor Wyndham Robertson, was a descendant of Pocahontas. Another New England scholar who had no great love for anything Virginian, Henry Adams, in 1867 attacked Smith's veracity. Of later defenders of Smith one of the ablest was Patrick Henry's grandson and biographer, William Wirt Henry. The controversy has gone on intermittently ever since, but historians no longer lose their tempers over it. The most effective attack on Smith's credibility has come from a Hungarian scholar, Lewis L. Kropf, who concludes that Smith had little or no part in the Transylvanian wars. He finds Smith so ignorant of Balkan geography that he does not believe the Captain was ever in that part of Europe. On the other hand, it should be noted that a portion of *The True Travels* had been printed by Purchas five years earlier. If the story was not fundamentally true, it seems hardly likely that Smith would have dared to dedicate the book to three English noblemen and to state that it was written at the request of one of the three, Sir Robert Cotton. Smith had enemies who surely would have welcomed an opportunity to prove him a liar.

Whatever Smith's shortcomings, there must have been something in him that prompted one of his followers to write the striking tribute which appears twice in *The Generall Historie*:

What shall I say? but thus we lost him that, in all his proceedings, made Iustice his first guid[e], and experience his second; ever hating basenesse, sloth, pride, and indignitie more then [than] any dangers; that never allowed more for him-selfe then his souldiers with him; that upon no danger, would send them where he would not lead them himselfe; that would never see us want what he either had, or could by any meanes get us; that would rather want then borrow, or starve then not pay; that loved actions more then wordes, and hated falshood and cous[e]nage worse then death; whose adventures were our lives and whose losse our deathes.

Whatever the truth of the story of the famous rescue—and Smith gave it only a few lines in a large book—there is no doubt that the Smith-Pocahontas story is one of our most cherished legends. No Vergil has arisen to make it the subject of a great epic; no Longfellow has told the pathetic story of the Indian princess's supposed love for the great Captain; but numerous poets, novelists, and dramatists have treated it since the English traveler John Davis made it the subject of a short story in 1803.

8
William Strachey

IN 1609, the year that Smith returned to England, William Strachey (1567?–1620?), the first Secretary of the colony, set out for Virginia in the *Sea Adventure* with Sir George Somers and Sir Thomas Gates. The ship was separated by a violent storm from the rest of the fleet and was wrecked in the Bermudas. After nine months the crew managed to put together two pinnaces from the wreck of the *Sea Adventure*, and in these they finally reached the half-starved colony at Jamestown. No fewer than five accounts of the Bermuda adventure were published. Shakespeare before he wrote *The Tempest* may well have read some of these, and some Shakespearean scholars think it probable that he read in manuscript Strachey's letter to a lady which was printed in *Purchas His Pilgrims* in 1625. This formal account was entitled A *true reportory of the wracke, and redemption of Sir Thomas Gates Knight; upon, and from the Ilands of the Bermudas. . . .* The family tradition suggests that Strachey may have known Shakespeare and told him of his experiences in the New World. Ariel's account of how on the king's ship he "flamed amazement" during the storm was perhaps suggested by a passage in Strachey's letter.

Of Strachey's life not many details are known, and it is difficult to distinguish him in the records from other members of the famous family who bore the same given name. He was probably the William Strachey who was matriculated at Emmanuel College, Cambridge, in 1585, and it was perhaps he who married Frances Foster in 1595. Before he sailed for Virginia he had been for a short time secretary to the British ambassador at Constantinople. Whether or not he knew Shakespeare, it is clear that he was acquainted with his patron, the Earl of Southampton. He was also a friend of John Donne. He contributed a commendatory sonnet to Ben Jonson's *Sejanus* (1605), and to him was addressed a Latin poem by Thomas Campion. In later life he was a member of "the Graies-Inne Societe."

He was in Virginia a little more than a year. He was apparently the editor of the Virginia *Lawes Divine, Morall and Martiall* (London, 1612), which are written in much better prose than is generally found in legal documents. Late in 1611 when Strachey left Virginia, "one of the goodliest Countries under the Sunne," he carried with him the materials he had collected for *The Historie of travaile into Virginia Britannia; expressing the cosmographie and commodities of the country, together with the manners and customes of the people.* There are three manuscripts of this work; one, dated 1612, is in the Bodleian Library at Oxford; another, 1618, is in the British Museum. The later of these, dedicated to Francis Bacon, was finally published in 1849 by the Hakluyt Society. A third and still earlier manuscript, now in the Princeton University Library, is being edited by Louis B. Wright for publication by the Hakluyt Society. Strachey had not been able to induce the Virginia Company or any patron to have the book published. He was so much discouraged that he never carried out his plan to enlarge the work, and the latter portions of the published work are inferior to the earlier. Nevertheless, *The Historie of travaile into Virginia* contains important materials and is far better written than most of the fairly numerous early accounts of Virginia. The colony, he writes, is "a nurse for soldiers, a practize for marriners, a trade for merchants, a reward for the good, and, that which is most of all, a business most acceptable to God, to bring infidels to his knowledge." He gives an excellent account of the Virginia Indians. Of Powhatan he writes:

He is a goodly old man, not yet shrincking, though well beaten with many cold and stormye winters, in which he hath bene patient of many necessityes and attempts of his fortune to make his name and famely great. He is supposed to be little less than eighty yeares old, I dare not saye how much more; others saye he is of a tall stature and cleane lymbes, of a sad aspect, rownd fatt visaged, with graie haires, but plaine and thin, hanging upon his broad showlders; some few haires upon his chin, and so on his upper lippe; he hath bene a strong and able salvadge, synowye, and of a daring spirit, vigilant, ambitious, subtile to enlarge his dominions. . . .

9

John Hammond

OF JOHN HAMMOND the little that is known is derived from his book *Leah and Rachel, or, The Two Fruitfull Sisters of Virginia and Mary-Land,* printed in London in 1656. He was in England when he published his book, but he had spent nineteen years in Virginia and two in Maryland, and he expected to return. Hammond was primarily interested in inducing the needy to migrate to the New World, where they could better themselves; and at the same time he hoped to refute misrepresentations of Maryland and Virginia. His subtitle is revealing: *With a Removall of such Imputations as are scandalously cast on those Countries, whereby many deceived Souls, chose [choose] rather to Beg, Steal, rot in Prison, and come to shamefull deaths, then to better their being by going thither, wherein is plenty of all things necessary for Humane subsistance.* The new land, he maintains, is "wholesome, healthy and fruitfull; and a model on which industry may as much improve itself in, as in any habitable part of the World; yet not such a Lubberland as the Fiction of the land of Ease is reported to be, nor such a Utopia as Sr. Thomas Moore hath related to be found out." The labor to which the indentured servants were put was lighter than that of English laborers, and the freedman when his term was out had the opportunity to become a land-holder himself. Hammond studied the wretched street peddlers in London crying "Matches, Smal-coal, Blacking, Pen and Ink, Thred-Laces, and a hundred more such kinde of trifling merchandizes," and felt like telling them that their condition was far below that of the meanest indentured servant in Virginia.

The other day [he writes], I saw a man heavily loaden with a burden of Faggots on his back, crying, Dry Faggots, Dry Faggots; he travailed much ground, bawled frequently, and sweat with his burthen: but I saw none buy any, neer three houres I followed him, in which time he rested, I entered into discourse with him, offered him drink, which he thankfully accepted of, (as desirous to learn the mistery of his trade) I enquired what he got by each burden when sold? he answered me three pence: I further asked him what he usually got a day? he replyed, some dayes nothing some dayes six pence; some time more, but seldome; me thought it was a pittifull life, and I admired [wondered] how he could live on it; And yet it were dangerous to advise these wretches to better their conditions by travaile, for fear of the cry of, a spirit, a spirit [kidnapper!].

And therefore I cannot but admire [wonder at], and indeed much pitty the dull stupidity of people necessitated in England, who rather then they will

remove themselves, live here a base, slavish, penurious life; as if there were a
necessity to live and to live so, choosing rather then they will forsake England
to stuff New-Gate, Bridewell, and other Jayles with their carkessies, nay cleave
to tyburne it selfe, and so bring confusion to their souls, horror and infamie to
their kindred or posteritie, others itch out their wearisom lives in reliance of
other mens charities, an uncertaine and unmanly expectation; some more ab-
horring such courses betake themselves to almost perpetuall and restless toyle
and druggeries out of which (whilst their strength lasteth) they (observing hard
diets, earlie and late houres) make hard shift to subsist from hand to mouth,
untill age or sicknesse takes them off from labour and directs them the way to
beggerie, and such indeed are to be pittied, relieved and provided for.

10
John Cotton

THE FIRST NOTABLE poem written in America—"Bacon's Epitaph, Made
by His Man"—grew out of Bacon's Rebellion in Virginia in 1676. This uprising, which had its counterparts in other colonies, was in part a revolt of
the lower orders against the little oligarchy of large-scale planters who had
begun to monopolize the government of the colony. Among the grievances
of the rebels were the Navigation Acts and the disfranchisement of men
who did not own land. At the prevailing low price of tobacco, small farmers
were finding it difficult to hold their own against the wealthy planters, who
were now relying more upon the labor of Negro slaves. The immediate occasion of the outbreak was the failure of Governor Berkeley and the Council
to protect the frontier against Indian attacks.

Nathaniel Bacon was a young Englishman of education and position with
a genius for leadership. For a time he had the support of men of all classes,
but the burning of Jamestown and the unfolding of his projected reforms
alienated the well-to-do. Bacon nevertheless carried everything before him,
but after his sudden death the rebellion quickly collapsed; and the vindictive governor put to death so many of the rebels that Charles II is said to
have remarked that the old fool had hanged in that naked country more
men than had been executed in England for the murder of his father.

The Rebellion and its aftermath occasioned a surprisingly large amount
of writing. Three of the numerous accounts deserve particular mention. In
1705 one T. M.—generally identified as Thomas Mathew, a merchant-
planter of the Northern Neck—wrote out for Sir Robert Harley his still
vivid recollections of events he had witnessed nearly thirty years before.
In "The Beginning, Progress, and Conclusion of Bacon's Rebellion" T. M.

painted a memorable picture of Bacon in Jamestown at the head of his men threatening to kill governor, Council, Assembly, and himself unless he was immediately granted his promised commission to fight the Indians, while the obstinate old Governor, baring his breast, repeated over and over: "Here! shoot me. 'Fore God, fair mark; shoot!"

In 1814 and again in 1866 the Massachusetts Historical Society published the account known as "The Burwell Papers" or "The History of Bacon's and Ingram's Rebellion." The manuscript, now in the library of the Virginia Historical Society, is in an eighteenth-century hand, and it lacks title page, signature, and the opening and closing pages. In content and in style it bears a marked resemblance to a briefer narrative, "An Account of Our Late Troubles in Virginia. Written in 1676, by Mrs. An. Cotton, of Q. Creeke." Her account is addressed "To Mr. C. H. [Christopher Harris] at Yardly in Northamptonshire," who had lived in Virginia. Evidence, mainly internal, which I have elsewhere presented, indicates that Mrs. Cotton's account is a condensation of "The Burwell Papers" and that the longer narrative was written by her husband, John Cotton of Queen's Creek near Williamsburg. Cotton was a planter who at the time of the Rebellion was a neighbor of Bacon's wealthy cousin, the elder Nathaniel Bacon, a member of the Council and a conservative. Cotton was obviously in a position to witness or to learn from participants the chief incidents of the uprising. His attitude, except when it is slightly cynical, is that of the impartial historian, and he never uses the first person. He is fully aware of the historical importance of the episode he depicts, and he writes like a Sallust narrating the story of Catiline's conspiracy. It is evident, however, that up to the burning of Jamestown his sympathies were largely with Bacon; that he had nothing but contempt for Ingram, who succeeded him; and that he disapproved of Berkeley's harsh treatment of the captured rebel leaders. Cotton's prose style is so artificial that it quickly wearies the reader unless he is hardened by much reading in Elizabethan prose. It is characterized by an excessive use of alliteration, balance, and antithesis coupled with many conceits and classical allusions. Here is a typical passage in Cotton's characteristically chaotic spelling:

But he [Major Lawrence Smith] perceueing that the Gloster Men did not weare (in there faces) the Countinances of Conquerors, nor there Cloathes the marks of any late ingagement (being free from the honourable Staines of Wounds or Gun shott) he began to hope the best, and the Gloster men to feare the worst; and what the properties of feare is, let [Owen] Feltham tell you, who saith, That if curage be a good Oriter, feare is a bad Counceller, and a worse Ingineare. For insteade of erecting, it beates and batters downe all Bullworks of defence:

perswadeing the feeble hart that there is no safety in armed Troops, Iron gates, nor stone walls.

Cotton's prose style is as artificial as that of Nathaniel Ward in *The Simple Cobler of Aggawam*, but it is distinctly less effective.[10]

"The Burwell Papers" contains two poems about Bacon which express diametrically opposite conceptions of the rebel leader: "Bacon's Epitaph, Made by His Man" and "Upon the Death of G. B. [General Bacon]." It is almost certain that Cotton wrote them both. In phraseology and style they resemble his prose, and they were obviously both written by the same poet. Taken together, the poems represent a kind of debate as to Bacon's character; it is as though the poet were expressing his own conflicting feelings about the man. The "Epitaph," which is really an elegy, is the better poem of the two. W. P. Trent and Louis Untermeyer have rated it as the best American poem written in the seventeenth century. As a poet the author clearly belongs to the metaphysical school, best represented in this country by the Puritan poet Edward Taylor. I quote the whole of it since it is not easily accessible to the general reader. The confusing punctuation and the erratic spelling have been modernized.

> Death, why so cruel? What! no other way
> To manifest thy spleen but thus to slay
> Our hopes of safety, liberty, our all,
> Which through thy tyranny with him must fall
> To its late chaos? Had thy rigid force
> Been dealt by retail and not thus in gross,
> Grief had been silent. Now we must complain
> Since thou in him hast more than thousands slain
> Whose lives and safeties did so much depend
> On him, their life, with him their lives must end.
>   If't be a sin to think Death bribed can be,
> We must be guilty. Say 'twas bribery
> Guided the fatal shaft. Virginia's foes,
> To whom for secret crimes just vengeance owes
> Deservèd plagues, dreading their just desert,
> Corrupted Death by Paracelsian art
> Him to destroy; whose well-tried courage such

---

[10] Howard Mumford Jones comments on Cotton's reading: "He has read *Scoggan's Jests* and the *Resolves* of Owen Feltham, Thomas Fuller and the Iliad; he refers to the Koran, *Reynard the Fox*, Scanderbeg, Euphues, 'Bellonies Bagpipe' and 'Marsses whisle,' the Copernican theory, 'the hoggs the devill sheard," the fables of Aesop, the astrolabe, three essential properties of a general, and the titmouse which became an elephant" (*The Literature of Virginia in the Seventeenth Century*, 1946, p. 43).

Their heartless hearts, nor arms, nor strength could touch.
　Who now must heal those wounds or stop that blood
The heathen made and drew into a flood?
Who is't must plead our cause? Nor trump nor drum
Nor deputations; these alas! are dumb
And cannot speak. Our arms, though ne'er so strong,
Will want the aid of his commanding tongue,
Which conquered more than Caesar. He o'erthrew
Only the outward frame; this could subdue
The rugged works of nature. Souls replete
With dull chill cold he'd animate with heat
Drawn forth of reason's limbec. In a word,
Mars and Minerva both in him concurred
For arts, for arms, whose pen and sword alike,
As Gato's did, may admiration strike
Into his foes, while they confess withal
It was their guilt styled him a criminal.
Only this difference does from truth proceed:
They in the guilt, he in the name must bleed,
While none shall dare his obsequies to sing
In deserved measures until time shall bring
Truth crowned with freedom and from danger free
To sound his praises to posterity.
　Here let him rest, while we this truth report:
He's gone from hence unto a higher court
To plead his cause, where he by this doth know
Whether to Caesar he was friend or foe.

11
Robert Beverley

THE SOUTHERN planter's way of life, like that of the British country gentleman, permitted the development of one's individuality even to eccentricity. John Randolph of Roanoke is the classic Virginia example; but Robert Beverley, or Beverly (about 1673–1722), the first native historian, is the earliest of importance. His father, Major Robert Beverley, an offshoot of the Yorkshire gentry, came to Virginia in 1663. He brought with him sufficient capital to buy land, and at his death in 1687 he owned fifty thousand acres. The elder Beverley supported Governor Berkeley against Nathaniel Bacon, but he afterwards became the leader of what might be called

a people's party in the colony. Certain large planters felt that he had betrayed the class to which he belonged.

The younger Beverley was educated in England, but he returned to Virginia by the time he was nineteen and was quickly initiated into governmental affairs. He served several terms in the House of Burgesses and became clerk of the House, of the Council, and the General Court. In 1697
he married Ursula Byrd, sister of William Byrd II. She died a year later and
he did not marry again. Becoming involved in litigation over an estate he
had bought, he went to England, where he remained for a year and a half
and finally lost his suit. It was during this visit that he wrote his *History and
Present State of Virginia* (1705, 1722).

While still in England, he wrote some indiscreet letters to Virginians attacking Governor Francis Nicholson and Robert Quarry, surveyor-general
of customs. He reported that Nicholson and Quarry had sent to England
reports which slandered Robert Carter, William Byrd II, and himself.
Virginians, he said, had been represented as "obstinate people of Commonwealth principles" and their House of Burgesses as "a pack of rude, unthinking, willful, obstinate people, without any regard to her Majesty or her
interest, and it's laid a crime to them that they think themselves entitled
to the liberties of Englishmen." When Beverley's letters were made public,
the Council tried to pacify the angry governor, but the outcome was that
when Beverley returned to Virginia, he retired to his plantation at "Beverley
Park" in King and Queen County and thenceforth took little active part
in political affairs. In 1716, when Governor Spotswood led his famous expedition across the Blue Ridge, Beverley entertained the party at "Beverley
Park" with wine of his own vintage and accompanied them to the Shenandoah Valley. In the year of his death he published *An Abridgment of the
Public Laws of Virginia* (1722).

It was accident that led Beverley to write his *History*. In the Preface to
the revised edition he explained the circumstances which led him to undertake it. He had been asked by his bookseller, Richard Parker, to look over
the material on Virginia and Carolina prepared for John Oldmixon's *The
British Empire in America*.

I very innocently (when I began to read) placed Pen and Paper by me, and
made my Observations upon the first Page, but found it in the Sequel so very
faulty, and an Abridgment only of some Accounts that had been printed 60
or 70 Years ago; in which also he had chosen the most strange and untrue Parts,
and left out the more sincere and faithful, so that I laid aside all Thoughts of
farther Observations, and gave it only a Reading; and my Bookseller for Answer,

that the Account was too faulty and too imperfect to be mended: Withal telling him, that seeing I had in my junior Days taken some Notes of the Government, which I then had with me in *England*, I would make him an Account of my own Country, if I could find Time, while I staid in *London*. And this I should the rather undertake in Justice to so fine a Country; because it has been so misrepresented to the common People of *England*, as to make them believe, that the Servants in *Virginia* are made to draw in Cart and Plow, as Horses and Oxen do in *England*, and that the Country turns all People black, who go to live there, with other such prodigious Phantasms.

In the Preface to his revised edition Beverley listed four pages of errors and corrections of Oldmixon's account of Virginia. It was, as I have before noted, such persistent misrepresentations of their country that led the proud Virginians to write much of what they published. In particular, they resented misleading accounts of the climate and of their treatment of slaves and indentured servants. Beverley, however, was honest enough to admit that Virginia had its annoyances and inconveniences; he sums them up as "Thunder, Heat, and troublesome Vermine." Under the last head he specifies frogs, snakes, mosquitoes, chinches, and "Seed-ticks, or Red-worms, by some call'd Potato-lice." "In Fine," he says, "if any one impartially considers all the Advantages of this Country, as Nature made it; he must allow it to be as fine a Place, as any in the Universe; but I confess I am asham'd to say any thing of its Improvements, because I must at the same time reproach my Countrymen with unpardonable Sloth. If there be any Excuse for them in this Matter, 'tis the exceeding Plenty of good things, with which Nature has blest them; for where God Almighty is so merciful as to give Plenty and Ease, People easily forget their Duty." In Virginia there were few rich men—the British merchants, he says, saw to that—and almost nobody suffered from actual want. "I remember the time," he writes, "when five Pound was left by a charitable Testator, to the Poor of the Parish he lived in; and it lay nine Years, before the Executors could find one poor enough to accept of this Legacy; but at last it was given to an old Woman. So that this may in truth be term'd the best poor Man's Country in the World." Hospitality was already a characteristic Virginia trait.

The Inhabitants are very courteous to Travellers, who need no other Recommendation, but the being human Creatures. A stranger has no more to do, but to inquire upon the Road, where any Gentleman, or good House-keeper, lives, and there he may depend upon being received with Hospitality. This good Nature is so general among their People, that the Gentry, when they go abroad, order their principal Servant to entertain all Visitors, with every thing the Plantation affords. And the poor Planters, who have but one Bed, will very often sit up, or lie upon a Form [bench] or Couch all Night, to make room for a weary Traveller, to repose himself after his Journey.

If there happens to be a Churl, that either out of Covetousness, or Ill-nature, won't comply with this generous Custom, he has a Mark of Infamy set upon him, and is abhorr'd by all.

The historical portions of Beverley's book, though better than anything that had previously appeared, have no special value today. The value of the book for the historian now lies in its excellent account of the Virginia Indians and of the government and way of life of the colony. His book and Hugh Jones's *The Present State of Virginia* give us the best accounts of Virginia life in the early eighteenth century. Beverley knew the Indians, and since he liked them he portrayed them more sympathetically than his predecessors had painted them.

The original edition of 1705 gave offense to certain planters and officials, and seventeen years later Beverley, somewhat mellowed by age, omitted or softened his criticism of individuals. As Louis B. Wright has pointed out, the earlier version, like that of Irving's *Knickerbocker's History of New York*, is better from the point of view of literature. In 1705 Beverley had severely criticized some of the Royal Governors, but in 1722 he toned down or left out most of these passages. Some of the omitted comments are shrewd. He had explained Governor Culpeper's method of getting the Burgesses to enact certain laws: "In these he had the art of mixing the good of the country with his own particular interest, which was a sure means of getting them passed." In referring to Culpeper's part in drawing up the act of pardon for those who had taken part in Bacon's Rebellion, Beverley commented: "But he put a sting into the tail of this law that justifies oppression whenever the people happen to fall into the hands of an ill governor. I mean the clause that imposes a penalty of five hundred pounds and a year's imprisonment upon any man that shall presume to speak disrespectfully of the governor. This is such a safeguard to tyranny, that let a governor commit never so many abuses, no person while he is there dare say a word against him; nor so much as go about to represent it to the throne of England for redress for fear of incurring a severe penalty." In the earlier edition Beverley had described Governor Nicholson as a tyrant ready to hang Virginians "with Magna Charta about their necks" if they protested on the ground of their natural rights. Loyal though he was to the crown, Beverley wrote always of Virginia as "my Country." He was, however, no uncultivated provincial. He had read widely in literature, ancient and modern, and in travel books, history, and geography. *The History and Present State of Virginia* is a minor but genuine American classic, and Louis B. Wright has good reason for charging our literary historians with neglecting it for inferior works by New England divines.

12

Hugh Jones

The Present State of Virginia (London, 1724), by the Reverend Hugh Jones (about 1670–1760), forms a useful supplement to Beverley's *History*. The author, however, was no planter or officeholder but a clergyman, a graduate of the University of Cambridge who came to the colony in 1716. He taught mathematics in the College of William and Mary, served as chaplain to the House of Burgesses, and was afterwards rector in various parishes until his death in 1760 at about ninety years of age. His book, written apparently during a visit to England, was designed in part to correct British misconceptions.

For though some may have perfect Information and true Notions of these Things; yet the generality of Mankind are utter Strangers to what I here specify, and entertain monstrous Thoughts concerning the Country, Lives, Religion and Government of the *Virginians;* so that there seemed a great Necessity for a Book of this kind; which I have made as plain and intelligible as I possibly could, and composed in the best Method that I could devise for the Service of the Plantations [colonies], more particularly *Virginia, Maryland,* and *North Carolina,* where I have been.

Like Beverley and Hammond, Jones took great pains to correct misconceptions of the lot of slaves and indentured servants. His book is full of useful facts and sensible suggestions for the improvement of the colony. The English clergyman, however, was not unaffected by Virginia notions of the other colonies: "If *New England* be called a Receptacle of Dissenters, and an *Amsterdam* of Religion, *Pensylvania* the Nursery of Quakers, *Maryland* the Retirement of *Roman* Catholics, *North Carolina* the Refuge of Run-aways, and *South Carolina* the Delight of Buccaneers and Pyrates, *Virginia* may be justly esteemed the happy Retreat of *true Britons* and *true Churchmen. . . .*"

The Virginians, he observes, modeled their way of life on that of the mother country. "The *Habits, Life, Customs, Computations, &c.* of the *Virginians* are much the same as about *London,* which they esteem as their *Home. . . .*" The better families in Williamsburg "live in the same neat Manner, dress after the same Modes, and behave themselves exactly as the *Gentry in London;* most Families of any Note having a *Coach, Chariot,*

Berlin, or *Chaise."* Of the Governor's balls and assemblies he wrote: ". . . I have seen as fine an Appearance, as good Diversion, and as splendid Entertainments in *Governor Spotswood's Time,* as I have seen any where else." Jones shared something of the Virginian's fondness for country life with its universal hospitality, its love of hunting, racing, and visiting. By the early eighteenth century the Virginia planter could hardly be induced to go anywhere by land except on horseback. "They are such Lovers of Riding, that almost every ordinary Person keeps a Horse; and I have known some spend the Morning in ranging several Miles in the Woods to find and catch their Horses only to ride two or three Miles to Church, to the Court-House, or to a Horse-Race, where they generally appoint to meet upon Business; and are more certain of finding those that they want to speak to or deal with, than at their Home."

Jones took a keen interest in his students and prepared texts for them when he could find none suitable. These young men impressed him as American college students still impress the academic visitor from overseas. Their minds were good, he found, but they were "generally diverted by Business or Inclination from profound Study, and prying into the Depth of Things." Consequently, their learning seemed to him "for the most Part . . . but superficial." "They are more inclinable to read Men by Business and Conversation, than to dive into Books, and are for the most Part only desirous of learning what is absolutely necessary, in the shortest and best Method."

13
William Stith

THE MOST SCHOLARLY of the Virginia historians was the Reverend William Stith (1707–1755), who was educated at the William and Mary Grammar School, where he later taught for several years, and at Queen's College, Oxford. It has been generally supposed that he was a native of Virginia, but in the Queen's College register he is entered as the son of "John Stith of the Virgin Islands." In 1752 he succeeded his brother-in-law William Dawson as President of the College in spite of the fact that Governor Dinwiddie opposed him as unorthodox and as a man of turbulent spirit who had tried to stir up the lower classes against the administration.

Stith's historical writing, however, was done at an earlier period while he was Rector of Henrico Parish, whither he had gone in 1738. It had seemed to him that a history of Virginia "must naturally be a great Satisfaction, and

even Ornament, to our Country." It would also, he wrote, be "a noble and
elegant Entertainment for my vacant Hours." *The History of the First
Discovery and Settlement of Virginia* was published by William Parks in
Williamsburg in 1747 and was reprinted in London in 1753. Stith covered
only the early years through 1624. The reception of the book was not such
as to induce him to complete the task he had set for himself. In his Appendix he confessed his surprise and mortification that Virginia gentlemen
"seemed to be much alarmed, and to grudge, that a complete History of
their own Country would run to more than one Volume, and cost them
above half a Pistole." Nevertheless, Stith could not reconcile himself to
omitting altogether certain important early documents which seemed to
him important as the guarantees to Virginians of the liberties, franchises,
and immunities of Englishmen.

Stith, in his own words, had set out "to give a plain and exact History
of our Country, ever regarding Truth as the first requisite and principal
Virtue in an Historian, and relating nothing without a sufficient Warrant
and Authority." The local records, when they were not lost, he had found
mangled and disordered. He had of course the historical works of Captain
John Smith, which though "vastly confused and perplexed," seemed to him
extremely valuable for the two years Smith was actually in Virginia. The
latter part of Smith's *Generall Historie* he justly regarded with some suspi-
cion. In addition, Stith had certain books and pamphlets and the papers of
his uncle, Sir John Randolph, who had planned to write "a Preface to our
Laws, and therein to give an Historical Account of our Constitution and
Government." He had also "a very full and fair Manuscript of the *London
Company's Records,* which were communicated to me by the late worthy
President of our Council, the Honourable *William Byrd,* Esq. . . . ." The
Virginia Company's records enabled Stith to view the establishment of the
colony from the English point of view—one greatly neglected for more
than a century after his time. In spite of his efforts to secure the basic documents, Stith lacked many materials which became available to modern historians—notably to Alexander Brown, a Confederate veteran who gave
most of his life to an intensive study of the very period covered by Stith.

Stith admired the historical works of Tacitus, Suetonius, and Bishop
Burnet, and he followed his sources closely—so closely as to cramp his narrative style. In the main, that style is concise and pedestrian; but occasionally, as in his account of the Indian massacre of 1622, it rises into something
like eloquence. As a specimen which illustrates his opinions as well as his
style, I quote a passage from his Preface in which he explains the freedom
with which he has treated the character of King James I:

And I take it to be the main Part of the Duty and Office of an Historian, to paint Men and Things in their true and lively Colours; and to do that Justice to the Vices and Follies of Princes and great Men, after their Death, which it is not safe or proper to do, whilst they are alive. . . . He [James I] was, at best, only very simple and injudicious, without any steady Principle of Justice and Honour; which was rendered the more odious and ridiculous, by his large and constant Pretensions to Wisdom and Virtue. And he had, in Truth, all the Forms of Wisdom; for ever erring very learnedly, with a wise Saw, or *Latin* Sentence, in his Mouth. For he had been bred up under *Buchanan,* one of the brightest Genius's and most accomplished Scholars of that Age, who had given him *Greek* and *Latin* in great Waste and Profusion, but it was not in his Power to give him good Sense. That is the Gift of God and Nature alone, and is not to be taught; and *Greek* and *Latin* without it, only cumber and overload a weak Head, and often render the Fool more abundantly foolish. I must therefore confess, that I have ever had, from my first Acquaintance with History, a most contemptible Opinion of this Monarch; which has perhaps been much heightened and increased, by my long studying and conning over the Materials of this History. For he appears, in his Dealings with the [Virginia] Company, to have acted with such mean Arts and Fraud, and such little Tricking, as highly misbecome Majesty.

14
William Dawson

In October, 1736, William Parks, publisher of the *Virginia Gazette,* brought out in Williamsburg a volume of some thirty pages entitled *Poems on Several Occasions. By a Gentleman of Virginia.* The sole copy of the original edition that survives is in the Boston Athenaeum, and it came from the private library of George Washington. The book has been twice reprinted (1920, 1930), and there has been considerable speculation about its authorship. The early date and the comparative excellence of the verse add to its historical importance. In 1937 the mystery of the authorship was solved by Harold Lester Dean. He noted that a poem—"To a Lady. On a Screen of Her Working"—which appeared in the *Virginia Gazette* for December 10, 1736, as by "a Gentleman of Virginia," also appeared in the same month in the *London Magazine* over the name of William Dawson, who was at that time Professor of Moral Philosophy in William and Mary College and who later became its President.[11]

[11] "An Identification of the 'Gentleman of Virginia,' " *Papers* Bibliog. Soc. Am., Vol. XXXI, Part II (1937), pp. 10–20.

William Dawson (1704–1752) was born in county Cumberland, and at the age of fifteen he entered Queen's College, Oxford. He came to Virginia in 1729, possibly through the influence of William Stith, who also studied at Queen's College. Dawson married Mary Randolph Stith, sister of the historian and a niece of Sir John Randolph. Governor Gooch, who hoped that Dawson would succeed James Blair as head of the Anglican Church in Virginia, wrote in 1739 to the Bishop of London: "Mr. Dawson . . . is a thorough Scholar, a good Christian, and Orthodox Preacher, in his Behaviour as much a gentleman as we anywhere meet with, and in all respects fitted for Ecclesiastical Jurisdiction. . . ." Oxford gave him the degree of Doctor of Divinity in 1747.

Although *Poems on Several Occasions* was printed in Virginia, there is nothing in the poems themselves to show that any of them were written there. In the Preface the author refers to them as "the casual Productions of Youth." The verses are obviously the work of a well-read young man who had studied at Oxford, who loved the theater although he did not wholly approve of it; and who had read with some care the poems of Milton, the Cavalier poets, Waller, and Pope. The versification is competent and the style graceful. When compared with other volumes by American poets before Freneau, *Poems on Several Occasions* takes high rank; but if we compare it with the work of the major American poets of the next century or the chief British poets of Dawson's own time, the poetry seems only competent eighteenth-century verse. "To Sylvia, on Approach of Winter" treats the *carpe diem* theme and is probably reminiscent of Herrick as well as Horace and even more of certain songs in Shakespeare's romantic comedies.

> COME, my *Sylvia*, come away;
> Youth and Beauty will not stay;
>   Let's enjoy the present now.
> Heark, tempestuous Winter's Roar,
> How it blusters at the Door,
>   Charg'd with Frosts, and Storms, and Snow.
>
> SEATED near the crackling Fire,
> Let's indulge our fond Desire,
>   Careless of rough *Borea's* Blast:
> Let us teach the blooming Youth,
> What Joys attend on Love and Truth;
>   How much they please, how long they last,

THE am'rous Warblers of the Grove,
That in sweet Carols chant their Love,
 Can only sing, whilst Spring inspires;
But let us show, no Age, no Time,
No warring Seasons, frozen Clime,
 Can damp the Warmth of our Desires.

15
The Virginia Gazette

MASSACHUSETTS HAD a printing press as early as 1639, but printing came later to the Southern colonies. From the Restoration until 1693, when the Press Restriction Act expired, printing in England was permitted only in London, York, Oxford, and Cambridge. The memory of the pamphlet warfare of the Puritan party upon church and king was still fresh in men's minds in 1671, when Governor Berkeley wrote: "I thank God there are no free schools nor printing [in Virginia] and I hope we shall not have these hundred years; for learning has brought disobedience, and heresy and sects into the world, and printing has divulged them. . . . God keep us from both!" In 1682 John Buckner, a merchant-planter, brought to Virginia a printer named William Nuthead; but the Governor forbade him to practice his profession, and Nuthead went to Maryland, where we find him at work from 1685 on.

William Parks (about 1698–1750), who came to Annapolis in 1726 with considerable experience in England to his credit, was the most important Colonial printer after Benjamin Franklin.[12] He was a bookseller and publisher as well as a practical printer, and he had literary taste and a wide knowledge of public affairs. In September, 1727, he launched the *Maryland Gazette*, the first newspaper printed in the South. He also published the works of the Maryland poets Richard Lewis and Ebenezer Cooke. In 1730 he opened a branch office in Williamsburg, and the next year he was living there. Among his more notable Williamsburg imprints are William Dawson's *Poems on Several Occasions* (1736) and William Stith's *The History of the First Discovery and Settlement of Virginia* (1747). In 1731 he issued proposals for a book one would like very much to see if it was ever printed: *The Virginia Miscellany, consisting of New Poems, Essays, and Transla-*

---

[12] Lawrence C. Wroth, *William Parks* (1926), *The Colonial Printer* (1931, 1938), and *A History of Printing in Colonial Maryland* (1922).

tions, on various Subjects. In August, 1736, Parks founded the *Virginia Gazette,* which he conducted until his death in 1750.

One of the first items that Parks brought out in Williamsburg was J. Markland's *Typographia. An Ode on Printing* (1730),[13] inscribed to Governor William Gooch, himself the author of a dialogue on tobacco. The author of this skilfully contrived tribute to the printer and the Governor was apparently the "John Markland, Attorney, New Kent [County]" listed among the subscribers to the *Collection of Acts in Force in Virginia,* which Parks printed in 1733. *Typographia* is an irregular poem in rhyme of the same type as Dryden's great ode, "Alexander's Feast." It is not a notable poem, but it is for a colonial a meritorious performance. The author obviously knew the ancient classics and the English poets, especially Milton and Dryden. The versification is handled with commendable skill; so also is the flattery of the governor, which is too effusive for modern taste. In orthodox fashion the poem opens with an invocation to the Muses:

> Ye NYMPHS, who o'er *Castalian* Springs,
>   With joint Command preside,
> Who trill the Lyre's sonorous Strings,
> Record the great and glorious Things,
> Of Godlike *Rulers,* matchless *Kings,*
>   And poetic Numbers guide;
>   Daughters of eternal *Jove,*
> Gently to my Assistance move. . . .

The last of the twelve divisions of the poem reads:

> Happy the *Art,* by which we learn
> The Gloss of Errors to detect,
> The Vice of Habits to correct,
> And sacred Truths, from Falshood to discern!
> By which we take a far-stretch'd View,
> And learn our Fathers Vertues to pursue,
>   Their Follies to eschew.
> And may that *Art* to latest Times proclaim
> Its PATRON's *Honourable Name.*
> As some *Sybillin* Book of old,

---

[13] My quotations are from the facsimile of the unique copy in the John Carter Brown Library, reproduced in 1926 by The Stone Printing and Manufacturing Company of Roanoke, Va. Gooch's dialogue, published by Parks in 1732, is entitled *A Dialogue between Thomas Sweet-Scented, William Oronoco, Planters, both Men of good Understanding, and Justice Love-Country, who can speak for himself.*

Had *Sybils* known the Times to come,
Wrapt in *Futurity's* dark Womb,
Would thus these happy Days have told:
"Revolving Ages hence,
"In Climates now unknown,
"A *Ruler's* gentle Influence
"Shall o'er his Land be shewn;
"*Saturnian Reigns* shall be renew'd,
"Truth, Justice, Vertue, be pursu'd,
"Arts flourish, Peace shall crown the Plains,
"Where GOOCH administers, AUGUSTUS reigns."

In the early eighteenth century news was scanty and difficult to obtain, and partly on that account newspapers printed a considerable amount of verse and informal essays—material which in the nineteenth century was much more likely to find its way into magazines. A large amount of the literary material printed in the various colonial papers was of course taken from British periodicals. The *South-Carolina Gazette*, founded in 1732 by Thomas Whitmarsh, one of Franklin's printers, borrowed heavily from the *Spectator* and the *Pennsylvania Gazette*. Parks's two newspapers borrowed more largely from the British successors of the *Tatler* and the *Spectator*. Local allusions in all three newspapers, however, indicate that much of the literary material was of American origin. All three gazettes frequently solicited contributions from their readers. For example, on January 17, 1745, Jonas Green, Parks's successor on the *Maryland Gazette*, announced: "We take this Opportunity of making Application to our Learned Correspondents, whose ingenious Productions, if [with] such we shall at any Time be favoured, will ever find a Place in this Paper, and lay the Printer under the greatest Obligations; provided whatever is transmitted of this Kind, be consistent with Sobriety and good Manners." On August 10, 1739, the *Virginia Gazette* gave as its reason for reprinting an essay from the *Guardian* that it had been disappointed in its expectation of assistance from "the *Gentlemen of this Country*, many of whom want neither Learning, or fine natural Parts, to qualify them for the Task. . . ."

If some scholar would collect and reprint the best of the anonymous materials found in the rare files of these newspapers, he would help to dispel the notion that Southern literature in colonial times was almost nonexistent. Too many still share Moses Coit Tyler's notion that Colonial newspapers have no literary importance. In his time it was extremely difficult to find the scattered numbers that survive. Now, however, many of the larger libraries have them available in photostat or microfilm, and there is little excuse for neglecting them. Miss Elizabeth Christine Cook, who carried her study of Colonial newspapers no further than 1750, closes her discussion of the *Virginia Gazette:* "Surely these facts are enough to dispel that faintly inquisitive lift of the eyebrow with which literary historians have often greeted any reference to Southern literature."

Among the better essays which appeared in the *Virginia Gazette* is a series of light social satires entitled "The Monitor," which are clearly of native origin.[14] With "The Monitor" in mind, "J," obviously a clergyman, on October 29, 1736, commended the press as "a natural and necessary Auxiliary to the Pulpit; 'Tis our Light-Horse, which, whilst we attack the main Body of Atheism, Profaneness and Immorality, makes excurtions abroad, picks up little straggling Parties of inferior Enormities, and, if I may use the Expression, reaches, within Pistol-shot, what escapes the Brunt of our Canons."

Possibly "J" had in mind the story of a prude which "The Monitor" had printed in the *Gazette* two weeks before. Jack Pamflino had become engaged to her in 1718. "The Day of Marriage being fix'd, honest *Jack* thought himself sure of his Mistress; but, unfortunately, [he] happen'd to praise the Fashion of the Ladies wearing their Stays low before; which exasperated the Virtuous Dame in such a Manner, that she declared, that the very Expression was indecent; This put her into another Phrensy, [she] discarded her Lover, never to see him more." The story ends:

In about Three Weeks after this Affair, she married an honest Country Gentleman, who unfortunately died a few Days after the Consummation of the Wedding.

The Lady, so disconsolate at the Loss of her Husband, was not to be comforted; her Affliction was insupportable; and, had it not been for another Lover which she accepted of in Three Days after the Funeral, she was resolv'd, like the *Ephesian* Dame, to have been interr'd with her dear Husband.

'Tis strange! we do not give our selves Leave to consult Nature a little more; we could never thus degenerate into the Stupidity of Brutes, nor become such refined Fools.

Much of the verse that appeared in the *Virginia Gazette* is light, clever, and satirical. Technically, it is often competent, but it is rarely poetry. As a specimen I give part of J. Dumbleton's "The Paper Mill," a printer's plea for rags to make paper out of:

---

[14] This series should not be confused with the Revolutionary essays by Arthur Lee which appeared under the same title.

Ye Fair, renowned in Cupid's field,
Who fain would tell what Hearts you've killed,
Each Shift decay'd lay by with care;
Or Apron rubb'd to bits at—Pray'r.
One Shift ten Sonnets may contain,
To gild your Charms and make you vain;
One Cap a Billet-doux may shape,
As full of Whim as when a Cap,
And modest 'Kerchiefs sacred held
May sing the Breasts they once concealed.
Nice Delia's Smock which, neat and whole,
No man durst finger for his Soul,
Turn'd to Gazette, now all the Town
May take it up, or smooth it down;
Whilst Delia may with it dispence
And no Affront to Innocence.[15]

A more ambitious poem is "The Choice of Hercules"—a typical eighteenth-century subject—which appeared on January 17, 1752. An introductory note reads as follows:

This Fable was composed by *Prodicus*, and is related by *Xenophon* in his *memorable Things of* Socrates. As it has been admired by all good Judges for upwards of two thousand Years, and is one of those plain, yet elegant Compositions that will please for ever; it is here cloath'd in a new Dress by a very eminent Hand, and retains all the native Elegance and Simplicity of the Prose Original, heighten'd with all the Graces of Poetical Ornament.

The poem, which is reminiscent of Spenser, Milton, and Thomson, is written in a metrical form adapted from the Spenserian stanza. The fourth and fifth stanzas, which characterize Virtue and Sloth, who calls herself Happiness, will serve to represent the entire twenty-seven:

The first, in native Dignity surpass'd;
Artless and unadorn'd she pleas'd the more:
Health, o'er her Looks a genuine Lustre cast;
A Vest, more white than new-fall'n Snow she wore.
August she trod, yet modest was her Air;
Serene her Eye, yet darting heav'nly Fire,
Still she drew near; and nearer still more fair,

---

[15] *Virginia Gazette*, July 26, 1744. The entire poem is reprinted in Rutherfoord Goodwin, "The Williamsburg Paper Mill of William Parks the Printer," *Papers* Bibliog. Soc. Am., Vol. XXXI, Part II, pp. 21–44 (1937).

More mild appear'd; yet such as might inspire
Pleasure corrected with an awful Fear;
Majestically sweet, and amiably severe.

The other Dame seem'd ev'n of fairer Hue;
But bold her Mien; unguarded rov'd her Eye;
And her flush'd Cheeks confess'd at nearer View
The borrow'd Blushes of an artful Dye.
All soft and delicate, with airy Swim
Lightly she danc'd along; her Robe betray'd
Thro' the clear Texture every tender Limb,
Height'ning the Charms it only seem'd to shade:
And as it flow'd adown, so loose and thin,
Her Stature shew'd more tall; more snowy-white her Skin.

16
William Byrd

WILLIAM BYRD (1674–1744), the second of his name, is after Benjamin
Franklin and perhaps Jonathan Edwards the most important of Colonial
writers. His father, William Byrd I, was the son of John Byrd, a London
goldsmith and a descendant of the Byrds of Broxon in Cheshire. The first
William Byrd came to Virginia in the early seventies to take over an estate
of eighteen hundred acres situated near the falls of the James. This estate
came to him from his mother's brother, Thomas Stegge, whose father, a
thrifty merchant-planter, had become a member of the Virginia Council
as early as 1644. William Byrd I married a young widow, Mary (Horsmanden) Filmer, daughter of a Cavalier officer who had brought her with him
to Virginia during the English Civil War. The elder Byrd was pious, shrewd,
and practical but not highly cultivated like his son. He was a member of
the Council and also Auditor and Receiver-General of the colony. He sent
his agents into the wilderness to trade with the Indians as far off as western
North Carolina. Living near the frontier, he at first supported his neighbor
Nathaniel Bacon in his war against the Indians; but when it became clear
that Bacon meant to reshape the colonial government, Byrd drew back from
open rebellion. When he died on December 4, 1704, he left to his son and
namesake twenty-five thousand acres of land and, in a sense, his social and
official position as well. Not many Virginians ever came into such an inheritance.

William Byrd II, who was born in the year John Milton died, was not so shrewd a businessman as his father—though he too acquired many acres —but he was far more highly cultured. By the time he was ten years old, he was in England being educated under the supervision of his grandfather Horsmanden, now back in England, at Christopher Glasscock's grammar school in Essex, where Oliver Cromwell had sent his sons. As part of his education for practical affairs, Byrd was sent to Holland. He made for London, however, as soon as he was permitted to return to England. Instead of going to one of the universities, he studied law at the Middle Temple from 1692 to 1695. In the latter year he was admitted to the bar, but he never practiced. During these years Byrd sowed his wild oats like any young English gentleman, but he was not altogether wasting his time. He loved the theater and he knew Wycherley, Congreve, and perhaps other playwrights. Among his friends were Charles Earl of Orrery and his son and successor John; the Duke of Argyle; Sir Hans Sloane, a prominent physician; and Sir Robert Southwell, under whose sponsorship Byrd was elected a member of the Royal Society at the age of twenty-two. Byrd was a popular social figure, and he made a point of associating with the best people. In a character sketch of himself—"Inamorato L'Oiseaux"—he notes the various professions that attracted him. Of the law he says: ". . . he was soon taken off by the rapine and mercenariness of that Profession. Then the Gaity of St James's made him fancy to be a Courteour: but the falsness and treachery, the envy and corruption in fashion there quickly made him abandon that pursuit." He had thoughts of becoming a soldier, but this step he was not permitted to take.

Returning to Virginia after an absence of about twelve years, Byrd was through his father's influence elected a member of the House of Burgesses. The next year, however, he returned to England with John Povey to lay before the Board of Trade an address from the General Assembly. Named by the Virginia Council as colonial agent in 1698, he remained in England until early in 1705, when news of his father's death called him home. Byrd was now thirty-one years old; and, with the exception of a year or two, he had lived in Europe since the age of ten. The contrast between London and Westover, or even Williamsburg, was probably a painful one; but there is little indication that Byrd grieved over the change. Virginia was another rural England; besides, he was a busy man trying to fill the conspicuous place held by his father. He succeeded his father as receiver-general at an increased salary but had the mortification of seeing the post of auditor given to another man. It was not until 1708 that he became a councilor and not until the last year of his life that the death of the aged and half-deaf Commissary Blair permitted him to become President of the Council.

In 1706 this most eligible of bachelors married Lucy Parke, the "Fidelia" of the letters. She was a daughter of Colonel Daniel Parke, who once tried forcibly to eject from a church pew the wife of Commissary Blair and who later as aide to the Duke of Marlborough carried to Queen Anne the general's dispatches announcing the great victory of Blenheim. Lucy Parke Byrd inherited something of her father's stormy temper, as Byrd's diary plainly shows. On Parke's death in 1710 Byrd made the great financial blunder of his life: he took over certain lands that he coveted with the understanding that he should pay the debts of his father-in-law. The debts proved to be much larger than Byrd had anticipated, and in spite of his large inheritance they kept him in cramped circumstances the remainder of his life and probably prevented his eventually settling in England.

Byrd's position as Councilor and Receiver-General brought him into active conflict with Alexander Spotswood, who became governor of Virginia in 1710. Since the death of Governor Berkeley over thirty years before, the Council had all but governed the colony. The councilors were men of wealth and ability belonging to families which in many instances had intermarried. They were in effect the untitled nobility of the colony. When the uncompromising Scotch governor undertook to reform what he considered abuses in the Virginia government, he came into conflict with Byrd and eventually with the other councilors as well. Right or wrong, the independent planters fought the royal governor as persistently as their successors resisted Lord Dunmore on the eve of the Revolution. Of Spotswood, Byrd wrote that one "must either be a slave to his humour, must fawn upon him, jump over a stick whenever he was bid, or else he must have so much trouble loaded on him as to make his place uneasy. In short, such a man must be either the governor's dog or his ass; neither of which stations suit in the least with my constitution." [16]

In 1715 the Spotswood controversy and private affairs took Byrd back to England; and there except for a brief visit to Virginia in the winter of 1720–1721 he remained until 1726. He hoped in vain to displace Spotswood and become governor of Virginia or, at another time, of Maryland. With

[16] The Board of Trade disliked to listen to any agents except those appointed by the royal governor. Byrd regarded Col. Blakiston, the governor's appointee, as the governor's "Solicitor, and not the Country's for he will act nothing in the world in prejudice of the Governor, tho' he do anything never so injurious to the country" (Ella Lonn, *The Colonial Agents of the Southern Colonies*, p. 213). Byrd was once rebuked thus by the Board of Trade: "We are surprised to find that any objection would be made to an Instruction of this Nature, since it can never be supposed that the Plantations had or could have the Power of making any Laws which might be prejudicial to the Trade & Navigation of this Kingdom, for whose Benefit & Advantage the Plantations were first settled and still are maintained" (*ibid.*, p. 375). Such an attitude was bound to provoke American resistance and ultimately rebellion.

him was his daughter Evelyn, a wit and a beauty, who had a brilliant social career and, but for her father's determined opposition, probably would have married a baronet (not the Earl of Peterborough, as legend has it). Lucy Parke Byrd, who joined her husband in England in the summer of 1716, died in November of smallpox. After her death Byrd spent much time and money on various mistresses while he was on the lookout for a second wife with personal charms and property. He was not, however, a very successful wooer. Lady Elizabeth Lee, a granddaughter of Charles II, to whom he wrote the "Charmante" letters in 1722, eventually married the poet Edward Young, the author of *Night Thoughts*. In May, 1724, Byrd married Maria Taylor, daughter of a moderately well-to-do gentleman in Kensington, in spite of her mother's opposition to the match.

During his long stay in London Byrd was presented at court, made many calls upon ladies, was a frequent visitor at the Spanish ambassador's, and was often to be seen at Will's and the Virginia Coffee Houses. He records in the secret diary that he saw many plays though he never tells us what they were, that he often fell asleep in church, that he visited Oxford and Tunbridge Wells, and that he saw much of his prominent English friends, among whom was Horace, or Horatio, a brother of the Prime Minister, Sir Robert Walpole. In spite of these activities and his sexual adventures with many loose women, he managed to do some writing and much reading in various languages.

In 1726 at the age of fifty-two Byrd returned to Virginia, but for several years he kept his apartments in Lincoln's Inn, hoping eventually to return. His last eighteen years, however, were spent in Virginia, where he died in 1744, the year also of Alexander Pope's death. It was the continued low price of tobacco, he wrote to John Earl of Orrery on July 20, 1732, that made it impossible for him to discharge his debts and return to England.

At least thirty of Byrd's seventy years were spent in Europe; nevertheless, he was in many ways a representative Virginian planter of the early eighteenth century, and he seems to have been contented enough at Westover. On July 5, 1726, soon after his final return from England, he wrote to Charles Earl of Orrery: "Your Ldsp [Lordship] will allow it to be a fair Commendation of a Country that it reconciles a Man to Himself. . . ." In this letter he notes the absence of beggars and criminals in the colony, comments on the superiority of the Virginia climate, and states that the colonists are allowed to govern themselves with little interference from England. He continues:

Besides the advantage of a pure Air, we abound in all kinds of Provisions without expence (I mean we who have Plantations). I have a large Family of my own, and my Doors are open to Every Body, yet I have no Bills to pay, and half-a-Crown will rest undisturbed in my Pocket for many Moons together. Like one of the Patriarchs, I have my Flocks and my Herds, my Bond-men and Bond-women, and every Soart of Trade amongst my own Servants, so that I live in a kind of Independence on every one but Providence. However tho' this Soart of Life is without expence, yet it is attended with a great deal of trouble. I must take care to keep all my People to their Duty, to set all the Springs in motion and to make every one draw his equal Share to carry the Machine forward. But then 'tis an amusement in this silent Country and a continual exercise of our Patience and Economy.

The leisure of the Southern planter was not then or later that which figures in popular legend, and Byrd's time and attention were absorbed by many duties and interests. At his death he owned no less than 179,440 acres of land in Virginia and North Carolina. The Westover estate alone might have occupied a less energetic man; but Byrd was everything a Virginia planter might become except perhaps a preacher—and he often talked and prayed with his slaves. He experimented with various methods of farming, gardening, and mining. He constructed one of the handsomest houses and laid out one of the most beautiful gardens in Virginia. He built up a library of nearly four thousand volumes, the finest if not the largest in the colonies, and he decorated the walls of Westover with portraits of distinguished English friends. He collected specimens for the Royal Society. He founded the cities of Petersburg and Richmond. His official duties, one would think, might fully have occupied a less active man. In addition to his duties as Councilor, Receiver-General, and Colonial agent, he found time to help run the dividing line between Virginia and North Carolina in 1728 and to survey the Northern Neck in 1736, when he was well past sixty. Only an exceptional man could have adapted himself, like Byrd, to London society and to life on the Carolina frontier. With all his other activities he found time for a good deal of reading and writing. He rose early and read before breakfast in Hebrew, Greek, or Latin or—as at various times he notes in his diary—in French, Italian, or Dutch. He wasted little time in such popular sports as fox hunting. In versatility and intellectual curiosity he reminds one of Jefferson and Franklin. On the one hand, he belongs with the witty, worldly writers of Queen Anne's time; on the other, he looks forward to Jefferson, Mason, and the Lees, building libraries and fine houses, contending with royal governors, and planning the future of a commonwealth.

Byrd looms today a more important figure in American literature than he seemed a decade or two ago. One reason for the slow growth of his reputation is the tardiness with which his works have been published, but some of our earlier critics and literary historians were inexcusably blind to his merits. Not until 1841, nearly a century after his death, was "The History of the Dividing Line" published when Edmund Ruffin brought out in Petersburg *The Westover Manuscripts*.[17] Books printed in the South in those days of controversy—and this one was badly printed—were little read outside the state in which they were published. Twelve years later, on February 19, 1853, Evert A. Duyckinck, busy preparing *A Cyclopaedia of American Literature*, wrote to John Esten Cooke: "What is there of Virginia Revolutionary poetry? You [in Virginia] have had much literature but the light has been under a bushel. E.g. Byrd of Westover whose MSS. would have made the fortune of a northern historical society. I showed a few passages to Washington Irving the other day, who appeared never to have heard of the book before; yet Byrd had in it virtually anticipated many of the best points of the Knickerbocker [*History of New York*], substituting North Carolinians for Yankees." [18]

In 1901 John Spencer Bassett brought out an edition of Byrd's *Writings* with an excellent biographical sketch; but he included few of Byrd's admirable letters, and he failed to print "The Secret History of the Line" although Lyman C. Draper had called attention to the manuscript in the library of the American Philosophical Society as early as 1851. "The Secret History" remained unpublished until 1929. In 1940 Professors Richmond C. Beatty and W. J. Mulloy brought out, under the title *William Byrd's Natural History of Virginia*, a translation of an account of Virginia which had appeared in a book printed in Switzerland, in 1737. In 1941 and 1942 two of the three

---

[17] Many persons seem to have read the "History" in manuscript. John Daly Burk used it and other writings of Byrd in his *History of Virginia* (see I, 102–104, 115–116). James K. Paulding read it, presumably at "Brandon," in 1816 and was particularly impressed by Bearskin's description of an Indian Heaven. "The style of this work," Paulding wrote, "is, I think, the finest specimen of that grave, stately, and quaint mode of writing fashionable about a century ago, that I have ever met with any where" (*Letters from the South*, 1817, I, 27–29).

[18] Cooke MSS (Library of Congress).
That indefatigable promoter of Southern literature, William Gilmore Simms, wrote of "The History of the Dividing Line" about two years after its first publication: "The style of the narrator is very simple, but very happy. His mind is not only clear and manly, but it is lively and ingenious. He is no dry relator of his experience—gives us no tedious details—appreciates at a glance, and with the true traveller's instinct the things and topics of interest, and passes, with light and easy pen, over those which, however necessary to the narrative, are yet so likely, in ordinary hands, to fatigue, and not inform, the reader. A frank, direct business tone, mingled happily with a playful temper, improves and freshens every page of this diary—for it is nothing more; and without aiming at effect, or indulging in sentimentality, the writer yet contrives to invest his unimposing subject with a charm that beguiles the reader onward with confidence in his companion which increases at every step" (*Magnolia*, N.S. II, 259–260 (April, 1843)).

known extant portions of Byrd's secret diary were published. The diary throws much light upon Byrd and his environment, and it is an important source of information for plantation life in Virginia. *Another Secret Diary* (1942), edited by Maude H. Woodfin and Marion Tinling, contains many new Byrd letters, a number of interesting "characters," some poems written during a stay at Tunbridge Wells in 1719, and A *Discourse concerning the Plague*, which had appeared in pamphlet form in London in 1721 as "By a Lover of Mankind." All this recently published material enlarges considerably the canon of Byrd's writings and suggests that the time is ripe for a new estimate of his literary significance. It is time also for a new biography and an edition of his writings which includes his letters.

Byrd's shorthand diary—he apparently kept it throughout his mature life—is a document of importance to the biographer and the historian, but it has in itself small literary value. It is mechanical in form and style, and it abounds in such formulas as: "I rose at 6 o'clock and read two chapters in Hebrew and some Greek in Josephus. . . . I said my prayers. I had good health, good thoughts, and good humor, thanks be to God Almighty." He is as frank as Samuel Pepys in recording intimate details of his personal life, but his diary lacks the qualities that make Pepys's diary literature. From it we learn many things: that Byrd was a good master, a hospitable friend and neighbor, a loyal supporter of the church though indulging in sexual irregularities, an inveterate health-faddist given to doctoring his family, servants, and friends. More important, however, is the fact that we see Byrd clearly as a cultivated man determined not to sink into the mere tobacco farmer. No, even if he must rise before daylight, he would not neglect his Hebrew, Latin, Greek, and French; and he would as far as possible keep up with the latest intellectual developments in London.

Byrd did considerable writing in England during his last stay there, particularly in the years 1715–1720. The writing he did in these years bears little relation to Virginia; almost all of it might pass for the work of an Englishman of the time—one of the lesser wits contemporary with Swift and Pope and Addison. Most of the known poems from Byrd's hand appeared in *Tunbrigalia* (London, 1719). They are only competent eighteenth-century verses, tributes to women in society, gracefully turned compliments with a touch of satire, for there is satire in almost everything that Byrd wrote.

The letters in *Another Secret Diary* are addressed chiefly to women whom Byrd knew. They are characterized by charm, gallantry, and a touch of the satiric. The letters which he exchanged with Sabina, a Miss Smith who almost made up her mind to marry Byrd in spite of her father's opposition, constitute an epistolary novel in miniature. It is a clandestine correspondence, marked by subterfuges, the use of invisible ink, the connivance of Sabina's sister and brother-in-law, and even the hint of a duel.

A *Discourse concerning the Plague, with Some Preservatives against It* (London, 1721) has been identified as Byrd's by references in the unpublished portion of his secret diary. It is, except for the poems and the *Natural History*, the only work of Byrd's printed during his lifetime. He wrote the pamphlet in February and March, 1721, during a brief visit to Virginia. News that the dreaded plague threatened England prompted Byrd to go over his numerous medical works and to list various remedies. He lists six methods to be adopted by the public—fasting and repentance are among them—and ten preventives to be adopted by individuals. The last of these reveals Byrd the planter, worried by the low price of tobacco and eager to enlarge the market for it:

Instead of all other amulets, and preferable to them all, we shall find a singular virtue against the Plague in fresh, strong, and quick-scented Tobacco. The sprightly effluvia sent forth from this vegetable, after it is rightly cur'd, are by nature peculiarly adapted to encounter and dissipate the pestilential taint, beyond all the antidotes that have been yet discover'd.

Among Byrd's lesser works we may mention "The Ephesian Matron," a free prose translation of the *Satyricon* of Petronius. The cynical attitude toward women is not uncharacteristic of Byrd's British contemporaries. Ribald enough for the Restoration wits is "The Female Creed," written about 1725. It is cynical and satirical, reminding one of Swift more than of other English writers of the time; and it shows considerable interest in popular superstitions. Much of the satire in it is directed at women whom Byrd knew, for the fictitious names he employs are often the same as those which appear in the letters and poems.

Of the newly discovered writings, those most likely to enhance Byrd's reputation are his "characters." This type of writing, associated with the name of Theophrastus, was cultivated in England in the seventeenth century by Bishop Joseph Hall, Sir Thomas Overbury, and John Earle and in France by La Bruyère and others. It had an important influence upon the early novel and essay. The earlier English character was a brief descriptive sketch of a personage who represented some quality or profession rather than an individual. Byrd's characters, however, though he was apparently familiar with the writings of his predecessors, are primarily portraits of actual persons, chiefly men. The names attached to the characters, usually in Italian, are fictitious, but in some instances Byrd has added the real name, as in "Cavaliero Sapiente Southwell" and "Duke Dulchetti Argyle." These two are rather flattering portraits of Byrd's prominent friends. The characters show a fondness for balance and symmetry and antithesis. For example, here is part of his portrait of "Dr Glysterio," whom Miss Maude Woodfin identified as Samuel Garth, author of a once popular poem, *The Dispensary:*

He is an eminent Physician at the Coffee house, a Poet at the colledge, a sloven at court, a Beau in the country, & a mad man every where. He's never so grave as at a Ball, nor so jocose as at a consultation. . . . He is beholden to the Muses and not to Apollo for all his practice: but he's in a fair way to loose it by the same method he got it, by being much a better Poet than a Physician.

Byrd's portraits of the country parson and the prude in his letter to Lucretia are among his best. They are as vividly drawn as the coach-load of similar types in Smollett's *Roderick Random* of a later period.

For the biographer the most interesting of Byrd's characters is "Inamorato L'Oiseaux," a self-portrait, apparently an early work. This longest of the characters is a portrait of Byrd primarily in the role of a lover. It is on the whole an illuminating document, and it indicates that the writer knew his own virtues and vices very well indeed. He was often, as he describes himself, an unlucky lover. "He woud look like a fool, & talk like a Philosopher, when both his Eye and his Tongue shoud have sparkled with wit and waggery." He considered himself less of a sensualist than a reader of his diary might infer. "He often frequented the Company of Women, not so much to improve his mind as to polish his behaviour. There is something in female conversation, that softens the roughness, tames the wildness, & refines the Indecency too common amongst the men. He laid it down as a maxime that without the Ladys, a schollar is a Pedant, a Philosopher a Cynick, all morality is morose, and all behaviour either too Formal or too licentious." Byrd's comment on his personal appearance suggests the well-known portrait by Sir Godfrey Kneller: "His Person was agreable enough, tho he had a certain cast of pride in his look, which clouded some of the grace of it." "His conversation was easy, sensible and inoffensive, never bordering either upon profaneness, or indecency. . . . He never coud flatter any body, no not himself, which were two invincible bars to all preferment. He was much readyer to tell people of their faults, than their fine qualitys. . . ." "His Religion is more in substance than in form, and he is more forward to practice vertue than to profess it." "Of all cheats in the world he has least charity for the Holy Cheat, that makes Religion bawd for his Interest and serves the Devil in the Livery of Godliness." Intellectual interests are not overlooked: "He has learning without ostentation. By

Reading he's acquainted with ages past, and with the present by voyaging
& conversation." Although Inamorato is a man of the world, "He loves retirement, that while he is acquainted with the world, he may not be a
stranger to himself. Too much company distracts his thoughts, and hinders
him from digesting his observations into good sense." Here, finally, is a
significant clue to Byrd's character: "He abhors all excesses of strong drink
because it wholly removes those Guards that can defend a man from doing
& suffering Harm. He's a great freind to temperance, because tis the Security
of all the other virtues."

In 1736 Byrd sold to a Swiss colonial agency for three thousand pounds
33,400 acres of land on the Roanoke River. The next year the Helvetische
Societät published in Switzerland a two-hundred page booklet entitled *Neu-
gefundenes Eden*, of which the Library of Congress possesses what may be
a unique copy. Among the miscellaneous materials in the book is the travel-
journal of the Society's agent, Samuel Jenner, whom Byrd entertained at
Westover. Jenner incorporated in *New-Found Eden* a long description of
Virginia written by Byrd which Jenner called "eine Kurze Beschreibung
von Virginia." In 1940 Richmond C. Beatty and W. J. Mulloy reprinted
this "short description of Virginia" with an English translation under the
title *William Byrd's Natural History of Virginia*.[19] What Jenner gives us
is a dry literal translation of Byrd, but he often interrupts to speak in his
own person. Whatever literary qualities Byrd's original manuscript had
rarely appear in the German translation or in Professor Mulloy's literal
version based on the German. Occasionally, however, one meets with a
sentence which has the Byrd hallmark, as "Wer bald verlangt zu sterben
gehe nur nach Carolina"—"Let him who wishes to die quickly go to Carolina." Byrd's account of his native colony reveals him as a sounder student
of natural history than his letters to the Royal Society. There are, however,
occasional passages which seem to testify rather to Byrd's credulity than
to careful observation. Of the green live oak he wrote: "The Indians press
or boil an oil from it which is as sweet as that from olives, but somewhat
brown in color. They make also from the acorns a chocolate which is as
good as that from cocoa. . . . I have myself tasted it and found no difference at all." Some of the more interesting passages deal with the social

---

[19] John Oldmixon, who had not mentioned Byrd in the 1708 edition of his *The
British Empire in America*, stated in the Preface to the 1741 edition that he was greatly
indebted to an account of Virginia "written with a great deal of Spirit and Judgment by
a Gentleman of the province. . . . This refers to the History of Virginia which was
written by *Col. Bird*, whom the Author knew when he was of the *Temple*, and the Performance answered the just Opinion he had of that Gentleman's Ability and Exactness"
(I, x–xi). Oldmixon presumably refers to a work now lost.

life of Virginia and supplement as well as confirm the accounts given by Robert Beverley and Hugh Jones. Parts of the book show Byrd as a booster for the colony; but if he wrote it to attract settlers, it is strange that he gives no account of the lands he wished to sell to the Swiss. The conclusion of the Swiss venture was tragic. Of the 250 Switzers who sailed for Virginia in 1738 nearly all were drowned when their ship was wrecked on the North Carolina coast.

In 1728 Byrd as head of the Virginia Commission joined with the North Carolina Commissioners in surveying the dividing line between the two colonies. Byrd left two quite different accounts of his experiences on the border. "The Secret History of the Line," first published in 1929, is shorter than the older version, but it contains certain documents lacking in the longer version. It was presumably written for circulation in manuscript among Byrd's Virginia friends. Employing only fictitious names, he was able to speak his mind freely about two of his Virginian associates, Richard Fitz-William and Alexander Irvine, who on all possible occasions sided with the Carolina Commissioners. "The Secret History" reveals Byrd's difficulties with some of his own men and describes their disgraceful conduct with women along the border. The satiric comments on North Carolinians, which form the best-known passages in the longer work, are conspicuously lacking.

"The History of the Dividing Line" has greater literary importance than anything else that Byrd wrote. Edmund Ruffin, who first published it, mistakenly inferred from the condition of the manuscript that Byrd had never intended to publish it. The fact, however, that Byrd asked Peter Collinson to make arrangements for plates to be used in illustrations of the flora and fauna of the border country makes it appear that Byrd meant to publish the book in England. The introductory portion, giving a brief history of Virginia, was obviously written for non-Virginian readers. On July 18, 1736, Byrd wrote to Collinson, who had asked to see the manuscript: "I owe it go's against me, to deny you Such a Trifle, but I have one Infirmity, never to venture anything unfinisht out of my hands." [20] Byrd offered to send his rough journal, but he added: "This is only the skeleton and ground work of what I intend, which may sometime or other come to be filled up with vessels and flesh, and have a decent skin drawn over all, to keep things tight in their places and prevent their looking frightful. . . . I must only desire

---

[20] *Va. Mag.*, XXXVI, 355 (Oct., 1928). Cf. *Writings*, ed. Bassett, p. lxxix. In 1736 Lord Egmont wrote in praise of the "History" and "A Journey to the Land of Eden" and urged Byrd to publish them. Byrd replied that he was always so busy with "some Project for improving our Infant Colony" that he had no time to prepare anything for the press (*Va. Mag.*, XXXVI, 217, July, 1928).

you not to suffer this journal to go out of your hands nor a copy of it unless Sir Charles Wager should have a fancy to see it." As a writer, Byrd may have been an amateur, like most Southerners who wrote, but his standards of excellence were those of a professional.

"The History of the Dividing Line" is much more than a series of day-by-day entries. Byrd added by way of introduction a historical sketch showing how—as he ruefully makes clear—Virginia by successive royal grants had been greatly reduced from its original size. The work has affiliations with various literary types: it is a travel book, a history, a nature book with information about animals, plants, and trees, and a collection of character sketches; it is also something of a satire aimed chiefly at the riffraff along the border. Occasionally it reminds one of William Bartram's *Travels* in Georgia and Florida but more often it suggests the diary in which Sarah Kemble Knight recorded her impressions of the Connecticut backwoodsmen she encountered on her journey from Boston to New York in 1704. It is an entirely different book from "The Secret History," which was intended for a very limited set of readers. The best-known passages are those in which Byrd pictures the inhabitants of "Lubberland." Here the Southern poor-white first emerges into literature to be forgotten until the nineteenth century, when he was played up by the Abolitionists as among the horrible by-products of slavery.

The shorter pieces—"Journey to the Land of Eden" and "A Progress to the Mines"—are also examples of Byrd's best and maturest work. In all these Byrd's writing has the best characteristics of the early eighteenth century: ease, urbanity, sprightliness, and charm. Here are no provincialisms or solecisms, no long lumbering sentences like those of contemporary New England divines. Few early American prose writers had Byrd's lightness of touch. Franklin at his best is a greater writer and Jonathan Edwards plumbs spiritual depths unknown to the master of Westover. Not, however, until we come to Washington Irving do we find an American writer who excels Byrd in those qualities that distinguish him from his contemporaries.

17
Samuel Davies

THE PRESBYTERIAN "Apostle of Virginia," Samuel Davies (1723–1761), was so unlike William Byrd that he seems to belong to a different place and time. Jonathan Edwards, whom Davies was to succeed as President of Princeton, referred to him as "a man of very solid understanding, discreet in his behaviour, and polished and gentlemanly in his manners, as well as fervent and zealous in religion." Patrick Henry described him as the greatest orator he had ever heard. A Delaware farmer's son, Davies was educated at Samuel Blair's "Log College" at Fagg's (or Fogg's) Manor. He was in Hanover County, Virginia, for six weeks in 1747, and the following year he returned to stay. The Great Awakening had begun to have some effect there before he came, but there was no other New Light congregation within two hundred miles. The Established Church was at a low ebb, especially in the western part of the colony. The time was ripe for evangelical missionaries, and Davies was probably the ablest of all who came South. Of his difficulties he wrote in 1759: "The rawness and inexperience of my youth, and the formidable opposition then made both by Church and State, when a dissenter was stared at with horror, as a shocking and portentous phenomenon, were no small discouragements in my way." An example of the extreme hostility toward dissenters found among orthodox Virginians appears in the satiric "Receipt to make an ANABAPTIST PREACHER in two Days Time," printed in the *Virginia Gazette*, October 31, 1771, ten years after Davies' death:

Take the Herbs of Hypocrisy and Ambition, of each one Handful, of the Spirit of Pride two Drams, of the Seed of Dissention and Discord one Ounce, of the Flower of Formality three Scruples, of the Roots of Stubbornness and Obstinacy four Pounds; chop the Herbs, pound the Seeds, slice the Roots, and bruise them altogether in the Mortar of Vain-Glory, with the Pestle of Contradiction, putting amongst them one Pint of the Spirit of Self-Conceitedness. . . . This will make the Schismatick endeavour to maintain his Doctrine, wound the Church, delude the People, justify their proceedings of Illusion, foment Rebellion, and call it by the Name of Liberty of Conscience.

Davies had difficulty in getting a license to preach, for the governor had issued a proclamation calling on magistrates "to suppress and prohibit . . . all itinerate preachers." In Williamsburg, however, where Davies argued his own case, he proved himself more than a match for Attorney-General Randolph and caused listeners to remark that an excellent lawyer had been spoiled to make a dissenting preacher. Davies led the fight in the colony for religious freedom and was able in 1754 to bring back from England the opinion of the British attorney-general that the Act of Toleration of 1689 applied to Virginia.

Davies was an indefatigable worker. He once noted that in a period of two months he had ridden five hundred miles and preached forty sermons. He preached at seven churches in five different counties and made excursions into still other parts of the colony. When he came to Virginia, he found profanity, gambling, cock-fighting, horse-racing, and excessive drinking all too common. Many people, he says, had discarded "serious religion as the badge of the vulgar." Almost single-handed, he built up a strong Presbyterian following in Piedmont Virginia, and he won converts without attacking the Established Church. He interested himself in the religious education of his followers, including the poorer whites and the Negroes, whose singing and religious enthusiasm impressed him. He wrote to London for Bibles, catechisms, Watts's *Psalms* and *Hymns* to distribute among the slaves. Years afterwards John Holt Rice, who preached in this part of Virginia, said he rarely found a member of one of Davies' congregations that did not have some standard religious books. "In fact," he says, "Davies's churches were schools in which the people were taught better things than the ancient sages ever communicated to their disciples." The founding of Hampden-Sydney College by the Presbyterians in 1776 was due in part to Davies' work.

In 1759 Davies reluctantly heeded the call of the church, which wished him to become President of Princeton, succeeding Jonathan Edwards, whom he had once tried to induce to come to Virginia. The move was unfortunate. Davies' health, which had been good while he rode the circuit in rural Virginia, failed, and he died in 1761 at the age of thirty-six.

Davies was one of the most eloquent of Presbyterian divines. His published sermons were often reprinted both in this country and in England. "Even today," writes W. W. Sweet, "they possess persuasiveness, solid content, logical development, and beauty of style." Particularly notable are the sermons he delivered in support of the French and Indian War. In a note to one of these comes the well-known allusion to a certain Virginia soldier who had taken part in Braddock's disastrous campaign: "I may point out to the public that heroic youth, Col. Washington, whom I cannot but hope Providence has hitherto preserved in so signal a manner, for some important service." Much of the power of Davies' sermons must have depended on his effective delivery. He and others were at that time developing a new type of oratory marked by naturalness, directness, warmth of feeling combined with dignity and a feeling for appropriate language.

The success of Davies and other evangelists was due in part to the fact that the movement they headed was social and political as well as religious. Under the leadership of Jefferson and Madison, the nonconformists and the yeomen were to overturn the Anglican oligarchy which had governed the colony and to make Virginia more democratic than it had ever been.

The Great Awakening produced many fine hymns, of which Charles Wesley's are the most memorable. Davies was the first American Presbyterian hymn-writer of merit. His "Lord, I am Thine, Entirely Thine" is still sung in the churches.

In the winter of 1751–1752 Davies published in Williamsburg his *Miscellaneous Poems, Chiefly on Divine Subjects, in Two Books. Published for the Religious Entertainment of Christians in General*. These poems compare not unfavorably with the better poems which appeared in the *Virginia Gazette*, but they aroused the scorn of a critic who under the pen name "Walter Dymocke Anonymous" contributed a mock-serious review in eight parts, beginning March 20, 1752, entitled "Remarks on the Virginia Pindar." This lengthy "encomium without Flattery," as its author called it, reads like a travesty on Addison's criticisms of *Paradise Lost*. It is ably written, but it is very unfair, for the reviewer pays no attention to context when he ridicules such lines as:

> Though Vanity is my Prerogative,

or

> For I, of all the Race that fell,
> Deserve the lowest Place in Hell.

Ironically the critic pretends to praise the poet "for his pious and laudable Attempt to banish the *Heathen Deities*" from his poems and defends him for his inconsistency in referring to "a Muse and a Nymph in the Body of his Book":

For, the Muse which our Author celebrates, was not one of those Virgin Deities, who used to ramble about on Visiting Days to the Houses or Garrets of Bards residing in the Heathen Country adjacent to *Parnassus*: Nor was the Nymph He eaks of that light Wench *Egeria*, whose Intrigue with *Numa Pompilius*, makes minent a Part of the Roman History. But the Muse and the Nymph whom ouchsafes to immortalize, are two honest Country Girls Natives of H——r over] in *Virginia*, (otherwise called the *Boeotia* of *America*.) They were nd bred in a certain gloomy Swamp; whose Bottom is covered with a *lux-Puddle*. Our Author remembers very well when they were born, and was rry at the Christening of them both.

ntributors came to Davies' defense, and he himself replied in manly ion on July 3 and 10. He stated that he had no objection to criticisms of book "as far as they relate only to my *poetical Character*," but he did ect to Dymocke's aspersion of his "*moral Character* . . . when I am accused of blasphemously transforming our adorable *Immanuel* . . . into an ndian Idolater. . . ." He urged the anonymous satirist: ". . . appear in your *proper Name* and *Character*, that the Innocent may not suffer by uncertain Surmises; and particularly that the Rev. Mr. *Cam,* upon whom your Remarks have been fathered, may no longer bear the Odium." President John Camm, of the College of William and Mary, if he was the critic, did not acknowledge authorship of "Remarks on the Virginia Pindar."

18
Virginia in English Literature

THE SETTLEMENT OF Virginia occasioned a large quantity of writing both in and outside the Jamestown colony. Not much of what was written in the colony itself was literary in intent. In the mother country, however, writers whose works are among the glories of the English Renaissance shared the common interest in the project of extending the English language and empire to the New World.

From the beginning many Englishmen seem to have held one of two antagonistic conceptions of America. One of these is well expressed in Bishop George Berkeley's "Verses on the Prospect of Planting Arts and Learning in America":

> Westward the course of empire takes its way:
> The first four Acts already past,
> A fifth shall close the Drama with the day;
> Time's noblest offspring is the last.

Another view is suggested by Samuel Johnson's impatient remark: "Sir, they [the Americans] are a race of convicts, and ought to be thankful for any thing we allow them short of hanging."

Among the few British writers who had any accurate knowledge of Virginia was Francis Bacon, who embodied much sage advice in his essay, "Of Plantations" (1625), written after the colony had survived early misfortune and mismanagement. A colony, he points out, is a long-term investment.

For the principal thing that hath been the destruction of most plantations [colonies], hath been the base and hasty drawing of profit in the first years. It is true, speedy profit is not to be neglected, as far as may stand [consist] with the good of the plantation, but no further. It is a shameful and unblessed thing to take the scum of people, and wicked condemned men, to be the people with whom you plant; and not only so, but it spoileth the plantation; for they will ever live like rogues, and not fall to work, but be lazy, and do mischief, and spend victuals, and be quickly weary, and then certify over to their country to the discredit of the plantation. The people wherewith you plant ought to be gardeners, ploughmen, labourers, smiths, carpenters, joiners, fishermen, fowlers, with some few apothecaries, surgeons, cooks, and bakers.

The best expression of the romantic view of the New World appears in the fine ode "To the Virginian Voyage," with which Michael Drayton sped John Smith and his companions on their way to Jamestown in 1606. For Drayton, as the following stanzas indicate, the golden age still prevailed in Virginia:

> You brave Heroique Minds,
> Worthy your Countries Name,
>   That Honour still pursue,
>   Goe, and subdue,
> Whilst loyt'ring Hinds
> Lurke here at home, with shame.
>
>   .   .   .   .
>
> And cheerefully at Sea,
> Successe you still intice,
>   To get the Pearle and Gold,
>   And ours to hold,
> VIRGINIA,
> Earth's onely Paradise.
>
> Where Nature hath in store
> Fowle, Venison, and Fish,
>   And the fruitfull'st Soyle,
>   Without your Toyle,
> Three Harvests more,
> All greater then your Wish.
>
> And the ambitious Vine
> Crownes with his purple Masse,
>   The Cedar reaching hie
>   To kisse the Sky
> The Cypresse, Pine
> And use-full Sassafras.
>
> To whome, the golden Age
> Still Natures lawes doth give,
>   No other Cares that tend,
>   But Them to defend
> From Winters rage,
> That long there doth not live.
>
>   .   .   .   .

And in Regions farre
Such *Heroes* bring yee foorth,
  As those from whom We came,
  And plant Our name,
Under that Starre
Not knowne unto our North.

And as there Plenty growes
Of Lawrell every where,
  APOLLO's Sacred tree,
  You it may see,
A Poets Browes
To crowne, that may sing there.

Drayton never went to Virginia, nor did John Donne,[21] who once sought appointment as Secretary of the colony; but George Sandys (brother of Sir Edwin Sandys, one of the liberal statesmen of the Virginia Company) spent some years as Colonial Treasurer at Jamestown. Drayton addressed a poem "To Master George Sandys, Treasurer for the English Colony in Virginia," in which these lines appear:

And (worthy GEORGE) by industry and use,
Let's see what lines *Virginia* will produce;
Goe on with OVID, as you have begunne,
With the first five Bookes. . . .
Intice the Muses thither to repaire,
Intreat them gently, trayne them to that ayre,
For they from hence may thither hap to fly. . . .

Sandys did find time in Jamestown to work on his translation of Ovid's *Metamorphoses*, but when he dedicated it to King Charles I he referred to it as "sprung from the Stocke of the ancient Romanes; but bred in the New-world, of the rudeness whereof it cannot but participate; especially having Warres and Tumults to bring it to light in stead of the Muses." It was, he said, "limn'd by that unperfect light which was snatcht from the howers of night and repose." Properly speaking, Sandys's Ovid belongs to Latin and to English literature, but under the Dewey system of classification used in many of our libraries his book is classified as "American Literature."[22]

21 Robert L. Hickey, "Donne and Virginia," *Philol. Quart.*, XXVI, 181–192 (April, 1947); Harold Cooper, "John Donne and Virginia in 1610," *Modern Language Notes*, LVII, 661–663 (Dec., 1942); and Stanley Johnson, "John Donne and the Virginia Company," *ELH*, XIV, 127–138 (June, 1947).

22 Richard Beale Davis, "Early Editions of George Sandys's 'Ovid': The Circumstances

The lyric poets shared the romantic view of Virginia, but the London dramatists seem to have regarded it as the last resort of fools and rascals. In Philip Massinger's *The City Madam* (1632) the villain proposes a voyage to Virginia to his sister-in-law and nieces. They protest:

> *Lady Frugal.* How! Virginia!
> High Heaven forbid! Remember, sir, I beseech you,
> What creatures are shipped thither.
>
> *Anne.* Condemned wretches,
> Forfeited to the law.
>
> *Mary.* Strumpets and bawds,
> For the abomination of their life,
> Spewed out of their own country.

The kind of tall stories with which sea captains lured prospective settlers on a Virginian voyage is suggested by a scene in the Blue Anchor Tavern in *Eastward Hoe*, a comedy by Ben Jonson, George Chapman, and John Marston, which was written and acted two years before the founding of Jamestown. Captain Seagull is speaking to Scapethrift in Act III, scene iii:

I tell thee, golde is more plentifull there then copper is with us; and for as much redde copper as I can bring, Ile have thrice the waight in golde. Why, man, all their dripping pans and their chamber pottes are pure gold; and all the chaines with which they chaine up their streetes are massie [solid] golde; all the prisoners they take are fetterd in gold; and [as] for rubies and diamonds, they goe forth on holydayes and gather 'hem by the sea-shore, to hang on their childrens coates, and sticke in their capps, as commonly as our children weare saffron guilt brooches and groates with hoales in 'hem.

Once fixed in the Londoner's mind, the unfavorable opinion of Virginia was to find expression in plays and novels written long after 1605. Mrs. Aphra Behn's *The Widow Ranter* (produced in 1690, the year after her death) deals with Bacon's Rebellion, but it is in large part a satire on Colonial attempts at self-government. The Governor's Council is made up of illiterate and incompetent rascals who have come to Virginia as indentured servants. What the colony needs most, in Mrs. Behn's opinion, is to be peopled with a well-born race!

---

of Production," *Papers* Bibliog. Soc. Am., XXXV, 255–276 (4th quarter, 1941) and "America in George Sandys' 'Ovid,'" *W.M.Q.*, 3rd ser. IV, 297–304 (July, 1947). In the 1632 edition Davis finds "frequent reminders that the work and its translator were intimately connected with the New World" (p. 299). See also Davis's "George Sandys, Poet-Adventurer," *Americana*, XXXIII, 180–195 (April, 1939).

A later writer who was at once abler and more deeply interested in Virginia was Daniel Defoe, who included important Virginian episodes in two of his best picaresque novels, *Moll Flanders* and *Colonel Jacque*, both published in the year 1722. What the fertile and practical mind of Defoe saw in Virginia and Maryland was a place where the pauper and the criminal could begin life all over again under auspicious circumstances. The nonconformist novelist had himself twenty years before been pilloried for writing *The Shortest Way with Dissenters*, and he had a genuine sympathy with victims of the social and economic order. In *Moll Flanders* Moll's mother thus explains how easily even criminals can rehabilitate themselves in Maryland and Virginia:

"When they come here," says she, "we make no difference [distinction]; the planters buy them, and they work together in the field, till their time is out. When 'tis expired," said she, "they have encouragement given them to plant for themselves; for they have a certain number of acres allotted them by the country, and they go to work to clear and cure the land, and then to plant it with tobacco and corn for their own use; and as the merchants will trust them with tools and necessaries, upon the credit of the crop before it is grown, so they again plant every year a little more than the year before, and so buy whatever they want with the crop that is before them. Hence, child," says she, "many a Newgate-bird becomes a great man, and we have," continued she, "several justices of the peace, officers in the trained bands [militia], and magistrates of the towns they live in, that have been burnt in the hand."

The extended Virginia episode of *Colonel Jacque* gives a much more convincing demonstration of the practicability of Defoe's scheme than any part of the earlier novel. An important minor episode is an indirect plea for a more humane treatment of the Negro slaves. In the English popular mind, however, Defoe's two novels, written more than a century after the founding of Jamestown, may well have strengthened the now prevalent notion that the colonists were a race of convicts.

The greatest of the poets of modern Wales, Gronow (or Goronwy) Owen (1723–1769), spent the last twelve years of his life in Virginia.[23] He was born to a humble family on the island of Anglesey. His worthless father and

[23] For Owen's life and writings, see Arthur Gray, "Gronow Owen in America," *W.M.Q.*, 2nd ser. XI, 235–240 (July, 1931); J. E. Lloyd's sketch in *D.A.B.*; and George Borrow, *Wild Wales* (Vols. XII–XIV of *The Works of George Borrow*, ed. Clement Shorter, 16 vols., London, 1923–1924), especially Vols. XII, chaps. xxx ff., and XIV, "The Welsh Bards." The Huntington Library has one of the twenty copies printed for Clement Shorter of Borrow's translation of Owen's "Ode to Lewis Morris." I am indebted to the late Tom Peete Cross for certain details drawn from an unpublished lecture on Owen.

his intelligent and devoted mother both died early. An eager student of Latin, Greek, and Welsh poetry, Owen attracted the attention of Lewis Morris, an admirer and collector of the older Welsh poetry; and through his instrumentality Owen was sent to Jesus College, Oxford. After graduation he took orders and, unable to find a place in Wales, he drifted from parish to parish in England as a poorly paid curate. Homesick for his native land, he continued to labor at poetry and scholarship. What is perhaps his greatest poem, "Vision of the Great Judgment," is said to have been written in a London attic in a time of extreme poverty and depression of spirit. In these years the poet took to drinking and began to quarrel with his friends.

In 1757, through the influence of the Earl of Powis, who had interests in Virginia, Owen was appointed head of the grammar school at William and Mary College. On their way to Virginia his wife and one of his children died, and he arrived a sad and embittered man. He is said, however, to have been a successful teacher. He married a sister of the president of the college, but she died soon afterwards. After two or three years Owen lost his position because he had taken part in a quarrel between students and townsmen. He became rector of St. Andrew's Parish in Brunswick County in southern Virginia, where he died in 1769.

The only surviving long poem of Owen's which seems to have been written in Virginia is a "Lament for Anglesey." The mood of the poem is like that of the famous Psalm in which an exiled Jew weeps by the waters of Babylon. While living in Brunswick County, Owen wrote that for nine years he had hardly ever heard the Welsh language spoken. It was not until the nineteenth century that many of his poems saw publication and attracted wide attention in Wales. Most of them are written in complex and difficult verse forms, practically impossible to render into English verse, and few of them have been translated. American and British scholars who have studied his poems, however, agree that along with Chaucer's contemporary, Dafydd ap Gwylim, Gronow Owen is one of the two greatest Welsh poets of all time.

Virginia was also the home during his last years of the minor Scotch poet, John Lowe (1750–1798), author of the ballad, "Mary's Dream." [24] He came to Virginia in 1773 as tutor to the children of George Washington's brother, John Augustine Washington. In later life he conducted an academy in

[24] There is an account of Lowe's life in Scotland and Virginia in R. H. Cromek, *Remains of Nithsdale and Galloway Song* (London, 1810), pp. 342–360. Numerous allusions to Lowe may be found by consulting the Index to Hunter Farish (ed.), *Journal and Letters of Philip Vickers Fithian, 1773–1774* (1943). Farish did not identify Lowe as the Scotch poet. See also William Meade, *Old Churches, Ministers and Families of Virginia* (1857), II, 185, and *Va. Mag.*, XXIX, 102–105 (Jan., 1921).

Fredericksburg, became a minister, and because of an unhappy marriage, it is said, gave way to dissipation which brought about his death. He was a friend of Philip Vickers Fithian, who many times mentions him in his diary.

A better Scottish poet, Thomas Campbell, had several near relatives in Virginia, and he himself very nearly embarked for that state to become tutor to the children of Patrick Henry.[25] Campbell's father and two uncles came to Virginia. Later the father returned to Scotland, where he engaged in the business of importing tobacco. Two of the poet's brothers also went to Virginia, but Thomas himself was dissuaded by an older brother from a similar journey. New opportunities which opened up in Scotland and the success of his poem *The Pleasures of Hope* (1799) caused him finally to give up his long-cherished plans to live in America. In later life Campbell said: "I love America very much—and I came very near being an American myself. My father passed the early portion of his life in Virginia. My uncle adopted it as his country; one of his sons was district-attorney under Washington's administration. My brother, Robert, settled in Virginia, and married a daughter [Sarah Henry] of your glorious Patrick Henry. Yes, if I were not a Scotsman, I would like to be an American."

MARYLAND

19
George Alsop

ALTHOUGH MARYLAND and Virginia were often on bad terms with each other, social and economic conditions were much the same in both. John Hammond in *Leah and Rachel* (1656) and Daniel Defoe in *Moll Flanders* (1722) and *Colonel Jacque* (1722) treated the two colonies as practically one.

A vigorous pamphleteer who stoutly defended Maryland against British misrepresentations was George Alsop,[26] who after some experience in the colony—part of it as an indentured servant—published in London in 1666 *A Character of the Province of Maryland*. The book was dedicated to Lord Baltimore, who probably hoped it would attract immigrants to the colony.

[25] Charles Duffy, "Thomas Campbell and America," *Am. Lit.*, XIII, 346–355 (Jan., 1942).
[26] Ernest Sutherland Bates wrote the sketch of Alsop in *D.A.B.* Alsop's book was reprinted in New York in 1869, in Baltimore in 1880, in Cleveland in 1902, and was included in C. C. Hall (ed.), *Narratives of Early Maryland* (1910).

Little is known about Alsop's life apart from what he tells us. In London he had served as some sort of apprentice. In 1658 at the age of twenty he came to Maryland, partly as a result of his hatred of Oliver Cromwell. His little book interested Moses Coit Tyler far more than most Southern writing of Colonial times. Nathaniel Ward's *The Simple Cobler of Aggawam* was, he thought, the only American book of the seventeenth century which could compare with it "for mirthful, grotesque, and slashing energy." Alsop wrote both verse and prose, but his prose is superior. Here is a fair specimen of his very individual style:

The Trees, Plants, Fruits, Flowers, and Roots that grow here in *Mary-Land.*, are the only Emblems or Hieroglyphicks of our Adamitical or Primitive situa-tion, as well for their variety as odoriferous smells, together with their vertues,. according to their several effects, kinds and properties, which still bear the Effigies of Innocency according to their original Grafts; which by their dumb vegetable Oratory, each hour speaks to the Inhabitant in silent acts, That they need not look for any other Terrestrial Paradice, to suspend or tyre their curiosity upon, while she is extant. For within her doth dwell so much of variety, so much of natural plenty, that there is not any thing that is or may be rare, but it inhabits within this plentious soyle. . . .

After the abandonment of St. Mary's, the original capital, which is so vividly described in Kennedy's *Rob of the Bowl* (1838), Annapolis became a social and cultural center comparable to Williamsburg. Jonathan Boucher describes it as it appeared to him on the eve of the Revolution: "It was then the genteelest town in North America, and many of its inhabitants were highly respectable, as to station, fortune, and education. I hardly know a town in England so desirable to live in as Annapolis then was." In the second quarter of the eighteenth century the little capital was a literary center of some importance. This was chiefly owing to the presence in the colony of the two poets Ebenezer Cooke and Richard Lewis and of the printer William Parks, who founded the *Maryland Gazette* in 1727. The books which Parks advertised and the literary materials which he printed in the *Gazette* suggest a comparatively high cultural standard. Among the original essays of the Addisonian type printed in the *Gazette* we may single out "Euphranor's" discussion of Taste or Decorum, which appeared on August 26, 1756. It would not be easy to find in English literature a more characteristic eighteenth-century pronouncement than the following: "The *true Taste* may be called, that Faculty of the mind, which discerns what is decent in *Company*, and elegant in *Arts*, what is just in *Society*, and beautiful in *Nature*, and the order of the World."

Some of the verse printed in the *Maryland Gazette* is as competently written as the prose. It includes of course types popular in contemporary England: satires, fables, elegies, didactic verse, and imitations or translations of the classics. Imitations of Spenser suggest that some Marylanders were keeping abreast of literary fashions in England. As a fair example of the *Gazette's* better verse I quote a portion of "Juba's" "To the Ladies of Maryland" (June 14, 1745):

> SHUN Affectation in your Air and Dress;
> The clipt, lispt Accent, and the prim set Face:
> Easy each Motion, natural and free,
> Not pinch'd with cramp, strait-laced Formality. . . .
> Affect to please the Men of Sense alone,
> And scorn the *Fopling Flutters* of the Town. . . .
> Fly Books; they'll turn your Head, and spoil your Charms;
> Philosophy your ev'ry Grace disarms;
> Yet deign to make the lighter Muse your Care,
> 'Twill form the Wit, and give the Debonnair. . . .
> Be neat, not nice; be rather clean than fine;
> And let plain Elegance around you shine.

20
Ebenezer Cooke

In LONDON IN 1708 there appeared a clever Hudibrastic satire on Maryland under the title *The Sot-Weed Factor: Or, A Voyage to Maryland. . . . By Eben. Cook, Gent.* The poem describes with some vindictiveness Ebenezer Cooke's (or Cook's) experiences and impressions while in Maryland. He gives a sarcastic picture of drunken planters and wrangling lawyers at a county court. After being robbed at an inn, he goes to the Eastern Shore, where he meets with a pious rogue.

> While riding near a Sandy Bay,
> I met a *Quaker, Yea* and *Nay;*
> A Pious Conscientious Rogue,
> As e'er woar Bonnet or a Brogue,
> Who neither Swore nor kept his Word,
> But cheated in the Fear of God;
> And when his Debts he would not pay,
> By Light within he ran away.

Turning to a lawyer for help, the poet finds himself victimized by another rascal. The poem concludes:

> May Canniballs transported o'er the Sea
> Prey on these Slaves, as they have done on me;
> May never Merchant's, trading Sails explore
> This Cruel, this Inhospitable Shoar;
> But left abandon'd by the World to starve,
> May they sustain the Fate they well deserve:
> May they turn Savage, or as *Indians* Wild,
> From Trade, Converse, and Happiness exil'd;
> Recreant to Heaven, may they adore the Sun,
> And into Pagan Superstitions run
> For Vengeance ripe . . .
> May Wrath Divine then lay those Regions wast[e]
> Where no Man's Faithful, nor a Woman Chast[e].

After such a blast as this, it is surprising to find Cooke returning to Maryland to live. When he came back we do not know, but on December 24, 1728, the *Maryland Gazette* printed "An Elegy on the Death of the Honorable Nicholas Lowe, Esq.," which was signed as "By E. Cook. Laureat." Possibly the Royal Governor had designated Cooke as Maryland poet laureate. In 1730 William Parks published in Annapolis a much revised edition of Cooke's first book under the new title *Sotweed Redevivus. Or The Planters Looking-Glass*. "By E. C. Gent." In revising the poem Cooke, now a loyal Marylander—unless some impostor had assumed his name— dropped most of the satiric hits at the colony and turned the poem into a discussion of the financial depression brought on by overproduction of tobacco. The situation seems quite modern. Although poetically inferior to the earlier version, *Sotweed Redevivus* deserves something better than Moses Coit Tyler's impatient summary: "The first poem has, indeed, an abundance of filth and scurrility, but it has wit besides; the second poem lacks only the wit."

When in 1731 Parks brought out a new edition of *Sotweed Redevivus*, the volume contained a new poem of some length: *The Maryland Muse: Containing I. The History of Colonel Nathaniel Bacon's Rebellion in Virginia. Done into Hudibrastic Verse, from an old MS.* The source of the narrative, as Lawrence C. Wroth has shown, is "The Burwell Papers," written presumably by John Cotton about 1676 but not printed until 1814. Cooke's sympathies are altogether with Governor Berkeley, and he ridicules Bacon and his followers much as Samuel Butler had done the Puritan party in *Hudibras*. Since the Revolution it has been difficult for an American to regard Bacon otherwise than as a hero and Berkeley as the villain of the historic episode. Cooke has some good passages but nothing in the way of poetry comparable to "Bacon's Epitaph, Made by His Man." I quote from the prefatory poem "To the Author," which is signed "H.J." but was presumably versified by Cooke himself:

> Old Poet,
>   As you may remember,
> You told me sometime in September,
> Your pleasant Muse was idly sitting,
> Longing for some new Subject fitting
> For this Meridian, and her Inditing,
> Worth Praise and Pence for Pains in Writing.
> I therefore (thinking it great Pity
> A Muse should pine, that is so witty)
> Have sent an old, authentick Book,
> For Her in Doggrel Verse to Cook;
> For since it never was in Print,
> (Tho' wondrous Truths are written in't)
> It may be worthy Clio's Rhimes,
> To hand it down to future Times.

21
Richard Lewis

A BETTER POET than Ebenezer Cooke was Richard Lewis, whose original verse is meditative and descriptive rather than satiric and narrative. Lewis was a schoolmaster who came to Maryland at least as early as 1725. He had attended Eton and possibly studied at Oxford. Apart from his published work and the fact that he was a teacher, we know little about him except that he was at one time clerk of one of the committees of the Maryland General Assembly. The governor seems to have been a patron of the schoolmaster poet. The first book published in Annapolis by William Parks was Lewis's translation of Edward Holdsworth's *Muscipula: The Mouse Trap, or The Battle of the Cambrians & the Mice* (1728). Holdsworth's Latin mock-heroic poem at the expense of the Welsh is carefully and competently rendered into English verse. The Preface indicates that Lewis was something of a scholar and literary connoisseur. In the poetic dedication to

Governor Benedict Calvert he contrasts the New World with the Italy which he had heard Calvert describe:

> There PAINTURE breathes, There STATUARY lives,
> And MUSIC most delightful Rapture gives:
> There, pompous Piles of *Building* pierce the Skies,
> And endless Scenes of *Pleasure* court the Eyes.
> While *Here*, rough Woods embrown the Hills and Plains,
> Mean are the *Buildings*, artless are the *Swains:*
> "*To raise the Genius,*" WE no Time can spare,
> A *bare Subsistence* claims our utmost Care.

Between the time when Lewis wrote his dedication and 1929, when Archibald MacLeish published his "American Letter," how many American authors and artists have lamented the artistic barrenness of the New World!

Lewis's most striking poem is his "Description of Spring. A Journey from Patapsco to Annapolis, April 4, 1730," which was four times reprinted in London periodicals in 1732 and 1733, thrice with appreciative critical comments. The English editors were obviously impressed by the novelty of the natural background described in the poem. It is one of the most notable of Colonial poems in spite of some echoes of Milton's "L'Allegro" and "Il Penseroso" and James Thomson's *The Seasons*, especially of *Summer* (1727). Lewis, like Milton, describes the sights and experiences of a single day. Pastoral scenes are interrupted by a spring thunderstorm. Although he lacked Wordsworth's marvelous descriptive power or ability to communicate deep feeling, Lewis managed to paint an effective picture of what he saw on an April day in Maryland over two centuries ago. Unlike so many of our other poets, he wrote as though his eye were on the objects he was trying to describe. The mockingbird and the hummingbird here apparently make their first appearance in American poetry. I quote the description of the mockingbird. If not so good as later poems by Richard Henry Wilde and Sidney Lanier, it is one of the best things of its kind in our early poetry.

> But what is He, who perch'd above the rest,
> Pours out such various Musick from his Breast!
> His Breast, whose Plumes a cheerful White display.
> His quiv'ring Wings are dress'd in sober Grey.
> Sure all the *Muses*, this their Bird inspire!
> And he, alone, is equal to the Choir
> Of warbling Songsters who around him play,
> While, Echo like, *He* answers ev'ry Lay.
> The chirping *Lark* now sings with sprightly Note
> Responsive to her Strain *He* shapes his Throat,

> Now the poor widow'd *Turtle* wails her Mate,
> While in soft Sounds *He* cooes to mourn his Fate.
> Oh sweet Musician, thou dost far excel
> The soothing Song of pleasing *Philomel!*
> Sweet is her Song, but in few Notes confin'd;
> But thine, thou *Mimic* of the feath'ry Kind,
> Runs thro' all *Notes!—Thou* only know'st them *All,*
> At once the *Copy—*and th' *Original.*

The poem closes with a description of the coming of evening, the appearance of the stars, and some pious, semi-Deistic reflections upon life, from which we learn incidentally that the poet was thirty years old when he wrote the poem.

22
Dr. Alexander Hamilton

ONE OF THE first Southern travelers to record his impressions of New York and New England was the witty, urbane, and accomplished Annapolis physician, Dr. Alexander Hamilton (1712–1756). He was born in Scotland and received his education at the University of Edinburgh, where his father, William Hamilton, was Professor of Divinity and Principal of the University. In 1739, when he was twenty-seven years old, Dr. Hamilton began the practice of his profession in Annapolis. He won a place for himself in the aristocratic circle of officials and large-scale tobacco planters who constituted the ruling class in the colony. He was a member of the lower house of the General Assembly in 1753–1754. In 1747 he had married Margaret Dulany. She was the daughter of the prominent and wealthy Daniel Dulany the elder and brother of the younger Daniel Dulany, who was in 1765 to publish what is probably the ablest of Colonial protests against the Stamp Act. Dr. Hamilton published some minor medical treatises, but his claim to a place in literary history rests upon his *Itinerarium*. After he completed his Northern journey in 1744, he gave the manuscript to an Italian friend, Onorio Razolini. The manuscript, now in the Huntington Library, remained in Italy for more than a century and a half. It was privately printed in a small edition by William Bixby in St. Louis in 1907 with an introduction by the Harvard historian, A. B. Hart. It was not published until 1948, when the University of North Carolina Press brought out an edition with an introduction and notes by Carl Bridenbaugh.

It was in 1744, three years before his marriage, that Dr. Hamilton made the four-month journey which took him as far north as York in what is now the state of Maine. His chief motive was the hope—actually realized —of improving his health; but he enjoyed traveling and in the *Itinerarium* he complained little of bad roads and other inconveniences of travel in the eighteenth century. Hamilton had a wide range of intellectual interests, which included science, natural scenery, men and women, manners, and to a certain extent politics. He traveled on horseback in fine clothes with a laced hat, a sword, and a Negro body servant. In the *Itinerarium* he often commented on inns and innkeepers. Many of the latter he found excessively alcoholic, but a Rhode Island tavern-keeper, he notes, persuaded him that it was unlawful to travel on the Sabbath. He makes frequent reference to the books he was reading. Among them were the *Iliad*, Shakespeare's *Timon of Athens*, and the comparatively recent *Joseph Andrews* (1742) of Henry Fielding, on the reading of which he made the comment that the time was well spent. In New York he heard "the first news of the death of our great poet Pope, full of glory tho not of days." In 1744 the Great Awakening was near its peak, and Dr. Hamilton, who was perhaps a Deist, had little sympathy with such manifestations of the movement as he saw. He was somewhat disturbed by the behavior of the parvenus whom he met. In the colonies the traditional sharp distinctions between the gentry and the lower classes were beginning to break down. Hamilton noted his dislike of the "narrow notions, ignorance of the world, and low extraction" of "our aggrandized upstarts in these infant countrys of America who never had an opportunity to see, or if they had, the capacity to observe the different ranks of men in polite nations or to know what it is that really constitutes that difference of degrees."

Dr. Hamilton had an eye for the other sex. He was struck by the number of handsome women in Boston; but, he wrote: "For rural scenes and pritty, frank girls, I found it [Newport] the most agreeable place I had been in thro' all my peregrinations." In Albany, however, he had written: ". . . their women in generall, both young and old, are the hardest favoured ever I beheld." Perhaps it was the Southern prejudice against the New Englanders that led him to write: "It is not by half such a flagrant sin to cheat and cozen one's neighbour as it is to ride about for pleasure on the sabbath day or to neglect going to church and singing of psalms." Of the Bostonians he wrote: "The middling sort of people here are to a degree disingenuous and dissembling, which appears even in their common conversation in which their indirect and dubious answers to the plainest and fairest questions show their suspicions of one another. The better sort are polite, mannerly, and hospitable to strangers, such strangers, I mean, as come not to trade among them (for of them they are jealous). . . . there is abundance of men of learning and parts; so that one is att no loss for agreeable conversation nor for any sett of company he pleases." In closing his *Itinerarium* Dr. Hamilton briefly summed up his impressions:

In these my northeren [*sic*] travells I compassed my design in obtaining a better state of health, which was the purpose of my journey. I found but little difference in the manners and character of the people in the different provinces I passed thro', but as to constitutions and complexions, air and goverment [*sic*], I found some variety. Their forms of goverment in the northeren provinces I look upon to be much better and happier than ours, which is a poor, sickly, convulsed state. Their air and living to the northward is likewise much preferable, and the people of a more gygantic size and make. . . .

In this itineration I compleated, by land and water, together, a course of 1624 miles. The northeren parts I found in generall much better settled than the southeren. As to politeness and humanity, they are much alike except in the great towns where the inhabitants are more civilized, especially att Boston.

SOUTH CAROLINA

23

The Historical Background

THE TWO CAROLINAS, which were one colony until 1729, developed in such different directions that by the time of the Revolution no two Southern colonies were more unlike. South Carolina became the most aristocratic and was long the most isolated of all the colonies. While the Carolinas were still undivided, the English philosopher John Locke wrote out for one of the Proprietors his "Fundamental Constitutions" for the province of Carolina. Locke's philosophy was to have a notable influence upon American political thought, but his scheme for a native nobility of Landgraves and Caciques with large landed estates never got thoroughly established in either colony. South Carolina, like Virginia and Maryland, developed her aristocracy out of other materials. Locke's provision for religious freedom, however, proved acceptable to the South Carolina settlers, who were as heterogeneous as those who came to any of the colonies. Cavalier gentlemen were few in numbers, but there were English dissenters, Scotch Presbyterians, French Huguenots, Puritans from New England, and—most influential of all—planters from the West Indies. These planters were chiefly responsible for a certain West Indian air that still lingers about houses in

Charleston and on the Low-Country plantations. They brought with them Negro slaves who spoke a dialect now known as Gullah, which Samuel Stoney describes as notable for "the barbarity of its grammar and the beauty of its rhythm."

The South Carolina Low-Country resembles Tidewater Virginia and Maryland in its numerous navigable rivers, which served as highways for the plantations situated on them. These rivers, however, were not generally deep enough for ocean-going vessels such as navigated the James and the Potomac. A huge triangle of the Low-Country comes to a point at Charleston, where the Ashley and Cooper rivers unite; and the Carolina planters sold their products in Charleston instead of shipping them direct to England. The little city consequently became for the Low-Country a political, social, and cultural capital such as Williamsburg and Annapolis never were for Virginia and Maryland. In effect Colonial South Carolina was a city-state dominated by rice and indigo planters and Charleston merchants. Not until after the Revolution was there any marked disposition to look down on the merchants. In the fading pages of the *South-Carolina Gazette* one may still see many an advertisement by merchants whose descendants were rated among the best in nineteenth-century Charleston society. Tidewater South Carolina had comparatively few yeomen and a high percentage of Negro slaves, for it was not believed possible to cultivate the land with white labor. Malaria, to which the slaves were almost immune, took a heavy toll among whites who remained on the swampy rice lands during the summer months. For this reason well-to-do planter families usually spent the months from May until November in Charleston, in the pine lands, by the seashore, or in Northern resorts—particularly Newport, Rhode Island. In the winter the planter families often came to Charleston to participate in the social life of the capital. Many of the planters were practically absentee landlords. Under these circumstances slavery was not the patriarchal institution that it was in the colonies to the northward.

By the middle of the eighteenth century the South Carolina planter type had developed out of the heterogeneous elements that had settled the colony. It was very definitely a Southern type, but it was characterized by a peculiar blend of the aristocratic and the democratic, the radical and the conservative. Dr. Joseph Brown Ladd, a Rhode Island poet who spent his last years in Charleston, wrote in 1785:

Among their neighbors, the Carolinians stand accused of haughtiness and insolent carriage. Nothing is apparently more true than this charge; nothing is really more false. Surrounded by slaves, and accustomed to command, they acquire a forward, dictatorial habit, which can never be laid aside. In order to judge of their dispositions, we must study them with attention. Courtesy, affability, and politeness form their distinguishing characteristics. For these, for exercise of hospitality, and all the social virtues, I venture to assert that no country on earth has equaled Carolina.

Charleston, by far the largest city in the South at this time, owed its social qualities mainly to the planters who owned houses there. These charming houses were built primarily for summer use with second-story galleries, or piazzas, to catch the prevailing breeze. Many of them were built with the gable end to the street and without front lawns. The gardens, enclosed by high brick walls, were at the back. The effect of exclusiveness was probably not altogether unintentional. Charleston was a seaport, full of sailors and strangers of all sorts in addition to the numerous Negro slaves. The town itself was enclosed by a wall in the years when South Carolina was a buffer state between the English colonies and Spanish Florida.

The charm of Charleston has had its effect upon visitors from the beginning, but it remained for the twentieth century to discover how excellent a contribution to American art the Low-Country made with its churches, its beautifully furnished houses, its wrought-iron gates, and its unsurpassed gardens. These in fact are more impressive than all but the best that the Low-Country has ever given to literature. The Magnolia Gardens inspired poems by Paul Hamilton Hayne and Amy Lowell, and a visit there led John Galsworthy to write in the *Century Magazine* for July, 1921: "A painter of flowers and trees, I specialize in gardens, and freely assert that none in the world is so beautiful as this. Even before the magnolias come out, it consigns the Boboli at Florence, the Cinnamon Gardens of Colombo, Concepcion at Malaga, Versailles, Hampton Court, the Generaliffe at Granada, and La Mortola to the category of 'also ran.' Nothing so free and gracious, so lovely and wistful, nothing so richly colored, yet so ghostlike, exists, planted by the sons of men." It is, he said, "the most beautiful spot in the world."

Charleston had a larger leisure class than any other American city. Many of the Low-Country planters sent their sons to England to be educated. In fact, South Carolina sent more students to the Inns of Court in London than any other colony. The ties which bound the colony to England were very close.

24

The Theater

IN THE EIGHTEENTH century Charles Town, as the city called itself until after the Revolution, had a distinguished theatrical history. Its first season was in 1735–1736, and in the latter year Charleston erected the third theater to be built in the colonies. Mainly responsible for introducing the drama to Charleston was the British actor-playwright Anthony Aston, who tells us that he arrived there "full of Lice, Shame, Poverty, Nakedness and Hunger:—I turn'd *Player* and *Poet*, and wrote one Play on the subject of the Country. . . ." [27] What Aston's American play was is not known; he had, however, been an actor before his arrival in Charleston. During the first three months of 1735 Charlestonians had an opportunity to see Otway's *The Orphan*, Dryden's *The Spanish Fryar*, and Colley Cibber's *Flora or Hob in the Well*, which was one of the earliest operas given in the colonies. The *South-Carolina Gazette*, which is our chief source of information, printed two prologues and an epilogue for *The Orphan*, all written by one who was not the least of Colonial poets. One infers from the epilogue, which is given below, that the players were hoping to build a theater and also that there were some persons in Charleston who objected to theatrical performances on moral grounds:

> By various Arts we thus attempt to please,
> And your Delight persue by different Ways;
> Nor from our numerous Imports judge it fit
> To banish Pleasure and prohibit Wit
> But while from *Britain's* wealthy Cities flow
> Much for Necessity and much for Show,
> From the old World in Miniature we shew
> Her choicest Pleasures to regale the new.
> For your Delight and Use has *Otway* wrote,
> And pow'rful Music tunes her warbling Throat,
> While other Objects entertain the Sight,
> And we, you know, can die for your Delight.

[27] Anthony Aston, *The Fool's Opera; or, The Taste of the Age. Written by Mat. Medley* [pseudonym for Aston]. *And Performed by His Company in Oxford. To which is prefix'd A Sketch of the Author's Life, Written by Himself* (London, [1731]), p. 20. Aston refers to himself: "You are to know me, as a Gentleman, Lawyer, Poet, Actor, Soldier, Sailor, Exciseman, Publican; in *England, Scotland, Ireland, New-York, East* and *West Jersey, Maryland,* (*Virginia* on both sides of *Cheesapeek,*) *North* and *South Carolina, South Florida, Bahama's, Jamaica,* Hispaniola, and often a Coaster by all the same. . . ." (p. 16).

Warm'd with th' Applause your Favour now bestows,
It may inspire the Merit you suppose;
If haply your continu'd Smiles produce
The *humble Fabrick* suited to the Use.
Then from the doubling Arch the Notes shall bound,
And Vaults responsive eccho to the sound:
Thence from their Graves pale Ghosts arising slow
Shall clear the injur'd and the guilty show.
From nobler Themes shall loftier Scenes appear,
And *Cato* urge what Senators may hear;
Or *Congreve's* Drama shake the laughing Dome,
With Wit unmatch'd by *Athens* or by *Rome.*

The little Term that Heaven to Mortals spares,
Is daily clouded with prolonging Cares;
Nor *real* Virtue blames with pleasing Strife,
To blend Amusement with the Shades of Life;
Wise, innocent, serene, she smiles at Ease,
Nor hanging Witches, nor abjuring Plays.[28]

25
Books and Reading

THE ADVERTISEMENTS of books in the *South-Carolina Gazette* indicate
that in Charleston poetry, fiction, and printed plays were much in demand.[29]
On February 12, 1753, appeared an advertisement of a "Large Collection
of curious, valuable and entertaining books" to be sold at auction. The
dealer flattered himself, he announced, "that, as this Collection will afford
equal Entertainment for the *Religious,* the *Learned,* the FAIR, the *Gay,*
and the *Young,* they will favour him with their Presence and Encouragement." Among the attractions offered were Fielding's *Tom Jones* and
Amelia, Smollett's *Peregrine Pickle, Don Quixote* (in English), *Adventures
of Miss Betsey Thoughtless, Adventures of a Creole, Adventures of a Valet,
Adventures of a Lap-Dog, Fair Adulteress,* Pope's *Essay on Man,* the
Spectator, the works of Spenser, Young, and Swift, the sermons of Dr. Isaac
Barrow, Fontenelle's *Plurality of Worlds,* and *The Oeconomy of Human
Life.*

[28] *South-Carolina Gazette,* Feb. 15, 1734/5. Quoted inaccurately in Eola Willis, *The
Charleston Stage in the XVIII Century* (1924), p. 14.
[29] Many of the books offered for sale are listed in Hennig Cohen, *The South-Carolina
Gazette, 1732–1775* (1953), chap. xi.

The Charleston Library Society was founded in 1748 by a group of young men who decided to make the books they owned more easily available to one another. The charter members included nine merchants, two planters, a schoolmaster, a peruke-maker, a printer, and a doctor. In 1754 the Society designated Robert Dodsley, the well-known London dealer, as its bookseller and asked him to send regularly the current magazines, reviews, and other papers. In 1778, when the Library was destroyed by fire, its collection numbered between five and six thousand books. It was strong not only in literature of the more serious kind but also in history, law, and science.

26
Alexander Garden and Samuel Quincy

THE ONLY COLONIAL writer from South Carolina whom Moses Coit Tyler found worthy of inclusion in his book was the Reverend Alexander Garden (1685?–1756), rector of St. Philip's Church in Charleston and head of the Anglican Church in the Carolinas, Georgia, and the Bahamas.[30] The irritable Scotch minister was greatly disturbed over the preaching of George Whitefield and its effect upon orthodox Anglicans under his jurisdiction. The tone of his Six Letters to the Rev. Mr. George Whitefield (Boston, 1740) was such as to justify Whitefield's remarking in his reply to Garden's first letter: "Both by your Conversation, Sermon and Letter, I perceive that you are angry overmuch." Garden used as the text for two of his sermons: "They who have turned the world upside down have come hither also." He referred to Whitefield's sermons as "a medley of truth and falsehood, sense and nonsense, served up with pride and virulence, and other like saucy ingredients."

More interesting than any of Garden's sermons is a "Letter from the Rev. Alexander Garden, about Whitefield and the Orphan House in Georgia—1742-3," which appeared in the New-England Historical and Genealogical Register for April, 1870. This reads in part:

I could now indeed wish, that my Pen ag^t W—d had run in somewhat smoother a Stile. But had you been here on the spot, to have seen the Frenzie he excited 'mong the People;—the Bitterness & Virulency wherewith he raved against the Clergy of the Chh of England in general;—& how artfully he labored to set

---

[30] Edgar L. Pennington, "The Reverend Alexander Garden," Hist. Mag. of Protestant Episcopal Church, II, 178–194 (Dec., 1933), III, 111–119 (June, 1934); George A. Gordon (ed.), "Letter from Rev. Alexander Garden," New-England Hist. and Geneal. Register, LIV, 390–392 (Oct., 1900).

the Mobb upon me in particular;—I dare say, you would have thought the Provoca°n enough to ruffle any Temper, & a sufficient Apology for the keenest Expressions I have used against him. And as to my putting the Eccles. Laws in Execution against him, my Conscience would give me no Peace had I neglected so bounden a Duty.

. . . .

As to the State of Religion in this Province, it is bad enough, God knows. Rome and the Devil have contrived to crucify her 'twixt two Thieves, Infidelity & Enthusiasm. The former, alas! too much still prevails; but as to the latter, thanks to God, it is greatly subsided, & even on the Point of vanishing away. We had here Trances, Visions, & Revelations, both 'mong Blacks & Whites, in abundance. But ever since the famous Hugh Brian, sousing himself into the River Jordan, in order to smite & divide its Waters, had his Eyes opened, & saw himself under the Delusion of the Devil, those things have dwindled into Disgrace, & are now no more.

An abler writer than Garden, who was his ecclesiastical superior, was the Reverend Samuel Quincy, a native of Boston, who in 1730 was ordained deacon and priest in the Anglican Church by the Bishop of Carlisle.[31] Where he was educated is not known. In 1733 the Society for the Propagation of the Gospel sent him to Savannah as its missionary. He gave up the position in the fall of 1735. John Wesley, who succeeded him, stated that the Georgia people regarded Quincy as a "good natured, friendly, peaceful, sober, just man," but his mission was apparently none too successful. He was ill much of the time, and he did not like the governor. "Religion," he wrote, "seems to be the least minded of any thing in the place. . . ." In 1742 he became Rector of St. John's at Colleton, South Carolina. In 1745 he was a missionary in St. George's Parish. A year or so later he was assistant pastor at St. Philip's in Charleston. Some of the vestrymen, we are told, objected to his weak voice. After two years he returned to Boston. There in 1750 he published *Twenty Sermons*. The last we hear of him is that in 1751 the Society for the Propagation of the Gospel would have sent him to St. Andrew's Church in South Carolina if his health had permitted.

Quincy's *Twenty Sermons* contains some admirable specimens of the homiletic art. They are scholarly, clear, logical, and forceful. The way in which he places the foundations of religion upon Reason and Nature shows that he had come in contact with the liberal thought of eighteenth-century

---

[31] Edgar L. Pennington, "The Reverend Samuel Quincy, S.P.G. Missionary," *Ga. Hist. Quart.*, XI, 157–165 (June, 1927); William Bacon Stevens, *A History of Georgia*, I (1847), 221, 321–322; "A Letter from Mr. Samuel Quincy to the Honorable Edmund Quincy, Esq.," *Mass. Hist. Soc. Collections*, 2nd ser. II, 118–119 (1814, reprinted in 1846).

England. "Christianity," he said, "is then a rational Religion, and those who deny that it can, or ought to be maintained upon rational Principles, do in Effect give it up. For is not Reason the only Faculty of the Soul that God has given us, to render us capable of Religion: And would Men persuade us to lay it aside, in order to become more religious? A monstrous Absurdity!" The doctrines of Christianity, as Quincy presents them, are thoroughly agreeable to "Men's natural Notions of Religion." "Corruption and Degeneracy among Christians" come from a failure to exercise the Reason, which frees us from "the Bondage of Superstition, Ignorance, and Prejudice." Our truest guide is "the Light of Nature and Revelation." Carl Becker, in tracing the development of ideas expressed in the Declaration of Independence, notes that in Quincy's sermons "we find the Nature philosophy fully elaborated."

Quincy vigorously attacks the Enthusiasts and Sectaries but in better taste than Garden had shown. In a footnote he refers to "the indiscreet Preaching (to say no worse) of Mr. *Whitefield* [by which], many were driven to downright Destraction, both in this Province and other Parts of the Continent." He points out that the Enthusiast "renounces his Reason, and believes implicitely without Examination." The Methodist ministers, who will allow no interpretations of the Bible but their own, take too literally the figurative language in which Jesus described religious conversion, and they fill weak minds "with infinite Fears and Jealousies concerning their spiritual State and Condition; about which they can receive no Satisfaction, but from the doubtful Opinions of their equally deluded Leaders. . . ."

27

The South-Carolina Gazette

THE BEST OF the secular literature of the province appeared in the *South-Carolina Gazette,* of which the Charleston Library Society possesses a remarkable file. The *Gazette* was founded in 1732 by Thomas Whitmarsh, one of Franklin's printers. With money and equipment furnished by Franklin, Whitmarsh had come to Charleston in 1731. After his death in 1733 Franklin sent as Whitmarsh's successor another of his Philadelphia associates, Louis Timothée, a French refugee, who in 1734 changed his name to Lewis Timothy. After Timothy's death in December, 1738, the *Gazette* was continued by his widow Elizabeth and their son Peter, who did yeoman service in bringing the colony over to the side of the Revolutionists. The *Gazette* was published during only a part of the Revolutionary period. When Peter Timothy was lost at sea in 1782, his widow Ann and their son Benjamin Franklin Timothy continued the *Gazette* under a slightly different name until September, 1802. Another newspaper of some importance of which few copies survive was Robert Wells's *South-Carolina and American General Gazette*, founded in 1758, which after the British captured Charleston was continued for nearly two years as the *Royal Gazette*.

The *South-Carolina Gazette's* chief literary importance is in the pre-Revolutionary years. In isolated Charleston the paper retained its literary features somewhat longer than most of its Northern contemporaries. In his first number, January 8, 1732, Whitmarsh, wishing as he said to intersperse the *Dulce* with the *Utile*, solicited from his readers "Essays, whether in Prose or Verse." As late as May 7, 1772, Peter Timothy was announcing that "All Articles of Intelligence, Essays, Poems, &c. from the Ingenious, will be thankfully received, and inserted gratis. . . ." (It was to be a long time before American editors of newspapers or magazines expected to pay for such materials.) When his subscribers failed to contribute, the editor reprinted essays from the *Spectator*, the *Idler*, the *World*, and other British essay series. A fair amount of what the *Gazette* published, however, originated in South Carolina. As early as August 16, 1735, Lewis Timothy published the first of three essays purporting to emanate from the Meddlers' Club, which show the influence of the *Spectator* and of Franklin's *Busy-Body* papers. The third essay in the series, "The Vice of the Bay," is an early example of social satire; it is directed against the "Sea Sparks" and their belles who were in the habit of promenading on what is now known as the Battery. "Cupid," says the satirist, "has shot more Darts on the Bay than in all Carolina." But there are, he believes, more respectable places than the Bay, "where every Jack Tarr has the Liberty to view & remark the most celebrated Beauties of Charles-Town. . . ."

The verse which appeared in the *Gazette* consists chiefly of humorous poems and elegies. Of the latter, which are usually bad, the best is one on John Mackenzie, a planter educated at the University of Cambridge who left a remarkably fine private library to the college which he hoped would soon be built in Charleston. I give the concluding lines of the poem, which appeared in the *Gazette* for May 30, 1771:

> To form the Man, both Art and Nature join'd
> Science and Nature both adorn'd his Mind:
> In CAM's instructive walls he Learning caught,
> Where ev'ry loyal Principle is taught;
> Then conversant in ancient classic Lore,

He catch'd the Flame which *Romans* had before;
There ev'ry nobler Virtue he imbib'd
What *Cato* did, and *Cicero* describ'd.

The *Gazette* was a suitable medium for short poems, but apparently not
every South Carolina poet was content to write lyrics and epitaphs. In the
Gazette for August 25, 1757, we find proposals for publishing by subscription "A Collection of POEMS, *On* various Subjects: By a Resident of SOUTH-
CAROLINA." The book was to be published as soon as a sufficient number of
subscriptions could be secured to pay for the printing. The *Gazette* gives
an *"Extract of a POEM, intitled INDICO, Being the First in the Collection."*
The planter-poet had written a long poem on the culture of indigo, modeled
presumably on Vergil's *Georgics*, and of the same type as popular English
didactic poems of the eighteenth century. He began by announcing his
theme:

The Means and Arts that to Perfection bring,
The richer Dye of INDICO, I sing.

The "Extract," of which I quote only a part, shows the writer to have been
an experienced indigo planter and not the least gifted of Colonial poets:

Begin when first bleak winter strips the Trees,
When Herds first shudder at the Northern Breeze,
'Tis Time the Walnut and the Cypress tall
And tow'ring Pride of verdant Pine to fall.
Arm'd with destructive Steel thy Negroes bring,
With Blows repeated let the Woodlands ring;
With winged Speed, the tim'rous Deer from far
Shall fly the Tumult of the Sylvan War,
When rattling Oaks and Pines promisc'ous bound,
And distant Groves re-eccho to the Sound.
Whilst the bright Flames shall seize the useless Log
For Brush and Trunks thy fertile Acres clog)
Then peaceful sleep—secure thy Herds shall be,
And leave to feast thy Country Friends and thee.
When midnight Wolves, impell'd by Hunger's Pow'r,
With fiercest Rage the darken'd Forests scow'r,
Scar'd by the dreaded Flames, they'll turn away,
And hideous howl when baulk'd of whist [wished] for Prey.

The diction of the poem is conventional, but the descriptive details are
chosen with some skill by a writer portraying what he has actually seen with
his own eyes.

The notion of a farm manual in verse, however, did not appeal greatly to Low-Country farmers. On November 24 of the following year one "Agricola," a friend of the poet, wrote to the *Gazette* enclosing another extract from "Indico," submitting it "to the Judgment of my Brother-Planters, whether his Reasoning is not agreeable to Philosophy and good Husbandry." "Agricola" added that the poem could not be published until additional subscriptions could be procured from London, "those here not amounting to the Expence of the Press." London's answer seems not to have been encouraging; and presumably the poems, like Parks's proposed *Virginia Miscellany*, were never published. When one recalls what has happened to so many Southern manuscripts of later date, it seems too much to hope that the indigo planter's poems will ever be found.

Among the numerous essays on various topics published in the *Gazette* the series entitled "The Humorist," printed in the winter of 1753–1754, stands out conspicuously. The essays are headed "Charles-Town" and are evidently the work of a local essayist. The assumed character of the author —a variant in the *Spectator* tradition—is summed up in the issue for February 19, 1754: "I have declared myself an Oddity, composed of strange Humours, full of Peculiarities; sometimes volatile, then solemn; sometimes flighty, at another Time sedate; one Minute in the Garret, and the next in the Cellar; I confess the Truth, indeed I am happy in the Opportunity." The Humorist discusses a variety of topics: friendship, theology, medicine, faculties of the mind, strange beliefs, children's tales, and literature. He discusses tragedy, descriptive verse, and criticism. The last number closes with the announcement that the Humorist "is become an Invalid, and as he loves Retirement must quit this foolish busy World, and please his vacant Hours with the secret Satisfaction of having intentionally displeased no one." "Of all the contributors to the Charleston gazettes," says Frederick P. Bowes, "he [the Humorist] alone seems to have possessed the wit, learning and urbanity that characterized an eighteenth-century man of letters."

NORTH CAROLINA

28
The Historical Background

NORTH CAROLINA history begins with the Lost Colony of Roanoke Island, which links the names of great Elizabethan seamen with that of

Virginia Dare, the first child of English parents born in the New World. Sir Walter Raleigh sent the first settlers in 1585 under the command of Sir Richard Grenville. In the winter that followed Sir Francis Drake took the discouraged settlers back to England. A second group of colonists came in 1587, but the war with Spain delayed until 1590 every attempt to send supplies to them. When John White returned to Roanoke Island in the latter year, he found no trace of the colonists except the word "Croatan" carved on a tree. The romantic episode has played a part in North Carolina literature of the twentieth century, most notably in Paul Green's *The Lost Colony* (1937), a historical pageant still annually produced on the island. John White's admirable watercolors were first reproduced in full and in color in Stefan Lorant's *The New World: The First Pictures of America* (1946), which also reprints Thomas Hariot's *A Briefe and True Report of the New Found Land of Virginia* (London, 1588).

Owing in part to the scarcity of good harbors, North Carolina developed no such cultural center as Charleston or even Annapolis or Williamsburg.[32] A large part of the colony was virtually a part of the Virginia back country. Among the early settlers there were some substantial Virginia planters who about the middle of the seventeenth century established plantations along the rivers of the Albemarle section. Along the Cape Fear River near Wilmington settled some planters from South Carolina and the West Indies. Among the immigrants from Virginia were refugees who after the death of Nathaniel Bacon fled from Governor Berkeley's vengeance. Others were debtors, indentured servants who had served their time, and small farmers who found it difficult to compete with large-scale planters employing slave labor. The North Carolina government unwisely encouraged the immigration of undesirables by exempting for five years newcomers from being sued for debts contracted outside the colony. In his "History of the Dividing Line" William Byrd satirized North Carolina as Lubberland. The unfortunate reputation of the colony as a sort of Boeotia—certainly not deserved—which the province early acquired lingered well into the nineteenth century. The great majority of the settlers were honest and industrious yeomen. They were, however, far from being homogeneous; among them were Highland Scots, Scotch-Irish, Germans, Moravians, Quakers, etc. In this

---

[32] Much the best source of information is James S. Purcell, Jr., "Literary Culture in North Carolina before 1820" (Duke University doctoral dissertation, 1950); but see also Guion G. Johnson, *Ante-bellum North Carolina* (1937); D. N. Lehmer, "The Literary Material in the Colonial Records of North Carolina," *Univ. of Calif. Chronicle*, XXX, 125–139 (April, 1928); Stephen B. Weeks, "Libraries and Literature in North Carolina in the Eighteenth Century," *Report* of Am. Hist. Assn. for 1895, pp. 177 ff.; and J. R. Masterson, "William Byrd in Lubberland," *Am. Lit.*, IX, 153–170 (May, 1937).

region of small farmers there was little intercourse between the eastern and the western sections of the province. In the east men looked to Norfolk or Petersburg or Charleston for their markets while in the west the closest ties were with western Virginia and Pennsylvania. There were no large towns in the colony. Schools were few and books comparatively scarce. Some of the well-to-do, however, had good private libraries. The colony had no printing press until 1749 and no newspaper until 1751, when James Davis founded the *North-Carolina Gazette* in New Bern. The *North Carolina Magazine*, which he established in 1764, was in substance a sequel to his *Gazette*; it was not a genuine magazine. The earliest North Carolina newspapers contain little material of literary importance. The great period in North Carolina literature comes of course in the twentieth century, when Thomas Wolfe, Paul Green, and many other writers contributed much to the brilliance of the "Southern Renaissance."

29
John Lawson

Both North and South Carolina figure largely in one of the best travel books of the eighteenth century. This is John Lawson's (d. 1711) *A New Voyage to Carolina, Containing the Exact Description and Natural History of that Country; Together with the Present State thereof and A Journal of a Thousand Miles, traveled thro' several Nations of Indians, Giving a particular Account of their Customs, Manners; etc. By John Lawson, Gent. Surveyor General of North Carolina, London: Printed in the Year 1709.* "I like," wrote James Russell Lowell in *A Fable for Critics:*

> I like, as a thing that the reader's first fancy
> may strike, an old-fashioned title-page,
> Such as presents a tabular view of the volume's
> contents.

The less accurate title used in some later editions was *The History of Carolina.*

Lawson begins his narrative by telling us that in the year 1700, when people were flocking to "the Grand Jubilee at *Rome*," he accidentally met with a widely traveled gentleman who assured him "that *Carolina* was the best Country I could go to; and that there then lay a Ship in the *Thames*, in which I might have my Passage." Lawson promptly embarked on the ship. He found Charleston, where he landed, a thriving town with fine streets and good houses and a busy trade. He notes that in the town are to be found "ingenious People of most Sciences, whereby they have Tutors amongst them that educate their Youth a-la-mode." "The Merchants of Carolina," he writes, "are Fair, Frank Traders. The Gentlemen seated in the country are very courteous, live very nobly in their Houses, and give very Genteel entertainments to all strangers and others that come to visit them." On December 28, 1700, Lawson, who by trade was a surveyor, began his thousand-mile journey through northern Carolina. His long opening chapter is given to describing this journey. Guided by Indians, he traveled through much of North Carolina that lies east of the mountains. He saw the Indians before contact with the whites had greatly altered their character. His second chapter is a description of Carolina, and his third and last is an excellent account of the Carolina Indians.

In 1708 Lawson was appointed Surveyor-General of the as yet undivided province. He was probably in England in 1709, when his book was first published. It was perhaps written at the suggestion of the Lords Proprietors, to whom he dedicated it. "I here present your Lordships [he wrote] with a Description of your own Country, for the most part, in her Natural Dress, and therefore less vitiated with Fraud and Luxury. A Country, whose Inhabitants may enjoy a Life of the Greatest Ease, and Satisfaction, and pass away their Hours in solid Contentment." Lawson returned to North Carolina in 1710 or 1711. On the recommendation of the General Assembly he had been appointed surveyor-general of the colony. He was also a director in Christoph Von Graffenried's project for settling a group of Swiss and Palatine immigrants in the vicinity of New Bern. In the fall of 1711 Lawson and Von Graffenried set out on an expedition to determine the navigability of the Neuse River. They were captured by Indians and while Von Graffenried was released, Lawson was put to death. If one may judge from his account of them in his book, the Indians had put to death one who took a much more kindly view of them than most English settlers.

In Dublin in 1737 Dr. John Brickell, who had lived in North Carolina, published *The Natural History of North-Carolina with an Account of the Trade, Manners, and Customs of the Christian and Indian Inhabitants*. There is some new material in the book, but Moses Coit Tyler was not far wrong when he called it "an extensive and very impudent plagiarism from John Lawson."

GEORGIA

30
The Historical Background

THE YOUNGEST OF the thirteen colonies was chartered in 1732—the year of George Washington's birth—under the auspices of General James Oglethorpe, who shared Defoe's belief that the New World offered an ideal place in which debtors and other unfortunates could start life over again unhandicapped by the past. The prohibition of rum and slavery, but not of indentured servants, distinguished it sharply from the other colonies. A few slaves were admitted in 1749, but it was long before slaves were as numerous in Georgia as in other Southern states. The dominant class there, as in North Carolina, was made up of small farmers and not large-scale planters. In the course of time Savannah became something of a cultural center, but the city has never been to Georgia what Charleston long was to South Carolina. Here in 1763 James Johnston began the *Georgia Gazette,* one of the last Colonial newspapers to be established. What is notable in the later literature of Georgia came not from the Savannah region but from Middle Georgia, which was settled largely by immigrants from Virginia and the Carolinas.

Among the mixed racial elements that came to Georgia the most remarkable was a small colony of New England Puritans who had settled at Dorchester in South Carolina shortly before 1700. In the 1750's it moved to the Midway region in Georgia. Here, as in New England, the church was the center of the community and the minister was its leading man. This section gave to Georgia a number of important ministers, educators, and political leaders so far out of proportion to its population that William Bacon Stevens in his *History of Georgia* referred to them as "the moral and intellectual nobility of the province." Abiel Holmes, the father of Oliver Wendell Holmes, preached for several years in Midway; and it may be that this fact explains in part the son's lack of sympathy with the antislavery movement.

31
Tailfer, Anderson, and Douglas

THE ONE NOTABLE piece of writing that came out of Colonial Georgia grew out of dissatisfaction with the government established by the trustees of the colony. Samuel Quincy, who had served two years as missionary at Savannah, wrote in 1735 that the merchants were "rapacious and dishonest" and the magistrate in charge "a most insolent and tyrannical fellow." He went so far as to suggest that apparently the trustees "designed to establish arbitrary government, and reduce the people to a condition little better than that of slavery." [33]

In 1741 there appeared a sizable pamphlet, printed in both Charleston and London, entitled A True and Historical Narrative of the Colony of Georgia. . . . The title page informs us that it was written "By Pat[rick]. Tailfer, M.D., Hugh Anderson, M.A., Da[vid]. Douglas, and Others, Landholders in Georgia, at present in Charleston, South Carolina." [34] Of the three Scotchmen who wrote all or most of the book little is known except that, dissatisfied with the Georgia government, they came to Charleston in 1740 and employed Peter Timothy to publish their scathing satire the next year. Dr. Tailfer, to whom the literary merits of the pamphlet are usually ascribed, was a prominent opponent of the Georgia authorities. He had been accused of cruelty to his servants, even of murdering one of them. The Georgian who supplied a Preface to the official reply to A True and Historical Narrative referred to it as "a narrative founded in lies and misrepresentations, projected and published by a few persons of no estate, and as little character, persons soured in their tempers, because not humored in their endeavors of subverting, or at least altering the constitution of a new settled colony . . . persons, who were under a necessity of banishing themselves from a colony, where, for their seditious and rebellious practices, and turbulent restless spirits, they were every day in danger of being called to account as stirrers up of discontent, and as incendiaries against the peace of the government. . . ."

Malicious the intent of Tailfer, Anderson, and Douglas undoubtedly was,

---

[33] In 1740 Rev. Alexander Garden wrote from Charleston: "Bad also is the present State of the poor Orphan House in Georgia; that Land of lies, & from wᶜʰ we have no Truth, but what they can neither disguise nor conceal.—The whole Colony is accounted here one great L——e from the beginning to this Day . . ." (Mass. Hist. Soc. Collections, 2nd ser. II, 118–119, 1814, reprinted 1846).

[34] The pamphlet was reprinted in Peter Force's Historical Tracts and in Ga. Hist. Soc. Collections, Vol. II (1842). The latter volume contains also an official reply by Benjamin Martyn, Secretary of the Georgia Trustees. The pamphlet is briefly discussed in M. C. Tyler, A History of American Literature, 1607–1765 (1878), II, 292–297.

Patrick Tailfer is mentioned as a doctor in Charleston in the South Carolina-Gazette for Dec. 27, 1735. Hugh Anderson's various activities from 1739 on as lecturer, teacher, and bookseller are mentioned in the Gazette. See Hennig Cohen, The South Carolina Gazette, 1732–1775 (1953), especially p. 124.

but they documented their pamphlet meticulously and at times ostentatiously assumed the attitude of judicial fairness. The conclusion to which
they direct their evidence is that "the poor inhabitants of Georgia are scattered over the face of the earth; her plantations a wild; her towns a desert;
her villages in rubbish; her improvements a by-word, and her liberties a
jest; an object of pity to friends, and of insult, contempt and ridicule to
enemies." They accuse the Georgia authorities of having misrepresented
the climate and soil, of exacting an extortionate quitrent, of not giving the
settlers permanent titles to the land, and even of misapplying funds. They
speak most feelingly, however, of the deprivation of Negro slaves and rum.
They see in the chief magistrate Thomas Causton a petty tyrant. They
even strike at Samuel Quincy's successor: "And now to make our subjection
the more complete, a new kind of tyranny was this summer [1737] begun
to be imposed upon us; for Mr. John Wesley, who had come over and was
received as a clergyman of the Church of England, soon discovered [revealed]
that his aim was to enslave our minds, as a necessary preparative for enslaving our bodies."

Many of the complaints are petty and probably all out of proportion to
the truth, but they are presented with considerable skill. The mocking dedication to Oglethorpe is one of the finest pieces of satirical writing in our
Colonial literature. If not quite worthy of Jonathan Swift, it is certainly not
unworthy of Benjamin Franklin or William Byrd. After giving Oglethorpe
all his proper titles, the authors begin:

As the few surviving remains of the colony of Georgia find it necessary to
present the world (and in particular Great Britain) with a true state of that
province, from its first rise to its present period; your Excellency (of all mankind) is best entitled to the dedication, as the principal author of its present
strength and affluence, freedom and prosperity: and though incontestable truths
will recommend the following narrative to the patient and attentive reader, yet
your name, sir, will be no little ornament to the frontispiece, and may possibly
engage some courteous perusers a little beyond it.

After protesting that they cannot hope to rival Oglethorpe's accustomed
flatterers, the authors hope "any deficiency of elegance and politeness" will
be pardoned on account of their sincerity and the importance of what they
have to say. They note that Oglethorpe has greatly improved upon the
customary methods of colonization. He has found out, "like a divine and
a philosopher," that the usual privileges of colonists are quite unnecessary
and that riches are merely "the *irritamenta malorum* . . . to pamper the
body with luxury, and introduce a long variety of evils."

Thus have you protected us from ourselves, as Mr. Waller says, by keeping all earthly comforts from us: you have afforded us the opportunity of arriving at the integrity of the primitive times, by entailing a more than primitive poverty on us: . . . as we have no properties, to feed vainglory and beget contention, so we are not puzzled with any system of laws to ascertain and establish them: the valuable virtue of humility is secured to us, by your care to prevent our procuring, or so much as seeing any negroes (the only human creatures proper to improve our soil) lest our simplicity might mistake the poor Africans for greater slaves than ourselves: and that we might fully receive the spiritual benefit of those wholesome austerities, you have wisely denied us the use of such spirituous liquors, as might in the least divert our minds from the contemplation of our happy circumstances.

The dedication continues:

Be pleased, then, great sir, to accompany our heated imaginations, in taking a view of the colony of Georgia! this child of your auspicious politics! arrived at the utmost vigor of its constitution, at a term when most former states have been struggling through the convulsions of their infancy. This early maturity however, lessens our admiration, that your Excellency lives to see (what few founders ever aspired after) the great decline and almost final termination of it. So many have finished their course during the progress of the experiment, and such numbers have retreated from the phantoms of poverty and slavery which their cowardly imaginations pictured to them, that you may justly vaunt with the boldest hero of them all,

—Like Death you reign
O'er silent subjects and a desert plain. BUSIRIS.[35]

[35] A *True and Historical Narrative*, II, 167. *Busiris* is a tragedy by Edward Young produced in 1719.

II

THE AMERICAN REVOLUTION

1765-1789

◇⊱⊰◇

1
The Historical Background

In the third quarter of the eighteenth century the type of civilization represented by the planters of Tidewater Maryland, Virginia, and the Carolinas reached its peak. The South in later times was to have a more widely diffused culture, but it was to produce few such men as the Southern statesmen of the Revolutionary era. These eighteenth-century planters were less provincial and more tolerant than their successors, and they had a firmer grasp of political and economic realities. As a class, they were admirably trained for the role they played on the national stage. They were well grounded in law, political science, history, and the classics; and as debaters, pamphleteers, and law-makers they were more than the equals of their British opponents. The seventeenth-century Southern planters had been largely actuated by the merchant spirit; they were none too scrupulous about the way in which they built up their plantations. In the middle of the next century, however, in the memorable words of Parrington, "A high sense of personal and civic honor became the hall-mark of the landed aristocracy, and for upwards of a hundred years this common code gave to Virginia an enviable distinction. Both in national and commonwealth politics her representatives were clean-handed and jealous to deserve the public faith reposed in them."

The great planters, however, were comparatively few in number. Their status had been in part attained at the expense of other classes, white as well as black. Wasteful methods of cultivation had begun to exhaust the once-fertile Tidewater soil. By modern standards the German settlers of the Shenandoah Valley were better farmers, for they were primarily interested in agriculture as a way of living rather than as a means of attaining prosperity and leisure. The planters loyally supported the Revolution, but it brought ruin to the majority of them. Many of their estates, even if not devastated by invading armies or Tory raiders or worn out by wasteful cultivation, were broken up and sold for debt. A few of the old families managed to hold their own, but most of the great planters of the early nineteenth century were to rise from the middle and lower classes.

In the years that followed the Revolution there arose misconceptions which obscure the actual life of the eighteenth-century planters. Defenders of slavery, Abolitionists, romantic historians, and careless writers of fiction painted a picture which still misleads the unwary. The wealthy planters were aristocrats, but they were no such nabobs as they often appear in legend and fiction. They were not only gentlemen but for the most part dirt farmers. The early nineteenth-century disposition to magnify them is seen in William Wirt's life of Patrick Henry, published in 1817. After reading a portion of the biography in manuscript, St. George Tucker had written to Wirt in 1815: ". . . I think the picture both of Governors, & Councillors' stile of living rather exaggerated. . . . Their *hospitality* was without Bounds: but there was not much pomp; & less of it, by far, than may be seen in Richm[on]d at this day. . . ."

An excellent account of the way of life of a great Virginia planter family is found in the journal and letters of Philip Vickers Fithian,[1] who in 1773 went to northern Virginia as a tutor in the family of "Councillor" Robert Carter, son of the great "King" Carter. Fithian, a graduate of Princeton destined for the Presbyterian ministry, found in Virginia much that surprised him. His friends and relatives had told him "That Virginia is sickly —That the People there are profane, and exceeding wicked—That I shall read there no Calvinistic Books, nor hear any Presbyterian Sermons—That I must keep much Company, and therefore spend as much, very probably much more Money than my Salary. . . ." He found Virginia more agreeable than he had anticipated and became greatly attached to the Carters and they to him. On August 12, 1774, he wrote to his Princeton friend John Peck, who was to take his place as tutor, concerning some of the differences between New Jersey and Virginia:

You will be making ten thousand Comparisons. The face of the Country, The *Soil*, the *Buildings*, the *Slaves*, the *Tobacco*, the method of spending *Sunday* among Christians; *Ditto* among the Negroes; the three grand divisions of time at the Church on Sundays, Viz. before Service giving & receiving letters of busi-

[1] Of the two editions, the more useful is *Journal & Letters of Philip Vickers Fithian, 1773–1774: A Plantation Tutor in the Old Dominion* (Williamsburg, Va., 1943), ed. H. D. Farish. The Introduction discusses Fithian and the Carter family and "Virginia during the Golden Age." John Rogers Williams, who edited *Philip Vickers Fithian: Journal and Letters, 1764–1774* (Princeton, N. J., 1900), was much more interested in Princeton than in Virginia. My quotations are from Farish's edition, which includes Fithian's catalogue of Carter's large library.

ness, reading Advertisements, consulting about the price of Tobacco, Grain &c, & settling either the lineage, Age, or qualities of favourite Horses 2. In the Church at Service, prayrs read over in haste, a Sermon seldom under & never over twenty minutes, but always made up of sound morality, or deep studied Metaphysicks. 3. After Service is over three quarters of an hour spent in strolling round the Church among the Crowd, in which time you will be invited by several different Gentlemen home with them to dinner. The Balls, the Fish-Feasts, the Dancing-Schools, the Christnings, the Cock fights, the Horse-Races, the Chariots, the Ladies Masked, for it is a custom among the Westmorland Ladies whenever they go from home, to muffle up their heads, & Necks, leaving only a narrow passage for the Eyes, in Cotton or silk handkerchiefs; I was in distress for them when I first came into the Colony, for every Woman that I saw abroad, I looked upon as ill either with the *Mumps* or Tooth-Ach!

Fithian, who came from a region of small farmers, was amazed at the wealth of some of the great Virginia planters. Robert Carter owned a number of plantations and at one time had five hundred slaves. He was, as Fithian learned, a very busy man, well read, and an accomplished musician. Fithian was particularly attracted to Mrs. Carter, who was a beautiful and cultivated woman. She was better read, her husband said, than the parson, and she astonished Fithian by her knowledge of governmental affairs. She surprised him, too, by what she said to him about slavery:

After Supper I had a long conversation with Mrs. Carter concerning Negroes in Virginia, & find that She esteems their value at no higher rate than I do. We both concluded, (& I am pretty certain that the conclusion is just) that if in Mr Carters, or in any Gentlemans Estate, all the Negroes should be sold, & the Money put to Interest in safe hands, & let the Lands which these Negroes now work lie wholly uncultivated, the bare Interest of the Price of the Negroes would be a much greater yearly income than what is now received from their working the Lands, making no allowance at all for the trouble & Risk of the Masters as to the Crops, & Negroes.

One reason why antislavery sentiment among Virginia planters in this period was so common is that many of them saw that the institution was no longer profitable. Slave labor was as a rule inefficient, and the Tidewater lands had deteriorated under a wasteful system of farming.

The Southern planters had more than one inducement to listen to Patrick Henry's stirring speeches. The balance of trade was running against the Southern colonies, and their bullion was going to London so rapidly that public credit seemed in danger. The land-hungry planters, now that the best lands east of the mountains had been taken up, were irritated by the British Proclamation of 1763, which forbade the taking up of land west of the Alleghenies. Still another circumstance that made them willing listeners to the call of the Revolution was their long-standing debts to British merchants. In many cases these debts had been inherited by the planters from their fathers and grandfathers until they felt enslaved to their British creditors. A century earlier in A *Discourse and View of Virginia* (London, 1663) Governor Berkeley had expressed his resentment that "forty thousand of these people [Virginia farmers] should be impoverish'd to enrich little more then forty Merchants, who being the only buyers of our *Tobacco*, give us what they please for it, and after it is here [in England], sell it how they please; and indeed have forty thousand servants in us at cheaper rates, then any other men have slaves. . . ." The size of these debts was enormous. In 1791 the British merchants submitted to their government claims in the Southern states totaling, with accumulated interest, £4,137,944, of which amount Virginians alone owed £2,305,408. To some debt-enslaved farmers a successful revolution may have seemed the only way out of their difficulties.

The American quarrel with the British ministry, however, was by no means merely a dispute over economic difficulties. The more intelligent Revolutionists were consciously contending for principles of British liberty more cherished in the reign of William and Mary, or of Victoria, than in that of George III. Until the last, some Americans hoped for the active support of British liberals. Richard Henry Lee in Virginia wrote to Samuel Adams in Massachusetts, April 24, 1774: "The truth is Sir, that we have only to be cool, firm, and united, to secure as well ourselves, as our fellow Subjects beyond the Water, from a Systematic plan of despotism, that has already fallen with a heavy hand on every part of the Empire." Lee failed to realize that the English governing classes, wealthy merchants and landowners—whether they happened to be Whigs or Tories—thoroughly approved the policies of the king's ministers.

The planters had learned from their fathers and grandfathers how to resist the encroachments of royal governors. As vestrymen in Anglican churches, they had fought for, and exercised, the right to elect their own ministers. They had read Locke and Montesquieu, and they were familiar with British law as well as their own colonial charters. They were for the most part loyal adherents to the Church of England, but they now made common cause with New England dissenters. They were also slaveholders, and Edmund Burke in his speech, "On Conciliation with America"—often to be quoted by Southern defenders of slavery in the nineteenth century—emphasized the effect of slavery on the masters:

There is, however, a circumstance attending these [Southern] colonies, which, in my opinion . . . makes the spirit of liberty still more high and haughty than in those to the northward. It is that in Virginia and the Carolinas they have a vast multitude of slaves. Where this is the case in any part of the world, those who are free, are by far the most proud and jealous of their freedom. Freedom is to them not only an enjoyment, but a kind of rank and privilege. Not seeing there that freedom, as in countries where it is a common blessing, and as broad and general as the air, may be united with much abject toil, with great misery, with all the exterior of servitude, liberty looks, amongst them, like something that is more noble and liberal. I do not mean, Sir, to commend the superior morality of this sentiment, which has at least as much pride as virtue in it; but I cannot alter the nature of man. The fact is so; and these people of the southern colonies are much more strongly, and with a higher and more stubborn spirit, attached to liberty than those to the northward. Such were all the ancient commonwealths; such were our Gothic ancestors; such, in our days, were the Poles, and such will be all masters of slaves who are not slaves themselves. In such a people the haughtiness of domination combines with the spirit of freedom, fortifies it, and renders it invincible.

2
Education

APART FROM William and Mary College, the Southern colonies had as yet no notable institution of learning, but this lack did not prevent the well-to-do planter from educating his sons. These young men were tutored at home or sent to an academy, and some of them went to Europe for education and travel. Charles Carroll attended a Catholic college in France. The Low-Country planters of South Carolina sent their sons in large numbers to the Inns of Court in London. James Madison went to Princeton, but it was not until after the Revolution that Southern students went in considerable numbers to Northern colleges. A few Virginians, notably Richard Henry Lee and Robert Munford, attended the excellent Wakefield School at Leeds in Yorkshire; but the great majority of Virginians went to William and Mary. Gaillard Hunt has noted that the little college counted among its alumni six of the eleven members of the 1773 Committee of Safety, eleven of the thirty-two men who drew up the Declaration of Rights, and four of the seven Virginians who signed the Declaration of Independence.

Too little is known of the William and Mary curriculum in the mid-eighteenth century. The college, however, was the earliest in America to establish a chair of modern languages when it engaged Charles Bellini in 1778. William and Mary had two great teachers in William Small and George Wythe, who was the first to hold a professorship of law in an American college. Wythe, a statesman in his own right, a classical scholar, and a gifted teacher, had a marked influence on Jefferson, Marshall, Clay, St. George Tucker, William Munford, and many others. As a place in which to study politics, the little college in Virginia had no superior in the American colonies.

3
Books and Reading

IT MAY SEEM strange that we know less about the reading of Virginia planters in this period than we know of what their predecessors read in the seventeenth century. The earlier period has been the happy hunting ground of antiquarians and genealogists, and many inventories of private libraries have been published. As one goes through the files of the Virginia historical magazines looking for materials, one finds less and less as he gets further away from the seventeenth century. With the exception of Douglas Freeman, the historians who have discussed the Revolutionary era have neglected the state of literary culture among even the great Virginians. The only significant figure whose reading has been carefully studied is Jefferson, and for this we are indebted chiefly to an American scholar born and educated in France, Professor Gilbert Chinard. For the other Southern states, we know even less than we know of Virginia.

In the Southern back country books were scarce. Jefferson and Madison were well supplied, but Patrick Henry and John Marshall had few. In the seaboard towns and on the larger Tidewater plantations, however, there was no scarcity of books. The Duc de la Rochefoucauld-Liancourt. who visited Virginia in 1796, found the common people perhaps more ignorant than elsewhere, but he added: "In spite of the Virginian love for dissipation, the taste for reading is commoner there among men of the first class than in any other part of America." Books in quantity were available at stores in Annapolis, Williamsburg, Charleston, and Savannah; and doubtless some planters ordered their books directly from England through their agents, as William Byrd had done half a century before.

One little-used source of information is the book advertisements in Colonial newspapers. These, unlike modern advertisements, are chiefly long lists of books recently imported from England and offered for sale at the printer's own bookstore. The advertisements do not of course tell us who bought the books, but they do indicate what the book merchant thought he could sell. He was doubtless guided partly by the local demand and partly by literary fashion in London. The books advertised varied from colony to colony but not very widely in either North or South. The literary taste of eighteenth-century Americans was much the same as that of their English contemporaries. Time of course had to lapse before the latest London fashion made itself felt in the colonies, as in English and Scottish towns and country places at a distance from London. In the American back country at all times literary fashions lagged behind those of the seaboard towns. If, however, we may judge from the books advertised in Southern newspapers, the lag in literary taste in these towns was not so great as it was to be at the turn of the century. One further point should be kept in mind: in the eighteenth century books did not go out of fashion in a few months, as they do now. In the last quarter of the century it was still good form to read the classics of the age of Queen Anne as well as the novels of Fanny Burney and the works of Johnson and Goldsmith. Men still referred to "Mr. Addison" and "Mr. Pope" as though they were speaking of their own contemporaries.

William Rind, publisher of the *Maryland Gazette*, carried a good stock of standard books. Charleston was an excellent book market. The chief Charleston bookseller, Robert Wells, had what was probably one of the two or three best bookstores in America. Even during the British occupation of Charleston, the *Royal Gazette*, edited by Wells's son, advertised substantial lists of books. The *Virginia Gazette* advertised extensive lists of books, especially in the early seventies, and as late as August 24, 1775, it was printing over four columns of titles of books to be sold cheap for cash. Few books were advertised in the *North-Carolina Gazette*, but the *Georgia Gazette* carried fairly numerous lists of books for sale by James Johnston, its publisher. After the outbreak of war, however, new books were in most places no longer available in quantity until after 1783.[2]

In the eighteenth century there were some subscription libraries in

---

2 For extensive lists of books, see the *Maryland Gazette* for July 31, 1760; the *Virginia Gazette* for Nov. 29, 1770; July 18, 1771; Sept. 17, 1772; June 10, 1773 (over 400 titles); and Nov. 25, 1775; and the *Georgia Gazette* for April 14, May 26, and Nov. 10, 1763; March 15, 22, 29, June 21, Oct. 18, and Dec. 6, 1764; and May 2 and 16 and Sept. 12, 1765. For advertisements in the *Royal Gazette*, see the numbers for March 10, June 2, Nov. 3 and 17, Dec. 29, 1781 (Library of Congress). See also Frederick P. Bowes, *The Culture of Early Charleston* (1942), pp. 66–67 and chap. iv, "Books, Libraries, Publications."

Southern towns but no public libraries in the modern sense of the term. The best library in the South was the collection of the Charleston Library Society, founded in 1748 by a group of young men who wanted more books to read than individually they were able to buy. In 1778, when most of its books were destroyed by fire, the Society owned between five and six thousand volumes. We are fortunate enough to know what books the Society owned in the early seventies, for the Library of Congress possesses two rare pamphlets bound together, both printed by Robert Wells. One of these is *A Catalogue of Books, Belonging to the Incorporated Charlestown Library Society, with the Dates of the Editions* (Charleston, 1770). The other is a catalogue (1772) of the private library of John Mackenzie, which he had turned over to the Society "for the Use of the College when Erected." Mackenzie's library (most of the books were burned in 1778) was a notable one, particularly rich in English literary classics and standard works in French. In the collection of the Charleston Library Society its members had available nearly every English classic—whether drama, poetry, fiction, or essay—from Chaucer down to Sterne. It included a larger proportion of French books than one would have found in Virginia or Maryland, and it included many books which do not appear in the numerous newspaper advertisements of the time.

The literary taste of the eighteenth century differed widely from that of the seventeenth. There was still no scarcity of religious books, but these had come to form a distinctly smaller proportion of the total. History, biography, travel, law, political science, philosophy, natural science, and belles-lettres all bulk proportionately larger. The interest in the ancient classics continues, but there is evident an increasing tendency to read them in translation. There was a notable increase in books with a Deistic tinge.

Among the more widely read authors were Locke, Swift, Bolingbroke, and Hume. Somewhat less commonly found were the third Earl of Shaftesbury's *Characteristicks of Men, Manners, Opinions, Times* (1711) and Algernon Sidney's *Discourses concerning Government* (1698). The Southern planter's conception of government owed much to these writers— especially to Locke's *Two Treatises on Government* (1690)—and something also to the prose works of Milton, Montesquieu's *Spirit of the Laws*, and the various works of Voltaire. These books embodied the liberalism of the Revolution of 1688, and were more highly regarded in America than in mid-eighteenth-century England. The influence of Rousseau seems not to nave been important in this period.[3]

[3] Charles E. Merriam, *A History of American Political Theories* (1903), pp. 89–92. In the *Virginia Gazette's* five longest lists of books Rousseau appears only three times,

The familiar essay of the *Spectator* type had a wide and long-continued vogue in the South. In a single issue, July 31, 1760, William Rind's *Maryland Gazette* advertised bound volumes of no less than seven series of periodical essays: *Spectator, Tatler, Guardian, Rambler, World, Adventurer,* and *Connoisseur.* The Charleston Library Society had, besides five volumes of Addison, eight bound volumes of the *Spectator,* four of the *Tatler,* two of the *Guardian,* and fourteen of the *Craftsman.* It also had complete runs of the *British Magazine,* the *Critical Review,* the *London Magazine,* and the *Universal Magazine.*

Although Americans in this period wrote little fiction, particularly in the South, they were apparently as eager to read novels as were the English. The moral objection to novel-reading was less evident than in New England or even in the South of the early nineteenth century. The novels of Richardson, Fielding, and Smollett were offered for sale repeatedly, and by 1770 novels of sentiment and seduction by lesser writers were widely advertised. The reading of plays, apart from Shakespeare, would seem to have been more common in Maryland and South Carolina than elsewhere. On July 31, 1760, William Rind advertised in his *Maryland Gazette* "a Variety of single Plays, among which are, Cleone, Douglass, Agis, Cato, Fair Penitent, Earl of Essex, Provok'd Husband, Barbarossa, Foundling, Brothers, Philoclea, Tamerlane, King *Richard* III, *Mackbeth,* Love for Love, &c." The Charleston Library Society had the plays of Shakespeare (in two editions), Beaumont and Fletcher, Dryden, Wycherley, Farquhar, Mrs. Behn, Cibber, Lee —and Gay's *The Beggar's Opera.*

When we turn to literature in foreign tongues, we find of course the Greek and Latin classics, along with dictionaries and textbooks; but German, Spanish, and Italian books are very scantily represented. There can be no doubt, however, that French literature was widely read both in the original and in translation. This is what we should expect when we remember that in eighteenth-century England every cultivated person was expected to read, and often to speak, French. In spite of the frequent wars between the two countries, Anglo-French cultural relations were fairly close until the outbreak of the French Revolution. In this country the alliance with France and the presence in America of cultivated French officers and travelers deepened the interest in all things French. Interest in

with "Rousseau's Eloisa" (twice) and "Rousseau's Works. 5 Vols." (once). *Emile* is listed twice in the *Georgia Gazette.* The Charleston Library Society had "Rousseau's New Eloisa" (London, 1761) in 4 vols. The *Royal Gazette* of Charleston advertised in 1781 "Oeuvres de Rousseau, 13 Tom." The *Social Contract* appears as a separate title only in the Mackenzie collection along with *Eloise* and *Emile,* all in translation.

French literature was perhaps keenest in Charleston but hardly less so in Virginia if one may judge from the advertisements in the *Virginia Gazette*. As late as 1797, when the excesses of the French Revolution had alienated many Americans, Washington wrote to his adopted son, George Washington Parke Custis, then a student at Princeton: "And the French language is now so universal, and so necessary with foreigners, or in a foreign country, that I think you would be injudicious not to make yourself master of it."

By far the most widely advertised French writer was Voltaire, who admired the English and had lived in England.[4] His three most advertised books were his life of Charles XII of Sweden, his book on England, and *The Age of Louis XIV*; but many other titles are found, usually in translation. *Candide* (1758), strangely enough, I have noted as a separate title only once—in the *Georgia Gazette* for May 26, 1763. The Colonial newspapers often advertised his works in English in thirty-five volumes or twenty-six in French. The first of Voltaire's works to be published in America was Beccaria's *An Essay on Crimes and Punishment*, with a Commentary by Voltaire, published by David Bruce in Charleston in 1777.

As one glances today at the names and titles of once-famous writers and books, it is not easy without an effort of the imagination to understand the eagerness with which intellectually keen Americans read them two centuries ago. But these books were to them as full of interest and new ideas as in the 1920's and 1930's young men and women found the new books by Beard, Parrington, Veblen, Bernard Shaw, and Oswald Spengler. The half-forgotten books that I have listed gave Jefferson, Richard Henry Lee, and the Rutledges of South Carolina, so to speak, the eyes through which they viewed the great political, economic, and cultural changes of their time. Without Locke, Sidney, Milton, Montesquieu, Voltaire—and perhaps I should add Cicero, Demosthenes, Livy, and Herodotus—it is conceivable that there might have been no Virginia Bill of Rights and no Declaration of Independence—at least in the form we have them. The books which nourished the founding fathers were, I dare say, more substantial fare than those on which most of our contemporary Washington legislators and bureaucrats have been fed.

[4] Mary-Margaret Barr's *Voltaire in America, 1744–1800* (1941) takes no account of Southern newspapers and libraries. An excellent study which does is Paul M. Spurlin's *Montesquieu in America, 1760–1801* (1940).

4
Political Writings

THE POLITICAL WRITINGS of Americans in this period are worthy of men brought up on Cicero, Montesquieu, and Locke. They bear comparison with the best that has come out of the mother country with the one exception of the speeches of the incomparable Edmund Burke. In belles-lettres, however, what survives is in general derivative. Although it is often competent writing in its kind, it is seldom the memorable expression of deep feeling or profound conviction. The most important literary figure of the period is Philip Freneau, who, although not a native, had a long and intimate connection with the South which served to make him more of a national poet than otherwise he would have been. There was as yet no place in America for the professional man of letters, as Freneau discovered to his sorrow. The nearest approach to a Southern man of letters was Robert Munford or St. George Tucker, but Williamsburg was too small to serve as a literary capital and Munford lived on a remote plantation. Charleston was an important theatrical center, but the merchants and planters who dominated the society of the little city were content with what they could import from overseas. There, as in other towns, cultivated Americans read English and French novels and plays, but it rarely occurred to them to write. Not until after the Revolution did it seem the duty of the cultivated classes to contribute to the much-desired "American" literature which the new nation felt it must have and speedily.

The Revolution set back the time when America would have a place for the professional writer. The man of letters flourishes in times of peace. A warlike age, as Abraham Cowley once said, may be good to write of but not to write in. The war interfered with education; it almost stopped the importation of books; it destroyed schools, libraries, and printing presses; and it impoverished many people. The Tories who were forced to leave the colonies came largely from the cultivated classes, the very classes that constitute the best patrons of literature and which most frequently supply the writers.

In all America there was, with the possible exception of Franklin, hardly a single publisher in the modern meaning of the word; but there were many printers whose primary task was to bring out pamphlets and newspapers. The newspapers of the period were not the "petty, dingy, languid, inadequate affairs" that Moses Coit Tyler considered them. One useful function which they performed was the publishing or reprinting of political essays, which were seldom the work of the editor. It has been estimated that in 1763 there were in the colonies twenty-one newspapers; in 1775 there were forty-two. Of the forty-two, fifteen were in New England, thirteen in the middle colonies, and fourteen in the Southern. On an average there was a newspaper for each sixty or sixty-five thousand persons, which is almost the exact average in our own time. The newspapers of Georgia and North Carolina published little original literary material, but the amount which appeared in the *Gazettes* of Maryland, Virginia, and South Carolina was considerable. The literary significance of these newspapers after 1750 has not been studied by any investigator comparable to Elizabeth Christine Cook, whose excellent study stops in the middle of the century.

In the field of belles-lettres American literary taste was satisfied with what could be imported from England, but not so with writings on political subjects. The best American writing of the Revolutionary period is political literature for the reason that English writers of the mid-eighteenth century gave no adequate expression to American thought. The political controversy—for every war is fought with pen as well as with gunpowder—called forth notable speeches, pamphlets, and official documents.

Political literature—one of the few genres in which American writing is not inferior to the English—occupies a somewhat uncertain place in our literary histories and our college curricula. Until recently it was regarded as comparatively unimportant; but nowadays with the rapid growth of courses in the history of American civilization its literary importance is perhaps in danger of being overstressed. Writing on political subjects, it would seem, if it is to endure, must possess substance, form, and beauty or, if it lacks the graces of style, be the forceful expression of important ideas. In the Revolutionary years American political writing reached a peak rarely since attained except in the best speeches and letters of Abraham Lincoln. In general the writings of our Revolutionary statesmen are worthy of the notable tribute which the elder William Pitt paid to the state papers of the First Continental Congress:

When your lordships look at the papers transmitted us from America, when you consider their decency, firmness, and wisdom, you cannot but respect their cause, and wish to make it your own. For myself, I must declare and avow that in all my reading of history and observation—and it has been my favorite study —I have read Thucydides, and have studied and admired the master-states of the world—that for solidity of reasoning, force of sagacity, and wisdom of conclusion under such a complication of difficult circumstances, no nation or body of men can stand in preference to the General Congress at Philadelphia. I trust it is obvious to your lordships that all attempts to impose servitude upon such men, to establish despotism over such a mighty continental nation, must be vain, must be fatal.

A British student of Anglo-American literary relations, the late George Stuart Gordon, wrote: "I am inclined to believe that the most magnificent irruption of the American genius into print is the literature of the American Revolution." He continued: "Nothing, indeed, that America has since done in literature, can equal that astonishing display of force. For the first, and almost the only time in the history of America all the powers of the American mind—legal, commercial, literary, political, oratorical—were directed to one end: the protection of national rights, and the expression of an ideal."

The political pamphlet had been a powerful weapon since the Martin Marprelate controversy in Queen Elizabeth's time. In the seventeenth century it had been a means of effective propaganda in the hands of the Puritans, and in Milton's *Areopagitica* it was the form taken by a literary classic. In the eighteenth century the satires of Swift, the dread of his Whig opponents, often appeared as pamphlets. In the Southern states the pamphlet was to be a favorite medium with political writers up to the time of the Civil War. In the eighteenth century the pamphlet was by no means the antiquated literary form which it seems now. It was an effective means of appealing to educated and influential men. Whether published separately or reprinted in the newspapers, pamphlets attracted the attention of leaders everywhere in the colonies and helped to provide a common basis in thought for political action. These pamphlets were usually forensic in form. They were formal arguments written in elevated language and addressed to men of intelligence. The more journalistic pamphlets of Thomas Paine were addressed to a wider audience and were tremendously effective. The South had no such pamphleteer as Paine.

The Revolutionary pamphlets tend to fall into two groups. The first were occasioned by the Stamp Act of 1765, and among the chief pamphleteers were John Dickinson, Richard Bland, and Daniel Dulany. The second group were occasioned by the closing of the port of Boston and the sequence of events that led to Lexington and Concord. A new group of pamphleteers which included Jefferson and Hamilton now contended that Parliament had no authority whatever over the colonies and that the king was the single link between them and Great Britain. Basing their case heavily on the doctrine of natural rights, the later pamphleteers prepared the way for the Declaration of Independence.

In the century of great letter-writers the colonies produced no writer comparable to Gray or Cowper or Horace Walpole, but the letters of Abigail

Adams and the letters which make up Jefferson's correspondence with her husband are not without the qualities which make for literary permanence. The letters of the statesmen, often only semiprivate, belong mainly to our political literature. This is especially true of the intercolonial correspondence of the Lees and the Adamses and of the rich materials gathered in Edmund C. Burnett's *Letters of the Members of the Continental Congress* (1921–1936). The letters of Jefferson and Hamilton, by which they kept in touch with party leaders in various parts of the country, must have been read by many others besides the recipients. Gamaliel Bradford recognized the literary value of such materials when he wrote to V. F. Calverton, May 14, 1931: "It has always seemed to me that here lies the real American literature, in the letters, diaries, personal narratives, which record the real experience of the race from the beginning. This stream widens and deepens with growing power and significance, so that the great American literature of the eighteenth century is the correspondence of Washington, Franklin, the Adamses, and a dozen others."

MARYLAND

5
Daniel Dulany

THE THREE POLITICAL writers to be discussed here—Daniel Dulany, Charles Carroll, and Jonathan Boucher—represent three widely different attitudes toward the Revolutionary cause. The oldest of the three, Daniel Dulany (1722–1797), brother-in-law of Dr. Alexander Hamilton, was the foremost of Maryland lawyers. He had been educated at Eton and at Clare College, Cambridge. He was Secretary of the province from 1761 to 1774. In October, 1765, he published in pamphlet form one of the ablest statements of the American position on the Stamp Act: *Considerations on the Propriety of Imposing Taxes in the British Colonies, for the Purpose of Raising a Revenue, by Act of Parliament.* The Maryland legislative houses had declared the Stamp Act illegal, and Dulany's pamphlet was an able statement of the political philosophy which had led to that action.

Dulany began by attacking the preamble to the Stamp Act: ". . . but what right had the commons of *Great Britain* to be thus munificent at the expence of the commons of America?—to give property, not belonging to the giver, and without the consent of the owner, is such evident and flagrant

injustice, in *ordinary cases*, that few are hardy enough to avow it. . . ."
The whole question of whether the imposition of stamp duties is "a *proper*
exercise of constitutional authority, or not, depends upon the single question, Whether the commons of *Great Britain* are *virtually* the representatives of the commons of *America*, or not?"

The right of exemption from all taxes *without their consent*, the colonies claim
as *British* subjects. They derive this right from the common law, which their
charters have declared and confirmed, and they conceive that when stripped
of this right, whether by prerogative or by any other power, they are at the same
time deprived of every privilege distinguishing free-men from slaves.

Dulany, arguing like the able constitutional lawyer that he was, effectually
refuted the claims of the advocates of the Stamp Act that Americans were
"virtually" represented in the British Parliament. English nonvoters, he admitted, were perhaps "virtually" represented, for they might ultimately become voters and their interests were the same as those of Englishmen who
were permitted to vote. Besides, if Parliament did not tax British nonvoters,
they would not be taxed at all whereas the colonists had their own taxing
bodies. The only way in which an American could become a voter in a
Parliamentary election was by going to England and ceasing to be an
American. Here is Dulany's summary of his whole argument:

If the commons of *Great Britain* have no right by the constitution to GIVE AND
GRANT property *not* belonging to themselves but to others, without their consent actually or virtually given; if the claim of the colonies, not to be taxed *without their consent*, signified by their representatives, is well founded; if it appears that the colonies are not actually represented by the commons of *Great
Britain*, and that the notion of a double or virtual representation, doth not with
any propriety apply to the people of *America*; then the principle of the *stamp
act* must be given up as indefensible on the point of representation, and the
validity of it, rested upon the *power* which they who framed it have to carry it
into execution.

Dulany vigorously attacked the British claim that if Parliament had no
authority to tax the colonies, then "the subordination and dependence of
the colonies, and the superintendence of the *British* parliament, can't be
consistently establish'd"; but he drew back from the obvious next step
which Jefferson and Henry found logical and necessary. Dulany, like John
Dickinson and John Joachim Zubly, was no real Revolutionist. He wrote:
"I would be understood: I am upon a question of *propriety*, not of power;
and, tho' some may be inclined to think it is to little purpose to discuss the
one, when the other is irresistible, yet are they different considerations;

and, at the same time that I invalidate the claim upon which it is founded, I may very consistently recommend a submission to the law, whilst it endures."

Having set forth his position, Dulany consistently held to it throughout the Revolution. Events moved too rapidly for him. He was denounced as a Tory, his estate was confiscated, and he was forced into seclusion.

6
Charles Carroll of Carrollton

In 1773 Dulany met his match in the youthful Charles Carroll of Carrollton (1737–1832), who was destined to outlive all the other Signers of the Declaration of Independence. In 1826 the British actor William C. Macready described Carroll at the age of eighty-nine as "retaining all the vivacity and grace of youth with the polish of one educated in the school of Chesterfield. In my life's experience," said he, "I have never met with a more finished gentleman. At his advanced age he kept up his acquaintance with the classics."

Carroll, educated at a Catholic college in Paris and at the Inner Temple in London, early espoused the patriot cause. On September 15, 1765, he wrote to Henry Graves: ". . . not all ye eloquence of Mansfield can persuade us that Englishmen by leaving their country to settle in these parts, thereby lose the privileges of Englishmen and the benefit of ye Common Law." Almost two years earlier, while still in Europe, Carroll had written to his father: "America is a growing country: in time [it] must and will be independent."

In 1773, while Jonathan Boucher was carrying on in the *Maryland Gazette* a controversy with William Paca and Samuel Chase, Daniel Dulany took the governor's side in a dispute over the latter's right to fix the fees of certain colonial officials—a right also claimed by the Maryland General Assembly. He published in the *Gazette* for January 7 of that year "A Dialogue between Two Citizens." His antipathy toward a certain type of Revolutionist appears in the comment of the Second Citizen, who is Dulany's mouthpiece: ". . . the blessings of Order, will still be preferred to the horrors of Anarchy; for to such must the principles of these men lead, who are fixed in their purpose, of opposing the Government at all adventures, and preposterously contend, that such a system is neither interest, nor faction, but genuine patriotism." On January 21 Dulany published "The Editor of the Dialogue," in which he undertook to mystify his readers as to the identity of the writer. In the same number "An Independent Free-man" protested that Dulany's sympathies all lay with his Second Citizen and that his First Citizen was a mere man of straw set up only to be borne down by the Tory arguments of his opponent.

Dulany had laid himself open to attack. Carroll saw his opportunity, and on February 4 he entered the controversy. Writing as First Citizen, he gave his own version of the original dialogue with telling effect. When Dulany, writing as "Antilon," asked who had assumed the title of First Citizen, Carroll replied: "A man, 'Antilon,' of independent fortune, one deeply interested in the prosperity of his country, a friend of liberty, a settled enemy to lawless prerogative." For the modern reader, both controversialists indulged too much in personalities, invective, and the pedantry of legal erudition. But in the eyes of many Marylanders Carroll had vindicated the cause of the patriots.

7

Jonathan Boucher

With one striking exception, the ablest of the Tory writers belonged to the Northern colonies. That exception was the redoubtable Anglican clergyman, Jonathan Boucher (1738–1804), grandfather of the English poet Frederick Locker-Lampson. The son of a village schoolmaster in county Cumberland, Boucher came to northern Virginia in 1759 as tutor to the sons of a planter. Ordained in 1762, he preached at various churches in Virginia and Maryland until September, 1775, when he returned to England. In The Reminiscences of an American Loyalist, not published until 1925, he quoted a characterization of himself given by the woman who later married him:

In person, inelegant and clumsy, yet not rough and disgusting; of a dark complexion, and with large but not forbidding features. Of a thoughtful yet cheerful aspect; with a penetrating eye, and a turn of countenance that invites confidence and begets affection. Manners—often awkward, yet always interesting; perfectly untaught and unformed, conformable to no rules, yet never unpolite; incapable of making a bow like a gentleman, yet far more incapable of thinking, speaking, or acting in a manner unbecoming a gentleman. Never knew a person of so low an origin and breeding with so high and improved a mind; a thorough gentleman as to internals and essentials, tho' often lamentably deficient in outward forms.

Boucher was an active and an able man, and he rose to prominence more rapidly than he could possibly have risen in England. "Determined always to raise myself in the world," he wrote, "I had not patience to wait for the slow savings of a humble station; and I fancied I could get into a higher, only by being taken notice of by people of condition. . . ." In addition to his preaching, he conducted a boarding school for boys, one of whom was Jacky Custis, the son of Martha Washington. Eventually Boucher, like nearly every other Southerner who prospered, acquired a plantation. In spite of abolitionist sympathies, he held slaves. In 1770 he became Rector of St. Anne's in Annapolis. He thus describes the important role which he played in the capital:

I was in fact the most efficient person in the administration of Government, though I neither had a post nor any prospect of ever having one. The management of the Assembly was left very much to me; and hardly a Bill was brought in which I did not either draw or at least revise, and either got it passed or rejected. . . . All the Governor's speeches, messages, etc., and also some pretty important and lengthy papers from the Council were of my drawing up. All these things were, if not certainly known, yet strongly suspected; and of course, though I really had no views nor wishes but such as I believed to be for the true interest of the country, all the forward and noisy patriots, both in the Assembly and out of it, agreed to consider me as an obnoxious person.

Boucher at first opposed the Stamp Act, but he quickly discovered that he had taken the wrong side and lined himself up with the conservatives. The self-made man, once he finds himself admitted to the class possessing privilege and power, is likely to prove a more uncompromising conservative than one to the manner born. "In America," says Boucher, "much execution was done by sermons." In spite of warnings and threats, he preached the most uncompromising Tory doctrine. "And for more than six months," he remembered, "I preached, when I did preach, with a pair of loaded pistols lying on the cushion; having given notice that if any man, or body of men, could possibly be so lost to all sense of decency and propriety as to attempt really to do what had long been threatened, that is, to drag me out of my own pulpit, I should think myself justified before God and man in repelling violence by violence." The patriots, however, were too strong for him. Militiamen finally took him from his church and escorted him to his home, and they played the Rogues' March as they went. Undaunted, Boucher preached again, but finally gave up and returned to England. There years afterwards he received some compensation for his confiscated American property.

In 1797, while Vicar of Epsom in Surrey, Boucher published thirteen of his Maryland sermons with a long Preface in a volume which he entitled *A View of the Causes and Consequences of the American Revolution*. Disturbed over the recent revolution in France, which he regarded as "one of the dreadful effects of the American revolt," he hoped that Englishmen and Americans would now listen to warnings which had gone unheeded in the 1770's. He dedicated the book to George Washington, whom he had known in this country and whose Farewell Address he had apparently read, saying: "I do not address myself to the General of a Conventional Army; but to the late dignified President of the United States, the friend of rational and sober freedom."

The published sermons (Boucher states that they are printed in much the same form as that in which they were delivered) show more power than his later writings. If he had been less uncompromising, Boucher might have made converts to his doctrine. "True liberty" he defined as "a liberty to do every thing that is right, and the being restrained from doing any thing that is wrong." "The word *liberty*, as meaning civil liberty," he said, "does not, I believe, occur in all the Scriptures." From the Bible he drew something very like James I's view of the divine right of kings. "The first father was the first king: and if . . . the law may be inferred from the practice, it was thus that all government originated; and monarchy is it's most ancient form." In a sermon "On Civil Liberty, Passive Obedience, and Non-Resistance," preached in Maryland in 1775, Boucher attacked the growing doctrine "that the whole human race is born equal; and that no man is naturally inferior, or, in any respect, subjected to another; and that he can be made subject to another only by his own consent":

The position is . . . ill-founded and false both in it's premises and conclusions. In hardly any sense that can be imagined is the position strictly true; but, as applied to the case under consideration, it is demonstrably not true. Man differs from man in every thing that can be supposed to lead to supremacy and subjection, *as one star differs from another star in glory*. It was the purpose of the Creator, that man should be social: but, without government, there can be no society; nor, without some relative inferiority and superiority, can there be any government. . . . On the principle of equality, neither his parents, nor even the vote of a majority of the society, (however virtuously and honourably that vote might be obtained,) can have such authority over any man.

That was Tory doctrine in 1775. Seventy years later, strange as it may seem, something very like it might be found in many of the speeches and pamphlets in which Southerners—and others—defended the institution of slavery.

VIRGINIA

In the Revolution the role of Virginia was a dominant one. The oldest and still the most populous of the colonies, it was also the largest in the territory under its control. Virginia, now at the climax of its remarkable development, sent many able men to the General Assembly, the Continental Congress, and the Constitutional Convention. History has made so much of Washington, Henry, Jefferson, and Madison that we have well-nigh forgotten the Lees, Mason, Bland, Wythe, the Randolphs, Pendleton, and a dozen others who in another age or region would have ranked with the best. The society which produced these men perhaps found in them its chief justification. The entire group should be studied as a whole and proper attention paid to their education, their reading, the development of their thought, their way of life, and their relation to the society in which they grew up. With the exception of Washington, these men were statesmen rather than soldiers; and for them the art of writing was a valuable accomplishment. They left behind some important official documents, pamphlets, letters, and at least some traces of great speeches.

8
George Mason

George Mason (1725–1792), who drafted the Virginia Declaration of Rights and the major portion of the state's first constitution, belonged to one of the most distinguished planter families of the Northern Neck. He was educated entirely by relatives and tutors. When he was ten, his father died; and Mason was brought up by his uncle and guardian, John Mercer of "Marlborough." Most of Mason's early reading was done in Mercer's library, which is said to have contained fifteen hundred volumes, a third of them on law. A partial list of Mercer's books, advertised for sale in Purdie and Dixon's Virginia Gazette for August 29, 1771, shows that the library was also rich in history, biography, books of a practical nature, and literature.[5] Although Mason was no lawyer, the proprietor of "Gunston

---

[5] Among the titles listed are *Paradise Lost, Paradise Regained,* and "Milton's Works. His Letters, &c. while minister, &c. in Prose. 2 Vols." One wonders what the Virginia Declaration of Rights may have owed to the *Areopagitica, Of Tenure of Kings and Magistrates,* and the *Defence of the English People.* A few other titles are "Select Plays. 16 Vols.," "Hume's Essays," "Dunciad," the *London Magazine,* 1732–1766, and 42 volumes of the *Universal Magazine.*

Hall" knew the principles of law and government better than most other members of the General Assembly. He managed efficiently his own plantation, which was practically a self-sufficient unit. He was modest and unambitious, and he consistently refused to become a candidate for Congress. As fully as any of his contemporaries except Jefferson, he represented the liberal spirit of the Age of Enlightenment and the rule of Reason. He favored on principle the disestablishment of the Anglican Church, and he was outspoken in his denunciation of slavery and the slave trade. The Virginia constitution of 1776, for which Mason was in large part responsible (Jefferson wrote the preamble), is one of the earliest and best examples of the written constitution. Mason also wrote the Virginia Declaration of Rights, which was clearly in the back of Jefferson's mind when he composed the Declaration of Independence. Here is a portion of it:

I. That all men are by nature equally free and independent, and have certain inherent rights, of which, when they enter into a state of society, they cannot, by any compact, deprive or divest their posterity; namely, the enjoyment of life and liberty, with the means of acquiring and possessing property, and pursuing and obtaining happiness and safety.

II. That all power is vested in, and consequently derived from the people; that Magistrates are their trustees and servants, and at all times amenable to them.

III. That government is or ought to be, instituted for the common benefit, protection, and security of the people, nation, or community; of all the various modes and forms of government, that is best, which is capable of producing the greatest degree of happiness and safety, and is most effectually secured against the danger of mal-administration; and that when any government shall be found inadequate or contrary to these purposes, a majority of the community hath an indubitable, unalienable, and indefeasible right, to reform, alter, or abolish it, in such a manner as shall be judged most conducive to the public weal.

Mason was a member of the Federal Constitutional Convention, but he refused to sign the Constitution, and in the Virginia Constitutional Convention he opposed ratification. He embodied his objections in a pamphlet, *The Objections of the Hon. George Mason, to the Proposed Foederal Constitution. Addressed to the Citizens of Virginia* (1788). His first and strongest objection was: "There is no declaration of rights. . . ." It was partly on Virginia's insistence that a bill of rights was embodied in the first ten amendments to the Federal Constitution. Mason objected to the Constitution also because it incorporated a compromise between New England and the lower South in its treatment of slavery and the tariff. Like Patrick Henry, he was afraid the Northern states would dominate the new nation. He prophesied: "By requiring only a majority to make all commercial and navigation laws, the five southern states (whose produce and circumstances are totally different from those of the eight northern and eastern states) will be ruined. . . ." In 1832 the South Carolina Nullifiers believed that Mason's predictions were being rapidly fulfilled.

9
Richard Henry Lee

WHEN THOMAS and Hannah (Ludwell) Lee died in 1750, they left behind them six sons, four of whom were to play no minor roles in the drama of the Revolution. Francis Lightfoot and Richard Henry both signed the Declaration of Independence, and William and Arthur served the patriot cause as colonial agents in England. The two to be discussed here are Richard Henry Lee (1732–1794) and Arthur Lee (1740–1792). The complementary roles they played are suggested by an unusual coincidence. In the spring of 1775 the lord mayor and the London aldermen— William Lee was one of these—presented to King and Parliament a remonstrance against the government's American policy. Not until after the Revolution did Richard Henry Lee, who had written the letter of thanks sent by the Continental Congress, discover that his brother Arthur had written the remonstrance.

In the little brick schoolhouse at "Stratford" the Lee brothers were taught in somewhat Spartan fashion by an able Scotch clergyman named Craig, who was treated like a member of the family. Afterwards Richard Henry Lee spent seven years at the Wakefield Academy at Leeds in Yorkshire, then presided over by the Reverend Benjamin Wilson. Robert Munford and Theodorick Bland, Jr., attended the same school. An advertisement in Rind's *Virginia Gazette* for November 23, 1769, describes the curriculum:

At the ACADEMY in *Leeds*, which is pleasantly situated in the county of *York*, in *England*, young Gentlemen are genteely boarded, and diligently instructed in English, the classics, modern languages, penmanship, arithmetick, merchants accounts, mathematics, modern geography, experimental philosophy, and astronomy, for Twenty Guineas *per annum*, if under twelve years of age, by Mr. *Aaron Grimshaw*, and able masters.

Drawing, music, and dancing, are extra charges. Due regard is paid to the Young Gentlemens health, morals, and behaviour.

In 1750 Lee and two older brothers, who were studying law in London, were called home by the deaths of their father and mother. He now devoted himself systematically to preparing himself for public life. Although he did not intend to become a lawyer, he studied law, political science, and history and made himself an expert on the British constitution. The writer who influenced him most was John Locke, but he studied also those other writers who had interpreted the political philosophy of the Revolution of 1688: Montesquieu, Grotius, Pufendorf, Cudworth, and others. We may be sure that he would have cared little for the books sanctioning the divine right of kings which were conspicuous in the library (burned in 1729) of his grandfather, the second Richard Lee. He was also a student of English literature (stressed at the Wakefield Academy), a subject which he rightly thought not sufficiently emphasized in the schools of his time. His favorite poets were Vergil, Milton, and, above all, Shakespeare.

Lee worked long and arduously to make himself an effective speaker. As an orator, he was excelled in Virginia only by Patrick Henry, who could not rival Lee's melodious voice, polished diction, or graceful gestures. In the Continental Congress Lee's hearers were struck by the fact that he kept his left hand wrapped in a black silk handkerchief, for through an accident he had lost all the fingers of that hand. Unfortunately, none of his speeches are extant. St. George Tucker, who heard both men at their best, missed in Henry "all the advantages of voice, which delighted me so much in the speeches of Mr. Lee—the fine polish of language which that gentleman united with that harmonious voice, so as to make me sometimes fancy that I was listening to some being inspired with more than mortal powers of embellishment—and all the advantages of gesture which the celebrated Demosthenes considered as the first, second, and third qualifications of an orator."

American political life would be immeasurably better off if we now had more men like Lee, who had prepared himself to be a statesman rather than a politician. It is not easy for a modern to understand how an aristocrat by birth and breeding—in apparent violation of the economic interpretation of history—could so continually take a liberal stand on so many public questions. As early as 1765 he wrote to Landon Carter that he hoped to see the "Demon Slavery" banished from America: "If I live to see that day, I shall be happy; and pleased to say with Sydney [Simeon], 'Lord now lettest thou thy servant depart in peace.'" [6] Still earlier, in 1759, he had pointed out the reason why some of the Northern colonies were surpassing the Old Dominion: ". . . with their whites they import arts and agriculture, whilst we, with our blacks, exclude both." Carter Braxton said of the New Englanders: "I hate their government—I hate their religion—I hate their levelling," but Lee was to say: "For my part, I must cease to live before

[6] *Letters*, ed. J. C. Ballagh, I, 11–12. For Simeon, see Luke 2:29.

I cease to love these proud Patriots with whom I early toiled in the vineyard of liberty." He once wrote to John Adams that he hoped eventually to live in Massachusetts: "The hasty, unpersevering genius of the south suits not my disposition, and it is inconsistent with my ideas of what must constitute social happiness and security."

Lee was in the House of Burgesses from 1758 to 1775. Apart from a speech on the slave trade, he took no very radical stand until the time of the Stamp Act crisis. He then vigorously supported Patrick Henry. He was active in carrying on correspondence with leaders in other colonies. He was in the Continental Congress from 1774 until 1780. John Adams thus summarizes one of Lee's speeches in Congress in 1774: "The rights [of the colonies] are built on a fourfold foundation; on nature, on the British constitution, on charters, and on immemorial usage. The Navigation Act, a capital violation." Lee served on important committees and drew up important documents. It was he that, at the behest of the Virginia Assembly, introduced in Congress the resolution—incorporated in the Declaration of Independence—"that these united colonies are and of right ought to be free and independent States." But for certain political jealousies, it seems, he would have been named as chairman of the committee which drew up the Declaration.

When ill health kept him out of public life, as it frequently did, Lee lived on his plantation at "Chantilly." As Colonel of the Westmoreland County militia, he fought in the battles of 1781 which ended in the capture of Yorktown. From 1784 to 1787 he was back in Congress, which elected him its president. He was a United States Senator from 1789 to 1792. He resigned after the first ten amendments (the Bill of Rights) had been added to the Constitution. He had declined an appointment to the Federal Constitutional Convention because he felt that his duties as Congressman would conflict with his duties as a member of the Convention.

He vigorously opposed the adoption of the Federal Constitution until it should include a bill of rights. Sick and unable to leave "Chantilly," he wrote letters to other leaders and published his views in two notable pamphlets which few modern students except Parrington appear to have read: *Observations Leading to a Fair Examination of the System of Government, Proposed by the Late Convention. . . . In a Number of Letters from the Federal Farmer to the Republican . . .* (1787) and *An Additional Number of Letters from the Federal Farmer to the Republican . . .* (1788).

Lee's analysis comes close to being a fair and dispassionate study of the new Constitution. He protests against the insistence of the proponents on precipitate haste in adopting it. "This subject of consolidating the states is new: and because forty or fifty men [who had been appointed to revise the old constitution, not to frame a new one] have agreed in a system, to suppose the good sense of this country, an enlightened nation, must adopt it without examination, and though in a state of profound peace, without endeavouring to amend those parts they perceive are defective, dangerous to freedom, and destructive of the valuable principles of republican government—is truly humiliating." Lee states his own position: "I wish the system adopted with a few alterations; but those, in my mind, are essential ones. . . ." He doubted the practicability "of consolidating the states, and at the same time of preserving the rights of the people at large. . . ." He disliked "that strong tendency to aristocracy now discernable in every part of the plan." "Every man of reflection must see, that the change now proposed, is a transfer of power from the many to the few. . . ." Lee's fundamental position was very much like that of Jefferson or Emerson: "The first maxim of a man who loves liberty should be never to grant to Rulers an atom of power that is not most clearly & indispensably necessary for the safety and well being of Society."

Even the House of Representatives seemed to him too little democratic, and he pointed out that the middle and lower classes would have little share in the levying of Federal taxes. Lee was no stranger to the economic interpretation of history, and he saw as clearly as Charles A. Beard the bias of the Federal Convention toward "aristocracy." "The few, the well born, &c. as Mr. Adams calls them, in judicial decisions as well as in legislation, are generally disposed, and very naturally too, to favour those of their own description." He placed his trust in the middle class. The following passage is as notable in its way as a similar one in Madison's tenth number of *The Federalist:*

One party is composed of little insurgents, men in debt, who want no law, and who want a share in the property of others; these are called levellers, Shayites, &c. The other party is composed of a few, but more dangerous men, with their servile dependents; these avariciously grasp at all power and property; you may discover in all the actions of these men, an evident dislike to free and equal government, and they will go systematically to work to change, essentially, the forms of government in this country; these are called aristocrats, m—ites, &c. &c. Between these two parties is the weight of the community; the men of middling property, men not in debt on the one hand, and men, on the other, content with republican governments, and not aiming at immense fortunes, offices and power.

In his second pamphlet Lee discussed these various classes in greater detail.

In a day when reaction had set in against Revolutionary democracy, Lee, like Jefferson and John Taylor, held fast to the earlier faith. To the argument that the Constitution should be forthwith adopted as it stood because it would be easy to amend it, Lee replied:

This is a pernicious idea, it argues a servility of character totally unfit for the support of free government; it is very repugnant to that perpetual jealousy respecting liberty, so absolutely necessary in all free states, spoken of by Mr. [John] Dickinson.—However, if our countrymen are so soon changed, and the language of 1774, is become odious to them, it will be in vain to use the language of freedom, or to attempt to rouse them to free inquiries: But I shall never believe this is the case with them, whatever present appearances may be, till I shall have very strong evidence of it.

10
Arthur Lee

ARTHUR LEE (1740–1792) championed the American cause as stoutly as his brother Richard Henry, but he was no more a democrat than Alexander Hamilton. Late in life he wrote: "The science of government is no trifling matter. It requires education and experience, it requires the habit of great worlds and great men, it requires the leisure which independent fortune gives and the elevation of mind which birth and rank impart. Without these you might as well attempt to make Sèvres china out of common earth as statesmen and politicians out of men bred and born in the sordid occurrences of common life."

At the age of eleven Arthur Lee was sent to Eton, where the students came predominantly from the English ruling class. After six years he returned to Virginia. Back in England in December, 1760, he met Samuel Johnson, whose advice he followed when he decided to study medicine at Edinburgh rather than at one of the English universities. After taking his M.D. degree in 1764, he spent a year in travel on the Continent. Although he disapproved of slavery in principle, he had in 1764 replied to Adam Smith's indictment of the American colonies in a pamphlet entitled *An Essay in Vindication of the Continental Colonies of America, from a Censure of Mr Adam Smith, in his Theory of Moral Sentiments* (London, 1764). Slavery seemed to Lee "absolutely repugnant to justice . . . highly inconsistent with civil policy," but he resented the charge that the slaves in Virginia were barbarously treated. "I have," he wrote, "travelled through most parts of Scotland and Ireland; and I can safely assert, that the habitations of the negroes are palaces, and their living luxurious; when compared with those of the peasants of either of these countries."

In 1766, after being elected a Fellow of the Royal Society, he returned to Virginia to practice medicine in Williamsburg, although he would have preferred to remain in England. He came to dislike his profession and in 1768 returned to London to study law at the Middle Temple. From 1770 to 1776 he practiced law in London. He wrote a series of political essays, "The Monitor," which his brother Richard Henry got published in Rind's *Virginia Gazette*. In general they resemble his friend John Dickinson's *Letters from a Farmer in Pennsylvania*, which includes a "Liberty Song," to which Lee had contributed a few lines. Some notion of Lee's argument appears in his summary: "I have proved, from the sentiments of the greatest men of all ages, and from histories of nations, how necessarily virtue, happiness and strength, attend a free government; and that weakness, vice, ignominy and wretchedness, are the unavoidable concomitants of [political] slavery." He strongly urged the need of a bill of rights. The high tone he adopted is suggested by the following passage:

Why, my friend, said a Gentleman the other day, do you employ your time in writing on Liberty, which may possibly bring you into some difficulties or danger; when you might use it so much more to your own emolument?—Because Liberty is the very idol of my soul, the parent of virtue, the nurse of heroes, the dispenser of general happiness; because slavery is the monstrous mother of every abominable vice, and every atrocious ill; because the liberties of my country are invaded, and in danger of destruction by the late acts of the *British* Parliament; because I would with joy be the sacrifice to the re-establishment of them, upon a sure and solid foundation.

Unlike most Southerners of later times, Lee was a cosmopolitan. While studying and practicing law in London, he greatly enjoyed music and the theater and the opportunity to mingle with cultivated men. He made many friends. Among these were John Wilkes and the Earl of Shelburne, a cabinet member who championed the American cause. Lovers of Boswell's *Johnson* will recall the dinner given by Dilly in 1776 at which Wilkes and the suspicious Johnson finally were brought together as a result of Boswell's scheming. Lee, whom the nearsighted Johnson did not recognize, was present. "Who is that gentleman, sir?" whispered Johnson to Dilly. "Mr. Arthur Lee" was the reply. "Too, too, too," muttered Johnson under his breath, for Lee was obnoxious to the author of *Taxation No Tyranny* both as a Whig and as an American.

In 1770 Lee became colonial agent for Massachusetts. Like his brother Richard Henry, he had a high regard for the Adamses of New England. Some of his writings in behalf of the Colonial cause appeared under the name "Junius Americanus," and he was at one time suspected of being the author of the famous "Junius" letters, now usually attributed to Sir Philip Francis. In trying to thwart the measures of the British ministry, Lee fully realized that the cause of American patriots was also that of British liberals. He urged English lovers of liberty to "cultivate the friendship of the Americans, who are pursuing the same sacred course of freedom. . . . The cause is common, let us be united in the attempt, the Liberties of both countries are embarked in the same bottom, the same storm that sinks the one, will overwhelm the other." Two of Lee's ablest pamphlet presentations of the American cause are *An Appeal to the Justice and Interests of the People of Great Britain* (1774) and *A Second Appeal . . .* (1775). These entitle Lee to something better than Moses Coit Tyler's impatient characterization of Lee as "a writer whose high literary reputation rests on no materials which can justify its revival at the hands of posterity."

In 1776 Lee was appointed, with Silas Deane and Benjamin Franklin, one of the commissioners to negotiate an alliance with France. The next year he was appointed commissioner to Spain. In the effort to negotiate a treaty with France, Lee's suspicious nature and high temper led him to distrust Franklin and to quarrel with Deane. This quarrel has tended to overshadow Lee's real services to the American cause.

Back in America in 1780, Lee served in the Virginia House of Delegates in 1781–1783 and 1785–1786, and in Congress in 1781–1784. He was one of the commissioners of the Treasury before Alexander Hamilton became Secretary in Washington's cabinet. He opposed ratification of the Federal Constitution, and he had gloomy forebodings about the future of the country. "Should I," he asked himself, "settle and remain among my friends in Virginia; should I retire to Kentucky; or return to England and enjoy in retirement there all that a country great in arts and sciences affords?" He had probably lived too long in Europe to be permanently happy in his own country. He finally settled on a plantation in Virginia and there, still a bachelor, he died at the age of fifty-two. John Adams, who had once complained that Lee's "prejudices and violent temper would raise quarrels in the Elysian fields, if not in heaven," wrote more judicially in 1819:

. . . Arthur Lee, a man of whom I cannot think without emotion; a man too early in the service of his country to avoid making a multiplicity of enemies; too honest, upright, faithful, and intrepid to be popular; too often obliged by his principles and feelings to oppose Machiavelian intrigues, to avoid the destiny he suffered. This man never had justice done him by his country in his lifetime, and I fear he never will have by posterity.

11
Patrick Henry

THE TURBULENT YEARS of the Revolutionary period brought opportunities which would not have come in times of peace. Had there been no Revolution, Patrick Henry (1736–1799), the back-country lawyer, would undoubtedly have risen to local prominence, but he could never have become what Byron in *The Age of Bronze* called him:

> the forest-born Demosthenes
> Whose thunder shook the Philip of the seas.

Hanover County, Virginia, in which Henry grew up—and in later years Henry Clay and Thomas Nelson Page—was in his youth a region of small farmers and dissenters. Hanover County was also for some years the home of Samuel Davies, whom Henry once declared the greatest orator he had ever heard. Henry's father, John Henry, who had come to Virginia from Aberdeen, Scotland, before 1730, was a first cousin of William Robertson, the Scottish historian. He was a man of some education and, according to Davies, more familiar with his Horace than with his Bible. He was county surveyor, presiding magistrate, and colonel in the Virginia militia. Patrick Henry's mother (born Sarah Winston) is described in William Byrd's "A Progress to the Mines" as "a person of a lively & cheerful Conversation, with much less of Reserve than most of her Countrywomen." She later became a Presbyterian and a member of Davies' church, but her husband and her famous son remained in the Established Church. Several of her relatives were effective speakers. In 1754 Patrick Henry married Sarah Shelton, a granddaughter of William Parks.

What education Patrick Henry got came chiefly from his father, under whose direction he read Vergil and Livy. He is described as fond of reading, but Sterne's *Tristram Shandy* is almost the only book he is known to have read in his youth. He was, however, well informed on many subjects and was by no means the ignorant natural prodigy that he seemed to Jefferson and William Wirt. After unsuccessful ventures in storekeeping and farming, he spent a month or two in the study of *Coke upon Littleton* and a digest of the Virginia Acts and then rode down to Williamsburg and applied for a license to practice law. The able lawyers who examined him found him deficient in knowledge of the law, but they were so impressed by his ability that they granted him the license. He enjoyed considerable success from the start. In a little over three years he had charged fees in no less than 1,185 suits—at the very time when, according to Wirt, he was unable to make a living by his new profession. In 1763 he made the first of his famous speeches at Hanover Court House in the Parsons' Cause, his father presiding.

When Henry took his seat in the House of Burgesses in the spring of 1765, he was almost unknown to the Tidewater planters who until that time had practically governed the colony. The Stamp Act was unpopular, but only a few—chiefly from the western counties—were inclined to resist. The young lawyer, now appearing in black suit and tie-wig, wrote out his famous resolutions on a blank leaf of an old copy of *Coke upon Littleton* and offered them to the astonished Burgesses. In these he maintained that the early settlers had brought to America all the rights of Englishmen; that these rights had been guaranteed by royal charters; and that the taxation of the people by their own representatives is the distinguishing characteristic of British liberty. The fifth of these resolutions—passed but later rescinded— read:

Resolved, therefore, That the General Assembly of this colony have the only and sole exclusive right and power to levy taxes and impositions upon the inhabitants of this colony, and that every attempt to vest such power in any person or persons whatsoever, other than the General Assembly aforesaid, has a manifest tendency to destroy British as well as American freedom.

In support of his resolutions Henry made one of the greatest speeches of his life. Thomas Jefferson, then a student in Williamsburg, heard the debate and in his old age wrote of Henry's oratorical powers: "They were great indeed; such as I have never heard from any other man. He appeared to me to speak as Homer wrote." Jefferson recalled that after the resolutions had been passed by a small majority, Attorney-General Peyton Randolph "came out at the door where I was standing, and said, as he entered the lobby: 'By God, I would have given 500 guineas for a single vote.'" Tradition has preserved little of Henry's speech except a single passage, which Wirt gives as follows:

It was in the midst of this magnificent debate, while he was descanting on the tyranny of the obnoxious act, that he exclaimed in a voice of thunder, and with the look of a god:—"Caesar had his Brutus—Charles the First, his Cromwell, and George the Third"—("Treason," cried the speaker—"Treason, treason!" echoed from every part of the house. It was one of those trying moments which is decisive of character. Henry faltered not for an instant; but rising to a loftier attitude, and fixing on the speaker an eye of the most determined fire, he finished his sentence with the firmest emphasis)—"*may profit by their example. If this be treason, make the most of it.*"

Wirt's version was approved by Jefferson and Judge John Tyler, who had both heard the speech. An earlier version, unknown to Henry's biographers and recorded in the journal of an unidentified French government agent, represents Henry as much more conciliatory in his manner:

Shortly after I Came in one of the members stood up and said he had read that in former times tarquin and Jul[i]us had their Brutus, Charles had his Cromwell, and he Did not Doubt but some good american would stand up, in favour of his Country, but (says he) in a more moderate manner, and was going to Continue, when the speaker of the house rose and Said, he, the last that stood up had spoke traison, and was sorey to see that not one of the members of the house was loyal Enough to stop him, before he had gone so far. upon which the Same member stood up again (his name is henery) and said that if he had afronted the speaker, or the house, he was ready to ask pardon, and he would shew his loyalty to his majesty King G. the third, at the Expence of the last Drop of his blood, but what he had said must be atributed to the Interest of his Countrys Dying liberty which he had at heart, and the heat of passion might have lead him to have said something more than he intended, but, again, if he said any thing wrong, he beged the speaker and the houses pardon. some other Members stood up and backed him, on which that afaire was droped.[7]

Henry's power over the Burgesses of the middle class is suggested by Judge Spencer Roane, whose father, a burgess from Essex County, "always came home in raptures with the man": "That a plain man, of ordinary though respected family, should beard the aristocracy by whom we were then cursed and ruled, and overthrow them in the cause of independence, was grateful to a man of my father's Whig principles. He considered Henry as the organ of the great body of the people; as the instrument by whom the big-wigs were to be thrown down, and liberty and independence established." It took something more than eloquence, however, to give Henry his position of leadership over such men as George Wythe, Richard Henry Lee, and George Mason, who wrote in 1774: "He is by far the most powerful speaker I ever heard. Every word he says not only engages, but commands the attention; and your passions are no longer your own when he addresses them. But his eloquence is the smallest part of his merit. He is in my opinion the first man upon this continent, as well in abilities as public virtues. . . ."

---

[7] "Journal of a French Traveller in the Colonies," *Am. Hist. Rev.*, XXVI, 745 (July, 1921).

In September, 1774, Henry took his seat as a member of the First Continental Congress. Here, too, he made a strong impression on all who heard him speak. The secretary, Charles Thomson, who took Henry for a Presbyterian clergyman, lost a unique opportunity to record for posterity the words of the great orator. John Adams, whom Henry greatly admired, has preserved a meager summary of what must have been a notable speech. One paragraph which suggests that Henry was in his best vein reads: "The distinctions between Virginians, Pennsylvanians, New Yorkers, and New Englanders, are no more. I am not a Virginian, but an American."

Henry's most famous speech, and perhaps his greatest, was delivered in the Virginia Convention which met in St. John's Church in Richmond. On March 23, 1775, he spoke in support of his own resolutions providing that "the colony be immediately put into a state of defence." Edmund Burke had delivered his great "Conciliation" speech in Parliament the day before. St. George Tucker, who heard Henry's speech, wrote long afterwards:

Imagine to yourself this speech delivered with all the calm dignity of Cato of Utica; imagine to yourself the Roman Senate assembled in the capital when it was entered by the profane Gauls, who at first were awed by their presence as if they had entered an assembly of the gods. Imagine that you had heard that Cato addressing such a Senate. Imagine that you saw the handwriting on the wall of Belshazzar's palace. Imagine that you had heard a voice as from heaven uttering the words, "*We must fight*," as the doom of Fate, and you may have some idea of the speaker, the assembly to whom he addressed himself, and the auditory, of which I was one.

Colonel Edward Carrington, who heard the speech standing outside the church looking through a window, is said to have exclaimed, "Let me be buried at this spot!"

This speech as given in condensed form by Wirt is found in many anthologies and is Henry's chief claim to a place in American literature. It has been frequently suggested that the speech represents Wirt's own very considerable oratorical powers rather than Henry's. It should be noted, however, that only in the closing paragraph does Wirt profess to give Henry's exact words. In order to make the speech read more effectively and serve as a declamation piece, anthologists have substituted the first person for the third throughout and have thus given the unwary reader the impression that Wirt was recording the entire speech as it was actually delivered. Wirt was not, like Henry's favorite historian Livy, inventing a suitable speech for a great occasion. He had the benefit of the written memoranda of men who had heard the speech, in particular of Tucker, Edmund Randolph,

Judge John Tyler, and Jefferson; but he did not realize how difficult it is for any one to recall the exact words he heard spoken thirty or forty years ago.

The speech as Wirt gives it has a sustained literary quality which Henry's recorded speeches in the Virginia Convention of 1788 do not have. Louis Mallory, who finds in Wirt's version "a conciseness, a lack of repetition, a polish, a poetic quality" which the later speeches do not possess, concludes that Wirt has given us only "the high points of the speech, those soaring moments when language, action, and emotion perfectly complement each other, moments that would naturally be fixed in the memory of the listener, and arranged them so as to give the impression that they alone constitute the speech." Oft-quoted though it is, the conclusion of the famous speech in Wirt's version still has the power to move its readers:

"It is in vain, sir, to extenuate the matter. Gentlemen may cry peace, peace, —but there is no peace. The war is actually begun! The next gale that sweeps from the north will bring to our ears the clash of resounding arms! Our brethren are already in the field! Why stand we here idle? What is it that gentlemen wish? what would they have? Is life so dear, or peace so sweet, as to be purchased at the price of chains and slavery? Forbid it, Almighty God! I know not what course others may take; but as for me," cried he, with both arms extended aloft, his brows knit, every feature marked with the resolute purpose of his soul, and his voice swelled to its boldest note of exclamation—"give me liberty, or give me death!"

Eloquence such as Henry's was a tremendous force in the General Assembly, but as soldier and as governor he did not greatly distinguish himself. As he grew older, he became more conservative and more provincial; in fact, he had never wholly shared in the Revolutionary idealism of Jefferson. In the Virginia Convention of 1788 he led the fight against ratification of the new Federal Constitution. The youthful James Madison was his principal opponent. The speeches which Henry made in the Convention— fully but none too accurately recorded—reveal flashes of the old fire, but something is gone.

Henry's objection to the Constitution was that it made the government not a "federal" Union but a "consolidated" one. He could find in the document no real check against Federal usurpation of the rights of the states. North and South, he pointed out, had different economic interests, and the Constitution left the five Southern states at the mercy of the eight in the North. The new government, he said, "squints toward monarchy": "Your president may easily become king." "This government," he said, "is not a Virginian but an American government." Once long ago he had said. "I am not a Virginian, but an American." Now he felt much as John Taylor of Caroline, John Randolph, Beverley Tucker, and John C. Calhoun would in time come to feel, that the Southern states were a minority section and in danger of domination by a more populous section with alien interests. "Suppose," he said, "the people of Virginia should wish to alter their government, can a majority of them do it? No, because they are connected with other men; or, in other words, consolidated with other states; when the people of Virginia at a future day shall wish to alter their government, though they should be unanimous in this desire, yet they may be prevented therefrom by a despicable minority at the extremity of the United States." In spite of Henry's eloquent protests, the Virginia Convention ratified the Constitution; but it was in part as a result of the insistence of Henry, Mason, and others that the Convention urged Congress to initiate the first ten amendments which constitute a Bill of Rights similar to that which Mason had drawn up for Virginia.

For a final generous estimate we may turn to John Adams, who, not wholly pleased by Wirt's biography, which seemed to him to belittle the role of Massachusetts in the Revolution, wrote to its author that he had always considered Henry "a gentleman of deep reflection, keen sagacity, clear foresight, daring enterprise, inflexible intrepidity, and untainted integrity; with an ardent zeal for the liberties, the honor, and felicity of his country, and his species."

12

Thomas Jefferson

THOMAS JEFFERSON'S (1743–1826) pen was one of his greatest assets, for he was neither a soldier like Washington nor an orator like Henry. And yet with the exception of his Notes on the State of Virginia (1784), which was not written for publication, he published no books. Indeed, in 1809, the year in which he retired from the presidency, he wrote that he saw nothing to encourage a publisher to bring out a collected edition of his works. His writings, which consist chiefly of official papers and private letters, seemed to him of no literary importance. It was, however, writing of this kind, and not poetry, drama, or fiction, that moved most deeply the minds of leading Americans in his time. There is far more vitality in the pamphlets, speeches, and letters of the Revolutionary statesmen than there is in the rather feeble beginnings of our drama and fiction.

Jefferson well represented, and thoroughly understood, both sections of his native Virginia. Through his mother, a Randolph, he was connected with the Tidewater planters, but he was reared in the western part of the colony and his father was an able product of the middle class. Although Jefferson's education and home surroundings were not those of a backwoodsman, the freedom and approximate equality of Piedmont society went far toward shaping his democratic creed, which was fixed long before he ever set foot in France.

In the Reverend James Maury's school he studied Greek and Latin for two years and then entered William and Mary College at the age of fifteen, the year after his father's death. In 1808 he wrote to his grandson concerning this critical period in his youth:

When I recollect that at 14 years of age, the whole care & direction of myself was thrown on myself entirely, without a relation or friend qualified to advise or guide me, and recollect the various sorts of bad company with which I associated from time to time, I am astonished that I did not turn off with some of them, & become as worthless to society as they were. . . . From the circumstances of my position, I was often thrown into the society of horse racers, card players, fox hunters, scientific & professional men, and of dignified men; and many a time have I asked myself, in the enthusiastic moment of the death of a fox, the victory of a favorite horse, the issue of a question eloquently argued at the bar, or in the great council of the nation, well, which of these kinds of reputation should I prefer? That of a horse jockey? a fox hunter? an orator? or the honest advocate of my country's rights?

"I would ask myself," says Jefferson, "what would Dr. Small, Mr. Wythe, Peyton Randolph do in this situation?"

To Dr. William Small, George Wythe, and Governor Francis Fauquier, Jefferson owed the best part of his education. The four met frequently around the Governor's table, and Jefferson enjoyed such intellectual society as few American college students have ever had access to. Fauquier was a well-connected, cultivated, widely traveled Englishman. He was a member of the Royal Society and was a particular admirer of Bolingbroke. Dr. Small was professor of mathematics in the College. When the chair of philosophy unexpectedly fell vacant, Small filled it temporarily. He was, says Jefferson, "the first who ever gave in that college regular lectures in Ethics, Rhetoric & Belles Lettres." George Wythe (1726–1806) was not only a great law teacher and legal scholar but one of the best classical scholars in Virginia as well. He also played his part in the General Assembly and in the Continental Congress. Among his pupils were Jefferson, John Marshall, Henry Clay, St. George Tucker, and many others who rose to at least local prominence. The wide variety of intellectual interests of Wythe,

Small, and Fauquier are all reflected in Jefferson, who had, like William Byrd and Benjamin Franklin, an eager intellectual curiosity that has been all too rare in Southerners of later times. He was intelligently interested in literature, language, music, architecture, education, agriculture, science, economics, law, and political science. Primarily of course he was a diplomatist, a statesman, a political thinker, and a consummate politician; but his other interests were genuine. There was little of the dilettante in his make-up; his varied interests were integral parts of the mind and personality of a great liberal whose high place in our history was not fully recognized until the administration of the second Roosevelt.

Jefferson was elected a member of the House of Burgesses at twenty-five, and he continued in the service of his state and country almost uninterruptedly until he was sixty-five. He was a member of the Continental Congress, Governor of Virginia, Minister to France, Secretary of State, Vice-President, and for eight years President of the United States. And yet, if we may believe his own words, he had no more love of office or power than Washington had. He wrote to John Melish on January 13, 1813: ". . . had it been a mere contest who should be permitted to administer the government according to its genuine republican principles, there has never been a moment of my life in which I should have relinquished for it the enjoyments of my family, my farm, my friends and books." But for the death of his wife in 1782, he might have remained in retirement for the rest of his life. A city-bred generation finds it difficult to credit the Virginia planters when they express a preference for their way of life above all others; and Jefferson, one must always remember, was a Virginia planter. He wrote to General Thaddeus Kosciusko, February 26, 1810:

I am retired to Monticello, where, in the bosom of my family, and surrounded by my books, I enjoy a repose to which I have long been a stranger. My mornings are devoted to correspondence. From breakfast to dinner, I am in my shops, my garden, or on horseback among my farms; from dinner to dark, I give to society and recreation with my neighbors and friends; and from candle-light to early bed-time, I read. My health is perfect. . . . I talk of ploughs and harrows, of seeding and harvesting, with my neighbors, and of politics too, if they choose, with as little reserve as the rest of my fellow citizens, and feel, at length, the blessing of being free to say and do what I please, without being responsible for it to any mortal.

Of his own county, Albemarle, he wrote to Jean Baptiste Say, March 2, 1815: "The society is much better than is common in country situations; perhaps there is not a better *country* society in the United States. But do not imagine this is a Parisian or academical society. It consists of plain, honest, and rational neighbors, some of them well informed and men of reading, all superintending their farms, hospitable and friendly, and speaking nothing but English."

Jefferson's views on government are best understood when seen against such a background as this. He long regarded great cities as "pestilential to the morals, the health and the liberties of men." On August 23, 1785, he wrote to John Jay: "Cultivators of the earth are the most valuable citizens. They are the most vigorous, the most independant, the most virtuous, & they are tied to their country & wedded to it's liberty & interests by the most lasting bonds." He wrote to James Madison, December 20, 1787: "I think our governments will remain virtuous for many centuries; as long as they are chiefly agricultural; and this will be as long as there shall be vacant lands in any part of America." Although Jefferson here and elsewhere anticipated by more than a century the frontier theory of Frederick J. Turner, he did not, any more than his contemporaries, foresee the enormous industrial development of this country. He was a practical politician and no doctrinaire, and in the White House he so far modified his position as to write: ". . . I trust the good sense of our country will see that its greatest prosperity depends on a due balance between agriculture, manufactures, and commerce. . . ."

Jefferson's view of human nature was that of many enlightened Europeans in his day, and it had much in common with that of Channing and Emerson. "I believe with you," he wrote to Dupont de Nemours, April 24, 1816, "that morality, compassion, generosity, are innate elements of the human constitution. . . ." In 1818 he wrote, in language that Godwin or Rousseau might have used: "It cannot be but each generation must advance the knowledge and well-being of mankind, not *infinitely* as some have said, but *indefinitely* and to a term which no man can fix and foresee." Ten days before his death he wrote: "The general spread of the light of science [knowledge] has already laid open the palpable truth, that the mass of mankind has not been born with saddles on their backs, nor a favored few booted and spurred, ready to ride them legitimately, by the grace of God."

Jefferson carried his devotion to freedom into every aspect of his thinking. He wrote to Benjamin Rush, September 23, 1800, in words that Shelley might have written: "I have sworn upon the altar of god, eternal hostility against every form of tyranny over the mind of man." In his famous epitaph —which made no mention of his eight years in the White House—he commemorated what he regarded as his most significant services to political, religious, and intellectual liberty: "Here was buried Thomas Jefferson,

Author of the Declaration of Independence, the Statute of Virginia for Religious Freedom, and Father of the University of Virginia."

The most unpopular form which Jefferson's devotion to freedom took was in religion. Some Virginia Anglicans never forgave him for his part in the disestablishment of their Church, and many New England clergymen looked upon him as an archatheist. Although he was under strong Deistic influences in his youth, his religion in later years was fundamentally Unitarian. On January 8, 1825, he wrote to Benjamin Waterhouse: "I am anxious to see the doctrine of one god commenced in our state. But the popul'n of my neighb'hood is too slender, and is too much divided into other sects to maintain any one preacher well. I must therefore be contented to be an Unitarian by myself, although I know there are many around me who would become so, if once they could hear the questions fairly stated." [8]

As a matter of fact, at that time the whole drift in the South was away from Unitarianism and Deism and toward a somewhat narrow orthodoxy. Although Jefferson had co-operated with the dissenters to bring about the disestablishment of the Anglican Church, he suffered so much abuse from them that on November 2, 1822, he wrote to Thomas Cooper, who was having his own difficulties with the orthodox:

The atmosphere of our country is unquestionably charged with a threatening cloud of fanaticism. . . . I had no idea, however, that in Pennsylvania, the cradle of toleration and freedom of religion, it could have risen to the height you describe. This must be owing to the growth of Presbyterianism. . . . In our Richmond there is much fanaticism, but chiefly among the women. They have their night meetings and praying parties, where, attended by their priests, and sometimes by a hen-pecked husband, they pour forth the effusions of their love to Jesus, in terms as amatory and carnal, as their modesty would permit them to use to a mere earthly lover.

Jefferson drafted the ordinance prohibiting slavery in the Old Northwest, and late in life wrote: "Nothing is more certainly written in the book of fate, than that these people [the slaves] are to be free. . . ." He was never able, however, to induce the Virginia Assembly to take measures looking toward emancipation. He did not foresee that in his old age slavery would

[8] This important letter, which is not in any edition of Jefferson's writings, was published in part in R. J. Honeywell, *The Educational Work of Thomas Jefferson* (1931), p. 92, and in Adrienne Koch, *The Philosophy of Thomas Jefferson* (1943), p. 27.

See also William D. Gould, "The Religious Opinions of Thomas Jefferson," *Miss. Valley Hist. Rev.*, XX, 191–208 (Sept., 1933). George Tucker, who knew Jefferson, wrote: "In the last years of his life, when questioned by any of his friends on this subject [his religious creed], he used to say he was 'an Unitarian'" (*Life of Jefferson*, 1837, II, 563).

become accepted as an institution to be defended on ethical and religious grounds; nor did he foresee that his native Virginia would reject much of the liberalism of the Revolution. His somewhat complacent optimism was temporarily dashed by the debate in Congress over the admission of Missouri as a slave state in 1820, but he did not live long enough to see the renewal of the conflict between North and South, to hear the doctrines of the Declaration of Independence denounced as glittering fallacies, or to see Lincoln and the Republican party use against the South his many condemnations of slavery. In April, 1857, William J. Grayson wrote in *Russell's Magazine:* "Mr. Jefferson has become a favorite statesman with the Abolition orators, and his opinion is perpetually quoted as overwhelming authority. Formerly, he was denounced in New York and New England as an arch Jacobin and preacher of false and dangerous principles in Morals, Politics, and Religion; now he is recognized there as the great Apostle of Freedom." A Southerner of a still later generation, Walter Hines Page, regarded the South's desertion of Jeffersonian liberalism as "one of the most disastrous apostasies of history."

Intellectually Jefferson was a cosmopolitan, but in all political matters he was intensely American. He envied Europe its fine arts, especially its music, but his stay in Europe served only to confirm him in the political stand he had taken in his youth. Shortly after his arrival "on the vaunted scene of Europe," he wrote to Charles Bellini, September 30, 1785: "I find the general fate of humanity here most deplorable. The truth of Voltaire's observation, offers itself perpetually, that every man here must be either the hammer or the anvil." In a letter to James Monroe shortly before the proclamation of the Monroe Doctrine, Jefferson wrote: "Our first and fundamental maxim should be, never to suffer Europe to intermeddle with cis-Atlantic affairs."

Jefferson was a student and a reader of books all his life, but he was not a bookworm. Fortunately, we know more about the books he read in his formative years than we know in the case of any of his Virginian contemporaries. His literary taste was in the main the taste of educated men of the later eighteenth century. In his youth and early manhood he read the Greek and Latin classics and the best of eighteenth-century English literature; but as he became involved in political activities, he devoted less attention to belles-lettres. By 1780 he had lost much of his liking for poetry, and in 1818 he thought that a great obstacle to education was "the inordinate passion prevalent for novels," which too often resulted in "a bloated imagination, sickly judgment, and disgust towards all the real business of life." Soon after Scott's *Ivanhoe* appeared in 1819, his daughter Martha, who had been fascinated by it, persuaded him to read it. He got no more than half-way through it and pronounced it the dullest and dryest reading he had ever experienced.[9] In his youth he had been passionately fond of Ossian, and he read and enjoyed the early Romanticists, but he cared little for the later and greater ones. He was moved by the Romantic melancholy of certain eighteenth-century writers, but he did not respond to the primitivism of Wordsworth and Rousseau. The glorification of the primitive was far more congenial to the urban population of the Old World than to the rural inhabitants of the New. His favorite authors were Homer, Euripides, Shakespeare, Milton, Bolingbroke, and Swift. He regarded Addison, Sterne, and Robertson as models in their respective fields. He admired Hume as a stylist but regarded his Tory principles as pernicious. The Greek and Latin classics seemed to him "models of pure taste in writing," and he read them even in old age.

Jefferson had little use for formal criticism. He wrote to William Wirt, November 12, 1816: "I have always very much dispised the artificial canons of criticism. When I have read a work in prose or poetry, or seen a painting, a statue, etc., I have only asked myself whether it gives me pleasure, whether it is animating, interesting, attaching? If it is, it is good for these reasons." This sounds strangely modern, but Jefferson was not altogether an impressionist. To Robert Skipwith, who had asked for a list of desirable books, Jefferson wrote, August 3, 1771: ". . . everything is useful which contributes to fix in the principles and practices of virtue." It did not greatly matter, he thought, whether Skipwith read history or fiction. Probably recalling his Aristotle and Horace, Jefferson wrote:

If the painting be lively, and a tolerable picture of nature, we are thrown into a reverie, from which if we awaken it is the fault of the writer. I appeal to every reader of feeling and sentiment whether the fictitious murther of Duncan by Macbeth in Shakespeare does not excite in him as great a horror of villany, as the real one of Henry IV. by Ravaillac as related by Davila? . . . . a lively and lasting sense of filial duty is more effectually impressed on the mind of a son or daughter by reading King Lear, than by all the dry volumes of ethics, and divinity that ever were written. This is my idea of well written Romance, of Tragedy, Comedy and Epic poetry.

[9] "Thomas Jefferson," *Southern Opinion* (Richmond), Oct. 3, 1868. This article was one of a series published by Professor Henry Tutwiler of the University of Alabama in the Mobile Sunday *Times*. Tutwiler, who had been a student at the University of Virginia, notes that Jefferson often had four or five students at Monticello for Sunday dinner, taking their names in regular order from the Proctor's books. It seems not unlikely that Edgar Allan Poe was among those who dined at Monticello in 1826. Poe, however, was no admirer of Jefferson.

The passages which Jefferson copied into his commonplace book in his youth indicate that his chief interest in Homer and Milton was not in their literary qualities (though he was by no means blind to these) but in other values. Homer, for instance, was the epitome of the wisdom of early Greek civilization. Jefferson, however, was sufficiently interested in literary technique to write out in some detail his "Thoughts on English Prosody: An Essay on the Art of Poesy."

Jefferson's "Essay on the Anglo-Saxon Language" resulted from a belief, going back to his early legal studies in Williamsburg, that Old English held the clew to the understanding of a multitude of legal terms. Hoping that the study of Anglo-Saxon would arouse in students the true British love of liberty, he insisted on its being taught in the University of Virginia. Believing that Bosworth and other Old English scholars had made Anglo-Saxon grammar and syntax unnecessarily difficult for the beginner, he proposed a simplified scheme of declensions and a normalized spelling.

Jefferson would have done better to establish a chair of English literature. He did not foresee how barren the study of Anglo-Saxon would become in the hands of the philologists. The historian of Jefferson's university, who regards the statesman's literary taste as meretricious, asks: "Is it the shadow of his comparative indifference to English literature, projected through the century which has followed, that explains the failure of the University of Virginia to produce successful authors in the normal proportion to successful lawyers, physicians, clergymen, engineers, and men of business?"

Jefferson had no literary ambitions and probably gave little conscious thought to stylistic problems. The merits of his writing are due to clear thinking and to constant practice in expressing his ideas in writing and in conversation. His style was modeled less on the ancient classics whose conciseness he admired than upon such eighteenth-century writers as Bolingbroke, Addison, and Hume. In his official writings he used a stately, full-dress style which—particularly in the Declaration of Independence—often rises to sonorous eloquence. His style lacks, even in his letters, the directness and homely simplicity of Franklin or Lincoln. He is inclined to be verbose, particularly in his letters. His comprehensive mind, like that of Walt Whitman or Henry James, was too frequently unwilling to abandon qualifying phrases and clauses, even in the interest of the conciseness which he admired in Tacitus and Sallust.

Nevertheless, Jefferson's phrasing often has a felicity of its own. Apart from Lincoln and Wilson, he has no rival as a writer among the men who have held the Presidency. Too many of our later statesmen have failed to cultivate the art of moving men by the use of written words. They have failed to realize that the ability to write—especially the art of simplifying complex issues and of summing them up in telling phrases—is a source of political power. What Jefferson most definitely lacked as a writer, says Carl Becker, was "a profoundly emotional apprehension of experience." His writing is often too placid and too full of something like complacent optimism. It is a style better suited to his day than to ours. Franklin's is a style less invalidated by the passing of time.

When Jefferson was selected to draft the Declaration of Independence, he had published only one work of importance, A Summary View of the Rights of British America (Williamsburg, 1774). Elected to the Virginia Convention of 1774, Jefferson had written the pamphlet hoping that the Convention would use it in the form of instructions to the delegates elected to the Continental Congress. Falling sick on the road to Williamsburg, he sent on what he had written. The document seemed too radical for the Convention, but some of the members had it published anonymously and gave it the title which it bears. Jefferson's argument is based not on the rights of the colonists as Englishmen but on natural rights and the right of expatriation. In his view the king is the one link that binds the colonies to England. Parliament, which had claimed the right to tax them, is practically ignored. The boldness and skill with which Jefferson developed this line of defense is undoubtedly a main reason why he was chosen to draft the Declaration. The document is addressed to the king and professes to have been "penned in the language of truth, and divested of those expressions of servility, which would persuade his Majesty that we are asking favors, and not rights." Daniel Dulany, Richard Bland, and John Dickinson had used no such language. George III and his ministers must have thought it insolent, particularly the closing paragraph, which reads in part:

That these are our grievances which we have thus laid before his majesty, with that freedom of language and sentiment which becomes a free people claiming their rights, as derived from the laws of nature, and not as a gift of their chief magistrate: Let those flatter who fear; it is not an American art. To give praise which is not due might be well from the venal, but would ill beseem those who are asserting the rights of human nature. They know, and will therefore say, that kings are the servants, not the proprietors of the people. Open your breast, sire, to liberal and expanded thought. Let not the name of George the third be a blot in the page of history. . . . The whole art of government consists in the art of being honest. Only aim to do your duty, and mankind will give you credit where you fail. No longer persevere in sacrificing the rights of one part of the empire to the inordinate desires of another; but deal out to all equal and impartial right. . . . This, sire, is the advice of your great American council, on the observance of which may perhaps depend your felicity and future fame, and the preservation of that harmony which alone can continue both to Great Britain and America the reciprocal advantages of their connection. . . . This, sire, is our last, our determined resolution; and that you will be pleased to interpose with that efficacy which your earnest endeavours may ensure to procure redress of these our great grievances, to quiet the minds of your subjects in British America, against any apprehensions of future encroachment, to establish fraternal love and harmony through the whole empire, and that these may continue to the latest ages of time, is the fervent prayer of all British America!

The Declaration of Independence is of course an American masterpiece in its kind, but it is often misunderstood by readers who forget that it is a war document. It is in the best sense propaganda, a statement of principles for which men were willing to fight. A later generation of Americans—especially in the South—came to regard it as full of glittering and specious generalities. They forgot that after he had written it, Jefferson returned to Virginia to see that those principles were incorporated into the laws of his native state. The Declaration has been criticized as unoriginal in both language and ideas. Richard Henry Lee thought it too much indebted to John Locke. Such criticism misconceives the purpose of the document. One might as accurately bring the same charge against Shakespeare's famous soliloquies (as in fact Bernard Shaw has done) or Gray's "Elegy" or the Gettysburg Address.

The merit of the Declaration is that it gives us, in Pope's phrase: "What oft was thought but ne'er so well expressed." Jefferson's assignment was to put together as forcefully and as persuasively as possible the new nation's charges against the King, for Parliament was to be quietly ignored. The wonder is that such a document, hackneyed from repetition in schools and political gatherings, should have the power to move men still. Better than any of his contemporaries, Jefferson gave memorable phrasing to what James Truslow Adams has called the American dream. Since the great nineteenth-century shift from an agricultural to an industrial economy, Hamilton's economic ideas have sometimes seemed sounder than Jefferson's; but American democracy owes more to Jefferson than to any other thinker. In a world in fear of totalitarian domination the ideal is still worth fighting for: "We hold these truths to be self-evident, that all men are created equal, that they are endowed by their Creator with certain unalienable rights, that among these are Life, Liberty and the pursuit of Happiness. —That to secure these rights, Governments are instituted among Men, deriving their just powers from the consent of the governed." [10]

[10] The Oxford Dictionary of Quotations (1941) prints ten quotations from Jefferson but nothing from the Declaration of Independence.

The one book that Jefferson published, *Notes on the State of Virginia*, was written in the winter of 1781–1782, with no intention of publication, in answer to a series of queries proposed to him by the Marquis of Barbé-Marbois, Secretary of the French Legation in Philadelphia. The query and answer form is somewhat mechanical, but no comparable scientific survey of the resources of any other state had yet been written by an American. The book is notable for its excellent descriptive passages, particularly of the Natural Bridge; for its bold indictment of slavery; and for an enlightened account of the Virginia Indians. Jefferson with considerable gusto wrote his refutation of the theory, sponsored by Buffon and Raynal, that on this side of the Atlantic Ocean Nature's productions are inferior to those of the Old World. To show what the aborigenes were capable of, he quoted the "speech" of Logan, the most eloquent piece of writing to come from an American Indian. The book gives us some notion of what Jefferson might have achieved if he had given his life to writing. But, as he wrote to J. Evelyn Denison on November 9, 1825: "Literature is not yet a distinct profession with us. Now and then a strong mind arises, and at its intervals of leisure from business, emits a flash of light. But the first object of young societies is bread and covering; science is but secondary and subsequent."

Jefferson's First Inaugural Address (1801) is a notable reaffirmation of his political creed, of what he termed "the essential principle of this government." His election was the result of a mild political revolution, and in memorable language he stated its significance. A century and a half have passed since he wrote the following passage, and yet it may be doubted whether any later writer has better stated the fundamental tenets of American democracy:

Equal and exact justice to all men of whatever state or persuasion, religious or political; peace, commerce and honest friendship with all nations, entangling alliances with none; the support of the state governments in all their rights, as the most competent administrations for our domestic concerns, and the surest bulwarks against anti-republican tendencies; the preservation of the general government in its whole constitutional vigor, as the sheet-anchor of our peace at home and safety abroad; a jealous care of the right of election by the people; a mild and safe corrective of abuses which are lopped by the sword of revolution, where peaceable remedies are unprovided; absolute acquiescence in the decisions of the majority, the vital principle of republics, from which there is no appeal but to force, the vital principle and immediate parent of despotism; a well-disciplined militia, our reliance in peace and for the first months of war, till regulars may relieve them; the supremacy of the civil over the military authority—economy in the public expense, that labor may be lightly burdened; the honest payment of our debts, and sacred preservation of the public faith; encouragement of agriculture, and of commerce as its handmaid; the diffusion of information and arraignment of all abuses at the bar of the public reason; freedom of religion, freedom of the press, and freedom of person, under the protection of the habeas corpus; and trial by juries impartially selected. These principles form the bright constellation which has gone before us, and guided our steps through an age of revolution and reformation. The wisdom of our sages and blood of our heroes have been devoted to their attainment; they should be the creed of our political faith; the text of civic instruction; the touchstone by which to try the services of those we trust; and should we wander from them in moments of error or alarm, let us hasten to retrace our steps and to regain the road which alone leads to peace, liberty, and safety.

For the modern reader, the letters of Jefferson offer matter more attractive than his official papers. He grew up in a century of great letter-writers, and he was a contemporary of Gray, Cowper, and Walpole. It was, as we are prone to forget, an age that had no telegraph, telephone, typewriter, locomotive, automobile, airplane, or radio. In America distances were great and roads were generally bad. Men and women wrote to one another about important matters and discussed them in detail. In the long intervals between legislative sessions political leaders discussed policies and outlined their views of what should be done. Their conversations are lost beyond recovery, but many letters remain, and they bring us closer to the great men of that generation than any other writings of the time.

Jefferson's letters run into the thousands, and many are still unpublished. Among the best are letters to his daughters and his Virginia friends, to his women friends in France, and to associates in the Democratic party. The letters to Mrs. Maria Cosway contain the deservedly famous "The Head and the Heart," a masterpiece and a very revealing document. But the most remarkable of Jefferson's letters are those which in old age he wrote to John Adams. The two men had become intimate friends in the Second Continental Congress, but in later years they were political rivals. At bottom the two men, outwardly so different, had much in common; and Benjamin Rush, who admired them both, had no great difficulty in persuading the two to resume their interrupted correspondence. Their letters, written between 1812 and 1826, are unlike anything else in our literature. The nearest parallel I can think of is the letters exchanged in old age between Justice Oliver Wendell Holmes and Sir Frederick Pollock. One can hardly imagine two ex-Presidents of rival parties in any later period writing letters like these. William Wirt compared the correspondence to the conversations which in the Elysium of the ancients the shades of the departed great held with one another. With unfailing wisdom, courtesy, and charm the two sages discussed old age, the books they were reading, their willingness to live life over again, and methods of selecting the best men for office. I quote as characteristic a passage from Jefferson's letter of August 1, 1816, which drew from Adams the equally characteristic comment: *"Festina lente,* my friend, in all your projects of reformation. Abolish polytheists, however, in every shape, if you can, and unfrock every priest who teaches it, if you can":

> I know nothing of the history of the Jesuits you mention in four volumes. Is it a good one? I dislike, with you, their restoration, because it marks a retrograde step from light towards darkness. We shall have our follies without doubt. Some one or more of them will always be afloat. But ours will be the follies of enthusiasm, not of bigotry, not of Jesuitism. Bigotry is a disease of ignorance, of morbid minds; enthusiasm of the free and buoyant. Education and free discussion are the antidotes of both. We are destined to be a barrier against the returns of ignorance and barbarism. Old Europe will have to lean on our shoulders, and to hobble along by our side, under the monkish trammels of priests and kings, as she can. What a colossus we shall be when the southern continent comes up to our mark! What a stand will it secure as a ralliance for the reason and freedom of the globe! I like the dreams of the future better than the history of the past,—so good night! I will dream on, always fancying that Mrs. Adams and yourself are by my side marking the progress and the obliquities of ages and countries.

Jefferson did not foresee any more than his contemporaries the enormous industrial development of the United States; but more than any one of them, he foresaw the time when this nation would be something like the world power it now is, and more than any of them he had faith in its future. He is in a double sense our greatest prophet, except possibly Walt Whitman. Two days after his death—he and John Adams died on the fiftieth anniversary of the Declaration of Independence, July 4, 1826— James Madison recorded his "assurance that he [Jefferson] lives and will live in the memory and gratitude of the wise & good, as a luminary of Science, as a votary of liberty, and as a benefactor of human kind." A century later Vernon Parrington concluded his chapter on Jefferson in a book which showed how strong the Jeffersonian tradition in our literature has always been: "Among the great thinkers of the constitutional period Jefferson remains by far the most vital and suggestive, the one to whom later generations may return most hopefully."

13
James Madison

JAMES MADISON (1751–1836), fourth President of the United States, made his home in Orange County, Virginia, not far from "Monticello," where his friend Jefferson lived. His father, although a large landholder, did not belong to one of the long-established families of the colony. While a mere boy, Madison read the *Spectator* with keen enjoyment. At the age of twelve he was sent to a school in King and Queen County kept by Donald Robertson, a younger brother of the Scotch historian and a cousin of Patrick Henry. Here he studied French and Spanish as well as the ancient classics. He received his final preparation for college at the hands of Thomas Martin, a Presbyterian minister who lived with the Madisons. Martin was a graduate of Princeton, and this fact is one of the reasons why, unlike other Virginia statesmen, Madison went North to complete his education. He entered Princeton as a junior and graduated in 1771. Among his classmates were Philip Freneau and Hugh Henry Brackenridge, and at this time Madison shared their keen interest in literature. The three were among the founders of the American Whig Society, which, like the Phi Beta Kappa Society at William and Mary, was founded for the purpose of cultivating friendship, morality, and literature. Here Madison had his first practice in writing essays and in debating questions of government, which were to become his dominant interest in life. He was undoubtedly affected by the Princeton atmosphere, which was strongly colored by Presbyterianism and Whiggism. He returned to Princeton for a year of postgraduate study of Hebrew and ethics under its able president, John Witherspoon; but, though his studies seemed to prepare him for the ministry, he did not enter that profession.

After his return to Virginia in 1772, Madison spent his time in study and in tutoring his brothers and sisters. As the outbreak of the Revolution drew near, his intellectual interests centered upon history and government. On January 24, 1774, he wrote to William Bradford, Jr.: "Poetry, wit, and criticism, romances, plays, &c. [formerly] captivated me much; but I began to discover that they deserve but a small portion of a man's time, and that something more substantial befits a riper age." Madison, however, kept to the end of his long life a keen intellectual curiosity about many subjects, including science. He had, in Jefferson's phrase, a "luminous and discriminating mind" and the ability to express his thoughts in "language pure, classical, and copious."

Madison was elected to the Virginia Convention of 1776, and from that time until his retirement from the Presidency in 1817 he held office almost continuously in either the state or the national government. He was active in Congress, which he entered in 1780; and he helped to put through the General Assembly Jefferson's statute for religious freedom. In the Virginia Convention of 1788 he was the ablest champion of the Federal Constitution, and in the debate he did not shrink from crossing swords with the redoubtable Patrick Henry. He was not regarded as an orator, but he was an able debater. "If convincing is eloquence," said John Marshall, "he was the most eloquent man I ever heard."

Madison's most distinguished service to the nation was rendered not in the White House but in the Federal Constitutional Convention of 1787. Here the quiet scholar-statesman stood out as one of the dominant figures, and the Constitution is probably more nearly his work than that of any other man. For at least three years he had systematically studied ancient and modern history with a view to determining the best form of federal government. He was seldom absent from the meetings of the Convention, and his *Journal of the Federal Convention* (1840) is an invaluable record of the proceedings of that body. He was a member of the committee on style appointed to put the finishing touches on the Constitution.

This is not the place for a discussion of Madison's political career. As Jefferson's Secretary of State, he succeeded to the presidency, as James Monroe was in turn to succeed him. Madison's eight years in the White House do not reveal him as a dominating figure. He had no desire to be a war president, but the high-handed policy of the British government and the incessant prodding of such young warhawks as Clay and Calhoun forced upon him a war which, as the outcome proved, he had been wise enough to try to avoid. As the British army approached Washington after defeating the American militia at Bladensburg, he and his wife, the fascinating Dolly Madison, were compelled to flee from the White House just before the British burned the Capitol.

A pleasanter subject for contemplation is Madison's last years at "Montpelier." With his plantation, library, friends, and his charming wife, he led a comfortable life except for the stream of visitors who nearly ate him, like Jefferson, out of house and home. Among those who have left illuminating accounts of Madison in old age are Harriet Martineau and James Kirke Paulding, who considered him "as emphatically THE SAGE of his time."

In 1798–1800, when Jefferson and Madison were drafting the Kentucky and Virginia Resolutions, both had come close to advocating Nullification. In his later years Madison, however, was intensely devoted to the Union. He denounced the South Carolina doctrine of Nullification, which he said, had "the effect of putting powder under the Constitution and Union, and a match in the hands of every party to blow them up at pleasure. . . ." Among his noblest words are his "Advice to My Country," which was written to be published only after his death: "The advice nearest to my heart and deepest in my convictions is, *that the Union of the States be cherished and perpetuated. Let the open enemy to it be regarded as a Pandora with her box opened, and the disguised one as the serpent creeping with his death wiles into paradise.*"

The debate over the admission of Missouri as a slave state prompted Madison in 1821 to write a brief allegory, "Jonathan Bull and Mary Bull," which was first published in the *Southern Literary Messenger* for March, 1835. It is not in itself an important work, but it is an interesting variant of the John Bull story which has apparently escaped the notice of students of that legend.[11] Madison's allegory presents a modified Southern view of the dispute between Jonathan [the North] and Mary [the South] over "a stain on her left arm" from an African dye [slavery], "which made it perfectly black, and withal somewhat weaker than the other arm." All this of course Jonathan had known at the time of their marriage and had then made no objection, but now he says: "White as I am all over, I can no longer consort with one marked with such deformity as the blot on your person." To which Mary responds that the stain is no fault of hers and that neither of them is able "to find out a safe and feasible plan" for removing it. The dispute is finally settled amicably and results "in an increased affection and confidence between the parties." Madison clearly did not recognize the 1820 crisis as the forerunner of a series of crises ending in disunion and civil war. In October, 1856, when the editor of *De Bow's Review* republished the allegory, he took occasion to point out that since Madison's time the South had become better enlightened as to both the benefits of slavery and the real intentions of Jonathan.

Madison's claim to a place in American literature rests upon his part in the writing of *The Federalist*. These essays, written by Madison, Hamilton, and John Jay, were first published in New York newspapers in 1787–1788 —most of them over the pseudonym "Publius"—and were quickly reissued in book form. Their primary purpose was to promote the ratification of the Constitution in the state of New York. Distributed to members of the conventions in New York and Virginia, they supplied facts and arguments to the supporters of the Constitution. The essays were hurriedly written with

[11] It is not mentioned in the late George E. Hastings' "John Bull and His American Descendants," *Am. Lit.*, I, 40–68 (March, 1929).

little consultation among the authors, and they were printed as rapidly as copy could be got to the printer. Inevitably *The Federalist* suffers from some repetition, careless phrasing, and inconsistencies. Nevertheless, these pamphlets have become a political classic. They have from the beginning been regarded as the best defense and interpretation of the Constitution and have figured as such in decisions of the Supreme Court.

Although it is known that Hamilton was the originator of the project and wrote more than half of the eighty-five essays, the authorship of certain numbers has been the subject of a prolonged controversy comparable to that over the identity of "Junius." The secret of the authorship was for more than a dozen years kept from the public apparently because to have revealed it would have embarrassed both Hamilton and Madison, who had each changed his stand on important questions connected with the Constitution. Hamilton, who valued other writings of his more highly, refused to permit the publication of the names of the authors in the 1802 edition. In July, 1804, however, just before his fatal duel with Aaron Burr, he left in the law office of Egbert Benson a written statement listing the sixty-three numbers which he claimed to have written. This list is in some respects obviously inaccurate, and it was apparently drawn up without a rereading of the essays. In 1810 all the eighty-five numbers appeared in Hamilton's collected works with the implication that he had written the great majority of them. Madison, then President, took no part in the controversy which began when some of his friends challenged the accuracy of Hamilton's list. In 1818, however, he lent his personal copy of *The Federalist*, in which he had indicated the author of each essay, to Jacob Gideon, Jr., who was to bring out a new edition in Washington in that year. Madison claimed that he had written Numbers 10, 14, 18–20, 37–58, and 62–63, a total of twenty-nine. Until after the Civil War, Madison's list seems to have been generally accepted as an accurate index to the authorship.

In the seventies and eighties, however, the reputation of Madison and other members of the Virginia Dynasty was at a low ebb, while Hamilton's fame was in the ascendant. The Constitution was now being reinterpreted to meet the demands of an industrial economy, and Hamilton's views fitted into the framework of the dominant Republican party. When Henry Cabot Lodge in 1886 brought out his edition of *The Federalist*, he resurrected the half-forgotten Benson list and credited Hamilton with having written the great majority of the eighty-five essays. In 1896 Edward Gaylord Bourne, a disinterested scholar, challenged Lodge's position with evidence difficult to refute, but Lodge made no changes in later editions. Soon afterwards Paul Leicester Ford came to Lodge's defense. Until recent years editors were content to accept the Lodge-Ford position without re-examining the involved and contradictory evidence.

In 1944 Professor Douglass Adair, of the College of William and-Mary, ably reviewed the whole question and reached the conclusion that the Gideon list, coming directly from Madison himself, is an accurate. index to the authorship of the disputed essays. The evidence which he presents —and it is cogently presented—is both internal and external. He points out that Madison, who began to write for *The Federalist* in November, 1787, remained in New York until March, 1788, although his Virginia friends kept writing him that if he did not soon return he might lose his seat in Congress in the approaching election. If he was not writing for *The Federalist*, it is difficult to see what was keeping him in New York. Furthermore, the essays claimed by Madison deal with just those topics which he was best fitted to discuss; and there are, as Adair points out, parallels between the disputed essays and Madison's acknowledged writings. Adair's conclusion, now generally accepted, is that Lodge and Ford built up an "elaborate structure of specious scholarship as a monument to a man [Hamilton] who did not in the least care to be remembered as 'Publius.' "

The plan of *The Federalist* was of course Hamilton's. He wrote the opening number and indicated in it the chief topics which were to be discussed. Jay, who had agreed to contribute, fell ill and wrote only five numbers (2–5, 64). Hamilton, busy with his law practice and apparently unable to secure other able collaborators, welcomed Madison as a contributor in spite of the fact that they were not intimate friends and were soon to become sharply divided on party lines. Jay had not been a member of the Constitutional Convention, and Hamilton had attended only the opening and closing sessions. He had, in fact, no enthusiasm for the new Constitution; he supported it only as the lesser of two evils. Madison, on the other hand, was at nearly every meeting of the Convention, and he was a recognized authority on certain subjects which must be discussed in *The Federalist*, particularly the historical background and the legislative functions of the new government. Hamilton, though an able writer, was primarily a practical politician who did not take political theory very seriously. Nor was he, like Madison, really interested in ideas as such. On the whole, then, as we should expect, Madison's essays—except for some of the more hurriedly written ones—are better than Hamilton's. The best are probably Numbers 10, 14, and 63.

It was not from Karl Marx, but from Aristotle and the tenth number of *The Federalist*, that Charles A. Beard says he learned the importance of the economic interpretation of politics. In explaining the diversity of interested "factions," Madison wrote the following passage, which needs only the substitution of a few such modern terms as "capital," "labor," and "pressure groups" to bring it up to date:

. . . the most common and durable source of factions has been the various and unequal distribution of property. Those who hold and those who are without property have ever formed distinct interests in society. . . . A landed interest, a manufacturing interest, a mercantile interest, a moneyed interest, with many lesser interests, grow up of necessity in civilized nations, and divide them into different classes, actuated by different sentiments and views. The regulation of these various and interfering interests forms the principal task of modern legislation, and involves the spirit of party and faction in the necessary and ordinary operations of the government.

Perhaps the most eloquent passage in *The Federalist* comes in the closing paragraph of Number 14, a passionate appeal for the Union which found an echo in the concluding paragraph of Lincoln's First Inaugural Address. Lincoln's eloquent conclusion is a reworking of a paragraph written for him by William H. Seward, who had recently made a study of *The Federalist*.[12]

Hearken not [wrote Madison] to the unnatural voice which tells you that the people of America, knit together as they are by so many cords of affection, can no longer live together as members of the same family; can no longer continue the mutual guardians of their mutual happiness; can no longer be fellow-citizens of one great, respectable, and flourishing empire. Hearken not to the voice which petulantly tells you that the form of government recommended for your adoption is a novelty in the political world; that it has never yet had a place in the theories of the wildest projectors; that it rashly attempts what it is impossible to accomplish. No, my countrymen, shut your ears against this unhallowed language. Shut your hearts against the poison which it conveys; the kindred blood which flows in the veins of American citizens, the mingled blood which they shed in defence of their sacred rights, consecrate their Union, and excite horror at the idea of their becoming aliens, rivals, enemies.

14
George Washington

THE GREATEST of the Virginians, George Washington (1732–1799), was a voluminous writer of letters and documents of the greatest historical importance, but only rarely does what he wrote bear the hallmark of literary

[12] Jay B. Hubbell, "Lincoln's First Inaugural Address," *Am. Hist. Rev.*, XXXVI, 550–552 (April, 1931).

excellence. In the thousands of his letters that survive, however, there are, in the words of Rupert Hughes, "gems of characterization, wisdom, passion, wit, tenderness, homely and exalted emotions vividly expressed." On the rare occasions when he was moved by intense feeling he wrote passages that have the power to move a modern reader. Such are the letter which he wrote on June 18, 1775, to his wife when the Continental Congress made him supreme commander of the new American army and the letter which he wrote on December 23, 1777, from Valley Forge to the President of Congress about his soldiers, who he felt were being scandalously neglected by Congress and the American people.

Washington's most notable literary achievement was of course the Farewell Address, not delivered as a speech but published in the newspapers in September, 1796, announcing his decision not to be a candidate for re-election. He was the first of many Presidents to avail himself of the assistance of a ghost writer. He had wanted to retire four years earlier and had gone so far as to ask James Madison to draw up a synopsis of what he felt should be embodied in an address to the American people. In 1796, however, his collaborator was Alexander Hamilton, who took greater pains with the Farewell Address than he had taken with most of his *Federalist* papers. The ideas are fundamentally those of Washington; the literary qualities are probably mainly Hamilton's. It should be remembered, however, that Washington sent Hamilton a draft to work on and that he altered or omitted a good deal that Hamilton wrote. The collaboration was more effective than could have been expected. There was considerable rewriting by both men. With Hamilton's aid the statesman was able to give memorable expression to the wisdom which long experience had taught him. It is unfortunate that posterity has chosen to forget his denunciation of "the baneful effects of the party spirit" and has elected to remember instead his warning against "entangling alliances"—the phrase is Jefferson's and not Washington's. When he wrote the Farewell Address, Washington had in mind not so much posterity as his own contemporaries. It was designed, he said, "in a more especial manner for the yeomanry of this country. . . ."

More impressive as literature than anything which Washington himself wrote is the large body of writing which his character and achievements have inspired in poets, novelists, and dramatists. For them he has been— at least till after the death of Lincoln—our supremely great man, our symbol of Americanism at its highest and best. To be sure, his earlier biographers and eulogists made him too perfect and too colorless to arouse one's warmest sympathies; and yet he is memorably portrayed in Cooper's *The Spy*, Thackeray's *The Virginians*, Lowell's "Under the Old Elm," and Paul

Leicester Ford's *Janice Meredith*.[12a] The late Douglas Freeman's monumental life of Washington, even though incomplete, will, it is to be hoped, enable future historians, novelists, poets, and dramatists to portray the great soldier and statesman more like the man he was than most of their predecessors have done.

15
Robert Munford

COLONEL ROBERT MUNFORD (1730?–1784) of "Richland" in Mecklenburg County, Virginia, was more nearly a man of letters than any other Southern writer of his time. He was the grandson of another Colonel Robert Munford who accompanied William Byrd on the excursion described in the "Journey to the Land of Eden." "An honester a man, a fairer trader, or a kinder friend, this country never produced," wrote Byrd: "God send any of his sons may have the grace to take after him." The playwright's father, still another Robert Munford, did not have the grace to take after the friend whom Byrd so greatly admired. This Robert Munford, who married Anna Bland, died in 1743, leaving his estate heavily mortgaged. On February 12, 1744, William Beverley of "Blandfield," son of the historian and husband of Anna Munford's sister Elizabeth, wrote to Richard Bennett:

It is now some months since my wife's sister Mrs Anna Monford has been left a poor distressed widow wth two sons and a daughter in very mean circumstances (I have taken Robert her Eldest son & Mr Lee her daughter Elizabeth) the House & 800 acres of Land where she lives being mortgaged to one Mr Theophilus Field for about £360 Sterling and no hopes of Redeeming it, without your kind assistance, for neither her Brothers nor myself have any Ready money to assist her, and before her Eldest son comes of age the Interest will eat it out, it is a very pretty seat on the navigable part of Appamattox River very Commodious for Trade. If you will be pleased to have Compassion on them and Redeem the Land I will take Care to have the Mortgage duly assigned to you and Recorded and then they will be in your own power who never fails to shew mercy to those who deserve it, as she does, who tho' her husband was a Sot & used her very Ill on all Occasions, yet she always behaved herself towards him on all accounts as a good & dutiful wife ought to do. . . .

[12a] See William Alfred Bryan, *George Washington in American Literature*, 1775–1865 (1952). This study was prepared as a doctoral dissertation at Duke University, but the author died on December 17, 1950, a few days before he had planned to take his final examination.

Most of the Munford estate, it appears, had to be sold to pay the husband's debts.

Robert Munford, the playwright, was born at "Wakefield" in Prince George County, not later than 1730. In the summer of 1750 William Beverley of "Blandfield" journeyed to England to put his own son and Robert Munford in the Wakefield School in Yorkshire, where Richard Henry Lee and one of his brothers were already in residence. The headmaster, John Clarke, known as "Little Aristophanes," was a good classical scholar and, as William Beverley noted in his diary, had the "character of a very worthy gent^n." Unlike some of his Virginia schoolfellows, Munford did not go to one of the English universities, perhaps because the diminished estate did not permit.

When Mecklenburg County in southern Virginia was organized in 1765, Munford was appointed county-lieutenant, and he held the post until his death in 1784. He was also for many years sheriff and justice of the peace. In 1782 he held ninety-one slaves, more than any other planter in the county. The proprietor of "Richland" belonged to the class of great planters who held most of the offices in eighteenth-century Virginia. He represented his county in the House of Burgesses or its successor, the House of Delegates, during the years 1765–1775, 1779, 1780–1781. His wife was his first cousin Anna (or Anne) Beverley, the daughter of William Beverley of "Blandfield." Their son William, to be discussed in a later chapter, also a poet and a playwright, was the first American translator of Homer's *Iliad*.

In 1758 Munford served as captain in the campaign which resulted in the capture of Fort Duquesne (Pittsburgh). His immediate superior was Colonel William Byrd III, whose son Otway was to marry Munford's daughter Ann. In August of that year he wrote to his aunt, Mrs. Theodore Bland: "Hon'd. Madm. I am well and lousie, but still your affect'e nephew, etc." In May, 1765, Munford spoke and voted for Patrick Henry's resolutions in opposition to the Stamp Act. In 1770 he signed the Williamsburg nonimportation agreement, and in 1774 he presided over a meeting of Mecklenburg freeholders who passed resolutions expressing sympathy with "our Distressed fellow subjects in the Town of Boston."

Although he served as a major during a part of the Revolutionary War, Munford, as his play *The Patriots* suggests, was no fiery Whig. In a letter which he wrote to William Byrd III on April 20, 1775, he expressed his disapproval of "the intemperate warmth displayed by the People" in Mecklenburg and feared the result would be civil war. He was determined, he wrote, "to make one Effort more" to bring the Mecklenburgers "to a due

Sense of the obligations both of Duty & allegiance that bind them to their Sovereign & to the preservation of civil order." "As our own loyalty begins to be suspected," he concluded, "it is high Time to speak out." Patrick Henry had delivered his great speech in St. John's Church nearly a month earlier, and Concord and Lexington had been fought the day before Munford penned his letter. The hour of final decision was at hand. His friend Byrd and his wife's brother, Robert Beverley, remained loyal to the crown, but Munford decided to support the Revolution.[13]

In 1798, fourteen years after Colonel Munford's death, his son William brought out in Petersburg, Virginia, A Collection of Plays and Poems, by the late Col. Robert Munford, of Mecklenburg, in the State of Virginia. The volume contains two plays—The Candidates and The Patriots—a readable translation of the first book of Ovid's Metamorphoses, and a few poems, of which the best is a mildly humorous narrative entitled "The Ram," in the manner and metrical form of Butler's Hudibras. Munford's literary reputation rests primarily upon his two comedies, both of which—though possibly never acted—antedate by over a decade Royall Tyler's The Contrast (produced in New York in 1787), generally regarded as our first comedy of any importance.

The earlier play, The Candidates, is less expertly written than The Patriots; but it has a greater historical interest because it is among the very few firsthand sources of information about elections in eighteenth-century Virginia. The opening sentence makes it clear that the play was composed soon after the death of Governor Botetourt on October 15, 1770. The play is preceded by a Prologue, written after the playwright's death "By a Friend" who refers to him as "Virginia's first and only comic son." The Prologue may have been written at the request of William Munford, who wrote from Richmond on November 10, 1792: "The players are in town, and I intend to get them to bring a farce of my father's writing upon the stage this winter." Both The Candidates and The Patriots were obviously written for the stage, but there is no proof that either was ever produced. There was, however, more theatrical activity in eighteenth-century Virginia than is generally supposed. Some time before 1798 the playwright's son William played a part in Farquhar's The Beaux' Stratagem and for this occasion wrote a prologue to be "Spoken at a Theatre in Mecklenburg County, where a

---

13 Colonel Munford commanded two battalions of militiamen from southern Virginia in the Yorktown campaign. The Huntington Library has an order to Munford issued by General Greene's aid-de-camp, Nathaniel Pendleton, which reads in part: "You will therefore be pleased to march the two battalions of militia from the counties of Lunenburg Mecklenburg & Brunswick, which I am happy to hear you expect to complete by the shortest route to Hillsborough . . ." (March 1, 1781).

company of Gentlemen acted for the amusement of the public." It may be that Robert Munford wrote his two comedies for similar occasions.

Historians of the drama have noted that in Ralpho, in *The Candidates*, the Negro comedian makes his first appearance. Ralpho, however, does not speak in Negro dialect and is no more realistically drawn than the conventional Jim Crow of the nineteenth-century minstrel stage. Munford was a contemporary of Goldsmith and Sheridan, the best British dramatists of the century, but *The Candidates* is earlier than their best comedies. The malapropisms of Ralpho can owe nothing to Mrs. Malaprop in Sheridan's still unwritten *The Rivals*. If we judge *The Candidates* by dramatic standards, we find the opening scene somewhat slow and the dialogue of the planter candidates much too stilted. A more expert workman would have infused the comic spirit more thoroughly into every scene in the play. As it is, the humor appears chiefly in the scenes in which those heavy drinkers, Sir John Toddy and the two Guzzles, appear. Nevertheless, when produced by the Williamsburg Players in 1949, *The Candidates* proved to be a better play than a reader would have anticipated.

In spite of the wide differences between elections then and now, the modern reader easily recognizes in the office-seekers certain characteristics that have not changed and that still provoke laughter. And—at least on the stage—the behavior of politicians is matter for laughter rather than for tears. In the first scene of Act II Sir John Toddy, prompted by his campaign manager, Guzzle, makes a point of greeting by name freeholders whom he does not know. All goes smoothly until he follows up his greeting to Roger Twist with: "I hope your wife and children are well." "There's my wife," replies Twist. "I have no children, at your service." Two other candidates, Strutabout and Smallhopes, have, like many a latterday candidate, no qualifications except a great yearning for the honors and emoluments of office. As one observes some of Munford's candidates resorting to bluster, rant, and the liberal donation of liquor, one wonders how such men as George Mason, Richard Henry Lee, and Munford himself ever got elected to the House of Burgesses. In the end the two best candidates are elected, but one of them in some disgust expresses his—and no doubt the playwright's —mind: ". . . well, I find, in order to secure a seat in our august senate, 'tis necessary a man should either be a slave or a fool; a slave to the people, for the privilege of serving them, and [or] a fool himself, for thus begging a troublesome and expensive employment."

In some respects early Virginia elections were quite unlike those of our time. There was no secret ballot. The voter called out the name of the candidate whom he favored, and the favored candidate, if present, said, "Thank you." Only property-holders could vote, and the electors in the county numbered only a few hundred. Still in the future was the day when Andrew Jackson would express the opinion that the common man was qualified to hold any office within the gift of the American people. There lingered in the colony something of the old English notion that offices were for the benefit of the gentry or, perhaps we should say, should be held by men of education and independent means. The wealthy planters were as a rule educated men and were often men of ability, the natural leaders of the country; and the smaller farmers looked up to them. In *The Candidates* Worthy and Wou'dbe are large-scale planters, each with a considerable following. These two have for some years represented their county in the House of Burgesses. When Worthy, tired of politics, announces that he will not stand for re-election, he leaves his friend Wou'dbe in difficulties. Sir John Toddy, an honest toper, proposes himself as running mate, but Wou'dbe rejects him as unfit for the office and later rejects with scorn the overtures of the insignificant Strutabout. The freeholders are confused by a malicious rumor that Wou'dbe has accepted Toddy as running mate. His election is uncertain until Worthy, in order to make sure of his friend's election, announces himself as once more a candidate. Two such distinguished gentlemen running together are unbeatable.

In the Virginia of Munford and Jefferson the freeholders accepted the prevailing class distinctions and chose their candidates from among the gentlemen planters. No wonder that Jefferson felt that the people in Virginia could be trusted with political power since they almost invariably chose gentlemen. By 1814, however, the situation had so greatly changed that Jefferson wrote to Adams that it was now difficult for a Randolph, a Carter, or a Burwell to get elected to office in Virginia. One of the most amazing scenes in the play shows Wou'dbe, at the very time he is soliciting votes, telling the yeomen that he will not commit himself to follow their wishes in supporting or opposing bills, but will use his own judgment. A candidate making Wou'dbe's speech today would probably be committing political suicide.[14]

The Patriots, a five-act comedy, is a better play. Since it includes allusions to the battles of Trenton and Princeton, it must have been written —or at least retouched—after January, 1777. It is a study of real and pretended patriots, a satire on the less admirable types of Revolutionist. Munford saw their shortcomings as clearly as Janet Schaw saw them in North

[14] George Wythe Munford, Col. Munford's grandson, published a novel, *The Two Parsons* (Richmond, 1884), which gives an excellent account of a Virginia election in the last decade of the eighteenth century. See especially pp. 208–209.

Carolina or John Trumbull in New England. The "doctrines of a state of nature and liberty without restraint" had intoxicated the weak and the unthinking. One Brazen, a member of the Committee of Safety, "is a violent patriot without knowing the meaning of the word. He understands little or nothing beyond a dice-box and [a] race-field, but thinks he knows every thing; and woe be to him that contradicts him!" Another obnoxious "patriot" is the recruiting officer, Captain Flash, a blustering, illiterate coward who thinks that "gaming and whoring are the two first qualifications of a soldier." In what is perhaps the best scene in the play the Committee meets to hear the charges preferred against three Scotchmen: M'Flint, M'Squeeze, and M'Gripe. When one of them asks what the accusations are, Colonel Strut, who has preferred the charges, replies: "The nature of their offence, gentlemen, is, that they are Scotchmen; every Scotchman being an enemy, and these men being Scotchmen, they come under the ordinance which directs an oath to be tendered to all those against whom there is just cause to suspect they are enemies." When M'Gripe asks for proof of his disloyalty, Brazen answers: "Proof, sir! we have proof enough. We suspect any Scotchman: suspicion is proof, sir." When Tackabout, a Tory at heart who poses as a ranting Whig, is told that he must accept a commission in the militia, he remonstrates:

Where is the man that has done more than I have? I have damn'd the ministry, abus'd the king, vilified the parliament, and curs'd the Scotch. I have raised the people's suspicion against all moderate men; advised them to spurn at all government: I have cried down tories, cried up whigs, extolled Washington as a god, and call'd Howe a very devil. I have exclaimed against all taxes, advised the people to pay no debts; I have promised them success in war, a free trade, and independent dominion. In short, I have inspired them with the true patriotic fire, the spirit of opposition; and yet you say it is expected I should do something.

The main plot concerns chiefly Trueman and his friend Meanwell, two sensible gentlemen who are suspected of being Tories—as probably Munford himself had been—because they do not rant and rave. Brazen tries to induce his daughter Mira to break her engagement with Trueman and marry Captain Flash. In the end he discovers that Trueman is a patriot and Flash a coward. After being finally cleared of suspicion, Trueman remarks: "I am not wiser or better than before. My political opinions are still the same, my patriotic principles unaltered: but I have kick'd a tory, it seems: there is merit in this, which, like charity, hides a multitude of sins." Even the patriot women do not escape Munford's satire. Isabella, who dearly loves a uniform, declares that she never saw an ugly officer in her life. Unfortunately for her, she discovers that her fiancé, Colonel Strut, whom she expects to make her a general's wife, is an arrant coward.

From such details as I have given, it is obvious that *The Patriots*, though it has every appearance of having been written for the stage, could hardly have been publicly produced in this country until after Munford's death. The subplot, which is distinctly less realistic than the main plot, recalls more than one British comedy, especially *The Beaux' Stratagem*. Meanwell's servant Pickle, whose lines are well turned, seduces by a mock marriage an honest farmer's daughter, Melinda. The ending of the play is pure romance and sentimentality. Secrets come to light: Melinda is revealed as by birth a Virginia lady and Pickle as a well-to-do English gentleman, and the marriage proves to be legal and binding. The speeches of the gentlemen in the play are stilted and often colored by such "sentiments" as this from Trueman which might have come from Joseph Surface in *The School for Scandal*: ". . . when suffering virtue is to be relieved, or innocence protected, the moments are too precious to be dedicated to ceremony." It is no wonder that Brazen finally breaks out, like Sir Peter Teazle, and exclaims: "I hate your high flown speeches, Mr. Trueman." *The Patriots* is a better play than many of "America's Lost Plays," which were reprinted a few years ago. Fortunately, both *The Patriots* and *The Candidates* have been republished in the *William and Mary Quarterly* and made available to scholars and to amateur actors looking for early American plays of dramatic and literary merit. Historians, too, will find that they record aspects of American life that have not been carefully investigated.

16
Nathaniel and St. George Tucker

After the Lees, the Tuckers are the most remarkable of Virginian families, for they have produced men of distinction in every generation since the Revolution. St. George Tucker (1752–1827), the founder of the Virginia family, was born in Bermuda. Two of his older brothers, Thomas Tudor and Nathaniel, also came to the United States. Thomas Tudor, who had studied medicine at the University of Edinburgh, was in his later years Treasurer of the United States. The three Tucker brothers all came to the American continent in 1771. St. George enrolled at the College of William and Mary. Thomas Tudor came to Charleston to practice medicine, and Nathaniel Tucker (1750–1807), whose father was at that time unable to send him to the University of Edinburgh, came to Charleston to study medicine in his brother's office. He was at one time hopeful of marrying a Carolina heiress, and he was more interested in the verses he was writing than he was in medicine. He wrote a descriptive and topographical poem, *The Bermudian*, in the manner of Goldsmith's "The Deserted Village." St. George Tucker and his Williamsburg friends read it in manuscript and gave it their enthusiastic approval. It was published in 1774 both in Edinburgh (with a London imprint) and in Williamsburg. Nathaniel Tucker hoped to find a profession as a man of letters, but although the British reviews were favorable, the sales in both countries were disappointing.

In the spring of 1775 Tucker was at last able to begin the study of medicine at the University of Edinburgh. There he made friends among men and women of literary taste, and early in 1776 he published *The Anchoret*, a religious and didactic poem. In 1777 he took his M.D. degree at the University of Leyden. In 1779 we find him practicing medicine at Malton in Yorkshire. In 1786 he settled in Hull, where in 1791 he married Jane Wood, the daughter of a local merchant. He died there in December, 1807. His friends in Hull brought out a new edition of *The Bermudian* in 1808.

Tucker, living in England, was deeply moved by the American war for independence. In 1783, the year in which the war came to an end, he began writing an allegorical epic poem in the Miltonic manner entitled *America Delivered*. It was to be in twelve books, but Tucker left it unfinished because he had discovered that it was too close an imitation of Milton and he saw no means of obtaining enough subscribers to pay the cost of publication. Nevertheless, the subject continued to fascinate him, and he wrote an allegorical masque entitled *Columbinus*, which is interspersed with lyrical passages. If the poem had been published, it would have anticipated Joel Barlow's *The Vision of Columbus* and Daniel Bryan's *The Mountain Muse*. Tucker also wrote a play intended for the stage, *The Queen of Jewry*, but he did not succeed in getting it produced or published.

In his later years Tucker was a devout Swedenborgian. For him, as he wrote, the writings of Swedenborg were the "only clue to a knowledge of the source and principles, consequently the nature of all things in the material world even, as well as the spiritual." He published translations from the Latin of no less than four of Swedenborg's books—translations which remained standard for years. Some of them were certainly read by William Blake, Wordsworth, Coleridge, and Southey. Perhaps, as Lewis Leary suggests, ". . . it is in these volumes, which fed poets whose verse does live, that Nathaniel inadvertently fashioned the small bark which has unobtrusively carried his literary influence to those distant shores of posterity toward which he had formerly looked with such longing. When he stopped trying, when he no longer worried about success, then he succeeded."

In the early 1770's St. George Tucker was studying law in Williamsburg with George Wythe. His geniality, wit, good sense, and personal charm won him many friends. Seeing no opportunity for the practice of his profession, he obeyed his father's injunction and returned to Bermuda. Before leaving Virginia, he had informed Peyton Randolph, who then presided over the Continental Congress, that in Bermuda there were large unguarded stores of ammunition. These were promptly seized by the Americans. Soon afterwards Tucker and some of his friends purchased a ship and used it in carrying salt from Turk's Island to Virginia. In 1778 he married Mrs. Frances (Bland) Randolph, the mother of John Randolph of Roanoke and the mistress of "Matoax" and other plantations. By her he had two sons, Henry St. George and Beverley, both of whom attained distinction as teachers of law. Tucker served in the Virginia militia at the Battle of Guilford Court House and in the Yorktown campaign.

When the Virginia courts reopened after the war, Tucker began the long-delayed practice of his profession. After his wife's death in 1788 he left "Matoax" and settled in Williamsburg, the better to educate the Randolph and Tucker children. In 1791 he married Mrs. Lelia Carter, daughter of Sir Peyton Skipwith, the proprietor of "Prestwoud" in Southside Virginia. The year before his second marriage he had succeeded George Wythe as professor of law at William and Mary; he resigned in 1804. From 1803 to 1810 he was a judge on the Virginia Court of Appeals. In 1813 he was appointed by President Madison Federal Judge of the Virginia district; he held the position for nearly fifteen years.

Tucker was a thoroughgoing "republican." In the closing years of the Revolution he became acquainted with some educated French officers; and for a time after the French Revolution his children when they wrote to him addressed him as "Citizen Tucker." In 1796 he published in Philadelphia a portion of his college lectures under the title A Dissertation on Slavery: With a Proposal for the Gradual Abolition of It, in the State of Virginia. The tenor of this unavailing plea to the Virginia General Assembly may be judged from the quotation from Montesquieu printed on the title page: "Slavery not only violates the Laws of Nature, and of civil Society, it also wounds the best Forms of Government; in a Democracy, where all Men are equal, Slavery is contrary to the spirit of the Constitution." Slavery appeared to Tucker, as to many other Virginians, "not only incompatible with the principles of [democratic] government, but with the safety and security of their masters." In Tucker's time, though almost no one defended slavery on principle, inertia and the complexity of the problem prevented the state from adopting the plan of gradual emancipation which Tucker had proposed. The next generation was to witness a radical alteration in the Southern attitude toward slavery. By 1820 Tucker's son Beverley had come to regard the Union as a curse and slavery as a blessing.

Tucker's reputation as a legal scholar rests upon his annotated five-volume edition—an early American edition—of Blackstone's *Commentaries*. This was long regarded, especially in the South, as an authoritative text. In an Appendix Tucker included a long discussion entitled "View of the Constitution of the United States," in which he upheld the view that the Union was a confederacy of sovereign states, each of which was still competent to resume all the functions which it had delegated to the Federal government. He also included a fifty-four-page Note "On the State of Slavery in Virginia," in which he again condemned the institution in no uncertain terms. Southern politicians of the next generation were to ignore his condemnation of slavery while they cited his endorsement of the right of a state to secede from the Union.

In Williamsburg Tucker was one of a circle of cultivated people several of whom could and did turn out excellent occasional verse or an essay. Tucker often exchanged verses of the lighter sort with John Page, William Wirt, George Tucker, and others. He is said also to have written essays and plays, and he probably contributed to Wirt's *The Old Bachelor*, although his part in it remains unidentified. Tucker's writings were never collected, and most of them were probably never published. Toward the end of his life he wrote to Mathew Carey asking him to make arrangements for a collected edition of his poems. Why they were not published is not clear. If they are ever collected and published, it will be evident that the Williamsburg circle produced a fair amount of light verse that is not unlike that of their contemporaries, the Connecticut Wits.

The longer poems that Tucker published are chiefly patriotic and political. *Liberty, a Poem; On the Independence of America* (Richmond, 1788) is said to have moved George Washington, whose poetic taste was none of the best, to remark that it was "equal to a reinforcement of 10,000 disciplined troops." More important are Tucker's satiric "Pindaric" odes on political topics of the 1790's. In these he modeled his style on that of John Wolcot, whose satirical verses, published in England under the name of "Peter Pindar," were widely read at the time. Part I of Tucker's *The Probationary Odes of Jonathan Pindar, Esq. A Cousin of Peter's, and Candidate for the Poet*

Laureat to the C.U.S. (Philadelphia, 1796) had already appeared in Philip Freneau's *National Gazette* in June, July, and August, 1793. Part II, written soon after Part I, was not printed earlier because Freneau had ceased publishing the *Gazette*. Parrington and others have wrongly ascribed the series of poems to Freneau. In introducing the poems in Part II, Tucker employed a not uncommon literary device somewhat similar to that later used in Wirt's *The Letters of the British Spy* (1803) and in Irving's *Knickerbocker's History of New York* (1809). By way of preface Timothy Touchpenny, an innkeeper, contributes a letter to Christopher Clearsight, who, like Lowell's Parson Wilbur of *The Biglow Papers*, annotates Jonathan's poems. In a letter we are told that the poet had come to his inn shabby and penniless, speaking of "a place called *Parnass*." The poet was soon afterward found drowned, and the innkeeper published the poems left in manuscript. The poems are anti-Federalist satires. Jonathan hits at the national bank, at speculation, at Alexander Hamilton and John Adams, whom he dubs "Daddy Vice." Tucker, like John Taylor and many another Southerner, feared the growing power of the Federal government. He foresaw a time when:

> A voice shall then be heard in Congress-hall
> STATES *are no* more—and WE are ALL in ALL!!!

Among the better poems are "To Liberty," "Cousin Jonathan to Cousin Peter," and "To Economy," which begins:

> Economy, penurious, griping Dame!
>   Though once a vot'ry to thy name,
>   In thee, no more, I put my trust,
> Since H***N [Hamilton] and K*X [Knox] have clearly shewn
> Where thou art found no good can e'er be done.

Better-remembered are James McClurg's "The Belles of Williamsburg," to which Tucker contributed a few stanzas, and his own "Resignation," which is said to have been a favorite of John Adams. I give the first of the three stanzas:

> Days of my youth,
>   Ye have glided away;
> Hairs of my youth,
>   Ye are frosted and gray;
> Eyes of my youth,
>   Your keen sight is no more;
> Cheeks of my youth,
>   Ye are furrowed all o'er;

Strength of my youth,
All your vigor is gone;
Thoughts of my youth,
Your gay visions are flown.

NORTH CAROLINA

17
Introductory

NORTH CAROLINA was largely a land of small farms. The western section, which was being rapidly settled by Scotch-Irish, German, and other elements, was still at least semifrontier. Schools were few and generally inadequate. There were cultured families and good private libraries in the seaboard towns and on a few large plantations. The best known of the colony's libraries was the Johnston library at Edenton. Belonging originally to Governor Gabriel Johnston, who married a daughter of Governor Eden, it passed to Johnston's nephew and James Iredell's brother-in-law, Samuel Johnston, who greatly enlarged it. As described by Stephen B. Weeks, the books were almost exclusively of English origin. Although its owners were all lawyers, the library contained a due proportion of ancient classics and British poetry, drama, fiction, essays, history, politics, biography, and travels. In Wilmington, we are told, "Every family possessed a collection of the best English authors, besides which there was a public library supported by a society of gentlemen, and styled 'the Cape Fear Library.'" Wilmington was the home of the eloquent William Hooper, Signer of the Declaration of Independence, son of a Boston clergyman, and educated at Harvard College. Here also lived Dr. John Eustace, who had some correspondence with Laurence Sterne, and Archibald Maclaine, who wrote some unpublished criticisms of Shakespeare. Most of these men were lawyers and officeholders, and they came to North Carolina from England, the Northern colonies, or the West Indies.

Printing came late to the colony. James Davis, who set up a printing press at New Bern in 1749, launched a *North Carolina Gazette* there in 1751; Andrew Stewart began another at Wilmington in 1764. After Yorktown, printing spread rapidly westward, as in Virginia. In the central section Hillsboro had a press in 1786, and Fayetteville a year or two later. In the western region there was a press in Salisbury in 1797 and one in Lincolnton in 1800.

The ships that plied between Northern and Southern ports constituted a cultural as well as a commercial link between the two sections, and a native of Charleston or Savannah might be more at home in New York or Boston than in the interior of his own state. Young men from the North sometimes saw a greater opportunity to better themselves in the less populous Southern states. William Hill Brown (1765–1793) of Boston, author of *The Power of Sympathy* (1789), spent the last year of his life in North Carolina.[15] An earlier Northern writer to visit the colony was Thomas Godfrey (1736–1763) of Philadelphia, who came to Wilmington as a factor in the spring of 1759. By November of that year he had completed *The Prince of Parthia*, generally regarded as the first American tragedy. After three years in the South he returned to Philadelphia but soon came back to Wilmington, where he died in 1763. In 1765 when his writings were published in Philadelphia, they carried the names of twenty-four North Carolina subscribers. A few of Godfrey's shorter pieces were obviously written in North Carolina. The following lines are an example:

> O come to *Masonborough's* grove
> Ye Nymphs and Swains away
> Where blooming Innocence and Love,
> And Pleasure crown the day.

> Here dwells the Muse, here her bright Seat
> Erects the lovely Maid,
> From Noise and Show, a blest retreat,
> She seeks the sylvan shade.

18
James Iredell

JAMES IREDELL (1751–1799), the son of a Bristol merchant and an Irish mother, was born at Lewes in county Sussex, England. A great-uncle who had lived in North Carolina got him an appointment as Comptroller of the Customs at Edenton; and at the age of seventeen the youth arrived in the colony. He managed to live on the fees of his office and sent his yearly salary of £30 to his invalid father. Edenton, a town of four or five hundred people, had in its neighborhood a number of cultivated lawyer and planter families. Iredell studied law under the direction of Samuel Johnston, whose

[15] Richard Walser, "The North Carolina Sojourn of the First American Novelist," *N.C. Hist. Rev.*, XXVIII, 138–155 (April, 1951).

sister Hannah he afterwards married. Hannah Johnston was the daughter of John Johnston, Surveyor-General of the province and a brother of Governor Gabriel Johnston, who is said to have contributed to the *Crafts-man*, one of the numerous English papers modeled on the *Spectator* and the *Tatler*. Iredell was a hard worker. He overcame an impediment in his speech and rose to be the foremost lawyer in the state. He was appointed state judge in 1777 and two years later Attorney-General. From 1790 until his death in 1799 he was Associate Justice of the United States Supreme Court. He was an active propagandist for both the Revolutionary cause and for the Federal Constitution.

Iredell's tastes were distinctly literary. He liked to read his favorite books aloud to his wife and her women friends and relatives, and on his frequent journeys from home he was unhappy if he had neglected to take a book with him. In 1770 he wrote in his journal of his great delight in the *Spectator*. The qualities which he thought made it superior to all other essays were "Strength of reasoning, elegance of style, delicacy of sentiment, fertility of imagination, poignancy of wit, politeness of manners, and the most amiable pattern of human life. . . ." He was fond of the novels of Richardson, Fielding, and Sterne and of Dr. Fordyce's sermons, with the reading of which Mr. Collins bored the younger Bennet sisters in *Pride and Prejudice*. Iredell was a serious reader. In his last illness he wrote to his wife from Philadelphia: "I wish you would send me my spectacles and the six last volumes of Gibbon." While he was reading *Sir Charles Grandison* —surely the dullest of Richardson's voluminous novels—he noted: "When I read a book that pleases me I do not inquire, is this what I *can* do, but is it what I *ought* to do?" In 1773 we find him writing in his journal: "In the afternoon went early to my office, and could not resist the temptation of reading a little in Clarissa [Harlowe], having the first volume in my pocket; began it yesterday at home, and read a little in it this morning at my office. . . . I am at a loss which most to admire,—the goodness of the author's heart, the fineness of his imagination, his elegant and admirable sentiments, or the uncommon strength and eloquence with which he expresses them, —and each character most excellently supported throughout." What young man of today would find enjoyment in *Clarissa Harlowe*? In maturer years Iredell's favorite writer seems to have been Edmund Burke. After the Revolution he wrote to his brother Arthur in England asking for everything that Burke had published since 1775 and "a general Catalogue of Books, with their prices."

Among the earliest of Iredell's writings are some verses and an anti-Deistic essay. His son-in-law, Griffith J. McRee, includes in his biography of Iredell many excellent letters which passed between Iredell, his brother Arthur, William Hooper, and Archibald Neilson, all good letter-writers. Iredell's letters, like those of most other patriot leaders, are full of lofty sentiment. On April 29, 1776, he wrote to Joseph Hewes: "I have now no thought or wish of going home [to England]. My mind is raised above the sordid idea of providing for myself. I am impatient to be attached to my friends in the noblest of all causes—a struggle for freedom. . . . I should not wish to survive the ruin of my country, and should think myself disgraced in pusillanimously deserting the support of her fallen fortunes." A generation later Archibald Murphey in reading the speeches and letters of the Revolutionary leaders was struck by "a style founded upon and expressive of exalted feeling." It is, he said, a "style of high thought, and of lofty, yet chastened feeling; and reminds the reader of the finest specimens of the compositions in Tacitus, and of the correspondence of Cicero and his friends after the death of Pompey."

Iredell's Revolutionary writings are chiefly pamphlets most of which, though not published in his lifetime, circulated widely in manuscript. His address "To the Inhabitants of Great Britain," dated September, 1774, is for a young man of twenty-three a remarkable document. Iredell bases his appeal on reason, justice, and the rights of British subjects guaranteed by colonial charters. If Parliament is to be permitted to control the colonies, he writes: "The charters granted by our Sovereigns, instead of being considered as pledges of the honor and sacred faith of kings, were a mere snare and delusion to induce our forefathers to come abroad, with the utmost difficulty, expense, and hazard, and for many years almost entirely at their own risk, to make out of the wilderness, by their own and their children's labor, a fine country for you to spoil in. You are the *real proprietors*, we only *tenants at will*, of these possessions." If the charters are not still in force, he asks: "What becomes of confidence in Government, of reliance on the most sacred contracts of state?" Then he adds with irony: "But your Parliament, I suppose, can do no wrong: they are immaculate, and none of their proceedings can ever cause any real injury to *us*; though you sometimes complain of them yourselves." If, he continues, our forefathers could have foreseen that the charters were to be violated·

No Sir Walter Raleighs would have been found to traverse unknown seas: no American empire would have been now the object of contention. Could our ancestors have foreseen the latent claims of a British Parliament lurking under all the fair promises and encouragements of a smiling king, would they have been deluded by the specious bait, to the destruction of their and their posterity's hopes? No. They would certainly have preferred a life of ease and security, though of indolence, at home: they would not have torn themselves from their friends and country to seek misery and slavery in a barbarous and hostile land.

After the war Iredell was a stout champion of the new Federal Constitution. In January, 1788, while *The Federalist* was still appearing in instalments, he published a pamphlet replying to George Mason's objections to the Constitution. Most of his other writings are on legal topics, and some of them have never been published. His biographer, however, did publish two excellent satirical pieces: "Creed of a Rioter" and "Marks of Aristocracy in Connecticut." The former gives Iredell's view of the social revolt of the lower classes against gentlemen and especially lawyers:

1. I am a sworn enemy to all gentlemen. I believe none in that station of life can possibly possess either honor or virtue. . . .

Lastly, I am of opinion that our affairs would prosper much better, if gentlemen who read and consider too deeply for us, were totally banished from all public business, and if those who neither read nor think at all (and consequently cannot injure us by the excess of those practices) were intrusted with the management of our present arduous concerns.

As a Justice of the Supreme Court, it was Iredell's duty to preside over Federal courts in various sections. In 1793–1795 he thus visited most of the New England states. Like other intelligent Southerners who visited that region before 1830, or after 1875, he found much to admire. The roads in Connecticut were bad, but he found little else to find fault with. From Boston he wrote to his wife, October 21, 1792: "I have constantly received the utmost distinction and courtesy here, and like Boston more and more. . . . It is scarcely possible to meet with a gentleman who is not a man of education. Such are the advantages of schools by public authority." New England hospitality he found "truly genuine, mixed with a cordiality and kindness that could not be mistaken." On May 7, he wrote from Springfield: "I was certainly intended for a New England man. I admire the people, the country, as much as our Southern people affect to despise them."

19
Janet Schaw

In 1921 Professor and Mrs. Charles M. Andrews published a manuscript which they had found in the British Museum, giving it the title *Journal of a Lady of Quality; Being the Narrative of a Journey from Scotland to the West Indies, North Carolina, and Portugal, in the Years 1774 to 1776.* The

Lady of Quality was Janet Schaw, a witty, intelligent Scotchwoman of perhaps thirty-five, who in February, 1775, came to the Wilmington region to visit a brother and remained until the middle of the following November. She described with appreciation a region which possessed "every gift of nature," but she was repelled by "a most disgusting equality" which she saw all about her. North Carolina was to her "this Noble country, which indeed owes more favours to its God and king than perhaps any other in the known world and is equally ungrateful to both. . . ." She mistakenly supposed all the better families in Wilmington to be loyalists. For the Revolutionists she had no sympathy whatever. It seemed to her that a few disgruntled men were for their own selfish ends stirring up a rebellion for which there was no excuse. In this, too, she was mistaken, but there is some truth in her description of how the rank and file were induced to join the Revolutionary militia:

At present the martial law stands thus: An officer or committeeman enters a plantation with his posse. The Alternative is proposed, Agree to join us, and your persons and properties are safe; you have a shilling sterling a day; your duty is no more than once a month appearing under Arms at Wilmingtown, which will prove only a merry-making, where you will have as much grog as you can drink. But if you refuse, we are directly to cut up your corn, shoot your pigs, burn your houses, seize your Negroes and perhaps tar and feather yourself. Not to chuse the first requires more courage than they are possessed of, and I believe this method has seldom failed with the lower sort. No sooner do they appear under arms on the stated day, than they are harangued by their officers with the implacable cruelty of the king of Great Britain, who has resolved to murder and destroy man, wife and child, and that he has sworn before God and his parliament that he will not spare one of them; and this those deluded people believe more firmly than their creed, and who is it that is bold enough to un-deceive them?

Miss Schaw was somewhat amused by the unmartial appearance of the militia, "2000 men in their shirts and trousers, preceded by a very ill-beat drum and a fiddler, who was also in his shirt and with a long sword and a cue at his hair, who played with all his might." When after the review one of the patriot leaders, Colonel Robert Howe, unceremoniously picked up a book she had been reading, she "reproved him with a half compliment to his general good breeding." When he admitted his fault and promised to submit to whatever punishment she might inflict, she asked him to read "that part of Henry the fourth, where Falstaff describes his company." When Colonel Howe began reading Falstaff's description of his ragamuffin soldiers, she says, he "coloured like Scarlet. I saw he made the application instantly; however he read it thro', tho' not with the vivacity he generally speaks; however he recovered himself and coming close up to me, whispered, you will certainly get yourself tarred and feathered; shall I apply to be executioner?" [16]

SOUTH CAROLINA

20
Introductory

In 1773, when Josiah Quincy, Jr., visited Charleston, that city was one of the four largest in the American colonies. The Massachusetts patriot had made the long voyage from Boston primarily for his health—Emerson was to make the same voyage for the same reason in 1826—but he hoped to be able to stimulate intercolonial correspondence on the part of Southern leaders. Quincy was not prepared for what he saw in Charleston. On March 1 he wrote to his wife: "I can only say in general, that in grandeur, splendour of buildings, decorations, equipages, numbers, commerce, shipping, and indeed in almost every thing, it far surpasses all I ever saw, or ever expected to see in America." At a concert sponsored by the St. Cecilia Society he found the music excellent. A French violinist, recently employed at a salary of five hundred guineas, was the best Quincy had ever heard. At the concert, he noted: "The gentlemen many of them dressed with richness and elegance, uncommon with us—many with swords on. We had two Macaronis present—just arrived from London. This character I found real, and not fictitious." In St. Philip's Church "A young scarcely-bearded boy read prayers, with the most gay, indifferent and gallant air imaginable: very few men and no women stand in singing-time. A very elegant piece of modern declamatory composition was decently delivered by another clergyman. . . ." The sermon lasted just eighteen and a half minutes by Quincy's watch. He found anti-British sentiment not uncommon, but he also discovered "A general doubt of the firmness and integrity of the northern colonies. . . ." The members of the Assembly, he found, were almost entirely well-to-do planters living in Charleston; the lower classes were not represented. The Councilors, judges, and other important officers were appointed from London. He wrote in his journal: "I heard several of the

---

[16] The passage to which Miss Schaw refers is probably *I Henry IV*, Act IV, scene 1; but *II Henry IV*, Act III, scene 2 would have been equally appropriate.

planters say, we none of us, when we grow old, can expect the honours of the State—they are all given away to worthless poor rascals."

In South Carolina Revolutionary reform did not proceed so far as in Virginia and North Carolina, but it resulted in the disestablishment of the Anglican Church and the abolition of primogeniture. Some were even eager to abolish slavery, notably Henry Laurens. Dr. Joseph Brown Ladd, a native of Rhode Island, wrote in 1785: "The most elevated and liberal Carolinians abhor slavery; they will not debase themselves by attempting to vindicate it."

The most active Revolutionary agitators in South Carolina were not planters but the merchants, Henry Laurens and Christopher Gadsden, and a blacksmith from New York, William Johnson. On June 12, 1777, Peter Timothy, proprietor of the *South-Carolina Gazette*, wrote to Benjamin Franklin: ". . . the Opposition to Tyranny here was raised by a single inconsiderable man here, under all the Discouragements imaginable, even Gadsden doubting whether it could be attempted." Abetted by Gadsden, Johnson organized the Charleston mechanics and regularly assembled them under a large live-oak tree in Mazyck's pasture outside the city. This Liberty Tree became so obnoxious in its association with radical activities that when the British captured Charleston, they burned it, as they had burned the one in Boston.

Peter Timothy, an ardent patriot, republished in the *Gazette* Hume's "Observations on the Liberty of the Press," John Dickinson's *Letters from a Farmer in Pennsylvania*, Thomas Paine's *Common Sense* and the *Crisis*; and he printed in addition whatever patriotic writing he could get from the South Carolinians. Of this there was a considerable amount, nearly all of it anonymous. The ablest writers were William Henry Drayton, Laurens, and Gadsden.

On September 21, 1769, Timothy printed in the *Gazette* "Philo Patriae's" poem "On Liberty-Tree," one of the best pieces of Revolutionary writing to come out of the colony.[17] With the local Liberty Tree in mind, the unknown poet hailed the live oak as peculiarly sacred to freedom:

> No Region boasts so firm a Wood,
> So fit to cut the Crystal Flood
> And Trade's wide blessings to convey,
> From Land to Land, from Sea to Sea.
> No Soil e'er grew a Tree so fair,
> Whose Beauty can with thine compare.
> Unmatch'd thy awful Trunk appears,
> The Product of an Hundred Years.

[17] Jay B. Hubbell (ed.), " 'On Liberty-Tree': A Revolutionary Poem from South Carolina," *S.C. Hist. and Geneal. Mag.*, XLI, 117–122 (July, 1940).

Thy graceful Head's bent gently down,
Which ever-verdant Branches crown.
Thro' thy twinn'd Foliage Zephyrs play,
And feather'd Warblers tune their Lay.

The poet restates the doctrine of natural rights:

Rights! which declare, "That all are free,
In Person and in Property.
That Pow'r supreme, when giv'n in Trust,
Belongs but to the Wise and Just.
That Kings are Kings for this sole Cause,
To be the Guardians of the Laws.
That Subjects only should obey,
Only submit to sov'reign Sway,
When Sov'reigns make those Laws their Choice
To which the People give their Voice.
That in free States, 'tis ever meant
No Laws should bind, without *Consent*;
And that, when other Laws take Place,
Not to *resist*, wou'd be Disgrace;
Not to *resist*, wou'd treach'rous be,
Treach'rous to Society.

This summary of the traditional doctrines of British liberty is less poetic
than the poet's conclusion:

Wide and more wide, may thy Domain,
O LIBERTY! its Power maintain,
Parent of Life! true Bond of Law!
From whence alone our Bliss we draw,
Thou! who dids't once in antient *Rome*,
E'er fell Corruption caus'd its Doom,
Reign in a *Cato's* godlike Soul,
And *Brutus* in each Thought controul;
Here, here prolong thy wish'd for Stay,
To bless and cheer each passing Day,
Tho' with no pompous Piles erect,
Nor sculptur'd Stones, thy shrine is deckt;
Yet here, beneath thy fav'rite Oak,
Thy Aid will all thy SONS invoke.
Oh! if thou deign to bless this Land,
And guide it by thy gentle Hand,
Then shall AMERICA become
Rival, to once high-favour'd *Rome*.

21
William Charles Wells

THE DEPARTURE from the colonies of cultivated Tory families, as I have noted before, marked a cultural setback, but no family that left the Southern colonies was comparable to that of Robert Wells (1728–1794). This Scotch bookseller and bookbinder from Dumfries came to Charleston in 1753. In 1754 he opened what was soon to become the best bookstore in the city, perhaps in all the colonies. He not only imported books but he bought private libraries and sold them at auction. In 1758 he founded Charleston's third newspaper, the *South-Carolina Weekly Gazette*, which in 1764 became the *South-Carolina and American General Gazette*. The Revolution temporarily divided his family, and his son John remained in Charleston to continue the *Gazette*. His daughter Louisa Susannah (Wells) Aikman wrote *The Journal of a Voyage from Charleston, S. C., to London Undertaken during the American Revolution*, published by the New York Historical Society in 1906. Another daughter, Helena (Wells) Whitford, published two novels after her return to England: *The Stepmother* (1799) and *Constantia Neville: or, The West Indian* (1800).

The most distinguished member of the family was Dr. William Charles Wells (1757–1817), who was born in Charleston. In 1768 he was sent to Dumfries to be educated. After two years and a half there he enrolled in the University of Edinburgh. In 1771 he returned to Charleston, where he was apprenticed to Dr. Alexander Garden, a noted physician and naturalist who is not to be confused with Whitefield's opponent, the Reverend Alexander Garden. In 1775 Wells went back to Edinburgh to continue the study of medicine. In 1780 or 1781 he came back to Charleston, now in British possession, on business for his father. His brother John, a loyalist, was publishing his father's newspaper under the title of the *Royal Gazette*. In 1782, when the British army evacuated Charleston, William Charles Wells and his brother John went to St. Augustine, where in 1783 and 1784 they published the *East-Florida Gazette*, "the first thing of the kind ever attempted in that country." In St. Augustine the versatile Dr. Wells managed a theatrical company and played certain roles himself.

Returning to England, he settled in London, where he devoted his time to medical practice and scientific research. *An Essay on Dew* (London, 1814; Philadelphia, 1838) won him the Royal Society's medal. Charles Darwin in a letter to Sir J. D. Hooker, written in October, 1865, said: "Talking about the 'Origin [of Species]' by Means of Natural Selection, a Yankee

[Charles L. Brace] called my attention to a paper attached to Dr. Wells' famous 'Essay on Dew,' which was read in 1813 to the Royal Society, but not (then) printed, in which he applies most distinctly the principle of Natural Selection to the Races of Men." In the fourth edition of *On the Origin of Species* Darwin gave due credit to Dr. Wells as one of the few who had anticipated his theory of evolution.

22
Joseph Brown Ladd

D<small>R</small>. L<small>ADD</small> (1765–1786), who died in Charleston at the age of twenty-two, was born in Newport, Rhode Island. He attended such schools as were available until 1775, when his father moved to a farm at Little Compton. Before this time the precocious boy had published in Solomon Southwick's Newport *Mercury* "An Invocation to the Almighty," which appears in his collected writings. Young Ladd disliked farm work and showed some ingenuity in avoiding it. "My head, sir," he said to his father, "and not my hands must support me." Clerking in a store proved no more congenial, and he was put to work in Southwick's printing office. While there, he wrote some satirical ballads. If he had only limited his victims to the quacks that infested the town, he might have escaped the difficulties he got into when he satirized the Reverend Samuel Hopkins, who complained to the boy's father. Young Ladd was taken from the printing office and at the age of fifteen placed under the tuition of Dr. Isaac Senter, for he had decided to become a physician. The youth had a passion for science as well as for literature, and he read widely in Dr. Senter's books and in what he could find in the Redwood Library in Newport. He studied philosophy, rhetoric, Greek, Latin, French, and even Hebrew, and for relaxation he read the English classics. The majority of his poems were written before he completed his education in 1783. "Amanda," to whom many of the poems are addressed, seems to have returned Ladd's affection; but the mercenary relatives who were her guardians, we are told, finding it profitable to manage her estate, refused to permit her to marry him. In 1783, having now a license to practice medicine, Ladd made the acquaintance of General Nathanael Greene, who urged the young doctor to try his fortune in the South. Some time in the spring of 1784 Ladd was in Charleston.

Nearly all we know of Ladd's life up to this time is found in W. B. Chittenden's biographical sketch, published in the *Literary Remains* forty-six years after the poet's death. For the last two or three years of Ladd's life, the Charleston newspapers, which Lewis Leary has carefully studied, furnish additional materials. Ladd found Charleston society congenial and the local newspaper hospitable; he published more than seventy of his contributions over the name of "Arouet." In 1785 he delivered the Fourth-of-July oration in Charleston. He set aside two hours each day to attend to penniless patients. He lectured on scientific subjects, and he published *An Essay on Primitive, and Regenerative Light*, and in August, 1786, *The Poems of Arouet*.

On October 14 of that year he printed in the Charleston *Morning Post* a communication in which he denounced one Ralph Isaacs as "a base, ungrateful villain." Isaacs would seem to have been a former Rhode Island friend of Ladd's. The reason for the quarrel is obscure, but Isaacs replied to Ladd's attack, branding him as a *"self-created Doctor,"* "a dangerous imposter," a coward, and a scoundrel. The result was a duel on October 20, in which Ladd threw away his fire but was mortally wounded by his opponent. He died on November 2, 1786.

Ladd's verses were extremely popular, not only in Charleston but throughout the nation. If we may judge by the poems which Mathew Carey reprinted in the *American Museum* in 1787–1788, Ladd's verses were in greater demand than those of Freneau, Francis Hopkinson, or the Connecticut Wits. His poems are easy, facile, and timely. They are a good index to what American readers liked in the closing years of the eighteenth century. They seem to the modern reader sentimental, pretentious, and imitative. Ladd had talent, but he was no poetic genius cut off in his young manhood like Chatterton or Keats or even Edward Coote Pinkney. The love poems show no deep feeling. The poet's excessive admiration for Ossian suggests that he saw little difference between Homer and the poetic prose of the Scotch schoolmaster whose "translations" from the Gaelic had earlier fascinated Thomas Jefferson. He was attracted to *The Sorrows of Young Werther*; Goethe's hero, it will be remembered, came at last to prefer Ossian to Homer. Ladd's verses do show a certain Romantic sensitivity to the beauties of nature and a scorn for the works of Dr. Johnson. As an example of Ladd's poetry at a fairly high level, I quote "What Is Happiness?"

> 'Tis an empty, fleeting shade,.
> By imagination made;
> 'Tis a bubble, straw, or worse;
> 'Tis a baby's hobby-horse;
> 'Tis a little living, clear;
> 'Tis ten thousand pounds a year;
> 'Tis a title; 'tis a name;

'Tis a puff of empty fame,
Fickle as the breezes blow;
'Tis a lady's YES or NO:
And when the description's crowned,
'Tis just *no where* to be found.

The *Literary Remains* includes part of Ladd's bombastic Fourth-of-July
oration, "Critical Remarks, on the Writings of the Late Dr. Johnson," and
a "View of Society and Manners in South Carolina," which shows none
of the too-common New England prejudice against Southerners.

GEORGIA

23
John Joachim Zubly

THE YOUTHFUL COLONY of Georgia, ruled by one of the best royal gover-
nors, Sir James Wright, had less cause for dissatisfaction than other colonies.
The chief Revolutionary writer there was the redoubtable John Joachim
Zubly (1724–1781), a Presbyterian clergyman of Swiss birth and education.
Called to Savannah from South Carolina in 1760, he built up a large and
influential church and accumulated considerable property. He was the chief
spokesman for the dissenters in their difficulties with the Established
Church. In 1766 he published a sermon, *The Stamp-Act Repealed*, and in
1769 *An Humble Inquiry into the Nature of the Dependency of the Ameri-
can Colonies upon the Parliament of Great-Britain*. While a member of
the Provincial Congress of Georgia, he published in 1775 *The Law of
Liberty: A Sermon on American Affairs, Preached at the Opening of the
Provincial Congress of Georgia* . . . (Philadelphia, 1775). In this sermon
Zubly contended that "Liberty and law are perfectly consistent. . . ."
Much more spirited than the sermon is the prefatory address "To the Right
Honourable William Henry, Earl of Dartmouth." Here Zubly speaks the
bold and fiery language of the Revolutionary agitator. He begins:

The question, My Lord, which now agitates Great-Britain and America, and
in which your Lordship has taken such an active part, is, whether the Parliament
of Great-Britain has a right to lay taxes on the Americans, who are not, and
cannot, there be represented, and whether the Parliament has a right to bind
the Americans in all cases whatsoever?

To bind them in ALL CASES WHATSOEVER, my Lord, the Americans look upon this as the language of despotism in its utmost perfection. What can, say they, an Emperor of Morocco pretend more of his slaves than to bind them in all cases whatsoever?

The Americans, he argues, are not idiots, and they are determined never to be slaves. He hints that the military resistance of Americans will be desperate:

The present dispute has made every American acquainted with, and attentive to, the principles of the Brittish constitution: In this respect, as well as in a strong sense of liberty, and the use of fire-arms almost from the cradle, the Americans have vastly the advantage over men of their rank almost every where else. From the constant topic of present conversation, every child unborn will be impressed with the notion: It is slavery to be bound at the will of another in all cases whatsoever; every mother's milk will convey a detestation of this maxim. Were your Lordship in America, you might see little ones acquainted with the word of [military] command before they can distinctly speak, and shouldering the resemblance of a gun before they are well able to walk.

Zubly represented Georgia in the Continental Congress of 1775; but clinging to the British constitution as the bulwark of civil liberties and believing the difficulties all due to the British ministers then in power, he disapproved of independence. A republic seemed to him—even though he had grown up in Switzerland—"little better than government of devils." Charged in Congress with outright disloyalty, he returned to Georgia, where he joined the Tories. In 1777 half his estate was confiscated, and he was banished from the state. He took refuge in South Carolina. In 1779, when British troops re-established the royal government, he returned to Georgia. He died two years later. "His crime," remarks Moses Coit Tyler, "was that of every man who begins as a political reformer and refuses to end as a revolutionist." There are eloquence and pathos in the appeal he addressed to the Grand Jury which indicted him in 1777:

I should be glad to know upon what principle, natural, humane, divine, moral, legal, equitable or conscientious, any jury upon oath, or any impartial Barbarian, could possibly condemn a man as an internal enemy, against whom no crime has been alledged, whose veracity is not disputed, and who offers solemnly to swear not to give any intelligence to, nor take up arms to assist an enemy, and in all things to do his duty as a good and faithful freeman of the State.

III

THE ERA OF GOOD FEELING

1789-1830

1

The Historical Background

IN 1789, when George Washington was inaugurated as the first President of the young republic, there was no "Solid South." Those who lived below the Mason and Dixon Line rarely thought of themselves as Southerners. They were, first of all, Virginians and Georgians and Marylanders, or they belonged to one of the Carolinas; after that, they were Americans. The experience of having fought the Revolution together made soldiers like John Marshall and statesmen like James Madison less provincial than their predecessors had been; but with the rank and file in North and South alike state pride was a more potent factor than it is anywhere today. Among the uneducated, ignorance of other sections was almost abysmal. The ties with England had been broken, but the process of making a real nation out of the thirteen separate sovereign states was to be a slow one. In the years 1789–1830 the Northern and the Southern states were often in marked disagreement on political questions, especially during the administrations of Jefferson and Madison. In the world of literature, however, I have found so many evidences of friendliness that I think I am justified in calling it "The Era of Good Feeling," a term which in historical usage is limited to the administration of James Monroe (1817–1825).

Before 1820 there was greater rivalry between East and West than between North and South. In that year the debate over the admission of Missouri as a slave state witnessed the first open clash between North and South. As hostility to slavery developed in the North, the Southern states, jealous of the fast-growing population and wealth of the North, began gradually to develop a unity of feeling; but this unity, hardly complete even in 1861, was a political accomplishment, and it was brought about in spite of great geographical and economic diversity among the Southern states. The South is no such natural geographical unit as the

Pacific Coast or New England, which seemed to Frederick J. Turner destined by its geographical position to provincialism.

Broadly speaking, there were two great areas in the South, each cutting across state lines: first, the lowlands of the Atlantic seaboard, the Gulf states, and the Mississippi Valley and, second, the uplands culminating in the great Appalachian range which cut through almost every Southern state east of the Mississippi. Beyond the Mississippi were the fertile lowlands and the Ozark Mountains, which were like a smaller Appalachian system. In the lowlands along the Atlantic seaboard the characteristic figure was the slaveholding planter or farmer, cultivating cotton, rice, or tobacco; in the uplands, more recently won from the Indians, the typical figure was the small farmer with few or no slaves, raising wheat, corn, cattle, and hogs and jealous of the Low-Country planter. The uplanders were Baptists, Methodists, Presbyterians, Lutherans, or followers of Alexander Campbell rather than Episcopalians. Many of them had come into the South from Pennsylvania and other Northern states, and in some cases they had closer ties with the North than with the Lowland South. On December 6, 1837, a Savannah physician, Richard D. Arnold, wrote to his wife from Milledgeville, the new Georgia state capital: "No two people separated by the barrier of a different language are more radically dissimilar than the low and up country people of this state." Dr. Arnold was more at home in Boston or New York than in Middle Georgia.

In the course of time, for the South has never been static, the slave plantation pushed its way into the Southwest and into the uplands to the foothills of the mountains. In the Piedmont regions the farmers often acquired slaves, took up the cultivation of cotton, and came to resemble the seaboard planter type. Not so the mountaineers, who remained almost isolated until after the Civil War. Before 1830, however, the Piedmont farmers contended vigorously with the still dominant lowland population for fuller representation in the state legislatures, for the extension of the suffrage, and for the removal of state capitals to central situations.

After the War of 1812 New England turned more and more to manufacturing. Meanwhile the invention of the cotton gin by Eli Whitney, while that Connecticut Yankee was tutoring on a Georgia plantation, turned the Lower South from a diversified agriculture to the indiscriminate raising of cotton. Southerners were content to buy manufactured products from New England as before the Revolution they had bought them from England. In the South trade was mainly in the hands of outsiders: Scotch merchants in Richmond, New York and New England factors in seaport cities further south, and Yankee peddlers everywhere. Like English country gentlemen, the Southern planters looked down upon businessmen. For a time cotton-raising was highly profitable, and the desire for new lands and slaves to till them was a powerful factor in promoting the rapid settlement of the Southwest. Meanwhile Northern traders, backed by Northern capital, bought up the cotton and sold the planters manufactured goods, making a substantial profit on both purchase and sale. Many a land-hungry farmer borrowed from Northern factors or merchants at a high rate of interest by pledging a cotton crop which had perhaps not yet been put in the ground.

Cotton quickly became the largest single item in America's export trade, but almost no cotton was carried overseas in ships owned in the South or manned by Southern seamen. The system known as the "cotton triangle" had developed.[1] New York businessmen diverted trade between European and Southern ports hundreds of miles out of the shortest course—sometimes ships stopped at New York going and coming—and exacted a heavy toll in commissions, freight charges, interest, insurance, and other profits amounting, so some have estimated, to forty cents on every dollar paid in Europe for the raw cotton. Beginning in the 1830's, Southern commercial conventions repeatedly protested against the system, but the chief result was increased Southern resentment rather than the adoption of practical measures.

The South complained of the tariff, which it believed responsible for the high prices of manufactured goods, and with some reason. Shortly before the "tariff of abominations" was passed by Congress in May, 1828, Daniel Webster received a letter from the wealthy New England manufacturer, Abbott Lawrence, who wrote concerning the amended tariff bill: "I must say I think it would do much good, and that New England would reap a great harvest by the having the bill adopted as it now is. . . . This bill if adopted as amended will keep the South and West in debt to New England the next hundred years." [2] Abbott Lawrence was one of the wealthy Massachusetts businessmen who paid Webster's debts in the expectation that he would represent their interests in Washington. Emerson's opinion of him is expressed in an entry in the *Journals* for May 23, 1846: "Boston or Brattle Street Christianity is a compound of force, or the best diagonal line that can be drawn between Jesus Christ and Abbott Lawrence."

In this period of declining Revolutionary liberalism the South was developing in the opposite direction from the North, especially New England.

[1] R. G. Albion, *The Rise of New York Port, 1815–1816* (1939), chap. vi, "The Cotton Triangle," and *Square-Riggers on Schedule* (1938), chap. iii, "Enslaving the Cotton Ports."

[2] Raynor G. Wellington, *The Political and Sectional Influence of the Public Lands, 1828–1842* (1914), p. 27, n. 5.

In the agricultural South the tendency was from a broad nationalism toward a sectionalism based upon the defense of slavery; in New England, now undergoing rapid industrialization, the national spirit was growing and provincial forces would become less powerful as the railroads linked New England to the country west of the Hudson. Daniel Webster became less the spokesman of a provincial New England and more the exponent of the new nationalism, while John C. Calhoun, who had been far more of a nationalist than Webster, became the champion of a minority section fighting on the defensive. In New England the industrial revolution loosened the grip of the conservative classes and paved the way for the development of isms of all kinds which were obnoxious to the South. The slave states, failing to heed Jefferson's repeated warnings about the evils of slavery, began to follow such new prophets as Thomas R. Dew and Beverley Tucker, who proclaimed slavery a positive good. The invention of the spinning jenny and the cotton gin had made slavery, moribund in Virginia, profitable in the Gulf states. The economic interpretation of history is by no means the only valid one, but it offers the most plausible explanation of the new Southern attitude toward slavery. The Declaration of Independence, now beginning to be labeled a collection of glittering fallacies, gave way to the Nullification Act of South Carolina. Thomas Cooper, beginning as a partisan of the French Revolution, became the South Carolina champion of state rights and Nullification. Beverley Tucker, son of St. George Tucker the advocate of gradual emancipation, became a leading advocate of secession and a defender of slavery on principle.

All that I have said is true, and yet it needs considerable qualification. The two democratic revolutions in politics led by Jefferson and Andrew Jackson each had its effect upon the South. Every Southern state except South Carolina rewrote its constitution to bring it into something like harmony with the principles of Jacksonian democracy. The Jackson movement has been seen too often as a movement which had vitality only in the West or in Eastern cities. Arthur M. Schlesinger, Jr.'s, highly praised *The Age of Jackson* (1945) grossly neglects the effect of the movement in the Southern states. In an article on "Democracy in the Old South" Professor Fletcher Green, an authority on Southern constitutional history, has pointed out that "The establishment of white manhood suffrage, the abolition of property qualifications for office holders, the election of all officers by popular vote, and the apportionment of representation on population rather than wealth, with periodic reapportionment, dealt a death blow to the political power of the landed, slaveholding aristocracy of the Old South." [3] With the one marked exception of Negro slavery, he points out,

3 "Democracy in the Old South," *Jour. So. Hist.*, XII, 17–18 (Feb., 1946).

the Southern states were politically as democratic in 1860 as their Northern sisters—more so than certain New England states. Long before the Civil War political power, in the South as in the North, had passed into the hands of the common man. Richard Henry Wilde, John Pendleton Kennedy, William Elliott, and Charles Gayarré were to find that being a gentleman was a handicap in a candidate for office.

A new generation of men came into power in the South after the Revolution. The political and intellectual leaders of the section from that time to the present have come principally from the middle classes and not from the old planter families. In Virginia, for example, the abolition of the laws of primogeniture and entail, the disestablishment of the Anglican Church, the debts to British merchants, the wasteful methods of cultivation, and the devastation of invading armies left many of the great planters in ruin. James Kirke Paulding, who visited Virginia in 1816, wrote of the old planter houses in his *Letters from the South* (1817): "A few of these ancient establishments are still kept up, but many of the houses are shut; others have passed into the hands of the industrious, or the speculating, whose modes of thinking, feeling, and acting, are totally different; and, with here and there an exception, nothing now remains, but the traditionary details of some aged matron, who lives only in the recollections of the past, of ancient modes, and ancient hospitality."

Many planters who had lost their estates began life anew in Kentucky or Alabama while new men rising from below bought farms and came into prominence. The new class gradually took on the ways of the old planters and sometimes intermarried with them. The Southern planter aristocracy was never a closed order, even in Low-Country South Carolina. Property, education, good manners, and ability could win admission to an upper class in the South as in the North, where the Colonial aristocracy had also suffered a decline. The tradition of the gentleman planter continued in modified form in the older Southern states; in the newer states to the westward the new rich planters were less influenced by the colonial tradition.

2

Religion

The Revolution, it is well known, brought a reaction against the Established Church, and after 1775 the Episcopal clergy were unpopular because so many of them had been Tories. They had neglected the lower classes and particularly the people in the sparsely populated western regions. In this period the influence of the Great Awakening continued, especially in Kentucky. In many instances the evangelical ministers came from the North; but the majority of them, whether native to the South or not, were men of little culture or breadth of mind. Their power was emotional rather than intellectual, and the camp meeting was a favorite method of conversion. There is much to be said for their zeal and energy, and perhaps no other form of religion could have made an impression on backwoodsmen; but among them there were few intellectual leaders comparable to James Blair, Samuel Davies, or the great New England divines. Intent upon denominational differences which seem to most persons of little consequence now, they argued endlessly over their creeds and rites and agreed only in denouncing Episcopalians, Unitarians, Deists, and atheists. In this period the Deists all but disappeared, and the Unitarians won only a scant foothold in the Southern states. The Presbyterians, who inherited a fine educational tradition from their Scotch predecessors, founded Hampden-Sydney College in Virginia in 1776. In the thirties and forties the Baptists and Methodists founded colleges in many Southern states. These denominations, and especially the Presbyterians, finally came to exert great influence upon the state universities. They prevented Jefferson from bringing Thomas Cooper to the University of Virginia, and they finally forced Cooper out of the presidency of the University of South Carolina. The South was very far from being the godless section which the Abolitionists were soon to proclaim it; but it had, one notes regretfully, too few such clerical leaders as William Ellery Channing and Theodore Parker, men of liberal views who were interested in literature and culture as well as in winning converts to their particular denominations.

In 1812 the able Presbyterian divine, John Holt Rice, the friend and biographer of Samuel Davies, noted the presence in Virginia churches of two types of ministers: "the Rational religionists, and the Evangelical preachers." "The former of these," he explained, "generally affect superior learning, and refinement, and taste: they dwell much on the small moralities of this world; they speculate in a very cool, philosophical manner on virtue, and the fitness of things, and the inconveniences of vice, &c. &c." Rice's own sympathies were obviously with the second class, who, he wrote, "are no enemies to true learning, to sound criticism, to refinement in taste, and to all the graces of literature; but they count every thing but loss in comparison with the excellency of the knowledge of Christ Jesus; and have determined to know nothing but Christ and him Crucified. . . . Hence the earnestness with which they insist on the depravity of man, his helpless condition, the necessity of regeneration, and of the influence of the Holy Spirit, the doctrine of justification by faith in Jesus Christ, and of the necessity of divine aid to enable us to persevere in the ways of holiness." [4]

As the evangelical churches grew in numbers and in power, Deism rapidly declined. The Deists had no organization and were not zealous to make converts; they could not compete with their opponents. In an address printed in the *Southern Literary Messenger* in November, 1836, Thomas R. Dew said, "Avowed infidelity is now considered by the enlightened portion of the world as a reflection both on the head and heart. . . . The Humes and Voltaires have been vanquished from the field. . . ." It is a singular circumstance that Dew and other defenders of slavery were orthodox members of the Protestant churches while the Deists of the eighteenth century had frequently denounced slavery.

There were Southerners who witnessed the growth of the new "Puritanism" with a certain bitterness. In 1831 Jesse Burton Harrison, who had studied at Harvard and in Germany, wrote to his friend Dr. Floriep at Weimar:

The whole Town [Lynchburg, Virginia] with scarce an exception is over-run with a fanatical religious spirit that employs all thoughts, interrupts all business, forbids all social parties, treats all dancing as the greatest of crimes (compassionate the necessities of my legs, so long used to the gallopade) and in fact is a "Schwärmerey" which leaves the English Evangelicals a thousand leagues behind. Could you see for a moment an American religious newspaper you would be amazed at the symptoms every where displayed by an age of barbarism rushing in upon us, an inroad of holy Vandals.[5]

As soon as Thomas Cooper's appointment as professor of chemistry in the University of Virginia was announced, John Holt Rice opened fire upon him in his *Evangelical and Literary Magazine* in January, 1820. Cooper wrote to Jefferson asking if he should resign his position. "I know," he wrote, "the inveteracy of the *odium theologicum*, & I dread to meet it at the close of life." Jefferson replied that the Baptists, Methodists, and Episcopalians were in general friendly to the University, and so also were the Presbyterian laymen. The Presbyterian ministers, however, he wrote, "are violent, ambitious of power, as intolerant in politics as in religion and want nothing but licence from the laws to kindle again the fires of their leader John Knox, and to give us a 2ᵈ blast from his trumpet." Cooper replied, July 1, 1820:

My opinion yet is, that the clergy will defeat all your schemes at Charlottesville, if you do not divide the professorships among them. . . . But the reign of

---

[4] From a letter written by Rice in 1812 to Theodoric T. Randolph, in William Maxwell, *A Memoir of the Rev. John H. Rice, D.D.* (Philadelphia, 1835), pp. 86–87.

[5] *Aris Sonis Focisque* . . . (privately printed, 1910), ed. Fairfax Harrison, pp. 126–127.

ignorance, bigotry and intolerance, is fast approaching: it will pass away, but not in my time. I have had too many melancholy occasions to remark, that in this country there is much of theoretical toleration, but far more of practical persecution; so much, that silence where public motives would urge to speak is forced upon every man who thinks on these subjects; and simulation & dissimulation become points of prudence, if not of duty.

Transylvania University at Lexington, Kentucky, though a state institution, finally came under Presbyterian control. In 1818, however, the liberals were in power, and they engaged as president Horace Holley, who gave up a prominent church in Boston to accept the position. During his administration Transylvania expanded its plant, established notable law and medical schools, and came to be regarded as by far the best of Western schools. Nevertheless, the Presbyterian clergy attacked Holley in sermons, newspapers, and anonymous pamphlets. They accused him of ridiculing "the distinguishing doctrines of the church," of degrading the Messiah to the level of Socrates and Zoroaster, of jesting at the Bible. He was charged with asking with reference to the Calvinist divines: "What do you think of those who go about the country like braying Asses, and telling God what poor Hell deserving scoundrels they are, and who burn brimstone under the noses of people?" Holley was an able man, and the memory of what he taught lingered long in the minds of his students, one of whom was Jefferson Davis. He was forced out in 1827. The view taken by Niels H. Sonne in his *Liberal Kentucky, 1780–1828* (1939) is: "The story of Kentucky Presbyterianism is the story of the ruthless destruction of every vestige of independent theological thought which might arise among the clergy, and even among the laity." The South had set its face against the religious liberalism which was so largely to motivate literature in the New England renaissance.

By the middle of the century a larger proportion of the Southern clergymen were college graduates, but—though they promoted many good causes —it cannot be said that they contributed much, either directly or indirectly, to the literature of the South. When William Hand Browne learned that Albert Taylor Bledsoe's *Southern Review* was about to become the organ of the Southern Methodists, he wrote to Paul Hamilton Hayne, October 19, 1870, that the result would be a marked decline in the quality of the *Review*. Most of the Methodist preachers, he wrote, were interested only in the peculiar doctrines of their sect. "For one man of general culture among them," he said, "interested in Science, Art, Literature, there are ten that see, hear, eat, drink, breathe nothing but Methodism with its narrow formularies and pietistic vocabulary."

3

Education

IN THE YEARS that followed the Revolution there was a growing interest in education. During the war years, however, there had grown to maturity a generation which had had few educational opportunities. It was no longer the fashion to send to England the sons of the well-to-do, and even educated Southerners were more provincial than the planters of the eighteenth century. Jefferson's great scheme for the education of the youth of Virginia was only in small part put into operation. The chief reliance was upon tutors, old-field schools, and academies. Writing to John Adams in 1814, Jefferson referred slightingly to "these petty academies . . . which are starting up in every neighborhood, and where one or two men, possessing Latin and sometimes Greek, a knowledge of globes, and the first six books of Euclid, imagine and communicate this as the sum of science. They commit their pupils to the theatre of the world, with just taste enough of learning to be alienated from industrial pursuits, and not enough to do service in the ranks of science."

Jefferson was certainly unjust to the better academies. William Gordon McCabe, who after the Civil War conducted a notable Virginia preparatory school, in 1888 had high praise for some of the academy teachers, especially "Old Parsons, who, although they had never heard of logaoedic rhythms, or the classification of the conditional sentence, could read Homer and Demosthenes without a dictionary and quote Horace with an apt felicity, which seems to have gone out with the last century." The most notable of all the Southern academies was that conducted in South Carolina by the Reverend Moses Waddel, who taught John C. Calhoun, A. B. Longstreet, Hugh S. Legaré, George McDuffie, William H. Crawford, James Louis Petigru, and many others who rose to prominence in South Carolina and Georgia. The academies became very numerous and, as graduates from the state universities and denominational colleges became available as teachers, their standards improved. It has been estimated that in 1860 the Virginia academies had 13,204 pupils and 700 teachers. In 1850 there were no less than ninety academies in distant Arkansas. There were still many as late as 1890 but in the twentieth century all but a few college preparatory schools disappeared.

The notable movement for the establishment of state universities had its chief strength in the South and, in later years, in the Western states. In this period were opened the University of North Carolina (1795); the

University of Georgia (1801), chartered as early as 1785; the University of South Carolina (1805), first called the South Carolina College; and the University of Virginia (1825), the most influential of them all. In its earlier years Jefferson's university was, after Harvard College, probably the best institution of its kind in the United States. It had an elective system long before Charles W. Eliot introduced a similar plan at Harvard. Under George Tucker at Virginia, Thomas R. Dew and Beverley Tucker at William and Mary, and Thomas Cooper at the South Carolina College, the work in history, law, economics, and political science was probably more thorough than could be found anywhere north of the Potomac. The emphasis upon the ancient classics was less exclusive than is generally supposed, and the interest in science and modern languages was greater. Education in the South was not nearly so unpractical as it seems to the modern mind; it was certainly not ill adapted to the training of leaders in law, politics, and theology. The teaching of English literature was still in its infancy as late as 1860, and American literature was taught only incidentally in the school readers. There were, however, lectures on belles-lettres, and considerable emphasis was placed on rhetoric and public speaking.

A favorite textbook was the Reverend Hugh Blair's *Lectures on Rhetoric and Belles Lettres*, first published at Edinburgh in 1783, but regarded in many schools as an authority half a century later. Thirty-nine editions of Blair's text were published in America before 1835. Blair took a middle position between Neoclassicism and Romanticism, but his sympathies inclined toward the former. He vastly overrated the importance of Ossian, and he failed to see the real significance of Robert Burns. For Blair, Shakespeare was a great genius, but his plays were full of artistic faults. Blair emphasized the ancient classics. He did not fully appreciate the importance of the novel, and he discussed the pastoral without perceiving that the genre was almost obsolete. He emphasized sensibility, reason, good sense, and good taste, which for him was reducible to two characteristics: delicacy and correctness. The stylistic qualities which he stressed were precision, variety, and simplicity. He had much to say about eloquence which must have found lodgment in the minds of young men ambitious of political distinction. He condemned false ornament and recommended good sense as the basis of all writing and speaking. The study of Blair's *Lectures* and other texts of the same kind probably had more to do with the literary conservatism of the South than the study of the ancient classics.

4

Books, Libraries, and Literary Taste

ONE WHO INVESTIGATES the state of literary culture in the South in this or any other period meets with the most contradictory assertions, often delivered in the most dogmatic manner. One tradition has it that every planter was a college graduate who owned a fine library in which the ancient classics predominated; and there is the rival tradition, which flourished like a green bay tree in circles hostile to slavery, that the average Southern farmer's library consisted of a newspaper, an almanac, and perhaps a Bible. The whole problem needs to be more fully investigated. The small farmers and the poorer whites were not a reading people then, and they are not now; and the statement holds true of some of the larger planters, especially the *nouveaux riches*. "How few of our families are *reading ones*, in the strict sense of the term!" wrote the discouraged editor of the *Southern Literary Messenger* in October, 1839. "Besides the newspaper, the Farmers' Register, the Sporting Magazine, and the year's almanac, a few trashy novels, constitute, it is feared, the major part of the libraries of our otherwise social, agreeable and hospitable country houses." The Southern aristocracy was rather social than intellectual; there was little counterpart to what Dr. Holmes called the Brahmin Caste of New England.

And yet the fact remains that the Old South was a book market of considerable importance. This is evident not only from the many newspaper advertisements of books but also from the numerous letters to Mathew Carey written by that most remarkable of book agents, Mason Locke Weems. With the coming of the steamboat and the railroad it was soon to become easier for the rapidly growing publishing houses in New York and Philadelphia to place their wares in the hands of Southern booksellers, who now ordered their books less often from London than in Colonial times.

The number of families with good private libraries was probably smaller in 1789 than in 1775 and certainly much smaller than in 1830, for the Revolution had hit hardest the cultivated classes. Books were far more plentiful in the towns and on the large plantations of the Tidewater region than they were in the uplands or west of the Appalachians. There were, nevertheless, even in the West, oases, so to speak, like Natchez and Lexington, where books were plentiful and the level of literary culture was high. Cultivated Virginia and Carolina families that had gone westward were still buying books. In the isolation of plantation life books were regarded as a necessity by many a planter family.

Let us begin with North Carolina, then looked upon by its neighbors as a backward state. There were cultured families and good private libraries in the seaboard towns and on a few large plantations, but further west the dearth of books seemed to some observers appalling. The Presbyterian minister Henry Pattillo, a protégé of Samuel Davies, living in the central part of the state, wrote in the Preface to his Sermons (1788): "And so affectingly scarce are good books, among the common people of these southern states, since the late war, that this little piece may compose the whole library in some houses its author has called at." Pattillo wished for "spelling-books, catechisms, testaments, and Watts's hymns" to give to pious slaves, but the Society for the Propagation of the Gospel no longer sent books from England. "I reside," he wrote, "an hundred miles from Petersburg, our center of trade, and nearest tide of water; and so am out of the way of books."

A third of a century later the situation had changed for the better. In 1827 Archibald Murphey, speaking at Chapel Hill, commented on his difficulty in finding books in the 1790's. At David Caldwell's academy in Guilford County he had found no school library and no students who owned any books except the usual texts.

> I well remember, that after completing my course of studies under Dr. Caldwell, I spent nearly two years without finding any books to read, except some old works on theological subjects. At length, I accidentally met with Voltaire's history of Charles the twelfth of Sweden, an odd volume of Smollett's Roderic Random, and an abridgement of Don Quixote. These books gave me a taste for reading, which I had no opportunity of gratifying until I became a student in this university in 1796. . . . At this day [1827], when libraries are established in all our towns, when every professional man, and every respectable gentleman, has a collection of books, it is difficult to conceive the inconveniences under which young men labored thirty or forty years ago.[6]

If Murphey had grown up in the eastern part of the state, he could have found an adequate supply of the best English, French, and American books. In New Bern, Halifax, Raleigh, and Fayetteville booksellers were advertising such books as early as 1790. For example in the years 1794–1797 in the little inland town of Halifax, A. Hodge was advertising works in law, religion, med-

---

[6] The Papers of Archibald D. Murphey (Raleigh, N. C., 1914), ed. W. H. Hoyt, II, 356.

About the time that Murphey entered the University at Chapel Hill, the two literary societies there bought their first fifteen books. Among these were Locke's Essay concerning Human Understanding, Mary Wollstonecraft's Vindication of the Rights of Woman, "Helvetius on the Human Mind," "Brown on Equality," and some standard works on law and history (Kemp P. Battle, History of the University of North Carolina, Raleigh, 1907–1912, I, 85).

icine, and literature which he had received from Philadelphia and New York. Among these were the works of Edmund Burke in three volumes, of Pope in six, Sterne in ten, and Swift in twenty-seven. There was also the "British Classicks" in thirty-nine volumes.

The most extensive advertisements appeared in the Raleigh *Register* of Joseph Gales, a cultivated Unitarian, who had fled prosecution in England for selling Paine's *The Rights of Man*. Gales got his books from London via Charleston as well as from Philadelphia and other Northern cities. On March 24, 1801, he listed 468 titles, in five columns, of books recently imported from England. The largest section consisted of law books, but there were also sections given to Divinity, Physic, History, Natural History, Philosophy, Politics, Voyages and Travels, Biography, Poetry and Dramatic Works, Novels and Romances, Juveniles, School Texts, etc. The list included four separate editions of Shakespeare and three of Pope besides *An Essay on Man* in separate form. He had also Bell's "British Poets" in fifty-four volumes and Bell's "British Theatre" in thirty-four.[7]

Other North Carolina dealers advertised books of much the same general character, including most of the British literary classics which were read in England in the late eighteenth century. It may be presumed that North Carolina literary taste lagged somewhat behind that in England; and yet "Wordsworth's Lyrical Ballads" was advertised in the Raleigh *Register* on November 7 and 21, 1803, and Lamb's little-read *Rosamond Gray* (1798) in the New Bern *Morning Herald* on October 1, 1807. The works of certain American writers—particularly Thomas Paine, Benjamin Franklin, and Joel Barlow—appear frequently in the book lists.

When we turn to Virginia, we find much the same books advertised in two Richmond newspapers: Samuel Pleasants' *Virginia Argus* and Thomas Ritchie's *Enquirer*. In 1800 and 1801 Pleasants listed the *Poems* of Philip Freneau, Royall Tyler's *The Algerine Captive*, and Mrs. Rowson's *Charlotte Temple* in addition to standard English works. In Richmond the poems of Scott, Southey, and Moore were offered for sale soon after their publication in England. It was in Richmond that William Ellery Channing, who had gone there in 1798 as tutor to the children of David Meade Randolph, first read the works of Rousseau, William Godwin, and Mary Wollstonecraft. Dr. Frank P. Cauble, after a study of advertisements in the Richmond *Virginia Argus*, noted that they "included nearly every well-known book which appeared during the eighteenth century in England and America." Mrs. Maria Derieux, the English-born wife of a teacher who lived at various

---

[7] For even longer lists of books, see the *Register* for March 30, 1802, and May 30, 1803. For further information, see James S. Purcell, Jr., "Literary Culture in North Carolina before 1820" (1950), an unpublished Duke University Ph.D. dissertation.

places in Virginia and North Carolina, kept a list of the 1,098 books which she read between May, 1806, and November, 1822. In these sixteen and a half years she read an average of more than sixty-six books each year. In western Virginia, however, books were so scarce that single volumes were passed from house to house as great treasures.[8]

The Library Society of Richmond, which printed a catalogue of its holdings in 1801, had few American books apart from Jefferson's *Notes on the State of Virginia* and histories of the state by Beverley and Stith. It had, however, many eighteenth-century English classics, including Johnson's English Poets in sixty-eight volumes and the works of Fielding in twelve and many series of periodical essays. It had some French works including Rousseau's *Confessions* and *Social Contract*.

The University of Virginia, which opened its doors in 1825, had a notable library. Jefferson had selected the books, but a few others had been added by 1828, when the Library published a catalogue of its holdings. It had little in the way of contemporary literature, but it was rich in law, history, science, medicine, and was fairly good in literature before 1800. The library records show that between 1825 and 1827 Shakespeare's works were borrowed 63 times; Dr. Johnson's, 42 times; Chesterfield's *Letters*, 21; *Don Quixote*, 20; Gibbon's *Decline and Fall of the Roman Empire*, 14. There was some demand also for the works of James Thomson, Voltaire, Bolingbroke, and Swift and for Butler's *Hudibras*, Pope's *Homer*, and Barlow's *The Columbiad.*[9] In 1828 the library owned 3,131 titles. Of these 348 were borrowed 849 times; only 11 per cent of the books were taken out of the library. The books borrowed most often were Robertson's *Charles V* and Marshall's *Washington*.

For contemporary English literature the students went to the Charlottesville booksellers, whose records tell a different story. The most popular writer by long odds was Byron; after him came Thomas Campbell and Thomas Moore. Favorite novels were *Don Quixote*, *Gil Blas*, and *Tom Jones*. There was some demand also for Johnson's *Rasselas*, the novels of Maria Edgeworth, and the *Spectator*. Strangely enough, the romances of Scott seem not to appear in the sales accounts of the local booksellers. By 1840 the authors

---

[8] James W. Alexander, *The Life of Archibald Alexander, D.D.* (New York, 1854), pp. 76, 108, 176–177. Dr. Alexander was the brother of William A. Caruthers' mother. In Southside Virginia he found Paine's *The Age of Reason* much read by young men. "Indeed," he said, "most of our educated and professional young men became Deists, or worse. Young lawyers openly reviled religion, and boldly attacked its serious professors" (p. 177).

[9] P. A. Bruce, *History of the University of Virginia* (1920), II, 204. See also II, 186 ff., 343–345.

most popular with the students were Bulwer-Lytton, Captain Marryat, and Mrs. Felicia Dorothea Hemans.

The years 1789–1830 were a period of slowly changing literary tastes. The drift was toward Romanticism, but the eighteenth-century classics were still widely read.[10] In Virginia, as in England, Scott, Moore, and Byron were almost immediately popular, but Wordsworth, Coleridge, Shelley, and Keats made their way much more slowly.

Whatever the condition of the South Carolina Up-Country, there can be no question that Charleston was well supplied with books. The best-known of several local booksellers was Orville A. Roorbach, whose *Bibliotheca Americana* is well known to scholars and collectors. Roorbach had bookstores in both Charleston and New York, and he often imported books directly from London.

The Charleston Library Society, which had in 1778 lost by fire most of its five or six thousand books, had less than one thousand in 1790; but by 1826, when the Society printed a catalogue of its holdings, it owned more than twelve thousand volumes. The collection was a remarkable one, but it was less rich in the ancient classics than one might have expected. Of the 339 pages which are given to the listing of book titles, 27 pages deal with theology, including a page on the controversy between Unitarians and Trinitarians; 39 pages with government and politics; 51 with arts and sciences; and about 95 with literature (including philology), besides numerous works of literary importance classified under other headings. The Society had a substantial collection of magazines, including practically complete sets of the *Gentleman's Magazine*, the *Edinburgh Review*, *Blackwood's Magazine*, and the *North American Review*. There was evident as yet no discrimination against Northern books. The Society's 1845 catalogue, as we shall see, tells a somewhat different story.[11] In 1826 the Society had 80 titles with Boston imprints and in proportion books and pamphlets published in New York, Philadelphia, and Baltimore. Thomas Paine, Philip Freneau, and Charles Brockden Brown were well represented, and the Library had nearly everything of importance that Irving and Cooper had published, including the two series of *Salmagundi*. There was nothing by Bryant, but there were books by a dozen other New England writers, including Timothy Dwight, Jonathan Edwards, Royall Tyler, Noah Webster, Joel Barlow, Robert Treat Paine, Abiel Holmes, William Ellery Channing, and Catharine Maria Sedg-

---

[10] Richard Beale Davis, "Literary Tastes in Virginia before Poe," W.M.Q., 2nd ser. XIX, 55–68 (Jan., 1939). Davis finds that Romanticism was a definite influence "a good decade before 1825."

[11] See pp. 359–360.

wick. Southern writers outside of South Carolina were not well represented.

The large proportion of works by early nineteenth-century British writers in the Society's Library contradicts the alleged conservatism of Charleston's literary taste. The Library had nearly everything published by Byron—including of course the Charleston, 1811, edition of his *English Bards and Scotch Reviewers*—Scott, Southey, and Joseph Priestley and much by Godwin, Moore, Campbell, Rogers, Jane Austen, and Charlotte Smith. There was, as one might expect, nothing yet by Shelley, Keats, or Carlyle; but Wordsworth and Coleridge are represented by *The Lyrical Ballads* (London, 1802), and *Christabel*. Hazlitt's only book is his *Lectures on the Comic Writers*.

There were at least half a dozen other library societies in the Low-Country. By 1830 there were twenty-one more in middle and upper South Carolina. "Library societies," says Frances L. Spain, "were found in communities with a well-established economy, a sense of permanency, and a cultured, refined society. Though there were only a few people of great wealth in South Carolina, there were many families in comfortable circumstances."

Beyond the Alleghenies good private libraries were fewer and farther between than on the seaboard. William Russell Smith (1815–1896) thus describes the situation in northern Alabama:

> When I was a boy, in the then wilderness of Alabama, there was no such thing as a library, at least within my reach or knowledge. The very nearest approach to a library consisted of a shelf of school books, rounded off at one end by the Holy Bible, at the other by a Methodist or Baptist hymn book. The contents of the shelf might thus be stated; Webster's Spelling Book, Pike's Arithmetic, The New York Reader, The COLUMBIAN ORATOR (the book of books to the aspiring young orator), the Rudiman's [Ruddiman's] Latin Grammar, Historia Sacra, the Greek Testament, and for higher students in English, Blair's Rhetoric.

Smith could have found the books he wanted in Mobile, or Natchez, or New Orleans, which since 1806 has always had good bookstores and some sort of library open to the public. There were some excellent private libraries in St. Louis—a thousand miles from the Atlantic coast—before there was a printing press or a public school in the town. In 1842 the Library of St. Louis University had at least five thousand books, of which two thousand had been acquired since 1829. John Francis McDermott comments: "In the village [St. Louis] in the wilderness, then, there were few and simple schools, no printing press [until 1808], no public libraries; yet the level of culture was high. The essential test of literary culture in an individual is the test of books, and there are data enough in probate records to show what Saint

Louisans read." The little town of Hannibal, in which Mark Twain grew up in the forties, had no dearth of books.

In Kentucky, which until 1792 was a part of Virginia, the most notable library was in Lexington, permanently settled first in 1779. The Lexington Library, begun in 1795–1796, had less than eight hundred volumes in 1803 but more than six thousand in 1837. In 1815 the Library had not only the narrative poems of Byron and Scott but even the anonymous *Waverley*, first published the year before. When Horace Holley visited Lexington in 1818, he found the Athenaeum "not yet furnished with many books, but well supplied with newspapers and the best periodicals." "I find," he added, "everything of this sort, which is valuable, from Boston and the other Atlantic cities."

Lexington, however, was not a typical Kentucky town. It was not only a cultural center, where educated Virginians lived; it was for some years a distribution center from which books were sold throughout the old Northwest. The advertisements in John Bradford's *Kentucke Gazette*, founded in 1787, show how rapidly Lexington became a book market. For the first three years the *Gazette* advertised few books except "Testaments, spelling books and primers" and "Watts's psalms and other books of divinity." By 1795, however, no less than three different booksellers were printing extensive book lists almost simultaneously in the *Gazette*.[12] If we may judge from these, the works of Thomas Paine were more widely read in Kentucky than elsewhere in the South. The books in demand in Kentucky may perhaps represent a slight lag in literary fashion as compared with Richmond and Charleston, but the Kentucky taste for political literature did not lean to the conservative side. Kentucky was a better market for English than for American books, but John Bradford advertised on June 27, 1795: "Bartram's Travels," "Columbian Muse," "Paine's Writings," and "American Theater."

In England in the first quarter of the nineteenth century the Romantic movement came to a climax in the work of the great poets, Wordsworth, Coleridge, Byron, Shelley, and Keats; in the historical romances of Scott; and in important works by such lesser figures as Hazlitt, Lamb, Landor, Moore, DeQuincey, and Campbell. To set over against these names, American literature has only Irving, Cooper, Bryant, and minor writers, chiefly from the North. The American Romantic movement reached its climax, after the accession of Queen Victoria, in the work of Emerson, Hawthorne, Melville, Thoreau, Longfellow, Poe, and Whitman.

[12] See, for example, the numbers for June 6 and 27 and July 25, 1795. For Deistic books sold in Kentucky, see Sonne, *op. cit.*, pp. 25–28.

Byron, Scott, and Moore were almost as immediately popular in America as in England, but in both countries Wordsworth, Coleridge, Shelley, and Keats had to wait long for anything like popular recognition. The last four writers presented difficulties to British and American readers reared on the neoclassical literature of the eighteenth century. In America a few eager and intelligent young men, like Bryant, Simms, Poe, and Pinkney, might discover these four great poets; but on both sides of the Atlantic the average reader was slow to adjust his taste to the new poetry. By 1830 the Romantic movement had definitely won its way, but in the preceding three decades American tastes and standards were a mixture of the Romantic and the neoclassical. In American writers in North and South alike one notes the influence of Addison, Swift, and Pope along with that of Gray and Collins and Cowper. Critical standards were drawn less often from the essays of Coleridge, Lamb, Hazlitt, and DeQuincey than from the British quarterlies, Hugh Blair's *Lectures on Rhetoric*, and Archibald Alison's *Essay on the Nature and Principles of Taste* (1790; reprinted in Boston in 1812). Men often read the more recent authors but praised the old. William Wirt, a transition figure in Virginia, in 1803 had high praise for the *Spectator*, but he referred to it as "thrown by, and almost entirely forgotten, while the gilded blasphemies of infidels [Godwin and Paine], and 'the noontide trances' of pernicious theorists, are hailed with rapture, and echoed around the world." There was as yet no appreciable lag in literary taste between South and North, as there was between the United States and England.

The vogue of Byron was enormous in both North and South.[18] His manner fascinated a whole generation, including such un-Byronic figures as Hugh Swinton Legaré. On July 1, 1823, the Richmond *Enquirer* stated: "If the number of British poets were reduced to three, they would present a rare and admirable combination—Scott—Byron—and Moore." Byron was widely read in Kentucky; and when the poet was informed of his vogue there, he wrote in his journal, December 5, 1813: ". . . the first tidings that have ever sounded like *Fame* to my ears—to be redde on the banks of the Ohio!"

In the first quarter of the nineteenth century literature and literary criticism were in both North and South chiefly the work of men in professional circles, and their readers belonged mainly to the cultivated classes

18 William Ellery Leonard, *Byron and Byronism in America* (1905), like so many other influence studies, pays slight attention to the southern half of the United States. In 1811 the first American edition of Byron's *English Bards and Scotch Reviewers* was published in Charleston; it was based upon the third London edition. Byron's literary conservatism may have had something to do with his long-continued popularity in the South.

whose economic and political ideas were conservative. After 1830 this was much less true in the North than in the South. William Charvat sums up the basic principles underlying critical writing in the years 1810–1835: Literature must not condone rebellion against the existing social and economic order or contain anything derogatory to religious ideals and moral standards. The critic was the watchdog of society, and he frowned upon writings that seemed to him egocentric or antisocial or unduly pessimistic. Art for art's sake was an outlandish notion—an attitude which accounted in part for the neglect of Poe in the years to come. These underlying assumptions help us understand why Americans completely accepted Scott, read Wordsworth and Coleridge with mixed emotions, and rejected Shelley and Keats.

In the United States the Romantic movement took a somewhat different form from that which it had taken in England or Germany or France. American writers shared the Romantic love of nature, and they were eager to proclaim the peculiar beauties of the forests, mountains, lakes, rivers, and prairies of the New World. They did not, however, respond warmly to the glorification of the primitive in the writings of Wordsworth and Rousseau. This was an essentially urban attitude, and in America the dominant occupation was still that of the farmer, whose practical experience in combatting nature made it difficult for him to view its influence as wholly beneficent. Americans in the seaboard states were beginning to idealize the Indian, but west of the mountains the settlers generally thought of the red man as a peculiarly wild beast who must be exterminated. American writers were eager to follow the lead of Scott, but it was difficult to write Waverley romances about a country whose brief history lacked the gorgeous trappings of England in the days of Elizabeth or Richard the Lion-Hearted. Americans tended to glorify the frontiersman, but in the South it was not the fashion to idealize the poor-white or sentimentalize over the lot of the slave. Political radicalism had made its way earlier in this country than in Europe, but it never proceeded to such extremes as in France. From the close of the Revolution till the rise of the extreme Abolitionists in the thirties, there seemed little for the radical young author to rebel against.

Before 1830 the force of Revolutionary liberalism had spent itself in the South; in New England radical isms of all kinds were just beginning to flourish. In 1840 Emerson wrote to Carlyle: "We are all a little wild here with numberless projects of social reform. Not a reading man but has a draft of a new community in his waistcoat pocket." The South was to have nothing corresponding to New England Transcendentalism. Indeed, few Southern readers were to understand what it was all about. Most Southerners were orthodox members of the evangelical churches, and they had no such background of Unitarian culture as nourished Emerson, Thoreau, and Margaret Fuller.

5
Sir Walter Scott and the South

THE SOUTH'S FAVORITE author, Sir Walter Scott, was well known as a poet before his first novel, *Waverley*, appeared in 1814. *The Lady of the Lake*, first published in May, 1810, was offered for sale in Richmond in September. *The Lay of the Last Minstrel* (1805) was reprinted in Savannah in 1811 and in Baltimore in 1812. *The Field of Waterloo* (1815) was reprinted in Lexington, Kentucky, in 1816. Scott's octosyllabic verse quickly became a favorite verse form of Southern poets.

Scott's historical romances were probably more widely read in the South than the poems of Byron and Moore or the novels of Bulwer-Lytton or G. P. R. James. They were also widely read in the Northern states and on the European continent. American publishers are said to have printed half a million copies of his novels in the nine-year period ending in 1823. Philip Alexander Bruce could find no evidence that students at the University of Virginia bought them, but there is abundant evidence that they were read in other parts of the South. John Pendleton Kennedy wrote in the *Red Book* in October, 1819: "Letters are now of such repute, that I am not bold in saying that most of our gentlemen read Reviews, and our ladies Waverly [*sic*]—only skipping the Scotch. . . ." In 1822 the *Virginia Evangelical and Literary Magazine* called the Waverley novels "wonderful performances" and their author "without doubt, the Shakespeare of Novelists." In the 1820's Scott was the most widely read of contemporary authors in St. Louis.[14]

Scott's vogue in the South was perhaps no greater than elsewhere, but it continued longer. Unlike so much later British and American literature, the Waverley novels contained nothing repugnant to the feelings of slaveholders. The father of Mary Noailles Murfree, says Edd Winfield Parks, "declared roundly that 'no education can be complete without a good knowledge of Scott,' and the twenty-two volumes of the Waverley novels which

---

14 John Robertson of Richmond wrote in his *Virginia: or, The Fatal Patent* (Washington, 1825): "The readers of the Waverly [*sic*] Novels, and we presume that will include all the readers this little work can hope to have ·. . ." (p. 63). One of Robertson's characters is borrowed from Scott's *Kenilworth*.

adorned his shelves were often in use. Mary disliked only *Ivanhoe.*" As late as April, 1860, *De Bow's Review* commented: "Johnson, and Burke, and Sir Walter Scott, should have statues in every Southern capitol. Thus would our youth learn what are the sentiments and opinions that become gentlemen and cavaliers." A few months later *De Bow's* returned to the subject: "Sir Walter Scott rescued us from pretentious inanity, and inaugurated the reign of nature, reason, and reality." In August, 1875, T. B. Kingsbury wrote in *Our Living and Our Dead* (Raleigh): "We say read Scott. He is the best *story-teller* the world possesses." Scott had probably been more widely read in the North than in the South, but long before 1875 his vogue had given way to Dickens and Thackeray and Bulwer-Lytton and George Eliot, who were also, incidentally, widely read in the South.

The literary influence of Scott's novels was of great importance to the emerging American literature of the early nineteenth century. The demand for a national literature became in fact practically a demand for American historical romances modeled on *Waverley* and its successors. Out of old elements Scott had created a new type of novel, the historical romance, and thus supplied a kind of pattern which could be adapted to the portrayal of American life. The American past was sadly deficient in the pomp and circumstance that marked the courts of Queen Elizabeth and Richard Coeur-de-Lion in *Kenilworth* and *Ivanhoe,* but the American Revolution and the Indian wars furnished matter for romance not inferior to the conflict between Highlander and Lowlander in Scott's novels. In the Southern states Caruthers and Simms found contrasting racial and social types not unlike those in the Waverley romances. In Virginia and South Carolina the novelists played up the Tidewater gentry as opposed to the cruder types of the backwoods. Sometimes the faithful slaves took the place of Scott's loyal retainers. Cooper and Simms could not read the Scottish novels without noting the striking resemblance of American Indians and frontiersmen to Scott's outlaws and Highland warriors. In *The Heart of Midlothian* (1818) Scott himself had suggested just such a parallel when he sent an outlaw from the Highlands to become chief of an Indian tribe in the United States. Writers bemoaning the literary barrenness of the American scene were struck by an episode in *Peveril of the Peak* (1822) in which an exiled English regicide suddenly appears from his hiding place to play the part of a military leader at a critical time in New England. If the Wizard of the North could find matter for romance in the supposedly drab American past, surely it was not impossible to write an American counterpart of *Waverley* or *Guy Mannering.*

Southern writers of fiction in many cases took over Scott's formula and often borrowed from Cooper at the same time. In 1824 Scott's popularity induced George Tucker to write *The Valley of Shenandoah,* and in the same year an unknown Virginian published a novel which in its title is clearly reminiscent of Scott, *Tales of an American Landlord: Containing Sketches of Life South of the Potomac.* Caruthers' *The Cavaliers of Virginia* (1835), Kennedy's *Horse-Shoe Robinson* (1835), and Simms's *The Partisan* (1835) all make use of methods employed by Scott and frequently of Cooper as well. The influence of Scott is discernible in the much later romances of Thomas Nelson Page. The Southern novelists would have agreed with Simms, who wrote in the *Southern Quarterly Review* for April, 1849: ". . . Scott is . . . more perfect, more complete and admirable, than any writer of his age. . . ."

There is no doubt that American writers of fiction—in the North as well as in the South—were heavily indebted to Scott for showing them how to treat native materials. That, however, is a very different matter from maintaining, as Mark Twain did in *Life on the Mississippi,* that Scott's romances had such a profound influence upon Southern life that "he is in great measure responsible" for the Civil War. Mark Twain was offended by the grandiloquent language of a New Orleans reporter, and the Mardi-Gras pageant reminded him of the Waverley romances, which were among his pet aversions. He wrote:

There [in the Southern states], the genuine and wholesome civilization of the nineteenth century is curiously confused and commingled with the Walter Scott Middle-Age sham civilization, and so you have practical common sense, progressive ideas, and progressive works, mixed up with the duel, the inflated speech, and the jejune romanticism of an absurd past that is dead, and out of charity ought to be buried. But for the Sir Walter disease, the character of the Southerner—or Southron, according to Sir Walter's starchier way of phrasing it— would be wholly modern, in place of modern and medieval mixed. . . . It was Sir Walter that made every gentleman in the South a major or a colonel, or a general or a judge, before the war; and it was he, also, that made these gentlemen value these bogus decorations. For it was he that created rank and caste down there, and also reverence for rank and caste, and pride and pleasure in them.[15]

Not many historians have agreed with Mark Twain's admittedly "wild proposition" that Scott is responsible for the Civil War; but Charles and Mary Beard, William E. Dodd, James Truslow Adams, H. J. Eckenrode,

---

[15] Chap. xlvi, "Enchantments and Enchanters." Van Wyck Brooks remarks: "Perhaps only a Southerner [like Mark Twain] could have been so angry with all these illusions of the Southern mind" (*The Times of Melville and Whitman,* 1947, p. 333). For the Southern tournament, which is older than *Ivanhoe,* see Esther J. and Ruth W. Crooks, *The Ring Tournament in the United States* (Richmond, 1936).

William B. Hesseltine, and others have endorsed the suggestion that Scott's romances altered the pattern of Southern life and character or believed that Southerners got their "chivalric" ideals from *Ivanhoe*.[16] Professor G. Harrison Orians and Miss Grace W. Landrum [17] have effectively refuted Mark Twain's charge, but few historians seem to have read their articles. In 1949 Dr. Rollin G. Osterweis—who had apparently read their articles —published his *Romanticism and Nationalism in the Old South*, in which Mark Twain's rash generalization became the basis of a lengthy interpretation of the mind of the Old South.[18] Osterweis claims to have read fifteen of the Waverley romances, but most other historians, I suspect, have read nothing but *Ivanhoe*. Osterweis's thesis is that the civilization of the Old South rested upon a tripod, "cotton and the plantation system forming one leg, Negro slavery a second." The third leg—the subject of his book—is "the chivalric cult," derived from Scott.

The theme from Abbotsford, then, was the glorification of the chivalric ideal, with its emphasis on the cult of manners, the cult of woman, the cult of the gallant knight, the loyalty to caste. Adjusted to local environmental features and reenforced by other "culture carriers," this imported notion was to emerge as the Southern cult of chivalry. In slightly differentiated forms, it permeated the several areas of the antebellum South. Virginia planters knew it as an all-pervading way of life. Carolinians flaunted the chivalric badge as the proud emblem of Southern nationality. In New Orleans, the cult had a flavor of joie de vivre. Along the Southwestern frontier the trappings of chivalry were cherished in a fierce, possessive, often crude fashion.

The historians seem not to realize that Northerners, Englishmen, Frenchmen, Germans, Italians, Spaniards, and Latin-Americans were all fascinated by *Waverley* and its successors without having their national char-

---

[16] Beard, *The American Spirit* (1942), pp. 295–298; William E. Dodd, *The Cotton Kingdom* (1919), pp. 62–63; H. J. Eckenrode, *Jefferson Davis* (1923), p. 11 and "Sir Walter Scott and the South," *No. Am. Rev.*, CCVI, 595–603 (Oct., 1917); Clement Eaton, *Freedom of Thought in the Old South* (1940), pp. 48, 317; James Truslow Adams, *America's Tragedy* (1934), pp. 95–96, 119–120; W. B. Hesseltine, *A History of the South* (1936), pp. 344–345; Francis B. Simkins, *The South Old and New* (1947), p. 55; W. J. Cash, *The Mind of the South* (1941), p. 65; Hodding Carter, *Southern Legacy* (1950), pp. 67–68. Many more names could be added to this list. In Thomas Wolfe's *The Hills Beyond* (1941), p. 322, Judge Robert Joyner, who is described as "perfectly aware of a fatal weakness in the Southern temperament—its capacity for romantic self-deception and mythology," denounces "Sir Walter Scott, fake chivalry, fake lords and ladies, fake ideals of honor, fake wooden columns on the houses. . . ."

[17] Orians, "Walter Scott, Mark Twain, and the Civil War," *S.A.Q.*, XL, 342–359 (Oct., 1941); Landrum, "Sir Walter Scott and His Literary Rivals in the Old South," *Am. Lit.*, II, 256–276 (Nov., 1930).

[18] Osterweis's book is discussed more fully in my review in *S.A.Q.*, XLVIII, 472–475 (July, 1949.)

acter transformed by reading them. They have likewise failed to realize that of Scott's thirty novels few of the better ones, apart from *Ivanhoe* and *The Talisman*, have anything to do with the age of chivalry.[19] Many of them may be classified as regional novels, and the best of them deal with Scottish life within the memory of his parents or his grandparents. Scott was a favorite author with Harriet Beecher Stowe. She was rereading his romances when she began *Uncle Tom's Cabin*. Was it the influence of *Ivanhoe*, which she read no less than nine times, that led her to write the novel which had so much to do with bringing on the Civil War? Perhaps after all her Hartford neighbor, Mark Twain, was right in thinking that Scott was "in great measure responsible for the war"!

I have found little in the comments of ante-bellum Southern critics and reviewers which suggests that Scott had anything to do with the creation of "rank and caste, and pride and pleasure in them." These writers often pointed out in his romances the very faults which latterday critics have condemned. Scott's influence, it is true, was a conservative one, as William Hazlitt was perhaps the first to point out; and he did, like other historical romancers, tend to idealize the past. His influence in the British Isles, however, led to no attempt to revive the age of chivalry.

The influence of Scott may have had something to do with the growth of the Cavalier legend, to be discussed in a later section, and perhaps with the increased use of the phrase "Southern chivalry"; but the Southern farmer had too keen a sense of realities to turn to *Ivanhoe* as a guide to living in the nineteenth century. His way of life would not have varied materially from its pattern—which was fixed before Scott was born—had Sir Walter never written a line. Slavery, tobacco, cotton, and a warm climate were far more important factors in determining his way of life than anything he read. And I may add that there is no simple formula—such as some Northern writers persist in looking for—which explains the complexities and contradictions of Southern life.[20]

What did the South learn from Scott? Perhaps there is no better answer than that given in Mrs. T. P. O'Connor's *My Beloved South* (1913): "Mark Twain said he [Scott] did measureless harm, more real and lasting harm,

[19] The historians have also failed to note that the age of chivalry figures in certain widely read romances by Scott's successors, G. P. R. James, Harrison Ainsworth, and Bulwer-Lytton—all widely read in this country without any profound influence on the lives of those who read them.

[20] The dangers that beset the social historian when he uses belles-lettres to document a thesis are brilliantly discussed in E. E. Stoll, "Literature No 'Document,' " *Mod. Lang. Rev.*, XIX, 141–157 (April, 1924) and Bernard DeVoto, "Interrelations of History and Literature," *Approaches to American Social History* (1937), ed. W. E. Lingelbach.

than any other individual who ever wrote. But what did he teach? Loyalty and self-sacrifice, a sense of obligation to your kinsfolk, chivalry, tenderness, and protection to women, honour and truth to your neighbour, courage and valour in battle, open-handed hospitality, and a sense of responsibility towards those dependent on you." Perhaps these are not the qualities most valued in an industrial age by young men who wish to get on in the world, but are they intrinsically less admirable than the traits of the leading characters in our twentieth-century fiction?

The Southern romancers who followed Scott took their cue from the Scottish novels. It was *Waverley*, *Rob Roy*, and *Guy Mannering* rather than *Ivanhoe* that enabled Caruthers, Kennedy, Simms, and Cooke to see the charm of the picturesque and the homely in the historic past and present of Virginia and South Carolina. The defenders of slavery were indebted not to Scott but to Aristotle, Burke, Carlyle, and the King James Bible. Caruthers, who owed much to Scott, was an advocate of intersectional good will who denounced the evils of slavery in language which might have come from an Abolitionist.

6
European Writers and the South: John Davis

Much of what the South has contributed to literature has come from the pens of outsiders, notably visitors from England, France, and the Northern states. These writers, in spite of the preconceptions they brought with them, sometimes vividly described aspects of life in the South which the writers of that section failed to remark as of particular interest. In the period we are studying, however, relations between England and the United States were at a very low ebb. The so-called paper war between the two countries was still going on, and Americans especially resented Sydney Smith's scornful question: "Who reads an American book?" British writers who belonged to the Whig party were in general more inclined to a sympathetic view of the new republic, but the oversensitive Americans were often displeased by the comments of such Whiggish writers as Sydney Smith. Poe was among the few who could find words of praise for Mrs. Frances Trollope's *Domestic Manners of the Americans* (1832), which greatly irritated many American readers. So also in the early 1840's did Dickens's *American Notes* and *Martin Chuzzlewit*, for they had regarded Dickens as friendly to America. Thackeray and other upper-class English visitors were to view American life more kindly, especially in the South, where in spite of slavery they often felt more at home than in the North. French visitors were, as we should expect to find them, more sympathetic than the English. They, however, sometimes noted that the Americans did not come up to their extravagant expectations. François René Vicomte de Chateaubriand in 1791 spent about five months in the United States and found materials which he later embodied in important works.[21] This disciple of Rousseau was disappointed to find Americans different from what he had been led to expect, and he took up the cause of the mistreated Indians. He saw considerably less of this country than one would infer from reading his *Travels* (London, 1828), and he borrowed a good deal from William Bartram's *Travels* and Gilbert Imlay's *Topographical Description of the Western Territory*. Gradually while he was living in exile in England, his imagination transformed his actual experiences into something strange and romantic. *Les Natchez* (1826) is a kind of romantic prose epic, with echoes of the Bible, Homer, and Ossian. His two short stories or prose poems, *René* and *Atala*—both of which are taken from *Les Natchez*—portray American Indians far more highly idealized than Cooper's Uncas or Simms's Sanutee. *Atala* is an idyllic story of the love of the young chieftain Chactas for the beautiful Indian maiden who gives the story its title. *René* pictures a melancholy, disillusioned European living among Indians in the American wilderness. Chateaubriand's America has always seemed too unreal greatly to interest American readers, but it left its trace upon Longfellow's description in *Evangeline* of the Mississippi River country which the New England poet had never seen.

The greater Romantic poets of England did not visit the United States, and in spite of a certain interest in this country their references to America often betray an amazing ignorance and insularity. William Wordsworth never came to America, but at the suggestion of his American friend, Henry Reed, he added to his *Ecclesiastical Sonnets* two mediocre poems in praise of the Pilgrim Fathers. In the 1840's, however, when the state of Pennsylvania stopped payment of interest on its bonds, some of which the poet had bought, he wrote the bitter sonnet "To the Pennsylvanians," which concludes:

> Renounced, abandoned by degenerate Men
> For state-dishonour black as ever came
> To upper air from Mammon's loathsome den.

[21] Gilbert Chinard, *L'Exotisme américain dans l'oeuvre de Chateaubriand* (Paris, 1912) and Chinard's edition of *Les Natchez* (1932) and E. K. Armstrong, "Chateaubriand's America," *PMLA*, XXII, 345-370 (1907).

Wordsworth and Coleridge eagerly devoured William Bartram's *Travels*, and the Pennsylvanian's descriptions of the Southern landscape had their effect upon *The Rime of the Ancient Mariner* and "Ruth." In his poems Wordsworth has much to say of the beneficent influence of nature, but in "Ruth" he suggests that all that was bad in the character of Ruth's faithless lover had been brought out by his sojourn in Georgia. The following stanzas are almost a parody of the beautiful poem describing Lucy's education at the hands of Nature—in England—beginning, "Three years she grew in sun and shower":

> Whatever in those climes he found
> Irregular in sight or sound
> Did to his mind impart
> A kindred impulse, seemed allied
> To his own powers, and justified
> The workings of his heart.
>
> Nor less, to feed voluptuous thought,
> The beauteous forms of nature wrought,
> Fair trees and gorgeous flowers;
> The breezes their own languor lent;
> The stars had feelings, which they sent
> Into those favoured bowers.

The most snobbish and supercilious of all British travelers who came to this country was the Irish poet, Thomas Moore, who visited the United States in 1804. On June 13 he wrote from Baltimore: "I am now dearest mother, more than three hundred miles from Norfolk. I have passed the Potomac, the Rappahannock, the Occoquan, the Potapsio [Patapsco?], and many other rivers, with names as barbarous as the inhabitants; every step I take not only *reconciles,* but *endears* to me, not only the excellencies but even the errors of Old England." A difficult traveler to please, truly! The Federalist lawyers in Richmond were not too bad, he thought, but the only literary society that Moore found congenial was in the undemocratic circle about Joseph Dennie, editor of the *Port Folio.* They flattered him; and so, he wrote: ". . . the only place I have seen, which I had one wish to pause in, was Philadelphia." No Romantic poet, however, could remain indifferent to the natural beauty of America. Alas! but it lacked, as he wrote from Saratoga, "any endearing associations of the heart (to diffuse that charm over it, without which the fairest features of nature are but faintly interesting). . . ."

In spite of his dislike of America, the facile Irish poet was long an American favorite, especially with Southern readers. They admired not only "The Lake of the Dismal Swamp" but also his sentimental lyrics and Oriental tales. *Lalla Rookh* had an important influence on Richard Henry Wilde, William Russell Smith, Alexander B. Meek, and Edgar Allan Poe.

Wordsworth was never in America and Moore remained only a few months, but John Davis (1774–1853?) liked the United States well enough to spend more than fifteen years (1798–1802, 1805–1817) here, most of them in Virginia. One might almost claim him as the first Southern novelist. "America," he once wrote, "is the country of my literary birth."

Davis, who was born in Salisbury, England, went to sea at the age of fourteen and was largely self-educated. Ten years later he came to the United States with an introduction from an earlier British traveler, Henry Wansey. Jefferson's *Notes on the State of Virginia*, he says, had taught him to think. Having decided to become a writer, he was shrewd enough to see that his best chance to make a name for himself lay in America. Here he would have access to a vast amount of unexploited literary materials of which European writers were ignorant.

Davis paid his way by tutoring and by doing hackwork for publishers, and he traveled on foot. In 1803 he published in Bristol, England, his *Travels of Four Years and a Half in the United States of America*, concerning which Robert Southey wrote from Keswick to John King on November 19, 1803: "He [Davis] is a vain man, and I should distrust his moral feelings, but most undoubtedly a man of great talents. By all means read his book; it will affect you in parts, and you will easily pardon the faults of a self taught man, struggling with poverty, and consoling himself with pride." For three months Davis was a tutor in a school which eventually became the College of Charleston. There he met a young Irish instructor of literary aspirations and some talent, Lucas George, who became his best friend. Not long afterwards Davis was a tutor at the Drayton plantation at "Coosahatchie." He collected the poems which first appeared in Peter Freneau's *South-Carolina Gazette* and published in Charleston the scarce and slender volume, *Poems Written at Coosahatchie*, which attracted a favorable notice in the *Port Folio*. In Virginia, Davis taught the children of planters in old-field schools and sentimentalized over the pretty girls. He lost one such position, he tells us, when it was discovered that one of his pupils wrote a better hand than the master. On his second sojourn in America he taught for a time in Petersburg, Virginia, where he saw something of the Irish-American playwright John Daly Burk. He married and returned to England in 1817. For many years he conducted a small stationery and book store in Winchester. He spent the last decade of his life in Charterhouse, pensioned under a provision made by Prince Albert for penniless men of letters.

In nineteenth-century English literature, so rich in great names, Davis's place is of no particular significance; but in the America of Dennie and Brown, of Wirt and Weems he bulks much larger. His *Travels*, twice reprinted in modern times, is an interesting book. In it he included a number of poems which show some feeling for nature in the New World. He included also the story of Pocahontas and the "Story of Dick the Negro," both of which show his awareness of important fresh materials.

Davis's best claim to a place among American writers is to be found in his novels, all based on American materials. Here we shall notice only the three versions of his Pocahontas story. The earliest appeared in his *Travels* in 1803. While teaching at Occoquan in northern Virginia, he had observed a party of Indians who had returned to visit the grave of one of their warriors. Among these was "an interesting girl of seventeen" who "appeared such another object as the mind images *Pocahontas* to have been." In the story of Captain John Smith and the Indian princess Davis felt he had made an important literary discovery. He concludes the story: "Thus have I delivered to the world the story of *Pocahontas*; nor can I refrain from indulging the idea, that it was reserved for my pen, to tell with discriminating circumstances, the tale of this *Indian* girl." In 1805 Davis published in Philadelphia an enlarged version entitled *Captain Smith and the Princess Pocahontas: An Indian Tale*. Later in the same year he expanded the novelette into a full-length historical novel, *The First Settlers of Virginia*. The Smith-Pocahontas story, however, suits the shorter form best; and in Davis's final version the Indian princess is off-stage most of the time. He did not solve a difficulty which was to confront the numerous writers who were yet to treat the theme: the big scene, the rescue of Smith, comes in the first act and the story ends anticlimactically with Pocahontas's marriage to the prosaic widower and tobacco planter, John Rolfe. It may be noted, however, that Davis's treatment of the theme had some influence upon James Nelson Barker's *The Indian Princess*, produced in 1808, the earliest of the Pocahontas plays and one of the earliest dramatic treatments of the Indian.

7
Southern Writers and New England

IN THIS ERA of intersectional good feeling when all our Presidents were drawn from Massachusetts and Virginia, New England and the Southern states were on friendlier terms than they were to be again for more than half a century. Southern visitors, like John Drayton, John Holt Rice, William Wirt, Lucian Minor, and Richard Henry Wilde, found much to admire in Yankeeland, as Richard Henry Lee and James Iredell had found before them. Before the Revolution Southerners and New Englanders had labored under many misconceptions of one another. Soldiers in Washington's army, like John Marshall, discovered that there were good and patriotic men in the Northern states. One Major Langhorne, lamenting the inferiority of Virginia to New England, drew from John Adams a "receipt for making a New England in Virginia—town-meetings, training days, schools, and ministers." As they worked together for independence, the Adamses of Massachusetts and the Lees of Virginia became greatly attached to one another. In the Constitutional Convention of 1787 Charles Cotesworth Pinckney of South Carolina confessed that he had come to Philadelphia with a prejudice against New Englanders but had discovered them to be "as liberal and candid as any men whatever." After 1830, as we shall see in a later section, New England and the South drew rapidly apart. The attitude of Emerson, Lowell, and Harriet Beecher Stowe was far less friendly than that of Bronson Alcott and James Gates Percival.

In the early nineteenth century Southern students began going in larger numbers to Yale, Harvard, and Princeton. John C. Calhoun and Augustus Baldwin Longstreet both graduated from Yale; both received honorary degrees from their alma mater; and both studied at a famous law school in Litchfield, Connecticut. Another Yale graduate, William Maxwell of Virginia, was a friend and poetic disciple of Timothy Dwight. Washington Allston and William Crafts were both graduates of Harvard. Allston, born on a South Carolina plantation, spent most of his mature life, when not living in Europe, in the neighborhood of Boston.

There were close commercial ties between New England and certain Southern coastal cities. Charlestonians liked to spend their summers in Newport. There was an active New England Society in Charleston. A. S. Willington, founder of the Charleston *Courier*, was a member; and so were William J. Grayson and James Louis Petigru, both native South Carolinians. Dr. Samuel Gilman, pastor of the Unitarian church in Charleston, and his wife, Caroline Gilman, who edited the *Southern Rose*, were both native New Englanders; and they formed a literary link between the two sections. Even after the Civil War a certain friendliness persisted. When the National Democratic Convention met in 1868, the delegates from Massachusetts and South Carolina marched down the aisle arm in arm.

There were many New Englanders in Baltimore. John Pierpont, who graduated from Yale in Calhoun's class, was once tutor in a Southern family and later was in the drygoods business in Baltimore with John Neal, a native of Maine, who tried both business and the law unsuccessfully in the same city. It was in Baltimore that Pierpont published his *Airs of Palestine* (1816) and that Neal received from Edward Coote Pinkney a challenge to a duel which he did not choose to accept. Jared Sparks, the future historian and Harvard professor, preached at the Unitarian church in Baltimore and was on friendly terms with Joseph and Winifred Gales in Raleigh.

John Drayton of South Carolina, who visited New York and New England in 1793, was impressed by the courtesy which young people in New England showed to travelers. In Boston, he wrote, "hospitality seems to be a national virtue." In New England, he noted, "Nobody is ignorant, and few are idle." On the eve of the American Revolution Josiah Quincy, Jr., had found Charleston to surpass Boston in many ways. Drayton, however, in 1793 found that Newport with a population of only six thousand had more shipping than Charleston with its ten thousand. Already Charlestonians were beginning to note that their beloved city was not sharing fully in the prosperity of the nation.

"New-England is *my country* as well as Virginia," wrote the able Presbyterian divine, John Holt Rice, after a visit to that section in 1822.[22] He found much to admire and commend to the readers of the *Virginia Evangelical and Literary Magazine*, which he edited; but he found the New England people so ill informed about the Old Dominion that he was "reminded . . . of the story of the Massachusetts girl who, in time of the revolutionary war, ran to the door to see the Virginia troops—after looking for a time, she exclaimed, with apparent disappointment, well, I *vow* mama, they are just like us!" Rice was impressed by the "frank and open-hearted hospitality" with which he and his friends were received in Boston. "There is," he wrote, "a particular ease and urbanity of manners, a graceful politeness and an elegant courtesy, which an observant stranger cannot but notice with pleasure." He found the rural New Englanders "more plain but not dis-

22 "A Journey in New-England," *Va. Evangelical and Lit. Mag.* [title varies], V, 350–358 (1822); VI, 7–14, 81–88, 133–144, 187–199, 255–261, 311–317 (1823).

agreeably coarse, nor are they rudely ignorant." "I am well persuaded," he said, "that the good *people* of the South and the North need only know each other, and carry on a free intercourse, to do away all local feelings of an unfriendly character. The collisions of ambitious politicians, the tricks of needy and unprincipled adventurers, and other things of a similar kind have created prejudices, which acquaintance will at once and entirely remove."

In 1829 William Wirt at the age of fifty-five went to Boston on legal business. He had lived in Maryland, Virginia, and Washington, where for twelve years he had been Attorney-General of the United States. After his return to the South, he wrote to his Virginia friend Dabney Carr a letter from Annapolis, August 3, 1829, which reveals to what extent provincial ignorance and prejudice had misled him:

. . . I think the people of Boston among the most agreeable people in the U.S. I suppose their kindness to me may have some effect on my judgment—but divesting myself of this as much as possible, I pronounce them as warm, as kind, as frank, as truly hospitable as the Virginians themselves—and in truth [they are] Virginians in all the *essentials* of character—I heard no *yankeeisms* in conversation except from a low Irishman— The gentlemen and the ladies of Boston speak & pronounce—english as purely as we do—and their sentiments are very much in the same strain, their literary improvements, *as a mass*, much superior— I expected to have found them cold, distant, shy, suspicious—I found them on the contrary, as open, as confiding, as playful, as generous as our own people— They have no foreign mixture among them—but are the native population the original english & their descendants— In this they resemble the best part of the population of Virginia—and I think are identical with them— Rely upon it, they are in republican principle and integrity among the soundest if not the very soundest of the people of the U. S.— You are not to judge of the mass by a few—and I speak of the mass—would to Heaven the people of Virginia & Massachusetts knew each other— What a host of absurd and repulsive prejudices w^d that knowledge put to flight—and how it w^d tend to consolidate the union, threatened as it is with so many agents of dissolution— My heart is set on bringing about this kno[w]ledge— How shall I effect it— If I write I shall be known and be supposed to have been bought up by a little kindness and flattery— I must think of this matter and do something to forward what I deem so important— be the consequences what they may—I believe the prejudices are all on our side— They resent what they suppose the contempt in which they are held by the people of Virg^a— Let them only believe that we view them with kindness & respect they will fly into our arms—I found it [so] in my own instance— They were su[r]prized by my courtesy and respect—did not seem to expect such a demeanour from a proud & high-hearted Virginian as they deemed me—and as they deem all Virginians— I do believe that they privately regard the Virginians as a superior people—and are gratified in being thought like them— Tho' they are far too proud to admit it in terms[?]— They are jealous too of the political ascendancy which Virginia has so long maintained and the proud superiority with which they suppose we look down upon them— Let them only understand that we regard them as equals and feel towards them real kindness, and they are ours— So I found it—and so I believe it will be found by every real gentleman and man of sense from the South who visits them— What a fool I have been to join in these vulgar prejudices against the yankees. I judged them by their pedlars—suppose they were to judge us by our blacklegs—it w^d be as fair—and yet how unjust & absurd w^d it be— [23]

Five years after Wirt's visit to Boston, Lucian Minor, a Virginia lawyer and a confidential adviser to the proprietor of the *Southern Literary Messenger*, journeyed through southern New England.[24] "Here," he wrote from Northampton, "is not apparent a hundredth part of the abject squalid poverty that our State presents. I have not seen a log house in New England; nor a dwelling-house without one or more glass windows. And nine tenths of the common farmhouses are painted." [25] As he turned his steps homeward, Minor wrote:

No other 6 weeks of my life have had compressed into them half so much excitement, or half so much interest. Those Northern States have very far the start of us Virginians, in almost all the constituents of civilization: yes further than my State pride will even now let me own without a struggle. They are more public spirited than we. They are more charitable—they possess better organized social and civil institutions. Their usages are more favorable to health, to virtue, to intelligence—and in their thorough, practical understanding of the word COMFORT . . . they are as far before us, as we are before the Hottentots or Esquimaux.

Great good—very great good—would result to Virginia or any other Southern State, if her farmers and planters, and their wives, would come often among

[23] This letter is given only in part and none too accurately in Kennedy, *Wirt* (revised ed., 1850), II, 237 ff. I have quoted from the original letter in the University of N. C. Library.

[24] James Russell Lowell (ed.), "A Virginian in New England Thirty-five Years Ago," *Atlantic Monthly*, XXVI, 162–179, 333–341, 482–492, 739–748 (Aug., Sept., Oct., and Dec., 1870); XXVII, 673–684 (June, 1871). Minor's letters, which had first appeared in the Fredericksburg, Va., *Arena*, had been reprinted in *S.L.M.*, Vol. I (1834–1835). Lowell, however, had the original manuscript and other materials not previously published, which were turned over to him by Minor's brother, Professor John B. Minor of the University of Virginia.

[25] XXVI, 333–334. Compare the impressions of the New Orleans-bred Grace King, visiting in Hartford in the 1880's: "The ride to Farmington and back in the public hack was exhilarating. The country was beautiful and prosperous, and every foot of land cultivated. No poverty was visible anywhere; no deserted plantations and tumbled-down dwellings; no poorly dressed children; in fact none of the features that marred the Southern country" (*Memories of a Southern Woman of Letters*, 1932, pp. 80–81).

the Yankees and observe their ways. Some things would be seen, to be shunned; but many more, to be imitated. I shall always preach up to my countrymen and countrywomen the utility of such a jaunt. I shall particularly exhort them to quit the great highways of fashionable touring—the steam and stage lines—and explore the simple, rural districts. . . .

In 1834 Minor could not visit Hartford without thinking of "the horrible convention, of 1814"; the idea of secession was still highly repugnant to a Virginian. Minor found that the Abolitionists were active, but in Boston and Cambridge he was assured that Garrison was regarded as only a miserable fanatic. So Minor, who was himself troubled about slavery, concluded that on the grave question "N. England is essentially sound: that the disposition is well nigh universal, to let us alone; to meddle not with the ulcer, which is too irritable for any but our own hands to touch."

Minor and his New England acquaintances failed to foresee that their sections were fast drifting further apart; that the Abolitionist conception of the South would win over the intellectuals; and that secession and civil war would come within less than thirty years. James Russell Lowell, who was to edit Minor's journal for the *Atlantic* in 1870 and 1871, would write often and bitterly about the South. After the war, however, he gradually changed his mind. When he read Minor's New England letters, he became greatly attracted to the Virginian's character and personality.

It is seldom [he wrote] that I have grown so intimate with a man I have never seen, seldom that I have had experience of so sweet, so equitable, or so well-balanced a nature as this. In reading these fading memorials; I have found myself sadly thinking: "And this was one of the class whom we have heard called barbarians by men who are proud to owe their culture to slaveholding Athens and Rome! This is one of the very persons whom our short-sighted statesmanship would exclude from all share in politics!"

After the Civil War Southern visitors to New England were, like Wirt and Minor, to discover to their great surprise that they had much in common with the New Englanders. On her first visit to New England in 1885 Mary Noailles Murfree wrote to her mother: "Where is the cold New England we have so often read about? Where are the frigid manners, the stern eyes, the aloof sympathies? I don't believe such Yankees exist. To quote Mrs. Betsy, there ain't none."

8
Northern Writers and the South

NOT MANY NORTHERN travelers of the better class visited the ante-bellum South. There were a few health-seekers, sportsmen, actors, and some Yankee teachers and preachers, but more numerous were the peddlers, overseers, and slave traders. It is not surprising that many Southerners held a low opinion of the New England Yankees. A few Northern writers came south and, though most of them disliked slavery, they were on the whole pleased with what they saw.

More deeply interested in the South than most Northern writers was the militantly American James Kirke Paulding (1778-1860), the intimate friend of Irving and collaborator with him in *Salmagundi*—the friend and admirer, too, of Madison and Calhoun. Paulding visited parts of the South in 1816 and the next year he published a gossipy two-volume *Letters from the South*, in which he said:

> One of the first things that strikes a Northern man, who flounders into Virginia . . . loaded with a pack of prejudices as large as a pedlar's, is, that he has, all life long, been under a very mistaken notion of the state of their manners. . . . Before I had been long in this part of the world, I discovered, to my great surprise, that the people were very much like other folks, only a little more hospitable. . . . Every day's experience, in short, convinces me, that the people of our part of the world have been much misled by the idle tales of travelling pedlars, sent out to buy tobacco and cotton, or by the unneighbourly arts of men, knowing better, but misrepresenting for party purposes.

Paulding read with delight the manuscript of William Byrd's still unpublished *History of the Dividing Line* He found the old Colonial houses in decay or in the hands of new families. Richmond he found given over to money-making like any Northern city. He gives a vivid picture of a degraded and unprincipled slave trader, but he found the planters lamenting slavery as "an evil that cannot be cured by immediate emancipation." He was one of the earliest travelers to show any interest in the songs of the Negroes. He was struck with the great difference between the Tuckahoes of eastern Virginia and the Cohees who lived west of the Blue Ridge. He found Southerners in great numbers migrating to trans-Allegheny regions. In his novel *Westward Ho!* (1832) he described a bankrupt Virginia family which began life all over again in Kentucky. In his lost play, *The Lion of the West* (produced in 1831), he introduced a racy Kentuckian, speaking in dialect and reminiscent of David Crockett.[26] In a later novel, *The Puritan and His Daughter* (1849), he contrasted Virginia and New England in Colonial times. Meanwhile he had written *Slavery in the United States* (1836) because, as he said, "the fanatics of religion and philanthropy" had circulated tales of abuses "equally vague as horrible, and in which neither time, place, nor names are specified, nor any clew given by which their truth may be tested" and which his own experience unequivocally contradicted. Here Paulding took the position to which he held during the remainder of his life—that slavery was not "an evil of such surpassing enormity as to demand the sacrifice of the harmony and consequent union of the states, followed by civil contention and servile war, to its removal."

In 1798 at the age of eighteen William Ellery Channing (1780–1842) went to Richmond as tutor to the children of David Meade Randolph, whom he had met in Newport, Rhode Island. Channing, who had just graduated from Harvard College, wished to earn money so that he could return to Cambridge to study theology. He remained in Virginia for a year and a half. Randolph, who built "Moldavia," the house which in 1825 Poe's foster father John Allan was to purchase for about fifteen thousand dollars, was at that time United States Marshal for the state of Virginia. At Randolph's home Channing met John Marshall and other prominent Virginians of both parties. More than once, it seems, the young tutor visited in the homes of Virginians not only in the city but on plantations, and he traveled about with the Randolphs during the summer. It was in Virginia that the young Federalist first became acquainted with intelligent members of Jefferson's party. After listening to debates in the General Assembly, he wrote: "The Virginians are the best orators I have ever heard."

In Virginia, though he did not cease to read the works of his favorite Francis Hutcheson, whom he had discovered in college, Channing read for the first time Mary Wollstonecraft's *Vindication of the Rights of Woman*, Rousseau's *Eloise*, and Godwin's *Caleb Williams* and *Political Justice*— books he might not have discovered so soon if he had remained in conservative Rhode Island. In Virginia Channing began to speculate about political and social problems with a freedom that would have shocked many of his New England friends. He even suggested that men should "destroy all distinctions of property" and "throw the produce of their labor into one common stock, instead of hoarding it up in their own garners. . . ." Like

---

[26] The play had some influence on Caruthers' *The Kentuckian in New-York* (1834). See N. F. Adkins' two articles: "James K. Paulding's *Lion of the West*," *Am. Lit.*, III, 249–258 (Nov., 1931) and "A Study of James K. Paulding's *Westward Ho!*" *Am. Collector*, III, 221–229 (March, 1927). See also Floyd C. Watkins, "James Kirke Paulding and the South," *Am. Quart.*, V, 219–230 (Fall, 1953).

Godwin and Jefferson, he believed that "virtue and benevolence are *natural* to man." But, he wrote: "I find *avarice* the great bar to all my schemes, and I do not hesitate to assert that the human race will never be happier then [than]—at present till the establishment of a community of property."

Channing found Deism rampant in Virginia. "Infidelity," he wrote, "is very general among the higher classes; and they who do not reject Christianity can hardly be said to believe, as they never examine the foundations on which it rests. In fine, religion is in a deplorable state." Channing began a thorough study of the evidences of Christianity. He was going through a spiritual crisis not suspected by his Virginia friends. As a result of intense study, brooding over his religious difficulties, and failure to care for his health, he was for the remainder of his life a chronic sufferer from ill health.

In letters to friends and relatives Channing compared Virginia and New England manners. He noted that the Virginians called one another by their first names: "They address each other and converse together with the same familiarity and frankness which they used to do when they were boys. How different from our Northern manners! There, avarice and ceremony at the age of twenty graft the coldness and unfeelingness of age on the disinterested ardor of youth." In another letter he wrote: "I believe I have praised the Virginians before, in my letters, for their hospitality. I blush for my own people, when I compare the selfish prudence of a Yankee with the generous confidence of a Virginian. Here I find great vices, but greater virtues than I left behind me. There is one single trait which attaches me to the people I live with more than all the virtues of New England. They *love money less* than we do. They are more disinterested. Their patriotism is not tied to their purse-strings. Could I only take from the Virginians their *sensuality* and their *slaves*, I should think them the greatest people in the world."

The passages which I have quoted from Channing's letters appear in the *Memoir*, published in 1848 by his nephew William Henry Channing, to whom Emerson addressed his well-known "Ode." The younger Channing, who was violently antislavery, believed that his uncle had praised the Virginians with "more enthusiasm than discrimination," and he felt it necessary to explain that Virginia had greatly deteriorated since the great Unitarian divine had lived in the Old Dominion.

While in Virginia, Channing wrote that his repugnance to slavery would alone prevent his settling in that state. He discovered, however, that the institution was "freely spoken of with abhorrence." After his return to New England, he received a letter from Mrs. Randolph in which she said: "I feel a great desire to quit the land of slavery altogether."

In spite of his dislike of slavery, it was more than thirty years after he left Virginia before Channing began writing antislavery pamphlets. In other words, his conscience troubled him most deeply at the time when his memories of Virginia had grown dim and when many other New Englanders were beginning to be deeply troubled over slavery. Channing, however, disapproved of the methods of the extreme Abolitionists, who were demanding immediate emancipation and were condemning slavery and slaveholder alike. Channing tried hard not to make that mistake, but at times he came near condemning all who held slaves. By 1842, the year in which he died, he had so far forgotten his youthful enthusiasm for Virginians that he could write of Richmond as "a licentious, intemperate city," in which "one spirit, at least, was preparing, in silence and loneliness, to toil, not wholly in vain, for truth and holiness."

In *New Connecticut: An Autobiographical Poem*, privately printed in Boston in 1881, Amos Bronson Alcott (1799–1888) gives us glimpses of the Southern planters as he had seen them more than half a century before while he was peddling almanacs and other wares in Virginia and the Carolinas. In this "New school of fine manners for the farmer's boy," he tells us:

> New England's customs find small favor here:
> A freer life, more opulent, less discreet,
> Far more restrained by courtesy than fear,
> E'en when the master and the menial meet.

When Alcott returned to his native Connecticut arrayed in broadcloth, on which he had spent his earnings, the rumor was: " 'No farmer now, but a fine gentleman.' " A fine gentleman Alcott undoubtedly was, and the Virginia planters recognized in him no ordinary peddler when they permitted him to read in their private libraries, which "were often voluminous and attractive." From Norfolk, Virginia, he wrote on March 19, 1820: "Hospitality is a distinguishing trait of the people, rich or poor. And their polished manners and agreeable conversation ingratiate the traveller at once in their favor. The planters in this section are largely an educated class,—gentlemen in the best sense of the word. I pass many an evening at their hospitable homes. It is a school of manners next to travelling abroad."

In later years, Alcott imagined that his fondness for the Virginians had prevented him from seeing the abuses of slavery: "The elegant refinement and gracious courtesy, of which I was enamored at the time, doubtless covered from my eyes the iniquities of the system." He still remembered, however, his surprise "at perceiving the kindest relations occasionally existing between mistress and maid," and he could recall no instance in which any Virginia planter had defended the institution of slavery during his sojourn on the banks of the York and the James.

Among the few New England writers who visited South Carolina in this era of intersectional good feeling we may single out the sensitive and eccentric poet, James Gates Percival (1795–1856), who sailed for Charleston in November, 1821. The Connecticut poet, physician, and scientist, with his tall, spare figure, thin face, and large dark-blue eyes, had already graduated from Yale, studied medicine, attempted suicide, and published a volume of poems. He went to Charleston as assistant to a none-too-competent botanical lecturer named Whitlow. Percival quarreled with Whitlow, hired a doctor's office, and put up a sign; but no patients came. He gave some lectures on botany and spent his leisure writing romantic verses. He was fortunate enough to become acquainted with William Crafts, the Gadsdens, the Elliotts, Samuel Gilman, who later introduced Percival to the Boston-Cambridge writers, and the New England-born A. S. Willington, who printed some of Percival's verses in the *Courier*. When Percival sailed for New York late in March, 1822, Willington printed in the *Courier* a eulogy of the poet, whom he thought "destined to outlive many generations after this in the annals of men." "We, in Charleston," he continued, "loved him for the artless simplicity, the delicate sensitiveness, the sweet timidity of his spirit and manner; and we admired the amazing fertility of his mind, always spontaneously pouring forth, as from an exhaustless spring, pure and beautiful and unearthly thoughts."

In January the Babcock brothers, who were from New Haven, had published in Charleston the first number of Percival's *Clio*. The success of *The Sketch Book* had suggested to Percival that perhaps poetry as well as prose might be successfully published in instalments. *Clio*, Number I contained two essays and about seventy-five pages of verse. These were all more strongly colored by Romanticism than anything to appear in Charleston before the early poems of Simms. In the second number of *Clio*, which he published in New Haven in August of the same year, Percival included some of the poems which he had written in Charleston. Among those that reflect his interest in the South are "Flower of a Southern Garden Newly Blowing," "The Coral Grove," "These Weeping Skies," and "There Is a Calm Lagoon," which begins:

> There is a calm lagoon,
> Hid in the bosom of a cypress grove;
> Around deep shade, above
> The tropic sun pours down the heat of noon.
> The aged fathers of the forest wave

Their giant arms athwart the gloom below,
And as the winds in fitful breathing blow,
Their rush is like the tide's resounding flow,
Or sighs above a maiden's early grave.
The long moss hangs its hair,
In hoary festoons, on from tree to tree.

When the third number of *Clio* appeared, Hugh Swinton Legaré, who had perhaps met Percival in Charleston, discussed it not unkindly in the *Southern Review* for May, 1828. He did not consider Percival "a man either of great genius or of profound sensibility." He saw in the volume "nothing more than a certain tender and poetic pensiveness, which, although a very pretty thing, is still very distinct from the agonies and energies of deep passion." He thought Percival at his best when "revelling in visions of Oriental magnificence, or painting (as he loves to do) the soft beauties and balmy fragrance of some delicious Southern climate." The acute Charleston critic had gauged Percival's merits to a nicety.

Even in the forties and fifties, when most Northern writers were under grave suspicion of hostility to the South, no one found any objectionable isms in Washington Irving. His writings found congenial and quick response in the South. With little loss of time the North Carolina newspapers reprinted in instalments *The Sketch Book* and *Knickerbocker's History of New York*. *The Sketch Book* bore a family resemblance to William Wirt's earlier *The Letters of the British Spy* and *The Old Bachelor*; and Irving's combination of humor, sentiment, and charm of style was as acceptable in the South as to readers in other sections. Furthermore, Irving had visited in the South and had many Southern friends. Two of his companions on travels in Europe had been Virginians, Joseph C. Cabell and William C. Preston. From Richmond, where he spent several weeks, he wrote in 1807: "I am absolutely enchanted with Richmond, and like it more and more every day. The society is polished, sociable, and extremely hospitable. . . ." He had friends, too, in South Carolina. From Columbia, when the Nullification excitement was approaching a crisis, he wrote: "It is really lamentable to see such a fine set of gallant fellows as these leading nullifiers are, so madly in the wrong." When Governor Hamilton gave him a warm invitation to return, Irving replied: "Oh yes! I'll come with *the first troops!*"

The most intimate of Irving's Southern literary friends was John Pendleton Kennedy, whose *Swallow Barn* (1832) owes something to *The Sketch Book* and *Bracebridge Hall*. Irving's liking for Kennedy extended to Kennedy's wife, his father-in-law, and to his niece Mary Kennedy, to whom he wrote some charming letters in his old age. He saw decided merit in Poe's short stories, which were so different from his own. He wrote in kindly fashion to an obscure North Carolina writer who had sent him a copy of an amateurish novel: "We [in the North] do not know sufficiently of the South; which appears to me to abound with material for a rich, original and varied literature." [27] Irving himself occasionally made use of Southern materials, as in "The Creole Village" in *Wolfert's Roost* (1855); and many a Southern reader must have been struck by the brief paragraph in which Irving pictured the Negro messenger who brought to Ichabod Crane an invitation to a party at the Van Tassels'.

James Fenimore Cooper, who was perhaps more widely read in the South than any writer of his time except Scott, found Southerners of his own class congenial. He understood the Southern planter, for he himself was a country gentleman and a large landholder. So also were his father, Judge William Cooper, and his father-in-law, who had actually owned slaves. In 1828 Cooper wrote in *Notions of the Americans*:

I am of opinion that in proportion to the population, there are more men who belong to what is termed the class of gentlemen, in the old southern states of America than in any other country in the world. So far as pride in themselves, a courteous air, and a general intelligence are concerned, they are, perhaps, quite on a level with the gentry of any other country, though their intelligence must necessarily be chiefly of that sort which is obtained by the use of books, rather than of extensive familiarity with the world. In respect to conventional manners they are not so generally finished as the upper classes of other countries, or even of some classes in their own, though I do not know where to find gentlemen of better air or better breeding throughout, than most of those I have met in the southern *Atlantic* states.

In 1827 Cooper went so far as to write a defense of American slavery for the *Revue Encyclopédique*.[28] It was not that he thought slavery right, but emancipation must be effected gradually. "The abolitionists," he wrote late in life, "beyond a dispute, have only had a tendency to rivet the fetters of the slave, and to destroy the peace of the country. Emancipation has not been extended a single foot by any of their projects; while the whole South has been thrown into an attitude of hostile defiance, not only towards these misguided persons, but to their innocent and disgusted fellow-citizens." Nevertheless, Cooper was repelled by the attitude of the Southern secessionists. He wrote to his old sailor friend, W. B. Shubrick: "The Southrons

[27] George H. Throop, *Bertie: or, Life in the Old Field* (Philadelphia, 1851), Preface.
[28] R. E. Spiller, "Fenimore Cooper's Defense of Slave-Owning America," *Am. Hist. Rev.*, XXXV, 575–582 (April, 1930). See also Max L. Griffin, "Cooper's Attitude toward the South," *Studies in Philology*, XLVIII, 67–76 (Jan., 1951).

are getting into a muss, especially you [South] Carolinians. With a population of less than half of New York town, they talk of fighting Uncle Sam, that long-armed, well-knuckled, hard-fisted old scamp, Uncle Sam."

In his first important romance, *The Spy* (1821), the setting of which is in Westchester County, New York, Cooper introduced a surprisingly large number of Southern characters. Among them are Captain Jack Lawton of the Virginia cavalry, a really notable portrait; Major Dunwoodie, the fictitious hero; and General Washington, thinly disguised as a Mr. Harper. Caesar, the faithful, humorous Negro house servant, is a very early example of a type common in later Southern fiction. It seems not unlikely that the success of *The Spy* suggested to Caruthers, Kennedy, and Simms that a Southern historical romance might be worth attempting. At any rate, Cooper's influence along with that of Scott is, I think, discernible not only in the scouts and the Indians of their romances but also in characters drawn from the gentry.

William Cullen Bryant's reputation in the South suffered little from his opposition to slavery since it rarely found expression in his poetry.[29] The first of Bryant's extended visits to the South came as late as 1843, and some of his friends had been afraid that his reception there would not be a cordial one. On his return to New York he wrote to R. H. Dana, Sr.: "Our visit to the South was extremely agreeable. New modes of life and a new climate could not fail to make it interesting, and the frank, courteous, hospitable manner of the Southerners made it pleasant. Whatever may be the comparison in other respects, the South certainly has the advantage over us in point of manners." It was perhaps at Simms's home at "Woodlands" that Bryant heard the Negroes singing at a corn-shucking and took pains to record a Jim Crow song in his "A Tour in the Old South." He was Simms's most intimate friend among Northern writers, and he wrote the essay on "Woodlands" which appeared in *Homes of American Authors* (1853). In 1856 he helped to make arrangement for Simms's lectures in New York which were so coldly received. Simms dedicated to Bryant his *Southern Passages and Pictures* (1839) and gave the poet useful letters of introduction to his Southern friends.[30]

---

[29] Max L. Griffin, "Bryant and the South," *Tulane Studies in English*, I (1949), 53–80. On Oct. 11, 1817, the Charleston *Carolina Gazette* reprinted the early incomplete version of "Thanatopsis" from the *No. Am. Rev.* for Sept., 1817, without mentioning the source. Bryant's short story, "The Marriage Blunder," has its setting in Louisiana.

[30] One of these presumably was Israel K. Tefft of Savannah, who in 1849 gave Bryant a copy of William Bacon Stevens's *A History of Georgia* with a request for the poet's opinion of it. See "A New Letter by William Cullen Bryant," ed. Jay B. Hubbell, *Ga. Hist. Quart.*, XXVI, 288–290 (Sept.–Dec., 1942) and John C. Guilds, "Bryant in the

In the years that followed the Civil War Bryant befriended Paul Hamilton Hayne and other penniless Southern writers. Two of these served as literary editors of the New York *Evening Post*: George Cary Eggleston and John R. Thompson, who was recommended by Simms for the position. Thompson, to his lasting credit, had written on the eve of the Civil War: ". . . the sins of Bryant, the editor, have not deadened us to the beauties of Bryant, the poet." [31]

9
Authorship in the Old South

BEFORE 1800 there was, outside of journalism, no place for the professional writer anywhere in the United States. Thomas Cooper accurately described the situation in *Some Information Respecting America* (Dublin, 1794):

With respect to literary men, it is to be observed that in America there is not as yet what may be called a *class* of society, to whom that denomination will apply. . . . Literature in America is an amusement only—collateral to the occupation of the person who attends, (and but occasionally attends) to it. In Europe, it is a trade—a means of livelihood. The making of books is there as much a business as the selling of books. No wonder therefore it is better done in Europe than in America; or that with their usual good sense the Americans should permit you to be their manufacturers of literature, as well as of crockery or calicoes.

In this period (1789–1830) a few Northern writers may in a limited sense be described as professional: Joseph Dennie, Charles Brockden Brown, Washington Irving, and Fenimore Cooper. Not one of these, however, was for an extended period of time wholly dependent upon his pen for a living. In the South there were many who wrote, but only journalists like Thomas Ritchie and A. S. Willington can be described as professional. The Southern towns and cities were too small and too widely scattered to serve as im-

South: A New Letter to Simms," *Ga. Hist. Quart.*, XXXVII, 142–146 (June, 1953). For an account of the 1849 visit, see Bryant's *Letters of a Traveller* (1850), Letters xliii–xlix.
    [31] *S.L.M.*, XXX, 72 (Jan., 1860). In the same month and year Hayne defended Bryant against the Richmond *Enquirer*, which had characterized him as "an inditer of mean doggerel." Hayne wrote: "Bryant is an Abolitionist, and his journal . . . an unscrupulous organ of his abominable creed; but it is simple justice to say that, unlike Longfellow, Whittier, Lowell, and a host of less distinguished bards, he has never polluted the works of his imagination by the introduction of the slavery question in any form" (*Russell's Mag.*, VI, 371, Jan., 1860).

portant literary centers, and on the plantations there was no place for authors by trade. Professional authorship is always something strange in the farmer's eyes, and he has scant respect for it even today unless the writer wins a Pulitzer prize or is called to Hollywood. At bottom few Americans anywhere except in New England have or have ever had real respect for a writer unless he made money by his profession. None of the arts except perhaps architecture played an important part in the planter's life. Without loss of face a planter might contribute occasionally to a farm journal or write an account of a hunting or fishing trip or turn out a political pamphlet; but poetry, drama, and fiction were in a different category. Literature in the form of library shelves filled with the works of Homer, Cicero, Shakespeare, Addison, Pope, Goldsmith, and even Franklin and Irving was worthy of respect; but contemporary writing was valued chiefly as an amusement unless it had some immediate practical application. For most planters, as for most readers in the leisure classes then and now, literature was not primarily a thing of beauty or an interpretation of the meaning of life.

The social status of the writer improved much more rapidly in the Boston area than anywhere else in the country. After moving from New York to Boston, Thomas Bailey Aldrich wrote to Bayard Taylor in 1866: "The humblest man of letters has a position here which he doesn't have in New York. To be known as an able writer is to have the choicest society opened to you. Just as an officer in the Navy (providing he is a gentleman) is the social equal of anybody—so a knight of the quill here is supposed necessarily to be a gentleman. In New York—he's a Bohemian! outside of his personal friends he has no standing."

To be known as a writer of verse or light essays was a handicap to a gentleman lawyer, like William Wirt or Hugh Swinton Legaré, or a Congressman, like Richard Henry Wilde. Edgar Allan Poe, who was a professional man of letters, never attained the social position of these men or even that of Simms, whose second wife was a planter's daughter. The Southern gentleman's attitude towards writing as a profession recalls the story of Voltaire's visit to William Congreve in old age, as the French author told it in his *Letters concerning the English Nation*:

Mr. Congreve had one defect, which was his entertaining too mean an idea of his own first profession, that of a writer, though it was to this he owed his fame and fortune. He spoke of his works as trifles that were beneath him, and hinted to me in our first conversation, that I should visit him upon no other foot than that of a gentleman. . . . I answered that had he been so unfortunate as to be a mere gentleman, I should never have come to see him; and I was very much disgusted at so unseasonable a piece of vanity.

In his *Autobiography* Joseph Le Conte tells a story which illustrates the Southern planter's reluctance to write for publication. Le Conte was a native of Georgia who studied at Harvard with Agassiz, taught at the University of South Carolina, fought in the Confederate army, and made a name for himself as a geologist at the University of California. While spending the summer of 1858 at Flat Rock, North Carolina, he had a remarkable conversation with Langdon Cheves, a planter from the South Carolina Low-Country.

We had both read that remarkable book Vestiges of the Natural History of Creation, published in 1844, and he had cordially embraced the idea of origin of species by transmutation of previous species, while I contrarily held to Agassiz' views of creation according to a preordained plan. We had it hot and heavy. When I brought forward the apparently unanswerable objection drawn from the geographical distribution of species and the manner in which contiguous fauna pass into one another, i.e., by substitution instead of transmutation, his answer was exactly what an evolutionist would give to-day—viz., that intermediate links would be killed off in the struggle for life as less suited to the environment; in other words that only the fittest would survive. It must be remembered that this was before the publication of Darwin's book [*On the Origin of Species*, 1859], and the answer was wholly new to me and struck me very forcibly.

Why did he not publish his idea? No one well acquainted with the Southern people, and especially with the Southern planters, would ask such a question. Nothing could be more remarkable than the wide reading, the deep reflection, the refined culture, and the originality of thought and observation characteristic of them; and yet the idea of publication never even entered their minds. What right had any one to publish unless it was something of the greatest importance, something that would revolutionize thought?

The ante-bellum Southern writers were with few exceptions amateurs, and many of them did not publish their work over their own names. Writing was an avocation for an occasional lawyer, doctor, minister, teacher, or planter; it was rarely resorted to as a means of making money. Writing for money, in fact, was not good form. Richard Henry Wilde gave away his poems to magazine editors who asked for them, and Philip Pendleton Cooke felt somewhat chagrined that he was unable to pay for the publication of his *Froissart Ballads*.

One "R.H.N.," who greatly admired Nathaniel Hawthorne, complained in the *Southern Quarterly Review* in April, 1853, that in the Northern states authorship was "fast becoming a trade" and authors were writing for money. That, he thought, was the wrong motive: "Its appeal is too low; it does not seek the adequate tribunal; it works only for the present, which is a fatal error, and it works for money; it is simply a trade among us, looking to market profits and pecuniary recompense, rather than to the utterance of new truths and the prosecution of a divine mission." How "R.H.N." expected Hawthorne and other American authors to live unless they were paid for what they wrote I do not know. Perhaps he thought that only men of independent means should write. Certainly we do not find among the Southern planters any one who followed "R.H.N.'s" advice and consecrated himself to "the prosecution of a divine mission," like Milton or Wordsworth or, perhaps I should'add, Edgar Allan Poe or Sidney Lanier.

It has been commonly said—Southerners themselves frequently said it —that the Old South had no publishers. The statement is true only in the limited sense that there were in the South no great commercial publishing houses like that of Harper & Brothers with its large facilities for the marketing of books. The South had its share of printers; but although they occasionally published books—which they did not know how to sell in large numbers—their chief business was the printing of newspapers, almanacs, and pamphlets.

In the years 1789–1830 there is evident an increasing tendency for the Southern writer to have his books published in Northern cities: New York, Philadelphia, and less frequently in Boston. Baltimore and Charleston published more books than other Southern towns or cities.[32] Until after the Second War with England, most American publishers except Mathew Carey in Philadelphia had been content with a local market for their books. Soon thereafter, however, the unprecedented demand for *Waverley* and its successors and a few years later for the novels of Dickens and Bulwer-Lytton brought about keen competition for a greatly enlarged American market. There was at that time no international copyright law to protect the rights of the British author, and in the cutthroat competition that developed, the largest profits went to the publisher with the most efficient methods of printing and distribution. When the publishing and marketing of books be-

[32] A check-list which I once made of works by Southern writers listed in Sabin's *Dictionary* for the years 1800–1835 included 216 titles in poetry, drama, and fiction. Of these 70 were published in the North, 125 in the South, 5 in England, and 16 at places not indicated. The distribution by states was: South Carolina, 40; Maryland, 35; New York, 33; Virginia, 31; Pennsylvania, 22; Massachusetts, 10; etc. See also the lists of printers and publishers, classified by states, in Charles Evans, *American Bibliography* (12 vols., 1903–1934). In *The Baltimore Book Trade, 1800–1825* (1953) Rollo G. Silver lists a large number of printers, publishers, and booksellers.

For a list of European books reprinted in the South in this period, see my Bibliography under "Printing and Publishing."

came a business requiring capital and skill, the Southern printers could no longer compete with such Northern houses as Harper & Brothers and Carey & Lea.

And yet, as we shall soon see, the impulse to write was felt by a surprisingly large number of Southerners. The published materials bulk larger than is generally supposed, and probably much was written that was never printed. There was much more writing in the towns and cities than on the numerous plantations; yet even in the cities the Southern writer suffered from isolation. New ideas did not reach him quickly. He rarely had literary friends on whose criticism and encouragement he could rely. He had at hand no suitable means of publishing, and he had little idea of the commercial value of what he wrote. The lack of a friendly circle of critical readers explains in part the extravagances and bombast in Daniel Bryan's epic of Daniel Boone as it explains the clumsy writing in John Taylor's shrewd discussions of political questions. Southern writers who traveled or lived abroad, like Richard Henry Wilde and Hugh Swinton Legaré, show fewer such defects.

In New England the clergy were, as Emerson said in 1837, "more universally than any other class, the scholars of their day." It was clergymen and teachers that gave New England its intellectual tone. In the South the dominant tone in society was set by the large-scale planters, but in intellectual matters it was generally the lawyers who took the lead. For young men not born to wealth or position, the law was the easiest path to distinction. William Wirt and Albert Pike are two examples of lawyers who largely educated themselves and from humble beginnings worked their way to professional distinction. The American lawyer was usually of middle-class origin, but his profession often brought him into intimate contact with men of wealth and position. It was only natural, therefore, that he should so often become the political representative of freeholders in the South. The effect of the study and practice of law, it is often said, is to make men conservative in their thinking. The planters, too, at least in the later years of the period, were a conservative class, and it was natural that the lawyers should so often represent their point of view in the state and national capitals. Often the successful lawyer was himself a planter. John Taylor of Caroline and John C. Calhoun were farmers, lawyers, and Congressmen. Among other writers who practiced law were Richard Henry Wilde, William Wirt, William Crafts, and George Tucker. Some of these men, used to much speaking in public, did not fully understand the differences between writing intended for the reader and writing meant to be carried home to an audience by the speaker's voice, gestures, and personality. The oral influence is strong in Southern literature, but it is seen to better advantage in the sketches of the humorists than in the addresses of lawyers and politicians.

Until after the founding of the *Liberator* in 1831, there was little agitation for a distinctively Southern literature.[33] National feeling was strong in the South, and Southern writers, like those in the North, resented the aspersions of British reviewers and travelers and debated the question of a national literature.

Early in the nineteenth century Virginians began to note with regret the literary backwardness of their commonwealth. In the *Virginia Evangelical and Literary Magazine* for March, 1819, John Holt Rice wrote: "Indeed we cannot find that, properly speaking, science and letters were ever cultivated in our state." In an address on "The Prospect of Letters and Taste in Virginia," in September, 1827, Jesse Burton Harrison found it almost incredible that the state had produced "not one poem, one history, one statue, one picture, one work of laborious learning to exhibit to the world. . . ." We know now that the literary history of Virginia was less barren than Rice and Harrison imagined. In the Preface to his novel, *Edge-Hill* (Richmond, 1828), James E. Heath refers to fiction as "this popular and alluring department of literature, hitherto so little cultivated south of the Potomac. We abound," he continued, "in able statesmen, and eloquent speakers, but in works of fancy we have few writers who have transcended the limits of a fugitive essay, or an humble duodecimo."

Various writers discussed the reasons for Virginia's backwardness in cultural matters, but the ablest analyses were written by George Tucker. In the *Virginia Literary Museum* (published at the University of Virginia) for November 4, 1829, he noted that law and medicine were the all-attractive professions and that few ever felt a desire for literary fame. "We have," he said, "written fewer (and perhaps worse) books and contributed less to the advancement of the arts, ornamental and useful, in Virginia, than in any country on earth equally civilized." "The time has arrived in Virginia," he concluded, "when the minds of our youth should expand to a nobler emulation than the mere scuffle after a law-suit or a case of bilious fever." Tucker had already discussed the subject in a fine essay "On the Low State of Polite Letters in Virginia" in *Letters from Virginia, Translated from the French* (Baltimore, 1816). Tucker noted that "the peculiar character

---

[33] For a fuller discussion of the general problem of a Southern literature, see Jay B. Hubbell, "Literary Nationalism in the Old South," *American Studies in Honor of William Kenneth Boyd* (1940), ed. David K. Jackson, pp. 175–220.

of the first settlers was not likely to give a literary turn to their successors." The Virginians were preoccupied with practical pursuits; they lived on scattered plantations; and they had no city "to draw them together to refine their manners and improve their tastes." Both the British authorities and the Virginians themselves had been backward in establishing libraries, schools, and colleges. The clergy, who in Europe had been "the greatest friends and patrons of learning and letters," had done little for the Ancient Dominion. The Revolution had been a great intellectual stimulus, but it had not turned men's minds to belles-lettres. Furthermore, in cultural matters Virginia was still a colony, and the taste of those who read was for foreign books and books on foreign themes. "Hence it is," Tucker concludes, "that while Virginia can show a long roll of her warriors and statesmen, she can give but a Flemish account of her poets and wits."

Edward W. Johnston, who discussed "American Literature" in the *Southern Review* of Charleston in August, 1831, frowned upon the demand for a national literature.[34] His article is a belated review of Samuel Knapp's *Lectures on American Literature* and Samuel Kettell's *Specimens of American Poetry*, both published in 1829. Johnston, like other Southern and Western reviewers, resented the way in which Knapp and Kettell had exaggerated "the early glories of New-England literature," but he made no counterclaim for the South. "We do . . . in the name of the good people of the planting States," he said, "utterly disclaim the having even the humble part, which is assigned us, in a separate school of writers, dignified with the title of 'American.'" To give up the British heritage seemed to the reviewer "the most singularly bold effort to advance the kingdom of Dullness that the world has ever yet beheld. . . ." Johnston argued from history that neither arts nor letters had ever flourished where Calvinism prevailed. The "general feeling of aversion to authorship" in the South, he maintained, was "for the greater part, precisely in proportion to good education and cultivated taste." If the reviewer correctly described the South Carolina attitude, it is no wonder that Charlestonians were lukewarm toward the claims of William Gilmore Simms and made both William Crafts and Hugh Swinton Legaré feel that their devotion to the law should not be interfered with by literary pursuits.

[34] VII, 436-459. Johnston, who was a teacher, was the older brother of General Joseph E. Johnston. He was the author of the memoir of Hugh S. Legaré included in the latter's *Writings* (1846). He often used the pen name "Il Secretario." In the Richmond *Semi-Weekly Examiner* for Aug. 29, 1851, he is satirized and compared to Squeers in Dickens's *Nicholas Nickleby*. The article in the *Southern Review* is similar to his "American Letters—Their Character and Advancement," *Am. Whig Rev.*, I, 575-580 (June, 1845).

10
Newspapers and Magazines

BEFORE THE REVOLUTION both North and South had sent to England for their books, but in the early nineteenth century Southerners began more and more to look to the Northern cities to supply them with reading matter not to be found in their local newspapers. Northern publishers with improved methods of printing and distribution sent to their agents in the South the works of Franklin, Paine, Charles Brockden Brown, Irving, and Cooper— all of which were frequently advertised by local booksellers in Southern newspapers. The publishers of some Northern magazines—especially the *Port Folio* of Philadelphia and the *North American Review* of Boston—advertised their new numbers in Southern newspapers and employed Southern booksellers as their agents. In intellectual matters the South was becoming more and more dependent upon the North.

The Old South had its share of newspapers, and some of them were excellent by the standards of the time. Jefferson thought Thomas Ritchie's Richmond *Enquirer* the best of American newspapers. The newspaper furnished reading matter to many more persons than the few Southern magazines. It continued the eighteenth-century practice of printing addresses, literary essays, and verse. In Richmond the *Virginia Argus* in 1803 brought out William Wirt's *The Letters of the British Spy* and a few years later the *Enquirer* printed his *The Old Bachelor*. The Charleston newspapers published verses by John Davis, Lucas George, and James Gates Percival and both essays and poems by William Crafts. After 1830 the chief literary importance of the newspapers is found in the numerous writings of the Southern humorists which ordinarily first appeared in that form.

From Franklin's *General Magazine* (1741) to Mathew Carey's *American Museum* (1787-1792) almost all our magazines were published in the North. Southerners contributed occasionally to the *American Museum* and to the *Port Folio* (1801-1827). The latter was in 1814-1816 edited by a North Carolinian, Dr. Charles Caldwell, who published in it some of George Tucker's early essays. From 1816 to 1827 the *Port Folio* was edited by John E. Hall and published by his brother Harrison Hall, both natives of Baltimore. John Earle Uhler has estimated that in Baltimore in the years 1815-1833 no less than seventy-two new magazines were announced for publication. The most notable of those that actually reached publication were *Niles' Weekly Register* (1811-1849), of great value to the historian, and the *Portico* (1816-1818), which is said to have printed still unidentified contributions from John Pendleton Kennedy. In Richmond were published the unimportant *National Magazine* (1799-1800) and John Holt Rice's *Virginia Evangelical and Literary Magazine* (1818-1828), primarily a Presbyterian organ. Charleston had the *South Carolina Weekly Museum* (1797-1798), but except for the *Southern Review* (1828-1832) the chief Charleston magazines belong to a later period. Savannah was the home of the unimportant Baptist *Georgia Analytical Repository* (1802-1803) and the *Ladies' Magazine* (1819), a very early example of a type that was to prove popular. Lexington had the *Medley* (1803), the earliest Western magazine of any importance, and the *Western Review and Miscellaneous Magazine* (1819-1821), but Cincinnati and Louisville were to become more important magazine centers of the West. Except for the *Southern Review*, which published many essays by Hugh S. Legaré, none of these magazines has much literary importance. The average Southern reader was satisfied with his books and newspapers; if he wanted a magazine, he was as likely to subscribe to the *Port Folio* or the *North American Review* as to one published in his own state.

In discussing the earlier writers of the South, I have arranged them according to the colonies or states in which they lived. In this period, however, it has seemed more advantageous to discuss separately the poets and the prose writers except for the few who appeared in the Western South. State feeling was still a strong force, but it was yielding somewhat both to national pride and to a feeling of closer ties with other Southern states.

11
John Taylor of Caroline

ALTHOUGH JOHN TAYLOR (1753-1824) is often the most tedious and prolix of writers, he deserves a place among Southern authors because he had something important to say and occasionally he said it in appropriate and telling phrases. He was a political and economic thinker of keen insight, a philosopher of Jeffersonian democracy, and a spokesman for the Southern planter's way of life. He regarded himself as primarily a farmer, but he impressed Thomas Hart Benton, who served with him in the Senate, as "the ideal of a republican statesman," "plain and solid, a wise counsellor, a ready and vigorous debater, acute and comprehensive, ripe in all historical and political knowledge, innately republican—modest, courteous, benevolent, hospitable—a skilful, practical farmer, giving his time to his farm and his books, when not called by an emergency to the public service—and returning to his books and his farm when the emergency was over."

Left an orphan at an early age, Taylor was brought up by his uncle Edmund Pendleton, who was himself one of the Virginia statesmen of the Revolution. Taylor was a student at Donald Robertson's classical school with James Madison before going to William and Mary. Afterwards he studied law with Pendleton. He came out of the Revolutionary War, in which he served with distinction, almost penniless owing in part to the depreciation of the paper currency. By the assiduous practice of law he made money and then set himself up as a farmer at "Hazelwood" in Caroline County on the banks of the Rappahannock. He was in the Virginia Assembly almost continuously from 1779 to 1800, and in the United States Senate, 1792–1794, 1803, 1822–1824.

Taylor disliked the financial policies of Hamilton and the judicial decisions of Marshall. Like Jefferson, he held fast to the doctrines of the Revolution, but he was also very jealous of the rights of the states. From time to time he expressed his views in pamphlets and in an occasional book, few of which had wide circulation. He had no literary ambition, and he wrote in desultory fashion as the inclination moved him or leisure permitted. His most important book, *An Inquiry into the Principles and Policy of the Government of the United States* (Fredericksburg, Virginia, 1814), was many years in the writing, and it was published three years after he had finished it. On November 8, 1809, he wrote to James Monroe: "My book! Yes, I have written one, so blotted and interlined by keeping onwards ten years in fits and starts, and finding upon going back a multitude of angles and windings to be streightened [sic]. . . . I think I shall print it if I live long enough to finish its correction (for I cannot copy it) and this has stopt for some months, and when it will end, I can not foresee." No wonder that John Randolph of Roanoke wrote of one of Taylor's pamphlets: ". . . for heaven's sake, get some worthy person to do the second edition into English."

Taylor's books were not timely enough to attract wide attention. He attacked John Adams's *Defence* nearly thirty years after its publication, and his criticism of *The Federalist* was equally belated. In some important ways, however, Taylor was too far ahead of his public to attract attention. He advocated agricultural reform long before Edmund Ruffin founded his *Farmers' Register* in 1833; and while Calhoun was still the ardent nationalist, Taylor expressed ideas on the tariff question, the indivisibility of sovereignty, and the necessity of a concurrent majority similar to those expounded in the South Carolina "Exposition" of 1828.

Perhaps the best expression of Taylor's ideas is found in *An Inquiry*, which Edmund Ruffin thought deserved to be called "The Philosophy of Free Government" and which James Kirke Paulding considered "the most profound political work" the age had produced. Southern secessionists made use of Taylor's ideas, but after the Civil War he was pretty well forgotten until William E. Dodd and Charles A. Beard began to write and talk about him. Beard places *An Inquiry* "among the two or three really historic contributions to political science which have been produced in the United States." The book is ostensibly a belated reply to Adams's *A Defence of the Constitutions of Government of the United States of America* (1787), but Taylor struck much harder at Hamilton than at Adams. He did not believe in the "natural aristocracy" of Adams, and he could discern no "natural political state." He regarded farmers as the soundest political element in the population of the country, and he feared the rising industrial "aristocracy" of the North, "the aristocracy of patronage and paper," "that political hydra of modern invention. . . ." This plutocracy of bankers, merchants, and manufacturers, who were preying upon the farmers, seemed to him to lack all the redeeming qualities of a feudal aristocracy.

Avarice and ambition being its whole soul, what private morals will it infuse, and what national character will it create? It subsists by usurpation, deceit and oppression. . . . Its acquisitions inflict misery, without bestowing happiness; because they can only feed a rapacity which can never be satisfied, and a luxury which cannot suppress remorse. In relation to private people, this system may only encourage idleness, teach swindling, ruin individuals, and destroy morals; but allied to a government, it presents a policy of such unrivalled malignity, as only to be expressed by saying, "the government is a speculator upon the liberty and property of the nation."

By helping to raise up a capitalistic class, based on the exploitation of farmers and workers through inflated public paper, bank stock, and a protective tariff, Hamilton seemed to Taylor to have created a basic conflict between agricultural interests, mainly Southern, and commercial interests, mainly Northern. The only remedy was to destroy special privilege and adopt a truly Jeffersonian policy.

If the passage quoted above sounds strangely modern, so also does Taylor's discussion of the way in which parties in power mislead men with words and phrases. "We lose truth in names and phrases," he says, "as children lose themselves in a wood, for want of geographical knowledge." "The aristocracy of superstition defended itself by exclaiming, the Gods! the temples! the sacred oracles! divine vengeance! and Elysian fields!—and that of paper and patronage exclaims, national faith! sacred charters! disorganization! and security of property!"

There is edification and safety in challenging political words and phrases as traitors, and trying them rigorously by principles, before we allow them the smallest degree of confidence. . . . That useful and major part of mankind, comprised within natural interests (by which I mean agricultural, commercial, mechanical, and scientifick; in opposition to legal and artificial, such as hierarchical, patrician, and banking) is exclusively the object of imposition, whenever words are converted into traitors to principles.

Like Washington and Whitman, Taylor feared the tyranny of wolfish political parties, which no system of checks and balances could hold in restraint. The doctrine of the party in power, he saw, is that its temporary government is the nation; and every party that comes to power preaches in a new form the old duty of passive obedience. Taylor saw hope only in the application of moral principles and political intelligence.

A political analysis alone, composed of moral principles, can reach and tame a beast, from which men flee to monarchy, because it lays waste and devours their rights with a thousand hands and a thousand mouths. . . . In legislation contrary to genuine republican principles, sustained by a dominant party zeal, lies, in my view, the greatest danger to the free form of government of the United States. . . . If, therefore, these essays should only prove, that it is the office of a republican government to protect, but not to bestow property, they may protract the period during which our government may remain the servant of the nation.

Taylor published three later books which are important for the political scientist but of less consequence to the student of literature: *Construction Construed, and Constitutions Vindicated* (Richmond, 1820); *Tyranny Unmasked* (Washington, 1822); and *New Views of the Constitution of the United States* (Washington, 1823). A much more widely read book was his *Arator: Being a Series of Agricultural Essays, Practical and Political* (Georgetown, D. C., 1813), which after going through six editions was republished by Edmund Ruffin in the *Farmers' Register* in 1840. Taylor was a successful farmer in a period of agricultural depression and an advocate of improved farm methods. The tariff he held partly responsible for hard times in Virginia, but the chief trouble was, he thought, that wasteful methods of growing tobacco had exhausted the soil. He was an early advocate of using special crops to improve the soil, the rotation of crops, the use of mould and manure and of what he termed "live fences." He condemned the prevailing practice of giving an overseer a share in the crops harvested rather than a fixed salary. He saw no danger to American government in a landed aristocracy because with cheap land to be had there could never be anything approaching a land monopoly. He had high praise for the virtues developed by farm life, but his picture of the life of the Southern planter is less attractive than that soon to be drawn in Kennedy's *Swallow Barn* (1832). Taylor regarded slavery as a misfortune for the Southern farmer, but it was an institution which, while capable of improvement, was not one which could be abolished. His attitude is a transitional one; he stands midway between Jefferson and Calhoun.

12
John Randolph of Roanoke

No OTHER STATE, and perhaps no other period in Virginia's history, could have produced that strange combination of qualities which one finds in John Randolph of Roanoke (1773–1833) or would have tolerated the eccentricities of this archindividualist and returned him to Congress year after year. "I am an aristocrat," he once said; "I love liberty; I hate equality." And yet Randolph could write to General Thomas Forman in 1814: "As to aristocracy it is an electioneering bug bear—the materials of it are not to be found in this country [Virginia]. . . . The old gentry have disappeared."

There was in eighteenth-century Virginia no more distinguished family than the numerous Randolph clan—his own branch boasted of its descent from Pocahontas—but in the early nineteenth century the first families were losing their property and their influence. Randolph himself found it difficult to pay off his family's hereditary debts to British merchants. Unlike the earlier Virginians, he was a *laudator temporis acti*: the great days had departed and the future was full of gloom. In 1814 he wrote to Forman: "I made a late visit to my birthplace. At the end of a journey through a wilderness, I found desolation & stillness as if of death—the fires of hospitality long since quenched—the hearth cold—& the parish church tumbling to pieces, not more from natural decay than sacrilegious violence. This is a faithful picture of this state from the falls of the great river to the sea-board." "The old families of Virginia," he wrote to a friend, "will form connections with low people and sink into the mass of overseers' sons and daughters. And this is the legitimate, nay inevitable, conclusion, to which Mr. Jefferson and his leveling system has brought us."

Of Randolph's father, who died in 1775, little is known except that, in the words of his son, he "left for some reason of his own this old family adage (*nil admirari*) and adopted *fari quae sentias* for his motto." His mother, Frances (Bland) Randolph, influenced him more profoundly than anyone else. "My mother," he said, "once expressed a wish to me, that I might one day or other be as great a speaker as Jerman Baker or Edmund Randolph! That gave the bent to my disposition." In 1778, ten years before her death, she married St. George Tucker, who was an excellent stepfather, although for no obvious reason Randolph came to hate him. In a well-known biography of Randolph which reveals a dislike of Randolph and Virginia, Henry Adams pictured the boy and his two brothers as growing up almost without discipline or instruction. As a matter of fact, St. George and Frances Tucker did their best to educate the children in the difficult years of the Revolution. In a letter to a nephew, February 16, 1817, Randolph gave some indication of what he had read in his youth:

I almost envy you [Ariosto's] Orlando. I would, if it were not Johnny Hoole's translation; although, at the age of ten, I devoured that more eagerly than gingerbread. Oh! if Milton had translated it, he might tell of

"All who, since, baptized or infidel
Jousted in Aspromont or Montalban,
Damasco, or Morocco, or Trebisond;
Or whom Bisserta sent from Afric shore,
When Charlemagne, with all his peerage, fell
By Fontarabia."

Let me advise you to

"Call up him, who left half told,
The story of Cambuscan bold."

I think you have never read Chaucer. Indeed, I have sometimes blamed myself for not cultivating your imagination, when you were young. It is a dangerous quality, however, for the possessor. But if from my life were to be taken the pleasure derived from that faculty, very little would remain. Shakespeare, and Milton, and Chaucer, and Spenser, and Plutarch, and the Arabian Night's Entertainments, and Don Quixotte [*sic*], and Gil Blas, and Tom Jones, and Gulliver, and Robinson Crusoe, "and the tale of Troy divine," have made up more than half of my wor[l]dly enjoyment. To these ought to be added Ovid's Metamorphoses, Ariosto, Dryden, Beaumont and Fletcher, Southern, Otway, Congreve, Pope's Rape [of the Lock] and Eloisa, Addison, Young, Thomson, Gay, Goldsmith, Gray, Collins, Sheridan, Cowper, Byron, Aesop, La Fontaine, Voltaire, (Charles XII., Mahomed, and Zaire;) Rousseau, (Julie,) Schiller, Madame de Stael—but, above all, Burke.

One of the first books I ever read was Voltaire's Charles XII.; about the same time, 1780–1, I read the Spectator; and used to steal away to the closet containing them. The letters from his correspondents were my favourites. I read Humphry Clinker, also; that is, Win's and Tabby's letters, with great delight, for I could spell, at that age, pretty correctly. Reynard, the fox, came next, I think; then Tales of the Genii and Arabian Nights. This last, and Shakespeare, were my idols. I had read them with Don Quixotte, Gil Blas, Quintus Curtius, Plutarch, Pope's Homer, Robinson Crusoe, Gulliver, Tom Jones, Orlando Furioso, and Thomson's Seasons, before I was eleven years of age; also Goldsmith's Roman History, 2 vols. 8vo., and an old history of Braddock's war. . . .

At about eleven, 1784–5, Percy's Reliques, and Chaucer, became great favourites, and Chatterton, and Rowley. I then read Young and Gay, &c.: Goldsmith I never saw until 1787.[35]

In this extraordinary list, by no means complete, we find about all of eighteenth-century English literature that anyone would think of reading today—and much besides. We miss the works of the so-called "Lake School," which, Randolph wrote in 1821, he had not read and did not expect to read. Scott's novels, however, delighted him. Claude G. Bowers is perhaps right in saying: "Had he [Randolph] been born in England, he probably would have aspired to a literary career; in America he turned to politics." His temperament was, as he knew, that of "the poet rather than of the public speaker." "For poetry," he wrote to a niece, "I have had a decided taste from my childhood, yet never attempted to write one line of it. I believe that I was deterred from attempting poetry by the verses of Billy Mumford [William Munford], and some other taggers of rhyme, which I heard praised . . . but secretly in my heart despised."

Randolph got his formal education, which was irregular, from Walker Maury's academy, William and Mary College, Princeton, and Columbia. In Philadelphia he studied law under his kinsman Edmund Randolph, then Attorney-General of the United States. In Philadelphia, then the national capital, he saw something of political life. Still earlier, while a student at Columbia College in New York, in his own words: "I had seen the old Congress expire and the new government rise like a Phoenix from its ashes. I saw the coronation (such in fact it was) of Gen. Washington in March, 1789, and heard [Fisher] Ames and Madison, when they first took their seats in the House of Representatives." Randolph had grown up a Deist, but in 1817 he became an orthodox member of the church. In 1813, when his house at "Bizarre" was burned, he wrote half ironically: "I lost a valuable collection of books. In it was a whole body of infidelity, the Encyclopaedia of Diderot and D'Alembert, Voltaire's works, seventy volumes, Rousseau, thirteen quartoes, Hume, &c."

[35] *Letters of John Randolph to a Young Relative* (Philadelphia, 1834), pp. 190–191.

Before Randolph entered public life in 1799, he had experienced a disappointment in love, shared in the "Gallomania" of his generation, had a part in a tragic family scandal affecting chiefly his brother Richard, and had recovered from an illness which left him impotent and had a determining influence upon his personality. He was not a happy man.

As a Republican candidate for Congress Randolph made his first political speech under difficult circumstances at Charlotte Court House in 1799. Patrick Henry, a candidate for the General Assembly on the other side, had just made the last speech of his life when Randolph rose to address the crowd. He held the attention of his audience and won his election. In Congress he quickly made a name for himself. During Jefferson's first administration he was majority leader of the House, but during the remainder of his career he was a free lance, an unmatched critic of both measures and men. The Capitol in Washington has seen orators come and go but never another speaker like Randolph. Francis W. Gilmer thus describes him:

The first time that I ever felt the spell of eloquence was when a boy, standing in the gallery of the capitol in the year 1808. It was on the floor of that house I saw rise, a gentleman, who in every quality of his person, his voice, his mind, his character, is a phenomenon among men. His figure is tall, spare, and somewhat emaciated: his limbs long, delicate, slow and graceful in all their motions; his countenance with the lineaments of boyhood, but the wrinkles, the faded complexion, the occasional sadness of old age and even of decripitude [sic]: possessing, however, vast compass and force of expression. His voice is small, but of the clearest tone and most flexible modulation I ever heard. In his speech not a breath of air is lost; it is all compressed into round, smooth, liquid sound; and its inflections are so sweet, its emphasis so appropriate and varied, that there is a positive pleasure in hearing him speak any words whatever. His manner of thinking is as peculiar as his person and voice. He has so long spoken parables, that he now thinks in them. Antitheses, jests, beautiful conceits, with a striking turn and point of expression, flow from his lips with the same natural ease, and often with singular felicity of application, as regular series of arguments follow each other in the deductions of logical thinkers. His invective, which is always *piquant*, is frequently adorned with the beautiful metaphors of Burke, and animated by bursts of passion worthy of Chatham.

James Kirke Paulding, who thought Randolph "the most extraordinary personage" he had ever known, wrote: "In short, in all the requisites of a great orator he has no superior; and in the greatest of all, the power of attracting, charming, rivetting the attention of an audience, no equal in this country."

Fearless and incorruptible, Randolph attacked real and imaginary abuses. He was right when he exposed the Yazoo fraud and perhaps when he attacked the young "War Hawks" who wished to plunge the country into a second war with England. When John Quincy Adams became President and selected Henry Clay as his Secretary of State, Randolph bitterly denounced the alliance "between Old Massachusetts and Kentucky—between the frost of January, and young blythe, buxom and blooming May—the eldest daughter of Virginia—young Kentucky—not so young, however, as not to make a prudent match, and sell her charms for their full value." It was, he said, a "coalition of Blifil and Black George," a "combination unheard of till then, of the Puritan with the black-leg." The famous bloodless duel with Clay was a direct result of this ill-advised accusation.

Some of Randolph's epigrams are worthy of the eighteenth-century British satirists: "England is Elysium for the rich; Tartarus for the poor." "A rat hole will let in the ocean." "Poverty, that nurse of genius, though she sometimes overlays it." "The most delicious of privileges—spending other people's money." "Life is not so important as the duties of life."

Randolph is a transition figure who stands midway between Jefferson on the one hand and on the other Calhoun and his own half-brother, Beverley Tucker. In his youth he was an enthusiastic Republican and an admirer of the French. In 1793 he begged St. George Tucker in vain to permit him to go to Europe and fight for the French republic. Like the elder Tucker, he disapproved of slavery. As he grew older, he became more conservative. Jefferson became for him "St. Thomas of Cantingbury." In his later years Randolph was an ardent defender of the rights of the states against a national government which threatened to become too powerful. He greatly admired the political philosophy of Edmund Burke. He did not like Calhoun, but it seems evident that the South Carolinian's later views of government owe something to Randolph, one of the first of many Southerners (and Northerners) to attack the doctrine of natural rights underlying the Declaration of Independence.

Yet Randolph cherished enough of Revolutionary liberalism to free his slaves at his death. There was some truth in Whittier's "Randolph of Roanoke":

> Beyond Virginia's border line
> His patriotism perished,

but he deserved to the full Whittier's praise:

> Bard, Sage, and Tribune!—in himself
> All moods of mind contrasting—
> The tenderest wail of human woe,
> The scorn like lightning blasting;

The pathos which from rival eyes
Unwilling tears could summon,
The stinging taunt, the fiery burst
Of hatred scarcely human!

Mirth, sparkling like a diamond shower,
From lips of life-long sadness;
Clear picturings of majestic thought
Upon a ground of madness;
And over all Romance and Song
A classic beauty throwing,
And laurelled Clio at his side
Her storied pages showing.[36]

Randolph's letters are excellent reading. His nephew, Dr. Theodore B. Dudley, published in 1834 many letters written to him along with a few addressed to another nephew, Tudor Randolph, in a volume entitled *Letters of John Randolph to a Young Relative*. Some of these are trivial and should not have been published, but others are worthy of Lord Chesterfield. They reveal a side of Randolph's nature hardly dreamed of by his associates in Congress. They are affectionate, considerate, full of wisdom and tenderness. On him the old ideal of the gentleman had a strong hold.

Do not . . . undervalue . . . the character of the *real* gentleman, which is the most respectable amongst men. It consists not of plate, and equipage, and rich living, any more than in the disease [gout] which that mode of life engenders; but in *truth*, courtesy, bravery, generosity, and learning, which last, although not *essential* to it, yet does very much to adorn and illustrate the character of the true gentleman. . . . Lay down this as a principle, that *truth* is to the other virtues, what vital air is to the human system.

Randolph saw plainly enough the faults of young Virginians in his time: conceit, a "petulant arrogance, or supine, listless indifference," "Indolence and indifference, the *maladie du pays* (of Virginia,). . . ." He even argued that "a decayed family could never recover its loss of rank in the world, until the members of it left off talking and dwelling upon its former opulence." Some of his own Randolph kin, he thought, would never thrive without first becoming "poor folks." He could write with worldly wisdom to the young about love and marriage:

[36] See Mary H. Coleman, "Whittier on John Randolph of Roanoke," *N.E.Q.*, VIII, 551–555 (Dec., 1935). James Kirke Paulding wrote: "Old Virginia was the goddess of his idolatry, and of her he delighted to talk. He loved her so dearly, that he sometimes almost forgot he was also a citizen of the United States" (*Literary Life of James K. Paulding*, 1867, pp. 241–242).

Rely upon it, that to love a woman as "a mistress," although a delicious delirium, an intoxication far surpassing that of Champagne, is altogether unessential, nay, *pernicious*, in the choice of a wife; which a man ought to set about in his sober senses—choosing her, as Mrs. Primrose did her wedding-gown, for qualities that "wear well." I am well persuaded, that few love-matches are happy ones. One thing, at least, is true, that if matrimony has its cares, celibacy has no pleasures. A Newton, or a mere scholar, may find employment in study: a man of literary taste can receive in books a powerful auxiliary; but a man must have a bosom friend, and children around him, to cherish and support the dreariness of old age.

In the "savage solitude" of his "Roanoke" [37] plantation in Southside Virginia Randolph must often have been tragically unhappy. On May 11, 1812, he wrote to Dudley, who had complained of being unhappy, that he shrank from the idea of going home: "Disappointed of every rational hope of my life—looking forward to nothing better in this world—my faculties jaded, and daily forsaking me—with recollections of the past which I would gladly dismiss for ever from my memory—it is for me, and such as me, to talk of being unhappy." In later years he shared his home with his half-brother Beverley Tucker, whose thinking he greatly influenced and not always for the better. St. George Tucker had openly advocated emancipation of the slaves, but his son was to be among the earliest defenders of slavery and secession. Of him it is truer than of Randolph that

> Beyond Virginia's border line
> His patriotism perished.

13
John Marshall

A VIRGINIAN WHO placed the welfare of the Union above that of his state was John Marshall (1755–1835), the biographer of Washington and the most famous of all justices of the United States Supreme Court. Through his mother, Mary (Isham) Marshall, he was related to Jefferson, the Randolphs, and the Lees. His father was not wealthy and he had little formal training, but he was a man of real ability. Marshall had two clergymen tutors, under one of whom he began to read Horace and Livy, but he completed them by himself. It was from his father, however, that he got the most important part of his early education. It was he who gave Marshall

---

[37] "Roanoke" plantation, which is not near the modern city of Roanoke, is in Charlotte County, in which Patrick Henry's "Red Hill" plantation is also situated.

an early taste for history and poetry, and for him Marshall transcribed Pope's *An Essay on Man* and some of the *Moral Essays*. In the winter of 1779–1780 at William and Mary College he attended George Wythe's law lectures and Bishop James Madison's lectures on natural philosophy.

Marshall had entered the army as first lieutenant in his father's regiment; he came out a captain. He carried strong Union sentiments into the army; and in the army, as he wrote in a sketch of his life for Justice Joseph Story, "I was confirmed in the habit of considering America as my country, and congress as my government." After serving in the Virginia legislature, as commissioner to France, and in Congress, he became John Adams's Secretary of State. In January, 1801, much to the displeasure of Jefferson, who had been recently elected President, Adams appointed Marshall Chief Justice of the United States.

In the twelve years of its existence the Supreme Court had not made its power felt strongly. It was Marshall who converted the Court into the powerful agency we know now. His decisions strengthened the power of the Federal government in many ways. Among his famous decisions are Marbury *vs.* Madison, in which the Court first claimed the power to declare unconstitutional an act of Congress; McCulloch *vs.* Maryland, in which he elaborated the doctrine of implied powers, thus limiting the powers of the states; Dartmouth College *vs.* Woodward, in which the Court declared that the charter granted to a private corporation was a contract which no state could invalidate; Gibbons *vs.* Ogden, in which the Court proclaimed in broad terms Federal control of interstate commerce. Such decisions paved the way for the industrial growth of the nation which Marshall did not fully foresee or perhaps desire.

Marshall could not write with the literary power and beauty of Justice Oliver Wendell Holmes, but some of his passages are in their own way memorable. I quote from his decision in Cohens *vs.* Virginia, in which the Supreme Court claimed the right to pass upon the verdict of a state court involving the validity of state legislation:

That the United States form, for many, and for most important purposes, a single nation, has not yet been denied. In war, we are one people. In making peace, we are one people. In all commercial regulations, we are one and the same people. In many other respects, the American people are one; and the government which is alone capable of controlling and managing their interests in all these respects, is the government of the Union. It is their government, and in that character they have no other. America has chosen to be, in many respects, and to many purposes, a nation; and for all these purposes, her government is complete; to all these objects, it is competent.

Marshall was probably ill advised when at the request of a publisher he undertook to write the life of George Washington. He found the enterprise much more laborious and less profitable than he had anticipated. The first volume was a history of the American colonies in which Washington rarely appeared. Parson Weems, who tried to sell the biography, complained of its length and its dullness. Marshall did not often succeed in making his portrait lifelike and vivid. Nevertheless, the book in spite of its Federalist bias contributed much to making Washington a symbol of national unity.

14
Mason Locke Weems

ALL THE WRITERS thus far considered wrote primarily for the educated, but Mason Locke Weems (1759–1825) was a pioneer writer for the uneducated and the young. The most remarkable book agent in our annals, he saw an opportunity for both author and publisher in potential purchasers who had been largely overlooked by his predecessors.

He was the nineteenth son of David Weems, and he was born in Anne Arundel County, Maryland; but almost nothing is known of his early life. In 1784 he was ordained in England as a priest in the Episcopal Church, and from 1784 to 1789 he was Rector of All Hallows in his native county. By 1794 he was selling books for the Philadelphia publisher Mathew Carey. For thirty years he sold books for Carey or for C. P. Wayne, the publisher of Marshall's *Washington*. In 1795 he married Frances Ewell. Their home was in Dumfries, Virginia, but he wandered over the Southern states preaching, fiddling, and selling books for the remainder of his life. He wrote to Carey in 1811: "I want to Enlighten, to dulcify & Exalt Human Nature —by GOOD BOOKS." He had written to Carey from Dumfries in 1796: "This country is large, and numerous are its inhabitants; to cultivate among these a taste for reading, and by the reflection of proper books to throw far and wide the rays of useful arts and sciences, were at once the work of a true Philanthropist and prudent speculator. For I am verily assured that under proper culture, every dollar that you shall scatter on the field of this experiment will yield 30, 60 and 100 fold."

Among his staples were Goldsmith's *Animated Nature*, Guthrie's *Modern Geography*, prayer books, and family Bibles. After two years' urging he induced Carey to put out a suitable family Bible, which proved to be a great success. "The Virginian," he wrote, "will give up his Tobacco & the Yankee his molasses for it." But Bibles were not his only reliance: "Of fine

Sentimental novels, entertaining histories &c. &c. I could vend a vast many."
Weems also sold the works of Godwin and Paine. Bishop Meade, who notes
that Parson Weems would pray with the Negroes at night in their owners'
houses and then fiddle for them by the roadside the next day, once found
Weems in a tavern at Fairfax Court House selling *The Age of Reason*.
When Meade remonstrated, Weems picked up the Bishop of Llandaff's
reply to Paine and said: "Behold the antidote. The bane and antidote are
both before you."

William Gilmore Simms in an essay on "Weems, the Biographer and
Historian" published some letters which indicate how Weems turned out
books which we should now call fictionized biographies. Colonel Peter
Horry, one of General Francis Marion's officers, placed a manuscript life
of the partisan leader in Weems's hands for revision, expecting only minor
changes. After keeping the manuscript a long while, Weems wrote to
Horry: "You have no doubt constantly kept in memory, that I told you I
must write it in my own way, and knowing the passion of the times for
novels, I have endeavoured to throw your ideas and facts about Gen Marion
into the garb and dress of a military romance." After the book had appeared,
the indignant Horry wrote to Weems:

A history of realities turned into a romance! The idea alone, militates against the
work. The one as a history of a real performance, would be always read with
pleasure. The other as a fictitious invention of the brain, once read would
suffice. Therefore, I think you have injured yourself, notwithstanding the quick
sales of your book. Nor have the public received the real history of General
Marion. *You have carved and mutilated it with so many* erroneous statements,
[that] your embellishments, observations and remarks, must necessarily be erroneous as proceeding from false grounds. *Most certainly 'tis not* MY history,
but YOUR romance.

Parson Weems knew his customers, and when he wrote his biographies
of great Americans and his sensational religious pamphlets, he capitalized
on that knowledge. Among his own best sellers were *Hymen's Recruiting
Sergeant, The Drunkard's Looking Glass,* and *God's Revenge against Adultery.* His lives of Penn and Franklin are, however, less colorful than his
Marion and *Washington.* He had discovered as early as 1797 that his customers wanted biographies of Revolutionary heroes. By the summer of 1799
he had some sort of book about Washington nearly finished. He wrote to
Carey, June 24, 1799, asking the publisher to print a piece called "The
Beauties of Washington." He said of it: ". . . 'tis artfully drawn up, en-
liven^d with anecdotes, and in my humble opinion, marvellously fitted 'ad
captandum gustum populi Americani'!!! What say you to printing it for

me . . . ?" When Weems heard of Washington's death on December
4, 1799, he proceeded to revise it. In January, 1800, he wrote to Carey:

I've something to whisper in your lug. Washington, you know is gone! Millions
are gaping to read something about him. I am very nearly prim^d & cock^d for 'em.
6 months ago I set myself to collect anecdotes of him. My plan! I give his history,
sufficiently minute—I accompany him from his start, thro the French & Indian
& British or Revolutionary wars, to the Presidents chair, to the throne in the hearts
of 5,000,000 of People. I then go on to show that his unparrelled [sic] rise &
elevation were owing to his Great Virtues. 1 His Veneration for the Diety [sic],
or Religious Principles 2 His Patriotism 3^d his Magninmity [sic]. 4 His Industry.
5. his Temperance & Sobriety. 6 his Justice, &^{c}. &^{c}. Thus I hold up his great
Virtues . . . to the imitation of Our Youth. All this I have lin^d & enliven^d with
Anecdotes apropos interesting and Entertaining. I have read it to several Gentlemen whom I thought good judges, such as Presbyterian Clergymen, Classical
Scholars, &^{c}. &^{c}. and they all commend it much. . . . We may sell it with great
rapidity for 25 or 37 Cents and it w^d not cost 10.

The pamphlet was printed several times in 1800, apparently first in Baltimore. When Weems became a salesman for Marshall's *Life of Washington*,
he ceased reworking his own life and tried to sell Marshall's. That five-
volume work was expensive and dull, and in Augusta in 1806 Weems
brought out a greatly enlarged version of his own biography—this time
with the story of the cherry tree. He was giving his customers the kind of
book most of them wanted. He had little pride in authorship; he wanted
something that would sell. There were something like forty editions before
Weems died in 1825 and probably more than forty since that time.

So much has been written about Weems's historical inaccuracies—which
are numerous enough—that his literary powers have been somewhat underrated. He had, as his letters show, an eye for a telling phrase. There is a
crude poetic and dramatic power in his descriptive passages; and the speeches
which, like the epic poets and the ancient historians, he put into the mouths
of his heroes are not lacking in eloquence. His widely read biography helped
to perpetuate among the masses down to our own time his conception of
Washington. He did his part to create a semilegendary national hero whose
name and fame would help hold together a union of diverse regions. The
liberties which he took with historical fact were such as Herodotus, Livy,
and Froissart assumed as the privilege of the artistic historian. William Russell Smith, who read the book in semifrontier Alabama at the age of ten,
contended that: "It was true to its great office and duty, and that was, to
make the American youth feel and believe with all his soul that Washington
was the greatest man that ever lived in all the annals of time, and that the

country he delivered was the greatest country on the globe." Perhaps, after all, Weems was no worse a sinner than some of our debunking historians and biographers of the 1920's and 1930's—better informed than Weems— who left their readers wondering whether American democracy was worth fighting to preserve.

15
William Wirt

WILLIAM WIRT (1772–1834), a central figure in the Virginia literary tradition, was born in Bladensburg, Maryland, just outside the District of Columbia. His father, who had come to this country from Switzerland about 1750, kept a tavern. William was the youngest of six children. Those who regard the Southern aristocracy as a closed circle will do well to consider the career of this almost self-made lawyer and gentleman. His father, Jacob Wirt, died when the son was only two years old, and five or six years later his German-born mother died. Thereafter Wirt never lived with any of the members of his family. His uncle and guardian, Jasper Wirt, sent him to a school in Georgetown and later to another in Charles County. The last and best school which he attended was that of James Hunt, one of the many Presbyterian ministers from Princeton who came South to preach and often to teach. In 1787, when the school was discontinued, it seemed that Wirt's education had come to an end; but the well-to-do Benjamin Edwards, who had seen promise in something Wirt had written, employed the fifteen-year-old youth to prepare for college his nephews and his son Ninian, afterwards Governor of Illinois. And so for nearly two years Wirt had the use of a good private library. He read widely in English literature of the seventeenth and eighteenth centuries, and he became a fair Latin scholar. He apparently knew no Greek, but he did know his Horace and his Cicero. In the fall of 1792, fearing tuberculosis, he went to Augusta, Georgia, for the winter. On his return he began the study of law at Montgomery Court House under William P. Hunt, a son of his old teacher; afterwards he studied under Thomas Swann.

In November, 1792, at the age of twenty Wirt, who in appearance is said to have resembled Goethe, moved to Culpeper Court House in northern Virginia, where as soon as he came of age, he began to practice law. ". . . his whole magazine of intellectual artillery, at this period," says his biographer John P. Kennedy, "comprised no other munitions than a copy of Blackstone, two volumes of Don Quixote, and a volume of Tristram Shandy."

The attractive young lawyer quickly made friends, and among them were Madison, Monroe, Dr. George Gilmer, Jefferson's nephew Dabney Carr, and Jefferson himself, who in 1799 wrote to John Taylor of Caroline: "He [Wirt] has lived several years my near neighbor, having married [Mildred] the daughter of the late Dʳ Gilmer. He is a person of real genius and information, one of the ablest at the bars in this part of the country, amiable & worthy in his private character, & in his republicanism most zealous & active." Dr. Gilmer's excellent library enabled the young lawyer to fill in some of the gaps in his reading. When Mildred Wirt died in September, 1799, the grief-stricken young attorney determined to begin life anew in Richmond. In spite of a fondness for drink to which he often yielded at this time, he became a notable figure in a remarkable group of lawyers, some of whom like himself came from poor families. In Richmond Wirt turned from Deism to orthodox Christianity. In 1802 the young Republican married Elizabeth Gamble, the daughter of a well-to-do Federalist merchant. Salmon P. Chase, who at one time studied law under Wirt's direction, wrote: "Mrs. W— is a lady of graceful manners, though, at times, a little tincture of aristocratic feeling makes a stranger somewhat uneasy in her society. She has a cultivated taste, and has displayed it in forming a Dictionary of the Floral language, which she intends yet to give to the world."

In the second year of his marriage Wirt was chosen to preside over one of the three chancery districts of the state. He now gave up the clerkship of the House of Delegates which he had held since 1799. Since his work as Chancellor lay chiefly in eastern Virginia, he moved to Williamsburg, where he became an intimate friend of St. George Tucker. Before long, however, he resigned his post and for two years practiced law in Norfolk. His law partner, the able Littleton Waller Tazewell, disapproved of the literary essays which Wirt published in the Richmond newspapers on the ground that they gave a man "a light and idle appearance, in the eye of the world, and might, therefore, injure [him] in [his] profession." By 1806 Wirt was back in Richmond, where he was soon to play an important part in the trial of Aaron Burr. A passage in a speech in which, in flowery language, he described how Burr had involved Blennerhassett in his conspiracy was long a favorite declamation piece with college students. Wirt disliked the acrimony of party politics and declined Jefferson's invitation to run for Congress, but he did serve a single term in the Virginia House of Delegates.

In 1817, the year in which his life of Patrick Henry appeared, he entered Monroe's cabinet as Attorney-General. He held the post throughout the administrations of Monroe and John Quincy Adams. He fulfilled his duties with some distinction although he was not a great legal scholar, like Hugh

Swinton Legaré, who afterwards held that post. After five years in the Attorney-General's office, Wirt wrote to John Holt Rice: "I am sick of public life; my skin is too thin for the business; a politician should have the hide of a rhinoceros, to bear the thrusts of the folly, ignorance, and meanness of those who are disposed to mount into momentary consequence by questioning *their betters.* . . ." After his retirement in 1829, he settled in Baltimore, where he became the friend of his future biographer, John Pendleton Kennedy. In 1832 Wirt, who was opposed to the re-election of Andrew Jackson, permitted himself to be nominated for the Presidency on the Anti-Masonic ticket. He had once been a Mason and had no enthusiasm for the party's anti-Masonic platform; but he was hoping for the support of the Whigs, who as it turned out were not willing to desert Henry Clay. Wirt carried only the state of Vermont. Two years later he died.

Wirt's literary activity was limited to the years in which he lived in or near Richmond, and it ended in 1817 with his appointment as Attorney-General. Richmond, which had become the state capital in 1779, was a small city in which commercial interests and political rivalries were strong. It had some excellent bookstores and newspapers, which were hospitable to those who wished to contribute. There were in Richmond a number of cultivated professional men, chiefly lawyers and journalists, who wrote essays for the local papers. More than any other person, Wirt furnished to these men the stimulus to write. After his departure for Washington in 1817, there was little literary activity in the city until the establishment of the *Southern Literary Messenger* in the year of Wirt's death.

The literary type which Wirt and his friends chiefly cultivated was the familiar essay, but their taste was less old-fashioned than is generally supposed. The authors most widely advertised in the local newspapers were Godwin, Southey, Byron, Moore, Scott, and Charles Brockden Brown. Wirt's own taste, though he admired Addison, ran chiefly to the later eighteenth-century writers: Gray, Young, Ossian, Sterne, and Burke. He had no enthusiasm for Dryden or Pope, and he disliked Johnson. He read with interest the early work of Irving and the *Edinburgh Review.* He cared little for Wordsworth, Coleridge, Shelley, or Keats; and in May, 1829, when Poe asked him to read "Al Aaraaf" in manuscript, he pleaded his "ignorance of modern poetry and modern taste" and suggested that the young poet seek "a better counsellor" than himself. His failure to appreciate the beautiful lyrics in Poe's poem, however, is less surprising than his lukewarm reception of Kennedy's *Swallow Barn* (1832), which was dedicated to him.

In August and September, 1803, Wirt printed anonymously in the Richmond *Virginia Argus* a series of ten essays which in the autumn of that year were republished as *The Letters of the British Spy*. He had begun the series to while away the anxious weeks which preceded the birth of a daughter, but he continued it because he found himself and his readers interested. The popularity of this slight work is today difficult to understand. The tenth edition, containing a biographical sketch by Peter Hoffman Cruse, appeared in 1832, and this edition, too, was often reprinted. There was a London edition in 1812. An imitator in the *Port Folio* in November and December, 1804, and January, 1805, published six instalments of "The British Spy in Boston."

Wirt had adopted the well-worn but effective device of an observer from the outside—a device which he employed to make some mild criticism of Virginian shortcomings. The primary topic of the book is eloquence, and the best-remembered portrait is that of the half-blind Presbyterian preacher James Waddell, done in the manner of Sterne. Wirt included also portraits of Governor James Monroe and Chief Justice Marshall and of two well-known Richmond lawyers: John Wickham and Edmund Randolph. Mrs. Marshall was exceedingly angry when she read Wirt's sketch of her husband in Letter V. Two fine American scholars, Lane Cooper and Vernon L. Parrington, misled by Marshall's physical resemblance to Jefferson, have mistakenly asserted that the book includes a portrait of the President.[38] Wirt had in fact planned to include Jefferson, but he discreetly changed his mind.

The *Spy* reflects the contradictions of a transition period. It is a mixture of early Romanticism and of Neoclassicism, of sensibility, sentiment, and piety, for Wirt, like most of his Virginian contemporaries, was recovering from the influence of Godwin and Paine. The criticism of the Virginian social order is extremely mild. Unlike his friends Jefferson and George and St. George Tucker, Wirt accepted slavery as a necessary part of the social order. His own estimate of the book was not a flattering one. On January 16, 1804, he wrote to Dabney Carr:

The letters bespeak a mind rather frolicksome & sprightly than thoughtful and penetrating; and therefore a mind qualified to amuse for the moment, but not to benefit either its proprietor or the world by the depth and utility of its researches. The style, altho sometimes happy, is sometimes, also, careless and poor; and still more frequently, overloaded with epithets; and its inequality proves either that the author wanted time, or industry, or taste to give it throughout a more even tenour. Yet these letters are certainly superior to the trash with which we are so frequently gorged through the medium of the press.[39]

[38] *C.H.A.L.*, I, 202; *Main Currents in American Thought*, II, 33.
[39] This letter is given in Kennedy, *Wirt*, I, 108–113; but here and elsewhere whenever possible I have quoted directly from the originals.

In 1804 and 1805 Wirt contributed to the *Rainbow* series of essays which appeared in the Richmond *Enquirer*. The initiator of this series, however, was not Wirt but the eccentric Scotch philosopher James Ogilvie,[40] then teaching in Virginia. Ten members of the Rainbow Association—Ogilvie, Wirt, George Tucker, Thomas Ritchie, George Hay, Meriwether and Skelton Jones, Peyton Randolph, and John and William Brockenbrough—were each in turn to contribute essays to the *Enquirer*. In 1804 Ritchie republished the first ten in book form as *The Rainbow; First Series*, but apparently the little book sold so poorly that he did not republish the later essays, several of which were written by persons not members of the Rainbow Association. The Rainbow essays are less attractively written, but many of them have more substance than *The Letters of the British Spy*. Richmond was regarded as a Federalist stronghold, but the lawyers, journalists, doctors, and teachers who made up the Rainbow Association seem all to have belonged to Jefferson's party and to have shared many of his liberal opinions.

In the fall of 1810 Wirt began printing in the *Enquirer* a series of essays entitled "The Sylph"; but finding the plan unmanageable, he dropped it for a new series, "The Old Bachelor," to which he and some half dozen of his friends contributed thirty-three numbers, most of which appeared in 1811. The essays were reprinted in book form in Richmond in 1814 and again in a more attractive format in Baltimore in 1818 in two separate editions. Less popular than the *British Spy*, *The Old Bachelor* contained, as Wirt knew, his best literary work. Wirt himself managed the enterprise and wrote most of the numbers, but there were contributions from George Tucker, Louis Hue Girardin, Richard E. Parker, Dabney and Frank Carr, David Watson, and probably St. George Tucker. John E. Hall, editor of the *Port Folio*, who had written the introduction for Fielding Lucas's edition of the *British Spy*, wrote to Wirt on September 2, 1816: "It is a little curious that I commenced an old Bachelor in the Baltimore papers about the same time that yours commenced his lucubrations." [41]

The contributions of Wirt's associates usually take the form of letters

[40] Richard Beale Davis, "James Ogilvie, an Early American Teacher of Rhetoric," *Quart. Jour. of Speech*, XXVIII, 289–297 (Oct., 1942). Ogilvie helped to spread the vogue of Godwin and Rousseau in this country.

For identification of the members of the Rainbow Association, see Jay B. Hubbell, "William Wirt and the Familiar Essay in Virginia," *W.M.Q.*, 2nd ser., XXIII, 136–152 (April, 1943).

[41] Goldsborough-Wirt MSS (Univ. of N.C. Library). It appears from Hall's next letter, Nov. 22, 1816, that Wirt asked Hall to send him something, presumably for a later edition of *The Old Bachelor*. See also "MS. Letter of Wm. Wirt," *S.L.M.*, XV, 698 (Nov., 1849).

addressed to Dr. Robert Cecil, the Old Bachelor, who is characterized by enthusiasm, sentiment, and moral purpose. Wirt's aim, as he phrased it, was *"virtuously to instruct, or innocently to amuse."* He hoped also "to awaken the taste of the body of the people for literary attainments," especially among the younger Virginians. The principal topic was to be education, but he tired of the series before he had adequately discussed it. His collaborators discussed oratory, patriotism, manners, avarice, gambling, and the mania for office. Character portraiture seemed to Wirt "much the liveliest and most impressive way of moralizing"; but he found to his chagrin that his readers were taking light satiric portraits as personal attacks on men living in Richmond. He was discouraged, too, by the little effect which the essays in the *Enquirer* seemed to produce. "I wrote in the hope of doing good," he confided to Dabney Carr, April 30, 1813, "—but my essays dropped, dropped into the world like stones pitched into a millpond—a little report from the first plunge—a ring or two rolling off from the spot—then in a moment all smooth & silent as before and no visible change to mark that such things had ever been." Writing to Carr in December, 1814, after *The Old Bachelor* had appeared in book form, he commented on the appearance in Baltimore of a fifth edition of the *British Spy* "while the O[ld]. B[achelor]. an infinitely better thing, slumbers comparatively unheeded & unknown!" In October, 1818, when Robert Walsh with abundant praise and some censure reviewed *The Old Bachelor* in the *Analectic Magazine,* Wirt was somewhat chagrined to find that Walsh had singled out as the best essay in the volume the thirty-third, written not by Wirt but by Major David Watson, a country gentleman from Louisa County, Virginia.

Meanwhile Wirt was still at work on his life of Patrick Henry, which was finally published in 1817, twelve years after he had undertaken the task. On September 17, 1805, he had written to Ninian Edwards that the success of the *British Spy* had induced him to consider undertaking in his leisure time "some little work . . . by which I may earn both money and fame." His original scheme called for a series of biographical sketches of eminent Virginians on the plan of Plutarch's *Lives.* The life of Henry was to be merely the first in a Virginia Plutarch, but Wirt did not for some time realize the magnitude of the difficulties which confronted him. He found the collection of materials a difficult task. He had never known the great orator, and the accounts given him by those who had were so contradictory as to confuse him. He admitted that he was never able to "embody him." In writing he disliked to be trammeled by matters of fact; it was, he said, "like attempting to run, tied up in a bag." Then there were aspects of Henry's life and character which did not lend themselves to effective narration or description. In particular, he felt, Henry was not notable as governor or soldier. As the biography drew near to its conclusion, Wirt looked forward with uneasiness to publishing it over his own name. He consulted various friends and asked Jefferson and others to read at least portions of the manuscript before he finally published it in Philadelphia under the half-apologetic title *Sketches of the Life and Character of Patrick Henry*. He had glossed over Henry's shortcomings, dwelt lightly on the years for which he had few factual details, and played up Henry's oratorical powers whenever possible.

As early as January, 1810, he had written to Jefferson: "Mr. Henry seems to me a good text for a discourse on rhetoric, patriotism and morals." In the end, however, Wirt's Henry proved to be a poor subject for a moral discourse intended for the young men of Virginia, for his hero is a prodigy who owes everything to native genius and nothing to industry. Wirt was too deeply influenced by Jefferson's conception of Henry as the lazy, idle, uneducated child of nature, whose one gift was the power to sway an audience. The book, though far from being the ideal biography, was a popular success. It went into its fifteenth edition in 1859; and others have appeared since then, including one as recently as 1903. It was, however, severely criticized in some quarters. John Adams objected that Wirt had slighted Massachusetts in always giving Virginia the leading role in the Revolution. Robert Walsh pronounced it "the Apotheosis of Patrick Henry & the Glorification of Virginia." John Taylor of Caroline referred to it as "a splendid novel," and John Randolph of Roanoke called it "a wretched piece of fustian." Even Peter Hoffman Cruse complained that "the hero . . . seemed more like the creation of a rhetorician, than a personage of history. . . ."

The best-remembered passage in the biography is the "Give Me Liberty, or Give Me Death" speech of March 23, 1775, which was first printed in the *Port Folio* in December, 1816. Wirt, himself an accomplished speaker, has been suspected of creating most of this speech out of his own imagination as Henry's favorite historian Livy might have done. The suspicion, however, is not quite borne out by what we know of Wirt's sources and the use he made of them. He had the benefit of the recollections of intelligent men who had heard the speech, particularly Jefferson, St. George Tucker, and Judge John Tyler. To Tucker he wrote: "I have taken almost entirely, Mr Henry's speech in the convention of '75 from you, as well [as] your description of its effect on you verbatim." He wrote to Dabney Carr, February 27, 1817: ". . . if [Edmund] Randolph's manuscript History of Virginia, which I have seen, shall ever come to light, you will discover that all I have said is Quaker drapery, compared with the account which he gives of the affair." [42]

It was not possible of course to recover the entire speech, and Wirt's account is only a fairly detailed synopsis which emphasized those oratorical flights which cling to men's memories. The speech is given in what readers of Caesar's *Commentaries* will remember as indirect discourse. Only in the memorable conclusion did Wirt feel that he could give Henry's actual words. One may be sure that Wirt's scanty factual materials lost none of their effectiveness in his handling of them.

Although no one reads his speeches now, Wirt was one of the great American orators of his time. Early in his career he yielded too often to the impulse to indulge in flowery language and to use phrases because they were music in his ear. "I have been often," he wrote to Francis Gilmer in 1818, "*very very* often, affected to tears by a mere succession of musical sounds, without any words or sentiments of song, to aid in producing the effect." It was the poetic passage about Blennerhassett and not the solidly reasoned and carefully documented analysis of the case that readers of his speeches in the Burr trial remembered. In later life Wirt was a severe critic of the kind of oratory that has come to be thought of as "Southern" although Southerners have certainly never had a monopoly of it. "Teach these young Virginians," he wrote to Gilmer, June 1, 1818, "by your example the insignificance of their affected swelling and rotundification of frothy sentences, and of their duplication, reduplication and infinite accumulation of cha[o]tic & confounding irish metaphors—I shall never enjoy any compliment that I may hear paid to you, unless it is accompanied by a compliment to the force as well as accuracy of your thinking." Salmon P. Chase, who regarded Wirt as Daniel Webster's great rival at the bar of the Supreme Court, praised him not only for "his fertile fancy and splendid imagination" but also for his "legal learning," "depth of thought," "power of argument, and splendor of genius . . . surpassed by none." Possibly if Wirt had lived in the perilous times of the Revolution, he might have been a formidable rival of Richard Henry Lee if not of the great Henry himself.

With Wirt literature was by necessity an avocation. After two years in the Attorney-General's office, he wrote to Dabney Carr, October 12, 1819: "I had always hoped to be able to retire from active pursuits at fifty and to spend the evening of my days in the bosom of my family, in literature, and a preparation for futurity— But now I have little hope of any thing

---

[42] Kennedy, *Wirt*, II, 20. Randolph's account of Henry's speech had been printed in the Richmond *Enquirer* for Sept. 2, 1815.

better than to toil on until actual decrepitude, or the superior vigor of the rising generation drives me from the bar." There was never a time when he felt able to support his expensive family on what he could earn from writing. Kennedy, who was inclined to blame Wirt for not devoting his whole time to literature, nevertheless followed Wirt's example. While Wirt's writings made his name well known, he felt that they were a handicap to him in his profession. In retrospect he was a severe critic of his own work. In a letter to Carr, February 15, 1815, he wrote:

Mine [my writings] have been only short and sportive excursions—exceedingly light & desultory—and I fear exceedingly frothy & flashy. I have written no sustained work—nothing which shews those masterly powers of investigation, of arrangement, of combination, of profound and great thinking, of the character of which I should be proud—and in which alone I should feel any satisfaction— such a work as Robertson's Charles the Vth, for example—or as Tacitus' annals; or Plutarch's lives, even would content me—is not this modest!

The then unfinished life of Henry, for which he hoped much, likewise failed to satisfy his own standards. In 1829 he wrote to Carr: "I ought either never to have written, or to have written more carefully." He was right in thinking that his writings brought him a greater reputation than he deserved, although the best of them, *The Old Bachelor*, was never to be fully appreciated.

16
Francis Walker Gilmer

FRANCIS WALKER GILMER (1790–1826), whom Jefferson described as "the best educated young man of our state," was the son of a friend and neighbor of Jefferson, Dr. George Gilmer, of "Pen Park" in Albemarle County. He was also a brother-in-law and particular favorite of William Wirt. One of his early teachers was the eccentric Scotch follower of William Godwin, James Ogilvie. After a year at William and Mary, Gilmer spent three years in Richmond studying under Wirt's direction. He practiced law for a year or two in Winchester, published *Sketches of American Orators* in Baltimore in 1816 and again in 1822, and assisted John Holt Rice in bringing out in Richmond in 1819 a new edition of *The True Travels* of Captain John Smith. (It was necessary to send to Maine for a copy of the original edition.) In 1824 at Jefferson's request Gilmer undertook the difficult assignment of going to England and selecting the first professors for the University of Virginia. He performed this delicate task with great skill and tact, and it is his chief claim to remembrance. He was struck by features common to England and Virginia. "The tone of manners in the higher walks" in England, he wrote, "is exactly what I have seen in Virginia." He was appointed professor of law in the University, but ill health prevented him from teaching.

In Virginia Gilmer long enjoyed a literary reputation which has its basis more in promise than in actual achievement. His published works include a speech or two, some interesting letters, a few pamphlets, and his *Sketches of American Orators*, which gives portraits of Wirt, John Randolph, Henry Clay, and John Marshall. The portraits are competently done in a manner somewhat resembling that of *The Letters of the British Spy*. Gilmer, however, was less given to rhetoric and bombast than Wirt. He had read the British classics from Shakespeare down to Goldsmith and Gray; he apparently did not care for the early nineteenth-century Romanticists, including even Scott. He knew French literature also; he read Turgot and translated portions of Rousseau, Quesnay, and du Pont de Nemours. He was a thorough Republican, and hated slavery as cordially as Jefferson.

17
George Tucker

ECONOMIST, essayist, biographer, and historian, George Tucker (1775–1861) was at once one of the best and one of the least-known Southern writers of his time. Our economic historians have rediscovered him, but his literary work is still neglected. Tucker was born in the first year of the American Revolution and until his death in the year of the attack on Fort Sumter he retained something of the liberalism of his friends Jefferson and Madison.

A kinsman of St. George Tucker, he was born on St. George's, the largest of the Bermuda islands, where his father Daniel Tucker, a merchant, was mayor of Hamilton. As a boy he had both animal spirits and intellectual curiosity. He was tutored in Latin, Greek, and mathematics, and he attempted a Latin ode at the age of eleven. He belonged to a literary society, which he christened the Calliopean, made up chiefly of persons older than himself. At an early age he read *Tom Jones, Roderick Random, The Vicar of Wakefield*, and *The Arabian Nights*—the last he read "by stealth." He was fond of history and of poetry, but he could find in Bermuda no waterfalls or mountains such as his favorite poets described, and presently Bermuda came to seem like a prison. Echoes of the far-off French Revolution stirred his democratic sympathies. While he was trying to decide whether to complete his legal studies in England or the United States, St. George Tucker's brother Thomas Tudor returned to Bermuda on a visit. His influence proved to be the deciding factor, and George Tucker came to the United States in 1795.

He graduated from William and Mary College in 1797 and in the same year married Mary Byrd Farley, a granddaughter of William Byrd. She died two years later. He studied law with St. George Tucker and in 1800 began to practice in Richmond. In 1802 he married Maria Ball Carter, a grand-niece of George Washington. In Richmond there were many able lawyers, many of them Federalists; but Tucker, who was a Republican, did not permit party feeling to keep him from making friends among the Federalists. He greatly admired John Marshall, whose political opinions were repugnant to Tucker's Republican friends. He had a part in the various literary enterprises launched by William Wirt and James Ogilvie. He was a member of the Rainbow Association and wrote some of the best essays in the three series published in the Richmond *Enquirer*.[43] In 1803, while *The Letters of the British Spy* was appearing serially in the *Virginia Argus*, Tucker under the pseudonym of "An Inquirer" replied in two letters to some of Wirt's ill-informed geological speculations. In a letter to Dabney Carr, June 8, 1804, Wirt wrote: "Tucker is a very handsome writer, in my opinion; &, what is more, he is a very good fellow . . . but, poor fellow, he is a better philosopher & writer than he is a lawyer or orator." Wirt conceded that Tucker had "a more intimate acquaintance with the subject; his style is more chaste and equal, and his compositions have much more of the philosopher and author." In this estimate Wirt was not far wrong, but Tucker's writings, substantial though they are, never appealed to the public like the *British Spy*. They lack the sentiment, the eloquence, the passion which might have made him a popular writer.

In 1806, believing that social life and cards were claiming too much of his time, Tucker left Richmond and moved to "Woodbridge" plantation in Pittsylvania County in Southside Virginia. There he found his neighbors plain and unpolished but civil and friendly. Although as commonwealth's attorney he was soon riding three hundred and forty miles each

---

[43] Tucker's earliest publication that I have seen is his *Letter to a Member of the General Assembly of Virginia, on the Subject of the Late Conspiracy of the Slaves; with a Proposal for Their Colonization* (Baltimore, 1801). This seems to be a second edition of a pamphlet first published in Richmond. Copy in possession of Charleston Library Society.

Tucker published over the pseudonym "Hickory Cornhill" some widely read verses attacking the game of loo, then extremely popular in Richmond (Samuel Mordecai, *Richmond in By-Gone Days*, Richmond, 1856, pp. 194–197).

month, he for the first time became a close student of the law. He also imposed on himself the task of writing every day on some "speculative subject." In 1813 he wrote ten essays which under the title of "Thoughts of a Hermit" appeared in 1814 and 1815 in the Philadelphia *Port Folio*, then edited by Dr. Charles Caldwell, a native of North Carolina. In 1822 he added five new essays and published the fifteen in Georgetown, D. C., as *Essays on Various Subjects of Taste, Morals, and National Policy.* In 1816 he had published in Baltimore the least-known of his works—if it is his—*Letters from Virginia, Translated from the French.*

Meanwhile in 1815 Tucker had been elected to the Virginia House of Delegates, where he served until 1818. In the latter year he sold his land at a profit and moved to Lynchburg, where he published an essay on banking. In 1819 he took his seat in the House of Representatives in Washington, where he served till March, 1825. Although he took part in the debate over the Missouri question, he was at that time, he says, more ambitious of excelling at chess than anything else.

The unprecedented popularity of Scott's romances stimulated Tucker to write a novel. In July and August, 1824, while on duty at various county courts, he wrote *The Valley of Shenandoah*, which was published in New York in the fall of that year. Charles Wiley, Fenimore Cooper's publisher, who brought out the hurriedly written story, allowed many typographical errors to slip through and soon afterwards failed in business. Tucker, who received no payment for the book, was not sure that it was ever put on sale. Although Tucker did not know it, a second edition was published in New York in 1828 besides one in London and still another in Germany. The story, he notes, ends unhappily and in a way to offend Virginian pride. He had planned to write a second novel; but James Madison, whom he greatly admired, had read *Essays on Various Subjects* and urged Jefferson to have Tucker engaged as a member of the University of Virginia faculty. Thus at the age of fifty Tucker became Professor of Moral Philosophy, and the new position gave an unexpected turn to his writing. He accepted the position because he thought it would give him more time for writing and because Charlottesville seemed a better place than Washington for his children. Tucker was now primarily interested in economics, but he gave lectures also on mental philosophy, morals, rhetoric, belles-lettres, and even grammar. Whatever his subject, he felt it his duty to investigate it thoroughly. Kindly and witty, he was well liked by his students. "Yonder goes dear old Tucker on Money and Banks," once exclaimed one of a group of students as Tucker rode by on horseback accompanied by his big dog Metaphysics. He did not enjoy the disciplinary measures which as chairman of the faculty he had to enforce.

In 1827 Tucker published in New York, under the pseudonym "Joseph Atterley," A Voyage to the Moon, which may have had some influence on Edgar Allan Poe, who the year before had been a student at the University. For a whole year in 1829 and 1830 Tucker and Dr. Robley Dunglison edited in alternate weeks the Virginia Literary Museum, and it seems that the two editors must have written most of the material they printed.[44] Its announced purpose was "to communicate the truth of science to the miscellaneous reader, and encourage a taste for polite literature." Much of the material was excellent, but there was little demand for such a magazine in Virginia or elsewhere in America. Even today university literary magazines require subsidies to keep them alive.

All but the very last of Tucker's later books were in the fields of economics, history, and biography. In 1837 he published what was for the time an admirable two-volume life of Jefferson. For the modern reader its chief advantage is that Tucker knew Jefferson and learned much about him from Madison and other friends of the sage of Monticello. In 1837 also he published The Laws of Wages, Profits, and Rent, Investigated. The Theory of Money and Banks followed in 1839. In 1843 came his important study of the 1840 census reports, Progress of the United States in Population, in which he pointed out the unexpected decline in the American birthrate. In a later edition he discussed the census returns for 1850. It is strange that such works should come out of the agricultural South rather than the growing industrial belt in the North. The full importance of these books was not recognized until long after Tucker's death.

Tucker retired from teaching in 1845. He was seventy years old; the other teachers were now much younger men; and since the resignation of Henry St. George Tucker, he had no very intimate friend in the faculty. Possibly he was influenced by the growing Southern reaction against the liberalism of Jefferson and Madison. His place was filled by the celebrated compiler of school readers and zealous advocate of temperance and piety, William Holmes McGuffey. Tucker settled in Philadelphia, where he had thought of going twenty-five years earlier. It seemed to him the best place for an old man who had nothing in particular to occupy him and who desired congenial intellectual companions. He was a member of both the American Philosophical Society and the Historical Society of Pennsylvania, which had their headquarters in Philadelphia. When he left Charlottesville, he had emancipated the five household servants who belonged to him. In old age he

44 Bruce, History of the University of Virginia, II, 346–350. The Museum published a series entitled "Americanisms," which was reprinted in The Beginnings of American English (1931), ed. M. M. Mathews, chap. ix.

retained his remarkable intellectual vigor. His later books—all published when he was past eighty—are *Political Economy for the People* (1859), *Essays, Moral and Metaphysical* (1860), and a four-volume *History of the United States* (1856–1857).

In the winter of 1860–1861—his third wife had died in 1859—he traveled extensively through the Southern states and witnessed the outbreak of a revolution with which he could not sympathize. In February, 1861, he wrote to Robley Dunglison from Savannah: "The state of public affairs is indeed gloomy, even to heart-sickening. People seem crazed in the fancies of imaginary evils, and of their strange remedies." In Mobile he was accidentally struck by a cotton bale as he was getting off a steamboat. He was taken to "Sherwood," the home of his daughter Mrs. George Rives in Charlottesville, and there he died on April 10, 1861, two days before the bombardment of Fort Sumter. He was perhaps fortunate to pass from the scene without witnessing the terrible war brought on, he thought, by men for whom he had scant respect: Southern fire-eaters, Northern sentimentalists and root-and-branch reformers, and political schemers from both sections— such at least they seemed to him.

Tucker's most important work, like that of Thomas Cooper or Walter Bagehot, of whom he reminds one, was done in the field of economics. "Tucker stands out as an acute thinker," says Joseph J. Spengler, "in a period when acuteness was conspicuously rare." "Economists have not forgotten him," writes John Roscoe Turner; "they never knew him. . . . He was too far in advance of contemporary thought to be appreciated; and his works were out of print long before they could have been justly appraised." He was the first Southern economist effectively to criticize the doctrines of Malthus and Ricardo. He might have been more widely known if he had, like Thomas Cooper, given economic backing to proslavery politicians; but while Tucker opposed the protective tariff, he supported the Whig doctrine of government control over money and banking.

Tucker's attitude toward slavery deserves special notice. While as a social historian he thought slavery had some good features in its influence on the masters, as an economist he employed Malthusian methods to show that slavery was an inefficient system of labor. It placed a stigma upon manual labor and it discouraged the development of manufactures in the South. He argued on economic grounds similar to those later developed by such scholars as Edwin R. A. Seligman, Walter P. Webb, and Charles W. Ramsdell that slavery was destined to ultimate extinction as an unprofitable institution in a region where the population was steadily growing denser. "And in this country," he wrote in 1837, "slaves would be worth little in the southern states on the Atlantic, if it was not for their greater value in the cotton and sugar growing states. As soon as those states are supplied with as many as can work their lands to advantage, the emancipation of slaves, occasioning but a small loss to any, and proving a positive gain to some, it will be impossible to prevent it." Again in 1843, while still living in Virginia, he spoke his conviction: "We may say of it [slavery], as of man: the doom of its death, though we know not the time or the mode, is certain and irrevocable."

The panic of 1857 hurt the sales of Tucker's longest work, his *History of the United States* (1856–1857). It was intended not so much as a defense of the South as a corrective of the bias of Northern nationalistic historians who, he thought, attached too little importance to regional affairs and the rights of the states. One is struck by Tucker's conception of the obligation of the historian: ". . . to make us acquainted with the progress of society and the arts of civilization; with the advancement and decline of religion, literature, laws, manners and commerce." The history, however, does not fully achieve Tucker's aim. An intelligent reviewer in *Harper's Magazine* in September, 1856, wrote after reading the first volume:

The materials of the work are derived, in a great measure, from contemporary documents, while little use has been made of the labors of other historians. . . . To the general reader, the execution of the work will seem too meagre and unadorned, too destitute of varied illustration, too skeleton-like in its rigid, unyielding frame-work. . . . Mr. Tucker has few of the qualities which give success to the popular writer. He makes no pretension to the graces of rhetoric. He never colours the exposition of facts by the glowing tints of imagination. . . . But he impresses one with a sense of his literary integrity and candor. . . .

The books on which Tucker's claim to literary consideration rests represent three different types, and only two of them were published over his own name. Even so, his colleague Dr. Robley Dunglison believed that Tucker's reputation as scholar and teacher suffered in Virginia from the fact that he was known to have written fiction. His literary essays are more substantial than those of William Wirt, but he never succeeded in hitting the popular taste as Wirt did. If he had given his whole time to literature and had published all that he wrote over his own name or a single pseudonym, he might in the course of time have built up for himself a reputation with the select few; but, like Wirt, he had a family to support and he was too lacking in literary ambition to follow such a course.

In his *Essays on Various Subjects of Taste, Morals, and National Policy* (1822) one finds an intellectual versatility which suggests Jefferson or Madison. Miscellaneous though the essays are, they all reflect the writer's genuine interests in literature, art, ethics, and economics. Most of them were written in wartime, but none shows any trace of hostility to England; and there is nowhere in any of his books much evidence of sectional feeling. Thoroughly just is Tucker's claim that he "has yielded to no opinion because it was fashionable, and has flattered no prejudice, either popular or local." A keen interest in economic problems is seen in the essays on banking, population, and national debts, but the literary reader will find metal more attractive in the essays which deal with literature and art. Among these are thoughtful discussions of beauty, style, simplicity in ornament, architecture, classical education, and the problem of a national literature. In the essay "On Duelling" he surprisingly takes the position that the institution "preserves, in undiminished force and purity, that courage, and courtesy, and generosity, and fidelity to engagements which our commercial habits, and possibly some of our political institutions, have a tendency to weaken." Tucker's taste was for the symmetry and simplicity of the classics, and he disliked extrinsic ornament.[45] He had none of Wirt's weakness for the sentimental or his love of rhetoric for its own sake. In the essay "On Style" he pointed out that the influence of the omnipresent public speaking in this country imparted "a declamatory style to our writers" and induced them to "strive to write beautifully, and eloquently, and pathetically, in which attempt they insensibly fall into mere rant and declamation." "On American Literature" is one of the sanest discussions of the much-discussed problem of a national literature.[46]

Edward Everett in the North American Review for January, 1823, rated Tucker's Essays as "no ordinary specimen of the literature of Virginia." "The characteristics of the essays throughout," he wrote, "are good sense, clear perception, absence of all dogmatism, and freedom from passion and a polemical spirit. There is no effort to astonish with brilliant paradoxes or overwhelm with arrogant declamation; and though many of the subjects of the essays have elsewhere led to angry controversies, our author has treated them throughout with the urbanity of a gentleman." "The style," he concluded, "is neither negligent nor painfully elaborate; but evinces at once ease and care. There is no parade or ornament, no affectation of plain-

---

[45] The author of Letters by a South-Carolinian (Norfolk, Va., 1827), p. 43, noted that Tucker's Essays were "written with elegance and spirit, and modelled on those of Hume." This book has been attributed to Richard Beresford and to Hugh Blair Grigsby.

[46] Tucker was to discuss the subject again in his "Discourse on American Literature: Delivered before the Charlottesville Lyceum, Dec. 19, 1837," S.L.M., IV, 81–88 (Feb., 1838). In his History of the United States, IV, 411, he once more commented on the alleged inferiority of the American intellect as a "hypothesis [which] has long slept in oblivion, or is remembered only to be laughed at, with the question once discussed in the French Academy, whether Germany could produce a work of genius!"

ness. . . . Should we name a fault in it, it would be its occasional languor."
Letters from Virginia, Translated from the French was published in Baltimore in 1816. Nowhere so far as I know did Tucker claim this book as his.
He failed to mention it in the list of his works which he sent to Rufus W.
Griswold in 1856.[47] The card catalogue of the New York Public Library
lists Tucker as the "supposed author" and gives as evidence: "Attributed
to George Tucker by Sabin, the Brinley catalogue, and M. Polock, the well-
known Philadelphia antiquarian and dealer, who knew Tucker personally;
the 'Letters' have also been attributed to William Maxwell and to J. K.
Paulding." Internal evidence seems to confirm the attribution to Tucker.[48]
The book attracted little attention. Had it been published twenty or thirty
years later, the heresy-hunters would have made a loud outcry over Tucker's
treatment of slavery. If he wrote the book—and I believe he did—he must
have known that it contained opinions which were becoming increasingly
unpopular.

Taking his cue perhaps from *The Letters of the British Spy*, Tucker
adopted the plan of presenting Virginia life through the eyes of a cultivated
young Frenchman who expects to realize in the Old Dominion if anywhere
his "hope of seeing a true republic, where the laws are made and administered
by the best men, only to promote the happiness of the people." But Virginia, much as he likes it, is not Utopia. Letter V describes in language full
of feeling a party of Negro slaves, among them a nursing mother, being taken
by a trader to North Carolina. "It cannot be Virginia that I am in," reflects
the young Frenchman. "They have landed me on some barbarous coast;
charming indeed at the first approach, but full of horrors upon a nearer
survey." The charge that the slaves have no feelings, he says, "is a libel upon
human nature, I had almost said, upon the Creator." Was Tucker, one wonders, describing his own reaction when he came to Virginia from Bermuda
at the age of twenty? Letter XI is an able, lawyerlike refutation of Jefferson's
suggestion, in his *Notes on the State of Virginia*, that the Negro's intellect
is inferior to that of the white man. Letter XIII is a satiric account of Virginia gourmands. Letters XIV and XV deal with Williamsburg and the

---

[47] *Passages from the Correspondence . . . of Rufus W. Griswold* (Cambridge, Mass.,
1898), p. 305. I have also seen a microfilm of the original letter, which is in the Boston
Public Library.

The New York Public Library and the Norfolk Public Library have copies of *Letters
from Virginia*.

[48] The attribution to Paulding is probably due to confusion with his *Letters from the
South* (1817). Prof. Leonard C. Helderman in a letter to me notes that certain passages
in the *Letters from Virginia* are "almost identical with some of his [Tucker's] established
writings."

College, where the French observer finds too little discipline among the students and notes that they have only recently banished from the library of their literary society the works of Thomas Paine. Infidelity, he learns, is on the wane, and Paine and Godwin are no longer favorite authors. Letter XXI is an excellent description of Richmond, where the higher classes, "chiefly of foreign extraction I believe," "generally live in a style of ambitious rivalship with one another, each endeavouring to surpass his neighbour in fashion and folly. . . ." He visits Yorktown and Jamestown, which tempt him to review a portion of Virginia's history. Letter XIX, as well written as any in the book, is a light satire, in the form of a dream, upon women; but some of the hardest hits are reserved for the New England Yankees pictured in Letter VI. *Letters from Virginia*, like the books of social criticism which James Fenimore Cooper had yet to write, was not calculated to please the sensitive readers of its time.

The Valley of Shenandoah (1824), Tucker's first novel and the first of importance written by a Virginian, resembles the Waverley novels— the popularity of which induced him to write it—only in its emphasis upon the regional background. The story itself is made up largely of conventional elements which go back through *The Power of Sympathy* and *Charlotte Temple* to Richardson's *Clarissa Harlowe*, but it is not a sentimental romance. Tucker's mind was primarily critical, and he had no special gift for narrative or dialogue. His avowed purpose was to present "to the public not only a faithful picture of the manners and habits" of Virginians in the year 1796—the year following his own arrival in Virginia—"but also an instructive moral to the youth of both sexes." The purpose of fiction, as he understood it, was "to supply to youth the wisdom and experience of age, and to mingle instruction with pure and rational amusement." This tale of the ruin of a once prosperous planter family is laid in the period when many debt-ridden plantations were passing out of the hands of their owners into those of men of inferior standing.

The plot, which we have compared to that of Richardson's most famous novel, vaguely resembles also that of Dreiser's *An American Tragedy*. A New York merchant sends his son Edward Gildon to the College of William and Mary to prevent his marrying a girl with no financial expectations. In Virginia, Gildon, who is a weakling rather than the conventional villain, meets Louisa Grayson, the sister of a college friend. After he has seduced the girl, he lacks the courage either to marry her—she is now poor—or to tell his father, who wants him to marry a wealthy New York woman. Louisa's brother follows Gildon to New York seeking to avenge his sister, and Gildon kills him. Louisa enters a convent, and the family estates are sold for debt,

This melodramatic story is told with many circumstantial details that savor of realism rather than romance. The background of plantation life, partly in the Tidewater but chiefly in the Valley, is faithfully described. There are excellent descriptions of barbecues, details of farm life, county-court proceedings. There is even a description of the auctioning off of the Grayson slaves—a scene that would be difficult to parallel in any other novel by a Southern writer. There is, finally, a remarkable contrast of the German and the Scotch-Irish settlers of the Valley. No other novel of Virginia includes so many typical aspects of the life of the state. There is no attempt to cast a halo over plantation life, no attempt to conceal unpleasant realities. Tucker had no part in the building up of the romantic plantation tradition.

A *Voyage to the Moon: with Some Account of the Manners and Customs, Science and Philosophy, of the . . . Lunarians* (1827) is closer to the tradition of *Gulliver's Travels* than to that of *Utopia*. The air of what Poe called verisimilitude is well maintained, and the pseudoscientific devices employed to convey Joseph Atterley and his Brahmin guide to the moon are ingeniously conceived. Poe, who certainly knew of the book, may have owed something to it when he wrote "The Unparalleled Adventure of Hans Pfaall"[49] and "Eleanora." Tucker's intent, mainly satiric, is not always clear or consistently maintained. The satire is directed at women's dress, the passion for gambling, the folly of asceticism, the incompetence of physicians, the pedantry of philosophers and pedagogues, the irrationality of fools, and the uselessness of most inventions. One finds a touch of beauty in the description of Gulgal, the sacred garden of roses, and of Okalbia, the Happy Valley. Okalbia was begun as a communistic enterprise with equal distribution of property; and although inequalities have arisen, the Okalbians are an intelligent and happy people. They live on quite undisturbed by Ricardo's fallacious theory of rent and in possession of some method of birth control which renders Malthus's fears of overpopulation ridiculous. The Brahmin's story of his life is a tale of passionate Oriental revenge, somewhat reminiscent of Byron and Moore, and it is out of key with the remainder of the book.

Before he retired from teaching, Tucker wrote another novel, still unpublished, which he entitled "A Century Hence: Or a Romance of 1941." It is the story of the unhappy love affair of Henry Carlton and Caroline Maunde, whose fathers, wealthy political rivals, are bitterly opposed to the match.

[49] In a long Note appended to the tale Poe refers to Robley Dunglison's long review of Tucker's *Voyage* in the *Am. Quart. Rev.*, III, 61–88 (March, 1828), but he does not specifically mention the book or attribute it to Tucker, whom he must have known in Charlottesville. The publisher of *A Voyage* was Elam Bliss, who four years later brought out Poe's *Poems*. See J. O. Bailey, "Sources for Poe's *Arthur Gordon Pym*, 'Hans Pfaal,' and Other Pieces," *PMLA*, LVII, 513–535 (June, 1942).

When Henry calls upon Caroline and finds her with the cousin whom her father wishes her to marry, he leaps to the conclusion that she is faithless to him and sets off on a European tour. Martinetta Greene, who wants Henry for herself, thwarts the efforts of Henry's friends to bring about a reconciliation. The story is unfolded in the leisurely manner of Richardson in letters written from various parts of the world by the lovers and their relatives and friends. The romance comes to a happy conclusion in the mid-Pacific, where in a melodramatic scene the hero rescues from a pirate ship the heroine and her grateful father. The letters show some understanding of the psychology of the jealous lover, but it is difficult to sympathize with one who plays so negative a role as Henry Carlton.

On this framework of letters written from various cities in America, Europe, and Asia Tucker has placed his forecast of the world of 1941. The capital of the United States is now Centropolis, a large city somewhere in the Middle West. There are forty-four states, and the population of the country is two hundred million. There has been a great development in the means of transportation. Swift packets now run from Manila to an Oregon port in eighteen or twenty days. One can travel still more speedily in the "flying cars," which are propelled by steam. Tucker had only a glimpse of the enormous industrial development of the United States. Although he hinted at the possible separation of the Pacific from the Atlantic states, he did not foresee the Civil War, the War with Mexico, or even the annexation of Texas. He did not of course predict the world war which would be raging in 1941. He did, however, foresee an expanded Russia, a "stupendous and ill cemented Empire," still ruled by a tsar, with a population of one hundred and sixty million which has engulfed Turkey, Greece, and Egypt and is threatening to overrun not only central and southern Europe but China as well. India has finally left the British Empire.

In Paris we learn of a notable improvement in educational methods. We see a class of boys of nine reciting in English, Latin, and Greek. The status of woman has greatly improved also. In Paris the majority of physicians are women, but only the older doctors are permitted to practice on patients of both sexes. France surprisingly is suffering from overpopulation, and among the remedies discussed is a law that would make it illegal for a woman to marry until her late twenties. Another proposed law would make it a penitentiary offense to propagate children unless one has the means of supporting them. Tucker was disturbed by the great multiplication of books, especially books on the subliterary level. In the London of 1941 the authors of popular novels hold themselves superior to those who write poetry, history, and scientific treatises. There are now so many books published—five thousand in English alone in a single year—that few read any of them. Instead they turn to the *Monthly Alembic*—soon to be published in New York as well as in London—in which a new book is summarized in no more than five pages.

"A Century Hence" everywhere reveals the vigor of Tucker's mind, but it is not a good novel. He gained nothing by placing the love story in 1941, and his forecast of the future continually slows up the story itself. The story has affiliations with pseudo-science fiction, with Utopian romances, and with such satires as *Gulliver's Travels*. Tucker is clearly following Swift when he ridicules the various devices displayed in London for making bread and alcoholic drinks out of sawdust. The book leaves one with the feeling that Tucker never quite decided what kind of novel he was trying to write. Why he did not publish it I do not know. It seems probable that no publisher would print it except at the author's expense. In the 1840's the market was flooded with ten- and twenty-five-cent reprints of English novels, and American publishers were reluctant to accept manuscripts, even those written by such popular novelists as Cooper and Simms.

Essays, Moral and Metaphysical (1860), Tucker's last book, was published in Philadelphia when he was eighty-five. Only a part of the book was new, for some of the essays had already been published in one form or another. In some respects it is the best expression of his ideas. The style is easy, always clear, a fitting garment for the thought, which is never feeble. "On Simplicity in Ornament" again reveals his taste for symmetry and simplicity. The subjects of the essays are highly varied. There is, for instance, "On the Siamese Twins," which suggests that Tucker was no mean psychologist. He had selected a list of questions which he asked the Siamese Twins separately so that neither could hear what he asked the other. The replies were not identical but were amazingly alike. Other essays discuss cause and effect, sympathy, the association of ideas, dreams, beauty, sublimity, the ludicrous, classical education, the love of fame, and "our belief of an external world." Even had the Civil War not been imminent when the book appeared, it could not have attracted wide attention. It bore no publisher's imprint, but it did carry the author's name. In some respects the collection seems an anachronism. The writers whom Tucker discusses or quotes belong to earlier periods: Alison, Blair, Burke, Hume, Dugald Steward, Berkeley, Longinus—the same writers he had quoted in the *Essays* of 1822. Among nineteenth-century authors he does mention Coleridge, Jeffrey, and Mill; but there is nothing to indicate that he had ever heard of Emerson, Hawthorne, Poe, Melville, Lowell, Carlyle, Tennyson, or Macaulay. In 1860 few but Tucker were interested in correcting the theories of writers and thinkers who had already receded into obsolescence. Tucker had been too long and too deeply absorbed in economic problems to keep abreast of literary movements. So it is likely to be with one with whom literature is only an avocation.

What Tucker lacked as a writer, as I have already suggested, was the power to arouse emotion. Once at least he wrote better than he knew. The Reverend Francis L. Hawks in the *New York Review* for March, 1837, published a long and bigoted attack on Tucker's life of Jefferson, in which he contended that Jefferson was a greatly overrated statesman, an atheist, and on the whole an evil influence. When Tucker learned of the review some time after its appearance, he wrote his spirited *Defence of the Character of Thomas Jefferson*. In the conclusion, which I quote in part, Tucker took his stand with the Revolutionary liberals as against the narrow orthodoxy of the evangelical denominations:

As for the consequences to Mr. Jefferson's reputation, we have but little fear. It is as safe from the effusions of clerical hate as the fixed star from the influence of earth's noxious exhalations. The river of his fame is rolling rapidly on to posterity, and it is as idle for the clergyman of the Church Journal to attempt to break its stream, as it would be for him to stay Niagara in its course, and hurl back its waters. He has erected for himself a monument broader and more imperishable than the largest of Egypt's kings. The Vandals of criticism cannot break it, nor stain its whiteness. It is in the hearts of millions of grateful people. His fame stands identified with the institutions of our country, and should they be destined to overshadow the earth, it will be cöextensive. The grandeur of his genius is for ever blended with the majesty of that period in the history of the human mind, when the great truth of man's capacity for self government was first discovered. Bacon's name is not more indissolubly connected with the emancipation of the human intellect from a false philosophy—Newton's with the great revelation in natural science—Columbus' with the discovery of this continent —than is that of Thomas Jefferson, with the proudest epoch in the history of human reason and human action.

18
Thomas Cooper

"A YOUNG MAN," said Thomas Cooper (1759–1839) to D. J. McCord when well past sixty, "must lay in a large stock of democracy, if he expects it to hold out to my age." As a young Englishman brought up in Manchester, he had protested against the slave trade, attacked the privileged orders of society, and espoused some of the doctrines of the French Revolution. In old age in South Carolina he was an advocate of Nullification and a defender of state rights. James Ogilvie wrote to Francis Walker Gilmer on February 4, 1814: "He [Cooper] has undergone as many metamorphoses as Proteus. . . . In the course of the last twenty years he has been farmer, lawyer, patriot, Belles-Lettres cognoscenti & professor of chemistry, to which shortly will be added Doctor in Medicine & Professor of Law." Yet Cooper in old age felt that he had consistently held to certain high principles. There is a clue in the closing paragraph of his Lectures on the Elements of Political Economy, first published in 1826: "In the year 1783, I published in England, a pamphlet in favour of parliamentary reform. . . . I have had some experience during this interval of near half a century; and my present opinions in old age, are not in exact conformity with those of my boyhood; but I trust they are equally in favour of the just rights of the people, against those who would abuse entrusted power."

Cooper was educated at Oxford, but he took no degree there, perhaps on account of an unwillingness to sign the Thirty-nine Articles. He practiced law, studied science and medicine, and interested himself in religion, philosophy, and reform. The wide range of his intellectual interests is reflected in his Tracts Ethical, Theological, and Political (1789). He was an active member of the Manchester Literary and Philosophical Society, to which also belonged James Watt the inventor and Joseph Priestley, Unitarian minister and discoverer of oxygen, who greatly influenced him. Priestley proposed Cooper's name to the Royal Society, which twice rejected him on account of his radical opinions. An intemperate pamphlet reply to Edmund Burke, who had denounced Cooper in the House of Commons, brought the threat of prosecution; and he fled to France, where for a short time he took an active part in the Revolutionary movement. Disgusted by the Reign of Terror, he came to America for a short stay. In 1794 he published Some Information Respecting America and in the same year settled at Northumberland, Pennsylvania, where Priestley, whose memoirs he was to write, was spending his last years. Cooper resumed the practice of law. An intemperate attack on President John Adams led, under the Sedition Act of 1798, to six months' imprisonment and a fine of four hundred dollars, which was finally repaid with interest to his heirs. From 1804 to 1811 he was a judge in the court of common pleas in the Fourth Pennsylvania District. He was now beginning to grow conservative in some respects, and a radical faction finally got him removed from office for "overbearing conduct."

Cooper now turned to teaching, which was to occupy him for the remainder of his life. He lost faith in many things but never in the power of education to change men's minds. He taught chemistry at Dickinson College, 1811–1815, at a salary of eight hundred dollars, and for part of that time he edited the *Emporium of Arts and Sciences*. He held the chair of chemistry and mineralogy at the University of Pennsylvania from 1816 to 1819. About this time at the instance of Jefferson, who regarded him as "the greatest man in America in the powers of the mind and in acquired information," he was elected professor of chemistry at the University of Virginia. Since the University was not to open its doors until 1825, he accepted—temporarily, he thought—a similar appointment in the South Carolina College (now the state university). When the Virginia Presbyterians began to attack him on account of his religious opinions, which were primarily Unitarian, he wrote to Jefferson: "Indeed I feel gloomy at the persevering, determined, unwearied march of religious intolerance among us. The clergy daily acquire more strength: they insinuate themselves among the females of the families, whose heads will not bend to their sway, & they exercise compleat controul over the ignorant every where." Although Jefferson tried to reassure him, Cooper remained in Columbia, where he became President of the College in 1820. In 1833, however, the clergy forced him out of his position even though he had done great service to the political leaders of the state. Cooper wrote little on strictly religious questions, but he could not conceal his contempt for the Calvinistic clergy, of whom he once said: "God forgive these ignorant and rancorous bigots, who form God after man's image, and choose the very worst model they can find, themselves." He was indiscreet enough to attack the clergy in his lectures and textbooks on economics.

Cooper was a vigorous writer and lecturer on many topics ranging from philosophy to science and politics. Woodbridge Riley, who gives him a chapter in his discussion of Materialism, notes that he was as much a nullifier in philosophy as he was in politics and comments on the surprising fact that he advocated Positivist doctrines several years before Auguste Comte. In science his chief importance was that he popularized the ideas and discoveries of other men.

The most important work he did while living in the South was in economics. With Thomas R. Dew at William and Mary College and George Tucker at the University of Virginia, Cooper was among the first Americans to lecture and write on the subject. In 1824 he recommended to the trustees of South Carolina College the appointment of a professor of political economy, and at their request he delivered the lectures which formed the basis of his textbook, already mentioned. He began by defining the study and carefully distinguishing political economy from politics. He defined his terms with the care of a modern scholar. In his attitude toward the tariff he took the orthodox Southern position. Although he pronounced slavery "undoubtedly the dearest kind of labour," he defended it on the ground that "the nature of the soil and climate . . . incapacitates a white man from labouring [in the Lower South] in the summer time."

Like other Southerners, he did not view with a friendly eye the industrial development taking place in the North. Pointing out the vast inequality in wealth in industrial England, he exclaimed: "God forbid this country should ever become an exporting, manufacturing country." He had little faith in such reformers as Robert Owen, whose schemes he thought would destroy "frugality and accumulation." He was opposed to universal suffrage, but he advocated, like Jefferson, "a full, complete, really free system of education of every grade, at the public expense, open to every citizen without exception, without money and without price." He repudiated the doctrine of natural rights, and he denounced the maxim: "The will of the majority ought to govern." Like John Taylor of Caroline and Calhoun, he defended the rights of minorities: "Let but the majority determine uncontrolled, what is for their own good, and decree it, then are the minority, in the strictest sense of the word, slaves." "The only safeguard in our confederacy," he said, "is the absolute inviolability of state sovereignty and state rights. . . ." He repudiated his friend Jefferson's doctrine of equality: "All men are said to be 'born free, equal and independent.' I know of no sense in which this ever was, or is, or can, or will be true."

Cooper was one of the ablest spokesmen for the Nullification doctrine of South Carolina. In a speech at Columbia, July 2, 1827, he said in attacking the tariff and Clay's American system: ". . . we of the South hold our plantations . . . as the serfs and operatives of the North: subject to the orders, and labouring for the benefit of the masterminds of Massachusetts, the Lords of the spinning jenny and Peers of the power loom!" Five days later he warned: "I have said that we shall, before long, be compelled to calculate the value of our union; and to inquire of what use to us is this most unequal alliance? by which the south has always been the loser, and the north always the gainer? Is it worth our while to continue this union of states, where the north demand to be our masters, and we are required to be their tributaries?" The slavery question, he predicted in 1838, would ultimately, like Aaron's rod, swallow up all other questions.[50] In 1836, un-

---

[50] In the Preface to the second (1830) edition of his pamphlet *Consolidation*, Cooper wrote: "All the evils of S. Carolina now complained of, were foreseen and foretold by *Patrick Henry* on the 4th of June, 1788, and on the subsequent days of Conventional debate."

able to attend a Fourth-of-July celebration to which he had been invited, the veteran advocate of state rights sent this grim toast: "The Memory of the Constitution of the United States." "History," says Dumas Malone, "cannot afford to disregard this prophet of secession, who valued union too little because he loved liberty too well."

19
William Crafts

In New England, as I have had occasion to note earlier, literary culture was largely in the hands of clergymen and teachers, while in the South it was most frequently the lawyers who supplied the intellectual leadership. They more than any other class gave to Southern writing its distinguishing characteristics. The two leading Charleston writers of this period, William Crafts and Hugh Swinton Legaré, were both lawyers. In their lives we shall see some of the difficulties which beset a lawyer whose real bent was toward letters rather than that austere mistress, the law. Apart from a common love of literature, however, the two men were very unlike. Crafts, half a New Englander, was a facile dabbler in literary trifles, indolent and somewhat vain; Legaré, a product of the Low-Country, was a genuine scholar and an indefatigable seeker after knowledge. Ten years the younger of the two, he lived to write a notable critical essay on Crafts' literary remains.

William Crafts (1787–1826) was the son of a Boston merchant who had settled in Charleston and married in his adopted city. The public-spirited merchant made a place for himself in Charleston. He served on the city council and in the state legislature. His precocious son began the study of Latin at the age of seven. Charleston schools were probably inferior to those of Boston, but Crafts had two clergymen teachers who were much above the average: Dr. Buist, a Scotchman reputed to have contributed to the *Encyclopaedia Britannica*, and a Bostonian, Dr. Gardiner, who after his pupil's death wrote that he had early "considered him as a most promising young man, of very amiable disposition, and fine talents, and [had] confidently predicted his future fame and fortune."

When Crafts entered Harvard College as a sophomore in the fall of 1802, he was struck by "the absurd ideas, which prevail too commonly at Cambridge with regard to the Southern States." His social gifts made him popular, and his facility in learning foreign languages enabled him to make a good record in his classes. In Boston he was impressed by the eloquence of the Reverend Joseph Buckminster and by the wit of Fisher Ames. In 1808, when he returned to Cambridge for his master's degree, he delivered to an enthusiastic audience an oration in what the scholarly Legaré declared to be execrable Latin. In 1817 Crafts delivered the Phi Beta Kappa oration at Harvard, choosing as his subject "The Influence of Moral Causes over National Character." Crafts was always loyal to Harvard, to which he once referred as "the only University which this country enjoys." He was ready enough to reply to Northern slanders on the South, but he was reluctant to concede that New England was in any way responsible for the growing bad feeling between the two sections. He did, however, quote the editor of the *Connecticut Journal*, who had made the charge that "the people of the South are false pretenders to most of the virtues"; and he admitted that he had heard "from the lips of Dr. [Timothy] Dwight himself" a statement to the effect that Southerners had no religion.

When at nineteen Crafts began the study of law in Charleston in the office of Ford and Desaussure, he possessed, according to Samuel Gilman, "a retentive memory . . . a fluency of expression, a gentlemanly address, a ready presence of mind, and a distinct and impressive elocution. . . ." He was equally facile whether he was composing a speech, an essay, or a poem. Dr. Gardiner thought that Crafts' comparative failure as a lawyer was due to "his contempt of money and [his] attachment to the Muses," but Legaré had a different explanation: ". . . nothing but his suicidal indolence and perverse vanity prevented his becoming able in business and debate." And again: "There was always something in his manner that reminded one of an under-graduate at a college exhibition." Legaré continued:

It is a mistake to suppose, that devotion to literary pursuits had any thing to do with it, and that, for the best of all reasons, viz. that Mr. Crafts never was devoted to literary pursuits, at least, after he came to the bar. "His favorite intercourse with the Muses," if by that is meant inditing sonnets for the newspapers, and songs for "festive occasions," may, indeed, have contributed to bring him into disrepute with men of business—but these effusions did him quite as little honor in the opinion of men of letters. The truth is, that so far from suffering by his reputation as a scholar, he was very much, if not mainly indebted to it, for his extraordinary popularity and success at the outset of his career. A felicitous allusion, an apt quotation, the elegance of his diction, and the various other graces of a classical education that adorned his style, were quite peculiar to him among his contemporaries, and contributed very much to secure for him the character, which he ever afterwards enjoyed, of *the* man of genius *par excellence*.

Although he attained no great success as a lawyer, Crafts' wit and charm made him socially popular, and he was in demand as a speaker for special occasions. He was ambitious for political honors; but although he served for a time in the state legislature, he was never elected to Congress, perhaps in part because his Federalist views were becoming increasingly unpopular in the state. Ill health and disappointments saddened his last years. He died at Lebanon Springs, New York, on September 23, 1826, and was buried in Boston. This was "the first time," remarks Samuel Gilman, "he had ever entered that city, without a heart beating high, in delightful expectation of the caresses, that were sure to await him, from an extensive and polished circle of friends." In a fragmentary poem on "Boston" Crafts had written:

> Seest thou yon shining dome
> That seems to hold a parley with the sky?
> Stranger rejoice—for thou hast found a home—
> Boston, the seat of courtesy is nigh;
> Of wealth and hardy enterprize, and mind—
> Of men enlightened—and of maids refined;
> And all that gives this lower world a zest,
> Is in that spot united and comprest.

Crafts published in Charleston two small volumes of verse, but most of his prose first appeared in the Charleston *Courier*, to which he was in his later years a frequent contributor. In his selection from Crafts' writings Samuel Gilman included eight speeches, of which the best are an address delivered before the New England Society of Charleston and a speech in the state legislature in defense of the Free School Act. The kindly Gilman found in Crafts' orations "a certain lyric strain"; but Legaré, a severer critic, found in them much of the prevalent tendency to "vapid, frothy, shallow declamation." Crafts seemed to him "as fond of conceits as the Seicentisti." There are, in fact, some good passages in Crafts' speeches, but there is also in them too much of that poetic bombast which is even today not unchar-acteristic of Southern orators.

The essays which Crafts printed in the *Courier* belong vaguely to the Ad-disonian tradition. Charleston readers were no more difficult to please than those of other American cities; and while many of the essays are gracefully written, they do not bear rereading. Among the better examples are "Literary Sparring," in which less skilfully than Irving he takes to task British re-viewers for libeling the United States; "Charleston," a description of the city in the summer when many of its inhabitants had fled northward; "The Theater"; and "Sullivan's Island" and "The Race Week," subjects also treated in his verse. As a specimen of Crafts' prose at its best I quote from "Sullivan's Island." He is describing the "little city of Moultrieville, the *Sybaris* of the South . . . the general resort of the indolent, and refuge of the invalid":

It is a state subsisting without a revenue—because taxes are unnecessary; without labour, for the soil can produce, and the inhabitants will do nothing. It is a city asleep for all the uses and purposes of life, except ease. It has no shops —no public library—no museum—no court house—no jail—and only recently a church. You can neither buy nor sell there—so there is no Bank. There is no traffic except of cake, which gets hard, and ice, which melts in its voyage from Charleston. There are no town meetings there, except a medley of carriages, chairs, cavalry, and pedestrians, collected in the evening at the cove, to witness the departure of the sun, and of the steam boat. There is no Custom House— there being nothing to collect but sand, which the wind gathers and disperses. They have no press, wherein they do suffer much imposition, being compelled to swallow the absurd crudities of the Charleston prints. They have a fort where they all resort, on the approach of a storm. Quere; would they do so on the approach of a battle? They have no fee-simple of the soil, their tenure being at the will of the State, and by courtesy of the air and the water. It is famous for crabs that are not aquatic, and fiddlers that make no music.

Crafts' slight body of verse has the same merits and faults as his prose: it suffers from too great facility and a lack of substance. His earlier model was Pope, but his later ideal seems to have been Thomas Moore. A number of Anacreontic love poems show the influence of Moore at its worst. With the exception of Moore and Byron, the British Romantic poets made little impression on him, and he seems quite unaware of Bryant. Among his better short poems are "To a Friend at Sea," "The Infidel Girl," and "A Dying Mother to Her Erring Daughter."

Somewhat more interesting are the two longer poems, "Sullivan's Island" and "The Raciad," which prompted the too partial Gilman to remark that in these poems Crafts had "rendered Sullivan's Island and the Charleston Race Course but little short of classic ground." Classic ground perhaps Sullivan's Island is; but if it is so, it is because of Poe's "The Gold Bug" and not Crafts' poetic description in the manner of Pope's *Windsor Forest*. "The Raciad" is an account of Charleston's Race Week somewhat in the vein of *The Rape of the Lock*. Two passages will serve to illustrate its quality:

> Soon as the sun proclaims the festal day,
> By judges destined for the glorious fray,
> The people's breast with furious madness glows,
> The flood-gates open—and the city flows!
> Coaches with fortune-hunters at their side,
> And gilded curricles, inflaming pride;
> The virgin, armed with beauty's keenest dart,
> The coxcomb, decked in all the tailor's art;
> The lawyer, anxious for a scene of strife,

The parson, going but to please his wife;
The horse, that late his tandem harness broke,
The mule, now first submitting to the yoke,
All leave alike the scene where dulness dwells,
And with collected streams the ocean swells.

. . . .

Here laugh the gay, and here the wise may frown,
The country lash the follies of the town:
The townsman here may quiz the country squire,
And joke his rudeness to his heart's desire.
The maid, whom time had spoiled of every grace,
May date her triumph from a lucky race.
The beau may gain the object of his life,
And to a curricle may owe a wife.
Hence too improved the horse's noble breed,
His strength, his stature, elegance and speed.
These in the racing calendar shall shine,
And even equal, blest Arabia, thine!

The lighter side of old Charleston supplied as attractive materials as
New York furnished to Irving or Boston to Dr. Holmes, but Crafts was
not their equal in talent. He belongs with St. George Tucker, Robert Treat
Paine, and the Hartford Wits in their lighter vein. Imitative and superficial
though he was, Crafts tried to portray a most interesting aspect of American life which the abler Southern writers who followed him left almost un-
touched.

20
Hugh Swinton Legaré

ONE OF THE BEST American examples of the scholar in politics is Hugh
Swinton Legaré (1797–1843), whose learning in the law was as profound as
that of Crafts was superficial. Ten years younger than Crafts, he was a
native of Charleston, born of French Huguenot and Scottish Covenanter
ancestry going back for something like a century in this country. His father,
Solomon Legaré, died early, leaving to the care of his widow two small
daughters and an infant boy. Mary (Swinton) Legaré was in her way as
remarkable a woman as Eliza Lucas Pinckney. She managed her estate and
reared her children well, and her approval always meant more to Hugh
Legaré than that of any other person. When he was about four years of age,
he was inoculated for smallpox. Infantile paralysis set in, and for a long time

his mother carried him on a pillow everywhere he went. Although he finally recovered, for years he hardly grew at all; and afterwards, while his body developed to normal proportions, his legs remained abnormally short. Seated, he was a fine figure of a man; but when he stood up, the disproportions of his body were immediately apparent. One result of these misfortunes was to make him shy, oversensitive, and almost morbidly melancholy; another was to develop in the youth, unable to take part in normal boyish sports, a love of books and a passion for intellectual distinction. What prompted Legaré throughout his life to "scorn delights and live laborious days" was not the desire for popular applause but "the aspiring after *excellence . . . for its own sake.*"

In his Charleston teachers Legaré was more fortunate than William Gilmore Simms. After his mother his first teacher was an Englishman by the name of Ward, who found him "a boy of high talents, fine taste and great industry." Dr. Simon F. Gallagher, a Catholic priest, aroused in the youth a love for Latin literature and eloquence. Legaré studied next in a Charleston high school (which later developed into the College of Charleston) under Mitchell King. When Legaré was about thirteen, his mother sent him to the famous Willington Academy of the Reverend Moses Waddel [51] in the Carolina Up-Country. Waddel, who married a sister of John C. Calhoun, taught such men as Calhoun, A. B. Longstreet, George McDuffie, William H. Crawford, and James L. Petigru. Young Legaré found most of the students uncongenial. He disliked the Spartan régime and developed a temporary aversion to Dr. Waddel, whom Legaré's first biographer describes none too sympathetically as follows:

A leading divine of the straitest of all sects [Presbyterian], he had then (about 1829) much of its antique formality and air of being buckled-up in rigour and precision—looking such as Cotton Mather must have looked, or as Dr. Samuel Parr turned Presbyterian. In his customary canonicals of dress, manners and countenance, he seemed terribly the austere polemic and the fierce pedagogue; and, in that day of very limited scholarship, shone as a sort of Aristarch of the South. . . . Beneath his severity of aspect and pedantry of style, however, he bore a heart full of simplicity and kindliness, a sound understanding, a firm temper and great rectitude of character.

Unjustly suspected of a part in a student conspiracy, Legaré begged his mother to let him come home; but she, realizing that the shy and sensitive boy must learn to get on with all sorts of people, steadfastly refused. In the end Legaré and Dr. Waddel learned to appreciate one another's better

---

[51] According to Ralph M. Lyon in *D.A.B.*, the name was pronounced *Waddle.*

qualities, and he acknowledged in later life that he owed to the Presbyterian divine his love of the Greek classics.

In December, 1811, Legaré entered South Carolina College as a sophomore. His most congenial friend and his only scholastic rival was his Virginian friend William C. Preston, who was afterwards to travel in the British Isles with Washington Irving and to study with Legaré at Paris and Edinburgh. South Carolina College was a new institution presided over by an able native of Massachusetts, the Reverend Jonathan Maxcy, who later became President of Brown University. Elected in 1804, Maxcy had assembled a competent faculty chiefly of Northern men. While in college and for years afterwards, Legaré studied something like fifteen hours a day. Paul Hamilton Hayne records a reminiscence from one of Legaré's college mates: "Often when returning with the jovial fellows of our class from ball or party, perhaps from a secret and less legitimate expedition, to our quarters, have I remarked Legaré's candle burning long after midnight, and heard his voice, in sonorous recitation, rolling over the campus. But the moment our noisy approach caught his ear, (if it happened that we dared be noisy,) the recitations ceased; the light, however, burned on; oh, he was indefatigable; nothing could wear him down." Legaré was devoting seven hours a day to his classes and about eight to his own private studies. He was spending many hours in the State Library, which then contained nine or ten thousand volumes. He was studying oratory, too, as assiduously as Demosthenes. The students called him "Cicero." He scorned all theatrical tricks. True eloquence, he affirmed in the words of Milton, "we find to be none but *the serious and hearty love of truth.*" In college Legaré was reading in French, Italian, and Spanish (German was to come later), and he was grounding himself in the English classics as well. His favorite English author was Milton, in whose austere character and elevated style he found much that was congenial. He graduated in December, 1814, at the head of his class. Perhaps it was his constant struggle with temperamental melancholy that prompted him to choose as the subject of his valedictory "The Influence of the Imagination on Human Happiness."

For three years after his graduation Legaré studied law in Charleston under the direction of Mitchell King, now a successful attorney. He was at this time by Charleston standards ready for the practice of his profession; but aiming always at the highest excellence, he determined, after the neglected fashion of Colonial Carolinians, to study abroad. He sailed for Bordeaux in May, 1818, with the intention of studying at the University of Göttingen, whither George Ticknor and Edward Everett—the first American students to go to Germany—had gone three years earlier. Inaccurate reports of revolutionary disturbances at Göttingen caused him, after a short stay in Paris, to proceed with his friend Preston to the University of Edinburgh. There he formed an enduring friendship with George Ticknor. His chief professional study was civil law (with lectures in Latin), but he was also reading widely in Italian literature. On February 15, 1819, he wrote to his mother that his stay in Europe had taught him "to be *an American*, to feel an interest in my country, and to be proud of my privileges as one of its citizens." He was ambitious to excel in his chosen profession, but, he added, "Still, (I must not deny it) I feel my old hankering after quiet and solitary studies; and it will really be painful to me to bid adieu to them forever." After some travel on the Continent, he returned to Charleston early in 1820. For the next two years he managed his mother's plantation on John's Island and served a term in the state legislature. The plantation was sold in 1822, and he settled in Charleston to practice law. Legaré must have been surprised to learn that prospective clients were suspicious of an overeducated young lawyer who had studied in Europe. Nineteen years later he wrote to T. C. Reynolds, an American student at Heidelberg: ". . . I have found my *studies in Europe* impede me at every step of my progress. . . . Our people have a fixed aversion to every thing that looks like foreign education. . . . Nothing is more *perilous*, in America, than to be too long *learning*, and to get the name of bookish." There were doubtless many things which the studious recluse had to learn before he became a successful lawyer.

Legaré was in the state legislature in 1821–1822, 1824–1830, and was attorney-general of the state in 1830–1832. (Meanwhile he had become the chief contributor to the short-lived *Southern Review*, 1828–1832.) With little admiration for Jefferson, Legaré was at this time a Democrat. For a time he supported the antibank, antitariff, and anti-internal-improvements policies of what eventually became the Nullification party; but though a strong advocate of state rights, he balked at Nullification. In the meantime he had shown his mettle at the bar of the United States Supreme Court in arguments that so impressed the Secretary of State, Edward Livingston, that he persuaded Andrew Jackson to offer Legaré the post of chargé d'affaires at Brussels. The triumph of the Nullification party in 1832 made him glad to accept it. On shipboard he tried to drive away his melancholy by reading in the original a Greek tragedy each day. In Brussels his salary was inadequate, but his duties were light and he found time to renew his legal studies with Savigny and to master German. On October 10, 1841, he was to write: "I am quite sure if I had gone to Gottingen, as I intended, in my youth, instead of going to Edinburgh, I might have dispensed with half the books I have since found to be unworthy of notice from a critical student.

The Germans are now, and have for some time past, been treating this very subject of the philosophy of society and legislation in a style peculiar to themselves, for they distance all other inquirers, both in vast and accurate research and in acute criticism."

During his four years in Brussels Legaré's thoughts were still often in Charleston. "If the Union should go to pieces," he wrote to I. E. Holmes, October 2, 1832, "it will be one hideous wreck,—of which, excepting New-England, no two parts will hold together." On April 8 of the following year he wrote to Holmes: "When I read your '[Nullification] Ordinance,' I rubbed my eyes to be sure if I was not in a dream. I could not believe it *possible* that such insolent tyranny was in the heart of any man. . . ." His friend James Louis Petigru—later to become known as the "Union Man of South Carolina"—wrote to him, July 15, 1833: "But nullification has done its work. It has prepared the minds of men for a separation of the States, and when the question is mooted again it will be distinctly Union or Disunion."

Charleston society seemed to Legaré immensely superior to that to be found anywhere else in America, even in Boston, but he saw signs of decay in the Low-Country. He wrote to Holmes in April, 1833: "I ask of heaven only that the little circle I am intimate with in Charleston should be kept together while I live,—in health, harmony and competence; and that, on my return, I may myself be enabled to enjoy the same happiness, in my intercourse with it, with which I have been hitherto blessed. *We* are (I am quite sure) the *last* of the *race* of South-Carolina; I see nothing before us but decay and downfall,—but, on that very account, I cherish its precious relics the more." After the Civil War Paul Hamilton Hayne was to quote Legaré's gloomy forebodings and speak of them as "A prophecy how dreadfully fulfilled!" On April 14, 1839, Legaré wrote from Charleston to Stephen Elliott, Jr.: "This City is said to be prosperous—relatively—I'm glad to hear it— tho' I think their prosperity is not in the way of morals or intellect. The South Carolina in which & for which I was educated, has some how or other disappeared, & left a *simulacrum* behind of a very different kind—which I don't understand, neither am understood by it."

Legaré returned to South Carolina in 1836 and was promptly elected to Congress as a Union Democrat. He showed his sympathy with the Whigs by taking a conservative stand on financial questions. At the expiration of his term, he returned to Charleston and at last built up a remunerative law practice. In the fall of 1841 he became Attorney-General in President John Tyler's cabinet and now for the first time found a full practical use for his legal erudition. Even yet, however, the sensitive scholar-statesman felt that many persons regarded him as an unpractical bookworm. Walking to the Capitol in January, 1842, to address the Supreme Court, he said to a companion: "It has been said that I am a mere literary man; but I will show them to-day whether I am a lawyer or not." He won his case.

Benjamin F. Perry, who shared Legaré's Unionist views, wrote in 1849: ". . . in my opinion he comes up nearer to the finished Orator than any man I ever did hear. . . . He had as fine a voice as I ever heard, & as complete controll of it. . . ." Mrs. St. Julien Ravenel remembered Legaré's musical voice. It was, she said, "an organ of many stops. He loved to read poetry aloud, and nothing could be finer than his tones in Manfred's soliloquy, or Dryden's 'long-resounding line.' "

On Webster's withdrawal from the cabinet, Legaré was made Secretary of State *ad interim* on May 8, 1843. His health, however, had begun to fail, and he was deeply saddened by the deaths of his mother and one of his two sisters. He went to Boston with the President in June to take part in the unveiling of the Bunker Hill Monument, and there he became critically ill. He died at the home of his friend George Ticknor on June 20, 1843. Soon afterwards Ticknor wrote to a friend: ". . . just as the country, divided about everything else, was beginning to look with great unanimity to him, from a perfect confidence alike in his talents, his principles, and his honor, —it was, indeed, just when he felt sure he was at once to 'burst out into sudden blaze,' that 'the blind Fury came, and slit the thin-spun life.' " [52] He was buried in Mount Auburn Cemetery in Cambridge, but fourteen years later his remains were reinterred in Magnolia Cemetery in Charleston.

The literary student is likely to condemn Legaré and men like him for not giving their best to literature. We should remember that it was not only Southerners who thought that a literary reputation was a handicap in the legal and other professions. John Quincy Adams, who in a later era might have been a man of letters, once wrote: "But there is no small number of very worthy citizens among us irrevocably convinced that it is impossible to be at once a man of business and a man of rhyme, and who, if they knew me for instance to be the author of the two pieces inclosed [verses for the *Port Folio*], would need no other proof that I ought immediately to be *impeached* for incapacity as a public servant." In his letter of October 10, 1841, from which I have quoted, Legaré wrote from Washington: "I could

---

[52] *Life, Letters, and Journals of George Ticknor* (7th ed.; Boston, 1877), II, 213. Ticknor had written in his journal on May 4, 1836: "His conversation is very rich. . . . He is a good scholar, with a good and rather severe taste; a wise and deep thinker. . . . I knew him very well at Edinburgh in 1819, and thought him then an uncommon person; but it is plain he has taken a much higher tone than I then anticipated" (*ibid.*, I, 488–489).

never reconcile myself to the idea of what is called a 'literary life'—that is, to a life contemplative and epicurean, however elegant, sloth, as contra-distinguished from one passed in the midst of the business of men, in promoting the great actual interests of society. Not to act on the minds of one's contemporaries, seems to me to be living in vain." Legaré would have agreed with Justice Oliver Wendell Holmes, who wrote in his *Collected Legal Papers* (1921): "But after all the place for a man who is complete in all his powers is in the fight. The professor, the man of letters, gives up one-half of life that his protected talent may grow and flower in peace. But to make up your mind at your peril upon a living question, for purposes of action, calls upon your whole nature."

Legaré's mind was that of a philosophical lawyer. His conception of the law was that which he ascribed to Cicero:

His idea is that laws are the recorded morality of nations, and law-givers the most effective teachers of virtue—that they give to the abstractions of philosophy, so to express it, a tangible and living form—clothe maxims, embracing the most important truths and the most refined ethics, with the awful authority of a public sanction, and bring their precepts to bear upon the conduct of life and the interests and business of mankind, with the plastic and controlling influence of a daily, permanent, and authoritative social discipline.

For one who held such beliefs, it was natural that Legaré, like most later Southern political figures, should fail to appreciate fully the economic forces that lie behind legislation. He was no reformer, and he had no high regard for Jefferson or Jackson. He had no use at all for "the hair-brained metaphysicians and empirical demagogues that brought France, at last, to the brink of ruin." "The maxim of the true statesman," he said recalling the motto of the Emperor Augustus, "is *festina lente*."

Most of Legaré's literary work appeared in the *Southern Review* (1828–1832). Charleston gentlemen admired the British quarterlies and after the launching òf the *North American Review* in 1815, felt a little jealous of Boston. As South Carolina found itself increasingly out of sympathy with the North, these gentlemen believed their state and section needed an organ. It perhaps never occurred to them that, as William J. Grayson was to write: "It is reversing the natural order of production to begin a Country's literature with a Quarterly Review. We should begin with books to be reviewed." In their prospectus the founders announced: "It shall be among our first objects to vindicate the rights and privileges, the character of the Southern States, to arrest, if possible, the current which has been directed so steadily against our country generally, and the South in particular;

and to offer to our fellow citizens one Journal which they may read without finding themselves the objects of perpetual sarcasm, or of affected commiseration."

The first editor was Stephen Elliott, banker and botanist. He was followed by Stephen Elliott, Jr., who later became an Episcopal bishop.[53] He in turn was followed by Legaré, who had been from the beginning the most voluminous contributor. Others who wrote for the *Review* were Thomas Cooper, Robert Y. Hayne, James L. Petigru, Dr. S. H. Dickson, Professor Henry Junius Knott, George McDuffie, William Elliott, Samuel Gilman, David J. McCord, and several others. When it was proposed to revive the *Review* in 1835, Legaré wrote to his sister from Aix-la-Chapelle: "I would not do again what I did for it before for any compensation. It has dimmed my eyes and whitened my hair (at least, helped to do so) before my time, and I am no longer capable of that sort of excitement,—besides various other reasons." The motives that impelled him to labor on the *Review* appear in a letter which he wrote to his friend Huger on November 21, of the same year:

My *immense labor* for the Southern Review, (which they saddled me with, as if it had been an hereditary estate,) do you think I went through so many nights (summer nights, too) of watching and toil, because I hoped to be spoken of with some terms of compliment in our own newspapers, or even by foreigners? If so, why don't I write *now*, when pressed to do so? No—no. I thought I could help to shew that people did not know what our race was:—I *felt* that, in speaking its language, I should be thought eloquent,—and I have not been mistaken. But I wrote as an American, and, especially, as a Carolinian. . . .

In reviewing Legaré's literary remains, George Frederick Holmes lamented "that Legaré has left no solid work behind him; that his remains are so scanty, and that they consist either of unfinished outlines, or disconnected essays. . . ." The essays are review-articles of the quarterly type, long, substantial, learned, and—for the modern reader—heavy and often tedious. American reviewers were seldom able to emulate the charm and sprightliness of Jeffrey, Sydney Smith, and Macaulay. Legaré more than once expressed a preference for "colloquial ease and simplicity," but he attained them only momentarily in his letters. In his *Eulogy* William C. Preston, who notes that Legaré wrote much as he spoke, thus characterizes his style: "His style is copious and elaborate; his sentences, in general, stately and measured and constructed with a view to harmony. It was, perhaps, originally formed on that of Dugald Stewart, and the writers of his school, who followed him

---

[53] Bishop Elliott was the father of Sarah Barnwell Elliott (1848–1928), author of *Jerry* (1891) and other novels.

in the Edinburgh Review. . . . There was, as he wrote more, a gradual approximation to a simpler elegance, the result of a more perfect art."

The essays in which Legaré was most at home were those on legal or classical subjects: "Classical Learning," "Roman Literature," "The Constitutional History of Greece," "Demosthenes, the Man, the Statesman and the Orator," "The Origin, History and Influence of Roman Legislation." [54] In literary matters he was ostensibly a classicist. He refused to "indulge in the pleasing day-dreams of perfectibility." He did not care for the French Romantic school, and while admiring Rousseau's "matchless style," he thought that never perhaps had a writer "exercised a more terrible influence." He thought the work of the English Romantic poets "all *bombastic*—even Wordsworth's, who loves such infantine simplicity." He upheld the idea of the Greeks: "Three things were considered as essential to all excellence, in a composition of genius, perfect unity of purpose, simplicity of style, and ease of execution—and it is in these things that the literature and art of Greece exhibit their matchless perfection." Legaré, however, was less the classicist than he thought, for in the middle of his essay on "Classical Learning" he proceeded to define poetry in Romantic terms which sound like the concluding paragraphs of Poe's "The Poetic Principle." He found the true spirit and essence of poetry "spread over the whole face of nature," "in every lofty sentiment, in every deep passion, in every bright vision of fancy," "in the still more mysterious connection between the heart of man and the forms and beauties of inanimate nature, as if they were instinct with a soul and a sensibility like our own. . . ." He had a great admiration for Byron—he regarded *Manfred* as the poet's masterpiece—and concluded the first of two essays on him:

> Upon the whole, excepting the two first places in our literature—and Pope and Dryden who are writers of quite another stamp—we do not know who is to be placed, all things considered, above Byron. We doubt between him and Spenser—but no other name is prominent enough to present itself to us in such a competition. His greatest rival, however, was himself. We throw down his book dissatisfied. Every page reveals powers which might have done so much more for art—for glory—and for virtue!

Legaré's criticism of literature—not adequately represented in his collected works—is always interesting and generally sound. His only conspicuous failure is seen in his extravagant estimate of Pollok's *The Course of Time*. He saw, however, as clearly as Macaulay, the worthlessness of the

[54] R. W. Emerson, who borrowed a copy of Legaré's *Writings*, found some good things in the essay on Demosthenes (*Journals*, VII, 243, Feb. 15, 1847; *Letters*, ed. R. L. Rusk, III, 373).

pretentious verses of Robert Montgomery. He estimated at their true weight
the novels and poems of Bulwer-Lytton. In "Sir Philip Sidney's Miscellanies," while he did not recognize fully the merits of Sidney's poems, he
wrote a notable appreciation of the "Defence of Poetry." As Sidney, he
thought, had defended poetry against the Puritans, so now it must be defended against the Utilitarians and other economists of the day. In "Jeremy
Bentham and the Utilitarians" [55] he recognized Bentham as "a most vigorous
and original thinker" who continually dressed up "plain matters in the
mysteries of artificial language," as economists still sometimes do. He saw
that Utilitarianism bore a close relation to the teachings of Epicurus. He objected vigorously to the Utilitarian proscription of poetry and eloquence. "Its
inevitable tendency, if not its avowed object, is to chill enthusiasm, to ex-
tinguish sensibility, to substitute wary, and even crafty calculation, for the
native goodness of an uncorrupted heart." In the eyes of the Utilitarians,
he complained, "A sin, a vice, a crime, is only an error in arithmetic—not,
perhaps, a very venial one, because it were a foul reproach not to know what
it is so easy to learn, the multiplication-table of this infallible school!" His
review of Scott's *The Fair Maid of Perth* contains a judicious appraisal of
the merits and shortcomings of one of the poorest of the Waverley novels.
His "Early Spanish Ballads" reveals alike Legaré's literary taste and his fine
scholarship.

Legaré's standards were high, and his estimate of American literature was
not flattering. On November 3, 1828, he wrote to a young contributor, Jesse
Burton Harrison, a Virginian who following his graduation from Harvard
was about to study in Germany:

I rejoice to hear you are going to Germany. . . . Let me exhort you to lay hold
of Greek and not to look back until you die. All other literature is wretched
in finish and elegance when compared with the Ionian. It is a hard thing to
acquire a competent knowledge of it, but every good thing is hard to be got.
The Irvings & Coopers & Percivals *et id omne genus* (of whom, by the bye,
you have a higher idea than I have) won't do. The soil must be properly
manured & broken up before it will produce a majestic & vigorous growth. I
think very little *entre nous* of those Northern smatterers. Dr. Johnson's notion
of the Scotch, that every man had a mouthful & no man a bellyful of knowledge,
applies to the trans Potomac people. They have yet to acquire the very rudi-
ments of scholarship. I never met a Northern man, except one or two, that had
any idea (& then not until he had been in Europe) what the word scholarship
means. You think no doubt very differently. You have, *I judge from your style,*

[55] *Southern Rev.,* VII, 261–296 (Aug., 1831). This essay effectively exposes John
Neal's ignorance of philosophy and the French language. Neal had published a translation of Dumont's edition of Bentham's *Principles of Legislation.*

been educated at Cambridge [Harvard]. But you will agree with me when you
have lived thirty years or so in the world. The Bostonians, however, are in a
fair way to improve, but, as for Philadelphia, New York, etc., "Souvenirs" [gift-
books and annuals] and such stuff will satisfy their tastes and their capacities
for some time to come.

Legaré's review of the literary remains of William Crafts is, as I have
noted, a model of critical analysis. Although he had known and loved the
most conspicuous writer his state had yet produced, Legaré showed not the
slightest disposition to overpraise Crafts on that account. He was quite as
impartial in his criticism of Irving, Cooper, Percival, and Bryant. In reviewing the *Life of Columbus*, he gave Irving full credit for his humor, his vivid
descriptions, and his charming style. He thought Irving at his best when
writing on American themes and rated *Knickerbocker's History of New
York* as "among the permanent monuments of our literature."

Legaré reviewed two of Fenimore Cooper's less known novels. He regarded *The Wept of Wish-ton-Wish* as a failure. Preferring the sea stories,
he thought that Cooper had "exhausted even his forest craft." Scott's Puritans seemed to him better-drawn than Cooper's. "Except in Leather-Stocking, his common Sailors, and his Indians—he has failed in the delineation
of character." Cooper seemed to him "rather an admirer of external nature,
than a close observer of human conduct in society. His inspiration is upon
him in the solitudes of the ocean and the wilderness, not in the crowded
haunts of men. Hence, his characters are at home in their collision with
savages and the mute and inanimate creation, but not in the companionship
of their fellows." Legaré reviewed Cooper's *The Bravo*[56] more sympathetically because, as he said: "It was our happy fortune to wander with
our author through many of the favourite scenes of Italy, and hence we can
both appreciate and vouch for his glowing descriptions." He believed the
book would sustain Cooper's reputation; and although he thought the story
should have ended sooner, he had high praise for even Cooper's women
characters.

In reviewing the *Poems* (1832) of Bryant, Legaré confessed that although
he had often heard Bryant's name mentioned, he had read none of his earlier
poems. The book struck him as "upon the whole, the best collection of
American poetry which we have ever seen." He had high praise for Bryant's
diction: "It is simple and natural—there is no straining after effect, no
meretricious glare, no affected point and brilliancy. It is clear and

[56] *Ibid.*, VIII, 382–399 (Feb., 1832). Legaré was struck with a certain resemblance
between the Venice of *The Bravo* and the declining Charleston of his own time (VIII,
398).

precise. . . ." "To say of a writer that his language is simple, natural, precise, idiomatic—and to add of what he writes that it is poetical, is to pronounce him one whom the gods have made a poet and who can make himself what he pleases. This is to us the charm of Mr. Bryant's verses. They flow spontaneously from a heart softened by the most touching sensibilities, and they clothe themselves in the very language which nature has adapted, and as it were consecrated to the expression of those sensibilities."

In the prose writers of this period we have noted the waning influence of Revolutionary liberalism and the gradual change in the Southern attitude toward slavery. In the poets, who are next to be considered, we shall remark the struggle between Neoclassicism and Romanticism and the gradual shift to new literary subject matter and literary values. The increasing conservatism in Southern thought, however, prevented most of the poets from being deeply influenced by that side of the Romantic movement concerned with changing the social and economic order. It will be noted that, as in the Northern states, the poets received less encouragement than the writers of prose.

21
Washington Allston

ALLSTON (1779–1843), the first American named for George Washington to rise to prominence, was born on a plantation on the Waccamaw River in South Carolina not far from Georgetown. The site is now a part of the Brookgreen Gardens. On both sides Allston was descended from ancestors who had settled in the province in the seventeenth century. His mother, the beautiful Rachel Moore, who lived to be painted by her son in 1809, was three-fourths French Huguenot. To please her parents, she became in 1775 the second wife of the wealthy planter, Captain William Allston. She had been in love with a cousin whom she believed to be dead. On one memorable occasion while her husband was away in General Francis Marion's little army, she was living in her "sea-shore house" when a ship was wrecked on the coast. The sole survivor, who sought shelter in her house, proved to be her lost lover. She fainted, and when she recovered, he was gone. Soon afterwards he died in Charleston of yellow fever. In 1781 Captain Allston came home from the Battle of Cowpens to die, poisoned, it was thought, by a trusted servant. The Allston house was once Cornwallis' headquarters. After the war Mrs. Allston, having married once, as she said, to please her parents, now married to please herself. Her second husband was Dr. Henry C. Flagg, chief of the medical staff in Greene's army and the son of a wealthy shipping merchant in Newport, Rhode Island. The marriage displeased her parents and friends, who considered Dr. Flagg's social position far below that of a Low-Country planter's daughter. Her father said she had "married a Yankee adventurer, and poverty should be her portion."

Meanwhile young Washington Allston's love for "the wild and marvellous" was being developed by the tales of witches and hags which the Negro servants told him. He had discovered a passion for drawing, and his first sketches were so good that Dr. and Mrs. Flagg were afraid the boy would disgrace them by becoming a professional painter. At the age of eight he was sent to Newport to be prepared for college by Robert Rogers. In Newport, Allston became acquainted with Edward G. Malbone, the miniature painter; William Ellery Channing; and Channing's sister Ann, whom he was to marry in 1809. In Newport he continued to make pictures, and he did more painting while in Harvard College, from which he graduated in 1800. One of his college friends, Leonard Jarvis, described Allston as

distinguished by the grace of his movements and his gentlemanly deportment. His countenance, once seen, could never be forgotten. His smooth, high, open forehead surrounded by a profusion of dark wavy hair, his delicately formed nose, his peculiarly expressive mouth, his large, lustrous, melting eye which varied with every emotion and his complexion of most beautiful Italian cast, smooth and colorless yet healthy, all blending harmoniously formed a face which was irresistibly attractive and which united with his gentle unassuming manners secured him the goodwill of all his classmates.

Practically self-taught as a painter, Allston studied the paintings of Robert Pine in the Columbian Museum in Boston and a copy of one of Van Dyck's portraits made by John Smibert years before. His early paintings show the influence of his reading in the Gothic romances and the poems of Churchill and Southey. Some of the subjects of early paintings were taken from Mrs. Radcliffe's *The Mysteries of Udolpho* and Schiller's *The Robbers*. He was writing verses, too, some of which appeared in the Boston *Centinell*. He was chosen class poet, and his poem, "Energy of Character," was regarded as a success.

After his graduation Allston returned to Charleston, which now boasted two miniature painters, Malbone and Charles Fraser. Dr. Flagg wished Allston to study medicine, but it was finally arranged that the young artist should study art in Europe. Allston disposed of part of his share in the family estates at a considerable sacrifice, and in May, 1801, accompanied by Malbone, he sailed for England. He found the English countryside "beyond my expectation, beautiful and picturesque," but London struck the young Federalist as made up altogether of "princes and beggars." In September, 1801, he was admitted to the Royal Academy, then presided over by another American, Benjamin West, who pronounced Allston's work full of promise. Allston admired West, Fuseli, and a few other painters; but as for most of the portrait painters, he wrote to Fraser in unusually emphatic language, "they are the damnedest stupid wretches that ever disgraced a profession." In the same letter, August 25, 1801, he said that he was "about (*mirabile dictu*) to publish a book." He was still writing verses, but he did not publish a book for some years. By this time he had discovered Spenser's *The Faerie Queene*, which inspired several of his paintings; and the verses contained in his letters show that his taste was influenced by the strong drift toward Romanticism. He wrote to John Knapp, August 24, 1803: "My profession will always be painting, but I have not serenaded the Muses so many cold wintry nights for nothing; they shall grant me a favor before I die."

In November, 1803, during a lull in the Napoleonic wars he went with John Vanderlyn to Paris, where he reveled in the works of art with which Napoleon was filling the Louvre. There he met William Hazlitt, then an art student and not yet the famous essayist. What interested Allston most was the poetry of color that he found in the paintings of Rubens, Titian, and others. In November, 1804, he settled in Rome. There he studied the great masters Raphael, Titian, Michael Angelo, and Da Vinci. In Rome he came to know Thorwaldsen, Washington Irving, and Samuel Taylor Coleridge. The youthful Irving was so fascinated by Allston that he seriously considered abandoning the law for painting. Many years later he wrote:

There was something, to me, inexpressibly engaging in the appearance and manners of Allston. I do not think I have ever been more completely captivated on a first acquaintance. He was of a light and graceful form, with large blue eyes and black silken hair, waving and curling round a pale expressive countenance. Everything about him bespoke the man of intellect and refinement. His conversation was copious, animated, and highly graphic; warmed by a genial sensibility and benevolence, and enlivened at times by a chaste and gentle humor.

More important for Allston was his friendship with Coleridge, of whom he wrote to William Dunlap years later: ". . . to no other man whom I have known, do I owe so much intellectually, as to Mr. Coleridge, with whom I became acquainted in Rome, and who has honored me with his friendship for more than five and twenty years. . . . It was there he taught me this golden rule: *never to judge of any work of art by its defects*; a rule as wise as benevolent; and one that while it has spared me much pain, has widened my sphere of pleasure." On June 17, 1806, Coleridge wrote to Allston: "To you & to you alone since I have left England, I have felt more, and had I not known the Wordsworths, should have loved & esteemed you *first* and *most*, and as it is, next to them I love & honor you." In 1822 Coleridge in a letter to a friend described Allston as a man of "high and rare Genius . . . whether I contemplate him in the character of a Poet, a Painter, or a philosophic Analyst. . . ." [57] So highly did Coleridge think of Allston's poem "America to Great Britain" that he included it in his *Sibylline Leaves* (1817) as the work of "an American Gentleman, a valued and dear friend." Allston painted two portraits of Coleridge, the later of which Wordsworth thought incomparably the best picture of the poet.[58]

In 1808 after an absence of seven years Allston returned to Boston. He married Dr. Channing's sister Ann, to whom he had long been engaged. Again we hear of his writing verses, and in 1811 he read a poem before the Phi Beta Kappa Society at Harvard. Later in the same year with his wife and a pupil, Samuel F. B. Morse, he returned to England. There he remained until 1818, experiencing no hostile treatment during the War of 1812–1815. He renewed his friendship with Coleridge, who was now back in England, and he won the esteem of Southey, Wordsworth, and Lamb, who like Coleridge, admired his poems and paintings. Certain lines in Wordsworth's "Composed upon an Evening of Extraordinary Splendor" were suggested by Allston's painting, "Jacob's Dream":

> Wings at my shoulder seem to play;
> But, rooted here, I stand and gaze
> On those bright steps that heavenward raise
> Their practicable way.

"In these lines," said Wordsworth, "I am under obligation to the exquisite picture of 'Jacob's Dream,' by Mr. Allston, now in America. It is pleasant to make this acknowledgment to a man of genius, whom I have the honor to rank among my friends."

In 1813 Allston published in London *The Sylphs of the Seasons, with Other Poems*, which was republished in Boston in the same year. On July 10 Morse wrote to his parents: "By the way, Mr. Allston has just published a volume of poems, a copy of which I will endeavor to send you. They are but just published, so that the opinion of the public is not yet ascertained,

---

[57] Earl Leslie Griggs (ed.), *Unpublished Letters of Samuel Taylor Coleridge* (1933), II, 305–306. The influence which Coleridge and Allston had upon each other's work deserves closer study than has yet been given to it.
[58] See Plates XII and XXX in Edgar P. Richardson, *Washington Allston* (1948).

but there is no doubt they will forever put at rest the calumny that America has never produced a poet."

As a painter Allston enjoyed considerable success in England, and possibly his artistic career might have been more distinguished if he had remained there. In 1818, however, shortly before his election to the Royal Academy, he returned to Boston. The death of his wife in February, 1815, had saddened him and made him lonely. He was homesick for America. He once said: "I know the faults of my country, and there are few Americans who feel them more than I do, or have less confidence in our form of government, but I cannot endure to hear my country abused by a foreigner. It makes my blood boil." Coleridge thought that Allston's wife was largely responsible for the artist's sensitiveness to British opinion and believed that he had made a mistake in returning to America.[59] In England, however, Allston had done much to correct the notions of America held by his British friends. Robert Southey in *The Vision of Judgment* spoke of the departing poet as

> he who, returning
> Rich in praise to his native shores, hath left a remembrance
> Long to be honour'd and loved on the banks of Thames and of Tiber:
> So may America, prizing in time the worth she possesses,
> Give to that hand free scope, and boast hereafter of Allston.

Allston brought home with him his unfinished canvas "Belshazzar's Feast," which he hoped would be his masterpiece; but, like Benjamin Haydon's "Triumphal Entry," it was destined never to be completed. Allston's final return to America by no means marks the end of his painting, as Van Wyck Brooks has suggested in *The Flowering of New England*. Mr. Brooks in 1936, I suspect, was still laboring under his early impression that the American environment is the worst in which any artist can live. In America, however, Allston did find less understanding of his art than he had found in Rome and London. Art, as it was best understood in New England, meant literature; and in 1818, as in 1808, when he returned from his first stay in Europe, Allston found himself stimulated rather to write than to paint.

[59] See Richardson, *Allston*, pp. 113–114. Maria Gisborne, who had spent the previous evening "with the great Coleridge," wrote in her diary on June 25, 1820: "He maintains his former admiration and partiality for Allston the painter; he regretted that his first wife, strongly attached to him, but illiterate and narrow minded, should have succeeded in filling his mind with prejudices, as to the injustice done to the Americans by the English, and to such a degree that with the strongest preference for England, he left that country to settle in America for ever" (from a photostatic copy of the original in the British Museum). Ann Channing Allston was neither illiterate nor narrow-minded, but she obviously resented the British attitude toward Americans.

In 1830 Allston allied himself with another prominent New England family by marrying Martha Dana, sister of the elder Richard Henry Dana. For the remainder of his life he made his home in Cambridgeport. In spite of his Southern birth and his long residence abroad, he became for Boston and Cambridge the beau ideal of the artist. He continued to paint, but he liked better to sit up until after midnight reading or talking with his friends. He enjoyed a reputation as the foremost living American painter. The Unionists in South Carolina wished him to paint a historical picture for Charleston, and others besought him to paint a panel in the Capitol in Washington; but political subjects did not interest him—and there was the unfinished "Belshazzar's Feast" which worried him. In another country and another phase of his artistic development it was difficult to recapture the right mood for completing it. He died on July 9, 1843. On July 21 Emerson wrote to his brother William: "Mr. Allston was buried the night of the full moon and I know not by what chance the funeral [was] so belated that when they came to the tomb it was evening & the moon shone full on the beautiful white statue as all who desired to see the body were permitted to do so."

In his "Cambridge Thirty Years Ago" James Russell Lowell left a memorable description of the aged painter and poet. He emphasized Allston's fastidious neatness, his refinement, the predominance in him of the spiritual over the physical. To him Allston was one of those rare spirits "whom Nature sends into the world to fill the arduous office of Gentleman." Seventeen years after Allston's death Longfellow wrote in a memorandum: "One man may sweeten a whole town. I never pass through Cambridge Port without thinking of Allston. His memory is the quince in the drawer, and perfumes the atmosphere."

Lowell pronounced Allston certainly "the greatest English painter of historical subjects." Later critics did not sustain the verdict of Allston's contemporaries. Poetic painting went out of fashion, and Allston's pictures came to seem an incongruous mixture of the pseudoclassical and the Romantic. There are indications, however, that there may be something like an Allston revival. Edgar P. Richardson's *Washington Allston: A Study of the Romantic Artist in America* (1948) is a brilliant and sympathetic study of the painter-poet. Allston's greatest influence, as Richardson points out, was not upon American painters but upon New England writers. There were few of them who did not know and admire him.

Allston's reputation as a poet was much less than his fame as a painter, and yet it was sufficient to induce Griswold in 1842 to dedicate to him *The Poets and Poetry of America*. Allston's writings represent a secondary impulse but a persistent one, and he wrote more in New England than in England or Italy. About half his poems were written after his final return to America in 1818. His poems are, like those of Blake and Rossetti, the work of a poetic painter. Not only do they reveal his love of form and color but they also indicate that, like Wordsworth, he tried to keep his eye on the object when he wrote. In prose as in verse he is usually at his best in descriptive passages or in passages interpreting paintings whether his own or those of some greater painter. One finds in his poems the tendency to reverie and the sense of the mysterious and the tragic which characterizes many of his best pictures. There is a certain distinction of style in all that he wrote. This it was that undoubtedly prompted Lowell to say that the really artistic spirit first came to expression in America in *The Sylphs of the Seasons*. One should not forget that Allston's little volume appeared eight years before Bryant published his *Poems* (1821) and four years before the unfinished "Thanatopsis" appeared in the *North American Review*. There was Freneau of course; but Freneau, while an important figure, was less the artist than Allston. Satire and propaganda play too large a part in Freneau's work just as an ingrained didacticism often mars the writing of Allston's New England successors.

When the definitive history of American poetry is written, Allston will have a definite place in it as a pioneer. Intrinsically, his poems are less important. To use his friend Coleridge's distinction, they have too much fancy and too little imagination. His verses are the work of a man of taste and sentiment rather than of a great poet. Some of the later verses strike a higher note. One of the best of these is "Art." "Gloria Mundi" and "The Atonement" have a certain religious mysticism that reminds one of Wordsworth. A few of the better poems—"Rosalie," for example—are interpretations of his own paintings. And yet he told Mrs. Jameson that the conception of this poem and of the painting, "Rosalie Listening to Music," as best he could recall, "had been simultaneous in his mind."

Allston was one of the first American poets to cultivate the sonnet form. As an example, I give his "Sonnet on the Group of the Three Angels before the Tent of Abraham, by Raffaele, in the Vatican." The elder Dana remarked of the poem: "How poetically philosophical . . . and how perfectly true it is when applied to his own works in the art." At least the sonnet suggests something of the delight with which the youthful Allston beheld for the first time the work of the Italian master.

> Oh, now I feel as though another sense,
> From Heaven descending, had informed my soul;
> I feel the pleasurable, full control

Of Grace, harmonious, boundless, and intense.
In thee, celestial Group, embodied lives
The subtile mystery, that speaking gives
Itself resolved; the essences combined
Of Motion ceaseless, Unity complete.
Borne like a leaf by some soft eddying wind,
Mine eyes, impelled as by enchantment sweet,
From part to part with circling motion rove,
Yet seem unconscious of the power to move,
From line to line through endless changes run,
O'er countless shapes, yet seem to gaze on One.

At first glance it seems that Allston's poems might have been wholly the work of an English poet who had never seen America. The scenery is oftener English or Italian than American. The poet's strong national feeling, however, comes out in "America to Great Britain," which is in effect a plea for "the moral union of the two countries" written long before the time of Winston Churchill or even of Henry James. Yet to Allston, who was impressed by Wordsworth's poems of childhood, the recollections of his own boyhood in the South Carolina Low-Country must have seemed worth cherishing.[60] There are echoes of them in his later paintings and in later poems, like "The Calycanthus," which he inscribed to his mother. Among the scenes of his childhood in South Carolina he recalls:

The aged Oak, whose moss-beard hoary
Waved to the fitful evening wind,
Was but the spirit of some Ogre, bound
In other shape, and doomed, for cruel thirst
Of infant's blood, to quit his form accursed,—
Then rooted to enchanted ground.

.   .   .   .   .   .

Ah, never will return those loving days
So loath to part,—those fond, reluctant rays
That seemed to haunt the summer's eve.
And, O, what charm of magic numbers
Can give me back those gentle slumbers
Those weary, happy days did leave,

[60] "The most important traits he derived from his South Carolina environment seem to have been a love of the magical acquired from the Negroes' ghost stories, a southern charm of manner, and the personal pride of a southerner of good family" (Richardson, *Allston*, p. 28). William Gilmore Simms, reviewing *Monaldi* in the *Magnolia* (N.S. I, 381, Dec., 1842), complained that Northern writers seldom mentioned the fact that Allston was born in South Carolina.

When by my bed I saw my Mother kneel,
And with her blessing took her nightly kiss?
Whatever Time destroys, he cannot this,—
E'en now that hallowed kiss I feel.

Allston's prose consists chiefly of a series of lectures on art, of which only four were completed and published, and *Monaldi: A Tale*, a Gothic novelette. *Monaldi* had been written for Dana's *The Idle Man* about 1822, but was not published before its appearance in book form in 1841.[61] Readers of Poe and Hawthorne will recall that in America the Gothic tradition continued down to at least the middle of the century. Allston's early reading provided him with conventional characters and stage properties. The setting is Mrs. Radcliffe's favorite background, Italy, which Allston knew better than she did. There are caverns, mountains, a beautiful heroine who is the incarnation of purity, two deep-dyed villains, revenge, and madness. In such a setting Allston has placed a story of jealousy, revenge, and insanity that makes one think of *Hamlet* and *Othello* as well as of *The Italian* and *The Monk*. *Monaldi* is the story of two artists: Maldura, who is a poetaster, and Monaldi, a great painter. In early life Maldura, who has talent but not genius, had dominated the passive but gifted Monaldi; in mature life Maldura is a failure as a poet while Monaldi as a painter enjoys great success. When Maldura learns that the beautiful Rosalia Landi, whom he had courted in vain, is the bride of Monaldi, he plans a revenge worthy of Iago. Through the instrumentality of the fascinating villain Count Fialto he drives Monaldi to jealousy and madness. In the end Maldura repents and takes refuge in a monastery.

So died Maldura; from whose miserable life may be learned this useful lesson: that without virtue, the love of praise is a curse; that distinction is the consequence—not the object, of a great mind; that it cannot be made so without the desire of supplanting; and that envy, jealousy, or any similar feeling—whatever the pursuit—may always be regarded by those who have them, as sure warnings that the true love of excellence is not in them—without which nothing great and permanent ever was produced.

Although Allston here points the moral much too directly for modern taste, one may doubt whether the didactic intent was uppermost in his mind when he wrote the tale. The best portions of it are the incidental comments on art and the descriptions of Rome and the Italian mountains. Italy and Italian art fascinated Allston's mind more than did either England,

[61] There was a second edition in Boston in 1856. Steele MacKaye dramatized it for the New York stage in 1872.

New England, or South Carolina. Italy was for him what it has been for
so many artists and writers from many lands since the time of Chaucer. If
Allston accomplished nothing more, he did at least cultivate in his countrymen—before Longfellow, Lowell, and Charles Eliot Norton—a love of the
art and the literature of the Old World.

22
William Munford

WILLIAM MUNFORD (1775–1825), the first American translator of the
Iliad, was born in Mecklenburg County in Southside Virginia. He was the
only son of Colonel Robert Munford, the Revolutionary poet and playwright, and of Anne (Beverley) Munford, a granddaughter of Robert Beverley the historian. Robert Munford died in 1784 leaving his "Richland"
plantation encumbered with debt. His son, who was a sickly child, was sent
first to an academy in Petersburg and, at twelve, to the Grammar School of
William and Mary College. In 1790 George Wythe, hearing that Munford
was about to leave school for lack of money, took him into his own home.
He supervised Munford's studies in Greek, Spanish, and Italian, and later in
law. In 1791, when Wythe became Judge in the Court of Chancery, he took
Munford to Richmond with him. More than any one else, Wythe was
responsible for Munford's lifelong interest in Homer. In 1793 Munford
returned to Williamsburg to attend the law lectures of St. George Tucker,
who also read the young poet's verses. For a time Munford practiced law
with some success in Southside Virginia. In 1798 he was elected to the House
of Delegates as a Republican and in 1802 to the State Senate, where he served
until 1806. In 1802 he married Sally Radford of Richmond. In 1806, having
been elected to the Privy Council, or Council of State, he moved his family
to Richmond, where he lived for the rest of his life. After five years he gave
up his post on the Privy Council to become Clerk of the House of Delegates,
a position which he held until his death in 1825. Until 1821 he edited and
published the decisions of the Virginia Court of Appeals. He also assisted Benjamin Watkins Leigh in bringing out in 1819 *The Revised Code
of the Laws of Virginia*. Those who knew Munford speak of the modesty,
gentleness, and integrity of the man. In early life he had been influenced by
the Deism which flourished in Williamsburg, but in mature life he was a
devout Episcopalian, a vestryman in the church, Recording Secretary of the
Virginia Bible Society, and an active participant in other religious and benevolent organizations.

In 1798, when he was only twenty-three years old, Munford brought out his father's literary remains in Petersburg and published his own *Poems and Compositions in Prose on Several Occasions* in Richmond. The ill-advised urging of friends is said to have led to the publication of this book, made up mainly of juvenilia. The reception was none too favorable, and Munford published no more of his literary work. As Beverley Tucker put it, ". . . the scholar and poet subsided into a professional drudge; and a name, which had seemed destined to stand high among the literary men of Virginia, is now [in 1846] known to the reading public only as it stands in the title page of ten volumes of Reports of the Judgments of the Court of‘Appeals." Although Munford occasionally printed verses in the Richmond newspapers, he gave the leisure of his mature years to a translation of the *Iliad*. During the last months of his life he was trying to make arrangements to publish his translation, but it was not until twenty-one years after his death that his widow and sons had the book published in Boston.

Munford's *Poems and Compositions in Prose* contains a tragedy and a number of juvenile poems and speeches, most of which should never have been published. The poems reveal some skill in light verse, a great fondness for Ossian, and a certain sympathy with Revolutionary France. The best of the poems and not unworthy of the elder Munford is "The Political Contest, A Dialogue. Written in 1798." The satire shows how difficult it was at that time in Virginia for a man of moderate opinions like Munford to mediate between partisans of the French and admirers of the British. Both agree in condemning the moderate man as

> A wretch who is of neither party,
> Nor in his own opinions hearty.

They proceed to drub him black and blue; and the poet points the moral:

> Thus moderation in these times,
> You see, is deem'd the worst of crimes.

The most significant piece in Munford's book is *Almoran and Hamet*, a tragedy "founded on an Eastern Tale of that name" by John Hawkesworth. This blank verse melodrama, which has certain Gothic and Oriental characteristics, was designed "to shew the evils of arbitrary power. . . ." In a rather naïve Preface to his book Munford indicates that his aim is the Horatian one, "on all occasions to mingle the useful with the pleasing." The story involves the unscrupulous efforts of Almoran, joint ruler of Persia with his brother Hamet, to deprive the latter of his throne and his fiancée. Almoran is aided by a "Genius" of supernatural powers who in the end turns out as evil an agent as the witches in *Macbeth* and leads him on to his undoing. Munford had had some amateur experience in acting, and a few scenes display some dramatic power. The rather high-flown language of the play shows an attempt to make use of what Munford called "the grand and splendid imagery of the East."

By 1804 Munford, who had been greatly influenced by the earlier English Romantic writers, seems to have turned back to the Neoclassicists for his models. His private library was markedly deficient in the works of his immediate contemporaries, the great British Romantic poets. His later verse, printed in local newspapers or surviving in manuscript, is chiefly occasional and humorous. Among the best are two unpublished Hudibrastic and anti-Federalist satires written in 1798, "The Richmond Cavalcade" and "The Richmond Feast." Other verses which survive are humorous addresses to friends and newspaper rhymes for the new year.

Munford, like many others who had read the *Iliad* in the original Greek, felt that Alexander Pope's translation was lacking in faithfulness. Pope, he said, had equipped Homer "in the fashionable style of a modern fine gentleman." Munford was well along with his own translation before he had seen William Cowper's, which he thought displayed Homer, like his Ulysses, "in 'rags unseemly,' or in the uncouth garb of a savage." In his own translation he aimed primarily at fidelity to the original. "The distinguishing traits of Homer's poetry," he justly stated long before Matthew Arnold wrote his essay "On Translating Homer," "are majestic simplicity of style, incomparable energy and fire of fancy and sentiment, with peculiar variety and harmony of modulation." These characteristics Munford tried as well as he could, working at night, to get into his own version. He was handicapped, however, partly because of his ignorance of German achievements in Homeric scholarship and partly by the eighteenth-century theory of translation, which involved a "more strictly moral aim, the cultivation of good manners, of propriety and decorum. . . ."[62]

Before Munford's *Iliad* was published in 1846, his son John journeyed to Boston to obtain a reliable critical estimate of it and to make arrangements for its publication.[63] Cornelius C. Felton, the Harvard classical scholar, examined the manuscript, advised publication, and promised to review it when published. In the *North American Review* in July, 1846, Fel-

[62] John W. Draper, "The Theory of Translation in the Eighteenth Century," *Neophilologus*, VI, 241–254 (1921).

[63] William P. Munford wrote to John Coles Rutherford, Oct. 3, 1845, that he was copying his father's translation with a view to having it published. "The facilities, afforded by the cheapness of publication, and the increased demand for the works of native authors, induce me to undertake the publication of this work which has so long been neglected" (Rutherford Papers, Duke University Library).

ton expressed the opinion that a translation of the *Iliad* coming from Virginia did more honor to that ancient commonwealth than all her political dissertations. "We have so long been accustomed to political talk from old Virginia," he wrote, "that a purely literary work, having no possible connection with 'the party,' strikes us as something unexpected, strange, and surprising." He regarded Munford's version as "rich and rhythmical, stately, and often remarkably expressive." Munford's versification, however, seemed to him sometimes monotonous, and his style less suited to "the homelier details of daily life" than to the battle scenes and descriptions of natural phenomena.

George Frederick Holmes, writing in the *Southern Quarterly Review*, noted that Munford had not had access to some of the best scholarly works on Homer, especially the German, but he thought the translation better than either Pope's or Cowper's. Munford would have been pleased with Holmes's verdict that the greatest merit of the translation was its fidelity to the original. It was, Holmes said, the only English translation "from which any idea can be formed of the manner, style, sentiment, and language of Homer. . . ." Holmes felt, however, that Munford's efforts in his Preface to prove that the study of the classics is not prejudicial to Christianity were somewhat ridiculous, as they undoubtedly are; and he complained that Munford in his notes had too often used Homer as "a text for the introduction of religious reflections" which were only "very genteel twaddling."

Not all the reviews were favorable. Had the book been published in the early 1820's—before the triumph of the Romantic revolt—the reception of the book would have been more favorable. Charles A. Bristed, writing in the *American Whig Review*, rated Munford's performance "just such a one as any educated man might execute who would take the trouble. . . ." In emphatic italics he asked: "*Why did Munford translate the Iliad, and why did his friends publish his translation?*" Yet Bristed also testified to Munford's fidelity to the original. No reviewer, however, credited Munford with the poetic power a great translator should have. I quote as a specimen the famous passage in Book VI in which Hector replies to Andromache, who has begged him to remain in the city and not imperil his life in the coming battle. It is one of the greatest passages in world literature, and no translation of course can do full justice to it.

> To her the mighty Hector made reply:
> All thou hast said employs my thoughtful mind.
> But from the Trojans much I dread reproach,
> And Trojan dames whose garments sweep the ground,
> If, like a coward, I should shun the war;

Nor does my soul to such disgrace incline,
Since to be always bravest I have learn'd,
And with the first of Troy to lead the fight;
Asserting so my father's lofty claim
To glory, and my own renown in arms:
For well I know, in heart and mind convinc'd,
A day will come when sacred Troy must fall,
And Priam and the people of renown'd
Spear-practis'd Priam! Yet for this, to me
No such concern arises; not the woes
Of all the Trojans, not my mother's griefs,
Nor royal Priam's, nor my brethren's deaths,
Many and brave, who, slain by cruel foes,
Will be laid low in dust, so wring my heart
As thy distress, when some one of the Greeks
In brazen armor clad, will drive thee hence,
Thy days of freedom gone, a weeping slave!
Perhaps at Argos thou may'st ply the loom,
For some proud mistress, or may'st water bring
From Messa's or Hyperia's fountain, sad
And much reluctant, stooping to the weight
Of hard necessity; and some one, then,
Seeing thee weep, will say, Behold the wife
Of Hector, who was first in martial might
Of all the warlike Trojans, when they fought
Around the walls of Ilion! So will speak
Some heedless passer-by, and grief renew'd
Excite in thee, for such a husband lost,
Whose arm might slavery's evil day avert.
But me, may then a heap of earth conceal
Within the silent tomb, before I hear
Thy shrieks of terror and captivity!

23
Daniel Bryan

IN THE EARLY years of the republic the urge to produce a national literature often took the form of an epic poem. That generation had been
brought up on Homer, Vergil, and Milton. It had not read the Waverley
novels, which were to give a new direction to American literary ambition.
Many there must have been who, like John Adams, writing to John Trumbull in 1785, hoped "to live to see our young America in Possession of an

Heroick Poem, equal to those the most esteemed in any Country." In that year Timothy Dwight published *The Conquest of Canaan*, and two years later Joel Barlow brought out *The Vision of Columbus*, which he eventually expanded into *The Columbiad* (1807). Charles Brockden Brown, before he fell under the spell of William Godwin, planned epics on Columbus, Cortez, and Pizarro. The "epic rage" was felt also in the Southern states, and Jefferson's friend, the Abbé Correa, an admirer of the Old Dominion, once said that if ever an epic poem should be written in this country, it would be in Virginia.[64]

In 1813 there appeared in Harrisonburg in the Shenandoah Valley a book bearing the title *The Mountain Muse: Comprising The Adventures of Daniel Boone; and The Power of Virtuous and Refined Beauty*. The author, as the title page informs us, was Daniel Bryan (1790?–1866), of Rockingham County, Virginia. He was the son of Major William Bryan and a brother of Allan Bryan, who became a lawyer of local reputation. He was also a relative of Daniel Boone, and he may have been named for the hero of his poem. Boone had married Rebecca Bryan, and his sister Mary was the wife of Rebecca's brother, another William Bryan. The Bryans are found with the Boones in Pennsylvania, in the Yadkin Valley in North Carolina, and in Kentucky. Some of the poet's relatives who had been in Kentucky with Boone in the early days may well have thrilled the youthful poet with tales of Boone's adventures. In 1806–1807 Daniel Bryan attended Washington Academy (now Washington and Lee University) in Lexington. He was a militia colonel in the War of 1812. From 1818 to 1822 he was in the state senate, where in 1821 he made a speech advocating the gradual emancipation of slaves. In 1826 he became postmaster in Alexandria, Virginia, a position he held for a quarter of a century. He seems to have been in some demand as a speaker on educational topics. The shorter of the two poems in *The Mountain Muse*—"The Power of Virtuous and Refined Beauty"—reads like a commencement oration for a girls' school. It is in fact a plea for the Anne Smith Academy.

The epic in which Bryan had hoped to immortalize his hero and himself has been forgotten, but students of Poe will recall a paragraph in "Autography" published in *Graham's Magazine* in December, 1841, which reads:

Mr. BRYAN has written some very excellent poetry, and is appreciated by all admirers of "the good old Goldsmith school." He is, at present, postmaster at

---

[64] "The Jefferson Papers," *Mass. Hist. Soc. Collections*, 7th ser. I, 190. The dullest of Southern epics is undoubtedly Richard Emmons' *The Fredoniad* (1827); the best is probably Judge Walter Malone's *Hernando De Soto* (1914).

Alexandria, and has held office for many years, with all the good fortune of a Vicar of Bray.

Among the few magazines that reviewed *The Mountain Muse* was the *Analectic Magazine*, and the reviewer may have been Washington Irving, who some time in that year (1815) gladly turned over to Thomas Isaac Wharton his uncongenial position as editor. The belated review begins:

A malicious critic—a Quarterly Reviewer, for instance, who felt inclined to amuse himself with hunting a wild American poet, could not wish a finer subject than this volume would afford him. It is full of all those faults which need nothing but a little exaggeration to be heightened into broad caricature, extravagance of metaphor, gorgeous description, loads of ornament, and epithet piled on epithet; the whole contrasted by many bald and prosaic lines.

After these remarks our readers will probably be a little surprised, when we add, that we have great respect for Mr. Bryan's poetical powers. The fact is, that though it would be difficult to select out of the poem fifty good lines together, without some glaring fault, it would be quite as difficult to find any dozen lines in continuity which do not contain some bold thought, some original view of nature, or some strong and glowing expression. This is, in short, an irregular and very faulty production of a mind capable of much higher efforts.

The kindly reviewer encouraged the author of this "wilding" to continue to write.

Thirteen years after the publication of *The Mountain Muse*, its author referred to that work as "the wild offspring of a rude and undisciplined fancy . . . disfigured by imperfections. . . ." He had, he said, been encouraged by injudicious friends to publish the book; and its unfavorable reception had "reared in the way of his Muse a barrier of prejudice which nothing but the current of Time . . . can effectually overthrow."

The Preface to *The Mountain Muse* suggests that the inhabitants of the Shenandoah Valley were as indifferent to contemporary poetry in 1813 as Philip Pendleton Cooke found them thirty years later. Bryan tells us that he had heard "expressions of astonishment . . . that a person in his circumstances should suspend his preparations for a profitable profession, to engage in the proverbially unfruitful employment of the Muse." For him, however, there had been no choice. "As well might it be ask'd," he declares, "why does the heedless Candle Fly, which has already scorch'd its wings in the flame, still flutter around it until it perishes?" He goes on:

Indeed the physical beauty and magnificence, combined with the moral and political enjoyments of this Land of elysium, are well calculated to inspire with poetic devotion, the bosom which has any native predisposition to the indulgence of imagination. Who, that has a soul susceptable [*sic*] of ennobling sensations, can ramble thro Columbia's forests, hear the roar of her rivers, gaze on the grandeur of her mountains, and muse on her glorious Liberties, without breaking forth into the rhapsodies of divinest enthusiasm?

The theme of the seven books of *The Adventures of Daniel Boone* is the exploration and settlement of Kentucky. This treatment of the frontier, the westward movement, and Indian warfare, it should be remembered, was published a decade before Fenimore Cooper brought out the first of the Leather-Stocking Tales. The poem is in the spirit of Bishop Berkeley's famous line: "Westward the course of empire takes its way." Boone is the hero

> whose valor laid the base
> Of Free Columbia's occidental States.

And he embodies the virtues most admired by the poet: courage, fidelity, generosity, humanity, and patriotism.

The epic is doubly unique in that it celebrates a living hero and that we know the hero's estimate of it. Some one who talked with Boone in 1818 when he was eighty-four years old wrote:

> I asked him if he had ever seen the book called the "Mountain Muse," written by Daniel Bryan? He said he had, and regretted that he could not sue him for slander; and added, that such productions ought to be left until the person was put in the ground. He took occasion to remark, that there was a small pamphlet [John Filson's *Kentucke*] that he had written some thirty years before, every word of which was correct to the best of his knowledge. The Colonel [Miller] observed that Bryan, in his book had made him a host—that he had killed a host of Indians. "But," said he, "I never killed but three that I claimed; but many was the fair fire I have had at them. . . ." [65]

Bryan and his literary contemporaries in America had the difficult problem of finding or adapting suitable literary forms in which to treat American life and landscape. "Thanatopsis" and *The Last of the Mohicans* were yet to come. The novel would seem to the modern reader more appropriate than the epic, but Scott's *Waverley* was still unfinished in 1813. Blair's *Lectures on Rhetoric*, which Bryan may have studied, gave much space to the epic and comparatively little to the novel. Dwight and Barlow had celebrated the exploits of Joshua and Columbus, and Robert Southey those of Joan of Arc.

[65] Draper MSS 7 C 43 (Wisconsin State Historical Society Library). A part of the passage is quoted in John Bakeless, *Daniel Boone* (1939), p. 394. Miss Alice E. Smith, Curator of Manuscripts, writes me that the passage is found in a manuscript in Lyman C. Draper's handwriting, presumably copied from an unidentified newspaper. For what seems to be the original of the story of the Lost Maid, Melcena, see Bakeless, *op. cit.*, pp. 34–35.

Bryan must have known of these epics even if he had not read them. It was natural that he should feel that Boone's heroic exploits required epic form and diction to give them dignity and weight. These he supplied with Miltonic machinery; and following the examples of Tasso and Spenser, he added a romantic love story. Bryan leaned heavily on Milton when he described the cloud-built Firmamental Hall, "High o'er the Alleganean Mountain-Heights," in which the guardian spirits of the Western Wild meet in "grand assemblage" to devise means for the settlement of Kentucky. Four of the spirits—Truth, Humanity, Zeal, and Enterprise—deliver speeches that are too reminiscent of *Paradise Lost*. It is Enterprise that suggests Boone for the great exploit and that later inspires the hero, brooding alone upon a mountain peak, to undertake the great adventure. Boone's various fights and escapes are described with some power, and the battle scene at the Blue Licks is probably the best in the book. The poet manages to suggest the bravery and cunning of his savages, but of the three Indian chieftains only Montour rises to the proportions suitable for a hero's antagonist. It is unfortunate for Bryan that a generation familiar with the somewhat Ossianic prose poetry of Cooper's Indian orators finds Miltonic diction peculiarly inappropriate in the mouth of an Indian. In an episode that recalls not Milton but Rousseau or Schiller perhaps, Bryan tells the story of the Allegheny Robbers and the Lost Maid, Melcena, whom Boone rescues from her kidnapers.

The diction of *The Mountain Muse* is at the opposite pole from that which has been most admired in the twentieth century. It is not the language of common speech but the highly Latinate language of Milton. Bryan had no more thought of divorcing poetry from rhetoric than Byron or Bryant or Shakespeare. He coined or adopted new words with the freedom of the Elizabethans or the youthful John Keats. Among his favorites were "nigrescent," "flosculous," "profluent," "lancinating," "demulcent," "constringent," "desultorious," "gratulant," "coajuvancy," and "deterged." Bryan's diction suggests that he had probably read *The Columbiad* and perhaps also *The Botanic Garden* of Erasmus Darwin. Like Barlow, he seems to have borrowed scientific terms from Darwin and to have invented others of the same kind.[66] Like Richard Dabney and the Connecticut Wits, he was influenced by the associationist psychology of David Hartley and probably also by Archibald Alison's *Essay on the Principles of Taste*.

[66] See Leon Howard, *The Connecticut Wits* (1943), pp. 310 ff. Bryan may also, like Barlow, have been influenced by Darwin's distinction between the language of poetry and the language of prose: ". . . Poetry admits of but few words expressive of very abstracted ideas, whereas Prose abounds with them" (*The Botanic Garden*, 3rd ed., London, 1795, II, 48).

The associating principle of mind,
That throws the thoughts with rapid power,
O'er all the mazy complicated chain
Of objects, which are link'd to the grand theme
That with sublime sensation swells the soul;
Boone now in all its forceful influence felt.

Bryan was a lover of nature, and his rhapsodies over the beauties of Kentucky make one wonder whether he had read Rousseau and Wordsworth as well as William Collins, to whom he refers. There is, however, nothing mystical in his view of the landscapes which he describes. He continually contrasts the forests of the New World with the cities of the Old. The story of Vulosko is one that might have appealed to Wordsworth or Byron. Vulosko describes his reaction to Europe, where he had been taken in boyhood:

Ashamed, disgusted, sick,
At sight of Perfidy, Corruption, Vice,
And Parasitic meanness, I return'd
To Carolina's uncorrupted shades. . . .

But even in Carolina, he found that:

the Hypocritic taint, the breath,
The *infectious* breath of Europe's poison'd sons,
Had reach'd Columbia's shores. To Solitude,
To Books, and to the instruction of my son
And daughter, therefore, did I turn for peace,
For consolation. These at times I've found.

Bryan's later poems are freer of faults than *The Mountain Muse*, but they are less interesting. If he began as an undisciplined Romanticist, he ended more nearly as a poet of "the good old Goldsmith school." In later years he published an occasional poem in the magazines. The most important of these is "The Mother and Daughter Land," a tribute to Coleridge and a plea for friendship between England and the United States. The poem is a reply to some lines which Coleridge had written in the album of a daughter of the American minister to England, John Barbour, a Virginian whom Bryan may have known.

In the year 1826 Bryan published two books of verse. He is hardly at his best in the lyrics of *The Lay of Gratitude, Consisting of Poems Occasioned by the Recent Visit of Lafayette to the United States* (Philadelphia, 1826), which appeared too late to be timely. A more interesting performance is *The Appeal for Suffering Genius: A Poetical Address for the Benefit of the*

Boston Bard; and The Triumph of Truth, a Poem (Washington, 1826).
The "Boston Bard" for whom Bryan made his appeal was Robert S. Coffin,
a poet-printer and the author of verses ranging from mediocre to execrable.
The poem is primarily a plea for more generous recognition of American
writers, and it was probably as much Bryan's own circumstances as Coffin's
that prompted him to write:

> Shall free Columbia share the deep reproach
> By which ungrateful lands are stigmatized,
> Nor aid her sons of genius whose bright thoughts,
> And arduous toils, illumine and advance
> Her march in virtue, liberty, and fame?

During the remaining thirty years of his life Bryan published little. In
1830 he brought out in Richmond a poem which two years earlier he had
read before the Literary and Philosophical Society of Hampden-Sydney
College: *Thoughts on Education in Its Connexion with Morals*. It is an
excellent Presbyterian discourse in verse in which the orator condemns war,
dueling, intemperance, avarice, profanity, faction, and party rage. Its poetic
level is suggested by:

> 'Tis Education's province then, no less,
> With moral treasures to enrich the heart,
> Than with its mental gems to store the head.

Daniel Bryan had outgrown his youthful tendency to extravagance, but
he had not fulfilled the promise which the *Analectic* reviewer had seen in
The Mountain Muse. In another age or region he might have developed
into a better poet, but his endowment was hardly sufficient to enable him in
any circumstances to become more than a very minor figure. Nevertheless
—to speak in the manner of Poe—had Bryan been a New England poet,
his memory would have been kept alive, at least in the anthologies of Kettell
and Griswold. As it is, only his tenuous connection with Poe has preserved
the memory of his name.

24
William Maxwell

WILLIAM MAXWELL (1784–1857) might almost be grouped with the
Connecticut Wits, although the scholars who have diligently studied the
Wits seem unaware of him. Born of Scottish parentage in Norfolk, Virginia,
he was sent to Wolcott, Connecticut, in 1797, to prepare himself for col-

lege under the Reverend Israel B. Woodward, a Yale graduate. Maxwell entered Yale as a sophomore and was graduated in 1820 in the same class as the South Carolina historian of diplomacy, William H. Trescot. In "The Yaliad," still preserved in manuscript in the Yale University Library, his classmate, Cyrus Pearce, spoke prophetically of Maxwell's future as "Solicitor General":

> To late posterity thy parts shall shine;
> And future orators, shall catch from thee,
> As from its native source, that majesty;
> That force of eloquence we seldom find:
> To grace the forum, & instruct mankind
> When as Solicitor you advocate,
> The course of Justice on behalf the State;
> The gaping Senators, admiring stand,
> To see you flutter and your arms extend.
> As when the greasy lamp, two thirds burnt out,
> Smokes, sputters, spitts, and throws the oil about;
> So Maxwell, when he speaks, profusely sputters,
> And thinks Hell trembles every word he utters.

Poor Pearce died a few weeks after his graduation and had no opportunity to see how well his classmates fulfilled his various predictions. Maxwell was a loyal alumnus of Yale. In 1807 he returned to receive his master's degree and read a poem entitled "A Word to the Fair." In July, 1856, only six months before his death, he wrote that his health would not permit him to go to New Haven to attend a reunion of his class. Obviously troubled by increasing ill feeling between the South and New England, he added: ". . . I earnestly wish to say some things to my friends of New England, which I flatter myself they would take kindly from me."

After studying law in Richmond, Maxwell began to practice in Norfolk in 1808. In September, 1827, he accepted a position as literary editor of the New York *Journal of Commerce*, but after a year he resigned and resumed his law practice in Norfolk. The Presbyterian divine James W. Alexander in 1827 characterized Maxwell as "the very best orator I know anywhere. . . . He is a [wealthy] bachelor, lives in good style, has an elegant library, is a most agreeable companion, and a finished scholar." Alexander added: "He is, though a native Virginian, the faithful and fearless champion of the oppressed Africans. For a publication of his on this subject, the Norfolk people menaced him with an application of tar and feathers. When he avowed himself the author of the paper, which was published anonymously, his opposers shrunk away before a character so universally revered."

Before 1838, when he became President of Hampden-Sydney College, Maxwell had served several years in the General Assembly, chiefly in the State Senate. In his later years he was a devout Presbyterian and an active member of the Virginia Bible Society and the Colonization Society. He had published in 1835 his *Memoir of the Rev. John H. Rice*, one of the best Southern biographies of the period. In 1844 he resigned his position at Hampden-Sydney and resumed the practice of law, this time in Richmond. The following year he was the unsuccessful rival of William Holmes Mc-Guffey for the professorship which George Tucker had resigned at the University of Virginia. In 1847 he took an active part in the revival and reorganization of the Virginia Historical Society. Until his death in 1857 he was its librarian and corresponding secretary, and he edited its organ, the *Virginia Historical Register*, from 1848 till 1853.

Maxwell's poetry belongs to his early manhood. He published in Philadelphia in 1812 a small volume of *Poems*, which with some omissions and additions was republished there in 1816. Among his poems are a few fables and sonnets and a considerable number of verses grouped under the head of "Lyric Notes," which show the influence of Thomas Moore. His "Ariadne to Theseus" is reminiscent of Pope's "Eloisa to Abelard." The growing strictness of the times in morals and conventions is probably responsible for his failure to reprint in 1816 "The Widow of Ephesus" and a jocular epistle "To William Wirt, Esq." Both volumes are dedicated to President Timothy Dwight of Yale, whom Maxwell admired both as man and as poet. The later volume contains no less than three poems addressed to Dwight, in one of which he is described as "First of Columbia's sons in Zion's sacred cause." "Wolcott," an elegy upon Maxwell's old teacher Woodward, shows an indebtedness to Dwight's "Greenfield Hill" as well as to Goldsmith's "The Deserted Village."

The most interesting of Maxwell's poems—appearing only in the 1816 *Poems*—is "The Bards of Columbia. An Epistle to the Rev. Timothy Dwight." It begins:

> How often will you ask me, dearest Dwight,
> When I can live at ease why don't I write?

In good eighteenth-century epistolary style Maxwell discusses the difficulties of the American poet. Like George Tucker, he complains that Americans who read prefer the imported product:

> Why yes! they read—but foreign bards alone,
> And have no sort of patience with our own;
> Thinking that poems, like Madeira wine,

Must cross the sea to mellow and refine.
And sure a fellow must be worse than frantic,
To write a song this side of the Atlantic,
In this vile clime, "beneath our shifting skies,
Where Fancy sickens, and where Genius dies."

Maxwell, however, has some hope that the future will be brighter than the
past or the present. He pleads for poetry which will do justice to American
scenery. He laments that

> proud Potomac, yet unknown to song,
> Pours his bright waves disdainfully along.

Maxwell's own efforts in this direction extend little beyond a sonnet on Lake
George and a poem on "The Natural Bridge." Except for his love of nature,
he seems to belong to the mid-eighteenth century rather than to the age
of Wordsworth and Scott and Byron. To judge from his epistle to Dwight,
he found poetry as little profitable as it proved to most of his American
contemporaries. He followed Dwight's example and devoted his later years
to pursuits that brought him a more substantial return. His verses, though
not of great merit, are better than some of those republished by Griswold
and the Duyckincks, who seem to have missed him. The unknown author
of *Letters by a South-Carolinian* (Norfolk, 1827), who devoted six pages
to Maxwell, wrote: "The poems of Mr. Maxwell have attained higher
celebrity abroad than at home; and in New England than 'in his own, his
native land.'"

25
Richard Dabney

THE LIFE OF Richard Dabney (1787?–1825) was as full of disappointments as that of any of his literary contemporaries. A first cousin of Meriwether Lewis, he was born in Louisa County, Virginia. Since he was one of
twelve children, his father, a planter of limited means, was not able to send
the boy to college. Dabney was educated at a local academy, where he probably learned Latin and Greek and perhaps French, but where the precocious
youth learned Italian is not known. He taught for a time in a boys' school
in Richmond, and he was seriously burned in the disastrous theater fire
of 1811. Opium was given to him to relieve pain, and he became addicted
to that drug and to the excessive use of alcohol as well. In 1812 he published
in Richmond a slight volume of *Poems*, which attracted little attention

and which he is said to have tried to suppress. Not long afterward he went to Philadelphia and tried to support himself by writing. He was able to earn approximately a dollar a day. He is said to have written the greater portion of Mathew Carey's *The Olive Branch* (1814). Carey, his principal employer, published in 1815 a revised and enlarged edition of Dabney's *Poems*, which attracted little more attention than his earlier book. A reviewer attributed to him Thomas Love Peacock's *Rhododaphne;* and although he denied having written it, it was often attributed to him. He returned to Louisa County in 1815 and again turned to teaching, but he seems to have published no poems in the last ten years of his life. His last years were saddened by mental and physical suffering, but he was still able to read and in a measure enjoy the pleasant social life of his native county. He is described as of an affectionate and guileless nature.

Poems, Original and Translated (1815) reveals Dabney as perhaps a better scholar than poet. The volume includes more than thirty translations from minor Greek, Latin, and Italian poets. His own poems show certain classical and Romantic influences; the latter are evident in a love of nature and an emphasis upon emotion and imagination. Dabney had a definite theory of poetry which in its stress upon unity seems to anticipate that of Poe. In some "Preliminary Remarks" prefixed to the *Poems*, he explains in rather pedantic language that his poems belong to "the denomination of Gnomique—a character of poetic composition, where the expression is limited to prominent and concise associations, in the train of thought, consequent on any simple emotion of taste, so as, by the preservation of unity, to prevent the force of that emotion from being diminished." He argues that "this unmingled and unique effect, is diminished by multiplied associations. . . ." To the type of poetry which he cultivated Dabney gave another name *"the moral miniature painting of poetry;* inasmuch as the exertions of the graphic art are generally restricted to a single point, in relation to time, and to a paucity of objects, in relation to expression." As his frequent use of the word "association" suggests, Dabney was indebted to Archibald Alison's *Essay on the Principles of Taste,* which he regarded as the supreme authority. Indeed, he was probably more deeply indebted to Alison than Daniel Bryan, George Tucker, the Connecticut Wits, or the early contributors to the *North American Review.*[67]

Dabney's theory is better than his practice, but some of his verses have a poetic quality. I quote his "Invocazione," which in idea anticipates Emerson's poem "The Enchanter." In a note Dabney explains that "the term

[67] R. E. Streeter, "Association Psychology and Literary Nationalism in the *North American Review,* 1815–1825," *Am. Lit.,* XVII, 243–254 (Nov., 1945).

Iris, bestowed on the faculty of association, acting under the influence of Memory and Imagination, is in allusion to the capacity, with which that mythological personage is invested by Homer and Virgil, as the medium of impulses produced on the human mind by superior intelligences."

Come Iris of the human mind,
And messenger, from soul to thought,
When fancy's magic chain to bind
Each heart connected link is sought—

Hills, on whose torrent-beaten side,
Thy solemn hues were ne'er reflected,
Where Nature's awful forms preside
Unheeded, unadmired, neglected—

Vales, on whose beauty-breathing breast,
Thy lighter colours ne'er were painted,
Where grace and charm for ever rest,
But soul and heart fore'er are stinted,

Await thy smiles—and from thy beam
Their hues appropriate each shall take,
And scenes, before unnoticed, seem
To grandeur, or to grace to wake.

High on the mountain's rocky side,
Shall sit, enthroned, the form of terror
While down, through frowning cliffs shall glide
The rapid torrent, breathing horror.

Low, in the bosomed vale, shall dwell,
Each charm in its appropriate place,
Each grove, each stream, each bower shall tell
Of beauty, soft delight, and grace.

26
John Shaw

Dr. John Shaw (1778–1809) was a Romanticist by temperament. "The son of a respectable gentleman," he was born in Annapolis and educated at St. John's College. He was a brilliant but unsystematic student. He had an uncanny facility in learning foreign languages and is said to have been able to speak fluently "all the European polished languages." An early poem modeled on Gray's "The Bard," "The Voice of Freedom," shows that Shaw in 1795 accepted the doctrines of the French Revolution. After his graduation in October, 1796, he began the study of medicine in Annapolis under Dr. John Thomas Schaaff. His love of travel and adventure led him after two years to sail as ship's doctor for Algiers. He remained for some time in Tunis. While on the Barbary Coast, he wrote a long poem called "The Wanderer"—of which he destroyed all but a few passages—in which he maintained "that genius was totally incompatible with prudence, and that superior abilities were a full excuse for extravagance and irregularity." Somewhat disillusioned by his experiences, he returned to Annapolis in 1800. The next year he started for Edinburgh to complete his medical education. Early in 1803, without having taken a medical degree, he went as physician to the Earl of Selkirk's settlement on St. John's Island in Canada. After recovering from typhus fever—he had two hundred patients down with it at one time—he returned to Annapolis early in 1805 to practice medicine there with Dr. Schaaff. In 1807 he married Jane Selby, to whom a number of his poems are addressed, and settled in Baltimore, which had by this time come to overshadow Annapolis. After a long illness he died of tuberculosis at sea while *en route* from Charleston to Barbados. He was only thirty-one when he died.

The moral drawn by his editor and biographer, John Elihu Hall, is: "Slow rises worth by poverty depress'd." The modern student is likely to attribute Shaw's failures to a restless and unstable temperament. Indecision and failure to discriminate among the many literary influences that played upon him perhaps kept him from developing an individual style. Among his poems, many of them published in the Port Folio, there are some brief translations from the Italian, Moorish, Greek, and Portuguese. He died too early to have discovered Byron, Shelley, or Keats; and I find no evidence that he knew Wordsworth or Coleridge; but there is abundant evidence that he knew Gray, Collins, Ossian, and Charlotte Smith. She probably supplied the model for his sonnets. Among his better poems are "The Pilgrim's Return," "A Midsummer Night's Dream," and a few specimens of light verse. Only one of his poems has shown sufficient vitality to hold a place in anthologies; and this "Song" is not wholly characteristic, for it is reminiscent of Shakespeare and the Cavalier lyrists. The first of the three stanzas is:

> Who has robb'd the ocean cave,
>   To tinge thy lips with coral hue?
> Who from India's distant wave,

For thee those pearly treasures drew?
Who, from yonder orient sky,
Stole the morning of thine eye?

27
Francis Scott Key

NATIONAL SONGS seem practically all to have been written by minor poets
—not by the Shakespeares and Miltons or even by the Poes and Whitmans.
The great poets often write superb patriotic poems, but they seem unable
to write poems like "The Marseillaise," "God Save the King," and "The
Star-Spangled Banner." And yet the great patriotic songs, as we shall note
again when we come to the songs of the Civil War, come from poets who
are not exactly amateurs. The author of "Maryland, My Maryland," for
example, wrote enough poems to fill a volume, some of them of distinct
merit. The author of "The Star-Spangled Banner" did not take his muse
very seriously, but he wrote a considerable amount of verse.

Francis Scott Key (1779–1843), the son of a lawyer who had been a
Revolutionary soldier, was born at Pipe Creek in western Maryland. He
graduated from St. John's College in Annapolis in the same class as Dr.
John Shaw. He studied law in Annapolis with his uncle Philip Barton Key,
who had held a commission in the British army during the Revolution. In
1801 Key and Roger Brooke Taney—who was to succeed Marshall as Chief
Justice of the United States in 1836—settled in Frederick Town to
practice law. There he married Mary Tayloe Lloyd; Taney married his sister
Anne Key. In 1805 he moved to Georgetown, where he took over his uncle's
practice. He proved himself an able lawyer and pleaded numerous cases before the Supreme Court.

From time to time he wrote verse, but his poems were left uncollected
until fourteen years after his death. He published a prose work *The Power
of Literature, and Its Connection with Religion* (1834). Some of his best
poems are religious lyrics; among them is the hymn "Lord, with Glowing
Heart I'd Praise Thee." Key was intensely religious and he rebelled against
the Deism represented by Thomas Paine; in 1814 he almost decided to give
up the law for the ministry. He was an admirer of Scott's martial verse, and
he gave some thought to the art of song-writing.

Although, like most other Federalists, he was opposed to the War of
1812, he fought, like John Pendleton Kennedy, in the disastrous Battle of
Bladensburg. A few days afterwards President Madison authorized Key and

John S. Skinner to visit the British fleet in the Chesapeake Bay under a flag of truce to ask for the release of the aged Dr. William Beanes. They succeeded in their mission but were detained aboard until after the attack on Fort McHenry. The fleet bombarded the fort with rockets and cannon while it lay out of range of the American guns. All through the long night of September 13–14, 1814, Key watched the bombardment with field glasses. Early the next morning while Dr. Beanes kept asking nervously: "Can you see the flag?" Key looked anxiously until a rift in the clouds showed the Stars and Stripes still flying. On the way back to Baltimore he finished a rough draft of the poem, which bears a resemblance to "The Warrior's Return," which he had written ten years earlier. He revised the poem that night. It was published in the Baltimore *Patriot*, September 20, 1814, and probably still earlier as a broadside. It was immediately popular and came to be regarded unofficially as the national anthem, although it was not until 1931 that Congress made the popular choice official. In 1934 the manuscript of the poem was sold to the Walters Art Gallery in Baltimore for $24,000. Key seems to have written the poem for the British air "To Anacreon in Heaven," to which it is still sung. The tune had been used in 1798 for a song entitled "Adams and Liberty." [68] While it is not a great poem, "The Star-Spangled Banner" is certainly not the poorest of national songs. The chief obstacles in the way of its wider use are that some of the lines are too full of consonants and the air has a range which is greater than the compass of the average voice.

28
Edward Coote Pinkney

EDWARD COOTE PINKNEY (1802–1828), the best of the Southern lyric poets before Poe, was born in London and lived there until he was eight years old. His father, William Pinkney, a distinguished lawyer and diplomat, was at that time ambassador at the Court of St. James; his mother was a sister of Commodore John Rodgers. As a student at St. Mary's College in Baltimore, young Pinkney is said to have won the admiration of his teachers. In the fall of 1815 he entered the United States Navy as a midshipman. He remained in active service until 1822 and did not resign his commission until 1824. He experienced little actual fighting though he took part in chasing pirate ships; but while in the Navy he saw something of Italy and northern Africa, the West Indies, and of both coasts of South America.

[68] On Aug. 4, 1803, the Raleigh *Register* published a patriotic American "Song" to the tune of "Anacreon in Heaven."

His father died in 1822, and though Pinkney retained his commission two years longer, he began studying law in Baltimore. He is described as handsome, chivalrous, and high-spirited. Though he seems never to have fought a duel, he was ready enough to invoke the code duello. He challenged John Neal, who in his novel *Randolph* (1823) had included a disparaging account of his father written in singularly bad taste; and when Neal declined to fight, Pinkney distributed about the city handbills committing "this Craven to his infamy." In 1824 Pinkney resigned his commission, began the practice of law, and married Georgiana McCausland. In 1823 he had published in Baltimore the fragmentary Byronic narrative *Rodolph*, and in 1825 he brought out his slender volume of *Poems*. In 1826 he was appointed Professor of Rhetoric and Belles Lettres in the struggling young University of Maryland but soon gave up a position that involved no teaching and carried with it no salary. Having no great success in the practice of law, he went to Mexico expecting to obtain a position in the Mexican navy under Commodore Porter. The expected position failed to materialize, and Pinkney returned to Baltimore afflicted with a disease which seems eventually to have brought about his death. In December, 1827, he became editor of the *Marylander*, a new semiweekly newspaper founded to promote the re-election of John Quincy Adams. After prolonged ill health, he died on April 11, 1828, at the age of twenty-six.

Although some of Pinkney's poems were to remain uncollected until 1926, he had even before his death begun to receive recognition as a poet. The *North American Review*, which often failed to review the works of writers who lived in the South, discussed both his slender volumes with discriminating praise. Anthologists promptly included a few poems which their successors have continued to reprint. Pinkney is not of course to be ranked with Keats and Shelley, whom he resembles in his early death, but in a few poems he achieved something like distinction. Poe, who was somewhat influenced by him, called him "the first of American lyrists."

Unlike many American writers, Pinkney was no mere local poet. Widely traveled and educated partly in England, he was quick to perceive new literary tendencies and to recognize the importance of new poets like Wordsworth as well as the far more popular Scott, Byron, and Moore. His reading was more extensive than one would expect of a young man who had entered the Navy at the age of thirteen. He knew something of the Greek and Latin classics, and he read French. He certainly knew Milton and Shakespeare, Dryden, Pope, Swift, and Sterne. There is, however, almost no evidence that he read the Cavalier poets, with whom he has often been compared. The dominant influences, according to his biographers, were those of Byron and in lesser degree Scott, Wordsworth, and Moore. He seems not to have been influenced by any American poets, even by those of his own state.

Pinkney's best poems contain a profusion of images derived alike from his reading and from the sea; they also have a music of their own and a lyric fire that suggests sometimes Shelley and sometimes Lovelace or Herrick. Many of his best poems are addressed to women, particularly Georgiana McCausland before and after their marriage. The best known is "A Health," still one of the finest toasts ever given in honor of a woman. The modern reader feels that both sentiment and diction are somewhat outmoded, but it suggests something of the semiworship of beauty in woman which we shall remark also in the poems of Poe and Richard Henry Wilde.

> I fill this cup to one made up of loveliness alone,
> A woman, of her gentle sex the seeming paragon—
> Her health! and would on earth there stood some more of such a frame,
> That life might be all poetry, and weariness a name.

Less well known but not inferior are "Serenade," "The Widow's Song," "Italy," "Elysium," and "Self-Esteem," which I quote in full:

> I know that perfect self esteem
> Is boyhood's most seductive dream:
> Like others, when my course began,
> I revelled in it,—but the man
> To whom experience betrays
> The sordor of life's miry ways,
> Feels that the hope is—Oh! how vain,
> To tread them through without a stain.

Among the poems first collected by Professor Mabbott and Captain Pleadwell, the most notable are "Self-Esteem," "The Beauty," "The Immortal," and "Melancholy's Curse of Feasts." Fragmentary and brief as are the new poems added to the Pinkney canon in 1926, they extend the scope of his verse and suggest that had he lived, he might well have made Bryant and Poe look to their laurels. "Melancholy's Curse of Feasts," though the mood is unusual for Pinkney, has a sureness of touch that represents him at his best.

> Pale, funeral flowers
> His drinking garlands twine;
> The star, named "Wormwood," fall
> On the grape's tears, his wine!

A lacrymary glass
To him his goblet be;
Along the lighted board,
No gladness let him see!

Hang shadowy skeletons
In his Egyptian halls;
Be dark handwritings traced
On his Assyrian walls!

Let each vase semble well
A cinerary urn;
Its fruit, to ashes like
The dead sea apples, turn!

Thus into wretched mirth
Of hours, his life compress,—
A miserable mass
Of grief and drunkenness.

29
Richard Henry Wilde

Richard Henry Wilde (1789–1847), author of the once-famous lyric "My Life Is Like the Summer Rose," was born in Dublin, Ireland. His mother, Mary (Newitt) Wilde, was the daughter of Tory refugees from America. His father was a wholesale hardware merchant and ironmonger. In 1797, when Richard was eight years old, the Wilde family came to Baltimore. The father's Dublin property was confiscated in the Irish rebellion of 1798; four years later he died. In 1803 young Wilde was working in a dry-goods store in Augusta, Georgia. Soon afterwards his mother came to Augusta and opened a general store, which she managed with the help of her son. Mrs. Wilde, who also wrote verses, had taught him to read. He may have learned a little Latin from a tutor in Baltimore, but his formal education was almost as scanty as Lincoln's. Years later he described his lack of preparation for his studies in Dante: "Never in my life having had the advantage of instruction in a school or from a tutor, more than a year altogether, and at distant intervals, I was wholly uneducated, except the fruits of my own acquirement, an imperfect knowledge of French, Spanish and Italian, a still slighter smattering of Latin, and such superficial acquaintance with the times, laws and history I was about to investigate, as might be gathered from a single perusal of a few modern histories." While still working in his mother's store, Wilde studied law and was admitted to the bar in March, 1809, a year before he came of age. He is said to have gone to a distant court to be examined so that in case of failure his mother would not hear of it. He soon became a very successful lawyer, eventually taking cases to the United States Supreme Court. By 1811 he was attorney-general of the state. He was elected to Congress in 1814 but was defeated two years later. He continued to practice law in Augusta through the year 1824. In February, 1819, he married Mrs. Catherine S. Buckle, who died in 1827. He filled a vacancy in Congress in 1825 and again in 1827. Wilde served with some distinction in the House of Representatives in 1815–1817 and from 1827 until March 3, 1835. In 1834 he led on the first ballot for Speaker of the House but was finally defeated by John Bell. In the election of that year Wilde was defeated, in part at least because he had opposed the measures of Andrew Jackson. He was deeply chagrined at the outcome of the election, and is said to have remarked that he had "found no party which did not require of its followers what no honest man should, and no gentleman would, do."

In June, 1835, Wilde went to Europe, and there he remained for five years. His health was poor; and he was, it seems, in love with a Kentucky beauty, Mrs. Ellen Adair White-Beatty, with whose two husbands he had served in the House of Representatives. He seems also to have had a distaste for the practice of law. As early as 1809 he had written:

> Or whether I shall waste my life
> Mid Courts and Law and care & strife
> Still slowly plodding o'er and o'er
> The same dull round I've trod before
> 'Till youth and joy and friendship fly
> And Love and hope and pleasure die.

After two years of travel in various European countries, he settled in Florence in 1837 for a stay of three years. Here he won the friendship of the American sculptors Horatio Greenough and Hiram Powers and of the youthful Charles Sumner.

The poetry of the Italian Renaissance fascinated Wilde more than anything else. In Florence he wrote the one book he was to publish: *Conjectures and Researches concerning the Love, Madness, and Imprisonment of Torquato Tasso* (New York, 1842), in which he maintains a somewhat romantic thesis with the skill of a practiced lawyer. Although as a scholarly treatise the book was fully up to the standards of the time, the reader of today is most impressed by the poetic merit of the translations from Tasso's poems. The following is one of the best:

> Three high-born dames it was my lot to see,
> Not all alike in beauty, yet so fair,
> And so akin in act, and look, and air,
> That Nature seemed to say, "SISTERS ARE WE!"
> I praised them all—but one of all the three
> So charmed me, that I loved her, and became
> Her bard, and sung my passion, and her name,
> 'Till to the stars they soared past rivalry.
> Her only I adored—and if my gaze
> Was turned elsewhere, it was but to admire
> Of her high beauty some far-scattered rays,
> And worship her in idols—fond desire,
> False incense hid—yet I repent my praise
> As rank idolatry 'gainst LOVE's true fire.

Wilde undertook a volume of translations from the Italian lyric poets with biographical sketches for which his son William Cumming Wilde, who completed the book, was unable to find a publisher. He laid aside the book unfinished to collect materials for "The Life and Times of Dante with Sketches of the State of Florence and of His Friends and Enemies," which was also uncompleted when he died.[69] After long and tedious delays he had managed to secure admittance to the Medicean archives in Florence. "Never, most assuredly," he wrote, "since I bivouacked in my boyhood amid a wilderness lately in the possession of the Indians, beside a rousing fire, the earth for my bed, the sky my canopy, a saddle for my pillow, and a blanket to cover me,—never since then did so deep a sense of my own insignificance and the enduring solitude of ages come over me as in my first visit to the Florentine archives." In his Preface to the unfinished book Wilde gives an interesting account of the many difficulties which confronted an untrained but determined investigator working with uncalendared manuscripts little known even to Italian scholars. Within his chosen period he proceeded line by line to examine all the available materials. In this way he made a number of discoveries which he regarded as important. If his book had been completed and published in his lifetime, it might have been a substantial contribution to Dante scholarship; but later scholars have found all that Wilde

[69] William Gilmore Simms had high praise for parts of the manuscript which Wilde had read to him (*Simms's Mag.*, II, 144, Aug., 1845).

found and a great deal more. The completed portions of the book form a detailed and very readable account of Dante's background in the social, cultural, and political life of Florence.

While engaged in his Dante studies, Wilde was able with the assistance of certain Italians to rediscover Giotto's forgotten portrait of Dante concealed underneath a coat of whitewash on a wall of the Bargello in Florence. Although an Englishman named Kirkup later claimed the entire credit for the discovery, it seems clear that Wilde was the prime mover in the undertaking. Washington Irving's account of the discovery, published in the *Knickerbocker Magazine* for October, 1841, seems to have been based on information supplied by Wilde himself.

Before the end of the year 1840 Wilde had returned to the United States. In January, 1842, he published his book on Tasso. Two years later he was admitted to the New Orleans bar. In 1846, somewhat against his wishes, he was made Professor of Constitutional Law without salary in what is now Tulane University. He died of yellow fever on September 10, 1847.

Charles C. Jones, Jr., thus describes the handsome poet:

He was an attractive specimen of physical and intellectual manhood. Six feet one inch in height, well proportioned, graceful, with an expansive forehead, black, flowing hair, an emotional mouth and bright eyes, cheerful in his disposition, dignified and yet affable in his address, brimful of anecdote, eloquent in speech, impressive in action and quick at repartee, he shone alike in legislative halls, at the bar, and in the social circle.

Wilde's singularly attractive personality is faintly suggested in A. B. Meek's "The Death of Richard Henry Wilde":

> As late I saw, I see him now!
>   His stalwart form, his graceful mien,
> His long, white locks, his smiling brow,
>   His eyes benignant and serene!
> How pleasant 'round the social hearth,
> When listening to his tones of mirth!
> What lessons of the good and true,
> The brave, the beautiful, he drew!

Among his contemporaries Wilde's reputation was very high, but it was based only in part upon his poems, which are still uncollected. He was one of the nine authors honored with engraved portraits in Griswold's *The Prose Writers of America* (1847). Wilde thought it was impossible for anyone to write great poetry in America, and he did not have a high opinion of his own verses. Like other lawyers and politicians North and South, he felt that a literary reputation was something of a handicap. Some of his Georgia friends found it impossible to understand how a man who had attained distinction as lawyer, orator, and congressman could abandon a successful career to spend five years in Europe and write a book on a forgotten poet like Tasso speculating which of three high-born ladies all named Leonora was the inspiration of his poems. Many of Wilde's poems, like those of Pinkney, Meek, and Poe, are addressed to women; and, again like those of these poets, they show the influence of Moore and Byron. This, however, does not tell the whole story, even when one adds the Southern semichivalric attitude toward women. Wilde shared the Italian Renaissance attitude which Jefferson B. Fletcher has called "the religion of beauty in woman."

One of Wilde's first published poems was "The Ocean Fight," which won a prize in a contest. It appeared in the Port Folio for August, 1815, over the pen name "Quevedo." [70] The famous poem variously known as "Stanzas," "The Captive's Lament," and "My Life Is Like the Summer Rose" seems to have been written about the same time. Just when or where it was first published is not known, but one of its first appearances was in a musical setting by Charles Thibault. It was printed in the Analectic Magazine for April, 1819. It was reprinted in The Columbian Lyre (Glasgow, Scotland, 1828), the editorship of which is attributed to Israel K. Tefft of Savannah.[71] It was again reprinted in Samuel Kettell's Specimens of American Poetry (Boston, 1829), together with some stanzas from the unfinished romantic epic of which it was a part. Captain Basil Hall reprinted it in his Schloss Hainfeld (1836) with the suggestion that its author was the Countess Purgstall. Wilde made no public claim to the authorship of the poem until 1834, when absurd charges of plagiarism were brought against him. Anthony Barclay, British consul at Savannah, in the spirit of fun, had translated the poem into Greek prose, arranged it to look like verse, added some erudite-seeming footnotes, and passed it off on men who knew some Greek as a translation from Alcaeus. By and by it got into print. In 1834 and 1835 two Catholic newspapers claimed the poem for a fictitious Irish poet Patrick O'Kelley. The North American Magazine in December, 1834, published an article entitled "Plagiarism" in which the poem was printed in English, Greek, and Latin. By this time Wilde, who was still in Congress, found the affair embarrassing and wrote to Barclay, then in New York, asking him to explain to the public that the poem was really his. On February 28, 1835,

[70] Port Folio, 4th ser., VI, 211–213. The 4th series was improperly numbered 3rd series. A poem by "Quevedo" appeared in the Port Folio as early as Feb., 1815.

[71] The Boston Public Library card catalogue attributes the volume to Tefft. The inclusion in this early American anthology of poems by the obscure George Robertson, Jr., of Savannah tends to confirm the attribution.

the *New-York Mirror* published an article by Barclay which in 1871 the Georgia Historical Society republished in pamphlet form. The Barclay article printed fragments of Wilde's unfinished epic and a letter from Wilde explaining the origin of the lyric:

The lines in question, you will perceive, were originally intended as part of a longer poem. My brother, the late James Wilde, was an officer of the United States army, and held a subaltern rank in the expedition of Colonel John Williams against the Seminole Indians of Florida, which first broke up their towns and stopped their atrocities. When James returned, he amused my mother, then alive, my sisters and myself, with descriptions of the orange-groves and transparent lakes, the beauty of the St. John's river and of the woods and swamps of Florida, a kind of fairy land—of which we then knew little except from [William] Bartram's ecstacies—interspersed with anecdotes of his campaign and companions. As he had some taste himself, I used to laugh and tell him I'd immortalize his exploits in an epic. Some stanzas were accordingly written for the amusement of the family at our meetings. That, alas! was destined never to take place. He was killed in a duel. His violent and melancholy death put an end to my poem; the third stanza of the first fragment, which alludes to his fate, being all that was written afterwards.

"My Life Is Like the Summer Rose" appears in Fragment IV. An Indian chief describes the sorrows of a white captive among the men of his tribe "many moons ago." The lyric is properly "The Captive's Lament." The captive was probably suggested by the fate of Juan Ortiz, a Spanish captive, who was later to become one of De Soto's guides on his journey to the Mississippi.

The lyric is one of the best of American fugitive poems. It is said to have won the praise of Lord Byron, whose influence is perhaps discernible in the poem. John G. Whittier wrote in 1885: "His [Wilde's] touching lyric was one of the first poems which attracted my attention when a boy. It is a perfect poem." It is not of course a perfect poem, but it is worthy of remembrance. I give the last of the three stanzas:

> My life is like the prints, which feet
>   Have left on Tampa's [72] desert strand;
> Soon as the rising tide shall beat,
>   All trace will vanish from the sand;
> Yet, as if grieving to efface
> All vestige of the human race,
> On that lone shore loud moans the sea—
> But none, alas! shall mourn for me!

[72] In the versions printed in *Schloss Hainfeld* and *The Columbian Lyre* "Tempe's" is substituted for "Tampa's."

Among the best of Wilde's published short poems are "A Farewell to America," "To the Mocking-Bird," and "To Lord Byron," all printed in Griswold's *The Poets and Poetry of America*. Among the unpublished poems there are many graceful complimentary verses addressed to women and some epistles, which are on the whole better. Many of the poems still in manuscript have dates appended to them, but few of the later poems show any appreciable poetic development. Wilde was lacking in literary ambition. In writing to Griswold he seemed much more eager to see his brother John's verses included than his own. After 1844 he seems to have written almost no verse. Some scholar, it is to be hoped, will yet collect Wilde's fugitive verses and publish them with a detailed memoir of his life.

Wilde's one published book of verse, *Hesperia* (1867), appeared, like William Munford's translation of the *Iliad*, long after verses of that kind had gone out of fashion. His son William paid Ticknor and Fields in Boston to publish the book two decades after the poet's death. The poem is an unfinished description of America in four cantos in the manner of Byron's *Childe Harold's Pilgrimage* and in the meter of *Don Juan*. It is addressed to La Signora Marchesa Manfredina di Cosenza, who is apparently a disguise for Mrs. White-Beatty. If we may credit Wilde's dedication, the poem was written for her eye alone and with no thought of publication. She had once suggested that he write a long poem, and years later at irregular intervals he had composed the four cantos mainly to recall scenes in some way associated in his memory with her. These verses, says the poet, "do not constitute a poem, for they have no plan." They are in fact held loosely together by the rather shadowy personage of the supposed author, "The Late Fitzhugh de Lancy, Esq." The poet toys with the Renaissance conceit of immortalizing his lady in verse, but he has no confidence in his own poetic powers.

> Even this frail record is not to survive,
> Foredoomed to dust while I am yet alive!

Not only does the poet lack confidence in his poetic talents but he also finds that "modern life, in America especially, is utterly commonplace. It wants the objects and events which are essential to poetry,—excludes all romance, and admits but one enthusiasm." America has landscapes which are as beautiful as those that surround Florence, but there are few historical and literary associations to humanize them. "Nature, however beautiful, is void" unless it is associated with "human action, passion, thought." (One is reminded of Thomas Moore's reaction to the American scene in 1804.)

Sweet as Egeria's, bore it but her name,
We have full many a grotto-guarded spring:
Streams not unworthy of Illyssus' fame,
Did classic recollections only fling
Grace on their urns,—mountains that well might claim
Eagles and poets of as bold a wing
As soared above Parnassus,—vales that vie
With Tempe, in the hues of earth and sky!

.   .   .   .   .   .

Could we our country's scenery invest
With history, or legendary lore,
Give to each valley an immortal guest,
Repeople with the past the desert shore;
Pass out where Hampdens bled or Shakespeares rest,
Exult o'er Memory's exhaustless store,
As our descendants centuries hence may do,—
We should—and then shall have—our poets too!

But now!—'tis true in this our day and land
All that is written perishes, alas!
Like feeble traces from the sea-beat strand,
Or evening's dews from morning's sunny grass:
Smote by the stroke of dull oblivion's wand,
As all have passed before us, we shall pass,
Nor leave one trace of us or ours behind,—
One glorious deathless monument of Mind!

The disillusioned poet, however, prefers poetry and hopeless love to a political career.

The spell dissolves that held me too a while
In bondage, 'mid the politician's throng:
It was not fame I courted, but THY smile,
And now I give my heart to love and song;
Wondering that toils so vain, and breath so vile,
And cares so base—falsehood, and fraud, and wrong—
Should e'er have held me captive for an hour
Among the slaves of party or of power.

The poet's skepticism includes even scientific knowledge and a belief in progress. One is reminded of Thoreau at Walden.

Alas! this "knowledge" our eternal vaunt,—
This half-refinement, and suburban show,—

This "Liberty" that chiefly serves to taunt
Others who know it not, nor wish to know,—
This vanity that boasts of all we want,—
This steam-borne "Progress" that finds Time too slow,—
What are they all? Gross, blind, ungoverned strength,
Iron-pent vapor which explodes at length!

Writing of the Carolina swamp country before the publication of *In Memoriam* or *On the Origin of Species,* Wilde noted that all nature is at war:

Such is the world, and hath been since the fall,
Life one long war among the things that live:
Each on the other preys, and man on all,
As if it were creation's plan to give
Existence endless, but in atoms small,
And ever-changing;—scorn superlative
Of individual life throughout we trace,
And watchfulness unceasing o'er the race.

It was not until 1850, three years after Wilde's death, that Tennyson published the lines:

Are God and Nature then at strife,
That Nature lends such evil dreams?
So careful of the type she seems,
So careless of the single life.

Hesperia ranges from Florida to Canada and westward to the Mississippi. The four cantos are entitled "Florida," "Virginia," "Acadia," and "Louisiana." The poet is better in describing natural scenes than battlefields. Canto III ends with a tribute to Boston such as few Southern poets would have written a decade or two later:

Here in the Bay State's capital I pause,
'Mid objects Time has rendered doubly dear
To all that reverence letters, arts, and laws;
With old Faneuil what glorious memories rear
Their shadowy forms, what pictures fancy draws
Of all his heroes! Cambridge too is near,—
Familiar Stewart [*sic*], Allston, Greenough's fame,
And Adams, Otis, Webster, Prescott's name!

As he approaches his conclusion, the poet reaffirms his lack of faith in American poetry, including his own:

My nameless, voiceless, tuneless song is o'er,
Avouching well, too well, what first I said,

We have no poetry! Upon this shore
Pan and Apollo and the Muse are dead;
This lay shall fade like all that went before,
While poppies and not laurels crown my head.

30
The Western South

THE FRONTIER furnished American writers with novel and abundant literary materials little known to their European contemporaries, but it supplied them with no literary technique for handling them. And the West was not a region in which a writer would choose to live; the readers were on the Atlantic seaboard or in Europe. Culturally, the frontier represents a reversion to a more primitive way of life in which literature and the fine arts have small place. The bulk of the Western population was uneducated, and those who could read were interested primarily in books of a practical kind or in religious writings with a marked sectarian bias. A considerable proportion of the backwoods population looked askance at schools, colleges, and educated ministers. The backwoodsmen could be reached best by political oratory or the emotional appeal of the circuit-rider and the evangelist with his camp meetings.

We have too often idealized the frontier, seeing in it a glorification of the primitive and a chief source of American democratic thought. Every Western state has idealized its early settlers in much the same way as Virginia and Massachusetts glorified the founders of Jamestown and Plymouth. Frederick J. Turner set the pace in 1893 with his influential essay, "The Significance of the Frontier in American History." In more recent years historians have re-examined Turner's hypothesis, and they now accept it only with considerable qualification.[73] In From Frontier to Plantation in Tennessee (1932) Thomas P. Abernethy has said that in Tennessee: "The frontier is most aptly characterized not by the cry of the frontiersman for more freedom, but by the cry of the speculator for more land. . . ." "The first offspring of

[73] See, for example, George W. Pierson's two articles, the result of an investigation undertaken for the American Historical Association: "The Frontier and American Institutions," New Eng. Quart., XV, 224–255 (June, 1942) and "American Historians and the Frontier Hypothesis in 1941," Wis. Mag. of Hist., XXVI, 35–60, 170–185 (Sept. and Dec., 1942).

The literary influence of the frontier is treated with considerable overemphasis in Lucy L. Hazard, The Frontier in American Literature (1927). My essay "The Frontier," in Norman Foerster (ed.), The Reinterpretation of American Literature (1928), pp. 39–61, needs some qualification in the light of subsequent research.

the West," he continues, "was not democracy, but arrant opportunism." Most of what is memorable in the literature which treats the early West was written on the Atlantic seaboard or in Europe, and the early writings of the Westerners themselves were often greatly influenced by a literary tradition established in the Old World. European Romanticists, who glorified the primitive and the natural, saw the Indian and the frontiersman as idealized figures set in the poetic background of the primeval forest. In French literature the Indian was highly idealized long before the time of Rousseau. So strong was the tradition that Chateaubriand, in spite of his five months in America, pictured the Natchez Indians as Rousseau might have painted them. In English literature, too, the Indian played a romantic role long before Thomas Campbell in 1809 paraphrased Logan's "Speech" in his *Gertrude of Wyoming*, turning eloquent prose into mediocre verse.

In America, however, it was many years before writers could accept the romantic view of the Indian. Charles Brockden Brown in *Edgar Huntly* (1799) painted his Indians as cunning wild beasts more dangerous than the panthers which Huntly hunted with tomahawk in hand. As the frontier slowly receded westward, however, men and women on the Atlantic seaboard, free at last from fear of the scalping knife, began to recognize the wrongs which the red man had suffered and to feel the pathos of his fate. The new point of view—European in origin—is well expressed in two essays in Irving's *The Sketch Book*, "Traits of Indian Character" and "Philip of Pokanoket." In 1823 Joseph Doddridge, who had spent much of his life on the Pennsylvania-Virginia frontier, published a play, *Logan: The Last of the Race of Shikellemus*, which gives an idealized portrait of the famous chieftain. In the same year Fenimore Cooper published the first of the Leather-Stocking Tales. *The Pioneers* is in the main a faithful description of life in a New York neighborhood just passing out of the frontier stage, but in it Cooper introduced those memorable characters, Chingachgook and Natty Bumppo. In 1826, when he published *The Last of the Mohicans*, he set his scene in the primeval forest a generation earlier and introduced in Uncas an ideal Indian warrior as brave and almost as chivalrous as Ivanhoe.

Not all Americans, however, accepted the romantic view of the Indian, and there was a literary reaction against the idealized red man. In his Kentucky story, *Nick of the Woods* (1837), Robert Montgomery Bird protested against Cooper's romantic red warriors and pictured the Indians much as Brockden Brown had seen them. Bird's view was that of the borderer: the only good Indian is a dead one. In 1832 the older Irving, after seeing the plains Indians, wrote in *A Tour on the Prairies*: "As far as I can judge, the Indian of poetical fiction is, like the shepherd of pastoral romance, a mere personification of imaginary attributes."

Some American writers who knew the West could not describe it without being influenced by the romantic tradition. In their nonfiction prose James Hall and Timothy Flint wrote realistically enough; but when they turned to fiction, they could not escape the influence of Cooper and Scott. Something of the romantic view is seen in James Kirke Paulding's *Westward Ho!* (1832), a story of Virginians in Kentucky, and in Beverley Tucker's novel of Virginians in Missouri, *George Balcombe* (1836). The romantic view appears also in the poems and prose sketches which Albert Pike wrote in Arkansas and New Mexico. It colors the poems and historical writings of Alexander Beaufort Meek in Alabama and the poems of Mirabeau Bonaparte Lamar, a romantic Georgian who became the second president of the Republic of Texas.

The central figure in the romantic tradition of the frontiersman is Daniel Boone. In 1784 John Filson, a New Jersey schoolmaster who lived in Kentucky, published *The Discovery, Settlement and Present State of Kentucke*, which paints a somewhat romantic picture of the new land for prospective immigrants. One section of the book, "The Adventures of Col. Daniel Boon," which the famous frontiersman himself approved as his autobiography, spread Boone's reputation far and wide. Gilbert Imlay included it in the 1793 edition of *A Topographical Description of the Western Territory*, where presumably Byron read it. Imlay's novel, *The Emigrants* (1793), which also paints a romantic picture of the frontier, was written in Europe for European readers. As we have seen, Daniel Bryan, who had read Filson's *Kentucke*, apotheosized the still living hero in an epic poem. It was probably the well-known story of Boone's later life that caused Cooper to place the scene of Leather-Stocking's last years on the Western prairie.

The most famous of all tributes to Boone appeared in 1823 in the eighth canto of Byron's *Don Juan*. The passage was included in the Brooklyn, 1823, edition of Filson's *Kentucke*; and here or elsewhere many an American must have read it.

> Of all men, saving Sylla the man-slayer,
>   Who passes for in life and death most lucky,
> Of the great names which in our faces stare,
>   The General Boon, back-woodsman of Kentucky
> Was happiest amongst mortals anywhere;
>   For killing nothing but a bear or buck, he
> Enjoy'd the lonely, vigorous, harmless days
> Of his old age in wilds of deepest maze.

> Crime came not near him—-she is not the child
> Of solitude; Health shrank not from him—for
> Her home is in the rarely trodden wild. . . .

"God made the country, and man made the town," writes Byron quoting William Cowper's famous line. Boone was "even in age the child/Of Nature."

> He was not all alone: around him grew
> A sylvan tribe of children of the chase,
> Whose young unwaken'd world was ever new
> Nor sword nor sorrow yet had left a trace
> On her unwrinkled brow, nor could you view
> A frown on Nature's or on human face;
> The free-born forest found and kept them free,
> And fresh as is a torrent or a tree.
>
> And tall, and strong, and swift of foot were they,
> Beyond the dwarfing city's pale abortions,
> Because their thoughts had never been the prey
> Of care or gain: the green woods were their portions;
> No sinking spirits told them they grew grey,
> No fashion made them apes of her distortions;
> Simple they were, not savage; and their rifles
> Though very true, were not yet used for trifles.

The Western states, however, were to develop a different literary tradition, and this is characterized by humor and satire rather than by romance and the glorification of Nature. In this tradition David Crockett plays a larger part than Daniel Boone. There were other types of frontiersmen than Boone and Leather-Stocking, and the East welcomed with delight the half-horse, half-alligator frontier boaster and teller of tall tales. Paulding introduced him to the New York stage in *The Lion of the West*, and Caruthers described a somewhat similar Western type in *The Kentuckian in New-York* (1834). Crockett's autobiography is in a different style from that of Boone's autobiography as recorded in Filson's *Kentucke*. Westerners were fond of story-telling, and they developed their own characteristic speech, which is closer to what we now regard as American than is found in Eastern writing of the period. The type of writing known as Western or Southwestern humor was being born, but it was not until after 1830 that it produced anything of more than temporary importance. Much of this humorous writing, as we shall see, came from men of education from the east of the Appalachians who were amazed and delighted at the incongruities of life in the new West. In the main it is realistic and satiric, and it recalls William Byrd's picture of the North Carolina Lubberland of 1728. The satiric note is conspicuous also in early Kentucky writing. Thomas Johnson's picture of pioneer Kentucky is no more flattering than Joseph Glover Baldwin's description of Alabama and Mississippi during the flush times of the 1830's.

There were in the new West a few towns, like Lexington, Nashville, and Natchez, in which a well-to-do and highly literate population quite early established schools, colleges, libraries, newspapers, and magazines little inferior to those in the older states. In New Orleans there was another cultural center of importance, but since it expressed itself in the French language and looked to Paris for its culture, it had no great influence on American writing, especially in these early years.

In the beginning there was little to distinguish Kentucky and Tennessee from Ohio and Illinois, but as the slave plantation spread westward, the Southwest differentiated itself from the Northwest. The Western South, however, never became quite like the seaboard South, even after it had built up towns and had established colleges, newspapers, theaters, and lyceums. Irving's friend William C. Preston, who visited the West in 1816, was struck by the differences between Virginia and Kentucky:

In Kentucky I made acquaintance with all the principal families, most of whom were variously connected with my own. . . . The principal inhabitants being well born Virginians, retained much of their native and early characteristics, modified, however, by some touch of influence from their new and raw condition. I will not say that the modification was a defect, for that might be a matter of taste and opinion, but it was different from a staid and settled society. The Browns and the Breckenridges and the Howards had lost a portion of Virginia caste and assumed something of Kentucky esteem, an absence of reticence and a presence of presumptuousness. Amongst persons of my own age, who were native to the state, there was a self-dependence not to say self-assertion, and ostentatious suppression of the smaller courtesies of life and minute observances of convention, which was not pleasant. When emigration to a new country takes place even in masses, civilization is not transported or preserved. . . . An old state of society cannot be propagated in a new country. A certain loss of civilization is inevitable.[74]

Until the opening of the Erie Canal in 1825, Kentucky was the chief thoroughfare to other parts of the West. The earliest settlers in the region

[74] *The Reminiscences of William C. Preston* (1933), ed. Minnie C. Yarborough, pp. 11–12. Cf. Abernethy, *op. cit.*, p. 284: "In the older society a man knew his status; in the new country he assumed it. Lineage counted for little in the West; wealth counted for much, and a 'gentleman' was known by his clothes."

north of the Ohio came from Kentucky or from Virginia and the Carolinas. Their influence in the development of the Middle West was very great, but unfortunately no Southern historian has written a companion volume to Lois Kimball Mathews' *The Expansion of New England* (1909) or Stewart Holbrook's *The Yankee Exodus* (1950), which study the role of the New Englander in the settlement of the West.[75]

Lexington, permanently settled in 1779, was the cultural capital of the Old Northwest until about 1825, when Cincinnati began to take its place. When the steamboat became a chief means of transportation, it was evident that Lexington had no such natural advantages as Cincinnati, Louisville, and St. Louis. Lexington had the first Western newspaper, the *Kentucky Gazette*, and in Transylvania University it had in the early 1820's the most influential Western institution of learning. "When Kentucky was still little more than a wilderness open to the attacks of savages," writes Ralph L. Rusk, "the Latin and Greek authors were on sale in Lexington." Although the town's population as late as 1840 was less than seven thousand, travelers who visited it spoke of it as the Athens of the West. In 1797 Samuel R. Brown had found there about fifty houses crudely built. The best farmers in the vicinity were living in log cabins and wearing hunting shirts and leggings. In May, 1816, he returned to find a large and beautiful town with a university, an academy for girls, and two bookstores.

The log cabins had disappeared, and in their places stood costly brick mansions, well painted and enclosed by fine yards, bespeaking the taste and wealth of their possessions. The leathern pantaloons, the hunting shirts and leggings had been discarded, for the dress and manners of the inhabitants had entirely changed. . . . The inhabitants are as polished, and I regret to add, as luxurious as those of Boston, New-York or Baltimore; and their assemblies and parties are conducted with as much ease and grace, as in the oldest towns of the union.[76]

[75] But see William C. Binkley, "The South and the West," *Jour. So. Hist.*, XVII, 5–22 (Feb., 1951) and the following articles by John D. Barnhart: "Sources of Southern Migration into the Old Northwest," *Miss. Valley Hist. Rev.*, XXII, 49–62 (June, 1935); "The Southern Element in the Leadership of the Old Northwest," *Jour. So. Hist.*, I, 186–197 (May, 1935); and "The Southern Influence in the Formation of Ohio," *ibid.*, III, 28–42 (Feb., 1937).

[76] Samuel R. Brown, *The Western Gazetteer; or Emigrant's Directory* (Auburn, N. Y., 1817), pp. 91, 93.

31
Thomas Johnson

THE BEST EARLY Kentucky verse is satiric, for frontier life had an ugly side particularly unpleasant to those immigrants accustomed to the comforts and the amenities of a settled society in the Eastern states. The satiric note is conspicuous in William Littell's *Festoons of Fancy*, published in Louisville in 1814; [77] and it characterizes the verses of Thomas Johnson, a Virginian who came to Kentucky when he was about twenty-five years old. As early as May 23, 1789, he advertised in the *Kentucky Gazette* a volume of original poems under the title *The Kentucky Miscellany*. If the book was then in print, it is the earliest book in English that was both written and printed in the West. The only copy of the book which survives, however, is the unique copy of the fourth edition, printed at Lexington in 1821, in the Durret Collection of the University of Chicago Library. The upper corner of each leaf of this thirty-six-page pamphlet is moth-eaten or torn off, leaving from three to six lines incomplete. In 1907 John Wilson Townsend reprinted in his *Kentuckians in Literature* many of the poems, which are now more difficult to decipher; but certain passages seemed to Townsend too obscene to reprint. In 1949 The Bluegrass Bookshop in Lexington reprinted Johnson's book with an introduction by Townsend in an edition of only fifty copies.

Practically nothing is known about Johnson except what may be inferred from his poems. From "The Mercer Election, for the Year 1787" it seems evident that he was in Kentucky by that date. He lived in Danville, at one time the state capital, which he described as

> Accursed *Danville*, vile, detested spot,
> Where knaves inhabit, and where fools resort.

We do not know the date of his birth or death or whether new poems were included in the later editions. Some of the poems, particularly the epitaphs, suggest that Johnson had read Burns, some of whose verses were reprinted in the *Kentucky Gazette* as early as November 8, 1797. At times Johnson's aversion extended to all Kentucky.

> I hate Kentucky, curse the place,
> And all her vile and miscreant race!

[77] Republished by the University of Kentucky at Lexington in 1940, with an Introduction by Thomas D. Clark, as the first in a series of "Kentucky Reprints."

Who make religion's sacred tie,
A mask thro' which they cheat and lic;
Proteus could not change his shape,
Nor Jupiter commit a rape,
With half the ease those villains can,
Send prayers to God and cheat their man.

Here as elsewhere Johnson's language is straightforward and unliterary. He paid his respects to the well-known Presbyterian divine David Rice in "On Parson R—e, who refused to perform divine service till his arrears were paid." Rice, it seems, had bought some land in the belief that his congregation would pay for it. While the sheriff was pressing him, communion day arrived. Rice caused a sensation by refusing to administer the sacrament on the ground that persons who refused to pay their debts had no right to communion. Johnson is said to have nailed a copy of his poem to the door of the church.

Ye fools, I told you once or twice,
You'd hear no more from canting R—e;
He cannot settle his affairs,
Nor pay attention unto pray'rs,
Unless you pay up your arrears.
O how he would in pulpit storm,
And fill all Hell with dire alarm!
Vengeance pronounce against each vice,
And, more than all, curs'd avarice;
Preach'd money was the root of all ill,
Consign'd each rich man unto Hell;
But since he finds you will not pay,
Both rich and poor may go that way.
Tis no more than I expected,
The meeting-house is now neglected—
All trades are subject to this chance,
No longer pipe, no longer dance.

Johnson's epitaphs are among his best poems. An "Epigram on William Hudson who Murdered His Wife" reads:

Strange things of Orpheus poets tell,
How for a wife he went to Hell;
Hudson, a wiser man no doubt,
Would go to Hell to be without.

And here is "A Grace Extempore, at Gill's Tavern":

> O Thou, who bless'd the loaves and fishes:
> Look down upon these empty dishes!
> By the same power those dishes fill;
> Bless each of us and curse old GILL.

In a gentler vein is "On Master Paulus Erwin's Little Bitch":

> Here lies the corpse of Little Cue,
> Whose heart was honest, good, and true,
> Why not preserve her mem'ry then,
> Who never yet like faithless men,
> Conceal'd in smiles a mortal spite,
> Nor fawn'd on them she meant to bite?

In "The Author's Hatred to Kentucky in General" Johnson included himself:

> Curs'd be the jilt that sins for pelf,
> And more accursed be myself!
> Who takes no council, mind no rules,
> And only live a jest for fools.

Finally, here is "The Author's Own Epitaph," which I fear gives too true a picture of the unhappy poet:

> Underneath this marble tomb,
> In endless shades lies drunken Tom;
> Here safely moor'd dead as a log
> Who got his death by drinking grog—
> By whiskey grog he lost his breath,
> Who would not die so sweet a death?

32
Wilkins Tannehill

LITERARY HISTORY is usually one of the last historical fields to be cultivated. Samuel Knapp published his *Lectures on American Literature* in 1829, but this is hardly to be dignified by the name of literary history. Not until 1849 did George Ticknor publish his admirable *History of Spanish Literature*. And yet in 1827 there had appeared from the press of John S. Simpson in Nashville, Tennessee, a book such as one would hardly in that year have expected to come from Boston or New York: Wilkins Tannehill's

(1787–1858) *Sketches of the History of Literature, from the Earliest Period to the Revival of Letters in the Fifteenth Century.*[78] In his Preface the author said of it: "It is an attempt by a *'backwoodsman'* to condense and comprise within a narrow compass [342 pages], the most prominent and interesting events, connected with the progress of literary and scientific improvement, from the earliest period through a long succession of ages, and amidst a great variety of circumstances." "Such as it is," he continued, "this volume appears before the public a candidate for patronage and favor, in the hope, that all due and reasonable allowances will be made for its defects, and that its merits will be faithfully appreciated, although proceeding from an individual unknown to fame, and issued from the press in the remote interior of the western country." Tannehill's compilation is no work of genius, but the emanation of such a book from the Tennessee which one associates with David Crockett has led me to bring together the scattered details of Tannehill's life and work that I have discovered, chiefly in the hope that some Tennessee scholar will make a thorough study of this pioneer literary historian.

Tannehill was born in Pittsburgh in 1787. His father, General John Tannehill, suffered financial reverses and died leaving his widow and children with few resources. Mrs. Tannehill's well-to-do brother, Charles Wilkins, took them into his home in Lexington, Kentucky, that cultural oasis in the frontier country west of the Appalachians. After the death of Charles Wilkins, Tannehill, who had gone to Nashville, took his mother and sister there to live with him. His sister's son, Charles Wilkins Webber, became a well-known author of books dealing with the Southwest, of which the best known is *Tales of the Southern Border* (1852). Tannehill was at one time cashier of the Nashville Bank and also one of a group of amateur players. He served on the Nashville board of Aldermen, 1813–1816, and was mayor of the city in 1825 and 1826. (Nashville was not incorporated until 1806). Tannehill was one of the founders of the Tennessee Historical Society in 1820, and he was chosen as its first secretary. He may have been a Unitarian, for in 1829 he was selling tracts for the American Unitarian Association. In 1839 he and W. T. Berry were operating an excellent bookstore. Tannehill was an active Free Mason. As Grand Master of the Cumberland Lodge in April, 1819, he welcomed General Andrew Jackson in a brief speech. He published a Masonic manual in 1824. Later he was a Whig and an admirer of

[78] Another remarkable book to come from the new West was Joseph Buchanan's *The Philosophy of Human Nature* (Richmond, Ky., 1812). See Woodbridge Riley, *American Philosophy: The Early Schools* (1907), Book IV, chap. iii, and Niels Sonne, *Liberal Kentucky, 1780–1828* (1939), chap. iii.

Henry Clay, but he was never a violent partisan. During much of his life he was a journalist, and he edited various newspapers in Nashville and Louisville, one of which was the Nashville *Orthopolitan*, founded in 1845. In 1848–1850 he was editor of the *Portfolio or Journal of Freemasonry and General Literature*. Tannehill is said to have become blind several years before his death in 1858. In reviewing his *Sketches of the History of Literature* in September, 1834, James Hall's *Western Monthly Magazine* said of him:

> Mr. Tannehill has long been known as a writer. . . . As editor of the Nashville Banner and subsequently of the Louisville Herald, he has furnished many valuable essays, elegant in their composition, and instructive in thought, which are probably doomed to the brief existence of newspaper articles. In the conduct of these journals, he also proved by example, that it is possible to conduct a political press, without violating the courtesies of civil and gentlemanly life. He has now, we understand, retired with the usual rewards of native literature —loss of property, and the indifference of the public.

The *Sketches* is of course a compilation, but it is not incompetently done. It covers, as he said, "an extensive field, one which we have not the vanity to suppose ourselves capable of exploring and fully unfolding." His book was designed particularly "for the benefit of those who have neither leisure nor opportunity to examine the subject more at large." The footnotes suggest that Tannehill must have owned certain books which he could hardly have found in any Tennessee public collection in the 1820's. He knew Latin, French, Italian, and probably a little Greek; but he knew no German and he gave scant attention to German literature. One of his twenty chapters, however, deals with the literature of the Arabians. He displays some taste and learning in selecting a variety of translations from Horace and other writers to illustrate his points, for he is not satisfied unless he can illustrate them by apt quotations. It is somewhat surprising perhaps that his discussions of Dante, Petrarch, and Boccaccio should be much better than his treatment of Chaucer. Many quotations from Byron show his fondness for that poet and his particular familiarity with the poems that deal with historic Italy and Greece. Presumably it was in Lexington, that Athens of the West, that Tannehill acquired his interest in literary history and some knowledge of world literature. When the history of American literary scholarship is written, Tannehill should have a small but honorable place in it.

IV

THE ROAD TO DISUNION

1830-1865

1
The Historical Background

THE THIRTY-FIVE years between 1830 and 1865 saw the publication of more American writing of high quality than any similar period in our literary history has seen except perhaps for the thirty-five years beginning about 1910. The earlier period was the golden age of New England, and during those years Emerson, Hawthorne, Thoreau, Longfellow, Lowell, Holmes, and Whittier published most of their best work. In New York Melville published all his best stories except *Billy Budd*, and Whitman by 1865 had written many of his finest poems. To match these names, the South has only such lesser figures as Simms, Kennedy, the Cookes, Hayne, and Timrod and its one major writer, Poe, who in 1837 had left the South to spend his last twelve years in Philadelphia and New York. Not all the Northern writers named above are now rated as major authors and some of them seem rather regional than national figures, but I do not wish any reader of this book to be under any illusion as to the comparable merits of the chief Northern and Southern writers of the period.

And yet there was a large amount of writing in the Southern states during these years, and the South did have a part in what the late F. O. Matthiessen called the "American Renaissance." The literature of the Old South seems today relatively more important than it seemed half a century ago. Even before the Civil War began, that literature was discredited in the North because it came out of the antiquated slavery regime. It remained for twentieth-century scholars to discover that Kennedy, Simms, Timrod, the Legarés, Chivers, and the humorists were more significant figures than the nineteenth-century Northern critics had supposed.

To understand this earlier Southern literature, one must be prepared to read much that even the Southerner now finds repugnant. It is pleasanter to read Paul H. Buck's *The Road to Reunion* than to follow the stony road which led to disunion and civil war. Today the defenders of slavery seem almost as antiquated as the seventeenth-century writers who championed the divine right of kings. Yet the writings of the Old South are an essential part of the nation's literature; and the scholar can no more afford to neglect them than he can afford to leave out of his view the literature of the Ohio Valley or the Pacific Coast. Too many literary historians in discussing American literature in the years 1830–1865 have made sweeping generalizations which may perhaps apply to New York and New England but which simply do not apply to the literature or the literary culture of the Southern states.

The literature of the South differs from that of the Northern states somewhat as the literatures of Scotland and Ireland have varied from the English pattern. One must never forget that Burns was a Scot, Yeats an Irishman, or Poe a Virginian. The South has been in and out of the main stream of American social and political development more than once. In the time of Washington, Jefferson, and Madison the Southern states were in the lead; in the period of Calhoun's ascendancy, however, some of the Southern writers practically repudiated the ideas which motivated the best Northern writing of the time. In the 1870's and 1880's, however, the South was once again to contribute notably to the national literature, as it has done once more in the twentieth century. In my discussions of the writers of the ante-bellum South I have tried to indicate traits and influences which were common to both sections of the country as well as those which belonged only to the South. Most of the earlier Southern literary historians and anthologists, it seems to me, made the capital mistake of treating the literature of the Old South as though it had only a tenuous connection with that of the states north of Maryland and Kentucky.

There is no single key—not even slavery, the most important—to the understanding of the mind of the Old South. Other important factors which must be borne in mind are the influence of Jacksonian democracy and the Southern revolt against the economic and cultural dominance of the Northern states. The South was not a thoroughly integrated part of the nation; too often it was a conscious minority. Southern resentment of the anti-slavery agitation and the failure of the South to share fully in the growth and prosperity of the nation hastened the development of a movement looking toward the creation of a separate nation with slavery somewhat reluctantly acknowledged as its cornerstone. The political results of this movement are well known, but its cultural and literary implications are not so well understood.

Andrew Jackson was a Southerner, like Calhoun, and the influence of the political movement which bears his name was by no means limited to the West or the Northeast, as one might infer from reading Arthur M. Schlesinger, Jr.'s, *The Age of Jackson* (1945). The constitutions of the Southern states were revised in the 1830's, and some of them were again revised before the Civil War. Many officeholders hitherto appointed by governors or elected by state legislatures were now elected by popular vote. Property qualifications for voting were abolished in all but Virginia and North Carolina, and property-holding as a requirement for office was wiped out in all but South Carolina and Louisiana. Massachusetts meanwhile continued until 1853 to apportion representation in her state senate on the basis of property, and Rhode Island until as late as 1888 kept a property qualification for both voting and officeholding. In the South the large-scale planters were shorn of most of their special privileges and political power. In the forties and fifties, as John Pendleton Kennedy, William Elliott, and Charles Gayarré discovered, being a gentleman was often a political handicap. So far as the white population was concerned, "government of the people, by the people, and for the people" was as much an actuality in the South as in the North.

Such was the political situation in the Old South as seen by a modern constitutional historian.[1] This, however, is not the picture painted by antislavery writers. Lowell wrote in "New England Two Centuries Ago" (1865):

There have been two great distributing centres of the English race on this continent, Massachusetts and Virginia. Each has impressed the character of its early legislators on the swarms it has sent forth. Their ideas are in some fundamental respects the opposites of each other, and we can only account for it by an antagonism of thought beginning with the early framers of their respective institutions. New England abolished caste; in Virginia they still talk of "quality folks."

In 1854 a reputable New England historian, Richard Hildreth, author of an early antislavery novel, wrote in his *Despotism in America*:

The Northern States of the Union are unquestionably Democracies, and every day they are verging nearer and nearer towards the simple idea and theoretic perfection of that form of government. The Southern States of the Union, though certain democratic principles are to be found in their constitutions and their laws, are in no modern sense of the word entitled to the appellation of

---

[1] Fletcher M. Green, "Democracy in the Old South," *Jour. So. Hist.*, XII, 3–23 (Feb., 1946). See also Green's *Constitutional Development in the South Atlantic States, 1776–1860* (1930). James Silk Buckingham noted in Southern writing "a singular admixture of the most opposite principles; especially of the most unbridled democracy, and an earnest defence of the institution of slavery" (*The Slave States of America*, London, 1842, II, 81).

Democracies: They are Aristocracies; and aristocracies of the sternest and most odious kind.

In *Miss Ravenel's Conversion from Secession to Loyalty* (1867) John William De Forest, who had spent several years in the South, put the following passage in the mouth of Dr. Ravenel, a Southerner who took the Union side in the Civil War:

"The pro-slavery South meant oligarchy, and imitated the manners of the European nobility. The democratic North means equality—every man standing on his own legs, and not bestriding other men's shoulders—every man passing for just what he is, and no more. . . . The polish of the South is superficial and semi-barbarous, like that of the Poles and other slaveholding oligarchies."

The Abolitionist legend of an undemocratic South so impressed the British economist, J. E. Cairnes, that although he had never been in this country, he wrote confidently in *The Slave Power* (1862):

To sum up in a few words the general results of the foregoing discussion:—the Slave Power—that power which has long held the helm of government in the Union—is, under the forms of a democracy, an uncontrolled despotism, wielded by a compact oligarchy. Supported by the labour of four millions of slaves, it rules a population of four millions of whites—a population ignorant, averse to systematic industry, and prone to irregular adventure. A system more formidable for evil, more menacing to the best interests of the human race, it is difficult to conceive.[2]

Lowell, Hildreth, De Forest, and Cairnes were historically wrong on almost every point in their analysis of Southern society. They were also, unlike the Southern proslavery writers, incredibly blind to the shortcomings of democracy in the industrial North. The Civil War silenced the Southern critics of the Northern plutocracy, and it was not until a generation after the war that Henry George, Edward Bellamy, and William Dean Howells demonstrated how short of the democratic ideal life in the Northern states had fallen.

Lowell, Hildreth, De Forest, and Cairnes saw the large-scale Southern planters as the chief villains, and the slaves and the poor-whites as the chief victims, of a vicious system. They quietly ignored the millions of independent yeoman farmers. The great planters were of course influential men in the same way that educated, well-to-do men are influential everywhere; but,

[2] *The Slave Power* (2nd ed., 1863), p. 103. For an effective refutation, see C. S. Boucher, "In Re That Aggressive Slavocracy," *Miss. Valley Hist. Rev.*, VIII, 13–79 (June–Sept., 1921).

like men of large property in other regions, they were as a rule the last to advocate anything likely to result in revolution.

In this and in all later periods the middle classes provided the South with most of its leaders in politics, literature, and the professions.[3] Conspicuous examples are Henry Clay, Andrew Jackson, John C. Calhoun, Jefferson Davis, Sam Houston, George McDuffie, Alexander H. Stephens, William Lowndes Yancey, Cyrus McCormick, Stonewall Jackson, William Gilmore Simms, Henry Timrod, John R. Thompson, Edgar Allan Poe, and nearly all other Southern writers of the period.

The Abolitionists regarded every slaveholder as an aristocrat and ignored the fact that half the slaves belonged not to planters but to farmers who worked in the fields beside their slaves. In 1860 only one Southern family in five owned any slaves. There were consequently thousands of small farmers who had no slaves and were probably unaware that there was any serious stigma attached to manual labor. The notion that the great planters monopolized all the best lands even in the Black Belt is an error. In his *Plain Folk of the Old South* (1949) Frank L. Owsley demonstrated from a study of surviving court records, tax lists, and census reports that the situation in the Lower South was far more complex. In the Black Belt as elsewhere the majority were farmers rather than planters. There were substantial farmers who employed hired labor and owned no slaves. Eighty per cent of the slaveholding farmers had no more than ten slaves and owned less than five hundred acres of land. In the Black Belt the great planter group constituted no more than 12 per cent of the slaveholders and they were much less numerous in other regions. In the 1850's Virginia, North Carolina, and Maryland were largely a region of small farms. Only 114 families in Virginia owned as many as one hundred slaves, and there were over a million white persons living in the state. In 1860 less than eleven thousand families in the entire South held as many as fifty slaves. E. Merton Coulter thus describes the situation in Georgia:

In 1860 there were 118,000 white families in Georgia, whereas only 41,000 held slaves. But the old plantation, mellow in fiction but too scarce in fact, could blossom forth only where there were about twenty or more slaves to do the work. Now in Georgia in 1860 there were only 6,363 families who could qualify, and credulity should not be stretched so far as to assume that all of these families lived in delightful mansions and read Shakespeare and Scott. The sad

---

[3] This was clearly pointed out in James D. B. De Bow's *The Interest in Slavery of the Southern Non-Slaveholder* (New York, 1860), p. 10. See also chap. xi of D. R. Hundley, *Social Relations in Our Southern States* (New York, 1860).

but inevitable conclusion follows that about 112,000 Georgia families were not presided over by Southern gentlemen and their accomplished ladies. Thus, for every family that might qualify for the planter aristocracy, there were about nineteen who had to be content to remain in the respectable middle class of farmers, tradesmen, and the professional men. . . .

Some of the planters were educated men who represented a high cultural level, but there were, particularly in the Southwest, many recruits to that class from lower economic and social strata. Among them were the rich and obnoxious "cotton snobs." The Southern farmer of this period had neither the culture, the breadth of view, nor the tolerance of the Virginia planter of the eighteenth century, particularly in matters that affected his religion or his slaves. The great planters, especially those sprung from the older families, were generally better educated, more widely traveled, and more tolerant, but they no longer dominated public opinion, even on political questions. In cultural matters the rise of the common man—in the North as well as in the South—was not an unmixed blessing. There was, for one thing, a notable decline in the level of artistic taste which is seen in the increasing popularity of subliterary novels.

The Abolitionist legend of the Old South bears a strange resemblance to the later Southern legend of a Golden Age before the Civil War. This, too, magnified the great planters and all but ignored the middle classes. In the confused period which followed the war the distinctions between great and small farmers became blurred, and well-to-do Southerners of middle-class origin often posed as descendants of large-scale planters. Historical romancers, like Thomas Nelson Page, George Cary Eggleston, Mrs. Burton Harrison, and Mary Johnston—all descended from prominent Virginia families—endowed their heroes and heroines with family trees as distinguished as their own. It is no wonder that it has taken modern historians so long to discover how few the great planters were in comparison with the smaller farmers.

The ante-bellum South had its legend-makers, too. The wealthy Southern planters of the thirties and forties were not as a rule descendants of the great planters of the eighteenth century, but they liked to think of themselves as continuing the aristocratic tradition, and they came to regard themselves as gentlemen born, descendants of the Virginia Cavaliers of the seventeenth century. The way of life of the Southern planters had from the beginning been modeled on that of English country gentlemen. As the tension between North and South increased, there was a growing disposition to regard Northerners, especially New Englanders, as descendants of low-born shopkeepers and fanatical Puritans. (In the same period Lowell and other New Englanders were playing up their Puritan ancestors as the real founders of American democracy and maintaining that most of what was good in the national character was of Puritan origin.[4]) English gentlemen had looked down upon men "in trade." As the Southern planters more and more often played up English Cavaliers as the ancestors and models of Southern gentlemen, they began, apparently for the first time, to talk about "Southern chivalry." Scott's *Ivanhoe* and chivalric romances by other British novelists probably had something to do with the extraordinary development of the Cavalier legend in the thirties and forties.[5]

The actual number of Cavaliers who settled in Virginia during the English Civil War and the Cromwell regime has been variously estimated, but it was certainly not the wholesale migration which was later supposed to have occurred, and the number that settled in other Southern colonies was inconsiderable. More of the great Virginia families were founded by merchants and sea captains than by country gentlemen.

Until after the American Revolution there was little disposition among Virginians to magnify the numbers or the importance of the Cavaliers who settled in the colony. In the early eighteenth century Robert Beverley the historian, son of an English country gentleman, wrote in his *History of Virginia:* "Several good Cavalier Families went thither [to Virginia] with their effects." [6] After the Revolution Virginians were no longer in close touch with English life and most of them were also ignorant of the history of their own commonwealth. They forgot that the term "Cavalier" had indicated not social status but merely political affiliation. All Cavaliers were now thought of as gentlemen or even noblemen, and it was supposed that they came over by the thousand. John Marshall mentioned "the great number of cavaliers, who, after the total defeat of their party in England, fled for refuge and safety to Virginia"; and John Daly Burk wrote: "The vigilant and severe government of the Protector, had compelled the cavaliers to resort in crouds to Virginia." The Virginia historian Hugh Blair Grigsby

[4] See, for example, George William Curtis's address before the New England Society in New York on Dec. 22, 1876, "The Puritan Principle: Liberty under the Law" in his *Orations and Addresses* (1894), I, 243–249. Thomas Wentworth Higginson wrote in 1867: "All the long, stern reign of Plymouth Rock and Salem Meeting-House was well spent, since it had this for an end,—to plough into the American race the tradition of absolute righteousness, as the immutable foundation of all" (*Atlantic Essays*, 1871, p. 46).

[5] The subject is discussed at greater length and with fuller documentation in my article, "Cavalier and Indentured Servant in Virginia Fiction," *S.A.Q.*, XXVI, 22–39 (Jan., 1927).

[6] *History of Virginia* (1722), p. 249. "Several" is also the term used by Governor Nicholson, Hugh Jones, and the English historian John Oldmixon.

protested against tracing "the distinguishing and salient points of the Virginia character to the influence of those butterflies of the British aristocracy"; but the legend grew steadily.

In *The Cavaliers of Virginia* (1835) and *The Knights of the Horse-Shoe* (1845) William Alexander Caruthers played up the Cavaliers as "the first founders of the aristocracy . . . the immediate ancestors of that generous, fox-hunting, wine-drinking, duelling and reckless race of men, which gives so distinct a character to Virginians wherever they may be found." Caruthers even turned Nathaniel Bacon's plebeian army into Cavaliers. In the final stage of the tradition, Southerners in all states became descendants of the Cavaliers. The tradition was in the mind of Robert Toombs when he said: "We [of the South] are a race of gentlemen." The Civil War seemed to Confederate poets and orators to represent the traditional antithesis of Puritan and Cavalier. The legend was impressed upon English visitors to Virginia, like G. P. R. James and Thackeray and, at a later date, Matthew Arnold; and it had something to do with widespread English sympathy with the Confederacy as representing a nation of gentlemen fighting against the descendants of vulgar Puritans and low-born immigrants from the European continent.

While Southerners were playing up the Cavaliers, they forgot about the numerous indentured servants who had come to the colonies. In 1786 Jefferson had estimated that not more than two thousand in all had come to Virginia. It remained for American historians to discover that soon after the Restoration Governor Berkeley had estimated that there were already six thousand in Virginia and that they were still coming over at the rate of fifteen hundred a year.

Northerners, however, were not so willing to forget the indentured servants who had come to Virginia—though they had little to say of those who came to the Northern colonies. Frederick Law Olmsted wrote: "Not one-tenth certainly, probably not one-thousandth, of the fathers of Virginia were of gentle blood. The majority of them were sold and bought as laborers." In 1864 Charles Sumner, who had no love for the South, devoted a fourth of a long political speech to a learned attempt to prove that the Virginians were descendants of convict servants of the most disreputable character.

The era of good feeling was approaching its end in 1818. Missouri's petition to be admitted as a slave state in that year brought violent protests from Northern Congressmen who feared the extension of slavery in the West or wished to break up a political alliance between Western and Southern farmers.[7] The immediate outcome was a compromise: Maine was admitted as a free state to balance Missouri. But the slavery question, having been brought into the open, was destined eventually to overshadow all other questions, as Thomas Cooper had predicted it would. John Quincy Adams wrote in his diary on January 10, 1820: "I take it for granted that the present question is a mere preamble—a title-page to a great, tragic volume." From Monticello on April 22 of the same year Jefferson wrote to John Holmes: ". . . this momentous question, like a fire bell in the night, awakened and filled me with terror. I considered it at once as the knell of the Union. It is hushed, indeed, for the moment. But this is a reprieve only, not a final sentence."

North and South were drifting steadily apart, and each blamed the other for forsaking the true American tradition. Neither section was clearly conscious of its own changed point of view, but it saw plainly enough the other's departure from its former stand. The agricultural South saw with alarm the threat of a hostile and more powerful industrial North, which seemed to hate alike slavery and slaveholder. The urban North was beginning to lose its ability to understand the attitude of the farmer, and it regarded slavery as a bar to industrial expansion. Antislavery agitation grew more violent and Southern resentment increased accordingly. The terms of the Compromise of 1850 were less acceptable to either section than those of the Missouri Compromise had been. In the North the stringent fugitive slave law of 1850 outraged the feelings of many persons, and the extension of slavery into the Western territories seemed to forebode disaster. Only a handful of men understood that beyond Missouri and eastern Texas slavery could never be profitable enough to warrant its extension there. The planters of the Lower South, dependent upon slave labor, had no sympathy with Jefferson's antislavery views. The new and violent Abolition crusade of Garrison, Phillips, and Weld seemed a direct incitement to slave insurrection, and it gradually silenced the voices of Southerners who hated slavery. Hostility to slavery was now a worldwide phenomenon, but the South had invested its capital in slaves and land and saw in emancipation not only financial ruin but the creation of an appalling race problem.

[7] "It [the Missouri controversy] made the question of sectional political power the paramount American issue, without regard to party. It pointed toward—indeed it was the last political step that led to—the abolition crusade. It demonstrated the vast advantages which might be derived from a union of the moral with the political, and marked the first combining of the two by the North in its fight against the slave power" (Albert F. Simpson, "The Political Significance of Slave Representation, 1787–1821," *Jour. So. Hist.*, VII, 334, Aug., 1941).

On the eve of the Civil War a Virginian, Dr. William H. Holcombe, summed up the momentous changes in each section's attitude which had come about in a generation:

It has not been more than twenty-five years since Garrison was dragged through the streets of Boston with a rope around his neck, for uttering Abolition sentiments; and not thirty years since, the abolition of slavery was seriously debated in the Legislature of Virginia. Now, on the contrary, the radical opinions of Sumner, Emerson and Parker, and the assassination schemes of John Brown, are applauded in *Fanueil* [sic] Hall, and the whole Southern mind with an unparalleled unanimity regards the institution of slavery as righteous and just, ordained of God, and to be perpetuated by Man.[8]

In the summer of 1857 a Southern planter who had been educated in New England revisited that section. Hitherto he had been a Whig and a Union man. On his return home he announced his change of mind in *De Bow's Review* in November, 1857, in an article entitled "South Side View of the Union." Twenty-seven years before, he said, he had attended in New England a meeting of a newborn organization calling itself "the society for the Abolition of slavery." "The wild glare of an unsettled brain," he remembered, "marked the countenances of most of those who conducted the meeting. . . . They dwelt much on its [slavery's] wrongfulness, and said some words, that made everybody stare and wonder if they were not clean 'daft,' about slaveholders being man stealers, thieves, and pirates. . . . When the exhibition was over, the assembly went away smiling and pitying the strange enthusiasts, who could embark in so hopeless an undertaking." But today, the disillusioned planter continued, "these men elect Congressmen; have Governors and Legislatures doing their behests; and (in spite of the concentrated conservatism of the whole nation) well nigh placed their candidate in the Presidential chair." It was not only politicians and demagogues, he told his Southern readers, that engaged in this agitation: ". . . quiet clergymen (messengers of peace) rave and froth when our institution is the topic. . . . from teacher and professor comes a steady and increasing stream of invective. . . . Even staid and conservative Yale . . . now fulminates against us amongst the loudest in angry popular assemblies, the lecture room and the magazine. . . . The aim is to excommunicate, to render us loathed and ignominious. Their cry is 'Delenda est Carthago.' " For the South, he concluded, there was left no remedy but secession.

The movement to establish a separate Southern nation came too late. Full economic autonomy was incompatible with the very nature of the

[8] "The Alternative: A Separate Nationality, or The Africanization of the South," *S.L.M.*, XXXII, 81 (Feb., 1861).

plantation regime. Economically, the status of the South was—and in many respects still is—that of a colony.[9] It was dependent on the outside world for its market and for much of its capital. A colonial economy is a debtor economy. Even if the Confederacy had managed to win the war, it could not have attained economic self-sufficiency without giving up much of what it had fought for. A victorious Confederacy would have continued to be a debtor region economically exploited by Northern or European bankers and merchants unless it gave up its dependence on agriculture—the basis of the social system which it fought to preserve.

The economic dependence of the South upon the industrial North in 1860 was much greater than most Southerners realized. Even educated men seemed to think that the Confederacy had the resources to win the war. They had unbounded faith in the power of King Cotton to bring about intervention by England and France. After the war the disillusioned General Richard Taylor wrote in his Destruction and Reconstruction (1879): "We set up a monarch, too, King Cotton, and hedged him with a divinity surpassing that of earthly potentates. To doubt his royalty and power was a confession of ignorance or cowardice. This potent spirit, at the nod of our Prosperos, the cotton-planters, would arrest every loom and spindle in New England, destroy her wealth, and reduce her population to beggary. The power of Old England, the growth of eight hundred years, was to wither as the prophet's gourd unless she obeyed its behests."

Commercial convention after convention from 1837 to 1859 protested against the "cotton triangle," the tariff, and other Northern methods of exploiting the Southern farmers, but the results were negligible. The planters with their contempt for business and businessmen had permitted Northern men to monopolize the marketing of their staples at a handsome profit and had likewise permitted the North to supply them with most of their manufactured products—again at a profit. Agitation increased Southern resentment at this economic dependence, but it did not change essentially the Southerner's way of life. It could and did, however, pave the way for secession.

The completeness of the South's dependence on the North was suggested by more than one speaker at the commercial conventions. For example, at the New Orleans convention of 1855 Albert Pike said:

From the rattle with which the nurse tickles the ear of the child born in the South to the shroud that covers the cold form of the dead, every thing comes to

---

[9] B. B. Kendrick, "The Colonial Status of the South," Jour. So. Hist., VIII, 3–22 (Feb., 1942); Walter P. Webb, Divided We Stand (1937); Rupert Vance, Human Geography of the South (1932), pp. 467 ff.

us from the north. We rise from between sheets made in northern looms, and pillows of northern feathers, to wash in basins made in the north, dry our beards on northern towels, and dress ourselves in garments woven in northern looms; we eat from northern plates and dishes; our rooms are swept with northern brooms, our gardens dug with northern spades, and our bread kneaded in trays or dishes of northern wood or tin; and the very wood that feeds our fires is cut with northern axes, helved with hickory brought from Connecticut and New York.[10]

At the commercial conventions the South's intellectual dependence upon the North was vigorously condemned. In 1845 James D. B. De Bow, estimating that Northern exploitation cost the South a hundred million dollars each year, asked: "Is there any reciprocity, sirs? Who of the North 'reads a Southern book?'—they have said this themselves sneeringly—who visits a Southern watering-place—attends a Southern College? . . . Great God! Does Ireland sustain a more degrading relation to Great Britain? Will we not throw off this humiliating dependence, and act for ourselves?"

There was no great outcry against Northern teachers, for after living in the South a few years most Northern men and women accepted the Southern point of view; but there was great dissatisfaction with Northern schoolbooks, which were usually the only texts available. A writer in De Bow's Review asked in September, 1852:

What is to be done with geographies that tell pupils "States are divided into towns and counties"? as if, out of New England, the use of town, as synonymous with parish, district, or township, was usual; that devote two pages to Connecticut onions and broomcorn, and ten lines to Louisiana and sugar? of histories that are silent about Texas? of first readers, that declare all spelling but Noah Webster's as "vulgar," and "not used in good society"? and of "speakers" that abound in selections from northern debates in Congress, and from abolition poets? [11]

One J. W. Morgan complained in De Bow's Review for April, 1860, that the history books used in Southern schools portrayed the early New England settlers "as a set of incorruptible patriots, irreproachable moralists, and most

---

[10] De Bow's Rev., XVIII, 524 (April, 1855). Similar passages are given in R. S. Cotterill, The Old South (1936), pp. 193–194; Herbert Wender, Southern Commercial Conventions, 1837–1859 (1930), p. 207; and John Fulton, Memoirs of Frederick A. P. Barnard (1896), pp. 121–122. Compare also Henry W. Grady's story of the "Pickens County Funeral," which he used repeatedly in the 1880's (Raymond B. Nixon, Henry W. Grady, 1943, p. 10).

[11] "Southern School-Books," De Bow's Rev., XIII, 262 (Sept., 1852). At the New Orleans Commercial Convention in 1855 the Reverend C. K. Marshall estimated that the Southern states each year paid to the North nearly five million dollars "as tribute money for books, education and abuse" (Wender, op. cit., p. 157).

exemplary models for future generations," while the Southern settlers were described "as a race of immoral reprobates, who have handed down all their vices and evil habits to their descendants of this day." Morgan could not see what benefit Southern boys and girls could possibly derive "from reading works wherein they are constantly informed that their fathers, and ancestors generally, for the last two hundred years, have been a heartless, cruel, bloody-minded set of robbers, kidnappers, and slave-whippers. . . ." [12]

Southerners complained that Northern school readers omitted Southern writers. Said one critic in the *Southern Literary Messenger* for December, 1858:

The verses of many New England bards are recited at Academy Exhibitions, and held up, with the pieces of Collins and Gray, as models of poetical composition, while the minstrels of South Carolina may in vain expect to obtain a hearing. If the poems of Bryant are far more widely esteemed than those of Simms, the result is due, therefore, not to their superiority so much as to the fact that they are in the hands of every schoolboy in the country beneath the lids of his Commonplace Book, while the only circulation enjoyed by the South Carolina verses, apart from the volumes in which they are brought out, is in the columns of the Southern newspaper.

The Duyckinck brothers' *Cyclopaedia of American Literature* (1855) was favorably received in the South, for its compilers had taken pains to seek the advice and assistance of their Southern friends, Simms, Cooke, and others; but Charles A. Dana's *Household Book of Poetry* (1857), which left out Simms, displeased the South Carolinians. In January, 1859, *Russell's Magazine*, anticipating a famous phrase of H. L. Mencken's, remarked that in Dana's book "the South is as quietly ignored, as if an intellectual Sahara did, in reality, stretch from Mason and Dixon's line to the waves of the gulf that washes the shores of Louisiana." Dana's sensible reply was that while he regarded Simms as "one of the most distinguished ornaments of

---

[12] "Our School Books," *De Bow's Rev.*, XXVIII, 436, 438 (April, 1860). For similar complaints, see John S. Ezell, "A Southern Education for Southrons," *Jour. So. Hist.*, XVII, 303–327 (Aug., 1951). For additional materials, see Edgar W. Knight, *A Documentary History of Education in the South* (5 vols., 1949–1953), V, 278–316.

Not all the histories that neglected the South were written before the war. A Northern traveler, Julian Street, wrote in *American Adventures* (1917), p. 106: "From my school history I gathered the idea that although Sir Walter Raleigh and Captain John Smith were so foolish as to dally more or less in the remote fastnesses of Virginia, and although there was a little ineffectual settlement at Jamestown, all the important colonizing of this country occurred in New England."

One of the most flagrant examples of this kind of provincialism that I have seen is Joe McCarthy's "Massachusetts: Where America Started," which appeared in *Holiday*, II, 34–49, 120–124 (June, 1952).

American literature," he thought his reputation would always "rest upon his prose works rather than his poems." Rufus W. Griswold's *The Poets and Poetry of America* (1842) did not please Southern reviewers any better than it pleased Poe. One critic suggested that the book should have been entitled *The Poets of the Northern States of the United States*. Beverley Tucker's reaction was unconventional: "We, in the South, forsooth, can hardly find the name of a southern man in Mr. Griswold's collection. 'Marry, and I am glad on 't. I'd rather be a kitten and cry mew, than one of those metre ballad mongers,' who are exhibited as the élite of American poets. . . .''

But it was not textbooks and anthologies alone that irritated Southern readers. In the fifties even the literary magazines of the North seemed hostile. The *North American Review* was on the whole friendly, but the *Atlantic Monthly*—which seemed a sectional organ masquerading in the guise of a national magazine—was hostile from the beginning. The *Southern Literary Messenger* found the *Atlantic's* first number "a fresh, clean, thoroughly respectable looking magazine" with "varied and entertaining" reading matter. There was nothing openly unfriendly to the South as yet, but, the *Messenger* predicted, "*cela viendra.*" The prophetic reviewer found the *Atlantic's* second number (December, 1857) bristling "with falsehoods against the Southern civilization." As a specimen, he quoted from Edmund Quincy's "Where Will It End?": "No antiquity hallows, no public services consecrate, no gifts of lofty culture adorn, no graces of noble breeding embellish the coarse and sordid oligarchy (the slave States) that gives law to us. And in the blighting shadow of slavery letters die and art cannot live." The *Messenger* might well have quoted Quincy further: "What book has the South ever given to the libraries of the world? What work of art has she ever added to its galleries?" The Bostonians of course had no high opinion of Poe or Simms, but Quincy might at least have remembered the poems and paintings of Washington Allston. James Russell Lowell, the editor who published Quincy's article, was himself to write of the civilization of the Old South in the *North American Review* in October, 1866: "There were no public libraries, no colleges worthy of the name; there was no art, no science,—still worse, no literature but Simms's: there was no desire for them." The Abolitionist legend of the Old South was to have an unfortunate influence upon those Northern writers who in the later nineteenth century were to write the political, social, and literary history of the United States.

Southern sensitiveness to outside criticism became extreme in the fifties. A writer in the *Southern Literary Messenger* for April, 1856, said:

There is a foolish soreness in our Southern fancies about having any blur or blemish pointed out in our society, which is absolutely childish. There is a certain class of minds who see in every effort of the kind, some imaginary thrust at the "peculiar institution." . . . we have met men who cannot bear to hear that there is good music in Rome, or good pianos made in Boston, and little of either in Virginia, because, forsooth, they think there is some slur cast upon the South.

Commenting on "Injustice to the South" in the *International Monthly Magazine* for December, 1851, Rufus W. Griswold wrote: "In politics, in religion, in letters, our friends beyond Washington will not believe us in the North capable of treating them with fairness. In literature we have constantly heard it alleged that success should never be dreamed of by an author who had the misfortune to be born the wrong side of Mason and Dixon's line." And yet, Griswold thought, if *The Scarlet Letter* had emanated from Charleston, it would have been as popular as it was coming from New England. He continued:

We have an amusing illustration of the [Southern] feeling on this point in the last *Southern Literary Messenger*. The amiable and accomplished editor [John R. Thompson] of that work counts among his personal friends as many northern gentlemen as have had ever opportunity to know him, yet he honestly believes us incapable of appreciating the genius of a poet from one of the tobacco, sugar, or cotton states. Introducing some pretty verses entitled *The Marriage of the Sun and Moon*, "by the late H. S. Ellenwood, of North Carolina," into his last number, he says:

"Had the gifted author been a native of Massachusetts, his name would be familiar as household words: as it is, we doubt whether one in ten of our readers has ever heard of it."

Griswold knew more about minor American authors than almost any of his contemporaries, and he had an effective reply:

He *was* a native of Massachusetts. His original name was Small, and he was born in Salem . . . at twenty-one had his name changed to H. S. Ellenwood; in 1820 emigrated to North Carolina. . . . We suspect that, in literature at least, all charges of "injustice to the South," are as ill founded as this.

Still unconvinced, Thompson replied in a private letter:

I remark your hit at me about "Injustice to the South." Nevertheless the fact is so, and the "Scarlet Letter" hailing from Charleston would have lined portmanteaus. Why can't [James M.] Legaré find a publisher? Depend upon it, if another De Foe should emerge from the pine-barrens of Carolina, with a

Robinson Crusoe under his arm, he would find an Edmund Curll in every book shop of Northern publication houses. Legaré is not De Foe, to be sure, but if he lived in New England it would be different.

In the thirties and forties Southern magazinists pleaded for a literature that would serve to justify the South in the eyes of its own citizens and the outside world, but the Southern public calmly went on buying Northern books, magazines, and newspapers. The politicians meanwhile thought they could protect Southern interests in Washington. It was the crisis of 1850 and even more the extraordinary vogue of *Uncle Tom's Cabin* (1852), in the Old World as well as the New, that revealed to Southerners the plight of the slave states. They were now arraigned before the civilized world without being able to make an effective defense. George Frederick Holmes in December, 1852, put before the readers of the *Southern Literary Messenger* the predicament in which the South now found itself:

The Southern population have checked and chilled all manifestations of literary aptitudes at the South; they have discouraged by blighting indifference, the efforts of such literary genius as they may have nurtured: they have under-rated and disregarded all productions of Southern intellect; and now, when all the batteries of the literary republic are turned against them, and the torrent of literary censure threatens to unite with other agencies to overwhelm them, it is in vain that they cry in their dire necessity, "Help me, Cassius, or I sink."

The demand for a distinctively Southern literature led to the establishment of numerous short-lived magazines, and it stimulated some persons to write and to publish; but it did not serve to make Southern literature *Southern* except in a rather superficial sense of the word. The sketches of the humorists, written without literary pretensions and generally first printed in the newspapers, are far more Southern than the great mass of the material printed in the literary magazines. The agitation, however, did probably succeed in raising somewhat the status of the author in the South. John R. Thompson, who as editor of the *Messenger* was in a position to know, wrote in December, 1857: "It is getting to be thought that a man, may perhaps, accomplish as much for the South by writing a good book as by making a successful stump speech."

One finds in the magazines frequent allusions to the obstacles to literary development in the South but few such thoroughgoing analyses as that which George Tucker had made or those which were to be made after the Civil War by Thomas Nelson Page and John Spencer Bassett. The non-literary Southerner undoubtedly applauded William Lowndes Yancey when he said: "Our poetry is our lives; our fiction will come when truth has ceased to satisfy us; and as for our history, we have made about all that has glorified the United States." The Southern magazinists, however, felt impelled to try to create a Southern literature. It was as though Sydney Smith's famous question had been: "Who reads a *Southern* book?" Southerners were being made to feel that their civilization must stand or fall by its literature rather than by any other test which might be applied to it.

Various writers pointed out that the South, having no professional authors except Simms, had to rely upon amateurs; that a literary reputation was a handicap to a professional man; that law and politics attracted the men who might have produced a Southern literature; that the South had no large cities to serve as literary and publishing centers; and, finally, that the Southern people would not buy Southern books or pay for the Southern magazines for which they had subscribed. What was probably the greatest handicap was put realistically enough by Simms: "No *purely* agricultural people any where, has ever produced a national literature; has ever triumphed in the Arts, *belles lettres*, or the Drama; though they have produced great orators, politicians, warriors, and even philosophers."

Hinton Rowan Helper was the one Southern writer who accepted the Abolitionist theory that it was the blight of slavery which prevented the South from creating an important literature. The Reverend S. J. Cassels answered this contention by an appeal to history: "The cause of this state of things cannot be found in the influence of slavery. Athens and Rome, at the very acme of literary fame, were surrounded by an almost infinite multitude of slaves." [13]

Cassels, however, failed to note a significant difference between the nineteenth-century South and ancient Rome and Athens. In the days of Pericles and Augustus slavery was accepted as the normal condition of thousands of human beings. Southern slaveholders were on the defensive in a world which condemned slavery as a relic of barbarism. They looked to their writers to defend the institution against attacks from the outside. Moreover, so sensitive were Southerners in this period that few writers were willing to attempt a faithful picture of life on a slave plantation. There was always the danger that an innocuous passage might be misconstrued by hypersensitive Southern readers or used as propaganda by the Abolitionists. No Southern writer dared to follow Thackeray and satirize the "cotton snobs," who were too often in the Northern mind confounded with Southern gentlemen.

[13] "Domestic Literature," *So. Presbyt. Rev.*, V, 7 (July, 1851), Cassels admitted, however, that "Probably . . . . at least two-thirds of what may pass for Southern literature has been produced by *adopted* citizens!" Cassels greatly exaggerated the number of Southern writers born outside the South.

The writers of the New South labored under even severer economic handicaps than their ante-bellum predecessors, but with slavery gone they could portray the life of their region with a freedom which Cooke and Simms did not have.

The most penetrating analysis of the difficulties of the Southern author was Henry Timrod's "Literature in the South," which appeared in *Russell's Magazine* for August, 1859. Timrod began by suggesting that the Southern author was "the Pariah of modern literature," for no author anywhere else had, he thought, such peculiar difficulties and so limited an audience. "He publishes a book. It is the settled conviction of the North that genius is indigenous there, and flourishes only in a Northern atmosphere. It is the equally firm conviction of the South that genius—literary genius, at least —is an exotic that will not flower on a Southern soil." If he published his book in the North, the South was indignant that he had not chosen a Southern publisher; but if he published his next book in the South, he found more than half the edition left on his hands. (Such was the actual experience of Timrod's friend Hayne.) If he gave a beautiful and truthful picture of Southern life, he was abused in the North; if he published a volume of poems of universal appeal but without Southern local coloring, his own people condemned him as lacking in Southern feeling. Southerners, said Timrod, were an educated people but provincial and not highly cultivated. Their tastes and standards were archaic, and they did not esteem their own writers. Not once but a hundred times had he heard "the works of the first of Southern authors [Simms] alluded to with contempt by individuals who had never read anything beyond the title-pages of his books." Timrod charged that, for all the outcry about a Southern literature, the South had neglected all its writers with the solitary exception of Poe.

"Southernism in literature," Timrod believed, had led to many absurdities, including the overrating of certain writers merely because they had selected Southern themes or backgrounds. He reminded his readers that Shakespeare was no less an Englishman when he wrote *Antony and Cleopatra* than when he wrote his plays on English history. True originality, he contended, "will be always found identical with true nationality." "It is, unfortunately," he insisted, "not in the power of a people to confer together and say, 'Come, now, let us arise, and build up a literature.'"

2
Education

IN THE THIRTY years preceding the Civil War the Southern states made rapid progress in education, but the advance was much less notable in the public schools than in the academies, denominational colleges, and state universities. The Jackson movement, which resulted in a widened suffrage, led to agitation for more and better public schools, but in some quarters there was strong opposition. There were some who believed that education was not properly the concern of the state, and there were many more who did not want to pay the heavier taxes necessary to establish the schools. Active supporters of the public school movement were William Crafts in South Carolina and Alexander Beaufort Meek in Alabama. It remained for the despised carpetbag regimes in the Reconstruction period to write statewide educational requirements into some of the state constitutions. Such public schools as were put into operation functioned better in the towns than in rural communities. According to the census of 1850, illiteracy among Southern whites was as high as 20.3 per cent, while in the Middle Atlantic states it was about three and in New England less than one.

The most notable account of the numerous old-field schools—they were not free public schools—is found in Richard Malcolm Johnston's "Early Educational Life in Middle Georgia" and in his novels and short stories. These schools had little in the way of equipment, and they varied from good to extremely bad. The teachers' pay was low, and until late in the period most of the teachers came from the North. In Middle Georgia many of them were from Vermont, the better ones from Middlebury College. The emphasis was upon spelling, declamation, and arithmetic. Reading was badly taught and geography was conducted without maps and often without blackboards. The teacher's motto might have been "No lickin', no l'arnin'," as in Edward Eggleston's *The Hoosier Schoolmaster*, which gives a memorable account of a school of the old-field type which flourished among the poorer Southerners who had migrated to Indiana.

Some of the old-field schools called themselves academies, but in general the term was restricted to those schools which taught Latin and Greek. In 1850 the Southern states had more than 2700 academies; there were about 1000 in New England and nearly 2100 in the Middle Atlantic states. After 1850 they began to decline in the North, but in the South they were still fairly numerous as late as 1890. After that date, as the public high schools became better and more accessible, most of them either went out of existence or became college preparatory schools for the sons and daughters of the well-to-do.

The academies performed to some extent the functions of the public high school, the college preparatory school, the normal college, and in some instances even the liberal-arts college. Some of them in fact developed into colleges. Among the variants of the academy type were military, manual labor, and denominational schools. Some of the academies, unlike the colleges and universities, were coeducational. Most of them were nonsectarian, but the religious emphasis was strong in nearly all of them. Apart from the local boards of trustees, there was no sort of supervising agency, and they varied from good to very poor. They served, like the colleges, to give training in public speaking; and in the selections used for declamation and reading the emphasis was upon patriotism and morals. They often emphasized more than the higher institutions not only practical subjects but also English and American literature.

Increased attention was everywhere being paid to the education of women, but, as William Charvat notes, while the best of the women's colleges were those in the Northeast, "the number of girls enrolled in them was negligible; whereas the South, which had forty-two of the fifty-six women's colleges established during the period [ending in 1870], was giving higher education to almost as many women as men." Among the colleges operated by religious denominations was Wesleyan College in Macon, Georgia—chartered in 1836 and taken over by the Methodists in 1839—the oldest college for women in the United States. Harry Stillwell Edwards, writing to Fred Lewis Pattee in 1914, attributed largely to the influence of this college Georgia's remarkable literary development in the later nineteenth century. Some Southern families still imported governesses from the North, and others sent their daughters to Northern schools. One of the best of these was Madame Chegaray's school in New York, where Constance Fenimore Woolson met many Southern girls. Somewhat later Mary Noailles Murfree attended the Chegaray school in Philadelphia.

At a meeting of the National Teachers' Association at Harrisburg, Pennsylvania, in August, 1865, the war just ended was described in typical Abolitionist language as one "of education and patriotism against ignorance and barbarism." The members of the Association would doubtless have branded as incredible any suggestion that in the Southern states the percentage of college-bred persons was higher than it was in the North. It was in fact, if we exclude the Negro slaves, almost two to one. In 1840 the 19 New England colleges had 2,857 students, some of them Southerners; the 80 Southern colleges had 6,608. Even counting the slaves, in 1840 the South had one college student for each 376 of its entire population, while the remainder of the country had only one for each 550 persons. During the next two decades college enrollment increased more rapidly in the South than in the North. In 1860, for example, the 23 Virginia colleges had a total of 2,824 students while Massachusetts' 8 had only 1,733, of whom some were Virginians. At that time Virginia was spending annually fifty thousand dollars more on her colleges than was being spent in the Bay State.[14]

The academic standing of many of the Southern colleges was low; but, if we except Yale, Princeton, and Harvard, which had many Southern students, it was none too high in the North and West. In those years huge sums of money were not required to found a college or a university, and it was easier then for the small college to compete with the larger ones. A good many Southerners, however, thought that Harvard, Yale, and Princeton were the best schools in the country. Southern students constituted from one-third to one-half the total enrollment at Princeton. In 1850 there were 115 Southern students at Princeton, 65 at Harvard, and 72 at Yale. As late as 1860 the number at Harvard and Princeton had not materially diminished, but at Yale the number had dropped to 33. In the 1850's, however, there was a strong sentiment against sending Southern students to Northern colleges, and enrollment in the Southern colleges notably increased.

The Southern colleges trained few scholars in the modern sense, but they contributed much to the widely diffused general knowledge noted by visitors from the outside. James Silk Buckingham, who had no love for slavery, noted that Northern youths often left school to enter business or a profession while sons of Southern planters not only remained in college longer but often went to Europe afterwards. This, he argued, sufficiently explained why "the gentlemen of the South are in general so much more thoroughly educated in the classic and polite literature, and so much more polished in their manners, than those of the North."

The Jacksonian era saw the beginnings of numerous denominational colleges. The movement received impetus from complaints that the state uni-

---

[14] Charles F. Thwing, A History of Higher Education in America (1906), pp. 254–257; Charles S. Sydnor, The Development of Southern Sectionalism, 1819–1848 (1948), pp. 303–304; E. M. Coulter, College Life in the Old South (1929), pp. 240–241; T. C. Johnson, Jr., Scientific Interests in the Old South (1936), p. 11 n.; William E. Dodd, The Cotton Kingdom (1919), pp. 111–114; Edward Ingle, Southern Sidelights (1896), chap. v; George Tucker, Progress of the United States . . . (1843), p. 144. The statistics given by these writers come chiefly from the U. S. Census reports for 1840, 1850, and 1860.

versities were too expensive, but there were other reasons. The Baptists and the Methodists had come to feel the need of educated ministers. These they could hardly look for from the state universities, which they believed were either tinged with rationalism or under Presbyterian control. The Baptists founded Georgetown College in Kentucky, Richmond College in Virginia, Mercer in Georgia, Wake Forest in North Carolina, and a little later others in the newer states of the Southwest. The Methodists founded Randolph-Macon, Emory, Wofford, and took over Union Institute, which eventually became Duke University. The Presbyterians, less numerous but earlier convinced of the importance of an educated ministry, had founded Hampden-Sydney in 1776. Davidson, Washington (now Washington and Lee University), and Oglethorpe, where Lanier studied, came later. The denominational colleges drew their students largely from the middle classes, for the large-scale planters preferred to send their sons to the state universities or to Northern colleges. Their academic standards were on the whole lower than those of the state universities, but there was no great difference in the studies pursued.

In this period the newer states of the Southwest established state universities so that by the early fifties nearly every Southern state east of the Mississippi had its state university, and the movement had already extended to the West, where the state university, aided by land grants, has had its greatest development. The University of North Carolina was indebted to Princeton and the University of Georgia to Yale for many methods and practices. After 1830 the University of Virginia had a great influence upon the newer state universities of the Southwest. The Southern state universities contributed greatly to establishing in this country both the idea of state responsibility for higher education—an idea accepted much more slowly in the Northern states—and the conception of a university as distinguished from a college.

Throughout this period many of the state universities were under fire from Presbyterians, Baptists, and Methodists. The latter two frequently charged that the Presbyterians and the Episcopalians controlled the state institutions. The Presbyterians in fact, when not able to establish or support their own institutions, did try to control some of the state universities. There was in these years no great objection on religious grounds to the teaching of science, but there was a loud outcry against all critics of revealed religion—particularly Thomas Cooper in South Carolina.

Before 1830 the faculties of most Southern colleges seem to have been made up chiefly of Northern men. Twenty years later there was a much larger proportion of Southern professors. Some of the Northern teachers who came south were notable men; for example, F. A. P. Barnard, who presided successively over the University of Mississippi and Columbia University. Notable also in his way was William Holmes McGuffey of the University of Virginia, compiler of school readers. Among the abler Southern teachers were Gessner Harrison, who taught the classics at the University of Virginia, and Joseph Le Conte, a geologist who taught first at the University of South Carolina and later had a distinguished career at the University of California. There were also a few notable German scholars; among them, George Blaetterman at Virginia and Francis Lieber at South Carolina. The German influence is seen in an emphasis upon teacher training and upon research. Among Southern scholars who studied at German universities were Thomas Woodrow, who taught Lanier at Oglethorpe, and the eminent Greek scholar Basil Lanneau Gildersleeve, a Charlestonian, who had a notable career at the University of Virginia and later at Johns Hopkins.

The college curriculum was still dominated largely by Greek, Latin, and mathematics, as it was at Yale as late as the 1880's when Wilbur Cross was a student there. There was, however, considerable criticism of the emphasis upon the ancient classics. More attention was now being given to science, especially in medicine and agriculture, to the modern languages, history, political science, economics, and law. English literature appears camouflaged under such headings as rhetoric, belles-lettres, mental and moral philosophy. The chairs of History and English were sometimes combined, as at the University of Virginia under George Frederick Holmes, whose chief interest was rather in sociology. In the denominational colleges English literature was often in the hands of retired clergymen. The teaching of English literature was probably as far advanced in the South as in the North, but the great development in that field was to come some years after the War between the States. American literature as a separate study was still unknown to the curriculum.

There was considerable improvement in methods of teaching through lectures, seminars, and laboratories; and there was a growing feeling that a college teacher should do research. A number of Southern educational and scientific journals were established, and the abler scholars often affiliated themselves with national organizations. In 1848 out of a total of 462 members of the Association for the Advancement of Science, 78 were from the South. A Savannah doctor, Richard D. Arnold, was the first Secretary of the American Medical Association. Southern scholars, however, were handicapped by inadequate libraries, isolation from other scholars, and criticism from religious leaders. Yet on the whole the Southern colleges and universities were more nearly on a par with the Northern than they have, with a few notable exceptions, ever been since that time.

The state university libraries were better than those of the denominational colleges, but they varied greatly in size and in quality. Two of the best were those at the University of Virginia and the University of South Carolina. There was not much attempt at correlation between library holdings and the curriculum except in the sciences, in which the universities did some of their best work. Many books in the university libraries were never borrowed. The borrowings, however, indicate considerable interest in literature, history, biography, and travel. More than one third of the books borrowed from the University of Georgia library in 1835–1836 were novels, of which the most popular was *The Last of the Mohicans*, closely followed by *The Spy*, *Tom Jones*, and several of Scott's romances. In 1847, however, the library catalogue listed nothing by Cooper, Scott, Poe, Kennedy, Simms, or Caruthers. The library at that time apparently did not even have a copy of Longstreet's *Georgia Scenes* or the *Southern Literary Messenger*. In 1856 the librarian of the University of South Carolina reported that for the preceding ten years one half of the books classified as belles-lettres which the students had borrowed were "novels, principally Scott, with whom too frequently Smollet[t] and Fielding were associated."

From the point of view of literary culture, the most remarkable feature of the Southern college or university was its literary societies. There were usually two, and every student was expected to join one of them. Often their libraries were larger than that of the college or university. In 1847, nine years after its founding, the society libraries of Davidson College contained twelve thousand books. The University of Virginia Library had only fifteen thousand books in 1860. The society libraries contained a much larger percentage of novels than the college and university libraries, but there was no special emphasis upon recent and contemporary fiction. The society libraries were at their best in the years before the Civil War. In the period which followed they were gradually taken over by the college and university libraries.

In these literary societies the future lawyers, ministers, Congressmen, and state legislators learned the art of debating and got some experience in declaiming and in essay-writing. Frequently the societies joined in an invitation to some prominent person to deliver an address. Many of the addresses were published—usually in pamphlet form but often in the magazines—with the statement that the societies had requested publication.

Much of the literature of the Old South consists of such addresses as A. B. Meek's *Americanism in Literature,* delivered at the University of Georgia in 1844. The literature of New England in this period also is made up in considerable part of addresses, like those of Emerson and Lowell. The address as a literary form now seems almost as old-fashioned as the pamphlet or the printed sermon of earlier times. Few of the Southern orators had Lowell's gift of humor or his lightness of touch, but most of them would have appreciated his definition: "An address is a species by itself—a cross between an essay and speech—tolerating, even inviting, more rhetoric than the one, less logic than the other and suggesting the touch of humour here and there that shall relieve without relaxing the attention of an audience."

The *Southern Literary Messenger* in May, 1849, reviewing "Four New Addresses," commented: "The number of such publications is Legion. . . . Baccalaureate addresses have become more plentiful than the berries of the laurel, and the autumnal leaves of collegiate orations strew the post routes of travel with more than Vallambrosan profusion." The college speech, said the reviewer, is "the *pièce de resistance* of literature." The orator, whether undergraduate or alumnus,

begins far back in the dim twilight of tradition, before Homer . . . had uttered the majestic poetry of the Iliad,—he gradually progresses to the palmy days of Athenian supremacy, looks at Rome pillaged by the Visigoth, does up the dark ages in very respectable gloom, traces the departure of the Moors from Spain, and after a few flourishes on the French Revolution, with some grandiloquence touching the guillotine, at last reaches America and, as in duty bound, glorifies her gloriously. So much for the matter. The ornaments to set it off, the tinsel of rhetoric and the pomp of metaphor, are also invariably the same in all. The old myths are revived. Pallas comes forth again from the front of Jove and Niobe weeps afresh. Then follow two quotations from my Lord Byron, with four paragraphs of "fine writing," made up of eagles, pyramids, and other trumpery of Mr. Charles Phillips, and the performance is ended "and your orator will ever pray, &c."

One reason for the literary pre-eminence of New England in this period was the intimate relationship between literature and institutions of learning, particularly Harvard College. Longfellow and Hawthorne were graduates of Bowdoin College in Maine, but the other leading New England writers were, with the exception of Whittier, Harvard graduates. Longfellow, Holmes, and Lowell taught there. Emerson lectured in Cambridge and Boston, and both he and Thoreau made good use of the Harvard library. There were other excellent libraries in the Boston area which made easier the historical investigations of Prescott, Motley, Parkman, and Bancroft.

Someone in many a Cambridge family had written a book; it was not so in Charlottesville, Tuscaloosa, Chapel Hill, or Charleston. Harvard graduates supported the *North American Review* and the *Atlantic Monthly*, but Southern planters never gave adequate support to the *Southern Literary Messenger* or the Charleston quarterly reviews. In New England the lecture lyceum brought such writers as Emerson and Lowell into a more intimate relationship with the men and women who read their books. There were lyceums in Southern towns and cities, but they did not flourish like those in the more densely populated North. In Boston the New England writers had close at hand publishers like Ticknor and Fields who stimulated them to write and who knew how to sell their books.

The Southern universities and colleges now and then called upon writers —especially if they were also eminent lawyers or politicians—for occasional addresses; but there was in the Old South no intimate relation between literature and educational institutions—nothing like the situation at Vanderbilt University in Nashville when the Fugitive poets and the Southern Agrarians were active there a quarter of a century ago. At Harvard College, as Edward Everett Hale wrote in *James Russell Lowell and His Friends,* "the whole drift of fashion, occupation, and habit among the undergraduates ran in lines suggested by literature." One finds nothing of the sort, for example, at the University of Virginia. Nor was there any Southern city—not even Charleston—of which it could have been said, as William Dean Howells said of Boston in his *Literary Friends and Acquaintance,* that "all talents had more or less a literary coloring" and "the greatest talents were literary," and again: "literature in Boston, indeed, was so respectable, and often of so high a lineage, that to be a poet was not only to be good society, but almost to be good family." Said David H. Strother ("Porte Crayon"): "I went to Richmond, and no one took any notice of me. I went to Boston and every one wished to have me to dinner. So I always go to Boston."

The Southern writers whom we shall consider were chiefly men who had studied at the state universities, in Northern institutions, or occasionally at a Presbyterian college. The great majority of Southern college graduates were planters. They took a keen interest in the world around them; they were well informed and they often traveled; but with few exceptions they wrote and published little. Well educated though many of them were, they gave scant encouragement to scholars or writers on other subjects than politics, farming, and perhaps such sports as hunting, fishing, and horse-racing.

The South nevertheless had its scholars, its scientists, and its historians; and some of them, in spite of great difficulties, managed to complete their investigations and publish their findings. I have mentioned the notable work of George Tucker and Thomas Cooper in economics and political science. Notable, too, was the work of the German-born Francis Lieber, who in spite of his dislike of slavery—which did not prevent his owning house servants—wrote his best books while teaching in the University of South Carolina. Interest in the sciences was widespread, as T. C. Johnson, Jr., has shown in his *Scientific Interests in the Old South* (1936); and there were competent scientific students scattered over the Southern states from Maryland to Louisiana. In medicine there were Robley Dunglison at the University of Virginia, Charles Caldwell at Transylvania, and Samuel Henry Dickson, who taught in medical schools in Charleston and Philadelphia. James Marion Sims of Alabama was one of the great surgeons of his time. Perhaps the most remarkable of the Southern scientists was Matthew Fontaine Maury, who had much to do with the founding of the U. S. Naval Academy and who by his study of winds and ocean currents made quicker and safer the course of many an American and European ship. I should perhaps have discussed at length the work of Maury and of John James Audubon, who spent much of his life in the South in the study of birds and animals. Audubon is remembered primarily for his admirable pictures in color, but he wrote incidentally some fine brief descriptions of life in the lower Mississippi valley.

Before the Civil War historical societies were founded in all the Southern states except Texas. The Massachusetts Historical Society dates from 1791; the oldest of those in the South, the Virginia Historical Society, was organized in 1831. The men most active in founding these organizations were professional men, notably lawyers; and a considerable proportion of them were born in the Northern states or were educated there.

Most of the Southern historians were born or were educated outside the South. William Bacon Stevens, whom the Georgia Historical Society commissioned to write a history of the state, was born in Maine. David Ramsay, the historian of South Carolina, was a Pennsylvanian and a graduate of Princeton. Of the Virginia historians, John Daly Burk was an Irishman, Hugh Blair Grigsby had studied at Yale, and Charles Campbell at Princeton. Albert J. Pickett, the planter who wrote a history of Alabama, had studied for two years in Cambridge, Massachusetts. Charles Gayarré, the ablest of them all, studied law for three years in Philadelphia and lived for even longer in Paris. The only accomplished writer among them was Gayarré, whose work will be discussed later; but the works of Pickett, Stevens, Grigsby, and Campbell, to name no others, have not yet been altogether superseded.

3

Books, Libraries, and Literary Taste

IN THE PERIOD we are studying, as in every other, one meets with contradictory assertions in regard to the state of literary culture in the South.
Some backward-gazing Southern writers exaggerated the culture of the Old
South, and some Northern writers, influenced by the Abolitionist tradition,
were reluctant to admit that the Southern planter was a reader of good
books, or indeed of any books. My own investigations have led me to the
conclusion reached some years ago by Grace Warren Landrum: "On the
whole, I believe the scantiness of books in the South and the consequent
lack of reading have been overemphasized."

There is evidence that the Old South was regarded as an important book
market, much more important than the South of the seventies and eighties.
The New York houses of Harper and Putnam sold many books in the South,
and so did the Philadelphia firm of J. B. Lippincott, whose business was
almost ruined by the outbreak of war in 1861. In Charleston and Nashville,
we learn from the veteran publisher J. C. Derby, John Russell and W. T.
Berry sold more fine books in proportion to the population than were sold in
other American cities. Derby also states that the largest sales of Audubon's
The Birds of America were in the South. Park Benjamin, who knew something about the book market, wrote in the *Southern Literary Messenger* for
December, 1848: "The people of the whole North (I speak of the mass)
seem amazed to find that Southern gentlemen are educated, and utter the
most *naif* surprise when told by Book-Sellers that far the most costly and
recherché portion of the invoices they receive from Europe, go to the curious
old houses on the banks of the James and Savannah, or to the far off bluffs
of the father of waters."

The English-born William C. Richards, who owned the University Book
Store in Athens, Georgia, stated in the *Southern Literary Gazette* for November 18, 1848, that while the masses of the Southern people had not been
readers of books: "A great change has taken place in the South in ten years.
We hazard the assertion that, notwithstanding the present scarcity of money,
there [will] have been, in the year 1849, ten times as many books bought and
read in Georgia, and contiguous States, as in the year 1839—and we believe
the increase to be steadily progressive." [15] It was, as Richards suggested, the

---

[15] *So. Lit. Gazette*, I, 222 (Nov. 18, 1848). The books which Richards advertised in
the *Gazette* were chiefly new books and reprints of standard works. In the first volume of
the *Gazette* he listed Melville's *Typee* (1846), Emily Brontë's *Wuthering Heights*

rapid development of the railroad and the steamboat that enabled Northern publishers quickly to place their wares in so many Southern bookstores.

In the 1850's, however, the situation was somewhat altered by the Southern feeling that many Northern books and magazines were hostile to the South. For a time Northern publishers feared to alienate Southern buyers. A Philadelphia publisher omitted Longfellow's antislavery poems from a collected edition for fear that it would not be acceptable in the South. A Boston publisher declined to print *Uncle Tom's Cabin* for much the same reason. But Ticknor and Fields and other Northern publishers discovered that they had in the North and the Northwest so many potential buyers for what would displease their Southern customers they could afford to run the risk of losing their Southern trade.

By 1850 the North had almost monopolized the book trade as well as the business of publishing books. As a result, Southern booksellers stocked their stores largely with what Northern houses sent them. It is not surprising, then, to find that the books advertised in Southern newspapers were much the same as those being offered for sale in Northern bookstores. The Southern booksellers advertised few Southern books and rarely indeed books printed in other Southern states than their own. The situation did not promise well for those who wished to build up a Southern literature. Simms and Hayne found that if they wanted their books to sell and be reviewed, it was necessary to have them brought out by prominent publishing houses in the North.

The practice of the Southern bookseller is illustrated by the list of new books which S. W. Whitaker advertised in the Wilmington, N. C., *Herald* for September 5, 1853: Thackeray's *Vanity Fair* (1848) and *Henry Esmond* (1852), Bulwer-Lytton's *My Novel* (1853) Hawthorne's *The House of the Seven Gables* (1851), and "Ik Marvel's" *Reveries of a Bachelor* (1850) and *Dream Life* (1851). These were all books being widely read in the North at that time. It was not Southern books that Whitaker was trying to sell. For those who imagine that Melville was not widely read in 1853, I note that Whitaker also advertised *Typee* (1846), *Omoo* (1847), *Mardi* (1849), *Redburn* (1849), *White-Jacket* (1850), and *Moby-Dick* (1851). Whitaker had perhaps not yet received the unpopular *Pierre* (1853).

A private library had gradually come to be regarded as an essential part

---

(1847), and Cooper's *Oak Openings* (1848). After a visit to Charleston Richards wrote: "The people of Charleston and the planters of the Sea-board are a reading people— if I may judge from the numerous and well-supplied bookstores in the city. Of these none is more attractive than Russel[l]'s, where you may be sure to find the latest editions, and the choicest novelties from New York, London, and Paris" (I, 393, April 21, 1849).

of the furnishings of the educated planter, lawyer, doctor, or clergyman. On a plantation it was more desirable to own books than it was in Northern cities where readers had access to public collections. The Northern city-dweller was close to bookstores, but the Southern farmer had to order books by mail or search for them on his infrequent visits to the nearest large town. In the South, however, the climate tempted booklovers from their libraries while in snowbound New England villages men and women found books a necessary resource on long winter evenings.

The available evidence does not bear out the traditional view that the Southern planter's reading was largely limited to the ancient classics, law, and the Waverley romances. The traditional view, strange to say, has been perpetuated by some modern historians, who are often severely critical of other Southern traditions. For example, William B. Hesseltine wrote in A History of the South (1936):

> The Southerner's preoccupation with defenses of his peculiar social and economic order was reflected in his own reading and writing. The educated planter found in a study of the classics an intellectual justification for the slave system. A study of ancient history taught him that the brilliant society of Athens and the power of Rome had been based upon human slavery. In addition the literary Southerner read the romantic historical novels of Sir Walter Scott, seeing in the Southern system a modern counterpart of the idealized feudal society of the Middle Ages. . . . Such writers as Dickens, who painted the horrors of the contemporary scene, found no place in the planter's library. When he read of modern subjects, the Southerner's tastes were likely to run to constitutional law and the elaborations of the doctrines of States' rights. His reading served but to impress upon his mind the essential propriety of the Southern ideal.

The picture which Professor Hesseltine paints is plausible, but it is wrong in almost every particular. His conclusions are very different from those of Professor Walton R. Patrick, who has carefully studied the evidence for the planters' reading in Louisiana for the years 1830–1860.[16] Patrick's findings are in brief that the state was a good book market and that the books offered for sale were mainly recent books. Almost every town and settlement had a bookseller or at least a merchant who sold books. New Orleans in the 1850's

[16] Walton R. Patrick, "Literature in the Louisiana Plantation Home Prior to 1861" (La. State Univ. dissertation, 1937). See also Patrick's "A Circulating Library of Ante-bellum Louisiana," La. Hist. Quart., XXIII, 3–12 (Jan., 1940); "Reading Taste in Louisiana, 1830–60" in Studies for William A. Read (1940), pp. 288–300; and Patrick and Cecil G. Taylor, "A Louisiana French Plantation Library, 1842," French-Am. Rev., I, 47–67 (Jan.–March, 1948). See also Roger P. McCutcheon, "Libraries in New Orleans, 1771–1833," La. Hist. Quart., XX, 3–9 (Jan., 1937).

had at least seven bookstores, and there were yet other stores that sold books. The small-town booksellers got most of their books from the dealers in New Orleans, who acted as agents for such Northern houses as Appleton and Company, Carey & Hart, and Harper & Brothers. The booksellers in their advertisements announced their ability to procure any book published in this country or in Europe, and they did an extensive mail-order business with planters in the rural districts. They also sold annuals, gift-books, and American and British magazines—particularly Leonard Scott's New York reprints of the *Edinburgh Review* and *Blackwood's Edinburgh Magazine*.

The book advertisements in the Southern newspapers do not suggest any deep devotion to the Greek and Latin classics, but they do indicate a lively interest in the novels of Scott, G. P. R. James, Disraeli, Bulwer-Lytton, Dickens, Thackeray, Dumas, George Sand, Eugene Sue, Fenimore Cooper, Joseph Holt Ingraham, Mrs. Caroline Lee Hentz, "Marion Harland," and Mrs. E. D. E. N. Southworth. The popular poets were Byron, Moore, and Mrs. Felicia Dorothea Hemans. There was still some demand for such earlier writers as Shakespeare, Milton, Bunyan, Goldsmith, Hume, Young, and the eighteenth-century novelists. Patrick's conclusion, which seems to me a sound one, is: "Unless one insists that booksellers advertised certain types of literature but actually sold other types—an idea contrary to logic —then the conclusion is inevitable that the estimate of ante-bellum literary culture made by Hesseltine and others of the same mind has no real basis in fact."

Was the literary taste of the South conservative, as has been so often asserted? There is some evidence that it was. The fact that Southerners bought and read the new books does not mean that they invariably liked them. In our own time thousands of readers buy and read the new books—it is the fashion to read the new books—but it does not follow that American housewives, for example, like all the new novels so widely advertised in the magazines and newspapers and boosted by the book clubs. In the 1850's there was no Book-of-the-Month Club or Literary Guild, but publishers, magazines, newspapers, and booksellers all combined to push the sale of new books.

The traditional view of the typical plantation library in the 1850's is given by George Cary Eggleston in *The First of the Hoosiers*. In that decade he and his brother Edward read widely in "well-stocked libraries" in rural Virginia which "included next to nothing of strictly modern literature, but . . . were rich in all the classics of our language." Somewhat similar is the situation as described by Sherwood Bonner, who was born in Mississippi in 1849. In *Like unto Like* (1878) she wrote:

Their reading was of a good, solid sort. They were brought up, as it were, on Walter Scott. They read Richardson, and Fielding, and Smollett, though you may be sure that the last two were not allowed to girls until they were married. They liked Thackeray pretty well, Bulwer very well, and Dickens they read under protest—they thought him low. They felt an easy sense of superiority in being "quite English in our tastes, you know," and knew little of the literature of their own country, as it came chiefly from the North. Of its lesser lights they have never heard, and, as for the greater, they would have pitted an ounce of Poe against a pound of any one of them.

The ancient classics were still highly prized in the South, but General Daniel H. Hill exaggerated the Southern devotion to them when he wrote in the *Land We Love* in May, 1866: "Probably no people on the globe ever prized so highly a knowledge of the ancient classics as did the planters of the Southern Atlantic States of the old thirteen. In their estimation, not to possess this knowledge was not merely proof of want of scholarship— it was an absolute demonstration of the want of gentlemanly breeding."

In many plantation libraries books had been handed down from earlier generations, and naturally they included the British classics which had been widely read in earlier periods. Henry Timrod, tutoring on South Carolina plantations in the 1850's, ridiculed the old-fashioned taste of certain planters:

There are scholars of pretension among us, with whom Blair's Rhetoric is still an unquestionable authority. There are schools and colleges in which it is used as a text-book. . . . Here Pope is still regarded by many as the most *correct* of English poets, and here, Kaimes [Henry Home Lord Kames] after having been everywhere else removed to the top shelves of libraries, is still thumbed by learned professors and declamatory sophomores. Here literature is still regarded as an epicurean amusement; not as a study, at least equal in importance, and certainly not inferior in difficulty, to law and medicine. Here no one is surprised when some fossil theory of criticism, long buried under the ruins of an exploded school, is dug up, and discussed with infinite gravity by gentlemen who know Pope and Horace by heart, but who have never read a word of Wordsworth or Tennyson, or who have read them with suspicion, and rejected them with superciliousness.

The North, too, we must remember, had readers of conservative tastes. Oliver Wendell Holmes would have seemed to Timrod somewhat old-fashioned, and Francis Parkman was as indifferent to Timrod's favorite poets, Wordsworth and Tennyson, as any Southern planter. The literary taste of those who lived in small towns or rural regions in New England and the Middle West would have seemed equally old-fashioned.

If there was an old-fashioned quality in the literary taste of Southern planters in the 1850's, there was far more of it in 1875, when Constance Fenimore Woolson, who grew up in Cleveland, Ohio, wrote to Paul Hamilton Hayne that cultivated people whom she had met in the Carolinas seemed barely to have heard of George Eliot or Bret Harte and knew nothing about Joaquin Miller or the Rossettis. On the other hand, she complained, these persons were always telling her of Southern authors of whom she had never heard—in particular "a cloud of women,—novelists, poets, &c&c, who are, or rather each one is 'the greatest genius of the day.' " By 1875 propaganda for Southern literature had come to have an appreciable effect. More important is the fact, however, that most Southerners living in 1875 had for fifteen years been too poor to buy many new books and thus had limited their reading mainly to the old books in their family libraries.

When we study the reading of the chief Southern writers of the period, we find that Simms, Poe, Kennedy, Chivers, John Esten Cooke, Hayne, Timrod, Bagby, and Meek—to name no others—knew the important American and English authors of their own time. Simms was a subscriber to the *Dial*, and he was one of the first American critics to see that Robert Browning was a great poet. If these writers failed to sing the praises of certain Northern authors, it was not from ignorance of their works or of their high standing in the North but because of their hostility to a slaveholding society. A large part of Southern conservatism in literary matters resulted not from ignorance of contemporary writers but from a dislike for the brand of literature put out by radicals and reformers who for the most part knew nothing about the South.

In spite of the widely scattered Southern population, the movement for the establishment of libraries open to the public made great progress in the 1850's. According to the U. S. Census returns in 1850, such Southern libraries owned 561,188 volumes. By 1860 there were five times as many books in the public libraries. In the 1850's the number of libraries grew in North Carolina from 4 to 263, in Virginia from 21 to 1350, in Georgia from 3 to 288, and in South Carolina from 16 to 193. To be sure, the number of volumes in most of these collections was small. In South Carolina, however, there was an average of one and one-half volumes to each white person, which was the same ratio as in Massachusetts. For the South as a whole the libraries contained perhaps a single volume for every two or three white persons. There were of course large areas where the rural and small-town population had no access to any public library.

The Charleston Library Society, which in 1826 had published a catalogue of its notable collection, in 1845 published a long list of books purchased since 1826.[17] The Society had bought many books, but in its purchases there is noticeable a new tendency to discriminate among Northern writers. One finds Timothy Dwight, Mrs. Sigourney, Prescott, Miss Sedgwick, George W. Curtis, and Bryant but not Emerson, Hawthorne, or even the popular Longfellow. There are a good many titles by Cooper, Irving, Bulwer-Lytton, G. P. R. James, Dickens, Scott, Marryat, Lever, and Ben Jonson but among Southern writers, nothing by Poe or Caruthers. There are at least eleven titles by Simms, who was not so neglected in Charleston as has been supposed. The library was strong in French literature, but it had few German books except "tales."

Outside of Charleston and Columbia, probably the best library in the state was in Beaufort. In 1802, when the local library society was organized, it had some two thousand volumes. When the city was captured by Union troops in 1861, the United States Treasury shipped the books to New York to be sold at auction. Salmon P. Chase, the Secretary of the Treasury, stopped the sale. "We do not war on libraries," he said. The New York Times also protested against the sale. Books still unsold were sent to the Smithsonian Institution in Washington, where they were destroyed by fire in 1868. The Congress in 1940 belatedly appropriated ten thousand dollars to indemnify the city of Beaufort for the loss of the books. The New York Public Library has a ninety-five page catalogue of the Beaufort collection, which lists 3182 separate titles, totaling perhaps ten thousand separate volumes in all. It was a very fine collection of books, and one that could not in 1940 have been replaced by ten times the sum appropriated by Congress.

The Richmond Library had fourteen thousand volumes in 1855. If one judges by the catalogue of its holdings printed that year, one must conclude that the taste of the Old South was very conservative indeed. The library was fairly strong in the ancient classics, though many of them appeared only in translation. It had also a good collection of French literature with many books in the original language. The works of Voltaire were conspicuous, but there was little of contemporary French literature and few German or Italian books, even in translation. The library had most of the British quarterly reviews but only the *Southern Literary Messenger* among American magazines. The works of the Elizabethan dramatists and the British Romantic writers were well represented, but contemporary English literature was neglected. There was a good deal of Bulwer-Lytton and G. P. R. James, a little of Carlyle, Macaulay, and Thackeray, but nothing

[17] *A Catalogue of the Books of the Charleston Library Society Purchased since 1826* . . . Vol. II [*sic*] (Charleston, 1845).

of Browning, Dickens, or even Tennyson. American literature in 1855 was represented by Irving, Cooper, Prescott, Catharine Maria Sedgwick, and Mrs. Sigourney, "the sweet singer of Hartford"; but there was nothing by Emerson, Hawthorne, Longfellow, Whittier, Holmes, Lowell, or even Bryant or N. P. Willis. Except for certain Virginiana, its Southern collection was poor. The library had Poe's *The Raven and Other Poems* (1845), but it had nothing by George Tucker, Caruthers, or William Byrd. John P. Little in his *History of Richmond* (1933), first published in the *Messenger* in 1851–1852, wrote: "The Library of the City is one of the most insignificant ones that could be collected in any place as large and prosperous as Richmond; it may be classed among the curiosities of the city, as it scarcely deserves mention as any thing else." So curious a collection must have owed a partial explanation to the idiosyncrasies of the individuals who built it up. Obviously, much of the reading of the Richmond writers—John R. Thompson, George W. Bagby, and John Esten Cooke—was done elsewhere.

The public and private libraries of the Old South were intended primarily to meet the needs of the cultivated classes; they were not adapted to the special needs of scholars. Hugh Blair Grigsby, a historian whose special interest was the Virginia constitutional conventions of 1776 and 1788, wrote of his difficulties to David L. Swain, August 20, 1857:

. . . we have absolutely nothing historical in Charlotte [Court House] or in Norfolk; not even a library of schoolbooks in either. Our public (State) records, such as they are, are not accessible, and I have always lived at least a hundred miles from their place of deposit [Richmond]. I am compelled to buy all my authorities; for what I cannot buy I cannot read. Depend upon it, historical researches and authorship in the South are a different thing from what they are in the North. On the score of printed materials we have absolutely nothing, while in this important respect the North abounds. I am now engaged on a history of the Virginia Convention of 1788. I have hardly a solitary life of any man who composed it, except Wirt's life of Henry, which is to the last degree superficial, though a worthy and clever book, and nobly patriotic in its aims. When I write my history, it will be almost as new a revelation about men and things as if it had dropped from the sky. There is not even a file of papers for 1788. Fortunately, I came into public life at one and twenty, and knew Madison, Monroe, Marshall, Judge Stewart &c. who were members of the Convention of 1788, and had conversed with intelligent men who were present at the scene. Moreover, I have saved many facts gathered in conversation for thirty years past, and know every thing in print which can throw any light upon my theme. It is a work of great labor notwithstanding. Of many of my greatest men it is impossible to know from their friends and descendants the slightest particulars. Now this is not the case at the North. There the current publications preserve much that would be invaluable to me which is now lost forever.

On December 21 of the next year Grigsby wrote to Jefferson's biographer, Henry S. Randall: "I have not written a line of my history of the Convention of 1788 for two months, but hope to begin my work in a week or two. The inducement to write with us is exceedingly faint. I have no congenial people to talk with; and I know that, when I finish my book, no bookseller [publisher] will take it, and I will be compelled to print it myself, and risk a thousand dollars, all the profits going to the bookseller instead of the [Virginia] historical society, for which I have written it."

Two of the most remarkable of American collectors lived in Savannah. They were Israel K. Tefft and Alexander A. Smets, both among the founders of the Georgia Historical Society in 1839. Tefft collected autographs of famous men and whenever possible portraits to accompany them. The Swedish novelist, Fredrika Bremer, pronounced him the greatest autograph-collector in the world. Smets, an Alsatian by birth, collected incunabula and other rare books, and he possessed some valuable manuscripts. Among the last was a manuscript containing some unpublished poems by Joseph Addison. The whereabouts of this manuscript is now unknown, but a few of the poems fortunately were published in ante-bellum Southern magazines. In *Modern Philology* for February, 1939, I reprinted all of them that I could find. The Library of Congress has the printed catalogues of both the Smets and the Tefft collections, which were sold in New York—Tefft's in 1867 and Smets's in 1868—when Southerners had to part with their most treasured possessions. The items listed are sufficient to make any collector envious. Smets's manuscript volume of Addison's poems, for which he had paid twenty-eight dollars was sold to one "Byron" for only five.[18]

In recent years Southern scholars and librarians discovered to their chagrin that for the past century important Southern books, manuscripts, and periodicals have been flowing steadily into Northern, and more recently into

18 Fredrika Bremer, *The Homes of the New World* (New York, 1854), trans. Mary Howitt, I, 339. See also "A Week among Autographs" in Samuel Gilman, *Contributions to Literature* (Boston, 1856), pp. 303–347, also in *The Poetry of Travelling in the United States* (New York, 1838), ed. Caroline Gilman, pp. 373–430. The article first appeared in Mrs. Gilman's *Southern Rose*. Tefft's collection, I am told, is now in the State Library in Albany, N. Y.

For Smets's library, see Jay B. Hubbell, "Some Uncollected Poems of Joseph Addison," *Modern Philology*, XXXVI, 277–281 (Feb., 1939) and the references given in the footnotes. The two most important of these are: [John R. Thompson], "A Library," *S.L.M.*, XVII, 630–636 (Oct.–Nov., 1851) and W. B. S[tevens]., "The Library of Alexander A. Smets, Esq. Savannah," *Magnolia*, III, 310–314, 363–367, 409–416, 464–472 (July, Aug., Sept., Oct., 1841).

Western, libraries. The Huntington Library in California has a rich collection of Virginiana in addition to a valuable Poe-Chivers collection. The important Southern materials owned by the Wisconsin State Historical Society were in a large measure procured almost without cost through the energy and foresight of Lyman C. Draper, who collected priceless materials at a time when few Southerners realized their value. The student of Southern history or literature frequently has to visit the great Northern libraries for important materials.

4

Publishing

It is one of the misfortunes of the South that it has no publishers," said the *Southern Quarterly Review* in April, 1854. "What is printed, thus fails of proper circulation." As a matter of fact, there was no scarcity of printing presses in the ante-bellum South, and there were Southern publishers. In his *Bibliotheca Americana* (1852) Orville A. Roorbach listed at least one hundred Southern publishers among the approximately five hundred and fifty in the entire country.[19]

The chief reason for the often-repeated complaint that the South had no publishers is that the Southern printers lacked the facilities and, as we now say, the know-how, for marketing their wares. William Wilberforce Turner wrote in *Jack Hopeton; or, The Adventures of a Georgian* (1860): "There is not a publishing concern in all this region which can give currency to a book, save, perhaps, some religious houses, and even these cannot bring a work into that general circulation which is gratifying to an author. No parallel to this case exists, or ever existed, in the wide world." Books printed in the South had only a local circulation; they were not read even in adjoining Southern states. The Virginian rarely saw a book printed in Charleston. The great mass of books offered for sale in Southern bookstores came, as I have noted, from New York, Philadelphia, Boston, and London. If the early editions of William Byrd's writings—Petersburg, 1841, and Richmond, 1866—had come out in New York, his reputation would have grown far more rapidly than it did. William A. Caruthers' first two novels, published by Harper & Brothers in New York, attracted far more attention than *The*

---

[19] According to Hellmut Lehmann-Haupt and others, *The Book in America* (1939), p. 100, the numbers of publishers found in six American cities in the years 1820–1852 were: New York, 345; Philadelphia, 198; Boston, 147; Baltimore, 32; Cincinnati, 25; Charleston, 15.

Knights of the Horse-Shoe, his best book, which was brought out in Wetumpka, Alabama. The novels which Simms published in Charleston, like those which John Esten Cooke published in Richmond, sold much less widely than those which came out in New York and Philadelphia. Southern writers learned from sad experience that if their books were to be widely circulated and reviewed, they must be published at the North.

Edmund Ruffin, who had published a few books and pamphlets in Petersburg, Virginia, explained in the *Farmers' Register* for August 1, 1838, why the Virginia printers were reluctant to publish books by Virginia writers. The Northern publishing houses, he said, had acquired a virtual monopoly of publishing books for the South. This they had brought about "by combining the *credit system* and the *puffing system."* The Northern publisher would send his books to the numerous Southern booksellers on consignment. If half of them were sold, the publisher lost nothing; if the dealer sold two-thirds of them, he made a profit. The publisher also took pains to send copies to the many Southern newspaper editors; and "for so small a bribe," said Ruffin, "these gentlemen rarely refuse to give in return a *puff,* or complimentary notice of the work, which serves to aid the sale." This system explains, he said, why only rarely will any Virginia printer "dare to publish a book for sale; and . . . every southern author, to get his work before the public, either for his honor or his profit, must, of necessity, submit to have it issued, and introduced to his own state, by a northern publisher, even though he could have the printing done as cheaply, and more faithfully at home." Discouraged though he was, Ruffin nevertheless brought out *The Westover Manuscripts* of William Byrd in 1841. He first, however, printed it serially in the form of supplements to the *Farmers' Register* before he issued it in book form.

There were complaints that Northerners would not read Southern books, magazines, and pamphlets and consequently did not understand the Southern position on controversial questions. In launching his own magazine in January, 1845, Simms frankly avowed "that the characteristics of the work are to be sectional, since, it is believed, that whether this were the case or not, no periodical of the country, not published at one of the great cities of the North, could possibly hope for the countenance of the public in their vicinity. Our experience," Simms continued, "is conclusive on this head. The Northern press claims to supply us in the South and West with all our literature, and will take none of ours in return."

Northern booksellers were reluctant to handle Southern magazines although booksellers in the South often acted as agents for the Northern magazines. Northern readers eagerly devoured Longstreet's *Georgia Scenes*

(Augusta, 1835) when Harper & Brothers republished it in New York in 1840; but when copies of his pamphlet, A Voice from the South (Baltimore, 1847), were sent to a New York dealer to be sold, they were returned by the next mail. Public opinion in the North, we are told, forced a New York publisher to cancel a contract to publish Grayson's The Hireling and the Slave.

It was not so much these circumstances, however, as the growing hostility of Northern publications to the South that created the demand for Southern publishing houses. Injustice to the South in the universally used textbooks written and published in the North greatly stimulated the demand for a Southern literature. It led the Southern Commercial Convention at its Memphis meeting in June, 1853, to pass a resolution: "Resolved, That this Convention earnestly recommends to the citizens of the States here represented, the education of their youth at home as far as practicable; the employment of native teachers in their schools and colleges; the encouragement of a home press; the publication of books adapted to the educational wants and social condition of these States, and the encouragement and support of inventions and discoveries in the arts and sciences, by their citizens." The Convention which met in Savannah in 1856 actually went so far as to appoint a committee to prepare a "series of books in every department of study, from the earliest primer to the highest grade of literature and science." The grandiose scheme accomplished no more than did Duff Green's plan in 1835 to publish a series of Southern textbooks. George William Curtis in Putnam's Magazine in February, 1857, asked why the South's most distinguished writer, William Gilmore Simms, was not a member of the committee. He pretended that the Convention had passed the following resolutions: "Resolved, That there be a Southern literature. Resolved, That William Gilmore Simms, LL.D. be requested to write this literature." Curtis ridiculed the notion that literature could be built upon slavery and pointed to William J. Grayson's The Hireling and the Slave as a horrible example.[20]

The Civil War, as we shall see, practically cut off the Confederacy from Northern and English publications and stimulated the demand for Southern publishing houses. For a year or two West & Johnston in Richmond and a few other firms brought out more books than had been published in the South in any similar period. As the war progressed, however, most of

[20] "Southern Literature," IX, 207–214 (Feb., 1857); W. P. Trent, William Gilmore Simms (1892), p. 246. Paul Hamilton Hayne wrote on Oct. 3, 1856, to Richard Henry Stoddard: "As for Putnam I nurse a very pretty hatred against the entire concern. It begun with loud protestations of nationality; it ends with abolitionism, & a studied contempt for everything Southern" (D. M. McKeithan, A Collection of Hayne Letter, 1944, p. 18).

these firms were forced out of business. Since 1865 publishing has been, for good or for evil, more than ever concentrated in the large Northern cities.

5
Southern Magazines

BEFORE 1800, as we have seen, there were almost no magazines published in the South. In the next twenty or thirty years the South had a minor part in the establishment of literary magazines; but in the main the Southern reading public, when not content with its newspapers and periodicals devoted to religion and farming, was satisfied to read the Northern and British magazines. In the earlier period (1789–1830) New York and Philadelphia magazines welcomed their Southern contributors. After 1830, however, the controversy over slavery began to affect the tone of many Northern magazines. Educated Southerners were quick to sense the note of hostility toward their section and their way of life. By 1850 many felt that no Northern magazine was really friendly to the South. In October, 1854, the *Southern Quarterly Review*, then edited by Simms, noted that the Northern magazines were becoming increasingly hostile. "Now we ask the people of the South," he wrote, "how long this state of affairs is to continue, how long do we intend to give thousands to Northern publications to defame us and undermine our institutions, when it is notorious that our periodicals are languishing for the want of hundreds."

The mortality rate among American magazines has always been high, but it was somewhat higher in Charleston than in New York or Philadelphia. It has always been easy to start a new magazine; the difficulty is to keep it going. The men and women who founded the ante-bellum Southern magazines were with few exceptions amateurs—and this at a time when the best Northern magazines were being conducted by experienced editors often backed by the capital, equipment, and skill of a publishing house which knew how to market its wares. The great Northern magazines were better printed and better illustrated than all but a handful of those published in the South. In December, 1861, the *Southern Monthly* of Memphis reluctantly admitted: "With no small feeling of chagrin, and some of shame, we are forced to confess that a well-illustrated magazine *cannot* yet be produced in the South." A few Southern editors, like William C. Richards and Joseph Addison Turner, actually had their magazines printed in Northern cities.

The Southern magazines were not founded upon any real demand on the part of the reading public. They were begun by men and women of literary interests who felt that the South needed a medium for Southern writing and a means of refuting Northern slanders and removing the stigma of cultural and intellectual inferiority. Unable as a rule to pay their contributors, the Southern editors had to rely on amateur writers who, even if they could write acceptably, were seldom to be counted on to contribute regularly. It was not difficult to get subscribers; the difficulty was to get them to pay. Charles Dimitry in 1870 thus summed up the chief reasons why Southern magazines failed: "Their epitaph may well be written: Died of an indisposition to disburse, and of an infliction of immature intellect." In saluting a new Southern magazine in April, 1853, the disillusioned Simms wrote in the *Southern Quarterly Review:*

We look with a feeling akin to pity upon each new publication of a periodical nature in the South; the experience of twenty-five years having long since satisfied us that the doom of the editor, self-invoked, is one of perpetually deluding hopes, great toil and anxiety, and certain mortification. No periodical can well succeed in the South, which does not include the *political* constituent. The mind of the South is active chiefly in the direction of politics. . . . The only reading people of the South are those to whom politics is the bread of life. . . . We are not, in fact, a reading people. We are probably, at best, only the pioneers for those, who will atone to letters and the arts hereafter, for our grievous neglect.

Simms, after founding or contributing to many Southern literary magazines, was now editing the *Southern Quarterly Review,* which survived partly because of its political appeal but even more because Simms was willing to edit it for little or nothing and to write a large part of its contents without compensation. Daniel K. Whitaker, when he founded the *Review* in 1842, had written grandiloquently: "Quarterly Reviews are the embodiment, so to speak, of the national mind on all great questions . . ." and again: "Ably conducted Reviews are the offspring of a high state of civilization, and are the best evidence now-a-days that can be furnished, of intellectual advancement and of the prevalence of a pure and elevated philosophy." `A quarterly review, however, was, as William J. Grayson pointed out, a poor method of stimulating a Southern literature. "It is," he wrote, "a head without a body, a portico without a temple. It is not Hamlet without the ghost, but the ghost without Hamlet." A dozen Southern books in a dozen years would, he said, "constitute the critic's harvest. . . . It is reversing the natural order of production to begin a Country's literature with a Quarterly Review. We should begin with books to be reviewed."

The weeklies and monthlies fared no better than the quarterlies. George W. Bagby, while editing the *Southern Literary Messenger,* wrote in July,

1860: "Southern patriotism never was proof against Northern newspapers and picture magazines. If the angel Gabriel had gone into the very heart of the South, if he had even taken his seat on the top of the office of the Charleston Mercury and there proclaimed the immediate approach of the Day of Judgment, that would not have hindered the hottest secessionist from buying the New York Herald and subscribing for Harper's Magazine."

The Southern editors knew too little of what prospective subscribers wanted in a magazine. The Southern farm journals were better adapted to their readers. One of the most successful was the *Southern Field and Fireside*, which was both a literary magazine and a farm journal. John R. Thompson in 1860 became its editor at a salary of two thousand dollars a year. George W. Bagby took Thompson's place on the *Messenger* at a salary of three hundred—and the *Messenger* was still among the best of Southern literary magazines. The editors were loud in their demand for a distinctively Southern literature, but most of the material they printed was of exactly the same kinds as appeared in the Northern magazines. Only slowly did it occur to the Southern editors that the sketches of the humorists, which usually first appeared in newspapers, were the most distinctively Southern writing of the period.

From what I have said the reader will conclude that most of what the Southern editors printed in their magazines is dreary reading. So it is, but so also is most of what appeared in the magazines printed in New York, Philadelphia, and Boston. There is dull reading even in the *Atlantic Monthly*, which had a corps of contributors not surpassed by any other magazine in this country since Lowell ceased to edit it in 1861. The general level of the writing in the better Southern magazines is much below that of the *Atlantic*, but still much that they printed might have appeared in the *Knickerbocker Magazine* or *Godey's Lady's Book* without making it any better or worse.

In spite of the strained sectional relations, Southern writers often sent their manuscripts to New York and Philadelphia magazines. For example, Caruthers, Albert Pike, Philip Pendleton Cooke, and James M. Legaré all contributed to the *Knickerbocker*. As intersectional tension grew more acute, however, the Southern writers sent more of their manuscripts to the magazines of their own region. A smaller number of Northern writers appeared in the Southern magazines. Among Northern contributors to the *Southern Literary Messenger* were James Russell Lowell, Frank R. Stockton, Thomas Bailey Aldrich, Donald G. Mitchell ("Ik Marvel"), Park Benjamin, and Lydia Huntley Sigourney. Northern writers who had come South to live, like Margaret J. Preston and Caroline Gilman, often became regular contributors to the Southern magazines.

Among the best of the Southern magazine editors were Hugh Swinton Legaré of the *Southern Review;* the English-born William C. Richards, who edited the *Orion* and the *Southern Literary Gazette;* Paul Hamilton Hayne, chief editor of *Russell's Magazine;* Edgar Allan Poe, John R. Thompson, and George W. Bagby, all of whom were on the staff of the *Southern Literary Messenger;* and William Gilmore Simms, who at various times edited the *Magnolia,* the *Southern Quarterly Review,* and the *Southern and Western Monthly Magazine and Review*—a title so clumsy that it is generally referred to as *"Simms's Magazine,"* a second title which appears on the covers. Since these and other Southern magazines are competently discussed in Mott's *History of American Magazines,* I shall turn to other matters. Much of my illustrative material, however, is drawn from the magazines, and some of the editors were themselves writers of sufficient importance to merit separate treatment, notably Poe, Simms, Legaré, Thompson, Hayne, and Bagby.

6

New England Writers and the South

In this period of growing intersectional ill will the relations between Northern and Southern writers were much less intimate and less friendly than they had been before Garrison founded the *Liberator* in 1831 and South Carolina declared the iniquitous tariff null and void in 1832. Simms and Bryant continued to be friendly in spite of their radical disagreement on the question of slavery, but it was not until after the Civil War that a notable friendship developed between Hayne and Whittier. Many Southern writers visited New York and some of them had friends among the New York writers, but few except Hayne and Chivers spent any appreciable time in Boston. Emerson spent the winter of 1826–1827 in the South and Lowell once visited a Harvard friend in Charleston, but most of the New England writers were never in the South or the Southwest. Mrs. Stowe, who lived for many years in Cincinnati, visited briefly in Kentucky. John W. De Forest saw much more of Southern life than Lowell, Emerson, or Mrs. Stowe, but the years he lived in South Carolina, Virginia, and Louisiana did not bring affection for the backward region which, he thought, had plunged the nation into the most disastrous war of modern times.

The New Englanders appear to have read few of the writings of Southerners, even those published in the North. Simms, who like Poe thought highly of Beverley Tucker's *George Balcombe,* wrote in the *Southern Quarterly Review* for April, 1849: "It would be difficult, perhaps, to find a single New-England press which has ever accorded the slightest acknowledgment to this publication, or a single New-England citizen who had ever read it. It lacked the necessary *imprimatur* from the banks of the Charles. The saline flavor from the Plymouth rock, would have secured for it a thousand paeans." Simms's own work met with scant appreciation from Hawthorne and Lowell and, like Poe's, was roughly handled in the *North American Review.* The attitude of the *Atlantic Monthly* under Lowell's editorship was hostile to the South from the beginning. Emerson read one or two of Hugh S. Legaré's essays, and Thoreau gave grudging praise to William Elliott's *Carolina Sports.* There is little to indicate that the major writers of New England knew the widely read sketches of the Southern humorists or paid any attention to serious literary defenses of the Southern position except perhaps to ridicule them. The Boston bookstores carried no displays of magazines and books published in the South.

And yet in the years following the Civil War Emerson, Lowell, Holmes, and Whittier all exerted themselves to promote reconciliation between the two embittered sections. In the new era of good feeling that followed Reconstruction, New England readers discovered in the writings of Thomas Nelson Page and George W. Cable a South that they had never really known. In the eighties and nineties the Southerners who visited New England came to a new appreciation of the better qualities of the people of that region.

Northern critics have often ascribed the Southern sensitiveness on the subject of slavery to a pathological condition. Perhaps they are right; but if so, the New England excitement over Abolition amounted sometimes to a kind of hysteria. Intelligent observers, like Channing, Alcott, and Emerson, who had spent months or years in the South without being really shocked by what they saw, years afterwards, without revisiting the South, came to regard slavery as a horrible institution and the South as a land of semibarbarians. Those critics who find difficulty in understanding why Calhoun and Simms shifted from nationalism to sectionalism should consider what happened to Channing and Emerson. Their attitude toward the South changed almost automatically as sentiment in New England developed into a loud and insistent demand for emancipation.

One fundamental reason for the antagonism between South and North was economic, and the great tragedy of American life resulted from the fact that industrialization was confined to one section of the nation and slavery to the other. The South was still a land of farms; the North was becoming more and more a region of cities and towns. The farmer and the city-dweller have always felt a certain antipathy to one another and have often misunderstood each other's way of life and thought. The urban and industrial North regarded the slaveholding South with increasing distrust. Slavery was a bar to industrialization and progress. Moreover, in a world that no longer condoned slavery, it was becoming increasingly embarrassing for the Northerner to defend a democracy in which millions were held in involuntary servitude. The Abolitionists were so preoccupied with the sins of the distant and alien South that they seldom noticed the many injustices in their own society, now being rapidly industrialized. They resented far more the Southern planter's exploitation of his slaves than they did the New England manufacturer's exploitation of child and immigrant labor.

In the years following the war which freed the slaves Garrison, Whittier, and Wendell Phillips were often compared to the Hebrew prophets denouncing the enemies of unrighteousness. Their cause had triumphed and American history was rewritten largely from their point of view. Latterday historians, however, have not dealt with them so kindly and have treated them rather as zealots and doctrinaires without any firsthand knowledge of the institution which they were condemning. Mrs. Stowe had perhaps seen a slave plantation, but apparently Garrison, Whittier, Lowell, and Phillips had not; and they were willing to believe anything they heard or read provided it were to the discredit of slavery and the slaveholder. Barrett Wendell, a New Englander of the New Englanders, wrote in *Stelligeri* (1893): "It is hiding the truth that, for all their noble enthusiasm, the Abolitionists, after the good old British fashion, directed their reforming energies not against the evils prevalent in the actual society of which they formed a part; but against those that prevailed in a rival society which they knew chiefly by hearsay." In 1934 the distinguished historian, James Truslow Adams, said in *America's Tragedy*: "They [the Abolitionists] made no allowance for their own error, no allowance for the historic process which had fastened slavery on the South, no allowance for the economic and social problems involved in emancipation, no allowance for the hundreds of thousands of honorable, kindly white masters who found themselves caught in the nexus of a type of civilization which the world was only suddenly beginning to denounce. As is the way of reforming zealots always, they struck out venomously at the morality of all who differed with them."

John R. Thompson, who lamented that the better people of North and South knew so little about one another, wrote in the "Editor's Table" in the *Southern Literary Messenger* for March, 1853:

As long as Northern opinion of us is gathered from the pages of Mrs. Harriet Beeches [sic] Stowe and the lips of such snivelling divines as her reverend brother —as long as the primers of the District Schools of Massachusetts present opposite the word "planter" the pleasing little wood-cut of a man lashing a negro to death, —as long as the editorials of Greely [sic] and the Evening Post concerning the South are received for truth; it will be idle to expect that any just estimate of the Southern character can prevail "beyond the Tweed." On the other hand, it will not seem surprising that the majority of the Southern people should entertain no very kindly feeling towards New England, when it is remembered that, with few exceptions, the only specimens they see of her inhabitants are the annual swarm of half-educated teachers and peripatetic venders of wooden clocks which she sends to seek a living between the Potomac and the Rio Grande. For one real scholar that comes to us from her colleges, (and it is remarkable that all of them are graduates of Harvard University,) we have a score who cannot speak their own language correctly; and as for the clocks scattered about the South in a condition of refractory dumbness, we would not undertake to compute their arithmetic, had we the abilities, in that line, of Joe Hume himself.

Fitz-Greene Halleck, who knew something about the Southern opinion of itinerant Yankees, thus alluded to them in his "Connecticut":

> Wandering through the Southern countries, teaching
>   The ABC from Webster's Spelling Book;
> Gallant and godly, making love and preaching
>   And gaining, by what they call "hook and crook,"
> And what the moralists call overreaching,
>   A decent living. The Virginians look
> Upon them with as favorable eyes
> As Gabriel on the devil in Paradise.

Almost the only Northern writer who before the Civil War took the trouble to acquaint himself with the Southern scene at first hand was Frederick Law Olmsted (1822–1903), a native of Connecticut, who spent fourteen months in the South and recorded his observations and reflections in A Journey in the Seaboard Slave States (1856), A Journey through Texas (1857), and A Journey in the Back Country (1860). Olmsted had eyes for many aspects of Southern life for which he had not been prepared by anything he had heard or read. He found far less of what he anticipated than he had found in England or on the European continent. He saw much less of planters of the best type than he saw of yeomen and the poorer whites, but he saw enough to write: ". . . there is less vulgar display, and more intrinsic elegance, and habitual mental refinement in the best society of South Carolina, than in any distinct class anywhere among us [in the

North]." Olmsted was more strongly impressed, however, by the provincialism and ignorance of the ordinary Southern farmer, who was so largely ignored by writers in both sections. The economist in Olmsted was shocked by wasteful agricultural methods, and he felt a certain crudity and cruelty underlying the amenities of Southern social life. His stay in the South did not dispel the notion, which presumably he had brought south with him, that the Southerners were in a pathological state of mind on the subject of slavery; and yet he wrote: "The people of the South are 'my people.' I am attached to them equally as to those of Massachusetts or Pennsylvania. I desire their prosperity as I do that of no other people in the world. I look upon slavery as an entailed misfortune which, with the best disposition, it might require centuries wholly to dispose of. I would have extreme charity for the political expedients to which it prompts a resort." During the course of the war Olmsted wrote to a friend: "Why do you want to be so savage with the Southerners? . . . I think the slaveholders stand higher in the rank of civilization . . . today than English merchants or New York politicians."

7

James Russell Lowell

Few Northerners suspected how distorted were the accounts of the South which came to their attention. Much as the scholarly James Russell Lowell (1819–1891) wrote about the Southern problem, he had apparently no desire to study the slave plantation at first hand. He was content to view the South through the dark glasses of the Abolitionists. To look at Lowell or Emerson from the Southern point of view is to discover marked limitations in the "national" quality of much New England writing.

In college Lowell had two intimate friends from the South: Charles Woodman Scates and John Francis Heath. Scates, whom Lowell once visited in Charleston, worked with him on the editorial board of *Harvardiana* and was worried by Lowell's idleness and apparent lack of purpose. Lowell was deeply attached to his Virginia friend John Francis Heath, who first brought Landor's *Imaginary Conversations* to the attention of the young poet. He urged Heath to launch an antislavery movement in Virginia. Heath, however, after spending several years in Europe, returned to meet death in the Confederate army in 1862.

In 1840 Lowell published twelve early poems in the *Southern Literary Messenger*. He was grateful for the editor's praise, but wished that he had been paid for his poems. Lowell's conversion to Abolition has often been attributed to the influence of his first wife, Maria (White) Lowell. Mrs. Lowell was a niece of Caroline Gilman, who from her home in Charleston was doing her best to promote a better understanding of the South in her native New England. In spite of his Southern friends, Lowell accepted un-critically the Abolitionist conception of the South. Richmond Croom Beatty, Lowell's biographer, quotes Poe's characterization of him as "simply a fanatic for the sake of fanaticism" and remarks too severely: "A shrewder appraisal of Lowell in his thirtieth year could hardly have been written."

New England opposition to the annexation of Texas occasioned Lowell's "The Present Crisis," in which—fortunately for Southern college orators with whom it was a favorite after the war—Texas is not specifically mentioned. In *A Fable for Critics* (1848) the poet inserted a passage as obviously out of place as:

> Forty fathers of Freedom, of whom twenty bred
> Their sons for the rice-swamps, at so much a head,
> And their daughters for—faugh! thirty mothers of Gracchi. . . .

The First Series of *The Biglow Papers*, for which the War with Mexico provided the occasion, contains some of the best American humorous writing before *The Autocrat of the Breakfast-Table*, but it includes such unabashed political propaganda that it hardly deserves a place in the collected works of a serious poet. In Number I Lowell hit at "Them thet rule us, them slave-traders":

> 'Twouldn't suit them Southun fellers,
> They're a dreffle graspin' set,
> We must ollers blow the bellers
> Wen they want their irons het. . . .

Ironically, in view of the stand he was to take in the Second Series, Lowell closed the poem by openly advocating secession:

> Ef I'd *my* way I hed ruther
> We should go to work an' part,—
> They take one way, we take t'other,—
> Guess it wouldn't break my heart;
> Man hed ough' to put asunder
> Them thet God has noways jined;
> An' I shouldn't gretly wonder
> Ef there's thousands o' my mind.

The Second Series of *The Biglow Papers*, published in the *Atlantic Monthly* during the Civil War, differs widely from the first except that it is equally severe in its denunciation of the South. Here the poet is no longer a pacifist; secession has become a heinous crime; and the flag is not an object of ridicule but of veneration. Numbers I and III are letters from that renegade forerunner of "Petroleum Vesuvius Nasby," Birdofredum Sawin, now married to a Southern widow though he already has a wife back in New England. In Number I he comments on Southern illiteracy:

> For folks in Dixie th't read an' rite, onless it is by jarks,
> Is skurce ez wut they wuz among th' oridgenle patriarchs;
> To fit a feller f' wut they call the soshle higherarchy,
> All thet you've gut to know is jes' beyund an evrage darky;
> Schoolin's wut they can't seem to stan'. . . .

In Number III Sawin comments again on the Southern pretense to intellectual achievements:

> . . . hain't we the literatoor an science, tu, by gorry?
> Hain't we them intellectle twins, them giants, Simms an' Maury,
> Each with full twice the ushle brains, like nothin' thet I know,
> 'Thout 't was a double-headed calf I see once to a show?

In the final number, published a year after Appomattox, Biglow's attitude toward the South was still harsh and unforgiving. Southerners were not to be trusted; they had no intention of living up to their oaths of allegiance; and they should not be readmitted to citizenship in a Union that was too good for them without further tests and impositions.

Before many years passed, however, Lowell came to have, in the words of Howells, "a great tenderness for the broken and ruined South, whose sins he felt that he had had his share in visiting upon her. . . ." In "Under the Old Elm," written in 1875, he held out the hand of reconciliation to Virginia.

8

Ralph Waldo Emerson

I trust that no admirer of Ralph Waldo Emerson (1803–1882) will think me lacking in appreciation for one of the wisest and greatest American writers because I have chosen him to illustrate the extent to which sectional controversy prevented the New England writers from understanding the ante-bellum South. This, I am thoroughly aware, is to present Emerson at his worst. At the same time, although my story ends on a note of reconciliation, Southern critics of Emerson seem more lacking in insight than they were when they discussed the work of writers from New York and Pennsylvania.

Much that Emerson wrote about the South and slavery was at odds with some of his most characteristic ideas. This inconsistency did not disturb the Concord sage, but it may disturb some of his admirers. He once referred to Abolitionists and other professional reformers as "an altogether odious set of people, whom one would shun as the worst of bores and canters." The only way to make the world better, he thought, was to make better the individuals in it, and he was echoing Jefferson when he said that "the less government we have the better,—the fewer laws, and the less confided power." It was useless to try to reform society by attacking a single abuse. In "New England Reformers" he said in 1844: "Do not be so vain of your one objection [to society]. Do you think there is only one? Alas! my good friend, there is no part of society or of life better than any other part. All our things are right and wrong together. The wave of evil washes all our institutions alike. Do you complain of our Marriage? Our marriage is no worse than our education, our diet, our trade, our social customs." Might he not logically have added: ". . . than African slavery on Southern plantations or industrial servitude in New England mills and factories"?

Soon after his graduation from Harvard in 1821 Emerson wrote to a friend in Baltimore: "You know our idea of an accomplished Southerner; to wit, as ignorant as a bear, as irascible and nettled as any porcupine, as polite as a troubadour, and a very John Randolph in character and address." Emerson's notion of the Southern character shows plainly some marks of the traditional New England conception, but it was based in part on an acquaintance with Southern students at Harvard. For a brief time he shared a room with a Charlestonian, John Gourdin, whom Dr. Holmes describes as showy and fascinating. The recognized leader of Emerson's class was another South Carolinian, Robert Woodward Barnwell, whom President Josiah Quincy remembered as the "first scholar of the class . . . a noble specimen of the Southerner, high-spirited, interesting, and a leader of men." We shall hear of Barnwell again.

Health-seekers from New England often went South to avoid the cold Northern winter. It was thus that Emerson, recently ordained as a minister, spent the winter of 1826–1827 in Charleston and St. Augustine. This journey into what he felt was a foreign country had no such determining influence as his European visit six years later. The verses he wrote and the entries in his *Journals* indicate that he thought of himself as an exile. The Catholic priests and the Methodist ministers whom he heard, or heard of, confirmed his low opinion of the state of religion in the South. He felt, however, no deep repulsion from slavery as yet. That, as with Dr. Channing, was to come some years after he had left the South. He did, however, note a certain incongruity between slavery and Christianity. In St. Augustine he wrote in the *Journals* that he had attended a meeting of a Bible society, of which the treasurer was the district marshal. By "a somewhat unfortunate arrangement" the treasurer had called a meeting of the society in the government house while a slave auction was being conducted just outside. "One ear therefore heard the glad tidings of great joy, whilst the other was regaled with 'Going, gentlemen, going!' And almost without changing our position we might aid in sending the Scriptures into Africa, or bid for 'four children without the mother' who had been kidnapped therefrom."

Emerson was impressed with the superiority of the manners of Charlestonians white and black, but the most memorable event of his winter in the South was his meeting with Prince Achille Murat, a nephew of Napoleon, now married to an American and living on a plantation near Tallahassee. When Emerson sailed for Charleston, Murat went with him, and they talked incessantly. In Murat, Emerson found what he had not believed to exist: "a consistent atheist" and as ardent a lover of the truth as himself. Murat must have done something to shake some of the young minister's provincial notions, but Emerson presumably saw in Murat not a highly intelligent Southern planter but a European intellectual.

For eight years after his return from the South one finds in Emerson's writings few comments on the South or slavery. His conscience apparently did not deeply trouble him about slavery until the antislavery controversy became acute. As time went on, men who owed much of their culture to slaveholding Rome, Greece, and Palestine began to denounce Southern slaveholders as representatives of a semibarbarous civilization. Then the serene and philosophic Emerson was swept along by the tide exactly like lesser men. In the New England of his day, however, no one would remind him that in "The American Scholar" he had said: "Is it not the chief disgrace in the world, not to be an unit . . . but to be reckoned in the gross, in the hundred, or the thousand, of the party, the section, to which we belong; and our opinion predicted geographically, as the north, or the south?"

By October, 1837, Emerson had come to view the Southern collegian much more critically. The young Southerner who came to Cambridge was "a spoiled child," "a mere parader," "a mere bladder of conceit." "Each snippersnapper of them all undertakes to speak for the entire Southern States." They were, however, he admitted, "more civilized than the Seminoles . . . a little more."

In 1846, when he wrote the memorable "Ode Inscribed to W. H. Channing," Emerson was still not willing to take to the Abolitionist platform, and he was not, like some of the extremists, willing to break up the Union. He wrote:

> What boots thy zeal,
> O glowing friend,
> That would indignant rend
> The northland from the south?
> Wherefore? to what good end?
> Boston Bay and Bunker Hill
> Would serve things still. . . .

The crisis of 1850 moved Emerson to begin calculating the value of the Union—something which Thomas Cooper had advised South Carolinians to do some twenty years earlier. The new and more stringent fugitive slave law moved him to write in the *Journals:* "This filthy enactment was made in the nineteenth century, by people who could read and write. I will not obey it, by God." Speaking in Concord in 1851, he said: "Under the Union I suppose the fact to be that there are really two nations, the North and the South." Some Southerners would thus far have agreed with him but probably not in leaping to the conclusion that "The Union is at an end as soon as an immoral law is enacted." Until the war came, Emerson was willing that the masters should at enormous cost to the nation be compensated for the loss of their property in slaves; but when he read his "Boston Hymn" on January 1, 1863, he said:

> Pay ransom to the owner
> And fill the bag to the brim.
> Who is the owner? The slave is owner
> And ever was. Pay him.

On May 19, 1856, Emerson's friend Charles Sumner delivered in the United States Senate a vitriolic tirade entitled "The Crime against Kansas," in which he shamefully abused Senator Andrew P. Butler of South Carolina. Butler's young kinsman Preston S. Brooks, a member of the House of Representatives, retaliated by striking Sumner to the floor with his cane. Many but by no means all Southerners defended Brooks, but in New England Sumner was regarded as a martyr. Emerson said in a Concord address:

I do not see how a barbarous community and a civilized community can constitute one state. I think we must get rid of slavery, or we must get rid of freedom. Life has not parity of value in the free state and in the slave state. In one, it is adorned with education, with skilful labor, with arts, with long prospective interests, with sacred family ties, with honor and justice. In the other, life is a fever;

man is an animal, given to pleasure, frivolous, irritable, spending his days in hunting and practising with deadly weapons to defend himself against his slaves and against his companions brought up in the same idle and dangerous way. Such people live for the moment, they have properly no future, and readily risk on every passion a life which is of small value to themselves or to others.

Emerson had come to accept the Abolitionist legend of a barbarous South. He had forgotten his friend Barnwell when he added: "The whole state of South Carolina does not now offer one or any number of persons who are to be weighed in the scale with such a person as the meanest of them all has now struck down." This is even more ungenerous than a passage in a letter written by William Gilmore Simms on the last day of 1860: "Charleston is worth all New England."

In November, 1859, Emerson referred to John Brown, then under sentence of death, as "that new saint, than whom none purer or more brave was ever led by love of men into conflict and death,—the new saint awaiting his martyrdom, and who, if he shall suffer, will make the gallows glorious like the cross." A truer estimate of Brown is found in a passage that Hawthorne, no lover of reformers, wrote with Emerson in mind: ". . . nor did I expect ever to shrink so unutterably from any apothegm of a sage, whose happy lips have uttered a hundred golden sentences, as that saying . . . that the death of this blood-stained fanatic has 'made the Gallows as venerable as the Cross!' Nobody was ever more justly hanged."

While the Southern states were seceding one by one, Emerson took the same position as Hawthorne and Whittier that the North was well rid of them and no compromise should be made to bring them back. The attack on Fort Sumter, however, affected Emerson and millions of other Northerners as the Japanese attack on Pearl Harbor affected a later generation. Now the secessionists must be punished and the Southern states forcibly brought back into a Union which they hated.

This brief survey needs to be somewhat qualified. Except in the case of Preston S. Brooks, Emerson did not denounce individual Southerners. He always gave the Southerners credit for courage. Two years after the war he could say: "Of course, there are noble men everywhere, and there are such in the South. . . ." He had to add, however: "But the common people, rich and poor, were the narrowest and most conceited of mankind, as arrogant as the negroes on the Gambia River; and, by the way, it looks as if the editors of the Southern press were in all times selected from this class." Emerson would have been surprised if someone had told him how large a number of these Southern editors were natives of New England.

The rest of the story shows Emerson and the South in a more pleasant light. On July 6, 1866, he wrote to his old friend Barnwell, urging him to attend a reunion of the class of 1821: "But I wish you to know that distance, politics, war, even, at last, have not been able to efface in any manner the high affectionate regard in which I, in common I believe with all your old contemporaries of 1817–21, have firmly held you as our avowed chief, in days when boys, as we then were, give a tender & romantic value to that distinction, which they cannot later give again."

In the spring of 1876 the two literary societies of the University of Virginia asked Emerson to deliver an address in Charlottesville as a part of the commencement program. Emerson, now seventy-three years old, had given up speaking in public; but he accepted the invitation, "thinking it of happy omen that they should send to Massachusetts for their orator." "The visitors," Emerson and his daughter, says J. E. Cabot, "were treated with every attention in the society of the place, there was no intentional discourtesy, but the Southern self-respect appeared to demand that they should be constantly reminded that they were in an oppressed and abused country. And the next day, at Emerson's address, the audience in general—mostly young women with their admirers, but also children, as well as older persons—seemed to regard the occasion chiefly as one for social entertainment, and there was so much noise that he could not make himself heard." Emerson probably could not at that time have made himself heard by the entire audience if there had been perfect quiet. Finding themselves unable to hear, the youngsters talked, as others were to do six years later when a Southern writer, George W. Cable, was delivering a commencement address at the University of Mississippi. Emerson's friends were somewhat indignant; but when Cabot asked him about his reception in Virginia, all he would say was: "They are very brave people down there, and say just what they think."

In Charlottesville Emerson met several persons who had read his books and expressed their pleasure in meeting him. The next day in the train for the North many of his fellow-travelers, on their way to the Philadelphia Exposition, asked to be introduced to him. Reconstruction was coming to an end, and the South, which had not been hospitable to many New England writers, was at last coming to accept Emerson as a contemporary classic. It had taken a long time, for it was difficult for any Southerner to understand the Unitarian-Transcendentalist background out of which Emerson's writings had grown. By 1877, however, Sidney Lanier, who had grown up in a Presbyterian home in Macon, Georgia, was writing to Bayard Taylor that he would like to discuss with him "Emerson, whom I have been reading all winter, and who gives me immeasurable delight because he does not propound to me disagreeable systems and hideous creeds but simply walks along high and bright ways where one loves to go with him—then I am ready to praise God for the circumstance that if corn were a dollar a bushel I could not with my present finances buy a lunch for a pony."

Emerson's writings, which were often misunderstood even in his native Massachusetts, held peculiar difficulties for Southern readers in the forties and fifties. One exasperated Southern reviewer wrote: ". . . Mr. Emerson writes in a language which even his own children cannot understand." Even yet Emerson's poetic, oracular, semiclerical language sometimes misleads the unwary reader. Then, too, Emerson had, as I have shown, his provincial side; and the Southern reader, who had his own provincialisms, was often repelled. Lowell thought Emerson the most American of our writers; few Southerners would have agreed with him. A not untypical reaction was that of Joel R. Poinsett, one of the ablest and most intelligent Southerners of his time. The Swedish novelist Fredrika Bremer records her experience with Poinsett in the late forties:

I wished to make him a little acquainted with my friends the Transcendentalists and Idealists of the North, and I have read to him portions of Emerson's Essays. But they shoot over the head of the old statesman; he says it is all "unpractical," and he often criticizes it unjustly, and we quarrel. . . . Mr. Poinsett is, nevertheless, struck with Emerson's brilliant aphorisms, and says that he will buy his works. It is remarkable how very little, or not at all, the authors of the Northern States, even the best of them, are known in the South. They are afraid of admitting their liberal opinions into the Slave States.

For orthodox Southerners Emerson was an exponent of heretical doctrines that were dangerous. By this time the Southern churches had broken with the Northern, which they regarded as tainted with rationalism and fanatical on the slavery question. In January, 1852, John Custis Darby of Lexington, Kentucky, published an article on "Ralph Waldo Emerson" in the *Quarterly Review* of the Southern branch of the Methodist Church. "Mr. Emerson," he said, "is the representative of the New England infidelity; at the head of which form of doctrines, stands Strauss of Germany." For Emerson, as for Strauss, he thought, biblical history had only a symbolic value. "Strauss receives the truth, but denies the record as genuine, authentic history. . . . There is no God; it is all a myth." "It is a favorite doctrine with him [Emerson] to praise and admire the doctrines and excellencies of all religions except Christianity; and if he name the latter, to disparage it by a comparison with the doctrines of Vishnu and the philosophy of Plato. Among his representative men, the only Christian he has chosen to introduce, is the good and the learned, but the deranged Swedenborg."

A curious example of the Southern religious objection to Emerson is found in the second novel of Augusta Jane Evans, *Beulah* (1859). Its popularity suggests that in other sections there were many readers who regarded Emerson as an infidel. Beulah, a studious orphan girl, "with a slowly dying faith," is reading books one would not expect a Southern girl to read—although Miss Evans herself had evidently read them.

It was no longer study for the sake of erudition; these riddles involved all that she prized in Time and Eternity, and she grasped books of every description with the eagerness of a famishing nature. What dire chance threw into her hands such works as Emerson's, Carlyle's, and Goethe's? Like the waves of the clear, sunny sea, they only increased her thirst to madness. Her burning lips were ever at these fountains; and, in her reckless eagerness, she plunged into the gulf of German speculation.

Somewhat later Beulah has a long conversation with her friend Cornelia Graham, a widely traveled young woman who is rapidly becoming an invalid. Cornelia has absorbed the "grim Emersonian fatalism" completely, but Beulah has come to the conclusion that "of all Pyrrhonists he is the prince."

Beulah took up one of the volumes, and turned the pages carelessly.
"But all this would shock a Christian."
"And deservedly; for Emerson's works, collectively and individually, are aimed at the doctrines of Christianity. There is a grim, terrible fatalism scowling on his pages which might well frighten the reader who clasped the Bible to his heart."
"Yet you accept his 'compensation.' Are you prepared to receive his deistic system?" Cornelia leaned forward and spoke eagerly. Beulah smiled.
"Why strive to cloak the truth? I should not term his fragmentary system 'deistic.' He knows not yet what he believes. There are singular antagonisms existing among even his pet theories."

When Cornelia replies, "I have not found any," Beulah points them out and adds: "His writings are, to me, like heaps of broken glass, beautiful in the individual crystal, sparkling, and often dazzling, but gather them up, and try to fit them into a whole, and the jagged edges refuse to unite."
Cornelia on her deathbed says: "Oh, the so-called philosophers of this century and the last are crowned-heads of humbugry [*sic*]! . . . . They mock earnest, inquiring minds with their refined infinitesimal, homeopathic 'developments' of deity; metaphysical wolves in Socratic cloaks. Oh, they have much to answer for!" She admits that she has finally lost faith in Emerson and Theodore Parker: "Emerson's atheistic fatalism is enough to unhinge human reason; he is a great, and I believe an honest thinker, and of his genius I have the profoundest admiration. An intellectual Titan, he wages war

with received creeds, and rising on the ruins of systems, struggles to scale the battlements of truth. As for Parker, a careful perusal of his works was enough to disgust me." In the end Cornelia dies without recovering her faith. Beulah is more fortunate, for her faith returns and so does her lover, who had vanished somewhere in China.

The fairest and ablest discussion of Emerson that I have found in the ante-bellum Southern magazines is Daniel K. Whitaker's "Transcendental-ism," published in the *Southern Quarterly Review* in October, 1842. It is a review of the first two volumes of the *Dial*. Whitaker had grown up in Massachusetts and, though he did not like it, he had some understanding of what Transcendentalism was. "The Transcendentalists," he wrote, "are the enemies of antiquity, and equally hostile to existing institutions, and prevaling [*sic*] systems in morals, in philosophy, and religion. They are the champions of change and reform in all things." Thus they endangered the entire social and economic order. The Transcendentalists had no philosophic system and were, as Whitaker perceived, united only "by sympathy of spirit." Their heresies were only "opinions that were prevalent previous to the time of Locke, and which appear to us to have been fully met, and triumphantly refuted, by that illustrious metaphysician." Whitaker indulged in no denunciation, but he mildly ridiculed a passage in one of Emerson's essays.

William Gilmore Simms was greatly irritated by Lowell's *A Fable for Critics*, which omitted all Southern writers except Poe. "This critic, for example," he wrote in the *Southern Quarterly Review* for October, 1849, "expends all his praise upon the children of the East. He finds no others in the country, or, if he does, he dismisses them with a scornful complacency. . . ."

Hear our satirist discourse on Emerson, whom he styles a "Greek head on Yankee shoulders," and you fancy him one of the most marvellous men that the world has produced. A parallel is run between him and Carlyle, greatly to the discredit of the latter. None less than Plato will content him for a comparison. . . . And all this said of a man who is really half-witted, and whose chief excellence consists in mystifying the simple and disguising commonplaces in allegory. One Mr. Alcott follows, of whom we know nothing. . . .

In July, 1850, writing in the same periodical nine months later, Simms wrote in a calmer mood:

Emerson is an able essayist, of a school too much on stilts, too ambitious of the mystical, to be always secure of the sensible and true. He is decidedly popular with the *Transcendentalists*, if we may recognize, by a term so dignified, a rather inflated race, who presume somewhat upon the fact that their place of birth is a few degrees nearer the rising sun than ours. Emerson aims to be a reformer, after the fashion of Carlyle; and no doubt has large merits, which might be available to common and beneficial use if they were less clouded and embarrassed with his affectations of the Delphic.

One of the fairest reviews is found in De Bow's review of The Conduct of Life in March, 1861, the month of Lincoln's inauguration:

Under this title, Ticknor & Fields publish in their usual attractive style, the most recent volume of the writings of Ralph Waldo Emerson. We do not profess to be among the admirers of that eccentric gentleman, either as a man or as an author, but we do not deny that he possesses talent of a high order, possibly it might not be improper to say, genius. In not only this last, but in all of his works, we find many striking and original thoughts, but they are generally clothed in a style affectedly, studiously, and elaborately involved and obscure. They are not "apples of gold set in pictures of silver," but rather like pearls embedded in a mudhole, which it requires much patient industry to find. The followers of Mr. Emerson, and we believe that their name is not legion in these latitudes, will find in "The Conduct of Life," the usual characteristics of their favorite.

Long after 1861 intelligent Southerners found a difficulty in appreciating Emerson. Even Paul Hamilton Hayne, who had met Emerson and was an admirer of his English Traits and some of his poems, wished, as he wrote to Mrs. Julia C. R. Dorr, May 16, 1882, "that his Essays were some of them clearer, and informed by a loftier spirit of Faith; instead of that vague species of half-Pantheistic philosophy, which after all, is pre-eminently unoriginal, a mere elaborated echo of the 'Neo-Platonism' of Alexandria in the 4th and 5th centuries." On April 15, 1895, Joel Chandler Harris wrote in reply to William Malone Baskervill's inquiry about his favorite authors that the book which had first attracted his attention and held it longest was The Vicar of Wakefield:

Apart from this, all good books have me interested more or less. But the queer self-consciousness of Emerson has never appealed to me as strongly as it has to some of my friends. This is not Emerson's fault, but mine. You cannot expect an uncultured Georgia cracker to follow patiently the convolute diagrams of the Over-Soul. I find Sir Thomas Browne far more stimulating (I hope I am not treading on your corns here. Confidentially, Emerson's attitude as the New England Bigod—if I may use so crude an expression—has amused me no little.) You see I am perfectly frank in this, presenting the appearance of feeling as proud of my lack of taste and culture as a little girl is of her rag doll. It may give you a cue.

Simms and Whitaker were not ashamed to admit a failure to see in Emerson a great writer; Harris was. By 1895 Southerners had come somewhat reluctantly to accept, as a part of the new order, the Northern rating of Emerson and other New England writers.

That was well enough, but one Southern scholar at least was disturbed because, as it seemed to him, Southerners were accepting also the low Northern estimate of the writers of the Old South. In 1899 Professor Charles W. Kent, of the University of Virginia, said in a commencement address at the University of Tennessee: "I venture the assertion that our Southern youth to-day are as familiar with the writers of the New England school as are the boys of Boston or of Concord, but the New England boys—alas! it is true of our Southern youth as well—are lamentably ignorant of the literature of the South." [21]

9

Harriet Beecher Stowe

THE EXTRAORDINARY vogue of Uncle Tom's Cabin (1852) was due only in part to the literary merits which that powerful story has, for it appeared at the time when a vast reading public was fully prepared for it. The Northern feeling of indignation and frustration had been raised to a new height by the stringent fugitive slave law which was a part of the Compromise of 1850. Disgust and exasperation filled the minds of sensitive Northern men and women, but in those minds there was only the vaguest picture of the slave plantation. Poets like Longfellow and Whittier had sentimentalized over the slaves as if they were African kings undergoing the humiliation of captivity and slavery, but their fictitious personages seemed almost as remote as Mrs. Behn's Oroonoko and Imoinda. The professed Abolitionists had raved endlessly about the wrongs of the slaves, but it was all unreal, for they obviously did not know what a plantation was like. What Mrs. Stowe did was to present a clear and coherent series of pictures which to those who lacked firsthand knowledge seemed extraordinarily vivid and lifelike. Uncle Tom's Cabin seemed to draw aside a curtain that concealed a veritable chamber of long-suspected horrors. Ten years later Abraham Lincoln was to greet

---

[21] The Revival of Interest in Southern Letters (Richmond, 1900), p. 7. Kent charged that Northern anthologists were still neglecting the Southern writers. He might have noted that in Parnassus (1874), which displeased Whitman's followers because none of the Good Gray Poet's poems were included, Emerson found a place for only two Southern poems: Randall's "Maryland, My Maryland" and Timrod's Magnolia Cemetery "Ode."

its author with: "So this is the little lady who made the big war!" Half a century after the book came out, George E. Woodberry was to write that *Uncle Tom's Cabin* was "the one book by which the old South survives in literature, for better or worse."

In all Southern literature there was nothing to counteract the impression made by *Uncle Tom's Cabin*. For years Southern novelists had avoided giving any detailed picture of slavery. The South, content in the main to get its reading matter from the outside, now paid the penalty for its inability to convince the world that Mrs. Stowe's picture was a biased and distorted one. The damage was done, and it was irreparable. Effective refutation came only, after slavery had been swept away, in the writings of Irwin Russell, Joel Chandler Harris, and Thomas Nelson Page, who presented a somewhat idealized but much more accurate picture. *Uncle Tom's Cabin* rankled in the minds of Southerners for half a century or more. Page's *Red Rock* and the melodramatic romances of Thomas Dixon were in part motivated by the desire to put Mrs. Stowe in her place. That she was a New Englander made her book all the more obnoxious.

Harriet Beecher Stowe (1811–1896) was born in Litchfield, Connecticut, where Calhoun and Augustus Baldwin Longstreet studied law and perhaps first heard secessionist doctrines from their teachers. Her father, Lyman Beecher, was a vigorous opponent of Unitarianism, and the atmosphere in which Harriet grew up was somewhat Puritan. Her father did, however, permit her to read the romances of Scott and some of the poems of Byron, and their influence is discernible in her fiction. She was reading the Waverley romances again just before she began writing *Uncle Tom's Cabin*. When as a child she heard the news of Byron's death, she went out into the fields and flung herself weeping down on a pile of new-mown hay and prayed for his forgiveness and salvation. For her, as for the youthful Tennyson, Byron's death was a great personal loss.

The blighting effects of slavery were early brought home to her in the person of an aunt who had married an English settler in Jamaica only to discover that he had a Negro mistress and a family of mulatto children. From 1832 to 1850 the Beechers lived in Cincinnati, whither Lyman Beecher had gone to become President of the Lane Theological Seminary. Calvinism, rapidly losing ground in New England, was still strong in the Middle West. In Cincinnati, just across the Ohio River from Kentucky, fugitive slaves were to be seen, and their tales moved the emotional Harriet. Theodore Weld, Abolitionist evangelist, was active in this region. Although he headed a secession of students from her father's seminary—they went to Oberlin —he influenced her conception of slavery. With him Abolition was a pas-

sion, a religion. She was no Abolitionist—at least not yet—but she read
Weld's book, *American Slavery as It Is: Testimony of a Thousand Witnesses*,
published by the American Antislavery Society in 1839. Weld had been in
the South, but his book was made up chiefly of advertisements of runaway
slaves and other materials which he and his assistants had copied from
Southern newspapers in the New York Commercial Reading Room. That
was the way the Abolitionists got much of their ammunition. There were
apparently no fact-finding commissions in those days. This book, which supplied much material (not acknowledged) in Dickens's *American Notes*
(1842),[22] is cited as an authority again and again in Mrs. Stowe's *Key to
Uncle Tom's Cabin* (1853). She told Weld's wife, the former Angelina
Grimké of Charleston, that she "kept this book in her work basket by day
and slept with it under her pillow by night, till its facts crystallized into
Uncle Tom's Cabin." Although she did not understand that a race problem
was involved in emancipation, Mrs. Stowe knew slavery better than most
of the professed Abolitionist authorities. She did at least know that while
slavery was a patriarchal institution in the border states, it was something
worse in the Deep South. She once visited for a few days in Kentucky, but
she stayed not on a plantation but in the little village of Washington.[23]
From her brother Charles, who was in New Orleans for a time, she heard
the story of the overseer with a fist like an oak burl who said: "I got that
knockin' down niggers." Which sounds suspiciously like a tall tale told for
the benefit of the credulous outsider.

Cincinnati had its literary notables, among them James Hall, editor of
the *Western Monthly Magazine*, but Mrs. Frances Trollope had left before
Harriet arrived there and Moncure Conway was not to launch the second
Dial until after she departed. Harriet, who had not been attractive to young
men, married in 1836 Dr. Calvin Stowe, one of the professors in the seminary.
As children followed one another in rapid succession, the professor's salary

[22] Louise H. Johnson, "The Source of the Chapter on Slavery in Dickens's *American
Notes*," *Am. Lit.*, XIV, 427–430 (Jan., 1943).

[23] In a letter to James Lane Allen, April 30, 1886, Mrs. Stowe claimed a fuller knowledge of the slave plantation than is generally conceded to her: ". . . with him [her
father] I traveled and visited somewhat extensively in Kentucky, and there became acquainted with those excellent slaveholders delineated in 'Uncle Tom's Cabin.' I saw
many counterparts of the Shelbys—people humane, conscientious, just, and generous,
who regarded slavery as an evil and were anxiously considering their duties to the
slave" (Allen, "Mrs. Stowe's 'Uncle Tom' at Home in Kentucky," *Century*, XXXIV,
857, Oct., 1887). Allen found a good deal of truth in her picture of slavery in Kentucky. He remarks: ". . . it was not the *character* of Uncle Tom that she greatly idealized, as has been so often asserted; it was the category of events that were made to befall
him" (XXXIV, 854).

became inadequate, and Harriet turned to her pen to supplement the family income. Her husband had faith in her writing. In 1840 he wrote to her: "My dear, you must be a literary woman. It is so written in the book of fate." In view of the coming Southern reaction to *Uncle Tom's Cabin*, it is interesting to note that on July 23, 1842, she published in the *Chicora*, a Charleston literary weekly, an article entitled "Let Every Man Mind His Own Business."

In 1850 the Stowes moved to Brunswick, Maine. Dr. Stowe was to teach at Bowdoin College and a little later at the Andover Theological Seminary. All was excitement in New England over the Fugitive Slave Law and Webster's Seventh of March Speech in support of the Compromise of 1850. Henry Ward Beecher came to Brunswick and added to Harriet's excitement over the slave question. Her sister-in-law wrote to her: "Hattie, if I could use a pen as you can, I would write something that will make this whole nation feel what an accursed thing slavery is." The story goes that Harriet read the letter to her children and then rose to her feet as though taking a solemn vow and said: "I *will* write something. I will if I live." But as yet she had no story to write.

In February, 1851, while attending a communion service, in a kind of trance she had a vision of Uncle Tom being beaten to death. She wrote down the episode, and when Dr. Stowe read it, he said: "Hattie, you must go on with it. You must make up a story with this for a climax. The Lord intends it so." She went on with the story. In later life she said many times: "The Lord Himself wrote it. I was but an instrument in His hand." The Lord, however, was somewhat slow and spasmodic in the dictating of it; and, unfortunately, she had at that time no one to revise and rewrite her copy as she had later when William Dean Howells labored over her contributions to the *Atlantic Monthly*. In March, she wrote to Gamaliel Bailey, editor of the *National Era*, which had printed a few of her shorter pieces, that she was now writing a longer story "embracing a series of sketches which give the lights and shadows of the 'patriarchal institution,' written either from observation, incidents which have occurred in the sphere of my personal knowledge, or in the knowledge of my friends." She added: "I shall show the *best side* of the thing, and something *faintly approaching the worst*." Her vocation, she said, was merely that of "painter." "There is," as she said, "no arguing with *pictures*, and everybody is impressed by them, whether they mean to or not." The *National Era* offered her three hundred dollars for what was to be a longish short story, and that was all it ever paid her for the full-length novel which she wrote. After the instalments had begun to appear—it ran from June 5, 1851, to April 1, 1852—she sometimes found it difficult to continue. She had to do much of her writing after she had put the children to bed. She got inspiration and new materials by visiting the antislavery reading rooms in Boston and by studying *American Slavery as It Is* and the narratives of fugitive slaves. After the death of Little Eva she had to go to bed for two days; it was like losing a child of her own. She took the novel to her sister Catherine's publishers in Boston, Phillips, Sampson and Company, but they refused it, it is said, for fear of losing their Southern customers. It was published by young John P. Jewett, who offered her a 10 per cent royalty (which she chose) or an equal share in the costs and the profits. Dr. Stowe asked the advice of Congressman Philip Greeley, who advised him against risking anything upon a novel that would offend not only Southerners but many persons in the North. Within five years half a million copies of the novel had been sold in the United States and perhaps twice as many in the British Isles. Since that time the figure has risen to something like three million for this country and double that for sales in all countries. Longfellow wrote in his journal on February 24, 1853: "How she is shaking the world with her Uncle Tom's Cabin! At one step she has reached the top of the stair-case up which the rest of us climb on our knees year after year. Never was there such a literary *coup-de-main* as this."

Mrs. Stowe was not prepared for the violent opposition which came from the South. She had addressed the novel to Southern readers, or imagined that she had; and, incredible though it seems, it was not Southerners but Abolitionists that she had expected to object to the story. The Lord had written the novel, and nothing could shake her faith in the accuracy of the picture. She thought she had been fair to the South. She had portrayed kind masters as well as cruel, and she had drawn two of her meanest characters —Simon Legree and Marie St. Claire—from her native New England. In the *Key to Uncle Tom's Cabin* she wrote: "Human nature is no worse at the South than at the North; but law at the South distinctly provides for and protects the worst abuses to which that nature is liable." She never understood, I am sure, the grounds on which Southerners objected to the novel, the net effect of which was to condemn, as Emerson, Lowell, and many others were doing, the civilization of the South as semibarbarous.

As a novel, *Uncle Tom's Cabin* has serious defects, which are due in part to the episodic manner in which it was composed. *Dred* (1856) has seemed to some critics a better novel. Her best work of course is in her New England stories. Here she was on sure ground, and she blazed a trail for the later New England local colorists. But none of her other stories has the power that lies in *Uncle Tom's Cabin*. It has become a kind of national saga, and Uncle Tom and Simon Legree live on like Leather-Stocking and Huckleberry Finn.

It was Mrs. Stowe's passionate feeling that raised the novel above the conventional sentimental, pious, didactic, and often sensational narratives written by women and largely for women readers. The story is at bottom melodrama seasoned with romance and propaganda. The plot, made up of two stories only loosely tied together, involves lust, illicit love, suicide, murder, and sadistic cruelty. These are the same elements which some present-day Northern readers delight to find in the novels of Erskine Caldwell, William Faulkner, and Lillian Smith, and which leave them certain that the South is still only half-civilized. Mrs. Stowe's style is uneven; it is often affected or bombastic; and the book is frequently offensively moralistic in tone. Its Negro dialect—in spite of Forrest Wilson's defense of it—seems to me atrocious and more often Yankee than Southern. Much of the effectiveness of the story is due to its pictures of broken homes. Here was something that American and English mothers could appreciate. If Uncle Tom always failed to restore his shattered home, Eliza finally re-established hers after she reached Canada. The Swedish novelist Fredrika Bremer, visiting the United States in 1850, had wondered that stories of fugitive slaves, which she found "full of the most intense interest," were not being treated in American fiction. She must have found the answer in the story of Eliza crossing the Ohio River on the ice with her baby in her arms. So full of exciting events was the novel that few noticed that the conventional love story was lacking.

Mrs. Stowe was aware of the richness of Southern life as literary material. In her Preface to *Nina Gordon* (the later title of *Dred*) she gave her artistic reasons for laying the scene of her story in the Southern states:

First, in a merely artistic point of view, there is no ground, ancient or modern, whose vivid lights, gloomy shadows, and grotesque groupings, afford to the novelist so wide a scope for the exercise of his powers. In the near vicinity of modern civilization of the most matter-of-fact kind, exist institutions which carry us back to the twilight of the feudal ages, with all their exciting possibilities of incident. Two nations, the types of two exactly opposite styles of existence, are here struggling; and from the intermingling of these two a third race has arisen, and the three are interlocked in wild and singular relations, that evolve every possible combination of romance.

Perhaps it was her reading of Scott that enabled her to discover a literary "mine whose inexhaustible stores have but begun to be developed." She was certainly aware of the value of the contrasting racial and national types of Louisiana twenty years and more before Cable appeared on the literary scene.

Joel Chandler Harris, who first read the novel in 1862, argued in 1904 that in spite of herself Mrs. Stowe had found a certain charm in the slave system. He wrote: ". . . all the worthy and beautiful characters in her book —Uncle Tom, little Eva, the beloved Master, and the rest—are the products of the system the text of the book is all the time condemning." The villain is an outsider. "The real moral that Mrs. Stowe's book teaches," Harris declared, "is that the possibilities of slavery anywhere and everywhere are shocking to the imagination, while the realities, under the best and happiest conditions, possess a romantic beauty and a tenderness all their own. . . ."

Frances Hodgson Burnett read the novel while she was a little girl in England, and it made her want to live in the South, even in wartime. In 1865 she realized her dream when her family settled in East Tennessee. She tells the story in her autobiography, *The One I Knew Best of All* (1893), which is written in the third person:

She did not in the least know what the war was about, but she could not help sympathizing with the South because magnolias grew there, and people dressed in white sat on verandas covered with vines. Also, there were so many roses. How could one help loving a place where there were so many roses? . . . One wept all through "Uncle Tom's Cabin" because they [the slaves] had not their "freedom," and were sold away from their wives and children, and beaten and hunted with bloodhounds; but the swarms of them singing and speaking negro dialect in the plantations were such a picturesque and loveable feature of the Story; and it was so unbearable to think of the plantations being destroyed, the vine-covered verandas disappearing, and the magnolias blooming no more to shade the beautiful planters in Panama hats and snow-white linen. She was so attached to planters, and believed them all—except the Legrees—to be graceful and picturesque creatures.

Moncure D. Conway, who had grown up in Virginia, read parts of the novel in the *National Era* without recognizing—in spite of his hatred of slavery—anything that was true of slavery in Virginia. After he had been driven out of Fredericksburg, however, he reread it with different eyes and concluded that *Uncle Tom's Cabin* was "a photographic representation of things going on in States farther south"—where, it seems, he had never been.

In the South of the early fifties *Uncle Tom's Cabin* was denounced in practically all the magazines and in many newspapers. It was regarded as a very unfair picture of slavery and a very offensive book. Reviewers resented Mrs. Stowe's tone of righteous Puritan superiority. She was meddling with matters that were none of her business, they felt—matters, too, that she really knew nothing about. They objected that she had played up isolated, untypical instances of cruelty and abuse. Louisa S. McCord, writing in the *Southern Quarterly Review* for January, 1853, saw in the novel all the old antislavery libels except that slaveowners were in the habit of fattening Negro babies for the soup pot. Mrs. Stowe, she said, had pictured a society of slaveholders "without heart, without soul, without intellect; a nation, too, (strange incongruity!) of cultivated human beings, so ignorant of right and wrong, so dead to all morality, that it were an insult to Deity, to believe in their existence." Mrs. Stowe, she said, did not know what a gentleman was, and she had made Southern ladies and gentlemen talk "rather vulgar Yankee-English" while her Louisiana Negroes all talked "Kentuck."

Mrs. McCord and many another Southern critic pointed out that no master with a thousand dollars invested in a slave would have permitted Uncle Tom or George Harris to be cruelly treated. They pointed out numerous other errors—errors, however, that only a Southerner was likely to notice. Mrs. Stowe had, for example, shown her ignorance of Southern social life when she represented the planter Shelby as receiving a slavetrader in his parlor. They objected that Mrs. Stowe was ignorant of the laws governing the treatment of slaves. They contended of course that the slaves were not unhappy, which was probably true of most of them, and that few of them cared anything about freedom, which was undoubtedly wrong. They resented most of all the assumption that intellectually and morally the Negro was the equal of the white man. They felt that Mrs. Stowe, like vast numbers of Northern critics then and now, had completely failed to understand that underlying slavery was a race problem which would remain to trouble the nation long after emancipation had come about.

Few Southern critics except Simms could read the book dispassionately enough to recognize its literary merits. He saw in the novel "a passionate power" and a remarkable "dramatic faculty." "She is, unquestionably," he wrote in the *Southern Quarterly Review* for January, 1854, "a woman of great inventive faculty, and 'Uncle Tom,' considered wholly aside from the slavery question, is a story of great and striking, though coarse, attraction. She has found it easier, as most persons have, to make a picture of bad passions and a vicious atmosphere, than one of virtue and purity. . . ."

If *Uncle Tom's Cabin* served no other purpose. it awakened many leading Southerners to the consequences of their section's having failed to produce a literature which would serve as a defense of the Southern way of life. The demand for this Southern literature became louder than ever. John R. Thompson took occasion to urge Southerners to support their literary magazines. "Never before," he wrote in the *Southern Literary Messenger* for January, 1853, "have the forces of fanaticism been so banded together to

compass the destruction of Southern interests." The duty of Southerners
to support their own literary organs, he pointed out, was now more impera-
tive than ever.

Years were to pass before many Southerners would even read *Uncle Tom's
Cabin*. Grace King apparently had not read it when she first saw Mrs. Stowe
at Hartford twenty years after Appomattox. Thomas Nelson Page, Thomas
Dixon, and other Southern writers made it their business to refute her libels
on the Old South. The book, however, as I have indicated, made a deep impression on the youthful Joel Chandler Harris. George W. Cable and Mark
Twain were friends of Mrs. Stowe, and directly or indirectly her treatment
of slavery had its influence upon *The Grandissimes* and *Huckleberry Finn*.
They saw, as she had seen, the strain of cruelty and violence in the life of
the western South. In the twentieth century Paul Green, T. S. Stribling,
William Faulkner, DuBose Heyward, Lillian Smith, and still other Southern writers have treated the Negro less in the manner of Thomas Nelson
Page than in that of Mrs. Stowe. Perhaps not all of them have read *Uncle
Tom's Cabin*, but they write as if they must atone for the guilt of an earlier
generation by glorifying the virtues of the primitive Negro and by picturing
the decadent descendants of the planter gentry as expiating the sins of their
slaveholding ancestors. Faulkner, for instance, in *Absalom, Absalom!* refers
to Appomattox as "that day when the South would realize that it was now
paying for having erected its economic edifice not on the rock of stern
morality but on the shifting sands of opportunism and moral brigandage."
In "The Bear" in *Go Down, Moses* Ike McCaslin praises the virtues of the
Negro:

"They are better than we are. Stronger than we are. Their vices are vices aped
from white men or that white men and bondage have taught them: improvidence
and intemperance and evasion—not laziness: evasion: of what white men had set
them to, not for their aggrandisement or even comfort but his own—. . . .
And their virtues— . . . [are] Endurance— . . . and pity and tolerance and
forbearance and fidelity and love of children— . . . whether their own or not
or black or not."

10
John William De Forest

JOHN WILLIAM DE FOREST (1826–1906) saw as much of Southern life
as Bronson Alcott—far more than Mrs. Stowe had seen—and the spectacle
fascinated him. He did not love the South, however, and he did not, like

the Transcendentalist philosopher and peddler, return to his native Connecticut arrayed in broadcloth to look like a fine Southern gentleman. In the years before the war De Forest traveled widely in Europe and the Near East, and he spent more than a year in Charleston. As an officer in the Union army he saw service in Virginia and Louisiana, and in 1866 and 1867 he was for fifteen months in the Freedmen's Bureau in Up-Country South Carolina. De Forest saw the South at the time when the people of the two sections hated one another most bitterly. For him, as for Lowell, the Southerners were a provincial, archaic people who by obstinately defending an antiquated and barbarous institution had inflicted a bloody war upon the only really civilized part of the nation and who consequently must somehow be made into good Americans. In spite of his experiences in the South, De Forest thought that the ante-bellum South had been ruled by a little oligarchy of wealthy planters. He disliked the Reconstruction policies of Andrew Johnson, who was only trying to carry out as best he could the wise and humane plans of Lincoln. When he first came to the Carolina Up-Country, his predecessor said to him: "The worst social feature is the poverty. There are numbers of old Negroes who are living on their bankrupted former masters. There are four hundred soldiers' widows in the district of Greenville, and six hundred in that of Pickens. You can imagine the orphans." Not long after, De Forest told the white families in Greenville that soon their finest houses would be in possession of the blacks. De Forest, however, soon found himself as much disillusioned about the ex-slaves as he had been by their former masters.

De Forest made use of his Southern experiences in *Miss Ravenel's Conversion from Secession to Loyalty* (1867), *Kate Beaumont* (1872), and *The Bloody Chasm* (1881). The first of these novels, republished in 1939, impressed Howells by its realism and power. In 1881, when the last of the three novels appeared, stories of reconciliation were the vogue. De Forest made use of the conventional love story of the Northern soldier and the Southern belle, but it is significant that he exaggerated rather than minimized the gulf of sectional hatred that separated the lovers.

De Forest collected and rearranged his various magazine articles with a view to publishing a book on his experiences with the Freedmen's Bureau; but the book remained unpublished until 1948, when the Yale University Press brought it out under the title *A Union Officer in the Reconstruction*. His general view of the Southern character is given in those chapters which he had published in *Harper's Magazine* in January and February, 1869, under the title "Chivalrous and Semi-Chivalrous Southrons." These chapters constitute one of the shrewdest appraisals of the Southern character ever written.

Yet, although there is no question of the intelligence or the honesty of the observer, the portrait emphasizes chiefly those Southern traits which most irritated Northerners of his time.

De Forest had no sympathy with the Southern contention that the war was due primarily to the aggressive designs of the North, especially his native New England. He quotes a Greenville farmer who said to him:

"They [the New Englanders] always were you know, the most quarrelsome people that God ever created. They quarreled in England, and cut off the king's head. They have been quarreling here ever since they came over in the *Mayflower*. They got after the Indians and killed them by the thousands. They drove out the Baptists and whipped the Quakers and hung the witches. Then they were the first to pick a fight with the old country. It's my opinion, Sir, and I think you must agree with me, that God never made such another quarrelsome set. What in h—ll he made them for passes my comprehension."

Since this seemed to him "better history" than he usually heard from Southerners, De Forest "let it pass without controversy." He found many Southerners who said to him: "I am glad the thing [slavery] is done away with; it was more plague than pleasure, more loss than profit." And yet these · farmers, filled with wrath at the way the slaves had been freed, would always add: "Damn the Yankees!"

The Southerners for De Forest represented a simpler type, "more provincial, more antique, more picturesque." They had, he thought, "fewer of the virtues of modern society, and more of the primitive, the natural virtues." They cared less for "wealth, art, learning, and the other delicacies of an urban civilization" and more for "individual character and reputation of honor." They were, he suggested, as different from other Americans as the ancient Spartans from the Athenians or the modern Poles from the Germans.[24]

The widely traveled De Forest felt acutely the provincialism of the average Southerner. In Up-Country South Carolina a farmer said to him: "I

[24] In an article entitled "Chivalrous Southrons" published in the *Southern Review*, VI, 96–128 (July, 1869), the anonymous author—probably Albert Taylor Bledsoe, the editor—conceded that De Forest's list of Southern characteristics was "striking." What he objected to was De Forest's attempt to make them seem ridiculous. It was all, he thought, a part of the attempt to "Northernise" the South. "The great defect of Northern civilization," he said, "is its materiality. It is of the earth, earthy; and ignores the spirituality of our nature. Its grand motive and object is the accumulation of money; and its prime boast is of the things money can buy—'the lust of the eye, the lust of the flesh, and the pride of life.' Mammon is its god; and nowhere has he more devout and abject worshippers, or has set up a more polluted civilisation than in the North. The whole spirit of Christianity," he concluded, "is opposed to this sort of civilisation" (VI, 109).

go first for Greenville, then for Greenville District, then for the up-country, then for South Carolina, then for the South, then for the United States; and after that I don't go for a thing. I've no use for Englishmen, Turks, and Chinese." Such an attitude was not confined to Up-Country farmers. Basil Lanneau Gildersleeve, a Charlestonian trained in a German university and the son of a Connecticut Yankee, was accustomed to saying: "I am a Charlestonian first, a South Carolinian next, and after that a Southerner."

The provincial Southerner's reaction to metropolitan life in the North is well suggested by De Forest's story of a young Kentuckian of good Virginian family who tried in vain to accustom himself to life in New York. "I can't stand this any longer," he finally said. "I can't respect myself when I am run against a dozen times a day by Irishmen, Jews, Yankees, and all kinds of busy people. I am of no consequence here; nobody cares whether I am a gentleman or not—whether I am angry or pleased; nobody values me as I know that I ought to be valued. I must go South again—go where there is more elbow-room—go where I can make myself known. I detest a city where seven hundred thousand people tread on my toes, and haven't a moment's leisure to apologize, and don't even know that my name is Peyton."

Before the war De Forest, like many another Northerner, had been irritated by the Southern disposition to defend slavery on every occasion. He tells with some relish the story of a South Carolina clergyman who on a steamer bound for Liverpool so continually expatiated on the happiness of the slaves that an Englishman who shared his stateroom finally said to him: "My dear Sir, if things are as you say, why not go back to South Carolina and become a slave?"

The South that De Forest saw after the war was bankrupt. Farmers were selling their land for a seventh of its prewar value; and some of them, unable to hire laborers, were themselves hiring out for seventy-five cents a day or for twenty-five cents with room and board. Nothing but the stay-laws and stay-orders, it seemed, prevented all the farms in the South from being brought under the auctioneer's hammer. Although the Southerners, he thought, had brought all these calamities upon themselves, still De Forest had some appreciation of the deep humiliation of a Southern lady forced to open a boarding house or become a house servant; and he had some pity for a gentleman who had once represented his country abroad but was now driven to open a beer saloon or accept rations from "low-downers" and Negroes. In the almost universal bankruptcy of the South, it seemed to De Forest, those Southerners who had once been honorable were now stooping to all sorts of trickery and chicanery in order to save their property. The "chivalrous Southrons" were fast becoming a race of Micawbers.

De Forest, a member of a socially prominent Connecticut family, had considerable admiration and respect for "high-toned gentlemen of the old Virginian or Carolinian school." They belonged to the leisurely caste which set an example to their inferiors. In the Up-Country after the war, however, De Forest was surrounded by small farmers rather than great planters of fine old families. The cotton plantation had come to the Up-Country late, and the few wealthy families were usually newcomers to the ranks of the aristocracy. They were only "semi-chivalrous." In the Greenville district there were also numerous sand-hillers, crackers, and other "low-downers" who were neither "chivalrous" nor "semi-chivalrous." In the foothills of the mountains De Forest found many Unionists, but they seemed to him ignorant and "half wild." The Greenville district was not the best place in which to study the really "chivalrous Southrons," and the Reconstruction era was certainly not the most propitious time for a Northern observer to be among them.

Among the Southern traits that most impressed De Forest was pugnacity, often leading to violence. The Southern code compelled even the clergyman to resent an insult and to fight a duel if necessary to vindicate his honor. The remarkable courage of the Confederate soldier, De Forest thought, was explained partly by his pugnacity and partly by the probability that if not killed in battle he would be killed in a fight. "The bullet-hole was a mere question of time," he cynically suggested, "and why not open one's arms to it on the field of glory?" The Southern planter, said De Forest, made an excellent army officer because his virtues and vices were remarkably like those of the professional soldier: "Notably brave, punctilious as to honor, pugnacious to quarrelsomeness, authoritative to imperiousness, generous to extravagance, somewhat formal in his courtesy, somewhat grandiose in his self-respect, there is hardly an agreeable or disagreeable trait in him which you cannot find in the officers of most armies." The Southerner's sense of honor, De Forest thought, showed itself at its best in the admirable honor system practiced in Southern colleges.

The "central trait of the 'chivalrous Southron'" was, in De Forest's estimation, "an intense respect for virility." The Southerner, he said, "will forgive almost any vice in a man who is manly. . . . If you will fight, if you are strong and skillful enough to kill your antagonist, if you can govern or influence the common herd, if you can ride a dangerous horse over a rough country, if you are a good shot or an expert swordsman, if you stand by your own opinions unflinchingly, if you do your level best on whisky, if you are a devil of a fellow with women, if, in short, you show vigorous masculine attributes, he will grant you his respect." That, too, De Forest felt sure, was the kind of man whom Southern women admired.

The literary culture of even the "chivalrous Southron" did not impress De Forest.

One of the mistakes of the "chivalrous Southron" was to suppose that he was a great reader, and well up to his age in science and literature. The truth is that while his reading was mainly good, it was venerable; he had a conservative taste for what had been considered improving and interesting by his grandfather; his shelves were loaded with the worthy though possibly heavy old "books which no gentleman's library should be without"; he was sure to own Hume, Robertson, Gibbon, Addison, Johnson, Goldsmith, etc. In theology he was strenuously orthodox, holding fast by the English fathers in biblical exegesis, and distrusting all Germans without knowing any thing about them. In science he was averse to admitting novelties, unless they went to show that the negro is not a human being, and so can not claim the benefit of the Declaration of Independence. In light literature he was cautious how he meddled with Northern, and even with English publications, lest he should unawares become entangled in some "ism."

Preoccupation with the defense of slavery, it seemed to De Forest, had dwarfed the Southern mind so that the Southerner had become incapable of thinking justly on any subject. There had been a vast decline in Southern writing since the time of Jefferson and Hugh S. Legaré, "in other words, since the intellect of Dixie ceased to be free." De Forest knew very little about the literature of the Old South, but what he had read seemed to him almost worthless. He wrote: "The romances of Dixie, produced under a mixed inspiration of namby-pambyism and provincial vanity, strong in polysyllables and feeble in perception of character, deserve better than any other results of human labor that I am aware of the native epithet of 'powerful weak.' The novelist evidently has but two objects in view: First to present the Southron as the flower of gentility; second, to do some fine writing for his own glory. Two or three works by Kennedy and . . . 'Marion Harland' [Mrs. Mary Virginia Terhune] are the only exceptions to this rule."

The "chivalrous Southron," as De Forest pointed out, had not been adequately treated in literature: "People have not described him; they have felt driven to declaim about him; they have preached for him or preached against him. Northern pens have not done justice to his virtues, nor Southern pens to his vices." De Forest proceeded to suggest the changes which would have to come about in Southern thinking before there would be a Southern literature worthy of the name:

Not until the Southerners get rid of some of their local vanity, not until they cease talking of themselves only in a spirit of self-adulation, not until they drop the idea that they are Romans and must write in the style of Cicero, will they be able to so paint their life as that the world shall crowd to see the picture. Meantime, let us pray that a true Southern novelist may soon arise, for he will be able to furnish us vast amusement and some instruction. His day is passing; in another generation his material will be gone; the "chivalrous Southron" will be as dead as the slavery that created him.

In his most kindly mood but still somewhat patronizingly De Forest concluded his article by suggesting how the victorious North should treat the defeated and bankrupt South, but he did not include the passage in his book:

How shall we manage this eccentric creature [the Southerner]? We have been ruled by him; we have fought him, beaten him, made him captive; now what treatment shall we allot him? My opinion is, that it would be good both for him and for us if we should perseveringly attempt to put up with his oddities and handle him as a pet. . . .

A little letting alone, a little conciliation, a little flattery even, would soothe him amazingly; and if united with good government would in the end be sure to reconstruct him as a quiet citizen and sound patriot. The Republican party, while firmly maintaining the integrity of the country and the great results of the war in the advancement of human freedom, ought to labor zealously for the prosperity of the South, treat tenderly its wounded pride, forget the angry past, be patient with the perturbed present, and so create a true, heart-felt national unity.

During the years of reconciliation and good will that followed upon President Hayes's withdrawal of Union soldiers from the South in 1877, Northern visitors, like Constance Fenimore Woolson and Maude Howe Elliott, took a more kindly view of the Southern character than De Forest had held. And when Mary Noailles Murfree and Grace King visited New England, they found the Yankees as kindly, as friendly, and as hospitable as Tennesseans and Louisianians. William Wirt and Lucian Minor had made a similar discovery when they went to New England in the early nineteenth century, but forty years of controversy, war, and Reconstruction had increased the barrier of ignorance and prejudice which separated the two sections.

In September, 1883, Joel Chandler Harris, who did not believe that the war was fought by two dissimilar peoples, visited rural New England to find out for himself "whether the people of New England were as different from the people of the South as the gentlemanly publicists of both sections are in the habit of claiming." The people whom Harris saw in rural New England—though De Forest would hardly have admitted it—bore a strong "family resemblance" to the familiar Southern types.

Here, waiting for me with smiles of welcome, were my old friend Major Joseph Jones, of Pineville, Simon Suggs, the Hon. Potiphar Peagreen, and all the rest of the characters who are identified with rural life in the South. Here, too, was Bud Stuckey, the Georgia Tacky, though what he was doing hanging barefooted around the little station of Bethel on the Vermont Central the Lord only knows. . . . He wore here the same striped shirt and red jeans trousers he used to wear in Georgia, and he had the same pale, watery blue eyes, the same straggling sandy beard, and the same habit of fingering his weak chin and mouth. And, then, when the train-boy, with true Southern accent, called out "Northampton," why should a group of E. W. Kemble's Georgia "crackers" be standing near the station? All this is more than I can make out, unless the leagues that stretch between Vermont and Georgia are a dream and sectionalism a myth.

"I have never been able to clearly understand," said Harris, "the real intent of the comparison that has been set up in literature and out of it between New England and the South. Neither side gives a fair view of the other."

Fortunately, although ignorance and prejudice have not been altogether dissipated, Southern and New England writers have done much to dispel such misconceptions as I have discussed. It is obvious now that New Englanders and Southerners had much more in common than writers from either section would admit during the long years of controversy, war, and Reconstruction. In *The Attack on Leviathan* (1938) Donald Davidson included an admirable essay, "Still Rebels, Still Yankees," which contains remarkably shrewd and kindly portraits of rural Vermonter and Georgian and emphasizes traits common to both regional types.

11
Southern Antislavery Writers

THE PRESSURE OF opinion in the Old South never succeeded in compelling all Southerners to think alike. It is significant, however, that most of the literary dissenters were from the upper South and even there found life so uncomfortable that many of them removed to the North.[25] In the forties

[25] There is much material in Clement Eaton, *Freedom of Thought in the Old South* (1940). See also J. S. Bassett, *Anti-Slavery Leaders of North Carolina* (1889); S. B. Weeks, "Anti-Slavery Sentiment in the South," So. History Assn. *Publications*, II, 87–130 (1898); and U. B. Phillips, "Economic and Political Essays in the Ante-bellum South," *The South in the Building of the Nation*, VII, 173 ff.

and fifties the South was immensely more intolerant of divergent opinions than it had been in the eighteenth century. The decay of religious liberalism, the rise to political power of the common man, and the ceaseless agitation of the Abolitionists accompanied if they did not bring on increasing intolerance.

I have already noted examples of religious intolerance in the striking cases of Horace Holley and Thomas Cooper. After 1840, however, religious heterodoxy was less objectionable than unorthodox views on the slavery question. In the Black Belt of the Deep South the white population was by 1860 practically a unit on the question of slavery; only in the upper Southern states was there any disposition to question the divine sanction of the institution. The heretics were rarely planters. For them the institution was a source of profit; it was also a matter of personal relations, not to be considered in the abstract. The most conspicuous antislavery planter was James G. Birney, who hated slavery as he saw it in Alabama, became an active Abolitionist, and eventually, after he had settled in the North, a candidate for the Presidency on the Abolitionist ticket. Those Southerners who refused to accept the orthodox view of slavery were usually ministers, teachers, journalists, or Quakers. The two whom I shall discuss at some length are Hinton Rowan Helper, a North Carolinian, and Moncure Daniel Conway, a native of Virginia. I must, however, devote a paragraph to each of two other antislavery writers from the same two states: Daniel Reeves Goodloe (1814–1892) and Samuel Janney (1801–1880), both of whom contrasted the intolerant South of their time with the Virginia of Jefferson and Washington.

Goodloe was a native of North Carolina who, finding his antislavery views unacceptable there, moved to Washington, D. C., where he was for a time editor of the National Era, in which Uncle Tom's Cabin first appeared. In 1858 he published The Southern Platform, a compilation of what earlier Southern leaders had said about the evils of slavery. His most notable work, however, was the pamphlet, Inquiry into the Causes Which Have Retarded the Accumulation of Wealth and Increase of Population in the Southern States (1846). Goodloe's strongest and most original argument was that the capital invested in slaves was largely wasted. The South, he calculated, had tied up in its slaves the enormous sum of $150,000,000 when one-fifteenth of that amount would have sufficed to hire the labor needed annually by the planters. "Slavery," he said, "merely serves to appropriate the wages of labor—it distributes wealth, but cannot create it."

Janney, who lived in northern Virginia, was a Quaker poet, teacher, and preacher who eventually published biographies of William Penn and George

Fox and a four-volume history of the Quakers. In 1849 President William A. Smith of Randolph-Macon College delivered in Leesburg a lecture in which he argued that slavery had biblical justification and was a good in itself. Janney published a detailed reply in the Leesburg *Washingtonian*. In 1850 he was tried on the charge that he had denied that "owners had right of property in their slaves." Janney won his case with a brilliant defense, but the presiding judge lectured him on his lack of discretion in meddling with so delicate a question as slavery. In addressing the jury, Janney had said: "And can it be that freedom of the press is so completely prostrated in Virginia that a native citizen of the county may not be permitted to answer an address thus publicly delivered in which were maintained doctrines at variance with the sentiments of Washington, Jefferson, Patrick Henry, and all the great statesmen of Virginia?"

Nothing irritated and embarrassed the Southern proslavery writers more than to have Lincoln and the Abolitionists continually remind them that Washington, Jefferson, and Madison had condemned slavery and secession. In "Virginia—The West" Whitman, noting that Virginians living in the Northwest were volunteering to fight to defend the Union, pictured the nation as addressing the Mother of Presidents:

> As to you Rebellious . . . why strive against me, and why seek my life?
> When you yourself forever provide to defend me?
> For you provided me Washington—and now these also.

12
Hinton Rowan Helper

GOODLOE'S PAMPHLETS had no appreciable effect upon the masses in either North or South, but there were many who read *The Impending Crisis of the South* (1857), in which another North Carolinian tried to turn against the slaveholding minority the six million Southern whites who owned no slaves. On his father's side Hinton Rowan Helper (1829–1909) was of German descent; his grandfather had spelled the name *Helfer*. His father owned a few slaves, but Helper himself had the characteristic German-American hostility to slavery, and he was also a violent Negrophobe. He graduated in 1848 from an academy in Mocksville, where one of his teachers was Peter S. Ney, a Frenchman whom some North Carolinians believe to have been Napoleon's famous marshal. After working in a store in Salisbury, Helper went to New York in 1850 and in 1851 to California. After three

years in the Far West he returned to North Carolina as poor as ever. In
The Land of Gold: Reality vs. Fiction (1855) he announced briefly his
recent discovery that slavery was a less profitable system of labor than freedom. His Baltimore publisher—Charles Mortimer, also publisher of the
Southern Quarterly Review—refused, so Helper afterwards said, to print
the book until certain passages about slavery were deleted. Helper was irritated, but having already spent four hundred dollars on the book, he
finally agreed to the changes demanded. Immediately he set to work on
The Impending Crisis of the South. He was determined to state his case
against slavery. "New England wives," he wrote in his Preface, "have written the most popular anti-slavery literature of the day. Against this I have
nothing to say; it is all well enough for women to give the fictions of slavery;
men should give the facts." Even in New York, however, Helper had been
unable, he says, to find a publisher who was willing to print the book for
fear of losing the Southern trade. After seven months he finally found a
book agent, A. B. Burdick, who was willing to bring out the book provided
that Helper would guarantee him against loss. For the first year or two
after its publication the book sold only moderately well. Then Horace
Greeley and others seized upon it as admirable Abolitionist propaganda—
all the more valuable as coming from a Southerner who detested the slave-
owning "oligarchy"—and the book sold something like a million copies. In
1859 it was republished in condensed form with a new section, for which
perhaps Helper was not responsible, consisting of extracts from the writings
of prominent Abolitionists. In spite of his hatred of the Africans, Helper
had been taken into the Abolition camp bag and baggage. He could now
hope for few readers in the South, where men are said to have been im-
prisoned for owning the book.

In 1861, President Lincoln, who was impressed by *The Impending Crisis*,
sent Helper as consul to Buenos Aires. Returning to the United States in
1866 with an Argentine wife, Helper found himself completely out of sympathy with the Radical party in Congress. They were bent upon placing
in power the Negroes whom he hated, and they cared little about the poorer
Southern whites whose cause he had championed. He expressed his views
in three books: *Nojoque* (1867), *Negroes in Negroland* (1868), and *Noon-
day Exigencies* (1871). His purpose in these books, as he expressed it, was
to write the Negro out of America and, if possible, into extinction. It was
the Democratic party and not the Republican that made political capital
of these books, especially the first of the three. Helper spent his later years
and seventy thousand dollars of his own money in promoting his favorite
scheme for a railroad which was to run from Alaska to the Straits of Magel-

lan. Finally at the age of eighty he committed suicide, declaring, "There is no justice in the world" and saying that he was "tired of living anyway."

In *The Impending Crisis* Helper undertook to prove by statistics taken from the census reports that it was Negro slavery and nothing else that was keeping the Southern states from enjoying an increase in wealth and population equal to that of the North. In the eyes of latterday economists he damaged his case by manipulating his figures and by making unfair comparisons. His animus against slaveholders—which was what endeared him to the Abolitionists—prevented his book from making any favorable impression in the South. Although he hated the slaves, Helper had swallowed *in toto* the Abolitionist legend of a slaveholding oligarchy that ruled the poorer whites with a rod of iron. He saw in the South "three odious classes of mankind; the slaves themselves, who are cowards; the slaveholders, who are tyrants; the non-slaveholding hirers, who are lickspittles." The fantastic remedy which Helper proposed was that the numerous nonslaveholders should organize their own party, refuse co-operation with the proslavery politicians, make slaveholders ineligible for office, place a tax of sixty dollars on every slave, and use the money thus raised to deport all Negroes to Africa. *The Impending Crisis* is not great literature, but it is effective pamphleteering. Helper's impassioned earnestness gives it power and sometimes eloquence.

Not the least effective portion of the book is the concluding chapter, "Southern Literature," where Helper follows the stock Abolitionist interpretation. Liberty and literature, he maintains, forgetting the Greeks, the Romans, and the Hebrews, are inseparable. Without education, mental freedom, and enterprise the South could never hope to have a literature of its own. It was ridiculous, he thought, for slaveholders to be crying for a sectional literature when their school texts were being written in the North and Southern books of all kinds were being printed in Northern cities.

Southern divines give us elaborated Bible arguments [for slavery]; Southern statists heap treatise upon treatise through which the Federal Constitution is tortured into all the monstrous shapes; Southern novelists bore us *ad infinitum* with pictures of the beatitudes of plantation life and the negro-quarters; Southern verse-wrights drone out their drowsy dactyls or grow ventricious with their turgid heroics, all in defence of slavery—priest, politician, novelist, bardling, severally ringing the changes upon "the Biblical institution," "the conservative institution," "the humanizing institution," "the patriarchal institution"—and then—have their books printed on Northern paper, with Northern types, by Northern artisans, stitched, bound and ready for the market by Northern industry; and yet fail to see in all this, as a true philosophical mind *must* see, an overwhelming refutation of their miserable sophisms in behalf of a system against which humanity in all its impulses and aspirations, and civilization in all its activities and triumphs, utter their perpetual protest.

13
Moncure Daniel Conway

Moncure Daniel Conway (1832–1907) was, though a native Virginian, an Abolitionist, a Unitarian, a Transcendentalist, and ultimately a freethinker—now best remembered as the editor and biographer of Thomas Paine. His life and works, like Helper's, do not figure conspicuously in older books on Southern literature. He was born in Stafford County, Virginia, and he grew up near Falmouth, which lies across the Rappahannock River from Fredericksburg. When he became aware of his own divergence from orthodox Virginian opinion, Conway regarded himself as a throwback to an earlier and more liberal generation of Virginians. Nevertheless, though it was long before he knew it, his mother detested slavery and his father considered it "a doomed institution." His paternal grandfather, John Moncure Conway, once took into his own home a Yankee peddler who had been bundled out of the only inn in the village because he took a walk one Sunday morning instead of going to church. The peddler was Bronson Alcott. The same grandfather was shocked when Conway's father was converted to the Methodist faith, which the older man regarded as a vulgar form of fanaticism.

Conway was sent to an academy in Fredericksburg, but the most valuable part of his education, he tells us, came from listening to the discussion of cases in the law courts and in his own home. As a boy he read the works of Bunyan, Maria Edgeworth, and Dickens, whom he once saw passing through Fredericksburg. He preferred the older British novelists to Scott. He was forbidden to read Byron. At Dickinson College in Pennsylvania— he entered at fifteen—"American literature," he says, "consisted of Poe, Longfellow, Bryant, Irving, Paulding, Cooper, Prescott, R. H. Dana, Bancroft, Sparks, N. P. Willis, Mrs. Sigourney, Caroline Lee Hentz, and a few others, chiefly women, whose verses were widely read." He could not find in any libraries available to him the works of the "new school of writers," by which he means Goethe, Emerson, Channing, Hawthorne, and George Sand. He persuaded the students at Dickinson to launch a magazine, and he edited the only five numbers that were published. "My only enthusiasm was for literature," he says, "but what channel was there in Virginia for that?

None." As a matter of fact, he had already written for the local newspaper, and was soon to contribute to the *Southern Literary Messenger* and the weekly Richmond *Examiner*, edited by his cousin John Moncure Daniel. It was in the columns of the *Examiner* that he first read anything of Hawthorne's.

After completing his college course, Conway went to Warrenton to study law. He did not at heart really wish to be a lawyer. He was, moreover, not in sympathy with what he calls "Young Virginia," by which he means men, like George Fitzhugh, who had come to defend slavery on principle. He was going through a spiritual crisis which he did not understand. After an illness, he came home in April, 1850, for a few weeks. One morning he went off to spend a day in the country, taking with him his old flintlock and a copy of *Blackwood's Magazine* for December, 1847. The title of the leading article was "Emerson," an unfamiliar name; and the very first extract—from Emerson's essay on "History"—"fixed itself in me like an arrow." New England Transcendentalism had reached Conway by way of Britain through a magazine over two years old. At the Fredericksburg bookstore he found "Emerson's Arithmetick" in stock but Emerson's *Essays* unknown. The obliging bookseller ordered the desired volume; and while Conway was reading it, he discovered that John M. Daniel had been writing about Emerson in the *Examiner*.

The influence of Emerson had something to do with Conway's abandoning the law and becoming a Methodist minister. As the nineteen-year-old preacher rode a Maryland circuit, he carried in his saddlebags an unusual assortment of books for a circuit rider: the Bible, Emerson's *Essays*, Watson's *Theology*, Carlyle's *Latter-Day Pamphlets*, Jeremy Taylor's *Holy Living and Holy Dying*, the *Methodist Discipline*, and Coleridge's *Aids to Reflection*. By his lawyerlike efforts to prove the soundness of his creed, he soon began to reason himself out of it. Contact with some Hicksite Quakers stirred his antislavery impulses, and he finally decided to enter the Harvard Divinity School. His father, noting the books that his son was reading, declined to assist him at Cambridge. Conway, however, managed to complete his theological course without serious difficulty.

On May 3, 1853, Conway wrote in his diary: "The most memorable day of my life: spent with Ralph Waldo Emerson!" The Concord sage, who influenced Conway more than any other man, introduced him to Oriental writings and later sent him to see Walt Whitman. In Boston, Cambridge, and Concord Conway met all the major New England writers. Indeed, so full is his *Autobiography* of the great men whom he met that one suspects him of being a "tuft-hunter." [26] Conway came to know and to like Thoreau, Holmes, Longfellow, Theodore Parker, and many others. He did not, however, get on well with Lowell, who seemed to him—as perhaps also he seemed to Edgar Allan Poe—too like "the 'Yankee' conventionalized in Southern prejudice."

In September, 1854, Conway became pastor of the influential Unitarian church in Washington. For a time the young radical was discreet, but early in 1856 he began to preach against slavery and in October in a "stormy session" a majority of the members voted to dissolve his connection with the church. Meanwhile his parents had been disturbed by rumors which came to them about his sermons and even more by a false report that in Boston he had tried to free the fugitive slave Anthony Burns, whose master lived in the vicinity of Fredericksburg. His father wrote to him that it would not be safe for him to come home. "These [antislavery] views," he wrote, "give me more uneasiness just now than your horrible views on the subject of religion, bad as these last are." When he did return to Falmouth, Conway was practically ordered out of town by the younger men. Feeling himself a martyr and an exile, Conway went back to Washington. In later life he admitted that this experience distorted his vision.

At Emerson's suggestion Conway had read *Leaves of Grass*, and in the late summer of 1855 he visited Whitman in Brooklyn. He was, so Whitman told him, the first person who had come to see him on account of his book. On a later visit Whitman said to him: "I have not met any one so charged with my ideas as you." Many of the ideas in question both men had undoubtedly got from Emerson. At this time Conway's creed was in his own words "the theism evolved from pantheism by the poets."

In November, 1856, Conway became pastor of a Unitarian church in Cincinnati. Here he found a much livelier interest in art and literature than had existed in Washington. He strengthened his ties with New England by marrying Ellen Davis Dana, whose parents belonged to prominent Massachusetts families. His acquaintance with a local group of freethinkers in Cincinnati led him to preach a sermon in defense of Thomas Paine. During the year 1860 he edited the second Transcendentalist magazine to be named

---

[26] Hamlin Garland wrote in his diary for June 4, 1905: "I have just finished Moncure Conway's book—a very interesting chronicle of great personalities. . . . I met him once, a harsh, unlovely person who related with gusto certain incidents in Lincoln's life which revealed his weak side, but the pictures he drew of Emerson, Carlyle, Hawthorne, and Tennyson were beautiful. His book is appalling, however. It is like watching a procession of noble men and women march into an abyss" (*Companions on the Trail*, 1931, p. 277).

the *Dial*. Among his leading contributors were Emerson and a new friend, William Dean Howells.

Conway wanted the slaves freed, but he did not want war, for war seemed to him "the apotheosis of brutality." The John Brown affair, however, swept him off his feet, as it did so many others. In later life he said that North and South had divided over a John Brown that neither side saw clearly for what he was. He blamed Lincoln, whose greatness he never fully recognized, for ordering Fort Sumter provisioned; and he never forgave the President and other leaders for not adopting his own impracticable scheme, which was that the President and the Congress should at once declare every slave in America free. If that were done, he thought, every Southerner would have to stay at home to guard his slaves. There could be no war, and what it would cost to wage war for one month would pay the owners the value of their emancipated slaves. Obviously, Conway no longer understood what was happening in his native Virginia, where two of his brothers were in the Confederate army. When Conway House, abandoned by the family, came within the Union lines, it was only his own portrait which prevented the house, where Whitman once nursed wounded soldiers, from being destroyed. Conway took the now masterless slaves of his father and settled them at Yellow Springs, Ohio.

In September, 1862, he returned to Massachusetts to join Frank Sanborn in editing a new antislavery organ, the *Commonwealth*. In April of the next year, at the urging of Wendell Phillips, he went to England to lecture and to convince the English of the rightness of the Union cause. His success was no greater than that of another Virginian, John R. Thompson, who a little later came to England in behalf of the Confederacy. Somewhat rashly Conway entered into correspondence with the Confederate agent, John M. Mason, another Virginian, and promised that if the Confederate States would emancipate their slaves, the Northern antislavery leaders would immediately oppose further prosecution of the war. When Mason discovered that Conway had no authority to make such a proposition, he published the correspondence in the London *Times*. Conway had been out-maneuvered. Perhaps now he understood the North as little as he understood the South. If he returned to America, he felt, he would stand alone. Even Emerson had come to respect war. And so when in June, 1863, Conway was offered the pastorate of the unorthodox South Place Chapel in Finsbury, he decided to accept and remain in London. Although he occasionally revisited America, he presided over South Place Chapel until 1884 and again from 1892 to 1897. He then returned to the United States, but his stay was brief. His wife died on Christmas Day, 1897. Not long after, he says, "Broken by personal bereavement, filled with horror by the reign of terror suffered by negroes in the South, alienated from my countrymen by what seemed to me a mere lynching of Spain,—my youthful visions turned to illusions,—I left for Europe." Finding England on the brink of the Boer War, he sought refuge in Paris. In the Preface to his *Autobiography*, published in 1904, he wrote: "One who starts out at twenty to think for himself and pursue truth is likely to discover at seventy that one third of his life was given to error, another third to exchanging it for other error, and the last third to efforts to unsay and undo the mistakes of the other two thirds." He had, as Bernard Shaw once remarked of Lady Astor, "come a long way from Virginia." He had progressed along the road from Unitarianism and Transcendentalism to rationalism and skepticism.

The best efforts of his later years were given to writing the life, and collecting the scattered writings of, Thomas Paine. He published a two-volume biography in 1892 and brought out in 1894–1896 a four-volume edition of Paine's works. These are his best claim to a place in American literary history. He found Paine's life and work obscured by the anathema which clung to his reputation. It was, Conway found, necessary more or less to rewrite the history of America, England, and France in Paine's lifetime in order to demonstrate the importance of the man's work. Later scholars have added materially to our knowledge of Paine, but Conway's work is still not altogether superseded. This, however, cannot be said of his other books, interesting though several of them are. His biographies of Hawthorne, Emerson, and Carlyle are chiefly valuable for his reminiscences of these men. He wrote both history and fiction dealing with Virginia, but he was not a good novelist and he was not a first-class historical writer.

In 1875 Conway revisited his old home and found evidence of wartime destruction on every hand. Conway House was now in the hands of Northern people, and the garden was running to weeds. His father, now advanced to "a sweet tolerance," welcomed home the prodigal son and even read with pleasure one of Conway's books. There was, however, in the New South no place for a writer of Conway's kaleidoscopic readiness to accept new ideas. It was perhaps easier for the later nineteenth-century South to bear with his attitude toward the Negro than to listen to his heterodox religious views, even though they were in large measure those of the Revolutionary leaders of his native state.

14
Defenders of Slavery

IT IS DIFFICULT to understand how Southerners, especially Virginians, whose ancestors in the late eighteenth century often deplored slavery as a great evil, managed to convince themselves that the outmoded institution was just and beneficent.[27] The plantation system, however, was not very unlike that which has flourished in warm climates all over the world. Wherever the whites in such regions have come into contact with a backward race of a different color, there has been some form of exploitation, and white men have vigorously defended it. In the South the fear of slave insurrections played a part, and so, too, did resentment of outside interference with what was regarded as a local institution, not subject to Federal control. What the antislavery agitators seemed never to grasp was that the problem of slavery was also a race problem. The Southern farmer could not imagine an agricultural system built upon the labor of free Negroes. He had had enough trouble with free Negroes, he thought, to be certain that wholesale emancipation would be a menace to civilization in the South. To the Southern slaveowner the spectacle of several millions of suddenly emancipated blacks was appalling; it was nothing less than revolution.

The economic motive, though not the only one, was a compelling one. The invention of the spinning jenny and the cotton gin helped to create an unprecedented demand for cotton, and the result was an extraordinary demand for slave labor in the new lands in the Lower South. Naturally, the price of slaves rose in Virginia and Maryland, where slavery had seemed on its way to extinction. In the Deep South every man thought his fortune lay in land and slaves and cotton. It is difficult for human beings to see evil in any source of profit to themselves—especially when the remedy suggested by outsiders seems a source of grave danger.

In the debate over the admission of Missouri as a slave state in 1819–1820 some Southern Congressmen defended slavery on principle. To Northern Congressmen this attitude seemed both new and ominous. In the 1830's the numerous Abolition petitions—many of them presented by John Quincy Adams—provoked a franker and more determined defense. In

---

[27] See W. S. Jenkins, *Pro-Slavery Thought in the Old South* (1935); Bibliography, pp. 309–358. The two chief collections of proslavery essays are William Harper and others, *The Pro-Slavery Argument* . . . (Charleston, 1852) and E. N. Elliott and others, *Cotton Is King, and Pro-Slavery Argument* . . . (Augusta, 1860).

1839 Calhoun spoke in the Senate: "But let me not be understood as admitting, even by implication, that the existing relation between the races in the slaveholding States is an evil—far otherwise; I hold it to be a good, as it has thus far proved itself to be to both, and will continue to prove so if not disturbed by the fell spirit of abolition." In 1858 James H. Hammond, son of a Northern teacher who had gone to South Carolina, expounded in the Senate a theory of society which was peculiarly repugnant to Lincoln and other Northerners of strong humanitarian feelings:

In all social systems there must be a class to do the menial duties, to perform the drudgery of life. That is, a class requiring but a low order of intellect and but little skill. Its requisites are vigor, docility, fidelity. Such a class you must have or you would not have that other class which leads to progress, civilization, and refinement. It constitutes the very mudsill of society and of political government; and you might as well attempt to build a house in the air, as to build either the one or the other, except on this mudsill.

Northern criticism sometimes led Southern proslavery writers to take in public a stand which did not altogether represent their private convictions. On July 23, 1847, Hammond wrote to William Gilmore Simms: "As to the thing [slavery] *per se*, I do not love it. I believe it a political and social blessing, taking government and society at large. As an individual, I would far prefer tenants to slaves. But that system is wholly impracticable now and abolition would be simply to *ruin* all things."

The basic Southern arguments for slavery had all been used before except perhaps the pseudoscientific thesis that the Negro belonged to a permanently inferior race. The proslavery writers appealed to Aristotle, to Roman law and practice, to the Bible, to the Church Fathers, to Edmund Burke, and finally to Thomas Carlyle. His *Frederick the Great* (1858–1865) appeared too late to have much influence, but they made much of Carlyle's earlier writings. The *Southern Quarterly Review* in July, 1850, stated that Southern newspaper editors should read Carlyle's *Latter-Day Pamphlets* and stop repeating Yankee denunciations of "one of their best friends and champions." [28]

The fatal "mistake that was made by the Southern defenders of slavery," said Lucius Q. C. Lamar in his oration on Calhoun in 1888, "was in regarding it as a permanent form of society instead of a process of emergence and transition from barbarism to freedom." For, said he, "Every benefit which slavery conferred upon those subject to it; all the ameliorating and humaniz-

[28] Moncure D. Conway states that Carlyle's Latter-Day pamphlet on the Negro question was suppressed in the Northern edition but was published in the South (*Autobiography*, I, 409).

ing tendencies it introduced into the life of the African; all the elevating agencies which lifted him higher in the scale of rational and moral being, were the elements of the future and inevitable destruction of the system." It is difficult, in the twentieth century, to understand why this was not obvious to men as intelligent as Calhoun, Beverley Tucker, Grayson, and Fitzhugh, who were not ogres but men as kindly and as upright in their private lives as Emerson, Channing, Lowell, and Whittier. It should be said, however, that apart from the writers whom I have named, few Southern writers of any literary importance devoted much of their time and energy to the defense of slavery.

From the nature of their position the proslavery writers were bound to be vigorous critics of the "free society" of the Northern states. They were convinced that society in the slave states was superior, and they saw more clearly than the writers of the North the glaring shortcomings of an industrial civilization. Indeed, apart from Thoreau and a few other voices crying in the wilderness, the Southern critics were the only American writers who denounced the industrial economy and its cultural, social, and moral consequences. The Southern proslavery writers contended that the Northern day laborer—himself a mudsill of a sort—was much more ruthlessly exploited than the Southern slave, who could expect his master to look after him in sickness and old age. It was of course as difficult for the Northern millowner to see the wrong in the system by which he profited as it was for the cotton planter to recognize the evils inherent in slaveholding.

The defeat of the South in the Civil War left Northern industrialism almost without critics among American writers. In the sixties and seventies Northern capitalists strengthened their economic control of the South and the West, and they have held it ever since. It was to be a decade or two before the North found in Henry George, Edward Bellamy, and William Dean Howells vigorous critics of its industrial civilization. It was to find many more such critics in the twentieth century, especially during the Great Depression, which discredited the big businessman as the key figure in our industrial economy. In the twentieth century the Southern Agrarians were to attack Northern ideals with some of the old arguments of Tucker, Grayson, and Fitzhugh and were to find themselves listened to almost as little as those forgotten defenders of slavery.

What Fitzhugh and Grayson objected to in the Northern way of life was for the most part just those traits which were being condemned by visitors from nearly every country in Europe. Like Mrs. Trollope, the proslavery writers found too many Americans in the Northern states materialistic, vulgar, ill-bred, ignorant of the art of gracious living. The Northern man, they thought, cared nothing for culture for its own sake, and he measured everything by its cash value. The Northerner had little appreciation of the past. He was too willing to throw overboard institutions and ideals while he welcomed new isms of every kind. He was blind to the shortcomings of his own society and eager to reform the people in another region whose ways he did not understand. The North, too, assumed that its own society was the American norm by which the society of the South was to be appraised. Then even more than now, however, the North was not disposed to listen to Southern critics of its ideals and its way of life.

15
John C. Calhoun

THE SOUTH CAROLINA champion of state rights, John Caldwell Calhoun (1782–1850), was not a great Low-Country planter but the son of a pioneer Up-Country farmer. He was a Puritan, not a Cavalier, type. Paradoxically, too, he was educated chiefly in Federalist New England, where in his youth secession doctrines were more commonly held than in the South.

His mother, Martha (Caldwell) Calhoun, was born in Charlotte County, Virginia, of Scotch-Irish parents. Patrick Calhoun, his father, whose forebears were Highland Scots, came to Pennsylvania in 1733 at the age of ten from northwest Ireland. Following the line of migration south along the Blue Ridge, he finally settled in the Abbeville district not far from the Georgia line. An able Indian fighter and a thrifty Presbyterian farmer, he served for about twenty-five years in the South Carolina legislature. His views of government were Jeffersonian: he thought the best government was that which permitted the largest degree of individual liberty compatible with peace and order.

In Calhoun's boyhood schools in the Up-Country were few. His early training, which was irregular, came partly from his mother. He was one of the earliest pupils of the Reverend Moses Waddel, the most famous of Carolina teachers and the husband of Calhoun's sister Catherine. In the winter of 1795–1796 Calhoun spent fourteen weeks reading in Waddel's library; the school had been suspended when Catherine Waddel died. Among the books that he read were Rollin's *Ancient History* in eight volumes, Voltaire's life of Charles XII of Sweden, and John Locke's *Essay concerning Human Understanding*. The last of these Calhoun studied at thirteen or fourteen with the same intense interest it had aroused in Jonathan Edwards at the same age. So thoroughly did the youth become absorbed in his studies that he was recalled to the farm on account of his health. The next four years he spent in farming, working with the slaves in the fields, hunting in his spare time, and since his father was now dead, gradually taking over the management of the farm.

In 1800, when John was eighteen, his older brother James came home to urge upon his somewhat reluctant mother that the youth be educated for a profession. John, saying that he would rather be a farmer than a half-educated lawyer, stipulated that he should be given a first-class education in college and law school. He now returned to Waddel's academy to prepare for college. In two years' time he was able to enter Yale as a junior with a good classical foundation. At New Haven the young Jeffersonian Democrat found himself in a hotbed of Federalists. His abilities, however, so impressed President Timothy Dwight, who hated Jefferson as though he were both an atheist and an anarchist, that he remarked that the young man had talent enough to be President of the United States and predicted that Calhoun would attain that high office. Calhoun was preparing himself for a political career. His commencement address, which he was too ill to deliver, dealt with "the qualifications necessary to constitute the ideal statesman."

After some study of law in South Carolina, Calhoun returned to Connecticut in 1805—possibly calling at Monticello on the way—to study in the famous Litchfield law school conducted by Judge Tappan Reeve and James Gould. Both these men were able teachers and extreme Federalists; Reeve, and probably Gould 'as well, at one time favored New England's secession from the Union. Calhoun at this time, however, was not in sympathy with secession doctrines. He was admitted to the bar in 1808 and quickly demonstrated his ability, but he had no great enthusiasm for the law either as a study or as a profession. In the same year he was elected to the state legislature. He was elected to the House of Representatives in 1810 and the next year began his nearly forty years of political life in Washington.

Before he took his seat in Congress, he was married in January, 1811, to Floride Calhoun (or Colhoun). Her father, John Ewing Colhoun, son of Patrick's brother Ezekiel, had studied at Princeton, practiced law in Charleston, and married Floride Bonneau, a wealthy planter's daughter. He died in 1802 shortly after taking his seat in the United States Senate. For several years his widow, an intelligent and cultivated woman who spent her summers in Newport, had taken a keen interest in the young law student and had helped him as only a sympathetic and intelligent older woman can to prepare himself for a notable career.

This is not the place in which to discuss Calhoun's long and distinguished career in Washington. He served in the House of Representatives, 1811–1817; as Secretary of War, 1817–1825; as Vice-President, 1825–1832; as Secretary of State, 1844–1845; and as Senator, 1833–1843 and 1845–1850. Calhoun's later career, identified with Nullification and state rights, has blurred the memory of the notable services which he performed in the House and as Secretary of War in Monroe's cabinet. Charles M. Wiltse's *John C. Calhoun, Nationalist* (1944) supplied a much needed account of the younger Calhoun. In 1816 he was, in his own words, "no advocate for refined arguments on the Constitution. The instrument," he said, "was not intended as a thesis for the logician to exercise his ingenuity on." In those years he supported internal improvements and even a protective tariff. He was not at this time, or ever, the "cast-iron man" that he seemed to Harriet Martineau. In 1824 William Wirt, also a member of Monroe's cabinet, wrote to a Virginia friend: "His is the very character to strike a Virginian;—ardent, generous, high-minded, brave, with a genius full of fire, energy, and light;—a devoted patriot—proud of his country, and prizing her glory above his life."

The fundamental change in Calhoun's political attitude came while he sat in the Vice-President's chair. The quarrel with Andrew Jackson, which ended his immediate hopes of becoming President, probably had something to do with the change. But there were other factors. Among them were the debate in which Robert Y. Hayne and not Calhoun argued with Webster over the nature of the Union. The North, now committed to industrialization, wanted a high tariff. The South, selling its staples in a world market but buying its manufactured goods from Northern factories protected from competition by a tariff wall, felt itself cheated and exploited, as in some degree it undoubtedly was. Pressure groups—no more scrupulous then than now—lobbied for a higher tariff which would still further enrich the manufacturers. As Calhoun wrote in the "South Carolina Exposition" of 1828: "No system can be more efficient [than the tariff] to rear up a moneyed aristocracy. Its tendency is, to make the poor poorer and the rich richer." The first effect, he pointed out, would be to impoverish the South; its second would be to impoverish the laboring classes at the North. Wages would sink below the subsistence level, and then, he said, "the contest will be between the capitalists and [the] operatives; for into these classes it must, ultimately, divide society." Karl Marx, it might be remarked, was only ten years old in 1828; but Madison and John Taylor of Caroline, not to mention Aristotle, had also known something about the effect of economic developments on politics.

The change in Calhoun's political attitude did not please all South

Carolinians. Hugh Swinton Legaré in Brussels wrote in 1834: "Nullification is, with him, it seems, what the French call an *idée fixe*,—a monomania, in short, he is, *quoad hoc*, stark mad. . . ." It was a pity, Legaré thought, that Calhoun's pre-eminent talents should be so misapplied, for, he said: "There is nobody to be compared with him in the management of *men* and affairs."

Some Northern historians have represented Calhoun as a vacillating and unprincipled politician conspiring to overthrow the Union because of disappointed ambition. In making this accusation these writers relied too heavily on the ill-founded and rancorous suspicions which John Quincy Adams confided to his famous diary, first published in 1870.

Calhoun's love for the Union was strong. In 1838 he wrote to his daughter: "In speaking of abolition, you say it is better to part peaceably at once, than to live in the state of indecision we do. This is a natural and common conclusion, but those, who make it up, do not think of the difficulty involved in the word; how many bleeding pores must be taken up in passing the knife of separation through a body politick (in order to make two of one), which has been so long bound together by so many ties, political, social, and commercial." Calhoun was not trying to break up the Union. He was trying to save it in the only way he thought it could be saved. Class and sectional legislation were undermining the loyalty of the Southern states. Loyalty to the Union, he saw, depended upon a feeling of security; and the South was now definitely a minority section, believing itself exploited by Northern commercial interests. Ceaseless antislavery agitation added still further to the Southern feeling of insecurity within the Union. Northern Congressmen, trying to upset the existing balance of power between the sections, were, he saw, making unscrupulous use of the moral crusade against the South. It was disillusioning to find that even Senators, as Calhoun saw them, cared little for truth and justice as compared with the economic interests or the emotional bias of their supporters and could not resist the pressure groups which were continually at their backs.

Calhoun fell back upon state sovereignty as the most effective Southern foundation for defense. Patrick Henry in the Virginia Convention of 1788 had warned that under the new Federal Constitution Virginia might find itself at the mercy of a hostile Northern majority. St. George Tucker in his edition of Blackstone had interpreted state sovereignty as justifying secession. John Taylor and Thomas Cooper had warned of the danger of an unscrupulous Northern plutocracy. Calhoun based his position, so he stated, primarily upon the Federal Constitution and the Kentucky and Virginia

Resolutions of 1798 and 1799, written by Jefferson and Madison in protest against the Alien and Sedition acts passed by a Federalist Congress.

As Calhoun saw it, the only way to preserve the Union was to give the minority state or section a veto over unfriendly legislation. The great danger now, he realized, was what Alexis de Tocqueville was soon to name "the tyranny of the majority." Calhoun's fear of the all-devouring political state was a natural reaction to what was happening in the North. What he had seen of the workings of the Washington government did not make him view with complacency the enormous concentration of power in the central government.

The complacent Northern assumption of the superiority of its own brand of civilization irritated Calhoun, as it irritated thousands of other Southerners. In a "Speech on the Reception of Abolition Petitions," February 6, 1837, he said:

. . . I appeal to all sides whether the South is not equal in virtue, intelligence, patriotism, courage, disinterestedness, and all high qualities which adorn our nature. I ask whether we have not contributed our full share of talents and political wisdom in forming and sustaining this political fabric; and whether we have not constantly inclined most strongly to the side of liberty, and been the first to see and first to resist the encroachments of power. In one thing only are we inferior—the arts of gain; we acknowledge that we are less wealthy than the Northern section of this Union, but I trace this mainly to the fiscal action of this Government, which has extracted much from, and spent little among us.

A decade later, February 19, 1847, he spoke with even stronger feeling as he contemplated a situation rapidly changing for the worse:

. . . I may speak as an individual member of that section of the Union. There is my family and connections; there I drew my first breath; there are all my hopes. I am a planter—a cotton-planter. I am a Southern man and a slaveholder—a kind and merciful one, I trust—and none the worse for being a slaveholder. I say, for one, I would rather meet any extremity upon earth than give up one inch of our equality—one inch of what belongs to us as members of this great republic! What! acknowledged inferiority! The surrender of life is nothing to sinking down into acknowledged inferiority!

Calhoun did not have the personal magnetism which drew people to Henry Clay, and his speeches lack most of the literary qualities which keep some of Webster's alive, but he had a better mind than either of his great rivals. When Clay accused him of making too finespun distinctions, he replied:

I cannot retort on the Senator the charge of being metaphysical. I cannot accuse him of possessing the powers of analysis and generalization, those higher faculties of the mind (called metaphysical by those who do not possess them) which decompose and resolve into their elements the complex masses of ideas that exist in the world of mind, as chemistry does the bodies that surround us in the material world; and without which those deep and hidden causes which are in constant action, and producing such mighty changes in the condition of society, would operate unseen and undetected. The absence of these higher qualities of mind is conspicuous throughout the whole course of the Senator's public life.

In the fields of politics and economics Calhoun was well informed, but he was not a great reader of books and he did not travel outside the United States. He read the British and American quarterlies, including the *Southern Review* (1828–1832), and he knew his Burke, Machiavelli, and Aristotle. He did not read novels—not even those of Dickens, whom he once met; he might have understood better the temper of the outside world if he had. He did not live to see the publication of *Uncle Tom's Cabin*, which made Southern leaders doubt whether Washington was the best place in which to defend slavery against the assault of the civilized world. Calhoun's mind was lacking in appreciation of the artistic; it is said on doubtful authority that the only poem he ever tried to write began with "Whereas"! He had a quick perception and a retentive memory, and he learned much from talking with other men. He thought deeply, and not all the conclusions he reached were typical of the South. He opposed the War with Mexico, for example. He was brought up a Presbyterian, but in his religious beliefs he was practically a Unitarian. His opinion of human nature was closer to that of Jonathan Edwards than to Jefferson's. He wrote to his daughter, March 7, 1848: "I hold the duties of life to be greater than life itself. . . . Indeed, I regard this life very much as a struggle against evil, and that to him, who acts on proper principle, the *reward is in the struggle, more than in the victory itself,* although that greatly enhances it."

Calhoun was primarily a speaker and only incidentally a writer. He found the writing out of his speeches for the printer a laborious task, but he discovered that he could express his ideas more concisely by so doing. His published speeches are clear, forceful, well organized, and logical. They have occasional moments of eloquence, but they lack the qualities which make Lincoln's later speeches so memorable. The appeal is to the reason rather than to the emotions, to the listener rather than to the reader, and to the intelligent rather than to the average man. He did not sufficiently appreciate the importance of reaching the general reader. He could address his Carolina constituents effectively, but he was at his best in the Senate. Like the Revolutionary statesmen, he appealed to the intelligent and the influential—not to the masses—and his strongest influence was on the political leaders of his own section.

Aside from the part he may have had in preparing a campaign biography, Calhoun's writings consist of speeches, letters, and two posthumous works: A *Disquisition on Government*, in which he hoped "to lay a solid foundation for political Science," and its sequel, A *Discourse on the Constitution and Government of the United States*. Calhoun feared that in government, progress would not keep pace with advances in material development and that the failure of political science to keep up with material progress would lead to revolutions which would slow down or even put a stop to progress in material things. What he only feared would happen has obviously happened and on a worldwide scale that would have appalled him had he lived to see it.

He did not live to revise either the *Disquisition* or the *Discourse*, but the two constitute a document as notable in its way as *The Federalist*; but not until long after the Civil War did students of political science realize its importance. The *Disquisition* shows how far Southern political thinkers had departed from the teachings of Jefferson. Calhoun did not believe that "all men are equal in the state of nature," for such a state "never did, nor can exist." Man's natural state, he argued, is "the social and political—the one for which his Creator made him, and the only one in which he can preserve and perfect his race." [29] It follows that since men are born into the social and political state, they are not born free and equal; they are born subject to parental authority and to the laws and institutions of a particular country. Security seems to him as important as liberty; and liberty, he writes, "is a reward to be earned, not a blessing to be gratuitously lavished on all alike;—a reward for the intelligent, the patriotic, the virtuous and deserving;—and not a boon to be bestowed on a people too ignorant, degraded and vicious, to be capable either of appreciating or of enjoying it." Nor is equality, except equality before the law, essential to liberty. Inequality is the necessary consequence of liberty, and it is at the same time the spur to progress. It is inequality that drives individuals to try to improve their condition.

Calhoun in his later years did not share Jefferson's, or Emerson's, optimistic view of human nature. The function of constitutional government, as he saw it, was to give stability to political institutions and particularly to

[29] Cf. the passage in Poe's "Marginalia" (Nov., 1844), *Works* (Virginia ed.), XVI, 6–7.

counteract "the tendency of government to oppression and abuse." "Those who exercise power and those subject to its exercise,—the rulers and the ruled,—stand in antagonistic relations to each other." The constitution of a state should give its citizens a means of resisting the encroachments of power. The right to vote is a first essential to the protection of the ruled.

But Calhoun feared the results of rule by a numerical majority. It would lead, he thought, to "corruption, disorder, and anarchy," which in turn would lead to an appeal to force, and that would finally bring on revolution and a radical change in government. The mature Calhoun saw as clearly as Madison had seen that every government has to deal with factions, with varied economic interests, each seeking special favors. The great diversity of such interests made it extremely difficult "to equalize the action of the government,—and the more easy for one portion of the community to pervert its powers to oppress, and plunder the other." The ballot alone could not prevent this tyranny of the majority. And just here Calhoun emphasized what seemed to him the most important and least understood principle of the science of government. The checks and balances provided in the Federal Constitution were not enough. What was needed was to give to each important interest or section "either a concurrent voice in making and executing the laws, or a veto on their execution."

And so Calhoun worked out his scheme for a concurrent majority as indispensable to prevent tyranny by the numerical majority. Under the party system it often happens, he pointed out, that the laws passed actually represent only a minority of the people. The old saying Vox populi vox Dei seemed to him anathema. It is folly, he said, to imagine that "the party in possession of the ballot-box and the physical force of the country, could be successfully resisted by an appeal to reason, truth, justice, or the obligations imposed by the constitution." "Neither religion nor education can counteract the strong tendency of the numerical majority to corrupt and debase the people." Jefferson had thought otherwise. As Calhoun pointed out, the idea of a concurrent majority was already a part of the Constitution, but the checks and balances which it provided were no longer sufficient to prevent the oppression of minorities.

In A Discourse on the Constitution Calhoun pointed out that the Federal Constitution had created not a nation but a federation. Reporters, he once complained, were always putting in his mouth the word nation when what he had said was Union. The Constitution was a compact between sovereign states, and the remedy for existing evils was to restore to the national government its federal character. But even more was it important to restore the equilibrium between the sections. Each section should be given a veto power. "Nothing short of this," he wrote, "can protect the weaker, and re-store harmony and tranquillity to the Union, by arresting, effectually, the tendency of the dominant and stronger section to oppress the weaker."

Calhoun's remedy for the tendency of the American majority to tyrannize over minority interests and sections was worked out partly of course to safe-guard slavery, but in some respects the tyranny of the majority today is a greater menace than it was in his time, and its influence is seen as clearly in social and cultural matters as in economics and politics. It is a problem to which our political leaders still give too little attention. On March 4, 1850, in Calhoun's last speech, which, since he was too weak to stand, Senator James M. Mason of Virginia read for him, he made his last and perhaps most eloquent plea for a solution that would give the South some assurance of its security within the Union. It was too late for a permanent settlement, although the Compromise of 1850 may have postponed war un-til the North had grown to such power that the South could not hope to win. The lines had been drawn. As Calhoun himself put it in his last speech:

Every portion of the North entertains views and feelings more or less hostile to it [slavery]. Those most opposed and hostile, regard it as a sin, and consider themselves under the sacred obligation to use every effort to destroy it. . . . Those less opposed and hostile, regard it as a crime—an offence against humanity, as they call it; and although not so fanatical, feel themselves bound to use all efforts to effect the same object; while those who are least opposed and hostile, regard it as a blot and a stain on the character of what they call the Nation, and feel themselves accordingly bound to give it no countenance or support. On the contrary, the Southern section regards the relation as one which cannot be destroyed without subjecting the two races to the greatest calamity, and the section to poverty, desolation, and wretchedness; and accordingly they feel bound, by every consideration of interest and safety, to defend it.

A few days before he died Calhoun said to Senator Mason:

The Union is doomed to dissolution; there is no mistaking the signs. I am satisfied in my judgment even were the questions which now agitate Congress settled to the satisfaction and with the concurrence of the Southern States, it would not avert, or materially delay, the catastrophe. I fix its probable occurrence within twelve years or three Presidential terms. You and others of your age will probably live to see it; I shall not. The mode by which it will be done is not so clear; it may be brought about in a manner that none now foresee. But the probability is it will explode in a Presidential election.

When William Gilmore Simms reviewed Melville's *Mardi* (1849) in the *Southern Quarterly Review* for October, 1849, he praised it briefly and then added: ". . . he spoils every thing to the Southern reader when he paints a loathsome picture of Mr. Calhoun, in the character of a slave-driver, drawing mixed blood and tears from the victim at every stroke of the whip. We make no farther comments." In Chapter CLXII Melville's voyagers visit "the extreme south of Vivenza [the United States]," where they see "under a burning sun, hundreds of collared men . . . toiling in trenches. . . ." Standing over them are men "armed with long thongs, which descended upon the toilers, and made wounds. Blood and sweat mixed; and in great drops, fell." The head overseer is "one Nulli; a cadaverous, ghost-like man; with a low ridge of forehead; hair, steel-gray; and wondrous eyes." Nulli tells them that the serfs have no souls and are content with their lot.

"Oro [God]! Art thou?" cried Babbalanja; "and doth this thing exist? It shakes my little faith." Then, turning upon Nulli, "How can ye abide to sway this curs'd dominion?"

"Peace! fanatic! Who else may till unwholesome fields, but these? And as these beings are, so shall they remain; 'tis right and righteous! Maramma champions it! *I* swear it! The first blow struck for them, dissolves the union of Vivenza's vales. The northern tribes well know it; and know me."

Truly, as Poe wrote in April of the year *Mardi* was published: "It [was] high time that the literary South took its own interests into its own charge." But what would he have said had he known that *Uncle Tom's Cabin* was still to come?

James Russell Lowell, like other antislavery writers, had no patience with the Southern interpretation of the nature of the Union. In Number V of *The Biglow Papers, First Series* he pictured "The Debate in the Sennit." I quote the first stanza:

> "Here we stan' on the Constitution, by thunder!
> It's a fact o' wich ther's bushils o' proofs;
> Fer how could we trample on 't so, I wonder,
> Ef 't worn't thet it's ollers under our hoofs?"
> Sez John C. Calhoun, sez he;
> "Human rights haint no more
> Right to come on this floor,
> No more'n the man in the moon," sez he.

When Lowell reprinted his rhymes in book form, he added a note by the pedantic Parson Wilbur in which presumably he gave his sober judgment of Calhoun:

Mr. Calhoun, who is made the chief speaker in this burlesque, seems to think that the light of the nineteenth century is to be put out as soon as he tinkles his little cow-bell curfew. Whenever slavery is touched, he sets up his scarecrow of dissolving the Union. This may do for the North, but I should conjecture that something more than a pumpkin-lantern is required to scare manifest and irretrievable Destiny out of her path. Mr. Calhoun cannot let go the apron-string of the Past. . . .

. . . .

Mr. Calhoun has somehow acquired the name of a great statesman, and, if it be great statesmanship to put lance in rest and run a tilt at the Spirit of the Age with the certainty of being next moment hurled neck and heels into the dust amid universal laughter, he deserves the title. He is the Sir Kay of our modern chivalry.

In a lecture, "Political Infidelity," which he delivered more than fifty times in 1864 and 1865, Lowell's friend, George William Curtis, said: ". . . Mr. Calhoun saw that the only safety and success of the Southern Policy lay in the demoralization of the national character. And to this tremendous and terrible task he devoted his life." "His brain," Curtis continued, "was the huge reservoir of rebellion, and all the floods of theories, arguments, and appeals which have reared [roared?] and rattled in the speeches of the Southern leaders and their Northern allies until they overflowed in civil war, are merely the few false principles of Calhoun filtered through baser minds and mouths." Later in the lecture Curtis said:

The two most illustrious fanatics in our history were John C. Calhoun and old John Brown. They represented the inevitable tendencies of American civilization. One died in his bed, honored and deplored as a great statesman. The other was hung upon a gallows, derided as a fanatic. The statesman struggles with his last strength to keep millions of human beings degraded. The felon stoops beneath the gallows, and, tenderly lifting a child of the degraded race, kisses her in the soft winter sun. Peace! peace! History and the human heart will judge between them. Both their bodies lie mouldering in the grave; whose soul is marching on? It was the fanaticism of abolitionism that has saved this country from the fanaticism of slavery. It was fire fighting fire. And the fire of Heaven is prevailing over that of hell.

Lowell and Curtis helped to shape the estimate of Calhoun which was to find expression in Northern histories of the later nineteenth century. In the twentieth century, however, historians have dealt more justly with him. In one of his most eloquent passages Vernon L. Parrington wrote a quarter of a century ago:

Lost faiths and repudiated prophets go down to a common grave. The living have little inclination to learn from the dead. The political principles of Calhoun have had scant justice done them by later generations who incline to accept the easy opinion that the cause which triumphs is altogether the better cause. What

Calhoun so greatly feared has since come about. He erected a last barrier against the progress of middle-class ideals—consolidation in politics and standardization in society; against a universal cash-register evaluation of life: and the barrier was blown to pieces by the guns of the Civil War.

16
Beverley Tucker

THE SON OF St. George and Frances (Bland) Tucker, (Nathaniel) Beverley Tucker (1784–1851), was a half-brother of John Randolph of Roanoke. He was a difficult child, moody, restless, with a feeling that he was thwarted and misunderstood. After being tutored at home, he entered the College of William and Mary, from which he was graduated in 1801. He studied law and practiced in Charlotte County with little success. A poor voice accounted in part for his comparative failure at this time. In 1809 he moved to "Roanoke," in the same county, where for several years he lived with John Randolph, "from whose eloquent lips," he was to write in 1845, "I have learned more than from all my own experience and reflection, and from all the men with whom I ever conversed, and from all the books I ever read." He did not share, however, Randolph's antipathy to slavery. After some experience as a soldier in the War of 1812, he moved in 1815 to Missouri. For a time he lived in a log cabin near Florissant and kept his office inside the stump of a huge sycamore tree. He was for years a judge in the northern district of the circuit court of Missouri. The effect of his fifteen years in Missouri was to intensify his love of Virginia. He became a Virginian of the Virginians; he conspicuously lacked Caruthers' desire to promote intersectional good will. His contacts with men from the North during the agitation over Missouri's admission to the Union made him something of a Yankeephobe. He carried his dislike of New England to its politicians, authors, schoolmasters, even to Webster's dictionaries and to New England speech. He is said to have urged the exclusion of all Yankees from Missouri; and, when asked how such a plan could be made feasible, replied that every newcomer ferried across the Mississippi should, as a shibboleth, be required to pronounce the word *cow*. All who said *keow* were to be debarred.

Tucker was one of the earliest Southern secessionists. In 1851, the last year of his life, he wrote to William Gilmore Simms that he had seen the Union as a curse in 1820: "I vowed then, and I have repeated the vow, *de die in diem*, that I will never give rest to my eyes nor slumber to my eyelids until it is shattered into fragments. . . . there is now no escape from the many-headed despotism of numbers, but by a strong and bold stand on the banks of the Potomac. . . . If we will not *have* slaves, we must *be* slaves." Tucker, however, always believed that peaceful secession was possible, and he was not a Nullifier.

Tucker returned to Virginia in January, 1833, and the next year he succeeded to the position once held by his father as professor of law at William and Mary. Here he came under the influence of Thomas R. Dew, one of the ablest of all proslavery writers. Tucker had in full measure his father's taste for literature, but he shared few of St. George Tucker's liberal opinions, especially on the subject of slavery.

It was Tucker and not Poe who wrote for the *Southern Literary Messenger* of April, 1836, the review of James Kirke Paulding's *Slavery in the United States* which until recently has been attributed to Poe. Here Tucker pointed out that attempts to reform society occur in cycles; and, he argued, whether these attempts are made in the name of religion or of fanaticism and irreligion, they tend to become attacks upon property rights. "Under such excitement, the many who want, band themselves together against the few that possess; and the lawless appetite of the multitude for the property of others calls itself liberty." To Tucker, as to other Southerners, the attack on slavery was but the precursor to attacks upon all other Southern rights. The disastrous results of emancipation in the West Indies, the Nat Turner insurrection in Virginia, and the increased violence of Garrisonian Abolitionists made him almost despair of the South's ability to resist a fanatical movement which he thought belonged to "the family of superstition." He pictured slavery as a patriarchal institution not to be understood by those who had not seen its nature at first hand. Tucker's defense, though he thought it novel, followed the usual pattern, which was to find its most memorable expression in Grayson's *The Hireling and the Slave*. For Tucker, himself one of the kindest of masters, slavery was no matter for abstract speculation. Like other Southern slaveholders, he could not visualize a social and economic order in which the childlike and affectionate but primitive and irresponsible Negroes were free. That way lay chaos.

Tucker and other Southern defenders of slavery admired Thomas Carlyle, but that admiration was not based upon *Sartor Resartus*—the publication of which in Boston, so Lowell thought, had set off the Transcendentalist uprising—but upon his disparaging comments on Negro emancipation in the West Indies and American Abolitionists. In an article on "The Nigger Question" (1849), which Tucker probably read, Carlyle wrote: "Yes, this is the eternal law of Nature for a man . . . this, that he shall be permitted, and if need be, compelled to do what work the Maker of him has intended by the making of him for this world!" In "Shooting Niagara: And After" (1867) he was to write: "Essentially the Nigger Question [in the United States] was one of the smallest. . . . The Almighty Maker has appointed him to be a Servant." On October 31, 1851, Carlyle replied to a letter he had received from Tucker:

> . . . I find it a settled conviction among rational Englishmen, which they frequently express in a careless way, that the Southern States must ultimately feel driven to separate themselves from the Northern; in which result there is not felt here to be anything treasonous or otherwise horrible. . . .
>
> For you and other men of sense and manfulness of spirit, who stand in the very coil of Negro complications, and feel practically that you must retain command of your servants, or else quit your place and task in the world I find it altogether natural that you should in silence resolve to front all extremities rather than yield to an extrinsic clamour of that nature, however big-voiced and sententious it become: in which quarrel too, what can I say, except "God stand by the right," which I clearly perceive you in part are!
>
> . . . .
>
> My notion is, that the relation of the white man to the black is *not* at present a just one, according to the Law of the Eternal; and though "abolition" is by no means the way to remedy it, and would be a "remedy" equivalent to killing it (as I believe); yet, beyond question, remedied it must be; and peace upon it is not possible until a remedy be found, and begin to be visibly applied. "A servant hired *for life*, instead of by the day or month": I have often wondered that wise and just men in your region (of whom I believe there are many) had not come upon a great many methods, or at least some methods better than those yet in use, of justly enunciating this relation, and relieving such asperities of it as become intolerable.

As the Civil War was nearing its close, Carlyle said to Moncure Conway: ". . . you will never see the whites and blacks in the South dwelling together as equals in peace."

Tucker held no public office in Virginia, but he had a strong influence through letters addressed to such men as Simms and Senator James H. Hammond of South Carolina and in essays in the newspapers which often appeared under his favorite pseudonym "A State Rights Man." He was a regular contributor to the *Southern Literary Messenger* from 1834 to 1847; and during Simms's editorship of the *Southern Quarterly Review* he contributed six articles, one of them a slashing review of Hugh Garland's life of John Randolph of Roanoke. At one time Tucker considered writing as a career, but none of his books was popular or profitable enough to make

professional authorship seem attractive. He came to feel that his best opportunity to make his ideas count was by impressing them upon his students.
In 1850, when secession seemed not impossible, he went to Nashville to
attend the Southern Convention as a delegate from Virginia. There he
made a notable speech which in 1862 West & Johnston reprinted in Richmond with the heading "Prescience." He argued that if the South should be
driven to secession, "there is no reason to apprehend that such a step
would lead to war." He stated that "the unequal operation of the Federal
Government" had robbed the South of seven hundred million dollars to
enrich New England. "And who cares for the South?" he said. "—What
is the South? An ass of the tribe of Issachar, 'bowed down between two
burthens'; thirty millions to be paid [annually] into the [Federal] treasury,
and twice as much more to go into the pockets of the Northern manufacturers."

In his later years Tucker, as he wrote to Simms, despaired of Virginia,
"sunk in the slough of democracy, which has no sense of honor, no foresight, and is never valiant but against its own instruments"; and so he turned
hopefully to South Carolina. "South Carolina alone can act," he wrote, "because she is the only State in which the gentleman retains his place and
influence, and in which the statesman has not been degraded from his post."
Tucker did not realize that in South Carolina the voters often chose candidates from the middle class in preference to a great Low-Country planter like
William Elliott.

Tucker carried his anti-Northern bias even into the realm of literature.
In a review of Macaulay's *History of England* he wrote in the *Southern
Quarterly Review* for July, 1849:

We [in the South] do read the writings of Irving and Prescott; such of us as are
not particular about truth in a history, read Bancroft; we sometimes spare
time and eyesight for one of Cooper's novels; but as to the rest, whatever favor
they may find with the shop boys and sempstresses of New-York, we beg to
assure Mr. Macaulay, that *our literary public* (if there be such a thing) heed
them no more than the twittering of so many hedge sparrows. Our reading men
are familiar with the best writers of England, and with some of those of France
and Germany, and try to keep up with the literature of the day. In doing this
they have little time to spare for those who write only because they think that
what they call America ought to have a literature *of its own*. We, here in the
South, are not aware of any such necessity. We are for *free trade*, and go for
getting what we want, of the best quality and at the cheapest market. Both
objects we think are best secured, by not taking any of the wares of our northern *brethren*, (qu. plunderers and slanderers?) whether mechanical, intellectual
or moral.

Tucker's published lectures not only throw light upon his political opinions, which influenced Abel P. Upshur and other writers, but are in themselves often notable writing of their kind, clear, forceful, and eloquent. He published *The Principles of Pleading* (Boston, 1846), a textbook, but he was at his best in *A Series of Lectures on the Science of Government* . . . (Philadelphia, 1845). Tucker's political views were a strange combination of the realistic and the romantic. For him Virginia was still a sovereign state, as it had been for his father. "Virginia," he said to his students, "is your country, and the country of your fathers. To her your allegiance is due. Her alone you are bound to obey."

Are not the names of Washington and Henry, and Jefferson and Madison, and Marshall and Randolph, all *her property?* Are not these her jewels; and shall she, unlike the mother of the Gracchi, pine, because others may outshine her in such baubles as mere *gold* can buy? Can you consent to throw these honours into common stock, and to share your portion in Washington with the French of Louisiana, and the Dutch of New York, and the renegades from every corner of the earth, who swarm their great commercial cities, and call themselves *your countrymen and* HIS! What fellowship have we with those who change their country with their climate? The Virginian is a Virginian everywhere. In the wilds of the west, on the sands of Florida, on the shores of the Pacific— everywhere his heart turns to Virginia—everywhere he worships with his face toward the temple of freedom erected here. To us, who remain, it belongs to minister at the altar—to feed the flame—*and, if need be, to supply the sacrifice.* Do this, and Virginia will again be recognised as the mother of nations. . . .

But even in Virginia Tucker found a great abatement in state pride: "That sentiment has passed away, and Virginia no longer claims to be regarded as a sun sole and self-poised, but is content to be looked on only as a planet of one great concentric system." Tucker was the uncompromising opponent of centralizing tendencies. He found no principle of corruption in a state government; but, like John Taylor of Caroline, he saw in the tremendous power of Federal patronage the source of much corruption. He feared the tyranny of the vicious and the ignorant, and he was, he wrote, "the last man in the world to contend for the divine right of majorities to do what they please." He scouted the fear of "the phantom of aristocracy," and placed his chief reliance in the small Virginia landholders. He thought that the right to vote should still be limited to freeholders. Such opinions can hardly have represented the Virginia of 1845. His ideas were more at home in South Carolina, as Tucker's correspondence with Simms and Hammond shows.

Tucker published three novels. The last and least interesting of these,

Gertrude, appeared serially in the *Messenger* from September, 1844, to December, 1845, but was never published in book form. It is a domestic, sentimental novel with the scene in Washington. It is in part a satire on marriages of convenience, and the story seems designed to show that the course of true love never runs smoothly. It lacks almost entirely the qualities that interest the modern reader in *George Balcombe* and *The Partisan Leader*, both written in a period of about four months in 1836 and published in the same year.

George Balcombe, published in New York by Harper & Brothers and rated by Poe and Simms as one of the best of American novels, is a mystery and adventure story of Virginia and Missouri. Simms, who knew the border country well, praised it as "a bold, highly spirited, and very graceful border story, true to the life, a fine picture of society and manners on the frontier —animated and full of interest." He added: "It lacked color or warmth of tone, wanting the softening effects of fancy, though not without imagination. Reason was his predominant faculty." The story reminded Poe of Godwin's *Caleb Williams*, but he did not remark the influence of Scott and Cooper, which is also noticeable. The plot, which involves an unconvincing villain and a missing will, is conventional; but there are some good scenes, chiefly in Missouri, which give the book some importance as an early picture of life in the West. The camp-meeting and courtroom scenes are well done, and there is a brief glimpse of Daniel Boone, whom Tucker may have seen. There is, however, not much local color in either the Virginia or the Missouri scenes. The minor characters are better than the major figures. John Keizer, a Virginia mountaineer, has a knowledge of woodcraft that recalls Leather-Stocking and Horse-Shoe Robinson. The picture of slavery is of course benevolent, and a certain glamour is thrown over the planter class. George Balcombe, the mouthpiece for Tucker's ideas, has traits that come from John Randolph and from Tucker himself. He is sagacious, accomplished, a mind-reader like Poe's M. Dupin, who is a later creation. On the whole, the book strikes the modern reader as a rather promising novel for a beginner; it is certainly not the work of one who has mastered his craft.

The Partisan Leader: A Tale of the Future was published in Washington in 1836 by Duff Green, but it bore only the imprint: "Printed for the Publishers, by James Caxton. 1856," and it carried the pseudonym "Edward William Sidney." The book appears to have been in some fashion suppressed, or at least Tucker thought so. He had put his warning in the form of a novel to get a wider audience than he could find by writing for Southern newspapers and magazines. Financially, the novel was a failure. Six or seven years later he openly admitted having written it, and in July, 1850, when he had hopes of getting it reprinted, he wrote to James H. Hammond: "I would rather be known, ten years hence, as the author of that book, than of any thing ever published on this continent." This prophecy of a coming civil war was reprinted in New York in 1861 as *A Key to the Disunion Conspiracy*. It was reprinted in Richmond in 1862 by West & Johnston, who advertised it in the *Messenger* as "A Novel, and an Apocalypse of the Origin and Struggles of the Southern Confederacy."

The idea of an impending civil war may well have come from John Randolph, who on March 17, 1832, when excitement over Nullification was high, wrote to William Wallace: "I look for civil war. You may live to see Winchester & Richmond in two different states. All south of the [Potomac?] river will join S. Carolina & if the Rope of Sand miscalled the Fedl. Govt. does not take Cuba somebody else will do it. We have no choice."

As a forecast of the Civil War of 1861–1865, *The Partisan Leader* was in many respects wide of the mark. Tucker's war is mainly an affair of guerrillas and is on a far smaller scale than the conflict which broke out in 1861. He was wrong in believing that the Virginia mountaineers would be conspicuously loyal to the Confederate cause. In 1849, as Tucker represented it, the states of the Lower South would be out of the Union, having peacefully seceded mainly on account of the iniquitous tariff rather than Northern agitation of the slavery question. When the novel opens, Martin Van Buren, now President in his fourth term, is trying to prevent Virginia from seceding and joining the Southern confederacy. The story is intentionally left incomplete, but it is clear that Virginia is to win her independence.

Tucker's friend, Abel P. Upshur, who reviewed the novel in the *Messenger*, had high praise for its literary qualities. Among modern critics Carl Van Doren is almost alone in praising Tucker's style. The narrative, weighted with propaganda, moves much too slowly. Tucker's Negro dialect is better than most of that written by his contemporaries because he realized that the intonation and exact pronunciation could not be represented by the conventional misspelling. Slavery is considerably idealized and pictured as an institution which the Yankee mind cannot understand. It should be remembered that the idealized picture of plantation life found in the stories of Thomas Nelson Page and many other later Southern writers had its beginnings in the work of Tucker, Grayson, and other ante-bellum writers.

Readers of the story tried to identify the originals of Tucker's characters. It may be doubted, however, whether "Mr. B—" is John C. Calhoun, for it was not until after 1836 that Tucker became an admirer of the South Carolina statesman. Christian Witt, however, has an original in a man named Saunders Witt; and the original of Schwartz is John Switzler, whom Tucker had known in Missouri. Tucker anticipated Cooke and Page and many another novelist when he represented the two Virginia brothers, Hugh and Bernard Trevor, as fighting on opposite sides. On reading Upshur's review, in which it was stated that the characters were painted from life, Tucker's brother Henry St. George—as distinguished a legal scholar as Beverley but no secessionist—canceled his subscription to the *Messenger*, believing that Hugh Trevor was intended as a portrait of himself. As a matter of fact, Beverley Tucker admitted in a letter to his brother that while he had had no intention of portraying either himself or his brother, during the writing of the story he had found it difficult to keep himself from using Henry St. George as a model.

Tucker's contributions to the *Messenger* include some poems of no particular importance, a translation of Goethe's *Iphigenia at Tauris*, a number of addresses, his novel *Gertrude*, and several important reviews, notably of William Munford's translation of the *Iliad* and Philip Pendleton Cooke's *Froissart Ballads*. Tucker, however, was not merely a contributor to the *Messenger*; he was, along with Lucian Minor and James E. Heath, one of the trusted advisers of Thomas Willis White, who owned it. He read manuscripts for White and even wrote an occasional review of the magazine to be printed in the newspapers. He came nearer than any others of the inner *Messenger* circle to fully appreciating the writings of Philip Pendleton Cooke and—what is more important—of Edgar Allan Poe.

Tucker, who read some of Poe's contributions before they appeared in print, was obviously impressed by the tales and even more by the book reviews.[30] Poe's penchant for the horrible disturbed him, as it disturbed White, Heath, and Kennedy, but he recognized the power in the early tales. In exchanging with Poe his notions about versification, Tucker commented on "that marvellous performance—'clapping Juba,'" which had already impressed the youthful Chivers. "The beat is capriciously irregular; there is no attempt to keep time to *all* the notes, but then it comes so pat & so distinct that the cadence is never lost." One wonders what influence, if any, Negro music had upon Poe. Apparently one of Poe's letters to Tucker is lost. In it he had suggested that White, misinterpreting something that Tucker had written him, had expressed some doubt of Poe's editorial ability. On January 26, 1836, Tucker wrote a long letter to White in which he said:

[30] Tucker wrote one letter to Poe and received at least two, one of which is apparently not extant. In addition, Tucker wrote two letters to White which the latter apparently read to Poe. The letter to Poe is in Harrison, *Poe*, II, 21–24. The letters to White are in the Griswold Papers (Boston Public Library). The earlier one, Nov. 29, 1835, is given in A. H. Quinn, *Edgar Allan Poe* (1941), pp. 234–238.

"That I have not admired all Mr. P's productions, as much as some others, and that his writings are not so much to my taste as they would be, were I (as would to God I were) as young as he, I do not deny. Thus much I expressed, and this so freely as to show, that, had I meant more, I would have said more. . . . I was equally sincere, I assure you, in what I said in his praise." Tucker went on to say that for his part he did not admire "Mrs. Sigourney & Co., or any of our native poets except Halleck," but that "Mr. P's review of the writings . . . of these ladies in your last number, is a specimen of criticism, which for niceness of discrimination, delicacy of expression and [all?] that shows familiarity with the art, may well compare with any I have ever seen." The youthful Poe, however, seemed to him somewhat "rash" in writing slashing reviews. The review of Fay's *Norman Leslie*, which Poe had held up as a horrible example of all that was bad in a popular novel, was objectionable only because Poe had attacked a rival editor. Tucker had not read Simms's *The Partisan*, but Poe in reviewing it, he thought, had been "less just, and less fortunate" than with *Norman Leslie*. "Mr. P's critical notices," he went on, "are very far superior to those which formerly appeared in the Messenger. In point of style and piquancy there is no comparison, and piquancy is indispensable in criticism."

Poe's review of *George Balcombe* appeared in the *Messenger* in January, 1837, after he had given up his editorial position. White, who had lost patience with his brilliant assistant, wrote to Tucker in April: "The truth is, Poe seldom or ever done what he knew was just to any book. He read few through—unless it were some trashy novels,—and his only object in reading even these, was to ridicule their authors. Read his eulogistic review of [George] Balcombe—which he penned only because he believed you were its author. He has scarcely selected a passage out of the two volumes which warrants the praise he has lavished on it. But enough of this—this mortifying subject."

In this instance at least White had wholly mistaken his man. Poe's review gives ample evidence that he had read the book, and the estimate he expressed was repeated long afterward when there was no point in his flattering its author. He singled out the best scenes for particular comment. "The general manner," he said, "is that of a scholar and gentleman in the best sense of both terms—bold, vigorous, and rich—abrupt rather than diffuse —and not over scrupulous in the use of energetic vulgarisms." "Its most distinguishing features are invention, vigor, almost audacity, of thought— great variety of what the German critics term *intrigue*, and exceeding ingenuity and finish in the adaptation of its component parts." In the year of his death Poe wrote: "Had the 'George Balcombe' of Professor Beverley

Tucker been the work of any one born North of Mason and Dixon's line, it would have been long ago recognized as one of the very noblest fictions ever written by an American." Poe was recalling Tucker's novel because he wished to hit at Yankee critics for their failure to appreciate the work of Southern writers, but there is no question of the high estimate he placed upon the book. Tucker and he belonged to different literary generations, and the Judge had not fully understood his literary aims, but Poe was grateful enough to write to Philip Pendleton Cooke in 1839 that Tucker was one of the three or four persons who had shown any real understanding of his work.

17

George Fitzhugh

GEORGE FITZHUGH (1806–1881), who defended slavery and attacked "free society," undoubtedly helped to bring on the "irrepressible conflict," but he was not the inhuman savage he must have seemed to Sumner, Garrison, and Lincoln. This absent-minded, none-too-successful lawyer, was a genial, kindly, and attractive man. He was born and reared in the same region in northern Virginia as that in which John Taylor had lived and where Moncure Daniel Conway grew to manhood. He was a descendant of William Fitzhugh, one of the great seventeenth-century Virginia planters. His grandfather, Colonel William Fitzhugh, had surrendered his commission in the British army and gone to prison rather than fight against his countrymen in the Revolution. His father was a doctor and planter with only four or five hundred acres. Fitzhugh attended a "field school," but he was largely self-educated. He knew Latin but not Greek, and he read widely but with little system until he was past forty. He read regularly *Blackwood's Magazine* and the *Edinburgh, Quarterly, North British,* and *Westminster* reviews, all in American editions put out by Leonard Scott and Company of New York. He had no such command of economic fact and theory as George Tucker or Thomas Cooper, but he had a shrewd, inquiring mind that grasped new ideas easily though it failed to see all their implications. He belonged to what Conway called "Young Virginia," for, as Conway put it, "it was the most scholarly and philosophical young men who discarded old Virginia principles and advocated slavery *per se*." "Young Virginia," as Fitzhugh saw, had something in common with Disraeli and other conservative representatives of "Young England" who were vigorously defending the landed aristocracy and the Established Church. It was the democratic revolutions of 1848 in Europe as well as Virginia troubles with free Negroes and the question of slavery in the territories newly won from Mexico that prompted Fitzhugh to publish in 1849 a pamphlet entitled *Slavery Justified*. 'This contains most of the ideas which he developed at greater length in his two books: *Sociology for the South, or The Failure of Free Society* (Richmond, 1854) and *Cannibals All! or, Slaves without Masters* (Richmond, 1857). Much of the material in these books was reworked from articles which Fitzhugh had published in the Richmond *Examiner* and, for his second book, from *De Bow's Review*.

In the fifties Fitzhugh was reading the British reviews and the works of American antislavery writers looking for materials which could be used to defend slavery or to point out the shortcomings of "free society." The vagaries of the Abolitionists had for Fitzhugh the same kind of fascination which thirty years ago Irving Babbitt and Stuart Sherman found in the writings of Greenwich Village radicals. In gentlemanly fashion Fitzhugh entered into correspondence with William Lloyd Garrison, who treated him rather badly. In 1855 during his one visit to the North he discussed with the antislavery Stephen Pearl Andrews methods for approaching the problem of slavery objectively and scientifically. In his books Fitzhugh drew most of his illustrations of the shortcomings of the industrial order from England rather than from the Northern states, partly because he did not wish to alienate Northern conservatives. There was some truth in his contention that the cause of Abolition was integrally related to all the other Northern isms of the time.

No one who reads a newspaper can but have observed that every abolitionist is either an agrarian, a socialist, an infidel, an anti-renter, or in some way is trying to upset other institutions of society, as well as slavery at the South. The same reasoning that makes him an abolitionist soon carries him further, for he finds slavery in some form so interwoven with the whole frame-work of society, that he invariably ends by proposing to destroy the whole edifice and building another on entirely new principles.

Fitzhugh was at this time still opposed to the reopening of the slave trade; and he did not, like Josiah C. Nott and others, play up the Negro as a permanently inferior race. In April, 1855, he wrote to George Frederick Holmes: "I assure you, Sir, I see great evils in Slavery, but in a controversial work I ought not to admit them." Fitzhugh was not in every respect a conservative; he supported the movement for educational reform in Virginia. He belonged to the right wing of the Democratic party and in 1857–1858 was a clerk in Washington in the office of Attorney-General Jeremiah S. Black. Unlike Calhoun, he had little faith in constitutional measures. "The power to construe them," he said, "is the power to nullify them." In his books he represented slavery as the remedy for the many evils that afflicted the "free society" of England and the Northern states. "A well-conducted farm in the South," he wrote, "is a model of associated labor that Fourier might envy." In almost Fascist fashion he attacked free speech, the freedom of the press, and freedom of religion along with free trade and laissez-faire economic doctrines. Carried away with his leading idea, he did not clearly understand what he was doing. He was, however, only anticipating Emerson, Seward, and Lincoln when he wrote: "One set of ideas will govern and control after awhile the civilized world. Slavery will every where be abolished, or every where be re-instituted." With an ill grace he attacked the Virginia Declaration of Rights, which had been drafted by his distant kinsman, George Mason. He quoted one of Jefferson's noblest utterances and remarked: "It would be far nearer the truth to say, 'that some were born with saddles on their backs, and others booted and spurred to ride them,'—and the riding does them good." In his attack upon Northern capitalism he went further than John Taylor had gone, so much so that in his economics he suggests Karl Marx. Like other proslavery writers, he was indebted to Aristotle; but not until April, 1855, did he discover that, as he wrote to George Frederick Holmes, he had adopted not only Aristotle's "theories, his arguments, and his illustrations, but his very words." "All these things which I thought original with me," he wrote, "I find in Aristotle. I am in a fix. If I did read him, I am a plagiarist. But if I write again, I'll make a clean breast and acknowledge my pseudo-learning is all gathered from Reviews. I never read a Socialist author treating his subject philosophically in my life. Newspapers, novels, Reviews, are the sources of my information."

Still greater was Fitzhugh's indebtedness to Thomas Carlyle, who glorified the Hero, scorned democracy, idealized work, and criticized emancipation in the West Indies. Carlyle did not approve of some of the uses to which the proslavery writers put his teachings, but he had only himself to blame if Fitzhugh printed on the title page of *Cannibals All!* a longish passage from "The Present Age," warning of the danger of loosening "by assiduous wedges in every joint, the whole fabric of social existence, stone from stone: till at last . . . it can . . . be overset by sudden outburst of revolutionary rage. . . ." Fitzhugh, however, was not uncritical of Carlyle. He wrote in 1860: "Carlyle is a man of genius, but he is reckless, rash, bold, original, affected, and half-ideal. He is right in saying 'the world is too little governed'; wrong in repudiating institutions, forms, ceremonies, or 'phantasms,' as he calls them, and relying on the government of mere force and the naked sword."

It is a remarkable coincidence that the two first American books to carry the word *sociology* in their titles should be defenses of slavery. One of course was Fitzhugh's *Sociology for the South*; the other was the work of a Mississippian, Henry Hughes, *A Treatise on Sociology*, and they both appeared in 1854. Fitzhugh had hesitated to use the newly coined word, half Latin and half Greek, but finally adopted it, he says, because the term was needed to describe the disease that afflicts "free society" and which is unknown in the South. The first really important American texts in sociology, however, were Lester F. Ward's *Dynamic Sociology* and *The Science of Society*, by Fitzhugh's friend Holmes; and they both appeared in 1883.

Fitzhugh was aware of some of his own literary shortcomings. He wrote to Holmes, October 12, 1854: "My Book has in a high degree the failing of the young Lawyer. It runs over the argument too often—but the subject is difficult and in part excuses this failing." He wrote in fact too much as a jury lawyer talks, repeating his main points, resorting to sarcasm, argument, quotation, and repetition to drive home his main points. His books are too diffuse and suffer from lack of thorough organization. Fitzhugh was an amateur who did not take himself very seriously as a writer. His books, however, are still readable and suggestive. His defense of slavery is more conventional and less interesting than his attack on the shortcomings of our young industrial civilization, which was fast ripening for such satiric treatment as it has received only since Mark Twain and Charles Dudley Warner published *The Gilded Age* in 1873. Fitzhugh argued that "As modern civilization advances . . . its tendency is to accumulate all capital in a few hands, cuts off the masses from the soil, lessens their wages and their chances of employment, and increases the necessity for a means of certain subsistence, which slavery alone can furnish, when a few own all the lands and other capital." That was in 1857. Not until 1879 was Henry George to publish his *Progress and Poverty*, in which he noted: "This association of poverty with progress is the greatest enigma of our times." All nineteenth-century science, invention, and machinery seemed to George only to have made "sharper the contrast between the House of Have and the House of Want."

In the spring of 1855 Fitzhugh received an invitation to lecture on slavery before a lyceum audience in New Haven, Connecticut. The invitation had come as a result of a suggestion made by Moncure Conway to Senator John P. Hale, of New Hampshire. And so Fitzhugh at the age of forty-nine, very much the provincial in some ways, paid his first visit to the North. In New York he visited the bookstores, had himself photographed, and ordered a copy of Aristotle's *Politics* with the results that have been noted. At Peterboro, New York, he visited his distant kinsman, Gerrit Smith, a wealthy philanthropist who supported temperance, women's rights, pacifism, prison reform, abolition of capital punishment, religious rationalism, and Abolition. In New Haven he delivered his lecture on "The Failure of Free Society" and was listened to courteously enough. He had come to New Haven to debate the slavery question with Wendell Phillips, but Phillips did not arrive till after Fitzhugh's lecture. The Virginian stayed over to hear the Abolitionist orator deliver a tirade against the churches, which were still mainly neutral on the slavery question. Fitzhugh's reaction was that Phillips' address was an "eloquent tirade against Church and State, Law and Religion. It was flat treason and blasphemy—nothing else." Samuel Foote, an uncle of Mrs. Stowe, drove Fitzhugh around New Haven to show that the city had no slums and was enjoying prosperity under a "free society." Fitzhugh admitted that he must modify his opinions on the subject of free labor, but after his return to Virginia he wrote:

But I was "carrying coals to Newcastle" in proving the "Failure of Free Society." They all admit that, but say they have plans of social organization that will cure all defects. *Truly* one half of them are atheists seeking to discover a "New Social Science," the other half Millennial anti-church, anti-law, and anti-marriage Christians, who expect Christ's kingdom on earth is about to begin. . . . I do not believe there is a Liberty man in the North who is not a Socialist.

As an advocate of Virginia or Southern nationalism, Fitzhugh was logically bound to champion the cause of a Southern literature, and in *De Bow's Review* in the late fifties he wrote much on literary topics. "It is all important," he wrote, "that we should write our own books. It matters little who makes our shoes." In *Sociology for the South* he had argued that since the Reformation the spirit of liberalism and commercialism had brought about a steady decline in "genius, taste and art." "There is not," he said, "a poet, an orator, a sculptor, or painter in the world. . . . Nothing now but what is gaudy and costly excites admiration. The public taste is debased." Debased the taste of the majority of readers, North and South, undoubtedly was, but Fitzhugh did not face the fact that the literature being produced in money-making, reformist New England—now that Poe was dead—far surpassed in quality what was being written in the South. In a series of articles in *De Bow's Review* Fitzhugh passed judgment on many of the world's writers, noting their deviation from the extreme Southern position much as a Nazi or Communist critic might do. With such a philosophical basis as conservative Southern thought afforded, an abler critic might have made a much stronger case against nineteenth-century literature written in English. It had weaknesses that seem rather glaring now. Joseph B. Cobb, of Mississippi, in his *Leisure Labors* (1858) pointed out weaknesses in Willis and

Longfellow with a critical acumen that Fitzhugh could not equal. Fitzhugh was shrewd enough, however, to see that much which passed for literature in his time, as in ours, was intended for readers who had the mentality of adolescents. He found Burke and Johnson congenial, but he did not care for the "low novels" of Fielding, Smollett, and Dickens. Among the few novelists whom he admired were Cervantes, Goldsmith, and Scott. He admired Shakespeare, but the radicalism of Milton's prose offended him. He was willing to admit that German literature was the best written in modern times, but to him it was suspect because New Englanders were so fond of it. He knew no German, but from his reading of Carlyle and Madame de Staël he concluded that it was the German spirit that had made society in Europe "a heaving volcano." He reserved his praise for the classics—they were safe enough—but knowing no Greek he preferred Vergil to Homer.

When the sections came to blows in 1861, Fitzhugh rather foolishly undertook to glorify war; but wiser men than he have often done the same thing. Even Emerson, as we have seen, was not exempt. By 1862 Fitzhugh had been forced to leave his home and was employed as a clerk in the Treasury department in Richmond. After the war he was for a time a court agent for the Freedmen's Bureau there. His attitude toward the new regime was vacillating, but he was not among those who refused to see any good in it. He wrote once more for the revived *De Bow's Review* and contributed a few articles in 1869 and 1870 to *Lippincott's Magazine*, which was not unfriendly to the South. In 1878, his wife now dead, he went to Frankfort, Kentucky, to live with his son. In 1880 he moved to Huntsville, Texas, to live with his daughter Mariella. His later years were saddened by insomnia and partial blindness. He died in 1881 practically forgotten in his native Virginia, which was now concerned with other matters than a philosophical defense of slavery.

18
William J. Grayson

WILLIAM JOHN GRAYSON (1788–1863), author of *The Hireling and the Slave*, was born in Beaufort, South Carolina. His father, who had been an officer in the American Revolution, died when young Grayson was ten years old. At twelve he was sent North to school. He had already developed a fondness for reading, but in the New York and New Jersey schools where he spent the next three years he found no books to read at a time when, as he says in his *Autobiography*, "I could have devoured a library." "The art of keeping school in the North," he says, "seemed to consist in making the most money with the least annoyance to teacher and scholar." Returning to South Carolina in 1803, he was prepared for college by two excellent New England teachers. They were brothers of Jonathan Maxcy, the President of South Carolina College, which Grayson entered in February, 1807. The basic studies in American colleges were then Latin, Greek, and mathematics; and Grayson presumably studied the *Iliad*, the *Odes* of Horace, Cicero's *De Oratore*, Longinus's *On the Sublime*, and Hugh Blair's *Lectures on Rhetoric*. The leaders of the class of 1809 were Grayson and his lifelong friend James Louis Petigru. Together they read Horace and Rabelais and agreed that Pope and Dryden were better poets than their Romantic successors, who were now beginning to be read in this country. Grayson's literary taste was somewhat conservative even in his youth.

Grayson, who came to regard the American college "as a sort of hybrid between the English high school and the University with the advantages of neither," remarks of himself: "I became a bachelor of arts with the usual inaptitude of the tribe for any definite or useful employment." Like most of his college friends, he had been educated as though he were to inherit a plantation and live a life of leisure. When it became necessary for him to earn a living, he found his range of choice quite narrow. "Men who pursue knowledge for its own sake and who are suddenly awakened to the necessity of seeking their bread," he says, "betake themselves commonly to one of two pursuits. They become authors or schoolmasters. But the South, fifty years ago, offered no field for authorship." And so Grayson became assistant to Dr. Brantly, the Baptist minister who presided over Beaufort College. In January, 1814, he married Sarah Matilda Somarsall, the daughter of a Charleston merchant. In 1822 he began the practice of law in Beaufort but soon found himself inclined to doubt the justice of his own causes—and with lawyers, he remarks, "Right, justice, truth are secondary considerations or rather no considerations at all." In the same year he was elected to the state house of representatives. Four years later he was elected to the state senate, from which he resigned in 1831 to become commissioner of equity in the Beaufort district. During the Nullification crisis he edited the Beaufort *Gazette*. Unlike William Elliott, he shared the beliefs of the Nullification party, but he was opposed to the extreme measures they adopted. In March, 1833, Grayson took his seat in the House of Representatives in Washington, which then contained two such different personalities as David Crockett and Richard Henry Wilde. Four years later he was defeated for re-election partly, he thought, because he was too proud to solicit votes or to treat voters with liquor. In August, 1841, he became Collector of Customs in Charleston, a post which he held for almost twelve years. In 1855, the year in which he wrote *The Hireling and the Slave* (1856), he bought "Fair Lawn" plantation near Charleston. In his memoir of Petigru he remarks: "It [buying a plantation] was the approved Carolina custom in closing every kind of career. No matter how one might begin, as lawyer, physician, clergyman, mechanic, or merchant, he ended, if prosperous, as proprietor of a rice or cotton plantation. It was the condition that came nearest to the shadow of the colonial aristocracy which yet remained." The ownership of a plantation colored his later writings.

Grayson had written verses while in college, but it was not until he was sixty-five that he began seriously to write poetry. His literary work brought him practically no money, but it gave him something congenial to do, for he liked to write. The establishment of *Russell's Magazine* in Charleston in 1857 brought together for the first time Grayson and the youthful editor Paul Hamilton Hayne, who describes him as a tall, erect, gray-haired man with an air of benevolence like that of a Moravian missionary. Grayson wrote the leading article for the first number—a reply to the *Edinburgh Review*'s attack on slavery—and became one of the regular contributors to the magazine.

Defender of slavery though he was, Grayson consistently opposed secession. He had no illusions as to what a conflict between South and North involved, and he regarded the Confederate political leaders as demagogues motivated by selfish interests and blind to the consequences of their own actions. During the dark days of the Civil War he wrote his *Autobiography* and a memoir of his friend Petigru, whose Unionist views he shared. He died in Newberry, South Carolina, on October 4, 1863, and was buried in Magnolia Cemetery in Charleston.

In 1850, when many South Carolinians were loudly clamoring for secession, Grayson addressed to Governor Seabrook a pamphlet in which he contended, to quote his own summary of the argument:

. . . that the Union is the source of peace prosperity and power to the Nation, and its dissolution would be followed by disorder, violence, and civil wars; that if the present Confederacy is broken up, the formation of any other would be difficult and its continuance impossible; that no causes exist to justify the destruction of the Union; . . . that the wrong of which we complain, comes from the people of certain States, and the appropriate remedy would be the cessation of social intercourse; . . . that the South wil[l] lose nothing by waiting, she is rapidly advancing in wealth, population, and power, and nothing can arrest her progress but the imprudence of her own people, and the rashness of her leaders.

Grayson ridiculed the secessionists' contention that a Southern confederacy could be expected to hold together. "If for this shadow and delusion, the mere dream of distempered imaginations," he wrote, "we let go the substantial blessings of law and order, and peace at home, and security from abroad, we shall most justly become a by-word among all nations." Most South Carolina newspapers ignored Grayson's pamphlet.

During the war that came eleven years afterwards Grayson wrote in his memoir of Petigru:

We flatter ourselves that our Southern Confederacy will present an example of truer amity, and closer and more lasting union. There is no just cause for the expectation; no warrant in history, reason, or our own experience. We think slavery will be a bond of union. Were not Sparta, Athens, Thebes, slaveholders, and constant and deadly enemies nevertheless? Will there be any lack among us of rapacious, unprincipled demagogues? Have we known the time when there have been no eager traffickers among us for power and office? In a word, is there no pride, vanity, or ambition in the Southern States?

Bitterly Grayson sums up the methods by which he thought secession had been brought about in South Carolina:

To induce the simple people to plunge into the volcanic fires of revolution and war, they were told that the act of dissolution would produce no opposition of a serious nature; that not a drop of blood would be spilled; that no man's flocks, or herds, or negroes, or houses, or lands would be plundered or destroyed; that unbroken prosperity would follow the ordinance of secession; that cotton would control all Europe, and secure open ports and boundless commerce with the whole world for the Southern States.

Nor did the Southern clergymen seem to Grayson more enlightened than the politicians. He wrote: "The most solemn compact between states is assailed by ambition and pride, and perishes 'as flax that falls asunder by the touch of fire,' and no pulpit censures, or protests, or dissuades."

Paradoxically, Grayson's proslavery sentiments made him a stronger advocate of the Union. What he said of Petigru's position is true of his own:

He was convinced that war, anarchy, military despotism, would inevitably follow a dissolution of the Union; that secession would impart to the Abolition party a power over slavery that nothing else could give them—a power to make war on Southern institutions, to proclaim freedom to the negro, to invoke and command the sympathy and aid of the whole world in carrying on a crusade on the Southern States. This was the long-sought purpose of the Abolitionists, which nothing but a broken confederation could enable them to reach. Secession threw into the abolition service the whole military power of the North. It forced into their ranks all parties of every description, Democrat as well as Republican. It secured to Seward's agents in Europe the ear of all its governments, who were prepared to regard Lincoln's proclamation of liberty to the negro as a sublime act of benevolence and wisdom.

Grayson is an extreme example of the conservatism of Southern literary taste, but his conservatism, like that of Dr. Holmes, was not due to ignorance of the literature of his time. When he wrote *The Hireling and the Slave*, he deliberately selected as his model the poetry of the eighteenth century. In his Preface he wrote: "The poetry of the day is, for the most part, subtile and transcendental in character. Every sentiment, reflection, or description is wrought into elaborate modes of expression from remote and fanciful analogies. The responses of the Muses have become as mystical and sometimes as obscure as those of more ancient oracles, and disdain the older and homelier forms of English verse." In his *Autobiography* he said: "I believe in Dryden and Pope, the nonsense of Bowles and his coadjutors and of Wharton [Warton] notwithstanding. I have faith in the ancient classical models, the masters directly or indirectly of all the great poets of modern times. My taste is too antiquated to fall into raptures over the metaphysical sentiment of Shelley, or the renovated pagan deities of Keats, or the Hindoo monsters of Southey." "The sin of modern poetry," he continued, "consists in exaggeration of sentiment, of passion, of description, of every thing. It wants simplicity and truth. It seeks to be sublime and becomes inflated. It strives to be deep and is obscure only. It strives after the new and the wonderful and sinks into the grotesque and unintelligible." William Cowper seemed to him a better poet than Wordsworth, in whose poetry he felt "an affectation of [the] love of nature rather than the genuine sentiment." In "What Is Poetry?" he attacked Wordsworth vigorously:

He was a sort of verse making machine all his life. He lived to manufacture verses. His morning and evening walks were taken to levy poetical black mail from every stock and stone, every shrub and flower, every bird and butterfly. —The daisy [primrose] that to Peter Bell was a daisy and nothing more, was to Wordsworth a very different and much more important object—it was a peg to hang verses upon. He turned over every pebble in his path to see if there might not be a stanza lurking beneath it. If he sat down on an occasional bench it produced a poem. If he visited a river it was made to rhyme. If he returned again to its banks it was forced to do double duty. Not an old thorn bush in his neighborhood escaped the general tax. Every creature within reach, asses and idiots, pedlars and prostitutes, brought grist to his indefatigable mill. He wrote with a sort of malice prepense. He walked to make verses. He traveled to make verses. He never thought of his bills but only of his rhymes. He looked on nature as a kind of poetical milch cow, which he was never tired of milking—a mass of raw material to be made up into metrical dresses.

It seemed to Grayson that modern writers had confused the arts and forgotten the lines that separate them. The bounds of prose and verse, he believed, should be kept distinct, and meter seemed to him the one characteristic that distinguishes verse from prose. "To omit verse in a definition of poetry," he said, "is to omit its distinctive property." He who wished to write poetry should remember that: "The four greatest names of English verse [are], Chaucer, Spenser, Shakespeare and Milton. . . ." Halleck is almost the only American poet whom Grayson mentions. The modern practitioner, he believed, should follow Horace's advice and give his days and nights to the study of the Greek masters. Grayson might have approved of the New Humanism had he lived to read the writings of Irving Babbitt and Paul Elmer More. Substantially, he said, there is in all the world but one literature—that belonging to the Greek literary tradition. Grayson's models, however, are clearly not Homer and Vergil but Goldsmith, Cowper, Crabbe, and Scott. He was a belated Neoclassicist.

This staunch supporter of the Union was one of the most vigorous defenders of slavery against Mrs. Stowe's attack, and The Hireling and the Slave (1856) is the most notable of many replies to Uncle Tom's Cabin. Slavery, he admits in his Preface, is not without its abuses, but it is as easily improvable as other institutions. "I do not say that slavery is the best system of labor, but only that it is the best for the Negro in this country." The problem, as only Southerners seemed to realize, involved not only economics and politics but race as well. Like every other Southerner, Grayson was irritated by the "malignant abuse" heaped upon slaveholders by writers who knew little about slavery and who in painting the institution as infamous showed an unscrupulous disregard for fact and common sense. On his Northern tour in 1817–1818 he had taken a Negro servant with him as far north as Boston; yet he had heard no word whispered against slavery. In those days the Bostonians had seemed to him far superior to New Yorkers and Philadelphians. Now the situation was vastly different. "The chief revilers of the slaveholder," he wrote, "are the people of England and the Eastern States. They are the parties who bought the Negroes in Africa, brought them to America, and left them in exchange for large sums of money. They made the system and enjoy the profits. Now that they can no longer carry on the trade, they slander the slaveholder of their own making." The time had come, he felt, as George Fitzhugh did, to carry the war into the enemy's country.

The defense of slavery, he noted, had taken almost every form except verse; and he thought that the subject admitted poetical dress. Perhaps also he hoped by demonstration to refute the Abolitionist contention that literature could not flourish in a slave society. Following the example set by Fitzhugh's *Sociology for the South* (1854), he presented contrasting pictures of the miserable Northern and British day laborers and the contented Southern slaves. He published the poem in Charleston in 1856 and made arrangements with a New York publisher for a new edition, but the pressure of Northern opinion, we are told, compelled the publisher to cancel the contract.

"Strip the subject [slavery] of cant," said Grayson, "and the negro slave is the peasant of the Southern States as comfortable, as joyous, as picturesque as any other." In a sense this was perfectly true, but Southern writers found it much easier to portray the happy life of the slave after slavery had disappeared. Irwin Russell, Joel Chandler Harris, and Thomas Nelson Page, using literary forms more acceptable to their readers, succeeded better than Grayson in painting a convincing picture. Grayson is at his best in describing the slaves at play, hunting 'possums or fishing or celebrating the Christmas holidays. His picture of the slaves at work is less convincing. Slavery in South Carolina, except perhaps on such plantations as Grayson's own, was hardly the patriarchal institution that it was in Virginia and Kentucky. Grayson of course employs the stock arguments. The slave has few worries. He is sure of care and protection in sickness and old age. Unemployment and hunger have no terrors for him.

If Grayson's picture of the happy slave seems lacking in power, this is by no means true of his picture of the British wage-slave. It was the English rather than the Northern attacks upon slavery that Grayson most bitterly resented, and his picture of the English day laborer is done with a power that reminds one of George Crabbe's pictures of unhappy English villagers:

> There, unconcerned, the philanthropic eye
> Beholds each phase of human misery;
> Sees the worn child compelled in mines to slave
> Through narrow seams of coal, a living grave,
> Driven from the breezy hill, the sunny glade,
> By ruthless hearts, the drudge of labor made,
> Unknown the boyish sport, the hours of play,
> Stripped of the common boon, the light of day,
> Harnessed like brutes, like brutes to tug, and strain,
> And drag, on hands and knees, the loaded wain:
> There crammed in huts, in reeking masses thrown,

All moral sense and decency unknown,
With no restraint but what the felon knows,
With the sole joy that beer or gin bestows,
To gross excess and brutalizing strife,
The drunken hireling dedicates his life:
Starved else, by infamy's sad wages fed,
There women prostitute themselves for bread,
And mothers, rioting with savage glee,
For murder'd infants spend the funeral fee;
Childhood bestows no childish sports or toys,
Age neither reverence nor repose enjoys,
Labor with hunger wages ceaseless strife,
And want and suffering only end with life;
In crowded huts contagious ills prevail,
Dull typhus lurks, and deadlier plagues assail,
Gaunt Famine prowls around his pauper prey,
And daily sweeps his ghastly hosts away;
Unburied corses taint the summer air,
And crime and outrage revel with despair.[31]

Few Northern or British readers, if Grayson had any, were willing to listen to Southern criticisms of the industrial order, which spelled "progress" for them. It was so much more satisfying to trouble about an accursed institution in the far-off semibarbarous states of the South than to investigate factories and slums nearer home. Only after the proslavery critics of the industrial order were forgotten did Americans in the North in appreciable numbers condemn child labor, long hours, low wages, and insecurity.

The Hireling and the Slave includes satiric portraits of Horace Greeley, Charles Sumner, and Harriet Beecher Stowe, all of which suffer from a readiness to believe malicious rumors. One wishes that Grayson had not charged Mrs. Stowe with writing Uncle Tom's Cabin for money. She seemed to him a "moral scavenger" who

hunts up crimes as beagles hunt their prey;
Gleans every dirty nook—the felon's jail,
And hangman's mem'ry, for detraction's tale,
Snuffs up pollution with a pious air,
Collects a rumor here, a slander there;
With hatred's ardor gathers Newgate spoils,
And trades for gold the garbage of her toils.

[31] The Hireling and the Slave, pp. 24–25. Cf. Wilfred Carsel, "The Slaveholders' Indictment of Northern Wage Slavery," Jour. So. Hist., VI, 504–520 (Nov., 1940).

Mrs. Stowe's motives were not mercenary, but "Snuffs up pollution with a pious air" is a palpable hit, and A *Key to Uncle Tom's Cabin* clearly reveals her as only too willing to print without investigation any slander on slavery that came her way. Grayson refers to the characters in her novel as

> Creatures in fancy, not in nature found—
> Chaste Quadroon virgins, saints of sable hue,
> Martyrs, than zealous Paul more tried and true,
> Demoniac masters, sentimental slaves,
> Mulatto cavaliers, and Creole knaves—
> Monsters each portrait drawn, each story told! [32]

Grayson's other poems call only for brief comment. In 1858 he published *The Country*, which in his *Autobiography* he describes as "a poem intended not so much to celebrate the charms of wood and field, so often celebrated before, as to sketch the changes through which our continent has passed from the rude hut and small clearing of the first settlers, to the fields, meadows and orchards, the farm houses and country seats of the present occupants." The long poem "Chicora" is an Indian story reminiscent of Scott's narrative poems and Thomas Campbell's *Gertrude of Wyoming*, published half a century before. Another long poem, "Marion," was published in *Russell's Magazine* in 1858, and also privately printed in Charleston. Grayson perhaps came nearest to writing poetry of a high order in a short lyric entitled "Threescore Years and Seven," in which he expressed his deep religious feeling. The poem concludes:

> I ask no scholar's lore, no poet's lyre,
>   Trophy nor wreath that conquerors display,
> Nor wealth, nor wit, nor eloquence desire,
>   Nor matchless wisdom, nor imperial sway,
>
> But faith—strong faith—that upward to the sky
>   In every ill unshaken, undismayed,
> Looks, like the eagle, with unblenching eye,
>   Steadfast and bright in sunlight and in shade.
>
> Let this be mine! and if the parting day
>   Grow dark, the wave seem black with winter's gloom,
> Fearless, though rough and perilous the way,
>   I tread the path that leads me to the tomb.

[32] *Ibid.*, p. 41. In a note (pp. 161–162) Grayson sarcastically observes that Mrs. Stowe overlooked among the horrors of slavery "the greatest of them all . . . the cannibalism prevailing in the Southern States." "It will be as authentic as the rest of her facts," he writes, "and as readily believed by her Northern and European readers."

19
The Civil War

SOUTHERNERS BORN in the twentieth century rarely talk or think about the Civil War or, as some prefer to call it, the War between the States. Few of the millions of men and women who lived through it are now alive, and many a young Southerner has never seen a Confederate veteran. Two world wars and the threat of a third have pushed the war out of our consciousness. It is no longer easy for even the Southerner to realize the magnitude of the contest or the bitterness engendered by it. Without some historical study it is difficult to realize that for half a century and more—from about 1830 to 1880 or later—the minds of men and women, especially in the South, were so largely occupied with the sectional controversy culminating in, but not ending with, the war itself. For a whole generation before the outbreak of the war many Southerners were either threatening to leave the Union or were trying to find a way to preserve slavery within the Union. After the war they were embittered and deeply troubled by the catastrophe which had come upon them. They were trying to restore their devastated farms and rebuild their ruined towns and at the same time were endeavoring to find the terms upon which they could live peaceably within a nation reunited by force. For the thoughtful Southerner in 1865–1875 American history since 1830 seemed mainly the tragedy of the suppression of the South.

In the Northern states the memory of the war faded much more quickly. When Mark Twain revisited the Lower South after an absence of over twenty years, he wrote in Life on the Mississippi (1883): "In the South, the war is what A.D. is elsewhere; they date from it. All day long you hear things 'placed' as having happened since the waw; or du'in' the waw; or befo' the waw; or right aftah the waw; or 'bout two yeahs or five yeahs or ten yeahs befo' the waw or aftah the waw. It shows how intimately every individual was visited, in his own person, by that tremendous episode. It gives the inexperienced stranger a better idea of what a vast and comprehensive calamity invasion is than he can ever get by reading books at the fireside."

This chapter is placed out of what may seem its proper chronological position to emphasize the tremendous influence upon Southern writers of the sequence of events from the founding of the Liberator in 1831 to the withdrawal of Union troops from the Southern states in 1877. In those years we have seen a few writers, like Beverley Tucker and George Fitzhugh, defending slavery and advocating withdrawal from the Union. A few writers, like Hinton Rowan Helper and Moncure Daniel Conway, hated slavery so much that they settled in the North before the outbreak of war. In William J. Grayson we found a writer who at the same time was a defender of slavery and an opponent of secession. There were many more who, like John C. Calhoun, tried hard to save both the Union and slavery. We shall see other writers, like William Gilmore Simms, shifting from Unionist to secessionist. We shall see still others who, like John Esten Cooke, Henry Timrod, and Alexander B. Meek, steadily opposed secession but when their states left the Union, loyally supported the Confederate cause. We shall also find Northern-born men, like Daniel K. Whitaker and Albert Pike, supporting the Southern cause throughout the war.

The war, as we shall discover, deprived the Southern writers of their literary market in the North. To some of them, notably Simms and Timrod, it brought poverty, suffering, and premature death. Sidney Lanier in 1865 emerged from a Federal prison with the seeds of tuberculosis in his lungs and only sixteen years to live. A whole generation of young writers like Harris and Cable were deprived of educational advantages such as Southern young men had had before 1861. We shall find them publishing their early writings in Southern magazines and newspapers which paid them little or nothing because as yet the Northern magazines were for the most part unfriendly to the South. We shall see the writers of the New South becoming thoroughly loyal to the Union and yet cherishing an idealized memory of the Old South of slavery and secession. We shall find them welcoming, with some reservations, literary influences from the outside on which too often the Old South had turned its back. We shall find Southern writers finally rediscovering the liberal tradition of the South of Washington and Jefferson. Since that time the South, in spite of some misgivings about the social, economic, and cultural ideals of the North, has been as loyal to the Union as any other part of the nation.

"The Civil War was certainly the greatest disaster in the whole of American history," said T. S. Eliot in Charlottesville, Virginia, in 1933; "it is just as certainly a disaster from which the country has never recovered, and perhaps never will: we are always too ready to assume that the good effects of wars, if any, abide permanently while the ill-effects are obliterated by time." Until after the First World War, such a verdict would have looked like sheer pessimism to most Americans; but in the twentieth century belief in the progressive evolution of society has declined, and one may now question whether the national unity is worth all that it cost in human lives, especially the lives of the finest and fittest young men in both sections.

Some modern historians find it difficult to see the Civil War as an "irrepressible conflict." The quarrel between South and North was chiefly over the extension of slavery into the Western territories, where soil and climate were alike unsuitable for cotton, tobacco, and sugar cane. In his Seventh of March Speech in 1850—for which Whittier bitterly denounced him in "Ichabod"—Daniel Webster maintained that the high and dry plains and the Rocky Mountains blocked the westward extension of the slave plantation. Beyond Missouri and eastern Texas there was no place for the slave plantation to go. Except in the newer states of the South, slavery was none too profitable; and there also in another generation or two it would have been seen for the wasteful institution it was. George Tucker had stated the case years before, but Calhoun and Davis and Sumner and Lincoln thought otherwise. If our ante-bellum statesmen on both sides had understood economic questions as well as their Revolutionary predecessors, they would have seen that war was neither the only nor the wisest solution of the problem. Writing in the *Mississippi Valley Historical Review* in September, 1929, on "The Natural Limits of Slavery Expansion," the late Charles W. Ramsdell said: "It [slavery] had reached its limits in both profits and lands. The free farmers in the North who dreaded its further spread had nothing to fear. Even those who wished it destroyed had only to wait a little while—perhaps a generation, probably less. It was summarily destroyed at a frightful cost to the whole country and one third of the nation was impoverished for forty years. One is tempted at this point to reflections upon what has long passed for statesmanship on both sides of that long dead issue. But I have not the heart to indulge them." [33] In May, 1860, when Alexander H. Stephens predicted a civil war, Richard Malcolm Johnston asked him why he thought war inevitable. Stephens replied: "Simply because there are not virtue, patriotism, and sense enough left in the country to avoid it."

By 1860 many Northern and Southern politicians had lost the ability to understand each other's position. For example, Stephens, who had known Lincoln in Congress years before, said of him after the war: "The Union, with him, in sentiment rose to the sublimity of a religious mysticism, while his ideas of its structure and formation, in logic, rested upon nothing but the subtleties of a sophism!" By 1860 the Abolitionist legend of the South as a land of Simon Legrees and planter barbarians with Negro harems had come to be accepted in the North by millions who did not consider themselves Abolitionists. William Lloyd Garrison had denounced the South as "one great Sodom" and Wendell Phillips had called it "one great brothel,

[33] "The Natural Limits of Slavery Expansion," *Miss. Valley Hist. Rev.*, XVI, 171 (Sept., 1929). See also Walter P. Webb, *The Great Plains* (1931), pp. 184 ff.

where half a million women are flogged to prostitution." The average Southerner, on the other hand, had come to think of the Northern people as
fanatics, money-grubbers, and political schemers embarked on a crusade
against him. The situation was highly explosive. In his *Autobiography*
Joseph Le Conte commented on how emotional and psychological factors
affected men who lived in South Carolina: "At first I was extremely reluctant to join in, and was even opposed to the secession movement; I
doubted its necessity and dreaded the impending conflict and its result. A
large number of the best and most thoughtful men all over the South felt
as I did; but gradually a change came about—how, who can say? It was
in the atmosphere; we breathed it in the air; it reverberated from heart to
heart; it was like a spiritual contagion—good or bad, who could say? But
the final result was enthusiastic unanimity of sentiment throughout the
South."

In the North many must have felt as Hawthorne felt when he wrote to
Horatio Bridge on the eve of war: "The States are too various and too extended to form really one country. New England is quite as large a lump of
earth as my heart can really take in." The great change in Northern feeling came almost overnight with the attack on Fort Sumter. It was like the
effect upon isolationist Americans of the Japanese attack on Pearl Harbor.
The attack on Fort Sumter accomplished one of its purposes, to bring Virginia into the Confederacy, but it aroused in millions of Northern men
and women a passionate devotion to the Union and the flag which most
of the Confederate leaders quite failed to understand. At a meeting of the
Confederate Cabinet in Montgomery, where the proposed attack on Fort
Sumter was being discussed, Robert Toombs, the Secretary of State, warned
Jefferson Davis that the attack meant war. "Mr. President," he said, "at
this time, it is suicide, murder, and will lose us every friend at the North.
You will wantonly strike a hornet's nest which extends from mountains to
ocean, and legions, now quiet, will swarm out and sting us to death. It
is unnecessary; it puts us in the wrong; it is fatal." [34]

Frank L. Owsley has argued that the fundamental cause of the war was
the extreme "egocentric sectionalism" of both South and North.[35] Each
section insisted that it was the real nation—that its interpretation of the
Federal Constitution was the only valid one. Professor Owsley finds "the
timeworn stereotype that the South was attempting the destruction of free
government and the North fighting to preserve it . . . very unrealistic and

[34] Pleasant A. Stovall, *Robert Toombs* (1892), p. 226.
[35] "The Fundamental Cause of the Civil War: Egocentric Sectionalism," *Jour. So. Hist.*, VII, 3–18 (Feb., 1941).

downright silly. . . ." Lincoln's statement at Gettysburg that the war was being fought "that government of the people, by the people, and for the people shall not perish from the earth," beautiful though it is, was, Owsley concludes, irrelevant. That was just what Southerners thought they were fighting for, too. "Their ideology was democratic and identical" with that of the North.

Perhaps the Southern position was never better summarized than by John H. Bocock in the *Southern Presbyterian Review* in April, 1869: "The thing on trial in the American Union, as Southern men thought, was *liberty* —constitutional liberty; the power of the States, the power of persons, to maintain all their constitutional rights, against all claims of power whatever; against the irresponsible constructions of the extent of its own powers by the Federal Government; against reckless and passionate majorities; against all overriding of rights which men in cooler moments established for their own guidance, and bound themselves by written constitutions not to override." Vernon L. Parrington found himself agreeing with Alexander H. Stephens, who, he says:

rightly insisted that slavery was only the immediate *casus belli*. The deeper cause was the antagonistic conceptions of the theory and functions of the political state that emerged from antagonistic economic systems. That the principle of local self-government should have been committed to the cause of slavery, that it was loaded with an incubus certain to alienate the liberalism of the North, may be accounted one of the tragedies of American history. It was disastrous to American democracy, for it removed the last brake on the movement of consolidation, submerging the democratic individualism of the South in an unwieldy mass will, and surrendering the country to the principle of capitalistic exploitation.

Unless one takes into account the psychological impact of the attack on the Stars and Stripes, it is difficult to understand why the North went to war. The seceding states would seem to have had as clear a right to self-determination as most of the clashing nationalities for which Woodrow Wilson spoke in 1918. Those Northerners who hated slavery had by secession got rid of the states which contained the great majority of slaves. What was the advantage of forcing back into the Union people whom they had come to distrust or hate? Was the dominant but unacknowledged motive a desire to punish and humiliate the rebels? John M. Daniel wrote in the Richmond *Examiner* for May 20, 1863:

What is the meaning of this cuckoo-cry of the North, that they are waging war to save the "life of the nation"? Is there no life for them except in a union with

the South? The Confederate States can support a national existence very well
by themselves; why cannot the North do likewise? And how unworthy of any
nation is the plea, that it must die a political death if they lose their association with another, which desires to get rid of the fellowship! Besides, even
if the plea were ever so well grounded, if the North were, indeed, a mere par-
asite incapable of self-existence, does that circumstance confer upon it any
moral right to yoke another people, alien and hostile, to an abhorrent association?

Yet much as one may sympathize with the cause of the Confederacy, no
intelligent person can today wish that the Lost Cause had triumphed. There
was no natural geographical boundary between North and South. There
would have been endless quarreling and perhaps war before the end of the
century. Other sections might have seceded to form new nations, and the
United States might now be a group of small nations like those of Latin
America. What would have happened to them in the twentieth century with
the rise of the great dictatorships?

The Confederate cause, as we see it now, was practically doomed from
the beginning. Few Southerners, however, understood that the Confederacy
lacked the industrial resources needed to fight a successful modern war. The
Confederate leaders fancied that cotton was indispensable to France and
England and discovered too late that those nations would not intervene to
stop the war. They did not see that even if in some miraculous manner the
Confederacy could have won the war, it would have found itself in economic
vassalage to some outside power. The planters would have been unwilling to
give up the agricultural economy for which they had fought in order to
build up the industrial machinery necessary to sustain the economic and
political independence of the new nation. And an industrial regime would
have brought an end to slavery.

The Confederacy, so Frank L. Owsley argued a quarter of a century ago,
died of state rights. The devotion to local patriotism and state sovereignty
made it impossible to keep in line eleven sovereign states, which had
seceded from a Union in which the Federal power had grown too great. If
the Confederate states had at the outset turned over to the new central
government all their soldiers and equipment, the victory at Bull Run might
perhaps have been followed by the capture of Washington and other Northern cities; but even during the last two disastrous years of the war the governors of Georgia and North Carolina were more concerned with resisting
political encroachment from Richmond than they were with actually winning the war. As in the Revolutionary War, men who were willing to fight for
the state in which they lived were not willing to fight in distant states. They

could not see that the only safeguard for the Lower South was to defeat the Union armies in the upper South.

The war, nevertheless, brought to the South a unity of feeling which it had never before possessed and which continued long after the end of the conflict. The manner in which the poor as well as the rich rallied to the Stars and Bars effectually refuted the Abolitionist notion that the South was under the control of an oligarchy of men who owned vast plantations and multitudes of slaves. It also dispelled the notion that the slaves were ready to rebel against their masters. The war became a second and more glorious war for independence. General Sherman wrote to his wife in 1864: "No amount of poverty or adversity seems to shake their faith: niggers gone, wealth and luxury gone, money worthless, starvation in view within a period of two or three years, and causes enough to make the bravest tremble. Yet I see no signs of let-up—some few deserters, plenty tired of war, but the masses determined to fight it out. . . ."

Yet even in wartime Southern unity was never complete. In South Carolina William J. Grayson and James Louis Petigru felt that the secessionists had betrayed the state into the hands of the Abolitionists. The mountaineers, who held few or no slaves, were too isolated to share fully in the movement for Southern independence. Their hostility or indifference made it easier for Sherman to drive a wedge between the Carolinas and the Gulf states. Southerners who had settled in the Northwest loyally supported the Union cause. Many Southern army and naval officers fought for the Union. Conspicuous among these were General George H. Thomas of Virginia and Admiral David Farragut of Tennessee. By the time war actually came, economic developments had made the border states less Southern than they had been even in 1850, when there had been much talk of secession. Lincoln's call for volunteers, issued after the fall of Fort Sumter, brought into the Confederacy North Carolina, Tennessee, Arkansas, and the major portion of Virginia; but Kentucky, Missouri, Maryland, and Delaware remained in the Union.

The Civil War was in many ways the first of modern wars, as European military observers quickly realized. The trench warfare around Richmond was not unlike that practiced in France and Belgium from 1914 to 1918. Both sides made use of balloons, torpedoes, ironclad fighting ships. It was also the first war in which the attempt was made on so large a scale to break down the morale of the civilian population. Sherman's raid through Georgia and the Carolinas and Sheridan's devastation of the Shenandoah Valley were less brutal than events of more recent occurrence in Europe; but they were brutal nonetheless, and it may be that, as James Truslow Adams has sug-

gested, these campaigns made Prussian generals aware of the efficacy of a
policy of *Schrecklichkeit* in overcoming the will of a nation to fight.

The first effect of the war upon writers in the Confederacy was to rein-
force the demand for a literature distinctively Southern. Now more than
ever before, they felt, the South must have its own literature. The Confederate States were a new nation with a unity of feeling that the old Union
had never had. The poets promptly rallied to the call. In "Ethnogenesis"
Timrod wrote in February, 1861:

> Hath not the morning dawned with added light?
> And shall not evening call another star
> Out of the infinite regions of the night,
> To mark this day in Heaven? At last, we are
> A nation among nations; and the world
> Shall soon behold in many a distant port
> Another flag unfurled!

The South was for the first time thrown upon its own literary resources.
The war and the blockade of Southern ports soon cut off the Confederacy
from Northern and European books, magazines, and newspapers. Editors
and publishers now foresaw a greatly enlarged market for Southern books
and magazines. Early in the war the Richmond publishers, West & Johnston,
tried with some success to give the South a publishing house such as it had
never had. On September 13, 1862, the *Southern Illustrated News* con-
gratulated Southerners that they would no longer be compelled to read
"the trashy productions of itinerant Yankees . . . but will, in future, have
Southern books, written by Southern gentlemen, printed on Southern type,
and sold by Southern publishing houses." On November 2 of the same year
the *News* made the surprising claim: "The publishing house of West &
Johnston, in this city, has issued more books from original MSS. during the
past year, than any firm in Yankee land, not excepting our friends Sharper
& Brothers, of New York." In February of the following year George W.
Bagby asserted in the *Southern Literary Messenger* that in the year 1862
West & Johnston had paid in royalties to Southern authors over fifteen thousand dollars, "more than *all* the publishers of the North ever paid in any
one year to Southern writers."

The books brought out by Confederate publishers are not a notable contribution to a Southern literature. Most of the books published by West &
Johnston were of a military nature or were in some way designed to forward the Confederate cause. Among their imprints are Augusta Jane Evans's
Macaria, James Dabney McCabe, Jr.'s, *The Aid-de-Camp*, and William Rus-

sell Smith's play, *The Royal Ape*, a scurrilous satire on Lincoln. West & Johnston also reprinted some of Mary Elizabeth Braddon's popular novels and they published in instalments a translation of Victor Hugo's recent *Les Misérables*, which led Confederate soldiers in Virginia to call themselves "Lee's Miserables." Among the books published by West & Johnston there are only nine that can be classed as belles-lettres, and there are only nine which bear the imprint of Goetzel and Company of Mobile and only seven among those published by Branson and Farrar in Raleigh.

The books published in the Confederacy do not suggest that Southern literary taste differed appreciably from that of Northern readers. The Southern houses were not reprinting Scott's historical romances or the Latin and Greek classics but novels that were attracting attention in the Northern states and in England. There were, for example, no less than five Confederate editions of one or another of Miss Braddon's sensational novels, four in Richmond and one in Mobile. The Confederate imprints include two of Bulwer-Lytton's novels, George Eliot's *Silas Marner*, and two titles by Charles Dickens, whose writings are so often said to have been unpopular in the South.

A number of new magazines were launched, and the old ones struggled on. By 1864, however, it had become extremely difficult to print and distribute any Southern magazine. Subscription prices had risen to the point where most readers were unable to pay them. New type, paper, and ink were difficult or impossible to get, and in Richmond the printers were sometimes taken from the presses to help man the defenses of the city. In its issue of January 23, 1864, the *Magnolia Weekly* estimated that in spite of the strenuous exertions of Southern writers, editors, and publishers the combined circulation of all the literary journals of the South did not equal the Southern circulation of Robert Bonner's *New York Ledger* before the outbreak of war. On February 27 of the same year the *Southern Punch* printed an editorial entitled "Are We a Literary People?" and answered its own question: "More in sorrow than in anger, we answer: it is to be feared we are not."

Among the better wartime magazines were Joseph Addison Turner's *Countryman* (1862–1866) in Georgia, the *Southern Monthly* (1861–1862) in Memphis, and the *Illustrated Mercury* in Raleigh. In Richmond, besides the *Southern Literary Messenger*, which survived until June, 1864, there were the *Magnolia Weekly* (1862–1864), the *Southern Illustrated News* (1862–1865), the *Southern Punch* (1863–1864), and *Smith & Barrow's Monthly* (1864). The *Magnolia Weekly* and the *Southern Illustrated News* more than all others received the support of such recognized men of letters as Simms, Hayne, Timrod, Thompson, Cooke, and Bagby. Well-known women writers responded to the call and new ones came forward to help build up a distinctively Southern literature. What the Southern editors printed, however, suggests that what their readers wanted differed little from what was being published in Northern magazines. Except for an ardent Confederate enthusiasm, there was little to distinguish Southern from Northern literary taste.

On November 22, 1862, the *Southern Illustrated News* printed Hayne's long poem, "The Southern Lyre," in which he called the roll of Southern poets, beginning with Poe. Some of the names were so little known that the editors said in an explanatory note: ". . . it is not remarkable that Southern readers should be ignorant of Southern writers when we remember that the Yankees have hitherto had the making of the commonplace books of Prose and Poetry, and have been careful to exclude from their pages all Southern effusions." The *Magnolia Weekly* published serially from October 17 to November 28, 1863, William Archer Cocke's hastily prepared "Sketches of Southern Literature." How far ignorance and sectional prejudice had blinded him may be inferred from his rhetorical question: "With the exception of Prescot[t] and [George] Ticknor, what great standard authors in literature, has the North produced?"

Not all Southern writers, however, lost their sense of literary values. Just before Cocke's "Sketches" began to appear in the *Magnolia Weekly*, its editor, James Dabney McCabe, Jr., contributed to the number for September 12, 1863, an editorial entitled "Literature the Property of the World," in which he said:

Many persons in the South, influenced by a just hatred of our foes, have made a fierce war upon the literature of the United States. . . . This is unjust. The literature of the North is by no means the exclusive property of that section—it belongs to the world. . . . The person who carries his hatred of the North so far as to wish to destroy what is great in its literature, must be influenced by the same feelings that caused the barbarians to destroy the works of art in Italy.

We may hold the writer an enemy, but his writings should be our friends. Because Irving was a Yankee, he is not the less fascinating, and the fact that Holmes is an Abolitionist does not diminish his wittiness. We cannot, if we would, withdraw our admiration from that which is great, and it is unjust to do so, even though it be the work of an enemy.

The Confederate newspapers printed a certain amount of literary material, but the best of it had already appeared elsewhere. An exception must be made, however, of the writings of "Bill Arp" and the poems of Henry Timrod. The spirited editorials which John Moncure Daniel printed in the

Richmond *Examiner* were widely admired—particularly by those who disliked the Confederate administration—but few of them can hold the reader now. An established feature of the Southern newspaper was the Poets' Corner, and the newspapers were the chief means of popularizing the best poems of the war. When the Southern supply of verse ran short, however, the editors printed the verses of British poets, including the recent work of Tennyson when they could find it. They even reprinted a certain amount of verse by the New England poets, usually without giving the name of the author.

The Northern literature of the war, unlike the Southern, came chiefly from men and women who had no personal experience of the war; and it was written in the main by authors whose names were already well known. This generalization, however, does not apply to Henry Howard Brownell, a Connecticut Yankee who once taught school in Mobile, where years later, attached to Admiral Farragut's flagship, he witnessed a famous sea-fight which he celebrated in verse. Brownell's war poems, though diffuse and filled with unpleasant epithets, are not often matched in power by the work of his Northern contemporaries. The best volume of poems to come out of the war was Walt Whitman's *Drum-Taps* (1865). The war came closer to Whitman than to other Northern poets since he lived in Washington during most of the war years. His poems are notably free from bitterness, and so are those in Herman Melville's *Battle-Pieces, and Aspects of the War* (1866). Among the more memorable war poems to come out of New England are Emerson's "Boston Hymn," Whittier's "Laus Deo," and Lowell's Harvard Commemoration "Ode." Lowell resurrected for the *Atlantic Monthly* our old acquaintance, Hosea Biglow, and made him a mouthpiece for doctrines strangely at odds with those he had expressed during the War with Mexico.

One of the best-known ballads to come out of the war was Whittier's "Barbara Frietchie," which was based upon a newspaper clipping sent to the poet by the Southern-born but violently anti-Confederate novelist, Mrs. E. D. E. N. Southworth. John Moncure Daniel in 1863, noting the Northern vogue of Whittier's ballad, wrote for the *Examiner* an editorial entitled "The Yankee Muse in History." "Verse," he wrote, "is stronger than prose, and history is powerless in competition with the popular ballad." "The uncultivated," he continued, "may pronounce this poem so much unadulterated nonsense, but the wise, the gifted, the good, know that it will outlive and disprove all histories, however well authenticated." The Confederacy faced the prospect not only of defeat on the battlefield but of having everything it fought for misinterpreted for the world by Northern poets and historians.

The Confederate War was fought not only with powder and bullets but with music and verse as well. Songs, ballads, and lyrics not only furnished an outlet for patriotic emotion but also played an important part in marshaling the scattered population of the South for war. The soldiers had their favorite songs, as all soldiers have; not content with borrowing whatever they could use, they sometimes wrote or adapted songs of their own. Behind the lines the women sang in their old-fashioned parlors and at local patriotic gatherings. More numerous, however, than the songs were the hundreds of poems which were quickly broadcast throughout the Confederacy by magazines, newspapers, and broadsides. Patriotic women clipped and pasted them in their scrapbooks or laboriously copied them by hand. In 1862 West & Johnston published the earliest anthology, War Songs of the South, compiled by "Bohemian" [W. G. Shepperson], a correspondent of the Richmond Dispatch. Other collections soon followed. After the war there were many more, of which the best was Simms's War Poetry of the South (1866). Two appeared in England: one in Liverpool in October, 1864, and a second in London in 1866. Even in the North there was enough curiosity about the poetry of the Confederacy to induce Frank Moore to bring out in New York in 1864 his Rebel Rhymes and Rhapsodies.

Many of the poems were published anonymously, and the early anthologists, like most of the later ones, made little effort to identify authors of individual poems. John Williamson Palmer's "Stonewall Jackson's Way" and "In Martial Manner" are even now often reprinted as "Anonymous." As "Anonymous" also usually reappears the Irish poet William Maginn's "The Soldier Boy," beginning: "I give my soldier boy a blade." An illustration of the prestige attached to the authorship of a popular war poem is seen in the claim made by two Southerners, Lamar Fontaine and Thaddeus Oliver, to having written "The Picket-Guard," beginning: "All quiet along the Potomac." The poem was almost certainly the work of a Northern poet, Mrs. Ethel Lynn Beers.[36]

Even in Federal prisons the Confederate poets were still active. At Camp Chase in Louisville the prisoners issued in manuscript a weekly entitled the Rebel 64-Pounder, or Camp Chase Ventilator. Colonel William Stewart Hawkins, of Nashville, was its editor, and Lamar Fontaine was a prolific contributor.

---

[36] Lamar Fontaine's claim was practically disposed of by Joel Chandler Harris and James Wood Davidson in the latter's The Living Poets of the South (1869), pp. 194–201.

The Civil War gave us little in the way of folk songs comparable to those of the cattle country or the Jacobite songs and ballads of Scotland. A few of the literary songs have been taken down by ballad-hunters from the singing of back-country singers of folk songs. Among these is Innes Randolph's "The Good Old Rebel." The *Southern Bivouac* in 1885 recorded some verses of a soldiers' favorite sometimes entitled "Billy Patterson." Every army corps is said to have contributed new stanzas. The genuine folk note is evident in the following stanza:

> Mars' Robert said, "My soldiers,
> You've nothing now to fear,
> For Longstreet's on the right of them,
> And Jackson's in their rear."

Another stanza, written after the Confederate disaster at Nashville, runs:

> You may talk about your Beauregard,
> And sing of General Lee,
> But General Hood, of Texas,
> Played hell in Tennessee.

The best Southern poems of the war came almost invariably from practiced writers of verse; but with the exception of Timrod, Thompson, and a few others, not from writers with an established reputation. The war poetry of the South is characterized by a passionate conviction of the rightness of the Confederate cause and often by a strong religious feeling as well. The diction is distinctly less literary than that of magazine poems of the forties and fifties. The Southern poet had at last an opportunity to express emotions that were common to all loyal Confederates; he was no longer a solitary dreamer but the spokesman for a nation in arms. The outside world had condemned slavery as a barbarous institution, but no suspicion that the Confederate cause was wrong colored his verses.

The poems reflect the changing emotions and events of the war. Secession and the beginning of hostilities brought such poems as Timrod's "Ethnogenesis," James Barron Hope's "The Oath of Freedom," and James Ryder Randall's "Maryland, My Maryland." In these is reflected the new-found unity of the Southern states and a passionate devotion to the Confederate cause. Important events of the war occasioned such poems as John R. Thompson's "On to Richmond," Francis Orray Ticknor's "Our Left," and Timrod's "Charleston." The heroes celebrated in Confederate verse are not Jefferson Davis and Alexander Stephens but soldiers; above all, those killed in battle: Ashby, Pelham, Stuart, and Stonewall Jackson. Toward the close of the conflict the longing for peace is seen in Timrod's "Christmas" and

Mrs. Preston's "When the War is Over," but the spirit of fight is evident to the last. It found expression in John Dickson Bruns's "The Foe at the Gates," written when the capture of Charleston seemed imminent.

> Ring round her! children of her glorious skies,
>   Whom she hath nursed to stature proud and great;
> Catch one last glimpse from her imploring eyes,
>   Then close your ranks and face the threatening fate.
>
> .   .   .   .
>
> From all her fanes let solemn bells be tolled;
>   Heap with kind hands her costly funeral pyre,
> And thus, with paean sung and anthem rolled,
>   Give her unspotted to the God of Fire.

The end of the war occasioned some of the finest poems: Augustus Julian Requier's "Ashes of Glory," Joseph Blyth Alston's "Stack Arms," Father Ryan's "The Conquered Banner," Daniel Bedinger Lucas' "The Land Where We Were Dreaming," and John R. Thompson's "Virginia Fuit." The plight of the defeated South in the humiliation and poverty of the Reconstruction period is nowhere better described than in Paul Hamilton Hayne's "South Carolina to the States of the North."

Reconciliation began more quickly than one would guess from the proceedings of the Congress in Washington. In 1867 a lawyer-poet in Ithaca, New York, read that in Columbus, Mississippi, Southern women had impartially placed flowers on the graves of Union and Confederate soldiers, and Francis Miles Finch wrote "The Blue and the Gray." In 1878 Father Ryan, one of the last to be reconciled, wrote "Reunited"; and James Russell Lowell, ten years after Appomattox, paid in his "Under the Old Elm" a notable tribute to Virginia as the mother of Washington.

Much as North and South hated one another in wartime, they were undergoing similar experiences and responding to them with much the same emotions. And so, ironically enough, the Confederate poems of the war, written to uphold the cause of a new and short-lived nation, seem now an integral part of our national literature. This Simms understood in September, 1866, when he wrote in the Preface to his *War Poetry of the South*: "Though sectional in its character, and indicative of a temper and a feeling which were in conflict with nationality, yet, now that the States of the Union have been resolved into one nation, this collection is essentially as much the property of the whole as are the captured cannon which were employed against it during the progress of the late war. It belongs to the national literature, and will hereafter be regarded as constituting a proper part of it, just as legitimately to be recognized by the nation as are the rival ballads of the cavaliers and roundheads, by the English, in the great civil conflict of their country."

Simms's words seem almost prophetic, but he could hardly have foreseen in 1866 what an inexhaustible storehouse for poetry and romance the Civil War was soon to prove. Walt Whitman, though he had earlier said that "the real war [would] never get in the books," wrote in 1879 in his "Death of Abraham Lincoln": "A great literature will yet arise out of the era of those four years, those scenes—era-compressing centuries of native passion, first-class pictures, tempests of life and death—an inexhaustible mine for the histories, drama, romance, and even philosophy, of peoples to come—indeed the verteber of poetry and art, (of personal character too,) for all future America—far more grand, in my opinion, to the hands capable of it, than Homer's siege of Troy, or the French wars to Shakspere."

The Civil War gave to the reunited nation not only songs and ballads comparable to those of the Roundheads, the Cavaliers, and the Jacobites; it gave American writers, especially in the South, a heroic age more memorable than the American Revolution. Lost causes have a way of acquiring a glamour not so easily attached to that of the victor. Twenty years after Appomattox even Northern readers were accepting the now fully developed romantic Southern legend of the war. In the eighties and nineties few American writers—except Henry James, who had deserted America for England—complained of the barrenness of American life, past or present, as material for literature. As the war receded into the past, it became evident that Cable, Harris, and Page had at their command richer literary materials than Simms, Cooke, and Kennedy had found in the Revolutionary War. Now even the newer Southern states, which had had no share in the Revolutionary drama, had a part in a heroic legend. Shiloh, Vicksburg, and Chickamauga had become magic names comparable to Bunker Hill, Valley Forge, and Yorktown while the fame of Lee, Jackson, Stuart, and Forrest overshadowed that of all the Revolutionary leaders except Washington.

In the New South the literature of England no longer satisfied even the conservative reader. England had not come to the rescue of the embattled Confederacy, and it had finally accepted the Northern interpretation of slavery, secession, and Civil War. The South must produce its own literature and it must justify the fateful course it had taken. More fortunate than most of their ante-bellum predecessors, the writers of the New South found in the eighties a large and sympathetic audience in the North. Aided by friendly and competent Northern magazine editors, who helped them to put their stories into acceptable form, they produced a body of literature superior to that— if we except Poe and two or three others—of the South in any earlier period.

20
Daniel Decatur Emmett

IN TIME OF war men have no scruples about appropriating the tunes of their enemies. Both "The Star-Spangled Banner" and "America" were written to English airs. The music of "John Brown's Body" seems originally to have been a camp-meeting song written by William Steffe, a South Carolinian. Both the words and the music of "Dixie" were the work of an 'Ohioan of Southern parentage. When he was told that the Confederates had adopted "Dixie," he is said to have remarked: "Yes: and if I had known to what use they were going to put my song, I will be damned if I'd have written it!"

Daniel Decatur Emmett (1815–1904), born in Mount Vernon, Ohio, was the son of a Virginia father and a Maryland mother. His education was scanty. After a few years as apprentice to a newspaper printer, he joined the army as a fifer. He is said to have enlisted at seventeen and to have been three times discharged as a minor. He was later connected with various minstrel troupes and he wrote many songs. One of his early hits was "Old Dan Tucker." In 1857 he was engaged by Bryant's Minstrels as musician and composer. On a Saturday in September, 1859, so the story runs, he was asked to have ready on the following Monday a new "walk-around" or "hooray" tune. He wrote the song on a dreary, rainy Sunday. The common showman's phrase "I wish I was in Dixie," it is said, suggested the theme. The music was not altered, but some changes were made in the words which accompanied it. "Dixie" soon afterwards made a hit in New Orleans when it was sung in connection with a performance of John Brougham's burlesque *Pocahontas, or The Gentle Savage*.

Whatever the original meaning of the word *Dixie*, the song soon became a favorite of the Confederates, soldiers and civilians alike. The words of the song were not too literary for the common soldier, and the merits of the tune are of course recognized everywhere. No other national air brings anything like the response that "Dixie" arouses in an American audience. Perhaps, as O. Henry suggested in "A Cosmopolite in a Cafe," it is more loudly applauded in the North than in the South. Before the Confederates adopted "Dixie," however, it had been used as a Republican campaign song at the convention which nominated Lincoln for the Presidency. Possibly this explains why just after Lee's surrender the President asked a band on the White House grounds to play the tune, saying that with the capture of the Confederate army "Dixie" had been captured, too.

21
John Williamson Palmer

Two of the best of the many poems that deal with that Southern Puritan and military genius, Stonewall Jackson—though their authorship was long in dispute—were written by John Williamson Palmer (1825–1906), a Baltimorean by birth.[37] After taking his M.D. degree at the University of Maryland, he joined the Gold Rush of 1849 and became, it is said, the first practicing physician in San Francisco. A year or so later he was in Hawaii, from which he sailed to the Far East, serving for a time as surgeon on a small East Indian steamer. Returning to this country, he gave up medicine and settling in New York devoted himself to literature and journalism. In *Putnam's Magazine* he published a series of tales of the mining camps which, says Professor Mott, "were quite in the earlier manner of Bret Harte, with his elements of literary allusion, local color, and sentimentalism." He published a volume entitled *Folk Songs* (1856) and wrote a play with the title *The Queen's Heart* (1858), which was successfully produced by James E. Owens. His Southern sympathies, however, were so strong that he finally joined the Confederate army. After the war he returned to New York, served on the editorial staffs of the Century and Standard dictionaries and reviewed books for the *Literary Digest*. His collected verse, *For Charlie's Sake and Other Lyrics and Ballads*, appeared in New York in 1901, five years before his death.

Palmer's collected poems include the two popular narrative poems, "Stonewall Jackson's Way" and "In Martial Manner," which under the title "The Brigade Must Not Know, Sir!" still appears as anonymous in most anthologies. They possess a vividness, a compression, and a power rare in the war ballads on either side. In 1891 Palmer wrote an account of the composition of "Stonewall Jackson's Way." He was in Oakland in September, 1862, not far from Antietam, where one of the great battles of the war was being fought.

Early on the 16th there was a roar of guns in the air, and we knew that a great battle was toward. . . . I knew that Stonewall was in it, whatever it might be; it was his way—"Stonewall Jackson's way." I had twice put that phrase into my war letters, and other correspondents, finding it handy, had quoted it in theirs. I paced the piazza and whistled a song of Oregon lumbermen and loggers that I had learned from a California adventurer in Honolulu. The two thoughts were coupled and welded into one to make a song; and as the words gathered to the

[37] See the sketch in *D.A.B.* by Allan Westcott. Palmer's account of the writing of "Stonewall Jackson's Way" is given in *The Photographic History of the Civil War*, IX, 86, 88; see also Francis F. Browne, *Bugle-Echoes*, p. 89.

call of the tune I wrote the ballad of "Stonewall Jackson's Way" with the roar of those guns in my ears. On the morrow I added the last stanza.

The account continues:

In Baltimore I told the story of the song to my father, and at his request made immediately another copy of it. This was shown cautiously to certain members of the Maryland Club; and a trusty printer was found who struck off a dozen slips of it, principally for private distribution. That first printed copy of the song was headed "Found on a Rebel Sergeant of the old Stonewall Brigade, Taken at Winchester." The fabulous legend was for the misleading of the Federal provost marshall, as were also the address and date: "Martinsburg, Sept. 13, 1862."

22

James Ryder Randall

THE AUTHOR OF "Maryland, My Maryland," James Ryder Randall (1839–1908), was the son of a Baltimore merchant. He was tutored by Joseph H. Clarke, who had taught Poe in Richmond, and he studied at Baltimore College, but illness prevented him from taking a degree. After some varied experiences he became in 1860 Professor of English and the Classics in Poydras College in Louisiana. An ardent secessionist, he hoped that Maryland would follow Virginia into the Confederacy. He was greatly excited when he read in the New Orleans *Delta* an account of the fighting in Baltimore between Marylanders and some Massachusetts troops passing through the city. One of his college friends had been killed. Of Randall's several accounts of the composition of the famous lyric, the best was written for Brander Matthews:

That night I could not sleep, for my nerves were all unstrung, and I could not dismiss what I had read in the paper from my mind. About midnight I rose, lit a candle, and went to my desk. Some powerful spirit appeared to possess me, and almost involuntarily I proceeded to write the song of "My Maryland." I remember that the idea appeared to first take shape as music in the brain— some wild air that I cannot now recall. The whole poem was dashed off rapidly when once begun. It was not composed in cold blood, but under what may be called a conflagration of the senses, if not an inspiration of the intellect. I was stirred to a desire for some way of linking my name with that of my native State, if not "with my land's language." But I never expected to do this with one single, supreme effort, and no one was more surprised than I was at the widespread and instantaneous popularity of the lyric I had been so strangely stimulated to write.

The circumstances were strikingly similar to those under which Julia Ward Howe a little later wrote "The Battle Hymn of the Republic." Randall's poem first appeared on April 26, 1861, in the *Delta*, in which he had published earlier poems. The editor of that paper, D. C. Jenkins, had sent Randall the poems of James Clarence Mangan; and the Irish poet's "Karamanian Exile" evidently suggested the unusual metrical form of Randall's poem. One stanza begins:

> I see thee ever in my dreams!
> Karaman!
> Thy hundred hills, thy thousand streams,
> Karaman, O Karaman!

Randall's poem found its way quickly to Baltimore and into the home of Wilson Miles Cary, headquarters for those in the city who sympathized with the South. While his daughter Jennie was trying to find a suitable song for a local glee club to sing, her sister Hettie suggested that she use the words of "Maryland, My Maryland." When her sister began reading the poem, Jennie Cary exclaimed, "Lauriger Horatius," and quickly mated the words to the old German air of "Tannenbaum, O Tannenbaum." The air had been introduced into the Cary household by Burton Harrison, who had learned it at Yale. A little later the Cary sisters were driven out of Baltimore, and Jennie Cary sang "Maryland, My Maryland" to the Maryland troops in Beauregard's army soon after the first Battle of Bull Run. The soldiers had asked to hear a woman's voice. When Jennie Cary, standing in the tent door, sang the lyric, the soldiers caught up the refrain and shouted: "*We* will break her chains! She *shall* be free! She *shall* be free! Three cheers and a tiger for Maryland!"

The air, beautiful though it is, does not measure up to the power and fire of Randall's poem. "Maryland, My Maryland" is one of the two or three finest lyrics that came out of the Civil War. Oliver Wendell Holmes is said to have pronouncd it the greatest of all war songs and to have added: "My only regret is that I could not do for Massachusetts what Randall did for Maryland." The quality of the poem is apparent in the closing stanzas, which are now rarely sung:

> Thou wilt not yield the Vandal toll,
> Maryland!
> Thou wilt not crook to his control,
> Maryland!
> Better the fire upon thee roll,
> Better the blade, the shot, the bowl,

Than crucifixion of the soul,
Maryland! My Maryland!

I hear the distant thunder hum,
Maryland!
The Old Line's bugle, fife, and drum,
Maryland!
She is not dead, nor deaf, nor dumb—
Huzza! she spurns the Northern scum!
She breathes! she burns! she'll come! she'll come!
Maryland! My Maryland!

Randall promptly enlisted in the Confederate army but was soon discharged on account of ill health. His later life was spent mainly in Augusta, Georgia, where he edited the *Constitutionalist*. For a time he was in Washington as correspondent for the Augusta *Chronicle* and private secretary to two Georgia Congressmen. He was an official guest of the state of Maryland at the Jamestown Exposition in 1907, and again in the year of his death the state paid honor to him as the author of one of the best of our state songs. His collected poems appeared in 1908, the year in which he died at the age of sixty-nine.

Although Randall is said to have lost a number of poems still in manuscript, he wrote other war poems which rank among the better poems occasioned by the conflict: "Pelham," "There's Life in the Old Land Yet," "The Battle Cry of the South," and "The Lone Sentry." After Appomattox he wrote "Memorial Day," "Our Confederate Dead," and "At Arlington," which he regarded as his best poem. His early poems, grouped under the heading "Sentimental and Miscellaneous," are immature and imitative— the kind of verses that but for the outbreak of war Randall would probably have gone on writing to the day of his death.

23

Henry Timrod

THE POETIC TALENT of Henry Timrod (1828–1867) was apparently inherited from his father, William Henry Timrod (1792–1838), himself a minor Charleston poet. William Timrod's father, Heinrich Dimroth, came to Charleston from Germany in the middle of the eighteenth century. Changing his name to Henry Timrod, he fought in the Revolution, prospered as a merchant-tailor, and finally set up as a planter. After his death his widow chose as her second husband a man who squandered the property accumulated by her first. William Timrod was destined by his mother for the law; but the bookish lad, imagining that a bookbinder must have access to many desirable books, ran away and apprenticed himself to one of that trade. Even when he had discovered his mistake, he refused to return home. Poorly educated as he was, he cultivated a passion for poetry—even to reading Shakespeare on the roof by moonlight when candles were not available. A fascinating talker, he gathered about him a group of clever young men of superior social station who came to hear him talk while he continued at his work. He edited a weekly, the *Evening Spy*, of which no copies seem to be extant. He wrote a poetic drama, the manuscript of which was lost, much to his son's regret, but several scenes from it were published in the Charleston magazines. In 1814 he published a youthful volume which in later years he regretted having allowed to be printed, *Poems, on Various Subjects*. Much of it is conventional eighteenth-century verse, but the Deistic sonnet "To Superstition" is somewhat better. There are two eclogues with Negro characters, "Morning" and "Noon," in which plantation life is treated in the manner of the Neoclassical pastoral but with some attempt to give the real speech of the Low-Country Negro. In "Noon" Sampy and Cudjoe stage a song contest about the charms of their sweethearts while the driver sleeps. Quasheboo, who sets himself up as judge, awards the prize to Sampy, but he first empties it of the New England rum which it contains. Five of William Timrod's later poems are preserved in Hayne's edition of Henry Timrod's poems. Among them are "To Time, the Old Traveller," which Washington Irving is said to have praised; a spirited anti-Nullification lyric beginning, "Sons of the Union, rise!" and "To Harry," addressed to his son Henry. As captain of the German Fusiliers of Charleston, William Timrod took part in the Second Seminole War, but hardships brought on tuberculosis, of which he died in 1838 when his son Henry was only ten years old.

Henry Timrod, who is after Poe and Lanier the best of the Southern poets, was born in Charleston on December 8, 1828, one year earlier than the date recorded on his tombstone. His mother, Mrs. Thyrza (Prince) Timrod, sent her son to Christopher Coates's school, where he occupied a seat next to that of his lifelong friend Paul Hamilton Hayne. There he showed Hayne his first attempt at verse-making, "a ballad of stirring adventures, and sanguinary catastrophe!" Seeing the two boys discussing the ballad, the unsympathetic one-eyed Yankee principal thrashed them both.

While Hayne attended the College of Charleston, Timrod—aided, it is said, by a friendly Charleston merchant named Ross—entered the University of Georgia in January, 1845. Ill health or lack of money led to his withdrawal a year and a half later. "A large part of my leisure at college," he told Hayne, "was occupied in the composition of love verses, frantic or tender. Every pretty girl's face I met acted upon me like an inspiration!" Some of these juvenile verses are said to have been published in the Charleston *Evening News* over a pseudonym which has not been identified.

Returning to Charleston, Timrod began the study of law in the office of James Louis Petigru. He soon found the law distasteful. On one occasion Petigru sent the absent-minded young poet on an errand to a factor. By and by Timrod returned to confess that he had totally forgotten the message he was to convey. "Why, Harry, you are a fool!" said the lawyer in his highest squeaking voice. And, Timrod added when he told the story to Hayne, "I would have been a fool to Mr. Petigru to the end of my days, even had I revealed in after-life the genius of a Milton or a Shakespeare!" Abandoning the study of law, Timrod renewed his classical studies—he was especially fond of Homer, Vergil, Horace, and Catullus—hoping for a place as a college teacher. Finding no such position, he became a tutor. For the next decade he taught in rural schools or tutored in planters' families in various parts of the Carolinas. The South Carolina communities now claiming Timrod are as numerous as the Greek cities which claimed Homer as a native son. Timrod's occupation—the kind usually reserved to some wandering pedagogue from New England or New Jersey—was not particularly congenial, but it was better than the law would have been. Though it kept him for much of the year away from his Charleston friends, it gave him some leisure for study and writing.

Beginning in January, 1849, Timrod contributed many verses over the pseudonym "Aglaus" to the *Southern Literary Messenger*, then edited by John R. Thompson, one of his staunchest admirers. In *Russell's Magazine* (1857–1860), edited by Hayne, Timrod found a medium for critical prose as well as verse. Early in 1860 the Boston house of Ticknor and Fields, which had already published two volumes by Hayne, brought out—presumably at Timrod's expense—his *Poems*, the only volume of his verse to appear in his lifetime. Timrod had carefully revised the best of his early poems, and he had high hopes of its success. There were a few favorable reviews, but the book did not sell as rapidly as its author had hoped. After his death in 1867 Simms induced the publishers to send him the remainder of the small edition so that he might sell it for the benefit of the poet's widow and sister. A reviewer, writing in *Harper's Magazine* for February, 1860, wrote what still seems a just appraisal of the book. He found in it "the indications of true poetical genius," considerable skill in versification, "a refined vein of sentiment," and genuine feeling. He closed with the prediction: "Mr. Timrod's name now comes before us for the first time, but he has given assurance in this volume that he will not remain a stranger in the walks of American poetry." Timrod had gone far toward perfecting his technical skill, but he had as yet little to say. His most common subjects were love and nature, but he also wrote of death, poetry, and literary fame. The only long poem in the volume is "A Vision of Poesy," a narrative in which, echoing Keats's "Endymion" and Shelley's "Alastor," he developed none too effectively his conception of the Poet. One stanza alone suggests the future author of "Carolina" and "The Cotton Boll":

> Before my power the kings of earth have bowed;
> I [Poesy] am the voice of Freedom, and the sword
> Leaps from its scabbard when I call aloud;
> Wherever life in sacrifice is poured,
> Wherever martyrs die or patriots bleed,
> I weave the chaplet and award the meed.

Timrod was born in the same year as Rossetti, Meredith, Tolstoy, and Ibsen, but he seems to belong to an earlier literary generation. It was the war that quickly developed into maturity Timrod's poetic talent; and yet this Southern Tyrtaeus was not a secessionist, was not an advocate of "Southernism in literature," and had as yet shown little interest in writing of the Southern scene.

After the outbreak of war Timrod returned to Charleston, where for a year he seems to have done some writing for one or more of the local newspapers. His early war poems, copied from newspaper to newspaper, soon brought him recognition as a significant Confederate poet. On December 10, 1861, he wrote to Rachel Lyons, "La Belle Juive" of his poems:

Most of my friends being absent from the city, I have, since my arrival, led almost the life of a hermit. Except an occasional stroll to the newspaper offices, I have gone *nowhere*. In this isolation I feel more than ever the inconveniences of the war. No new books, no reviews, no appetizing critiques, no literary correspondence, no intellectual intelligence of any kind! Ah! it is a weary time! To volunteer is now the only resource against utter *ennui*. The Camp is *life*. Thither flow exclusively all the currents of thought and action, and thither, I suppose, I must betake myself if I would not die of a social and intellectual atrophy. I only await the return to the city of some recruiting friends, to see what Mars will do for one of the humblest votaries of Apollo. If I can get a satisfactory position, you may soon sing "The Minstrel has gone to the wars." . . .

I do wonder whether this damnable war will ever end.

On March 1, 1862, Timrod enlisted in Company B of the Twentieth South Carolina Regiment. He was assigned as clerk to regimental headquarters, but even the clerical work proved too much for his frail health. After an interval, with the permission of his commanding officer, he joined the Army of the West as correspondent for the Charleston *Mercury*. He arrived just in time to be caught in the retreat from the Battle of Shiloh, which the death of Albert Sidney Johnston had converted from victory to defeat. Timrod, in Hayne's words, "staggered home, half blinded, bewildered, with a dull red mist before his eyes, and a shuddering horror at heart." A little later he became assistant editor of the Charleston *Courier*. Toward the close of the year 1862 Theodore D. Wagner, a well-to-do businessman, C. G. Memminger, Confederate Secretary of the Treasury, and others promoted a plan for bringing out in London a handsome edition of Timrod's poems. Frank Vizitelly, war correspondent of the London *News*, had offered to supply illustrations. Timrod set to work revising his poems and had them set up in type. The corrected proofs were sent to England (John R. Thompson's poems were sent at the same time), but they were apparently lost in the blockade. Thus vanished Timrod's last chance of seeing his best poems appear in book form. To the end of his life he hoped in vain to see a collected edition of his poems.

With the financial assistance of Wagner, Timrod obtained an interest in the Columbia *Daily South Carolinian* and with it the post of associate editor. His primary task was to write editorials and to review such new books as were available. He began work on the paper in January, 1864, and in February he married an English girl, Katie Goodwin, whose brother George had married Timrod's sister Emily. The best of his love poems are addressed to Katie. During his few remaining years Timrod did not write many poems, but he published in the *Carolinian* some editorials which throw light upon his conception of the relations of war to literature.

The last years of Timrod's life are among the saddest in our literary history. When Sherman's army approached Columbia, Timrod went into hiding, knowing that his writings had made him obnoxious to the Federals. The burning of Columbia almost ruined him financially. Ill from tuberculosis and at times unable to work at all, he could not find permanent employment of any kind. He and his wife both tried unsuccessfully to find places as tutors, but in the universal poverty of the South few families had any money to pay tutors. He wrote for the newspapers, which paid him little or nothing, and for a short time he held a clerical position in the office of Governor Orr. He published a few poems in two of the postwar magazines, the *Southern Opinion* of Richmond and *Scott's Monthly Magazine* of

Atlanta. In the summer of 1865 he had asked his friend Richard Henry Stoddard to try to sell some of his poems to editors of the New York magazines. These men expressed sympathy for the unfortunate Southern poet,
but they would have none of his poems. Had he lived a few years longer,
he might, like Hayne, have been able to overcome the hostility to Southern
writers.

In his last two or three years Timrod was in desperation endeavoring to
support not only his wife and mother but the family of his widowed sister.
Only the assistance of friends and the sale of the family furniture and silver
saved them from outright starvation. On March 30, 1866, Timrod wrote to
Hayne:

You ask me to tell you my story for the last year. I can embody it all in a few
words—beggary, starvation, death, bitter grief, utter want of hope. . . . Both
my sister and myself are completely impoverished. We have lived for a long time
and are still living on the gradual sale of furniture and plate. We have eaten two
silver pitchers, one or two dozen forks, several sofas innumerable chairs and a
bedstead. . . . My days of verse, I am afraid are over! I have written but one
brief poem in the last three years. God knows what has come over or overcome
me—I begin to fear that my poetry was but the effervescence of youth, and
that I have survived its power to bubble and sparkle. Or perhaps there is nothing
to blame but the damned drudgery and worse things through which I have passed.

I not only don't write verse now, but I feel perfectly indifferent to the fate
of what I have written. I would consign ever[y] line I ever wrote to eternal
oblivion for one hundred dollars in hand.

Timrod did not starve, but the want of proper and sufficient food had its
effect upon his weakened constitution. Simms and his Columbia friends,
almost as poor as Timrod, helped him with loans and gifts of whatever they
had. In search of a better climate, he twice visited Hayne at "Copse Hill" in
the Georgia pine barrens but found only temporary improvement. The end
came on October 7, 1867. Edgar Allan Poe had died on October 7 exactly
eighteen years before.

Hayne promptly claimed the privilege of collecting Timrod's poems and
writing a memoir of his friend; but it was not until 1873 that he found it
possible to publish such a volume. Hayne's editorial work was competent and
the memoir is perhaps still the best account of Timrod's life, but Hayne took
unwarranted liberties in revising those portions of the letters that he included in the memoir. In one instance he published as from a single letter
passages taken from two separate letters. Timrod's letters, which are simple
and direct, seemed to Hayne too unliterary to represent the poet, and he
translated parts of them into his own more ornate style.

Timrod's friends were loyal to his memory. Thirty years after his death the Timrod Memorial Association placed a stone over his grave in Columbia, erected a bust in Charleston, and brought out an edition of his poems. In 1928 Colonel Henry T. Thompson, son of one of his old friends, published in Columbia a biography entitled *Henry Timrod: Laureate of the Confederacy*.

The loyalty of South Carolinians to Timrod's memory is a pleasing testimony to the vitality of his poetry in that state, but the crowning of Timrod as "the Poet Laureate of the Confederacy" has not promoted the growth of his reputation outside of the South. It has made him seem much more the local poet than he was. He deserves to be read and studied not as a local poet but as an American poet of power and originality who shared experiences which, broadly speaking, were those of the American people during the four most critical years of our history. It is true that most of his best poems deal in one way or another with the war, but if he had lived another twenty years, these would have bulked no larger in his collected works than do the war poems in Whitman's *Leaves of Grass*.

The chief reason for the comparative neglect of Timrod in our literary histories was not, as his Southern admirers often maintained, an antipathy to the Confederate poet but simply the lack of adequate sources of information about the man and his work. In the early 1940's Southern scholars began at last to make amends for their long neglect of the poet. There is still no adequate biography and no collected edition of his writings, but the critic and literary historian may find much relevant material in my *The Last Years of Henry Timrod* (1941), Guy A. Cardwell's *The Uncollected Poems of Henry Timrod* (1942), and Edd Winfield Parks's *The Essays of Henry Timrod* (1942).

Timrod's attitude toward the poetic art was not that of the amateur. He had taste, intelligence, ambition, and industry. He formed his style upon the best models he knew. He read both the ancient and the British classics as well as the chief poets of his own time, but the writers who influenced him most were Milton, Wordsworth, and Tennyson. The influence of Wordsworth was the strongest and the most congenial. He wrote one poem which might almost pass for one of Wordsworth's own, the sonnet beginning:

> At last, beloved Nature! I have met
> Thee face to face upon thy breezy hills. . . .

The Tennyson influence, not always happy, is seen too often in the early poems in a fondness for sentiment and verbal embroidery. "To Marie" seems like a weak echo of "Locksley Hall"; "The Arctic Voyager," a better poem, is too obviously reminiscent of "Ulysses"; and "Hark to the Shouting Wind" borrows inappropriately the metrical pattern of "Break, Break, Break." In the war poems, however, there are few discernible echoes of other poets; there the style and manner are indisputably Timrod's own.

Timrod's theory of poetry is expounded in his critical prose, which consists chiefly of three articles in Russell's Magazine—"The Character and Scope of the Sonnet," "What is Poetry?" and "Literature in the South"— and "A Theory of Poetry," which was delivered as a lecture at Columbia early in 1864. Timrod twice attacked William J. Grayson's definition of poetry as primarily metrical language. In his lecture he gave much of his time to a refutation—the only good one—of Poe's contention that there is no such thing as a long poem. Using for illustration Paradise Lost, which Poe had singled out for criticism on this score, he demonstrated conclusively the fallacy underlying Poe's reasoning. Timrod's view of the nature and function of poetry is close to that of Wordsworth. His definition of poetry, however, is somewhat reminiscent of Keats and De Quincey: "I think when we recall the many and varied sources of poetry, we must perforce confess that it is wholly impossible to reduce them all [as Poe had done] to the simple element of beauty. Two other elements at least must be added; and these are power, when it is developed in some noble shape, and truth, whether abstract or not, when it affects the common heart of mankind." [38]

The war, as I have said, matured Timrod's poetic talents, and it gave him for the first time deep emotional experiences that he could express in verse —emotional experiences which he shared with thousands who had not read his earlier poems. In his war poems there is little verbal embroidery, little echoing of other poets, and no trace of sentimentality. He had found his true substance and form. His war poems, many of which deal only indirectly with the war, express the various emotions of a people engaged in a war for their existence as a nation. When the first Confederate Congress met in Montgomery, he wrote the stately ode, "Ethnogenesis," celebrating the birth of a nation. In another ode, "The Cotton Boll," he found the inevitable symbol of the new nation. "Carolina" and "A Cry to Arms" are passionate appeals comparable to Burns's "Bannockburn" and Campbell's "Ye Mariners of England." "Ripley" is an elegy written in the spirit of Wordsworth's "The Happy Warrior." "The Unknown Dead" is a better poem than the many of our time dealing with the Unknown Soldier's tomb in Arlington Cemetery. "Spring," certainly one of Timrod's three or four best poems, uses the war only as a dark background for a description of the approach of the lovely Carolina Low-Country spring. "Charleston" reflects a mood not

[38] For Timrod's discussion of the problem of a Southern literature, see p. 344.

of defiance and hate but of calm assurance that whatever the outcome of the threatened siege, the city will acquit itself in the hour of trial in a manner worthy of its history and traditions. The most perfect of all his poems is the "Ode" (in the Horatian sense) sung at the memorial exercises at Magnolia Cemetery on June 16, 1866—not 1867, as generally stated. Professor G. P. Voigt discovered in the Charleston *Courier* for July 23, 1866, a new version of the poem revised by its author but included in no edition of his poems. Here is the poem, as appropriate as Emerson's "Concord Hymn" and as perfect as William Collins's "Ode" beginning: "How sleep the brave who sink to rest / By all their country's wishes blest!"

> Sleep sweetly in your humble graves,
> Sleep, martyrs of a fallen cause;
> Though yet no marble column craves
> The pilgrim here to pause.
>
> In seeds of laurel in the earth
> The garlands of your fame are sown;
> And somewhere, waiting for its birth,
> The shaft is in the stone!
>
> Meanwhile, your sisters for the years
> Which hold in trust your storied tombs,
> Bring all they now can give you—tears,
> And these memorial blooms.
>
> Small tributes, but your shades will smile
> As proudly on those wreaths today,
> As when some cannon-moulded pile
> Shall overlook this Bay.
>
> Stoop, angels, hither from the skies!
> There is no holier spot of ground
> Than where defeated valor lies,
> By mourning beauty crowned!

24
Francis Orray Ticknor

THE PARENTS OF Dr. Francis Orray Ticknor (1822–1874) were both natives of Connecticut, but they were married in Savannah, where the father, Dr. Orray Ticknor, practiced medicine. Soon after their marriage the Ticknors moved to Fortville in Jones County, where Francis Orray was born only a few months before his father's death. Somewhat later the mother removed to Columbus in the same state. In 1835 Ticknor was sent to a boys' school in Pittsfield, Massachusetts, kept by the Reverend R. M. Chapman, whose curriculum included English, Latin, Greek, French, mathematics, drawing, and singing. Ticknor received his medical education in Philadelphia and New York and then spent a year in his mother's birthplace, Norwich Town, Connecticut. When in 1844 he began to practice medicine in Muscogee County, Georgia, he found the life of a country doctor oppressively lonely. In 1847 he married Rosalie Nelson, who belonged to a well-known Virginia family. Ten years later the Ticknors settled at "Torch Hill," a plantation on the Chattahoochee River not far from Columbus. The house commands an impressive view of a long expanse of the beautiful river which was later to flow through the lines of Sidney Lanier's best-known poem. Here Ticknor lived for the remainder of his life, practicing medicine, cultivating evergreens, roses, and fruit trees, planning mechanical improvements, for he had the ingenuity of a Connecticut Yankee, and cultivating music and poetry principally for the entertainment of himself and his friends. From time to time he wrote on horticultural subjects for the *Southern Cultivator*. Many of his poems were written on prescription blanks while he was in the saddle riding long distances to see his patients. He did not take himself very seriously as a poet, and in spite of Paul Hayne's appreciative letters (their correspondence began in 1869) he probably did not realize that his poetic talents were considerable. He printed his verses in the *Southern Cultivator, Church Register*, and *Land We Love*, and in various newspapers; but they did not appear in book form until five years after his death. The best of his poems were written during and soon after the Civil War, in the course of which he worked in various hospitals in and near Columbus. As in the case of Timrod, the war matured his poetic talent, and his best poems deal with the war. The Reconstruction regime depressed him so much that on January 17, 1867, he wrote to General D. H. Hill that he was thinking of moving to Northeast Texas. "The prospect here," he wrote, "is appalling. I predict a wilderness in two years." Nevertheless, he remained at "Torch Hill" until his death, which was due to his visiting patients before full recovery from illness.

Edmund Clarence Stedman wrote to Mrs. Paul Hamilton Hayne, April 24, 1881, after reading some of Ticknor's poems: "The man was, within his limits, a born poet—there is no doubt of it." Little is known of Ticknor's reading or of the poets whom he admired. He did not care for the kind of verse that was most popular when he wrote to Hayne on March 26, 1871: "As for me, I am quite content to relegate the aesthetic exaltation of this present America to Bret. Harte and the composer of Shoo fly! Anything heavier would break its back." He added, however: "But that's cynical!" The poet whom Ticknor most resembles is Browning. At his best he has something of Browning's power, compactness, and vivid colloquial diction. Though he wrote competent tributes to several of the Confederate leaders, the best of his poems is "Little Giffen," which he came near destroying thinking it too true to be good poetry.[39] This ballad first appeared in General Hill's magazine, the *Land We Love*, in November, 1867. It has for its subject the story of one of Dr. Ticknor's wartime patients, a sixteen-year-old Confederate soldier, Isaac Newton Giffen, son of a blacksmith in East Tennessee. In September, 1863, Dr. and Mrs. Ticknor took him from a Columbus hospital to "Torch Hill," where with the aid of a faithful black mammy they nursed him back to health. In March, 1864, Giffen left to rejoin the army and was never heard from again.

> "Johnston pressed at the front," they say;—
> Little Giffen was up and away!
> A tear, his first, as he bade good-by,
> Dimmed the glint of his steel-blue eye.
> "I'll write, if spared!" There was news of fight,
> But none of Giffen—he did not write!

In a different vein is "The Virginians of the Valley," from which I quote the concluding stanza:

> We thought they slept! the sons who kept
> The names of noble sires,
> And slumbered while the darkness crept
> Around the vigil fires.
> But still the Golden Horse-Shoe Knights
> Their Old Dominion keep,
> Whose foes have found enchanted ground,
> But not a knight asleep.

[39] "Little Giffen" was reprinted in *Burke's Weekly for Boys and Girls* (Atlanta), IV, 138 (Oct. 29, 1870) along with Ticknor's "William Nelson Carter" under the heading "The Boy Knights." A headnote, apparently written by the poet, suggests a parallel between the two dead Confederates and Sir Galahad. These and many other poems by Ticknor appeared under the title "The Midnight Cross in Idylls." The general arrangement and notes on other poems suggest that Ticknor had planned to publish them in book form and, failing to find a publisher, had printed them in *Burke's Weekly*.

25
Abram Joseph Ryan

ABRAM JOSEPH RYAN (1838–1886), whose poems were widely read in the dark days that followed Appomattox, was born in Hagerstown, Maryland. Some time in the ten years that preceded his birth his parents had come from Clonmell in Ireland to Norfolk, Virginia. Not long after his birth they were in St. Louis, where Ryan entered the Christian Brothers' School. He attended Niagara University, where he studied under the Vincentian fathers. He became a priest in 1856. He taught for a time at Niagara University and at the diocesan seminary at Cape Girardeau, Missouri. In September, 1862, he joined the Confederate army as a chaplain. In shriving the dying and carrying wounded soldiers off the battlefield, he revealed uncommon physical courage. He is even said on occasion to have seized a musket and fought beside the men in gray. At the Gratiot prison in New Orleans he ministered to victims of smallpox when no other minister would undertake the task. In that city Father Ryan was once summoned to appear before the notorious General Ben Butler to answer the charge that he had refused to bury a dead soldier because he was a Yankee. He defended himself by saying: "Why, I was never asked to bury him and never refused. The fact is, General, it would give me great pleasure to bury the whole lot of you." After the war he lived for a time near Beauvoir, Mississippi, where he knew Jefferson Davis. Ryan was among the irreconcilables until 1878, when the yellow fever epidemic of that year brought money, nurses, and physicians from the North. Then he wrote "Reunited."

A popular lecturer wherever he went, Ryan was nearly always on the move. He was stationed for a few years at Augusta, where he edited the *Banner of the South*. In New Orleans at one time he edited a Catholic weekly, the *Star*. He was at various times stationed in Biloxi, Mississippi; at Nashville, Knoxville, and Clarksville, Tennessee; at Macon, Georgia; and at Mobile, Alabama, where he made his longest stay as pastor of St. Mary's Church from 1870 to 1883. In 1882 he published a beautifully written book of devotions entitled *A Crown for Our Queen*. He left unfinished a life of Jesus. He died in 1886 at a Franciscan monastery in Louisville. He was buried in Mobile, where a monument was erected to his memory with dimes given by Southern school children.

Father Ryan had no high regard for his verses; he did not like to call them poems. They were, he said, "written at random—off and on, here, there, anywhere—just when the mood came, with little of study and less of art, and always in a hurry." It was only after persistent urging by Hannis Taylor that he agreed to permit them to be published in book form. Some of his religious poems—"Song of the Mystic," "The Seen and the Unseen," and "De Profundis"—compare favorably with much of our religious verse, but his best poems were devoted to the Lost Cause. "In Memory of My Brother" and "In Memoriam—David J. Ryan, C.S.A." commemorate a younger brother killed in the war. The best known of his poems are "The Conquered Banner" and "The Sword of Robert Lee." His great admiration for Lee appears also in "Sentinel Songs," which concludes:

> Ah! Muse, you dare not claim
> A nobler man than he,
> Nor nobler man hath less of blame,
> Nor blameless man hath purer name,
> Nor purer name hath grander fame,
> Nor fame—another Lee.

The duty of the Southern poet was, he felt, to keep alive the memory of the Confederacy.

> When falls the soldier brave,
> Dead at the feet of wrong,
> The poet sings and guards his grave
> With sentinels of song.

In the same poem he speaks of his own verses:

> I sing with a voice too low
> To be heard beyond to-day,
> In minor keys of my people's woe,
> But my songs will pass away.
>
> To-morrow hears them not—
> To-morrow belongs to fame—
> My songs, like the birds', will be forgot,
> And forgotten shall be my name.
>
> And yet who knows? Betimes
> The grandest songs depart,
> While the gentle, humble and low-toned rhymes
> Will echo from heart to heart.

Ryan's best and most famous poem, "The Conquered Banner," first appeared in the *Freeman's Journal* of New York on May 19, 1866, over the pen name of "Moïna." This pseudonym led Simms to ascribe the poem to a New Orleans writer, Mrs. Anna Peyre Dinnies, who employed the same pen name. Francis F. Browne in *Bugle-Echoes* (1886) quoted a portion of a letter from Ryan in regard to the writing of the poem: "I wrote 'The Conquered Banner' at Knoxville, Tenn., one evening soon after Lee's surrender, when my mind was engrossed with thoughts of our dead soldiers and dead cause. I never had any idea that the poem, written in less than an hour, would attain celebrity. No doubt the circumstances of its appearance lent it much of its fame. In expressing my own emotions at the time, I echoed the unuttered feelings of the Southern people; and so 'The Conquered Banner' became the requiem of the Lost Cause."

The most conspicuous literary influence in Father Ryan's poems is that of Edgar Allan Poe. In them one finds a somewhat similar melancholy tone, a verbal melody akin to Poe's—although he occasionally reminds one of Swinburne—and a fondness for reiterated rhymes.

> Furl that Banner, for 'tis weary;
> Round its staff 'tis drooping dreary;
> Furl it, fold it, it is best;
> For there's not a man to wave it,
> And there's not a sword to save it,
> And there's not one left to lave it
> In the blood which heroes gave it;
> And its foes now scorn and brave it;
> Furl it, hide it—let it rest!

26
Innes Randolph

In 1910 John A. Lomax printed in his *Cowboy Songs* what he took to be a genuine folk ballad which the cattlemen sang under the title "I'm a Good Old Rebel." The cowboy singers had preserved only four stanzas, with some verbal differences, of Innes Randolph's (1837–1887) "The Good Old Rebel," a rather bitter expression of Southern feeling in the months that followed upon Lee's surrender. The poem still appears as anonymous in most anthologies. Here is the first stanza as Randolph wrote it:

> O I'm a good old rebel,
> Now that's just what I am;
> For the "fair land of freedom,"
> I do not care a damn;
> I'm glad I fit against it,

I only wish we'd won,
And I don't want no pardon
For anything I done.

Randolph wrote what must have seemed to him far better poems, but this is the only one that ever got any real response from the public. His poems remained uncollected until 1898—eleven years after his death—when they were published in Baltimore with a Preface written presumably by his son Harold, who said of him: "Born and brought up in Virginia at a time when the old-fashioned, narrow ideas concerning the 'pursuits proper for a gentleman' held full sway, he was not permitted to turn his attention to music, painting, sculpture or literature, in any one of which, with proper training, he might have accomplished great things." The proper career for a Randolph was of course law or politics, and Innes Randolph studied law.

He was born in Winchester in the Shenandoah Valley. During the war he was a captain of engineers on "Jeb" Stuart's staff and one of the most accomplished members of the Mosaic Club in Richmond. For three or four years after Appomattox he lived in Richmond. He then went to Baltimore to practice law. There he drifted into journalism, writing for the Baltimore *American* editorials, book reviews, articles on art, and music and dramatic criticism. He was an amateur actor of some talent, and he took the leading role in the operetta, *Bombastes Furioso*, staged by the Wednesday Club. Sidney Lanier was a member of the Club and one of Randolph's most intimate friends. Randolph showed his understanding of poetry and music when he defended Lanier's much criticized "Centennial Cantata." At the poet's funeral he was one of the pallbearers. Remembered if at all as a friend of Lanier, Randolph deserves to be studied in his own right.

Among the poems written soon after the close of the war one of the best is "John Marshall," in which, like John R. Thompson, Randolph reflects the chagrin of proud Virginians whose state had now become "Military District No. 1." In the *Poems* (1898) there are four pages of "Vignettes," brief poems in irregular rhythms, most of which give the writer's impressions of travel in Europe. When they were composed is not clear, but since Randolph died in 1887, they were certainly written before the poems of Stephen Crane and the Imagistic free verse of the twentieth century. Here are two of them:

A low, hanging full moon,
Yellow gleams falling on the sombre plain,
Glint of white cottages,
Silvery trunks of birch trees
And tall spires of poplar

Casting dark shadows along
The flat French highway.

An orchestra rising wild, impetuous
Pleading, passionate,
For lovers Tristram and Isolde
Clasped in a kiss—
Silent—
The violin voices speaking for them
To those who can listen.

It is a far cry from a song sung by Texas cowboys to lines that would have
done no discredit to "H.D." or Amy Lowell. Innes Randolph's poems, says
his son, "are indeed but the irrepressible outpourings of a naturally poetic
and artistic nature," but perhaps our literature would have been considerably richer if he had been able to devote his life to literature rather than to
law, war, or journalism.

27
John Pendleton Kennedy

In the early years of the nineteenth century, when John Pendleton
Kennedy (1795–1870) was growing into manhood, his native Baltimore
was emerging from the village stage into a thriving commercial town. Its
society was more homogeneous and more aristocratic than it was to become
in his later years. As the town grew, newcomers of various types poured
in; among them were French refugees; Scotchmen, Irishmen, and Dutch-
men. The successful merchants, seldom natives of Baltimore, were usually
immigrants from Britain, Holland, or New England. As the little city became more of a center of commerce and manufacturing and less exclusively
a market for tobacco, mercantile interests came to dominate those of the
planters. Baltimore was slowly becoming a part of the industrial North,
and its atmosphere was becoming distinctly less Southern than it had been
in the eighteenth century. These changes in his native city had their effect
upon Kennedy, whose point of view gradually became less Southern and
more national.

Although Baltimore had in Kennedy's youth, as he wrote in "Baltimore
Long Ago," "its fine old gentlemen, and its accomplished lawyers, divines
and physicians, and its liberal, public-spirited merchants," it was never a
cultural or literary center comparable to Boston. Kennedy was to learn that,

as he once wrote, "fine writing falls on the business world like water on a duck's back." The few men who wrote and published books were chiefly lawyers, journalists, or New Englanders living temporarily in Baltimore. Among the last were John Neal, Jared Sparks, and John Pierpont. On January 18, 1843, Emerson wrote to his wife from Baltimore: "I learn that a very large proportion of the people in active professions are Yankees." Emerson records the somewhat inaccurate answers his Baltimore friends gave to his inquiries: " 'Have you any libraries here?'—'None'—'Have you any poet?'—'Yes; Mr [John N.] McJilton.'—'Who?'—'Mr McJilton.' 'Any scholar?'—'None.' Charles Carroll the Signer is dead, & Archbishop Carroll is dead, and there is no vision in the land." If Emerson's Baltimore friends mentioned Kennedy, he probably forgot him since he attached little importance to novels.

Kennedy's background and temperament made the law less uncongenial than journalism would have been. The ablest and most respected of the Baltimore intellectuals were lawyers. Among the distinguished members of the Baltimore bar were Luther Martin, Generals Harper and Winder, William Wirt, and William Pinkney. To Pinkney's daughter Charlotte, sister of the poet, Kennedy was for a short time engaged. William Wirt, who spent his last years in Baltimore, probably came nearer to being Kennedy's model than any other man. He dedicated his first book to Wirt, and in 1849 he published a two-volume biography of his friend. Consciously or not, he followed in Wirt's footsteps in law, political life, and in literature. Wirt, who thought highly of Kennedy, once recommended him to President Monroe as "a scholar and a gentleman—intelligent, liberal and enlightened. . . ."

In Kennedy were united two ancestral strains less antagonistic than a later generation likes to imagine: the Scotch-Irish merchant and the Virginia planter. His father, John Kennedy, came from Ireland soon after the Revolution. From him the novelist is said to have derived his "relish for humor and [his] love of friends." Intellectually Kennedy is supposed to have owed more to his mother, Nancy Pendleton, who belonged to a widespread and distinguished Virginia family. Among Kennedy's cousins were the Cooke brothers, Philip Pendleton and John Esten. Another relative was David H. Strother ("Porte Crayon"), who illustrated the second edition of Swallow Barn. Nancy Pendleton's home was in Martinsburg in Berkeley County (now in West Virginia) at the northern end of the Shenandoah Valley. The most influential of Kennedy's Virginia relatives, after his mother, was his uncle Philip Pendleton, of whom he wrote in 1828: "I think [him] the first man in point of talents, acquirements and manners that I have ever been acquainted with." "Mr. Pendleton," writes Henry T. Tuckerman, "was a genuine specimen of the old school Virginia gentlemen, a Federalist of the strictest pattern, and one of those rural lords of the manor, so well described in 'Swallow Barn,' easy-going, warm-hearted, intelligent, with intense local pride, tenacity of opinion, and a kind of philosophical *dolce far niente* habit characteristic of the landed gentry of his State." This conservative planter, whose sympathies during the Civil War were with the Union, followed his nephew's career with sympathy and pride, but he never hesitated to state their points of disagreement. After reading one of Kennedy's addresses, he wrote: "I dare say that, like old Polonius, I have attained to a plentiful lack of wit, but I beg leave to say that the address of yours before the Mechanics' Institute is, in my judgment, an admirable one, tasteful and appropriate in the highest degree, albeit it contains, as it inevitably must, some fuss and fustian about the dignity of labor."

In 1804 an unfortunate speculation by a business partner involved Kennedy's father in difficulties which in 1809 resulted in bankruptcy. The Kennedy family now lived the year round at "Shrub Hill," their small country place near Baltimore; and a farm in Virginia belonging to his mother became the chief support of the family. In 1820 Kennedy's parents settled on this farm, which was situated near Charlestown in Jefferson County (now in West Virginia). Kennedy remained in Baltimore, but during most of his life he spent a month each summer visiting his numerous Virginia relatives. He was fond of country life, and he liked to travel. The deaths of his father in 1826, of his mother in 1854, and of a favorite brother Andrew, a Virginia planter, in 1858 weakened in some degree his ties with the Old Dominion; but even the Civil War, in which most of his kinsmen took the Southern side, did not wholly sever them.

Meanwhile, in spite of his father's financial difficulties, Kennedy's education had not been neglected. He attended a Baltimore academy presided over by a Mr. and Mrs. Priestley. William Sinclair, the original of Parson Chub in *Swallow Barn*, was Priestley's chief assistant and eventually his successor. Sinclair was a Presbyterian minister of Irish birth who according to Kennedy "had been private tutor and companion to Lord Castlereagh, the Prime Minister, by whom in the time of the Irish rebellion, he was very badly treated. . . ." "He was," says Kennedy, "a good scholar, with the kindest heart and the most attractive simplicity of character." Sinclair's Academy was combined with another to form Baltimore College, from which Kennedy graduated with the first class in 1812. His literary taste was developed mainly from his study of the ancient classics and the English writers of the eighteenth century. In an autobiographical sketch he describes his studies:

> I worked hard during these years to accomplish myself in a whole circle of science and learning. I studied Greek a whole winter, by rising before daylight; I read Locke, Hume, Robertson—all the essayists and poets, and many of the metaphysicians; studied Burke, Taylor, Barrow; worked at chemistry, geometry, and the higher mathematics, although I never loved them; made copious notes on all the subjects which came within my study; sketched, painted (very badly), read French, Spanish, and began German; copied large portions of Pope's translations of Homer, and wrote critical notes upon it as I went along; in short, I thoroughly overworked myself through a number of years in these pursuits. . . .

He had begun to write very early; and, though he was shy about appearing as an author, he was already dreaming of literary fame. "Essays, treatises, notes, journals, farces, poems, travels, pencil sketches, paintings—what author ever was prouder of his collection!"

After his graduation Kennedy drifted naturally into the law, which he studied first under his uncle Edmund Pendleton, and afterwards under Walter Dorsey. Meanwhile the War of 1812 had interrupted his legal studies and brought on a martial fever in Kennedy as in other youthful Baltimoreans. He was fond of the pomp and circumstance of military life. He saw action at the Battle of Bladensburg, where although he ran away like the rest of the militiamen, he bore off on his shoulders a comrade with a broken leg.

When in 1816 he began the practice of his profession, Kennedy found it uncongenial. His real taste was for letters and politics. Preferring the business side of the legal profession to active practice, he became a trustee for various estates and counsel for local banks. In his early years he lived with three other young bachelors, one of whom, Peter Hoffman Cruse, shared his literary interests. Together the two published anonymously at fortnightly intervals in 1819–1820 a periodical in the *Spectator* tradition called the *Red Book*. "This little book," they said in their Preface, "comes before the publick eye, the careless offspring of chance, unsupported by patronage and unadorned by the tinsel of name or fashion. . . . It possesses this advantage, that let the world slight it as it may, it will always be *red*—a greater favour, surely, an author could not wish." The little pamphlets were made up chiefly of light verse by Cruse and of light and satirical sketches and essays by Kennedy. Cruse published some delightful adaptations from Horace under the title "Horace in Baltimore." Kennedy's part in the *Red Book* was distinctly promising. The plan of the work was in the Addisonian tradition with some echoes from Swift. Kennedy had obviously also read Irving's

Salmagundi, Knickerbocker's History, and such numbers of *The Sketch Book* as had appeared. In one of his stories, "The Recollections of Mr. Bronze," he described a country family of good birth but unprogressive and poorly educated who had sunk to the status of "a very respectable family, old settlers in these parts." The material is similar to that of *Swallow Barn,* but the author's attitude is not sympathetic.

Kennedy was elected to the Maryland Legislature in 1820 and served for three years. He was known as an advocate of internal improvements. He was an admirer of Henry Clay, of whom he saw a good deal after his election to Congress in 1838. Through the influence of William Wirt he was in 1823 offered the post of Secretary of the American Legation in Chile, but his approaching marriage led him to decline it. Early in 1824 he married Mary Tennant, daughter of a prosperous shipping merchant in Baltimore. She died a few months later. In 1829 he married Elizabeth Gray, to whom he wrote many delightful letters. Her father, Edward Gray, was a wealthy manufacturer of Irish birth and Whig views in politics, whom Washington Irving thus characterized: "Mr. Gray is a capital specimen of the old Irish gentlemen—warm-hearted, benevolent, well-informed,. and, like myself, very fond of music and pretty faces, so that our humors jump together completely." Kennedy regarded his father-in-law as "the tenderest, lovingest, most considerate man, full of the finest impulses and most generous qualities I have ever found."

Kennedy meanwhile had been giving many of his evenings to writing, and in 1832 he published *Swallow Barn, or A Sojourn in the Old Dominion,* which is still his best-known work. The book had been a long time in the writing. Kennedy had noted in his journal on October 19, 1828: "On Saturday I recommenced my Swallow Barn on the new plan, and finished the first chapter." He read the manuscript chapter by chapter to his friend John H. B. Latrobe, who notes that parts of both *Swallow Barn* and *Horse-Shoe Robinson* were often rewritten. Since the manuscript was not long enough to make a two-volume book, Kennedy rather awkwardly included a forty-five page sketch of the life of Captain John Smith. The reviews were favorable, but Kennedy's profits on the first edition of two thousand copies were only $782.59, very far short of paying for a house costing over $15,000 which he built in 1834. He did not heed the advice of A. H. Everett, who wrote in the *North American Review* for April, 1833, that the author should "withdraw his attention from other objects, and devote himself entirely to the elegant pursuits of polite literature, for which his taste and talent are so well adapted. . . ." In fact, though his publisher was calling for a revised edition by 1835, Kennedy waited until 1851 to bring out a second edition.

In 1832 our only successful professional authors were Cooper and Irving. Kennedy had no notion of giving up a certain income from law and business for the meager rewards of writing. He could mildly censure Wirt for not giving his time and energies to literature, but he apparently adjudged himself by a different standard. Irving once wrote to Mrs. Kennedy that her husband took pride "in showing the world that a literary man can be a man of business."

Swallow Barn was a venture in the eighteenth-century tradition being kept alive by Wirt, Irving, and others. *Horse-Shoe Robinson*, which followed three years later, is a full-length historical novel in the manner of Cooper and Scott. Kennedy dedicated the American edition to Irving, whom he had first met in 1832, and the English edition to Samuel Rogers, the friend of many American writers. His friend Latrobe wrote the song beginning, "You may talk as you please of your candle and book." *Rob of the Bowl* (1838), though it brought Kennedy twice as much money as *Swallow Barn*, seems to have attracted less attention than its predecessors. His later publications include *Quodlibet* (1840), a brilliant satire on Jacksonian Democracy; *Memoirs of the Life of William Wirt* (1849); a number of addresses; a few essays and sketches; and a superb historical short story, "A Legend of Maryland."

In 1853, when Irving advised him "to write diligently now for a few years on some good work," Kennedy replied that he was "preparing such an enterprise in the plan of a work intended to give a history of the political and social condition of this country during the ten years preceding the revolution." This *magnum opus* never came to completion. Kennedy's health was not robust; Baltimore made many claims upon him for addresses and other public services; he was fond of social life and of travel; he was financially independent—no wonder he found his literary ambitions flagging.

In 1838, the year of *Rob of the Bowl*, Kennedy was elected to Congress on a protectionist platform. He was the first Whig Congressman elected from his district, and he served for three terms (1839–1840, 1841–1845). While in Congress, he was at various times chairman of committees on commerce and international copyright, and he was instrumental in getting an appropriation which enabled Samuel F. B. Morse to demonstrate the value of his new invention, the electric telegraph. In 1846 he lost his seat in Congress, but he was once more elected to the Maryland House of Delegates, which promptly chose him as its Speaker. In 1852 President Fillmore appointed him Secretary of the Navy. In that capacity Kennedy's best-remembered act was the sending of Commodore Perry's expedition to Japan.

By the time his term expired in 1853, Kennedy, like Wirt and Wilde before him, had grown tired of political life and disgusted with politicians. "Do you remark," he wrote to Philip Pendleton, "how lamentably destitute the country is of men in public station of whom we may speak with any pride? We have, with very few exceptions, no man of eminent ability, none of high accomplishment, none of lofty sentiment, in any conspicuous position. How completely has the conception and estimate of a *gentleman* been obliterated from the popular mind! . . . What a miserable array of charlatans and make-believe statesmen and little clap-trap demagogues and mock gentlemen manufactured out of blackguards, are everywhere in the lead!"

Kennedy had no sympathy with the South Carolina secessionists, but he had a high regard for the gentlemen of the Palmetto State. He wrote to his South Carolina friend, Judge G. S. Bryan on January 12, 1860:

South Carolina is always paramount in the congregation of the elect, and most to be admired in the true nobleness of its aristocracy. The gentleness and refinement of high breeding, attract such instant regard, when brought into contrast with the vulgar ostentation which seeks to supplant it, and which is everywhere so obtrusive and ambitious an element of what claims to be our upper society, that I more than ever regret the sectional spirit which keeps the real gentry of our country, North and South, so distinctly apart, and prevents such missionaries as your old families can supply, from uniting with their kindred classes "across the line," to inspire a national esteem for the elegancies of character, love of what is good, scorn for what is base, purity of taste, and contempt of all make-believe.

Kennedy regarded slavery as essentially a temporary institution. Although he pictured it half sympathetically in *Swallow Barn*, he believed that slavery was keeping the Southern states from fully enjoying the benefits of industrial and commercial expansion. He could not see that slavery justified either genuinely honest affection for it or vehemently honest indignation against it. "The wrath that is stirred against it, and the patriarchal beauty that is claimed for it," he wrote in December, 1860, "are both offsprings of excited imaginations." The Abolitionist movement seemed to him "a moral epidemic . . . like St. Anthony's Dance in the fourteenth century. The fancy of getting up 'a great abomination,' in order to turn it to account as a topic of popular preaching, is as old as the first consecrated cobbler."

When the Civil War broke out, Kennedy took the Union side without hesitation. He denounced South Carolina's secession as "a great act of supreme folly and injustice passed by a set of men who have inflamed the passions of the people and driven the State into an enterprise which history will record as the most foolish of blunders as well as the most wicked of crimes." After the war he republished in book form a series of articles which he had written for the Washington *National Intelligencer*, calling the book *Mr. Ambrose's Letters on the Rebellion* (1865). They are among the ablest statements of the Union position, but they are thoroughly partisan and show little sympathy for the Confederacy.

Kennedy had a gift for making friends, and he valued the friends which his books made for him. His first literary friends were Southerners, like Cruse, Wirt, his Cooke cousins, John R. Thompson, and Simms. With the New England writers he had little contact before 1841, when he met Longfellow in Philadelphia. He first visited Boston in 1847. In 1863 Harvard gave him the LL.D. degree, and in the same year Dr. Holmes invited him to a dinner with the Saturday Club, writing: "You will be welcome either as man of letters or statesman." He was on excellent terms with Holmes, Longfellow, Lowell, and Prescott, but it may be doubted whether in literary tastes he had much in common with Emerson, Thoreau, Whittier, or Hawthorne. His most congenial literary friend was Washington Irving. Their period of greatest intimacy began in 1853. It is worth noting that what Kennedy wrote after 1832, the year he first met Irving, bears less resemblance to Irving's writings than his earlier work. Irving's fondness for Gray and the Kennedys appears in a letter of March, 1856: "My dear Kennedy, my intercourse with you and your family has been a great sweetener of the past few years of my existence and the only attraction that has been able to draw me repeatedly from home."

Kennedy's relations with Edgar Allan Poe were less intimate, but he befriended the penniless young genius at a crucial time in the very beginning of his career. Long afterwards Poe wrote: "Mr Kennedy has been at all times a true friend to me—he was the first true friend I ever had—I am indebted to him *for life itself*." Wirt, it will be remembered, had failed to see any conspicuous merit in "Al Aaraaf," but Kennedy was one of the three judges who awarded to Poe the Baltimore *Saturday Visiter's* fifty-dollar prize for his "MS. Found in a Bottle." Kennedy wrote in his journal for November 11, 1833:

> In July last I was appointed, together with John Latrobe & Dr Miller, a committee, by the editor of the Saturday Morning Visiter to decide upon a prize tale and poem. Early in October we met for this purpose and having about a hundred tales and poems. The prize for the tale we gave to Edgar A. Poe, having selected that call[ed] "A MS. found in a bottle" from a volume of Tales furnished by him. The volume exhibits a great deal of talent, and we advised him to publish it. He has accordingly left it in my possession, to show it to Carey in Phil—a

On hearing of Poe's death in October, 1849, Kennedy wrote in his journal: "It is many years ago, I think perhaps as early as 1833 or '34, that I found him in Baltimore in a state of starvation. I gave him clothing, free access to my table and the use of a horse for exercise whenever he chose; in fact brought him up from the very verge of despair." He got Poe his position on the *Southern Literary Messenger*, where his writings soon began to attract attention. Although Kennedy discerned Poe's great talents, he had no great fondness for the kind of writing Poe was doing. In recommending Poe to the proprietor of the *Messenger*, he stated that Poe was "highly imaginative, and a little given to the *terrific*." He added: "He is at work upon a tragedy [*Politian*], but I have turned him to drudging upon whatever may make money. . . ." After some months he wrote to Poe: "You are strong enough now to be criticized. Your fault is your love of the extravagant. Pray beware of it. You find a hundred *intense* writers for one *natural* one." After Poe's death Kennedy pronounced him "an original and exquisite poet, and one of the best prose critics in this country."

With William Makepeace Thackeray, Kennedy was more congenial, for Thackeray loved the eighteenth-century classics and he was a gentleman of the kind dear to the Marylander's heart. They first met on Thackeray's earlier visit to the United States in 1852–1853. On his second visit in 1855–1856 Thackeray mentioned in a letter "Mr. J. P. Kennedy, exceedingly pleasant, natural and good-natured; and he has introduced me to a club— O Gods such a dreary club!" They discussed Thackeray's projected American sequel to *Henry Esmond*, and Kennedy lent him some books on the Revolution. *Swallow Barn*, if Thackeray read it, would have been much more valuable to him. He asked Kennedy for some pertinent facts about George Washington, who was to appear in *The Virginians*; but when Kennedy gave him the traditional account, he interrupted him somewhat testily and said: "No, no, Kennedy, that's not what I want. Tell me, was he a fussy old gentleman in a wig? Did he take snuff and spill it down his shirt front?" Kennedy took Thackeray on a visit to his brother Andrew in Virginia so that the British novelist might see something of plantation life for himself.

He met Thackeray for the last time in Paris in 1858, while *The Virginians* was appearing in instalments. On September 26 Kennedy wrote in his journal:

Thackeray calls to see me, and sits an hour or two. He is not looking well. He tells me he has need of my assistance with his Virginians,—and says Heaven has sent me to his aid. He wants to get his hero [George Warrington] from Fort Duquesne, where he is confined a prisoner after Braddock's defeat, and to bring him to the coast to embark for England. "Now you know all that ground," he says to me, "and I want you to write a chapter for me to describe how he got off and what travel he made." He insists that I shall do it. I give him a doubtful promise to do it if I can find the time in the thousand engagements that now press upon me on the eve of our leaving Paris. I would be glad to do it if circumstances will allow.

Tuckerman, who printed this paragraph in his life of Kennedy in 1871, failed to find in Kennedy's journal any further mention of the matter, and years later John H. B. Latrobe, writing a sketch of Kennedy for *Appleton's Cyclopaedia of American Biography*, stated that Kennedy had told him he had written the fourth chapter of the second volume of *The Virginians*. In the years that followed there was some controversy over what if anything Kennedy had actually written. It is obvious to the American reader of the episode in question—which, incidentally, covers somewhat more than one chapter—that Kennedy could hardly have made Thackeray's mistake of referring the making of maple sugar to the autumn of the year. Edward M. Gwathmey has apparently set the controversy to rest for all time, for he found in Kennedy's journal four pages overlooked by Tuckerman. Kennedy in a conversation gave Thackeray the information he desired and later put it into writing. On October 3, 1858, Kennedy noted: "I write nearly all the morning preparing notes for Thackeray—an outline of the chapter he wants—and in making a rough map of illustration." Five years later, hearing of Thackeray's death, he wrote: "[He] got me to write him a sketch for a chapter in the *Virginians*, which I did and he afterwards partially incorporated it in the book."

Kennedy's literary tastes, as shown for example in his letters to Poe, were conservative. Although he believed in progress, he had no great sympathy with reformers and people with a "mission." He had, like his Southern friends, no enthusiasm for Socialism, Abolition, or Transcendentalism. He was not in sympathy with certain newer modes of writing. He wrote to Judge G. S. Bryan in 1854: "We have so much *intensification* of late, such gushing emotions in such excruciating words, such a distillation of wonderful quintessences in such incomprehensible alembics of thought, and such a rattle and roar of poetical locomotives, that the man who will recall the art back to the domain of common sense, and restore the human heart to its old place in the human economy, and render it, once more an honest and intelligible viscus, will be, I think, entitled to a general vote of thanks, and, if he get his deserts, be made Vice-President, at least, in the Republic of letters."

Kennedy was not a literary critic, and he never formulated his literary creed. He did, however, suggest his conception of history and historical romance in the opening paragraphs of "A Legend of Maryland." That conception almost certainly owes something to Scott's romances and perhaps also to Macaulay's essay on "History." After some comments on the dullness of the conventional history which deals only with governmental development, legislation, wars, treaties, and statistics, he continues:

But that which makes history the richest of philosophies and the most genial pursuit of humanity is the spirit that is breathed into it by the thoughts and feelings of former generations, interpreted in actions and incidents that disclose the passions, motives, and ambition of men, and open to us a view of the actual life of our forefathers. When we can contemplate the people of a past age employed in their own occupations, observe their habits and manners, comprehend their policy and their methods of pursuing it, our imagination is quick to clothe them with the flesh and blood of human brotherhood and to bring them into full sympathy with our individual nature. History then becomes a world of living figures,—a theatre that presents to us a majestic drama, varied by alternate scenes of the grandest achievements and the most touching episodes of human existence.

In "A Legend of Maryland," as in *Horse-Shoe Robinson* and *Rob of the Bowl*, Kennedy wrote like a very human antiquarian, interested in the people of a past age and in what was vital and picturesque in their life and environment.

James Russell Lowell, who published "A Legend of Maryland" in the *Atlantic Monthly*, noted that Kennedy the man and the author possessed much the same qualities:

He was in the highest sense a genial man. He had a singular gift for companionship, for being something better than his books, and his finer qualities were lured out by the sympathy of the fireside. He was excellent in anecdote and reminiscence. His talk had just that pleasant suspicion of scholarship in it that befits the drawing-room, and never degenerated to the coarser flavor of pedantry. . . . He had the somewhat rare excellence of being playfully earnest; and, though he had strong convictions, never made them the scourge of other men.

Lowell did not find Kennedy "a man of genius in the creative sense of that somewhat elastic word"; he placed him "in the company of authors who simply know how to be agreeable." Of his books Lowell said:

They are refined, manly, considerate of our grosser apprehensions; they attempt no solution of the problem of the Infinite (as it is called); they abound in cheerful pictures of natural scenery; and they will have a real value for the historian, from their lively notices of manners already remote. Perhaps the strongest impression they leave upon the mind is that they were written by a gentleman, a profession of greater consequence than is generally conceived.

Swallow Barn (1832), which bears a family resemblance to Wirt's *The Letters of the British Spy* and Irving's *Bracebridge Hall*, is not a novel but, as Kennedy himself described it, "a series of detached sketches linked together by the hooks and eyes of a traveller's notes. . . ." "There is," he said, "a rivulet of story wandering through a broad meadow of episode." The book is in fact a more faithful picture of Virginia plantation life than a romantic novel could possibly have been.[40] Kennedy knew that life like a native Virginian, but he could also view it with the perspective of an outsider. He made no attempt to throw over the planters that aura of glamour which is found in the stories of Caruthers, Cooke, and Page. The homely simplicity of that life appealed to Kennedy; and he managed to get into his book something of the "mellow, bland, and sunny luxuriance of her [Virginia's] old-time society—its good fellowship, its hearty and constitutional *companionableness*, the thriftless gayety of the people, their dogged but amiable invincibility of opinion, and that overflowing hospitality which knew no ebb. . . ." Except for the practical omission of all types but the planters, the lawyers, and the slaves, *Swallow Barn* remains the best picture of Virginia life in the early nineteenth century.

Horse-Shoe Robinson (1835) is a full-fledged historical romance covering parts of Virginia and the Carolinas and culminating in a vivid description of the Battle of King's Mountain. With the exception of Cooper's *The Spy* (1821), it was the first really notable romance of the Revolution and was the first to deal with the war in the South. In his Preface Kennedy commented on the fact that thus far "only the political and documentary history of that war has been written," leaving its romantic and picturesque features to writers of fiction. The novel includes a number of exciting incidents to which Kennedy does full justice, but his usual method of narration is too leisurely to please the modern reader.[41] The range of characters

---

[40] It is surprising that Wirt had little enthusiasm for the book. He wrote to Dabney Carr, May 23, 1832: "Pray have you seen a new work called 'Swallow Barn' which is dedicated *to me*. It is said to be by John P. Kennedy, a right merry young lawyer of this place. It is a *sort* of a novel, of which the scene is laid in Virginia—but it is a *non descript* sort of a novel—very little incident—& a great deal of what is called sketches of characters —It is said to be much puffed in Philadᵃ There[?]— But it is too much like Paulding's conceited style for my taste—too much verb[i]age & too little matter—a light, trifling, fantastic style—flippant & smart enough—but no deep and strong drawing or solemnising [?]— This is *entre nous*—for as I am complimented by the dedication, it wᵈ seem ungrateful in me to decry the work—but to you I say whatever comes uppermost."

[41] In his review of the revised edition of the novel, Simms wrote: "Mr. Kennedy is not distinguished as a raconteur. His merits lie in portraiture of character, and, especially,

includes a Tory Virginia planter and his daughter, who is of course a patriot, a rustic Carolina maiden and her lover, partisans on both sides, and certain British and American officers, notably Tarleton and Marion. Major Butler, the conventional hero, is quite as colorless and ineffective as that other Butler in Scott's *The Heart of Midlothian.* The one memorable character is the "woodland hero" Horse-Shoe Robinson himself, who plays a role similar to that of Cooper's Leather-Stocking and Simms's numerous scouts.

For this character Kennedy professed to have a model. In the Introduction to the 1852 edition he described in some detail his own brief acquaintance with Galbraith Robinson, with whom he had spent an evening in western South Carolina in the winter of 1819. Robinson's adventures had supplied him with two interesting episodes which are not, however, integral parts of the romance: how he escaped from Charleston and how he took the five Scotchmen prisoners. These, says Kennedy, "the reader will find preserved in the narrative . . . almost in the very words of my authority." Kennedy claims to have "retained Horse Shoe's peculiar vocabulary and rustic, doric form of speech." He concludes the Introduction by giving Robinson's reaction to the novel when a friend of Kennedy's read it to him in extreme old age on the banks of the Tuscaloosa: "It is all true and right—in its right place—excepting about them women, which I disremember. That mought be true, too; but my memory is treacherous—I disremember." All this, as John Robert Moore has suggested, sounds less like fact than fiction; but there can be no doubt that Robinson was an actual person. He died near Tuscaloosa, Alabama, on April 28, 1838, at the age of seventy-eight. Alexander Beaufort Meek, who knew him, praised him in "The Day of Freedom" as one whose chivalrous deeds were comparable to those of Douglas and Percy. Of Kennedy's novel, which he greatly admired, he wrote:

> Romance hath wreathed,
> With flowery fingers and with wizard art,
> That hangs the votive chaplet on the heart,—
> His story, 'mid her fictions, and hath given
> His name and deeds, to after time.[42]

---

in a happy perception of the piquant and the humorous. . . . The true attraction of the work lies wholly in the character of 'Horse-Shoe Robinson'" (*S.Q.R.,* VI, 204, July, 1852). He found some shortcomings in dialect, history, and geography.

[42] *Songs and Poems of the South* (New York, 1857), p. 232. See also William Russell Smith, *Reminiscences of a Long Life* (Washington, 1889), I, 332 n.

Kennedy wrote in his journal on Feb. 7, 1830: "Invited Warren R. Davis of South Carolina M.C. to dine with me to-day. He is an old acquaintance made while I was in Pendleton District in 1818. I want to get the story of Horse Shoe Robinson from him."

Horse-Shoe Robinson is certainly one of the finest characters in our early fiction. Courageous, honest, resourceful, athletic, the blacksmith scout and protector of his friends is more alive than any other character that Kennedy created.

Rob of the Bowl (1838) is a historical romance of a somewhat different type. It tells the story of the conflict between Protestant and Catholic, and the scene is laid in Maryland's first capital, St. Mary's. In the hands of Simms or Cooke the plot would have turned into melodrama, but Kennedy chose rather what Parrington calls "the vein of the cavalier romantic." He worked up his màterials with close attention to historical accuracy even in the matter of archaic speech, and the story is told with charm and lightness of touch. Kennedy brought together a rare assortment of characters —too many in fact: Rob himself, a gentlemanly blackguard, who having lost his legs has had the stumps bound in a bowl; his lost son Albert Verheyden, aristocratic young clerk to the Governor; a swaggering pirate, who like the clerk, loves the beautiful Blanche Warden; Garret Weasel, the garrulous innkeeper, and his termagant wife; and many others.

Kennedy's only other important venture into fiction—except the delightful "Legend of Maryland," which has affinities with Rob of the Bowl—is Quodlibet (1840), written as propaganda for the Whig party in the year of a Presidential election. This satire on Jacksonian Democracy skilfully hits off the Democratic hatred of aristocracy and social superiority of the Whigs, its canting phrases, its fustian, demagoguery, and buncombe. It is ably written, but it is very partisan and, for the modern reader who does not know the political background, impossible to appreciate fully. Kennedy was giving to his party talents that should have been given to literature.

After the death of William Wirt in 1834, the Wirt family asked not only John Quincy Adams and Salmon P. Chase but also Washington Irving to write a biography of the distinguished lawyer. When all of them declined, the family, at the suggestion of Chase, asked Kennedy to write it. The Memoirs of the Life of William Wirt (1849; revised edition, 1850) is a substantial two-volume life and letters. In some respects the task was congenial, but portions of the biography are dull, as official biographies generally are. The book includes many valuable letters, but Kennedy's versions often lack the raciness of the originals. He should have made more of Wirt's literary activities, and he slighted The Old Bachelor, which he did not appreciate at its full value. Wirt's life before his second marriage in 1802 is treated too sketchily, and the first wife is shuffled off the scene much too quickly. Kennedy, knowing the second Mrs. Wirt and her children, probably found it difficult to give a full and accurate picture of Wirt in the early years when he drank too freely and was fond of practical jokes.

Kennedy's first book is his best—not because it is better written than the others but because in *Swallow Barn* he described the life which he knew well from observation and experience. In his historical romances, excellent though they are, he was attempting to portray life in earlier periods which he could never know intimately. His place in American literature rests upon the books which he published in the 1830's. In his later years he made vague plans for books which were never written. "He was," as Parrington has well said, "a man of letters rather than a lawyer, and if he had eschewed politics and law and stuck to his pen our literature would have been greatly in his debt. Few Americans of his day were so generously gifted; none possessed a lighter touch."

28
William Alexander Caruthers

Dr. WILLIAM ALEXANDER CARUTHERS (1802–1846) was a Virginian and he was immensely proud of his native state, but he was a Virginian of a different sort from Beverley Tucker and George Fitzhugh. They defended slavery on principle. Tucker was one of the earliest of Southern secessionists and Fitzhugh was a vigorous critic of the ideals of "free society." Caruthers hated slavery and did his best to promote intersectional good will.

Caruthers was born in Lexington in the Valley of Virginia. In later times Lexington was to be the home of Margaret Junkin Preston, Matthew F. Maury, Stonewall Jackson, and Robert E. Lee. There were few slaves in the Lexington area, and religious, cultural, and commercial ties with the North were stronger than in Tidewater Virginia. In the memorable debate on slavery in the Virginia General Assembly in 1832 almost all the representatives from west of the Blue Ridge advocated measures looking toward emancipation. In this debate Samuel McDowell Moore, who represented Rockbridge County, in which Lexington is situated, spoke of slavery in language that Jefferson or St. George Tucker might have used. Slavery, he said, had an "irresistible tendency . . . to undermine and destroy every thing like virtue and morality in the [white] community." It had the effect of causing the whites to feel that manual labor was "degrading and disreputable."

"That all men are by nature free and equal" is a truth held sacred by every American, and by every Republican throughout the world. And I presume it cannot be denied in this Hall, as a general principle, that it is an act of injustice, tyranny, and oppression, to hold any part of the human race in bondage against their consent. . . . The right to the enjoyment of liberty, is one of those perfect, inherent and inalienable rights, which pertain to the whole human race, and of which they can never be divested, except by an act of gross injustice. . . . Liberty is too dear to the heart of man, ever to be given up for an earthly consideration. . . .

Of Caruthers' life until recently very little was known. Now, thanks to the researches of Curtis Carroll Davis, we know probably as much as will ever be known. He came of Presbyterian Scotch-Irish stock which had come early into the Shenandoah Valley. His father was a well-to-do merchant and a leader in the community. His mother, Phoebe (Alexander) Caruthers was a sister of the able Presbyterian minister, Archibald Alexander, who once taught in a theological seminary at Princeton, New Jersey. Caruthers attended Washington College in Lexington in the years 1817–1820 but left without taking a degree. The College had only forty or fifty students, but it had able teachers in mathematics and the classics, which were the core of the curriculum. Caruthers joined a literary society and had some experience in debating, and he probably read many books not assigned by his professors. While in college, he witnessed Jim Piper's feat of climbing the Natural Bridge, which supplied the material for Caruthers' best-known magazine article. Having made up his mind to study medicine, he enrolled in the medical school at the University of Pennsylvania, where nearly half the students were from the Southern states. He took his M.D. degree in 1823. His thesis subject, *Magnolia Tripetala*, suggests an interest in botany. In Lexington, where he lived from 1823 to 1829, he practiced medicine and took an active part in the Masonic lodge. He also married—the exact date is not known—Louisa Gibson of Savannah, where the doctor was to spend the last years of his life. If, as I suspect, his heroines were modeled upon his wife, Louisa Caruthers was small, blonde, and blue-eyed.

In the years 1830–1836 Dr. Caruthers was practicing medicine in New York City. He appears to have played his part manfully during the cholera epidemic of 1832. These years in New York were the period of his greatest literary activity. He contributed to the *Knickerbocker Magazine*, which was favorably disposed toward his work; but if he formed close relations with any of the well-known New York writers, that fact has not yet come to light. In June, 1834, Harper & Brothers brought out his first novel, *The Kentuckian in New-York*, and in the following January his second and most popular work, *The Cavaliers of Virginia*. His third and best novel, *The Knights of the Horse-Shoe*, was at least begun before he left New York. The family tradition is that in New York Caruthers spent more than he earned. Certainly he changed his residence there oftener than one would expect a successful physician to do. In 1837 he settled in Savannah, and in that city he spent the last nine years of his life. He was the friend of William Bacon Stevens, the historian of Georgia; of those two remarkable collectors, Israel K. Tefft and Alexander A. Smets; and of Richard D. Arnold, the first Secretary of the American Medical Association. He helped them organize the Georgia Historical Society in 1838; he served on the Board of Aldermen from 1841 to 1844; and he gave occasional lectures on temperance and on scientific subjects. By 1838 he had completed *The Knights of the Horse-Shoe*, but he had to rewrite it after the manuscript was destroyed in a fire that burned his house. After first appearing in 1841 as a serial in a Savannah magazine, the *Magnolia*, it was finally brought out in book form in 1845, not this time by Harper & Brothers in New York but in Wetumpka, Alabama, where it was published by a Virginian acquaintance, Charles Yancey. The result was that his best novel got only one review and attracted little attention. Unlike his other novels, however, it has several times been reprinted since his death. Caruthers planned a sequel and also a novel of contemporary Georgia life, but his only important later work is a three-part story, "Love and Consumption," which appeared in the *Magnolia* in 1842. In the summer of 1846 he went to Marietta in northern Georgia in the vain search for improved health. He died there of tuberculosis on August 29 in his forty-fourth year.

Caruthers was a Presbyterian, a Whig, an optimist, and an enthusiastic believer in the manifest destiny of the American republic. Like many another western Virginian, he had no liking for slavery, and he frankly admitted its abuses. And yet he was among the first to picture in fiction the aristocratic society of Colonial Virginia. He turned to historical romance slightly earlier than either Kennedy or Simms. His writings show clearly that his favorite books were Shakespeare's plays, the Bible, and the Waverley novels. There was some influence, too, from Byron and the Gothic novelists. To American writers he rarely refers. For Caruthers, the proper field of fiction was romance. "As the civilized world departs from nature and becomes more enslaved to the conventional laws of society," he wrote in 1842, "just in the same proportion will the choicest spirits of that world become slaves to the ideal; and this is the true reason why ours is such a novel-reading age." He was aware, however, that, as he phrased it, "there is a bastard romantic vein in some minds which idealizes after its own morbid visions all the stern realities of life, but these," he added, "are not the genuine children of song and romance." There is a sentimental strain in Caruthers, but—except in *The Kentuckian*—it is clear that his master was Scott. "We thank God," he wrote,

that we have lived in the days when those tales of witchery and romance were sent forth from Abbotsford, to cheer the desponding hearts of thousands, and tens of thousands. He not only threw a romantic charm around the scenes of his stories, but he has actually made the world we live in more lovely in our eyes. The visions which his magic wand created before our youthful eyes, rise up in every hill and vale in our own bright and favored land. Who is there that has not, ere now, found his imagination clothing some lass, as she burst upon his view from a mountain defile in full canter, with the imperishable vestments of *Die Vernon?* [48]

It was apparently the Scottish novels and not *Ivanhoe* that interested Caruthers most. He wished to do for the rich and romantic past of Virginia what Scott had done for his native Scotland. Another motive was the desire to help create a literature characteristically Southern. In *The Kentuckian* one of his characters writes: " 'Tis galling to our southern pride, I grant you, that we should be a mere appendage, in the eyes of a foreigner, to a people who are totally dissimilar to us. We must brook it until we can outdo them, in literature at least."

The Kentuckian in New-York, or, The Adventures of Three Southerns is a novel of contemporary life in South and North. It is epistolary in form and very little influenced by the Scott tradition. For the most part, it is a mixture of the sentimental, the lachrymose, and the Gothic, with the conventional happy ending at the altar. We follow the fortunes of two young South Carolinians on their way from Virginia to New York. With them journeys Montgomery Damon, a Kentucky drover who though a minor character gives the title to the novel. To complicate the story, Caruthers sends a young Virginian to South Carolina to undergo adventures and to lose his heart to a blue-eyed heroine. The Kentuckian was obviously suggested by David Crockett, now a well-known personage in the East. There are echoes also of Nimrod Wildfire in James K. Paulding's play, *The Lion of the West*, which Caruthers presumably saw in New York in the autumn of 1832. The story of *The Kentuckian* is not unskilfully unfolded, but what interests the modern reader is chiefly Caruthers' contribution to intersectional good will—even though, as Dr. Davis estimates, this extends to only

---

[48] *The Knights of the Horse-Shoe* (1845), II, chap. xx. The passage was omitted from the 1928 edition.

fifteen out of nearly four hundred and fifty pages . Cooper in *The Spy* (1821) had included a number of Southern characters, chiefly from Virginia, but he had confined his setting to Westchester County, New York. Caruthers ranges from South Carolina to New York and even brings in incidental glimpses of the regions beyond the Appalachians. With Southern readers in mind Caruthers wrote:

Every southern should visit New-York. It would allay provincial prejudices, and calm his excitement against his northern countrymen. The people here are warm-hearted, generous, and enthusiastic, in a degree scarcely inferior to our own southerns. The multitude move as one man, in all public-spirited, benevolent, or charitable measures. Many of these Yorkers are above local prejudices, and truly consider this as the commercial metropolis of the Union, and all the people of the land as their customers, friends, patrons, and countrymen.

Nor is trade the only thing that flourishes. The arts of polished and refined life, refined literature, and the profounder studies of the schoolmen, all have their distinguished votaries,—I say distinguished, with reference to the standard of science in our country.

Caruthers noted the increasing wealth and prosperity of the North and the comparative poverty of the Southern seaboard. He was disturbed by the agitation over the slavery question which had become much more bitter after his removal to New York: "The more I see of these northern states, the more I am convinced that some great revolution awaits our own cherished communities. . . . A line of demarkation . . . is now drawing between the slave and free states, I fear. God send that the disease may be cured without amputation, and before mortification takes place."

The young Virginian who visits South Carolina is Caruthers' chief spokesman on the subject of slavery. He declares himself "no *abolitionist*, in the incendiary meaning of the term," but he is greatly disturbed by what he has seen in South Carolina, where slavery is not the patriarchal institution he has known in Virginia.

The poor of a slave-country [he writes] are the most miserable and the most wretched of all the human family. The grades of society in this state are even farther apart than in Virginia. Here, there is one immense chasm from the rich to the abject poor. In the valley of Virginia, or in the country where you are, there are regular gradations. The very happiest, most useful, and most industrious class of a well-regulated community, is here wanting. Their place is filled up by negroes; in consequence of which, your aristocrats are more aristocratic, and your poor still poorer. The slaves create an immeasurable distance between these two classes, which can never be brought together until this separating cause be removed.

In his second volume Caruthers again noted the wide difference between slavery in the border states and in the Deep South:

With us [in Virginia] slavery is tolerable, and has something soothing about it to the heart of the philanthropist; the slaves are more in the condition of tenants to their landlords—they are viewed as rational creatures, and with more kindly feelings. . . . Here slavery is intolerable; a single individual owning a hundred or more, and often not knowing them when he sees them. . . . The slaves here are plantation live-stock; not domestic and attached family servants, who have served around the person of the master from the childhood of both. . . . Here, besides your white overseers, you have your black *drivers;*—an odious animal, almost peculiar to the far south. It is horrible to see one slave following another at his work, with a cow-skin dangling at his arm, and occasionally tying him up and flogging him when he does not get through his two tasks a day.

Such outspoken revelation of the abuses of slavery we shall hardly find in the writings of any of Caruthers' Southern contemporaries. He had no solution to propose for a problem which could only be solved with the aid of time and Providence. The Negroes if freed would constitute a mob more dangerous than the mobs of Northern cities, which also, he thought, boded no good for the future. After his removal to Savannah, where anti-slavery sentiments were extremely unpopular, Caruthers had little to say about the abuses of slavery.

In his later novels Caruthers turned to a field less likely to arouse controversy, Colonial Virginia. In *The Kentuckian* he had commented on the Tidewater region of his native state: "Poor, exhausted eastern Virginia! she is in her dotage. Her impassable roads protect her alike from the pity and contempt of foreign travellers; but with all her weakness, with all the imbecilities of premature age upon her, I love her still." A realistic treatment of the rundown Tidewater country did not appeal to Caruthers and would undoubtedly not have pleased many Southern readers, but a historical romance picturing that region in its heyday with the glamour and local coloring of the Waverley novels—that would be something worth doing. Cooper had shown how Scott's methods could be adapted to American materials, and in *The Spy* he had painted in Captain Jack Lawton a dashing Virginia cavalryman. In Colonial Virginia there were Cavaliers and backwoodsmen, faithful servants, Indians, and even Puritans; and there, too, were those picturesque neglected figures Nathaniel Bacon and Alexander Spotswood. Virginia had begun to look backward and glorify the past. The Cavalier legend had developed to the point where men imagined that the Colonial population was made up of English gentlemen and nobles—the more numerous indentured servants had been all but forgotten. Even Bacon's ragamuffin army was in Caruthers' imagination made up of Cavaliers. Caruthers' second novel bears the title *The Cavaliers of Virginia, or The Recluse of Jamestown. An Historical Romance of the Old Dominion.* In the Cavaliers Caruthers saw "the first founders of the aristocracy which prevails in Virginia to this day . . . the immediate ancestors of that generous, fox-hunting, wine-drinking, duelling and reckless race of men, which gives so distinct a character to Virginians wherever they may be found." Bacon of course is a Cavalier hero opposed to the villainous Berkeley, but Caruthers had not lost his democratic sympathies: he was one of the first to picture the Virginia rebel as a forerunner of George Washington and the rebellion as a premature struggle for independence. Into the story Caruthers introduced a mysterious figure, "the recluse of Jamestown," who turns out to be one of the Regicides who had ordered the execution of Charles I.[44] Caruthers told his rather melodramatic story well, but he took great liberties with historical fact, particularly in his treatment of Bacon. The book, curiously enough, was reviewed more unfavorably in the *Southern Literary Messenger* than in any Northern magazine. The reviewer, James E. Heath, was himself the author of a historical novel of Virginia, *Edge-Hill* (Richmond, 1828), but he took Caruthers to task for making of Bacon "a kind of half frantic, inconsiderate stripling—something of a dandy—but more of a wild and reckless lover, whose thoughts were principally occupied by his 'Ladye love'; and but slightly, if at all, by the wrongs of his suffering country." Heath objected also, we may note, to Caruthers' use of Gothic elements, as he was to object to the same kind of materials in the stories of Edgar Allan Poe. Before he published his next novel, Caruthers took the precaution of consulting Charles Campbell, the ablest of the ante-bellum historians of the state.

The Knights of the Horse-Shoe; A Traditionary Tale of the Cocked Hat Gentry in the Old Dominion has certain melodramatic elements, but it is Caruthers' best-constructed novel. The plot is handled more skilfully and there is more of local color. The central figure of Governor Spotswood is an attractive one, and Caruthers makes the most of the romantic expedition beyond the Blue Ridge. Caruthers, however, made a mistake when he permitted his best book to be published in Wetumpka, Alabama. The only review the novel is known to have received was a brief and belated one, and it came from the *Southern Quarterly Review* in Charleston. It was presum-

---

[44] Caruthers is not mentioned in G. Harrison Orians, "The Angel of Hadley in Fiction," *Am. Lit.*, IV, 257–269 (Nov., 1932). Caruthers had perhaps read Scott's *Peveril of the Peak* (1823), Vol. I, chap. xiv, which is one of the sources of Hawthorne's "The Gray Champion," first published in the same year and month as *The Cavaliers of Virginia.*

ably written by the editor, Daniel K. Whitaker, the Massachusetts-born ex-minister who became an indefatigable promoter of Southern magazines. "We are glad to see," he wrote, "that this work is issued from a Southern press,—a bold step for any author to take nowadays who wishes to be popular." After some slight praise the reviewer feebly concluded: "What we particularly like in this work is, its truth and fidelity, its nice discrimination of character, and its pure and graceful style. We have not, for some time past, read a better moral—certainly not from the pen of any American writer. . . . From such hands, we need not fear that anything will proceed, calculated to injure the morals of the age, or corrupt public sentiment." The *Southern Literary Messenger* in Caruthers' native state made no mention of *The Knights*—perhaps never received a copy of it. Obviously Charles Yancey, who published it, lacked the facilities for distribution that Harper & Brothers had used in promoting and selling Caruthers' earlier novels. Harper & Brothers did bring out an edition of the novel but not until 1882, when Caruthers had been dead for thirty-six years.

29

Philip Pendleton Cooke

PHILIP PENDLETON COOKE (1816–1850) was born in Martinsburg in what is now West Virginia; and he spent most of his short life in the northern part of the Shenandoah Valley, where some of the best Tidewater families had settled after the Revolution. His father, John Rogers Cooke, was a lawyer and—with Madison, Marshall, and others—one of the framers of the Virginia Constitution of 1830. His mother Maria (Pendleton) Cooke was a daughter of Philip Pendleton, a favorite uncle of John Pendleton Kennedy. Cooke was a cousin of Kennedy and a nephew of Philip St. George Cooke, who was a Union general in the Civil War. John Esten Cooke, the novelist, was a younger brother. Like any normal Virginia country boy, Cooke spent much of his time in hunting and visiting, but he also read widely and at an early age published verse and prose sketches in the Winchester *Republican*. After studying at an academy, he entered Princeton at fifteen; both his father and his grandfather had studied there. In college he spent much time in reading the older English authors, among whom Chaucer and Spenser are specifically mentioned. In 1833 and 1834 he contributed a few poems to the newly established *Knickerbocker Magazine* under the pseudonyms "Frank Beverley" and "Erroll Conway." He was graduated in 1834; he had entered as a sophomore and completed the course in two years, but he took no honors.

At Winchester, where his parents now lived, he began the study of law under his father's supervision. He practiced a little, but the profession proved uncongenial, and he had too many other interests to make a success of either law or farming. He entered fully into the social life and sports of the lower Valley, and he was noted for his exploits as a hunter. At twenty he married Willie Anne Burwell—she died nearly half a century after her husband—against the opposition of members of her family, who rightly thought that he would not prove a good provider. In later years he lived at "The Vineyard," which was his wife's property but which was managed by her uncle Nathaniel Burwell.

Cooke's letters to his father give us glimpses of the social life of the Valley, tell us something about his fits of writing, mention "outbreaks of temper," and reveal almost continuous financial difficulties. At one time he seriously thought of moving to Missouri. In these years the Valley farmers were always complaining of hard times; and Cooke, unable to make ends meet, was again and again driven to borrowing money from his father, who was himself in difficulties from having in the old Virginia fashion been too ready to endorse notes for his friends. He wrote to his father on November 28, 1842: "I have already assured you, and now assure you again, that my greatest vexation in life is the not being able to do without your assistance in pecuniary matters. There is a striking and offensive impropriety in my taking my support, at twenty six, from my father. The young of the eagles (of which high breed I persuade myself I am come) feed themselves when their wings are old enough, and so does every other animal, when matured, except that good for nothing creature a 'Virginia gentleman.'" The Cookes, however, were not the only old family that seemed sinking in the social and economic scale. He wrote to his father, December 29, 1840: "It is lamentable to see the old families of the land, the first in gentility & *caste, reduced*; to see their descendants gradually sinking by marriage & association into humbler classes; and to see *mine* thus would break my heart." It was natural that Cooke should choose to write first of the romantic European past rather than of the Virginia of his own time.

In a letter to Rufus W. Griswold John Esten Cooke wrote on June 6, 1851: "My brother's tastes ran most toward the old poets and prose writers; —The 'dearest books' as Sir Walter Scott says, in his Library were a fine English edition of Chaucer in 14 vols and Lord Berner's [sic] Froissart also English in four large volumes. Keats Shelley and Coleridge were also favourites with him; not Southey or Byron. When the [Froissart] Ballads were published he had not seen Tennyson but his poems afterwards were favourites with him—more especially the 'Morte D'Arthur' and 'Ulysses.' " To this list should be added the *Edinburgh Review*, the *Spirit of the Times*, and the poems and romances of Scott, which probably helped to kindle Cooke's interest in the age of chivalry.

Unlike his younger brother, Philip Cooke received no literary encouragement from friends and neighbors. Even his indulgent father appears to have written him that in this country the writing of poetry would bring him neither wealth nor honors. Cooke once wrote to Griswold:

What do you think of a good friend of mine, a most valuable and worthy and hard-riding one, saying gravely to me a short time ago, "I wouldn't waste time on a damned thing like poetry; you might make yourself, with all your sense and judgment, a useful man in settling neighborhood disputes and difficulties." . . . I am wasting my letter with these people, but for fear you may think I am chagrined or cut by what I abuse them for, I must say that they suit one half of my character, moods, and pursuits, in being good kindly men, rare table companions, many of them great in field sports, and most of them rather deficient in letters than mind; and that, in an every-day sense of the word, I love and am beloved by them.

It was fortunate that Cooke, who knew nothing about the marketing of literary wares, numbered among his friends Kennedy, Griswold, Poe, and John R. Thompson. The launching of the *Southern Literary Messenger* in 1834, the year he graduated from Princeton, provided a suitable medium for his verse, essays, and prose fiction. Among the pen names he used was "Larry Lyle," which the *Messenger* editor at first mistook for "Zarry Zyle." His long essay on "English Poetry" attests his knowledge of the older British poets and indicates that for an amateur he was making a serious study of the English classics.

Cooke perhaps first heard of Poe through Kennedy, who had known him in Baltimore as early as 1833. At any rate Cooke was among the very first to recognize the high quality of the early stories which Poe was publishing in the *Messenger* in 1835 and 1836. Some time in 1835 he wrote of Poe: ". . . he is the first genius, in his line, in Virginia. And when I say this, how many other States are included—certainly all South of us." About this time Poe was praising Cooke's contributions to the *Messenger*, and he was still praising Cooke's poems ten years later in the *Broadway Journal*. On September 21, 1839, Poe, then living in Philadelphia, wrote to Cooke that he valued his opinion more highly than that of any man in America. "You read my inmost spirit 'like a book,'" he continued, "and with the single exception of D'Israeli, I have had communication with no other person who does. Willis had a glimpse of it—Judge [Beverley] Tucker saw about one half way through—but your ideas are the very echo of my own." Some passages in Cooke's letters, it seemed to Poe, showed an unusual insight into what he was trying to accomplish in his poems and stories. In 1845 Poe asked Cooke to write an article supplementing Lowell's article on Poe which had appeared in *Graham's Magazine* for February, 1845. Cooke's "Edgar A. Poe" eventually appeared in the *Messenger* in January, 1848.

Since Lowell's article had emphasized Poe's poems, Cooke gave most of his space to the tales, which he discussed with more intelligence than most of his contemporaries. He noted that Poe, like Defoe, had a "peculiar talent for filling up his pictures with minute life-like touches—for giving an air of remarkable naturalness and truth to whatever he paints." In Poe's "MS. Found in a Bottle," he said, "we have a story as wild as the mind of man ever conceived, and yet made to sound like the most matter-of-fact veracious narrative of a seaman." Poe "deals with mysteries of 'life and death,' dissects monomanias, exhibits convulsions of soul—in a word, wholly leaves beneath and behind him the wide and happy realm of the common cheerful life of man." "Defoe," said Cooke, "loves and deals always with the homely. Mr. Poe is nervously afraid of the homely—has a creed that Beauty is the goddess of the Poet:—not Beauty with swelling bust, and lascivious carriage, exciting passions of the blood, but Beauty sublimated and cherished by the soul—the beauty of the Uranian, not Dionean Venus."

With a genuine admiration for Poe's extraordinary achievements, Cooke, like many another reader since his time, could not help wishing that Poe had peopled some of his tales with real persons engaged in thoroughly human activities.

For my individual part, having the seventy or more tales, analytic, mystic, grotesque, arabesque, always wonderful, often great, which his industry and fertility have already given us, I would like to read one cheerful book made by his *invention*, with little or no aid from its twin brother *imagination*—a book in his admirable style of full, minute, never tedious narrative—a book full of homely doings, of successful toils, of ingenious shifts and contrivances, of ruddy firesides —a book healthy and happy throughout, and with no poetry in it at all anywhere, except a good old English "poetic justice" in the end. Such a book, such as Mr. Poe could make it, would be a book for the million, and if it did nothing to exalt him with the few, would yet certainly *endear* him to them.

Such a book Poe, alas! never wrote and probably never could have written —certainly not in 1848 when Cooke published his article

In spite of Poe's encouragement, Cooke had in 1835 resolved to give up poetry. In December of that year he wrote to Beverley Tucker, who had also given him some encouragement, that it was impossible to combine poetry and law:

As a lawyer reputation and fortune await me. . . .

As an author (*of poetry*) a painful fear of the world's censure—a restless ache of mind—a morbid yearning after the high place among men—(painful, all painful, during their unquiet life, and terrible when failure follows them) await me. I would not live that shrinking and sensitive and cowering existence for —*success*. And what chance would there be of this. Even Wn. Irving was 'wretchedly poor for years'—a type of temporary failure *in prose*. But look at our Poets. Bryant (the master of them all) has sheltered himself from starvation behind the columns of a political newspaper.

When Poe some years later asked Cooke to send something for Burton's *Gentleman's Magazine,* Cooke after several months finally wrote: "My wife enticed me off to visit her kins-people in the country, and I saw more of guns & horses and dogs than of pens and paper. Amongst dinners, barbecues, snipe shooting, riding parties &c. I could not gain my brains into the humour for writing to you or to any body else." He hoped occasionally to send a contribution, but, he added:

. . . I cannot promise anything like the systematic contribution which I was guilty of in White's case, for the "madness of scribbling" which once itched & tickled at my finger-ends has been considerably cured by a profession & matrimony—money-cares and domestic squabbles—buying beef & mutton, and curing my child's croups, colicks, &c. The fever with which I was afflicted has given way to a chill—or, as romantic young persons say, "The golden dream is broken." [45]

For several years Cooke wrote little, but in 1843, owing to the persistent urging of Kennedy, he set to work on a volume of ballads based partly on Froissart's *Chronicles.* He wrote to Kennedy: "The poems are going on with that alternation of fervid execution and half desponding, half loathing after-feeling, which has cut off so many of my pieces in past times, like the story of the Bear and the Fiddle—in the middle. I think, however, I am doing sure work on them." After sending the manuscript to Griswold, who was to see it through the press, he wrote to him, January 20, 1847: "The Froissart Ballads sent you are certainly not in the high key of a man warm with his subject, and doing the thing finely; I wrote them with the reluctance of a turkey hunter kept from his sport—only Mr. Ky's urgent entreaty & remonstrance whipped me up to the labour." But for Kennedy and Griswold and perhaps Poe, *Froissart Ballads, and Other Poems* would probably never

[45] Poe, *Works,* XVII, 49. Poe wrote to Cooke, Sept. 21, 1839: "You need not attempt to shake off or to banter off Romance. It is an evil you will never get rid of to the end of your days. It is a part of yourself—a portion of your soul" (*Works,* XVII, 53–54).

have appeared. It was brought out by Carey & Hart in Philadelphia early in 1847. In accepting the publishers' offer of a 10 per cent royalty, Cooke wrote to Griswold: "Indeed I am somewhat mortified that my limited means and family obligations make it impossible to issue the book at my own charge." The sales were disappointing to the author, for he made only a hundred dollars off the edition, and the book was never reprinted. In "Literature in the South," published in *Russell's Magazine* in August, 1859, Henry Timrod wrote: "While our centre-tables are littered with the feeble moralizings of Tupper, done up in very bright morocco; and while the corners of our newspapers are graced with the glibly versified common-places of Mackey, there is, perhaps, scarcely a single bookseller in the United States, on whose face we should not encounter the grin of ignorance, if we chanced to inquire for the Froissart ballads of Philip Pendleton Cooke."

In the three remaining years of his life Cooke did a great deal of writing, but it was very largely in prose. He left unfinished a long prose romance, *The Chevalier Merlin,* which was appearing serially in the *Messenger.* In the *Messenger* also appeared a number of still uncollected short stories. "These tales," wrote John Esten Cooke, "were the commencement of a series which were to dramatize the whole history and manners of Va. & Virginians."

While hunting in January, 1850, Philip Cooke waded into the icy Shenandoah River to retrieve a wounded duck. Pneumonia followed, and he died shortly afterwards in his thirty-fourth year. A month later Griswold wrote to John R. Thompson: "So P. P. Cooke, the finest poet that ever lived in Virginia—one of the finest that have written in our day—is dead." Griswold notoriously underrated Poe, but there were Southern writers whose merits he fully appreciated.

Froissart Ballads contains seventeen poems, eleven of which are classed as Miscellaneous. Apart from the "Proem," only three of the seven narrative poems are actually taken from Froissart: "Orthone," "Sir Peter of Bearn," and "Our Lady's Dog." "The Story of Ugolino" is from Dante's *Inferno,* and "The Master of Bolton" and "Geoffrey Tetenoire" are of the poet's own invention. The appeal that Cooke found in Lord Berners' translation of Froissart is suggested in the "Proem":

> In the wells
> Ot Froissart's life-like chronicles,
> I dipped for moving truths of old.
> A thousand stories, soft and bold,
> Of stately dames, and gentlemen,
> Which good Lord Berners, with a pen

Pompous in its simplicity,
Yet tipt with charming courtesy,
Had put in English words, I learned;
And some of these I deftly turned
Into the forms of minstrel verse.

The stories are all told with some narrative skill and charm of style.
Cooke's model, as he wrote to Beverley Tucker, March 29, 1847, was John
G. Lockhart's *Spanish Ballads*. He added: "I wrote them all after the proem,
and they assumed a shape and look very different from the original design,
and are, in fact, only *ballads*, by courtesy of the most liberal interpretation
of the word—as Scott's poem of Branksome was a *Lay*. . . ." Of "Geoffrey
Tetenoire" he said:

I never was satisfied with the *tone* of that poem, and now you let me into the
secret reason of my dislike of it. I have told an old ballad tale in the manner
of the pretty, thought-diluting, modern school of versifiers. . . . I dashed off a
prose sentence containing the rapid outline of the story, with some honest old
ballad feeling in my blood at the time, but wrote it many months afterwards in
the hurry of completing my book for print, and when all feeling of the sort was
gone.

In spite of Cooke's depreciation, "Geoffrey Tetenoire" has considerable
power, but in its meter and diction it suggests Macaulay's "Horatius" as
well as the Robin Hood ballads of an earlier day. The longest of the ballads
—"The Master of Bolton"—is the story of a penniless young English gentleman who in the time of the Black Prince goes to France and with his good
right arm wins for himself broad acres and the hand of his lady. The story,
however, probably derives more from Scott's *Ivanhoe* and *Quentin Durward*
than from anything in Froissart. Cooke did not subscribe to Griswold's
notion that an American poet should deal mainly if not exclusively with
native materials, and he followed the practice of older poets from Chaucer
to Dryden in borrowing suitable plots wherever he could find them. One
of his best ballads, still uncollected, "The Murder of Cornstalk," is a story of
Dunmore's War with the Indians.

Of the Miscellaneous Poems "Florence Vane" was the popular favorite.
It is in the melancholy, half-sentimental vein of Moore, Byron, and Richard
Henry Wilde. J. C. Derby, the publisher, has preserved John Esten Cooke's
account of the composition of the poem:

Mr. Cooke once told me that when his brother was eighteen or twenty, he fell
in love with his cousin, Evelina Dandridge—"Florence Vane." He often rode
his fine black horse, "John Randolph," on moonlight nights fifteen miles to see

her. He would throw nosegays into her window and ride home again. Of this boy and girl passion nothing came. He went to college, she to spend the winter in Richmond. There she became engaged to and married R. M. T. Hunter, subsequently the eminent Virginian statesman. His brother also married in his turn Miss Burwell of the Valley. It was after his marriage that he wrote "Florence Vane." It came to him he said whilst he was walking in the garden listening to his young wife seated in a window singing.

What most impresses the reader of today in the poem is its music.

> Thou wast lovelier than the roses
> In their prime;
> Thy voice excelled the closes
> Of sweetest rhyme;
> Thy heart was as a river
> Without a main;
> Would I had loved thee never,
> Florence Vane.

A few of the Miscellaneous Poems, like "Life in the Autumn Woods," reveal the poet as aware of the beauty of the landscape of his native Virginia, but it was in prose rather than in verse that Cooke chose to write of the Old Dominion.

His longest prose work, the unfinished *The Chevalier Merlin*, is based largely on that widely read eighteenth-century classic, Voltaire's life of Charles XII of Sweden. "Edgar A. Poe," wrote John Esten Cooke, "declared in the hearing of the writer that *The Chevalier Merlin* was less a novel than a poem and that no one but Cooke could have written it." The story contains some of Cooke's best writing in prose.

In a three-part article on "Living Novelists," published in the *Messenger* in 1847, Cooke, now that he had turned to prose fiction, had something to say about modern practitioners of the art. He overrated Disraeli, but he was clear about the limitations of Bulwer-Lytton and G. P. R. James. He found Bulwer's style "Painfully ornate, ambitious. (a fatal fault of style,) full of circumlocution introduced evidently for the sake of music, and where natural often slovenly." His own ideal was: "Write clearly, go by the nearest way to your meaning, use words of distinct, well understood signification, abjure ornament as a separate quality, but where it comes as a natural grace make it welcome. . . ." Dumas impressed him as a "literary manufactory," but he liked his good sense, humor, and skill in dialogue. James, he thought, moralized too frequently and failed to vary his plots sufficiently. Possibly thinking of himself as well as of James, Cooke said that the British novelist had "an inexhaustible relish for the ancient chivalric life—as poets, and romancers, misled by the glitter of its ornaments have feigned it to have been." He rated Cooper as "the most creative, and most dramatic of our novelists—and the only true *poet* amongst them. . . . We can think of no novelist, save Scott, who has conceived so many characters so well." Cooke was not only a far abler critic than his brother, but with the exception of Poe and Simms and Hugh S. Legaré probably the best critic among the Southern writers of his time.

Like Poe and Henry James after him, Cooke was apparently trying to learn the art of fiction by studying the practice of other writers and by writing stories himself at the same time. Of his four long Virginia stories—they are what the French call *nouvelles*—each too long for a single number of the *Messenger*, "John Carper, the Hunter of Lost River" suggests the influence of Cooper. In turn, it probably influenced John Esten Cooke's first novel *Leather Stocking and Silk* (1854). It is based upon an incident recorded in Samuel Kercheval's *History of the Valley of Virginia*, and it pictures the frontier region in the time of the Revolution. The three other stories—"The Two Country Houses," "The Gregories of Hackwood," and "The Crime of Andrew Blair"—deal chiefly with the planter society of the lower Valley. Kennedy and Caruthers had already done something to make Virginia a popular background in fiction, but Cooke pictures a different part of Virginia. Taken together the three stories present what seems on the whole —barring certain melodramatic incidents—a faithful picture. The planter families in these stories all suffer from financial troubles and seem sinking into the level of the socially inferior. The protagonist in "The Gregories of Hackwood" is an accomplished gentleman ruined by the lust for gold. "The Crime of Andrew Blair," perhaps the most powerful of the three, is in Cooke's words "a study of a respectable planter with a criminal past" which in some ways recalls Godwin's *Caleb Williams*. Andrew Blair instead of fighting an honorable duel with Colonel Pellew, with whom he has quarreled, murders him. He is seen, however, by Jack Herries, the poor-white son of "an old witch of a woman," and Herries blackmails Blair into lending him the money with which to buy Pellew's estate. Eventually he tries to marry his son Tom to Blair's niece and heiress, Minny, so that he will not have to pay the debt. Minny reluctantly agrees to marry Tom, who drinks to excess and is something of a fool. Eventually Tom's better qualities —presumably inherited from his mother—win out, and Minny, who has nursed him back to health, loves and marries him. "The Crime of Andrew Blair" is not very expertly told. At the beginning of the eighth chapter Cooke confessed to his readers: "When I began this history it was with the purpose of developing the progress of a nature in some respects well-gifted, from a single crime [murder] to which unrestrained passions in an evil hour propelled it, to remorse and eventual ruin. I found myself very early beguiled into a love-story, and thrown quite out from my original design." In completing the story he returned to his original plan, threw the love story into the background, and placed the emphasis upon Blair's confession of guilt and death. Cooke's story suggests correctly, I think, that there was no such gulf between social classes in Virginia as one would infer from the stories of Thomas Nelson Page. Cooke's stories also show that he was not blind to the strain of violence in Southern life which has figured so conspicuously in recent fiction.

At the time of his death Cooke was still not expert in handling his plots, but his treatment of dialogue, character, and description is good enough to justify the reprinting of his stories. If he had lived, he would have written better stories and poems. He had more talent than his younger brother, whose romances have been far more widely read than the *Froissart Ballads*. What he needed was the kind of criticism and encouragement that he might perhaps have got if he had lived among his literary contemporaries in Charleston, or, better, in Boston or New York. And yet when one remembers how few helpful critics Melville, Hawthorne, and Whitman found in their formative years, one wonders whether an urban environment might not have been worse for Cooke than that he found among the planters and hunters of the Valley.

30
John Esten Cooke

JOHN ESTEN COOKE (1830–1886) was born in the Shenandoah Valley, which he has done more to celebrate in fiction than any other writer. His brother Philip, fourteen years his senior, was too old to be a close boyhood companion; but there were younger brothers and other playmates white and black, and Cooke's early years were those of almost any normal country boy. In Richmond, to which his parents moved when he was ten, he studied at an academy and took an active part in a literary society, the members of which were impressed by his early attempts at essay-writing. At sixteen, like his brother Philip before him, he began the study of law under the direction of his father. He had hoped to enter the University of Virginia, but his parents were unable at that time to send him; and when the family's financial situation improved, Cooke withdrew in favor of his brother Edward. Although he liked the law no better than Philip, he managed to obtain his license and became a partner of his father, who had regarded him as a rather idle student. Cooke's notebooks, says his biographer, show that his supposed idleness consisted chiefly in taking an active interest in lectures, concerts, and plays; in keeping himself informed on political and literary subjects; and in a certain amount of the normal social life of a young man. The light reading to which his father objected included Carlyle, Dumas, Irving, Emerson, and Poe. He was interested in Virginia history, and Kercheval's *History of the Valley of Virginia* was a favorite book. Cooke was already taking notes on his reading, and in his own fashion he was, like Robert Louis Stevenson, playing "the sedulous ape" to his favorite authors by writing imitations and burlesques. He seems to have cared little for Dickens, but he met and liked Thackeray, who said to him: "If I were you I would go on writing. Some day you will make a fortune. Becky Sharp made mine. I married early and wrote for bread." [46] Cooke was considerably indebted to Irving, and at his best his writing has something of Irving's charm and graceful lightness of style. But Cooke also liked Dumas and the sensational stories of Charles Reade and Wilkie Collins, and he did not always distinguish between the literary and the subliterary. He found Susan B. Warner's *The Wide, Wide World* "one of the most delightful of books." Cooke wrote verse as well as prose, but as he wrote to Griswold, October 24, 1855: "The plain field of prose is my walk, and in this I trust I may one day do something not unworthy of the family. My brother was essentially a poet, and I am essentially—however feebly—a dramatist."

Cooke was from the beginning a prolific writer, and he was soon contributing verse, essays, sketches, and stories to the *Southern Literary Messenger*, *Putnam's*, and *Harper's*. He wanted to give up the law and devote his whole time to writing, but literature seemed an uncertain means of support, and so he repeatedly resolved to stop writing. His Richmond friends, however, unlike the planters in the Valley who had advised his brother to give up poetry, urged him to make literature his profession. This friendly advice he was reluctant to take, and for several years law and literature divided his energies. On April 24, 1851, he wrote to Griswold that he wanted a publisher for a novel which was to be a sequel to Dumas's *De Mauleon:*

My name could not under any circumstances appear as the author and this you will perceive after a simple word of explanation. I am a practising attorney, just commencing the life of a business man, and, some of my numerous scribblings

---

[46] Derby, *Fifty Years*, p. 405. Of Cooke's several accounts of his interview with Thackeray, perhaps the best is "An Hour with Thackeray," *Appletons' Jour.*, VII, 248–258 (Sept. 1879).

in the Messenger & elsewhere have unavoidably been identified. My evident policy is therefore to live down these trifling literary productions, and to gain a reputation for practical prosaic business talent. The reputation then of a writer of an extended work would be almost fatal to me—how much more of a *French* work, a sequel to M. Dumas'!

With what he made from his law practice and his writing Cooke was, with strict economy and by remaining a bachelor, able to support himself and eventually to pay off his father's debts, which he had assumed as a matter of honor.

Among Cooke's earliest writings were two unpublished romances dealing with medieval France—a background which was later to fascinate Sidney Lanier and James Branch Cabell. His interest in the Middle Ages was perhaps first aroused by his reading in Froissart's *Chronicles* and in his brother's *Froissart Ballads*. In his youth, however, Kennedy and Simms were exploiting the rich Southern background of the Revolution in the South, and his older brother had shifted his center of interest from the age of chivalry to nineteenth-century Virginia. In later life Cooke wrote: "My aim has been to paint the Virginia phase of American society, to do for the Old Dominion what Cooper has done for the Indians, Simms for the Revolutionary drama in South Carolina, Irving for the Dutch Knickerbockers, and Hawthorne for the weird Puritan life of New England."

In 1852 Cooke began his first serious effort as a romancer with *Leather Stocking and Silk; or, Hunter John Myers and His Times*. The fire which caused so many of Herman Melville's books to go out of print prevented Harper & Brothers from publishing the novel until 1854. This story of the Shenandoah Valley, suggested by his father's account of the actual John Myers, owes its title to Cooper, but its method derives in the main from Irving. It was, he wrote to Griswold, May 21, 1855, "a story of Martinsburg in which I tried to *weave up* a number of traditions, and odd characters I had heard talked of, and to give a picture of 'provincial' life. Almost every character is more or less founded on fact." That Cooke's literary aim in this story of provincial life was not very high is suggested by a sentence in his Preface: "If the book be found entertaining, and (above all else) the spirit of it pure, the writer will be more than satisfied."

In 1853 Cooke laid aside the half-finished *Fairfax* to begin writing what has proved to be his best romance, *The Virginia Comedians* (1854). He wrote the two volumes at top speed, sometimes turning off as many as a hundred pages of manuscript in a single day. He wrote three novels in the year 1854, and he was still practicing law. *The Virginia Comedians* is a story of Williamsburg and its vicinity in the years immediately preceding the

Revolution, and the leading historical personage is Patrick Henry, whose portrait owes much to William Wirt's biography. Cooke's fondness for the theater led him to make much of the company of actors who under the lead of Lewis Hallam had enjoyed a brief but notable success in the little Virginia capital. Cooke's actress friend Kate Bateman was the model for Beatrice Hallam, who fails to return the love of the sophisticated young aristocrat, Champ Effingham. Cooke wrote to Griswold, May 28, 1855, that the novel was "intended to be a picture of our curiously graded Virginia society just before the Revolution." "The book," he continued, "is profoundly demo-catic, and American—the aristocracy whom I don't like, getting the worst of it." Cooke, however, though less the aristocrat than his brother, could not help casting a glamour over some of the planter families, but his yeomen are well drawn. Negroes and poor whites he was never able to treat with much success. Like Thackeray's *The Virginians*, Cooke's romance breaks in two in the middle and becomes two separate stories, which with *Henry St. John, Gentleman* (1859) may be regarded as a trilogy. Cooke thought of himself as writing in the spirit of a social historian, imaginatively recon-structing a great period in American history. As a social historian of Vir-ginia, he is markedly inferior to Ellen Glasgow.

Cooke tried his hand at other types of fiction. In *Ellie* (Richmond, 1855), which he wrote in a month, he published a social tract, reminiscent of Dickens, attacking the shallowness of the genteel life around him and asking the reason for the poverty in the lower circles in Richmond. A reviewer in *Putnam's* wrote in September, 1855: "He must try again, and write about ancient Virginia, not that of the present day." Cooke was discovering not only that books published in the South did not sell but also that American readers were little interested in social studies of contemporary life.

In addition to contributing numerous articles to various magazines and occasionally editing the *Messenger* so that his friend John R. Thompson could enjoy a vacation, Cooke wrote articles on Jefferson, Irving, and others for *Appleton's Cyclopaedia*. He and Thompson planned to bring out an an-thology, *The Poets and Poetry of the South*, designed doubtless to counter-act the New England bias in their friend Griswold's *The Poets and Poetry of America*. Perhaps it was just as well that the outbreak of war stopped this project, for, as Cooke wrote to Kennedy: "I fear the volume . . . will in-clude some sad trash, and I am all the more anxious to have matter which will neutralize the bad." Neither Cooke nor Thompson knew enough about the earlier Southern writers, even in Virginia, to compile what might have been a respectable anthology.

Cooke suffered somewhat from lack of contact with the best American writers of his time. He knew G. P. R. James, who was for some years British consul in Norfolk and Richmond. He formed friendships with Griswold, Duyckinck, Stedman, and Thomas Dunn English; but he seems to have known none of the important New England writers.

Cooke did not admire Poe nearly so much as his brother Philip had done. He did, however, in 1852 send to *Harper's* a poem, "A Vision of E. A. Poe," which the editor returned with a note written in the third person stating that he"dislikes the subject—and therefore would prefer not using it in the mag⁼." Cooke knew Poe only slightly during the last sad years when the poet revisited Richmond in 1848 and 1849. Like Thompson and John M. Daniel, he found it difficult to recognize in the rapidly breaking magazinist one of the three or four great American writers of the time. He regarded Poe's critical writings as "some of the fiercest, most savage, and most unfair literary criticism ever published in America." He wrote an essay on "Poe as a Literary Critic" which remained unpublished until 1946, when it was brought out by the Edgar Allan Poe Society of Baltimore.[47] Its chief value is in Cooke's account of Poe's lecture on "The Poetic Principle," delivered in Richmond in 1849. Cooke and Thompson came close to agreeing with Griswold's notorious characterization of Poe. In April, 1854, the *Messenger* reprinted from the London *Critic* a savage attack on Poe, and it was apparently Cooke who wrote the editorial introduction to this article while Thompson was on a vacation.

When the Civil War broke out, Cooke was thirty-one years old. He was already a successful romancer and had written a better book than he was to write during his remaining twenty-five years. In reviewing *Henry St. John, Gentleman* (1859), Simms had complimented Cooke on having selected for himself a rich field and for treating it capably, but he suggested that the romancer needed to develop considerably before he could do full justice to his theme. The *Messenger* reviewer found in this romance all of Cooke's characteristic excellences and faults. "The chief merit of it," he said, "is to be found in the faithful and minute reproduction of the social habitudes of a past age," but the plot he thought was "singularly ill-contrived" and the characters lifeless. "Mr. Cooke writes too fast and publishes without proper revision." Cooke, however, would probably not have developed into a really important writer even had the war not interrupted his work. His friend George W. Bagby, the humorist, criticized him more severely than Simms had done, for Bagby was a realist. Cooke, he thought, had eyes only in the back of his head, and they were covered with rose-

[47] Cooke, *Poe as a Literary Critic* (Baltimore, 1946), ed. N. Bryllion Fagin. Mr. Fagin's Introduction is inadequate. See my review in *Am. Lit.*, XVIII, 345–346 (Jan., 1947).

colored goggles of enormous magnifying power. "The respectable gentlemen and ladies who were buried down at Williamsburg about eighty years ago, were, I doubt not, very nice people; but they are too dead for my taste." Bagby could not understand how "such a set of homely, selfish, money-loving cheats and rascals as we are, should have descended from such remarkably fine parents. No doubt it is very good noveling, but I swear it is wretched physiology." Even Thomas Nelson Page, who himself threw a halo of glamour over the Virginia planters, thought that Cooke, Caruthers, and Simms all pictured the life of the South as reflected through the lenses of Scott and G. P. R. James: "They dressed their gentlemen in wigs and ruffles and short clothes and their ladies in brocades and quilted stomachers and flashing jewels; housed them in palaces and often moved them on stilts with measured strut as automata strung on wires and worked, however, skilfully, from behind the scenes. They spoke book-English and lived, if they lived at all, in slavish imitation of generations gone. . . . It was generally well done, often admirably done, but it was not real."

Cooke had little interest in the perpetuation of slavery and he did not share in the growing hatred of the North, but the election of Lincoln converted him into a secessionist. He fought throughout the war without receiving a single wound. As a sergeant he had charge of a gun at Bull Run, and on the field of Appomattox, it is said, he buried his silver spurs to keep them from falling into enemy hands. During much of the war he was a cavalry officer on the staff of General J. E. B. Stuart, who had married his cousin; and in that capacity Cooke led an adventurous life and came to know the generals of the Army of Northern Virginia. Intermittently he kept a diary, which contains a vivid account of what he saw and did during the Seven Days' Battle north of Richmond. The diary also records the fact that Cooke found time for a good deal of writing, most of which was published in Confederate newspapers and magazines. In the winter of 1864 he sent fifteen sketches to the *Cornhill Magazine*, but they were apparently lost in the blockade. In 1863 he brought out a hastily written life of Stonewall Jackson, of whom he had seen a good deal. J. C. Derby, who knew Cooke, writes: "He remembers stopping at one time in the middle of a sentence to go and get shot at by a party of blue cavalry. Most of the MS. was sent off as written, but his satchel with the remainder was captured with his toothbrush and prayer-book."

Although Cooke never suspected it, his published criticism of the Confederate administration appears to have kept him from being promoted to the rank of major on the recommendation of Stuart and Lee. The story told by George Cary Eggleston of how Stuart recommended Cooke for promotion is eminently characteristic of the great cavalry commander:

"You're about my size, Cooke," Stuart said, "but you're not so broad in the chest."

"Yes, I am," answered Cooke.

"Let's see if you are," said Stuart, taking off his coat as if stripping for a boxing match. "Try that on."

Cooke donned the coat with its three stars on the collar, and found it a fit.

"Cut off two of the stars," commanded Stuart, "and wear the coat to Richmond. Tell the people in the War Department to make you a major and send you back to me in a hurry. I'll need you tomorrow."

Adventurous as his life was, Cooke found the war on the whole a rather dull affair. The books he mentions reading in wartime are chiefly biography and fiction. He had particularly high praise for Hugo's Les Misérables, published in instalments in Richmond. On March 13, 1864, he wrote in his diary: "I have just finished 'Jean Valjean' the last of the Wretched, Infinitely mournful book!—with a pathos in these last pages too deep for tears. What a genius! Nothing in any literature is greater than some of these pictures." "Why," he continued, "should I try to write in the lifetime of my master? I sit in my tent by the dying fire and consider myself a nobody."

On February 11, 1865, Cooke outlined in his diary the philosophy which he had developed in the course of the war:

How to make manhood and age happy? Here it is.

Avoid *passion*, that is, not feeling (have as much as possible) but wearing, tearing *passion*. Be calm, steady, moderate. Make the most of simple pleasures, and small enjoyments. First and foremost cultivate hygiene. Half of the ills of life spring from want of exercise, irregularity in eating or drinking—late hours etc. *Be regular*—be calm: be a philosopher. If anybody says "The Yankees are charging us!!!" with all the horrours in his voice ask "Where did you say they were?" Get in the saddle but keep cool.

Don't be flustered. Don't hate or envy. They are dark sins— They are also *unhealthy*. Nothing is more wholesome than kindness. Be kind to all, and of modest Simplicity—not humble, not proud: courteous: the considerate gentleman.

. . . .

Make God the first and last.

"My first thought on the surrender," wrote Cooke, "was to go to Amelia [County]—get my two horses fat on grass—sell them—then to N. Y.—write, and look Paris-ward." On second thought, however, he decided to return

to the Shenandoah Valley, where he had relatives; he had not lived there
since the age of ten. For a year or two he lived at "The Vineyard" with the
widow and children of his brother Philip. He had come out of the war
practically penniless, but he was exceptionally fortunate in securing commissions from Northern publishers. In the summer of 1865 he began writing
for the New York World, and the next year the Appletons brought out his
revised life of Jackson. He wrote in his diary in March, 1867: "Hope to become the writer of the South, yet! Big ambition." By March, 1873, he had
made thirteen thousand dollars with his pen.

Of the seven books which he wrote dealing with the war not one is the
book he should have written—a plain, straightforward account of what he
had experienced, for no other writer on either side had seen so much of
what was really memorable. His lives of Jackson and Lee are hurriedly written accounts of battles rather than substantial biographies. Wearing the
Gray (1867) is made up chiefly of newspaper sketches written in wartime,
and Hammer and Rapier (1870) is a series of articles first published in the
Old Guard as "The Battles of Virginia."

Cooke was the first important novelist to treat the Civil War in fiction.
Surry of Eagle's-Nest (1866) and its sequel Mohun (1869) cover most of
the great battles of Lee's army. Hilt to Hilt (1869) is a story of John S.
Mosby's guerrillas. Surry was written in six weeks; Cooke was still too facile
and too uncritical of his work to become a great novelist. He told George
Cary Eggleston that he saw in modern warfare "nothing heroic or romantic
or in any way calculated to appeal to the imagination!" The war was too
close for him to see it through the romantic haze in which it was wrapped
for Thomas Nelson Page. In Cooke's imagination the Revolution was still
the romantic period in Virginia's history. In his Civil War novels he felt
it necessary to adopt "the Reade-Collinsish style of mystery and sensation"
and to import into rural Virginia outlandish villains who figure in plots
made up chiefly of the outworn machinery of mystery and intrigue. Perhaps because of the inferior periodicals which alone would accept his work,
he found in his later years it was generally his poorer novels that paid him
best. In Surry and Mohun history and fiction refuse to blend, and in consequence each novel breaks into long sections in which historical and
fictitious events are treated separately. No writer of Cooke's ability, however, could treat such fresh and interesting materials as the battles and
leaders of Lee's army without accomplishing something better than I have
suggested. His pictures of Ashby, Pelham, Stuart, and Jackson are memorable. In the flood of Civil War literature it is not easy to find anything better
than Cooke's best historical passages. His account of the war—and this

explains in part his success—is remarkable for the almost complete absence of bitterness toward the North. In some respects his romances set the pattern for later Civil War fiction, notably in picturing a Virginia family divided by the war. His own family supplied the model. Kennedy and other relatives took the Northern side. His uncle Philip St. George Cooke, a Union general, had in 1862 tried in vain to head off the Confederate cavalry, led by the General's son-in-law "Jeb" Stuart. General Cooke's only son and two nephews—John Esten and Nat, son of Philip Pendleton Cooke—were all in the Confederate army.

In 1867 Cooke married Mary Frances Page, and the match prompted George Cary Eggleston to remark that by this step the novelist "had married into all the good [Virginia] families he didn't belong to himself." "He remained to the end," says Eggleston, "the high-spirited, duty-loving man of honor that I had known in my youth [in Richmond]; he remained also the gentle, affectionate and unfailingly courteous gentleman he had always been." On March 16, 1877, Paul Hamilton Hayne wrote to Cooke that Mrs. Hayne considered him "one of the very few real Southern gentlemen, left to show what the manners & morale of the South once were!"

Cooke's wife brought as her dowry a farm known as "The Briers," and in gardening as well as in writing Cooke sought relief from the gloom of Reconstruction Virginia. "Politics, and city and public life seem to me the merest farces," he wrote. "Literature and gardening are the really philosophic pursuits of life." In spite of his attempts to use modern farming methods, however, Cooke found that it took the income from his books to balance the budget.

In *The Heir of Gaymount* (1870), a book which cost him much labor, he tried to do something similar to what Ellen Glasgow was to do much more successfully in *Barren Ground*: to show how by scientific methods a planter could make money out of an estate reduced to forty acres. A part of the prescription was: "Come down to small things, above all, to *work*." Cooke, however, could not even here keep out mystery and sensation: it is a buried treasure, discovered by solving a cryptogram in Poe-like fashion, that gives the planter his financial independence. If in *The Heir of Gaymount* Cooke resorted to such devices, it can easily be imagined what he did in *Out of the Foam* (1872), which in the manuscript he had entitled *The Wolves of Pembrokeshire*. "The sort is not literature," he wrote, "and Reade invented it to make money. I am in want thereof, and I write the *Wolves* to sell, as I would raise wheat or corn, or make coats if I were a tailor. I follow 'the fashion'—when I should set it! . . . I have attempted a style and treatment not natural to me, and I do not propose, D. V. ever again to return to it.

. . . 'Out of the Foam' is mere melodrama." Not long before his death Cooke wrote:

I still write stories for such periodicals as are inclined to accept romance, but whether any more of my work in that field will appear in book-form is uncertain. Mr. Howells and the other realists have crowded me out of popular regard as a novelist, and have brought the kind of fiction I write into general disfavor. I do not complain of that, for they are right. They see, as I do, that fiction should faithfully reflect life, and they obey the law, while I can not. I was born too soon, and am now too old to learn my trade anew. . . . Besides, the fires of ambition are burned out of me, and I am serenely happy. My wheat-fields are green as I look out from the porch of "The Briers," the corn rustles in the wind, and the great trees give me shade upon the lawn. My three children are growing up in such nurture and admonition as their race has always deemed fit, and I am not only content, but very happy, and much too lazy to entertain any other feeling toward my victors than one of warm friendship and sincere approval.

The passage just quoted is characteristically generous, but Cooke was too ready to concede the field to the realists and to admit that romance represents an inferior mode of writing. He should have recalled *The Odyssey*, *As You Like it*, *The Heart of Midlothian*, and *The Last of the Mohicans* and reminded himself that the taste for romance, temporarily in abeyance, was certain to return. In fact, under the leadership of Stevenson, it had already begun to revive before Cooke's death. By using the romantic materials of Colonial Virginia in *Justin Harley* (1874) and *Canolles* (1877), the old-fashioned romancer had anticipated Mary Johnston in *Prisoners of Hope* (1898) and *To Have and To Hold* (1900). He never, however, quite succeeded in equaling *The Virginia Comedians*, published when he was only twenty-four. He had failed to develop into the writer he had promised to become. In later years his inventiveness flagged, and he repeated incidents and resorted still oftener to the tricks of tawdry melodrama. In *The Virginia Bohemians* (1880), however, he employed with partial success the newer methods of the local colorists, and in *My Lady Pokahontas* (1885) he treated with charm a theme which Thomas Dunn English had urged upon him years before.

Two of Cooke's historical works deserve mention: *Stories of the Old Dominion* (1879), written partly for his own children, and *Virginia: A History of the People* (1883), which he wrote for Houghton Mifflin's "American Commonwealths" series. On reading the latter book Edmund Clarence Stedman wrote to Cooke: "The narrative is clear, synthetic, fluent, and vivid in every way; Virginians and all other Americans owe you a debt for this graceful and scholarly work." By present-day standards Cooke's history is not to be described as scholarly, for here, as in his romances, Colonial Virginia is seen through a golden mist; but it is written with all the charm and skill of Cooke at his best, and when he is at his best there are few American historians who write with half his charm. The century following the Revolution, however, is only sketched; except for the Civil War years, the later history of Virginia did not lend itself to Cooke's romantic method of treatment. After his death in 1886 Thomas Nelson Page, Mrs. Burton Harrison, and his friend Eggleston were to discover for readers in North and South alike that Virginia plantation life in the 1850's was as attractive a background as that which Cooke had portrayed in his romances of the American Revolution.

31
John R. Thompson

JOHN REUBEN THOMPSON (1823–1873) was one of the few professional literary journalists of the Old South. His life illustrates the great difficulties which encompassed the Southern magazine editor. He was born and brought up in Richmond; but his father, a merchant, was a native of New Hampshire and his mother, Sarah (Dyckman) Thompson, belonged to a well-known New York family. After attending various schools in Richmond, Thompson spent a year in a preparatory school at East Haven, Connecticut, and then entered the University of Virginia. After two years he returned to Richmond and for the next two years studied law in the office of John A. Seddon. Although he practiced law for a short time, his real interests, like those of his friend John Esten Cooke, were all social and literary. At twenty-four he bought the *Southern Literary Messenger* from Benjamin Blake Minor, and he edited it from 1847 until 1860. Like Poe before him, he wanted to make the *Messenger* a national literary magazine of high quality and not a forum for political debate. In the 1850's, however, he found it impossible to keep the *Messenger* out of controversial questions. *Uncle Tom's Cabin* seemed to him the basest of all attacks upon the South, and he condemned it emphatically. And yet, though Thompson was a stout champion of a distinctively Southern literature, the *Messenger* under his editorship was less obviously sectional than any of its Charleston contemporaries. In January, 1860, in the last year of his long service as its editor, he wrote in the "Editor's Table" that the *Messenger* had not been obnoxiously sectional, like certain magazines of the North. He continued: "We have endeavoured to cultivate kindly feelings between the two divisions of the country, believing that in the Republic of Letters at least there should be no strifes and bickerings. . . . The magazine has been prompt to recognize the highest merit alike in all quarters of the land, and the sins of Bryant, the editor, have not deadened us to the beauties of Bryant, the poet."

Thompson was on friendly terms with many of the lesser Northern writers, especially in New York City, and he numbered among his contributors Richard Henry Stoddard, Thomas Bailey Aldrich, Park Benjamin, Rufus W. Griswold, Donald G. Mitchell ("Ik Marvel"), and Frank R. Stockton, who made his literary debut in the *Messenger*. Under Thompson's editorship the *Messenger* played an important part in the development of such Southern writers as Hayne, Timrod, and James Barron Hope. Although he knew Poe and published some of his writings in the magazine, he did not fully appreciate the man whose work had made the *Messenger* for the first time a magazine of importance. He was unable to see any merit in Whitman's *Leaves of Grass*. The *Messenger* ignored the first two editions of that epoch-making book, but after the third edition appeared, Thompson wrote in the *Southern Field and Fireside* for June 9, 1860: "Five years ago we recollect to have seen the first edition of it, and to have made up our mind that if it did not proceed from a lunatic, it was designed as a solemn hoax upon the public." [48]

Thompson himself contributed to the *Messenger* an occasional poem and reviewed books with taste and discrimination. He wrote now and then for *Harper's*, the *Literary World*, the *Knickerbocker*, Griswold's *International Monthly Magazine*, and after the war *Appletons' Journal*, *Harper's*, and the *Albion*.

In the winter of 1851 Thompson went to Charleston in the interests of the *Messenger* and became acquainted with Hayne and Timrod, both already contributors. On hearing of Thompson's death in 1873, Hayne described to Margaret J. Preston his first sight of Thompson:

How vividly I recall his appearance! Just 26 [he was 28] years old, slightly, but elegantly formed, with a manner far quicker & more vivacious, than it was in after life,—dressed in the height of the prevailing mode, with light-twilled pantaloons, and a blue coat, brass buttoned,—he shone upon us "hobbledehoys" —a somewhat radiant vision of a man, partly *littérateur*, and partly dandy! We liked him none the less, however, for this touch of the *petite mâitre* [sic],—and from that spring morning in the month of May 1849 [February, 1851]—when his

---

48 "A New American Poem," *So. Field and Fireside*, II, 20 (June 9, 1860). Thompson's article brought him a letter from Hayne in which the poet said: "Your critique upon Mr *Walt Whitman delighted* me beyond measure!" (D. M. McKeithan, *A Collection of Hayne Letters*, p. 127).

acquaintance was made—until the end of T's career—I, at least, can affirm that our friendship continued uninterrupted, growing warmer, despite many a year of separation. . . .

On May 11, 1850, Thompson wrote to A. L. Taveau: "I have sunk so far $5000 in endeavoring to give the Southern people a magazine worthy of their fame and their intellectual standing. . . . I think it merits a better fate than bankruptcy, while thousands of dollars are sent by Southern men to pay Northern magazines to abuse them. . . . Shall it die, to the shame of the Southern people?" In December, 1851, Thompson wrote to Griswold of his difficulties:

. . . the Messenger is almost "gone." I look into the future to see nothing but disaster; my affairs are really so much embarrassed that the sale of my library hangs over me like an impending doom and with no coryphaeus of the [re]d-flag fraternity like Keese to "knock down" my darlings. Four years of hard labour find me in debt my small patrimony exhausted and myself utterly unfitted for any sort of employment. I have followed the will-o'-the wisp, literary fame, into the morass and it has gone out, leaving me up to the armpits in the mud. Eh bien, I snap my fingers and whistle care down the wind!

Thompson sold the magazine to the firm which had printed it and up to 1860 continued to edit it for a small salary. In 1860 solely for financial reasons he accepted at $2000 a year the editorship of the *Southern Field and Fireside*. George W. Bagby succeeded him as editor of the *Messenger* at $300 a year.

The *Southern Field and Fireside*, combining the functions of a farm and home journal with those of a literary magazine, was comparatively prosperous. Unhappy at leaving Richmond, Thompson found Augusta, he wrote to Kennedy, "a very stupid provincial town." By the end of 1860 he had resigned his position and gone North in search of literary employment. Kennedy secured for him a position on the Baltimore *American*, but the war was now at hand. After Thompson had returned to Richmond, he wrote to Kennedy: "Our town is threatened with invasion by Lincoln's armies—my parents, my widowed sister, my home is here, every consideration of filial and patriotic duty would oblige me to remain and share in the fate of my native Virginia, apart from any convictions I might entertain of the original folly of secession." In Richmond Thompson served as Assistant Secretary of the Commonwealth and as librarian of the State Library; in 1863 he edited the *Record*; and he wrote for various other periodicals.

In the summer of 1864 he ran the blockade and joined the Confederate colony in London. He found employment on the *Index*, a weekly which had been established by Henry Hotze to present the Confederate cause to the British people. He found Tennyson, Carlyle, and other writers friendly; and he contributed, according to his own statement, to *Blackwood's, Punch, London Society*, and the *Standard*. He remained in London for a year after Appomattox and would have done well to remain longer, but he was homesick for Virginia. He arrived in Richmond in the autumn of 1866 to find the situation there much worse than he had anticipated. In April of the following year, convinced that there was no hope of employment for his pen in the South, he made his way to New York, where many Southerners were gathering.[49] The Confederate colony in New York welcomed Thompson, and he presently found employment on the *Albion*, a weekly with pro-English leanings. In May, 1868, he became literary editor of Bryant's *Evening Post*—a position to be held later by that Indiana-born ex-Confederate, George Cary Eggleston. Edmund Clarence Stedman had introduced Thompson to Bryant, and Simms had written to Bryant in his behalf. Thompson soon became one of the best-liked men on the *Post's* staff. Bryant later wrote of him: "He had read so variously, observed so minutely, and retained so tenaciously the results of his reading and observation that he was never at a loss for a topic and never failed to invest what he was speaking of with a rare and original interest. His fund of anecdote was almost inexhaustible, and his ability to illustrate any subject by apt quotation no less remarkable."

Meanwhile, Thompson's health—he had tuberculosis—grew steadily worse. He managed to keep himself going by drinking whisky on his doctor's orders. Early in 1872 his condition was so serious that Bryant took him to Cuba, the Bahamas, and Mexico so that he might escape the rigorous New York winter. In February, 1873, the *Post* on the advice of Thompson's physician sent him to Colorado. His place as literary editor was filled temporarily by another Southerner, James Wood Davidson. In Colorado Thompson's health failed to improve. He returned to New York, where he died on April 30, 1873. His last literary undertaking was an unfinished review of Hayne's edition of their friend Timrod's *Poems* (1873), which be-

---

[49] The Richmond weekly *Southern Opinion* on Oct. 3, 1868, copied from the New York *Evening Mail* a brief article in which it was stated that there were perhaps 25,000 Southerners in New York. Among the writers mentioned were Thompson, Edward A. Pollard, and James D. McCabe, Jr., of Richmond; A. J. Requier and J. C. Nott, of Mobile; and Miss Sally Marshall, of Kentucky. The *Mail* remarked of Thompson: "There is John R. Thompson, of Virginia, well and widely known as a most accomplished journalist, lecturer, poet, and critick. He resides in the city; but is over the country lecturing a good deal."

gan: "One of the truest and tenderest poets of America was Henry Timrod of South Carolina."

Thompson's life, like that of Timrod, was full of literary disappointments. The war prevented the completion of "The Poets and Poetry of the South," on which John Esten Cooke was collaborating with him. A fire destroyed the entire edition of his travel book, *Across the Atlantic*. In 1863 he sent his poems with Timrod's through the blockade for publication in London, but the manuscripts were never heard of again. Shortly before his death he again collected his poems and appointed as literary executor Richard Henry Stoddard, who seems to have lost the manuscript. Finally, in 1920, nearly half a century after his death, John S. Patton, Librarian of the University of Virginia, brought out an edition of his poems with a brief memoir.

Thompson was a writer of excellent occasional verse but, as he well knew, not the poet that Timrod was. He wrote to Griswold, December 21, 1849: ". . . I do not think I have any *right* to a place among our Poets. . . ." A few of his war poems—notably "Music in Camp," "The Burial of Latané," "Ashby," and "Lee to the Rear"—are equal to all but the best of Confederate war poems. Better still is his "Virginia Fuit," published in the *Old Guard* for May, 1867, in which he pictures the desolation which on his return from England he found in Reconstruction Virginia—now reduced to the status of Military District No. 1. A few of his lighter poems, like "The Window-Panes at Brandon," are charmingly done, and there are some good passages in his rhymed orations: "Washington," "Virginia," and "Poesy: An Essay in Rhyme." A passage in the first of these—written in 1858 for the unveiling of Crawford's statue of Washington in the Capitol Square in Richmond—contains some of his best lines. Timrod borrowed the stanza form for his "Charleston."

> Not queenly Athens, from the breezy height
>   Where ivory Pallas stood,
> As flowed along her streets in vestures white
>   The choral multitude—
>
> Not regal Rome, when wide her bugles roll'd
>   From Tagus to Cathay,
> As the long triumph rich with Orient gold
>   Went up the Sacred way—
>
> Not proud basilica or minster dim,
>   Filled with War's glittering files,
> As battle fugue or Coronation Hymn
>   Swept through the bannered aisles—

Saw pageant, solemn, grand or gay to view,
    In moral so sublime,
As this which seeks to crown with homage due
    The foremost man of Time!

Thompson was one of the many Southern magazinists who were calling for a Southern literature, but he could not see the poems and stories of Edgar Allan Poe as the answer to the demand. He saw Poe on his visits to Richmond in 1848 and 1849 when the poet was far from the man he had been when he left the *Messenger* in 1837. In October, 1850, in reviewing *The Literati* in the Richmond *Whig*, Thompson made a point of defending his friend Griswold's notorious memoir of Poe: "As far as we are capable of judging (and we had some intercourse with Poe at one period of his life), the record is truthful. . . ." In a lecture on Poe, privately printed in 1929 in an edition of only one hundred and fifty copies, he said: "I cannot now . . . call up the image of Poe as I knew him, without seeing him, as I once did, in a barroom, endeavoring to give a maudlin explanation of 'Eureka' to a circle of ruffianly fellows who had never heard of the Newtonian system or the law of gravitation, though they had often illustrated it by gravitating to the gutter." "The fanciful, speculative and abstruse reasoning of 'Eureka,' hiccupped in the language of the philosophers" disgusted the fastidious Thompson.[50] As editor of the *Messenger*, he had welcomed Poe as a contributor and been somewhat disappointed in what Poe sent him.

As time passed, he came to realize that Poe was a greater writer than he had thought him. He became something of a collector of Poe manuscripts, and to him we owe the text of " 'O Tempora! O Mores!' " perhaps the earliest specimen of Poe's verse that survives. Poe's case, he came to feel, called for "a larger and more liberal charity than is ordinarily extended to the infirmities of genius." "He had extraordinary genius, but he lacked sympathy," he said; "he was not selfish, but he did not enter warmly into the affairs of others who were ready to befriend him; he was capable of generous and chivalrous actions, but a wayward impulse made him neglectful of the inexorable duties of life."

I love to think of him as he appeared during the two months which immediately preceded his death, a quiet, easy, seemingly contented and well-bred

---

[50] *The Genius and Character of Edgar Allan Poe* (privately printed [Richmond], 1929), ed. J. H. Whitty and J. H. Rindfleisch. The quotation from the Richmond *Whig* appears on p. 57. The *So. Field and Fireside*, II, 212 (Nov. 24, 1860), gave a brief account of Thompson's lecture and printed an extract of some twenty lines. What changes he made in it after that time are not known. From the manner in which Thompson refers to an article which appeared in the *Edinburgh Review* in 1858, I infer that his lecture was written soon afterwards.

gentleman, conversing for hours with an opulence of language and of thought that was his alone, projecting new enterprises in literature, and now and then reading aloud some favorite verses of Tennyson and of Longfellow with an inflection and an emphasis that made the exercise as delightful as a sonata of Mozart. I mention Longfellow because I have heard Poe more than once recite the poem commencing: "The day is done, and the darkness," with something of enthusiasm, a fact which is enough to show that with all his faults, envy, that most despicable trait of the literary pretender, was no part of his nature.

Thompson did not think highly of Poe's critical writings. They lacked, he thought, "that vital element of sympathy which must enter into literary judgments," and he did not have complete confidence in the critic's honesty. He thought that Poe stirred up controversy because "he found the excitement of wrangling absolutely necessary to his mental equipoise . . . he kept on exchanging hard blows with others that he might not turn upon his own consciousness." "As a writer of stories Poe," he said, "was undeniably the most original and marvellous narrator that has ever enriched English literature with his creations." His tales were not healthy, but they possessed an amazing verisimilitude. What impressed Thompson in Poe's poems was "the charm of versification." He was "the Beethoven of language," but he was "mechanical to the last degree in the construction of his poems. . . ." In all that Poe wrote Thompson felt the strain of melancholy which for him always suggested, I think, the poet on the eve of a sordid and tragic death in Baltimore. In July, 1856, Thompson in a long poem "Virginia," which he read at William and Mary College, had lamented that there was no great Virginian poet:

> No favored son, created for all time,
> For thee has ever 'built the lofty rhyme'. . . .

He first paid tribute to the lamented Philip Pendleton Cooke and then he turned to Poe whose

> genius sought "a wild, weird, clime,"
> Beyond the bounds of either space or time,
> From whose dim circuit, with unearthly swell,
> A burst of lyric rapture often fell,
> Which swept at last into a strain as dreary
> As a lost spirit's plaintive *Miserere*;
> Unhappy POE, what destiny adverse
> Still hung around thee both to bless and curse!
> The Fairies' gifts, who on thy birth attended,
> Seemed all with bitter maledictions blended;
> The golden crown that on thy brow was seen,

Like that Medea sent to Jason's queen,
In cruel splendor shone but to consume,
And decked its victim proudly for the tomb.

32
Edgar Allan Poe

THE GREATEST OF all the Southern writers, Edgar Allan Poe (1809–1849),
was such an anomalous figure among American authors that his major
literary contemporaries, particularly in New England, failed to understand
him. The critics, too, until recent times wrote about him with less discernment than about more typical authors. The writer who is first and always
the artist is a type better understood in Europe than in America, where
literature not devoted to practical ends or to the inculcation of moral
principles has always been suspect. In our country, too, the author—in
disregard of known facts in the lives of many Old World writers—was
expected to be a man of irreproachable character. Poe was held up as a
horrible example of the unprincipled man of genius, or he was treated as
a lonely artist dwelling intellectually in a

wild weird clime that lieth sublime,
Out of SPACE—out of TIME.

Here we are primarily concerned with Poe's connections with the South.
This obviously is to take a partial view of the life and work of a writer who
admittedly had little interest in describing the Southern scene. There are,
however, too many discussions of Poe in which little attention is paid to
his Southern upbringing, his Southern friends and associates, or the Southern sources of his thought. "Northern critics and biographers," wrote Hervey
Allen, "seem, largely, to have forgotten that Edgar Allan Poe was a Southerner raised in the South." "I am a Virginian," Poe wrote to Frederick William Thomas in 1841; "at least I call myself one, for I have resided all my
life, until within the last few years, in Richmond."

If we do not count his five boyhood years in England, all but one of Poe's
first twenty-eight years were spent in the South. It was there that he formed
his literary taste and his views of society; there, too, that he mastered the
various crafts of critic, poet, and writer of tales. There also he edited his
first magazine, made his earliest literary friends, and received his first important recognition. When early in 1837 he left Richmond for the North,
he was approaching the peak of his powers. New York and Philadelphia
were more important literary centers than Richmond and Baltimore, but

they were little more disposed to recognize his greatness or even to pay him the equivalent of a decent salary. Wherever Poe lived, his lot was, in the words of Hardin Craig, that of "an unfortunate Southern gentleman, sensitive in temperament, cursed by poverty, illness, bereavement and plain hard luck, born at an unpropitious time in the development of our literature, always endangered and ultimately victimized by bad habits (with pride and other human weaknesses to help them on), but who was, nevertheless, noble and generous by nature, industrious, and intellectually as keen as one of his own Saracenic blades."

Poe's mother was an English actress, but his father, an actor of more ability than is generally supposed, belonged to a Maryland family that had seen somewhat better days. He was born, ironically enough, in Boston. Another Virginian, born to a different heritage, Robert E. Lee, was two years old on the day (January 19, 1809) that Poe was born. A few days before the death of Elizabeth Arnold Poe, Samuel Mordecai, the future historian of Richmond, wrote from that city to his sister, November 2, 1811: "A singular fashion prevails here this season—it is—charity—Mrs. Poe, who you know is a very handsome woman, happens to be very sick, and (having quarreled and parted with her husband) is destitute[.] The most fashionable place of resort, now is—her chamber—and the skill of cooks and nurses is exerted to procure her delicacies." When Mrs. Poe died on December 8, Edgar, an orphan boy of less than three years, was taken into the home of John and Frances (Valentine) Allan. They never, however, legally adopted him. Allan, himself an orphan, had his good qualities, and for a time he was fond of the boy; but he was hardly "that benevolent Virginian gentleman" whom Barrett Wendell imagined as trying to adopt Poe "into the gentler social classes of America." He was a narrow-minded and obstinate Scotch merchant with illegitimate children whose existence he tried to keep from the knowledge of his wife. He even tried to provide for them in a will that completely ignored the youth who had been reared in his home with the expectation of becoming the merchant's heir. A more unfortunate guardian for a youthful artistic genius it would be difficult to imagine. Nor was Frances Allan the ideal mother or wife. Her letters and Allan's mention frequent sick headaches and other illnesses which her husband thought largely imaginary. If she was the devoted mother that most of Poe's biographers have represented her as being, it is strange that in her letters she almost never mentions him—strange, too, that Poe, who writes to Allan but not to her, rarely mentions her in his letters. She may have spoiled the boy by giving him too much pocket money, but it is recorded that Poe, although he often visited in the homes of his boy friends, rarely asked them to his.

His boyhood worship of Jane Stith Stanard, to whom he paid tribute in "To Helen," suggests that Frances Allan was not the devoted mother so often imagined.

The Allans sent the boy to good academies in Richmond and during their stay in London placed him in John Bransby's excellent school at Stoke Newington. It is worth noting that Poe, like Robert Munford and Edward Coote Pinkney before him, owed in part to his English education his freedom from certain provincial attitudes toward life and literature. He quickly showed his native bent by writing verses, most of which are lost. Among the very earliest that survive is " 'O Tempora! O Mores!' " a satire on a dry-goods clerk named Pitts. By the time he was seventeen, he had discovered some of the writers who were to influence him most: Milton, Moore, Byron, and Coleridge. All of these except Milton were widely influential among the Southern writers of his time. If Poe was already dreaming of a literary career rather than the gentlemanly practice of law, there seemed little likelihood that he would ever have to live by his pen, for in 1825 Allan inherited a large sum of money from the elder William Galt.

Poe spent most of the year 1826 at the newly opened University of Virginia, where were gathered 177 young Southerners, many of them with too much pocket money and too little discipline. His academic record was excellent, and there is nothing against him in the University's books. The courses for which he registered and the books he borrowed from the library indicate an interest in foreign languages, literature, and history. His professors—all foreign-born—contributed to the widening of his intellectual interests beyond those of the average American college student. He was undoubtedly reading the English Romantic poets, and *Tamerlane*, composed under the spell of Byron, must have been at least partly written before he left the University.

The year in Charlottesville was not a happy one. Poe was disturbed over news of difficulties at home, for by this time Frances Allan must have known of her husband's infidelity, and, still more, by the strange silence of Sarah Elmira Royster, to whom he had become engaged before he left Richmond. The girl's parents, knowing that Allan did not now intend to make Poe his heir, intercepted the lovers' letters and persuaded Elmira to marry an older man whose future seemed secure. As if Poe did not already have sufficient troubles for a single year, his guardian—if we may accept the detailed account in Poe's letters to Allan—had not given him enough money to pay his necessary college expenses. He took to gambling in the hope of winning enough to pay his bills and, losing, plunged deeper into debt. When Poe returned to Richmond in December, there was a violent quarrel.

Allan not only refused to let him return to Charlottesville; he refused to pay his debts—including at least one debt for clothing—which are said to have amounted to two thousand dollars or more. Poe's social status as the son of actors and the foster son of a Scotch merchant had probably given him a feeling of insecurity long before. Now he must have felt *déclassé*. If he could not pay his debts of honor, how could he mingle freely with the sons of gentlemen planters?

Somehow the Byronic young poet made his way to Boston, where he published *Tamerlane and Other Poems* (1827). This is the most famous collectors' item in American literature; but although it treats the now familiar themes of love, beauty, pride, and the death of a beautiful woman, it gives few indications of poetic genius. Under stress of necessity, Poe enlisted in the United States Army, giving his name as Edgar A. Perry. Part of the next two years he spent at Fort Moultrie near Charleston. At the end of his period of service he had risen to sergeant major and his superiors testified to his good habits and to his competence. He procured his discharge with the hope that he would be able to enter the Military Academy at West Point. In 1829 he published in Baltimore, where he was then living, *Al Aaraaf, Tamerlane, and Minor Poems.* William Wirt, whom Poe had asked to read "Al Aaraaf" in manuscript, was able to make nothing even of the beautiful song to Ligeia, which is among the best lyrics Poe was ever to write.

After some delay Poe entered West Point late in June, 1830. Meanwhile Frances Allan was dead and her husband was on the point of marrying again. There was no longer any hope of an inheritance in Richmond. The West Point routine became a bore. Many of the students were younger or less mature than Poe, and he did not have the leisure he had had in the regular army. He learned to his disappointment that his previous service would not reduce the time necessary to secure his commission as lieutenant, and he probably concluded that even with a commission it would be difficult to live on a lieutenant's pay. If he remained in the army, he would probably be sent to some post remote from books, writers, and publishers. If he was to accomplish the lofty purposes for which he was made, it was high time that he was giving his energies to literature. In March, 1831, he was court-martialed and dismissed for persistent failure to attend the required exercises. John Allan had refused to give him permission to resign, and Poe had taken the most obvious method of freeing himself from a way of life that had grown meaningless and unbearable. He made his way to New York, where he brought out a third volume, *Poems* (1831). This book, published when Poe was only twenty-two, contains half of the finest poems he was ever to write, though none of them are in their final form. Since he now had no home in Richmond, he went to Baltimore, where in genteel poverty he lived with his aunt, Mrs. Maria Clemm.

Poe's three volumes of verse failed to attract attention or to bring him royalties; hence he decided that if he was to earn money by writing he must turn to prose. Apparently he studied the tales in *Blackwood's* and other magazines while he was writing his earliest stories. On April 30, 1835, he wrote to the proprietor of the *Southern Literary Messenger*, who had disliked the subject of "Berenice": "The history of all Magazines shows plainly that those which have attained celebrity were indebted for it to articles *similar in nature—to Berenice*—although, I grant you, far superior in style and execution. I say similar in *nature*. You ask me in what does this nature consist? In the ludicrous heightened into the grotesque: the fearful coloured into the horrible: the witty exaggerated into the burlesque: the singular wrought out into the strange and mystical." Poe had made up his mind to cultivate what he was later to call the grotesque and the arabesque. Editors and readers were to complain of the "Germanism" and "gloom" of his subject matter, but he never varied far from the path which he had marked out for himself. His conception of beauty, it should be remembered, included the horrible. "Even out of deformities," he said, the imagination "fabricates that *Beauty* which is at once its sole object and its inevitable test."

In 1832 Poe submitted some of his stories to the Philadelphia *Courier* in competition for a prize. The *Courier* printed some of the tales, but it awarded the prize to Delia Bacon, who was later to espouse the strange theory that the plays of Shakespeare were written by Francis Bacon. The next year Poe competed for two prizes offered by the Baltimore *Saturday Visiter*. The twenty-five-dollar prize for the best poem was given to John H. Hewitt, though Poe had submitted "The Coliseum"; but the committee of judges awarded the prize of fifty dollars for the best story to his "MS. Found in a Bottle." The committee, moreover, urged the young author to publish all of "The Tales of the Folio Club." "These tales," they said, "are eminently distinguished by a wild, vigorous, and poetical imagination, a rich style, a fertile invention, and varied and curious learning." The ambitious and industrious young writer had finally emerged from obscurity; his poverty, however, was to cling to him to the last.

One of the three judges was John Pendleton Kennedy, who though he moved in a circle remote from Poe's, recognized the gentleman in the shabbily dressed young man and befriended him in various ways. He advised him to lay aside his unfinished poetic tragedy, *Politian*, and write what would be more immediately profitable. He recommended him to Thomas W. White, who had founded the *Southern Literary Messenger* in 1834, after Poe had left Richmond. Poe began to write for the magazine and to send White practical suggestions for its improvement. In 1835 he went to Richmond as White's editorial assistant. In that capacity he read proof, corresponded with contributors, wrote critical notices of new books, looked after the office routine, and performed even more menial services. White was by trade a printer with little education who was trying to run a literary magazine with such editorial assistance as he could get from capable amateur writers like James E. Heath, Lucian Minor, and Beverley Tucker. He once offered the editorship to Minor, but he was never willing to make Poe anything more than an editorial assistant.

Poe published in the *Messenger* tales and poems that won the admiration of Tucker and Philip Pendleton Cooke, but it was only by his book reviews that he attracted wide attention. Where he had served his apprenticeship as a reviewer is not known, but from the outset he was master of a vigorous critical method which owed much to a study of Coleridge and the British quarterlies. He could not prevent White from printing much inferior material in the body of the magazine, but in his reviews he soon made it evident that here at last was an American critic with the equipment and the courage to appraise by nonprovincial standards the work of poetasters and sentimental novelists accustomed to indiscriminate praise. His standards were too high to please his contemporaries, but he was not lacking in the editorial intuition for what would attract attention to the magazine. When he dissected Theodore Fay's pretentious and widely advertised *Norman Leslie,* he must have known that his review would attract attention in New York, for Fay was one of the editors of the *New-York Mirror.* During his connection with the *Messenger,* according to Poe's estimate, the circulation of the magazine rose from seven hundred to over five thousand. It was largely through his work that a struggling Southern monthly had become for the moment the best literary magazine in the United States. White, however, never gave him a free hand in accepting or rejecting manuscripts; and though Poe had probably saved the *Messenger* from early extinction, he was not willing to let it be stated in his columns that Poe was its editor. He finally made up his mind to part with Poe, but the poet's occasional drinking was not the determining factor. White wrote to Beverley Tucker on December 27, 1836: ". . . I am cramped by him in the exercise of my own judgement, as to articles I shall or shall not admit into my work. It is true that I neither have his sagacity, nor his learning—but I do believe I know a handspike from a saw." No, the *Messenger* was his private property, and he would run it to suit himself. He must have been very stupid, however, if he did not know that he could never find another editor of Poe's competence. Poe, for his part, seeing the profits of his labors going into the proprietor's pockets, had begun to dream of founding a magazine of his own. Like many another Southern writer since his time, he believed that he would fare better in one of the Northern cities. It was already obvious that the important literary centers would be found in the North. There perhaps he would find more time, too, for the creative work he wished to do.

We shall not follow in detail the varying fortunes of the young Southern writer in Philadelphia and New York. He was soon to write better poems and tales, and he was to make clearer his critical standards; but when he left Richmond in 1837, at the age of twenty-eight, he was no novice but a master of his craft. "Ligeia," certainly one of his best tales, appeared the following year.

Richmond, Poe's home during most of his formative years, was a city of less than twenty thousand people—too small to support any professional writers except newspapermen—but it was the capital of a large and important state and it was a center of trade and manufacture. The testimony of travelers who visited Richmond does not bear out William Crary Brownell's notions in regard to "the half savage, half aristocratic society" in which Poe grew up. James Kirke Paulding, Washington Irving, Albert Gallatin, William Ellery Channing, Kennedy, Thackeray, and others testified to the intelligence and charm of Richmond society. The city had excellent newspapers, schools, private libraries, and bookstores which sold standard books and the latest importations from British as well as American publishers.

Among the well-to-do there were three important classes: the planters, the professional men, and the merchants and manufacturers. The planters, who either lived or visited in the city, gave society a tone which served in part to counteract the narrowness of men engaged in commercial pursuits. There were also the members of the state legislature, employees of the state, lawyers, doctors, ministers, and newspapermen. Before William Wirt left the city in 1817, there had been considerable literary activity among the Democratic lawyers and journalists, but in Poe's mature years the chief Virginia writers were living in other parts of the state.

Richmond, it is too often forgotten, was an important center of trade. Ships came up the James and took on loads of coal and agricultural products brought down the James River Canal from the back country. In Poe's time

there was surprisingly little social discrimination against the Scotch merchant families, the Galts, the Allans, the Ellises, and the Mackenzies, who
constituted the social circle in which Poe moved in his earliest years. Extant
letters of the Allans, Galts, and Ellises are marked by a combination of
Scotch religiosity and thrift that at least one reader has found oppressive.
Perhaps Poe also found it so. John Allan was something of a social climber,
but he was not wealthy until late in life. In 1825 he bought for $14,950
"Moldavia," a fine house originally owned by David Meade Randolph, who
in 1798 had employed William Ellery Channing as a tutor for his children.
The Allans, in later years certainly, were received in the homes of some of
the best families of the city. Frances Allan was the orphan daughter of a
small planter. Poe's connection with the planter tradition—of which he
made almost nothing in his writings—came chiefly through her and her
sister Ann Valentine. It was surely to them that he owed the best part of
his breeding; and that his manners were those of a gentleman we have the
emphatic testimony of Kennedy, Graham, Willis, Mrs. Whitman, Mrs.
Osgood, Mrs. Richmond, and many others. He had the courtesy, reserve, and
pride of the Southerner which were not always understood in Philadelphia
and New York.

The age in which Poe lived was, especially in New England, an age in
which literature was valued as an instrument of reform. He had little sympathy with reformers trying to make the world over, and he was too much
the pessimist to share the optimism of Emerson and Lowell, who expected
of poor human nature more than in its ordinary varieties it seems capable of
producing. There were other Southerners who shared Poe's attitude toward
the gospel of Progress. An anonymous reviewer of Herbert Spencer's *Social
Statics* wrote in the *Quarterly Review* of the Southern Methodists in April,
1856: "The doctrine of perfectibility was a dream of the last century; it is a
folly in this. . . . Man remains essentially the same throughout the shifting career in which he is exhibited by history." He added: "Optimism of any
kind is always a mark of intellectual imbecility."

The critics who have bemoaned Poe's indifference to reforms have not
reckoned with the conservative influences which played upon him in his
youth. Richmond was predominantly Whig, though the state was usually
Democratic; and Poe though not a party man certainly preferred the Whigs
to the Jacksonian Democrats. He was an admirer of John Marshall, but
there is almost nothing to suggest that he admired Jefferson or subscribed to
his liberal opinions, except in religion. He grew to manhood in a time of
Southern reaction against Jeffersonian liberalism when the leading classes
in Virginia were becoming alarmed by the isms emanating from New Eng-

land. Even after Poe, following his break with Allan, had left Richmond, there is nothing to indicate that he held any radical opinions about society. In this he was a typical Southerner of his time. If Poe distrusted political democracy, he was only thinking what men like Beverley Tucker and Calhoun were saying more emphatically than he did. It should be noted that it was not Poe but Beverley Tucker who reviewed James Kirke Paulding's *Slavery in the United States* in the *Messenger* for April, 1836. Harrison's inclusion of it in the Virginia Edition of Poe's writings has led critics and biographers to belabor Poe for a review he did not write and for opinions he may not have held.

The South of Poe's time was not tolerant of political or religious heterodoxy; yet it permitted the development of one's individuality, even to eccentricity. And Poe was primarily an individualist. He wrote to Lowell on July 2, 1844: "I cannot agree to lose sight of man the individual in man the mass." He was certainly no democrat except in so far as the republic of letters was concerned. He denounced Charles Lever's "blind and grovelling worship of mere rank," and he resented in Griswold's anthology what he thought was a discrimination in favor of writers who had wealth or social prominence.

One finds in Poe, as in Richard Henry Wilde, Edward Coote Pinkney, Thomas Nelson Page, Sidney Lanier, and Mark Twain, something akin to the Renaissance literary worship of woman as embodying the spirit of beauty and goodness. It is seen in his love of Virginia Poe, which George Graham described as "a sort of rapturous worship of the spirit of beauty which he felt fading before his eyes." It is seen in his "Hymn" to the Virgin Mary and in his belief that the most poetical topic in the world is the death of a beautiful woman, perhaps even in his laudatory reviews of Mrs. Osgood and Mrs. Browning. The Southern semichivalric glorification of woman— greatly exaggerated in the legend—is only a partial explanation, though Poe's notions about the position of woman were definitely Southern. In the 1850's Paul Hamilton Hayne, visiting John R. Thompson in the *Messenger* office in Richmond, saw some Poe manuscripts and letters. Writing of the experience afterwards to Essie B. Cheesborough, he said:

> One of the latter [the letters] especially struck me: Poe says, (speaking of his experience in the matter of friendship) that almost all his *male* friends had at one period, or another, deserted him: "Just," he remarked "when I most needed aid and sympathy from them, they turned upon me, some with a civil sneer, others with brutal, outspoken rudeness, and left me struggling in the mire, unpitied, lonely, desperate. But women do not argue logically as to one's merits or demerits;—they follow certain heart instincts more profound sometimes than

the deductions of philosophy, and so, (God eternally bless them!) they have been angels of mercy to me, and have tenderly led me from the verge of ruin, while men stood aloof and mocked." [51]

Poe had few close friends among men, but women were invariably fascinated by him. The memory of kind and beautiful women who had loved him haunted him all his life. There was his mother, who died before he was three years old; Mrs. Stanard, his first "Helen," whom he lost in boyhood; Sarah Elmira Royster, who married another; Frances Allan, who died when he was twenty; and above all there was Virginia, by the fear of whose death he was haunted for years before she died. After her death he displayed a morbid craving for the love and sympathy of women, particularly Sarah Helen Whitman and Annie Richmond. In "The Poetic Principle" when he enumerated the things which "induce in the Poet himself the true poetical effect," he gave the climactic position to woman's love and beauty:

He feels it in the beauty of woman—in the grace of her step—in the lustre of her eye—in the melody of her voice—in her soft laughter—in her sigh—in the harmony of the rustling of her robes. He deeply feels it in her winning endearments—in her burning enthusiasms—in her gentle charities—in her meek and devotional endurances—but above all—ah, far above all—he kneels to it—he worships it in the faith, in the purity, in the strength, in the altogether divine majesty—of her *love*.

For Poe, the principle of poetry was "the Human Aspiration for Supernal Beauty," and "Love—the true, the divine Eros—the Uranian, as distinguished from the Dionaean Venus—is unquestionably the purest and truest of all poetical themes."

Among American writers Poe and Henry James are the best examples of the man of letters. Our other writers have too often been artists and something else besides. "Depend upon it after all, Thomas, literature is the most noble of professions," wrote Poe in the last year of his life. "In fact, it is about the only one fit for a man. For my own part there is no seducing me from the path. I shall be a *littérateur* at least, all my life; nor would I abandon the hopes which still lead me on for all the gold in California." If Poe had inherited Allan's wealth, he might, like James, have taken refuge in London or Paris, where the artist was a less lonely figure than anywhere in the United States. There was in his time outside journalism only the scantiest room for the professional writer—least of all in the South and the West. Nearly all other Southern—and most Northern—writers were ama-

[51] MS "Recollections of Paul H. Hayne" (1886) in the Duke University Library. Hayne is presumably quoting from memory a lost Poe letter. It is worth noting that immediately after quoting the passage given in the text, Hayne added: "Ah! he was right."

teurs for whom literature was an avocation, not a means of livelihood. Poe aspired to be a professional writer, but none of his books brought him money. A single copy of *Tamerlane* has been sold for more money probably than Poe ever got from all he wrote. His first ambition had been to be a poet, but his poems did not pay, and only toward the end of his life did one of them, "The Raven," attract wide attention. For a living he turned to the magazines. By editing them or writing stories and book reviews for them he could earn a scanty living. (British magazines were being reprinted in New York and sold at the low price of four yearly subscriptions for eight dollars.) The main reason why the publishers of American magazines paid anything at all to their contributors was that their readers demanded short stories and other materials which could not in sufficient quantity be pirated from abroad.

The lot of the magazinist was a hard one. In June, 1844, Poe wrote to Charles Anthon that he had been "so far essentially a Magazinist [illegible] bearing, not only willingly but cheerfully, sad poverty and the thousand consequent contumelies and other ills which the condition of the mere Magazinist entails upon him in America, where, more than in any other region upon the face of the globe, to be poor is to be despised." In another mood, however, Poe, weary of working for Graham, who was making money from his magazine, wrote to Thomas, July 4, 1841, that he would be glad to accept a government clerkship—"even a $500 one—so that I [may] have something independent of letters for a subsistence. To coin one's brain into silver, at the nod of a master, is to my thinking, the hardest task in the world."

Had Poe been born half a century later, he would have been able to earn a substantial living by writing for the magazines; but in his time he was doing well when *Graham's Magazine*, which boasted of its liberality to its contributors, gave him four or five dollars a page for his exquisite prose while N. P. Willis was getting eleven. Professor Mott estimates that in the year 1843, when he was at the peak of his achievement, Poe's writings brought him only about three hundred dollars. And Poe was a hard worker. No idle Bohemian could have turned out by the time he was forty the materials comprised in the fifteen volumes of his collected works. He was one of the ablest magazine editors of his time; but he was never adequately paid, never had a wholly free hand in his editorial policies, and always saw the lion's share of the profits go into the pockets of the owner.

In February, 1836, Poe reviewed in the *Messenger* a book that prompted him to express his resentment at society's treatment of the artist. This was *Conti the Discarded*, by the London music critic, poet, and novelist, Henry

F. Chorley, who was all his life interested in the relations of artistic genius to society. In his Preface Chorley said that he had long looked "with painful interest on the unreckoned-up account of misunderstanding and suspicion which exist between the world and the artist. I have grieved when I have seen the former disposed to degrade Art into a mere plaything, to be enjoyed without respect and then cast aside, instead of receiving her high works as among the most humanising blessings ever vouchsafed to man by a beneficent Creator." Chorley's stories deal with musicians; but Poe, drudging for White in an indifferent Richmond, felt keenly that Chorley's indictment applied to writers in America as well as to musicians in England:

We repeat it—our whole heart is with the author. When *shall* the artist assume his proper situation in society—in a society of thinking beings? How long shall he be enslaved? How long shall mind succumb to the grossest materiality? How long shall the veriest vermin of the Earth, who crawl around the altar of Mammon, be more esteemed of men than they, the gifted ministers to those exalted emotions which link us with the mysteries of Heaven? To our own query we may venture a reply. Not long. Not long will such rank injustice be committed or permitted. A spirit is already abroad at war with it.

Poe was at this time far more hopeful of finding a place for himself as an artist in American society than he was ten years later when in the only extant letter to his wife he wrote: "You are my *greatest* and *only* stimulus now, to battle with this uncongenial, unsatisfactory, and ungrateful life."

If in 1836 Poe looked at what the chief Southern writers were doing for a living, he could have found little to encourage him to hope for a place in the South where the artist would receive honor and earn a decent living. Kennedy was soon to desert literature for law, business, social life, and politics. George Tucker was Professor of Moral Philosophy at the University of Virginia and was now more concerned with economics than with literature. Beverley Tucker was publishing two novels in 1836, but his primary concern was with law and politics. William Maxwell had given up poetry for law, journalism, and teaching. Caruthers had published two of his three novels and was about to settle in Savannah to continue the practice of medicine. Daniel Bryan was postmaster at Alexandria. Philip Pendleton Cooke, unsuccessful both as lawyer and as planter, was intermittently writing poetry in spite of the apathy of his foxhunting friends. The only Southern writers who might be called professional were the well-to-do Chivers and Simms, who in 1836 was raising his social and financial position—as Poe had certainly not done—by marrying a planter's daughter. So far as authorship was concerned, the South was still in the status of a colony. The leading publishing houses and magazines were in the North.

To be sure, the situation there was not much better, for hardly one of the chief American writers of the time was able consistently to earn a living by his pen. This, however, Poe probably did not yet know.

Poe might have been happier if he had remained in Richmond. Boston was beginning to honor its writers, but in Philadelphia and New York the professional writer had no standing. Edmund Clarence Stedman in 1890 spoke to an interviewer about Fitz-James O'Brien and others who were writing in New York a decade after Poe's death:

> There was a pathetic side to those days. If many of these men were living now, as some of them are, with equal wit and romance and ambition in their way, they would be in society, have cheerful homes, belong to clubs, have stable if not handsome incomes—in short, lead the lives of other successful professional men. As it was, the pace, the hard work, the irregular income together killed off many of them. No other such list of names that I remember could show such a death roll within fifteen years from that period—from '59 to '63. That was New York's Bohemian Olympiad.

In the North Poe found himself not in the social circles which included an Irving, a Cooper, or a Longfellow but in the world of Griswold and the Literati. What impressed Poe's biographer, George E. Woodberry, about this shabby world was "the mean literary poverty of the time, its atmosphere of impecuniosity, of little pay for the best work, of a log-rolling and subsidized criticism and feeble product; its environment of gossip and scandal, its deficient integrity, its undeniable vulgarity, its Grub-Street and Dunciad populace with the disadvantages of a large female immigration into these purlieus. . . . If oblivion could have been the lot of such literary mortality as is here disclosed, it would have been nothing to be sorry for. . . ."

Here was no place for the artist with ideals of perfection. Poe's mature books paid no better than his early ones. He tried to make his stories more marketable by treating topics of current interest, but he would not stoop to the writing of "namby-pamby love tales." In this alien world he found himself compromising his own ideals. He himself indulged in logrolling tactics. He edited the verses of poetesses for pay. He ridiculed Griswold as a man whose intellect he despised and then tried to make up with him, for Griswold was in a position to further his literary aims. The great critic stooped to literary gossip in "The Literati" instead of writing the critical history of American literature which he had planned. He got into a libel suit with Thomas Dunn English and as a result all his personal failings were advertised to the world. No wonder that late in life he said to Mrs. Weiss in Richmond: "You must not judge of me by what you find me saying in the magazines. Such expressions of opinion are necessarily modified by a thousand circumstances, the wishes of editors, personal friendship, etc." In 1851 Chivers, who had not compromised his ideals, wrote to Griswold: "You are very much mistaken if you suppose that I endorse everything that Poe did. He married the Venus Urania in early life; but afterwards committed adultery with the Venus Pandemos." Poe, however, never sank quite so low as his enemy, English, who wrote to John Esten Cooke on January 25, 1859, explaining why he was writing for Bonner's *New York Ledger:* "I write because it pays. I own to you that I am living in a state of literary prostitution—and deal out my favors to all who appear with heavy purses." English insisted, however, that he would not sell his opinions.

"How dreadful is the present condition of our Literature!" Poe wrote to Lowell in March, 1844. "To what are things tending? We want two things, certainly:—an International Copy-Right Law, and a well-founded Monthly Journal, of sufficient ability, circulation, and character, to control, and so give tone to, our Letters." Poe wanted a magazine of his own, as he wrote to Philip Pendleton Cooke, August 9, 1846, "in which the men of genius may fight their battles; upon some terms of equality with those dunces, the men of talent." Failing to find a backer for his projected *Penn Magazine*, Poe evolved another and more grandiose scheme which he outlined in the letter to Lowell from which I have quoted. It was to be a magazine owned by, and filled exclusively with the writings of, the best living American authors. Each writer was to make an initial investment of two hundred dollars. "A nominal editor to be elected from among the number. How could such a journal fail?" Lowell, still smarting from the failure of the *Pioneer*, which had left him in debt, did not even trouble himself to reply to Poe's proposal. Most biographers except Quinn have regarded the project as visionary, but the success in our century of the Playwrights' Theatre, of musicians' unions, and book clubs suggests that Poe may have been simply a hundred years ahead of his time.

The first important recognition of Poe's literary talents came from writers in his own section, but the great majority of Southern readers of the *Messenger* failed to see in his work more than competent magazine writing. Significant appreciation came, as I have shown elsewhere in these pages, from Kennedy, Beverley Tucker, Philip Pendleton Cooke, Chivers, Simms, and James M. Legaré; but the owner of the *Messenger* and James Heath and Lucian Minor, upon whom White depended for editorial advice, all apparently failed to see in Poe more than the competent literary journalist. Beverley Tucker, who, like these men, belonged to an older generation, came nearer to discerning Poe's exceptional ability. Younger Virginia writers like John R. Thompson, John Esten Cooke, and John M. Daniel, who knew

Poe only in the late forties, recognized him as a writer of great talent, but until after his death they could not see in the victim of bad habits one of the really great American writers of all time.

Poe, furthermore, was not the kind of writer for which the South was clamoring. He was indifferent to the Southern scene in his fiction, and he did not devote himself to a defense of the Southern civilization. He wrote no Southern historical romances, like Simms and Cooke, and he had no interest in glorifying the Southern plantation. There was, nevertheless, something Southern in Poe's genius, which is perhaps best expressed in the words of Ellen Glasgow in A Certain Measure: ". . . Poe is, to a large extent, a distillation of the Southern. The formalism of his tone, the classical element in his poetry and in many of his stories, the drift toward rhetoric, the aloof and elusive intensity,—all these qualities are Southern. And in his more serious faults of overwriting, sentimental exaggeration, and lapses, now and then, into a pompous or florid style, he belongs to his epoch and even more to his South."

The first American writers and critics to recognize Poe's importance were, as I have indicated, Southerners; and yet apart from these few, Poe's work was no better appreciated in the South than in Philadelphia or New York. It was not until after his death in 1849 that Southerners began playing him up as a great Southern writer maligned by Griswold and neglected by Northern critics. The Civil War strengthened this tendency, and in the seventies and eighties Poe was often held up as an example of unappreciated Southern genius. It must be said, however, that those who praised him often showed little understanding of the significance of his work. Poe was Southern on one side only. He was, as I have said, an urban, not a rural, type; a professional, not an amateur writer; an artist, not a glorifier of the plantation tradition. His influence, however, is perceptible in certain important Southern writers, particularly Paul Hamilton Hayne, Sidney Lanier, Lafcadio Hearn, John Banister Tabb, James Branch Cabell, and, I think, DuBose Heyward and Conrad Aiken. It is also obvious in Vachel Lindsay, born in Springfield, Illinois, of Southern parents. Southern writers of fiction—like Fitz-James O'Brien and Ambrose Bierce and other writers from the West and the North—learned something from Poe's technical mastery of his craft, but until the twentieth century they rarely followed him into the region of morbid psychology.

In Poe's mature years New England and the South, each of which had inherited many misconceptions of the other, were drifting further and further apart. Poe shared in a measure the Southern distrust of New England, but he laid it aside when he met a New Englander whom he liked or whose writings he admired. No sectional prejudice prevented him from quickly recognizing the merits of Longfellow, Lowell, and Hawthorne, all of whom at one time or another he praised quite as highly as they deserved. While still living in Virginia, he lamented the Southern prejudice against New England. In fact, all his expressions of hostility to that section were written while he was living in the North. In Philadelphia and New York, as we often fail to remember, there were many to whom the New England authors looked like a mutual admiration society which recognized no writers so unfortunate as to live west of the Hudson River or farther south than New York. Eighteen years after Poe's death George Henry Boker in Philadelphia wrote to Paul Hamilton Hayne in Georgia: "According to the Yankee creed, Longfellow, Lowell, Holmes, Emerson and Whittier are the only poets in America, and also the only poets that New England will permit to exist."

It was while living in the North that Poe came to see the literary product of New England as a sectional literature masquerading in the guise of a national literature. In his projected *Penn Magazine* he planned to promote a literature in which all sections would share. In the *Broadway Journal* in 1845 he was, as he wrote during the so-called "Longfellow War," trying to open the eyes of the New Englanders "to certain facts which have long been obvious to all the world except themselves—the facts that there exist other cities than Boston—other men of letters than Professor Longfellow—other vehicles of literary information than the 'Down-East Review.' " He boasted that his "friends in the Southern and Western country" were taking up arms in his cause—"and more especially in the cause of a national as distinguished from a sectional literature." He wrote to Daniel Bryan in 1842: "I shall make war to the knife [in the *Penn*] against the New-England assumption of 'all the decency and all the talent' which has been so disgustingly manifested in the Rev. Rufus W. Griswold's 'Poets & Poetry of America.' " Lowell's *A Fable for Critics*, he charged, practically ignored all but New England writers. The American literary capital, he insisted, should be not Boston but New York. Bostonians, we may be sure, did not take the suggestion kindly. Twenty-five years after Poe's death Edmund Clarence Stedman said in an interview that the "literary metropolis" was rapidly shifting from Boston to New York. Soon afterwards his friend Thomas Bailey Aldrich wrote him that literary Boston was in an uproar. "Gad," he said, "these Bostonians are not thin-skinned on the subject—they haven't any skin at all!"

Poe in short had an excellent case against literary New England, but unfortunately he handled it so badly that he gave offense to New England writers without being able to rally to his cause the literary forces of other sections. His charges of plagiarism gave offense to those who did not understand that what he had in mind was not moral obliquity but a spirit of imitativeness. There was in Poe's make-up something of what he called "the imp of the perverse." For him, as he once confessed, "the most exquisite of sublunary pleasures" was "the making a fuss, . . . the 'kicking up a bobbery.'" With his peculiar sense of humor it seemed good sport to attack Longfellow as a plagiarist, to poke fun at the *North American Review*, and to laugh at Boston as the "Frogpond." Perhaps at the time all this seemed good journalistic copy for the *Broadway Journal*, but Poe's attacks simply scandalized the New England literati. Too vulnerable himself, he made the capital mistake of offending Rufus W. Griswold, another literary New Englander; and Griswold avenged himself by writing a memoir—regarded as authoritative for a whole generation—in which he pictured Poe as just the unprincipled man of genius that New Englanders would regard with horror. Poe was the one black sheep in the American literary flock. Our literature has had enough of them since his time to make up for any deficiency we may have had in comparison with the writers of other nations; but there are still people who shudder, as it were, when Poe's name is mentioned. Edith Wharton has a story entitled "Autres Temps, Autres Moeurs . . . ," the point of which is that society, having condemned a woman for an offense against its standards—in this case leaving her husband and running away with another man—never reconsiders her special case even when that particular offense ceases to be regarded as a heinous sin. Poe as the unprincipled man of genius was placed quite outside the national literary tradition.

There was a wide gulf between Poe's conception of the literary art and that held by the New Englanders. He was primarily an artist who for a living followed the unprofitable occupation of a magazinist. As an artist he was not in sympathy with many of the writings of the professors, lyceum lecturers, and professional reformers, to whom literature was not so much an art as a means of accomplishing some nonliterary aim. To such a critic as he the New England writers with the exception of Hawthorne seemed when judged as literary artists inferior or at least very uneven. His criticism of Longfellow, which is really craftsman's criticism of a high order, must have seemed to the New England poet entirely too personal and ungentlemanly. What the New England writers really wanted was praise and not criticism. Even Hawthorne could not write about Poe or even write to him without belittling the function of the literary critic. And Poe was at that time Hawthorne's stoutest champion. Lowell came finally to understand that, as Poe charged, he was confusing the function of poetry with that of preaching, but he resented the charge of plagiarism and even in his later years continued to underrate Poe's work on the ground that his character was bad.

Poe failed conspicuously to foresee that for half a century after his death the New England point of view, or something akin to it, would dominate American criticism.[52] Our early canon of Great American Writers was mainly a New England creation. For New England not only produced a good half of what was important in our literature between 1830 and 1870, but it also gave us many of our critics, anthologists, magazine editors, literary historians, and teachers of English. Of many of these we may say as Woodrow Wilson in 1894, fresh from a reading of Frederick J. Turner's memorable essay on the frontier, said, in "The Course of American History" of New England historians in general: "From where they sit the whole of the great development [of the United States] looks like an Expansion of New England." (In the same address Wilson noted that for Southern writers American history was chiefly "the history of the Suppression of the South.")

Even when it finally dawned upon the New England critics that in Europe Poe was regarded as one of the very greatest of American writers, they clung tenaciously to their original estimate. As in the case of Walt Whitman, they did not like the poet's European sponsors: Baudelaire with his *Fleurs du mal* and English writers of the so-called "Fleshly School." As late as 1893 Edmund Gosse wrote: "It is understood that Edgar Allen [sic] Poe is still unforgiven in New England." In January, 1901, William Dean Howells wrote in the *North American Review*:

> The great New Englanders would none of him [Poe]. Emerson called him "the jingle-man"; Lowell thought him "three-fourths [three fifths] fudge"; Longfellow's generous voice was silenced by Poe's atrocious misbehavior to him, and we can only infer his slight esteem for his work; in a later generation Mr. [Henry] James speaks of Poe's "very valueless verses." Yet it is perversely possible that his name will lead all the rest when our immortals are duly marshalled for the long descent of time.

In an article in the *North American Review* for October, 1846, Longfellow's intimate friend C. C. Felton reviewed with scant praise the tales of William Gilmore Simms, which he nevertheless found better than Poe's short stories; these he assigned to "the forcible-feeble and the shallow-profound school." On December 15 of the same year Poe wrote to George W. Eveleth: "The Frogpondians (Bostonians) have badgered me so much that I fear I am apt to fall into prejudices about them." In October, 1852,

[52] This subject is discussed in greater detail in my concluding chapter.

Thomas Holley Chivers, then in Boston, wrote to W. D. Ticknor to ask whether the publisher would allow his imprint to be used on Chivers' projected life of Poe. Presumably Ticknor's reply, which seems to be lost, was similar to that which Chivers received from another Boston publisher two years later. That publisher, B. B. Mussey, wrote that Philadelphia was a better place in which to bring out such a book. "Mr. Poe," he added, "was not as popular in Boston as he was in some of the Cities south of us."

In the autumn of the same year, 1854, Paul Hamilton Hayne, dining with a group of New England writers in the Albion House in Boston, found himself forced to dissent from the New England estimate of Poe. When a discussion arose as to the comparative merits of Poe and an unnamed New England poet, only a stray New Yorker who happened to be present dissented from the general verdict that Poe was by much the inferior of the two.[53] Hayne, who was only twenty-four years old, kept discreetly silent, but when pressed for his opinion, gave it that Poe was the most original genius in American literature. "At this," he remembered twenty years later, "the very air appeared to grow thick with a demurrer of argument, expostulation, sarcasm, and invective." In 1874, when he told the story in the Louisville *Argus*, Hayne reiterated his conviction. "I *was* right!" he said.

The following year, a quarter of a century after Poe's death, a monument was finally erected over his grave in Baltimore. For the ceremonies the generous Whittier wrote that "the extraordinary genius of Edgar A. Poe is now acknowledged the world over. . . ." Even Bryant, who ten years earlier had refused to contribute to the erection of a monument to Poe on the ground that he had heard too much about the man Poe "to be able to join in paying special honor to his memory," now relented sufficiently to write an epitaph in which he referred to Poe as

> distinguished alike
> for originality in the conception,
> skill in word-painting,
> and power over the mind of the reader.

[53] Bronson Alcott wrote in his diary for Oct. 14, 1854: "Dine at the Albion with Emerson, Lowell, Whipple, Dwight, Hayne (of South Carolina), and [Horatio] Woodman; and we arrange to meet there fortnightly hereafter for conversation" (George Willis Cooke, *John Sullivan Dwight*, 1898, pp. 238–239). If this is the dinner to which Hayne refers, the unnamed New England poet was probably Longfellow, Holmes, or Whittier. Perhaps the question of Poe's merits came up at "a large dinner party in Boston about the year 1854-5, at which Longfellow and Lowell were present," which Hayne mentioned in a letter to Mrs. Julia C. R. Dorr, May 16, 1882 (*S.C. Hist. and Geneal. Mag.*, LII, 209, Oct., 1951). In that event the unnamed poet must have been Holmes or Whittier, whose literary reputation in Boston was not nearly so high as it would be a few years later. See also Hayne's letter to Lowell, April 5, 1885, in D. M. McKeithan (ed.), *A Collection of Hayne Letters* (1944), pp. 104–105.

Nevertheless, the New England attitude toward Poe continued to be unfavorable. The anthologists of that section were markedly less hospitable than those of other sections. There were exceptions of course. Professor Charles F. Richardson of Dartmouth, who had lived for some years in other sections, edited Poe's works not unsympathetically. More representative, however, was the view taken by Professor Henry A. Beers of Yale in An Outline Sketch of American Literature (1887), intended mainly for Chautauqua readers. "The defect of Poe was in character . . . ," he wrote. "If he had had the sweet home feeling of Longfellow or the moral fervor of Whittier he might have been a greater poet than either."

In 1893 the Critic, a New York literary weekly, took a poll of its subscribers to determine the ten greatest American books. First place went to Emerson's Essays with 512 votes and second to The Scarlet Letter with 493, but nothing by Poe got as much as 20 votes.[54] In a letter to the Critic Edmund Gosse expressed his astonishment at the neglect of "the most perfect, the most original, the most exquisite of the American poets." The exclusion of Poe seemed to him "extraordinary and sinister." "If I were an American," he wrote, "I should be inclined to call it disastrous. While every year sheds more lustre on the genius of Poe among the most weighty critical authorities of England, of France, of Germany, of Italy, in his own country prejudice is still so rampant that he fails to secure a paltry twenty votes. . . ." In a poll of twenty-seven specialists in American literature taken in 1949 Poe with 143 points came within a single point of tying Hawthorne for first place among American authors.

When the first election to New York University's Hall of Fame took place in 1900, Poe failed to win a place. Both Whittier and Lowell were elected before Poe was finally admitted in 1910. The London Spectator commented: "The preference of Whittier to Poe is remarkable, if literary genius is to be taken as a test of merit. It seems to indicate that character is regarded as an indispensable passport to the Hall of Fame. . . ."[55] When Poe was finally voted in, Walter Hines Page aptly remarked: "Edgar Allan Poe might be described as the man who made the Hall of Fame famous. He made it famous for ten years by being kept out of it, and he has now given it a renewed lease of fame by being tardily admitted to it."

The speeches and writings occasioned by the Poe Centenary in 1909 made it clear even in New England that Poe was a major American writer. For the Centenary the Irish poet William Butler Yeats wrote that Poe was "certainly the greatest of American poets, and always and for all lands a great

---

[54] For the results of the poll, see the Critic, n.s. XIX, 341 and 357 (May 27 and June 3, 1893). Gosse's letter appeared in n.s. XX, 78 (July 29, 1893).

[55] For this and other comments, see Current Literature, XXXIX, 614 (Dec., 1905).

lyric poet." And Thomas Hardy wrote: "Now that the lapse of time has reduced the insignificant and petty details of his life to their true proportion beside the measure of his poetry, and softened the horror of the correct classes at his lack of respectability, that fantastic and romantic genius shows himself in all his rarity."

The effect of changing literary taste and standards upon Poe's reputation may be noted in the successive comments of three New England critics, George E. Woodberry, William Crary Brownell, and Barrett Wendell. I shall use Wendell to illustrate the change. In a commencement address on "American Literature" delivered at Vassar College in 1893 the Harvard professor of English pronounced Poe "fantastic and meretricious throughout." "As one knows him better," he said, "one does not love him more." Wendell believed that, as he said, "only New England has expressed itself in a literary form which inevitably commands attention from whoever pursues such inquiries as ours." In 1900 Wendell published a delightfully written *Literary History of America*, which Fred Lewis Pattee, a native of New England and a graduate of Dartmouth College, has said should have been entitled "A Literary History of Harvard University, with Incidental Glimpses of the Minor Writers of America." In his 530 pages of text Wendell could spare only 15 pages to a chapter on "The West" and only 20 to "Literature in the South." He did, however, devote about 75 pages to the New York writers, 15 of them to Poe. Wendell still regarded Poe as somewhat "meretricious" but admitted that "genius he certainly had." The New England writers were, as Wendell makes only too clear, gentlemen of good family, but Poe seemed to him "always a waif and a stray, essentially a Bohemian." In a letter to Dean L. B. R. Briggs, President Charles W. Eliot of Harvard complained of a certain snobbishness in Wendell's point of view: "Wendell's frequent discourse on the subject of birth and descent seems snobbish in an American, and will cause many people to underestimate his judgment and good sense." Poe had complained years before that Griswold included in his anthologies many writers whose only claim was their wealth or superior social position. In 1909 Wendell journeyed down to Charlottesville to deliver the principal address on the evening of January 19 as part of the University of Virginia's observance of the Poe Centenary. Here Wendell for the first time conceded to Poe a high place among American writers. Perhaps during his year at the Sorbonne he had been impressed by Poe's "constantly expanding fame," or possibly he was trying to say what the amenities of the occasion seemed to require; and yet when he revised and republished the address later in the year he made no essential change in what he had said in Charlottesville. He said: "Not only all of us here assembled, not only Virginia, and all New

York, and all New England, and all of our American countrymen beside, but the whole civilized world instantly and eagerly recognize the certainty of his eminence." "So long as the name of America shall endure, the name of Poe will persist, in serene certainty, among those of our approved national worthies." He praised the poet's "consummate craftsmanship" and his "supreme artistic purity" and said nothing about his meretriciousness. That Wendell had found a new perspective on American literature—nine years after publishing his *Literary History*—is suggested by his reversal of his 1893 estimate of the literature written in his native New England. "The literature of New England, in brief," he now said, "American though we may gladly assert it in its nobler phases, is, first of all, not American or national, but local."

Since the Poe Centenary more than one of our literary historians have had difficulty in finding for Poe a place in the national literary tradition. In *The World of Washington Irving* (1944) Van Wyck Brooks suggested that the main stream runs through the New England Transcendentalists and their heirs, including Walt Whitman. He made a place in the national tradition for Jefferson, whose reputation was for many years, like Poe's, lower in New England than elsewhere, but he found it difficult to fit Poe into it.

Our historians in trying to define the national literary tradition have failed to use the inductive method. The definition must include all major American writers, for the literary tradition is largely of their making. One simply cannot afford to omit an author of Poe's intrinsic merits and wide influence. If by such tests he does not belong to our literary tradition, who does? One of his chief claims to our attention, it seems to me, is that his writings have forced us to broaden our conception of our literary tradition beyond what it would have been if the old New England point of view still dominated the study of our national literature.

If Poe were living now, he would, I think, maintain that in this country literature as an art is still imperfectly understood and appreciated. In my opinion he would be right. Literary critics and historians—it is perhaps an English and American defect—still generally underrate the importance of technical mastery over the artist's medium. It is not so in the other arts, where mastery of one's craft is regarded as the first essential. Judged purely as artists, how few of our major American writers ever attained a consistent mastery of the forms they cultivated! Hawthorne, Henry James, and Poe were first-rate artists, but Emerson, Melville, Whitman, and Mark Twain only at intervals succeeded in expressing what they had to say in a form which is the inevitable expression of the view of life which each of them held. *Moby-Dick* and *Huckleberry Finn* and "Out of the Cradle Endlessly

Rocking" are masterpieces, but what is one to say of the numerous mediocre works which these writers published in their maturer years?

If Poe's subject matter does not interest the critic—and often it does not —he may find compensation, if he cares for the art of writing, in a few poems and tales which are as nearly perfect as anything else yet written on this continent. If, finally, Poe is found not to measure up to the supreme literary artists of the Old World, it is yet something of great importance to our often feeble and sprawling nineteenth-century literature that we had one poet, critic, and short-story writer who consistently maintained toward his work the attitude of the great artist. For Poe was that if nothing else. When such another appears, let us hope that he will find a better understanding and appreciation of his achievement than the living Poe found in either South or North.

33
Thomas Holley Chivers

THE SCANTY LITERARY reputation which Thomas Holley Chivers (1807?–1858) [56] had won by the time of his death quickly faded away. Even Miss Louise Manley, who indiscriminately collected Southern writers for her anthology, *Southern Literature* (1895), failed to include him. "Had he been of the North," remarks S. Foster Damon, "the literary coteries there would surely have pruned and preserved him. Had he come but a little later, his technique would have been better, and would have found a prepared public. But time and space were against him."

It was the perennial interest in Poe that led scholars to rediscover him, and these by and by began to realize that he was worthy of study in his own right. The late Lewis Chase, who had long studied Poe, went to the Huntington Library to examine the Poe-Chivers papers and came away with a passion for Chivers. It was through his efforts that the remainder of Chivers' manuscripts were placed in the Duke University Library. Since 1930, when Damon published his *Thomas Holley Chivers: Friend of Poe*, anthologists and literary historians have conceded him a small niche in the American literary Pantheon. Apart from a certain likeness to Poe, Chivers is a unique figure in the literature of America.

[56] Chivers' daughters told Rufus W. Griswold that their father was born in 1807 and the date on his tombstone indicates that he died in his fifty-second year; but S. Foster Damon finds evidence in certain of Chivers' poems that the year of his birth was 1809 (*Thomas Holley Chivers: Friend of Poe*, 1930, p. 30 n.).

He was born on a plantation in Washington County, Georgia, where he spent a happy childhood. The music of verse appealed to him early. At the age of seven he read with delight Cowper's "The Rose" in a Webster spelling book. While still in his teens, he married a cousin, who, believing slanderous reports that came to her ears, as he thought, deserted him and refused to permit him to see their child. The impassioned young poet could not fail to note the parallel between himself and Byron, whose wife also deserted her husband; and, like his favorite poet Shelley, Chivers was ready enough to believe himself persecuted. After two years in Transylvania University, he won his M.D. degree with distinction in 1830.

A well-to-do planter's son, Dr. Chivers had no need to practice his profession. A period of wandering in the West and North followed until 1835, when he returned to Georgia. By this time he had printed two of his eleven volumes of verse: *The Path of Sorrow* (Franklin, Tennessee, 1832) and *Conrad and Eudora* (Philadelphia, 1834). The first of these reveals how deeply his wife's desertion affected him. The second is the earliest literary treatment of the Kentucky tragedy which was later to figure in Poe's *Politian*, Simms's *Charlemont* and *Beauchampe*, and Robert Penn Warren's *World Enough and Time*. In March, 1835, the recently founded *Southern Literary Messenger* declined some of his poems in a printed notice—not written by Poe—which reads in part: "We question whether the Doctor will find the lancet and pill-box of more profit in that warm region [Georgia] to which he has emigrated, than the offerings of his prolific muse." Although he printed many of his verses in newspapers and magazines, Chivers was to receive little encouragement from any source South or North. Simms in reviewing Chivers' *The Lost Pleiad, and Other Poems* in "*Simms's Magazine*" in October, 1845, wrote: "We have long known Dr. Chivers, through his writings, as a man of real talent, and very delicate fancy. He possesses a poetic ardor sufficiently fervid, and a singularly marked command of language. But he should have been caught young, and well-bitted, and subjected to the severest training. . . . Never was a poet more luckless in the direction of his wing. His judgment fails him in the choice of topics. . . . As an artist, Dr. Chivers is yet in his accidence."

In 1855 Chivers wrote to James M. Smythe, who was proposing to launch a Georgia literary magazine:

I once had stronger hopes than ever burned in your bosom, for the mental aggrandizement of my native State; but they have all been dissipated into the wide abyss of eternity by the sad experience that there is no such thing in the South as a popular love for any thing that has a tendency to glorify the life of the soul either in time or in Eternity. . . . Your Political papers are not supported, then how can you expect to publish a *Literary* one—the most hazardous enterprise in the world? What you want is a *Literary Public*—just the kind of Public which never was nor ever will be, in the South—unless the times should undergo a most miraculous palingenesis.

In New York in 1837 Chivers married a Massachusetts girl of eighteen, Harriette Hunt.[57] It was a happy marriage until it was made sad by the deaths of most of their children. For years the Chiverses moved about from place to place, living mainly in hotels in Northern cities. He thought New Haven the most beautiful city in the world, and in spite of its Abolition activities he liked Boston. From time to time he brought out a volume of poems or a play. Only two of his books, *Eonchs of Ruby* (1850) and *Virginalia* (1853), bear the imprints of publishing houses. On April 5, 1856, he wrote to Charles R. Rode explaining that a number of his writings had not been published—

because I am not acquainted with any Publisher who has education enough to talk even in the vernacular of common politeness in regard to them; and I feel a million times too proud to ask one to do it, or even suffer the impertinent formalities of a negotiation. The truth is, they were not written with an Eye to publication, but as a felicitous outpouring of that oversoul of passion, which if suffered to remain dammed up, would effectually damn me to utter distraction. In fact, nothing I ever wrote was written for the Public—which is a Beast —a Hydra—with countless heads and myriads of Horns—outheading—outhorning—even the great Whore of Babylon herself.

From 1845 to 1850 the Chiverses were in Georgia. They spent the next five years in the North, but in 1855 the tense sectional feeling that had developed in that region brought him back to Georgia, where he died three years later, December 19, 1858. In describing his death Mrs. Chivers wrote to a friend: "On Saturday the 18th at 11 oclock he asked the time of day. we told him. He says, *To-day is the anointing day of the Poets in Valhalla.* I said to him Dr. are you going to be there. He says 'I AM, I AM' in the most emphatic manner." His last words were: "All is perfect peace with me."

Chivers had been reared a Baptist, but in later life he was deeply interested in spiritualism, Swedenborgianism, Fourierism, and Transcendentalism. He was in fact a Transcendentalist of his own school. He was an interested reader of the *Dial*. After asking for Poe's opinion of that magazine, he wrote to Poe: "I cannot say that I like very much your *dis*like of Transcendentalism. All *true* Poetry is certainly transcendental—although it is the

[57] Damon gives the name as *Harriet* and states that the name is so spelled on her tombstone, but the Duke University Library has a letter addressed to Louis F. Wilson Andrews, Dec. 20, 1858, in which she signs her name Harriette Hunt Chivers.

beautiful expression of that which is most true." That was in 1844. On August 27, 1840, he had written a long letter to Poe in which he discussed Transcendentalism at considerable length. He noted that those who found fault with the *Dial* knew "nothing of the power of language in the reflection of ideas, which are the twilight presence of God living in the soul."

And what is Revelation but Transcendentalism? It is the effect of inspiration. What then is inspiration, if it is not the power given to the soul to recognize the beautiful of a truth which is transcendent in its nature, when compared with other truths? We may convey the idea of a heavenly truth by an earthly one— that is, we may make an earthly truth the representative of a truth beyond expression. This shows the power of language. This shows that language has a higher office than to manifest the relations which subsist between us and the external world—although our knowledge comes therefrom. We may express the existence of a truth which is beyond expression.

In *Search after Truth* (1848) Chivers wrote: "Matter is perceived by the senses of the body, ideas by the mind. The senses cannot form an idea; they cannot perceive the soul of God; yet we have ideas of them both. Therefore, in spite of Locke, all knowledge does not come through the senses." Chivers, "long aware of his subconscious mind," says Damon, "identified it with Eternity, or Heaven."

These beliefs had an important influence upon his conception of the function of poetry. In the Preface to *Nacoochee* (1837), published the year after Emerson's first book, *Nature*, which Chivers had probably not seen, he wrote: "Poetry is the power given by God to man of manifesting" "the wise relations that subsist between him and God." "Poetry is the soul of his [man's] nature, whereby, from communing with the beauties of this earth, he is capable of giving birth to other beings brighter than himself. . . ." "Poetry," he continued, "is that crystal river of the soul which runs through all the avenues of life, and after purifying the affections of the heart, empties itself into the Sea of God." The poets, he said in the Preface to *Memoralia* (1853), are *"the Revelators of the Divine Idea through the Beautiful."*

But Chivers, unlike the Transcendentalist Jones Very, did not expect the Over-Soul or the Holy Ghost to dictate to him perfect poems. Poetry, he said in his Preface to *Memoralia*, "consists in a perfect unition of . . . Passion and Art—a pure body united to a pure soul. . . ." Like Poe, he sought for novel and suitable metrical mediums for his ideas. The refrain of a poem, he said in the Preface to *Virginalia* (1853), "is not only an ornament, but an essence—a life—a vitality—an immortal soul—not a mere profane appendage. . . ." For him, as for Poe, music was essential to poetry. Some of his poems are primarily exercises in verbal melody, but he often tried to create a magical or hypnotic effect by the use of sounds and images. He delighted in creating new and musical words like *ouphantic, acerbitous,* and *oblectation.* It is not surprising that he had an influence not only on Poe but also upon Swinburne and Rossetti. He anticipated some of the theories of the French Symbolists, who knew Poe's work if not his.

Hervey Allen has suggested that the music of Poe's poems owes much to the songs of the Negroes which he heard in his boyhood. It was these "melancholy harmonies and strange rhythms" which became "the foundation for his weird imaginings and the strange 'new' cadences which he was to succeed later on in grafting upon the main stream of English poetry."

I do not know how much truth there is in Allen's suggestion, but Chivers was much interested in the rhythm of Negro folk songs. After quoting a Negro song with its refrain of "Too, Mark, a-Juba!" he wrote: "There is no such rhythm as this in Greek Poetry—nor, in fact, in any other Nation under the sun. There is no dance in the world like that of Juba—the name of that [illegible] provoking jig which accompanies this recitative—the very climax of jocularity—being as far above the Pyrr[h]ic as the Tarantula [tarantella?] in provoking laughter accompanied by irresistible shouts of uproarious hilarity." Chivers had long thought, he said, of writing "a paper on the various rhythms of the Aethiopians compared with those now in use of the Caucasian race—descriptive of the different idiosyncrasies of the two races—their peculiar modes of passionate expression are as essentially different in every respect, as their complexions. . . ." "The Homeric expression was spondaic—like the ponderous tread of a mighty army of Elephants —compared with that of the Aethiopians, which is generally Satyric, or lively. The English people write Hymns and funeral elegies; the Aethiopians —trochaic, Drinking-Songs giving a better knowledge of the two nations than can be found either in tradition or History. . . ."

In a letter of March 12, 1853, Chivers gave the text of a "Corn Song" which he says he wrote, before he entered Transylvania in 1828, to be sung by his father's slaves at a corn shucking. If the song is not rather a genuine folk song, Chivers has succeeded marvelously in capturing the rhythm and diction of the type. "If you could only hear it sung, as I have," he writes, "at the middle hour of the night, by a great Chorus of three hundred of the best bass voices that ever thundered lofty peals of passionate joy to the omnipresence of the immaculate Silence filling the canopy of Heaven with the Bacchanal unsilence of the Refrain—you would be more than delighted."

> Jinny had de black eye—
> Jinny was de gal!
> Oh! Jinny had de black eye—

Jinny was de gal!
Jinny was my darling!
· Jinny was de gal!
Oh! Jinny was my darling—
Jinny was de gal!
Git away de Cawn, Boys!
Git away de Cawn!
Oh! git away de Cawn, Boys!
Git away de Cawn!
Jinny took to sighing—
Jinny was de gal!
Oh! Jinny took to sighing—
Jinny was de gal!
Jinny had de heart-ache—
Jinny was de gal!
Oh! Jinny had de heart-ache—
Jinny was de gal!
Git away de Cawn, Boys!
Git away de Cawn!
Jinny lem me kiss her—
Jinny was de gal!
Oh! Jinny lem me kiss her—
Jinny was de gal!
Jinny said she lubbed me—
Jinny was de gal!
Oh! Jinny said she lubbed me—
Jinny was de gal!
Git away de Cawn, Boys!
Git away de Cawn!
Jinny! wat de matter?
Jinny is de gal!
Oh! Jinny! what de matter?
Jinny is de gal!
Jinny! I am dying!
Jinny! aint you, gal?
Oh! Jinny! I am dying!
Jinny! kiss me, gal!
Git away de Cawn, Boys!
Git away de Cawn!
Git away de Cawn, Boys!
Shuffle out de Cawn!

Chivers is the most uneven of poets. He often did not know his best from his worst, and so he could revise his poems without improving them. In this respect he is very unlike Poe. Chivers had little sense of humor. In one of his best poems, "To Allegra Florence in Heaven," he included the stanza which has so often been held up to ridicule:

> As an egg, when broken, never
> Can be mended, but must ever
> Be the same crushed egg forever—
>   So shall this dark heart of mine!
> Which, though broken, is still breaking,
> And shall never more cease aching
> For the sleep which has no waking—
>   For the sleep which now is thine!

Here Chivers quite unconsciously parodied his own work. He had ideas about art, but his critical sense often left him when he came to judge his own poems. His poems are weak in structure; they lack compression. He pads his lines; he is often obscure; he repeats favorite words and images; and he lacks emotional restraint. As a result, while there are fine passages in many of his poems, he has few poems which are without serious flaws. James Russell Lowell once said "that Dr. Chivers had been wont to send him his books, and he read them aloud to his classes as illustrations of the shell of Shelley." [58]

As an example of Chivers at his best I give his "Apollo," which may be reminiscent of Shelley but is certainly not in the Poe manner.

> What are stars, but hieroglyphics of God's glory writ in lightning
>   On the wide-unfolded pages of the azure scroll above?
> But the quenchless apotheoses of thoughts forever brightening
>   In the mighty Mind immortal of the God whose name is Love?
> Diamond letters sculptured, rising, on the azure ether pages,
>   That now sing to one another—unto one another shine—
> God's eternal scripture talking, through the midnight, to the Ages,
>   Of the life that is immortal, of the life that is divine—
> Life that *cannot* be immortal, but the life that is divine.
>
> Like some deep impetuous river from the fountains everlasting,
>   Down the serpentine soft valleys of the vistas of all Time,
> Over cataracts of adamant uplifted into mountains,
>   Soared his soul to God in thunder on the wings of thought sublime.

[58] Edmund Clarence Stedman wrote to Col. J. Q. Adams, July 3, 1888: "Dr. Chivers was a crazy poet, but he had an ear for melody." On Sept. 15 of the same year Stedman wrote that Chivers "was a blind devotee of Poe,—a sort of Poe-run-mad!" He added that he thought Swinburne and Bayard Taylor both had copies of Chivers' *Eonchs of Ruby.*

With the rising golden glory of the sun in ministrations,
  Making oceans metropolitan of splendor for the dawn—
Piling pyramid on pyramid of music for the nations—
  Sings the Angel who sits shining everlasting in the sun,
  For the stars, which are the echoes of the shining of the sun.

Like the lightnings piled on lightnings, ever rising, never reaching,
  In one monument of glory towards the golden gates of God—
Voicing out themselves in thunder upon thunder in their preaching,
  Piled this Cyclop up his Epic where the Angels never trod.
Like the fountains everlasting that forever more are flowing
  From the throne within the centre of the City built on high,
With their genial irrigation life forever more bestowing—
  Flows his lucid, liquid river through the gardens of the sky,
  For the stars forever blooming in the gardens of the sky.

Somewhat more in the Poe manner is Chivers' "The Fall of Usher," which
is a brief elegy on Poe:

"Thou art gone to the grave!" but thy spirit is shining,
  And singing afar in the REALMS OF THE BLEST;
While the living are left by thy cold grave reclining,
  And mourning for thee while they long for thy rest—
  Left mourning for thee while they long for thy rest!

. . . .

"Thou art gone to the grave!" where the Violets are springing,
  And feeding upon thee above the damp sod,
Now thy Pandemos mourns, while thy spirit is singing,
  And drinking delight from the FOUNTAINS OF GOD—
  With thine ULLALUME lost from the FOUNTAINS OF GOD.[59]

The literary relations between Chivers and Poe are complicated by the
fact that each influenced the other and that both of them were working
toward similar ends and using similar means. Both, for example, were in-
dependently attracted to the angel Israfel; both were striving for verbal
melody and musical magic. In *Graham's Magazine* for December, 1841,
Poe referred to Chivers as "at the same time one of the best and one of
the worst poets in America." But he noted "an indefinite charm of sentiment and melody" in even the poorest poems and added that there were
"as fine individual passages to be found in the poems of Dr. Chivers as in
those of any poet whatsoever." "His productions," he said, "affect one as
a wild dream—strange, incongruous, full of images of more than arabesque

---

[59] See also Chivers' poem "Coelicola," *Peterson's Magazine*, XVII, 102 (Feb., 1850);
another lament for Poe.

monstrosity and snatches of sweet, unsustained song." Poe was somewhat more favorable when, after meeting Chivers, he reviewed *The Lost Pleiad* in the *Broadway Journal* for August 2, 1845. "In a word," he said, "the volume before us is the work of that *rara avis*, an educated, passionate, yet unaffectedly simple-minded and single-minded man, writing from his own vigorous impulses—from the necessity of giving utterance to poetic passion—and thus writing *not* to mankind, but solely to himself. The whole volume has, in fact, the air of a rapt soliloquy."

Chivers had met Poe in New York in the spring of 1845, when "The Raven" was extremely popular. He states that Poe was at that time intoxicated, but two days later they had a long talk. Poe, he discovered, greatly admired Tennyson, who was not a favorite with Chivers, and thought Horne's *Orion* a better poem than *Paradise Lost*. He apparently surprised Chivers by belittling Shelley and by arguing that poetry should have little to do with passion. Most of the letters that passed between the two poets were written by Chivers. Poe's interest in the Georgia poet was due in part to the hope that Chivers might be willing to put up money needed for Poe's projected magazine. But I do not think Poe was consciously insincere when he wrote to Chivers, July 22, 1846: "Your professions of friendship I reciprocate from the inmost depths of my heart. Except for yourself I have never met the man for whom I felt that intimate *sympathy* (of intellect as well as soul) which is the sole basis of friendship." Chivers knew Poe's weaknesses but he knew also that Poe was a great genius. He was interested in the man and the poet, not in Poe the magazine editor, and on February 21, 1847, he wrote to Poe: "If you will come to the South to live, I will take care of you as long as you live—although, if ever there was a perfect mystery on earth, you are one—and one of the most mysterious."

After Poe's death in October, 1849, Chivers planned to bring out a book which would convince the American people that Poe was a great poet. Two Boston publishers whom he approached declined to accept his proposed "biography." The Chivers manuscripts in the Huntington Library, however, show that what he had planned was a book of selections from Poe's writings with a critical and biographical introduction which would include some of the letters which Poe had written him. In 1952 Richard Beale Davis brought out *Chivers' Life of Poe* in a well-edited volume which makes available in full for the first time materials which are important for an understanding of both poets.

In the years following Poe's death Chivers was more deeply influenced by Poe's poetry than ever before. Simms, who also admired Poe's writings, wrote to Chivers, April 5, 1852: "Give him up as a model and as a guide. He was a man of curious genius, wild & erratic, but his genius was rather curious than valuable—bizarre rather than great or healthful." Chivers, his pride in his own originality deeply wounded, replied: "I am the Southern man who taught Mr. Poe all these things." The poems which Simms thought imitative, he said, had all been published before "The Raven," which was taken from them. To Augustine Duganne he wrote, December 17, 1850: "Poe stole all his *Raven* from me; but was the greatest Poetical Critic that ever existed."

Foster Damon has, I think, somewhat overestimated the influence of Chivers on Poe: "Chivers's priority in these things—idea, meter, refrain, and something of atmosphere—is unquestionable." The question of Poe's indebtedness to Chivers and other poets is of course an aesthetic and not a moral question. Many of his borrowings have been pointed out, and yet they are all assimilated, transformed into something original and Poesque. And poor Chivers' best claim to fame—except for the very few lovers of his poems—is that he contributed something to the making of "The Raven."

34
James M. Legaré

James Mathewes Legaré (1823–1859) was one of the best Southern poets of his time; yet his name does not appear in the *Dictionary of American Biography* or in Parrington's notable discussion of Southern writers. Until Curtis Carroll Davis began his investigations, very little was known about Legaré apart from his one published volume, *Orta-Undis, and Other Poems* (Boston, 1848). He was a kinsman of Hugh Swinton Legaré, whose death occasioned one of his best poems. His father, John D. Legaré, was librarian of the Agricultural Society of South Carolina and editor of the *Southern Agriculturist* and its successor, the *Southern Cabinet*. In later life he was postmaster at Aiken. James Legaré, who was born in Charleston, attended the city schools, the College of Charleston, and St. Mary's College in Baltimore. In 1843 he began the study of law in the office of James Louis Petigru, but he was apparently no more interested in the law than two future pupils of Petigru, Paul Hayne and Henry Timrod. His main interests were literature, painting, and mechanical invention. He was among the young Charleston writers whom Simms advised and encouraged, and some of his early prose and verse appeared in *"Simms's Magazine"* in 1845.

In the spring of 1848, soon after the publication of *Orta-Undis*, Legaré settled in Aiken—not for the society there, as he explained in a letter to John

R. Thompson, but on account of the fine dry climate. He had tuberculosis. For a time he tried to earn a living by his pen. In May, 1850, he wrote to Thompson that he had no regular income except what his writings brought him. He had paid William D. Ticknor and Company of Boston to bring out his volume of poems. Most of the five hundred copies were sent to booksellers in South Carolina and Georgia but not many copies were sold. In November, 1849, Legaré wrote to Thomas Powell that except for three poems in it he was somewhat ashamed of the book. He planned to bring out a second volume of poems. In 1851 Thompson wrote to Griswold: "Why can't Legaré find a publisher?" The reason why the second volume of poems never appeared was probably the inability of the poet to pay the printer's bill and not, as Thompson thought, the Northern prejudice against Southern writers.

Legaré tried to earn a living by writing prose fiction for the magazines. He published no less than sixteen articles, chiefly fiction, in nine different magazines, ten of them in Northern periodicals. He was trying his hand with some success at all the popular types of fiction: Western stories, romances of adventure, satirical stories, and even the domestic sentimental stories so popular with women readers. His best story perhaps was the "Story of the Hà-Hà," which Thompson published in the *Southern Literary Messenger* in July, 1850. In March, 1851, *Graham's Magazine*, boasting of its regular contributors, said: "Graham, at least, thinks he has a class of young writers now, who ask no odds in a fair encounter: Lowell, Read, Legare, Godman, Whipple, Fields . . . form a galaxy unequalled in ability, we will venture to say, by any corps of writers engaged for any other magazine in the world." After 1855 Legaré seems to have written almost nothing. After his death *Harper's Magazine* in the midst of the Civil War published his "Cap-and-Bells: A Novel in Ten Chapters" (December, 1863; January, 1864), but the author's name appeared only in the indexes to the annual volumes.

In the late forties Legaré became interested in invention, which seemed to promise eventually a larger income than writing had brought him. He sank into various projects all that he could earn by painting or giving lessons in drawing. For one year, he wrote to Senator James H. Hammond, "I even tried a class of 'finishing' young ladies, but these last occupied more time than I could spare, and had to be relinquished." He had a cottage and a workroom, or laboratory, near his father's house in Aiken, where he and his wife took their meals. By 1858 he was a confirmed invalid. In a long letter to Hammond, May 15, 1859, he asked the Senator to assist him in marketing some of his inventions.

About twelve years ago my attention was first accidentally directed to mechanical invention, and after some years of vague and useless experiment—for the most part given to a search after Perpetual Motion, that Syren of inventors . . . I at length settled down upon a conclusion which I have not since abandoned, viz: of making the principle of the hydrostatic paradox, a *motive*, rather than as now employed, a *passive*, power. In endeavouring to realise this idea the past ten years of my life have been consumed. . . . Some of these [repeated] failures are dreadful to look back to; as when after a long series of successful experiments backed by a no less promising series of figures, the results of many months of thought and study, by a single final calculation or by the unlooked-for result of some final experiment, I would find the invention I had thought on the point of being perfected, only a heap of mental rubbish, and myself bankrupt in purse and, as it seemed to me, in mind.

One of the four inventions which Legaré considered successful was a dual air engine which would use only one-sixth of the coal consumed by a steam engine. Another was "a light, cushionless easy reading-chair." He took out two patents covering an improved plastic cotton, which in combination with other ingredients, was "capable of being worked up by hand without the use of moulds, & so converted into furniture of solid or open patterns and decorations of buildings, and into fire & water proof roofing." [60] Perhaps if Legaré had lived and been able to promote his inventions, he might have made enough money to justify the time and labor he had spent on them. Or perhaps there was, on the eve of the Civil War, no demand for plastics. In the field of invention, as in authorship, the Southerner was too far from his market. At last, I fear, Legaré regarded himself as a failure both as a writer and as an inventor.

Orta-Undis, and Other Poems was reviewed more or less favorably in at least seven different magazines. *Holden's Dollar Magazine* noted that the "distinguishing qualities of Mr. Legare's poetry are chasteness of sentiment, classical tone, and correctness," but it saw none of "those flashes of genius which at once impress the reader with the presence of a new and true poet." William C. Richards, the English-born editor of the *Southern Literary Gazette*, though he wished to praise the work of a Southern poet and a contributor to his own magazine, disliked the Latin title of the volume. The poems, he thought, had grace, delicacy, and originality, but they seemed to him "marked by a studied quaintness—amounting to a positive affectation."

Legaré's own estimate of the poems was not extravagant. He wrote to John R. Thompson in November, 1849, that he claimed for them "no merit

[60] *De Bow's Rev.*, XXV, 215–216 (Aug., 1858), reprinted from the Charleston *Courier* Legaré's "New and Important Uses of Cotton."

but earnestness. I have," he continued, "been critically accused of affectation, but except in a few instances, I think with little justice. For at least
one thing is certain, I write only when touched to the soul or moved by
some more transient emotion—and all I say is verily out of my heart." In the
same letter he stated that if he should visit the North, he wanted to meet
Philip Pendleton Cooke and "Ik Marvel" (Donald G. Mitchell). He added:

And so poor Poe is dead—his poems rank first among my pet books, those
almost-sacred few kept on a small shelf apart from my mere library volumes, and
(sometimes one, & sometimes another) companions of long rambles through the
woods. I felt far more grieved at his death than I would at that of many a relative; for I *do* love genius in whatever shape manifested, and best of all in a true
poet. Both before and since his death, I have earnestly maintained his case
against such "small people" as have no charity for the failings of great men. . . .

Legaré was, like Poe, an ardent admirer of Tennyson's poems. He was also,
it would seem, a classical scholar. The poem which gives the title to his
his volume—placed at the end in the modern fashion—is in Latin. Legaré
and Walter Savage Landor, who also wrote verse in Latin, come near the end
of a long English tradition which goes back through Milton to the medieval
poets.

Legaré's poems were inspired chiefly by love and nature. The nature
poems show that he was a close observer of natural phenomena and had
something of the skill which we should expect of a painter in describing what
he saw. One of his longer poems, "Thanatokallos," was written to refute the
unchristian view of nature and death expressed in Bryant's "Thanatopsis."
The love poems, most of them apparently inspired by his wife, Anne
(Andrews) Legaré, show sincere feeling with rare traces of the sentimentality
which marred the work of the many Southern imitators of Thomas Moore.
Occasionally one finds a conceit worked out so elaborately as to suggest
artificiality. His poems reveal a more careful and competent workmanship
than those of all but three or four of his Southern contemporaries. "On the
Death of a Kinsman," written in June, 1843, when he heard that Hugh S.
Legaré was dead, has an admirable opening stanza, rather above the level
of the four which follow:

> I see an Eagle winging to the sun—
> Who,sayeth him nay?
> He glanceth down from where his wing hath won,—
> His heart is stout, his flight is scarce begun,—
> O hopes of clay!

"Last Gift," presumably addressed to his wife, shows us the Southern poet trying his hand at the old Petrarchan convention of the power of poetry to immortalize a woman's beauty and goodness:

Illustrious thy name shall be
To all who love in future years:
These little songs I sing to thee,
            Thy tears,
Thy many griefs will I bequeath
To uncreated heirs.

Now, hidden are the quiet ways
That bring thee to my bosom nigh;
And when is spent thy term of days,
            Thou'lt die:
Then shall thy virtues live in praise
That riches cannot buy.

Night shall descend upon thy eyes,
Thy lips no more repeat my name;
But all the virtuous and wise
            Shall claim
Thee for their sister:—*See*, they'll say—
Her whom he raised to fame!

I quote in conclusion "To Jasmines in December," which appeared only in the *Literary World* for May 26, 1849:

Young jessamines that bloom as sweet
As if it now were May,
Though crisp brown leaves beneath the feet
Hide all the forest way,
I pray you soft my darling greet,
And in her bosom say:

Bloom freshly on, thou sister fair,
While pleasant Spring remains,
And while the Autumn's yellow hair
Is plaited thick with grains;
For soon will Winter, white and drear,
Encamp upon these plains.

But if thou art not, Love, inclined
To perish with the rest,

When birds may scarce warm shelter find,
Then blossom out thy best.
And surely one true heart I'll find
To wear thee on his breast.

And for thy perfume's sake, unstirred
He'll front the icy sleet,
The icy sleet of worldly words,
And gather round his feet
In fancy, Spring again, and birds
With carols high and sweet.

Yes, make his winter mild again,
And bring him back his May,
And though in prison cell, all men
Will envy him the day.
Not fetters, but a sceptre!—then
The baffled crowds will say.

35
William Elliott

Among the handful of gentleman farmers in the South who wrote any-thing of literary importance William Elliott (1788–1863) was one of the most gifted. He was a nephew of Stephen Elliott, botanist, banker, and one of the editors of the *Southern Review*; and he was a cousin of Stephen Elliott, Jr., who in 1831 tried to persuade him to devote himself entirely to literature. Elliott was born in Beaufort, South Carolina, in a family which owned half a dozen Low-Country plantations, some of which his widowed mother continued to manage until her death in 1855. With such a back-ground as this, one would hardly expect Elliott to become as he in fact did a vigorous opponent of Nullification and secession or an advocate of manu-facturing and of scientific farming as opposed to the one-crop system of the cotton plantations.

Elliott was educated at Harvard College. Ill health compelled him to leave at the end of his junior year when he was at the head of his class, but the Col-lege gave him "the unsolicited compliment of an honorary [A.B.] degree" in 1810. When he returned to South Carolina, he devoted himself to the management of some of the family plantations, to politics, agricultural im-provements, and to sports. In 1814 he was elected to his father's old seat in the lower house of the state legislature. He served there or in the state senate most of the time until 1832. He also served one term in the U.S. House of Representatives.

In the South Carolina state legislature he developed an antipathy to the lawyer politicians who wrangled while men of better sense sat still and were bored by technical arguments. He disliked the protective tariff, but he could not see that it was primarily responsible for the state's economic difficulties, and he was firmly opposed to Nullification, like his friends Joel R. Poinsett and James Louis Petigru. His newspaper articles in opposition to Nullification prompted Petigru to write: "You really are the only man that has caught the secret of Swift and can make one scream with laughing, while your own gravity is maintained all the while to admiration."

In 1832 Elliott resigned his seat in the state senate rather than support the Nullification policies desired by his constituents. He then published an impassioned *Address to the People of St. Helena Parish* defending his own position and pointing out fallacies in the stock arguments that the high tariff was the sole cause of the state's economic difficulties. "You will remember my friendly caution, and look back with regret," he said. "But . . . when you have struck forward the ball of revolution, can you prescribe its path, and regulate its motion?" The *Address* betrays irritation that the masses were no longer willing to follow the advice of a great planter, the traditional leader in his own community. Like his contemporaries, Kennedy and Gayarré, Elliott was discovering that the Southern masses no longer preferred great planters as their representatives. For Robert Barnwell Rhett, the secessionist fire-eater, Elliott had nothing but contempt. He wrote to his wife in 1851: the secessionists "prostrate themselves before this bellowing mooncalf and swallow all his fatuities as oracles. One who has gulp of this would swallow a haystack." Elliott's political career ended in the 1830's, but he continued to be a keen observer of political developments. He believed in slavery, but until 1860 he opposed secession. From time to time he expressed his views in pamphlets or newspaper articles.

To the *Southern Review* in 1829 and 1830 Elliott contributed excellent reviews of Scott's *Anne of Geierstein* and Gifford's edition of the writings of Ben Jonson. These make it clear that he was well-read in the Elizabethan drama and the early English novel; they also show that he had a keen relish for good descriptive writing and for dramatic effect. In 1850 he printed anonymously in New York a five-act tragedy in blank verse entitled *Fiesco*. He wrote to his wife: "I am also printing my tragedy—for private presents to my literary friends—it is without a name, and is a dead secret. It has talent —*I know*—but it does not become *me!* Therefore it comes forth as an illegitimate!" It was not desirable that a great planter should be known as

the author of a poetic drama. In his Preface Elliott gave his historical
sources, stated that he had not read Schiller's play of the same title, and
indicated that although he had scrupulously adhered to the three unities of
time, place, and action, his judgment told him that he had sacrificed much
by so doing. The play deals with the unsuccessful attempt in 1547 of Fiesco
to usurp the place of his uncle as Chief of Genoa. *Fiesco* is a good specimen
of the poetic drama in the Elizabethan tradition. Some of the scenes are
reminiscent of *Julius Caesar* and *Romeo and Juliet*. The play has some
poetic merit, but like nearly all other poetic plays of the nineteenth century
in English, it is a closet drama and not suited to the stage.

Elliott's scanty reputation rests upon a single book, *Carolina Sports by
Land and Water* (Charleston, 1846), which has been reprinted at least four
times including a London edition in 1867. The book was put together from
sportsmen's narratives (not all written by Elliott) contributed to the Charleston newspapers, the *American Turf Register*, and the *Southern Literary
Journal* under the pseudonyms "Piscator" and "Venator." Later narratives
printed under the same pen names appeared in the Charleston newspapers
and are still uncollected. Elliott, who shared with the publishers the expense
of the illustrated edition of *Carolina Sports* which Derby and Jackson
brought out in New York in 1859, thought highly enough of the book to
write to his wife: "I think that if any thing that I have written will live after
me it will be these 'Sports.' . . . At the worst they can only drop into
oblivion, but should they acquire notoriety, it will be a sort of legacy of
honor to my posterity who need not then be ashamed of claiming descent
from old 'Venator.' " The great planter would not publish a poetic drama
under his own name, but he was not ashamed to be known as a writer of
sportsman's sketches.[61]

The contents of *Carolina Sports* are almost equally divided between fishing and hunting, in both of which Elliott was a recognized expert. He concluded the book with an excellent defense of sport—and incidentally of
the theater and the dance—entitled "Random Thoughts on Hunting."
Hunting, he thought, made men more manly as well as more athletic. "The
sports of a country," said Elliott's reviewer in the *Southern Quarterly Review*, "are somewhat akin to its ballads, and these, as Fletcher of Saltoun
thought, are of more importance than its laws." The Southern passion for
hunting had perhaps a greater influence upon character and manners than

[61] For Henry D. Thoreau's comments on *Carolina Sports*, see his *Journals*, XX, 315–
319. Thoreau's biographer, Henry S. Canby, remarks: "If he had been able to disregard
the ugly fact of slavery, Thoreau would have found the plantation life of the old South
in closer accord with his philosophy than Concord ways of living" (*Thoreau*, 1939, p.
483 n.).

Elliott realized, although he once remarked: "Assuredly, there is no such preparatory school for war. . . ."

Elliott gave some thought to the literary qualities demanded in stories of fishing and hunting. "The sportsman, who gives a true description of his sports," he said, "must be an egotist." There is no escape from this necessity. When accused of want of repose in his writing, he replied that the lack was intentional: "*Celerity of movement* is the play—whether in the field or in the narrative!" [62] He appreciated his advantage in dealing with unhackneyed materials. Of drum-fishing he said: "Isaac Walton knew nothing like this—if he had, he must have disdained all smaller fry—and have abandoned the impaling of minnows, and the enticement of trouts, to indulge in the superior pleasure of drum-fishing." Elliott's longest chapter deals with devil-fishing, which, he declared, is "in fact, whale-fishing in miniature." The dangerous pursuit of the large and fleet devilfish was a favorite diversion of the planters in the vicinity of Port Royal Sound. Harpooning a devilfish was almost as dangerous and as exciting as whaling. At his best Elliott has something of the gift of vivid description and absorbing narrative that make memorable Melville's *Moby-Dick*. A more careful artist, however, would have rewritten the long chapter on devilfishing, which is put together from various newspaper narratives by Elliott and probably other sportsmen.

Elliott's hunting stories deal chiefly with deer and wildcats and remind us that the South was a great hunting region to which men came from the Northern states and from England. The hunts are described with gusto and animation, and the writer manages to communicate to the reader much of his own enjoyment of the adventures he describes. Four sketches which deal with Elliott's plantation at "Chee-ha" furnish interesting glimpses of plantation life. There are semiscientific chapters on South Carolina birds and animals which are the objects of sport. The best sketch in the whole volume is probably "The Fire Hunter," which is in effect a short story. An overseer named Slouch, with Pompey the plantation messenger to assist him, goes deer-hunting at night on his master's plantation in defiance of the law and of the absent owner's orders. The story comes to its tragic conclusion when Slouch in the light of a pine torch mistakes the eyes of a mule for those of a deer and shoots the mule's rider, who turns out to be Pompey's brother

[62] Elliott presumably did not agree with Simms, who in a letter to Elliott, March 7, 1849, suggested that "all that was necessary to make our Carolina Sports popular was such an incorporation with its details of the Social and Domestic Life of the Parishes, as would absolutely carry the reader to the scene, and supply the relief which is always essential in works whose chief object is exciting event and lively action" (Simms, *Letters*, II, 493).

Toney. Description and dialogue are handled with skill comparable to that of the local colorists of a later generation. Had Elliott given himself seriously to literature of this kind, he might well have made Simms look to his laurels.

36
Charleston

THE SOUTH WAS too large and too diverse to have such a literary capital as Boston was to New England, but Charleston was a literary center of greater importance than Baltimore, Richmond, Savannah, Mobile, or New Orleans. In the 1850's it had a kind of renaissance, cut short by the war, in which the leading figures were Simms, Hayne, Timrod, and Grayson. Its chief organ was *Russell's Magazine* (1857–1860), a sectional rival of the *Atlantic Monthly*, founded somewhat later in the same year.

Charleston, which in the eighteenth century had been one of the four largest American cities, had in 1840 a population of only 24,780. By 1860 its population had grown to 40,522, but nearly half its inhabitants were Negro slaves. As they watched the rapid growth of New York, Philadelphia, and Boston, Charlestonians attributed their city's slow growth and its lack of prosperity to the tariff and other discriminatory actions of the Federal government. The city became a hotbed of secessionist sentiment. As the first state to secede from the Union, South Carolina became an especial object of Northern antipathy. During the Civil War William J. Grayson wrote in his *Autobiography:* "Our Northern brethren have an especial hatred for this city. It is a nursery of treason, a trumpeter of sedition, a nest of rebels, an exact counterpart of the Boston of 1774 that insulted the dignity of King George and threw his tea into the river. The People of Massachusetts do not appreciate the resemblance." On December 18, 1864, the Chief of Staff in Washington, General Henry W. Halleck, wrote to General Sherman, then on his march through Georgia: "Should you capture Charleston, I hope that by *some accident* the place may be destroyed, and, if a little salt should be sown upon its site, it may prevent the growth of future crops of nullification and secession." When Sherman left Savannah, the Charlestonians expected him to lead his army directly to their city, but he surprised them by marching to Columbia instead.

Political leadership had passed from the Low-Country and the old planter families. Calhoun was an uplander; Hammond was the son of a Northern schoolmaster; Preston was a Virginian; George McDuffie was the orphan son of Up-Country parents. Of the chief Charleston writers only Paul

Hamilton Hayne belonged to one of the city's first families. Grayson and William Elliott came from the Beaufort region. Daniel K. Whitaker, the founder of the *Southern Quarterly Review*, was a Massachusetts Yankee. Timrod belonged to a middle-class family of merchant stock which Charleston's aristocrats looked down upon.

It is not easy to generalize about Charleston, for the little city was full of paradoxes. Its social tone was set by the Low-Country planters, who left commerce and business in the hands of outsiders, chiefly men from the North. A Charleston gentleman might be a banker or a factor, but he could not without loss of caste be a mere merchant. In other parts of the South, however, a merchant's social standing might be as good as a planter's. Charleston was a city of clubs, and apart from political questions, it was tolerant of individual differences. New Englanders, Irishmen, Germans, Jews, Unitarians, and Catholics mingled more freely than in many Northern cities. In Charleston, where men grew excited when one mentioned Garrison's *Liberator*, Francis Asbury Mood and his brothers in the late forties paid their way through the College of Charleston by conducting a school for the children of free Negroes. Their most advanced class studied the same subjects—including Tacitus and Homer in the original Latin and Greek—as the senior class in the College of Charleston.[63]

"Nobody understands the South Carolinian," wrote Walter Hines Page from Charleston on March 18, 1899. The North Carolinian added: "This is the only Southern city that I know of where white women of good social station teach negro schools and lose nothing thereby. The women of 'blood' do that here. Yet in the same town Northern women who teach in negro schools cannot obtain even the slightest social recognition." "Yet," he went on, "the old blue blood clings fast to its social idols; and there are women in good society here—the very best society—who sew for negroes; and they never see the negroes! Neither will they see or ever admit to their houses the whites for whom they sew."

In the period we are studying the Grimké sisters, who had turned Abolitionist, were gone—one of them married Theodore Weld—but Charleston tolerated and honored James Louis Petigru, "the Union Man of South Carolina," who in no uncertain terms spoke his mind about the folly of secession. Charleston was, as I have suggested, a cosmopolitan place. It had an active New England society, and native South Carolinians like Grayson and Petigru felt honored when invited to join it. Charleston was hospitable

[63] C. C. Cody, *The Life and Labors of Francis Asbury Mood* (Chicago, c. 1886), pp. 75–79. The school had a library and a debating society. In Raleigh a Negro, John Chavis, prepared the sons of North Carolina planters for college.

to Samuel Gilman, the New England-born pastor of one of the few Unitarian congregations south of Baltimore. Charlestonians often traveled in the North and in Europe. They frequently spent their summers in the North, and intersectional marriages were not uncommon. Many Charlestonians had attended New England colleges or secondary schools. Politics aside, the residents of the city often had stronger ties with Northern cities than with the Up-Country regions of their own state. And yet in political matters the state was, now that the cotton plantation had extended into the uplands, almost of a single mind; and the chief spokesman of that mind was John C. Calhoun.

There is abundant testimony to the charm of Charleston society and to the cultivation of its citizens. "In' my travels," wrote Emerson's friend Achille Murat, "I have found the society of Charleston by far the best, both here as well as on the other side of the Atlantic. There is nothing wanting either as regards finish, or elegance of manners. . . . she abounds in real talents, and is as far above pedantry as insignificance." [64]

James Silk Buckingham, who had no love for slavery wrote: "A taste for literature is more prevalent here [in Charleston] . . . than in most of the American cities; and there appeared to me to be a much more general acquaintance with the popular writers of Europe among the society of Charleston than in that of Boston, with less of pretension." "Reading constitutes, in fact, the principal recreation with all classes in Charleston," wrote the actor Louis Tasistro. "Novels, memoirs, books of travel, scientific tracts of all sorts and sizes, and historical compositions, are seized upon with the greatest avidity as soon as they are issued from the press, and still the public appetite, never satisfied, is constantly craving for more." [65]

In Charleston, wealth and family counted for much, but a certain degree

[64] *America and the Americans* (New York, 1849), trans. Henry J. Steele of Bradfield, p. 17; see also p. 247. This book is a translation of Murat's *Esquisse moral et politique des États-Unis de l'Amérique du Nord* (Paris, 1832). Murat's book attracted far less attention in France—and America—than Tocqueville's *Democracy in America*, for the Anti-Bonapartists controlled the French press in 1832. Professor A. J. Hanna comments: ". . . as Murat admired Charleston, so Tocqueville extolled the virtues of that 'hub of the solar system' located on Massachusetts Bay. The influence of Boston was to triumph; that of Charleston to recede" (*A Prince in Their Midst*, 1946, p. 237). See also pp. 176 ff., 233 ff.

[65] *Random Shots and Southern Breezes* (New York, 1842), II, 138. Tasistro comments on the popularity of Hart's Circulating Library, much frequented by Charleston women. It had, he says, "one of the best collections, both of old and modern books, English and foreign, to be found in America." At the time Tasistro was in Charleston, the books most in demand were George Combe's *Notes on the United States* and Bulwer-Lytton's *Night and Morning*.

of cultivation was indispensable. Frederick A. Porcher in "Southern and Northern Civilization Contrasted," published in *Russell's Magazine* for May, 1857, said: "The Southern gentleman regards education not as a means to a fortune, not as a resource against want, not as a step to a profession, but as thing desirable in itself." Literature and the arts were graceful aids to refined living. To take them seriously enough to give one's life to trying to create them—as Washington Allston had done and as Simms and Timrod were doing—was another matter, as it still is in the homes of many well-to-do Americans today. The culture of Charleston was less creative than that of Boston. Charlestonians had a taste for literature, but their little city was no literary market like Boston, New York, or Philadelphia.

Too much has been made of the exclusiveness of Charleston society, particularly in its treatment of Simms. There, as everywhere else in the United States, it was always possible for men of talents and cultivation to rise in the social scale by making money, attaining influential position or office, or marrying daughters of established families. Simms, who knew his Charleston and loved it, had something to say of its society in two of his little-known books—little known because they were published only in Charleston. In *Father Abbot* (1849) he notes that Charleston society consists of two communities which for twenty years have been in conflict. One class consists of those who work for a living and have in the eyes of the other no social consequence. Of the other class he says: "Its people could boast of a *past*. They could look back with pride to their ancestry, many of whom occupied an acknowledged place in our annals. They had been accustomed to wealth,—had all the advantages of social training and education, and could assert those graces of manner which require leisure and society as well as education and wealth." Simms paid his tribute to those who had all that wealth, good breeding, and education could give, but he maintained that the old families had made too many sacrifices to refinement and social grace. "The secret," he said, "is to refine our manners without forfeiting our strength." In *The Golden Christmas* (1852) Simms gave an enlightening account of the Low-Country aristocracy both in Charleston and on the plantations. The book includes a keen satirical portrait of one Madame Girardin, who believed that "there was some secret virtue in her blood that made her very unlike, and very superior to other people"; but Simms makes it clear that there were very few like her and that persons of no family background were to be seen in the best social circles—for there was more than one—in Charleston. There were doubtless many places in the city where a man of Simms's character and talents was welcome.

37
William Gilmore Simms

WILLIAM GILMORE SIMMS (1806-1870) rather than Poe is the central
figure in the literature of the Old South. He knew personally most of the
Southern writers of the time, and he more than any other man stimulated
them to write and to publish. But he was a national as well as a sectional
figure, and he was the most important literary link between North and
South. He had many friends in the Northern cities, where most of his books
were published, and he had until 1860 more readers in the North than in
his own section. In consequence, students of American literature, whether
their chief interest is in poetry, fiction, drama, or criticism, find themselves
continually running across his writings or allusions to his activities. So few
read his books today, however, that one is likely to forget his great historical
importance. His letters, now being published by his granddaughter, Mrs.
Mary C. Simms Oliphant, and others, are making it more than ever evident
that he was a national figure who deserves closer study than he has been
given.

"My family was a good one—the paternal side from Ireland, the maternal
from Virginia," wrote Simms to his New York friend, James Lawson, on
December 29, 1839. He added:

My immediate ancestors were poor. My father was unfortunate in business. My
mother died while I was an infant in the arms of the nurse. I had two brothers
who died about the same time. The ruin of his concerns, the death of his wife &
these two Children, seriously affected the spirits of my father, who emigrated to
the Southwest, a discontented & forever wandering man. He was a volunteer from
Tennessee under Jackson, in the invasion of the Creek nation & Seminoles, and
formed one in the Western Army against the invaders of New Orleans. He was
a man of great energy & enthusiasm of character, a lively & playful temper—
full of humour, and no small poet in the acceptation of those days.

Simms's maternal grandfather, John Singleton, was a captain in Marion's
army. His great-grandfather was one of the forty prominent citizens of
Charleston who when the British captured Charleston, were seized as
hostages and kept for three years on a prison ship at St. Augustine. Although
Simms's father failed in business, he was not financially ruined. When he
left Charleston he still owned 569 acres of land in the Edgefield District,
and in Mississippi he acquired a plantation and slaves. Simms inherited from
his mother two houses in Charleston and about twenty-five slaves. His

maternal grandmother, he thought, had not managed his inheritance skilfully. This "stern though affectionate" grandmother, after the death of her first husband, married a Massachusetts Yankee, Jacob Gates.

Mrs. Gates had lived through the exciting period of the British occupation of Charleston, and her stories first aroused in Simms an interest that eventually led to the writing of his Revolutionary Romances. She sent him to both free and private schools—all of which he thought were poor—and later apprenticed him to a druggist, hoping that eventually the boy would become a physician. Loneliness and recurrent illness had made him an omnivorous reader. To escape his grandmother's watchful eyes, he read until late at night with his book, a candle, and his head all hidden in a large box so that she, seeing no light coming from his room, would think him asleep. Two of his boyhood favorites were *The Pilgrim's Progress* and *The Vicar of Wakefield*, but his earliest ambition was to be a poet. Charleston was well supplied with bookstores, and young Simms soon discovered the Romantic poets, Byron, Scott, Wordsworth, Moore, and even Keats—the Elizabethan dramatists were presumably a later discovery—and he began to write reams of facile verses in imitation of these British poets. Somewhat prematurely, too, he began to publish them, at first in the Charleston newspapers and later in several small volumes. Hugh S. Legaré liked some verses that Simms had written in praise of the Ashley River and said to the youthful poet: "Yes, sir, it deserves to be sung in high heroics. It is a noble and *poetical* river." Few other Charlestonians, however, cared for Simms's verses. On November 1, 1830, Simms wrote from Charleston to James Lawson: "You can have no idea of the general dearth of letters prevailing among us, and indeed, it is not a strong epithet to say as I have said before, with us & in our city, a man betraying the most remote penchant for poetry, is regarded as little less than a nuisance."

When he was about eighteen, Simms abandoned the uncongenial drug business and began to study law. It was perhaps before this time that he made the long journey to Mississippi to see his father, who had some years earlier tried unsuccessfully to have the boy entrusted to his care. This was the first of several visits to the Southwest, the background of his Border Romances. On these visits the future author of *The Yemassee* and *Border Beagles* saw more of Indians and frontiersmen than it was ever Fenimore Cooper's good fortune to see. On this first visit Simms's father tried to induce him to settle as a lawyer in the West and assured him of a seat in Congress in ten years. He warned his son that in Charleston without friends, family, or fortune he could never achieve success in any occupation. "*Charleston!*" he exclaimed, "*I know it only as a place of tombs!*"

Young Simms, however, returned to Charleston, where in 1826 he married Anne Malcolm Giles. A year later he was admitted to the bar, and for a short time he practiced with some success. The call of literature, however, was too strong. By 1830 he had published five small volumes of verse, written a play or two and helped to edit several magazines and newspapers. One of these was a miniature literary weekly, the *Album*, published in the last half of the year 1825. On January 1, 1830, appeared the first number of the daily *City Gazette*, owned and operated by Simms and E. S. Duryea. Simms unfortunately had invested in the newspaper what was left of his inheritance from his mother. His opposition to Nullification cost him many subscribers and made enemies for him. In 1832 he sold his interest in the paper at a loss and found himself saddled with a debt that plagued him for many years.

In 1832 his wife died—his father and his grandmother were already dead —and the lonely young widower left Charleston, where the Nullifiers were in full control. He made his way somehow to Hingham, Massachusetts, where he prepared for the press what William Cullen Bryant thought the best of his longer poems, *Atalantis* (1832). In New York he met Bryant, whose poems Simms had praised in print some years before; and he made friends among New York writers, editors, and publishers. He was to keep in touch with them by frequent visits to the North. Many of his New York friends belonged to the "Young America" group, composed chiefly of Democrats who strongly advocated a national literature. On December 29, 1839, he wrote to James Lawson: ". . . I am a Democrat of the Jackson School, a State rights man, opposed to Tariffs, Banks, Internal improvements, American Systems, Fancy Rail Roads, Floats, Land Companies, and every Humbug East or West, whether of cant or cunning. I believe in the people, and prefer trusting their impulses, than the craft, the cupidity & the selfishness of trades & Whiggery."

In 1833 Simms made a novel, *Martin Faber*, out of "The Confessions of a Murderer," a short story he had published in the *Southern Literary Gazette* in November, 1829. This somewhat Godwinesque novel enjoyed only a moderate success, partly because of a superficial resemblance—suggesting plagiarism to some minds—to a recent English novel that Simms had not seen. His second novel, *Guy Rivers: A Tale of Georgia* (1834), had a good run. Cooper had shown that it was possible to make native materials the basis of a popular romance. In *Guy Rivers* Simms uncovered fresh American materials in semifrontier northern Georgia, which the recent discovery of gold had brought before the public eye. At this time Simms had no competitor in the novel of anything like his own talents except Kennedy, who wrote only two historical romances. Cooper had published no very popular novel since *The Prairie* (1827) and was in 1834 prematurely announcing to his countrymen that he would write no more works of fiction.

A young writer's inventive faculty is often more active than that of the more mature author. In *Guy Rivers* (1834) Simms had published the first of his Border Romances. In the next year he brought out his first Colonial Romance, *The Yemassee*, and *The Partisan*, the first of his Revolutionary Romances. *The Yemassee* is the book by which Simms is best known, for it is the only one of his many books that continues to be reprinted. This historical romance contains some effective scenes, but those who read nothing else by Simms are likely to conclude that he is only a second-rate Cooper. His Indian characters are less striking than Cooper's but they are closer to the historical Indian.[66]

Although Simms sometimes forgot that his proper task was to write historical fiction rather than romantic history, his best work is probably to be found in his seven Revolutionary Romances. These are: *The Partisan* (1835); *Mellichampe* (1836); *The Kinsmen* (1841), later entitled *The Scout; Katharine Walton* (1851); *The Sword and the Distaff* (1852), afterwards known as *Woodcraft; The Forayers* (1855); and *Eutaw* (1856). The series suffers from the long interval between its planning and completion. The last two, which contain some of Simms's best writing, are really a single novel in two volumes. *Woodcraft*, which Van Wyck Brooks regards as the best, is perhaps most likely to interest the modern reader.

Meanwhile in 1836 had come one of the most important events in Simms's life, his marriage to Miss Chevillette Roach, whose father owned two plantations in the Barnwell district, halfway between Charleston and Augusta. From now on, although he also had a house in Charleston, most of Simms's life was to be spent at "Woodlands," an estate of nearly three thousand acres. He was now a member of the planter class, and from this time on Simms's point of view was somewhat colored by his new connections.

Both his way of life at "Woodlands" and his method of writing, as Paul Hamilton Hayne describes them, remind one of Scott and in less degree of Cooper, both country gentlemen:

For a whole morning have I sat in that pleasant library, a book before me, but watching every now and then the tall, erect figure at the desk, and quick, steady passage for hours of the indomitable pen across page after page—a pen that rarely paused to erase, correct, or modify. At last, when the eternal scratch, scratch became a trifle irritating, and this exhaustless labor a reproach to one's

---

[66] Simms protested against the "noble savage" as portrayed by Chateaubriand and others in a long poem, "Chilhowee, the Indian Village," which appeared in the *Old Guard*, VII, 148–152 (Feb., 1869).

semi-idleness, Simms would suddenly turn, exclaiming, "Near dinner time, my boy; come, let's take a modest appetizer in the shape of sherry and bitters."

At dinner he talked a great deal, joked, jested, and punned, like a school-boy freed from his tasks; or, if a graver theme arose, he would often declaim a little too dogmatically and persistently, perhaps, to please those who liked to have the chance of wagging their own tongues occasionally. At such periods it was impossible to edge in the most modest of "caveats." Still, Simms could be a charming host, and was, *au fond*, thoroughly genial and kind-hearted. His dictatorial manner, to some extent, originated, I have thought, in the circumstances of his early life.

The first impression which Simms made upon John Pendleton Kennedy, who was a Whig, was distinctly unfavorable. It is given in an unpublished letter to Mrs. Kennedy from Patapsco, June 28, 1840:

Who do you think dined here today?—Guy Rivers. . . . He is tall, well made, not handsome in feature, amazingly pedantic, Sir Oracle in conceit, a thorough Loco [Democrat], and shortsighted in every sense. [Kennedy's note: "wears glasses."] He talked *literary* but fortunately I had not read or believed I had not, any of the books he wanted me to criticize, and shuffled off every imputation of scholarship he was pleased to presume in my favour. I abused Bryant to him for being *political*, and spoke of his editing a party newspaper as altogether derogatory to his fame. I was not overnice in my phrase in this matter—and after all, discov[ered?] that my new friend himself,—who, by the by, claims to be a poet,—was also, or had been, a party hack editor. I cant say I took *very* viol[ently?] to him. . . . I think the tribe, *author*, is not altogether the best of the Twelve of Israel.

Other men of letters more quickly rated Simms at his true value. Kennedy's cousin, John Esten Cooke, found him "a hearty, cordial, open-hearted man—a capital companion, and true as steel. It is refreshing," he added, "to meet now and then such a 'high pressure steamboat' as he is— it stirs my languid pulse, and wakes me from my indolence, and reveries. . . ." William Cullen Bryant, who twice enjoyed the hospitality of "Woodlands," said of Simms in the chapter on "Woodlands" which he wrote for *Homes of American Authors* (1853): "His manners, like the expression of his countenance, are singularly frank and ingenuous, his temper generous and sincere, his domestic affections strong, his friendships faithful and lasting, and his life blameless. No man ever wore his character more in the general sight of men than he, or had ever less occasion to do otherwise."

Simms, who thought that he was less popular in Charleston than in other parts of the state and less in the state than out of it, wrote to Lawson in the important letter of December 29, 1839, from which I have quoted:

My mind was of a very uncompromising sort, my temper exceedingly earnest & impassioned, and my pride, springing, perhaps, something from the feeling of isolation in which I found myself at an early age—without father or mother, brother or indeed, kindred of any kind—was always on the look out for opposition and hostility to those claims of my intellect which I believed to be well founded and which I also well knew, would never be anywhere more jealously resisted, than in a proud, wealthy & insulated community. . . . My reserve, under these impressions became hauteur, and I arrived very soon at a con sciousness to which few young & ambitious minds ever attain, that I could never be, in my native place, what I might be elsewhere. . . . No man took pains to ask whether my opinions were sound, or not: it was enough that he knew they were spoken by a mere boy,—one without family, friends or fortune, and one, too, who had never recieved a Classical Education—that venerable humbug which perhaps, has ruined more minds than it ever made scholars; and substitutes in the minds of most a habit of silly logic-chopping, instead of one which enables the pupil to address himself to the true studies and the serious businesses of life which are before him.

In an article on Simms published in *Appletons' Journal* in July, 1870, Hayne explained more clearly than elsewhere why Simms met opposition from certain Charleston intellectuals:

At that period there were in Charleston a number of persons distinguished for scholarship and ability. They were mostly men of mature age, elegant, refined, aristocratic, the graduates of first-class colleges in New England or Europe, who looked upon literature as the choice recreation of gentlemen, as something fair and good, to be courted in a dainty, *amateur* fashion, and illustrated by *a propos* quotations from Lucretius, Virgil, or Horace. In fact, with them literature meant simply and exclusively the classics. That any man ignorant of the dead languages, who could only read Homer through the medium of old Chapman or Pope, and whose acquisitions generally were confined to the masterpieces of his own vulgar mother-tongue, should aspire to the honors of *any* of the Muses, seemed monstrous and absurd. The sole arbiters of taste in a comparatively small provincial town, they treated the maiden effusions of our author with good-natured contempt.

What Hayne suggests is that Charleston gentlemen, like those who wrote for the *Southern Review*, to which Simms was not a contributor, held themselves superior to this rather aggressive, self-educated merchant's son and ridiculed his early efforts in verse and fiction. Charleston intellectuals were in general not enthusiastic advocates of an American literature, and they held a low opinion of the novel as a literary form.

Whatever certain Charleston aristocrats may have thought of him, Simms's character and talents had by the time he was thirty won him a place in one of the better Low-Country families. His wide correspondence and the dedicatory letters prefixed to his books are sufficient to prove that he stood on excellent terms with many of the state's leading citizens and with distinguished men, like Beverley Tucker, outside of South Carolina. He was eventually, it seems, made a member of the St. Cecilia Society— the supreme social honor open to a Charlestonian.

Simms was not content—any more than Scott or Cooper or Kennedy— to be merely a successful romancer. He wrote verse, criticism, essays, plays, short stories, biographies, histories. There are times when he seems, like N. P. Willis or H. L. Mencken, primarily a journalist rather than a man of letters. He even served a term in the state legislature, like other country gentlemen, and came within a single vote of being elected lieutenant-governor.

Too much of his time and energies went into the effort to give Charleston a magazine which should be both a literary medium for Southern writers and an organ for the defense of Southern institutions. Would any great creative artist have undertaken such a task? When Bliss Perry in his auto-biography, *And Gladly Teach,* came to speak of his own editorship of the *Atlantic Monthly,* he quoted as the chapter motto a sentence from Edward Fitzgerald: "The power of writing one fine line transcends all the Able-Editor ability in the ably-edited universe." Simms's editorial ventures were not even financially profitable, for his meager salary was not promptly paid—probably never paid in full—and his publishers did not know how to market their wares efficiently. In November, 1845, in announcing his ap-proaching retirement as editor of *"Simms's Magazine,"* he wrote: "It has never rewarded us in a pecuniary point of view. Were money the object, we could always have wrought more profitably in a dozen other occupations. We have aimed at something more. We have struggled, if possible, to urge and to provoke the South, into intellectual and literary exertions of her own—to indicate just standards of judgment in general literature, and to bring out the domestic genius in the various provinces of belles lettres and the arts." On November 9, 1854, shortly before he gave up the editorship of the *Southern Quarterly Review,* he wrote to Evert Duyckinck of his diffi-culties with his publisher: "The fellow is at once a fool and scamp. (Entre nous) He has put into the last number an article (Petrarch's Laura) which I had rejected as unpublishable, and has introduced another (on Harper's & Putnam's magazines[)], which I had never seen, and of which I wholly disapprove. With such an impertinent, how can I get on?"

As he grew older and as his extraordinary energy began to flag, Simms was often despondent. On May 26, 1852, his friend and neighbor D. F. Jamison wrote to George Frederick Holmes that for two years Simms had given way to a morbid depression of spirits.

He says he has laboured for the wind—that his works are not appreciated, as he reasonably expected they would be—especially in South Carolina for whose people he has written everything. I am sorry to admit that the last charge is too true. His more laboured compositions and his occasional contributions to the periodical press, all sell at the North and what is more to him, excite attention and call forth praise or blame, while at home they do not sell and come and go unnoticed.

. . . .

Simms, I admit has some faults. They proceed from a pardonable literary vanity, but he has some right to be vain. He has made himself, not only without the aid, but in spite of others. He is a fine animal, and my esteem and admiration of him as a man and an author have increased in exact proportion with the intimacy of my acquaintance with him.

Over a year later, Simms, still laboring on the *Southern Quarterly Review*, wrote to Holmes:

I am still a most unhappy drudge, fettered to the desk, as the galley slave to his oar. . . . That I am compelled to work incessantly, & mostly in vain, is a necessity which will finally overcome any will, and subdue the elastic in any spirit. I am in debt, my family increases, my resources diminish, and every hope upon which I persuade myself to build, seems doom'd to disappointment. . . . A literary man, residing in the South, may be likened to the blooded horse locked up in the stable, and miles away from the Course, at the moment when his rivals are at the starting post. Do what we may, it is impossible in such cases, that we can stand any chance of success. My true policy is to live in one of our great northern cities. Yet my wife is an only child; her father is in declining health & years; she cannot leave him, and I cannot separate from her & my children, except for a brief period. I am thus compelled to remain here, & in my stable, when I ought to be speeding over the track. My labours here are profitless. The Review does not pay me.

On October 30, 1858, in a time of grief and bitterness, Simms recalled his father's warning many years before:

Thirty odd years have passed, and I can now mournfully say the old man was right. All that I have [done] has been poured to waste in Charleston, which has never smiled on any of my labors, which has steadily ignored my claims, which has disparaged me to the last, has been the last place to give me its adhesion, to which I owe no favor, having never received an office, or a compliment, or a dollar at her hands; and, with the exception of some dozen of her citizens, who have been kind to me, and some scores of her young men, who have honored me with a loving sympathy and something like reverence, which has always treated me rather as a public enemy, to be sneered at, than as a dutiful son doing her honor. *And I, too, know it as a place of tombs.* I have buried six dear children within its soil! Great God! what is the sort of slavery which brings me hither!

As early as April 30, 1842, Simms had written to James H. Hammond: "I have always been, from my first consciousness, a marked man—set aside and very much distinguished by the scourge." Eighteen years later we find him writing to William Porcher Miles: "I have been overworked; I have been unsuccessful all my life; my books fail to pay me; I am myself a failure! In S.C. I am repudiated."

Simms was in fact far from being "repudiated" in his native state, but there were still Charlestonians who underrated his achievements. John R. Thompson in the "Editor's Table" of the *Southern Literary Messenger* for October, 1859, wrote: "A notable discussion is going on in the newspapers of Charleston, S. C., the point at issue being whether Mr. William Gilmore Simms can write good English. We shall expect to hear soon that the good people of Boston are in doubt as to Mr. Longfellow's acquaintance with the alphabet, and that the London *Athenaeum* is perplexed about Sir Edward Bulwer-Lytton's familiarity with the auxiliary verbs. When will the people of the South learn to know and honour their worthiest literary men?" Paul Hamilton Hayne wrote in *Russell's Magazine* for November, 1857: "Nowhere, probably, in the Union has he [Simms] been honored with less of encouragement and appreciation, than in the city of his birth, and among the people of the very State whose traditional and revolutionary annals, whose society, institutions, scenery and peculiar phases of life, and character, he has done more than any other, to describe, perpetuate, and defend. It is an old story, but not on that account the less melancholy."

Doubtless Simms had to fight his way up in Charleston. He must have taken a grim pleasure in the story of Lord Morpeth, who had inquired in Charleston for Simms only to be told that he was not considered such a great man in Charleston. "Simms not a great man!" the noble Lord exclaimed; "then for God's sake, who is your great man!" Simms, however, had his admirers in Charleston. In *The Hireling and the Slave* (1856) William J. Grayson mentioned "Simms, who is always at home in Southern scenes and scenery—never so strong as when his foot is on his native soil, and *facile princeps* in Southern song, history, and story." In far-off New Orleans *De Bow's Review* in August, 1861, praised "William Gilmore Simms, to whom Southern literature is more indebted than to any man living." In May, 1859, the *Southern Literary Messenger* said: "Mr. Simms occupies a position in the eyes of the Southern people which is most enviable. The chivalric gentleman—the accomplished scholar—the untiring defender of the South, and all its rights and interests—he is everywhere recognized as one of our most worthy citizens, and distinguished ornaments."

What Simms wanted was such recognition as generally comes only to a great writer in old age or after his death. While preparing a two-volume edition of his poems, he wrote to Evert Duyckinck, November 24, 1853: "I flatter myself that my poetical work exhibits the highest phase of the Imaginative faculty which this country has yet exhibited, and the most philosophical in connection with it." Not even Simms's most intimate friends and admirers could agree with such a mistaken estimate as that. Hayne wrote to Margaret J. Preston not long after Simms's death that Simms's delusion that he was "a Great Poet, of the rugged Elizabethan type of genius" always gave him a feeling of "pity & dismay."

Simms, like Hayne and too many other Southern writers, imagined that if he had made his home in New York, Boston, or London, he would have quickly won fame and fortune. The failure of certain Charlestonians to recognize Simms as a great writer had much less to do with his social origin than Professor Trent thought. Hayne, born to wealth and social position, found Charleston no more disposed to recognize his claims than it had been to acknowledge those of Simms or Timrod. Their friend George Henry Boker belonged to a wealthy family which stood high in Philadelphia, but that city steadily refused to attach any importance to his poems and plays. In more recent times New York society showed no greater willingness to recognize the literary merits of Edith Wharton, who was to the manner born. Hayne liked to imagine that if Simms had lived in old or New England, he would have been much more highly honored than he was in Charleston. Yet even in Boston, where some authors were highly honored, no single writer of any eminence among Simms's contemporaries made his living wholly by writing. In every country and every century the pen has been an uncertain means of earning a livelihood, and authors have lived and died without adequate recognition from their contemporaries. Our own century, which thinks itself so much more discerning, waited for many years before it recognized the claims of Dreiser, Frost, and Robinson. Lowell's biographer, Richmond Croom Beatty, found himself disgusted by the "servile tributes to Lowell and New England from authors in other regions," each complaining "that the writer's own environment was hostile to him, that he was misunderstood, that there was nothing about it to inspire him." Southern writers seemed to Beatty "especially culpable in this regard." "The view," he thought, "was part of that flabby derivativeness that was blinding them fatally to the literary material lying at their own doors. It accounts for a great deal that is worthless and secondhand in the work of the early poets of the South."

It should be noted that Simms, whose books had brought him approximately six thousand dollars in 1835, was earning considerably less in the forties and fifties. There were too many cheap books, especially pirated British novels, on the American market. On August 16, 1841, he wrote to Hammond: ". . . Irving now writes almost wholly for magazines and Cooper & myself are almost the only persons whose novels are printed—certainly, we are almost the only persons who hope to get anything for them. From England we get nothing. In this country an Edition now instead of 4 or 5,000 copies is scarce 2,000. My Damsel of Darien was 3,000. My Kinsmen not more than 2,000; and it is seldom now that the demand for novels carries them to a 2d. Edition." It is no wonder that Simms was so long in completing the series of Revolutionary Romances. He wrote to James Henry Hammond, December 24, 1847:

My residence in South Carolina, is unfavorable to me as an author. I lose $2000 per annum by it. Our planting interests barely pay expenses and my income from Literature which in 1835 was $6000 per annum, is scarce $1500 now, owing to the operation of cheap reprints which pay publishers & printers profits only & yield the author little or nothing. . . . Here [in the South] I am nothing & can be & do nothing. The South don't care a d—n for literature or art. Your best neighbour & kindred never think to buy books. They will borrow from you & beg, but the same man who will always have his wine, has no idea of a library. You will write for & defend their institutions in vain. They will not pay the expense of printing your essays.

Simms had not taken the advice which Hammond had given him in a letter of May 10, 1845:

I know it is only a notion of yours writing for money. But if you were compelled to support yourself by your pen, you would be justified, with your abilities, to imitate the old masters, & live on crusts, that you may have abundant leisure to think thoroughly, & write composedly. To penetrate again and again the inmost recesses of your subject, explore every turn & nook until it is as familiar as your daily food, & then to draw it in bold outline adding only *essential* detail, & to paint with strong, broad, harmonious, & concentrated colour. There is no other way to produce a great work. And you ought to be put to death if you do not set about producing one.

Professor Trent has given a very unsympathetic account of Simms's various activities in defending slavery and promoting secession. The truth of the matter would seem to be that the biographer was in 1892 a radically reconstructed young Southerner who felt it his duty as a historian to set Charleston and the South right as to the merits of the long sectional controversy. In recent years Northern historians have dealt more kindly with Simms and his fellows. Simms was honest in supporting these causes, and he knew that in promoting them he was injuring the sale of his books in the North, his chief market. There is a better reason for condemning Simms's propagandistic writings; namely, on the ground that they took time and energy that should have gone into the writing of romances. But Simms, being the man he was, could no more stay out of the controversy than Milton could devote his time to writing an epic when his country was undergoing a revolution.

In the late forties Simms became a zealous defender of slavery and the rights of the states. John W. Higham has argued that the marriage of the merchant's son to the daughter of a Low-Country planter explains Simms's shift from Unionist to secessionist.[67] The explanation ignores the fact that in these years many another Southerner, whether merchant, professional man, or planter, underwent a similar change in his political opinions. Simms had married Chevillette Roach in 1836, but it was years later that he became a secessionist. In discussing his new political stand, Simms wrote on May 1, 1847, to James H. Hammond: "Perhaps, I should have arrived at my conclusions without your aid, if I had not, after my repudiation 20 years ago as a Union man, dismissed as much as possible from my mind the consideration of subjects over which it appeared to me I was destined to have no control." In October, 1854, when Simms printed in the Southern Quarterly Review an article by a planter who belittled the merchants and magnified the planters, he protested in a three-page note: "It is a mistake to ascribe the intellectual greatness, or the political success, the eloquence, or the virtues of the South, to agriculture exclusively. . . . Our great men have not been simply planters." The planters were, as Simms well knew, largely indifferent to the Southern literature he was doing his best to promote. In June, 1837, a year after his marriage to Chevillette Roach, he had published in the Southern Literary Journal an article entitled "Country Life Incompatible with Literary Labor," in which he said: "To hunt, to ride, to lounge, and to sleep,—perhaps to read a few popular novels conducing to repose,—is the sum and substance of our country performances." Simms is reported on one occasion to have said: "No, sir, there will never be a literature worth the name in the Southern States, so long as their aristocracy remains based on

[67] "The Changing Loyalties of William Gilmore Simms," Jour. So. Hist., IX, 210–223 (May, 1943).

so many head of negroes and so many bales of cotton." Simms had, I think, a smaller share in building up the glamorous legend of the slave plantation than Caruthers, Grayson, or Beverley Tucker.

When the war came, Simms at the age of fifty-five was too old to join the Confederate army, in which his son and namesake served. He sent in suggestions for the military defense of Charleston, and he did his best to help his friends Hayne and Timrod when they were in financial difficulties. The war had cut him off from his literary market in the Northern cities, but he wrote for the short-lived wartime magazines and he supplied martial lyrics to the Charleston newspapers.

There was one moment when the discouraged and aging novelist felt that South Carolina appreciated what he had done for the state. After his house was burned in 1862, his friends and admirers promptly raised $3600 to rebuild it. In his letter of thanks, printed in the Charleston *Mercury* for July 8, 1862, he said that the many offers of help which had come to him proved "in the most conclusive manner, that I have not lived or labored in vain— that the forty years of my life which I have devoted to the fame and interests of our people—their reputation and securities—have not failed to win their confidence, their affection and esteem."

During Sherman's northward march through the Carolinas Simms's home was again burned and with it his library of over ten thousand volumes. He was not at "Woodlands," however, but in Columbia when Sherman came through. A youthful Union lieutenant came to the house where Simms and his children were staying and said: "Sir, I have enjoyed too much pleasure from your books not to feel grateful. You belong to the Union, and I have come to see if I can render you any service." Soon after Sherman's army left Columbia, largely destroyed by fire, Simms published in the devastated city a pamphlet which is one of his most powerful pieces of writing, *Sack and Destruction of Columbia, S. C.*

Turning now to journalism for a living, he worked on the Columbia *Phoenix* and then on the *Daily South Carolinian*, which was soon moved to Charleston. It was here that John Townsend Trowbridge, who had read Simms's romances as a boy, found him "a man of sixty, with shortish iron-gray hair and roughish features,—not at all my idea of a great writer who could harrow up the souls of boy readers." Simms was quite ready to talk to Trowbridge about the damage the Yankees had inflicted upon his state. In *My Own Story* (1903) Trowbridge wrote:

"Charleston, sir," he [Simms] said, with a level fixity of look, "was the finest city in the world; not a large city, but the finest. South Carolina, sir, was the flower of modern civilization. Our people were the most hospitable, the most accomplished, having the highest degree of culture and the highest sense of honor, of any people, I will not say of America, sir, but of any country on the globe. And they are so still, even in their temporary desolation."

On December 8, 1868, Simms wrote to Joseph Henry: "My property, save my land, is all destroyed. One day I was the owner of $150,000 in slaves, lands, &c. I have nothing now, but what I can extract, from what Ben Jonson styles 'Brain Sweat.' " On June 15, 1865, Simms had described his circumstances in a long letter from Columbia to his old New York friend, Evert Duyckinck:

You have probably been apprised already of the destruction of my house and plantation, by your army under Sherman. The house had been recently rebuilt. It is completely destroyed; all my furniture, and—my library!—not a volume was spared. You can form, from what you know, a sufficient idea of the value of the collection which numbered some 10,700 vols. My carriage house, stables, kitchen, barns, machine house, threshing house, wagons, implements of husbandry,—all shared the same fate. Eighteen mules & horses were carried off, and how many head of cattle, hogs, poultry destroyed, it is impossible to say. Thirty-one of my Negroes were carried off. Some 45 remain, of whom 5 are over 70, as many over 60, and perhaps 10 are children less than 10 years of age. Their provisions were all taken from them, and they, like myself, are almost destitute. There are 17 now at work on the place, but these, without tools, implements, mules, wagons &c. will hardly be able to earn their bread. . . . It is . . . impossible for me at present even to get back to my plantation, lacking equally in money & the ability to walk. The pedestrian is now with us almost the only traveller. . . . I am, under these circumstances, constrained to ask what my friends in New York & elsewhere can do for me. . . . I wish you next to inquire into the condition of my copyrights, and ascertain what is due me on the sale of my books, upon which I have not for five years received one copper. . . . And I could wish to have some books sent me, through John Russell, of Charleston. I have had nothing to read for 4 years. . . . I am a widower and have buried 9 out of 15 children. My hair & beard are quite white, and I am verging on 60, but I am healthy, comparatively vigorous, & with my children present ever to my eyes, I feel that I have many years of good work in me yet,—If my friends will help to rescue me from my shackles. Excuse this hurried epistle, which is written *stans pede in uno* & with the momentary expection [*sic*] that it will be called for. Besides, all my old familiar conveniences of desk, table, portfolio, good pens &c. are gone. I am literally the inhabitant of a garret such as Grub Street would recognize from family likeness, & such as Goldsmith so well describes.

In June, 1866, Simms went to New York and remained in the North for three months trying to re-establish connections with editors and publishers.

A few of his old friends stood by him. With their help eventually he found a few publishers—none of the first class—that were willing to pay for what he might write. To the *Old Guard*, a "Copperhead" monthly, he contributed some poems and two serial novels, *Joscelyn* in 1867 and *The Cub of the Panther* in 1869, neither of which was republished in book form. The pay was small, and Simms practically killed himself through excessive work.

In February, 1869, he wrote to Hayne: "I do not now write for fame or notoriety or the love of it, but simply to procure the wherewithal of life for my children; and this is a toil require [requiring] constant labor. My recent illness is simply the consequence of a continued strain upon the brain for four months, without the interval of a single day. In that time I wrote near two thousand pages note paper of manuscript on two works, to say nothing of an immense correspondence and numerous asides at the call of friends, etc." Simms had even taken the time to write, presumably without pay, his recollections of early nineteenth-century South Carolina writers. These were published in a new Charleston magazine, the *XIX Century*, which in June, 1869, hailed him as "Dear, genial, generous, sturdy old Carolina Gentleman —'one of ye olden time.'" Simms in New York had obtained advances on three novels as yet unwritten. He completed two of them but broke down on the third. He died on June 11, 1870, and was buried with due honors in Magnolia Cemetery, at the consecration of which he had read a poem twenty-one years earlier.

In 1878 a monument surmounted by Ward's bronze bust of Simms was erected in Battery Park in Charleston. A decade later his New York friend, James Grant Wilson, visited Charleston. In company with Mayor William A. Courtenay he drove to Magnolia Cemetery, where he found Simms's grave unmarked except for the name SIMMS carved on the granite coping that surrounded it. Wilson said to Courtenay that "if the distinguished author's Southern friends were indisposed to honor his memory by erecting a suitable monument to mark the resting place of the first and foremost of their writers, [he] would undertake to collect the requisite amount from among his many admirers and friends in the North." The next year Wilson received a letter from Courtenay in which he said: "When you again visit Charleston you will find the grave of your friend Simms covered by an appropriate and handsome monument."

Simms tried his hand at nearly every type of writing popular in his time. Much of it quickly lost the temporary value it had. Most of his newspaper and magazine pieces, usually written in a hurry, are still uncollected and probably few of them will ever be reprinted. He wrote too rapidly and published too much. Altogether he published something more than eighty books. "I find it much easier," he said, "to invent a new story than to repair the defects of an old one." Admitting the shortcomings of the too-hastily written *The Partisan*, which Poe had roughly handled, he defended himself by saying: ". . . the finish of art can only be claimed by a people with whom art is a leading object. No other people are well able to pay for it—no other people are *willing* to pay for it. . . ." All of this may be true, but I cannot believe that Poe, Hawthorne, and Henry James ever relaxed their standards because the reading public failed to see the difference between their best and their second best. I hasten to add, however, that when new editions of his novels were called for, Simms gave them more extensive revision than is generally supposed. When he sent some of his novels to Beverley Tucker in May, 1849, Simms wrote: "They were written most of them at an extremely early age, & under the pressure of necessities which left me too careless of any but present & momentary considerations. You will find them wanting in symmetry and finish, and grossly disfigured by errors of taste and judgment." In September of the same year he wrote to James H. Hammond: "It was in writing the most of these works that I *acquired my education*, such as it is." In another mood he had written to George Frederick Holmes, January 26, 1844: ". . . fame does not so much follow polish & refinement as Genius—not so much grace and correct delineation as a bold adventurous thought."

Simms was not a great critic, but he was a man of sense and intelligence and, as his numerous prefaces show, he thought much if not profoundly about the literary art. We are not bound of course to accept his theories of the function of the novelist, but we shall understand his work better if we have some knowledge of what he was trying to do.

Like Hawthorne, he was careful to distinguish between the romance and the novel. In dedicating one of the later editions of *The Yemassee* to Dr. S. H. Dickson, he wrote: "The modern Romance is the substitute which the people of the present day offer for the ancient epic. The form is changed: the matter is very much the same. . . . The domestic novel . . . is altogether a different sort of composition." The romance, he thought, partook of the characteristics of both novel and epic poem. "It does not confine itself to what is known, or even what is probable. . . ." "It invests individuals with an absorbing interest—it hurries them rapidly through crowding and exacting events, in a narrow space of time—it requires the same unities of plan, of purpose, and harmony of parts, and it seeks for its adventures among the wild and wonderful."

In his romances Simms took over the pattern first developed by Scott and later adapted by Cooper to American materials. Simms in turn adapted it to the portrayal of guerrilla warfare in Revolutionary South Carolina and to outlaw activities in the old Southwest. He was more indebted to Scott than to Cooper. His numerous scouts are as good as all but Cooper's best, but they live and fight in the swampy region of the Carolina Low-Country, which is very unlike the primeval New York forest of *The Deerslayer* and *The Last of the Mohicans*.

Simms's best work, it is generally agreed, was done in the seven Revolutionary Romances. Unlike the Leather-Stocking Tales, the series was planned in advance. After publishing *The Partisan* in 1835, however, Simms proceeded in 1836 to add as an afterthought *Mellichampe*, the poorest of the seven. *The Scout* (1841) suffers from Simms's fondness for the melodramatic. *Katharine Walton* (1851) is the only one which describes Charleston in detail. Twenty-one years elapsed between the publication of the first and the last of the series. *Woodcraft* (1852), *The Forayers* (1855), and *Eutaw* (1856) are more carefully written than *The Partisan* and *Mellichampe* and are the best of the series. Simms's best character, Captain Porgy, who has a certain resemblance to Falstaff, plays a leading role in *Woodcraft* and has a minor part in other books in the series.

At his best Simms is as good as Cooper, but he sometimes forgets that his readers' primary interest is not in South Carolina history but in men and women undergoing exciting adventures. Unlike Scott and Cooper, he often fails to keep his leading character at the front of the stage. If, however, one is willing to read the series as a whole—or even the last two or three—the total effect is impressive, and one has no feeling, such as when one reads only *The Yemassee*, that Simms is a second-rate Cooper. The seven romances constitute a kind of epic of the American Revolution. In spite of the melodramatic episodes, a sense of reality pervades these books. Simms took great pains to make his general picture accurate, and he must have been pleased when William Hickling Prescott in 1859 said in an address in Charleston: "I cannot refer to [the American Revolution] without acknowledging the debt which I think the State owes to one of her most distinguished sons, for the fidelity with which he has preserved its memory, the vigor and beauty with which he has painted its most stirring scenes, and kept alive in fiction the portraits of its most famous heroes."

In his dedication to *Katharine Walton* (1851) Simms stated that when he wrote *The Partisan*, no one but himself seemed to think the materials worth writing about. "My friends," he said, "denounced my waste of time upon scenes, and situations, and events, in which they beheld nothing latent —nothing which could possibly (as they thought) reward the laborer. Now,

South Carolina is regarded as a very storehouse for romance. She has furnished more materials for the use of art and fiction, than half the states in the Union." One is reminded of Francis Parkman undertaking to write the story of the conflict between France and England for the possession of a vast American empire and finding that even his own family regarded the subject as merely a contest among bushrangers for the possession of a wilderness.

The pattern of historical romance gave full play to Simms's love of incident and of picturesque border fighters, but it did not permit full play to his bent toward realism, which was strong. Simms's temperament was robust. He had in full measure what we call gusto, and he had no more sympathy than Poe with the sentimentality which was so conspicuous a trait in the women novelists of the time. In 1841 he published in the *Magnolia*—which had begun life the year before as the *Southern Ladies' Book*—a three-part story entitled "The Loves of the Driver," in which he described the futile attempts of a Negro driver, or foreman, to seduce the squaw of a worthless Indian vagrant. Readers of the *Magnolia* immediately protested to the editor that the story was not only in bad taste but positively immoral. In defense of his story Simms wrote in the *Magnolia*:

It is a tale of low life—very low life—that is true. Elegant people,—very elegant people, I mean,—revolt, I very well know, at mere human interests when they do not relate to the fortunes and movements of other elegant people. There is nothing surely very attractive in Negroes and Indians; but something is conceded to intellectual curiosity; and the desire is a human, and very natural one, to know how our fellow beings fare in other aspects than our own, and under other forms of humanity, however inferior.

Simms deplored the "mock modesty" of the readers of the *Magnolia*. "We are reluctant, in very nice society," he wrote, "to call things by their proper names. We dare not speak of legs, or thighs, in the presence of many very nice ladies. . . ." He insisted that there was nothing immoral in his story. "A writer," he said, "*is moral only in proportion to his truthfulness.*"

Simms would, I think, have protested vigorously against the fundamental assumption of his biographer, Professor Trent, that "nobility is that quality of a romance which is essential to its permanence." For nobility of character Simms had as high regard as any other writer, but he felt it his duty to picture men and women as they are. To those who objected to the oaths which he placed in the mouths of some of his characters he replied that he could not alter for the better the backwoodsman's vocabulary. To those who objected to his realistic treatment of certain characters in the first of the Revolutionary Romances, he replied: "The low characters predominate in the

'Partisan,' and they predominate in all warfare, and in all times of warfare, foreign and domestic. They predominate in all imbodied armies that the world has ever known." As the Border Romances show, Simms saw as clearly as William Faulkner or Robert Penn Warren the strain of violence in Southern life—in life in all lands, for that matter—the strain of violence and disorder which sentimental readers and writers have always been disposed to ignore.

On the question of morality in fiction, Simms in the Advertisement to *Mellichampe* (1836) took the position which Thackerary was to take in his Preface to *Pendennis* (1850) and George Eliot in Chapter XVII of *Adam Bede* (1859). He wrote:

The question which propriety may ask, having the good of man for its object, is—"Has the novelist made vice attractive, commendable, successful, in his story? Is virtue sacrificed—are the humanities of life and society endangered, by the employment of such agents as the low and vulgar? Is there anything in the progress of the vicious to make us sympathize with them—to make us seek for them?" . . . perhaps [he added sarcastically], if, instead of naked vulgarity and barefaced crime, I had robed my villains in broadcloth, adorned their fingers with costly gems, provided them liberally with eau-de-Cologne, and made them sentimental, I should have escaped all objections of this nature.

When Sara Josepha Hale declined to accept Simms's *Vasconselos* for serial publication in *Godey's Lady's Book*, he acquiesced in her decision, but he felt it necessary to explain his own position in a letter which he wrote to her on October 15, 1849:

Of an intense and passionate temperament myself, delighting in deep tragedy, and the sternest provocations to the passions, I have learned to distrust my own judgment in such matters, and gladly give ear to the suggestions of a more deliberate method and a calmer mood. I do not think that Vasconselos would ever be considered an immoral story. It is one of dark & terrible imaginings and will, I think, prove one of the wildest interest and the most intense power. It is a tale of crime, but not of voluptuousness, & none of the scenes would have embodied an argument for, or an inducement to sensuality. On the contrary, crime, as in the Holy Scriptures, would be shown, almost entirely, in its griefs, its glooms, and its terrible penalties. So much for my defence of my story *per se*. But I do not argue for its appropriateness to the publication which, like yours, appeals so *intensively* to the more delicate sensibilities of your *sex*. I cheerfully accept your decision and will endeavor to supply its place with another [*Katharine Walton*] to which, I pledge you, no exception can possibly be taken.

Simms's theory of the relation of plot to character, as he stated it in *The Golden Christmas* (Charleston, 1852), is admirable: "The artist does not make events; they make themselves. They belong to the characterization. The author makes the character. If this be made to act consistently,—and this is the great necessity in all works of fiction,—events flow from its action necessarily, and one naturally evolves another, till the whole action is complete. Here is the whole secret of the novelist." Like many another novelist, Simms did not always live up to his theory. He was, for one thing, too fond of melodramatic situations and events. He created many excellent minor characters but no one major figure comparable to Leather-Stocking or Uncas or Long Tom Coffin of Nantucket. His best characters are his scouts, and these are in their way admirable. Like Cooper, he was less happy with his ladies and gentlemen, and they seldom come to life in his stories. He was more successful with his Negro characters than any other Southern writer before Joel Chandler Harris, Irwin Russell, and Mark Twain, but there are too few of them.

In addition to his historical romances, Simms wrote several novels and short stories which in a letter to Rufus W. Griswold he characterized as "the moral imaginative." (Griswold's son printed the phrase as "novels imaginative.") To this category belong *Martin Faber* (1833), *Carl Werner* (1838), *Confession* (1841), *Castle Dismal* (1844), and many of the short stories in *The Wigwam and the Cabin* (1845–1846). Of somewhat the same type are *Beauchampe, or The Kentucky Tragedy* (1842) and *Charlemont* (1856), which Simms referred to as "Border Domestic Novels." The last two novels make use of a famous Kentucky murder story that figures in Poe's *Politian*, Chivers's *Conrad and Eudora*, numerous forgotten plays and novels, and, much more recently, Robert Penn Warren's notable *World Enough and Time* (1950).[68]

Of his attempts at fiction in "the moral imaginative" vein, Simms said in a letter to Griswold written on December 6, 1846: "These publications, forming in all some ten volumes, were marked chiefly by the characteristics of passion & imagination—by the free use, in some cases, of diablerie and all the machinery of superstition, & by a prevailing presence of vehement individuality of tone & temper. They constitute, in all probability, the best specimens of my powers of creating & combining, to say nothing of a certain

[68] *Beauchampe*, with some additions, was republished as two novels, *Beauchampe* becoming a sequel to *Charlemont*. Arthur H. Quinn has straightened out the confused relations between two novels in his *American Fiction* (1936), p. 122 n. 2.

For other treatments of the Kentucky tragedy, see Arthur H. Quinn, *A History of American Drama . . . to the Civil War* (revised ed., 1943), pp. 260–261, and W. R. Jillson, "The Beauchampe-Sharpe Tragedy in American Literature," *Ky. Hist. Soc. Register*, XXXVI, 54–60 (Jan., 1938). Quinn and Jillson do not mention Mary E. MacMichael, "The Kentucky Tragedy. A Tale—Founded on Facts of Actual Occurrence," *Burton's Gentleman's Mag.*, II, 265–271 (April, 1838).

intensifying egotism, which marks all my writings written in the first person." Simms wrote more clearly of his aims in the Introduction to the 1856 edition of *Confession*. By that time he realized that most of his readers preferred his romances of adventure to his psychological novels. In *Confession*, he said, "The attempt is made to analyze the heart in some of its obliquities and perversities; to follow its toils, pursue its phases, and to trace, if possible, the secret of its self-deceptions, its self-baffling inconsistencies, its seemingly wilful warfare with reason and the sober experience. . . . It belongs, somewhat, to the class of works which the genius of Godwin has made to triumph in 'Caleb Williams,' even over a perverse system." "Success, of a popular kind," he noted, "is rarely possible in any work of fiction where events, which naturally speak for themselves, are mostly rejected from use; where the whole history depends for development upon the silent progress of the thoughts, and sentiments, and emotions—the passions themselves working as undercurrents of moods and feelings—moods which look, but speak not, and feelings that boil for ever in fiery fountains, but are never suffered to overflow!" These novels, stemming like the tales of Poe and Hawthorne from the Gothic tradition, William Godwin, and Charles Brockden Brown, are psychological studies of morbid moods and the complexes of troubled introverts. Perhaps the reading public was right in preferring Simms the romancer to Simms the psychological novelist of crime and introspection, but that does not excuse students of the American novel from grossly neglecting his many attempts at psychological fiction. He deserves recognition along with Hawthorne and Poe as a forerunner of Henry James and William Faulkner and Robert Penn Warren. Poe, as we shall see, thought Simms was at his best when he abandoned historical romance for "the moral imaginative" novel.

Simms's short stories are less read than his novels, but some of them are worthy of remembrance. In structure they are looser and more leisurely than Poe's, and in substance and suggestiveness they do not compare favorably with Hawthorne's. There are over sixty of them. A good many are the product of his earlier years, but the best of them are as good as his romances. They cover a wide range: the Indian, the Negro, the pioneer. Some of the best were reprinted in *The Wigwam and the Cabin* in 1845–1846, but the later ones are still uncollected. "How Sharp Snaffles Got His Capital and His Wife," printed in *Harper's Magazine* in October, 1870, is an admirable example of the tall tale. It is worthy of Johnson Jones Hooper or George W. Harris, and it is better than anything in Simms's earlier venture in the tradition of Southern humor, *As Good as a Comedy; or The Tennessean's Story* (1852).

The Golden Christmas (1852) was apparently suggested by Simms's reading of the revised edition of Kennedy's Swallow Barn which appeared in 1851. It was published only in Charleston, and partly for that reason it attracted little attention. In the year in which Uncle Tom's Cabin appeared perhaps no Northern publisher thought his readers would care for so unexciting a story of social life in Charleston and on Low-Country plantations. The Golden Christmas is not on the whole so good as Swallow Barn, but it is good enough to suggest that if Simms had got any real encouragement to write novels of contemporary Carolina life, he might have continued to explore an extraordinarily rich field. He might conceivably have written other books which would interest the modern reader more than his historical romances of a South Carolina that he could never know at first hand.

Simms's plays are just promising enough to suggest that if he had possessed a more intimate knowledge of the theater and had seriously devoted himself to dramatic writing, he would have written important plays. One of his plays prompted Thomas Holley Chivers to write: "I have received and read your Drama, and find it the best thing I have ever seen of yours—in fact, I am now puzzled to know why you should ever have worn out your faculties in writing Novels."

A few of Simms's many poems have points of interest. The references to his boyhood suggest that Mrs. Gates, who brought him up, was not a very congenial or understanding grandmother. "The Edge of the Swamp" is a powerful and vivid description of a characteristic feature of the Low-Country landscape. His only really popular poem was "The Lost Pleiad," which he says was "written between my eighteenth and twentieth year." On May 28, 1859, he printed a much enlarged and revised version of the Southern Field and Fireside.[69] In his shorter lyrics Simms strove for verbal melody, like Pinkney, Chivers, Poe, and other Southern poets of the time. Poe was particularly struck by the "Indian Serenade," which first appeared in The Damsel of Darien (1839). In July, 1846, he asked: "By the way, how happens it, in the melodious stanza which follows . . . that the sonorous Samana has been set aside for the far less musical and less effective Bonita?" The stanza originally read:

> 'Tis the wail for life they waken
> By Samana's yielding shore—
> With the tempest it is shaken;
> The wide ocean is in motion,
> And the song is heard no more.

[69] I reprinted the revised version of "The Lost Pleiad" in my American Life in Literature (revised ed., 1949), I, 366–368.

Simms's later criticism is uncollected, but in 1846 (dated 1845) he published two volumes under the title *Views and Reviews in American Litera-ture, History, and Fiction*, one of which contains what Bryant thought was the best essay on Fenimore Cooper that he had seen. Simms's conception of the duty of the critic as he stated it in *Egeria* is well-phrased: "Justly to discriminate, firmly to establish, wisely to prescribe, and honestly to award —these are the true aims and criteria of criticism." He was by no means blind to the merits of his New England contemporaries, but though he had high praise for Hawthorne and Longfellow, he had no enthusiasm for Emerson or Lowell. He was far ahead of most critics and readers when in the *Southern Quarterly Review* for September, 1850, he wrote of Robert Browning: "Browning is no common verse-maker. He is a writer of thought and genius, of peculiar and curious powers as an artist; subtle, spiritual, and singularly fanciful, and, though as yet perhaps unacknowledged, is one of the master minds of living European song. . . . He will grow slowly in public esteem, and, finally, when his peculiar phraseology shall become familiar to the ear, it will compel an admiration which is very far from general now."

Simms, who in 1842 described himself as "an ultra-American, a born Southron, and a resolute loco-foco," was for many years as stout a champion of an American literature as Emerson or James Kirke Paulding. In asking Paulding to accept the dedication of *The Damsel of Darien*, Simms wrote on June 16, 1839: "The original literature of a Nation is no less important to its interests, than its valour and its virtue. . . ." He condemned Edward W. Johnston's article in the *Southern Review* which maintained that British literature was sufficient for all our purposes. "Shall America," he asked, "be only an echo of what is thought and written under the aristocracies beyond the ocean?" He wrote in the *Magnolia* for December, 1840: "The literature of a nation is, in plain terms, the picture of its national character —the distinct embodiment of its moral aims; its political achievements; the taste which it loves to indulge, and the amusements which it enjoys. It is noble or base, according to the moral standards which graduate these exercises."

Although Simms was a persistent advocate of a distinctively Southern literature, he saw it as also an important part of the national literature. He was an American as well as a South Carolinian and a Southerner. The fullest expression of his view of the problem of an American literature is found in an essay—inspired by A. B. Meek's *Americanism in Literature* (1844)— which he published in the First Series of his *Views and Reviews*. He was troubled by what he thought was a lack of American feeling in certain Northern writers, especially in New England. On July 15, 1845, he wrote to Evert Duyckinck:

If the Authors of Am[erica]. will only work together we may do wonders yet. But our first step will be to disabuse the public mind of the influence of English & Yankee authorities. *Every thing depends on this.* The latter have done more than anything beside to play the devil with all that is manly & original in our literature. They have, curiously enough, fastened our faith to the very writers who, least of all others, possess a native character. Such is Longfellow, a man of nice taste, a clever imitator,—simply an adroit artist. W. Irving is little more than a writer of delicate taste, a pleasant unobtrusive humor, and agreeable talent. Miss [Catharine Maria] Sedgwick is a better fellow than either, yet not a woman of genius. In imaginative endowment, these are all feeble.—Yet, these are thy gods,—Oh! Israel!

Another war with Great Britain, Simms suggested, would "take us out of our leading strings." "It is," he continued, "through our political & social dependence [on England], in great degree, that the national mind suffers. . . . With every struggle with European nations shall we better know ourselves, & rise more into self-respect. Self Esteem will take the place of vanity, and even a sound drubbing will help our manliness."

Simms's final view of the problem of a national literature is seen in the Dedication which he wrote in 1856 for *The Wigwam and the Cabin:* "One word for the material of these legends. It is local, sectional—and to be *national* in literature, one must needs be *sectional.* No one mind can fully or fairly illustrate the characteristics of any great country; and he who shall depict *one section* faithfully, has made his proper and sufficient contribution to the great work of *national* illustration." Simms may have been wrong, but if so his theory coincided with just what his New England contemporaries were doing. Most later Southern writers of fiction write as though their theory was similar to that of Simms; and when, like Ellen Glasgow and Thomas Nelson Page, they shift their setting to the North or the West, one immediately feels the lack of an intimate knowledge of their materials. The Northern novelist, too, unless he has long lived in the South portrays not the actual but a conventionalized Southerner. Many of the well-known Middle-Western novels of the twentieth century are, properly speaking, regional or sectional novels. Many Northern literary critics, however, have insisted that the novelist's canvas should not be limited to the life he knows most intimately. We are still haunted by a desire for the impossible Great American Novel. As recently as 1950, in an address at the University of Pennsylvania, James A. Michener said: "Certain critics think that we shall have discharged our responsibility when we have compiled a healthy collection of regional novels. I cannot think so. Probably the most overrated aspect of our current literary scene is the so-called Southern Renaissance. It is true that most of our best writers happen to be Southerners, but the morbid and inverted little books they produce simply do not add up to a national literature." Simms's novels and romances, however, are neither "morbid" nor "inverted," and in one or more of them he touched upon the life of nearly every state in the South.

At the time of his death in 1870 Simms's reputation was much lower in the North than it had been in the 1840's. Nothing that he published after *Eutaw* (1856) added anything to his reputation, and most of his later writings never appeared in book form. After the emergence of Bret Harte, Mark Twain, Howells, Henry James, and Cable and the other writers of the New South, his writings all seemed old-fashioned. Even in the 1880's, when Southern stories were again in vogue, there was no Simms revival, even in the Southern states. Northern critics remembered him as a rabid proslavery writer who had written popular romances of the subliterary variety. Some of his books, however, continued to be reprinted from old plates down almost to the appearance in 1892 of W. P. Trent's biography of Simms. They were read, one infers, chiefly by boys and by unsophisticated readers who liked old-fashioned romances of adventure better than the new realistic fiction. Even the revival of historical romance in the 1890's did not bring Simms's books back into circulation, as one might have expected that it would; nor has the drift to realism led twentieth-century readers to resurrect them. For the past sixty years only *The Yemassee* has remained in print, and this is perhaps largely due to its use as a text in Southern schools and colleges. Only in the historical perspective do Simms's books seem important now. And yet they would seem to deserve a better fate than the obscurity into which they have fallen.

In recent years scholars have shown considerable interest in Simms's life and writings, but most of our literary historians seem not to know quite what to make of him and, one suspects, few of them have read more than one or two of his books. When in 1900 Barrett Wendell published his *Literary History of America*, he had read Trent's biography and *The Yemassee* but apparently nothing else. The later literary historians have read the notable chapter on Simms which Parrington in 1927 included in his discussion of "The Mind of the South," but some of them seem to have read little else. Historically, Simms is so important that he must be discussed by any one who tells the story of our literature, but few of our literary historians besides Van Doren, Quinn, Leisy, and Cowie have had the industry and the patience to read widely enough in his novels, romances, poems, plays, and miscellaneous writings to form any adequate conception of his literary achievement. Many discussions of Simms are still based largely on Trent, Parrington, and *The Yemassee*. One can visualize the historian, knowing that he must say something about Simms and with the whole of American literature to cover in some fashion, sorting out his notes on *The Yemassee* and trying somehow to reconcile the discordant estimates which he finds in Trent and in Parrington. The result is not a synthesis but an amalgam.

If Simms lacked genius such as Poe had, he certainly had talent and industry. In his best books one is impressed by his fertility of invention, his power, his variety, and by the sense of reality in them. In their individual scenes his Revolutionary Romances often seem as effective as Cooper's in the Leather-Stocking Tales. He failed, however, to create any one great character comparable to Cooper's best. What was it that Simms lacked? Perhaps it was a keener sense of style and literary form and a passion for perfection such as Poe and Hawthorne had. Simms, like Hawthorne, owed much initially to the Waverley romances, but he did not, like the author of *The Scarlet Letter*, work out his own individual pattern of historical romance, one that at once best suited his own gifts and the materials he wished to present. Similarly, when Simms ventured into the domain of William Godwin and Charles Brockden Brown, he did not develop an individual artistic medium which suited his talents, as Poe did. Simms wrote some of the best short stories of his time, but again they suffer from comparison with those of Poe, Hawthorne, and Irving. Simms had something of the power and intensity of Melville, but in him we miss the conjunction of time, writer, and theme which enabled Melville to produce a masterpiece in *Moby-Dick*. Simms never had the stimulus of close personal relations with such an artist as Hawthorne, who was Melville's neighbor during much of the writing of *Moby-Dick*. There was in the Charleston of Simms's time no sympathetic writer or critic of genius to hold him to his best, and the standards of publishers and editors were too low. The one great Southern critic, Poe, did not care for Simms's historical romances and did not until late in life realize the significance of Simms's work. Simms's ventures into psychological fiction are of only historical interest, for his knowledge of the workings of the subconscious mind seems to us too superficial. Today we should like Simms better if he had continued to explore the vein he opened in *The Golden Christmas*, but ante-bellum Southern readers were little concerned with literary descriptions of plantation life and Simms had too little to say about the numerous slaves upon which the attractive social life of Charleston and the Low-Country was based. The Civil War matured the talent of his friend Timrod and gave him the great theme which he was best fitted to treat, but in 1861 Simms was too old to adapt his technique to a wartime epoch so different from the American Revolution.

The man Simms was greater and more worthy of admiration than any of his books. I have expressed opinions which are at variance with those of my former teacher and friend, William Peterfield Trent, but I do not think that anyone who studies Simms can disagree with the estimate of the man which Trent wrote sixty years ago:

> Yes, Hayne was right. The man Simms "is worthy of all honor." Whether as a literary toiler, working successfully under most harassing conditions; whether as misguided patriot, striving for what he believed to be his section's good; whether as a defeated, worn-out spirit, laboring to relieve the distresses of his children and his friends, the man Simms ceases to be a mere man and assumes proportions that are truly heroic. His State may still point to her Calhouns and McDuffies, and his section may point to politicians and soldiers, contemporary lights that have cast and still cast him in the shade; but it is doubtful whether South Carolina, or indeed the whole South, has produced in this century a man who will better stand a close scrutiny into his motives and his life-work than William Gilmore Simms.

Simms's relations with Edgar Allan Poe deserve some discussion for the light they throw upon the two chief writers of the Old South. In the *Messenger* for January, 1836, Poe offended Simms by the rough handling he gave *The Partisan*. In his conclusion he pronounced the romance "no ordinary work," but the remainder of the review was in a different key. He began by noting that Simms had already published several books. "Mr. Simms," he said, "either writes very well, or it is high time that he should." This he followed with two pages in poor taste ridiculing Simms's four-line dedication of the book to his friend Richard Yeadon. The brash young editor, looking for popular and extravagantly puffed authors, had mistaken his man. Poe had in fact, apart from *The Bride of Lammermoor*, little liking for historical romances. Although he praised some of Simms's historical portraits, he thought the fictitious characters were all bad. He pronounced Lieutenant Porgy, one of Simms's best characters, "a most insufferable bore." He found fault with Simms's diction and sentence structure, even with his grammar. Poe's review has prejudiced later critics of Simms. It remained for Parrington in 1927 to point out that Simms at his best was really a master of a racy and masculine English prose style and not the slipshod writer that some of Poe's successors have maintained.

A recently published letter from Simms to Evert Duyckinck, March 15, 1845, gives his mature estimate of Poe as well as his first reaction to Poe's review of *The Partisan:*

I am glad that you think and speak well of Poe, which [Cornelius] Mathews was not disposed to do though I tried to open his eyes to the singular merits of that person. Poe is no friend of mine, as I believe. He began by a very savage attack on one of my novels—The Partisan. I cannot say that he was much out in his estimate. In some respects, as a story for example,—& in certain matters of taste & style, that was one of the very worst of the books I have ever written. Poe's critique, however, paid little heed to what was really good in the thing, and he did injustice to other portions which were not quite so good. Besides, he was rude & offensive & personal, in the manner of the thing, which he should not have been, in the case of anybody,—still less in mine. My deportment had not justified it. He knew, or might have known, that I was none of that miserable gang about town, who beg in literary highways. I had no clique, mingled with none, begged no praise from anybody, and made no condition with the herd. He must have known what I was personally—might have known—& being just should not have been rude. What should we think of an executioner who mocks the carcass after he has taken off the head. I tell you all this to satisfy you of my sense of verities. I do not puff the man when I say I consider him a remarkable one. He has more real magnetic power than 99 in the 100 of our poets & tale writers. His style is clear & correct, his conceptions bold & fanciful, his fancies vivid, and his tastes generally good. His bolder efforts are impaired by his fondness for *detail* & this hurts his criticism which is too frequently given to the analysis of the inferior points of style, making him somewhat regardless of the more noble features of the work. But, I repeat, he is a man of remarkable power, to whom I shall strive some day to do that justice which a great portion of our public seem desirous to withhold.[70]

In November, 1839, when Poe reviewed *The Damsel of Darien* in Burton's *Gentleman's Magazine,* he said: "The novel now published is, in our opinion, a much better book [than *The Partisan*]; evincing stricter study and care, with a far riper judgment, and a more rigidly disciplined fancy." "The defects of the 'Damsel of Darien,'" he said, "are few, and seldom radical." When he came to particularize, however, Poe charged Simms with "the sin of imitation—the entire absence of originality." "The style of our novelist," he said, "has improved of late, but it is still most faulty." He found

---

[70] Duyckinck MSS (New York Public Library), quoted by permission. The passage appears in *The Letters of William Gilmore Simms,* II, 42–43. Almost all of my quotations from Simms's letters are from manuscripts which I had examined before the publication of the *Letters.*

some of Simms's images repellent, and he hinted at "awkward or positively ungrammatical phrases" in Simms's dedication to James Kirke Paulding.[71]

In December, 1841, Poe briefly reviewed Simms's *Confession* in *Graham's Magazine*. "In general," he said, "Mr. Simms should be considered as one giving *indication*, rather than *proof* of high genius. . . . So far, with slight exceptions, he has buried his fine talent in his themes. He should never have written 'The Partisan,' nor 'The Yemassee.' . . . His genius does not lie in the outward so much as in the inward world. 'Martin Faber' did him honor and so do the present volumes, although liable to objection in some important respects. We welcome him home to his own proper field of exertion—the field of Godwin and Brown—the field of his own rich intellect and glowing *heart*."

In December, 1844, Poe wrote: "Mr. Simms has abundant faults—or had; —among which inaccurate English, a proneness to revolting images, and pet phrases, are the most noticeable. Nevertheless, leaving out of the question Brockden Brown and Hawthorne, (who are each a *genus*,) he is immeasurably the best writer of fiction in America. He has more vigor, more imagination, more movement and more general capacity than all our novelists (save Cooper) combined."

In reviewing Simms's *The Wigwam and the Cabin* for *Godey's Lady's Book* in January, 1846, Poe noted that in his first novel, *Martin Faber*, Simms had given "evidence of genius, and that of no common order."

Had he been . . . a Yankee, this genius would have been *immediately* manifest to his countrymen, but unhappily (*perhaps*) he was a southerner, and united the southern pride—the southern dislike to the making of bargains—with the southern supineness and general want of tact in all matters relating to the making of money. His book, therefore, depended entirely upon its own intrinsic value and resources, but with these it made its way in the end. The "intrinsic value" consisted first of a very vigorous imagination in the conception of the story: secondly, in artistic skill manifested in its conduct; thirdly, in general vigour, life, movement—the whole resulting in deep interest on the part of the reader. These high qualities Mr. Simms has carried with him in his subsequent books; and they are qualities which, above all others, the fresh and vigorous intellect of America should and does esteem. It may be said, upon the whole, that while there are several of our native writers who excel the author of "Martin Faber" at particular *points*, there is, nevertheless, not one who surpasses him in the aggregate of the higher excellences of fiction.

[71] If the review of *Border Beagles* in the *Gentleman's Magazine* for Sept., 1840, is Poe's, he did not apparently suspect that the anonymous author was Simms. He disapproved of the subject matter of the book. "The amplification of the details of villany [sic]," he said, "is a degradation of the intellect, and its effect upon the mind of the reader is to render him familiar with any grade of vice."

A year earlier Poe had written of Simms: "His merits lie among the major and his defects among the minor morals of literature." It had taken the critic a long time to come to something like a just estimate of Simms's merits and shortcomings. The writers of the Old South, I may add, were not the mutual admiration society which they must have seemed to certain Northern critics—nor for that matter were the great New Englanders, though they now seem to us strangely oblivious of writers in other sections.

In a note on the *Stylus* Simms wrote in the *Magnolia* for June, 1843: "Mr. Poe is well calculated to conduct a literary magazine. He is acknowledged as one of our best writers and critics. If any fault is to be found with him, it is in the latter capacity. He is, we fancy, not unfrequently tempted into the utterance of a smart thing, without troubling himself to ask if it be a just one. But the error may well find its excuse, in a day of such lamentable magazine puffery as the present, and we may forgive an occasional wrong to real genius,—which can most generally revenge itself,—in consideration of the great service done to the literary community by the stern conviction, to punishment, of a cloud of fools." Twice in the year 1845 Simms praised Poe in his own magazine. In reviewing Poe's *Tales* in December, he spoke of "the fine artistic stories of Mr. Edgar A. Poe,—a writer of rare imaginative excellence, great intensity of mood, and a singularly mathematic directness of purpose, and searching analysis. . . . Certainly, nothing more original, of their kind, has ever been given to the American reader." Simms, however, complained that in "The Gold Bug" Poe had been "grievously regardless" of its locale when he placed "rocks and highlands in and about Sullivan's Island."

In the summer of 1846 Poe, living now in the Fordham cottage, was publishing "The Literati" in *Godey's Lady's Book* and becoming involved in his quarrel with Thomas Dunn English. His invalid wife was to die on January 30 of the next year. In July Poe wrote to Simms asking for something which he could use in his controversy with English. On the thirtieth of that month Simms, then in New York too busy seeing a book through the press to go out to Fordham, wrote a long letter to Poe, full of admirable advice which the poet did not—perhaps at that time could not—take:

I note with regret the very desponding character of your last letter. I surely need not tell you how deeply & sincerely I deplore the misfortunes which attend you —the more so as I see no prospect for your relief, and extrication but such as must result from your own decision and resolve. . . .
. . . Your resources from literature are probably much greater than mine. I am sure they are quite as great. You can increase them, so that they shall be ample for all your legitimate desires; but you must learn the worldling's lesson

of prudence;—a lesson, let me add, which the literary world has but too frequently & unwisely disparaged.

Simms, who had urged Godey to ask Poe to write for the *Lady's Book*, continued: "I hear that you reproach him. But how can you expect a Magazine proprietor to encourage contributions which embroil him with all his neighbors? These broils do you no good—vex your temper, destroy your peace of mind, and hurt your reputation." Simms concluded his long letter: "As a man, as a writer, I shall always be solicitous of your reputation & success. You have but to resolve on taking & asserting your position, equally in the social & the literary world, and your way is clear, your path is easy, and you will find true friends enough to sympathize in your triumphs."

On March 20, 1867, Simms wrote to John R. Thompson that Redfield the publisher wished Thompson to write a biography of Poe to accompany "a new edition of Edgar." Simms added: "That you are the very person to do such a work better than any body else, I have no question. Still the task, in his case, is a very difficult one, since all biography should be written *con amore*, and the poor fellow was perpetually upsetting his own buckets of milk, to the great disgust of friends & admirers. Still, you could do it, without violating the truth, and yet with some softening of its harsher aspects." Perhaps it is just as well that Thompson, who had not considered Griswold's Memoir unjust, did not undertake the task.

38
Women Writers

THE HIGH-WATER mark of American literary achievement came in the years 1830–1865; and yet, paradoxically the same period saw a definite decline in the level of literary taste. Regardless of what the literary critics might say, the reading public preferred Joseph Holt Ingraham, Sylvanus Cobb, Jr., Lydia Huntley Sigourney, and Mrs. E. D. E. N. Southworth to Emerson, Hawthorne, and Poe. It preferred Robert Bonner's *New York Ledger* to the *Atlantic Monthly* and the *Southern Literary Messenger*. Since the time when Parson Weems had published his fictionalized biographies of great Americans for the young and the half-educated, the reading public had expanded enormously, and the expansion was mainly on the subliterary level. Editors and publishers had discovered a more remunerative market among the intellectually immature. The literary critics, whether Northern or Southern, were for the most part conservatives who viewed the situation with increasing alarm, but they had as little control over what the masses chose to read as the editors of the *Saturday Review* have in our age of cheap editions and pulp magazines. Bradford A. Booth's study of the annuals and gift-books shows that the major American writers could not compete for popular favor with Mrs. Sigourney, who is credited with 225 contributions, while Longfellow had only 46; Hawthorne, 33; Simms, 29; Emerson and Holmes, 25 each; and Lowell, only 24, less than the forgotten Charleston poetess, Mary Elizabeth Lee, who had 26. Poe had only 15. Of the nine most popular contributors only one was a man—Nathaniel P. Willis, who had 94.[72]

By 1850 women had come to form a much larger part of the reading public than had been the case in 1800. They had also come to form a proportionately larger percentage of those who wrote. It hardly follows, however, that, as some have thought, the decline in literary taste was due to women readers. It happens to be true that many of the most popular writers on the subliterary level were women. Not until after 1865, with the exception of Mrs. Stowe, did an American woman attain such literary distinction as after that date Sarah Orne Jewett, Emily Dickinson, Charles Egbert Craddock, and others won with their pens. Why this was so, I do not know; there is no way of knowing when literary geniuses will be born or whether they will find the nurture that will bring them into their full powers.

On January 19, 1855, Nathaniel Hawthorne wrote to his friend and publisher W. D. Ticknor: ". . . America is now wholly given over to a d—d mob of scribbling women, and I should have no chance of success while the public taste is occupied with their trash—and should be ashamed of myself if I did succeed." Hawthorne might well hesitate to bring out a new romance, for the consulate at Liverpool was proving more remunerative than fiction-writing had been. In the 1850's Mary Jane Holmes and Augusta Jane Evans were selling their books by the thousand, and the success of a writer was coming more and more to be judged by his ability to make money. The situation was no better in 1879 when Helen Hunt Jackson wrote to Moncure D. Conway that he had much better stay in London than return to the United States. Men in American "financial circles," she said, regarded literature as "an uncommonly poor way of making a living." "If they had to take their choice between being Mrs. Southworth and Hawthorne they would be Mrs. S.,—unhesitatingly; she has written fifty-nine novels and made a fortune,—*that* is worth while."

The number of Southern women who took to writing in the forties and fifties is very considerable. In fact, there were at this time more women than men among Southern writers who could be classed as professional. The

<hr>

[72] "Taste in the Annuals," *Am. Lit.*, XIV, 299-302 (Nov., 1942).

Dictionary of American Biography includes a surprisingly large number of them. In *The Living Writers of the South* (1869), James Wood Davidson listed 75 women and 166 men. He left out "Fadette" and some others who were not willing to appear under their actual names. Southern women may have been a little slower than their Northern sisters to seek fame or fortune by the pen, for the South had no large cities and the industrial revolution had not materially changed the status of women in the slave states. And yet, for that very reason, writing was one of the few occupations open to a Southern woman, for until after the Civil War even teaching was not a highly esteemed profession.

The ante-bellum Southern woman is not to be confused with the heroines of popular romances. She was usually a capable person, and her education was not nearly so impractical as is often imagined. She was much more likely than the Northern woman to have attended a college. President Josiah Quincy of Harvard was surprised to discover that "The fashionable ladies of the South [including Calhoun's daughters] had received the education of political thought and discussion to a degree unknown among their sisters of the North." In Southern private schools and colleges women were given some training in writing essays, and they were in the habit of writing numerous letters to relatives and friends.

A number of the best Southern women writers were, like Mrs. Caroline Gilman and Mrs. Caroline Lee Hentz, of Northern birth and education; but some of the most successful were, like Augusta Jane Evans and Eliza Ann Dupuy, born and educated in the South. In the main, the women writers, like the men who wrote, belonged to the urban South. Few of them were wives or daughters of planters. Most of them were either teachers or wives or daughters of teachers, journalists, ministers, lawyers, physicians, or businessmen.

Most of the writers of verse must have written because they liked to write and wished to see their verses in print, but with many of the prose writers the dominant motive was economic. Maria Jane McIntosh and Eliza Ann Dupuy turned to writing because they had lost their property. Mrs. Southworth, whose marriage had proved unhappy, wrote to supplement her meager income as a teacher. She turned to writing, she said, at "the time when I found myself broken in spirit, health, and purse—a widow in fate but not in fact—with my babes looking up to me for a support I could not give them. It was," she continued, "in these darkest days of my *woman's* life, that my *author's* life commenced."

Southern women could not fail to note in the books and magazines which they read the increasing part played by Northern and English women, and some of them were tempted to emulation. Writing then as now seemed to call for little in the way of capital besides a supply of pen, ink, and paper. If relatives or friends disapproved, it was easy to hide behind a pseudonym. If Southern magazines would not pay for their work, they could send their manuscripts to Bonner or Godey, who could and did pay. Even during the Civil War Eliza Ann Dupuy, whose sympathies were Confederate, continued to publish serials in the *New York Ledger*. In *Beulah* (1859) Augusta Jane Evans attributed to her heroine an experience that may well have been her own. Beulah submits a manuscript to the editor of a Southern magazine and surprises him by asking to be paid for it. "I happen to know," she says, "that northern magazines are not composed of gratuitous contributions; and it is no mystery why southern authors are driven to northern publishers. Southern periodicals are mediums only for those of elegant leisure, who can afford to write without remuneration. With the same subscription price, you cannot pay for your articles. It is no marvel that, under such circumstances, we have no southern literature." Beulah becomes a regular and a paid contributor.

The unprecedented success of *Uncle Tom's Cabin* in 1852 impressed Southern women with the tremendous power of the pen, and a number of them made what seemed to them replies appropriate to their sex. The outbreak of the Civil War in 1861 supplied new motives for the Southern woman to write for publication. Now more than ever the South must have its own literature, and many of the men who wrote were in the Confederate army. Women who had published nothing before were now glad to send their work to the newspapers or to the *Weekly Magnolia* or the *Southern Illustrated News*. Writing under the pen name "Refugitta," Constance Cary Harrison began her long literary career by contributing to these two Richmond magazines. At the end of the war the universal poverty of the South turned still more women to writing, and some of them wrote noteworthy accounts of their wartime experiences.

The general use of pseudonyms suggests that there were in the South many who, like Hawthorne, thought "ink-stained women . . . without a single exception, detestable." "The feeling which disposes a woman to see her name in print," wrote Beverley Tucker, "is hardly less meretricious than that which makes her show her ankles." To Paul Hamilton Hayne, who had written that Margaret J. Preston thought highly of his poems, Dr. Francis Orray Ticknor wrote in reply, March 26, 1871: "I am of course (humbly) proud of Mrs. Preston's good opinion. I have always admired her, because I thought I could see, through her 'Poetry' the noblest of God's writings, a *good* Woman. In such (to me) the ability to Rhyme seems almost a blemish! it is *worse* than paint—say Bismuth—on a Lily." Mrs. Caroline Gilman, when nearly sixty, commented on the great change that had come about in women's attitude toward appearing in print. When she was about sixteen, still living in Massachusetts, she heard that some verses of hers had appeared in a newspaper. ". . . I wept bitterly," she writes, "and was as alarmed as if I had been detected in man's apparel."

In England and the Northern states many of the women who wrote were hiding their identity behind pen names and writing without the approval of friends and relatives. George Eliot and Mrs. Browning used pen names. Emily Dickinson's unwillingness to publish was due at least in part to the fear of offending relatives and friends.

> Publication is the auction
> Of the mind of man,

she wrote, and she could not bear the thought of having her mind put up for sale to the public. In the South there was at least one Southern writer, Mrs. Mary Scrimzeour Whitaker, who scorned the use of a pseudonym as a foolish species of affectation; and another, Mrs. Julia L. Keyes, would probably not have published her verses if her husband had not himself seen to their publication.

Even after American women had demonstrated their ability to write, by commercial standards, as successfully as men, there was still a marked condescension toward women writers. This is obvious in the rather scandalous way Hawthorne and Lowell wrote about Margaret Fuller. In the *Southern Field and Fireside* for January, 1860, Mrs. Mary E. Bryan published an article "How Should Women Write?" [73] in which she protested against some of the limitations imposed upon the female writer. Above all, she must not be unfeminine. She was free to "fustianize over" the beauties of nature and the claims of orthodox religion, but she must not write of great social and moral problems. Yet even if she stayed within the prescribed limits, she was liable to ridicule.

If she writes of birds, of flowers, sunshine, and *id omne genus*, as did Amelia Welby, noses are elevated superbly, and the effusions are said to smack of bread and butter.

If love, religion, and domestic obligations are her theme, as with Mrs. Hentz, "namby-pamby" is the word contemptuously applied to her productions. If, like Mrs. Southworth, she reproduces Mrs. Radcliffe in her possibility-scorning romances, her nonsensical clap-trap is said to be "beneath criticism"; and if, with

[73] I, 276 (Jan., 1860), reprinted in *Southland Writers*, II, 664–668, from which my quotations are taken.

Patty Pepper, she gossips harmlessly of fashions and fashionables, of the opera and Laura Keene's, of watering-places, lectures, and a railroad trip, she is *"pish"*-ed aside as silly and childish; while those who seek to go beyond the boundary-line are put down with the stigma of *"strong-minded."*

In spite of the handicaps under which the woman writer labored, there were Southern women who felt that they simply had to write. Mrs. Louisa S. McCord, the wife of a South Carolina newspaper editor, wrote to William Porcher Miles in 1848: "It is to me more than amusement,—it is an absolute comfort, an almost necessity, to put my fancies upon paper. . . ." and again: "Although I have been pushed back in every possible way, & have myself endeavoured for many a long year to crush my own propensities," she said, still she had to write. "An effortless life, is, to a restless mind, a weary fate to be doomed to; and as no other door is open to me, I may as well push on this." In a later letter she thus commented on Miles's criticism of her play, *Caius Gracchus:* "As to my productions being *closet dramas,* what else can a Woman write? The *world of action* must to her be entirely a closed book."

The place which Southern women writers made for themselves they made in spite of the disapproval of literary critics and often of timid and skeptical publishers. The editor of the *Southern Literary Messenger,* John R. Thompson, after reading for a Richmond publisher the manuscript of "Marion Harland's" first novel, reported that it would not be safe to publish it except at the author's risk. That book, *Alone* (1854), sold a hundred thousand copies. A New York publisher refused the manuscript of her *Common Sense in the Household* (1871) because he did not believe it would make a marketable book. Neither, we are told, did the Scribners, who published it and sold a hundred thousand copies. Perhaps no businessmen with something to sell know less about the cash value of their wares than publishers—unless it be theatrical producers—but publishers did finally learn that women could write books that were profitable to handle. Augusta Jane Evans is said to have made a hundred thousand dollars from the sales of her books, which may well be more than Poe, Emerson, Melville, Whitman, Hawthorne, and Thoreau all combined made from theirs. But the most successful of all women writers, with the possible exception of Mrs. Stowe, was probably Mary Jane Holmes (1825–1907). She was born in Massachusetts. It was after her marriage and removal to Kentucky that she wrote her first novel, *Tempest and Sunshine, or Life in Kentucky* (1854). The aggregate sales of her novels ran to more than two million copies. In paper covers her novels were sold by the thousand on steamboats and on the trains. She attained her extraordinary popularity without resorting, like Mrs. Southworth and others, to the sensational. She aimed at writing stories which could be read aloud in the family circle. The didactic motive bulks large in the work of the women writers, who in their own way were as eager to elevate as was Emerson—or E. P. Roe.

In a sense the work of these successors of Parson Weems and Anne Royall is "beneath criticism." It is, however, a phenomenon of importance to the cultural historian, like the school readers of William Holmes McGuffey. One cannot draw an arbitrary line separating the literary from the subliterary. Both kinds of writing were subject to much the same influences, and those who wrote what we call literature were often influenced by those who did not. In *The Sentimental Novel in America* (1940) Herbert Brown has demonstrated that even our major novelists were affected by the strain of "sensibility" stemming from Richardson's novels of the eighteenth century. In the nineteenth century the blight of the "genteel" mars the work of men as well as women writers. It is found in Longfellow as well as in Mrs. Stowe and Mary Jane Holmes, and it is found in such later writers as James Lane Allen and Thomas Nelson Page. And there are other strains from the subliterary that made their way into the work of Poe, Hawthorne, Howells, Mark Twain and, we may add, Tennyson and Dickens.

Although the major literary influences came from later British writers, one notes traces of the influence of the *Spectator*, sentimental comedy, and the novels of Richardson, Fanny Burney, and Maria Edgeworth. The Southern women poets were influenced by Scott, Byron, Moore, and Tennyson, especially in their sentimental and didactic moods. There was also the influence of Elizabeth Barrett Browning; Mrs. Bryan regarded her *Aurora Leigh* as "the greatest book of this century . . . because of the moral grandeur of its purpose." But the most influential poet was, I think, Mrs. Felicia Dorothea Hemans. She and Mrs. Lydia Huntley Sigourney, "the sweet singer of Hartford," helped greatly to popularize a kind of debased Romanticism among readers who did not care for the far greater poems of Wordsworth, Shelley, and Keats. In the fiction of the women writers one still finds the influence of Gothic romances, which also affected the work of Poe and Hawthorne. The women writers read of course the Waverley romances and the novels of Dickens and Thackeray. From these and the novels of Charles Reade and Wilkie Collins they drew whatever catered to the love of the sentimental and the sensational. Charlotte Brontë's *Jane Eyre* (1847), with its Byronic hero Rochester, its Gothic elements, and its appeal to readers of lacrymose proclivities, perhaps had a greater influence on the women writers than any other single novel of the century.

Constance Fenimore Woolson, who lived in the South in the 1870's, in letters to Paul Hamilton Hayne expressed her opinion of the subliterary novels of Southern women writers. In one of them she said that an aunt of hers adored Augusta Jane Evans's *Infelice* and added: "As a side remark, —have you, O, *have* you read 'Infelice'? What in the world *can* any cultivated reader see in that mass of words, words, words?" Of the stories of Frances Christine Fisher ("Christian Reid") and other Southern women she wrote:

They have seemed to me exaggerated in style, and too full of a certain spirit, which I can best describe perhaps by saying that their heroes are always [too] "knightly,"—for the real life of to-day. Now I was at Madame Chegaray's school in New York City just before the breaking out of the war, and my school mates were all Southern girls, of fine old families too; their mothers and their grandmothers had been to the same school before them. . . . These girls were charming to me for the very simplicity of their manners; they were delightfully and naturally well-bred, from the ends of their curls down to their pretty little high-arched feet. But, Mr Hayne, they were very simple in their manners and notably so in their talk. They used to talk to me by the hour of their homes, their parents, brothers, *and* lovers,—and—well, it was not at all like "The Daughter of Bohemia," "St Elmo," "The Household of Bouverie," and other novels I have read since.

The inflated style of many Southern writers—men as well as women—served, as Miss Woolson clearly saw, to misrepresent the chief charm of Southern life, its homebred simplicity and naturalness. Even the later Southern writers, like Thomas Nelson Page, frequently mislead the unwary reader when they convert plantation houses into mansions and the simple farmers and their wives into lords and ladies to the manner born.

Space will not permit detailed discussion here of more than two of the women writers of the Old South. The subject deserves a book. Among the more interesting figures who would appear in it are Mrs. Caroline Gilman, Mrs. Caroline Lee Hentz, both born in New England; Amelia Welby, perhaps the best of the poets promoted by George D. Prentice, the Louisville wit and journalist; Mary Elizabeth Lee, the sentimental Charleston poetess; Mrs. E. F. Ellet, who made trouble for Poe; Madame Octavia Le Vert, the Southern beauty, who had a literary *salon* in Mobile; Mary Bayard Clarke ("Tenella") of North Carolina; Sue Petigru King, daughter of "the Union Man of South Carolina"; Maria Jane McIntosh, of Georgia and New York; Lucy Virginia French of Memphis, Tennessee; Mary Ashley Townsend of New Orleans, whose pen name "Xariffa" is one of the queerest; and perhaps the strangest writer to come out of the South, the Jewish poet and actress Adah Isaacs Menken, who became notorious for her representation of

Byron's Mazeppa, riding practically naked on horseback on the stage, and
was the mistress of various European literary and artistic notables.

39
Augusta Jane Evans Wilson

AUGUSTA JANE EVANS (1835–1909) was a Southerner by birth, education,
residence, and sympathies. She was born in Columbus, Georgia, which was
at different times the home of Mirabeau B. Lamar and Francis Orray
Ticknor. Her father was a merchant of planter background. Her mother was
the sister of John Howard, who built the first of many cotton mills eventually
to be erected at the falls of the Chattahoochee. In 1841 Matt Evans's business ended in bankruptcy, and in 1845 he took his family to Texas. On the
long journey Mrs. Evans helped to pass the time by telling Augusta stories
of great writers. Not long after the Evanses settled in San Antonio the War
with Mexico began, and Augusta's recollections of her four years in Texas
were to be colored by the unrest and violence of the period. In 1849 the
Evanses left Texas and settled in Mobile, Alabama, where the father became a not too successful cotton factor. What education the precocious
daughter received came largely from her mother and from miscellaneous
reading in a large family library.

At the age of fifteen Augusta Evans began writing her first novel, *Inez:
A Tale of the Alamo* (1855). Not sure that her parents would approve, she
took into her confidence only a slave named Minervy, who supplied the oil
needed to make possible Augusta's midnight labor on the manuscript. When
her mother finally learned of the still unfinished novel, she agreed not to tell
the father until it was completed. On Christmas morning in 1854 Augusta
presented to her father as a gift the neatly copied and completed manuscript.
It was probably her uncle, Augustus Howard, who paid Harper & Brothers
to publish the book. This story of love, war, and religion, colored by anti-
Catholic feeling, was no great popular success, but the vogue of her later
novels was so great that it was often reprinted. Few critics praised it. The
Southern Quarterly Review, then edited by Simms, said of it in April, 1855:
"There is not a natural character, and scarcely a natural phrase in the whole
volume." Other reviewers were to find similar faults with her later novels.
In 1875, when she published *Infelice*, Miss Evans indicated her opinion of
literary critics by quoting in her Preface from Disraeli's *Lothair*: "Tomorrow
the critics will commence. You know who the critics are? The men who have
failed in literature and art."

Miss Evans mailed the manuscript of her second novel, Beulah (1859), to D. Appleton and Company. When they declined it, she went to New York to look for a publisher. She took the manuscript to J. C. Derby of Derby and Jackson, who in 1854 had published "Marion Harland's" successful first novel, Alone. With her was her cousin, Colonel John W. Jones, who in case Derby also rejected the manuscript planned to hurl at the publisher's head one of his own books. Derby took the precaution of having his own family read the manuscript. Their verdict was favorable. The manuscript was accepted, and Beulah sold more than twenty thousand copies within a year.

When she revisited New York in the fall of 1859, Augusta Evans met the pious young journalist, James Reed Spaulding, who had been so deeply impressed by his reading of Beulah that he wanted to meet the author. They were immediately attracted to each other. There was a tentative engagement conditioned upon the approval of her parents. In the summer of 1860 Spaulding went to Mobile to ask formally for Augusta's hand. He was accepted, but a few months later she decided that the political differences between them were too great, and she broke off the engagement.

Augusta Evans was an enthusiastic secessionist. She reproved Mrs. L. Virginia French for trying to prevent the secession of Georgia, and after the outbreak of war she censured "Marion Harland" for not siding with her native Virginia. In 1859 she had published in the Mobile Daily Advertiser a series of articles in which she contrasted Northern and Southern literature, altogether to the advantage of the latter. In the North literature, she thought, was a purely commercial product, and at the same time the Yankees were debasing the function of literature by using it for unworthy political purposes.

During the war Augusta Evans did all that she could to promote the Confederate cause. She visited the troops as near the front line as she could get. She nursed wounded soldiers at Camp Beulah, which was named of course for her novel. From June, 1862, to March, 1863, she devoted every spare moment to the writing of Macaria, which she hoped would strengthen the Confederate will to victory. During the winter General Beauregard took the time to write out for her use a full account of the first Battle of Bull Run. In 1863 West and Johnston of Richmond published the novel on crude wrapping paper. General George H. Thomas, commanding a Union army in Tennessee, pronounced the book "contraband and dangerous" and ordered to be burned all copies that could be found among his soldiers. Meanwhile the author had sent through the blockade a copy of the novel to J. C. Derby, who arranged with J. B. Lippincott of Philadelphia to bring out a Northern edition. Derby soon learned that a less scrupulous publisher in New York, Michael Doolady, was already reprinting *Macaria* and had no intention of paying a royalty to the "arch rebel" who had written it. Derby sent to Philadelphia for Lippincott, and the two gave Doolady his choice of paying a royalty to the author or of competing with a rival edition to be immediately printed by Lippincott. Doolady consented to pay a royalty. And so it happened that when in the summer of 1865 Augusta Evans, her family now practically bankrupt, came to see Derby in New York, she learned for the first time that the Doolady edition had made money for her. In New York she was, as she wrote, "surprised at the kindness and courtesy shown me wherever I went."

In 1866 Miss Evans abandoned her plan to write a history of the Confederacy and returned to fiction. *St. Elmo*, which appeared in December of that year, proved to be the most popular of all her novels. Hotels, steamboats, cigars, a popular brand of punch, and even towns are said to have been named for the novel. *St. Elmo* was published by G. W. Carleton and Company, which had taken over the business of Derby and Jackson. For the copyright of her next novel, *Vashti* (1869), Carleton paid the author fifteen thousand dollars. The book sold so well that Carleton, though he had bought the manuscript outright, paid Miss Evans royalties on the book for many years. Carleton once wrote to her from Agra in India: ". . . today I saw a Parsee boy reading a London edition of *Vashti*—here—here! miles and miles up the jungles of interior India—within a stone's throw of the amazingly beautiful Taj Mahal, surrounded by magnificent, half-ruined palaces, tombs and temples, barbaric mosques, wild monkeys and venomous snakes, turbaned Mohammedans and naked Hindoos. . . ."

In 1868 Miss Evans had married the elderly and well-to-do Colonel Lorenzo Wilson and thenceforth made her home at "Ashland," one of the finest houses in the vicinity of Mobile. Colonel Wilson proudly displayed to friends the fifteen-thousand-dollar check which his wife had received for *Vashti*, but he tried to prevent her from working too hard at her writing. Until after his death in 1879, she published comparatively little. Perhaps, impressed though he was by the success of her books, Mr. Wilson did not quite approve of his wife's writing novels.

Beulah (1859), which appeared in the same year as *Adam Bede* and the *Origin of Species*, is an excellent example of the attitude of American orthodoxy toward Unitarianism, Transcendentalism, and rationalism. Beulah is a studious orphan girl "with a slowly dying faith" reading Emerson, Carlyle, Goethe, and other writers of whom orthodox Protestants disapproved. It was, however, apparently a reading of Poe's *Eureka* that launched both

Beulah and her creator upon this "sea of Cosmogonies." For a time, as I
have noted elsewhere,[74] Beulah thought she had found a sound creed in
Emerson, but in the end she reached the conclusion that "Emerson's works,
collectively and individually, are aimed at the doctrines of Christianity."

The better literary critics labeled Miss Evans's novels unnatural and
pedantic. A parodist suggested that the trouble with the heroine of *St. Elmo*
was that she had swallowed an unabridged dictionary. Miss Evans's formula
owes much to *Jane Eyre*. Her heroine is usually an ambitious orphan girl
of deep religious feeling and great intellectual precocity. Her mission in life
is to convert from infidelity to faith the Rochester-like hero. In *St. Elmo*
Edna Earl, the novelist-heroine, is advised not to attempt to elevate or
educate her readers. Her reply is: "But, sir, how many habitual novel-readers
do you suppose will educate themselves thoroughly from the text-books to
which you refer? . . . do you not regard the writers of each age as the custodians of its tastes, as well as its morals? . . . At all events I wish to risk
it. I would rather sink in the effort than live without attempting it." And
attempt it both heroine and author did, and the author took immense satisfaction in the letters she received from reclaimed infidels and from culture-
hungry young people who asked her what books they ought to read.

St. Elmo (1866), Miss Evans's greatest popular success, treats among
other problems authorship as a career for a woman. The book presumably reflects some of its author's experiences, and it certainly makes clear her literary
aims. Edna Earl, the orphan granddaughter of an uneducated blacksmith
from the vicinity of Lookout Mountain, is taken into the home of the
wealthy and cultivated Murray family in Columbus, Georgia, and there she
makes the most of her superior educational opportunities. Ambitious to
succeed as a writer, she sends a manuscript to Mr. Manning, editor of a high-
brow New York magazine. Though somewhat impressed, he returns it with
the comment that the subject is entirely beyond her powers or those of any
other woman. He suggests that she burn the manuscript and write "sketches
of homelife—descriptions of places and things that you understand better
than recondite analogies of ethical creeds and mythologic systems, or the
subtle lore of Coptic priests."

When her first published article appears anonymously in Manning's
magazine, Edna has the mortification of hearing the brilliant, cynical, disillusioned St. Elmo Murray pronounce it "Pretentious and shallow! A tissue
of pedantry and error from beginning to end. . . ." She goes to New York
as a governess in order to be near publishers and editors. There a minister
warns her against "literary females," who, he suggests, would do better to

[74] See pp. 381–383.

earn their bread "at the wash-tub, or in the dairy, or by their needles." St. Elmo, now realizing that he is in love with Edna, goes to the metropolis and begs her to marry him. "My darling," he entreats, "you are not strong enough to wrestle with the world; you will be trodden down by the masses in this conflict, upon which you enter so eagerly. Do you not know that '*literati*' means literally the branded? A bondage worse than Roman slavery! Help me to make a proper use of my fortune, and you will accomplish more real good to your race than by all you can ever accomplish with your pen, no matter how successful it may prove." Edna, however, is a determined young woman—quite unlike the heroines of so many later Southern novels. Merely to amuse her readers seems to her ignoble. ". . . her high standard demanded that all books should be to a certain extent didactic, wandering like evangels among the people, and making some man, woman, or child happier, or wiser, or better—more patient or more hopeful—by their utterances." Manning, her editor friend, warns her that her readers expect her to "help them kill time not improve it." He tells her that she misapprehends the spirit of the age and that novels are not the proper medium for teaching morality or the elements of the sciences. Edna, however, regards writers as custodians of the tastes and morals of the age; and if she is wrong, she had rather fail than not try to elevate her readers. Her first book is severely handled by the literary critics.

Newspapers pronounced her book a failure. Some sneered in a gentlemanly manner, employing polite phraseology; others coarsely caricatured it. Many were insulted by its incomprehensible erudition; a few growled at its shallowness. To-day there was a hint of plagiarism; to-morrow an outright, wholesale theft was asserted. Now she was a pedant; and then a sciolist. Reviews poured in upon her thick and fast; all found grievous faults, but no two reviewers settled on the same error.

Here Miss Evans is apparently giving her own experience. Edna's book sold so rapidly that the publishers could scarcely supply the demand. It went through twenty editions in a short time. No wonder that Edna Earl—like her creator—thought so little of the literary critics.

In the end, however, Edna, nearing a breakdown, gives up her career to become the wife of St. Elmo Murray, now an ordained minister. Just before the wedding he says to her: "To-day I snap the fetters of your literary bondage. There shall be no more books written! No more study, no more toil, no more anxiety, no more heart-aches! And that dear public you love so well, must even help itself, and whistle for a new pet. You belong solely to me now, and I shall take care of the life you have nearly destroyed, in your inordinate ambition." A twentieth-century novelist would have closed the

romance in another key. Undoubtedly Miss Evans knew that no other ending would please her readers, but then one remembers that only a year or
two later she married Lorenzo Wilson and temporarily gave up her own
career. Nevertheless, in *St. Elmo* she had challenged the assumption that
women had no place outside the home. Not until 1913, when Mary Johnston
published *Hagar* and Ellen Glasgow *Virginia*, was any woman novelist
seriously to bring into question the traditional conception of the Southern
woman.

Perhaps the experience of Robert Selph Henry, visiting in the Tennessee
mountains, may help one to understand the vogue of such novels as *St. Elmo*.
In a mountain home he found a dozen novels, including *St. Elmo* and Mary
N. Murfree's *In the Clouds*, a story of the Tennessee mountains. When
asked about Miss Murfree's novel, the old lady, who had named one of her
daughters after the heroine of *St. Elmo*, said: "Mister, I can go right out into
these here hills and see people like that and hear talk like that. Now when
I waste my time and eyesight reading, I want something worth my while, that
will teach me something—like *St. Elmo*."

A confusion of literary values is seen in some of the comments of reviewers
in Southern magazines of the sixties and seventies. In reviewing *St. Elmo* in
Scott's Magazine of Atlanta in March, 1867, John Shirley Ward of Nashville, though he objected to Miss Evans's pedantic style, ended on this high
note: "With a fancy bold and fervid—with an imagination as warm and
luxurious as the breath of the orange groves of her own sunny land—with
a taste cultivated and refined by a thorough knowledge of classical and
modern belles-lettres—with a genius as versatile as De Stael's and as spiritual
as Hannah More's—we are ready to crown her Queen Regnant of Southern
Literature." In the same month in the recently revived *De Bow's Review*
"P. S. R.," a woman, pointed out the chief faults of *St. Elmo* with considerable force. The book was not "a fair sample of the manners, customs,
and conversation" of the Southern people. The conversation in *St. Elmo*
seemed indeed "a continual advertisement of the contents of the author's
private library." She pronounced one of St. Elmo Murray's impassioned
speeches "a farrago of false sentiment and conceit," which it undoubtedly is.
The few original ideas in the book were "overwhelmed with an avalanche of
ancient and modern lore" and lost their identity "in a sea of classical quotations." Bombast, said "P. S. R.," "weakens the force of her arguments,
pedantry mars the effect of the most thrilling scenes, and so overdrawn and
unnatural are the characters introduced that they fail to live, move, and have
their being, remaining to the end but the creations of an ill-regulated and
heated fancy."

In a brief review of *Vashti* A. B. Stark in the *Home Monthly* of Nashville in January, 1870, stated that he once had some hope that Augusta Evans would write a book "which would honor our Southern literature," but he no longer had any such expectation. "The persons in *Vashti*," he noted, "all speak in the same style. The pauper girl, who glories in hating all study, never speaks without making a most startling display of learning. . . . The personages all quote poetry in season and out of season. They all quote Lessing with astonishing familiarity." Stark noticed that the quotations from Maurice de Guérin all had been culled from Matthew Arnold's essay. He concluded: "It would be ungracious to dismiss the book without commending its high morality and earnest religion. Why will she persist in damaging her power for good by disgusting people with her fantastic fustian?" In the same magazine for April, 1870, one "F. F." compared *St. Elmo* with Fanny Burney's *Evelina*, which the writer found far superior. The story of *Vashti* was "utterly beyond the range of probability." "She makes so evident a display of her learning, by such constant and uncalled-for allusions beyond the range of all but the most diligent encyclopedists, [that] the conclusion forces itself upon the mind that the knowledge of books is not hereditary in her family. She has not yet become accustomed to such dazzling stores of wisdom, but betrays awkwardness as well as ostentation in the use of her riches." Like the reviewer in *De Bow's*, "F. F." urged Miss Evans to lift her eyes from her books and study the people around her. In the May, 1870, number *Vashti* found a defender in the Rev. H. A. M. Henderson, D.D., who dared to "challenge the critical acumen" of both "F. F." and the editor of the *Home Monthly*.

The vogue of the subliterary novels of Southern women seemed to Hayne, Lanier, and William Hand Browne a chief obstacle in the way of those who wished to create a really worthy Southern literature. The subliterary is still with us today, and in a democracy it is likely to be a permanent menace to the wide recognition of what is truly great in literature. Nor is the subliterary limited to prose fiction. The South has given American literature some of its worst poets, too. One of them was J. Gordon Coogler of Columbia, South Carolina, who wrote the two-line epigram:

> Alas for the South! Her books have grown fewer;
> She was never much given to literature.

40
Margaret Junkin Preston

Mrs. Margaret J. Preston (1820–1897), best of the Southern poets of her sex, was born in Milton, Pennsylvania, and she spent the first twenty-eight years of her life in the North. She came of Scotch Covenanter stock on both sides. Her father was the able Presbyterian minister, Dr. George Junkin, founder and President of Lafayette College at Easton. During her girlhood Margaret read widely under the guidance of her parents and received private instruction from members of the Lafayette faculty. The books she read and studied were chiefly those prescribed for boys and young men. She learned Greek from her father. Excessive use of her eyes after an illness so weakened her sight that for years she had to give up reading entirely, and much of her writing was done on the grooved apparatus devised for the blind. Nevertheless, she managed to read the chief British and American writers of her time. Until the failure of her eyesight, art had interested her more than literature. She laid aside brush and pencil, but her interest in art shows in the subject matter of her verse, and it had some influence on the technique of the poems which she designated as "cartoons."

In 1848 Dr. Junkin became President of Washington College (now Washington and Lee University). In the little college town of Lexington the Junkins found congenial friends among "the visiting Virginians," as she once designated them from their most marked characteristic. Among those whom she came to know in Lexington now or later were Matthew F. Maury, Robert E. Lee, and Stonewall Jackson, whose first wife was her sister Eleanor Junkin. Meanwhile Margaret Junkin had been publishing stories and poems in various newspapers, magazines, and annuals, occasionally winning a prize. In 1856 she published anonymously her only novel, *Silverwood: A Book of Memories*, written primarily to preserve the memory of a brother and sister who had died. She refused her publisher's offer of an additional two hundred dollars if she would permit the use of her name on the title page.

In 1857 Margaret Junkin married Major John T. L. Preston, Professor of Latin in the Virginia Military Institute and one of the founders of that institution. She had long vowed that she would never marry a widower, but now she had married one with seven children. Major Preston, who had known Poe in his boyhood in Richmond, belonged to one of the most prominent families in the state and owned a fine house in Lexington over which Margaret, who did not like to give orders to servants, had to preside. Her husband's cousin, Senator William C. Preston of South Carolina, the friend of Irving, at first looked with some disfavor on her as a woman who appeared in print and noted "the little Yankee's want of style and presence." It was not long, however, before he discovered her finer qualities. Referring to her learning and her small size, he once said: "She is an encyclopaedia in small print!"

For some time after her marriage Mrs. Preston wrote little because, as she later remarked in her husband's presence, Major Preston "did not in his heart of hearts approve of his wife's giving any part of herself to the public, even in verse!" Major Preston eventually became one of the warmest admirers of her poems and, one suspects, one of her best critics. On October 8, 1870, he wrote to Paul Hamilton Hayne: ". . . the poet is the true reflex of the *woman*. Her choice of subjects is but the explication of her nature. Yes, my little wife is as full of faith and reverence as ever was any daughter of Jerusalem: the Greek hardly excelled her in love of the beautiful: she is as true and trustful as Lady Hildegarde; as simple as a ballad, and as intense as a sonnet."

The outbreak of the Civil War brought about an unhappy division in the Junkin family. Her brother John became a surgeon in the Union army, and her father and a sister returned to the North. She, however, shared the political views of her husband, who, though he opposed secession, went with his state and served with distinction in Jackson's army. Mrs. Preston suffered much from divided sympathies. On June 3, 1862, she wrote in her diary: "When I am compelled to hear scorn and loathing predicated of everything *Northern* (as must continually be the case), my heart boils up, and sobs to itself. But I must be silent." Somewhat later she had the trying experience of having her house pillaged by Northern soldiers who swore at her while her husband and stepsons were away in the Confederate army.

She wrote a few war lyrics which were quickly gathered up in the anthologies that began to appear even during the war. In the winter of 1864–1865 her husband, now Colonel Preston, wrote to her: "I send you a little poem ["Wee Davie"] which is making a great stir here in Richmond: it is rather a pretty thing, but you could do something much better in the same line." She accepted the challenge and in the intervals of her household duties she dictated to her stepdaughter by the light of an open fire the long poem, *Beechenbrook: A Rhyme of the War*. After reading the manuscript to enthusiastic army officers, Colonel Preston paid $2600 in Confederate money for an edition of two thousand copies. All but fifty copies were destroyed in the fire that followed Lee's evacuation of Richmond, but admirers made many manuscript copies of the poem. When it was republished in

Baltimore in 1866, *Beechenbrook* sold seven or eight thousand copies. The poem deals with typical wartime hardships and tragedies, but the subject was too close to the poet for the most effective treatment of the theme.

In the omnipresent "honorable poverty" of Reconstruction Virginia Mrs. Preston published poems and reviews in various Southern magazines and newspapers and in an occasional Northern magazine, like *Lippincott's*, which was not inhospitable to Southern contributors. In 1870 J. B. Lippincott and Company brought out her *Old Song and New*. In her diary for February of that year she referred to the circumstances under which she collected and revised the poems included in that volume: "All kinds of interruptions—housekeeping—children—callers, &c. And I am writing just in the midst of it. Surely it is the pursuit of literature under pressure of difficulties." On July 11 of the preceding year she had written to Paul Hamilton Hayne:

Congratulate yourself, my dear sir, that you are a *man*, and are thus free from the thousand petty housewifely distractions that fill up the life of a wife and mother! I smile to myself, many a time, on reading the letters of literary correspondents, who seem to imagine that my days are devoted to literary pursuits, and that *the stylus* is my appropriate symbol: when if they could look in upon me, they would see company to breakfast, ditto to dine, ditto to tea,—they would find a row of cookery books adorning my store-room shelves—they would find me deep in the mysteries of Sally-Lund, or lemon tartlets, or orange-ice, or cream-sponge (your good wife will understand all this, if you do not!) and so my days go by.

One need not lament that Mrs. Preston gave first place to household duties. Had she been a great poet, like Emily Dickinson, she would have managed somehow to free herself from such handicaps or have written great poetry in spite of them. During her lifetime she published three more volumes: *Cartoons* (1875), *For Love's Sake* (1886), *Colonial Ballads, Sonnets and Other Verse* (1887). A summer in Europe in 1884 led her to give her impressions of the trip in her last prose work, *A Handful of Monographs* (1886).

In the postwar years she paid her tribute in verse to many British and American poets, and with some of them she carried on a semiliterary correspondence. Some of her best letters are addressed to Paul Hamilton Hayne, whom she never saw. After her husband's death in 1890, she sold her house and lived with a son in Baltimore. She was now partially paralyzed. She disliked living in a large city, but she managed to preserve her serenity and her interest in the life about her. On May 29, 1897, she died in her sleep, just as she had expressed the wish to do in the poem, "Euthanasia," written a short time before.

James A. Harrison, who knew her well, thought that Mrs. Preston's masters were Tennyson, Longfellow, and the Brownings. Tennyson at least she could read critically. Of one of the later *Idylls of the King* she wrote to Hayne: "Now *don't* you think the limpid wine has been well drawn off, and we are getting down (just ever so little) towards the lees?" She thought Swinburne too sensual; and, like many women, she disliked Whitman. The influence of Robert Browning would seem to be the strongest in her poems. It is seen in her character portraits, for which she often used the dramatic monologue form, and it is frequently seen in her employment of the colloquial style. She had in common with Browning a keen interest in painting and sculpture. In sentiment she most resembles Longfellow. The forms in which her best work was done are the sonnet, the ballad, and the dramatic monologue. Some of her sonnets and devotional pieces are good, but her best poems are character portraits. Her instinct for the best way to tell a story often failed her, but she had an eye for character. She wrote with more vigor and sincerity than most of the Southern poets of either sex, but she wrote too rapidly and her diction often lacks individuality and expressiveness. Her feeling, however, is genuine; it is sentiment rather than the too prevailing sentimentality of the period.

Like Longfellow, she loved Old World art and romance. Like Browning, she loved Italy and Italian art—above all, the artists whose lives were written by Vasari. "Greek stories, literature, &c.," she wrote to Hayne, "have an irresistible attraction for me. But I think it a most unprofitable and *unattainable* path to attempt." Like many another American of her time— especially in the South and West—she was deeply disturbed by the growing religious doubts of the later nineteenth century, even though she had modified her own Calvinistic creed. In "Prophets of Doubt" she praises Mrs. Browning as almost the only British poet free from doubt. To the other poets she says:

> Keep then your sad negations, iced
> With darkness, doubt, and frore despair;
> Bind up your vision, and declare
> That no Evangel has sufficed,
> (Despite the faith of myriads dead,)
> Upon your deviate paths to shed
> The light ye seek: But leave *us* CHRIST!

Mrs. Preston never took herself very seriously as a writer. "Poetry," she wrote to Hayne, "has been only my pastime, not the occupation or mission of my life. . . . I think I can truly say that I have never neglected the concoction of a pudding for the sake of a poem, or a sauce for a sonnet. Art is a jealous mistress and I have served her with my left hand only." In "Artist-Work" she wrote:

> Hours winnowed of care, soft-cultur'd, studious ease,
> Days hedged from interruption, and withdrawn
> Inviolate from household exigence,—
> Are not for women,—at least for wives and mothers. . . .

They must
> catch suggestions of the beautiful,
> For Love, true Artist, to idealize
> In living frescoes on the walls of home.

There were times, however, when she must have resented restrictions put upon what women could write. In "Woman's Art" (in *Cartoons*) she told with feeling the story of a woman of Bologna who, forbidden to carve in marble, was given a cherry-stone to carve and out of it fashioned a work of art that outlived the creations of her male contemporaries.

41
The Old Southwest

Before 1820 there was little to differentiate the northern states of the Old West from those south of the Ohio River. As the cotton plantation pushed its way westward, however, the states in the lower Mississippi Valley came more and more to conform to the pattern of the seaboard slaveholding states. Well-to-do planters with their slaves came into the Black Belt, and the frontier population for the most part moved still further westward or settled in the poorer regions of the hill country.

In his journey through the back country in the 1850's Frederick Law Olmsted noted that he did not see a thermometer, a copy of Shakespeare, a piano, or an engraving. The people were friendly, but everything seemed temporary and makeshift, even the houses in which the farmers lived. The great mass of the Southern farmers, it would appear, had little interest in education or matters pertaining to literary culture.

The best culture of the Southwest was to be found on the larger plantations in the Black Belt and in such cultural centers as Mobile, Tuscaloosa, Nashville, Natchez, and New Orleans. Here at least there was no lack of educated men, of books, and of general intelligence. Some settlers of the better class of planters from Virginia and the Carolinas had moved to the Gulf states. There is no finer specimen of the Southern planter than Thomas

Dabney, who rather than sell his slaves left Virginia in the thirties to settle in Mississippi. In his daughter's biography, *Memorials of a Southern Planter* (1887), Susan Dabney Smedes has vividly portrayed for us as admirable an example of the Virginia gentleman as can be found in all the literature of the Old Dominion. In closing his review of this book in the *Nineteenth Century* for December, 1889, William E. Gladstone wrote: "Let no man say, with this book before him, that the age of chivalry has gone, or that Thomas Dabney was not worthy to sit with Sir Percival at the 'table round' of King Arthur."

One of the most remarkable of Southern cultural oases was Natchez, center of a rich farming region to which cultivated young men had come from many parts of the Union. One of the newcomers to this region was Joseph Holt Ingraham, who in 1835 published his first book, *The South-West. By a Yankee*. His numerous novels were still to be written. Ingraham, a native of Portland, Maine, considered Natchez society not surpassed by that of any other region in the United States. "Perhaps no state," he said, "—not even Virginia herself, which Mississippi claims as her mother country—could present a more hospitable, chivalrous, and high-minded class of men, or more cultivated females than this, during the first few years, subsequent to its accession to the Union [in 1817]." There were, according to Ingraham, good schools in the towns, but on the plantations education was likely to be somewhat neglected. Two-thirds of the planters' children were being educated outside the state. The majority of the ministers were graduates of Princeton. The population of the Southwest was, as Ingraham saw it, more frankly commercial than that of the older Southern states. "A plantation well stocked with hands," he said, "is the *ne plus ultra* of every man's ambition who resides at the south." Every young lawyer, doctor, journalist, and minister felt the mania for owning a broad plantation. There was no scarcity of books in the plantation libraries, but in such a society only a few who had come into the region from the Atlantic seaboard felt any desire to write. There was no place for any but the amateur author. With few exceptions the best writers were humorists.

Such magazines as were published in the Southwest, with the remarkable exception of *De Bow's Review* in New Orleans, were short-lived and poorly supported. There was no dearth, however, of newspapers, and these to a certain extent fulfilled the functions of magazines. Mrs. Rhoda Coleman Ellison's excellent study, *Early Alabama Publications* (1947), shows that the newspapers published more literary materials than one would have supposed. The American poets, she discovered, were never so popular as the English, and Southern poets were less often reprinted than the Northern.

The Alabama editors, however, were much more interested in native fiction than in the work of any British writer except Scott, who was "the fiction god of ante-bellum Alabama idolatry, even while he was still called 'the Great Unknown.' "

42
Joseph Holt Ingraham

THE STUDENT WHO imagines that the only American novels which were widely read in the 1840's were those of Cooper and Simms should glance at Lyle H. Wright's bibliography, *American Fiction . . . 1774–1850*. There he will find that the "Yankee" who in 1835 published *The South-West* anonymously was also the author of no less than 70 of the 765 novels which appeared in a single decade. And yet literary historians often do not even mention the name of Joseph Holt Ingraham (1809–1860). He grew up in Portland, Maine, and is said to have attended Bowdoin College; and yet Longfellow, a native of Portland and a graduate of Bowdoin, appears not yet to have met him when Ingraham dedicated to him his first novel, *Laffite* (1836). Longfellow wrote to a friend in 1838: "He is tremendous—really tremendous. I think he may say that he writes the worst novels ever written by anybody. But they sell; he gets twelve hundred dollars apiece." In his journal for April 6, 1846, Longfellow described Ingraham as a "young, dark man, with soft voice." The poet added: "He says he has written eighty novels, and of these twenty during the last year; till it has grown to be merely mechanical with him. These novels are published in the newspapers. They pay him something more than three thousand dollars a year." No other novelist North or South was consistently earning as much as that in the 1840's.

In 1832 Ingraham had become professor of languages in Jefferson College near Natchez, Mississippi. Not long afterward he married the daughter of a planter. In 1836 he published his first novel, *Laffite; or, The Pirate of the Gulf*, a semihistorical romance. In Lafitte—to follow the more common spelling of the name—and in Creole New Orleans Ingraham had discovered a picturesque background. He had also apparently worked out a formula for his numerous later novels.

In his last phase Ingraham was an Episcopal clergyman, and he wrote religious novels, of which the best known is *A Prince of the House of David* (1855). He is said to have used the income from his religious novels to buy up the copyrights of his earlier romances and withdraw them from circulation. In the 1850's we find him preaching or teaching at Nashville and at various other towns in Tennessee, Alabama, and Mississippi. He was killed at Holly Springs, Mississippi, by the accidental discharge of a gun. One of his last books, *The Sunny South; or, The Southerner at Home* (1860), deals with the experiences of a Northern governess in the South and was written to promote better understanding between the sections.

His son, Prentiss Ingraham (1843–1904), became an even more prolific writer of what were soon to be called dime-novels. He is said to have written more than two hundred novels about Buffalo Bill and on one occasion to have written with a fountain pen in a day and a night no less than thirty-five thousand words.

43
Alexander Beaufort Meek

THE MOST CONSPICUOUS literary figure in ante-bellum Alabama was Alexander Beaufort Meek (1814–1865). Of Scotch-Irish descent on both sides, he was born in Columbia, South Carolina; but when he was about five years old, his father, who was at various times doctor, druggist, and Methodist minister, moved to Tuscaloosa, Alabama. William Russell Smith, who knew Meek well, gives us a glimpse of him as "a bright-eyed, fair-headed boy—a lean, tall stripling of ten or twelve years old, limber as a fishing-rod and fleet as an arrow." As a boy he carried to school newspapers hidden in his hat, for he found the verses and tales contained in them more fascinating than his Greek and Latin texts. He had some local reputation as a poet before he entered the University of Georgia—then presided over by Moses Waddel —from which he transferred to the newly opened University of Alabama in Tuscaloosa. He graduated in 1833. He attained some distinction in many fields, but he was too versatile and too unambitious to give himself entirely to either literature, journalism, law, or politics. He practiced law with some success but gave it up to serve in the Indian war in Florida, where he was much impressed by the semitropical scenery. He was at one time a probate judge and was of course ever afterwards known as Judge Meek. He served with some distinction in the state legislature, where his greatest achievement was in the promotion of a public-school system for Alabama. Before this time, however, he had gone to Washington in 1845 as Assistant Secretary of the Treasury. A year later he was Federal attorney for the Southern district of Alabama. He now moved to Mobile, where he made his home for several years. He was for a time editor of the Mobile *Daily Register*. He clipped most of his news items, other than local, from the metropolitan dailies and wrote his daily editorial, which before printing he read aloud to his friend Thaddeus Sanford, the owner of the paper. The newspaper work was not particularly congenial. Mobile under the influence of Madame Octavia Le Vert aspired to be a literary and cultural center. On November 22, 1851, Meek wrote to Simms: "Hereabouts, our mental atmosphere, like the interior of a Gin room, is impregnated almost entirely with Cotton. But we have a few Sardinians that have not defiled their garments." [75]

Meek was in demand as an orator, and his published work includes a number of speeches delivered chiefly to college audiences. He was a Jacksonian Democrat; he was, however, an admirer of Webster and he had an antipathy to the doctrines of Calhoun. In "The Day of Freedom," a long poem which he read in Tuscaloosa on July 4, 1838, he gave his conception of the Union:

> What, though each Star that on our banner shines,
> Moves in its orbit with a sovereign sway,—
> With laws, with institutions of its own,—
> Yet 'round one common centre all converge,
> And each, upon its golden pathway wheels
> With sympathetic harmony and force
> And equipoise sublime. Strike but one orb
> From its appointed place, or rudely dim
> Its purity and light, and soon the whole
> Great frame-work of the sky, would madly whirl
> In dire confusion and disaster vast.

Meek went into secession unwillingly along with his party and state. He died at Columbus, Mississippi, on November 1, in the year in which the war came to an end.

In appearance Meek was a striking figure, handsome, well-proportioned, six feet four inches in height. "In the parlor," says William Russell Smith, "he was superb; on the streets, he was genial, social, and cheerful; as a friend, he was warm and candid; as an acquaintance, he was cordial." Long a bachelor, he was a favorite with women, and many of his lyrics are addressed to them. He once wrote to Simms, who thought him lazy: "My sympathies are all literary, though my habits are anything else." *Russell's Magazine* in January, 1858, complained that Meek had not given his best to literature, his real vocation: "He gave too much to society; too much to partisan politics; too much to inferior considerations, moral and material. He was just the man to have concentrated all his force upon literature, and made

---

[75] Charles H. Ross, "Alexander Beaufort Meek," *Sewanee Rev.*, IV, 419 (Aug., 1896). By "Sardinians" Meek means natives of Sardis, not Sardinia. See Revelation, 3:4.

himself and his people famous. Why did he not do this? Why did he leave literature for politics—for society? Why did he give up for party what was meant for mankind?" Meek, however, if we may judge from his slowness in bringing out a volume of his poems, had some suspicion that they were less important than his friends considered them.

Like his friend Simms, Meek was a strong advocate of Americanism in literature. He believed that an American author should write about his own country, with a special emphasis upon the region he knew best. He considered Kennedy's *Horse-Shoe Robinson* not inferior to the best of the Waverley novels, and his admiration for Cooper extended even to such unpopular books as *Homeward Bound* and *Home as Found*. He first formulated his ideas in the *Southron*, a literary monthly which he edited and published in Tuscaloosa during the first six months of 1839. In his "Introduction Salutatory," which was subtitled "Southern Literature," he argued from literary history that southerly regions are the natural home of literature; that the scenery of the South is unsurpassed; and that the slave plantation not only supplied Southern writers with leisure but also furnished literary materials comparable to the peasantry and country gentry of Europe. The *Southron*, although Meek found a few able contributors, failed after six months, presumably from lack of support. The failure of his magazine was perhaps in his mind when in 1841 he delivered his college oration on "Jack-Cadeism and the Fine Arts," an attack upon the utilitarian spirit and a defense of literature and the fine arts.

"Prithee Poins!" did you not speak of such a thing as Southern Literature? Like the sounding of a bell in a vast wilderness, we have heard the faint chimes of a scattered few, who would awaken us to an elevated devotion. They have been the neglected prophets and apostles of an impracticable creed. The Jack-Cadeism of the day has quenched their vestal fires. "Hang him with his pen and ink-horn about his neck," has been the constant verdict of our backwoods' juries.

The young Southerner, he once said:

may spend night and day in any kind of dissipation suited to his taste, make every grocery in his neighbourhood ring with his Bacchanalian shouts, and other improving and intellectual amusements, of a like nature, with little injury to his reputation; but if it be once known that he cultivates any branch of general literature, especially poetry, he must bid adieu to all hopes of success. Poetry and nonsense are regarded as convertible terms; dunces pass him with a sneer and the half uttered exclamation, "Yes, I'd write poetry"; maidens titter, unless perchance he may have indited sonnets to their eyebrows; old men shake heads at him, and prefer to entrust their lives, fortunes and souls to some dull machine. . . .

In 1844, when the University of Georgia honored him with a master's degree, he delivered an address on "Americanism in Literature," which Simms reviewed with high approval. In 1851, sharing the common feeling that the South must have its own literature, he wrote to Simms: "I am convinced we cannot have *Home* Independence of any kind, in Commerce, Manufactures, Politics, or what not, until we have Home Independence of *Mind*. This is the *end* at which the great Southern Reformation should begin; and Consul Baylors and Macon Conventions would do more in striving for it, than by all the Cotton-monopolies and State fairs they can conceive." Meek's maturest expression of his literary creed appears in the Preface to his *Songs and Poems of the South* (New York, 1857):

The poetry of a country should be a faithful expression of its physical and moral characteristics. The imagery, at least, should be drawn from the indigenous objects of the region, and the sentiments be such as naturally arise under the influence of its climate, its institutions, habits of life, and social condition. Verse, so fashioned and colored, is as much the genuine product and growth of a Land, as its trees or flowers. It partakes of the raciness of the soil, the purity of the atmosphere, the brilliancy of its skies, its mountain pictures, and its broad sweeps of level and undulating territory. The Scenery infuses itself into the Song; and the feelings and fancies are modulated by the circumstances amid which they had their birth.

Such was Meek's creed. It probably never occurred to him that Johnson Jones Hooper and Joseph Glover Baldwin, in writing their humorous sketches of Alabama and Mississippi, were producing work which was both American and Southern in a sense in which his poems were not. His themes were American, but his literary models were the British Romantic poets, particularly Scott, Byron, and Moore. Of the influence of Moore's almost forgotten *Lalla Rookh* upon Meek and himself, William Russell Smith had much to say:

Of all the books of poetry appearing in my time, in the depth of its impression on my sensitiveness, and its hold upon my heart, I may say that "Lalla Rookh" was *the* book. It was a "thing of beauty and a joy forever." "The Light of the Harem" glowed in every cottage, and flashed on every center-table. The book was the pocket companion of the boys and the bosom darling of the girls. . . .

I have reason to know that this book took possession of Meek. He mastered all its beauties, and was especially fond of memorizing and quoting its more striking passages. From a mere dreamer at the shrine of the muses he became at once a full-grown worshiper and a vigorous worker.

The half-breed heroine of Meek's *The Red Eagle*, Smith went on to complain, is "The Light of the Harem" all over again: "In the tone and cast of melody, in the flowing drapery flung round the breathing development of his fancy, it is still the 'Light of the Harem.' " Meek could not help seeing the Southern landscape through the eyes of the British Romanticists. A number of his Southern songs are reminiscent of the opening lines of Byron's *The Bride of Abydos:* "Know ye the land of the cypress and myrtle . . . ?" Meek comes nearest to originality when he writes of the sun, moon, stars, and sky. Even his best poems suffer from too great a profusion of images and an excess of ornament. Among the better poems are "The Fated City" (Pompeii), "The Death of Richard Henry Wilde," and "Balaklava." The last of these has some good lines but it suffers inevitably from comparison with "The Charge of the Light Brigade." Meek's poem was widely copied, partly because it had been attributed to the English poet Alexander Smith. His long poem, *The Red Eagle*, was the result of a lifelong interest in the American Indian and the early history of the Southwest. Meek saw epic possibilities in the story of Weatherford, or the Red Eagle; but the style of the poem is too often lyric rather than epic, and the hero is represented too much as lover and too little as warrior. Meek was following not Milton or Homer but Moore and Scott and, in his conception of the red man, Cooper and Simms. The poem is nevertheless—though this is not high praise—one of the best long narrative poems written in the South in the period.

Meek left unpublished at his death a history of Alabama, on which he had worked intermittently for years. If we may judge from Meek's one long prose work, *Romantic Passages in Southwestern History* (New York, 1857), the history was not a sober jogtrot narrative. *Romantic Passages*, in which the story of Weatherford is told again, contains a number of historical sketches among which we may mention "The Southwest: Its History, Character, and Prospects"; "Claims and Characteristics of Alabama History"; and "The Pilgrimage of De Soto." Meek had an eye for the picturesque and the effective, and he had a keener concern for the factual than one might infer from the title of his book; and yet his conception of history is a blend of fact with romance, like that of the youthful Charles Gayarré. As a historian, he was an amateur, as he was in everything he undertook. The amateur spirit is a fine thing in its place, but the great drawback in ante-bellum Southern literature is that it is the work of talented amateurs who seldom gave to it the full devotion and tireless industry that characterize a writer like Edgar Allan Poe.

Among the lesser writers of the Southwest whom I cannot discuss at length there is Meek's friend, the equally versatile William Russell Smith (1815–1896), whom I include in the hope that some Alabama scholar will study his career and his writings. Born at Russellville, Kentucky, of parents of

Virginia descent who died early, he was brought up in Tuscaloosa. He studied at the University of Alabama, where two of his teachers were F. A. P. Barnard, later president of Columbia University, and Henry W. Hilliard, who taught English and eventually became a United States Senator. Before he left college, Smith had published in Tuscaloosa a volume of poems, *College Musings, or Twigs from Parnassus* (1833), of which the only extant copy is in the Harris Collection in the Brown University Library. He studied law but, like Meek, he had too many other interests to give his full time to the law. He fought in the Creek War, edited a magazine called the *Bachelor's Button* (1837–1838), which expired after the sixth number, contributed to Meek's the *Southron*, served as mayor of Tuscaloosa, edited several newspapers, became a circuit judge, and was a member of Congress from 1851 to 1857. In a speech in Congress on January 18, 1856, he said: "I am a southern Democrat, and yet I denounce the doctrine of secession in all its phases—in all its aims, and even in all its abstractions." In the convention that took Alabama out of the Union he denounced secession as "the tocsin of war and the death-knell of slavery." He was a Confederate soldier, a member of the Confederate Congress, and for a brief time president of the University of Alabama. In 1879 he moved to Washington, where he lived in a house which was finally torn down to make room for the new Supreme Court building. There he edited the *Central Law Journal* and followed his wife into the Roman Catholic Church. His published writings include a novel, *As It Is* (Albany, 1860); a play about Lincoln, *The Royal Ape: A Democratic Poem* (Richmond, 1863); and a *Key to the Iliad* (Tuscaloosa, 1871). His best poem is probably "The Uses of Solitude," but by far his most interesting work is his *Reminiscences of a Long Life* (1889), of which only the first volume was published. It is an exceptionally interesting autobiography which throws much light on Alabama history and cultural conditions.[76]

44

Mirabeau B. Lamar

MIRABEAU BUONAPARTE LAMAR (1798–1859), the second President of the Republic of Texas, is an important military and political figure in the history of the new Southwest, but as a poet he belongs to the Old South. There were two sides to Lamar's personality, but only one of them—and that inadequately—is reflected in his verses. He was as dashing a cavalryman as

[76] There is a brief biography by his daughter, Anne-Easbey Smith, *William Russell Smith of Alabama* . . . (Philadelphia, 1931).

Turner Ashby or "Jeb" Stuart, but he was too reserved and too unpractical
to be a consistently successful politician. Among his intimate friends he
was companionable and communicative, but his deeper feelings he kept to
himself. They rarely found expression even in his verses. Many of these are
tributes to women, for like Poe and Richard Henry Wilde he tended to
glorify and idealize woman. His *Verse Memorials* (1857) is hardly the kind
of book that one would expect to come from the Southwestern frontier.

Lamar's father, a Georgia planter, was the descendant of Huguenot
refugees. Mirabeau attended two Georgia academies, but his education was
rather desultory. "It has not been," he once wrote, "my good fortune to
wander far in the labyrinth of letters." Ancient history fascinated him, and
Gibbon was among his favorite writers. The British poets whom he liked
best were Dryden, Pope, Churchill, and of course those general Southern
favorites, Moore, Byron, and Scott.

Lamar tried his hand at various occupations with no great success. At one
time he was a merchant in Cahawba, Alabama, where at another time he
published a newspaper. In many parts of the South a planter's son lost little
in respectability by being a merchant; in Charleston he might have lost
caste. Lamar tried journalism again and again. He studied law in preparation for a political career, and he was for a time private secretary to the
Georgia governor. He served one term in the state senate; but when his wife
died in 1833, he gave himself up to grief, destroyed the poems he had addressed to her, and declined to stand for re-election. He was deeply moved
in the summer of 1834 by the suicide of his brother Lucius, father of the
statesman who bore the same name. There was a strain of melancholia in
the Lamar family. Lamar himself once wrote: "I never pass by a graveyard
without stopping to peruse these pathetic records of bereaved friendship and
affection."

It was with a feeling akin to desperation that Lamar set out for Texas
in June, 1835. Soon after his arrival in the little town of Washington he
made a speech in which he advocated the independence of Texas. He returned to Georgia to make final arrangements for a permanent removal to
Texas. There he heard of the fall of the Alamo, and he hurried back to take
part in the Texas War for Independence. He joined the retreating army as
a mounted volunteer not long before the decisive Battle of San Jacinto.
In a preliminary skirmish two of Lamar's comrades were surrounded by
Mexicans. Like a knight of romance, he rushed to the rescue, killed one
of the Mexican lancers, and put the rest to flight. He then rode coolly in
front of the Mexican lines back to his own squad. The story has been somewhat embroidered in Texas legend, but it appears that on the following day

Lamar was proclaimed colonel of the cavalry—sixty men in all. Out of consideration for the regular officers, he declined the honor, but on their insistence he finally accepted the post. Like other Texans, he played his part manfully in the decisive Battle of San Jacinto, in which Texas avenged the massacre at Goliad and the murder of the defenders of the Alamo and won her independence.

From this time Lamar's rise was incredibly rapid. In less than two weeks he became Secretary of War, and within a month the Cabinet made him commander of the army. He resigned, however, when he discovered that the soldiers were resentful that they had not been consulted before the appointment was made. Four months after San Jacinto Lamar was elected Vice-President, and in October, 1836, he was inaugurated along with President Sam Houston. Meanwhile Lamar's friend Porter in Eatonton, Georgia, had written: "All your life, Mirabeau, you have bemoaned the quiet spirit of our age and seemed to have renounced all hope of jostling your way up fame's proud summit. But there you are."

In 1838 Lamar succeeded Houston as President of Texas. His threats of making war on Mexico led Anson Jones, the Massachusetts Yankee who was to become the last President of Texas, to write: "Gen. Lamar may mean well. I am not disposed to impugn his intentions—he has fine belles lettres talents & is an elegant writer. But his mind is altogether of a dreamy, poetic order. A Sort of political Troubadour & Crusader, wholly unfit by habit or education for the active duties & the every day realities of his present station. Texas is too small for a man of such wild visionary 'vaulting ambition.'"

Lamar was an idealist with visions of the future of a great republic. He wished, he said in his inaugural address: "To awaken into vigorous activity the wealth, talent and enterprise of the country, and at the same time to lay the foundation of those higher institutions for moral and mental culture, without which no government on democratic principles can prosper, nor the people long preserve their liberties." Financially, Lamar's administration was a failure, partly because Houston had left grave financial problems for his successor to wrestle with. Lamar, however, laid a foundation for later achievements. He made plans for a public-school system and a state university. He was the only approach to a patron of the arts and letters in Texas. He himself collected materials for a history of Texas that he was never to write.

When his term of office was over in 1841, Lamar, saddened by the death of his daughter, an only child, retired to his plantation on the Brazos. In 1844, when he went to Washington to plead for the annexation of Texas, he visited in Philadelphia and New York. In Mobile he renewed his acquaintance with Madame Octavia Le Vert, in whose drawing room he met Richard Henry Wilde, whose "My Life Is Like the Summer Rose" had been frequently reprinted in Texas newspapers. In Mobile also he met Wilde's friend, Alexander B. Meek. On Meek's front porch the two poets read together much of the manuscript of Meek's Songs and Poems of the South, which when it was published in 1857, carried the dedication: "To Gen. Mirabeau B. Lamar, Ex-President of Texas, The Soldier, Statesman and Poet. . . ." His Mobile friends rekindled in Lamar an interest in literature.

In the War with Mexico Lamar was Inspector-General in the army of General Zachary Taylor. He distinguished himself at the Battle of Monterey. He was unable to get himself transferred to General Scott's army, which was to capture the Mexican capital; and he spent the latter part of the war with the Texas Mounted Volunteers in protecting the border from Comanche raiders and Mexican marauders.

At the end of the war Lamar retired to his plantation. In 1851 he married Henrietta, the daughter of the Irish-born poet and preacher, John Newland Maffitt. In 1855 he returned to Georgia hoping to borrow money to pay some of his debts. In New Orleans he was elected President of the Southern Commercial Convention. In Mobile he listened while Alexander B. Meek read aloud his poem, The Red Eagle, which seemed to Lamar "a poem of great merit abounding in gorgeous imagery."

In 1857 Lamar was appointed Minister to Nicaragua and Costa Rica at a salary of ten thousand dollars a year. At last it seemed as though he would be able to free himself from the incubus of debt. He proceeded alone to Nicaragua, where he wrote that favorite of the anthologists, "The Daughter of Mendoza." After twenty months in Central America, with his financial situation greatly improved, he returned to Texas, hoping to spend the remainder of his life peacefully on his plantation. Friends and relatives were preparing to celebrate his return home with the merriest of Christmases when he died suddenly of a heart attack on December 18, 1859.

Just before his departure for Nicaragua, Lamar had published in New York his Verse Memorials, and had sold some of his Texas land to pay the printer's bill. The diffident poet had agreed to publish his poems only after long urging on the part of Mrs. Lamar and Meek. Verse Memorials is a slim volume, for Lamar had selected for publication only those poems reminiscent of some person or occasion. Many of them are courtly compliments to women, "spontaneous effusions" written in a lady's album. In this respect they resemble many of the poems of his friends Wilde and Meek, who in some verses addressed to the second Mrs. Lamar referred to her husband as:

one who is his country's pride—
To whom the blended wreaths belong
Of valor, statesmanship, and song. . . .

In "Home on the Brazos," which is a poetic introduction to *Verse Memorials*, Lamar wrote:

O Gentle ladies, gay and bright,
For you—and you alone—I write;
And if my verse should fail to please,
For want of your own native ease,
You must your faithful bard forgive,
Whose songs are not designed to live. . . .

· · · · ·

Such is the nature of my lays—
Plain, simple strains in Beauty's praise;
Designed at first for those fair friends
Whose memory with my being blends,
And now sent forth to find their way
To minds congenial, grave or gay.
Oh, could their simple tones impart
One throb of joy to woman's heart,
The bard would find, for all his toil,
An over-payment in her smile.

Knowing only the poems in *Verse Memorials*, William P. Trent wrote in 1905: "This volume is probably the most extraordinary repository of extempore effusions addressed by a gallant gentleman to lovely ladies to be found in the whole range of our literature. The belles of nearly every important Georgia town and of the chief cities of the other Southern states are celebrated in easy stanzas, and Mexican beauties and Northern poetesses are not neglected."

In 1938, when Philip Graham published *The Life and Poems of Mirabeau B. Lamar*, he added considerably to the number and the range of Lamar's poems from a diligent search among manuscripts and newspaper files. He found few, however, that will enhance the reputation of the poet. Not many of Lamar's poems reveal deep feeling. The following stanza, from a poem written in memory of his first wife, begins well but soon imagery and idea become conventional:

She was all beauty, melody, and mirth—
A spirit bright, that gladdened soul and eye;
But as the fair and cherished things of earth,
Whose sweetness links them to their kindred sky,

Are always first to wither and to fall—
So perished she, the loveliest of them all.

The ladies to whom Lamar addressed his verses were too easy to please, and so also were such literary friends as Meek and Madame Le Vert. A better than average specimen is the first stanza of "In Deathless Beauty," addressed to his second wife before their marriage:

O Lady, if the stars so bright
Were diamond worlds bequeathed to me,
I would resign them all this night,
To frame one song befitting thee;
For thou art dearer to my heart
Than all the gems of earth and sky;
And he that sings thee as thou art,
May boast a song that can not die.

Lamar was not without talent; and if he had been intimately associated with other writers and given his best to literature, he would occupy a larger place in our literature than that of "The Poet Laureate of Texas." In one or two of his early humorous poems he perhaps came nearer to writing something memorable than in any of his complimentary verses to the ladies. In a "New-Year's Address" to the readers of the Cahawba *Press*, hurriedly written in December, 1821, he described a country dance in a manner that seems almost to anticipate Irwin Russell's memorable description of the dance in "Christmas-Night in the Quarters." That, however, was not the kind of verses which the Southern ladies wished written in their albums.

45
Theodore O'Hara

THE MOST NOTABLE poem occasioned by the War with Mexico and after Timrod's "Ode" perhaps our finest martial elegy, "The Bivouac of the Dead," was written by the soldier-journalist-poet, Theodore O'Hara (1820–1867). O'Hara's mother, Helen (Hardy) O'Hara, was a Kentuckian of Maryland descent. His father, Kean O'Hara, an Irish Catholic, had fled from Ireland after the failure of the rebellion of 1798. Until his death in 1851 the elder O'Hara taught in various Kentucky academies. Theodore, who was probably born in Frankfort and not in Danville, as is often stated, passed his boyhood in the Kentucky capital. He received his education in schools conducted by his father and in St. Joseph's College, where he was for a short time instructor in Greek. He studied law in the office of Judge William

Owsley, who was later Governor of Kentucky. One of his closest friends was John C. Breckinridge, who became Vice-President under Buchanan and was afterwards a Confederate general. After practicing law for a short time, O'Hara took a minor post in the Treasury department in Washington. Soon afterwards he was on the staff of the Frankfort *Yeoman*. The remainder of his life was divided chiefly between army life and journalism.

He served as a captain in the War with Mexico, and in August, 1847, he was breveted major for "gallant and meritorious conduct in the battles of Contreras and Churubusco." In 1850 he joined in Lopez' unsuccessful attempt to free Cuba and was wounded. It seems unlikely, however, that he had any part in Walker's filibustering expedition to Nicaragua. In 1852 he was one of the editors of the Louisville *Times*. In 1855–1856 he was in the U. S. Army again. From 1857 to 1860 he was editor of the Mobile *Register*. In November, 1860, regarding civil war as inevitable, he organized the Mobile Light Dragoons. He fought through the war but never received a command such as his military experience would seem to have justified. He was on the staff of Albert Sidney Johnston when that general fell at the Battle of Shiloh. He was later on the staff of General Breckinridge. After the war he was a cotton factor in Columbus, Georgia, but a fire quickly ruined his business. Until his death in 1867, he lived on a plantation near Guerry-ton, Alabama. In 1874 the Kentucky state legislature ordered his remains reinterred in the State Cemetery at Frankfort, where rest the Kentucky soldiers celebrated in his best-known poem. O'Hara is described as handsome and soldierly in appearance, witty, and accomplished. He was in demand as an orator and delivered enough addresses to fill a volume.

It would seem that some of O'Hara's poems are lost. Those on which his reputation rests are two in number. "The Old Pioneer" was probably written in September, 1845, when the remains of Daniel Boone were reinterred in the State Cemetery at Frankfort. The tone and meter are similar to those in his most famous poem, but the style is less mature.

"The Bivouac of the Dead" was occasioned by the reinterment in the State Cemetery of Kentucky soldiers killed at the Battle of Buena Vista, which took place on February 22 and 23, 1847. O'Hara may not have been in this battle, and he was certainly still in Mexico on July 20, 1847, when a great public funeral was held in Frankfort. There is no truth in the story that O'Hara, being asked the day before to read a poem written for the occasion, sat up all night in order to have his elegy ready. O'Hara returned to Frankfort in 1848. The poem was written to be read at the dedication of the monument (completed on June 25, 1850) erected in memory of all Kentucky soldiers killed in the various battles of the Mexican War. The earliest known text of the poem had twelve stanzas and it appeared in 1858 in the Mobile *Register,* then edited by the poet. Later versions printed during O'Hara's lifetime embody minor revisions. In 1875 George W. Ranck published a version with only nine stanzas which the poet's sister had found among his manuscripts. This she rightly took to be O'Hara's final version of the poem. In its revised form the poem is a distinctly better work of art, but there are still readers, especially in Kentucky, who prefer the poem in its earlier form. In revising the poem, O'Hara was apparently trying to eliminate local allusions and descriptive passages so that the elegy, now purely lyrical, might have a more universal application. He substituted "Sons of our consecrated ground" for the earlier "Sons of the Dark and Bloody Ground," much to the displeasure of some Kentucky readers. Perhaps O'Hara revised the poem so that it might be made applicable to soldiers killed in the Civil War. Stanzas from the poem are inscribed on many war memorials, particularly on monuments to the Confederate dead (there are no less than nine at Gettysburg), and it has often been included in anthologies of poems of the Civil War.

O'Hara's style, which is quite individual, owes something perhaps to Gray and Collins and even more to William E. Aytoun's *Lays of the Scottish Cavaliers.* Aytoun's book was not published until 1849, but some of his poems had appeared several years earlier in *Blackwood's Edinburgh Magazine.* Soldiers who served with O'Hara in Mexico remembered hearing him recite Aytoun's "Edinburgh after Flodden" and "The Burial March of Dundee." The opening and closing stanzas of "The Bivouac of the Dead" in O'Hara's final version are as follows:

> The muffled drum's sad roll has beat
>   The soldier's last tattoo;
> No more on life's parade shall meet
>   The brave and daring few.
> On Fame's eternal camping-ground
>   Their silent tents are spread,
> And Glory guards with solemn round
>   The bivouac of the dead.
>
> .   .   .   .   .
>
> Yon marble minstrel's voiceless stone
>   In deathless songs shall tell,
> When many a vanished age hath flown,
>   The story how ye fell;
> Nor wreck, nor change, or winter's blight
>   Nor Time's remorseless doom,
> Shall dim one ray of holy light
>   That gilds your glorious tomb.

46
Joseph Beckham Cobb

AMONG THE VERY few Southern planters who wrote anything that belongs properly in the field of literature, Joseph Beckham Cobb (1819–1858) is one of the most interesting. He was a member of a distinguished Georgia family, and he was the son of Senator Thomas W. Cobb. He was educated at Moses Waddel's academy at Willington, South Carolina, and the University of Georgia. In 1838 the wealthy planter was living in Noxubee County, Mississippi. In 1844 he removed to Columbus, where he wrote editorials for the Columbus Whig and looked after his large plantation, "Longwood," a few miles from town. He died at the age of thirty-nine leaving property valued at $177,000. Cobb apparently had some political ambition, but in a state that was preponderantly Democratic he failed of election to Congress although he served a term or two in the state senate.

Cobb contributed to the American Whig Review, which in February, 1851, printed an engraved portrait of him as frontispiece of Volume XIII. He published three books, of which only the last rises far above the general level. The Creole: A Story of the Siege of New Orleans (Philadelphia, 1850) makes it clear that Cobb lacked the gift for narrative which enabled George W. Cable a generation later to portray so memorably the life of the Creoles of Louisiana. Mississippi Scenes (Philadelphia, 1851) was dedicated to Augustus Baldwin Longstreet, who was a friend of the Cobb family. This collection of essays and sketches, however, is closer to Irving and the British essayists than to Southern humorous writing. The book showed some promise, but Cobb's talent lay in criticism and not in creative writing. In 1858, the year of his death, he published in New York Leisure Labors; or, Miscellanies Historical, Literary and Political, portions of which had already appeared in the American Whig Review. Of the seven essays in the book, one deals with the Georgia statesman, William H. Crawford; another with Thomas Jefferson; and two others with "Slavery and the Slave Trade in the District of Columbia" and "Union or Disunion." The eloquent conclusion of the last of these makes clear Cobb's view of the chief political issue of the 1850's:

In conclusion, fellow-citizens, I am unable to see any thing so ominous in the present aspect of our national affairs as will authorize us to go about banding and marshalling the States for a crusade against the action of the General Government—especially under the lead of such Hotspurs as I perceive to be at the head of the resistance forces. I am a Southerner by birth and education—a

Southerner in pride of land and in feeling—a Southerner in interest, and by every tie which can bind mortal man to his native clime; and I shall abide the destinies of the South. But I venerate the Federal Constitution. *I love the Union.* I love the first for its beneficent protecting influence and power; I love the last for its proud and glorious association with all that is dear to an American heart.

In the Abolitionist view the great planters were a small oligarchy who ruled the Southern masses with a rod of iron, and they were doing their best to break up the Union. Cobb, however, was typical of the wealthy Whig planters; they wanted no revolution. He saw clearly—as James Louis Petigru and William J. Grayson saw—that secession would leave the South powerless to preserve the very institution—slavery—which the secessionists sought to preserve by leaving the Union.

Cobb's sober estimate of Macaulay's extravagantly praised *History of England* shows his indifference to the popular estimate. He recognized Macaulay's real abilities, but he had little patience with his partisan bias and his fondness for the romantic and the sensational. But it is as a critic of two popular American writers—N. P. Willis and Longfellow—that Cobb is at his best. Intelligent Southerners had an intellectual background which should have enabled them to see better than other critics the defects of the popular American literature of the North, but most of them apparently accepted that literature—unless it came out of New England—at the value placed upon it by those who advertised or puffed it in Northern newspapers and magazines. Already in the 1850's, even in the South, the reading public was being made to feel that unless one read the new books, its taste was old-fashioned and crude. Today of course the situation is far worse than in 1858. Cobb singled out Willis and Longfellow as two extremely popular and extravagantly overrated American authors. The lack of an international copyright law, he pointed out, had played into the hands of American publishers, who lived by pirating the works of British writers and by puffing certain American poets and magazinists. Though he lived in remote Mississippi, Cobb saw as clearly as Poe in New York or Philadelphia how the system worked. "Nobody will doubt, we imagine," he writes, "but that Mr. Willis has acquired his poetical notoriety by means of a systematic and well-directed course of magazine and newspaper puffing; for no sane person, we are persuaded, can read his poetry, and trace the same to any merits he possesses in that line." Willis assumes that he is a great author and poses as one. Publishers and magazine editors "are justly answerable for the ascendency of that herd of venal pretenders to literary excellence, whose daily flip-flap from job presses not only discourage meritorious and independent competitors, but have created such disgust for home literature as to divert the interest of our truly tasteful and literary people across the waters, and to sicken them at the sight of an American work."

American poets, it seemed to Cobb, should make more of the American scene.

Our rhymers are full of every other kind of poetry save that which alone is open to them. They are eternally inditing silly verses about every-day silly things —are lavishing pretty words in the sickly attempt to retouch and embellish Scriptural incidents [a hit at Willis]—making sonnets about flowers, and cigar-girls, and pigeon-nests; or else, like Mr. Longfellow, are running a wild-goose chase to catch up insipid fragments of German or Swedish verse, for which the reading portion of their own countrymen care about as much as they care for a translation of Merlin, or a reprint of Henry the Eighth's Defence of the Roman Church. And yet these venal pretenders are called *poets*, have admiring coteries, assume a puny arrogance of air and manner, and, now and then, flaunt over to England, that, after begging a reluctant moiety of praise from one or two writers anxious to court American favor, they may prop their petty productions by exhibiting a transatlantic puff.

For Longfellow, Cobb had once some hope.

No one can doubt but that he is a man of practical sense, of very considerable talent, and of high and enviable attainments as a scholar; yet we see the strong evidences of nature's inconsistency in his condescension to father poems which might have *graced* the Dunciad, and which, for bad taste and tame composition, might stand comparison with the shallowest specimens of the American school.

No one but Poe and Margaret Fuller pointed out so clearly faults which are now obvious in Longfellow's poorest—and often most popular—poems. Cobb was not disturbed by the antislavery poems, and he found something to praise in "The Skeleton in Armor" and *The Spanish Student;* but he found "A Psalm of Life" "dull and commonplace, full of examples of bad taste and bad grammar." *Evangeline* seemed "Dull, stiff, and tiresome, more apt to induce a comfortable siesta than to excite admiration." These estimates Cobb frequently, somewhat in Poe's manner, defended by detailed criticism, especially in the case of Willis, of the poet's grammar and use of words. Cobb's own style is not especially felicitous, but his critical ability transcended that of all but a few Americans who set up as critics in the 1850's. One would like to have his estimate of Southern writers and the widespread demand for a distinctively Southern literature. There was room for deflation there, too.

47
Albert Pike

ALBERT PIKE (1809–1891), one of the strangest and most fascinating figures in the literature of the South, was born in Boston on December 29, 1809, the year which also witnessed the births of Poe, Holmes, and Lincoln. When he was four years old, his parents moved to Newburyport, where his father, a shoemaker, died eleven or twelve years later. Young Pike attended the public schools in Newburyport and an academy in Framingham. He had planned to complete his education at Harvard College. ". . . in August, 1825," he says, "I passed an examination and entered the freshman class at Harvard. To earn money for my board and tuition at college, it was neces-sary that I should teach, and at the same time pursue my studies. I did so for six months, that fall and winter, at Gloucester, and returned home and studied there, fitting myself to enter the junior class. But when I went to Harvard, in the fall of 1826, to enter that class, and had passed the examina-tion, I was informed that to enter that class, I must pay the tuition-fees for the two years, Freshman and Sophomore. I declined to do so, and after-ward educated myself, going through the junior and senior classes, while teaching." [77] Before leaving New England for the West in March, 1831, Pike taught at Gloucester, North Bedford, Newburyport, and Fairhaven, where, so he wrote to Griswold, he wrote most of his "Hymns to the Gods." The earlier ones first appeared in N. P. Willis's *American Monthly Maga-zine* in Boston.

It was from reading Coleridge that Pike discovered that he was a poet.

> this "annciente rime"
> Hath shown my powers to me—both [hath?] waked the tide
> Of poetry, which lay within my soul.
> Henceforth I know my fate. . . .

The reading of Coleridge had awakened in him, it seems, not only a love of poetry but also an interest in the supernatural, which afterwards made him a student of the Vedic hymns. Under the influence of Coleridge, Shelley, Keats, Byron, and Scott, he contributed numerous Romantic verses to the

[77] John Hallum, *Biographical and Pictorial History of Arkansas*, I (Albany, 1887), 216. Hallum, whose admiration for Pike was extravagant, rates him as "the ripest scholar America has yet given to the world" (I, 106), as "the greatest of American poets" and as "the Homer of America, the Zoroaster of modern Asia, a profound philosopher, a great jurist, a great philologist, a profound ethnologist, and a great statesman . . ." (I, 222).

lesser New England magazines. One of the earliest that Miss Susan B. Riley discovered is "The Maniac's Song to the Cloud," which was printed in the *Bower of Taste* for November 1, 1828, and which suggests the influence of Shelley. "The Ice-Ship," which John Neal printed in the *Yankee and Boston Literary Gazette* for February 19, 1829, occasioned an editorial note: "For *such* poetry we are always ready to make room. N." [78]

What Pike's literary career would have been had he remained in Massachusetts one can only conjecture. Perhaps he would not have given up his literary ambitions so easily as he did in Arkansas. Like many another New Englander, he had begun to look westward. He lost his position in a Newburyport school, he tells us, because he had demanded an assistant. He adds: "Ostensibly, they turned me out of the grammar school because I played the fiddle on Sunday." His daughter writes:

Although he never in later years referred to it with any expression of bitterness, he lived constantly in an atmosphere of restraint when a boy; for he was by heredity and by nature a thinker, a student and a poet; large-minded, highstrung, sensitive, chivalrous, munificent, communicative with those he loved, but reserved to strangers and uncongenial persons; ambitious and conscious of his powers, yet diffident and modest; easily depressed by unkind words and sneers, but steadfast in his determination to do something, to be a power in the world. Thrown with rigid Puritans, who had little toleration for sentiment, and scorned poetry and "flowery Talk," as they called everything imaginative and ideal, it is not to be wondered at that he longed to breathe a freer air, to lead a wider life than the purely materialistic one of wage-earning and eating and drinking, with no thought of greater things, no interchange of ideas, no aspirations towards intellectual development.

Pike's early poems suggest that he was in love with a wealthy girl to whom the penniless poet was too proud to propose marriage.

In March, 1831, Pike set out for the West. He had planned to go to Tennessee, but he did not care particularly where he went. By boat, by stage, and on foot he made his way to Albany, Buffalo, Cleveland, Cincinnati, and on south to Nashville. Finding no opening there, he went on to St. Louis, where he joined a trading expedition bound for Santa Fé under Charles Brent, later Governor of New Mexico. Before the party reached Taos in November, Pike had experienced such hardships as intense cold, hunger, and thirst. He worked for a time in a store in Santa Fé. He joined a trapping expedition and visited the Staked Plains. He found the plains country bar-

---

[78] "The Skeleton Hand," signed "P," in the same magazine (I, 72–73, Aug., 1829), has been attributed to Poe by J. A. Harrison and J. H. Whitty, but Pike seems to me probably the author.

ren and sometimes depressing but saw also much to admire in the scenery of the West, and he was interested in the Mexicans and Indians whom he saw. In old age he remembered this as one of the happiest periods in his life. Though he had no books with him, he was still writing poetry. In Boston in 1834 appeared the only book he ever formally published, *Prose Sketches and Poems. Written in the Western Country*. Pike was in fact a pioneer in the literary treatment of the Southwest, and the book contains some promising prose sketches of Indians and Mexicans and some poems which reflect the impression which the Southwest made upon a very Romantic young poet. When a New England reviewer complained that the book was in "too gloomy and melancholy a vein," Pike replied: "Part of that book I wrote in a foreign country, while traveling about alone, among men of a different language—part in the lodge of an Indian,—part in the solitude of the mountains; in the loneliness and danger of the desert; in hunger and watching, and cold and privation—part in the worse loneliness of a school-room,—all in poverty, trouble, and despair. It is easy to *imagine* a desolation of the heart: I *know* what it is."

Pike was in the Territory of Arkansas as early as December, 1832. For a time he split rails and worked on a farm. Then he taught school. In July, 1833, he was teaching his second school on Little Piney Creek in "a small log house, with a fire-place the width of one end—no floor—no boarding, or weather boarding—a hole for a window, and one for a door." He was paid half in cash and half in pigs. Robert Crittenden and Jesse Turner, finding that Pike was the author of poems appearing in the Little Rock *Arkansas Gazette*, went to see him, and they urged Crittenden's brother-in-law, Charles P. Bertrand, the owner of the newspaper, to employ Pike as assistant editor. This he did. Pike settled in Little Rock in October. In the fall of 1834 he married Mary Hamilton and with her help bought the *Advocate*. He became its editor in January, 1835. He published or republished in the *Advocate* much of his own prose and verse. Besides writing much of what the paper contained, he tells us: "I got the news, set the type, did the press work, and hustled for subscriptions." When after two years and a half he sold the newspaper, he found it impossible to collect money due him for subscriptions.

Meanwhile Judge Lacey of the Little Rock bench had offered to give him a license to practice law. When Pike replied that he knew no law, the judge remarked: "Well, you are not like a doctor. You cannot kill anybody through want of knowledge." While he was still with the *Advocate*, William Cummins, hoping perhaps that the newspaper might forward his political ambitions, offered to make Pike his law partner. Pike accepted and with his license in hand studied hard—for many years he slept only five or six hours out of the twenty-four and devoted many hours to study—and soon he was riding the circuit. He became in time a very successful lawyer. He built in Little Rock a fine house which ultimately became the residence of another Arkansas poet, John Gould Fletcher.[79] Arkansas was admitted to the Union in 1836, and Pike soon became one of the leading lawyers in the state capital. He never ran for office. If he had political ambitions, he remembered that he was a Whig in a Democratic state and that he was too sensitive to endure the mudslinging of a political campaign.

He had by this time lost much of his early desire for literary fame. Perhaps he was too easily discouraged, or possibly his poetic activity had been chiefly the emotional expression of a lonely and unhappy young man. Perhaps his wife, who is said to have preserved only one of the many poems he wrote to her, was not in sympathy with his writing. He had apparently come to the conclusion that poetry was a handicap to a young man who wished to get on. In "To the Planet Jupiter" he had written:

> Alas! to him,
> Whose eye and heart must soon or late grow dim,
> Toiling with poverty, or evils worse,
> This gift of poetry is but a curse,
> Unfitting it amid the world to brood,
> And toil and jostle for a livelihood.
> The feverish passion of the soul hath been
> My bane.

In 1854 when Pike reprinted in Nugae some of his poems in revised form for private distribution, he said in his Preface: "I am too conscious of their great defects not to know that they would be of no value or interest to any other person in the world [than a few friends and relatives]; and not to be aware that, if I were to publish them for sale, I should justly incur the wrath of all critics and reviewers, who might think that they were worthy of any notice at all. I am not rash enough to incur their just vengeance." In vain the editor of the Knickerbocker Magazine protested that such poems were too good not to be given to the world. Pike published some verse and prose in the Knickerbocker, but he had ceased to take himself very seriously as a poet. Even the encouragement of "Christopher North" (Professor John Wilson), who with flattering comments published the "Hymns to the Gods" in Blackwood's Magazine for June, 1839, did not induce the poet to give himself unreservedly to poetry. Pike, however, did not cease writing.

[79] See Fletcher's poem "The Ghosts of an Old House" in Goblins and Pagodas (1916) and in Preludes and Symphonies (1922).

One of his later poems, "To Isadore," later entitled "The Widowed Heart"—published in the *New Mirror* for October 14, 1843—probably had some influence on Poe's "The Raven." [80] Like Chivers and Poe, he often strove for musical effects. The most popular of his later poems, "Every Year," is somewhat in the didactic and sentimental vein of Longfellow. Pike also contributed some humorous "Anecdotes of the Arkansas Bar" to William T. Porter's *Spirit of the Times*. Among his prose contributions to the *Knickerbocker* is a series of essays in the Addisonian tradition entitled "The Walking Gentleman." "My purposes are," he announced, "to discuss, under the title which I have assumed, all subjects that may offer themselves to me, or be suggested; to lash the follies and faults of mankind; to apply the caustic of contempt to vice, and to hold up virtue for approval and imitation. Nor shall I be always grave and serious. I propose to relax at times into a laugh; to give here a satire and there an essay." "I am," he added, "neither poet nor philosopher, transcendentalist nor politician." One could hardly ask for a more typical statement of the purpose of the Addisonian essay. One passage suggests the intellectual loneliness in which Pike lived in Arkansas:

There but two things for which I, who live on the sunset side of the Mississippi, envy you, my beloved KNICKERBOCKER, and those others of taste and leisure who walk Broadway. These two are books and music. In the little out-of-the-way village where I vegetate, the arrival of a rare book is like the coming into port of a rich argosy to its owner. . . . Bacon, Shakespeare and Ben Jonson, Chaucer and Spenser, Beaumont and Fletcher, Froissart and Monstrelet, Massenger [sic], Ford, Middleton, and others of the glorious old demi-gods, in all the beauty of London type grace my shelves. Montaigne smiles philosophically on Rabelais. . . .

As Pike grew older, he cared less for the British Romantic poets, who had inspired his early poems, and much more for the writers of the sixteenth and seventeenth centuries. In 1852 he expressed a great fondness for Francis Bacon, Sir Thomas Browne, Owen Felltham, and the Elizabethan dramatists.

To resume the story of Pike's life. When the Mexican War broke out, he raised a company of militia and served with some distinction under Zachary Taylor. He afterwards fought a bloodless duel with Colonel John

---

[80] Entitled "Isadore," the poem had already appeared in the *Magnolia*, II, 109 (Feb., 1843). In a letter printed in [John Tomlin], "The Autobiography of a Monomaniac," *Holden's Dollar Mag.*, II, 719 (Dec., 1848), Pike states that the grief expressed in the poem had no basis in fact—except a fear that his wife might die. In the same letter Pike stated that his best poem was "Ariel."

For the possible influence on "The Raven," see R. S. Forsythe, "Poe's 'Nevermore': A Note," *Am. Lit.*, VII, 447–448 (Jan., 1936).

Roane, who took offense at Pike's criticism of his regiment. On April 20, 1855, he wrote to his friend John F. Coyle that he was going to New Orleans. He continued:

I am weary of Arkansas—weary and worn out, and must get out into the world, *somewhere*. It is nothing to me that I am in a Minority here; because I have no tendency towards office; but I am sick of the constant squabbling and snarling that goes on around me, and of the antediluvian notions of Boobydom. The government of the State is in the fullest sense of the word a Booby-ocracy, and itself lies supine like a lean sow in the gutter, "with meditative grunts of much content," waiting for the good time to come when railroads, school houses and other public improvements will build themselves, and nobody have it to pay for. That's their idea of the Millenium [*sic*].

He moved to New Orleans, but after three years he returned to Little Rock. The New Orleans courts met at an inconvenient time for Pike, who had each year to go to Washington to look after the interests of the Choctaw Indians.

The increasing hostility between South and North proved a great trial to Pike, who had written of himself in "Taos" as one "Who has been, is, will ever be, New England's son." In 1856 he made an appeal in a pamphlet entitled *Letters to the People of the Northern States*, which is one of the best statements of the moderate Southern point of view. Thoroughly aware of the economic rivalry between North and South, Pike notes that the North has now won economic control of the Northwest. While admitting that slavery had its abuses (Pike's only slaves were house servants), he maintains that Southerners are no less humane and are quite as intelligent as Northerners. Slavery, he admits, is an evil "as great cities are an evil; as the concentration of capital in a few hands, oppressing labor is an evil"; but freeing the slaves will not remedy the situation altogether. The evils of slavery "are the same evils that environ pauperism, ignorance, a low grade of intellect, and an over-crowded population, everywhere." With real eloquence he states his own difficult position:

I speak for the interest that I and my children have in this mighty question. *They* are natives of the South, but *my* heart-allegiance is divided. Born almost in the shadow of Faneuil Hall; educated in the free-schools of Massachusetts loving still her clear brooks and green hills, that when a boy I loved so well; claiming, as a part of my inheritance as an American, an interest in the glories and the soil of all the revolutionary battle-fields of New England; owing all that I am, and all that I and my children ever shall be, to the institutions and influences of the Union, under whose flag I have fought, and its honor aided to defend; long denounced in the South for approving the compromise of 1850, and almost odious there, as an extreme Union-man, in times when those who loved popularity were not eager to be so classed; and my heart clinging alike to the North and the South—to the soil with which the ashes of my father, my brother, and my sisters have mingled, and to the land to whose bosom I have committed the dead bodies of my children; how can I look upon the strife, the antipathies, the bitterness, and the hatred, ominous of disaster, of the North, and the South, without the profoundest sorrow and the gloomiest apprehension.

After the secession of South Carolina late in 1860, Pike saw clearly that Arkansas must choose the side upon which it would fight; and he ably advocated secession on constitutional grounds in another pamphlet, *State or Province? Bond or Free?* A recent speech in the United States Senate by Charles Sumner led him to write:

A person who speaks for Massachusetts in the Senate has lately arraigned the Southern States as "the Barbary States of the Union,' before the bar of the world, and impeached the courage, the honor, and the decency of all their people, in stilted Ciceronian sentences, steeped with gall and bitterness, and reeking with malignant falsehood. No one should have replied a word. And when his State formally, and with the intention of branding the insult in upon the South, endorsed his harangue and made it her own, either *her* Senators should have been expelled, or those of all the Southern States, ought, in strict justice to their constituents, to have withdrawn from that desecrated and dishonored chamber.[81]

The "malignant falsehoods" of Sumner and his kind explain in part why so many adopted Southerners like Pike went with the states in which they lived. He wrote for the tune of "Dixie" a lyric beginning: "Southrons, hear your country call you!" which in literary quality surpasses Dan Emmett's better known verses. Robert Toombs, the Confederate Secretary of State, commissioned Pike to negotiate a treaty with the Southern Indians. When General Van Dorn, in violation of the terms of the treaty, incorporated the Indian soldiers under Pike's command in the Confederate army, Pike protested to President Davis. He was overruled and had to resign his commission as brigadier general. For a time he camped out on the Red River, but later in the war he served on the Arkansas Supreme Court. After Appomattox he lost most of his property by confiscation but managed to save his library. In fear of being charged with inciting the Indians to revolt against the national government, he spent a short time in Canada. In a letter from Washington, December 4, 1888, Pike wrote to Fanny M. Scott:

[81] P. 29. Copy in the Library of Congress. Sumner's speech, "The Barbarism of Slavery," was delivered in the Senate on June 4, 1860.

My property in Little Rock was confiscated and the United States has in its Treasury nearly $2,000 of the money paid for it. I have accepted nothing of the government but permission to go home, when I was in Canada. I was indicted for treason, and dared them to bring me to trial, and refused to agree to pay the cost, when they offered to dismiss the case, if I would do that. I have had nothing to ask the government for, since the war, and it is welcome to the poor pittance of $8 a month that [they] offered to give me as a soldier of the Mexican war. I live in this Country, just as I should in France, obeying the laws, claiming no rights as a citizen, and looking on its political squabbles without feeling the slightest interest in them. I am an old Whig, and neither Democrat nor Republican. Above all, Fanny, I am a Mason, and as such a citizen of the world; and I am an old man, now become indifferent to most things.

In 1866, when he left Canada, Pike went to Memphis, where he practiced law with General Charles W. Adams and wrote for the Memphis *Appeal*. In 1868 or 1869 he settled in Washington, where he spent the remainder of his life. He worked on the Washington *Patriot* until 1870, and eight or nine years later gave up his law practice to devote himself to Masonic work and to a study of the sacred writings of the East.

Pike had joined the Masons in 1850 and had risen rapidly; as early as 1859 he became Sovereign Grand Commander of the Supreme Council for the Southern Jurisdiction. By 1880 he was the foremost Scottish Rite Mason in the world. Among the Masons the fact that Pike had been a Confederate soldier seemed not to matter. When some time after the war Robert Toombs urged him to stand for the Senate, Pike replied that he could accomplish more for the good of humanity and for his personal satisfaction through his work as a Mason. He was now content to pour his poetic gifts and his scholarship into purely Masonic writings. Besides composing forms for special ceremonies and making many speeches, he rewrote the Scottish Rite ritual from the fourth degree through the thirty-third. Only Scottish Rite Masons of course are in position to judge the literary qualities of their ritual; obviously it has deeply impressed them. Since his death they have brought out a bibliography of his works and printed a considerable portion of the manuscripts which he left behind him. In his honor they have set aside in their temple in Washington a memorial room filled with portraits, books, manuscripts, and mementoes; and they have erected a statue in the city. "When I am dead," Pike once wrote, "I wish my monument to be builded only in the hearts and memories of my brethren of the Ancient and Accepted Scottish Rite." [82]

[82] *Gen. Albert Pike's Poems*, p. 3. In his unpublished essay, "Of My Books and Studies" Pike wrote: "I have written for an Order, that extends over the world. In its

In his old age Pike's chief literary enthusiasm was for the Vedic hymns; these, too, were hymns to the gods. His *Lectures of the Arya*, which the Scottish Rite Supreme Council published in 1873, represent the fruits of a study which he had undertaken with no notion of delivering lectures on the subject. "Nothing in the field of study," he said, "has ever so much interested me, as this endeavor to penetrate into the adyta of the ancient Aryan thought, to discover what things, orbs, principles or phenomena, or potencies of Nature our remote ancestors worshipped as Gods; and what their Deities really *were*, in the conception of the composers of the Vedic hymns." The subject fascinated him as it hardly fascinated even the New England Transcendentalists. The self-taught scholar apologized for his lack of the thorough scholarship which would entitle him to speak with assurance about the meaning of doubtful passages, but his poetic insight and his indefatigable industry to a certain extent compensated for his lack of scholarship in the field. The lectures are an excellent introduction to the subject.

The great bulk of Pike's poems were written when as a young man he was fascinated by Coleridge, Byron, Shelley, and Keats.[83] It was their poems that he reprinted in the *Arkansas Advocate* and imitated in his own verses. Coleridge supplied the original impulse, but the influence of Shelley and Byron was stronger. In a poem entitled "Shelley" he rated these two as the best of the modern poets. The influence of Shelley is obvious in the long poem "Ariel," which he considered his best poem. So much was Pike under the spell of the Romantic poets that he continued to echo them while traveling in the West with no books accessible to him. No wonder that he never quite managed to find his own individual idiom.

The best of his early work is his "Hymns to the Gods." The first two— the hymns to Neptune and Juno—are said to have been written in 1828 when he was only nineteen. Others were composed in 1829 and 1830, but the hymns to Mars, Minerva, and Flora are said not to have been written until 1845. Coleridge aroused in Pike a fondness for the supernatural, but it was presumably Byron, Shelley, and Keats that stimulated his interest in Greek mythology. Keats's *Endymion* perhaps supplied the immediate stimulus that led to the writing of the hymns. On August 15, 1838, Pike sent

Rituals, Lectures and various offices, I have endeavoured to 'stir up' the Brethren now living, 'and those that may follow us, to an earnest endeavour of noble actions' and the practice of morality and virtue, the faithful performance of life's duties, the faithful observance every where, in the market and the forum, at home and among men, of the laws of Truth, Justice, Right and Toleration."

[83] The poets celebrated in Pike's "The Progress of Poetry" (*Am. Monthly Mag.*, I, 644, Dec., 1829; II, 603, Dec., 1830) are Byron, Scott, Coleridge, Shelley, Keats, Wordsworth, Moore, Campbell, Southey, and Crabbe.

a group of the hymns to *Blackwood's Edinburgh Magazine* with a letter which read in part: "I would fain believe them worthy a place in your inestimable Maga, which regularly reaches me *here*, two thousand miles from New York. . . ." The hymns were published in *Blackwood's* the following June with the following introductory note: "These fine hymns, which entitle their author to take his place in the highest order of his country's poets, reached us only a week or two ago—though Mr Pike's most gratifying letter is dated so far back as last August: and we mention this, that he may not suppose such compositions could have lain unhonoured in our repositories from autumn to spring. . . ." [84] "Christopher North" was overenthusiastic in his praise, but unless he had seen some of Bryant's poems, he is not likely to have seen better verses by an American poet. Bombastic and verbose though the hymns may seem to the modern reader, they have some beautiful images and a sonorous rhythm not unpleasing to ears that can tolerate the union of poetry and eloquence. "To Neptune" begins:

> God of the mighty deep! wherever now
> The waves beneath thy brazen axle bow—
> Whether thy strong proud steeds, wind-wing'd and wild,
> Trample the storm-vex'd waters round them piled,
> Swift as the lightning-flashes, that reveal
> The quick gyrations of each brazen wheel;
> While round and under thee, with hideous roar,
> The broad Atlantic, with thy scourging sore,
> Thundering, like antique Chaos in his spasms,
> In heaving mountains, and deep-yawning chasms,
> Fluctuates endlessly; while through the gloom
> Their glossy sides and thick manes fleck'd with foam,
> Career thy steeds, neighing with frantic glee
> In fierce response to the tumultuous sea—
> Whether thy coursers now career below,
> Where, amid storm-wrecks, hoary sea-plants grow
> Broad-leaved, and fanning with a ceaseless motion
> The pale cold tenants of the abysmal ocean—
> Oh, come! our altars waiting for thee stand,
> Smoking with incense on the level strand!

The later poems are written in a simpler style, but in them, too, there is ample evidence of Pike's striving after verbal melody. "The Widowed Heart" may well have suggested to Poe the metrical form and the refrain of "The

---

[84] *Blackwood's*, XLV, 830 (June, 1839). Pike's "To the Mockingbird" appeared in the same magazine, XLVII, 354 (March, 1840). Some of the "Hymns to the Gods" were reprinted in the *Knickerbocker* in 1850 (Vols. XXXV and XXXVI).

Raven," although many other influences went into the creation of that musical and melancholy poem. I quote the first and last stanzas:

> Thou art lost to me forever!—I have lost thee, Isadore!
> Thy head will never rest upon my loyal bosom more;
> Thy tender eyes will never more look fondly into mine,
> Nor thine arms around me lovingly and trustingly entwine,—
> Thou art lost to me forever, Isadore!

> . . . .

> Thou art gone from me forever;—I have lost thee, Isadore!
> And desolate and lonely I shall be forever more:
> Our children hold me, Darling, or I to God should pray
> To let me cast the burthen of this long, dark life away,
> And see thy face in Heaven, Isadore!

48
Charles Gayarré

In the first half of the nineteenth century history was still—as it had been since the time of Herodotus—a branch of literature and not the "science" that some men wished to make of it. The writing of history has come to be, for both better and worse, almost a monopoly of university professors, at least in the United States. The books written by university scholars show a great advance in accuracy and thoroughness, but too often also a marked decline in literary quality.

Until after the mid-nineteenth century, most historical works were written by educated men who had wealth or leisure. Such were Robert Beverley in the eighteenth century and in the nineteenth, Prescott, Motley, Parkman, and Gayarré. The earlier historians were not cloistered scholars but men who played their part in the public life of their times. Irving, Motley, and Bancroft held important diplomatic appointments. These men, moreover, did not limit their writing to history. Irving was better known for his essays and stories than for his historical writings. Parkman and Motley each published a novel, and Prescott wrote lengthy essays upon Cervantes, Scott, and Charles Brockden Brown.

Charles Étienne Arthur Gayarré (1805–1895), the best of the early Southern historians, resembles these writers in more ways than one. He was an educated and traveled planter-lawyer of independent means who held important offices in the state and nation and who also tried his hand at the novel and the drama. Except for his interesting character study, *Philip II of Spain* (1866),[85] he limited his historical writing to Louisiana.

Few of the Southern writers of this period were men of distinguished families. Gayarré, however, could boast of descent from ancestors as eminent as any that came to Louisiana. His great-grandfather, Don Esteban Gayarré, who came to Louisiana in 1766 to take over the colony for the Spanish crown, was a younger son of a family in Navarre which had been ennobled in the ninth century. His mother was the daughter of Étienne de Boré, who as the discoverer of a process for granulating sugar became a sort of patron saint of Louisiana. Étienne de Boré belonged to a Norman family which had been raised to the nobility in the sixteenth century, and before he came to Louisiana in 1772 he had served as a *mousquetaire* under Louis XV. Gayarré was naturally proud of his inheritance, but he was neither a snob nor an insulated Creole. He is one of the most attractive figures in our literary history. Grace King describes him in old age as "an impressive figure, very tall," "majestic, in his high satin stock that held his head inflexibly erect." "His face was of great intellectual beauty, with high forehead, clear blue eyes, slightly thinning dark hair, a mouth of slightly ironic lips. It was the portrait of an aristocrat and littérateur."

Gayarré spent his boyhood on Boré's plantation, which he was to describe in "A Louisiana Sugar Plantation of the Old Régime," published in *Harper's Magazine* in March, 1887. As a boy he listened to the guns during the Battle of New Orleans and at eleven o'clock at night heard the cry of a galloping horseman shouting "Victory!" After the battle General Jackson is said to have visited the Boré plantation and to have patted the young Gayarré on the head. Gayarré was educated at the Collège d'Orléans, which he was later to describe in his novel, *Fernando de Lemos* (1872). In 1826–1829 he was studying law in Philadelphia. In 1830 he published his *Essai historique sur la Louisiane.* This was for the most part only a translation of Judge François Xavier's history, which Gayarré wished to make available to Creoles who could not read English.

Meanwhile Gayarré had been elected to the state legislature at the age of twenty-four. There he successfully fought a proposal to expel from the state

[85] Paul Hamilton Hayne complained that Gayarré's New York publisher, W. J. Widdleton, without consulting the author, omitted a passage in this book in which Gayarré had called attention to the marked resemblance between Philip's proclamation against the Moors of Granada and Lincoln's proclamation against the Southern rebels. Hayne commented: "A beautiful example of that boasted reverence for liberty of thinking and writing, which is being continually enunciated in certain hyperborean regions!" (*Southern Bivouac*, N.S. II, 111 n., July, 1886).

all free persons of color. In 1832 he was appointed attorney-general and a year later he became presiding judge of the New Orleans city court. In 1835, when he had just reached the constitutional age of thirty, he was elected to a six-year term in the United States Senate. To his bitter disappointment ill health compelled him to resign the position. He had bronchial asthma, and his physician advised him to go abroad. In Paris he regained his health and met many interesting people, including King Louis Philippe, who during his period of exile had visited Gayarré's grandfather Boré. The King said to Gayarré: "I do not wish to be a prophet of evil, but you [Americans], as a people, have conflicting interests and ambitions and unappeasable jealousies. You have the Puritans in the North and the Cavaliers in the South, Democracy with its leveling rod, and Aristocracy with slavery raising its haughty head in the other section and creating a social elegance, a superiority of breeding, and race, which must incite the intense hatred of your antagonists. Hence, deadly conflicts, political convulsions and social transformations."

During his eight years in France Gayarré's interest in history revived, and he collected important documents. Many of these found a place in his two-volume *Histoire de la Louisiane* (1846–1847), which covered the period 1492–1770. Both the documents and Gayarré's editorial comments appeared in French. It seemed to him fitting that the story should be told in the language of those who had played so notable a role in colonial history.

Meanwhile in 1846 Gayarré had become the Louisiana Secretary of State, a post he was to hold for seven years. In 1847 he persuaded the state legislature to appropriate two thousand dollars to be used in copying from the Spanish archives documents relating to Louisiana. The Spanish authorities were slow to facilitate the work until Gayarré on a visit to Spain called upon the Minister of Foreign Affairs, who greeted him as a kinsman of one of the first families in Spain and promised him every assistance in his researches.

In 1853 Gayarré was an unsuccessful independent candidate for the U. S. House of Representatives. Believing that he had been fraudulently cheated of election, he relieved his feelings by writing *The School for Politics: A Novel* (1854), of which there were three American editions and one in France. Gayarré was too close to the election to see it objectively; and although he stated that all the characters were fictitious, readers identified Dunder Blunder Beckendorf with Pierre Soulé and Randolph with Dunbar, the victorious candidate in the election. Gayarré had even less talent for fiction than John Hay or Henry Adams, who were each to write a political novel some thirty years later. Gayarré's reaction to politicians and political conditions was like that of John Pendleton Kennedy, who noted in the fifties that there were few gentlemen in important political positions. Through the character of Lovedale, Gayarré explained the methods by which demagogues got themselves elected to office:

. . . shake hands with every low fellow you meet—the dirtier the better; dress shabbily—affect vulgarity—learn to swear as big and as loud as possible—tap every man affectionately on the shoulder—get drunk once a week—conspicuously, mind you—in some well known tippling establishment—become a member of every one of those associations which spring up daily in New Orleans—spout against tyrants, aristocrats, and the rich—above all, talk eternally of the poor oppressed people and of their rights—drop entirely the garb, manners, and the feelings of a gentleman—and you may have the chance of a triumphant election. . . .

Perhaps Gayarré's last historical work seemed to him to represent a rather dull and arid type of scholarship. At any rate, when he prepared the series of lectures which he published in *Romance of the History of Louisiana* (1848) and three later volumes, he swung to the opposite extreme. Gayarré had read Irving, Cooper, and Simms and doubtless also the French historians and romancers, but the dominant influence here would seem to be that of Sir Walter Scott. The Waverley romances had a powerful influence upon the writing of history in this country and in England. Scott, as Macaulay pointed out in his essay on history, had shown the historians how by using methods and materials which they had neglected it was possible to bring to life men and women whose way of life had been forgotten. Scott's success had also shown that there were many persons with an interest in the past whom the historians had failed to reach. The influence of Scott is seen in the histories and historical romances of most English, American, and French writers of the early nineteenth century. In the Preface to his new book Gayarré wrote:

The number of those who have read Tacitus, Hume, Gibbon, or Clarendon, is comparatively small, when opposed to those who have pored with delight over the fascinating pages of Walter Scott. To relate events, and, instead of elucidating and analyzing their philosophy, like the historian, to point out the hidden sources of romance which spring from them—to show what materials they contain for the dramatist, the novelist, the poet, the painter, and for all the varied conceptions of the fine arts—is perhaps an humbler task, but not without its utility. . . . Through the immortal writings of Walter Scott, many have become familiar with historical events, and have been induced to study more serious works, who, without that tempting bait, would have turned away from what appeared to them to be but a dry and barren field, too unpromising to invite examination, much less cultivation. To the bewitching pen of the wonderful magician of her romantic hills, Scotland owes more for the popular extension of her fame, than to the doings of the united host of all her other writers, warriors, and statesmen.

Of Gayarré's lectures one might say what Nathaniel Hawthorne said of Simms's lectures, in *Views and Reviews*, on "American History, as Suited to the Purposes of Art":

. . . they abound in brilliant paragraphs, and appear to bring out, as by a skilfully applied varnish, all the lights and shades that lie upon the surface of our history; but yet, we cannot help feeling that the real treasures of his subject have escaped the author's notice. The themes suggested by him, viewed as he views them, would produce nothing but historical novels, cast in the same worn out mould that has been in use these thirty years, and which it is time to break up and fling away.[86]

In 1851 Gayarré set himself to work seriously at the task of writing the history of Louisiana. He now wrote in English because he had discovered that thus he could reach a much wider circle of readers. His *History of Louisiana: The French Domination* (2 vols., 1854) covered the period to 1769, and its sequel, *History of Louisiana: The Spanish Domination* (1854), brought the story down to 1803. His *History of Louisiana: The American Domination* (1866) covered the years 1803–1816; a supplemental chapter in the form of annals sketched the period 1816–1861. In the Preface to his third series of lectures, *Louisiana: Its History as a French Colony* (1852), Gayarré had written:

The four lectures which I delivered on the "Poetry or Romance of the History of Louisiana," and which are reproduced in the preceding volume as an introduction to a composition of a more grave nature, I looked upon at the time as *nugae seriae*, to which I attached no more importance, than a child does to the soap bubbles which he puffs through the tube of a tiny reed, picked up by him for the amusement of the passing hour. But struck with the interest which I had excited, I examined with more sober thoughts the flowery field in which I had sported, almost with the buoyancy of a school-boy. Checking the freaks of my imagination, that boon companion with whom I had been gamboling, I took to the plough, broke the ground, and turned myself to a more serious and useful occupation.

Gayarré once calculated that he had spent at least thirty thousand dollars upon his history of Louisiana. It brought him, however, the high compliment

[86] Randall Stewart (ed.), "Hawthorne's Contributions to *The Salem Advertiser*," *Am. Lit.*, V, 331 (Jan., 1934). Much the same verdict might be passed upon A. B. Meek's *Romantic Passages in Southwestern History* (1857), which is probably indebted to both Simms and Gayarré.

which George Bancroft bestowed upon him when he called it "an authentic history such as scarce any other [state] in the Union possesses." Certainly none of the other Southern historians of his time produced a history which equals Gayarré's in thoroughness, skilful interpretation, or in artistic presentation.

Gayarré's novels, *Fernando de Lemos: Truth and Fiction* (1872) and *Aubert Dubayet, or The Two Sister Republics* (1882), are of no great importance except for the light they throw upon their author. Even the friendly Hayne could find little to praise in the earlier novel, but he greatly overrated the second, which is a historical novel of the American and French Revolutions.

On the eve of the Civil War Gayarré was planning to leave Louisiana and live in Spain, where he expected to work in the Spanish archives. He had property valued at four hundred thousand dollars, and his wife had brought him another hundred thousand. He had already converted the bulk of their properties into cash when the threat of war caused him to feel that he was abandoning his state at a critical time. He remained in Louisiana and invested most of his money in Confederate bonds and currency. As a matter of honor both Gayarré and his wife in 1863 refused to take the oath of allegiance during the notorious General Ben Butler's occupation of New Orleans—even though taking the oath was the only way to escape poverty. They lived mainly by the sale of furniture, plate, and family portraits. Gayarré managed to earn a little money by writing and by lecturing; once at least he had to borrow money to buy the clothes in which he appeared on the lecture platform. Edward C. Wharton used to bring along a couple of loaves of bread when he came to see Gayarré, who would say: "I thank you, sir, but I can never eat charity bread." Wharton's invariable answer was: "Well, you may be a very great writer, but as a man you're a very great fool; and even if you want to starve yourself, you've got no right to refuse to let your wife eat."

Gayarré had played a prominent role in political affairs before the war, but he was no favorite with the leaders of the Democratic party in later years. In 1873 he ran once more for Congress and vigorously attacked the carpetbag regime, but he lost the election. From 1873 to 1876 he was reporter to the state supreme court. In 1886 Paul Hamilton Hayne, writing an article on Gayarré for the *Southern Bivouac*, wrote to the old statesman: "I am going to give your Louisianians 'particular hell' because of their conduct towards you." Gayarré replied: "My dear friend, don't be too hard on our poor Louisianians. They *mean* well, I believe, but as to *action*, they know no better than what they do." Even the Democratic administration of

Grover Cleveland turned down Gayarré's application for a naval office in New Orleans. He had hoped for an appointment as a man of letters rather than as a politician. He wrote to Hayne: "I belong to no ring, to no association of any kind; I am not a professional patriot, I do not steal, drink whiskey, chew tobacco, stuff ballot boxes, nor command the votes of a thousand bog trotters. What chance have I to get one single drop of the national cocoanut milk? Better buy a Lottery Ticket. Washington nowadays could not be elected or appointed, if alive, turnkey to jailbirds." All this of course was long before the spectacular rise to power of Huey Long, but even before the Civil War there had been a marked decline in the quality of men elected to office in the South. Aristocrats of the caliber of Gayarré or the Revolutionary statesmen of Virginia were not the kind of men whom the enlarged electorate chose to send to either the state or the national capitals.

Beginning in 1876, when he lost his reporter's job, Gayarré wrote many articles for magazines and newspapers. By this time Northern magazines were becoming hospitable once more to writers from the South. In November and December, 1877, the *North American Review* published "The Southern Question," in which Gayarré gave a forceful statement of the Southern view of Reconstruction. Of his three articles in *Harper's Magazine* the best is "A Louisiana Sugar Plantation of the Old Régime." Gayarré, though he needed the money, did not relish writing for pay. He wrote to Mrs. Hayne on July 1, 1885: "I do not know of a more miserable condition than that of being compelled to think and write for bread. It is a prostitution of the intellect of man—a profanation of the soul—the enslavement of all our faculties. . . . Write to please the taste of King Multitude, and therefore dip the pen in black and fetid liquid of the street sewer—that inkstand of the Devil!"

The notable correspondence between Gayarré and Hayne, who never saw one another, was occasioned by an article which the former had published in reply to George W. Cable's "The Freedman's Case in Equity," one of a series to be republished in *The Silent South* (1885). Both men resented Cable's attitude toward the South and particularly his "Abolitionist" views of the Negro problem. In addition, Gayarré as a Creole resented the treatment of his race in Cable's stories. He wrote to Hayne:

This Cable, although accidentally born in Louisiana, is a true Yankee, who publicly wrote to Mrs. Beecher Stowe that it was only in the North that he felt at home. This sneak, miserable in the utmost degree as a writer, is a most acute man of business who excels in the art of advertising himself. . . . He is a literary jobber, and he trades, as an author, after the fashion of the quack who puffs his "Jacob's Oil" or his "Brown's Iron Bitters" in every newspaper by drawing largely on what Bismarck calls the "reptile fund." . . . Cable, as a writer, is indubitably a prodigious humbug, a phenomenal fraud, but as a dollar scraper, as the chaser of the very shadow of a shilling round every corner, he is a genius. In the pursuit of a dime the gates of Hell could not prevail against him. I do not believe that I do injustice to the insect.

Gayarré, who had read of Cable's books only *The Grandissimes,* was of course unjust to Cable; and so was Hayne, who had apparently read none of them. They belonged to an older generation, and while they wanted friendly relations with the North, they were both largely "unreconstructed" in their political views. In the North Cable and not Gayarré was now the recognized authority on Louisiana. It was Cable who was asked to write the article on New Orleans for a new edition of the *Encyclopaedia Britannica.* Cable had also published the semihistorical work, *The Creoles of Louisiana* (1884). For Gayarré it was too much that this *parvenu* writer of fiction should pose as the historian of Louisiana. He had refused Cable's request that he review *The Grandissimes* (1880) because the novelist could not name two Creole families with whom he was intimately acquainted. In a lecture, *The Creoles of History and the Creoles of Romance* (1885), Gayarré forcefully presented the Creoles' case against Cable. The novelist had falsified history when he suggested that some of the great Creole families were descended from immigrant harlots. Cable had represented his Creole characters as speaking not the excellent French they really spoke but "the broken English of the negroes of Virginia, the Carolinas, Georgia, etc." Cable's crowning insult, however, was his repeated insinuation that there was an infusion of Negro blood in the best Creole families. No wonder that, as Edward Larocque Tinker puts it, "The Creoles considered Cable more loathsome than a Carpetbagger; called him a renegade scalawag; and when they mentioned his name they spat." Henry W. Grady, who replied to Cable in the *Century,* which had printed Cable's article, could admit shortcomings in the South's handling of its problems; but Gayarré and Hayne were among the scattered few that could never be fully reconciled to the new regime. Gayarré outlived his friend, who was a quarter of a century his junior, and died in 1895 in his ninety-first year. During his last years his chief support had come from a group of Louisiana women, headed by the mother of Grace King, for whom he was always the greatest of the writers of Louisiana.

49
The Humorists

THE OLD SOUTHWEST, as we have seen, had its poets, its novelists, its historians, and its literary magazines. Its most distinctive literary achievement, however, is to be found not in such books as A. B. Meek's *Songs and Poems of the South* or in such magazines as the *Southron,* but in the sketches of humorists like Longstreet and Hooper. The unpretentious humorous pieces which were published in newspapers, almanacs, and in the sportsman's magazine, Porter's *Spirit of the Times,* come nearer to being a regional literature than the more "literary" pieces which were being printed in magazines busily promoting a literature of the South. In the 1850's, however, the magazine editors admitted to their pages the sketches of Longstreet, Baldwin, and Bagby. In 1860 Bagby became editor of the *Southern Literary Messenger.* The humorists revealed an aspect of Southern society which had been largely overlooked since William Byrd had satirized the motley population of the North Carolina border in the early eighteenth century. Literature had been written too largely for and about gentle folk. Caruthers introduced the Crockett-like Montgomery Damon into *The Kentuckian in New-York,* but his primary interest was in the cocked-hat gentry of Colonial Virginia.

Before the Southwestern states settled into something like the prevailing Southern pattern, social distinctions such as obtained in Virginia and the Carolinas hardly existed. The froth and dregs of society were much more conspicuous than the solid, unpretending farmers of the better sort. In the topsy-turvy life of the frontier the ignorant and the incompetent thought themselves as good as anybody else. The frontiersman was often a jack at all trades. In the border country where no one knew or cared much about a man's past it was easy for a quack to set up as a physician or for a peddler to turn preacher or merchant. There was on the surface an excess of vulgarity, pretension, and humbuggery; there were fools in plenty and sharpers and rascals to fleece them. Even after the true frontiersmen had gone further west, there remained in the Southwest a rare and unexploited field for the humorist with an eye for character and a gift for telling a story. In the Southwest there were incomparable materials for a "folk literature," which were eventually to find their most memorable embodiment in Mark Twain's *Huckleberry Finn.* The humorists were, as Henry Watterson put it in *Oddities in Southern Life and Character* (1882), chroniclers of "the nether side of Southern life:" They pictured the good old times of muster days and quarter-racing, before the camp-meeting and the barbecue had lost their power and their charm; when men led simple, homely lives, doing their love-making and their law-making as they did their fighting and their plowing, in a straight furrow; when there was no national debt multiplying the dangers and magnifying the expenses of distillation in the hills and hollows, and pouring in upon the log-rolling, the quilting, the corn-shucking, and the fish-fry an inquisitorial crew of tax-gatherers and detectives to spoil the sport and dull the edge of patriotic husbandry.

The writers who exploited these abundant materials were not backwoods-men nor were they historical romancers or women writers of sentimental fiction. They were generally young fortune-seekers from the older states, and a large proportion of them either came from the Northern states or had been educated in the North. These young journalists, sportsmen, doctors, soldiers, planters, and lawyers were moved to mirth and not to tears by what they saw. They were seldom ambitious of literary distinction, and many of them wished to remain anonymous; but they were not uneducated men, and many of them knew their Shakespeare, their Cervantes, and their Addison and Irving. They wrote primarily to share with their own kind the humor of the backwoods.

As the frontier receded, the humorists found within the Southwest itself an audience which relished what had now become a literary tradition. Many a Southern newspaper had its own humorous writer, and all of them re-printed freely from other newspapers. The humorous sketches of Northern and Western writers were copied in many a Southern daily or weekly. American humor is not of course limited to the South. One of the pioneers in the field was Seba Smith from Maine, who began publishing his letters from "Major Jack Downing" as early as 1830. His letters and the nearly con-temporary *Georgia Scenes* of Augustus Baldwin Longstreet are among the earliest and most influential of all the humorous sketches.

The man who did most to promote the work of the Southern humorists was a Yankee from Vermont, William Trotter Porter (1809–1858). After his graduation from Dartmouth College, he taught for five years in Virginia and Georgia, and he more than once revisited the South, chiefly in connec-tion with sporting events. Many of the best humorous sketches of the South appeared first in his *Spirit of the Times*. He compiled two excellent collec-tions: *The Big Bear of Arkansas* (1845) and *A Quarter Race in Kentucky* (1846). In his preface to the earlier collection Porter announced:

A new vein of literature, as original as it is inexhaustible in its source, has been opened in this country within a very few years, with the most marked success. Up to the period when the publication of the first American "Sporting

Magazine" was commenced—at Baltimore, in 1829—and which was immediately followed by the publication, in New York, of the *"Spirit of the Times,"* there existed no such class of writers as have, since that recent day, conferred signal honour on the rising literature of America . . . the novel design and scope of the "Spirit of the Times" soon fixed attention; and ere long it became the nucleus of a new order of literary talent.

Some of the humorists were influenced by the orthodox English and American humorous literature more deeply than Porter thought, but their sketches bear no close resemblance to the work of Swift, Irving, or Kennedy. In the beginning at least oral influences counted for more than all others. Southerners, like other Americans, have long delighted in swapping stories. In the South there were—and still are—many skilful raconteurs, and many a good story never written down was told around county court houses, country stores, in barrooms, on steamboats, or at the dinner table. Some of the stories that got into print had been told repeatedly until the authors when they sat down to write them out had little to do but to record them in the language in which they had been first told. The published stories are sometimes slow in getting under way, but for the most part they are straightforward, vivid, and marked by the flavor of local speech and a full appreciation of individuality of character. The South, like other rural regions, is and long has been rich in character; and in the period which followed the Civil War it supplied abundant materials for local colorists, like Richard Malcolm Johnston and Joel Chandler Harris.

The Negro, though he figured prominently on the Northern minstrel stage, played only a minor part in Southern humorous writing until after his emancipation. The rich vein of Negro humor had impressed English visitors like John Bernard and Thackeray, but the ante-bellum Southern writers made little use of it. An exception is a book written by a Georgia county clerk, an admirer of Longstreet, Francis James Robinson, *Kups of Kauphy: A Georgia Book, in Warp and Woof. Containing Tales, Incidents, &c. of the "Empire State of the South," with a Slight Sketch of that Well-known and Eccentric "Colored Gemman," OLD JACK*—(Athens, Georgia, 1853).[87]

The chief butt of the ante-bellum humorists is the poorer and more ignorant whites, who are by no means all to be classed as "poor-whites." Every state had its crackers, hillbillies, or backwoodsmen as well as numerous

---

[87] There is a copy of this rare volume in the Duke University Library. Old Jack was an actual personage, a waiter who worked in a hotel at Madison in Morgan County "whose remarkable politeness and singular manner of expression, have made him one of the lions of middle Georgia" (George White, *Statistics of the State of Georgia*, Savannah, 1849, p. 435).

yeomen farmers, who were themselves often intense individualists and who frequently had a keen relish for a story or a practical joke. The leading characters of the Southern humorists are more local in type than those of the Northern and Western writers. Strangely enough, the Southern humorists show comparatively little interest in politics. Burlesque is occasionally found, as in William P. Brannan's "The Harp of a Thousand Strings," and satire makes its appearance, but the humorist rarely made fun of anything in which many of his readers believed. The Primitive or Hardshell Baptists who might have taken offense at Brannan's burlesque sermon were not numerous enough to give the writer any concern.

The Southern humorists as we see them now were in their own fashion pioneer realists, and they wrote of large areas of American life which could not be faithfully presented in the romantic and sentimental types of poetry and fiction then in favor with the public. They were also early local colorists, and they exerted an influence by no means negligible on the better-known writers who emerged in the seventies and eighties. In Virginia, for example, the line runs from George W. Bagby through Thomas Nelson Page. In Middle Georgia Richard Malcolm Johnston and Charles Henry Smith ("Bill Arp") stand midway between Longstreet and William Tappan Thompson, on the one hand, and Joel Chandler Harris and Harry Stillwell Edwards, on the other. The later writers possess more enduring qualities of style and technique, but they too often fall victims to a sentimentality which is rare indeed in the earlier humorists. The tradition of Southern humor of course culminates in Mark Twain, who grew up in a slaveholding town on the banks of the Mississippi.

I have space for only eight of the Southern humorists, but there are many more who wrote at least one excellent sketch or story. Among these are Henry Clay Lewis, who published *Odd Leaves from the Life of a Louisiana Swamp Doctor* (1850) under the pseudonym of "Madison Tensas"; John B. Lamar, a Georgia planter whose "The Blacksmith of the Mountain Pass" is said to be the source of Dickens's "Colonel Quagg's Conversion"; Thomas Bangs Thorpe, author of "The Big Bear of Arkansas" and other fine sketches; Colonel C. F. M. Noland, a West Point graduate from Virginia who settled in Arkansas; Hamilton C. Jones, the author of "Cousin Sally Dilliard" and "A Quarter Race in Kentucky"; T. A. Burke, who edited *Polly Peablossom's Wedding and Other Tales* (1851); and H. E. Taliaferro, who under the pen name of "Skitt" published *Fisher's River (North Carolina) Scenes and Characters* (1859). Nor must I fail to mention William Gilmore Simms's venture into the field in *As Good as a Comedy; or, The Tennesseean's Story* (1852), which is not so good as his historical romances. His "How Sharp

Snaffles Won His Capital and Wife," published in *Harper's Magazine* in October, 1870, is good enough to have been written by any of the Southern humorists.

One of the forgotten Southern humorists created a character who now belongs to folklore. Charles Napoleon Bonaparte Evans, who for many years edited and printed the Milton, North Carolina, *Chronicle*—a newspaper that perhaps never had more than a thousand subscribers—published from time to time letters from Jesse Holmes the Fool-Killer reciting his untiring efforts to clear the region of fools.[88] Evans printed a woodcut, none too good, showing the Fool-Killer holding in his hand the white-oak club with which he mauled his victims. On those occasions when he met an obnoxious person who was obviously no fool, he sent for his coworker, the Rascal-Whaler. In Evans's hands the conception is generally better than the execution, but the letters were interesting enough to be copied by other newspapers in North Carolina. O. Henry, whose mother was a relative of Evans and who had visited in Milton, gave the Fool-Killer wider currency in his short story, "Jesse Holmes, the Fool-Killer," but he somewhat distorted the creator's conception of the character. A fool-killer appears also in Ambrose Bierce's *Black Beetles in Amber* (1892), and still others figure in George Ade's *Fables in Slang* (1900) and Stephen Vincent Benét's short story, "Johnny Pye and the Fool-Killer" (1937). These stories are important enough to make it worth while to remember the name of the obscure journalist-philosopher who created the Fool-Killer, but when I think of what Swift, Cervantes, Molière, or Mark Twain might have made of him, I am inclined to hope that Jesse Holmes will some day reappear in a notable comic epic in prose or verse.

50
David Crockett

DAVID CROCKETT (1786–1836) became the center of so many legends, comic and heroic, that it is difficult to get at the actual Tennessee backwoodsman whom his neighbors sent to Congress in 1827. In the legends he is the champion bear-hunter; the practical joker who sells a single coonskin to the same storekeeper a score of times; a "ring-tailed roarer" who as a

---

[88] Jay B. Hubbell, "Charles Napoleon Bonaparte Evans: Creator of Jesse Holmes the Fool-Killer," *S.A.Q.*, XXXVI, 431–446 (Oct., 1937). James Larkin Pearson, whom Governor William B. Umstead appointed Poet Laureate of North Carolina in August, 1953, once conducted a paper in the northwestern part of the state entitled the *Fool-Killer*. I have not seen Helen Eustis' recent novel, *The Fool Killer* (1954).

fighter rivals Mike Fink, the hero of the keelboatmen; the central figure in tall tales ·like those which celebrate the exploits of Paul Bunyan, idol of the lumberjacks, or Pecos Bill, the greatest cowpuncher of them all. Crockett is also of course one of the heroes who died in the Alamo fighting in the Texas War for Independence.

Kennedy's friend, John H. B. Latrobe, who met Crockett in December, 1833, recorded his impressions of the Congressman: "Colonel Crockett is a tall muscular man of a good face rather, and one whom, dressed in a ploughman's frock with a flail over his shoulder, we would esteem a good representative of that class; or who, to meet him in the woods with a rifle on his shoulder and clad in deer skin, we would say was a proper hunter. Dressed in the clothing of a gentleman and occupying a seat in the National Legislature, he is as much out of his element as he well can be." Latrobe added: "They say that Colonel is shrewd and sensible. Maybe so, but he is ignorant and vulgar." Latrobe was repelled by Crockett's boasting that when he was appointed justice of the peace, he did not know how to write his name.

William J. Grayson, who sat in Congress with Crockett and Richard Henry Wilde, was struck by the contrast between the two: "One [Crockett] was stout and clumsy in person with a blotchy fair complexion and light eyes, ungainly in dress and manners; the other dark of good figure with black eyes, easy, sprightly, engaged [engaging?], in conversation and still more a poet." Grayson continues: "He [Crockett] was a dull, heavy, almost· stupid man, in appearance. I never heard him utter a word that savoured of wit or sense. To judge from his features one would have supposed such an event impossible. Yet by some freak of fortune he became the reputed author of innumerable queer sayings and stories, a man of infinite joke, an incarnation of frontier oddity, a sort of Western Joe Miller. He was a good natured, kind hearted man and a general favourite in the house . . . but he was the last man in the house that a stranger would have pitched upon as a wit and humourist."

Lucian Minor was also struck with the difference between the actual Crockett and the legendary figure he became while in Congress. In June, 1834, Minor saw Crockett in the rotunda of the Capitol with some ladies who were looking at the pictures and statues there. "The Col.," he wrote in his journal, "played the tame bear very quietly, for the ladies; and he seemed to be a pet. I was disappointed at finding him so tame. He should always appear in character—i.e. with hunting shirt and tomahawk—moccasins and leggings of deerskin with the hair on. As it is, he looks like any Christian: you would never suppose him to be the man what can wade the Mississippi, tote a steamboat, whip his weight in wildcats, grin the bark off an oak-knot, —swim further, dive deeper, and come out drier, than any other man in the Western Deestrict."

Crockett was born in Greene County, Tennessee, in 1786 and spent most of his life in the mountains of East Tennessee until he was twenty-five years old. He was in Middle Tennessee by 1811. He fought in the Creek War and rose to the rank of sergeant. In later years he lived in West Tennessee. He was in the state legislature in 1821–1822. He was elected to Congress in 1827 from a district in western Tennessee where there were many squatters who wanted the taxes kept low and were afraid of being dispossessed of their lands. Crockett broke with Andrew Jackson and was defeated in 1831. He was re-elected in 1833 and again defeated in 1835. Then came his journey to Texas and the final scene at the Alamo.

Crockett's break with Jackson gave the Whigs, who were handicapped by the aristocratic Federalist tradition which their party had inherited, a chance to play up this picturesque man of the people. In 1834 he made his triumphal "tour to the north," where he was treated as a national figure. Crockett probably never realized how he was being used by the Whigs for party purposes, and when soon afterwards he failed of re-election in Tennessee, he was rather bitter.

Crockett resented the unauthorized *Sketches and Eccentricities of Col. David Crockett, of West Tennessee* (1833), but it prompted him to write *A Narrative of the Life of David Crockett. Written by Himself* (1834), in which he stated that the unknown author of the earlier book had put into his mouth "such language as would disgrace even an outlandish African" and in other respects had done him "much injustice." Crockett may possibly have had something to do with *An Account of Colonel Crockett's Tour to the North and Down East* (1835) and perhaps also with *The Life of Martin Van Buren* (1835), a satirical campaign biography which has been attributed to Augustin S. Clayton, a Georgia Congressman and a friend of Augustus Baldwin Longstreet. He could not of course have written *Colonel Crockett's Exploits and Adventures in Texas* (1836), which may have been written by Richard Penn Smith. How far the legend has departed from actuality is suggested by the following passage from the *Sketches and Eccentricities of Col. David Crockett*. Crockett is supposed to be writing of his first visit to Washington:

. . . I was *rooting* my way to the fire, not in a good humour, when some fellow staggered up towards me, and cried out, "Hurrah for Adams!" Said I, "Stranger you had better hurrah for hell, and praise your own country."

Said he, "And who are you?"

"I'm that same David Crockett, fresh from the backwoods, half-horse, half-alligator, a little touched with the snapping-turtle; can wade the Mississippi, leap the Ohio, ride upon a streak of lightning, and slip without a scratch down a honey locust; can whip my weight in wild-cats,—and if any gentleman pleases, for a ten-dollar bill, he may throw in a panther,—hug a bear too close for comfort, and eat any man opposed to Jackson."

In the Crockett almanacs which were published from 1835 to 1856, first in Nashville and then in New York, Boston, and other cities, the Crockett legend underwent still further development. Tall tales and folk stories of various kinds were attached to the Tennessean until he became the center of something like an American comic epic. The various unknown authors of the almanacs gave their imaginations full sway. Here one meets the typical frontier boast expressed in extravagant, earthy or semipoetic language, flavored by a dialect that is largely unreal.

The American tall tale is at least as old as the time of Benjamin Franklin, who in 1765 wrote to the editor of a British newspaper that the Canadians were preparing for "a Cod and Whale Fishery" in the Great Lakes region:

Ignorant People may object that the upper Lakes are fresh, and that Cod and Whale are Salt Water Fish: But let them know, Sir, that Cod, like other Fish when attack'd by their Enemies, fly into any Water where they can be safest; that Whales, when they have a mind to eat Cod, pursue them wherever they fly; and that the grand Leap of the Whale in that Chase up the Fall of Niagara is esteemed, by all who have seen it, as one of the finest Spectacles in Nature. Really, Sir, the World is grown too incredulous.

One of the almanac writers put into the hero's mouth the story of "Crockett's Wonderful Escape up Niagara Falls." Davy was taking a nap at the foot of Niagara Falls on the back of his pet alligator, "Long Mississippi," when the British troops surrounded him and thought they were about to capture him.

But by all go-ahead-itiveness they were most tarnally mistaken, for I jist tickled up the old alligator with my toe, twisted his tail around my body, put my thumb to my nose, an' we walked up the great hill o' water as slick as a wild cat up a white oak. . . . By way of a parting salute, my alligator sent such a cloudburst of old Niagara's water upon 'em, that they all cut stick like so many half drowned turkies from a spring shower, thinking that the hull entire cataract was coming to baptise 'em Christians and Republicans. My pet an' me shot up the rapids about as fast as a roughshod rocket, and landed on Uncle Sam's side, amid a salute of five hundred double barrelled rifles in honor of Colonel Crockett and his amphibious pet cataract navigator.

This is a far cry from Crockett's own *Narrative*, which is written in a straightforward and homely style with an individuality of its own. In his Preface Crockett admitted that a friend had looked over his manuscript and that "some little alterations have been made in the spelling and grammar"; but he insisted, it was *his* book:

> But just read it for yourself, and my ears for a heel tap, if before you get through you don't say, with many a good-natured smile and hearty laugh, "This is truly the very thing itself—the exact image of its Author,
>
> DAVID CROCKETT."

Here, as in the work of the later Southern humorists, we find that colloquial manner which now seems so much more American than the style and diction of Hawthorne, Emerson, and Poe. It was in the Old Southwest running westward from Kentucky, Tennessee, and Georgia that there developed, in the words of George Philip Krapp, "an Americanism of expression strongly colored and highly flavored, racy of the soil and the people," which reached its peak in the work of Mark Twain.

51
Augustus Baldwin Longstreet

MIDDLE GEORGIA is the birthplace and home of the raciest and most original kind of Southern humor," wrote William Malone Baskervill, following a clew given him by Joel Chandler Harris. "In this quarter native material was earliest recognized and first made use of. A school of writers arose who looked out of their eyes and listened with their ears, who took frank interest in things for their own sake, and had enduring astonishment at the most common. They seized the warm and palpitating facts of everyday existence, and gave them to the world with all the accompaniments of quaint dialect, original humor, and Southern plantation life." That was the proper way for a professor of English to write half a century ago. What Harris had written to Baskervill was this: "By-the-by, if you will take a map of Georgia, pick out Putnam county, and then put your finger on the counties surrounding it—Morgan, Greene, Hancock, Baldwin, Jones and Jasper—you will have under your thumb the seat of Southern humor. Major Jones's Courtship belongs to Morgan county. Colonel Richard Malcolm Johnston's characters to Hancock. Unc' Remus was in Putnam. Simon Suggs was a native of Jasper. Polly Peablossom was from Baldwin. Jonce Hooper went to school in Monticello (Jasper), when a boy, and there saw Simon Suggs." To Middle Georgia belong also Charles Henry Smith ("Bill Arp"), Harry

Stillwell Edwards, Francis Orray Ticknor, and Sidney Lanier. Middle Georgia was primarily a land of small farms rather than of big plantations. Slaves were not numerous in the early nineteenth century, and farmers who owned them worked in the fields beside them. In this region frontier characteristics lingered longer than in other seaboard Southern states except Florida.

Augustus Baldwin Longstreet (1790–1870) was the uncle of the Confederate General James Longstreet and the father-in-law of Lucius Q. C. Lamar; he was also the author of *Georgia Scenes*. He was born in Augusta in 1790, only a few years after his parents had come to Georgia from New Jersey. His father, William Longstreet, it is said, successfully demonstrated a steamboat he had invented only a few days after Robert Fulton. Longstreet attended three of the same schools as Calhoun had attended a few years before. He prepared for college under Moses Waddel at the famous Academy, which he has well described in *Master William Mitten* (Macon, 1864), graduated from Yale in 1813, and studied law at the famous school at Litchfield, Connecticut. At Calhoun's suggestion, Yale gave him an honorary LL.D. degree in 1841. Longstreet practiced law successfully and was from 1822 to 1825 judge of the superior court. In the years 1834–1836 he was editor of the Augusta *State Rights Sentinel*. Some of his Georgia sketches first appeared in that newspaper, and it was the *Sentinel's* press that in 1835 issued *Georgia Scenes, Characters, Incidents, etc., in the First Half Century of the Republic. By a Native Georgian.*

In 1837 Longstreet was converted to the Methodist faith and in 1838 he became a Methodist minister. From this time on, although really proud of the great popularity of the hastily written *Georgia Scenes*, he sometimes felt that it was not the kind of book by which a minister should be known. After Harper & Brothers republished it in 1840 with illustrations by E. H. Hyde, *Georgia Scenes* enjoyed a great vogue in the North. During the latter part of his life Longstreet was a college president, serving in succession at Emory College in Georgia, Centenary College in Louisiana, the University of Mississippi, the University of South Carolina, and again at the University of Mississippi. Longstreet was well educated, but, if we may believe Joseph Le Conte, "not in any sense a cultured man." He was, however, a shrewd observer and an accomplished raconteur. His political views were strongly Southern, and he gave them forceful expression in two pamphlets directed mainly to Northern readers who probably never saw them: *Letters on the Epistle of Paul to Philemon or The Connection of Apostolical Christianity with Slavery* (Charleston, 1845) and *A Voice from the South: Comprising Letters from Georgia to Massachusetts* (Baltimore, 1847).

The first Georgia "scenes" appeared in the Milledgeville *Southern Recorder* in the fall of 1833, but in 1834 Longstreet transferred the series to his newly acquired *States Rights Sentinel* in Augusta. As a young lawyer riding the circuit, Longstreet had been a delighted observer of Georgia rural life in the more primitive districts and had often entertained his friends with stories about his experiences, for he was an accomplished mimic. He discovered that in their printed form they pleased equally well. In later years he said that he had written *Georgia Scenes* to fill a gap in the state's history, covering a period in which "the society of the Southern States underwent almost an entire revolution." The book, he said, "has been invariably received as a mere collection of fancy sketches, with no higher object than the entertainment of the reader, whereas the aim of the author was to supply a chasm in history which has always been overlooked—the manners, customs, amusements, wit, dialect, as they appear in all grades of society to an ear and eye witness of them."

There is nothing to indicate that Longstreet had read the "Major Jack Downing" letters of Seba Smith, which had begun to appear in 1830. He was writing rather in the general Addisonian tradition, and his intention was in part that of the moralist. Longstreet was more of a realist than Caruthers, Kennedy, or Simms, who were writing historical romances in the 1830's. In the Preface to the 1835 edition he maintained the fidelity of the picture he painted. The sketches, he said, "consist of nothing more than fanciful *combinations* of *real* incidents and characters; and throwing into those scenes, which would be otherwise dull and insipid, some personal incident or adventure of my own, real or imaginary, as would best suit my purpose. . . . Some of the scenes are as literally true as the frailties of memory would allow them to be."

One would hardly have supposed that the youthful Edgar Allan Poe, who had ripped to pieces Simms's *The Partisan* in January, 1836, would two months later find anything worthy of high praise in *Georgia Scenes*, but he hailed it "as a sure omen of better days for the literature of the South." "Seriously," he wrote, "—if this book were printed in England it would make the fortune of its author." He treated it as a humorous masterpiece and a vivid and accurate account of "the manners of our South-Western peasantry." Poe commented on nearly every sketch in the book and quoted extensively from several of them. He overpraised "The Debating Society," but he rightfully picked "Georgia Theatrics," "The Fight," "The Horse-Swap," and "The Gander-Pulling" as among the best in the book. He did not fail to see that one of Longstreet's finest characters is Ransy Sniffle, that misshapen victim of malaria and hookworm, "who, in his earlier days, had fed copiously upon red clay and blackberries" and who "never seemed fairly alive except when he was witnessing, fomenting, or talking about a fight."

"The Militia Company Drill," which pleased Poe, was written not by Longstreet but by his friend, the versatile Connecticut-born Oliver Hillhouse Prince. In 1882 the New York *Critic* pointed to the striking resemblance between Prince's farcical sketch and Chapter XXIII of Thomas Hardy's *The Trumpet Major* (1880). In the Preface to the 1895 edition Hardy stated that the chapter in question was based upon C. H. Gifford's *History of the Wars Occasioned by the French Revolution* (London, 1817), II, 968–970. Somewhere the British compiler had picked up—presumably from an American newspaper—Prince's sketch even before Longstreet included it in his *Georgia Scenes*. The *Critic* printed the Hardy and the Prince versions in parallel columns but inadvertently transposed the authors' names at the top of each column. A British writer in the London *Daily News* who undertook to show how great an improvement Hardy's version was over the crude American original unwittingly argued that Prince's version was better than Hardy's.

Georgia Scenes was so popular that in Longstreet's later years the editors of Southern magazines were continually importuning him for more stories. Some of his uncollected sketches were reprinted in *Stories with a Moral Humorous and Descriptive of Southern Life a Century Ago* (Philadelphia, 1912). An interesting Confederate imprint is another story with a moral, *Master William Mitten: A Youth of Brilliant Talents Who Was Ruined by Bad Luck* (Macon, 1864). The story, written as a warning to indolent youths and overindulgent mothers, had been printed serially in the *Southern Field and Fireside* in 1859. Except for its account of Moses Waddel and his famous school, the book has little to recommend it. As James Wood Davidson said of it: "In attempting to adorn a moral, he has spoiled a tale; not much of a one, it is true, but still,—a tale." Longstreet's later writings made little impression, but *Georgia Scenes* led many a Southern humorist to recognize the rich materials lying all around him.

52
William Tappan Thompson

THE CREATOR of that most representative of Southern comic figures, "Major Jones," was not like Longstreet a native Georgian. William Tappan Thompson (1812–1882) was born in Ravenna, Ohio. His father was a Virginian and his mother an Irishwoman. He attended the district schools in

Ohio, but at an early age he was on the staff of the Philadelphia *Daily Chronicle*. In the early 1830's he was assistant to Dr. James D. Wescott, Secretary of the territory of Florida, and was studying law in Wescott's office. He returned to journalism and was for a time with Longstreet on the Augusta *State Rights Sentinel*. He was editor of two Georgia literary magazines and then for some years with Park Benjamin on the Baltimore *Western Continent*. In 1850 he founded the Savannah *Morning News*, on which he worked for many years. In 1870 he gave Joel Chandler Harris a position on the *News*.

Thompson had written sketches of Florida and Georgia rustics before the first of the Major Jones sketches appeared in June, 1842. In 1838–1841 he had edited the semimonthly *Augusta Mirror*, the first purely literary magazine published in Georgia. Longstreet assisted him during a part of the year 1840. In 1842 Thompson combined the *Mirror* with the *Family Companion* of Macon, edited by Mrs. Sarah Lawrence Griffin; but the two co-editors did not get on, and in August, 1842, Thompson left Macon to launch the weekly *Southern Miscellany* in the little town of Madison. The first of the Major Jones letters had appeared in the *Family Companion and Ladies' Mirror* in June, 1842. Thompson had thought so little of it that he published it anonymously. Surprised at the attention which it attracted, he continued the series in the *Southern Miscellany*, but he apparently had no notion of republishing the Major's letters until a Colonel Jones, who lived in Madison, insisted that they be brought out in book form at his own expense. The first edition of *Major Jones' Courtship* was printed in Madison in 1843, and the only extant copy known is in the Duke University Library. There was no Philadelphia, 1840, edition such as is listed in several reference books.

Professional journalist though he was, Thompson knew no more about dealing with publishers of books than other Southern writers. The Philadelphia house of Carey and Hart offered to republish the book and asked what royalty he expected. As Thompson himself wrote to Salem Dutcher in 1866:

Had they [Carey & Hart] asked me for the Mss., I would have freely given it then, so little confidence had I in the success of the book. I returned for answer that five cents per copy would satisfy me, fearful that any higher price would bluff them off. They promptly accepted my terms and "Maj. Jones Courtship" became the first book of Carey and Harts Humorous Library. During the first year of its publication I received, at five cts. per copy, $750 and thinking it had had its run, I the same year accepted $250 for the copyright entire, making the sum of $1000 received for what I would have freely given to any publisher. I have the best assurances that if I had retained the copyright it would have yielded at least $2500 at 5 cts. per copy yearly to the present time.

Major Jones' Courtship was published in Philadelphia in May, 1844, with twelve illustrations by F. O. C. Darley. Fifteen thousand copies were sold within a year. By 1852 eighty thousand copies had been sold. There were two pirated editions in England, and many of the letters were reprinted in anthologies. What the total circulation of the sketches amounted to, no one knows, but it was one of the most popular books of its time.

Thompson was no doubt influenced by Longstreet, with whom he was associated on the *Sentinel* and the *Mirror*, but he was also influenced by the "Major Jack Downing" letters of Seba Smith. He abandoned the Longstreet-Irving-Addison method of telling a story and, adopting the epistolary form of Seba Smith, he wrote his stories in the Georgia rustic dialect. The original of Major Jones is said to have been a man named Wall who actually lived in the village of Pineville. The Major is not to be confused with the poor-whites; properly speaking, he is not a Georgia cracker, either. He is a substantial yeoman farmer who owns a few slaves. He is kindly and naïve, and he is the butt rather than the perpetrator of jokes, like Simon Suggs and Sut Lovingood; but he is also, like "Bill Arp" and Joel Chandler Harris's Billy Sanders, a homely crackerbox philosopher. Like his creator, he is a Whig, and he names his first-born Henry Clay. Thompson makes him the medium for Whig propaganda and for satire on woman's fashions, dandies' dress, especially long whiskers and "soaplocks," and heavy drinking. The Major hates pretense and ridicules the farmers who move into town to spend the winter— that, he says, is "a fool quality notion." In one sketch Thompson describes Jack C——, a Negro hotel waiter and well-known wit, who is the central figure in Robinson's *Kups of Kauphy*. Thompson's women characters receive more attention and are better drawn than those in most books by the Southern humorists. Old Mrs. Stallions [Stallings] and her daughter Mary, whom the Major marries, are among the best. The following passage suggests the way Southern country girls were brought up even after the Civil War. Before Miss Mary Stallions went off to the Female College in Macon, "she used to be jest as plain as a old shoe, and used to go fishin and huckleberryin with us, with nothin but a calico sun-bonnet on [her head], and was the wildest thing you ever seed." After she had been at college nearly a year, she came home. When the Major called, "she made a sort of stoop over and a dodge back, like the little galls does to the school-marm, and said 'Good evenin, Mr. Jones,' (she used to always call me jest Joe.)" The Madison, 1843, edition, from which the following paragraph is taken, differs slightly from the later texts:

She didn't say much, but was in a mighty good humor and laughed a heap. I told her I never seed such a change in any body, nor I never did—why, she didn't look like the same gal—good gracious! she looked so nice and trim—jest like some of them pictures what they have in Mr. Graham's magazine, with her hair all combed down longside her face, as slick and shiny as a mahogany burow. When she laughed she didn't open her mouth like she used to, and she set up strait and still in her chair, and looked so different, but so monstrous pretty! I ax'd her a heap o' questions, bout how she liked Macon, and the Female College, and so forth; and she told me a heap bout 'em. But old Miss [Mrs.] Stallions and Miss Carline and Miss Kesiah, and all of 'em kep all the time interruptin us so we couldn't say nothin much, axin bout mother—if she was well, and if she was gwine to the Spring church next Sunday, and what luck she had with her soap [making], and all sich stuff, and I do believe I told the old woman more 'n twenty times that mother's old turkeyhen was settin on fourteen eggs.

53
Johnson Jones Hooper

JOHNSON JONES HOOPER (1815–1862), the creator of "Captain Simon Suggs," was born in Wilmington, North Carolina. He was the grand-nephew of William Hooper, a Harvard graduate and one of the Signers of the Declaration of Independence. Through his mother he was a descendant of Jeremy Taylor, "the Shakespeare of divines." His father divided his activities among business, journalism, and the law. By 1832 he was poor and blind and unable to send his youngest son to college. In 1835 Johnson, who had already shown some talent for humorous writing, went to La Fayette in East Alabama to study law in the office of his brother George. The remainder of his life was devoted to law, journalism, and politics. Thanks to the researches of William Stanley Hoole, we know more about his various activities than is known of most of his Southern literary contemporaries.

In 1842 Hooper married Ann Brantley, daughter of a well-to-do merchant and planter. Alexander B. Meek dedicated to her his poem, "The Rose of Alabama." In the summer of 1843 Hooper printed in the *East Alabamian* a humorous piece based upon his own experience, "Taking the Census in Alabama." On September 9 of that year William T. Porter reprinted it in the *Spirit of the Times* with a compliment to its author. "This Hooper," he wrote, "is a clever man, and we must enlist him among the correspondents of the 'Spirit of the Times.'" In January, 1845, Porter reprinted the first of the Simon Suggs stories and suggested that Hooper was hiding his "light under a bushel" by writing for a local newspaper. Porter was about to publish his first collection of humorous writing, *The Big Bear of Arkansas* (1845), but he managed somehow to squeeze into it Hooper's "How Simon Suggs Raised Jack." Porter doubtless had a hand in inducing the Philadelphia publishers, Carey & Hart, to bring out Hooper's first book, *Some Adventures of Simon Suggs, Late Captain of the Tallapoosa Volunteers*, which appeared late in the summer of 1845. "This," said Porter in his notice of the book, "is the best half dollars worth of genuine humor, ever enclosed between two covers!"

Almost at a bound Hooper had become one of the most popular of American humorists; but as he grew older and became an important figure in Alabama politics, he came to feel that his reputation as a humorist stood in the way of his advancement. There is a story which although not fully authenticated illustrates his feeling. While he was sitting next to Albert Pike at the Southern Commercial Convention of 1856, the audience, impatiently waiting for the nominating committee to bring in its report, called on Hooper for a humorous speech. He resented the implication that he was nothing more than a teller of funny stories and refused to speak.

Until his death in 1858 Porter promoted Hooper's reputation in every possible way and often urged him not to neglect his humorous writing for political activities. He even took the trouble to purchase for his Alabama correspondent guns and other things which were not so easily obtainable in Alabama. The *Spirit of the Times* not only gave a nationwide audience to Hooper and other Southern humorists; it was also one of the links which still bound the Southern states to the Union. Soon after Porter died, Hooper wrote to Thomas Bangs Thorpe, now coeditor of the *Spirit*: "To many of us here in the South, we have been accustomed to regard the 'Old Spirit' as the single remaining link which bound us in kindly feeling and sympathy to New York. . . ." In its issue of January 14, 1860, the *Spirit*, much disturbed by the danger of disunion, paid its tribute to the Southern humorists: "Some of the best things, always the most original, produced in this country, are the results of Southern pens. For more than a quarter of a century the columns of the 'Spirit' have teemed with the finest specimens of writing, overflowing with wit and sentiment, playful and profound, a large part of which is destined to become permanent specimens of real American originality, for which we have been largely indebted to Southern correspondents."

Hooper included a few more Simon Suggs stories in *A Ride with Old Kit Kuncker*, published in Tuscaloosa, Alabama, in 1849 and reissued in Philadelphia two years later by A. Hart under the title, *The Widow Rugby's Husband*. In 1856 Hooper brought out in New York a serious book, *Dog and Gun; A Few Loose Chapters on Shooting*, only a part of which had been written by Hooper himself. In 1859 he supplied a long introduction for Woodward's *Reminiscences of the Creek, or Muscogee Indians*—an anticlimactic close to a literary career which had begun so auspiciously.

In his later years Hooper had become increasingly interested in politics. He was for many years an ardent Whig. The dissolution of that party left him somewhat at sea. He was for a short time a member of the American, or "Know Nothing," party. In the fifties he became an enthusiastic supporter of the avowed secessionist, William Lowndes Yancey. In 1861 he became Secretary and Librarian of the Confederate Congress and also private secretary to the Secretary of War. He died in Richmond on June 7, 1862, in the midst of the Seven Days' Battle on the outskirts of the Confederate capital.

Like all the other Southern humorists, Hooper was familiar with Longstreet's *Georgia Scenes*. In fact, Young Coats in "The Dirtiken" in *The Widow Rugby's Husband* is so like Ransy Sniffle that Hooper remarks that "he might well pass for that worthy's twin brother." Hooper's book has an advantage over Longstreet's in that it chronicles the adventures of a single leading character. And Simon Suggs, who is said to have won the praise of Thackeray, who surely knew about rogues, is the prince of rascals. Each episode, complete in itself, recounts the triumph of rascality over innocence and unsophistication. Simon begins as a "bad boy" by cheating at cards his own father, a Georgia Hardshell Baptist preacher, and continues his shifty career in Alabama. His greatest exploit perhaps is in raising a collection at a camp meeting by pretending conversion. This story was obviously in the mind of Mark Twain when he wrote Chapter XX of *Huckleberry Finn*.

Unlike Longstreet, Hooper usually leaves the moral to the discernment of the reader. Simon's aphorisms suggest a philosophy suitable to the "flush times": "It is good to be shifty in a new country."—"Mother-wit can beat booklarnin' at *any* game."—"There is no telling which way luck or a half-broke horse will run." Ostensibly the *Adventures* is a campaign biography and, though it is little concerned with politics, it concludes with a plea to the voters to elect Suggs sheriff: "His military services; his numerous family; his long residence among you; his gray hairs—all plead for him! Remember him at the polls!"

Hooper's model for Simon Suggs seems to have been one Bird Young, an early settler in Tallapoosa County who had come from Georgia at the age of sixteen. He is said to have been somewhat disturbed to find some of his experiences put into print. Joel Chandler Harris, who owed much to the ante-bellum Southern humorists, wrote on April 15, 1895, to William Malone Baskervill:

Jonce Hooper went to school in Monticello (Jasper [County]) when a boy, and there saw Simon Suggs. When he went away and wrote his book, some one in Monticello heard of it. When Mr. Suggs came to town this conversation occurred: "Squire Suggs do you remember Jonce Hooper—Little Jonce?" "Seems to me I do," replied Mr. Suggs. "Well, squire," said the other, "little Jonce has gone and noveled you." Mr. Suggs looked serious. "Gone and noveled me!" he exclaimed. "Well I'll be danged. Gone and noveled me! What could 'a' possessed him?" [89]

54
Joseph Glover Baldwin

JOSEPH GLOVER BALDWIN (1815–1864), whom W. P. Trent regarded as the best of the Southern humorists, was born near Winchester in the Shenandoah Valley, where his father operated a small cotton and woolen factory. After reading law in an uncle's office, Baldwin at the age of twenty-one decided to try his fortune in the booming Southwest, that "legal Utopia" where litigation and politics were among the chief amusements of the motley population. And so, as Baldwin put it, he "turned his back upon his country and put all to hazard—*videlicet*, a pony valued at $35, a pair of saddle-bags and contents, a new razor not much needed at that early day, and $75 in Virginia bank bills." What the young lawyer found in the Southwest he was vividly to describe in *The Flush Times of Alabama and Mississippi* (New York, 1853):

The condition of the country may be imagined:—vulgarity—ignorance—fussy and arrogant pretension—unmitigated rowdyism—bullying insolence, if they did not rule the hour, *seemed* to wield unchecked dominion. The workings of these choice spirits were patent upon the face of society; and the modest, unobtrusive, retiring men of worth and character (for there were many, perhaps a large majority of such) were almost lost sight of in the hurly-burly of those strange and shifting scenes.

Even in the professions were the same characteristics visible. Men dropped down into their places as from the clouds. Nobody knew who or what they were, except as they claimed, or as a surface view of their characters indicated. Instead of taking to the highway and magnanimously calling upon the wayfarer to stand and deliver, or to the fashionable larceny of credit without prospect or design of paying, some unscrupulous horse-doctor would set up his sign as "Physician and Surgeon," and draw his lancet on you, or fire at random a box

[89] Jay B. Hubbell (ed.), "Letters of Uncle Remus," *Southwest Rev.*, XXIII, 222 (Jan., 1938). Harris was mistaken in thinking that Hooper went to school in Georgia.

of his pills into your bowels, with a vague chance of hitting some disease unknown to him, but with a better prospect of killing the patient, whom or whose administrator he charged some ten dollars a trial for his markmanship.

A superannuated justice or constable in one of the old States was metamorphosed into a lawyer; and though he knew not the distinction between a *fee tail* and a *female*, would undertake to construe, off-hand, a will involving all the subtleties of *uses and trusts!*

Baldwin practiced law at DeKalb, Mississippi, and later in Gainesville, Livingston, and Mobile in Alabama. In 1844 he was elected to the state legislature, but as a Whig candidate for the House of Representatives in 1849 he was defeated. In 1853 he published in New York *The Flush Times of Alabama and Mississippi* and in 1855 *Party Leaders*, containing sketches of Jefferson, Hamilton, Jackson, Clay, and John Randolph. Once more Baldwin decided to try life in a new country and by 1854 he was established in California, where some years later he became associate justice of the state supreme court. There he died in 1864, much troubled, it is said, by the War between the States and his inability to communicate with his parents in Virginia.

Unlike the other Southern humorists, Baldwin was not content to publish his sketches in a country newspaper. He sent some of them back to Virginia to be published by John R. Thompson in the *Southern Literary Messenger* in 1852 and 1853. With Thompson he journeyed to New York to make arrangements with D. Appleton and Company to bring them out in book form. Within six months twenty thousand copies are said to have been sold, and there were many later editions in New York and San Francisco. His *Party Leaders* attracted much less attention. "California Flush Times," which appeared in the *Messenger* for November, 1853, seems to be the first sketch in a projected volume that was never completed.

Baldwin's sketches are essays and character sketches rather than short stories. The incidents, most of which take place in the courtroom, are legal anecdotes. The dialogue is scanty and the digressions are numerous. One would guess that Baldwin's models, if he had any, were not Longstreet or even Irving or Addison but Charles Lamb, and perhaps Charles Dickens. There is the same gusto, whimsy, and keen eye for incongruity which one finds in the *Essays of Elia* and *Pickwick Papers*. *The Flush Times* is in the main a lawyer's book; many of the best characters are lawyers or their clients, and the number of legal terms is enough to trouble the lay reader. Among Baldwin's characters rascals and jokers predominate, and the humor often turns on their various escapades and the shrewd shifts to which they resort. Conspicuous among them is Ovid Bolus, "a natural liar, just as some horses are natural pacers, and some dogs natural setters." Another is Simon Suggs, Jr., a rascal who does credit to his sire. There is in the book a good deal of legal autobiography, and often actual persons and incidents are only thinly disguised under new names.

Some of Baldwin's sketches were directed primarily to Virginian readers. There were many Virginians in the Southwest. "Patriotism," said Baldwin, "with a Virginian is a noun personal. . . . It makes no odds where he goes, he carries Virginia with him. . . . [Horace's] 'Coelum non animum mutant qui trans mare currunt,' was made for a Virginian. He never gets acclimated elsewhere; he never loses citizenship to the old Home. . . . He may breathe in Alabama, but he lives in Virginia." In "How the Times Served the Virginians" Baldwin vividly described the misfortunes of the Virginia planters when the crash came in the panic of 1837:

In the old country, a jolly Virginian, starting the business of free living on a capital of a plantation, and fifty or sixty negroes, might reasonably calculate, if no ill-luck befell him, by the aid of a usurer, and the occasional sale of a negro or two, to hold out without declared insolvency, until a green old age. His estate melted like an estate in chancery, under the gradual thaw of expenses; but in this fast country, it went by sheer cost of living,—some *poker* losses included—like the fortune of the confectioner in California, who failed for one hundred thousand dollars in the six months keeping of a candy-shop. But all the habits of his life, his taste, his associations, his education,—everything—the trustingness of his disposition—his want of business qualifications, his sanguine temper—all that was Virginian in him, made him the prey, if not of imposture, at least of unfortunate speculations. Where the keenest jockey often was bit, what chance had *he?* About the same that the verdant Moses had with the venerable old gentleman, his father's friend, at the fair, when he traded the Vicar's pony for the green spectacles. But how could he believe it? How *could* he believe that that stuttering, grammarless Georgian, who had never heard of the resolutions of '98, could beat him in a land trade? . . . .

If he made a bad bargain, how could he expect to get rid of it? He knew nothing of the elaborate machinery of ingenious chicane,—such as feigning bankruptcy—fraudulent conveyances—making over to his wife—running property—and had never heard of such tricks of trade as sending out coffins to the graveyard, with negroes inside, carried off by sudden spells of imaginary disease, to be "resurrected," in due time, grinning, on the banks of the Brazos.

The new philosophy, too, had commended itself to his speculative temper. He readily caught at the idea of a new spirit of the age having set in, which rejected the saws of Poor Richard as being as much out of date as his almanacs. He was already, by the great rise of property, compared to his condition under the old-time prices, rich; and what were a few thousands of debt, which two or three crops would pay off, compared to the value of his estate? (He never thought that the value of property might come down, while the debt was a fixed fact.) He lived freely, for it was a liberal time, and liberal fashions were in vogue, and it was not for a Virginian to be behind others in hospitality and liberality. He required credit and security, and, of course, had to stand security in return. When the crash came, and no "accommodations" could be had, except in a few instances, and in those on the most ruinous terms, he fell an easy victim. They broke by neighborhoods. They usually endorsed for each other, and when one fell—like the child's play of putting bricks on end at equal distances, and dropping the first in the line against the second, which fell against the third, and so on to the last—all fell; each got broke as security, and yet few or none were able to pay their own debts! So powerless of protection were they in those times, that the witty H. G. used to say they reminded him of an oyster, both shells torn off, lying on the beach, with the sea-gulls screaming over them; the only question being, *which* should "gobble them up."

55
George W. Harris

For the humorist, a varied life which brings him into contact with many kinds of people is more valuable than an acquaintance with many books, particularly if he lives among people who are adept at telling stories. George Washington Harris (1814–1869) was born in Allegheny City, now a part of Pittsburgh, but he grew to manhood in Knoxville, Tennessee. He was a reader of books, but his formal education was scanty. He was at one time or another apprentice to a jeweler, operator of a metal-working shop, manager of a sawmill, postmaster, railroad man, and at two separate times a steamboat captain. His experiences, like those of Mark Twain, acquainted him with many types of human character.

Knoxville lies in the Tennessee Valley between the Cumberland and the Great Smoky mountain ranges. The mountain population lived in what has been called a retarded frontier. They have perhaps been more misrepresented in American fiction than the people of any other Southern region—and that is saying a good deal. Harris was struck by the picturesqueness and individuality of the mountain people, but his treatment of them is unlike that in the as-yet-unwritten romantic stories of Mary Noailles Murfree. A comparison of her "The Dancin' Party in Harrison's Cove" with his two sketches of mountain dances illustrates the different ways in which the romantic local colorist and the humorist treat similar materials.

Harris attempted no large-scale picture of the mountain people. His purpose was accomplished by singling out one striking character whose practical jokes were to be recounted in the mountain vernacular by the joker himself. The first of Harris's full-length sketches was printed in the *Spirit of the Times* in 1845. It was not until 1854, however, that Sut Lovingood made his appearance. He often appeared in the Nashville newspapers in the later 1850's, but it was not until 1867 that *Sut Lovingood's Yarns* was published in New York. Sut, one of the earliest "bad boys" in American literature, is a "queer looking, long-legged, short-bodied, small-headed, white-haired, hog-eyed, funny sort of a genius" who calls himself a "nat'ral born durn'd fool." He thus characterizes himself:

Fustly, that I haint got nara a soul, nuffin but a whisky proof gizzard, sorter like the wust half ove a ole par ove saddil bags, *Seconly,* that I'se too durn'd a fool tu cum even onder millertary lor. *Thudly,* that I hes the longes' par ove laigs ever hung tu eny cackus, 'sceptin' only ove a grandaddy spider, an' kin beat *him* a usen ove em jis' es bad es a skeer'd dorg kin beat a crippled mud turkil. *Foufly,* that I kin chamber more cork-screw, kill-devil whisky, an' stay on aind, than enything 'sceptin only a broad bottum'd chun. *Fivety,* an' las'ly, kin git intu more durn'd misfortnit skeery scrapes, than enybody, an' then run outen them faster, by golly, nor enybody.

Harris's spelling of the mountain dialect leaves something to be desired. His use of "du," "intu," "ove," "lor," etc., suggests that he was too much influenced by Lowell or other writers of New England dialect.

Sut is, like Huckleberry Finn, a person whose reactions are natural and spontaneous. The people whom he particularly dislikes, those who are the victims of his practical jokes, are deceitful and strong-minded women, circuit-riders, lawyers, sheriffs, dandies, politicians, temperance workers, to name only the chief. Above all, he hates hypocrisy. Among the circuit-riders he hates most Old Bullen, who makes and sells bad whiskey. Harris, whom Walter Blair regards as the best of the Southern humorists, is a writer for men and not for women. Miss Jennette Tandy, whose favorite was "Bill Arp," was obviously embarrassed by some of the Lovingood stories. For narrative skill and figurative language Harris is certainly one of the best. "For vivid imagination, comic plot, Rabelaisian touch, and sheer fun," says Franklin J. Meine, "the *Sut Lovingood Yarns* surpass anything else in American humor."

56
George William Bagby

THE BEST OF the Virginia humorists was George William Bagby (1828–1883), a doctor who gave up medicine for journalism and aspired to be a serious essayist rather than a humorous writer in dialect. His father was a pious and none too successful merchant in Lynchburg, Virginia. His mother was the daughter of a planter in Buckingham County, where Bagby was born. She died when he was a small boy, and he lived with an aunt in Cumberland County two miles from the nearest neighbor. After some experience in old-field schools, his father sent him to the reputable Edgehill School at Princeton, New Jersey. Its principal at that time was John S. Hart, author of an essay on *The Faerie Queene* and later professor of Rhetoric and English Language in Princeton University. At Edgehill Bagby read the *Penny Magazine* and then or soon afterwards learned to love Dickens, Lamb, and Irving, the writers who seem to have influenced him most. After completing his sophomore year at Delaware College, he began at eighteen the study of medicine at the University of Pennsylvania, where Caruthers had studied some years earlier. Receiving his M.D. degree in 1849, he began the practice of his profession in Lynchburg.

He quickly developed a distaste for medical practice and began writing essays for the local newspapers. Early in 1853 he became one of the editors of the Lynchburg *Express*. In 1856 the paper failed, and Bagby's health broke down. He had returned from his eleven years in the North with chronic dyspepsia. He spent a year recuperating on an uncle's plantation in Prince Edward County. He had meanwhile begun to contribute to Northern magazines. In December, 1856, he published in *Harper's Magazine* "The Virginia Editor," a burlesque character sketch of the fire-eating, dueling, swaggering Southern journalist, which was doubtless taken too literally by many Northern readers. From December, 1857, to March, 1859, he was in Washington, where he wrote regularly for the New Orleans *Crescent* and the Memphis *Eagle and Enquirer*.

While he was reporting political developments in the national capital, it occurred to Bagby, who was fond of colloquial English, that the humorous methods of the dialect writers might once more be employed to good effect. "The Letters of Mozis Addums to Billy Ivvins" ran in the *Southern Literary Messenger* from February to December, 1858, and to the surprise of both author and editor (John R. Thompson) proved a decided popular success.

In later years Bagby wrote: "I literally 'woke up and found myself famous,' much to my annoyance, for I was then ambitious to succeed in quite other and more elevated fields of literature. But the public would have its way. From that day to this I have gone by the name of 'Mozis,' and I am sure that, directly and indirectly, these letters have paid me better than all my other writings put together." Bagby wrote "literally hundreds of papers, letters, and skits in this dialect."

Mozis Addums is a very provincial rustic from the backwoods of Southside Virginia who goes to Washington with a perpetual motion "skeam" and writes of his adventures in the national capital. Much of the humor is of the slapstick variety, but Mozis is occasionally the medium for some shrewd criticism of "Kongris" and the "Supreame Kote." Of "Kongris" he says: ". . . uv all peepul on the fase uv the erth to talk, and talk, and talk, and do nuthin, they is the beet."

And Kanzis, Billy,—goodness nose I wisht it wuz berrid under Willis's mountin. I do think it's enuf to maik a man cuss out and quit the humin famly which has heerd what I has on this drottid subjick; constunt, Billy, without no sessashin furuver and furuver mo. Nar a tiem has I gone to Kongris, but straitway a man upriz and pode foth the viles uv his rath on Kanzis, howlin at it like a houn when you blow the hon fer dinner, yelping at it like a fice when he sees a straindge nigger cummin in the yard.

Back in Richmond in 1859, Bagby became librarian for the Virginia Historical Society, the Richmond Library Association, and the Mechanics Institute; and as if he did not have enough to do, he wrote editorials for several Richmond newspapers and contributed much to the *Messenger*. To supplement his meager income from these various sources, he began lecturing to lyceums and similar organizations in Virginia towns. His "Apology for Fools" and his readings from Mozis Addums were popular, but his net earnings were small. In June, 1860, he succeeded John R. Thompson as editor of the *Messenger* at a salary of three hundred dollars a year. He edited the magazine until January, 1864. More aggressive than Thompson, he declared for a Southern Confederacy in December, 1860 (months before Virginia seceded), though the step cost him his Northern subscribers and some of those in the Southern states as well.

In his editorials and reviews Bagby showed a strong distaste for the imitative and the sentimental in Southern writings. He attacked John Esten Cooke, as we have seen, for overidealizing the Virginia of the eighteenth century. He maintained that "many weak and trashy productions receive undue praise at the hands of Southern critics, merely because they are written and published South of the Potomac." He urged Southern poets to "quit straining at the heroic and the historical, kick Tennyson and all other models into the middle of next week . . . and come right down to the soil that gave them birth." When some young women asked him to encourage them by publishing their articles, he replied that the sooner the majority of scribblers were crushed out, the better for them; those who could not be crushed out were the only persons likely ever to write anything worth while.

What Bagby wanted was a home-grown Southern literature made up of writings which smacked of the soil. This was a sound editorial policy, but Bagby found it difficult to secure such writers as he wanted. The best that he discovered was the North Carolina humorist Harden E. Taliaferro ("Skitt"). Southern magazines, Bagby thought, might succeed if they had the capital to enable them, like the Northern magazines, to print pictures and pay five dollars a page for articles; but, he complained, the best Southern writers had been "bought up by the newspaper capitalists at the North," and Southern readers preferred illustrated magazines or the British reviews.

When the Civil War broke out, Bagby was thirty-three years old and almost an invalid, but he joined a Lynchburg company and took part in the Battle of Bull Run. In the summer of 1861, however, he was discharged as physically unfit for active service and returned to Richmond. The *Messenger* continued to appear in spite of rising prices and the scarcity of paper and ink. In 1863, the year of his marriage to Lucy Parke Chamberlayne, he became an associate editor of the Richmond *Daily Whig* and wrote occasional editorials for John M. Daniel's *Examiner*, besides writing for the *Southern Illustrated News* and for various newspapers outside of Richmond. After the first six months of the war, he had little hope that the Confederacy could win its independence. Like Daniel, he was a severe critic of Davis's administration. Early in 1864 he gave up his position on the *Messenger*, which survived a few months longer under the editorship of Frank H. Alfriend.

The end of the war brought no relief from Bagby's difficulties. Finding little profit in writing for Virginia newspapers, he went to New York in 1865, but eye trouble forced him a few months later to return to Virginia. For two or three years he published in Orange County his own weekly, the *Native Virginian*. He wrote occasionally for the New York *Evening Post* and the *Southern Magazine* in Baltimore. Beginning in 1869, he published a number of articles in *Lippincott's Magazine*—one of the few Northern periodicals then hospitable to Southern writers—under the pseudonym of "Richard B. Elder." In 1870 he became the State Librarian. In 1878, when the Readjusters turned him out of the State Library, he took to the lecture platform once more. The best known of his lectures, "The Old Virginia Gentleman," printed as a pamphlet in 1877, was prepared to help raise funds for the Virginia Historical Society. In this lecture the realist is seen more or less consciously idealizing the slaveholder and his way of life. Bagby found it difficult to reconcile himself to the new order of things, but his last public address, "Yorktown and Appomattox," delivered at Trenton, New Jersey, in 1882, is conciliatory. He died on Thanksgiving Day of the following year.

In spite of his Northern education, Bagby was as thoroughly Virginian as any of his contemporaries. "Enough for me," he wrote in 1880, "if, dying, I shall be so fortunate as to leave behind me some descriptions of Virginia and her people which the children of my friends will take pleasure in reading after we are gone." Circumstances militated against the fulfilment of his early ambitions and made of him a newspaper man and a humorist on a level below his wish. His newspaper writings were ephemeral. His Mozis Addums letters are inferior to the best of Longstreet and Hooper, and they are much more "dated." The humor of such pieces as "My Vile Beard" no longer appeals, and "Bacon and Greens," though it has its good points, smacks too much of the popular entertainer. His essays are rambling and uneven, but the colloquial style in which they were written is often effective. The best of them all, "John M. Daniel's Latch-Key," is a superb character portrait of the most interesting Southern journalist of the time; it is a classic that deserves a place in future anthologies of Southern writings.[90]

57
Charles Henry Smith, "Bill Arp"

THE FATHER OF Charles Henry Smith (1826–1903), who made famous the name of "Bill Arp," was a New England Yankee; his mother was a Southern woman of Irish extraction. Smith attended a manual-labor school, worked in his father's store in Lawrenceville, and spent three years at the University of Georgia before his father's illness called him home. In 1849 he married Mary Octavia Hutchins, the daughter of a judge, who soon suggested to his son-in-law that he needed an assistant in his law office. After three months study of Blackstone, Smith was admitted to the bar.

[90] Bagby complained that "The chapter on John M. Daniel in Cooke's last novel, 'Mohun,' is made up mainly of scissorings from the 'Latch-Key' and no credit given" (King, Bagby, p. 110 n. 20).

In 1851 he moved to Rome, Georgia, where he practiced law until the outbreak of the War between the States. He served on the staffs of Generals Bartow and Anderson until 1863, when failing health caused him to be transferred to Macon to preside as judge advocate over a military court. After the war he resumed the practice of law, served as state senator, 1865–1866, and as mayor of Rome, 1868–1869. In 1877 he moved to a plantation, "Fontainebléau," near Cartersville. In 1888, his children now grown, he moved into Cartersville, where he lived the remainder of his life. The combination of lawyer and planter was not an uncommon one.

The letters from "Bill Arp" were first published in the Rome *Confederacy*, but after the war they were for many years a feature of the Atlanta *Constitution*, which included in its staff Henry W. Grady and Joel Chandler Harris. The first of the "Bill Arp" letters was written in April, 1861. Before printing it, the author read it aloud to some friends whom he met on the streets in Rome. Among the listeners was one William Arp, an illiterate ferryman, an intermittent drinker, and though a small man the champion fighter in his district. He was not, however, a poor-white in the usual meaning of that word. The following conversation took place between Arp and Smith:

"'Squire, are you gwine to print that?"
"I reckon I will, Bill," said I.
"What name are you gwine to put to it?" said he.
"I don't know yet," said I; "I haven't thought about a name."
"Well, 'Squire," said he, "I wish you would put mine, for them's my sentiments."

In the earliest of "Bill Arp's" letters to Abe Linkhorn, Arp is represented as a Yankee sympathizer, somewhat comparable to David Ross Locke's copperhead, "Petroleum V. Nasby." Gradually, however, the character changes until Bill Arp is a thoroughgoing Confederate who will bet on Dixie to his last dollar. A fair specimen of the letters to Lincoln is the following paragraph from the letter of December, 1862:

Mr. Linkhorn, sur, our peepul git more stubbern every day. They go mighty nigh naked, and say they are savin their Sunday clothes to wear after we have whipped you. They just glory in livin on half rashuns and stewin salt out of their smoke house dirt. They say they had rather fight you than feed you, and swear by the ghost of Calhoun they will eat roots and drink branch water the balance of the time before they will kernowly to your abolition dyenasty. Chickahominy! what a job you have undertook!

Bill Arp's fighting spirit is still high even after Sherman's march through Georgia. "Spose Sherman did walk rite thru the State. Spose he did. Was enybody whipped? Didn't the rebellyun just klose rite up behind him, like shettin a pair of waful irons? . . . He'll have to go over that ground sevrul times yet, and then sell out and move away."

The best-known of the letters was that addressed to Artemus Ward on September 1, 1865, in the dark months that followed Appomattox. Bill Arp was endeavoring to adapt himself to the new regime; he was all for peace but first he must "say sumthin." What he said expressed what many a Southerner wanted to say.

I ain't no Bo Konstrikter, but I'll be hornswoggled if the talkin, and the writin, and the slanderin hav got to be all done on one side eny longer. Sum of your foaks hav got to dry up or turn our foaks loose. It's a blamed outrage, *so called*. Ain't your editers got nuthin else to do but to peck at us, skwib at us, and krow over us? Is evry man what can write a paragraf to konsider us as bars in a kage, and be always a jobbin at us to hear us growl? . . .

But *I'm* a good Union man *so called*. *I* ain't a gwine to fite any more. *I* shan't vote for the next war. *I* ain't no gurilla. I've dun tuk the oath, and I'm gwine to keep it, but as for my bein subjergated, and humilyated, and amalgamated, and enervated, as Mr. Chase says, it ain't so—nary time. I ain't ashamed of nuthin, neather—ain't repentin—ain't axin for no one hoss, short-winded pardin. Nobody needn't be a playin preest about me. I ain't got no twenty thousan dollars. Wish I had; I'd give it to these poor widders and orfins. I'd fatten my own numerus and interestin offspring in about two minits and a half. They shouldn't eat roots and drink branch water no longer. Poor unfortinate things! To cum into this subloonery world at sich a time. There's Bull Run Arp, and Harper's Ferry Arp, and Chickahominy Arp, that never seed the pikturs in a spellin book. I tell you, my frend, we are the poorest peepul on the face of the yearth—but we are poor and proud. We made a bully fite, selah, and the whole Amerikan nation ought to feel proud of it.

In *Bill Arp, So Called* (1866) Smith dropped the humorous misspelling. It was, he believed, demoralizing to the English language and, besides, as he said, "no wit is good that will not bear to be correctly written." But the tradition was too strong for him; a few years later he permitted the letters to be reprinted in their original form. "Josh Billings's" "Essa on the Muel," it will be remembered, had no vogue when it first appeared, in the conventional spelling.

Smith's later letters are less satirical. Bill Arp is now the good-humored, industrious farmer who talks about his family, friends, farm life, and social conditions in Georgia. He has become a genial homely philosopher and an advocate of reconciliation between North and South.

Like John Esten Cooke, Hayne, and Richard Malcolm Johnston, who published his first Georgia stories during the war, Smith is a link between the Old South and the New. On the one hand, he looks back to William Tappan Thompson and Longstreet. Two of Bill Arp's adventures recall Longstreet's "The Fight," and his descriptions of gander-pulling and other local customs look forward to the Southern local colorists. Joel Chandler Harris's Billy Sanders, the cracker humorist and philosopher, is almost like a reincarnation of Bill Arp. Although one of the last of the Southern humorists, Smith is one of the best and perhaps the kindliest of them all. There is in him little of the bitterness and scurrility which mar the work of "Petroleum V. Nasby." Miss Jennette Tandy suggests that "None of the Northern satirists except Lowell reach Bill Arp's literary level." Possibly, but "Artemus Ward" seems to me equally good; and Longstreet, Hooper, Baldwin, and George W. Harris in their different ways were not inferior to the creator of "Bill Arp."

58
The Literature of the Old South

As one looks back upon the Old South from the vantage point of another century, one is struck by the failure of the earlier native writers to make full use of rich materials which have since been explored by the writers of the New South or by their successors in the present century. Until Mrs. Stowe attacked the plantation system and war and emancipation destroyed it, most Southern writers failed to appreciate the uniqueness and the charm of the social life built upon it. Not until 1904, when Ellen Glasgow published *The Deliverance*, was there a Virginia novel which dealt with the cultivation of the staple for which the state is best known. In *The Reign of Law* James Lane Allen has described the hemp fields of Kentucky, but there is still no very notable novel about the cotton plantation. The Southern writers neglected the yeoman farmer, and for the most part they still neglect him. The farmer of American fiction is a Western type, and yet Georgia, Alabama, or Texas might have served as well as Wisconsin or California for the setting of Hamlin Garland's *Main-Travelled Roads* or Frank Norris's *The Octopus*. The older Southern writers saw the poor-white —when they condescended to notice him at all—as a comic type; they left it to Ellen Glasgow and William Faulkner to explore his possibilities as a serious, often a tragic, character.

Above all, the earlier Southern writers failed to realize the literary possibilities of the Negro. It was a Northern composer, Stephen Collins Foster, who working in the pseudo-Ethiopian musical tradition created the first memorable American songs. The earlier Southern writers neglected the rich folklore of both whites and blacks. A later generation of Southerners learned from British folklorists that the traditional folk songs of the Southern Appalachians had value both as music and as literature. The Negro spirituals went unrecorded until certain Northern educators in the Carolinas took the trouble to write down and publish their words and music.

For this neglect it is idle to blame Kennedy and Simms and Cooke; they had not been taught that these things were of any literary importance. The North was neglectful of its own folk materials in these years. Longfellow was interested in such materials but only when they were available in books. No one in those days thought it worth while to collect American versions of "Barbara Allen" or the backwoodsmen's tales of Mike Fink and Paul Bunyan. The scholars were almost as blind as the novelists. Half a century ago John A. Lomax as a freshman brought to the University of Texas a manuscript collection of cowboy songs and ballads. A professor of English to whom he showed them—one who knew the value of the British popular ballads—told him they were worthless, and he burned them. Some years later Harvard University, on the urging of Barrett Wendell and George Lyman Kittredge, gave Lomax a fellowship so that he could go back to the cattle country and once more collect the songs he had burned.

The neglect of rich literary materials must be attributed only in small degree to a deficiency of talent in the Old South. Most men who write see, especially in the beginning, only what they have learned from other writers to see. As a consequence, there are always marked limits to the value of literature in any period as a mirror of its life. One must never take a Restoration comedy or *In Ole Virginia* or *Tobacco Road* as a rounded picture of life at a given place or time. Fashion and the taste of the reading public set severe limits upon what a writer may portray and how he may picture it. No one would have cared for Faulkner's novels in the 1840's, and no writer would take William Gilmore Simms as a model now. Certain aspects of Southern life are faithfully mirrored in Kennedy's *Swallow Barn* and Simms's *The Golden Christmas*, but what their readers most delighted in was historical romances. It was difficult for men writing under the spell of Scott, G. P. R. James, and Bulwer-Lytton to deal adequately with contem-

porary life. Hawthorne, who had begun as a follower of Scott, found it, by
his own confession, extremely difficult to treat the New England life of
his own time. He could write nothing comparable to the realistic novels of
Anthony Trollope, which he greatly admired. In the slaveholding South
it was safer for the novelist to throw his story back into the past. Hence it
is that when we look for an adequate picture of Southern life in all its
aspects or in more than one period, we can never find it in any single work
of fiction. The nearest approach to a complete picture is the series of novels
in which Ellen Glasgow wrote her "social history" of Virginia in the period
from 1850 to 1940. Simms, who might have undertaken a similar task for
South Carolina, chose to write primarily of historical epochs which he
could never know at first hand. The picture of contemporary Southern life
as we have it in the writings of Caldwell, Faulkner, Wolfe, and others is
incomplete, too, for in addition to the blind spots common to their generation, they have had to write what Northern editors and publishers have
thought their non-Southern readers would be willing to buy.

Whatever the intrinsic worth of the literature of the ante-bellum South,
there can be no question, I am certain, of its historical importance. That
literature was a genuinely American product even though some of our older
historians neglected it from a belief that the South was not in any full sense
a part of the nation. Much of it was at one time or another widely read in
the Northern states. Many a reader north of the Potomac enjoyed Wirt's
The Letters of the British Spy; the novels of Caruthers, Kennedy, Simms,
and John Esten Cooke; Longstreet's *Georgia Scenes*, Baldwin's *Flush Times*,
and other sketches by Southern humorists. Discriminating lovers of books
read the poems of Edward Coote Pinkney and Henry Timrod. And the
undiscriminating read the novels of Mrs. E. D. E. N. Southworth and
Augusta Jane Evans.

There were, however, Southern writers whose work was little known in
the North: the essays of George Tucker, the poems of James M. Legaré
and Thomas Holley Chivers, and the writings of William Byrd. Northern
readers seldom looked into even the best of the Southern literary magazines,
and with a few exceptions they ignored the great mass of writing published
in defense of slavery and the rights of a minority section.

There was, as I have shown, more and better writing in the Old South
than is generally supposed. In its way the South of the mid-nineteenth
century had a share in the "American Renaissance" even though its only
major writer was Poe. No future literary historian, I hope, will write as
Barrett Wendell wrote in 1900: "Up to the Civil War, the South had

produced hardly any writing which expressed more than a pleasant sense that standard models are excellent."

The writers and readers of the New South were far too willing to acquiesce in the traditional Northern estimate of the valuelessness of the ante-bellum literature. The traditional estimate went almost unchallenged by our literary historians until twentieth-century scholars began simultaneously puncturing the inflated reputations of many better-known Northern writers and discovering a new importance in some of the writers of the Old South. Louis B. Wright told us that Beverley's *History of Virginia* is a neglected classic, more significant than the sermons of New England divines; and he and Maude H. Woodfin by their discovery of new materials added considerably to the literary stature of William Byrd. Many scholars have had a hand in rescuing from the hands of prejudiced biographers and politicians the reputation of Thomas Jefferson, who has come into his own only in the last thirty years. Lewis Chase and S. Foster Damon have pronounced Poe's friend Chivers an important poet in his own right. Thomas Ollive Mabbott has rated Timrod and Pinkney higher than did the older literary historians. Walter Blair, Jennette Tandy, Napier Wilt, Franklin J. Meine, and Constance Rourke (none of them Southerners) have found a new significance in the writings of the Southern humorists. Parrington in 1927 made students of American literature aware of such forgotten figures as Beverley Tucker and William Alexander Caruthers. George Tucker has been rediscovered by the economists, but our literary historians still know little about him. William Elliott's *Carolina Sports by Land and Water* is still read by an occasional lover of hunting and fishing, but students of our literary history seem never to have heard of him. Poe, Mark Twain, and Lanier are the only older Southern authors who can be said, in any proper sense of the word, to have had genius; but there were many who had talent —John Pendleton Kennedy, for example, who if he had given his whole time and energy to writing, might have made for himself a more important place among American novelists.

European students have found our literature less interesting on the whole than our history. Our statesmen, our soldiers, our businessmen, our inventors, our financiers, and our manufacturers outrank our writers. In a list of the ten or twelve greatest Americans probably no single writer would find a place. Our literature is hardly the best index to American achievements. This is even more emphatically true of the South, which has produced no writer who measures up to the stature of Washington or Lee. A better measure of the worth of that region may be found either in the soldiers and statesmen it has given to the nation or in its social life, which was its chief pride and joy.

The literature of the Old South, as I have had occasion frequently to note, came not from the many educated planters but from the numerically much smaller classes in the little Southern towns and cities. The planters, like English country gentlemen, looked down upon artists and writers. The town people to a great extent shared this attitude. Many of them had been brought up in the country and shared in large measure the farmer's view of life. Their prosperity like his depended upon the market price of cotton, tobacco, and sugar. Even in the twentieth century Ellen Glasgow noted a certain scorn of local literary talent among cultivated people in so large a city as Richmond. It is not surprising, then, to find that many of the older Southern writers were born in the North or born in the South of Northern parents or were educated in those parts of the North where to be known as a writer was less of a handicap than it was south of the Potomac. In America, as in England, the men who wrote our greatest books were not country gentlemen but generally middle-class and professional men from the towns and cities.

Until the sectional controversy became acute, the Southern planters were satisfied to get their reading matter—except for their newspapers and farm and religious journals—from England or the Northern states. Until the publication in 1852 of *Uncle Tom's Cabin,* they did not take seriously the warnings of Southern magazinists that the South must have its own literature. What the gentlemen farmers and their wives and daughters chiefly wanted was the British classics and novels which did not probe too deeply into contemporary problems. The planters had an appreciation for humor and eloquence, for history and biography. They did not limit their reading to eighteenth-century classics, as has been so often asserted, but read with delight the romances of Scott, Bulwer-Lytton, and G. P. R. James; and they relished the novels of Dickens for their humor and character if not for their pleas for reform. They read the poems of Pope, Byron, Campbell, Moore, and Tennyson. Mrs. Hemans, Mrs. Browning, and Mrs. Sigourney were favorites with women readers. Cooper and Irving were widely read, but the New England Transcendentalists and Abolitionists were regarded as radical reformers unfriendly to the South.

After the liberal influence of the American Revolution died away, the planters had little enthusiasm for that large segment of English and American literature which was intended to change the social and economic order. Moncure Conway's devout father was shocked by his son's heterodox opinions about slavery and religion just as that respectable-minded country gentleman, Sir Timothy Shelley, had been when his eldest son became a flaming prophet of a world made over according to the program of the French Revolutionists. Southerners in town and country alike cared little for the writings of Rousseau, Shelley, and Godwin or, among American writers, Emerson, Lowell, and Whittier. In the Old South one finds no Whittier, no Emerson, no Thoreau, no Whitman. Conway and Helper migrated to the North, where the upheaval created by the industrial revolution had made an environment in which advocates of change felt more at home.

A scholarly Englishman once asked me why it was that the Old South failed to produce the kind of literature which in Europe is associated with an aristocratic social order. Why, he asked, did the South produce nothing comparable to Congreve's *The Way of the World* or Pope's *The Rape of the Lock?* Why, he might have asked, did the Old South produce so little that is comparable even to what Dr. Holmes was writing in aristocratic Boston? Certainly, apart from a few minor pieces from the pens of William Byrd and William Crafts, the Old South produced little of this type of writing.

Perhaps the planters were satisfied with such lighter literature as they could import from England; and yet there was, I think, another reason. The Southern social order—apart from slavery—was at bottom no more aristocratic—in spite of the Cavalier legend—than that of Boston, New York, or Philadelphia. The overwhelming majority of Southern writers after the Revolution were of middleclass origin. There was, if we except Charleston, probably more aristocratic feeling in some Southern urban social circles in 1900 than there was in the Old South at any time after 1800. The best examples of "aristocratic literature" to come out of the South are Ellen Glasgow's *The Romantic Comedians* and *They Stooped to Folly*, and the disenchanted romances of James Branch Cabell. These have the lightness of touch, the wit, and the sophistication which one associates with Pope and Congreve and Dr. Holmes.

In spite of the popularity of contemporary Southern fiction, it is not the fashion nowadays to praise many things that are typically Southern. The urban American is likely to be somewhat intolerant of any marked variation from the national pattern, especially in rural areas. And yet perhaps a time may come when the values of the Southern way of life will be better appreciated than they are now. The finest product of the Old South was not its cotton or tobacco or its literature but its men and women. The Southern planter had his shortcomings, only too evident now, but he had his virtues also, and some of them are of a kind all too rare in the America of the twentieth century. By comparison we are a restless, uprooted people without strong local attachments and often without close personal ties. The Southern planter was an independent farmer living among lifelong friends and kinsmen. He could afford to take time to be neighborly, hospitable, friendly to strangers and to pay some attention to the amenities of life. He had a freedom to live as he pleased and a personal integrity less commonly found in a world where most men are employees having their actions controlled by their superiors and living in fear of losing their jobs. In the South of today the qualities which we used to call Southern are all too rare. The South seems no longer to breed men like Washington, Jefferson, Lee, Lucius Q. C. Lamar, or Thomas Dabney.

Something of the charm, the leisureliness, the homelike simplicity of the older Southern way of life is expressed in its literature—often inadequately, for, as I have said, that literature is often not the best index to the quality of its culture. I suppose I have read as much of that literature as anyone else is likely to read again. I have found myself more deeply interested in it than I anticipated. I have come to feel a strong personal admiration for certain writers. Kennedy, Simms, George Tucker, and Charles Gayarré, for example, were not great writers, but they were men of talent and they were in themselves admirable examples of the Southern civilization at its best. I should like for others to know them better.

The literature of the older South may have a definite value for the serious reader of today for the very reason that it deals with a society so different from that in which he lives. It gives the modern urban American a point of reference for understanding the good and bad features of the world of today. To read *Swallow Barn*, *Woodcraft*, or *In Ole Virginia* is like making a visit to some foreign country from which the traveler returns to look at his own land with sharpened critical eyes.

The Old South has been described as the last outpost of feudal Europe. Perhaps in one sense it was, and yet the social order of the Old South was an indigenous product, and so was the literature which sprang out of it. The American of the present time, whose sense of the past is often dull, may acquire a better understanding of his own place in the scheme of things by acquainting himself with the rich past of his own country. In that past for over two centuries the Southern states held nearly half the American population, and their part in the making of the American nation was proportionately large. I hope that every American who reads in this book will come to a better understanding of the American past and of his own relation to it.

V

THE NEW SOUTH

1865-1900

1
The Road to Reconciliation: The North

In that fateful spring of 1865 the great tragedy of the Civil War moved rapidly to its close. Atlanta had fallen; Sherman had marched to the sea and then turned northward through the Carolinas. Grant broke through the Confederate lines around Petersburg. Lee abandoned Richmond and on April 9 he surrendered the remnant of the Army of Northern Virginia. On April 26 Johnston surrendered his army to Sherman near Durham in North Carolina, and in Texas on May 26 the last important Confederate army, under Kirby Smith, laid down its arms. The Southern will to fight was gone. The newly created nation which only four years earlier Timrod had so proudly hailed in "Ethnogenesis" and "The Cotton Boll" was dead. In "The Conquered Banner," written when he heard the news of Lee's surrender, Father Ryan well expressed the despairing mood of the defeated Confederacy:

> Furl that Banner, softly, slowly!
> Treat it gently—it is holy—
>   For it droops above the dead.
> Touch it not—unfold it never,
> Let it droop there, furled forever,
>   For its people's hopes are dead!

Meanwhile, on Good Friday President Lincoln, born in Kentucky of Virginian parents, had been struck down by the assassin's bullet. Almost immediately he was canonized in the North as the Great Emancipator and the Savior of the Union. Lincoln was fortunate in his death, for he was not, like Woodrow Wilson, doomed to live to see his plans for peace frustrated by little and vindictive men. Lincoln's death, as it seemed to Walt Whitman in 1879, was one of "those climax-moments on the stage of universal Time, where the historic Muse at one entrance, and the tragic Muse at the other, suddenly ringing down the curtain, close an immense act in the long drama of creative thought, and give it radiation, tableau, stranger than fiction." In the same lecture, "Death of Abraham Lincoln," Whitman said: "Have you never realized it, my friends, that Lincoln, though grafted on the West, is essentially, in personnel and character, a Southern contribution?" Years, however, were to pass before a new generation of Southern writers would follow Whitman's cue and portray Lincoln as a product of the South.[1]

An even longer time was to elapse before the greatness of Lee was widely recognized in the North. When ten years after the war Lowell paid his tribute to Virginia in "Under the Old Elm," he still regarded Lee as a traitor to his country. Melville had been more generous in his poem, "Lee at the Capitol," published in the year that followed Appomattox; and in 1868 or 1869 Albion W. Tourgée wrote the noble estimate of Lee's character which appears in Chapter XXXI of his 'Toinette (1874). Eventually two New Englanders were to write what are among the finest of all tributes to the great soldier who died in 1870. In 1902 the younger Charles Francis Adams, who had fought against him, wrote "Shall Cromwell Have a Statue?" a plea that the state of Virginia should be permitted to place a statue of Lee in the national Capitol beside that of Washington. In 1912, when Gamaliel Bradford published his admirable portrait of Lee, he entitled it *Lee the American*, I suspect, to counteract the impression suggested by Thomas Nelson Page's *Robert E. Lee: The Southerner* (1908).

The sermons preached in Northern churches on that black Easter Sunday which followed Lincoln's death appealed not to the Christ of love and forgiveness but to an avenging Jehovah. "The great body of Northern clergymen," says Paul H. Buck in *The Road to Reunion*, "passed through the experience to a result disastrous to any hope of reconciliation. The defeat of the South came more than ever to signify a moral victory. The ability to understand, much less to sympathize, with the problems of Southern life grew more impossible. The feeling that a moral crusade for the regeneration of 'rebeldom' was necessary became henceforth a fixed article in the creed of the Northern churches." Such also was the reaction of Northern journalists, Abolitionists, and political leaders. After late in the summer of 1865 General Lee was elected president of little Washington College, Wendell Phillips said in a speech at Cooper Union: "If Lee is fit

---

[1] See, for example, Joel Chandler Harris, "The Kidnapping of President Lincoln" in *On the Wing of Occasions* (1900); Thomas Dixon, *The Southerner* (1913); and Roy P. Basler, *The Lincoln Legend* (1935), pp. 239–241. Walter Malone, Maurice Thompson, and John Gould Fletcher wrote poems about Lincoln which are much above the average. See also in this connection Vachel Lindsay, *The Litany of Washington Street* (1929).

to be president of a college, then for heaven's sake pardon Wirtz and make him professor of what the Scotch call 'the humanities.' " [2] When Emerson learned that Lee had surrendered to Grant, he wrote in his journal: " 'Tis far the best that the rebels have been pounded instead of negociated into a peace. They must remember it, and their inveterate brag will be humbled, if not cured." He continued: "General Grant's terms certainly look a little too easy, . . . and I fear that the high tragic historic justice which the nation, with severest consideration, should execute, will be softened and dissipated and toasted away at dinner-tables." Had Emerson so soon forgotten the wise words of the dead statesman who had said in his Second Inaugural Address: "With malice toward none; with charity for all . . ."?

Literate Northerners were confirmed in their notions of the South by reports which presumably competent observers brought back from the late Confederacy; but Sidney Andrews and John Townsend Trowbridge when they crossed the Potomac saw chiefly what they had come to look for in the "barbarous" region of Abolitionist legend. The South must now be civilized and Americanized. Lowell wrote in the *North American Review* in October, 1866: "Is it not time that these men were transplanted at least into the nineteenth century, and, if they cannot be suddenly Americanized, made to understand something of the country which was too good for them, even though at the cost of a rude shock to their childish self-conceit?" The South was made to feel that it must remain a conquered country, that its ideals were altogether un-American, and that nothing would satisfy the victorious North but repentance and a complete about-face in its beliefs and its way of life. It was as though the South had had no part in framing the Declaration of Independence or the Federal Constitution. John R. Thompson, returning from England late in 1866 to his native state, now "Military District No. 1," wrote in "Virginia Fuit:"

> *Consummatum*—the work of destruction is done,
> The race of the first of the States has been run,
> The guile of her foes finds her triumph at last,
> And VIRGINIA, like Poland, belongs to the past.

A decade later another Virginian, George W. Bagby, said to newspapermen in Charleston: "The end of the struggle at Appomattox was but the beginning of another and much more desperate struggle—the object of which

---

[2] *Nation*, I, 546 (Nov. 2, 1865). The *Nation* had already made its own protest in an editorial entitled "General Lee as an Instructor of Youth" (I, 329, Sept. 14, 1865). Henry Wirz, who was in charge of the Confederate prison at Andersonville, Ga., was tried by a military commission and hanged for alleged atrocities in his treatment of Union soldiers.

is the conquest of your most cherished ideas in politics, religion and social order—the rearrangement of the very molecules of your brain—the facing about of your inmost soul—no less. This is the new 'irrepressible conflict,' which, like the old, will bring us all to grief, years hence."

A year after Appomattox Herman Melville, his great novels all but forgotten by a fickle reading public, appended to a volume of poems, *Battle-Pieces*, a prose "Supplement," which contains wiser words about Reconstruction than came from anyone but Lincoln. The task of reconstruction, Melville thought, called for "little but common sense and Christian charity," and its success depended "not mainly on the temper in which the South regards the North, but rather conversely." While Northern ministers, journalists, and politicians were calling upon the defeated Confederates to repent, Melville asked:

But what exactly do we mean by this? . . . the only penitence now left her [the South] is that which springs solely from the sense of discomfiture; and since this evidently would be a contrition hypocritical, it would be unworthy in us to demand it. Certain it is that penitence, in the sense of voluntary humiliation, will never be displayed. . . . It is enough, for all practical purposes, if the South have been taught by the terrors of civil war to feel that Secession, like Slavery, is against Destiny; that both now lie buried in one grave; that her fate is linked with ours; and that together we comprise the Nation.

Melville, who had read British history and literature to some purpose, foresaw a time when Southerners would

be yielding allegiance to the Union, feeling all their interests bound up in it, and yet cherishing unrebuked that kind of feeling for the memory of the soldiers of the fallen Confederacy that Burns, Scott, and the Ettrick Shepherd felt for the memory of the gallant clansmen ruined through their fidelity to the Stuarts —a feeling whose passion was tempered by the poetry imbuing it, and which in no wise affected their loyalty to the Georges, and which, it may be added, indirectly contributed excellent things to literature.

Could any one in 1866 more accurately have predicted the state of mind in the New South which was less than twenty years later to find memorable expression in the war stories of Thomas Nelson Page? In the eighties Northern readers had so far forgotten their resentment as to enjoy the work of Southern writers who combined loyalty to the Union with tender memories of the Lost Cause.

Reconstructing a conquered country was a novel experience for American political leaders, and the result had most of the salient elements of both tragedy and farce. Long before President Hayes in 1877 withdrew the last of the Union soldiers from the South, many intelligent Northerners had come to realize the unwisdom of the whole plan and were aware of the incompetence or corruption of the carpetbaggers and scalawags who were misgoverning many of the Southern states. By this time Edward King and other Northern observers had published accurate and sympathetic accounts of what Southerners were thinking and doing. It was now clear that the South had accepted in good faith the end of slavery and secession and desired only to be allowed to rebuild its economy and to find its proper place within the framework of the nation. Lowell, who on many occasions had written bitterly about the South, wrote on November 20, 1868, to E. L. Godkin, editor of the New York *Nation:*

I confess to a strong sympathy with men who sacrificed everything even to a bad cause which they could see only the good side of; and, now the war is over, I see no way to heal the old wounds but by frankly admitting this and acting upon it. We can never reconstruct the South except through its own leading men, nor ever hope to have them on our side till we make it for their interest and compatible with their honor to be so. At this moment in Virginia, the oath required by the new Constitution makes it impossible to get a decent magistrate.[3]

In 1868, however, the Reconstruction Congress was in no mood for conciliation. The Republican party—which in Southern eyes was still only a sectional party—had thrown aside Lincoln's humane and intelligent plans for the South and branded as disloyal the Northern Democrats, especially after they had welcomed ex-Confederates back into the party's ranks. The Republican party, which glorified Lincoln's memory in part at least to serve its own selfish ends, kept itself in power by disfranchising the ablest white Southerners, by giving the ballot to illiterate ex-slaves, and by waving the "bloody shirt" before every election. To make matters worse, Northern educators and officials who, often with the best intentions, came south to help civilize the native "barbarians" contrived to widen the gulf between the freedmen and their former masters and thus to make more acute a race problem not solved by emancipation. The Southern view of Reconstruction was well expressed by Joel Chandler Harris in an editorial in the Atlanta *Constitution* in January, 1882:

In the whole history of politics there is not a parallel to the terrible blunder committed by the Republican leaders in inaugurating, after the war, their

---

[3] *Letters* (1893), ed. C. E. Norton, II, 5. On Oct. 9, 1876, Lowell wrote to Mrs. Sophia Bledsoe Herrick: "We are deliberately trying to make an Ireland of the South, by perpetuating misgovernment there" (*ibid.*, II, 183).

Southern policy. It was a policy of lawlessness under the forms of law, of disenfrancisement, robbery, oppression and fraud. It was a deliberate attempt to humiliate the people who had lost everything by the war, and it aroused passions on both sides that were unknown when the war was in actual progress. It banished for years the hope of reconciliation, delayed the natural progress of the country, and put an end, for the time being, to commercial prosperity in both sections. . . . History will justly charge to this policy all the demoralization at the South and the desperate efforts to resist it.[4]

While the Reconstruction Congress was trying by force to make the South conform to the national pattern, Northern men of letters were beginning to use their influence to promote friendlier relations between the sections. On January 4, 1868, less than three years after the close of the war, Oliver Wendell Holmes wrote to a Southern editor, Alexander P. Morse: "It is evident that there is a returning feeling of literary fellowship." He added, however, that in writing to Morse he found it difficult to separate the "two characters" united in the person of the son of an old friend who was at the same time the editor of a Southern periodical of which Holmes disapproved: He wrote:

But you must remember that the "lost cause" is *to us* a crushed rebellion; that, *to us*, its true source was a great national wrong trying to perpetuate itself; that in this belief our children and friends have died, so that the whole North is still in mourning; and that *to us* such poems as "The Confederate Dead," such pieces as "The Confederate Flag," are only a reopening of all the old wounds, not profitable to any, but entirely unwelcome to those who want to make all whole again as soon as time will let them.

Northern men of letters, however, soon held out friendly hands to Paul Hamilton Hayne and other Southern writers who were willing to meet them halfway. On March 17, 1870, Whittier wrote to Hayne: "I think the time is near at hand when Charleston & Boston—long centres of opposing ideas—both in advance of their respective sections . . . will understand each other better & do justice to each other. At any rate, their literary men should have no prejudices." Four years later Hayne wrote to Moses Coit Tyler: "Yes: a new epoch is dawning upon this long distracted land. At all events, in the pure, serene, beautiful realm of Art, there must soon be no division between North and South. The few scholars, writers, thinkers, of

---

[4] Julia C. Harris (ed.), *Joel Chandler Harris: Editor and Essayist* (1931), pp. 64–65. The orthodox view of Reconstruction held in the South ignores the milder and more intelligent regimes that governed Virginia and some other states, and it gives the Reconstruction state governments no credit for introducing some educational and other much needed reforms.

which my own unfortunate section can boast, are being drawn daily more closely towards their Northern brethren,—brethren now in reality and not in name alone." Longfellow gave encouragement and advice to Sherwood Bonner of Mississippi, his one-time amanuensis, and in 1878 she dedicated to him her novel, *Like unto Like*. William Cullen Bryant, Evert Duyckinck, and George Henry Boker tried to help Simms and other Southerners to re-establish their connections with Northern editors and publishers. Emerson in his old age made the long journey to Virginia because it seemed to him significant that students in a Southern university desired a speaker from New England. Bayard Taylor befriended Lanier in many ways. Lowell in 1875 held out the hand of reconciliation to Virginia in "Under the Old Elm" and a little later, reading the ode in Baltimore, brought tears to the eyes of men who had fought in the Confederate armies:

> Virginia gave us this imperial man . . .
> What shall we give her back but love and praise
> As in the dear old unestranged days
> Before the inevitable wrong began? . . .
> If ever with distempered voice or pen
> We have misdeemed thee, here we take it back,
> And for the dead of both don common black.
> Be to us evermore as thou wast then,
> As we forget thou hast not always been,
> Mother of States and unpolluted men,
> Virginia, fitly named from England's manly queen!

In the late seventies the Northern reading public began to rediscover the South as it was revealed by a new generation of Southern writers of fiction and soon found it as fascinating as the new West described by Bret Harte and Mark Twain. It was in fact a far richer field than the California gold mines. Newly established Northern magazines—notably *Lippincott's* and *Scribner's Monthly*—were much more hospitable than the *Atlantic Monthly* or *Harper's Magazine*, both of which by 1875 were falling into line. Irwin Russell, Sherwood Bonner, Joel Chandler Harris, Mary Noailles Murfree, James Lane Allen, Kate Chopin, Grace King, and Thomas Nelson Page found themselves able—without doing violence to their beliefs—to write about life in the South in a manner acceptable to readers in the North and West. In the eighties the South was the most popular setting in American fiction. As an editor of *Scribner's Monthly* put it, "The South was in the literary saddle in those days." In December, 1888, Albion W. Tourgée, who after an experience in trying to reconstruct North Carolina had published *A Fool's Errand* (1879), wrote in the *Forum* that American literature had become "not only Southern in type, but distinctly Confederate in sympathy." He added: "A foreigner studying our current literature, without knowledge of our history, and judging our civilization by our fiction, would undoubtedly conclude that the South was the seat of intellectual empire in America, and the African the chief romantic element of our population." Thomas Wentworth Higginson, a New England Abolitionist and partisan of John Brown who had commanded a Negro regiment during the war, actually shed tears as he read Page's "Marse Chan," in which a former slave describes the glories of the old plantation life, the epic days of the war in Virginia, and his grief at the death of his young master fighting in a war for the preservation of his right to hold Negroes in slavery. The new generation of Southern writers had accomplished what their predecessors had never been able to do: they had induced Northern readers to accept a picture of Southern life far more faithful than that of the Abolitionist poets and propagandists. Northern readers would have none of Grayson's *The Hireling and the Slave,* but they eagerly devoured Page's *Red Rock* (1898), which was in effect a reply to *Uncle Tom's Cabin,* published nearly half a century earlier.

The Hayes-Tilden controversy, which at one time threatened the unity of the nation, ended in the most important of all the sectional compromises. Hayes was declared elected to the Presidency with the understanding that he would withdraw the Union troops from the Southern states. When this was done early in 1877, the last of the corrupt state political machines collapsed and white Southerners regained control. The quiet work of reconciliation proceeded much more rapidly from this time onward. The inauguration of Cleveland in 1885 gave Southern politicians for the first time since 1861 a place in the national administration. Any lingering doubt of the South's loyalty to the Union was quickly dispelled when in 1898 old Confederate soldiers like Fitzhugh Lee and Fighting Joe Wheeler and thousands of young Southerners volunteered to drive the Spaniards out of Cuba. Long before this time the majority of Northerners had come to accept in large part the Southern view of the Negro problem. The North had met the South halfway. In the eighties and nineties the majority of the intelligent in both sections had come to an understanding based upon minimizing points of disagreement and emphasizing alike their devotion to the Union and the new social and economic order. Even though the Compromise of 1877 was to prove somewhat unstable, as Cable was soon to discover, the change which had come over both sections was an amazing one; and the achievement owed far more to the work of the men of letters than to that of the politicians. Let us now return to the very different South of 1865 and view the sequence of events as they were seen from below the Mason-Dixon Line.

2
The Road to Reconciliation: The South

Having appealed to the sword and lost, most Southerners quickly interpreted the verdict as meaning the end of both secession and slavery. Within a few years most of them came to recognize that emancipation was certainly a benefit to the whites and probably to the ex-slaves as well. Those who had never liked the "peculiar institution" could now speak their minds with impunity. But the fulminations of Northern journalists, politicians, and preachers aroused deep resentment. Southerners felt that their section was being made the whipping boy for the sins of the whole nation; and though they now saw the supreme folly of putting their trust in King Cotton and secession, they were no more repentant than "Bill Arp," who thus addressed "Artemus Ward" in 1865: "I ain't ashamed of nuthin, neather— ain't repentin—ain't axin for no one hoss, short-winded pardin. . . . We had good men, grate men, kristyun men, who thot we was right, and many of them hav gone to the undiskivered kountry, and hav got a pardin as is a pardin. When I die I am mighty willin to risk myself under the shadder of their wings, whether the klimate is hot or cold. So mote it be. Selah!"

Not long after Appomattox Mrs. Cornelia Spencer, whose parents had been born and reared in the North, wrote from North Carolina to a New England spinster friend of positive opinions who had visited in Chapel Hill before the war: "I seem to be addressing you on the other side of a great gulf—a gulf at one time impassable, but which has been bridged over, and which I do humbly and heartily pray may be filled up some time or other. Not yet, and not now, but some day, in God's own good time." She added: "I believe that the lying that was done by the newspaper press on both sides was enough to sink the whole continent to perdition. I look back aghast now to think what lies we swallowed about you, and I look on aghast to see what lies you swallowed about us."

Southerners, as I have said, resented the Reconstruction regime as an attempt to "Americanize" them, to make them conform to what still seemed to them a sectional pattern. It graveled them that a rival section of the country with its mongrel population of Yankees and foreigners, so they thought, should monopolize to itself the name of "American" and deny it to the region which had produced Washington, Jefferson, Lee, and Andrew Jackson. The commercial-industrial-urban ideal, which seemed to have as its basis money and exploitation, made little appeal to the old-fashioned Southern planter. The mind of the conservative Southerner of middle age, trying in some manner to justify the course his section had taken with such disastrous consequences, was thrown back upon the past. That past began to seem in retrospect a kind of Golden Age. In some respects he was now more intensely and more consciously Southern than his fathers had been. For a decade a main activity of the Southern mind—apart from the struggle for a living—was given to the defense of the Southern interpretation of American history. Most of all, Southerners resented having their own history written for the world to read by partisan Northern historians who attributed the "Rebellion" to a gigantic conspiracy which never had any existence outside of their own minds, who denounced the Southern way of life as barbarous and un-American, and who treated the proud South as a problem child which must be taught the elementary principles of decent living by an alien and hostile North.[5] In *The Coming of the Civil War* (1942) Avery Craven wrote: ". . . the Northern explanation of events [in the years 1830–1865], as evolved by Von Holst, Schouler and McMaster, became the orthodox history of the period. Textbooks followed their interpretation and gradually even the South itself accepted them as 'sound' and 'unbiased.' What Jefferson Davis had said would constitute the South's most serious loss became a reality; the victor was writing the history of the War for future generations."

What Southerners wanted, however, was not an accurate and impartial history but justification of the course the South had taken since 1830. Not for a generation would more than an occasional Southerner be able to agree with Walter Hines Page that when the South turned its back upon the liberalism of Jefferson to follow Calhoun and Davis, it had been guilty of one of the most dangerous apostasies in all history. It was to be more than one generation before many Southerners could agree with Joel Chandler Harris, who wrote in the Atlanta *Constitution* for January 17, 1880: "The disastrous and demoralizing mistake that the Southern people made after the surrender was in refusing to take their old slaves into their care and confidence instead of allowing them to be manipulated into a mechanical

---

[5] See, for example, Albert Taylor Bledsoe, "School Histories of the United States," *So. Rev.*, III, 155–179 (Jan., 1868); T. B. Kingsbury, "History Perverted" and "The South Must Write Its Own Histories," *Our Living and Our Dead* (Raleigh), II, 170–175 (April, 1875) and 300–305 (May, 1875); and Thomas Nelson Page, "The Want of a History of the Southern People," *The Old South* (1892).

and false sympathy with the intolerable policy of the carpet-baggers. The Southern people have made other political mistakes since, but this was altogether the most disastrous. In a manner, we held the poor blacks responsible for the shock that their emancipation gave to our social organism. This was human nature, perhaps, but it was the most deplorable blunder that Southern human nature ever made."

Meanwhile there was growing up in the South a younger generation which more quickly adapted itself to the changed social and economic order. The large plantations were being sold for debt and divided into small farms, for large-scale farming seemed impracticable with free Negro labor. The drift was to the towns and cities, and young men no longer looked forward to the owning of a large plantation as the *summum bonum*. Business and the professions were more attractive. The young and the more adaptable of the older men turned their energies to business, trade, manufacturing, or to a more scientific farming. Southern Bourbon and Northern capitalist and expert began to exploit untapped natural resources. And so there gradually emerged a New South which did not altogether please older Southern writers like Gayarré and Hayne. It was chiefly the younger men of the South who worked out in their thinking a compromise, not merely political, which, unstable though it was, enabled them to meet the North halfway and to live on friendly terms with the rest of the nation.

The common ground on which a New South and a New North could meet was suggested in Lucius Q. C. Lamar's historic eulogy of Charles Sumner, delivered on April 28, 1874. As a newly elected Congressman from Mississippi, Lamar had found in Washington a marked distrust of himself and his Southern colleagues. In an important unpublished letter written on September 3, 1874, Lamar explained at length to Clement C. Clay why he had made his plea for reconciliation. "It was dictated by no *pseudo* 'magnanimity,'" he said. In Washington Lamar had discovered that what the Southern Congressmen said "*never reached the masses of the North.*" He had talked with many Northern Congressmen in order to find out "whether there was any point upon which they could be approached successfully by the South—to ascertain if there was any ground upon which harmony, concord, peace & justice between the sections could be established." What he discovered was not encouraging. "I found among the new Englanders & a few N[orth]. Westeners," he said, "creatures egotistical, monstrously harsh . . . & contemptuous for the suffering people of the South. But such was not the spirit of even the *Republicans* in the North West, & there were some exceptions among the New Englanders." What Lamar looked for was an opportunity to make a speech to which the Northern people would listen and "listen with something of a feeling of *sympathy*. I thought," he continued, "the death of Sumner was such an occasion. . . . *Every word said about him, on the occasion of his funeral, would be read all over the North, especially among those classes who have never given us a hearing.*" Lamar knew that in eulogizing a man so deeply hated in the South as Sumner he was in danger of losing all Southern support. "But," he wrote, "I felt that the time had come for me to stake my political life." Disregarding the many bitter things which Sumner had said about the South, he made his eloquent appeal and concluded in words which, old-fashioned though they seem now, thrilled all who heard them:

. . . I see on both sides only the seeming of a constraint, which each apparently hesitates to dismiss. The South—prostrated, exhausted, drained of her lifeblood, as well as of her material resources, yet still honorable and true—accepts the bitter award of the bloody arbitrament without reservation, resolutely determined to abide the result with chivalrous fidelity; yet, as if struck dumb by the magnitude of her reverses, she suffers on in silence. The North, exultant in her triumph, and elated by success, still cherishes, as we are assured, a heart full of magnanimous emotions for her disarmed and discomfited antagonist; and yet, as if mastered by some mysterious spell, silencing her better impulses, her words and acts are the words and acts of suspicion and distrust.

Would that the spirit of the illustrious dead whom we lament to-day could speak from the grave to both parties to this deplorable discord in tones which should reach each and every heart throughout this broad territory: "My countrymen! *know* one another, and you will *love* one another!" [6]

There were Southerners who in 1874 regarded Lamar as disloyal to his own section, and there were Northerners who did not respond to his appeal when they read it in the newspapers. A few years after Hayes's inauguration, however, reconciliation and friendship were to become the vogue in both North and South. It was in the 1880's that Henry W. Grady, too young to have fought for the Confederacy, reaped a harvest of good will for the New South by his speeches in Boston and New York. There was, however, noth-

---

[6] Edward Mayes, *Lucius Q. C. Lamar* (Nashville, 1896), p. 187. See also Wirt A. Cate, *Lucius Q. C. Lamar* (1935), chaps. 1 and ix. Sumner was not the only antislavery spokesman whom Lamar praised. Sherwood Bonner "in one of her letters . . . tells how when still a girl she was surprised and stirred to thought by L. Q. C. Lamar, who told her that of American poems he thought the finest were Whittier's poems on slavery" (B. M. Drake in *Southern Writers*, II, 84–85). Lamar when he wrote his speech had presumably not read Whitman's lines:

"Over the carnage rose prophetic a voice,
Be not dishearten'd, affection shall solve the problems of freedom yet,
Those who love each other shall become invincible,
They shall yet make Columbia victorious."

ing essentially new in what Grady had to say to his Northern audiences; and this he well knew when in 1886 he began his address to the New England Society in New York:

"There was a South of slavery and secession—that South is dead. There is a South of union and freedom—that South, thank God, is living, breathing, growing every hour." These words, delivered from the immortal lips of Benjamin H. Hill, at Tammany Hall, in 1866, true then, and truer now, I shall make my text to-night.

To ultraconservative Southerners, like Albert Taylor Bledsoe, William Hand Browne, and Charles Colcock Jones, Jr., the attitude of Grady and Lamar seemed like a betrayal of the past. Even Paul Hayne, who had counted a number of Northern writers among his friends, could write to Margaret J. Preston on June 12, 1869:

The South that we knew is dead, beyond chance of resurrection. And the South to be, will prove the bastard offspring of Yankee thrift upon S° Necessity, a mere Monster, fat it may be, & puffed up with vanity, & greed, shining with a rank material oiliness,—but no more like the grand old South, of chivalrous, & majestic memory, than Sancho Panza swilling the wine, and stuffing the rich food of Barrataria, is like Raleigh, coursing in silver armor before Queens, & Emperors, or one of Arthur's knights seeking the San Grail!

In much the same strain is a letter to Hayne, written on July 19, 1870, by William Hand Browne: "Great God! it makes my blood boil in my veins when I think of the South flinging away just the priceless jewels of which no force can deprive her: her individuality, her Southern character, her Southern honor. Bayard, asking Bourbon to spare his life and make him a sutler in his army, where there is likely to be good pickings!" [7]

Now more than ever the irreconcilables in the poverty-stricken South felt that their section was being exploited by Northern capitalists. In November, 1866, an anonymous contributor to *De Bow's Review* contrasted the old "slaveholding aristocracy of the South" with "the moneyed aristocracy of the North-East." [8] Slaveholders, he admitted, had exploited their Negro slaves. "For this sin, if sin it were," he said, "the South has suffered most

[7] Both letters are in the Hayne Collection in the Duke Univ. Library. On May 19, 1885, Hayne wrote to Charles Gayarré: "In the 'young South,' so-called, I observe a growing tendency towards contempt for the Past, & a truckling spirit, so far as Yankee ideas, & Yankee prejudices are concerned." For the views of Charles Colcock Jones, Jr., and other conservatives, see John D. Wade, "Old Wine in a New Bottle," *Va. Quart. Rev.*, XI, 239–252 (April, 1935).

[8] "The Two Aristocracies of America," n.s. II, 461–465 (Nov., 1866). The thesis of the article is similar to that of many earlier Southern writers and speakers; it also anticipates in some respects the thesis of Walter P. Webb's *Divided We Stand* (1937).

grievously, and, if Radical rule be continued, must in the future suffer still more grievously." The slaveholders at least, he contended, had been honest and incorruptible, and in Congress they had never sought to make a profit out of the people of the North. At the same time, when no tariff protected the agricultural products of the Southern farms, Southerners were buying Northern manufactures "with forty per cent. added to their open market value by protective legislation."

The defeat of the South, the anonymous writer pointed out, had placed both the South and the West under the control of the Northern Plutocracy. "Aristocracy!" he exclaimed, "why the world has never seen an aristocracy half so powerful, half so corrupt, so unprincipled, and rapacious, nor one-tenth so vulgar and so ignorant, as the moneyed aristocracy of the North-East." Most of the natural resources of the nation, he pointed out, were in the South and the West; and yet by "financial legerdemain" more than two billion dollars each year were being "transferred from the pockets of the laboring producers of the North-West and of the South to the capitalists, the idle non-producers of the North-East."

This new aristocracy that has arisen on the ruins of the slave aristocracy knows no distinctions of race or color; it tyrannizes over and robs them all alike. The National debt belongs to this new aristocracy; most of the State and Corporation debts are due to them; the Banks all over the Union, in great part, are owned by them; so are the Railroads and Canals, and the factories of various manufactures, and the great mercantile interest is theirs. Through all these agencies they tax agricultural and working interests of the nation. . . . Does not North-Eastern capital now tax white labor more heavily than ever masters taxed negro slaves? . . . Is not the Federal Government in their hands, and do they not employ it as a mere engine to tax, fleece, rob, and exploit the South and the North-West?

The obvious remedy was for the South and the West to "combine to check the aggressions and mitigate the cruel exactions" of the Northern Plutocracy. In 1866, however, the Western farmers had no intention of aligning themselves with Southern farmers who had held slaves. In the North no one in 1866 cared to listen to Southern criticism of the way business was being conducted in the "Gilded Age" by the "Robber Barons." The New South of the 1880's, developing industries of its own with the aid of Northern capital, was to be far less critical of Northern business than the unknown writer in De Bow's Review.

It is difficult to make a sound generalization about the South or Southern literature without ignoring numerous and important exceptions. My division of Southerners into those who wished to keep the heritage of the Old South and those who advocated the new order is an artificial one. In fact, most Southerners except the intransigents hoped to have it both ways. They cherished the memory of the Old South and made a cult of the soldier in gray, but this did not prevent them from leaving their farms and going to live in towns or cities or from asking Northern capitalists to come south and build railroads and factories. Southerners idealized the old regime without being aware that, if they could by some miracle have brought it back, they would not have liked it. They failed to see also that in the new industrial order some qualities much admired by the gentlemen planters would come to seem archaic and unworthy of imitation.

3

Authorship in the New South

At the end of the war the South, now without publishing houses or magazines of its own, was once more reduced to the intellectual status of a colony. Southern booksellers, as of old, were restocking their shelves with books sent them by Northern publishers, including the wartime publications of the writers of New England. One typical conservative reaction to Northern writing of the sixties was that of Albert Taylor Bledsoe, who wrote in the *Southern Review* for April, 1867: "Literature in the North, especially in New England, like the Roman 'judgment,' 'fled' early, and the Everetts, and Bancrofts, and Motleys, and Lowells, and Holmeses, and Bryants, and Longfellows, who once, in our day of delusion, we thought were men of genial letters, all joined the Great Crusade, and preached and sang the Gospel and Psalmody of bloody War."

Once more the Southern schools were reduced to using the prejudiced Northern textbooks, now more unacceptable than ever.[9] Educated Southerners, reading the new books, magazines, and newspapers that emanated from Boston and New York, felt that the worst pang of defeat came from seeing the North give to the world its biased account of American history during the preceding half-century. It was galling to see Lee and Davis branded as traitors, to see Simms labeled as the South's only writer and a tenth-rate writer at that, to see slaveholders branded as barbarians and their former field hands hailed as the only hope of the fallen Confederacy. The

---

[9] "We will not use an inferior book because it is prepared by a Southern man. Yet, in the departments of history, literature, and moral philosophy, it is almost impossible to find an acceptable text-book written by a Northern man" (*Home Monthly*, Nashville, IV, 51, Jan., 1868)

South, in sentiment now more of a unit than it had ever been before the war, saw itself haled before the bar of civilization and once again left without an adequate defense. There was no longer any hope that the South would ever become a separate nation, but there was nevertheless an insistent demand that the South must have its own literature. Paul Hayne wrote too hopefully in *Scott's Monthly* in September, 1866: "Overthrown in our efforts to establish a political nationality by *force of arms*, we may yet establish an intellectual dynasty more glorious and permanent by *force of thought*." Much Southern writing was now frankly sectional and designed as a literature of defense, for if some Northern writers had seemed hostile in the fifties, practically all of them seemed so in the next decade.

The lot of the Southern writer had never been a happy one, but in the lean years of the late sixties it was pitiable indeed. Cut off from any literary market in the North when there was only the vestige of one in their own section, Simms, Timrod, and Hayne came close to starvation. From the devastated city of Columbia Timrod wrote in July, 1865, to Richard Henry Stoddard in New York:

I begin to see (darkly) behind that *Divine* political economy which has ended in the extinction of slavery and the preservation of the Union; and I am prepared to discharge in good faith the obligations which I assumed upon taking the oath. . . . I have been reduced by the destruction of this town to the most abject poverty. There is no possibility of my procuring employment here of any sort. Literature is an unattainable and undesirable luxury. . . . With what reception would a Southerner meet in New York? Could I hope to get employment there in any capacity whatever? Hack writer of a newspaper, editor of the poet's corner of some third-rate journal, grocer's clerk—nothing would come amiss to me that would put bread in the mouths and a roof over the heads of those whom I love best in the world.

In his letter Timrod enclosed some unpublished poems, which Stoddard tried in vain to place in Northern magazines.

The more professionally minded writers who survived the war were not so hopeful as the many amateurs of establishing a Southern literature. They looked northward. Sherwood Bonner, however, was the only important Southern writer to settle in Boston. Most of them preferred New York or Baltimore. In the latter city, where sympathy with the Confederacy had been strong, Richard Malcolm Johnston, Father Tabb, Innes Randolph, Albert Taylor Bledsoe, and eventually Sidney Lanier found a more congenial environment. Baltimore, however, was not an important literary market, and after the death of Kennedy in 1870 it had no native writers of importance. The newly established Johns Hopkins University, at which

Lanier lectured, had in its faculty Basil Lanneau Gildersleeve, an ex-Confederate who was perhaps the greatest of all American Greek scholars. Johns Hopkins also attracted some able Southern students, like Woodrow Wilson and W. P. Trent, both of whom were to find important positions in Northern universities. Simms, Bagby, and Hayne, recognizing the literary predominance of New York, visited that city in the effort to establish connections with editors and publishers.[10] Lanier, often though he tried, was never able to establish himself in New York. More fortunate were John R. Thompson and George Cary Eggleston, each of whom served as literary editor of Bryant's *Evening Post*.

Thompson, who had returned to Richmond from England late in 1866, wrote to a friend on April 1 of the next year: "Having satisfied myself beyond all question that there is no career for me here, no hope of employment even, I am just on the eve of departure for New York, where I shall remain *en permanence* if the fates are propitious. I have nothing certain before me, and only go to 'breast the blows of circumstance, and grapple with my evil star.' The Bohemian life is dreary enough in the prospect of it, and my heart is sad almost unto breaking in sundering the tie that binds me to Virginia, but I must get to work and the sooner the better."

While living in New York, Thompson found himself censured in the South as disloyal because he had published an article in *Harper's Magazine*. Mrs. L. Virginia French defended him: "When we have a commodity to sell, we *will* sell to the highest bidder. We may deprecate the *necessity* of selling the best brains of the South to *Harper*, which for years past has undergone torments to prove that the South *has no brains at all*—but is it not a splendid contradiction to this theory that 'Harper' now buys Southern brains at higher rates than the South itself is willing to accord them?" [11]

After the war authorship in the South, like manual labor and teaching, became a more respectable occupation than it had been in the forties and fifties. "The pursuit of letters," wrote the editor of the *Land We Love* in February, 1867, "is not now a recreation, but an earnest effort for a livelihood." Men and women, especially women, turned desperately or hopefully to writing, which seemed to require no capital or equipment except pen, ink, and paper. Professor Trent remarks in his life of Simms: "Those who fancied that they could write spent almost their last penny for paper and scribbled away quires of pathetic trash. Then they bought a stamp and mailed a letter to Simms, begging that he would get their books published."

---

[10] *De Bow's Rev.*, N.S. III, 215 (Feb., 1867), estimated that twenty thousand Southerners had removed to New York since the war.

[11] "Pen-Feather," *Land We Love*, VI, 148 (Dec., 1868).

Many of these writers were women who hoped for such success as had come to Augusta Jane Evans and Mrs. E. D. E. N. Southworth. A few of them eventually published memorable accounts of their wartime experiences. The generals, too, took up the pen to recount the heroic deeds of their soldiers or perhaps to explain their reverses. And of course the orators published in pamphlet form the speeches of which they were proudest.

A severe Southern critic, Mrs. Cornelia Spencer, wrote in March, 1866: "Literary projects seem to abound among us these days. Magazines, newspapers, books—one needs a fortune to subscribe to half. I do not think very highly of American literature even at its best, but Southern literature is the feeblest attempt, the very weakest dilution and rinsings." The year before she had written: "Oh beloved and Sunny South, Land that I love, more now in the day of humiliation, woe, and ruin than ever before, thy day of regeneration and renovation will never dawn till thou hast learned to dig deep, and lay thy foundations broad and firm—learned to educate thy children thoroughly—learned to distinguish gold from gilding, silver from tinsel."

There were in the South, as before the war, numerous printers who occasionally brought out a book which few of them knew how to market efficiently, but there were no real publishing houses. There were, however, a few publishers in Northern cities, notably New York, who were willing to print books by Southern writers, primarily for what was left of the old Southern market. Among these was Van Evrie, Horton and Company, publishers of the *Old Guard*, who in 1870 brought out John Esten Cooke's *The Heir of Gaymount*. A house with a better standing, D. Appleton and Company, published Cooke's biographies of Lee and Jackson in 1866 and 1870. Hurd and Houghton in 1867 published Lanier's *Tiger-Lilies* at his expense. Simms's *War Poetry of the South* (1866) was published by Richardson and Company, which tantalized Timrod with vain hopes that they might publish his poems. Probably G. W. Carleton and Company published more important Southern books in the sixties and early seventies than any other New York house. In an article on "Northern Publishing Houses" which appeared in the Richmond *Southern Opinion* on October 3, 1869, the firm is described as practically a Southern publishing house. Carleton brought out Cooke's *Fairfax* (1868), *Hilt to Hilt* (1869), *Hammer and Rapier* (1870), and *Out of the Foam* (1871). The house also published James Wood Davidson's *The Living Writers of the South* (1869) and Augusta Jane Evans's later novels. She described Carleton to J. C. Derby as "Verily, a Prince of Publishers!" Other New York publishers who brought out Southern books were the Metropolitan Record Office and E. J. Hale and Son. The Hales, who were North Carolinians, published Hayne's edition of Timrod's *Poems* (1873) and his own *The Mountain of the Lovers* (1875). It was a Philadelphia house that published Mrs. Mary Tardy's *Southland Writers* (1870) and in 1872 brought out a new edition of her collection under the title *The Living Female Writers of the South*. In the late seventies the great Northern houses began to discover that it was profitable to publish Southern fiction for Northern readers. The success of George W. Cable's *Old Creole Days*, published by the house of Scribner in 1879, demonstrated that it was possible for a Southern writer to find a nationwide audience provided that he expressed no opinions that were repugnant to Northern and Western readers.

A Northern economist or sociologist of literary tastes surveying the Southern scene in 1875 would probably have noted the absence of just those factors that seem indispensable if a region is to produce an important literature. The South was still predominantly a rural region, and it was now poorer than ever before. Illiteracy was high and its schools and colleges were more than ever inferior to those of the North. The Southern literary centers had disintegrated and most of the ante-bellum writers were dead. The South had few literary magazines and no publishers, and its newspapers were praising the shoddy novels of subliterary writers rather than the poems of Hayne and Lanier. Southern writers lived at great distances from one another and from the literary centers of the North. Few Northern publishers and magazine editors were as yet hospitable to Southern writers, and some of these writers had not yet discovered that it was possible for them to write for Northern readers without doing violence to their own convictions. And yet an important literature did emerge from certain states of the late Confederacy. What is the explanation of this paradoxical situation?

The Northern magazine editors who published the writings of the younger Southern authors had a very simple explanation. Slavery had prevented the Old South from producing an important literature. The emancipation of the slaves had released the creative energies of the South. William Dean Howells, reviewing Trent's life of Simms in *Harper's Magazine* in June, 1892, wrote: "Had Simms been born now, in an impulsive, generous society, which has dropped feudalism and slavery . . . there is every reason to believe that he would hold a front rank among American novelists. There was never such another demonstration in history of the effect of social emancipation upon literature as has been furnished by the band of brilliant Southern writers since the war of secession. . . ."

Howells' explanation is too simple to be wholly convincing. In spite of slavery, Simms had held a "front rank" among American novelists of his time. The existence of slavery was in itself no obstacle to literary development in the South. As Southern apologists frequently noted, Athens in the great age of Pericles and Rome under the Emperor Augustus had held many slaves. Their presence in fact was in large part what enabled some of their masters to devote their leisure to literature and the fine arts.

And yet there was one great difference which the Southern proslavery writers overlooked. The Greeks and the Romans accepted slavery as the normal and natural condition of many human beings. The South, on the other hand, although its treatment of its slaves was more humane than that of Greece or Rome, was consciously trying to preserve an antiquated economic and social order in the face of world opinion and in defiance of the traditional liberalism of the older South of Washington and Jefferson. Attacked as a semibarbarous region by a world which had outgrown slavery, the South, knowing that for the most part its slaves were not being cruelly treated, endeavored to justify holding them in bondage by an appeal to the Bible, the church fathers, Aristotle, Burke, Carlyle, and to a pseudo science which held the blacks to be an inferior race. The Southern writer, after his section had committed itself to the defense of slavery on principle, found it difficult to accept those liberal and humanitarian ideas which were among the strongest forces in the contemporary literature of England and the Northern states. He could no longer write freely of the daily life of his own region. He must either undertake to defend the status quo or else take refuge in historical romance that dealt with the past. He could not describe the daily life on a Southern plantation without laying himself open to criticism on the part of hypersensitive Southern readers who might fancy some deviation from the orthodox position. He might also unwittingly supply materials for Abolitionist propagandists scanning everything in print for evidence damaging to slavery. He could not satirize the rich and crude "cotton snobs" as Thackeray would have done or fill his novels with pleas for reform as Dickens was doing. It was safer to write of the past than of the present, and so Caruthers, Simms, Cooke, and Kennedy gave their best efforts to historical fiction.

The Civil War put an end to unrealistic dreams of a separate Southern nation, and emancipation opened the doors of the South to literary and cultural influences which had played little part in ante-bellum Southern writing. The Southerner, chastened by defeat, felt that he had to establish new relations with the outside world. As Lowell pointed out in his wartime essay, "The Rebellion," one of the more immediate results of the struggle was "to disabuse the Southern mind of some of its fatal misconceptions as to Northern character. They thought us," he said, "a trading people, incapable of lofty sentiment, ready to sacrifice everything for commercial advantage,—a heterogeneous rabble, fit only to be ruled by a superior race."

Calamity and change are great stimulants to thinking. Extreme conservatives, like William Hand Browne and Albert Taylor Bledsoe, clung closer than ever to the ideals of the past, but many young Southerners found this an impossible position. Some of them, indeed, like Cable, Mark Twain, Walter Hines Page, and W. P. Trent, settled the question for themselves by accepting almost *in toto* the Northern interpretation of war and emancipation. It is significant that all of these men eventually settled in the North. For Southerners like Harris, Johnston, and Thomas Nelson Page such desertion of their own people was an impossible solution. They tried to preserve the best in the ideals of the Old South and at the same time to adjust themselves as best they could to the new order. The writers of the New South were thoroughly loyal to the Union and felt all their interests bound up in it. They were glad that the slaves had been freed. They welcomed the new cultural and literary influences. They were not willing, however, like some of the Southern émigrés to the North, to repudiate the Southern past.

The New South was in fact less "New" than is generally supposed. The South was still a traditional society, and its ideals could not be wholly reconciled with those of an industrial civilization—and the North was now more than ever committed to industrialization and incessant changes in the social and economic order. Lanier was shocked by the Northern exploitation of labor, and he had little sympathy with the woman's rights movement. There is in stories of the Old South by Harris, Page, and others much implicit contrasting of the ideals of the Southern planter with those of the Northern industrialist. Explicit criticism of Northern ideals, even in the eighties and nineties, would hardly have been acceptable from a Southern writer.

The writers of the New South had a point of reference such as most Northern writers did not have. The South of the eighties and nineties was, as Donald Davidson has said of the South since the First World War:

. . . a traditional society which had arrived at a moment of self-consciousness favorable to the production of great literary works. A traditional society is a society that is stable, religious, more rural than urban, and politically conservative. Family, blood-kinship, clan-ship, folkways, custom, community, in such a society, supply the needs that in a non-traditional or progressive society are supplied at great cost by artificial devices like training schools and government agencies. A traditional society can absorb modern improvements up to a certain point without losing its character. If modernism enters to the point where the society is thrown a little out of balance but not yet completely off balance, the moment of self-consciousness arrives.[12]

War and Reconstruction brought changes which forced the young Southern writers into an examination of their whole cultural heritage. Much the same situation is to be found in the South of the twentieth century; and, like Lanier and Harris, William Faulkner, in Davidson's words, awoke "to realize what he and his people truly are in comparison with what they are being urged to become."

4

Southern Magazines

THE MIND OF the postwar South is well reflected in the numerous literary and semiliterary magazines founded between 1865 and 1880. The historian of American magazines has treated them all too casually, and the literary historians have practically ignored them. One of the best, the Richmond weekly *Southern Opinion* (1867–1869), is not even listed in the revised edition of the *Union List of Serials* or in F. L. Mott's *A History of American Magazines*. Many of my readers, however, will recall O. Henry's amusing burlesque, " 'The Rose of Dixie.' " The editor of the *Rose of Dixie* was Colonel Aquila Telfair, and its motto—unconsciously adapted from Lincoln—was "Of, For, and By the South." The Colonel refused all the high-priced manuscripts offered him by a Northern agent, a booster and a hustler who told him: "You can't successfully run a magazine for one particular section of the country." Finally, the editor, reconciled to making some concession to his backers' desire for a wider circulation, reprinted the "Second Message to Congress . . . By a Member of the Well-Known BULLOCH FAMILY OF GEORGIA, T. ROOSEVELT."

O. Henry, writing forty years after the Civil War, could laugh at the postwar magazines, but in the sixties and seventies educated Southerners took them seriously. They were often the only medium available to older Southern writers. More important, however, is the circumstance that their faded pages contain some of the early writings of such men as Sidney Lanier, Richard Malcolm Johnston, and Walter Hines Page. When the younger Southern writers discovered that they could write acceptably for *Lippin-*

[12] "Why the Modern South Has a Great Literature," *Vanderbilt Studies in the Humanities*, I (1951), 12. For comment on Davidson's address by two Southern sociologists, see Howard W. Odum and John Maclachan, "Literature in the South: An Exchange of Views," *Hopkins Rev.*, VI, 59–87 (Winter, 1953).

cott's Magazine and *Scribner's Monthly* without doing violence to their con-victions—and be well paid for what they wrote—the day of the Southern sectional magazine was drawing to a close. Richard Malcolm Johnston, who had permitted the *Southern Magazine* in Baltimore to publish his Dukes-borough tales for nothing, was told by the editor of *Harper's Magazine* that he would have published these stories and paid for the privilege. Joel Chand-ler Harris, a newspaperman in Atlanta filling a column in the *Constitution* with Negro folk stories, discovered that a New York publisher was willing to bring them out in book form and pay him a royalty. Ironically, the mag-azines and newspapers which had helped to develop the younger Southern writers found that they could not compete for their work with the great metropolitan magazines of the North.

We may single out half a dozen of the better magazines to represent the various types. The earliest, *Scott's Monthly* (December, 1865–December, 1869), was founded by an Atlanta minister, W. J. Scott, who was later to write that he saw in 1865 that the South needed not only "industrial re-organization" and "political reconstruction" but also "beyond all else, literary elevation and enfranchisement." The magazine numbered among its contributors Hayne, Timrod, Maurice Thompson, and Sidney Lanier, who probably received nothing for what they wrote.

The *Land We Love* (May, 1866–March, 1869), begun in Charlotte, North Carolina, was edited by General Daniel H. Hill. It was one of the more successful of Southern magazines, partly because its editor did not rely exclusively upon unpaid contributions. General Hill was shrewd enough to see that a purely literary magazine would win too few subscribers, and so he gave the *Land We Love* the subtitle: "A New Monthly Magazine De-voted to Literature, Military History, and Agriculture."

The Richmond *Eclectic* was launched in November, 1866, by Moses D. Hoge and William Hand Browne. In January, 1868, it was rechristened the *New Eclectic* and moved to Baltimore with Lawrence Turnbull and Fridge Murdoch as editors. The next year Browne returned as coeditor. In 1869 Margaret J. Preston wrote to Paul Hamilton Hayne that during the first year of their connection with the magazine the Turnbull brothers had lost five thousand dollars in the effort to maintain it. In April, 1869, the *New Eclectic* absorbed the *Land We Love,* and in December it became the official organ of the Southern History Association. In January, 1871, it be-came the *Southern Magazine.* Its last issue was that of December, 1875. Hayne, who was one of its ablest contributors, wrote to Mrs. Preston on January 15, 1872, that the *Southern Magazine* came "nearest to the right ideal standard" of a "really thoughtful and comprehensive 'organ' of our intellectual progress and learning." Browne was a scholar with considerable critical ability and strong prejudices. He and the magazine played an important part in the development of Sidney Lanier. Browne's letters to Hayne throw light upon his hopes and his editorial difficulties. On July 30, 1870, he wrote: "I want the new South, so far as it may be new, to be distinctly and essentially the *South*, and not a bastard New England." On October 20 of the same year he wrote that the magazine had "a very good subscription list, if all would pay; but our trouble is," he added, "they take the magazine and won't pay for it, maugre all our duns and bills." On March 25, 1872, explaining his inability to pay his contributors, Browne wrote: "If we had but 10,000 circulation (and what is that out of 8,000,000 [Southern] people?) we could give such prices to contributors as would bring the best work of the best men. . . ."

The *Southern Review* (January, 1867–July, 1879) of Baltimore was edited by the redoubtable Albert Taylor Bledsoe, to whom General Lee is said to have remarked: "Doctor, you must take care of yourself; you have a great work to do; we all look to you for our vindication." Bledsoe was a West Pointer who had practiced law in Springfield, Illinois, where he had known Lincoln, and had later been a professor of mathematics and finally become a Methodist minister. As with Charles Colcock Jones, Jr., his years of living in the North had only made him more Southern in his outlook. Among his more important books are his *Essay on Liberty and Slavery* (1856) and *Is Davis a Traitor?* (1866). The *Southern Review* was never a financial success, even when in 1871 it became the official organ of the Southern Methodists, and Bledsoe was in part dependent upon his daughters, who taught school. He died in December, 1877. His daughter, Mrs. Sophia Bledsoe Herrick, who had been her father's able assistant since 1875, continued the *Review* for a year and a half. The last two numbers were published in Richmond under the editorship of C. J. Griffith. Meanwhile the Southern Methodists had decided to revive their own *Quarterly Review*. From 1879 to 1906 Mrs. Herrick was on the editorial staff of *Scribner's Monthly* and its successor, the *Century Magazine*, where she gave expert counsel to Thomas Nelson Page and other Southern writers. In later years she developed far beyond her father's thinking. James Russell Lowell addressed some of his finest letters to her. Bledsoe, who wrote most of the articles printed in the *Review*, distrusted democracy, defended slavery and secession as constitutional rights, and regarded industrialism as an enemy of religion. Not many Southern writers were so uncompromising in their attitude toward the new regime.

The *South-Atlantic* (November, 1877–1882?) of Wilmington, edited by

Mrs. Cicero Harris, professed to be "A Monthly Magazine of Literature, Science, and Art," but of science and art the *South-Atlantic* printed very little. Bledsoe was working in the tradition of the old *Southern Quarterly Review*, but the *South-Atlantic* had a different model, which is suggested in the issue for April, 1878: "If we never succeed in imparting to it the vigor and varied excellence of the [*Southern*] *Literary Messenger*, in the palmy days of Poe, Thompson and White (the scholarliness and brilliance of that periodical in the first half of its existence, is almost the despair of magazinists), we yet may do something to foster the literary spirit and contribute to the convenience of writers and people of taste and culture in this section."

The *Southern Bivouac* (September, 1882–May, 1887) of Louisville was one of the last literary magazines devoted to the Lost Cause. After the demise of the *Southern Magazine* in 1875 it became the organ of the Southern History·Association, and it published some important historical materials. From 1885 to 1887 it was much more of a literary magazine than it had been. Of especial interest is Hayne's three-part article on ante-bellum Charleston published in 1885. The *Century Magazine* bought the *Southern Bivouac* in 1887 because, it is said, its editors wanted a clear field for the publication of war papers. On April 26 of that year Margaret J. Preston wrote to William Malone Baskervill: "I was sorry to see that the Southern Bivouac had gone down, as all its predecessors have done; and that we are now actually without a printed sheet in the South that can be called literary. . . . The truth is our people do not care for home-wares. They prefer the foreign product."

Most of the editors of these magazines were amateurs and were new to the business of conducting a magazine.[13] The printers who published them were no more proficient in marketing their wares than their predecessors in ante-bellum times. In 1881 Lafcadio Hearn, then living in New Orleans, pointed out that, to be successful, a Southern literary magazine would have to be issued by a stable publishing house such as the South did not have. Such a firm, he said, could use its magazine to discover new writers and to advertise its wares, and by republishing in book form materials which had appeared in the magazine it could reduce the cost of typesetting. In this manner, he said, the "publishers of *Harper's Monthly* and *Scribner's* [*Monthly*] *Magazine*, have utilized these periodicals to great advantage in their business."

The Southern editors made their appeal to the educated and not to the

---

[13] It should be noted, however, that those veteran editors, James D. B. De Bow and Daniel K. Whitaker, both once more tried their hands at conducting quarterly reviews in New Orleans.

masses, who if they were readers bought the more sensational pictorial magazines of New York. The educated Southerner, if he was able to subscribe
to a magazine, soon learned to prefer the better-written and better-printed
magazines of the North. Often he chose instead to subscribe to a British
magazine. He could subscribe for a whole year to American editions of
Blackwood's and four British quarterlies for fifteen dollars. In spite of a
strong antipathy to Northern products of all kinds, there was—after 1870
at least—less demand for a sectional literary magazine than there had been
in the forties and fifties. In the year 1867, when the *Atlantic Monthly* had a
circulation of fifty or sixty thousand, *Scott's Monthly* could claim only
five thousand. The more successful *Land We Love* was claiming twelve
thousand but complained that many subscribers had not paid for the magazine.[14] In May, 1870, the editor of the *Home Monthly* in Nashville announced that of all the Southern magazines so hopefully launched in 1866
his was the sole survivor. In November, 1877, the *South-Atlantic*, disregarding Bledsoe's *Southern Review*, claimed that it was "the only literary magazine published in the Southern States." Professor A. B. Stark, the editor of
the *Home Monthly*, must have expressed the feeling of chagrin and disillusionment of other editors when he wrote in his valedictory in June, 1870:
"We have given to it four of the best years of our life, without remuneration.
. . . Instead of the kind words and gratulations we expected at the end of
that long period of unpaid toil, we have received coldness, indifference, and
finally defeat. We leave the field to others of the five thousand men of
whom each man believes firmly that *he*, with his tact, and genius, and
energy, can accomplish what all previous adventurers have failed in—the
pecuniary success of a monthly magazine in the South."

The truth of course is that apart from local newspapers and farm and
religious journals, there was little demand for Southern periodicals—at
least by the time that many Southerners were able to pay for such things.
Even if the editors and publishers could by something like a miracle have
put out a magazine comparable to *Harper's* or the *Atlantic*, they would still
have been only amateurs when it came to marketing their product. Like
their predecessors in the Old South, they paid little if anything for what they
published, and they seldom paid promptly. Southern writers with any professional ambition quickly discovered that some Northern magazines paid
promptly and well. As early as December, 1868, Mrs. L. Virginia French was

---

[14] F. L. Mott, *A History of American Magazines*, III, 46 nn. In Jan., 1869, the *Home
Monthly* gave some estimates of circulation which had been issued by an advertising
agency. The *Atlantic Monthly* had 50,000; *Godey's Lady's Book*, 106,000; the *Nation*,
6,000; the *Round Table*, 7,000; etc.

insisting with some feeling in the *Land We Love* upon the right of a Southern author to sell his wares to the highest bidder in North or South. Of the old plea, much used by Southern editors before and after the war, that a Southern writer "*ought*, as a matter of duty, to write 'for the support of Southern literature,' " she said: "That string has been played upon until, to use an expressive vulgarism, it has literally 'played out.' "

General Hill undertook to find out what magazines the Southern people were buying in 1868. In one Southern city, he discovered, the ratio of Northern magazines sold to Southern was eight to one. That was the best showing he had found. In another Southern city, he said, the ratio was two hundred and forty to one.[15] The editor of the *Home Monthly*, referring to General Hill's figures, estimated that in most Southern towns the combined circulation of all Southern magazines was less than that of *Godey's Lady's Book* or Bonner's *New York Ledger*.[16]

The editors of the Southern magazines, directing their appeal to the cultivated classes, were not particularly unfriendly to the quality magazines of the North except perhaps to *Harper's Magazine*. Their chief complaint was that the Southern masses were buying "the lighter, frothier periodicals of the North." "The masses want chaff and garbage," complained the editor of the Nashville *Home Monthly*. In May, 1868, T. C. DeLeon in an article on "Demoralized Weeklies" stated that on a recent railway journey in the South he had heard newsboys at every station calling out "*Stetson's Dime* [*Illustrated*]!" and "*La-ast Sensation!*" Professor Mott quotes with approval from DeLeon's characterization of such sex-and-crime sensation periodicals: "Vilest among those that are all vile;—very Arch-Bestials in a carnival of beastiality [*sic*] are the latest born among them—'*Stetson's Dime Illustrated*' and the '*Last Sensation.*' . . . They are veritable 'Bibles of Damnation.' . . . " A few months later General Hill, who had published DeLeon's article, summed up his own opinion of the less offensive of Northern pictorial magazines: "These belong invariably to three classes, the trashy, the sensational and the libelous. Bonner's *Ledger* is the type of the first class; *Leslie* and *Day's Doings* of the second; and *Harper* [*Harper's Weekly*] of the third. The first is simply worthless, the second is licentious, and the

---

[15] *Land We Love*, V, 371 (Aug., 1868). Hill did not include political, agricultural, or religious magazines, for which there was apparently a greater demand. Some of these occasionally published literary materials.

[16] V, 274–276 (Oct., 1868). According to the *Home Monthly*, the editor of the Trenton, Tenn., *Weekly Gazette* on a recent visit to Nashville had discovered that the dealers in that city had sold 525 copies of the *New York Ledger*, 216 of *Harper's Magazine*, and 87 of the *Atlantic Monthly* but only 67 copies of the *Land We Love*, 13 of *De Bow's Review*, and 12 of the *New Eclectic*.

third slanderous to the last degree." The Virginia poet-editor, James Barron Hope, sadly commented on the failure of Southern readers to support their own magazines: "We see upon our streets, in our shops, in our offices, in our cars, on our steamboats—everywhere, pictorial papers, printed mainly in New York, which are eagerly bought; while the *Land We Love*, the *Banner of the South*, and numberless other meritorious publications, are supported only by a small class of our people. This is a humiliating reflection, but nevertheless true.—Our people prefer the spread-eagle literature and the leg-pictures to the inspirations of our poets, or the best reflections of our thinkers."

The South was being "Americanized" with a vengeance. The tide was running against the intellectual aristocrat, who valued good taste and restraint. No wonder that conservatives like Bledsoe, Browne, Jones, and Gayarré felt that the integrity of the South was being threatened by this deluge of unsavory lowbrow printed matter emanating from the North. Perhaps the editors of the *Atlantic Monthly* felt that the cultural integrity of New England was also imperiled.

The literary taste of the cultivated Southerner was relatively more old-fashioned in 1875 than it had been in 1840. Earlier magazine editors had taught him to distrust the literary radicalism of New England. The Civil War had in large measure cut him off from current Northern and British literature. He had thus missed reading Matthew Arnold, for example. After the war he was seldom able to buy many new books, and so he was thrown back upon the classics in his own private library. After living for two years in the South, Constance Fenimore Woolson wrote to Paul Hamilton Hayne in 1875 that she was puzzled by the ignorance among educated Southerners of Bret Harte, Joaquin Miller, George Eliot, and the Rossettis. She was still more puzzled by the Southern praise of writers, like Henry Lynden Flash and Mrs. Cornelia Jordan, of whom she had never heard.[17]

The standards of those who reviewed books in the Southern magazines were, as we should expect, somewhat archaic. We find the reviewers attacking the realism of Howells and opposing to it sometimes the creed of the Romanticists and at other times that of the Neoclassicists. People in trouble do not want too much realism in their fiction. "It is allowable," wrote one Southern reviewer, "to be lotus-eaters when we can neither bear, nor amend the present." Scott's romances were still read and Tennyson was still the

---

[17] "Some New Letters of Constance Fenimore Woolson," ed. Jay B. Hubbell, *New Eng. Quart.*, XIV, 717–718 (Dec., 1941). See also her unsigned article, "Literary Taste in the South," *Atlantic Monthly*, XLII, 245–247 (Aug., 1878).

favorite English poet. The Romanticist conception of literature served as a bulwark against what was detestable in the Northern philosophy of life. Said "C. H." in the *New Eclectic Magazine* in November, 1869: ". . . we need something which shall be marked by our distinctive modes of thought, our peculiar order of civilization, tinged as it is with much of the beautiful and the heroic lost to Europe in the lapse of ages since feudal chivalry prevailed. And we need something which may plant itself firmly in opposition to the modern spirit of agrarianism, the modern spirit of centralisation in all organized society, whether of Church or State, and the modern temper of Pharisaic meddlesomeness."

Yet in April of the very year these words were printed the *Home Monthly,* announcing that the *Land We Love* had been absorbed by the *New Eclectic,* commented mournfully: "One by one our Southern contemporaries leave us. It seems that we might appropriately write over the portal by which every Southern magazine enters life, the melancholy line of the Roman poet: *Débemur morti nos nostraque.*"

As the Northern literary magazines became increasingly hospitable to Southern writers, the Southern magazines declined and dropped out one by one. After the Reconstruction regime came to an end in 1877, there was no great need for a distinctively Southern magazine. In June, 1881, Joel Chandler Harris wrote in the Atlanta *Constitution:* "The idea that there is a disposition either in Boston or New York to ignore acceptable literary matter because it happens to be from the pen of a Southern writer is absurd." If the Southern writer, he suggested, would only rid himself of his outworn romantic trappings and his provincial point of view, he would find that he had an advantage over Northern and Western writers in his peculiarly rich materials.

Lafcadio Hearn while he was living in New Orleans had something to say about the much-discussed question of a Southern literature. He held that the chief handicaps of the talented Southern writer were "the indifference and neglect of the *Southern people* themselves and the absence of intelligent and impartial criticism." He took the Southern newspapers to task for praising the widely read shoddy "Southern novels," mostly the work of women writers.[18] To be successful, a Southern magazine would have to be issued by a publishing house and "Any tendency toward SOUTHERNISM in the con-

[18] The Southern newspapers not only overpraised the popular subliterary novels but gave scant recognition to important books, like Hayne's edition of Timrod's *Poems* (1873). See, for example, Jay B. Hubbell (ed.), *The Last Years of Henry Timrod* (1941), pp. 66–67 n., and Grace King, *Memories of a Southern Woman of Letters* (1932), p. 336.

duct of the magazine would render it ridiculous and finally kill it." "No real literary success," he said, "can be purely local; no work of veritable merit can be of merely sectional interest."

And yet, while as Hearn saw it, the establishment of a Southern literary magazine was no solution of the problem of the Southern writer, the problem still remained, even in the 1880's. The Southern writers were isolated from one another, and were far removed from the important literary centers, and so, he said, were "dependent mainly upon alien criticism and the opinions of a foreign public for the formation of our own estimates of our own products." The Southern writer did not enjoy "the advantages of a generous competition or the mighty power of mutual admiration." "It is hard to estimate," he continued, "the influence of that power in building up the reputations of men of real genius—like Holmes and Longfellow and Whittier of the elder, or Howells and Aldrich and that much over-praised author, Mr. Henry James, of the younger generation. It has not been the work merely of critics or publishers that has made the fame and fortune of these men, nor has it been owing only to what they have done for themselves. They have *built each other up*." There was, Hearn said, "no *virus* of diabolical malignity" in the indifference of Northern editors, publishers, and critics to the unknown Southern writer. Nevertheless, he said, "The Eastern magazines are largely supported by rings of writers through which it is not easy for a novice to break. . . . A great deal of importance is attached to a name, and far too little to the intrinsic merit of contributions." The editors were interested primarily not in literary quality but in what would appeal to their readers.

There was much truth in Hearn's shrewd diagnosis. Nevertheless, the younger Southern writers achieved an astonishing success in the eighties and nineties. In September, 1881, *Scribner's Monthly* in an editorial article entitled "Southern Literature" saluted the writers of the New South: "We welcome the new writers to the great republic of letters with all heartiness. New England has many advantages, but New England is no longer king. Her great literary school is dying out. . . . The South and the West are hereafter to be reckoned upon in making up the account of our literary wealth, and the North will welcome with no stinted praise and no niggardly hand the best that the South can do." This was generous praise indeed. In January, 1885, the author of an article on "Recent American Fiction" in the *Atlantic Monthly* suggested that the literary historian of the future would probably "take note of an enlargement of American letters at this time through the agency of a new South. . . . We have had our laugh," he said, "at the florid, coarse-flavored literature which has not yet disappeared at the South, but we are witnessing now the rise of a school which shows us the worth of generous nature when it has been schooled and ordered."

Like the *Atlantic*, *Scribner's Monthly* held a very low opinion of ante-bellum Southern writing, which it said was characterized by "floridness of style, sentimentality of material, and an unmistakable provincial flavor." "It was not widely accepted [in the North]," it said, "because it did not deserve to be." The Old South had lacked the conditions of "broad sympathy and catholic culture" only under which literature of lasting value could be produced. It was the war that had made possible the development of the new school of Southern writers: "The experiences of the war and the sad years of poverty and trial that followed them were great educators. It is to the everlasting credit of the Southern people that they so received this terrific discipline that they have emerged from it purified, exalted, catholic, and armed with noble purposes. It was in this discipline, and in the birth of new ideas and new sympathies consequent upon the issues of the war, that the new literary spirit was born."

Scribner's Monthly, in praising the New South at the expense of the Old, was expressing what had become and has since remained the conventional view of the literature of the Old South. Forgetting Greece and Rome and Palestine, Northern critics assumed that literature and slavery were incompatible. Thomas Nelson Page in an able essay on "Authorship in the South before the War" practically admitted that the literature of the Old South was, apart from political writings, of little consequence. He was at great pains, however, to refute the notion that "the want of a literature at the South was the result of intellectual poverty." Writing in the *Southern Bivouac* for September, 1885, Paul Hamilton Hayne complained that even within the South there was a disposition "to find the whole department of Southern *ante-bellum* literature a desert of antiquated rubbish, with nothing of permanent beauty or power from dismal Dan to barren Beersheba." Hayne must have found his conviction confirmed just two months later. In the November number of the *Southern Bivouac* Professor Charles Forster Smith wrote in an article on "Southern Dialect in Life and Literature": "What a world of distance between the 'Georgia Scenes' and 'Major Jones's Courtship,' the best of the old-time tales, and the stories of Craddock and Harris." Smith found the Sut Lovingood yarns "dreadfully tiresome," and the Simon Suggs stories seemed to him almost as bad. Not until the twentieth century were American scholars willing to question the accepted opinion and study afresh Southern writing in the earlier nineteenth century.

It remained for Parrington and others to discover the liberalism of Caruthers, the realism of Simms, and the vitality of the sketches of the Southern humorists.

5

Southern Writers and Northern Magazines

In 1865 there was probably only a single literary magazine in the entire North that would knowingly have printed an article by any Southerner except a repentant Confederate willing to accept the Northern view upon controversial issues. That was the New York *Old Guard* (1862–1870), edited by Charles Chauncey Burr, who was born in Maine.[18a] This "Copperhead" monthly, which was violently anti-Lincoln, anti-war, and anti-Abolitionist, was in the late sixties almost the only Northern magazine open to Cooke, Simms, and Hayne.

One of the first young Southern writers to have her stories accepted by Northern magazines was Frances Hodgson Burnett of Knoxville, Tennessee. As early as 1868 she found *Godey's Lady's Book* hospitable. Charles J. Peterson printed her stories in *Peterson's Magazine* and occasionally sent one of her stories to an editor who could pay more than he could afford to pay. Early in 1872 she began to contribute to *Harper's* and *Scribner's Monthly*. Her early success is to be attributed in part to her English birth and to the fact that her stories were laid in the British Isles. When Southern themes became popular, she began writing about life in the South.

Until 1875 or even after, the *Atlantic Monthly* and *Harper's* were regarded in the South as distinctly hostile. Much more hospitable were some of the newer New York and Philadelphia magazines. The *Round Table* (1863–1869) published two of Lanier's poems in 1866 and ten more in the next two years. When John Esten Cooke hailed the establishment of the *Galaxy* (1866–1878), a New York rival of the *Atlantic*, he pronounced *Harper's* "sectional and dull"; the *Atlantic* seemed to him "a New England coterie affair altogether." Cooke, however, found O. B. Bunce of *Appletons' Journal* (1869–1881) more helpful than any other Northern editor. *Appletons'* published four of his articles in its first year and many thereafter. Cooke had contributed to *Harper's* before the war, but it was not until 1876 that any of his later writings appeared there.

In 1868 the Philadelphia house of Lippincott, which before the war had sold many books in the South, established *Lippincott's Magazine* (1868–

[18a] See my article in *PMLA* for Sept., 1954, "Charles Chauncey Burr: Friend of Poe."

1916) with John Foster Kirk as editor. Almost from the beginning the magazine was exceptionally friendly to Southern writers. It never enjoyed the vogue of *Scribner's Monthly*, but in its earlier years it did more than any other magazine to encourage the writers of that section. Among its contributors were Simms, Hayne, Bagby, Mrs. Preston, Frances Hodgson Burnett, and that once-ardent defender of slavery, George Fitzhugh. In 1874 and 1875 *Lippincott's* printed two early pieces by Mary Noailles Murfree under the pseudonym "R. Emmet Dembry." It was not until 1878 that the *Atlantic Monthly* began to publish her stories over the pen name of "Charles Egbert Craddock." *Lippincott's* most notable service was to Sidney Lanier, whose "Corn" and "The Symphony" appeared first in its pages. In 1877 the house of Lippincott published the only volume of his poems to appear during Lanier's lifetime.

Scribner's Monthly (1870–1930), which became the *Century Magazine* in 1881, was a national magazine in a sense in which *Harper's* and the *Atlantic* were not until after 1875. Its editors and publishers succeeded in doing what Poe had only dreamed of doing with his projected *Penn Magazine*; they reached out into the West and the South for new readers and new writers. *Scribner's Monthly* published more of the better writings of the New South than any of its contemporaries. Among its editors were Josiah Gilbert Holland, a New Englander who had taught school in Richmond and Vicksburg; Richard Watson Gilder, from New Jersey; and Robert Underwood Johnson, from Indiana. Among their assistants was Mrs. Sophia Bledsoe Herrick, whom Johnson has characterized as "an intellectual woman of keen literary perceptions" and "One of the wisest and best women I ever knew." It was Mrs. Herrick, who had lived in the South, who put into acceptable shape Page's stories, "Marse Chan" and "Meh Lady." Among *Scribner's Monthly's* significant discoveries were Page, Irwin Russell, and George W. Cable.

In 1873, realizing that the South was an important part of the nation, the *Monthly* sent Edward King, accompanied by the illustrator, J. Wells Champney, on a journey of more than twenty-five thousand miles to write a series of articles on "The Great South." The series ran to about four hundred and fifty pages with an engraving on almost every page, and it cost the magazine more than thirty thousand dollars. As printed in the magazine and later republished in book form, King's articles were effective in promoting better intersectional relations. King showed no interest in such unreconstructed Southern writers as Bledsoe and Browne, but he took great pride in his discovery in New Orleans of a young warehouse clerk named Cable, who had begun to write about the Creoles of Louisiana. Most of the stories which the house of Scribner published in *Old Creole Days* (1879) were first printed in the magazine.

The *Century's* attitude toward its Southern contributors was explained in a letter which Gilder wrote in 1886 to the editor of a Southern periodical who had objected to the magazine's printing the Nicolay-Hay life of Lincoln: "The great force and utility of the 'Century's' attitude toward the South rests on the fact that we are national and antislavery in our views and have been so from the beginning. It is of no particular utility to the South to have a Southern periodical manifest hospitality to Southern ideas, but it is of great use that a Northern periodical should be so hospitable to Southern writers and Southern opinion, and should insist upon giving a fair show to Southern views even when they were not altogether palatable to our Northern readers, among whom, of course, is our greatest audience." Southern writers were admitted to the *Century* and other Northern magazines with the distinct understanding that they were not to defend slavery or secession or express sentiments unfriendly to the North. Gilder had occasionally to delete from manuscripts passages revealing an "unreconstructed" point of view. "In return," as S. C. Chew has well said, "he and his readers tacitly accepted the Southern writers' assumption of the racial inferiority of the Negro and the Negro's contentment with his lot in a feudal society where the 'quarters' were loyal to the 'great house' which watched over them."

Such was the understanding upon which the literature of the New South was based. The spirit in which the better writers of the South accepted these limitations is well described in the words of another *Century* editor, L. Frank Tooker:

But this is the significant thing about the appearance of these people in a Northern magazine: the old bitterness that had marked the work of the writers of defunct magazines of the South was gone. Gone, too, were the truculence, the provincial spirit, and much of the old sentimentalism that had from the first marked all the writers of what they themselves were wont to call "our beloved Southland." Welcomed by a Northern magazine, these new authors had met these advances with the characteristic courtesy and tact of the South, which ignore all differences of opinion between hosts and guests. Thus tacitly barred from any expression of the old hostility, and softened in spirit by gratitude, their literature blazed a new path in America—a path marked by the most pronounced local color, irradiated by humor and tender romanticism.

During Lowell's editorship (1857–1861) the *Atlantic Monthly* was regarded in the South as an organ of the antislavery party in New England. Even after the war, under the editorship of James T. Fields and William

Dean Howells, it was considered in New York and Philadelphia as primarily a New England affair, not hospitable to contributors who lived west of the Hudson River or as far south as New York City. For its Southern materials the *Atlantic* relied heavily on heterodox Southerners, like Moncure Conway or Nathaniel Shaler, or on Northern observers like Sidney Andrews or Thomas Wentworth Higginson. In the December, 1867, number Higginson repeated the old Abolitionist explanation of the alleged literary poverty of the South: "What graces might there not have been in that Southern society before the war? Here and there in its midst were to be found ease, affluence, leisure, polished manners, European culture,—all worthless; it produced not a book, not a painting, not a statue; it concentrated itself on politics, and failed; then on war, and failed; it is dead and vanished, leaving only memories of wrong behind." [19]

Paul Hamilton Hayne, who had been an *Atlantic* contributor before the war, had to wait until 1872 before the magazine would accept one of his later poems, and Howells rejected many of them. Mark Twain, the friend of Howells, was admitted early, but he came before the public not as a Southern but as a Western writer. Something like a break in Howells' editorial policy came in the second half of the year 1874 with the serial publication of George Cary Eggleston's "A Rebel's Recollections." In November of the next year appeared Eggleston's charming and too little-known essay, "The Old Régime in the Old Dominion," which at Howells' request he had expanded to twice its original length. Eggleston of course, though he had fought in the Confederate army, was a native of Indiana and a brother of the well-known author of *The Hoosier Schoolmaster* (1871). The first of many stories by Mary Noailles Murfree, "The Dancin' Party at Harrison's Cove," was published in May, 1878. Miss Murfree's relations with Howells were impersonal, but she regarded his successor, Thomas Bailey Aldrich, who had lived in the South, as not only the greatest of magazine editors but as an intimate personal friend. She found him and his circle anything but the cold, undemonstrative New Englanders she had expected to meet in Boston. Among the more notable articles which the *Atlantic* printed under Aldrich's editorship was Basil Lanneau Gildersleeve's "The Creed of the Old South," a classic of its kind which first appeared in the January, 1892, number. Walter Hines Page's "Study of an Old Southern Borough" had been published in May, 1881. In the late nineties the North Carolina–born Page became editor of the *Atlantic*. He banished rolltop desks from the editorial office so that letters had to be answered promptly.

[19] Higginson, *Atlantic Essays* (1871), p. 47, reprinted with slight changes from the *Atlantic Monthly*, XX, 754.

He examined the manuscripts which had been accepted by his predecessor, Horace E. Scudder, and returned many of them to their authors—one of these was Sarah Orne Jewett—because he felt that if the *Atlantic* was to survive, it must appeal to a wider audience. As a means of boosting its circulation, he printed in serial form Mary Johnston's melodramatic romance of Colonial Virginia, *To Have and To Hold.*

In 1873–1874 *Harper's Magazine* published a series of articles on "The New South" by Edwin DeLeon pointing out commercial opportunities for Northern businessmen, but DeLeon obviously was not permitted to comment on Southern grievances. When Charles Dudley Warner visited New Orleans in May, 1885, he learned from the King family that *Harper's* had not been "a welcome visitor to New Orleans since the Confederate War. . . ." It was partly through the influence of Warner, who presided over the "Editor's Drawer," 1883–1894, and in 1894 took over the "Editor's Study" from Howells, that *Harper's* became hospitable to Southern writers. Grace King, a discovery of Warner's, dedicated to him her first book, *Monsieur Motte* (1888) in recognition of his services to Southern writers. In May, 1887, *Harper's* featured a long article by Charles W. Coleman, Jr., entitled "The Recent Movement in Southern Literature" and illustrated it with photographs of twelve prominent writers. Grace King, the youngest of the twelve, wrote long afterwards: "For a young writer . . . to be included in *Harper's* pages was equivalent to the presentation of a débutante at Court. The writers who were thus presented never, in truth, forgot the honor." For Grace King and James Lane Allen, Henry Mills Alden, who edited *Harper's* for many years, was always the greatest of American editors and a close personal friend.

The debt which the literature of the New South owes to the editors of Northern literary magazines is much greater than is generally realized. The younger writers of the South were in the main self-educated even if, like Lanier, they had attended a college. Some of them got into literature through the newspaper office, like Harris and Mark Twain. Some of them, like Richard Malcolm Johnston and Thomas Nelson Page, were such accomplished storytellers that their friends urged them to write out and print their stories. Richard Watson Gilder, hearing some of the Negro stories of F. Hopkinson Smith, urged him to write them out for the *Century.* The result was *Colonel Carter of Cartersville* (1891), originally planned as merely a setting for stories to be told by the Colonel's colored servant Chad.

In their earlier years the Southern writers seldom had a literary friend to whom they could turn for advice and criticism. They did not know the literary catchwords of the day. What training they got they received largely from the editors who found their early work promising. The assistance which Maxwell Perkins gave to Thomas Wolfe, Scott Fitzgerald, and other Scribner authors is well known, but we have forgotten that it was of much the same kind that Alden and Warner of *Harper's* gave to Grace King and James Lane Allen and that members of the *Century* staff gave to Cable, Page, and Harris. Even greater of course was the expert assistance which Howells gave to Mark Twain. The Northern editors tried hard to impress upon writers from the South and the West the importance of literary form, originality, sincerity, good taste, and a national point of view. It was the golden age of the American literary magazine, and the Northern editors, recognizing the literary possibilities of Southern materials, did their best to help gifted amateurs to master their craft and thus become professional writers, able to support themselves by the pen.

Many of the letters from Northern editors to their Southern contributors are models of their kind. Better, however, than any letters were the conferences in editorial offices, to which the Southern writers journeyed when possible. On May 19, 1891, Cable was begging Robert Underwood Johnson to come to Northampton so that he could read a manuscript aloud to him. "Don't you see what I want?" he wrote. "It's the infinite advantage of your running comment and seriatim treatment!" Such comments, he said, were much more valuable than any letter of editorial criticism. Extant published and unpublished letters from Southern writers testify abundantly to their grateful appreciation of the help they got from their editor friends. After Gilder's death Frances Hodgson Burnett wrote: "I could imagine no pleasure more keen to one born with the story-telling habit than to sit and tell a growing story to Richard Gilder, led on and on by the mere luring gleam in the extraordinary eyes no one who knew him well will ever forget." Of Gilder, Cable wrote: "I think he was peculiarly an author's editor, and not merely a publisher's. He never dealt with one's literary products merely as wares for the market, but with their source, the author, and with his pages as things still hopefully in the making."

Never before or since was the American author's relation with editor and publisher more intimate. In these days of the literary agent an author may never unless by chance see the editors and publishers who print what he writes. In his Introduction to *In Ole Virginia* in the Plantation Edition of his writings Thomas Nelson Page recorded his obligations to Charles and Arthur Scribner, who, he said, "had the courage to back an unknown young writer twenty years ago and have by their kindness, liberality, and wisdom since then uniformly helped him in so many ways that the business relation has long been quite eclipsed by that of a delightful friendship."

The standards to which the Northern editors and publishers held Cable, Harris, and Page do not now seem very high, but except for Sidney Lanier probably no Southern writer had any higher artistic aims than those held up to him by Alden, Gilder, and Charles Scribner's Sons. Again excepting Lanier, no Southern writer had any clear conception of literature as an art. "A Southerner," writing in the New York *Evening Post* in 1887, stoutly maintained that merely to aim at "the standard of an editor's or a publisher's acceptance is not to aim high, but low—is not to create what will be priceless in the treasure-house of abiding literature, but what is simply marketable in a market where it is often necessary to buy some very bad things." [20]

From our vantage point in the mid-twentieth century it is not difficult to see the shortcomings of the literature of the New South, but they were apparent to few Southerners in 1887, when its writers were at the peak of their popularity. So remarkable, however, was the discernment of the anonymous "Southerner" who wrote for the *Evening Post* that I shall summarize his chief criticisms. The author was, I think, Walter Hines Page, who was at that time employed by the *Post*.

The "Southerner" felt that the writers of the New South were suffering from the excessive praise which American critics habitually bestow upon our native writers. The tendency to overpraise, he said, "is not due to disingenuous puffery, though that may be one element; it is not due to the pushing of the publisher's business, though that may be a second; it is not due to any phase of literary log-rolling, though that may be a third." American criticism, he insisted, "exaggerates the magnitude of native literary achievements—makes too much reputation and success out of two small a performance—and annually crowns so many authors with laurel that it is hardly worth one's while to be crowned at all. To the world of letters in other lands, as to the next generation of their own countrymen, they might as well have been crowned with the hickory or the sycamore."

The "Southerner" doubted whether the Northern novelists were good models since they were cultivating "little social fields" instead of picturing on a broad scale American life as it was found in the Northern states. While

[20] "Literature in the South," reprinted in the *Critic*, X, 322–324 (June 25, 1887), was occasioned by Charles W. Coleman, Jr.'s article, "The Recent Movement in Southern Literature," *Harper's*, LXXIV, 837–855 (May, 1887). In the "Editor's Study" in *Harper's*, LXXV, 641 (Sept., 1887) Howells maintained that the standard upheld by American magazines was "a very high standard." He did not share "A Southerner's" admiration for Poe as a critic. Poe, he said, "with great talent, had a perversity, arrogance, and wilfulness that render him wellnigh worthless as a censor of others' work, and a mechanical ideal that disabled him from doing any very noble work of his own."

the Southern writer's materials were incomparably rich, he noted, yet the only figures that had been memorably portrayed were the Creole, the mountaineer, and the Negro, "not one of which is a central, commanding, historic American type." The new Southern writers had "as yet never so much as touched the great passionate heart of Southern character." He did not expect "a single truly great novel of Southern life" until the Southern writers either discovered new methods for themselves or took "the scope and model of their art from other than the Northern novelist," whose realistic methods seemed to him too cold, analytical, and trivial.

"Northern critics," said the "Southerner," "cannot judge Southern literature. They cannot judge its local color, its landscapes, its dialects, its types of character, its environment of circumstance, its play of passion, its sentiments, its phases of morals and of faith." What the writer of the New South needed most was a Southern critic who "while fostering, encouraging, teaching" would urge "patience, modesty, humility, independence, and the loftiest, vastest ideals that it is possible for the Southern writer to form through a study of the world's great works of fiction. If," the "Southerner" concluded, "no living Southern critic can help him to these ends, let him go back to Poe, and take from his critical writings a certain standard of originality, contempt of mediocrity, and passion for beauty." The New South unfortunately had no critics with higher standards than those of the Northern editors and publishers. Lanier profited from his study of the older English writers, but not until the emergence of Ellen Glasgow and James Branch Cabell did the South have a novelist who had formed his standards by a study of the great European writers of fiction.

6
Northern Writers: Constance Fenimore Woolson

So great was the popularity of stories of the South in the eighties and nineties that many Northern writers were induced to try their hands at Southern stories, usually with a wartime setting and with reconciliation as a prominent motif and featuring an intersectional love story. The vogue is a potent witness to a new era of good feeling, but it drew some writers away from those areas which they knew best and led them to try to portray life in a region where formulas have no great value. This hardly matters in the case of subliterary novelists, like the popular E. P. Roe, who after a visit to Richmond published *Miss Lou* (1888), but the fashion affected more important writers. One who has read Sarah Orne Jewett's delightful stories of decaying New England coastal towns can understand her strong sympathy with the defeated South; and "The Mistress of Sydenham Plantation" (1888) and "A War Debt" (1895) are, except for the wretched Negro dialect, admirable short stories. But when Mary Wilkins Freeman, apparently at her publisher's suggestion, temporarily abandoned her hard-bitten New England farmers and small-town people to write *The Heart's Highway* (1900), the result was disastrous. No one was less fitted to write a romance of Colonial Virginia in the manner of Mary Johnston. Bret Harte, lecturing in the South in 1874, found himself moved to sadness and sympathy by what he saw, but the most conspicuous of his Southern characters, the dueling, reckless Colonel Starbottle, might have been borrowed from some forgotten melodrama.

There were writers in the North who had a more intimate knowledge of Southern life, and some of them proceeded to make capital of it. Frank R. Stockton and Thomas Bailey Aldrich wrote stories of the South not inferior to their general level of excellence. Albion W. Tourgée, who had lived for some years in North Carolina, used in *A Fool's Errand* (1879) and *Bricks without Straw* (1880) some of his own experiences in trying to reconstruct the South. Mrs. Cornelia Spencer recorded in her diary a more judicial appraisal than most Southern readers were capable of making: "I have just read Tourgée's *Fool's Errand*. It is very smart, and the only book on this phase of the South and North that presents a true picture. He has done it very well. Tells the truth as nearly as a Carpetbagger and a Tourgée could be expected to do. I think he tried to be fair."

The theme of intersectional reconciliation became popular on the American stage, but one finds little that is now convincing in the Southern characters or background of Bronson Howard's *Shenandoah* (1888), William Gillette's *Secret Service* (1896), James A. Herne's *Griffith Davenport* (1899), or Clyde Fitch's *Barbara Frietchie* (1898). In *Shenandoah* a Northern brother and sister are early in 1861 about to marry a Southern sister and brother. When Fort Sumter is attacked, they instantly become enemies; but almost as soon as the last gun is fired at Appomattox, they rush into each other's arms. It is as though the war were a trivial incident and Reconstruction a thing unknown.

The moral of the intersectional plays and novels was, though hardly in the sense intended by Chaucer's Prioress, *Amor vincit omnia*. Some of the Northern writers carried the motif so far that it became ridiculous. After spending six months in the South Maude Howe Elliott, a daughter of Julia Ward Howe, published a novel, *Atalanta in the South* (1886), in which one of her characters remarks: "If I were President of these United States

I should legislate to the end of amalgamating the too-cold Northern and the over-hot Southern blood." The result, he thought, would be the finest race of men since Adam.

The Southern novelists also overworked the theme of reconciliation. A year or two before his death in 1922 Grace King told Thomas Nelson Page of the difficulties she was having with a novel. "He brightened up. 'I know, I know,' he said. 'That was the fault they found with one of my novels. And I had to remedy it to get it published. Now I will tell you what to do; for I did it. Just rip the story open and insert a love story. It is the easiest thing to do in the world. Get a pretty girl and name her Jeanne, that name always takes! Make her fall in love with a Federal officer and your story will be printed at once! The publishers are right; the public wants love stories. Nothing easier than to write them. You do it. You can do it. Don't let your story fail'!"

The Northern conception of Southern life was by 1890 a strange blend of somewhat incongruous elements drawn from Stephen Collins Foster's songs, *Uncle Tom's Cabin*, *In Ole Virginia*, and the Uncle Remus stories. In the eighties and nineties, too, some Southerners could at last read Mrs. Stowe's novel without being emotionally disturbed, and were unconsciously absorbing some elements of the Northern conception of the South. In May, 1896, the youthful William Sydney Porter printed in the Houston *Post* a story, not in his collected works, entitled "Vereton Villa," [21] in which in delightful fashion he burlesqued Northern stories of the South and at the same time unconsciously made ridiculous certain aspects of the Southern legend of the Old South.

No follower of conventional literary patterns was Constance Fenimore Woolson (1840–1894), the earliest Northern writer of fiction who after the war treated Southern life with sympathy and knowledge. A grandniece of James Fenimore Cooper, she was born in New Hampshire and brought up in Cleveland, Ohio; and her earliest stories dealt with the Lake Country. After her father's death in 1869 her home in Cleveland was broken up. From 1873 until her departure for Europe in 1879 she lived with her invalid mother, spending much of each year in Florida, Georgia, Virginia, or the Carolinas. In her second year in the South she began to write about it in sketches, poems, and short stories. The shorter pieces which she published in Northern magazines from 1874 on may well have had something to do with opening the pages of these magazines, especially *Harper's*, to the Southern writers. Some of her best sketches deal with Florida, at that time

[21] *O. Henry Encore* (1939), ed. Mary Sunlocks Harrell, pp. 119–129.

beginning to attract Northern visitors, but the best of her short stories are about South Carolina in the Reconstruction period. She was greatly attracted to the well-bred but almost penniless gentlemen and ladies of Charleston. Until she came South, she wrote to Paul Hamilton Hayne in July, 1875, she had not understood the pride of the South Carolinian or the "cause and reason" for that pride. In the South she discovered that the war was not the "thing of the past" which it had become in the North. In 1880 she reprinted ten of her Southern stories in *Rodman the Keeper: Southern Sketches*. These eventually attracted the attention of Henry James, whose work she admired. In February, 1887, James wrote of the "high value" he found in these stories, "especially when regarded in the light of the *voicelessness* of the conquered and reconstructed South." [22] "She loves the whole region," he said, "and no daughter of the land could have handled its peculiarities more indulgently, or communicated to us more of the sense of close observation and intimate knowledge." James, I may add, had read so little of American fiction that even after a visit to Richmond in 1904 he could still write in *The American Scene* (1907) of the Civil War as "the social revolution the most unrecorded and undepicted, in proportion to its magnitude, that ever was. . . ."

Miss Woolson was something of a realist with "a horror of 'pretty,' 'sweet' writing"; and she was an admirer of George Eliot, Thomas Hardy, and Ivan Turgenev. As a writer she felt herself so alone that in a letter to Hayne she spoke of herself as a "Philistine" because, she said, "I do not seem to belong to anybody, or any class. The Boston writers, young and old, hang together; the New York journalists and magazine people have their own creed; and the southern, ditto." What a commentary on the disunity of American literature in 1876!

Miss Woolson's best work, as Van Wyck Brooks maintains, deals with the South rather than with Europe or the Lake Country. "Rodman the Keeper," first published in the *Atlantic Monthly* in March, 1877, will serve to illustrate her treatment of the Reconstruction South. After the war John Rodman, a New England soldier, returns to the South as custodian of a national cemetery in which fourteen thousand Union soldiers lie buried. It is too far away to attract Northern visitors, and white Southerners of course will not go near the place. Finally, Rodman finds a proud one-armed Southern veteran sick and starving, and he takes him to his cottage to care for him. Miss Woolson thus describes the situation which follows:

[22] *Partial Portraits* (1888), pp. 179–180. The essay first appeared in *Harper's Weekly*, XXXI, 114–115 (Feb. 12, 1887).

Then began a remarkable existence for the four: a Confederate soldier lying ill in the keeper's cottage of a national cemetery, a rampant little rebel coming out daily to a place which was to her anathema-maranatha, a cynical, misanthropic keeper sleeping on the floor and enduring every variety of discomfort for a man he never saw before,—a man belonging to an idle, arrogant class he detested,—and an old black freedman allowing himself to be taught the alphabet in order to gain permission to wait on his master,—master no longer in law, —with all the devotion of his loving old heart.

One can only be thankful that the tragic theme was handled by a sincere and competent artist like Miss Woolson and not by any one of the numerous sentimental writers who would have devised an intersectional romance culminating in the marriage of a proud Southern beauty to a Northern hero in blue.

"King David," which appeared in *Scribner's Monthly* in April, 1878, is a story which at that time perhaps no Northern magazine would have accepted from a Southern writer. It is the story of the failure of a well-meaning New England idealist, David King, who starts a school for Negroes in Jubilee Town. The ignorance, the shiftlessness, and the drunkenness of the blacks are responsible for his defeat. His brightest pupil, the "Captain," becomes the leader of a band of unruly blacks and arouses their passions by means of liquor and inflammatory literature obtained from an unscrupulous Northern carpetbagger. "A little learning is a dangerous thing" and good intentions are not enough for those who plan to make over the life of a region which they do not fully understand. Such is the point of the story.

Three of Miss Woolson's five novels have their setting in the South, but there are important Northern characters in all of them. *For the Major* (1883), probably the best of her novels, has its setting in western North Carolina. *East Angels* (1886) has a Florida background. *Horace Chase* (1894) has scenes in both Florida and North Carolina. A fourth novel, *Jupiter Lights* (1889), makes use of three of her favorite settings: the Lake Country, the South, and Italy. Miss Woolson was conscious of her limitations as an outsider. She showed, for example, no clear understanding of certain mountain types that Mary Noailles Murfree was beginning to portray. In her Preface to *Rodman the Keeper* she made only this modest claim for her Southern stories: "As far as they go they record real impressions; but they can never give the inward charm of that beautiful land which the writer has learned to love, and from which she now severs herself with true regret."

7

The Literature of the New South

THE LITERATURE of the New South, like that of the Old, owes little to the New England literary tradition. Robert Underwood Johnson, who as an editor of the *Century Magazine* had done much for many a Southern writer, recognized this fact and in his *Remembered Yesterdays* (1923) put forward a theory which the literary historians have generally overlooked:

These [Southern] writers and their successors have excelled in the direct narrative style. I account for this by the fact that the South was not affected by the subtleties of Emerson or Lowell or by the other transcendental influences of New England literature. These did not come into its ken for those influences were related for the most part to the Abolition movement. Rather, the writers of the South derived their style from Thackeray, Macaulay, Addison, and the other essayists of the Spectator type. This made them, first of all, good storytellers and as a tendency, if not as a school, they are worthy the attention of the historian of literary America.

In discussing "Literary Taste in the South" Constance Fenimore Woolson had noted as early as 1878 that Southern readers did not know the New England writers who contributed to the *Atlantic Monthly*. "Not that Southerners of the best class are unliterary," she said; "in one way they are more literary than we are, for they have the old English essayists, dramatists, and poets at their tongues' end, and quote voluminously and well. But they seem never to have come down farther than about the middle of the last century; there they stop with their quotations."

Perhaps it is fortunate that, as Johnson suggested, no Southern author wrote his stories in the style of Emerson's essays or Lowell's or modeled his novels upon Holmes's *Elsie Venner*, Longfellow's *Kavanagh*, or Sylvester Judd's *Margaret*. The Southern writers admired Hawthorne, but they rarely if ever imitated him. On the other hand, they undoubtedly owed something to Irving and Cooper, who belonged to an earlier era of intersectional good feeling. The poets who influenced Hayne and Lanier were, except for Poe, English poets, not American. Irwin Russell modeled his "Christmas-Night in the Quarters" not on Whittier's *Snow-Bound* but upon Burns's "The Jolly Beggars." I do not think that even the twentieth-century writers of the South owe much to the New England literary tradition.[23]

23 Katherine Anne Porter, whose style has been much admired by other writers of fiction, describes her early reading in Texas: "My reading until my twenty-fifth year was a

What Johnson and many literary historians have failed to realize, however, is the immense debt of some writers of the New South to their predecessors in the Old South. It is in a sense true that the Southern local colorists were following a broad trail blazed by Bret Harte, but they were more deeply indebted to the Southern humorists of an earlier period. In Virginia George W. Bagby had a direct influence upon Thomas Nelson Page, who edited a volume of selections from Bagby's writings and praised him as a Virginia realist. In Georgia, A. B. Longstreet and William Tappan Thompson influenced Charles Henry Smith ("Bill Arp") and Richard Malcolm Johnston; and all four of these writers had some influence on Harry Stillwell Edwards and Joel Chandler Harris. Harris served his apprenticeship under Joseph Addison Turner, a writer of humorous sketches and a magazine editor who helped him with his early contributions to the *Countryman*. Mary Noailles Murfree perhaps never read *Sut Lovingood's Yarns*—though Mark Twain certainly did—and she was probably shocked if she did read them, but in them George W. Harris had been the first writer of importance to draw a leading character from the Southern mountains which play so large a part in her work. The tradition of Southern humor reached its culmination in Mark Twain, who in his Mississippi River books was both the humorist and the local colorist, exploiting popular Southern materials, like his friends Joel Chandler Harris and George W. Cable.

The historical romance flourished more vigorously in the Old South than in New England. Except for Hawthorne, that section had little part in the movement to which Caruthers, Kennedy, Simms, and Cooke devoted most of their efforts. The South, particularly since the Civil War, has been more conscious of the past than the North, and the local-color stories of the New South have strong affiliations with the historical romance. Cooke was the first to write important historical novels with a Civil War setting; and in his picture of a Virginia family divided by the war he hit upon an effective situation which became a stock in trade with writers of fiction and drama. Many of the later Civil War novels were the work of Virginians or of men and women with Virginia connections, although the best seller of them all, *Gone with the Wind*, was written by a Georgian in more recent times. One finds in the historical romances of Mary Johnston and even in Margaret Mitchell's famous novel some of the same melodramatic elements that marred the work of Caruthers, Cooke, and Simms. The numerous Southern women writers who emerged in the forties and fifties continued to write

---

grand sweep of all English and translated classics from the beginning up to about 1800. Then I began with the newcomers, and found new incitements" (*Twentieth Century Authors*, 1942, ed. Stanley J. Kunitz and Howard Haycraft, pp. 1118–1119).

after the war, and their influence is seen in the work of the women writers who followed them. There is no sentimental strain in the stories of Kate Chopin or the novels of Ellen Glasgow, but few other Southern writers of fiction of either sex were wholly free from it. In the later nineteenth-century writers of fiction one finds all too frequently the same extreme religious conservatism, the same unrestrained didactic impulse, and the same emphasis upon the genteel rather than upon the real.

The memorable idyllic picture of the old Southern plantation which Northern readers admired in the stories of Page, Mrs. Burton Harrison, and George Cary Eggleston was not the new thing which they probably thought it was. Much the same picture can be found in books which few Northerners would read: Grayson's *The Hireling and the Slave*, Beverley Tucker's *The Partisan Leader*, and the novels which Southern women wrote in reply to *Uncle Tom's Cabin*. Only after slavery was dead did Southern writers find a formula for portraying the slave plantation in a manner acceptable to Northern readers. Then Harris, Page, and many others won wide acclaim with books which were in some measure designed to correct Mrs. Stowe's picture of the Old South. The new school aimed, in Harris's words, at giving their work "the flavor of localism" rather than "the peculiarities of sectionalism." Their work, as Albion W. Tourgée saw clearly, was "distinctly Confederate in sympathy," but it was not reactionary, like Thomas Dixon's *The Leopard's Spots* (1902) and *The Clansman* (1905). The younger writers, unlike their predecessors, played up the Negro as an important element in Southern life, and they handled his dialect more skilfully than Poe or Kennedy or Simms or Mrs. Stowe. From 1880 until H. L. Mencken published "The Sahara of the Bozart" in 1920 few outside critics accused the New South of the literary poverty which they had found in the Old.

Long before 1900 the writers of the New South had done their best work. The vogue of local color had given way to historical romance on one side and on the other to that form of realism which was coming to be called naturalism. Writers and editors alike were finding themselves baffled by changes in the taste of their readers. The editors of the *Century Magazine*, which had done so much for the writers of the New South, found themselves faced with the disintegration of their old reading public and with an inability to understand what the new public really wanted. One of the *Century* editors, L. Frank Tooker, looked back wistfully to the eighties and nineties when

comfortably assured in our own minds that we had arrived at the perfection of literary form, we were thoroughly resolved to keep our heritage unsoiled.

The structure of the poem and the good taste of the short story or novel were bound by the rules of regularity as rigidly as the entasis of the columns of the Parthenon was governed by the formulae of the craftsman who shaped them. Imagination and fertility of thought might be as dynamic as one chose, but form and good taste were static.

By 1900 the writers of the New South, like their contemporaries in other sections, found themselves struggling, often without success, to keep pace with the changing taste of the reading public. In the twentieth century readers of books and magazines were little interested in regional manners and dialectal varieties of American speech. In metropolitan areas readers had little interest in the past and were losing their ability to understand the rural mind. When Whittier's *Snow-Bound* had to be annotated for high school and college students, what could be done for readers who had never seen a cow or a horse and who knew nothing about the growing of cotton or tobacco? The new generation in the South was less inclined to live in the past, and the glamour had faded from plantation belles and heroes in gray jackets. The qualities of the Southern planter-gentleman no longer seemed worthy of imitation; they did not fit into the social life of an urban civilization. Younger Southern writers, like Ellen Glasgow, Mary Johnston, and James Branch Cabell, followed Cable's lead, perhaps unconsciously, and pointed out flaws in the gentleman's code of behavior. After them were to come Erskine Caldwell, William Faulkner, and Lillian Smith, who were to seem more nearly akin to Harriet Beecher Stowe than to Thomas Nelson Page.

The literature of local color now seems to many critics like an eddy rather than a part of the main stream of the national literary tradition. More nearly central, as we see them now, were Howells, Mark Twain, Henry James, Stephen Crane, and Frank Norris—forerunners of Dreiser, Lewis, and Hemingway. Sidney Lanier now seems overshadowed by Emily Dickinson and Walt Whitman.

For the taste of the present generation, the literature of the New South seems too local, too romantic, and too sentimental. It produced no great novels except *Tom Sawyer, Huckleberry Finn,* and possibly *The Grandissimes.* Its treatment of the Negro, vivid though it was, has not seemed wholly satisfactory in the days of Roosevelt and Truman. Except perhaps for "Free Joe" and some of the Uncle Remus tales, Negro readers have not cared for stories that moved to tears such old-fashioned New Englanders as Annie Fields, Henry Ward Beecher, and Thomas Wentworth Higginson. The Negro of the Southern writers seems now too much the funny man, too seldom a tragic figure, and too often merely an accessory to the white man. The later Southern writers have not concerned themselves greatly with the planter gentry—except perhaps to portray them as decadent. What most interests the sophisticated reader now is the poorer whites and mal-adjusted persons of all classes. Until the literary fashion changes, it will be difficult to make a judicial appraisal of the writings of the New South. A later generation may well find them better than they seem today. Certainly, the scholars who are busy in reinterpreting the work of Cable, Harris, Allen, Page, and Lanier have not found them uninteresting or unimportànt.

In spite of the great popularity of Southern stories, the fiction writers of the New South were restricted both by literary fashion and by the prejudices of their Southern readers, which they themselves shared in some degree. They were not free to draw a complete and accurate picture of the life of their section. Even if, like Cable, they could bring themselves to expressing opinions repugnant to their Southern readers, they still had to please the Northern editors and publishers who printed their work. It is then not surprising that they wrote oftener of the romantic past than of the troubled present. Even when they did not place their stories in an ante-bellum back-ground, they dealt in the main with character types which represented the Old South rather than the New: the faithful ex-slave, the Southern belle torn between loyalty to the Confederacy and love for a soldier in blue, and the gentleman planter struggling with poverty and holding on to his archaic ideals in an alien social and economic order. The writers of the New South rarely treated the wandering free Negro, the Negro small farmer, or the educated Negro who followed a profession. They rarely wrote of the rising poor-white, the sturdy yeoman farmer, or of urban types like the merchant, the banker, and the manufacturer.

The failure of writers of fiction to depict the life of the middle classes is not of course limited to the fiction writers of the South. The upper mid-dle class, in which the novelist finds most of his readers, is seldom interested in seeing its own life faithfully portrayed in fiction, even when it is done as expertly as in the novels of Howells and Jane Austen. It is far more interested in the doings of the rich and socially important and in the lives of the poor and the humble. In a discussion of "The National Element in Southern Literature," published in the *Sewanee Review* for July, 1903, John Bell Henneman quoted with approval the passage which follows from a letter which Miss Marie Whiting, a minor Virginia writer, had written to him more than ten years before:

There is a splendid opening for somebody in Southern literature—a field un-touched so far as I know. I speak of the want of any adequate representation of typical Southern life of *to-day*. We have stories of society-folk who live in the

South—they live there, that is all, for "society" is pretty much the same the world over; the very rich kill time in much the same way in all large cities or in all summer resorts or winter hotels or palatial country residences. Then we have the dialect stories in every form and shape—they represent the very poor or the very ignorant. But who has told of the great middle class, the blood and fiber and heart and brain of the body corporate? Who has written of the life of small and large towns, of the countryside, of the people who are distinctive and individual, yet who speak the King's English and read some more or less —who are neither marvels of wealth and culture, nor monstrosities of poverty and ignorance? If such people exist, have they not their life, and shall not some one arise to see its pathos and its beauty?

The one Southern novelist who has on any large scale memorably depicted the lives of unromantic Southerners of the great middle class, urban as well as rural, is Ellen Glasgow. The younger novelists of the South have concerned themselves chiefly with the primitive, the dispossessed, and what most Southern readers regard as perverts and degenerates. Is it any wonder that Northern visitors to the South still find that Southern life does not conform to the notions which they have derived from fiction?

In the chapters which follow I have tried to suggest how seven writers of the New South in their various ways made use of their rich inheritance. I have also tried to point out their indebtedness to their predecessors in ante-bellum times, to indicate how they arrived at something like a national point of view, to reveal some of the difficulties they confronted in becoming successful authors, and to suggest the different ways in which they treated life in the South. My discussion of the seven writers will, I hope, make it somewhat easier for the student to understand the conditions under which James Lane Allen, Mary Noailles Murfree, Grace King, and other Southerners managed to make their individual contributions to American literature.

8

Paul Hamilton Hayne

Paul Hamilton Hayne (1830–1886) is an important literary link between the Old South and the New. He was the intimate friend of Simms, Timrod, Grayson, and John R. Thompson; but, unlike these men, he lived long enough to witness the rise of Lanier, Cable, Harris, and other writers of the younger generation. When Simms died in 1870, Hayne inherited his position as chief literary representative of the South. Few of the younger

Southern writers failed to receive from him letters of encouragement and criticism. He also played an important part in the process of reconciliation between Northern and Southern writers. He was the personal friend of Longfellow, Whittier, Edwin P. Whipple, Richard Henry Stoddard, and other Northern writers at a time when the two sections failed most completely to understand one another. And yet he had little sympathy with the New South and remained in some respects unreconstructed to the end of his life. He was born in Charleston, South Carolina, in 1830. He died at "Copse Hill" near Augusta, Georgia, in 1886. His life-span was the same as that of his friend John Esten Cooke and also of Emily Dickinson. Cooke and Hayne probably never heard of her, for few of her poems were in print when she died; but she is now rated as a major American poet, and their works—well-known in their time—are almost forgotten.

Unlike Timrod and Simms, Hayne was born to wealth and high social position in Charleston. His father, an officer in the United States Navy, died when Paul was only two years old. The responsibility for his upbringing devolved upon his mother, Emily McElhenny Hayne, who taught him to love poetry. Until her son was nine, she had the support of his distinguished uncle, Robert Y. Hayne, who in the month (January, 1830) of the poet's birth had defended the South Carolina view of the Constitution in debate with the redoubtable Daniel Webster. The private school which Paul Hayne attended was reputed to be one of Charleston's best, but Christopher Coates, the one-eyed Yankee principal, seemed to Hayne to unite "the morals of Pecksniff with the learning of Squeers." In this school began his friendship with Timrod, whose seat was next to his. He graduated in 1850 from the College of Charleston, the oldest of America's municipal colleges.

As early as 1845 Hayne had published verses in the Charleston *Courier* over the pseudonym "Alpheus"; "Basil Ormond" was another pen name. In the fall of 1851 he was writing for the short-lived secession organ, the *Palmetto Flag*, of which his private library (now in the Duke University Library) contains what seems to be a unique file. In 1852 he married Mary Middleton Michel, granddaughter of a distinguished French surgeon who had seen service under Napoleon. In those years Hayne was ostensibly studying law with Timrod in the office of James Louis Petigru, but he cared as little for the law as Timrod or James M. Legaré, and he was giving most of his time to poetry and literary journalism. In May, 1852, he became assistant editor of W. C. Richards' *Southern Literary Gazette*. In the next year he took over this weekly as the only means of getting eight hundred dollars due him, perhaps as unpaid salary. By this time Hayne, as he put it in a letter to his wife, was sure that, no matter how he was to earn his living, a literary career was to be his "doom." Early in 1856 he became corresponding editor of the Washington *Spectator*, another short-lived literary weekly. He was the chief editor without pay of *Russell's Magazine*, which, launched a few months before the *Atlantic Monthly*, struggled through six volumes from April, 1857, to March, 1860. It was modeled upon *Blackwood's* and was meant to be, in Hayne's words, "an exponent of Southern genius both in literature & politics." *Russell's*, however, had no such corps of contributors as that which was making a notable success of the *Atlantic*. It had few subscribers outside of South Carolina; and though Hayne made a lecture tour in the interest of the magazine, it never received adequate support. Among its Northern contributors were Richard Henry Stoddard and the assistant editor, George C. Hurlbut. Hayne wished *Russell's* to be primarily a literary magazine, but he was not able to keep the magazine out of the controversy over slavery. Although *Russell's* was one of the best Southern magazines of its time, it was primarily a medium for Charleston rather than Southern opinion.

Meanwhile Hayne had published three volumes of verse. Early in 1855 Ticknor and Fields in Boston brought out his *Poems*. Of the edition of five hundred copies, for which Hayne paid the publishers $180, over a hundred were sold in Charleston; but there was little sale elsewhere. It is highly probable that he was censured for publishing a book in the North. Two years later—again at his own expense but this time in Charleston—he brought out his *Sonnets, and Other Poems*. Two years afterwards he wrote to Stoddard that of the three hundred copies printed more than one hundred "now burden the shelves of my library." [24] Concluding that if his poems were to receive any critical attention, he must publish them in the North, he took his third volume, *Avolio* (1859), to Ticknor and Fields.

Hayne had visited Boston in 1853 and returned in the fall of the next year to see his first book through the press. He made the acquaintance of Lowell, Fields, Holmes, Longfellow, Dana, and Whipple. It was to Whipple, whom he once described as "a father to me" and whom he always regarded as the most catholic of critics, that he dedicated *Avolio*. After his return to Charleston, Hayne felt more keenly than ever his isolation in the South. He wrote in 1860 to no less than three Northern friends—R. H.

[24] Hayne to R. H. Stoddard, Aug. 28, 1859. The originals of Hayne's letters to Stoddard are in the New York Public Library, by whose permission I quote. In Hayne's letters there are many underscorings very difficult to reproduce in print. Except where they represent italics, I have not tried to reproduce the underscorings in the original letters. When, however, I have quoted from printed letters the originals of which I have not seen, I have followed the printed version.

Stoddard, R. H. Dana, Jr., and Horatio Woodman—in language which, if known, would have made Charlestonians regard him as disloyal. He wrote to Woodman on August 19, 1860—only four months before South Carolina seceded from the Union:

> I love Boston. Some of the happiest days of my existence were spent there.
> As for Charleston, & So. Carolina generally—let me say to you, which I should not say to almost any other—that a more unfortunate home for an Artist (whatever his degree!) could not be found in the broad circle of Christendom!
> The people are intensely provincial, narrow-minded, and I must add—ignorant. Literature they despise. Poetry they look upon as the feeble pastime of minds too effeminate to seek manly employment. . . .
> If the opportunity ever presents itself, I shall take a final farewell of the South, and "pitch my tent" not far from "Bunker Hill."

Writing in much the same mood to Dana on January 5, 1860, Hayne had said: "You will not deem me unpatriotic in confessing to the general indifference of the South upon all subjects connected with the imaginative Arts. The literary workman—, above all—, the Poet, is terribly isolated here."

It was only for the writers of New England, however, that Hayne cared, for he disliked the general run of Boston humanity. South Carolinians, he wrote home from Boston, had no idea how rampant the Yankees were on the slavery question. Once at least, however, Hayne found himself at variance with the New England writers whom he admired. That was on the memorable occasion when at a dinner in the Albion House he found himself almost the only defender of the genius of Edgar Allan Poe.[25]

Hayne's early poems and prose writings indicate that he was following Stoddard's advice to ground himself thoroughly in the British poets and in a few literary critics like Coleridge. The poets who seem to have influenced him most are Wordsworth, Moore, Keats, Shelley, Tennyson, and Poe. The slighter influence of Morris, Swinburne, and Rossetti came later.

Hayne was a belated Romanticist. He was an exact contemporary of Emily Dickinson, but his early poetry belongs in the same category as that of Stoddard, Stedman, Aldrich, and Taylor. Theirs is for the most part a poetry divorced from actual life; it is poetry for the parlor, and it deals chiefly with books, dreams, and illusions. Of the poets named probably only Stedman ever understood the significance of Whitman. They were all in love with verbal melody, with sweet-scented adjectives, with the picturesque and the remote. They preferred to write of classical or medieval times, and they had a weakness for the Oriental and the sentimental. There

[25] See p. 546.

was perhaps more excuse for cultivating this type of poetry in conservative Charleston than in Philadelphia or New York. Hayne's early poems have little to do with the South of his day; even the nature poems, unlike the best of his later verses, are too generalized to suggest the actual South. Hayne was no more of a reformer than Poe, and he had little interest in ideas apart from literature. He had, like Lanier, a marked dislike for the ideals of "trade." He reminds one of the earlier William Morris, who described himself as a "dreamer of dreams, born out of my due time." He was a painstaking craftsman with a certain pale distinction of style but with little of importance to say. His best work, early or late, appears in his sonnets, which are said to have won the praise of Tennyson. After his friends Longfellow and George Henry Boker, he was perhaps the best American sonneteer of his time.

The secession of South Carolina put an end to Hayne's dreams of settling in Boston. He was for a time on the staff of Governor Pickens, and for the rest of his life was known as Colonel Hayne. He was stationed at Fort Sumter, but after a year his frail health compelled him to resign from the army. He wrote as a patriotic duty a number of war poems, but he knew they were not nearly as good as Timrod's. In wartime he published poems of various kinds in the Charleston newspapers and in the Richmond magazines, the *Magnolia Weekly* and the *Southern Illustrated News*. The war matured Timrod as a poet, but Hayne felt it as hostile to all his intellectual interests. He wrote to Clara Dargan on March 27, 1864: "This war is becoming intolerable, especially to those not actively engaged in the field. All social, & intellectual pleasures have been ruthlessly destroyed. For myself, I can only say, that the war seems to me like a gloomy, & terrible episode in existence; One cannot think calmly; the sympathies, fears, passions of the heart being abnormally excited, there is hardly any chance left for that cool, consistent mental action, essential to Artistic success."

During the long siege of Charleston a bombshell set fire to his home; the house was destroyed. His fine library and the family silver—valued at ten thousand dollars—had been sent to Columbia for safe keeping. Nearly everything was lost there when the "civilized Tecumseh," as Hayne called General Sherman, passed through the state capital. A few of his books were saved, but he lost some valuable Poe manuscripts which John R. Thompson had given him.[26] Hayne once received a letter from a New Yorker who said that he had several pieces of the Hayne family plate and would like to know

[26] In her Introduction to Hayne's *Poems* (1882) Margaret J. Preston referred to the library as totally destroyed. The Duke University Library, however, has about 150 books which belonged to Hayne before the war. For an account of Hayne's library, see

the meaning of the crest and motto. The New Yorker did not offer to return the stolen silver.

At the close of the war Hayne was a refugee in Georgia and was almost penniless. Stocks and bonds and Confederate currency were worthless, and the banks had failed. In July, 1865, he was in Augusta, Georgia, writing for the *Constitutionalist*, but a few months later his health broke down. Seeing no future for himself and his family in Charleston, he bought eighteen acres of uncultivated land in the pine barrens sixteen miles west of Augusta. Here in what might be called a lumberman's shack, badly planned and badly built, he lived from April, 1866, until his death twenty years later. He called the place "Copse Hill," but in other moods it became "Hayne's Roost." With him were his wife, his mother, and his son William Hamilton, who was to become an even more minor poet than his father. There was also the Negro family servant Edmund, whom Hayne is said to have taught to read Vergil in Latin. Here Hayne did his writing standing by a desk which had been improvised out of a carpenter's work bench. He kept his books—few at first—in cases made out of packing boxes, which his wife decorated with pictures clipped from magazines. He had determined to live by writing, supplementing his meager income by a little gardening. Here at least he was free from the rent and the taxes which he would have had to pay in Charleston or any other city. For some months he almost starved. The ephemeral Southern magazines that sprang up after Appomattox—and they were many—were able to pay him little or nothing, and few Northern magazines were as yet willing to publish the work of an ex-Confederate. He found that he had to write chiefly prose in order to earn a little leisure to write verse. The Richmond weekly, *Southern Opinion*, awarded him a prize of one hundred dollars for the best poem dealing with the recent war, and its editor, H. Rives Pollard, employed him to review books. In a short time, however, Pollard was killed, and the bulk of Hayne's salary was never paid. He reviewed books for General Hill's the *Land We Love* and for Father Ryan's the *Banner of the South*. He also wrote for the two chief Baltimore magazines, Albert Taylor Bledsoe's *Southern Review* and William Hand Browne's *New Eclectic*, soon to be rechristened the *Southern Magazine*. He conducted literary columns for various newspapers and asked Northern publishers to send him their new books for review. On April 25, 1869, he wrote to Simms: "Fame, posthumous renown, & 'a' that

---

his "Charles Gayarré," *So. Bivouac*, N.S. II, 108 (July, 1886). He still had, he wrote, a "forlorn remnant of a 'noble army of martyrs,' destroyed by fire a quarter of a century since, in the luckless capital of South Carolina."

& 'a' that,' I must leave to my intellectual betters; content if the cupboard is never *wholly* empty, & the demi-john of Rye or Bourbon gives out a sound, not *too* manifestly hollow. . . ." Hayne's last years were a continual struggle with poverty and chronic ill health.

The first of the Northern magazines to accept his work after the war were the *Old Guard*, the *Round Table*, and the *Galaxy*. After a few years, with the help of such Northern friends as Stoddard, Boker, and Taylor, he succeeded in placing poems in *Appletons'* and *Lippincott's*. He had published three poems in the *Atlantic Monthly* while Lowell was editor, but it was not until September, 1872, that Fields and Howells would print any of his later work. To have a poem published in the *Atlantic* was quite a triumph for a Southern writer in 1872; it was then difficult enough for anyone outside of New England to break into its pages. Hayne complained that Howells cared only for poems of a Wordsworthian stamp, and he felt somewhat bitter when the *Atlantic* rejected his powerful narrative poem, "Cambyses and the Macrobian Bow" because the dénouement—more tragic than in the analogous William Tell story—was too horrible for Howells' taste. Howells would accept none of Hayne's poems after 1876, and it was not until 1884, when Aldrich was editor, that Hayne had another poem published in the *Atlantic*. Although Howells found some of Hayne's poems unacceptable, he was pleased by the friendly letters which came to him from "Copse Hill." On January 2, 1873, he accepted a poem for the *Atlantic* and thanked Hayne for the photograph which he had asked for: "You have a good, kind, sensitive face, on which I like to look and feel that you are my friend; and I should know you for a poet anywhere."

In these later years Hayne brought out—apparently at his own expense—two more volumes of poems: *Legends and Lyrics* (1872) and *The Mountain of the Lovers* (1875). In 1873 after many delays he finally succeeded in finding a publisher for Timrod's poems with the memoir of his friend who had died nearly six years before. There was a final volume of Hayne's *Poems* (1882), which though labeled "Complete Edition," does not include all of his published poems; and there are numerous later poems still uncollected. The 1882 volume was appropriately dedicated to Colonel John G. James, President of the Texas A. and M. College, who had made its publication possible by getting two hundred subscriptions in advance, many of them from the North. Hayne did not see the proof sheets of the book; and when it appeared, he discovered that the Lothrop Publishing Company of Boston had made some mistakes in the arrangement of the poems and had omitted some materials that he had planned to include.

Perhaps Hayne's later work might have been better if he had been able to live in one of the large Northern cities where he could have found intellectual stimulus and companionship; and yet the advantages of metropolitan life had no miraculous effect upon the work of such poets as Stoddard, Stedman, Taylor, and Aldrich. At a time when the main drift of American life was toward the city, Hayne had chosen to live in the Georgia pine barrens. He explained the reason for his choice in a letter to Margaret J. Preston, April 9, 1872: "In any town whatever, I should have no choice but to become a local Editor or Clerk in some mercantile establishment—a molasses & Bacon store probably—, whilst here I am free—as the clouds & the rain, and if the great advantages of intellectual attrition are denied me,—at all events, I have nature as a friend, and those undisturbed opportunities for commune with her, and with the noble minds of the Past. . . ."

Isolated as he was, Hayne found consolation and stimulus in his extensive correspondence with other writers. Among his Northern correspondents were Stoddard, Holmes, Longfellow, Whipple, Whittier, Taylor, Stedman, and Bryant. From England came letters from Swinburne, Jean Ingelow, Richard Blackmore, and the blind poet Philip Bourke Marston. Among his Southern correspondents were Sidney Lanier, Margaret J. Preston, Maurice Thompson, John Esten Cooke, Charles Gayarré, and various forgotten writers, chiefly women. His most extensive correspondence was with Mrs. Preston, but fifteen of the most interesting letters he received came from Constance Fenimore Woolson, then living in the South and rediscovering for Northern readers the charm and reality of Southern life. Many of these writers Hayne was never to meet; he never saw Miss Woolson, Mrs. Preston, Gayarré, or Lanier. Many Southern writers were almost as isolated as Hayne himself. Maurice Thompson, an ex-Confederate living in Indiana, wrote to him: "I have never seen a *literary* man or woman!"

Hayne cultivated and valued his literary friendships, as well he might. Moses Coit Tyler in Ann Arbor, Michigan, laboring over *The Literary History of the American Revolution*, wrote to Hayne on January 15, 1881: "You seem to be almost unique among the men of this time in still indulging in the luxury of downright friendship, and in having the boldness to say so. You are the sort of fellow that would have been understood by Sir Philip Sidney and Ned Spenser and Will Shakespeare, who were not ashamed to love their manly friends and write love letters to them. I must say that I cannot help being on rather better terms with myself for finding delight in a nature like yours, a nature that seems almost an anachronism in our cynical and mercenary age." Hayne had the happy faculty of adapting his letters to the persons to whom he was writing, and he never hesitated to indulge in downright flattery when he wrote to influential persons. In his letters to Holmes, Lowell, and Whittier he had little to say of Southern grievances but much about the growing good will between the two sections. With some of his Southern correspondents, particularly Charles Gayarré, he discussed freely their common dislike of Northern politicians and their difficulties in pleasing Northern editors, publishers, and critics. His desire for reconciliation was genuine; but, like many another Southerner, he was irritated by the Northern assumption—now more complacent than ever—of the wrong-headedness and cultural inferiority of the defeated South. He was not in sympathy with the dominant trends of the New South, which seemed to him abandoning nearly everything for which the Old South had stood.

Among his correspondents there was a Southern writer more unreconstructed than Hayne. This was William Hand Browne, editor of the *Southern Magazine*, who wrote to Hayne from Baltimore, July 30, 1870: "I look forward to the threatening *Yankeeisation* of the South with unspeakable dread and abhorrence. It would not matter so much if the prospect was that of being Anglicised, Gallicised, Teutonised, or Feejeeised; but to be infected with the Yankee soul—the Yankee spirit—great heavens!" If Southerners had adequately supported Browne's magazine, he might not have written to Hayne as he did on September 11, 1871: "And I rage internally when I see our Southern people—my brothers and yours—meekly admitting the Yankees' claim to have all the culture, all the talent, all the genius of the country. . . . And I rage tenfold when I see our people—aye, our women and maidens—taught to hanker after the works of Mrs. Stowe, that Pythoness of foulness; Lowell, the twice-branded hypocrite; Whittier, the narrow bitter Puritan, Alger, the dish-washer of maudlin mysticism, and the rest of that shabby crew." Hayne, however, loved and admired Whittier; and he had too much sense to permit Browne to induce him to promote a plan for a "Southern Literary Guild," the purpose of which was to combat "the Yankeeisation of the South" and to protect the joint interests of Southern writers.

Experience had taught Hayne that if he was to live by his pen he had little to expect from the South. He wrote to Bayard Taylor, June 16, 1875: "Alack! almost all my readers are found North of the Potomac. . . . Why, from my native city of Charleston, I find that they have—, with tremendous effort,—succeeded in ordering just 15 *copies* (!!) of my vol!" On November 1, 1876, Miss Woolson wrote to Hayne that she had searched in vain for his *Legends and Lyrics*, published four years before, in bookstores in Charleston, Charlotte, Charlottesville, Baltimore, and Norfolk. As before the war,

Southern booksellers were taking what the New York publishers were sending them and were paying little attention to the works of Southern writers. The publishers of *Legends and Lyrics* and of Hayne's edition of Timrod's *Poems*, E. J. Hale and Son, were North Carolinians doing business in New York but obviously unable to compete with the larger houses. Even from Southern leaders, Hayne wrote to Mrs. Preston, January 16, 1873, the Southern writer could expect "nothing—unless it be contumely, and a thinly-veiled contempt." Northerners had a respect for literature and took a real pride in their writers, but the Southern poet was "at the mercy of every pert editorial puppy who can compose five grammatical sentences. . . ." The New South, he felt, had learned nothing from the experience of the Old. He had written to Mrs. Preston a year earlier, January 24, 1872: "After all, Dear Friend, is it not too mournfully true, that our thrice unfortunate section & people, owe much of their present humiliation, misery, and slavish bondage, to their own short-sighted policy, and wretched materialism in the Past? They despised Art, Imagination, Literature; discouraged every native aspirant after things spiritual and partly thro Literature, (think of 'Uncle Tom's Cabin'!) the death blow to their nationality, & fame was given! And they are a People who never learn; never take warning from past errors!" Hayne complained too much—much more than his friend Lanier—but it is impossible not to sympathize with him, for he struggled against great difficulties.

Hayne had to face even the disapproval of some of his own relatives. None of them, apart from his own immediate family, he confided to Mrs. Preston, January 18, 1873, cared two straws whether he lived or starved. They regarded him, he thought, as "a 'wool gathering,' un-practical, impecunious visionary, who has somehow broken faith with his family traditions—for you must know that the Haynes pride themselves upon what they call their 'clear common sense,'—which means, briefly, their blindness to all the fair world of imagination, & the graces of the highest spiritual culture." There were moments doubtless when Hayne would have agreed with Whipple, who once wrote to him that the South was "the worst place, this side of New Zealand, for poets and romancers," or with Bayard Taylor, who wrote: "Son of the South as you are, I must tell you that the South is no home for a born poet. It will be 50 or 100 years before Literature can take root in your soil. The very feelings and interests which make you the *most* Southern are just those which impede the growth of true Art among you. Don't be offended!—God knows, I write this in sorrow. And I don't mean you, personally, but your public: this you will take for granted. The *readers* are here in the North."

For Southern writers the decade 1865–1875 was the most difficult of all periods. In the North few editors, publishers, or readers had any real interest in anything being written about the South unless it was based upon the assumption that the South had been wrong on every fundamental question involved in the war. George W. Cable, whom Hayne condemned without reading his books, could please his Northern readers, for he had turned Abolitionist *after* the war, but Hayne could not stoop to professing opinions that he did not hold. Southern magazines could pay little or nothing for what they printed. Most educated Southerners were too poor, or thought they were, to buy books and magazines; and when they did buy, it was generally, as before the war, books and magazines imported from the North. In all economic matters the literary South was now more dependent upon the North than ever before.

Hayne's literary taste was somewhat old-fashioned, but he read the works of the newer writers, English as well as American. He was impressed by the poems of William Morris and Swinburne, but he could see nothing in Walt Whitman. Bret Harte and Mark Twain seemed to him vulgar, as they seemed to some older writers in New York and New England. He did not care for the realism of Howells. No wonder that he found it difficult to place his old-fashioned poems in Northern magazines which were publishing the writings of a younger generation which he did not really understand. He had grown up in an age when poetry was more widely read, and he was not able or willing to turn to writing local-color fiction or cultivate other literary types in demand. His friend Lanier was finally able to attain a measure of success by adapting his form and content to the needs of the new age, but Hayne was too unadaptable and too lacking in genius to succeed where so many of his contemporaries were failing.

As Hayne read the Northern and Southern magazines, looking for promising young writers of the South, he was, like Lanier, disturbed by the indiscriminate praise of the subliterary novels of Southern women. In June, 1874, he published in the *Southern Magazine* "Literature at the South: The Fungous School," in which he expressed his opinion of those untrained and feeble writers who got attention by "local influence and patronage . . . the *claquement* of friends and allies, and the blatant commendation of the press (generally the provincial press). . . ." He ridiculed "Mrs. Duck-a-Love's 'pathetic and passionate romance, that marvellous revelation of a woman's famishing heart'" and "Mrs. General Aristotle Brown's 'profound philosophic novel, in which metaphysical acumen and a powerful grasp and clear comprehension of the knottiest social problems of our time are combined with dramatic capabilities seldom equalled, and never surpassed, in the literature of the present or any other age." Mrs. Duck-a-Love's romance on examination proves to be an example "rather of bosh than beauty"; and Mrs. General Brown's novel is "an exponent of effervescing commonplace, with much fizz, fussiness and froth, and the smallest conceivable undercurrent of good sense or suggestive thought—in conception shallow, in taste tawdry and pretentious, and in style baldly ungrammatical. . . ." There was no hope, he thought, for better things until Southern scholars and thinkers had the courage to discourage instead of applauding such trash.

In 1873 with his son William, Hayne revisited Baltimore, Philadelphia, New York, and Boston. He hoped to find a better market by personal contact with editors, publishers, and creative writers. He was away from home five months, for his stay was prolonged by a dangerous illness. In desperation he applied for financial help to some of his Southern editor friends. All he got from William Hand Browne was a lecture on the business incompetence and chronic impecuniosity of poets. Some of the Northern literary friends who came to his rescue were Longfellow, Stedman, Moses Coit Tyler, and Bryant, who lent or gave him one hundred and fifty dollars. Without the assistance they gave, he thought, he would have died. Some time after his return to Georgia, he wrote to Mrs. Preston, May 12, 1874: "I frankly confess, that with the South, I,—as a literary man,—have done forever! No longer shall I attempt, to the utmost verge of my humble ability to sustain her periodicals, extend her knowledge of art,—defend her people, vindicate her character!" "The only real art-friends," he added, "(excepting, of course, some very dear personal friends like yourself), I ever found, are Northern men. . . ."

Hayne was of course too thorough a Southerner to keep his vow. He may have contributed less willingly to Southern magazines—now reduced in numbers—but he was prompt to encourage a new literary talent, like that of Lanier. Like Simms, Hayne overrated the Southern indifference to his work. In 1879, when he returned to Charleston for medical treatment, he was surprised to find himself known and honored for his poetry. He wrote to his wife: "It is the old story of the Greek Poet, who scorned by the Athenians in his youth, returned (when old and sick), to be crowned with the laurel, and surfeited with the honey of Hymettus!—Still I confess these honors are not ungrateful."

In his later years Hayne noted the rapid rise of new writers, North and South and West, who overshadowed him. He was perhaps a little envious even of Lanier's success. He thought he found editors and publishers increasingly indifferent even to his best work. In a pessimistic moment he wrote to his Vermont friend, Mrs. Julia C. R. Dorr, December 11, 1885:

As a Southerner, *always, always* have I been at a strange sort of disadvantage; and now that the "old South," is being abused, undervalued, sneered at, right and left, my being true to our Poets and our Traditions,—has shut the door almost hermetically, against further literary recognition. To be candid, my compeers (at the North), in *private* correspondence, *do* rank me very high; but they seem actually afraid to endorse their estimate in *print*.

There are times when I am placed, almost outside of National Literature. Stedman in his "Twilight of the Poets" speaks of "my people's" appreciation, as if I belonged more to a locality than the Country at large, while B[ayard]. Taylor in his "Echo Club," refers to me as if I belonged to another country altogether; and these examples I could multiply.

As a matter of fact, Hayne's poems were still appearing in the better Northern magazines, but he felt increasingly out of sympathy with the literary tendencies of the time. In 1885 Southern fiction was near the peak of its popularity, but local-color stories in Negro dialect were not what Hayne wished to write; and he sensed in the work of the younger writers, even in Lanier, a certain condescension toward both the writers and the ideals of the Old South. Even more than some of his New England contemporaries, he found it difficult to adapt his writing to the taste of a new age.

Hayne did not fail completely, however. He carefully studied the natural scene about him, and Howells showed his discernment by printing in the *Atlantic Monthly* some of the later poems which deal with the rather desolate country about "Copse Hill." Some of Hayne's later poems— notably "A Summer Mood," "Voices of the Pines," "Forest Pictures," and "Glorified Mists"—played a part in leading Lanier to give up his unfinished "The Jacquerie" and turn to the Southern scene of his own time.

Most of Hayne's poems, early or late, were too remote from life to interest readers even in Georgia or South Carolina. The narrative poems are frequently involved or overdecorated. Hayne's taste was for the ornate; he could not resist the temptation to touch up Timrod's letters before he published them. In his later years he dreamed less of poetic fame and wished, he wrote, "to come near and rouse the great heart of humanity—to elevate, comfort, and console the lives of [his] fellow creatures." But his training and his technique did not permit him to reach the thousands who read "The Village Blacksmith" and "A Psalm of Life." William Hand Browne, after rereading many of the poems in *Legends and Lyrics*, wrote to Lanier: "Hayne has great tenderness and delicacy, and often rare beauty of expression: what he lacks (entre nous) is strength. He rarely lets fly a thought that strikes to the heart like an arrow, or sticks in the memory like a fishhook."

One later poem of Hayne's, however, goes straight to the mark and is not wanting in strength. It is his "South Carolina to the States of the North" with its significant subtitle "Especially to Those That Formed a Part of the Original Thirteen." The poem is an impassioned protest against the injustice of rule by carpetbaggers and scalawags kept in power by Union soldiers. It begins:

> I lift these hands with iron fetters banded:
> Beneath the scornful sunlight and cold stars
> I rear my once imperial forehead branded
> By alien shame's immedicable scars;
> Like some pale captive, shunned by all the nations,
> I crouch unpitied, quivering and apart—
> Laden with countless woes and desolations,
> The life-blood freezing round a broken heart!

As a Southerner, Hayne was in his later years a curious combination of the old and the new. If one reads only his letters to older Southerners like Gayarré and Mrs. Preston, he seems wholly "unreconstructed." He had no enthusiasm for the New South or for American democracy in its newer phases, and Northern politicians seemed to him contemptible rascals and vulgarians. He had no respect for President Grant, but the assassination of Garfield moved him to write a memorial sonnet. Like Father Ryan, he was deeply moved by the aid which a generous North extended during the yellow fever epidemic of 1878. He wrote a poem about Hiram H. Benner, a young Northerner who lost his life during the epidemic, and about the same time he composed "The Stricken South to the North," which he dedicated to Dr. Holmes, and a New Year's poem which he significantly entitled "Reconciliation."

Long before he wrote these poems, however, Hayne had done his best to promote better relations between Northern and Southern writers. In a letter to Whittier he expressed the wish "that henceforth all jealousies, all unworthy prejudices may be annihilated, between North and South." "As for Literature," he said, "it has no sections." It is somewhat surprising to find that in the years that followed the Civil War Hayne found himself most attracted to Whittier. He wrote to Mrs. Preston on April 15, 1873: "Ah! the grand old man!! A fanatic, all his life, and yet so profoundly sincere; hating what he deemed crime, but ever tender towards the supposed Criminal!" When in 1877 he wrote a poem for Whittier's birthday, "To the Poet in Whittier," he made it clear that his poem was, as he said, "addressed to Whittier the Poet, not Whittier the Politician!"

By the standards of his own time Hayne's poems were good, and the workmanship was almost always competent. If they are forgotten now, it is partly because for those who like the kind of poetry he wrote there is too often a better poem by another Romantic poet on a similar theme. His "Avolio," rewritten and rechristened "The Vengeance of the Goddess Diana," suggests comparison with a later poem, William Morris's "The Lady of the Land." Occasionally, however, Hayne holds his own with better poets. In "The Story of Glaucus the Thessalian," although he seems not to have known it, he retold the Greek legend which also supplied the basis of Lowell's "Rhoecus" and Landor's "The Hamadryad." Hayne's poem is too much the parlor piece—particularly if one reads his prelude—but he does not obtrude an incongruous moral, as Lowell assuredly does. "The Hamadryad" is the best poem of the three, but Landor selected a version of the legend inferior to that used by Lowell and Hayne. In commenting upon Hayne's poem, Lanier praised "the fine spirit-of-green leaves, which makes the poem so dainty and shady and cool."

When he heard of Hayne's death, Whittier wrote to Mrs. Hayne, July 10, 1886: "He leaves an honored name behind him. A true gentleman, a generous unselfish friend, a poet whose pure, lofty verse is now known & loved wherever the English language is spoken—he will have a place in the Valhalla of the country, with Longfellow & Bryant & Taylor who while living were his friends." This is the partial verdict of a friend. Longfellow, Bryant, Taylor, and Whittier himself are no longer rated as great poets. Hayne did not succeed in writing poems that posterity would not willingly let die. He did manage, however, to achieve a position as the representative poet of the South in his own time. He was doubtless happier and more useful to his generation than he would have been if he had been a local editor, like his friend James Ryder Randall, or a merchant like still another friend, Henry Lynden Flash, in New Orleans. In an early poem, "The Will and the Wing," he had expressed an ideal to which he had remained steadfastly true although when he wrote the lines he did not know what his devotion to poetry would cost him:

> Yet would I rather in the outward state
> Of Song's immortal temple lay me down,
> A beggar basking by that radiant gate
> Than bend beneath the haughtiest empire's crown!

9

Sidney Lanier

ALTHOUGH SIDNEY LANIER (1842–1881) grew to manhood in the Middle Georgia of Johnston and Harris, he was, like Poe and Cable, a product of the urban rather than the rural South. Macon, which was his home until after 1873, was a commercial and educational center of some importance. In Mercer it had a Baptist college for men and in Wesleyan a pioneer college for women—older than the woman's colleges of the North. Lanier's parents were devout Presbyterians, and the social life of the town was sobered by what seems like a mild form of Puritanism.

Lanier was a gifted and attractive youth who combined the normal interests of an adolescent boy with a twofold passion for music and poetry. He read the romances of Scott and Bulwer-Lytton, Le Sage's *Gil Blas*, and the *Chronicles* of Froissart, which had fascinated Philip Pendleton Cooke in Virginia. Lanier's "Southern chivalry," in so far as it had any literary sources, probably owed more to Froissart and Tennyson than to Scott or any of the Southern novelists whom he may have read. Among his favorite poets were Shakespeare, Keats, and above all Tennyson.[27] Carlyle and Ruskin influenced his thinking about the relation of art to morals. In middle life he was to discover the treasures of the older English poetry. Poe was an early idol, and Lanier's earliest verses, which have not been preserved, are said to have been romantic and gloomy. Longfellow's *Hyperion* interested him because of its German background; but, like most other Southern writers, he owed little to the major writers of New England and New York. Somewhat belatedly, however, he became aware of the significance of Emerson and Whitman.

When he was fifteen, Lanier's parents sent him to Oglethorpe, a Presbyterian college in Milledgeville some thirty or forty miles from Macon. By the standards of the time Oglethorpe was better than the "farcical college" which Lanier once called it. After his graduation in the spring of 1860, he returned in the fall as a tutor at a salary of $550. He now found a congenial intellectual companion in Milton H. Northrup, a New Yorker who had graduated from Hamilton College and come to Milledgeville to take charge of the Oglethorpe Academy. The finest and strongest influence of Lanier's early years, however, came from young Professor James Woodrow, who

[27] See, for example, "Retrospects and Prospects," *Works*, V, 296–297. Compare also pp. 283–284 with the passage in Tennyson's "To the Queen" which describes the theme of the *Idylls of the King* as "New-old, and shadowing Sense at war with Soul."

had studied for a short time under Louis Agassiz at Harvard and afterwards taken his doctor's degree at the University of Heidelberg. The two spent many hours together discussing science, religion, and German philosophy and literature. Lanier's interest in science and his modernist religious views undoubtedly owed much to this teacher who after Lanier's death was officially censured for heresy.

On the eve of the war Lanier was thinking of following in Woodrow's steps and going to Heidelberg to prepare himself for a professorship. He was troubled by his passion for music. In a diary now lost he wrote:

I am more than all perplexed by this fact: that the prime inclination—that is, natural bent (which I have checked, though) of my nature is to music, and for that I have the greatest talent; indeed, not boasting, for God gave it me, I have an extraordinary musical talent, and feel it within me plainly that I could rise as high as any composer. But I cannot bring myself to believe that I was intended for a musician, because it seems so small a business in comparison with other things which, it seems to me, I might do. Question here: "What is the province of music in the economy of the world?"

In ante-bellum Georgia, as in many parts of the United States then and now, music was regarded as a delightful pastime, not as a respectable profession. Perhaps Lanier's final choice of literature rather than music for his creative work came from the conviction that in poetry he could better express whatever message he had for mankind.

The outbreak of war in the spring of 1861 postponed the time when it would be necessary to choose a profession. After the election of Lincoln he was "a full-blooded secessionist," and with his beloved younger brother Clifford he enlisted in the Macon Volunteers. Although they fought in some of the great Virginia battles, the brothers found, like Cable, Cooke, and Gildersleeve, much time for reading in the lulls between campaigns. In 1863 while stationed at Fort Boykin in Tidewater Virginia, they became acquainted with the family of General John Hankins, who lived at "Bacon's Castle"; and Sidney fell in love with Virginia Hankins, who, he wrote to his father, had "the best-cultivated mind I've seen in a long time." Together they read Mrs. Browning's *Drama in Exile* and perhaps other books which he read in wartime: Mrs. Browning's *Aurora Leigh*, Bailey's *Festus*, Augusta Jane Evans' *Macaria*, and Hugo's *Les Misérables*. He was also reading Carlyle, Novalis, Richter, and Longfellow's *Hyperion*, and he was paraphrasing or translating lyrics by the German poets. In the winter of 1863–1864 he began his novel, *Tiger-Lilies* (1867). In January he sent two chapters to his father and wrote: ". . . gradually I find that my whole soul is merging itself into this business of writing, especially of writing poetry—. I'm going to try it: and am going to test, in the most rigid way I know, the awful question whether it is my vocation—."

In the summer of 1864 Lanier was transferred to the Signal Service and not long afterwards he was captured while running the blockade and sent to the Federal prison at Point Lookout in Maryland. There he found a friend and lover of music and poetry in John Banister Tabb, whom he was to meet again in Baltimore after the war. The Federal prisons may not have been as deplorable as those in the Confederacy which were so bitterly denounced in the North, but they were bad enough. When Lanier was released in February, 1865, he was a sick man. A month later he had made his way to Macon to discover that his mother was dying. The sixteen years that were left to him now were to be a long struggle with disease, poverty, and misfortune. Few artists ever lived at a time or in a region more unfavorable to the artistic life than the South of the late sixties and early seventies. It was the eight years following his release from prison that Lanier had in mind when in August, 1875, he wrote to his new friend, Bayard Taylor: "I could never describe to you what a mere drought and famine my life has been, as regards that multitude of matters which I fancy one absorbs when one is in an atmosphere of art, or when one is in conversational relation with men of letters, with travellers, with persons who have either seen, or written, or done large things. Perhaps you know that with us of the younger generation in the South since the War, pretty much the whole of life has been merely not-dying!"

The young soldier-poet who had come home afflicted with tuberculosis found poverty, stagnation, and gloom everywhere about him. First, he must find some means of making a living. He tried tutoring; he worked in a hotel in Montgomery (a well-to-do grandfather before the war had owned several hotels); he was principal of an Alabama academy; he tried for a professorship in the University of Alabama. Again and again his health broke down and he had to give up his work, recuperate, and make a fresh start. In 1867 he published *Tiger-Lilies*, which did not bring the success he had hoped for. In the same year he married Mary Day, as loyal and devoted a wife as ever poet married; and in 1868, with a family to provide for, he decided that the practical thing to do was to study law and practice with his father. In that year also he determined to give up writing except as an avocation to be pursued in any leisure time he might have. He would have to live his poetry rather than write it. Fortunately, "Life and Song," in which he recorded his resolution, proved more popular than any other poem he had written.

Lanier was singularly free from the bitterness and hatred that marked both North and South in the late sixties. In 1869 he wrote in "Nirvâna":

I slew gross bodies of old ethnic Hates
That stirred long race-wars betwixt states and states;
I stood and scorned these foolish dead debates,
    Calmly, calmly, Nirvâna.

In May, 1866, he had responded cordially to a letter from his Northern friend Northrup: "The two margins of the great gulf which has divided you from me seem approaching each other: I stretch out my hand across the narrowing fissure, to grasp yours on the other side." "Our literary life," he continued, ". . . is a lonely and somewhat cheerless one; for beyond our father, a man of considerable literary acquirements and exquisite taste, we have not been able to find a single individual who sympathized in such pursuits enough to warrant showing him our little productions. So scarce is 'general cultivation' here!" He told Northrup that, "thirsty to know what is going on in the great Art-world" up North, he had subscribed to the *Round Table*. The policy of this New York literary weekly seemed not unfriendly to the South, and Lanier sent the editors some of his poems. They printed two of them without his name in July, 1866, and during the next two years they published ten more.

Lanier was little impressed by the Southern magazines which appeared in the late sixties, and he had nothing but contempt for the sentimental novels which Southern women were writing. On May 26, 1873, he wrote to Paul Hayne: "God forbid we [in the South] should really be brought so low as that we must perforce brag of such works as 'Clifford Troupe' and 'Heart Hungry': and God be merciful to that man (he is an Atlanta Editor) who boasted that sixteen thousand of these books had been sold in the South!" The magazine *Southern Society*, which had listed his name among its contributors, provoked this comment in December, 1867: "What a horribly jejune and altogether pointless affair is the 'Southern Society,' of Baltimore! My name was published as a contributor: but I shall certainly send nothing to such a set of asses." Meanwhile in the spring of 1867 Lanier had met in Montgomery the editor of *Scott's Monthly* who was to print his prose piece, "The Three Waterfalls," and his poems, "The Raven Days" and "Life and Song," probably without ever paying anything for them.

During these years Lanier, though he was a vigorous critic of the Reconstruction policies of Congress, was rapidly coming to see himself as primarily an American rather than a Southern writer. In his Furlow College Address of June 30, 1869, he denounced a certain insidious evil, which, especially since the war, has been the bane and poison of all our humble artistic endeavor here in the South. I mean the habit of inviting purchasers to buy artists' works, *simply* because they happen to be Southern artists. I mean the habit of regarding our literature as *Southern* literature, our poetry as *Southern* poetry, our pictures as Southern pictures. I mean the habit of glossing over the intrinsic defects of artistic productions by appealing to the Southern sympathies of the artist's countrymen. . . . How ignoble must be the ambition of that artist, whether he be poet, painter, musician, sculptor, or architect, who could consent to palm off the crudities of his indolence upon the patronizing good-nature of his countrymen! . . . For, the basis of it is hate, and Art will have nothing to do with hate.

By 1869 Lanier had written the best of his early poems. As early as February, 1861, his father had found in his son's verses evidence of "quick poetical sympathies, a rich fund of imagery . . . & a clever knack of versification." He had noted also an undue fondness for what in Shakespeare's time were called "conceits." In January, 1864, Lanier, planning to try his hand "at the *terse* way of writing," wrote: "I have frequently noticed in myself a tendency to the diffuse style—; a disposition to push my metaphors too far, employing a multitude of words to heighten the *pat*-ness of the image, and so making of it rather a *conceit* than a metaphor. . . ." In November, 1869, he was urging Virginia Hankins, who had sent him some of her verses: "Be, I pray you, merciless with yourself, in the matter of rejecting all weak or ignoble or common-place expressions or similes." He was ready enough to admit the redundancy of his prose writings, but, he wrote to Mary Day in 1867: "There is no single poem of mine which is not as simple in diction, in word-arrangement, and in thought, as any ballad of Burns'." That was an ideal which he often failed to live up to. Some of his earlier poems, however, have a directness and a simplicity less often present in the later poems. What Lanier needed most in his Macon years was such a discerning and friendly critic as he found in Bayard Taylor ten years after his release from Point Lookout.

Knowing that poetry was unlikely to furnish him a livelihood, Lanier staked much on the sale of *Tiger-Lilies*. He had begun the novel in 1863, but it was not until March, 1867, that he completed it. He took the manuscript to New York, borrowed four hundred dollars from a Northern cousin, and paid to have it published in the fall of that year. The book drew favorable comments from Simms, Hayne, and Joel Chandler Harris, but not more than eight hundred of the one thousand copies printed were ever sold, and Lanier found himself the poorer by two or three hundred dollars. The writing of novels seemed to offer no escape from Macon into the "great Art-world" where he longed to be. A year and a half after its publication he pronounced it a "foolish book . . . of a foolish boy." A sounder estimate is that contained in a letter which his brother Clifford wrote to William Malone Baskervill, September 21, 1896: "It is a welter of suggestions tossing in the mind of a young man passing thro the 'Sturm und Drang' period: It is eccentric as a meteoric sky in August. It is a mesh of roots from which perfect flowers grew. . . . It is not thought-out, but poured-out, like the lead fused in a ladle for bullets by the hunter. It is a phantasmagoria, of one who wakes from the nightmare of the Civil War." Tiger-Lilies has some good scenes, but it is a romantic, immature work, a medley of Lanier's interests in music, poetry, and German philosophy combined with his recollections of the Tennessee mountains and the battlefields of Virginia. It is, like Keats's Endymion and Emerson's Nature, full of ideas and themes which its author was to treat more successfully in his maturer years. If Lanier had chosen to write humorous local-color stories of Middle Georgia, like Richard Malcolm Johnston, he might have produced a book that would sell. His experiments in the cracker and Negro dialects leave one in little doubt that he might have made a place for himself in prose fiction.

Early in 1869 Lanier wrote to Virginia Hankins that he had given up all thought of literature as a profession "through a deep conviction that, as matters go at present, it is too narrow for elbow-room, and too hampered by provincialism and sect, for that large view which one would wish to take. . . ." In April, 1870, he wrote to Paul Hayne: "I've not put pen to paper, in the literary way, in a long time. How I thirst to do so, how I long to sing a thousand various songs that oppress me, unsung,—is inexpressible. Yet, the mere work that brings bread gives me no time." He published no poems in 1869, only two in 1870, and none in 1872 and 1873. Yet he was trying through a literary agency to market a volume of essays, mostly unwritten; and he was working intermittently on "The Jacquerie," a historical romance in verse dealing with a popular uprising in medieval France described in Froissart's Chronicles.

Meanwhile the poems he had already published had been read by a few discerning persons who were now urging him to write more poems. The most notable of these was Paul Hamilton Hayne, who wrote to Lanier some time in 1868 praising a poem which he had seen, presumably in the Round Table. Although the two poets, both living in Georgia, never met, they exchanged many letters of encouragement and often made specific suggestions for the improvement of each other's poems. The story of their literary friendship, however, is too complicated to discuss here.

In March, 1869, Lanier's "Nirvâna" appeared in the Baltimore Southern

Magazine, which both Lanier and Hayne regarded as the best of the regional magazines; and in the same month Lawrence Turnbull, traveling in the South in the interests of the magazine, stopped in Macon to see the young lawyer and urge him to become a regular contributor. Lanier was pleased even though Turnbull could not promise to pay for what he might print. He gave his impression of Turnbull in a letter to his wife: "A noble, quiet, handsome, beetle-browed, slender, gray-eyed fellow, he: and was like a revelation unto me from some other world: for he cometh out of the atmosphere of letters, and of men of scholarly lives, and carrieth the air thereof with him." Turnbull's visit perhaps caused the harassed young poet to look longingly toward Baltimore, where three years later he would find employment and friends who shared his love of music and literature.

In Macon his health deteriorated. In the years 1868–1873, which were given over to the law, he was too sick half the time to work. Again and again he had to leave Macon for a more suitable climate. It was apparently on such a journey in March, 1871, that he first visited Brunswick and saw the marshes of Glynn. His health again broke down in March of the following year. He spent the summer at Alleghany Springs in Virginia, but in the fall it was evident that he could not spend the winter in Macon. In November he made the long journey to Texas alone. With him went a newly-acquired volume of Chaucer's poems and *The English Classics: A Historical Sketch* by Richard Malcolm Johnston and William Hand Browne, who in Baltimore were soon to become two of his closest friends.

Among the German musicians in San Antonio, as he told his wife in a memorable letter, Lanier discovered that he was "a master of the flute." In the spring he made the eventful decision to give up the law and as soon as practicable to "get to New York and go at my true labor. For," as he wrote to his brother, "I will never be at rest at all until I so arrange my life as to get myself some leisure to write some books that now burn in my heart: I *must* write them. . . ." In September, 1873, he went to New York "armed only with a silver Boehm flute, and some dozens of steel pens." He was unable then or later to find permanent employment in New York; but amateur musician though he was, in Baltimore he managed to secure the position of first flutist with the Peabody Symphony Orchestra. His salary of sixty dollars a month, however, was not sufficient to warrant his bringing his family to Baltimore.

It was his flute and not his pen that enabled Lanier to live north of the Potomac. In a letter to a Baltimore friend, Edward Spencer, April 1, 1875, he wrote: "Things come to me mostly in one of two forms,—the poetic or the musical. I express myself with the most freedom in the former *modus:*

with the most passionate delight in the latter. Indeed I ought to say that, *apud me*, music is, in my present state of growth, rather a passion than a faculty: I am not its master, it is mine." The letters which the poet wrote to his wife reveal a passionate delight in the music which he heard and played. And so when his anxious father suggested a return to Macon and the law office, Lanier, "full of energy, full of unwritten music, full of un-rhymed poetry," replied in a memorable letter:

My dear father, think how, for twenty years, through poverty, through pain, through weariness, through sickness, through the uncongenial atmospheres of a farcical college and of a bare army and then of an exacting business-life, through all the discouragements of being born on the wrong side of Mason-and-Dickson's line and of being wholly unacquainted with literary people and literary ways,— I say, think how, in spite of all these depressing circumstances and of a thousand more wh[ich]. I could enumerate, these two figures of music and of poetry have steadily kept in my heart, so that I could not banish them! Does it not seem to you, as to me, that I begin to have the right to enroll myself among the devotees of these two sublime arts, after having followed them so long and so humbly and through so much bitterness?

Baltimore, to which many Southerners flocked after the war, was not a literary center of importance, and Lanier was not there among his peers. He did, however, find friends who shared his love of music and literature. Among them were Richard Malcolm Johnston, Father Tabb, Innes Randolph, Edward Spencer, and William Hand Browne. Browne, who was at various times librarian and professor at Johns Hopkins, published some of Lanier's best prose in the *Southern Magazine*; and it was he and Johnston who directed Lanier's attention to the older English poetry which gave him a truer conception of his art. In Baltimore also Lanier was to find a friend in Daniel Coit Gilman, President of the newly-founded Johns Hopkins University, where eventually the poet was to become Lecturer in English Literature.

Lanier's real career as a poet—although half his poems were already written—began in the summer of 1874, which he spent in Georgia. Leaving "The Jacquerie" unfinished, he turned from the past to the present and wrote of the land and the people whom he knew best. He found what seemed to him a suitable medium in the odelike irregular poem in rhyme. In July and August he wrote "Corn," which in some ways anticipates his essay on "The New South." The poem celebrates not King Cotton and the great plantation but the independent small farmer who properly rotates his crops and grows corn rather than cotton. The publication of "Corn" in *Lippincott's Magazine* in February, 1875, brought Lanier his first hard-won success as a national poet. He could now write, too confidently, to Virginia Hankins:

". . . your friend's *status* as a poet is fixed,—and he will not go on the farm to plough and reap waste memories of failures." "Corn" brought him two new friends in Charlotte Cushman, the actress and singer, and Gibson Peacock, editor of the Philadelphia *Evening Bulletin*, who was to do more than any other person to help Lanier to attain a national reputation.

Lanier's success, however, was not unalloyed with disappointment. Knowing that he had written an important poem, he had submitted "Corn" under favorable auspices to the *Atlantic Monthly*, which had just begun to be hospitable to Southern writers. Howells did not find the poem "successful." "The reader," he wrote, "would be mystified as to its purpose and meaning; and would hardly know how or why to connect the final bit of narrative with the preceding apostrophes. Neither is striking enough to stand alone." In a memorable letter to Edward Spencer, April 1, 1875, Lanier told how, chagrined though he was, he attained through an indescribable mystical experience alone in a room in Brooklyn the conviction that whether he was a great poet or a small one, his business in life was to make poems. "Since then," he added, "it has not occurred to me to doubt about my sort of work."

Even in its first form "Corn" was an exceptional poem, and Howells clearly did not recognize its merits. George Parsons Lathrop, who had been assistant editor of the *Atlantic*, told L. Frank Tooker that "He had never understood Mr. Howells's tests of availability in poems . . . he thought them erratic and not understandable." Lanier was a self-taught and somewhat undisciplined poet whose sense of proportion was always likely to fail him in his longer works, as it had failed him in *Tiger-Lilies*. He now wisely submitted his manuscript to his friends Hayne and Judge Logan E. Bleckley of Atlanta; and with the benefit of the detailed criticisms which they (and perhaps others) gave him, he reworked the poem. When *Scribner's Monthly* found it too long, he sent it to *Lippincott's*, which gave him fifty dollars for it. This magazine and the house which issued it had been exceptionally hospitable to new writers from the South. In the years 1875–1877 *Lippincott's* printed no less than thirteen of Lanier's poems—including his long Centennial "Psalm of the West," for which he received three hundred dollars— and in 1877 the house of Lippincott republished ten of them in the only volume of his poems to appear in the poet's lifetime. After 1877 Lanier published most of his poems in *Scribner's Monthly* and the *Independent*. Richard Watson Gilder of the former, himself a poet, thought highly of Lanier's later poems. William Hayes Ward, editor of the *Independent*, though he never met the poet, became one of his champions and wrote the memoir which appeared in the posthumous edition of the *Poems* (1884), edited by Mrs. Lanier.

In March, 1875, Lanier wrote "The Symphony," which though by no means his best poem, is for his thought perhaps the most significant. Here he combined his love of poetry and music in an ode in praise of music and love which is at the same time an indictment of "The Age of Trade." The poverty which he had seen in Northern cities shocked Lanier. In April, 1874, while on a concert tour in Wheeling, he had written to his wife: "O how I do abhor these trade-matters, as they are carried on here. God, to see the great stalwart men, in these acres of rolling-mills, sweating, burning, laboring, with only enough time betwixt tasks to eat and sleep in,—far too little time to wash in! Why should this be so? The men who own these mills do not so: they have plenty. It is not well, it cannot be well, that a hundred men should die in soul and body, in order that one man should live merely in body."

Lanier's antipathy to the ways of big business and mass production has been ascribed to the influence of Carlyle and Ruskin. This, however, is to overlook the obvious fact that many another Southern visitor to the North, even in the twentieth century—Thomas Wolfe, for example—has reacted much as Lanier did. Those old critics of the urban-industrial-commercial ideal, the proslavery writers, were silent or dead, but antipathy to the industrial regime was still strong in the South. "The Symphony" is a protest which does not fit into the ideology of the Marxist or any other type of reform, but it is a notable pronouncement to which one cannot find a parallel in the work of any other important American poet of the time.

Gibson Peacock directed the attention of Bayard Taylor to "Corn" and "The Symphony." After he had read the latter poem, Taylor wrote to Peacock: "I hail in the author a new, rightfully anointed poet, in whom are the elements of a great success." The two poets met in the summer of 1875 and almost immediately became intimate friends. Bayard Taylor's reputation has faded and he no longer seems an important poet. He was, however, a skilful craftsman and more the man of letters than any one whom Lanier had yet met. In August, inviting Lanier to a celebration in New York of Goethe's 126th birthday, he wrote: "I am heartily glad to welcome you to the fellowship of authors, so far as I may dare to represent it. . . ." He took the younger poet to the Century Club, where he met some of the better-known writers of New York. Charlotte Cushman invited him to visit her in Boston and made much of him. In Cambridge he called upon Longfellow and Lowell, who was to write after Lanier's death: ". . . the image of his shining presence is among the friendliest in my memory." Both poets treated Lanier with characteristic courtesy and kindness, but neither, it seems, quite recognized the significance of his poetry.

The year 1875 was Lanier's *annus mirabilis*. Through Taylor's influence he was appointed—in part because he was a Southern poet—to write the cantata for the Philadelphia Exposition of the following year. He wished "to make it as large and as simple as a Symphony of Beethoven's." Profiting greatly from Taylor's criticism, he completed the poem in time. "The Centennial Meditation of Columbia," written to be set to music by Dudley Buck, pleased both the composer and the conductor; but, printed in advance without its musical setting, it aroused much unfavorable criticism. Judged purely as a poem, it is not one of Lanier's happiest performances. His appointment as a Southern poet had pleased Lanier, but he was not pleased by the uncritical defense in certain Southern newspapers. He considered cheap any success which depended on local pride.

Lanier, who had so longed for the society of men of letters, was not greatly impressed by most of the American writers whom he met, including the eminent New Englanders. He was now, however, discovering the significance of Emerson, whose theory of the function of the poet so closely resembled his own. In 1878, apparently for the first time, he read carefully Whitman's *Leaves of Grass*. The book, he wrote to Taylor, who had lent him a copy, "was a real refreshment to me—like rude salt spray in your face —in spite of its enormous fundamental error that a thing is good because it is natural, and in spite of the world-wide difference between my own conceptions of art and its author's."

In North and South alike Lanier was irritated by the "hoofed Stupidity" of "these poor crude people who pretend to judge my art." The masses, he complained, were reading not the poems of Bayard Taylor but those of Josiah Gilbert Holland, one of whose poems seemed to Lanier "merely a clever piece of joinery." Of the thin verses in *The Masque of Poets* (1878)— in which he had unwisely permitted "The Marshes of Glynn," perhaps his finest poem, to be first published—he wrote to Gibson Peacock: "The truth is, it is a distressing, an aggravated, yea, an intolerable collection of mediocrity and cleverness. . . . If these gentlemen and ladies would read the old English poetry—I mean the poetry before Chaucer . . . they could never be content to put forth these little diffuse prettinesses and dandy kickshaws of verse."

Harris, Page, and Cable sometimes found it difficult to please the Northern magazine editors who published their stories. Lanier, a poet in an age of prose fiction, was not interested in writing local-color stories; and he found some of the Northern editors besides Howells too obtuse to understand his aims and methods. Dr. Holland impressed Lanier as "a man of unusual generosity, warmth of heart, and goodness," but Holland, the editor of *Scribner's Monthly*, was another matter. In October, 1874, Lanier wrote to his wife:

Now, as I said, there is absolutely no method by which an Artist can get to the people, save through these men [Northern editors and publishers]: except by money, which I have not: and therefore I know, and am adequately prepared for, all the disappointments that await—not *me*, but thee, dear loving Heart, in my behalf. If I were like Bret Harte, or Mark Twain, and the others of this class of wonderfully clever writers, my path would be easy: but what would I give for such success? I can not dream any fate more terrible to me, than to have climbed to their niche,—the ledge where Lowell, and Holmes, and that ilk, rest—and to find *that* my highest and ultimatum.

When the editors of *Scribner's Monthly* changed the Negro dialect in their joint production, "The Power of Prayer," he wrote to his brother Clifford: "The amount of pure jackass-ism which exists among these editor people is a thing that no man can credit until he has had a little to do with them." He felt a difficulty even when writing his serious poems. Of "My Two Springs," a tribute to his wife, he wrote to her: "Of course, since I have written it to print, I cannot make it such as *I* desire, in artistic design: for the *forms* of today require a certain trim smugness and clean-shaven propriety in the face and dress of a poem, and I must win a hearing by conforming in some degree to these tyrannies,—with a view to overturning them in the future." Yet, as he wrote to his wife on another occasion: ". . . the more I am thrown against these people here [in New York], and the more reverses I suffer at their hands, the more confident I am of beating them finally." Lanier's disillusionment with magazine editors and "merely clever" writers was somewhat like the experience that still awaited the youthful Ellen Glasgow, who in New York was to discover that "in America, and perhaps everywhere, literature was regarded not as an art, not even as a profession, but as a business." Of a reception of the Authors Club, she wrote in *A Certain Measure*: ". . . instead of the ripe wisdom I had expected to gather from the bearded meteors of our literary firmament, I listened, with incredulous amazement, to an animated discussion of the prices paid by the leading magazines."

It seems ironic if not tragic that the success of Lanier's poems brought him a commission to write a guide book to Florida and led to his preparing for boy readers abridged versions of Malory, Percy, Froissart, and the *Mabinogion*. In his last extant letter to Hayne, November 19, 1880, Lanier suggested half seriously that his prolonged illness "arose purely from the bitterness of having to spend my time in making academic lectures and boy's-books— pot-boilers all—when a thousand songs are singing in my heart that will certainly kill me if I do not utter them soon." [28] Perhaps in such moments he recalled his early poem, "June Dreams, in January," in which "the hungriest poet under heaven" asks:

> "Why can we poets dream us beauty, so,
> But cannot dream us bread?"

For his early poems, half his total output, Lanier seems to have been paid nothing. His later poems brought him only about twelve hundred dollars. His later prose writings brought him much more but not enough to keep him from "economic harassment." It was an age of prose, and if, as I have suggested, he had spent his energies upon local-color stories, he could have earned an adequate income. Perhaps too much has been made of his "poverty." It is true that his medical and travel expenses were heavy. It is true also that he was not very provident in money matters and his wife was by her own admission not a thrifty housekeeper. It is not pleasant to think of their selling his flutes and her wedding silver; but to the lasting credit of the poet's father and brother it must be said that they loyally made up the comparatively small difference between his income and his expenses, althought he was chagrined by the necessity of calling upon them. If his life could have been prolonged for a decade or two, some of the projects of which his mind was full would probably have led to a larger income. In spite of the obstacles which confronted him, he did manage to produce a handful of poems which give him a secure place among the American poets. While he was dying at Tryon in North Carolina in September, 1881, *Scribner's Monthly* in an editorial article saluting the writers of the New South, said of him: "Sidney Lanier is a rare genius. No finer nature than his has America produced. His work is not popular, nor is it likely to become so, for his mind is of an unusual cast and his work is of an exceptional character. . . . The world of American letters will unite with us in the hope that the delicacy of his health will not interfere with the full unfolding and expression of his power."

It had been only seven years since Lanier had really begun his poetic career. In that time he had written "The Revenge of Hamish," "A Ballad of Trees and the Master," "The Song of the Chattahoochee," and "The Marshes of Glynn" and its companion poems, which for many readers added a new beauty to the Georgia coast country so unlike anything else celebrated in American poetry. In his Macon period he had written "Life and Song"

[28] And yet Lanier, an important pioneer in the field of adult education, was greatly interested in his lectures and in the wide reading involved in preparing them; and he longed for a professorship at Johns Hopkins which would bring him an adequate income and free him from the necessity of writing pot-boilers.

and "Nirvâna," which are as good as all but the best of his later poems. He is not as great a poet as Whitman, whose background and methods were so different, or Emily Dickinson, whose name he probably never heard; but if we leave aside these two, Lanier was beyond question the most important American poet to emerge in the later nineteenth century.

One cannot help admiring the man Lanier and sympathizing with him in his struggle to be the great poet he felt he might become; and yet regretfully one concludes that he never fully understood his own endowment and his limitations. On August 1, 1876, Bayard Taylor wrote to Hayne: "He is a charming fellow, of undoubted genius, and I think will make his mark. In him the elements are still a little confused, but he will soon work into clearness: power he has already." Lanier did not quite fulfil the promise which Taylor saw in "Corn" and "The Symphony"; the elements were still a little confused even at the end of his brief literary career. In spite of his study of the English classics and of the technique of verse, he remained fundamentally an improviser, a poet of impressive fragments, not an expert craftsman like Poe tirelessly revising a poem until it became the perfect embodiment of a thought. His feverish reading in science, fiction, and poetry had no great effect upon the poems he composed. He believed in the prophetic function of the poet, but what most impresses those who read his verses is not his message but the word music and the magical pictures of the Georgia coast country. It is a hard thing to say, but one feels in some of Lanier's poems the strained language and the tumult of emotions in the breast of a sick and harried man. He might have written as Melville wrote of his own difficulties to Hawthorne: "The calm, the coolness, the silent grass-growing mood in which a man *ought* always to compose,—that, I fear, can seldom be mine. Dollars damn me; and the malicious Devil is forever grinning in upon me, holding the door ajar. . . . What I feel most moved to write, that is banned,—it will not pay."

Lanier's ties with the South were close, and he never lost interest in its people and its problems. He was no "desouthernized Southerner" such as Howells considered Mark Twain to be; and yet he was a thoroughly national poet, and he attained his national outlook earlier than most of his Southern contemporaries. He praised the early work of Harris and Cable and he gave excellent advice as well as encouragement to Tabb and Johnston. He could, however, be severely critical of the South. On June 8, 1870, he wrote to his brother: ". . . it really seems as if any prosperity at the South must come long after your prime and mine. Our people have failed to perceive the deeper movements underrunning the time; they lie wholly off, out of the stream of thought, and whirl their poor old dead leaves of recollections round and round, in a piteous eddy that has all the wear and tear of motion without any of the rewards of progress."

Lanier was in a more hopeful mood when in October, 1880, he published in *Scribner's Monthly* an essay on "The New South" which helped to give currency to the phrase. Not inclined to throw a glamour over the old plantation regime, he hailed the rise of the small farmers and advocated, as in "Corn," the raising of other crops than cotton. He noted with approval the emergence of ex-slaves as owners of small farms and thought that this new development might solve the race problem. He had only scorn for those shiftless farmers "who scratched the surface for cotton a year or two, then carelessly abandoned all to sedge and sassafras, and sauntered on toward Texas. . . ." As he penned the conclusion of the essay, there came to his mind's eye a picture of the Middle Georgia which he loved:

It is a land where there is never a day of summer nor of winter when a man cannot do a full day's work in the open field; all the products meet there, as at nature's own agricultural fair; rice grows alongside of wheat, corn alongside of sugar-cane, cotton alongside of clover, apples alongside of peaches, so that a small farm may often miniature the whole United States in growth; the little valleys everywhere run with living waters, asking grasses and cattle and quiet grist-mills. . . . . It is the country of homes.

Lanier's literary career in some ways resembles that of Poe, whose poems in early life had fascinated him. He would not, however, have viewed kindly those critics who have suggested that the chief value of his poems, like Poe's, lies in their music rather than in the ideas which they express. His later estimate was that Poe "did not *know* enough . . . to be a great poet." What he had in mind apparently was the Emersonian or Wordsworthian conception of the poet as a religious seer—the phrase is Charles Anderson's— "in charge of all learning to convert it into wisdom." [29] He might perhaps have added that Poe was too lacking in healthy human interests to attain the rank to which as an artist he was entitled. Poe and Lanier were both products of the urban rather than of the plantation South; and both were repelled by the uglinesses and injustices which industrialism was bringing to the Northern cities. Each was in a special sense a lover of the beautiful, and in each there was something for which the phrase "Southern chivalry" is not quite the right word. It is more nearly what Jefferson B. Fletcher has called "the religion of beauty in woman." Both writers found it difficult to get their best work published, especially their poems, and each had to do

[29] See the entire passage in Anderson's Introduction to Lanier's *Poems* in *Works*, I, xxiv.

much hack-writing to make a bare living. Each had looked to the cities of the North in the hope of meeting congenial men of letters and of being better paid for his work. Both were in large measure disappointed, and both were somewhat disillusioned by what they saw of literary society and by the ways of editors and publishers. Lanier, however, never stooped to log-rolling and such other expedients as Poe made use of in New York. Neither poet felt completely at home in the Northern states. Each of them, how-ever, managed in spite of poverty, ill health, and misfortune to write a handful of exquisite poems which the discriminating will not willingly let die, and Poe left behind him some admirable short stories which certain critics have thought greater than his poems. Each died at about the age of forty with perhaps his finest works still unwritten, while most of their great Northern contemporaries lived to be old men. Both Poe and Lanier were, in the memorable phrase which Shelley applied to Keats, dead at the age of twenty-six, "inheritors of unfulfilled renown." Poe was more gifted than Lanier, but his personality was less attractive and he was less admirable as a man. The South has never taken Poe to its heart as it did Lanier.

A brief consideration of the literary relations between Lanier and Hayne, the two chief Southern poets of the period, may serve to illustrate in part the debt of the New Literary South to the Old. Until Lanier met Bayard Taylor in the summer of 1875, Hayne was his most intelligent and sympa-thetic adviser. The period of their closest relationship extended from 1868 until 1873, when Lanier went to Baltimore, where he found new literary friends. The two poets had much in common. Both were suffering from poverty and sickness, and both were longing for some sort of communion with other writers.

At the time their correspondence began, Lanier had renounced poetry as a vocation and was hard at work on his law books. He could not, how-ever, remain indifferent to Hayne's glowing praise of his earlier work or to his urging to follow it up with something new. The two poets were soon sending one another their poems, and each gave the other the expert as-sistance of a practicing craftsman. Partly as a result of Lanier's criticism, Hayne's nature poetry came closer to the life of his own day. Lanier's debt to Hayne's poetry and criticism was considerable, but by 1875 he had entered upon a new phase of his poetic career as a national poet, leaving Hayne behind. Lanier became one of the chief spokesmen of the New South, but Hayne still clung to the Old. Strange as it may seem, the two poets, both living in Georgia less than a hundred miles apart, never saw one another. Hayne, who was by twelve years the older of the two, once asked Lanier to edit his literary remains, little thinking that he would out-live the younger poet by five years.

In 1868, when the correspondence began, both poets were reading the *Round Table*. This is the explanation of the curious circumstance that it was in a New York magazine that Hayne first saw one of the poems of his fellow Georgian. He had also read Lanier's novel by the time he wrote the following passage in his "Literary Notices" for the Richmond weekly, *Southern Opinion*, April 11, 1868:

> A young authour has recently arisen at the South, for whom we venture to predict a brilliant future. Our allusion is, to Mr. Sydney Lanier, of Macon, Ga., whose novel of "Tiger Lillies," is (with many glaring faults), the most original, and thoughtful tales [sic] we have read for a long time.
>
> Mr. Lanier is an accomplished musician, and a quaint, fanciful poet, as the following lines ["Barnacles"] will show. . . .

Hayne wrote Lanier a letter which has not survived, but its tenor may be judged by a second letter of December 5, 1868, in which he praised "The Ship of Earth," which he had read in the *Round Table*. He urged the younger poet to contribute his part to the building up of the literature of the South: "We have here, at the *South*, so few men of *your* order of ability, & learning, that really you *must* do 'your devoirs' to the *uttermost*, & in elevating yourself, elevate your *Section*." On October 30 of the following year he wrote: "For Heaven's sake don't allow 'Tiger Lilies' to be your *first* & your LAST *work!* Exert the genius God hath given you." Fearing perhaps that Lanier would think him guilty of flattery, he wrote on January 10, 1871: "God knoweth, we have but few poet-artists, South;—shall we not hail them when they appear?" He added that Southern writers "ought, & must stick together; encourage each other's efforts, and support each other's Fame!" That Hayne's estimate of Lanier's early poems was very high is evident from a letter which on January 16, 1873, he wrote to Margaret J. Preston. Lanier, he said, possessed "a very rare & original genius, and if Consumption spares his life for a decade to come, he will make a mark in our Literature." Hayne was enthusiastic about those parts of "The Jacquerie" which Lanier had sent him. He admired "Nirvâna" so much that he sent a copy of the poem to William Morris, whom both poets ad-mired. He thought so highly of Lanier's craftsmanship that early in 1873 he begged him to "rewrite" a poem which had given him much trouble, "In the Pine Barrens—Sunset."

Lanier for his part found Hayne's high praise "no ignoble stimulus." In the last of his extant letters to Hayne, November 19, 1880, he wrote: "I do not, and will not, forget the early encouragements which used to come from you when I was just daring to think of making verses." He found much to admire in Hayne's poems: their music, their pictorial quality, and the poet's antipathy to "Trade." He praised "Daphles" and other poems dealing with times and places remote from the Reconstruction South. He had not yet learned—what Hayne was only in part to learn—that the life and landscape of the contemporary South were a richer field. Yet he apparently made this discovery while studying Hayne's poems. He was struck by a new note in Hayne's "A Summer Mood," which he read aloud to Jefferson Davis and other friends. In his *The Mountain of the Lovers* (1875) Hayne included some poems in his new manner which Lanier had read and praised; among them, "Voices of the Pines," "Forest-Pictures," and "Glorified Mists."

Hayne gave Lanier excellent advice when he wrote him on October 10, 1874: "I have read your *Sonnets* very *attentively. Parts, I like well*; but frankly, the *general effect* does not impress me pleasantly. A certain exaggeration of tone, & imagery; an over-lushness, & over-ripeness, (so to speak) of sentiment,—*ultra* Tropical, somewhat clog one with sweets. . . . Drop the *Sonnet, my boy, (it don't pay)*, and compose more pieces like your glorious 'Corn.' " Hayne helped in the revision of "Corn," and he found it "a poem after mine own heart." He urged Lanier to take it North with him, and he sent letters of introduction to certain writers who he thought might assist Lanier in placing it to advantage. On October 23, 1875, he wrote to Lanier: "With pride no less than pleasure, I hail your really brilliant success in Literature." He was perhaps a little envious when he added: "You may thank God . . . that you are wholly independent of your own Section." There are Southerners, he said, who "can't understand that Lanier, being a Georgian, has, or could have any real claim to artistic distinction!"

Hayne, however, was still too conservative a Southerner to enjoy the centennial poem which *Lippincott's Magazine* had commissioned Lanier to write.

Ah! would to heaven Lanier, that I could agree with the triumphant prophecies of a grand future for America which flash & blaze throughout your wonderful "Psalm of the West"!

But I can't! These U[nited] States are to my mind, a collection of fast rotting States, bound to a Centralized Fraud, the stench whereof is rising to the very heavens!

Soon after Lanier's death Hayne wrote to Mrs. Preston: "The man possessed (I think) unquestionable genius, thwarted by constitutional, or organic eccentricity of imagination; yet *au fond* genuine!" In June, 1882, he published in *Harper's Magazine* "The Pole of Death—To the Memory of Sydney Lanier."

In January, 1875, the *Southern Magazine* belatedly published Lanier's review of Hayne's *Legends and Lyrics* (1872). In "Paul H. Hayne's Poetry" Lanier did not take into consideration the poems in Hayne's newer manner which had most impressed him. The article contains high praise for certain poems, but it points out two of Hayne's most common shortcomings—they are in lesser degree Lanier's also, as he was beginning to recognize: "a frequently recurring *lapsus* of thought, in which Mr. Hayne falls into trite similes, worn collocations of words and commonplace sentiments" and a "diffuseness, principally originating in a lavishness and looseness of adjectives." Hayne expressed his gratitude for Lanier's "wonderful critique," "the subtlest & most searching review ever suggested by my verses."

Lanier, as his review and his letters both show, was greatly impressed by the melody and pictorial beauty of Hayne's "Fire-Pictures." This poem, slightly reminiscent of Poe's "The Bells," is in the irregular rhymed form of which both Poe and Lanier were perhaps too fond. Of the lines quoted below, Lanier wrote: "I am quite in friendly earnest,—and you know I *love* music!—when I tell you, dear Mr. Hayne, that I do not know of anything, of the same style, in our language which is so beautiful as this passage. The flow of the melody is unbrokenly perfect: and the interfusing of the exquisite nature-picture with the one-passion of the two *human* hearts makes an *inner* music dwelling in the *material* music wh[ich]. enchants me beyond measure."

> Ah! the fire!
> Gently glowing,
> Fairly flowing,
> Like a rivulet rippling deep
> Through the meadow-lands of sleep,
> Bordered where its music swells,
> By the languid lotos-bells,
> And the twilight asphodels;
> Mingled with a richer boon
> Of queen-lilies, each a moon,
> Orbèd into white completeness;
> O! the perfume! the rare sweetness
> Of those grouped and fairy flowers,
> Over which the love-lorn hours
> Linger,—not alone for them,
> Though the lotos swings its stem

With a lulling stir of leaves,—
Though the lady-lily laves
Coy feet in the crystal waves,
And a silvery undertune
From some mystic wind-song grieves
Dainty sweet amid the bells
Of the twilight asphodels;
But because a charm more rare
Glorifies the mellow air,
In the gleam of lifted eyes,
In the tranquil ecstasies
Of two lovers, leaf-embowered,
      Lingering there,
Each of whose fair lives hath flowered,
Like the lily-petals finely,
Like the asphodels divinely.

Some of the lines which so pleased Lanier might be quoted as his own without arousing suspicion, particularly:

Like a rivulet rippling deep
Through the meadow-lands of sleep.

They suggest that for good or ill Lanier's indebtedness to Hayne's poetry may be only less than that he owed to Hayne's criticism of his verses.

10
Richard Malcolm Johnston

THE CLOSE KINSHIP of the local colorists of the New South with the ante-bellum Southern humorists becomes clearer as we contemplate the career of Lanier's friend, Richard Malcolm Johnston (1822–1898). In his earlier years he was a contemporary of Longstreet, Thompson, and Hooper; in his later period he was the friend of Joel Chandler Harris, who was more than twenty years his junior. He began by writing for his own amusement sketches modeled on those of Longstreet and Thompson; in his old age he was selling local-color stories of Middle Georgia to Northern magazines. The amateur writer had finally become a professional.

Johnston was born on his father's Middle Georgia plantation of "Oak Grove" near Powelton, the "Dukesborough" of his tales. His fun-loving father at the age of thirty-five had given up cardplaying, dancing, and fox hunting to become an unsalaried Baptist preacher. In his later life Johnston recalled Sunday as a day on which play was forbidden and his father and mother read no books but *The Pilgrim's Progress* and the Bible. There was something almost Puritan in Southern rural life after the decline of Deism in the early nineteenth century. Most of the teachers in the old-field schools which Johnston attended came from Vermont. One of these was his model for Lucius Woodbridge in *Old Mark Langston*. In 1841 Johnston graduated from a manual-labor institute which later became Mercer University. In 1844 he married Mary Frances Mansfield, whose father, a native of New Haven, Connecticut, kept a tailor's shop in Sparta, where Johnston was practicing law at the time. The twenty years between his graduation and the outbreak of the Civil War were divided between law and teaching. As a lawyer he spent what leisure time he had in reading the Latin and English classics and in writing occasionally for his own amusement. His third and last law partner was Linton Stephens, a half brother of Alexander H. Stephens, whose biography Johnston and William Hand Browne were to publish in 1878. Johnston was a tall, rather slender man, highly social and genial by nature, and fond of humor and young people. Grace King, who met him as a dinner guest in New Haven, describes him as "a typical Southerner in voice and language . . . erect of figure, with white hair and moustache, a genial, witty, unaffected talker, full of good stories, interesting to everybody. My heart went out to him at once." Johnston early acquired a reputation as an exceptionally gifted teller of stories. Among the Georgia lawyers riding the circuit the art of storytelling was as highly valued as it was in the Illinois of Lincoln's young manhood. Johnston, like Mark Twain and Thomas Nelson Page, managed to impart to his writing something of the naturalness and freshness of the raconteur.

It was the great vogue of Longstreet's *Georgia Scenes* that led Johnston to write his first humorous sketches. Some time in 1857, he says, he published in Porter's *Spirit of the Times* "A Georgia School in the Old Times," later rechristened "The Goosepond School." In 1858 it was reprinted in the *Georgia Temperance Crusader*. "Judge Mike and His Court" appeared in the *Southern Field and Fireside* in January, 1863; and in 1864 Stockton and Company, the publishers of this Augusta magazine, brought out under the pseudonym "Philemon Perch" his first book, *Georgia Sketches from the Recollections of an Old Man*. Johnston's stories of Middle Georgia life as it was before the coming of railroads show clearly the influence of both Longstreet and Thompson. His "The Various Languages of Billy Moon," "The Humors of Jacky Bundle," and "King William and His Armies" are all reminiscent of Longstreet's "The Fight"; and his "The Expensive Treat of Colonel Moses Grice" resembles Thompson's "The Great Attraction."

For the four years which preceded the Civil War Johnston was teaching English literature in the University of Georgia. He was one of the earliest and ablest of the American pioneers in that field. Not finding a suitable text for his students, he wrote *The English Classics: A Historical Sketch* (Philadelphia, 1860), which as revised by Johnston and William Hand Browne was republished in 1872 under the title *English Literature: A Historical Sketch*. In Baltimore Johnston published two volumes of literary and historical essays which reflect his wide reading but are otherwise of little importance. In later life he often lectured on English literature at the Peabody Institute and elsewhere; and he occasionally gave readings from his stories, on one occasion with Mark Twain.

When the war began, Johnston, who was no secessionist, resigned his position in the University of Georgia and opened a boarding school for boys near Sparta. The freeing of the slaves at the end of the war brought him a feeling of relief from a great responsibility, but he was much annoyed by the behavior of the freedmen and was pessimistic about the future of the state in the new regime. His loss in property due to war and emancipation he reckoned at fifty thousand dollars. After the death of his beloved daughter Lucy he removed to Baltimore in June, 1867. In a beautiful rural setting on the outskirts of the city he opened the Pen Lucy School for Boys. About forty of his Georgia students had followed him. After he joined the Roman Catholic Church in 1875 the school gradually declined. In 1883 he gave up the school and moved into an apartment in Baltimore. After the breakup of the school, the family was largely supported by his daughters, who taught school. Their father, one of them was to remark later, "never knew the value of a dollar."

Before the war Johnston had written chiefly for his own amusement. After his removal to Baltimore he sometimes wrote to alleviate a feeling of homesickness for rural Georgia. He permitted the editors of the *Southern Magazine* to print some of his older and newer sketches. "It never occurred to me," he says, "that they were of any sort of value." In 1871 and again in 1874 the Turnbull brothers, who published the *Southern Magazine*, brought out his *Dukesborough Tales*. In the preface to the 1871 edition he wrote: "These Sketches, which I have ventured to call TALES, were drawn partly from memories of incidents of old times, but mostly from imagination, were written for the sake of my own entertainment, in the evenings when I had nothing else to do." The spirit in which he wrote them is suggested by the dedication "to the Memories of the Old Times: The Grim and Rude, but Hearty Old Times in Georgia." At some unspecified time, he tells us in his *Autobiography*, a copy of *Dukesborough Tales* came into the hands of Henry Mills Alden, who expressed surprise that Johnston had been paid nothing for them. He would, Alden remarked, have been glad to print them in *Harper's Magazine* and he would have paid for them. In 1883 Harper & Brothers brought out an enlarged edition of *Dukesborough Tales*, and then for the first time Johnston prefixed his own name to them. Other Southern writers were discovering that there was a market in the North for stories which, in a desire to support a "Southern literature," they had been giving away to editors of Southern magazines. Amateur writers began to think of becoming professionals, and one by one the Southern literary magazines ceased publication.

Johnston, however, was slower than Lanier or Cable to turn to writing in earnest. It was not until he was fifty-seven that he published his first story in a Northern magazine. This was "Mr. Neelus Peeler's Conditions," which appeared in *Scribner's Monthly* in June, 1879. Sidney Lanier, who once taught for an hour a day at the Pen Lucy School, sent the story to the *Monthly*, and it was Lanier who gave to Johnston the first check he ever received for a story. Before this time Johnson had received encouragement and criticism of a sort from Alexander H. Stephens, William Hand Browne, and the Turnbull brothers; but it was perhaps from Lanier—who, it will be remembered, had published a novel—that Johnston first learned about writing fiction for the Northern literary market. He gave Johnston the kind of craftsman's criticism which Cable, Harris, and Page got from the editors of *Scribner's Monthly* or its successor, the *Century*.[30] In a letter dated November 6, 1877, Lanier gave his reaction to "Mr. Neelus Peeler's Conditions" in its unrevised form. After noting some verbal lapses, he pointed out that the action of the story did "not move fast enough during the *first* twenty-five pages, and the *last* ten, to suit the impatience of the modern magazine man." In general, however, Lanier found the story "exquisitely funny," and the "reproduction of the modes of thought and of speech among the rural Georgians" impressed him as "really wonderful." Lanier is also said to have suggested Johnston's writing his first novel, *Old Mark Langston* (1883); and on his deathbed he wrote to ask: "Tell me how the novel fares,—for I shall brood anxiously over each character." Johnston, for his part, shared his friend's love of music and poetry. He declared "The Marshes of Glynn" to be "the greatest poem written in a hundred years."

Johnston published more than eighty short stories; two novels: *Old Mark Langston* and *Widow Guthrie* (1893); and two novelettes: *Ogeechee Cross-*

[30] It is probable that Mrs. Sophia Bledsoe Herrick of the *Century* staff helped Johnston to put his stories into acceptable form. See her article, "Richard Malcolm Johnston," *Century*, XXXVI, 276–280 (June, 1888).

Firings (1889) and *Pearce Amerson's Will* (1898). In the early nineties he decided to look for another occupation. "I did not like," he says, "the idea of continuing at story telling down to the very grave." Perhaps he felt that he was now only repeating himself or perhaps he had grown tired of revising his sketches to suit the demands of editors who wanted well-constructed short stories. At any rate, he did not think highly of fiction-writing as a profession. His Georgia friends got him a place in the U. S. Department of Labor, which he soon gave up for a much more congenial position with W. T. Harris, the U. S. Commissioner of Education. For the Commissioner's *Reports* for 1894–1895 and 1895–1896 he wrote a long and illuminating essay on "Early Education in Middle Georgia." Outside of his own sketches there is nowhere so good an account of the old-field schools and academies of the South.

Even in his later years Johnston was still primarily, as some of his reviewers saw, a writer of humorous sketches rather than a creator of artistically constructed short stories. Among the best of his short stories are "Moll and Virgil" and "Mr. Absalom Billingslea." His novels are rambling and episodic, like those of his friend Harris, and the best parts are those in which his characters speak the colloquial language of Middle Georgia. In "Mr. Fortner's Marital Claims" he introduces an irrelevant anecdote by saying that "although it may not have much to do with the story," he will tell it anyway. When plots of some complexity were called for, he was likely to fall back upon a forged will, a mistaken identity, or a convenient death. For him, as for Longstreet and Harris, character was more important than plot. He never regarded a story as finished, he says, "until I could plainly see my characters." [31] The two he liked best were Mr. Bill Williams and Old Mr. Pate, each of whom figures in several stories.

There is much humor but little tragedy or pathos in Johnston's fiction. The Negro has no great part in his stories, but neither has the aristocratic planter of the type described in Page's *In Ole Virginia* and *Red Rock*. Johnston's best characters are middle-class farmers not essentially different from those in Hamlin Garland's *Main-Travelled Roads*; and the farmer is a type which, when we consider the millions whom he represents, has been given an astonishingly small part in American fiction. Johnston's writings,

[31] On Oct. 2, 1897, not long before he died, Johnston wrote to William Malone Baskervill: "One after another old Scenes rose in my recollection, and I reproduced them, with many elaborations & inventions such as occurred to me to harmonize with them. There is far more of invention in the stories than is generally believed, perhaps because (for giving greater verisimilitude) I have introduced myself so often into them. This was wholly imaginary & as was the creation of 'Mr Bill Williams' and 'Mr Pate' " (Baskervill MSS, Duke Univ. Library).

like those of his friends Harris and Lanier, are singularly free from bitterness and hatred. The South has produced a number of writers who surpassed Johnston as a writer of fiction, but few of them had so genial and attractive a personality as he. "My father's personality," said one of his daughters, "was greater than his writings."

11
Joel Chandler Harris

JOEL CHANDLER HARRIS (1848–1908) always insisted that he was a "cornfield journalist" and not a man of letters. His success, he said, was "a lucky accident," and his function as author of the Uncle Remus tales was merely that of a recorder. Yet as a boy he had filled scrapbooks with his writings, and in his youth he served an apprenticeship to the editor of a unique literary weekly. As a newspaperman he read widely and dreamed of some day writing a novel. No man was better prepared to put into memorable language the fading folk tales of the Negro, whom he knew better than did any of his white contemporaries. Their success brought a belated opportunity to fulfil his early ambition to write novels and short stories about the social life of the South. He did not like to be labeled a humorist; yet his indebtedness to the earlier Georgia humorists is very clear. He read also the stories of his friend Richard Malcolm Johnston, with whom in 1884 he was collaborating on a play that was never finished. Like Johnston, Harris remained to the end of his life primarily a writer of character sketches rather than a creator of well-constructed novels and short stories.

Harris was born in the little town of Eatonton in Middle Georgia, which, he often said, was as democratic in its social life as any other part of the United States. The red-headed, freckle-faced, undersized boy was fond of fun and practical jokes, but he was also a lover of books. He was all his life painfully shy and often lacking in self-confidence. His mother, Mary Harris, had fallen in love with an Irish day laborer and in spite of strong family opposition had gone off to live with him. When he deserted her and their child, she settled in Eatonton with her mother and earned a living by sewing. She concentrated her affections and her hopes on her only child. Friends enabled her to send him to the Eatonton Academy for a few years. One of the books which she read aloud to him was The Vicar of Wakefield. It kindled in him a desire to write stories in which the principal character silences all opposition by crying "Fudge!" His early reading included also the Arabian Nights and the Grimm brothers' fairy tales.

When he was thirteen, Harris saw in a newly-established weekly, the *Countryman*, an advertisement which read: "WANTED—An active, intelligent white boy, fourteen or fifteen years of age, is wanted at this office to learn the printing business." He immediately applied for the position, and in a few days the editor and proprietor, Joseph Addison Turner, took him to the plantation of "Turnwold," nine miles away in the country. Here young Harris learned to set type, and he soon began to write for the *Countryman*. At first, he says, he set up his articles directly "from the 'case' instead of committing them to paper . . . thus leaving no evidence of authorship!" In Turner's well-stocked library he read the English classics. At "Turnwold," too, he acquired an intimate knowledge of rural life, animals, children, and Negroes of all ages. Here also he learned from the lips of the older slaves many of the folk tales which were to make him famous.

Joseph Addison Turner (1826–1868), whom Harris once called a "miscellaneous genius," was a well-to-do planter, lawyer, and writer who owned a hundred slaves and possessed a library of perhaps two thousand volumes.[32] Close by lived his brother, William Wilberforce Turner, author of the novel, *Jack Hopeton and His Friends* (1860), who had a library as large as his brother Joseph's. Joseph Addison Turner was a kind master who even in wartime had no fear of a slave insurrection. He was a religious liberal and, like Harris, not a member of any church. He published a cotton planter's manual, two volumes of poems, and contributed to many Southern and a few Northern magazines. At twenty-two he began his editorial career with *Turner's Monthly*, which he discontinued after a few issues. In 1860 he published a few numbers of the *Plantation*, a quarterly which he had printed in New York. His third venture, the *Countryman* (1862–1866), was the only magazine ever edited and printed on a Southern plantation. "Our aim," said the editor in an early number, "is to model our journal after Addison's Little Paper, The Spectator, Steele's Little Paper, The Tatler, Johnson's Little Papers, The Rambler and The Adventurer [Idler], and Goldsmith's Little Paper, The Bee. . . . It is our aim to fill our Little Paper with Essays, Poems, Sketches, Agricultural Articles, and choice miscellany." [33] It was, the editor said, "entirely foreign to

[32] For Turner's life and writings, see two articles in *American Notes & Queries*, V, 115–119, 131–135 (Nov., Dec., 1945): "Joseph Addison Turner: Publisher, Planter, and Countryman" and "The 'Countryman': A Lone Chapter in Plantation Publishing." In the *Countryman*, XXI, 20–23 (Feb. 13, 1866) Turner published a sketch of his life which in 1943 was reprinted in Emory University Sources and Reprints Series I as *Autobiography of "The Countryman"* with an informative Introduction by Thomas H. English.

[33] *Countryman*, I, 10 (May 6, 1862). For an account of Turner's magazines, see

the nature of a Southern gentleman to advertise himself, or to drum for subscribers." Nevertheless, he added: "I have got my consent to advertise— but to drum, never!" Strange to say, even in wartime the weekly attained a circulation of two thousand, enough to make it self-sustaining. In the fall of 1862 Turner printed in the *Countryman* his long poem, "The Old Plantation," in old-fashioned heroic couplets and confessedly modeled upon Goldsmith and Gray. It certainly owes something to "The Deserted Village" and perhaps also to Grayson's *The Hireling and the Slave*, an earlier defense of the slavery regime. Turner's best writing, however, is in his "Goose-Quill Essays," in which his feeling for humor found expression. A driving force behind Turner's literary ventures was suggested in the *Countryman* for January 12, 1864: "My aim, from the beginning, has been to contribute my mite to the creation of a separate and distinct Southern literature. From my youth up, I have hated yankees, and yankee literature." Again, he wrote: "I do emphatically wish us to have a Southern literature. And prominent in our books I wish the negro to be placed." Yet Turner, even when the war had reduced him to poverty, could write in the *Countryman* in June, 1865: "Reunion—Henceforth we desire to know no North, no South, no East, no West, but one common country."

Such was the editor and such the magazine on which Harris served his apprenticeship. Harris lived in the house of the foreman of the printing shop, and by a fire of lightwood knots he read books borrowed from the Turners' libraries after others had gone to bed. It was not long before the editor began to take an interest in Harris's writing. Still preserved in a scrapbook is Turner's criticism of a manuscript which Harris had submitted. The young writer, said the editor, was wasting his time in replying to an article which was "contemptible and beneath criticism." Next, he noted in Harris's writing a "want of unity and condensation." He closed with this excellent advice:

In writing hereafter, 1st select a good—a worthy subject.
2nd, stick to that subject.
3d, say what you have to say in as few words as possible. Study the "nervous condensation" which you so much admire in Captain Flash.
All this is for your good.

An Eatonton woman in whose early writing Turner had found promise has said that on one occasion Turner laid one hand upon her head and another

---

Bertram H. Flanders, *Early Georgia Magazines* (1944). Many of Harris's contributions to the *Countryman* are reprinted in Robert L. Wiggins, *The Life of Joel Chandler Harris* (1918).

on young Harris's and said to them: "You will do the writing for the South that I shall be unable to do." In 1892, when Harris published *On the Plantation*, a half-fictitious account of his life at "Turnwold," he appropriately dedicated it "To the Memory of Joseph Addison Turner, Lawyer, Editor, Scholar, Planter, and Philanthropist."

The best of Harris's writings in the *Countryman* are little essays not unlike some of the miscellaneous editorials which he was to write for the Atlanta *Constitution* and *Uncle Remus's Magazine*. He also wrote verses which reveal the influence of Poe, and he attacked Griswold as a prejudiced biographer of the poet. Following the example of "Bill Arp," he addressed a letter to Lincoln in the cracker dialect, signing it "Obadiah Skinflint." He appears, however, not to have written about Negroes or to have attempted the Negro dialect.

It was on "Turnwold" plantation, however, that Harris came to know the Negro so well that Thomas Nelson Page could write in 1895: "No man who has ever written has known one-tenth part about the negro that Mr. Harris knows. . . ." [34] The "forlorn and friendless boy" discovered a strange sympathy with the Negro slaves. It was almost as though he were one of them. They understood him and befriended him so that under their influence his shyness melted away. His illegitimate birth seemed not to matter. It would have been different if he had been the son of a great slaveholder like Turner or perhaps if he had lived in Turner's house. In *On the Plantation* Joe's sympathies are with the runaway slave Mink rather than with the owner (not Turner) or the overseer who has been cruel to him. Harris could understand, as few slaveholders could, the slave's desire for his freedom. At "Turnwold" the future author of "Free Joe and the Rest of the World" witnessed the homely tragedy which he was briefly to describe in the last chapter of *On the Plantation*:

In a corner of the fence, not far from the road, Joe found an old negro woman shivering and moaning. Near her lay an old negro man, his shoulders covered with an old ragged shawl.

"Who is that lying there?" asked Joe.

"It my ole man, suh."

"What is the matter with him?"

"He dead, suh! But, bless God, he died free!"

The two pathetic old slaves had left their master and followed in the wake of Sherman's army, each of them to die after a few days of the freedom they had longed for.

[34] "Immortal Uncle Remus," *Book Buyer*, XII, 645 (Dec., 1895). Harris once told Walter Hines Page that he could translate Emerson into the Negro dialect.

Harris's critics and biographers have noted his kindly comments—for a Southerner—on *Uncle Tom's Cabin*, which he read at "Turnwold" in 1862. Here is one of them: "It was never discovered, until after the war, that Mrs. Stowe's attack upon slavery was a practical and genuine defense of the Southern slave owner. She painted him as merciful, almost imprudently lax in his discipline. The monsters in her book are of Northern birth, a fact that is not very flattering to our versatility." For Mrs. Stowe's birthday in 1883 Harris wrote to the *Atlantic Monthly*: "I owe a great deal, in one way and another, to the author of Uncle Tom's Cabin. In 1862, when quite a youngster, I chanced to get hold of a copy of the book, and it made a more vivid impression upon my mind than anything I have ever read since." This reading of *Uncle Tom's Cabin* may have had a good deal to do with Harris's attitude toward the Negro and slavery.

At "Turnwold" Harris learned to understand the cracker farmers, some of whom, hearing that their wives and children were without food, deserted from the Confederate army and came home. Moreover, the sight of Sherman's soldiers carrying fire and destruction through the countryside and followed by droves of cows, horses, and mules stolen from the farmers of Middle Georgia dispelled from Harris's mind, as he said, "the glamour and romance of war."

The last issue of the *Countryman*, printed by Harris's own hands, appeared on May 8, 1866. Now eighteen, he had to seek other employment. For a short time he was in Macon, where he may have met Lanier. For six months he was secretary to William Evelyn, editor of the New Orleans *Crescent Monthly*, one of the numerous Southern literary magazines that sprang up after the war. In 1867 he was in Forsyth, Georgia, setting type and writing humorous paragraphs for the *Monroe Advertiser*, a county weekly owned by James P. Harrison, whom he had known at "Turnwold." In Forsyth Harris lived with the Harrisons. Mrs. Harrison and particularly her sister-in-law, Mrs. Georgia Starke, and little Nora Belle Starke were kind to the shy and self-conscious youth, who had not hitherto really known any cultivated women of the upper class. He was already, it seems, "nursing a novel in his brain," and Mrs. Starke encouraged him to write. She thought highly of his verses; and so did James Wood Davidson, for whose *The Living Writers of the South* (1869) Harris prepared the index. He also helped Davidson to discredit Lamar Fontaine's claim to the authorship of "The Picket Guard," actually written by a Northern poet, Mrs. Ethel Lynn Beers. In a brief sketch of Harris, included in the book, Davidson wrote: "Of our young writers,—writers of energy, hope, and ability, who promise to become men of mark in letters,—there are few, if any, that rank higher than Chandler Harris."

After three years in Forsyth, Harris became associate editor of the Savannah *News* at a salary of forty dollars a week. His chief task was to write humorous paragraphs; these were soon widely copied in other Georgia newspapers. In Savannah Harris's chief was Colonel William Tappan Thompson, who years before had written the "Major Jones" sketches which Harris greatly admired. Thompson, it appears, thought highly of Harris's own writings and predicted a future for him. In 1873 Harris married Esther LaRose of a French Canadian family. Shortly before his death in 1908 he was to follow her into the Roman Catholic Church.

In 1876, while Harris was dreaming of eventually going to "that shining Sodom called New York," an epidemic of yellow fever caused him to take his family up to Atlanta, where soon afterwards he became one of the chief writers for the *Constitution*. Under the direction of Evan P. Howell, Henry W. Grady, and Harris the *Constitution* quickly won recognition as the most progressive newspaper in the South. Charles Henry Smith, though he did not live in Atlanta, was still writing for the *Constitution* under the name of "Bill Arp." One function of a newspaper editor, as Harris saw it, was "mowing down the old prejudices that rattle in the wind like weeds." He was no orator like Grady, but he perhaps accomplished more in the long run to promote reconciliation and to forward the ideals of the New South.

In the *Constitution* Harris published hundreds of editorials, a few stories, and a novelette, "The Romance of Rockville," which he probably lacked the courage to submit to a Northern publishing house. It is a rather conventional and poorly constructed story with a few good scenes and two or three well-drawn characters. But whatever plans Harris may have had for novels or short stories were temporarily laid aside when the Uncle Remus tales, to which he had attached little importance, made him one of the best-known of American writers and caused people to regard him as an authority on the Negro.

Until after the Civil War, American writers almost wholly neglected the rich treasury of the Negro's folk songs and legends.[35] William Cullen Bryant, who visited the South in 1843, was impressed by the singing of Negro workers in a Richmond tobacco factory, and he recorded a Jim Crow song which he heard sung at a corn shucking, apparently on Simms's plantation, "Woodlands." Mrs. Stowe had given the Negro major roles in *Uncle*

---

[35] For an exception, see Jay B. Hubbell, "A Persimmon Beer Dance in Ante-bellum Virginia," *S.L.M.*, n.s. V, 461–466 (Nov.–Dec., 1943).

Tom's Cabin and *Dred*, but she made little of his songs and folk tales. Possibly Harris had seen the spirituals which in 1867 certain Northern carpetbaggers had published in *The Slave Songs of the United States*. He had certainly seen William Owens' "Folk-lore of the Southern Negroes" in *Lippincott's Magazine* for December, 1877,[36] which suggested to him that Negro folklore was a matter of some importance. Like Thomas Nelson Page, he read with keen interest the dialect poems which, beginning in January, 1876, Irwin Russell was publishing in *Scribner's Monthly*. One can imagine his delight when he read in "Christmas-Night in the Quarters" Booker's ballad telling the story of Ham's invention of the banjo—which is also a folk tale that explains why the opossum has no hair on his tail. Many white Southerners had heard these animal stories told by Negro uncles and mammies in their childhood, but it had not occurred to them that it might be worth while to record them.

In September, 1866, a writer in *Scott's Monthly*, of Atlanta, commented on the rare narrative powers of a Negro "maumer" (mammy) who in the old days told to white children animal stories in the expressive but difficult Gullah dialect. "Ah!" he wrote, "how intently we used to listen to those charming stories, told with such gusto and Gullah grace, such animation and enthusiasm, such pantomimic illustration and imitative power!" He continued: "And as for the grand and humorous series of 'Buh Rabbit, Buh Wolf, and Buh Buff,' what printed account could do justice to her telling of them? Tone, emphasis, gesture, dialect, dramatic action would all be lost. 'Tis a pity, too, they cannot be printed." He retold but not in dialect the old mammy's Legend of the Lard Lady, who came too close to a hot fire and dissolved on the hearth. Here was an opportunity lost by one who desired to help create a genuine Southern literature. Fourteen years later thousands of people in the North as well as in the South were reading *Uncle Remus: His Songs and His Sayings*. In a later volume Harris even dared to include the Daddy Jack stories in a modified Gullah dialect.

As early as January, 1877, Harris was printing in the *Constitution* a few songs in Negro dialect, some of which were either folk songs or adaptations of songs he had heard the Negroes sing. Some time in the year 1878 Sam W. Small, who had been writing a column in Negro dialect revolving about the doings and sayings of "Uncle Si," left the *Constitution*, and Harris was asked to continue the feature. He declined but offered to provide a substitute. In that year and the next he printed character sketches of Uncle Remus

---

[36] XX, 748–755. Possibly he had also seen in *Lippincott's* Thaddeus Norris, "Negro Superstitions" (VI, 90–95, July, 1870). Norris summarized the Tar Baby story but not in dialect. The version he used is quite different from Harris's.

along with an occasional animal story. The Tar Baby story appeared in July, 1879, and was widely copied. Harris at first attached little importance to the stories. The first, he said, "was written out almost by accident, and as a study in dialect." He had no idea that he had created one of the great characters in American fiction.

Harris would never have had the courage to look for a Northern publisher, but the New York house of D. Appleton and Company sent to Atlanta its veteran representative, J. C. Derby, a friend of Southern writers, with the offer to make a book of Uncle Remus's stories. Together Derby and Harris went through a file of the *Constitution* and selected the proverbs, songs, and stories included in *Uncle Remus: His Songs and His Sayings* (1880). For the next quarter of a century the sales of this book alone averaged four thousand copies a year. Northern magazines began asking for more of the stories, and *Nights with Uncle Remus* followed in 1883. The series ran to six volumes in all. When his memory began to fail him, Harris appealed to friends to send him outlines of stories which he had forgotten or never heard. William Tappan Thompson and Harry Stillwell Edwards were among the first to respond; Mark Twain was another. For a time Harris made a study of the literature of folklore, but he finally came to the conclusion that the one important thing was to embody the legends in the language of the old-time plantation Negro.

It was characteristic of Harris to make little of the literary qualities of the tales, as he did in a letter to Mark Twain: "I am perfectly well aware that my book has no basis of literary art to stand upon; I know it is the matter and not the manner that has attracted public attention and won the consideration of people of taste at the North; I understand that my relations toward Uncle Remus are similar to those that exist between an almanac-maker and the calendar; but at the same time I feel very grateful to those who have taken the old man under their wing." [37] Of his leading character Harris said to an interviewer: "He was not an invention of my own, but a human syndicate, I might say, of three or four old darkies whom I had known. I just walloped them together into one person and called him 'Uncle Remus.' You must remember that sometimes the negro is a genuine and an original philosopher."

In answer to inquiries, Harris explained why the rabbit and not the fox, as in European folklore, is the hero: "It needs no scientific investigation

[37] *Life and Letters*, p. 168. In his reply Mark Twain said: "In reality the stories are only alligator pears—one eats them merely for the sake of the dressing" (*ibid.*, pp. 169–170). Mark Twain gave Harris the plot of "A Ghost Story," which he himself retold in "How to Tell a Story."

to show why he (the negro) selects as his hero the weakest and most harm-
less of all animals, and brings him out victorious in contests with the bear,
the wolf, and the fox. It is not *virtue* that triumphs, but *helplessness*; it is
not *malice*, but *mischievousness*." Brer Rabbit is an animal Til Eulen-
spiegel, playing merry pranks on his enemies. There is in the tales, however,
a good deal of what Oscar Wilde called "slave morality, the worst in the
world." The methods which Brer Rabbit uses to get the better of his foes
are similar to those used by the slave to wheedle something out of his master
cr overseer or to escape punishment for his misdeeds. Brer Rabbit has no
scruples about cheatmg or lying. There is a cruel, savage streak in him; he
will even burn his enemies alive. Perhaps all this explains why Harris never
told or read the stories to his own children. Now and then Uncle Remus
reminds the little boy to whom he tells them that one must not judge the
creatures by human moral standards. There are other implications which
Harris did not attempt to explain. Occasionally Uncle Remus takes a sly
dig at the white man's busyness or his questionable ways of making money
or getting ahead in the world.

   And yet the general effect of the stories in their framework is to glorify
the plantation regime, in which for Harris the romantic element was the
Negro slave rather than the master. He was less prone to idealize the relation between master and slave than Thomas Nelson Page; but he, too, had
a part in throwing a glamour over the slave plantation. When he printed
his earliest folk tales in the *Constitution*, Harris had in mind only readers
in the South. Probably Derby called his attention to passages which might
give offense to Northern readers. As John Stafford has pointed out,[38] there
are significant differences between "A Story of the War" as published in
the first of the Uncle Remus volumes and the *Constitution* version entitled
"Uncle Remus as a Rebel: How He Saved His Young Master's Life." In the
earlier version Uncle Remus, seeing a Yankee soldier about to shoot his
young "Marse Jeems," had "disremembered all 'bout freedom" and shot the
Union soldier. In the book, however, the Union soldier loses only an arm.
Moreover, Miss Sally nurses him back to health and marries him; and thus
the Yankee soldier becomes the older "Marse Jeems," the father of the little
boy to whom Uncle Remus relates the story in the presence of a visitor
from the North. When we turn to *Nights with Uncle Remus*, however, we
find that the little boy's father is not the Yankee soldier. It all becomes a
little confusing. Again, in "Aunt Fountain's Prisoner" and in other stories
Harris followed the literary fashion of marrying a Southern planter's daugh-

   [38] "Patterns of Meaning in *Nights with Uncle Remus*," *Am. Lit.*, XVIII, 89–108
(May, 1946).

ter to a Union soldier, thus suggesting to Northern readers that a man from beyond the Potomac was sometimes good enough to marry a Southern lady.

Outside of the Uncle Remus stories Harris's most striking treatment of the Negro is found in "Free Joe and the Rest of the World" (1884), one of its author's favorites. This tragic story of a free Negro in slavery times, "a black atom, drifting hither and thither without an owner, blown about by all the winds of circumstance, and given over to shiftlessness," could hardly have been written by any other Southern writer of the nineteenth century except perhaps George W. Cable.

Harris was well aware that emancipation of the slaves had given a new freedom to the Southern writer. In February, 1881, he wrote in the *Constitution:* "The Southern Thackeray of the future will doubtless be surprised to learn that if he had put in an appearance half a century sooner he would probably have been escorted beyond the limits and boundaries of our sunny Southern clime astraddle of an indignant rail." Thackeray was free to criticize the society in which he moved, but the writer of the Old South was not permitted to "draw an impartial picture of Southern civilization, its lights and its shadows." Harris, however, added truthfully enough that such limitations "fitted perfectly and exactly the inclinations and ambitions of the writers themselves." Still, he thought, these limitations explained why the Southern writers of fiction were "all romancers."

Harris assured his Southern readers in 1881 that there was among Northern editors and publishers no disposition to discriminate against any writer because he lived in the South. The chief difficulty the Southern writer had to face, he thought, was that of ridding himself of his self-consciousness, his sectional prejudices, and his fondness for the outworn trappings of romantic fiction. The writer's materials must be those of the region he knew best, but his point of view must be national. He made a sharp distinction between "sectionalism," which he condemned, and "localism," which seemed to him "the very marrow and essence of all literary art." In defending the outraged Bostonians against the charges of provincialism in Henry James's *Hawthorne,* Harris went so far as to propound his own theory "that no enduring work of the imagination has ever been produced save by a mind in which the provincial instinct was the controlling influence." Harris, though he liked James's earlier novels, regarded him as "the most delightful literary snob of the period." Among his favorite authors were Montaigne, Sir Thomas Browne, and Goldsmith. He cared little for Emerson and most of the older New England writers.

In 1885 the *Century Magazine,* in which Harris had published some of his stories, offered him a contract for whatever he might write that would have enabled the underpaid journalist at the age of thirty-seven to give up the newspaper grind and devote all his time and energy to literature. Too unsure of his creative powers, he made the mistake of declining the offer. Fifteen years later he accepted a similar offer from the McClure Phillips Company and at last left the *Constitution*. He was by that time past fifty, too old to master the structure of the novel. In 1907, as though he felt he had to get back into journalism, he founded *Uncle Remus's Magazine*, which lingered on for several years after his death in 1908.

Even before he had published *Nights with Uncle Remus* (1883), Harris was sending to Northern magazines stories in which the chief characters were white. Some of the best of these were republished in *Mingo* (1884) and *Free Joe* (1887). His first book-length story was the semifictitious *On the Plantation* (1892), but *Sister Jane* (1896) was his first real attempt at the novel since the immature "Romance of Rockville."

While he was writing stories for the Northern literary market, Harris profited from the advice he received from editors and publishers. On December 16, 1881, he wrote to Robert Underwood Johnson of the *Century*: "If your kind letters fail to get good work out of a fellow, it isn't in him." The Northern magazines wanted well-constructed short stories, and Harris was, as he soon came to realize, primarily a writer of character sketches. On March 22, 1883, he wrote to Johnson that he had "endeavored to carry out to the letter every suggestion" for the revision of "At Teague Poteet's" (which finally appeared as a two-part story in May and June), but he added: "At the same time, I would be glad for you to believe that I made no attempt to write a story, much less a novelette. My plan was merely to write a sketch in characterization of one phase of life in the mountains of North Carolina." To his eldest daughter he wrote on April 1, 1896: ". . . I can't write a long story. I put all my strength in the episodes and leave the thread of the main story hanging at loose ends." Johnson thought that if circumstances had been more favorable, Harris might have written "novels of distinction," but writing any long story was difficult for a man who could write only in the evening after a day's work in the newspaper office. Like some of the older Southern humorists, Harris often prolonged his introductory passages unnecessarily, and he sometimes failed to close at the right moment. In "Trouble on Lost Mountain" too much of the introduction is concerned with the difficulty between Abe Hightower and Sheriff McLendon which has little to do with the particular story which Harris has to tell. "Where's Duncan?" and "Balaam and His Master" each has an excellent opening paragraph, but in each case it comes not at the beginning but on the third page of the story.

There were times when Harris rebelled against the editors' suggestions in regard to structure. In November, 1894, he wrote to E. L. Burlingame of *Scribner's Magazine* about a three-part story which he had submitted: "The affair represents a good deal of hard work, but not in the direction of giving it *literary form*. There is something so painful in modern literary form—outside of Mr. [R. L.] Stevenson's inimitable stories—that I have forsworn all efforts in that direction. . . . My whole aim has been at *life* and *character*, and I have purposely left the *style* to take care of itself." After he had abandoned newspaper work, Harris wrote the novel *Gabriel Tolliver* (1902) to please himself. He was untactful enough to say in his Preface: "Let those who can do so continue to import harmony and unity into their fabrications and call it art. . . . I [am] powerless to twist individuals and events to suit the demands or necessities of what is called art." It is no wonder that the reviewer in the *Nation* found *Gabriel Tolliver* a "very poor work, rambling, shuffling . . . without characterization, form, or style."

Harris was to remain to the end primarily a writer of sketches like the Georgia humorists before him. He was no doubt right in thinking that the editorial demands for a well-made story showed too little appreciation of character. In a later period Sherwood Anderson, Ruth Suckow, and others were to rebel against the stereotyped short story and write character sketches without much regard to plot. If Harris had been a better artist or if he had lived at a later time, he might perhaps have worked out an artistic form which would have embodied his best qualities: humor, characterization, and a sympathy for the poor and the distressed. As it is, he is uniformly at his best when he places his story in the mouth of an unlettered narrator and writes in the dialect of the plantation Negro or the Georgia cracker.

There was a certain duality in the mind of Harris the writer, and he occasionally commented upon it. In an important letter to his eldest daughter, March 19, 1898, he said: "You know all of us have two entities, or personalities." One part of his mind, he said, wrote editorials for the *Constitution*, but it was the "other fellow" who wrote the best scenes in his stories. ". . . when night comes," he wrote, "I take up my pen, surrender unconditionally to my 'other fellow,' and out comes the story, and if it is a good story I am as much surprised as the people who read it." It was obviously this "other fellow" that Harris did not fully understand who wrote "Free Joe," the best of the Uncle Remus tales, and the most striking episodes in his other fiction. It was the "other fellow" who best understood the plantation Negro and the Georgia cracker and who could speak for them, as for example, Thomas Nelson Page could not. The "other fellow" had in fact a certain scorn for the Southern aristocrat and indulged occasionally in a "sly thrust at the pompous life of the Old South." [39] The "other fellow" preferred to write in dialect and disliked the editorial style of the Atlanta *Constitution*. The "other fellow" was guiding Harris's pen when he created Billy Sanders, who first appeared in "The Kidnapping of President Lincoln" in *On the Wing of Occasions* (1900). In Harris's short story this Georgia humorist belongs to the despised class of overseers. But when at the suggestion of Walter Hines Page, Harris resurrected Billy Sanders and converted him into a commentator on current events for the *World's Work*, possibly as a rival of "Mr. Dooley," he gave us only another—and a second-rate—"Bill Arp." Most of what Harris put into the mouth of Billy Sanders in the *World's Work* and *Uncle Remus's Magazine* is sensible enough, but it is the work of Editor Harris and not the "other fellow" who had created Uncle Remus.

Harris is remembered for the best of the Uncle Remus tales. How long will he be remembered, I wonder? The folklorists will always find his work important, but few persons at the present time, even in the South, can read the Negro dialect with any facility. The Negroes have never had much enthusiasm about Uncle Remus; he seems to them too subservient to the whites. There is another difficulty which confronts the urban child of today: he knows too little about country life. He has probably never seen a rabbit or a fox and, like some of Walt Disney's illustrators, he thinks that "goobers" grow on bushes or trees and not underground like potatoes. This difficulty, alas! is not limited to children or to those who live outside the South. It has rendered much of the literature of rural America almost meaningless to those who live in towns and cities. Every teacher of English knows that city-bred boys and girls often fail to understand *Snow-Bound* and *Main-Travelled Roads*. They have their difficulties, too, with such masterpieces of English literature as "The Cotter's Saturday Night" and *A Winter's Tale*.

In spite of the difficult dialect, the Uncle Remus tales are still a classic in children's literature and will, I hope, be read as such for many years. An occasional adult will no doubt discover that they contain something which only the mature reader understands and enjoys. Harris would have been quite content, I think, with the reputation he has at the present time. In an edition of Uncle Remus dedicated to A. B. Frost, the illustrator who, he said, "breathed the breath of life into these amiable brethren of wood and field," Harris wrote:

---

[39] So at least Walter Hines Page thought in 1881 when he first met Harris (Burton J. Hendrick, *The Earlier Life and Letters of Walter Hines Page*, 1928, p. 152). Mrs. Julia C. Harris omits this portion of Page's article.

I seem to see before me the smiling faces of thousands of children—some young and fresh and some wearing the friendly marks of age, but all children at heart—and not an unfriendly face among them. And while I am trying hard to speak the right word, I seem to hear a voice lifted above the rest, saying: "You have made some of us happy." And so I feel my heart fluttering and my lips trembling and I have to bow silently, and turn away and hurry back into the obscurity that fits me best.

12
Thomas Nelson Page

MORE THAN his fellow Southerners, the Virginian is regarded as a glorifier of times past, perhaps because—as a Virginian might reply to such a charge—his state has a longer and more magnificent past to boast of. Thomas Nelson Page (1853–1922) was among the writers of the New South the stoutest defender of the old regime. Like most of the other Virginian writers of fiction, he belonged to a family with a distinguished ancestry, and, like them, he gave his heroes and heroines a line of ancestors comparable to his own. The great days of the Nelsons and the Pages, however, had come in the last half of the eighteenth century. "Oakland" plantation in Hanover County, where he was born, was not a prosperous estate in the fifties. Hanover County, which is north of Richmond, lay directly in the path of invading Union armies, and it was fought over repeatedly by the soldiers of McClellan, Grant, and Lee. John Esten Cooke, to whom Hanover County was a familiar battleground, saw little that was romantic about the war; but Page, who was only twelve when the war ended, always saw it as a romantic Virginian epic age. He looked back upon the old regime as a near approach to the Golden Age and regarded Reconstruction as a betrayal of the state and the social class to which he belonged.

Page was a student at Washington College while General Lee was its president. After studying law at the University of Virginia, he practiced law for two years in Hanover County. Then at the age of twenty-three he gladly accepted a place in the office of a cousin, Henry T. Wickham, who was attorney for the Chesapeake and Ohio Railroad. Page was ambitious, eager for position and power, and not averse to seeing his name in print. Owning and operating a Virginia farm were not his ambition. In Richmond, where he had relatives and soon made many friends, he became known as a skilful raconteur. So impressed were some of his listeners with his stories of the old plantation and his command of the Negro dialect that they suggested that he ought to write them out and publish them. Irwin Russell's dialect poems, which were appearing in *Scribner's Monthly* in 1876, suggested a method. Page's "Uncle Gabe's White Folks" was published in the *Monthly* in April, 1877. Although his best work was to be done in prose rather than in verse, Page had thus early discovered his most effective mouthpiece in the faithful ex-slave who boasts of his old master's wealth and grandeur.

> "Fine ole place?" Yes, suh, 't is so;
>   An' mighty fine people my white folks war—
> But you ought ter 'a' seen it years ago,
>   When de Marster an' de Mistis lived up dyah;
> When de niggers 'd stan' all roun' de do',
> Like grains o' corn on the cornhouse flo'.
>
> "Live' mons'ous high?" Yes, Marster, yes;
>   D' cut 'n' onroyal 'n' gordly dash;
> Eat an' drink till you could n' res'.
>   My folks war n' none o' yo' po'-white-trash;
> Nor, suh, dey was of high degree—
> Dis heah nigger am quality!

In Page's stories the emphasis is upon the loyalty of the slave to a kindly master, of the planter to his state and to his code of honor, and upon the glorification of woman. Later he added the theme of sectional reconciliation. His chief characters belong to two classes: the great planters and the faithful house servants, who looked down on the field hands and the "po'-white trash." His best Negro characters—Sam of "Marse Chan" and Billy of "Meh Lady"—are faithful ex-slaves. He did not treat the typical freedman with distinction, and his Negro women are on the whole inferior to his men. Rarely did he portray the numerous field hands or the Southern small farmers or the poorer whites.

In 1881 *Scribner's Monthly* accepted Page's offer to write an article on Yorktown for the centennial of Cornwallis's surrender. In 1881 also the magazine accepted his most famous story, "Marse Chan," but the story remained unpublished until April, 1884, by which time the *Monthly* had become the *Century Magazine*. The editors were apparently fearful of printing so long a story written almost entirely in Negro dialect. It appears also that they found it necessary to delete certain passages which did not relate directly to the love story.

"Marse Chan" had its genesis in a letter, shown to Page by a friend, which was found on the body of an uneducated Georgia private killed in one of the great battles around Richmond. The letter was from his sweetheart, who told him that she had discovered that she loved him after all and added that if he could get a furlough and come home, she would marry him. She concluded: "Don't come without a furlough, for if you don't come honorable, I won't marry you." In theme and narrative method, as Page himself acknowledged, "Marse Chan" owes something to "Envion," a story which his friend Armistead C. Gordon had published in the *South-Atlantic* for July, 1880.[40] The theme, however, continued to haunt Page until in 1894 he published "Little Darby," which is essentially the same story, this time with Virginia poor-whites as the chief characters. He felt, as he wrote to Arthur H. Quinn, "that it was due to that class that I should testify with whatever power I might possess, to their devotion to the South."

In January, 1886, Page published in *Harper's* "Unc' Edinburg's Drowndin'," which he was inclined to think his best story. On December 31, 1885, Joel Chandler Harris wrote to Page that he would rather have written this story and "Marse Chan" than "everything else that has appeared since the War—or before the War, for that matter." Richard Watson Gilder also had high praise for "Unc' Edinburg's Drowndin'." In a letter to Page, January 19, 1886, he said: "I take off my hat to you for that. It is dramatically perfect, and in detail it is a most extraordinary reflection, through the mind and dialect of that old darky, of an interesting and complete society. It is an exquisite story."

In June, 1886, the *Century* published "Meh Lady" and paid Page two hundred and fifty dollars for it. Remembering Lessing's *Minna von Barnhelm*, Robert Underwood Johnson of the *Century* staff had suggested the love story of the Union soldier and the Virginia planter's daughter—a theme which was a conventional one in 1886. Page's handling of it, however, is far superior to that found in so many stories by Northern writers who had little understanding of Southern life. Page was doing his part to promote better relations between South and North, but it is perhaps significant that in "Meh Lady" the Union soldier turns out to be the son of a Virginia kinsman.

"Marse Chan," "Meh Lady," "Unc' Edinburg's Drowndin'," and three other stories were republished in book form in *In Ole Virginia* (1887). *Two Little Confederates*, the best of his stories for young people, appeared the next year. *The Burial of the Guns* followed in 1894. These books were widely read and were highly praised by Northern reviewers, but it was not until 1890 or after, that Page regarded his writing as being as important as his law practice. "Even now," he wrote in *The Old South* (1892), "the Southerner will not believe that a man can be a lawyer and an author." James Lane Allen had written to Page on October 16, 1889: "I cannot submit to the

[40] See Page's Preface to Gordon's *Envion and Other Tales of Old and New Virginia* (New York, 1899).

idea that you will allow the law or any other claim to separate you from literature. . . . I shall count it a loss if Southern literature is not to have from you some novels of Virginia life." Page had not found the writing of short stories particularly profitable, and he was already struggling with his first novel, Red Rock, which was not to be published until 1898.

The death in December, 1888, of Page's wife, Anne Bruce Page, was a great blow to him. She had encouraged him to write and had been an intelligent critic of his writings. After her death he visited Europe and on his return devoted much of his time and energy to lecturing and to giving readings from his stories. In 1893 he married the wealthy Mrs. Florence Lathrop Field, a sister-in-law of Marshall Field. They made their home in Washington in a handsome house built for Mrs. Page by McKim, Mead, and White. Page abandoned his law practice and gave up lecturing. He spent many of his summers in Maine and made only infrequent visits to Virginia. He was now more interested in politics than in writing. A friend of Theodore Roosevelt, he defended the President against Southerners who had bitterly criticized him for inviting Booker T. Washington to dine with him in the White House. In 1913 President Woodrow Wilson sent Page to Italy as Ambassador, and Page served in that capacity throughout the First World War. One of his last books was Italy and the World War (1920).

Page's best work had been done during his Richmond period, but he continued to publish with undiminished popular success for several years after his removal to Washington. In 1898 he published Red Rock, much of which had been written as early as 1885. Of his difficulties with his first novel Page wrote to Arthur H. Quinn:

. . . after having written a third or more of the novel I discovered that I had drifted into the production of a political tract. I bodily discarded what I had written, and going back beyond the War, in order to secure a background and a point of departure which would enable me to take a more serene path, I rewrote it entirely. I had discovered that the real facts in the Reconstruction period were so terrible that I was unable to describe them fully, without subjecting myself to the charge of gross exaggeration.

The story gave not only Page but also his literary advisers much trouble. Perhaps he should never have attempted a novel. He doubtless felt, however, like his contemporaries, that the novel was not only a more remunerative but also a more important literary form than the short story. If Page never mastered the art of construction in the longer form, he failed as Bret Harte, Harris, and nearly every other local colorist failed when they attempted to handle a long and complicated story. Red Rock begins effectively, but soon the story begins to bog down. Reconciliation is one of its themes, but this time Page varies the situation by having a Northern girl and not a Union soldier as a leading character in the love story.

Gordon Keith (1903) drew much unfavorable criticism, but it was a popular success, partly because it deals, somewhat sentimentally, with the New South rather than the Old. The opening sentence, however, is typical of Page's point of view: "Gordon Keith was the son of a gentleman." *John Marvel, Assistant* (1909)—his last novel except for the posthumous unfinished *The Red Riders* (1927)—reveals a very different Page. The setting is for the most part not Virginia but a great Midwestern city. It is essentially a problem novel—a type that Page had professed to detest—and it is a medley of Page's interests in his Washington period: social reform, politics, racial intolerance, etc. One of the leading characters is a Jewish reformer. There is also the son of a Virginia gentleman who never amounts to anything until he discovers that he must rely on his own exertions and not upon the achievements of his distinguished ancestors. *John Marvel* is not a good novel, but it reveals a Page who had become at last national in his outlook upon American life.

The library at "Oakland" did not contain many new books, and Page was never a great reader. In his earlier years he was fond of Scott's historical romances,[41] Cooper's Leather-Stocking Tales, and French romances. He was fond of Addison, Steele, and Goldsmith. His father's favorites were Pope, Goldsmith, and Boswell's life of Dr. Johnson. Page was little influenced by any writer of the North or the West. He read Poe and the romances of his father's friend, John Esten Cooke; but in later life he censured Cooke for seeing "the life of the South through the lenses of Scott, and his imitators." He acknowledged a debt to the dialect poems of Irwin Russell and the Virginia stories of his friend Armistead C. Gordon. To the pioneer work of the Virginia humorist, George W. Bagby, he confessed "an unending debt of gratitude," for Bagby, he said, had "opened his eyes to the beauty that lay at hand and whispered into his ear the charm that sang to his soul of the South." [42] But Bagby, though he loved Virginia no less than Page, was far more the realist, and it seems probable that some of the humorist's sketches —"Bacon and Greens," for instance—seemed to Page not only unromantic but also in poor taste.

In his Richmond period Page wrote comparatively little, but he revised

[41] Page's friend, the Virginia novelist, Mary Greenway McClelland, wrote to him, Aug. 12, 1888: "Like yourself, I can truly say that of all my teachers I owe most to Sir Walter Scott."

[42] See the Preface to Page's edition of *The Old Virginia Gentleman and Other Sketches* (1911).

with care the stories he published. Nearly everything he printed after *Red Rock* shows evidence of hasty writing and inadequate revision. He grew more reluctant to follow the suggestions of his literary advisers and publishers. His usual method in the earlier years was to tell his story to friends before he put it on paper. When the story was written down, he would read it aloud to a group of sympathetic listeners, watching carefully their reaction to every part of the story. In his later years he too often forgot the advice which he once gave to a nephew who wanted to write: "Write what you know about; write what you feel deeply as to; write as you feel; write simply, clearly, sincerely, and you will write strongly."

Like other writers of the New South, Page owed much to his Northern editors and publishers, especially Richard Watson Gilder, Robert Underwood Johnson, and Charles Dudley Warner. On his frequent visits to New York he learned from them something about literary style and structure as well as about what the reading public wanted. Nevertheless, they found it necessary to revise and condense his stories, for Page, like Harris, when left to himself was more likely to write a sketch than a carefully plotted short story. His *Pastime Stories* (1894), written for the "Editor's Drawer" department of *Harper's Magazine*, are frankly anecdotes rather than orthodox short stories. Two of Page's most helpful literary advisers were Southern women: Mrs. Bessie Pascal Wright, an editorial reader for Harper & Brothers who as Mrs. T. P. O'Connor was to dedicate to Page her *My Beloved South* (1913), and Mrs. Sophia Bledsoe Herrick of the *Century* staff, who had served her apprenticeship on her father's *Southern Review* in the 1870's. Mrs. Herrick wrote to Page on August 29, 1885:

There is a quality in your work, I think (if my thinking is worth anything to you)—which is like that in nobodys else. . . . If you only select your material wisely I do not think, in your own line, there is any one living who can touch you. But I sometimes think you do not quite see the limitations of your art. Art is not a literal transcript of nature. It must be true, not so much really, as ideally. And that requires the power of selection, the self restraint which can leave unsaid many good things. In *Marse Chan* the material was in excellent shape, it was a charming story. Where it had to be shortened I cut it with positive pain—it was so exquisite from beginning to end. In *Meh Lady* the form was not so good; the incidents & treatment were [in] no way inferior, but it lacked proportion & perspective. It was a little panoramic I think.

Gilder in a letter of January 19, 1886, pointed out a "grave defect" in Page's "A Soldier of the Empire": ". . . there is no climax, therefore no story. It is too much like a story for a sketch, but *as* a story it lacks dramatic completeness such as all your other stories have had."

E. L. Burlingame, the editor of *Scribner's Magazine*, pointed out two defects in the first version of Page's "No Haid Pawn." Severing the head of a man being hanged seemed to the editor "unnecessarily repellent without increasing the force of the story." He asked: ". . . ought not the dimly suggested connection of the runaway negro & his booty with the climax, to be brought out just a shade more, for the sake of the average rather inattentive reader?" Another editor, Mrs. Mary Mapes Dodge, in accepting *Two Little Confederates* as a serial to be run in *St. Nicholas*, stipulated that the six introductory chapters should be condensed to a single instalment by "shortening the general descriptions, cutting the amusing hen-house episode. . . ." She added: ". . . the account of the Yankee raid . . . must necessarily be pruned for St. Nicholas. To leave it in entire, as it now reads, would quite prevent the story, I fear, from being the olive branch you desire it to be."

Of all the writers of the New South except Hayne, Page was the staunchest defender of the old regime. He disliked the phrase "New South" because it seemed to imply an invidious comparison with the Old South and a desertion of its ideals. In December, 1887, he wrote to William Hamilton Hayne, son of the poet: "The New South is in my judgment only the Old South with slavery gone and the fire of exaction on its back." Some of the essays and addresses in Page's *The Old South* (1892) are in effect replies to Grady's addresses on the New South. When compared with Cable's *The Silent South* (1885), Page's *The Negro* (1904), with its rather defiant subtitle, "The Southerner's Problem," seems today somewhat reactionary, even to Southerners.

Northern misconceptions of Southern life and character irritated Page, and much of his earlier work was designed to refute them. *Red Rock* (1898), in spite of his change of plan, was in effect a belated reply to *Uncle Tom's Cabin*, which had appeared forty-six years earlier. And yet Page found a large and sympathetic audience waiting for him in the North. He once told Edwin Mims that the city of Boston bought more of his books than the entire state of Virginia. Mrs. Annie Fields, widow of the Boston publisher, James T. Fields, wrote to Page from Venice in May, 1892: "I have been reading your 'Gray Jacket' with my eyes full of tears." She added that her friend Sarah Orne Jewett had also read the story and "felt it deeply." Mrs. Stowe's famous brother, Henry Ward Beecher, shed tears when Mrs. T. P. O'Connor read "Marse Chan" to him. Thomas Wentworth Higginson, who had also shed tears over that story, wrote to Page in September, 1892: "I have been reading your 'Old South' with much interest & occasional disagreement."

For some Northern readers, I suspect, "Marse Chan" and "Unc' Edinburg's Drowndin' " were stories of a vanished way of life so remote in time and space that they had a romantic charm. Or perhaps these stories recalled to readers in huge Northern cities memories of a simpler life they had known or heard their parents or grandparents speak of. In *Lady Baltimore* (1906) the Philadelphia novelist, Owen Wister, suggests the charm which old Charleston had for him. A Northern visitor remarks: "And these ladies of yours—well, they made me homesick for a national and a social past which I never saw, but which my old people knew. . . . In their quiet clean-cut faces I seem to see a reflection of the old serene candlelight we all once talked and danced in—sconces, tall mirrors, candles burning inside glass globes to keep them from the moths and the draft that, of a warm evening, blew in through handsome mahogany doors; the good bright silver; the portraits by Copley and Gilbert Stuart; a young girl at a square piano, singing Moore's melodies—and Mr. Pinckney or Commodore Perry, perhaps, dropping in for a hot supper!" "Such quiet faces," Wister continues, "are gone now in the breathless, competing North: ground into oblivion between the clashing trades of the competing men and the clashing jewels and chandeliers of their competing wives—while yours have lingered on, spared by your very adversity."

To Page's Southern readers, "Marse Chan," "Meh Lady," and *Red Rock* were not merely good stories but historical documents which justified the slave plantation and made the Lost Cause seem in many ways the right one. Mrs. Paul Hamilton Hayne wrote to Page on May 10, 1888, that she and her son William were following his literary career with keen interest. "Our sacred past," she said, "we felt to be safe in your keeping." Page's friend William W. Archer wrote from Richmond, May 27, 1887: ". . . you have been the first Virginian to catch the attention of the outside world, and force its audience [to listen] while you told the story truthfully and pathetically, of 'Ole Virginia.' . . ." Molly Elliot Seawell spoke for other Virginia writers when she wrote to Page in December, 1888: "Every body who writes about Virginia now must follow your lead. . . ."

Page of course did not create the plantation literary legend. Before the Civil War Kennedy, Caruthers, Beverley Tucker, Cooke, Thackeray, and G. P. R. James had made the Virginia plantation a part of our literary tradition. Page, however, went far beyond most of them in idealizing the plantation life. Much more true to fact are the charming and too little-known *Sketches from Old Virginia* (1897) of Arthur Granville Bradley, an Englishman who lived in rural Virginia in the Reconstruction period. So far did Page carry the tendency to idealize the past that later Virginia writers reacted against him in his own lifetime. Mary Johnston's *Hagar* (1913) is a protest on the part of the New Woman of the South against the code of

"Southern chivalry" which motivated Page's heroines. In *The Rivet in Grandfather's Neck* (1915) James Branch Cabell went so far as to burlesque the story of "Meh Lady." [43]

Only six years after the publication of *Red Rock*, Ellen Glasgow in *The Deliverance* (1904) treated again but in very different fashion the central situation in Page's novel. In each story an overseer has acquired by fraudulent methods the master's plantation and mansion, and the master's family have, ironically enough, no place left to live in except the overseer's cabin. What chiefly interested Page was the gross injustice done to the planter's family, and he had of course to blame it upon villains, Northern carpetbaggers and Southern scalawags, who were not gentlemen to the manner born. In *The Deliverance*, however, there is no disposition to glorify the planter class or the slavery regime. What interested Miss Glasgow was exactly what would have interested Hawthorne: how the various characters in the story reacted to the changed conditions. In the planter's blind and invalid widow, who has never been told that the Confederacy lost the war or that she is now almost a pauper living in the overseer's cabin, Miss Glasgow, as she tells us in *A Certain Measure*, saw "not one old woman groping, blind and nourished by illusions, through a memorable epoch in history, but Virginia and the entire South, unaware of the changes about them, clinging with passionate fidelity, to the ceremonial forms of tradition."

Southern historians have shown that the great planters were always comparatively few in number and that not all of them were admirable characters. As long ago as 1908 a Southern historian, William E. Dodd, said in a review of Page's *The Old Dominion: Her Making and Her Manners* (1908): "A note which runs through all that Mr. Page has ever written is evident here also: the judgment and the language are too frequently those of one who supposes character to be absolutely determined by status. All heroic characters are gentlemen; the villains are outside the charmed circle. This is not life; it is not even ante-bellum Virginia life."

Page's stories and the point of view they represent are out of fashion now even in his native state. The pendulum has swung away from romance and sentiment. It is not the modern fashion to portray gentlemen and ladies or, perhaps one may even say, honest and decent persons in the upper class of any society. In a recent survey of contemporary Southern fiction a Southern scholar has shown that in twentieth-century novels by Southerners the

---

[43] See pp. 158–159 of the New York, 1925, edition. Cabell wrote in *Let Me Lie* (1947): "When these books [Ellen Glasgow's early novels] were written the ghost of Thomas Nelson Page still haunted everybody's conception of the South, keening in Negro dialect over the Confederacy's fallen glories" (p. 241).

gentleman plays a sorry role indeed.[44] That there were Southern gentlemen worthy of admiration is evident to anyone who knows something about Southern history or who has read a life of General Lee or Lucius Q. C. Lamar or Susan Dabney Smedes's life of her father, Thomas Dabney. Not many will ever care to read or reread Page's novels, but at some time in the future perhaps, when readers of fiction have grown weary of stories of Southern perverts and degenerates, a few may turn back to Page's early dialect stories, which even Ellen Glasgow could praise as "firm and round and as fragrant as dried rose-leaves. . . ."

13

George W. Cable

WHEN THE Creoles of New Orleans found themselves portrayed for Northern readers in a manner repugnant to their sensitive natures, they denounced George Washington Cable (1844–1925) as a "Southern Yankee," an Abolitionist at heart, who had wilfully misrepresented their speech, their manners, and their morals so that he could sell more of his books to Northern readers. In other parts of the South many persons read with pleasure his *Old Creole Days* (1879) and *The Grandissimes* (1880); but when in the middle eighties Cable began airing in Northern magazines his heretical views on the Negro question, he provoked widespread condemnation. From all over the South came the cry: "He is none of us."

The notion that Cable was a "Southern Yankee" now seems absurd. He had been born, brought up, and educated in Louisiana, which is more remote from New England than any other Southern state except Texas. On his father's side he could trace his ancestry back to the Old Dominion. He had fought in the Confederate army. He had written his best books while living in New Orleans; and if *Old Creole Days* and "Madame Delphine" are not Southern literature, what is? Cable did not remove to New England until he was a famous writer forty years old. Surely he was right when in 1893 he said at an Authors Club dinner in New York: "Southerners' utterances to the contrary, I am—after being first of all an American citizen— a Southerner. . . ."

Cable was alleged to have inherited his Puritan traits from his mother, who though born in Indiana belonged to a family originally from New England—as if somehow human nature in that region must be essentially dif-

44 C. P. Lee, "Decline and Death of the Southern Gentleman," *Southwest Rev.*, XXXVI, 164–170 (Summer, 1951).

ferent from that in the Deep South. More than one writer whom I have discussed in this book had one or both parents of Northern birth and yet escaped the imputation of being a "Southern Yankee." Cable's mother was a stern and devout member of one of the evangelical churches, but so were the mothers of Johnston, Lanier, and Mark Twain. If Cable was a "Southern Puritan," so were Stonewall Jackson and thousands of other men in every state in the South. And if Cable chose finally to live in New England, so did Sherwood Bonner, Walter Hines Page, and Mark Twain. Long before them Richard Henry Lee had wanted to live there rather than in his native Virginia. It is better to regard Cable as one of the first Southerners of his generation to return to the liberalism of Jefferson, who detested slavery as thoroughly as the little Louisianian.

Cable's chief offense against the South was that he had deliberately violated what Southerners understood to be the meaning of the Compromise of 1877. They had accepted the end of slavery and of secession with the understanding that the Negro was the Southerners' problem and the North would not again interfere. When Cable began writing in Northern magazines about "civil equality," they thought he was deliberately stirring up trouble. It seemed to them that he was advocating "social equality," perhaps even miscegenation. On the race question the New South was intolerant and uncompromising. The now Solid South did not care to be reminded that there had always been natives of that region who on one issue or another had refused to conform to prevailing opinion. There are—in part because of Cable's courageous stand—many more of them today.

Cable, like Poe and Lanier, had no intimate connection with plantation life, and in his fiction he made less use of the plantation tradition than Harris or Page. He was an urban product and a businessman, and he lived in the largest commercial center in the South. His father, the elder George Washington Cable, who was born in the Shenandoah Valley in 1811, was the descendant of one Jakob Kobell, who a century earlier had left the Rhine valley to escape religious persecution. The descendants of German dissenters were as a rule hostile to slavery; and when Cable's grandparents, while his father was still a child, moved to southern Pennsylvania, they freed their slaves. About 1830 they settled in Indiana, where in 1834 the elder Cable married Rebecca Boardman.

Cable's father, from whom the novelist is said to have derived his sense of humor and fun, was a not very successful businessman. Once at least he allowed himself to be cheated by business associates. In New Orleans he attempted various enterprises, including a wine store and a lumber and brickmaking concern. He also sold supplies to steamboats and invested heavily in two boats which were burned in the winter of 1849–1850. From this time he never prospered; and when he died in 1859, he left the family almost without resources. During much of their married life Rebecca Cable and the children had to live with relatives in Indiana.

When his father died, young Cable left school and went to work stamping boxes in the customs office. He was now his mother's chief reliance, and doubtless she spurred him on, all the more determined that he should succeed where his father had failed. With her Presbyterian creed she must have felt a certain scorn for the easygoing ways of the Louisiana planters and especially for the pleasure-loving Creoles, who held themselves superior to "*Américains*" of the merchant class. Rebecca Boardman Cable, as her son described her, was "an heroic spirit" whose chief traits were intellectual ambition, "a keen relish for social relations," and a certain "moral austerity." She was fiercely intolerant of the "spirit of indolence, whether it leaned toward ease or pleasure." Such a woman would have no patience with idle theater-goers or with pleasure-seekers who attended bullfights and quadroon balls. The youthful Cable, it is obvious from his stories, also felt a certain scorn for luxury-loving Creoles and easygoing Southern planters. In later life when his zeal for reform had cooled, he was more tolerant of such people. In 1893 when at the age of forty-nine he spoke at a meeting of the Authors Club in New York, he could even mildly ridicule what he referred to as the "Pentalogue": "Thou shalt not smoke. Thou shalt not drink. Thou shalt not play cards. Thou shalt not dance. Thou shalt not go to the theatre. On these five commandments hang all the law and the prophets."

The Cables were loyal Confederates. After the capture of New Orleans in 1862, his sisters refused to take the oath of allegiance and were ordered out of the city. They took along with them their eighteen-year-old brother, who was so diminutive in stature that the Union guards did not suspect his actual age. He enlisted in the Confederate army and served until the end of the war. One old planter who saw the little cavalryman is said to have exclaimed: "Great heavens! Abe Lincoln told the truth. We *are* robbing the cradle and the grave!" Like Sidney Lanier and John Esten Cooke, Cable found time for reading during the lulls between campaigns. The following passage in *The Cavalier* (1901) is obviously autobiographical:

But my unsoldierly motive for going to head-quarters kept my misgivings alive. I was hungry for the gentilities of camp; to be where Shakespeare was part of the baggage, where Pope was quoted, where Coleridge and Byron and Poe were recited, Macaulay criticised, and "Les Misérables"—Madame [Octavia] Le Vert's Mobile translation—lent round; and where men, when they did steal, stole portable volumes, not currycombs.

Cable was an idealist with a peculiarly logical mind that would eventually carry him far beyond the bounds of orthodox Southern opinion. If his memory is to be trusted, he had been puzzled at the age of nine, while memorizing the Declaration of Independence, "to know how men could declare such ideal truths and yet hold other men in slavery." At about the same age he read *Uncle Tom's Cabin*. When the war broke out, secession seemed to him "a dreadful thing." While he was in the army, it was rumored that Robert Toombs and Alexander H. Stephens were threatening to take Georgia out of the Confederacy. The report prompted Cable to remark to his soldier friends: "This shows me that we are fighting to establish a scheme of government that will work our destruction as sure as we succeed. We shall go to pieces as soon as we are safe from outside enemies." Such an idea was to be no part of the Solid South's legend of the Lost Cause. Cable had practically anticipated the thesis which Frank L. Owsley was to develop in *State Rights in the Confederacy* (1925), published in the year of Cable's death.

At the close of the war Cable returned to New Orleans, he says, without any feeling of loyalty to the Union and without seeing "any unrighteousness in fighting for slavery." The unwisdom of secession, however, was very clear to him, and he rebelled when Southern newspapers began saying that the right of secession had been ended by the defeat of the Confederacy. Had there ever been such a right? he wondered. He proceeded to investigate the question. He looked for the answer, however, not in the speeches and writings of Calhoun but in New England authorities: Justice Story's *Commentary on the Constitution* and George Bancroft's *History of the United States*. In the end he concluded that the doctrine of secession had no constitutional basis and had been devised solely to safeguard the institution of slavery—and slavery in Louisiana, as Mrs. Stowe had represented it, was not the patriarchal institution that it was in Kentucky and Virginia.

The presence in Louisiana of Northern politicians determined to "Americanize" the defeated South no doubt served to remind Cable that there were two sides to controversial questions. He abhorred the current Southern references to "our black peasantry." For his private maxim he chose: "There is no room in America for a peasantry." In a letter signed "A Southern White Man" he printed in a New Orleans newspaper a protest against segregating blacks from whites in the schools and on the horsecars. All the while he was actively engaged in various reform projects in his native city. Even while writing his second book, *The Grandissimes* (1880), he was, he has said, still "very slowly and painfully guessing out the riddle of our Southern question." He finally concluded that slavery was a great wrong which had few of the redeeming features which Southern writers like Harris and Page were claiming for it. He had gone completely over to the extreme Northern position on the Negro question.

Like many another writer of the South and West of his time, Cable was largely self-educated and not without the deficiencies of those who have educated themselves. Somehow or other, however, he managed to find the books which were to direct his writing in the right direction. We know a good deal about the books that Cable read, but unfortunately in many instances we do not know when he read them. The situation is complicated both by the inexactness of his memory and by certain statements in the biography written by his daughter, Mrs. Biklé. She tells us that in his youth he was forbidden to read novels; and she states that he did not rid himself of his prejudice against fiction until he read George MacDonald's *Annals of a Quiet Neighbourhood* (1866). If there ever was such a prohibition, it must have been withdrawn early, for in his farewell "Drop Shot" column in the New Orleans *Picayune*, July 9, 1871, he defended novel-reading on the ground that fiction often teaches excellent morals. The "Drop Shot" column makes it clear also that Cable knew something about the standard British authors, including the novelists, and—what is surprising—the great New Englanders as well. He had, for instance, learned to love Whittier's poems while still a mere boy. References in the "Drop Shot" column to Swinburne, Taine, Bret Harte, and Mark Twain suggest that he was trying to keep abreast of contemporary literature. It is significant that he read *Scribner's Monthly* from its first number, published in November, 1870. Cable owed less to the writers of the Old South and more to the New Englanders than any of his contemporaries whom I have discussed.

When Fred Lewis Pattee asked Cable about his early reading, the novelist replied, July 21, 1914: "Yes, I read some French literature and believe it had its influence on me, though not so much as Dickens, Thackeray, Poe or Irving. My Frenchmen were Hugo, Merimée and About. I also read many of the old *Relations* of the priest explorers and much other French matter of early historical value." Cable's memory, as I have said, is often inaccurate. I cannot reconcile his inclusion of Thackeray among writers who had influenced his earlier writings with his statement in a letter to Robert Underwood Johnson, April 12, 1880: "As for Thackery [*sic*] I hope to read him this summer. Have never read more than a few lines of his." Cable added that he had no favorite author.

In his letter to Professor Pattee, Cable failed to mention a writer who certainly had an important influence upon his writings—the Louisiana historian, Charles Gayarré. Even as late as 1914 Cable did not care to mention the critic who had attacked *The Grandissimes* with such bitterness. Yet it was Gayarré's history of Louisiana that supplied Cable with both important materials and a point of view which no Louisiana romancer could possibly overlook. Under the heading "Materials for Poems" Cable wrote in the *Picayune* for February 25, 1872:

Louisiana's brief two centuries of history is a rich and profitable mine. Here lie the gems, like those new diamonds in Africa, right on top of the ground. The mines are virgin. Choctaw legends and Spanish adventures may be found overlying each other in profuse abundance. Only one man, if I know aright, has culled among these nuggets. The historian of Louisiana—like that Indian hunter of Potosi who, in chasing after the living things of the ground's surface, unearthed its silver with the upturning of a sapling—in following the annals of colonization, has uncovered the mines of romance. But the half, I am sure, has not been told. . . .

Is it any wonder that when a friend urged him to go to California for local color, Cable replied that he had discovered in New Orleans "a mine of literary materials of which none of us had been aware"?

In the letter to Pattee from which I have quoted Cable wrote: "It would give me much pleasure to tell you just how I came to drop into the writing of romances but I cannot; I just dropt. Money, fame, didactic or controversial impulse I scarcely felt a throb of. I just wanted to do it because it seemed a pity for the stuff to go so to waste." Here again perhaps Cable's memory is not to be trusted. It is evident, however, that the desire to write was strong in him. After he had lost his post as reporter on the *Picayune* because he had refused to attend a theater to report a play, the editor persuaded him to write some historical sketches of New Orleans churches and charities. He was soon absorbed in the history of the city, and it was not long before he was trying his hand at romantic local-color stories laid in ante-bellum Louisiana. Cable's readers do not always remember that *Old Creole Days* and *The Grandissimes* all have their chronological setting in ante-bellum Louisiana, with dates ranging from 1803 to 1850. It was the old regime and not the new that fascinated Cable as it fascinated Harris, Page, and Johnston. Unlike them, however he persisted in introducing into his stories of the Old South a bias and a point of view alien to the period. The result was a loss not only in verisimilitude but eventually in artistic power as well. Fortunately, it was not until after he had written his best books that Cable came to realize how effective a means of promoting reform his fiction could be.

Cable has often been represented as bursting upon the American literary scene like a meteor, but the acclaim he won with *Old Creole Days* and *The Grandissimes* came only after more than a decade of writing, and it was preceded by repeated failures to interest the house which eventually published these books. In 1871 he sent to Scribner, Armstrong and Company a roundup of clippings from his "Drop Shot" column in the *Picayune*. Roger Burlingame, who tells the story in *Of Making Many Books* (1946) remarks that the unknown warehouse clerk who wrote them "came from the dark and very dubious South and his paper was operated by 'Rebels.' Neither he nor it had any standing in the Northeast and New Yorkers had little means of discovering that in New Orleans, Cable was a veritable Alexander Woollcott of his era." After keeping the manuscript for two months, the firm returned it even though Cable had offered to pay the printing costs himself.

Four years later Cable tried again. He sent a group of short stories, some of which had already appeared in *Scribner's Monthly*, and offered to furnish a list of five hundred subscribers. Blair Scribner wrote to Cable: ". . . the *times* are not particularly promising and collections of short stories are almost always unsalable." That was what publishers were telling Poe and Hawthorne thirty years earlier. *Old Creole Days* was not published until 1879, and it was published then only because—without Cable's knowledge —his friend H. H. Boyesen, whom he had not yet met, had guaranteed the publishers against financial loss on the book. Among the titles which Cable had suggested for the book was "*Jadis*." Apparently no one in the publishing house knew the meaning of this appropriate and expressive French word, and Cable had to explain that it means "*once*, in the fairy-tale sense; 'once upon a time,' or 'in old times.' "

Meanwhile Edward King, writing for *Scribner's Monthly* his articles on "The Great South," had visited New Orleans in the winter of 1872–1873 and met Cable. Not long afterwards he sent some of Cable's stories to the editors of the *Monthly*. On July 22, 1873, he wrote to Cable that he had read " 'Sieur George" to the editor: ". . . it trembled in the balance a day, and then Oh ye gods! was accepted! I fancy I can see you waltzing around the office of the venerable cotton brokers, shouting the war-cry of future conquest! Courage!" On August 29 Richard Watson Gilder wrote to King: "He is a genius & ought to know it. If he's a *man*, it won't hurt him to know it, but will spur him up." At the same time Gilder wrote to Cable: "Go to work in good earnest and high faith in yourself—work as religiously as if you had already Bret Harte's reputation—& perhaps you may have one as lasting."

Cable was after Lanier the first important new writer to emerge from what in 1877 Boyesen referred to as "the literary Sahara of the South," and the editors of *Scribner's Monthly*—soon to become the *Century Magazine*— made the most of their discovery. Josiah Gilbert Holland wrote to Cable on September 25, 1880: "You have made a field and are its only occupant." Although Joseph Holt Ingraham, Simms, and others besides Mrs. Stowe had written stories of Louisiana before Cable, it was reserved for him to make. American lovers of romance fully aware of the peculiar richness of the New Orleans background. Nowhere else in America could a novelist have found such picturesque types representing contrasting civilizations. To visitors from the North, New Orleans had the charm of an Old World city; it was more like Paris than New York or San Francisco. It was perhaps the reading of Cable's early stories that in 1877 drew to New Orleans that devotee of the exotic, Lafcadio Hearn.

In their letters to Cable his Northern editor friends gave him much advice and encouragement; and on his visits to New York, especially in 1881, they introduced him to Northern writers. On that visit Cable met Howells, who soon afterwards wrote to John Hay: "By the way, do you read Cable's books? . . . And Cable is himself the loveliest and loyalest ex-rebel that lives." In Hartford Cable met Charles Dudley Warner, Mark Twain, and Harriet Beecher Stowe, with whom, he wrote, he had "a long, & to me delightful, talk about the South." On June 9, 1882, unable to attend a birthday celebration in honor of Mrs. Stowe, Cable wrote a letter which, when it was published, infuriated Southern conservatives like Hayne and Gayarré and displeased even liberals like Henry W. Grady. In that letter Cable said: "To be in New England would be enough for me. I was there once,—a year ago,—and it seemed as though I never had been home till then. . . . I can only send you, Blessings on the day when Harriet Beecher Stowe was born." In Southern eyes that was perilously close to treason. Cable was being taken into the New England camp bag and baggage. By 1884, when he removed to New England, the South was ready to disown him. New Yorkers and New Englanders, on the other hand, had no difficulty in fitting Cable into their literary tradition. On April 12, 1884, when the New York weekly, the *Critic*, printed its list of "Our Forty Immortals," Cable was ranked twelfth among living American writers, two places ahead of Mark Twain.

Like Harris and Page, Cable had found the Northern magazine editors difficult to please. Holland and Gilder were enthusiastic about the stories which they accepted, but most of these seem to have been considerably revised before publication. *Scribner's Monthly* rejected "Dr. Goldenbow," "Hortensia," and "Ba'm o' Gilly," which was apparently never published anywhere. They declined "Bibi" as too horrible, and so did Howells when Cable submitted it to the *Atlantic Monthly*. It finally became the Bras-Coupe episode in *The Grandissimes*. Holland and Gilder also rejected "Posson Jone'," certainly one of Cable's finest stories, presumably because they feared the effect upon their subscribers of an intoxicated Protestant preacher. Eventually Edward King succeeded in placing it in *Appletons' Journal*.

On March 31, 1875, after reading the manuscript of "Madame Délicieuse," in which he had found "a lot of little awkwardnesses," Gilder wrote to Cable: "You bother me. Your conception of character is strong—artistic—your style is bright and witty—your plots are generally good—your field is all your own—and I consider your stories a great acquisition to the monthly—but you lack in the capacity to edit yourself. This is the only thing that makes me fear for your literary future." It was not until later that Gilder discovered that in Cable the artist was being threatened by the propagandist.

For several years, beginning in February, 1877, Cable received many admiring and encouraging letters from the Norwegian-born novelist, Hjalmar Hjorth Boyesen, who in a review of *The Grandissimes* was to name Cable "a literary pioneer . . . the first Southern novelist (unless we count Poe a novelist) who has made a contribution of permanent value to American literature." (Boyesen's sweeping condemnation of the literature of the Old South represents the prevailing Northern view in 1877.) Boyesen had been from the first impressed by "a superb grip on reality" which he thought he saw in Cable's short stories. When Cable outlined for him the plot of *The Grandissimes*, Boyesen replied: "Yours is going to be the kind of novel which the Germans call a 'Kulturroman,' a novel in which the struggling forces of opposing civilizations crystalize & in which they find their enduring monument." Boyesen wanted Cable to give his entire time to writing; but, being himself still a bachelor, he hesitated to advise Cable, who had a mother, a wife, and five children to support, to give up his business connections. He did, however, go so far as to write: "It is time now that the South should be represented in our literature by a genuine author, a genius *par la grace de Dieu*. And you are the man."

Cable considered making literature his profession for many months before he made the final decision. On January 3, 1878, he wrote to Boyesen: "I ought to be writing. A man ought to keep invested the talents of gold that God has given him as well as the talents of silver. I can write better than I can do anything else. Business is distasteful to me. I love literature; I'm no Samson in it, it's true; but so much the more it doesn't follow that I should have my eyes punched out & go to grinding corn in this Philistia of a country." Apparently the editors of *Scribner's Monthly* encouraged him to devote all his time to writing. On December 24, 1879, Cable wrote to Robert Underwood Johnson of the *Scribner's Monthly* staff: "Literature, as a profession, may be nearer to me now than ever before & I want your people to be ready to say what my expectations may reasonably be in that direction." It was not, however, until October 8, 1881, that after another visit to the North, he wrote to Howells: " 'The last link is broken'—I have resigned from my secretaryship in the cotton exchange and closed up my office. Nothing now for offense or defense but my grey goose quill!" When Roswell Smith of the Scribner firm heard the news, he wrote to Cable: "I confess I look with apprehension on your giving up your salaried position. Literary work is too precarious and the best work pays too little.—I do not see how you can possibly live by your pen." Cable, however, was soon to discover that the lecture platform offered a sure means of supplementing what he could earn by writing.

Now that he was free to write a second novel, Cable made what he later called "an odd digression" from the field of belles-lettres. For a creative writer of Cable's talents it was a very odd digression indeed. He accepted a commission from a Federal agency to help George E. Waring prepare a historical report, which in condensed form was published in Washington as *History and Present Condition of New Orleans* (1881). He also accepted a commission from the Superintendent of the Census to make a study of the Acadians in Louisiana. The editors of the *Century*, disappointed that he seemed to be abandoning fiction, suggested that he use the materials to make a book. They published it serially in the magazine in 1883, and the next year it appeared as *The Creoles of Louisiana*. The editors of the *Century*, however, had expressed their thorough dissatisfaction with the manuscript as Cable first submitted it, and for a time he considered severing his connection with the magazine. Cable was now less interested in writing artistic fiction than in using his pen to promote the various reforms which interested him. When Gilder read the manuscript of "Bread," which was eventually published as *Dr. Sevier* (1884), he wrote to Cable, February 1, 1882:

To me it is the least good work you have ever done. And yet it has in it some of your best work, and it is free from your greatest fault—namely confusion. . . . It seems to me that in the present story (if it is a story) your heart has got the better of your head. . . . The reader feels that it is a "put up job";— that the characters are dragged from misery to misery in order that the writer can preach his theories through them. . . . You have turned your mind lately so completely into philanthropical work that for the time being you have lost your sense of art.

The deterioration of the artist in Cable had already progressed very far indeed. He was to write nothing during the remaining forty-odd years of his life as good as "Madame Delphine" (1881).

Meanwhile Cable had discovered that lecturing, singing Creole songs, and reading his stories from the platform were more profitable and less laborious than writing and rewriting stories which must pass the gauntlet of editor and publisher. He gave his first public address at the University of Mississippi in June, 1882. "Literature in the Southern States" was a vigorous plea for a national point of view. "We have been," he said, "already too long a unique people. Let us search provincialism out of the land. . . ." He did not object to the author's choosing Southern subjects. "Only," he insisted, "let them be written to and for the whole nation. . . ." Joel Chandler Harris had expressed much the same view in the Atlanta *Constitution* a year earlier, and Lanier had before 1875 come to regard himself as a national rather than as a sectional poet. The accounts of Cable's address printed in Southern newspapers suggest that the audience was pleased with it and Cable's letters give one a similar impression; but some of the men who heard Cable speak told Professor David H. Bishop years later of a disturbing incident which took place in Oxford. Most of the audience, it seems, were unable to hear what Cable was saying, and so the young men and women began talking to one another just as the young people in Charlottesville six years earlier had talked while Emerson was speaking. Sitting on the speakers' platform was the Reverend C. K. Marshall, who had delivered the commencement sermon the day before. He was so displeased by what Cable had said that, without asking the permission of the presiding officer, he leaped to his feet and in a booming voice told the audience what Cable had said and then and there denounced as heretical the opinions which Cable had expressed.

In March of the next year, while lecturing at the Johns Hopkins University in Baltimore, Cable discovered how effective his own stories were when he read them aloud to a sympathetic audience. In 1884 on an invitation from Mark Twain he joined forces with the great humorist in what in a letter to his wife Cable once facetiously referred to as "the old highway-robbery business." It has been generally supposed that Cable was by much the less popular member of the team; but Fred W. Lorch, who in 1952 retold the story of the 1884–1885 tour from the abundant newspaper accounts, reached a different conclusion. By 1884 Cable had become an accomplished platform performer, and he was as well known to his audiences as Mark Twain. He was also a controversial figure whom audiences were eager to see and hear. In *Dr. Sevier*, published in September, 1884, he had boldly stated that in the Civil War the cause of the North was a "just" one. "The Freedman's Case in Equity," which appeared in the *Century* in January, 1885, provoked a storm of protest from the South. When Cable in June, 1884, had delivered a commencement address at the University of Alabama, the local press for the first time, he says, "met my utterances entirely without commendation." Cable was hoping "that, behind all the fierce conservatism of a noisier element there was a silent South needing to be urged to speak and act." In Southern eyes, however, what Cable had done was to violate the Compromise of 1877, by which Southerners understood that the North would not again interfere with the treatment of Negroes in the South. Northern indifference to the Negro question irritated Cable also, and so he spoke out boldly. The South interpreted his demand for "civil equality" as a demand for "social equality," perhaps even for erasing the color line completely, and labeled him an "Abolitionist" and a "Southern Yankee." He was at the same time, as I have noted, being thoroughly assimilated into the New York–New England literary tradition as a worthy successor to Garrison, Channing, Emerson, Lowell, Whittier, and Harriet Beecher Stowe. Whittier, for example, said to Cable in November, 1883: "I have read all thy stories, and I like them very much. Thee hast found an untrodden field of romance in New Orleans, and I think thee a writer whom we have so long waited to see come up in the South."

The lecture tour was a financial success for both members of the team, but Mark Twain's close association with Cable left him with mixed feelings of admiration and exasperation. Cable had irritated him by reading the Bible aloud to him and by refusing to travel by public conveyances on Sundays. As the tour ended, Mark Twain wrote to Howells that his association with Cable had taught him that "Cable's gifts of mind are greater and higher than I suspected." But, he added: "You will never, never know . . . how loathsome a thing the Christian religion can be made until you come to know and study Cable daily and hourly. Mind you I like him; he is pleasant company; I rage and swear at him sometimes, but we do not quarrel; we get along mighty happily together; but in him and his person I have learned to hate all religions." Mark Twain once in his exasperation is said to have called Cable a "Christ-besprinkled, psalm-singing Presbyterian."

Even Southern liberals like Henry W. Grady found altogether unacceptable the views of the Negro question which Cable was freely expressing in Northern and not Southern periodicals. Conservatives like Hayne and Gayarré regarded him as a traitor to the South. Cable, as I have suggested, owed much to Gayarré's historical studies of Louisiana; and it was a debt which he never adequately acknowledged anywhere in print. In Northern eyes it was now the author of *The Creoles of Louisiana* and not Gayarré who was the historian of Louisiana. It was to be Cable and not Gayarré who was asked to write the article on New Orleans for the *Encyclopaedia Britannica*. Is it any wonder that the penniless and exasperated Gayarré, trying with little success to live by his pen, wrote in a newspaper article which fell under Cable's eyes: "Why wait . . . until Mr. Cable has copied my statements and republished them as his own?" Cable in fact had indicated his indebtedness to Gayarré in numerous footnotes in his *History and Present Condition of New Orleans*, but the government editor had deleted them. Yet if Cable had really cared to indicate his indebtedness to the historian, he could have expressed it in one or another of his various books and articles.

"The Freedman's Case in Equity" moved Gayarré to reply in the New Orleans *Times-Democrat* in January, 1885. Cable, he thought, was trying to erase the color line completely. He wrote: "Mr. Cable seems to wish to bring together, by every possible means, the blacks and whites in the most familiar and closest friction everywhere, in every imaginable place of resort, save the private parlor and the private bed-chamber, into which, for the present, a disagreeable intrusion may not be permitted. . . ." Gayarré admitted that Cable had "talent" and suggested that one perhaps might admire him "if he had the modesty to assume a less lofty tone of moral and intellectual superiority in his dictations over a vast number of his fellow-citizens, whom, in the face of the world, without the least hesitation and without the least sign of regret, he proclaims as guilty of the basest malignancy, the most systematic tyranny, and the most drivelling imbecility." In Cable's pleas for reform Gayarré detected the same tone of righteous Puritan superiority that had seemed so obnoxious in *Uncle Tom's Cabin*. Of his purpose in writing *The Grandissimes* Cable has said: "I meant to make 'The Grandissimes' as truly a political work as it has ever been called. . . . My friends and kindred looked on with disapproval and dismay, and said all they could to restrain me. 'Why wantonly offend thousands of your own people?' But I did not intend to offend."

On April 25, 1885, Gayarré delivered at Tulane University a lecture, *The Creoles of History and the Creoles of Romance*, in which he attacked Cable's various insinuations that the Creoles had African blood in their veins. Of Cable's fiction Gayarré seems to have read only, and not very carefully, *The Grandissimes*. Cable had asked him to review this book, but Gayarré had declined, he states, because its author could not name two Creole families with whom he was intimately acquainted. In his lecture Gayarré attacked Cable's assertion that ". . . the pilgrim fathers of the Mississippi Delta were taking wives and moot wives from the ill specimens of three races." In his indignation Gayarré had forgotten that he himself had written of "the promiscuous herd of thieves, prostitutes, vagabonds, and all sorts of wretches of bad fame who had been swept together, to be transported to Louisiana."

The Creoles looked to Paris and not to London or New York. Their culture was French. American literature as it came to them from the Northern states seemed prudish; it lacked color and warmth. For all of Cable's reading in French literature, his fundamental aims were very un-French. The sex morals of the Creoles had a continental freedom repugnant to Cable, and they resented his pictures of quadroon balls, which were in fact far from being the romantic affairs that Cable made of them. In the eyes of the proud and sensitive Creoles the *"Américains,"* especially those of the merchant class to which Cable belonged, were vulgar outsiders, pushing and ill-bred. The Creoles understood better the aristocratic Southern planter.

To be portrayed unsympathetically by an outsider, by a "Southern Yankee," was intolerable. As Cable himself said, "A Creole never forgives a public mention." The Creoles' resentment mounted with the publication of each new book by Cable, for, as they rightly saw, he portrayed them less and less favorably in each new story. "Madame Delphine" was peculiarly offensive. In that story a Negro woman of the quadroon caste manages to get her daughter, who is seven-eighths white, across the color line. When in 1883 this story was included in a new edition of *Old Creole Days,* the Louisianians were certain that in the eyes of Cable and his Yankee readers the proud Creoles had Negro blood in their veins. This insinuation was even harder to bear than Cable's representing men who prided themselves on their excellent French as speaking broken English. It is eighty-one years since Cable's first story appeared in *Scribner's Monthly,* but there are still Creoles who have not forgiven Cable.

Louisiana readers saw in *The Grandissimes* satiric thrusts which were likely to escape the Northern reader. In that book, for example, Cable ridicules the Creoles' "ancestral, perennial rebellion against common sense" and again: "Those Creoles have such a shocking way of filing their family relics and records in ratholes." The Creole men, as Cable paints them, are proud, vain, ignorant, boastful, quarrelsome, fond of gambling and of quadroon mistresses. His Creole women, on the other hand, are beautiful, fascinating, amiable, and vivacious. When James Barrie was in New Orleans in 1896, several Creole ladies warned him against accepting Cable's account of the Creoles as accurate. Barrie's reply was that he "supposed it must be so, no ladies in the flesh could be quite so delicious as the Creole ladies of Mr. Cable's imagination." There was in the author of *Old Creole Days* a certain susceptibility to the voluptuous such as one feels in the sage and serious Spenser's description of the Bower of Bliss in *The Faerie Queene.*

In July, 1884, the Cables left New Orleans for a long stay in Simsbury, Connecticut. The next year they settled permanently in Northampton, Massachusetts. The reasons that Cable gave for leaving Louisiana were his wife's poor health, the need to be closer to editors, publishers, and the audiences to whom he lectured and read his stories. He desired also, he says, to study American life in other sections. He never admitted that Southern hostility, which had become acute in 1884, had anything to do with his change of residence, but one wonders. On January 24, 1880, he had written to Robert Underwood Johnson: "I see no good reason why I should leave Louisiana; why should I? What advantage is supposeable?" In his later years Cable was only at long intervals to revisit New Orleans.

In New England Cable gave much of his time to the promotion of Home-Culture Clubs and to teaching Sunday School classes. In 1891 he published *The Busy Man's Bible*. In later life he modified his stern religious creed much as Lanier had done some years earlier. He also modified his theory of the function of the novel. In April, 1900, he wrote to Waitman Barbe: "A novel's most obvious aim—the aim which should never for a moment be evidently directed by any other purpose—should be to entertain, not to inform." It cannot be said, however, that the adoption of his new theory resulted in the writing of better novels.

Cable's new theory of the function of fiction seems to have come during the writing of *John March, Southerner* (1894). When in August, 1890, Gilder read the manuscript of that novel, he is said to have wrung his hands in despair. He had found it "a tract, not a story." He had been hoping that Cable could work off his preoccupation with reform in addresses and essays and keep his novels free from propaganda. Even after Cable had worked hard to meet Gilder's criticisms, the editor found in it "less charm" than in any of Cable's earlier stories. *John March* did not seem to him "to have its origin in a deep sense of art."

In January, 1894, Cable published in the *North American Review* "After-Thoughts of a Story-Teller," which contains the best statement of his later views of the function of the novel. In concluding the article, he suggested the ideal he thought he had aimed at in *John March, Southerner:* "A pleasing story of the heroic in imagined lives; truth of the passions and affections, not advocated, but portrayed; a book with every page good prose, and each of its chapters, as a chapter, good poetry; a book able to keep you—not me, merely—always emotionally interested, and leave you profited; a story written for all readers, to all, and at none. I should call that a good novel, but alas!—" Alas, indeed! Cable had come much closer to that ideal when he wrote *Old Creole Days. John March*, though it contains some shrewd criticism of Southern life, is not a good novel. It is the work of a reformer rather than of an artist. Cable, moreover, had made the mistake of forsaking Louisiana and placing his setting in a part of the rural South that he did not know intimately.

In "After-Thoughts of a Story-Teller" Cable, who had won fame as the local colorist of Creole Louisiana, expressed his new theory that the novelist's choice of a setting for his story is unimportant. "Truth is," he said, "the only discovery worth making in this direction is not a new field of romance with geographical or chronological boundaries, but the fact that the field of romance is wherever man is, and its day every day; that wherever in place or time there is room—and where in the habitable earth is there not?—for wars of the heart against environment, circumstance, and its own treasons, there is the story-teller's field; and though old as Nineveh or as hard trodden as Paris, it will be, to his readers, just as fresh or stale, as small or great, as his individual genius, and no more." In the abstract Cable's theory is admirable, and it is admirably expressed, for he still had the gift of style. But what Cable and so many of the local colorists of his time failed to see was that though the materials of romance are everywhere to be found, the individual novelist can rarely portray effectively anything but the life he has intimately known in his formative years. As a writer of fiction Cable was never completely at home anywhere except in his native Louisiana.

Cable's deterioration as an artist, which so greatly disturbed the editors of the *Century*, has troubled every critic who has discussed his work. It has been suggested that his loss of creative power was due to his removal from the region which he knew best, but Cable's best books had all been written three years before he removed to New England. They had all been written in fact by the time he was free to devote himself entirely to literature. Cable's decline in power disturbed William Malone Baskervill, who in his *Southern Writers* (1897) placed Cable in "the class of thoroughgoing men, actuated by thoroughgoing logic, lovers of abstract truth and perfect ideals, and it was his lot to be born among a people who by the necessities of their situation were controlled by expedience. They were compelled to adopt an illogical but practical compromise between two extremes which were logical but not practical." This cast of mind explained to Baskervill why Cable gave "a prejudiced, incorrect, unjust picture of Southern life, character, and situation. This domination of one idea," Baskervill concluded, "has vitiated the most exquisite literary and artistic gifts that any American writer of fiction, with possibly one exception, has been endowed [with] since Hawthorne. . . ." Baskervill, who would probably have approved of Cable's later theory of the function of fiction, did not live to read the later novels.

Howells, writing in *Harper's Magazine* in October, 1888, took another view: "It is the conscience of Mr. Cable that gives final value to all he does." The Southern condemnation of Cable, he thought, was "narrow-minded,

the censure of a people who would rather be flattered than appreciated."
A somewhat similar view has been expressed much more recently by Cable's
Swedish biographer, Kjell Ekström, who maintains that Cable's deterioration as a novelist was due to the fact that "being no longer fired with a
reformatory zeal, he was unable to create really moving literature." The
difficulty with Ekström's theory and those of other critics is that it does
not explain the decline in the quality of Cable's work in the years 1882–
1894, when he was still deeply concerned with reforms. A similar ·decline
in artistic power is seen in nearly all of Cable's local-color contemporaries.
In nearly every instance the writer's first book is his best, and it is a book
of short stories rather than a novel. Few of them indeed wrote novels of
any distinction. Was Van Wyck Brooks right when in "The Literary Life
in America" (1922) he maintained that there is something in the American
environment which prevents the writer from developing his full poten-
tialities?

Whatever be the explanation of Cable's decline, it seems clear that the
delicate balance between the love of beauty and the desire to make over
the world which one finds in *Old Creole Days* is less in evidence in *The
Grandissimes* and has practically disappeared in *John March, Southerner.*
Cable's best work was done before his attitude toward the Southern problem had hardened into a fixed creed. His best work was done while he was
young, ambitious, and enthusiastic and while he was willing to be guided
by the editors of *Scribner's Monthly*, whose sense of literary form was
keener than his. His first two books angered the Creoles, but other Southerners were enthusiastic about them. After he had published "The Freedman's Case in Equity" in January, 1885, the South practically disowned
him. I believe that Southern condemnation had a profounder effect upon
Cable than he was ever willing to admit. He was no longer one of his own
people, and the life of the slaveholding South had little attraction for him.
By the time he had lost his deep concern with the Southern problem and
had altered his theory of fiction, the literary fashion had shifted away from
romantic local-color stories of the Old South. He was by training a romancer
and not a realist, and he was unable to write successful realistic studies of
contemporary American life in the manner of Howells. The time for new
stories like those in *Old Creole Days* was long past. I do not wish, however,
to be understood as regarding Cable's later novels—which are not discussed
here—as uninteresting or altogether unimportant.

When Richard Watson Gilder visited New Orleans in 1885, he asked
the youthful Grace King, the intimate friend of Gayarré, to explain to him

"the inimical stand taken by the people of New Orleans against Cable and his works." "I hastened to enlighten him," she wrote in her autobiography, "to the effect that Cable proclaimed his preference for colored people over white and assumed the inevitable superiority . . . of the quadroons over the Creoles. . . ." The people of New Orleans, she added, felt that Cable had "stabbed the city in the back . . . in a dastardly way to please the Northern press." Gilder listened "with icy indifference" and remarked: "Why, if Cable is so false to you, why do not some of you write better?" Grace King took this as a challenge and the very next day she began her first novel, *Monsieur Motte* (1888).

Many of the Creoles, as I have said, never forgave Cable; indeed, some have not forgiven him even today. Elsewhere in the South, however, the antipathy to Cable was disappearing long before he died in 1925. Grace King, who met Cable in New Orleans about five years before he died, came to understand him at last. This is the story as she told it to an interviewer from the Boston *Transcript*:

> I understand him now. I would say he wrote too well about the Creoles. He wanted to read something of his at a meeting of our Historical Club. Some of the members objected, but we finally made arrangements. He captured the audience. Everybody rushed up and shook hands with him. Many of us never dreamed the day would come when we would shake hands with Cable. He told us a little story of a Confederate who served in the war and was wounded. It was beautifully written and really the most compelling little incident I have ever heard. The hall was packed. When he finished everybody stood up, and I never heard such applause. I am glad that at last he got that compliment from New Orleans. He deserved it, not only as tribute to his genius, but as compensation for the way we had treated him. I am glad. He is an old man, very picturesque, very sad, with beautiful manners.[45]

Before Cable's death in 1925 Ellen Glasgow, Mary Johnston, and James Branch Cabell had begun to follow his example and were attacking Southern traditions in literature and in life with a freedom which among the writers of the New South only Cable had dared to claim. They were to be quickly followed by T. S. Stribling, Paul Green, Julia Peterkin, Erskine Caldwell, William Faulkner, and others who would seem to conservative Southerners to belong to the tradition of Cable and Mrs. Stowe rather than that of Thomas Nelson Page and Grace King. Cable was an important literary pioneer. His attack upon Southern conservatism hastened the time when

---

[45] Robert Tallant, *The Romantic New Orleanians* (1950), pp. 303–304. There were few Creoles in Cable's audience.

Southern writers would be able to describe the life of their region with the freedom which had prevailed in the days of George Tucker, Jefferson, and Madison.

14
Mark Twain

IT WAS AS a humorist from the Far West of Bret Harte that Samuel Langhorne Clemens (1835–1910) won his early reputation, and ever since that time critics and literary historians, with some important exceptions, have treated him as a product of the Western frontier. And yet it was not until he was twenty-six years old that—after a few weeks as a Confederate soldier—he went to Nevada and for the first time saw the frontier. He did not live in the South after 1861, but his three best books—*Tom Sawyer*, *Life on the Mississippi*, and *Huckleberry Finn*—all deal with life in the Old South. It is no mere coincidence that these books appeared at the time when the South was becoming the most popular background in fiction. It was while living in the South that Mark Twain formed his literary taste and made his earliest experiments in writing. It was there, too, that he learned the art of the storyteller from men with whom storytelling was a favorite pastime. He kept his "Southern drawl" to the end of his life. He read the sketches of the old Southern humorists, and traces of their methods can be found even in his masterpiece, *Huckleberry Finn*. Like Cable, Page, and Harris, he owed much to the literary advice and encouragement of Northern editors and writers, notably William Dean Howells, and like them he found his best materials in the vanished life of the Old South.

In his later years Mark Twain rarely referred to himself as a Southerner, and Howells, who knew him only after he had left the South and the West, described him in *My Mark Twain* as "the most desouthernized Southerner I ever knew." [46] What Howells had in mind was Mark Twain's complete acceptance of the Northern interpretation of the meaning of the Civil War and emancipation. In this respect Mark Twain was a not uncommon type: the Southerner who after the war had gone North or West and discovered that he was no longer primarily a Virginian or a Missourian but an American. Southerners who lived in the North, like Walter Hines Page and

[46] There is some confusion in Howells' use of geographical terms. In the sentence quoted above he wrote: "The part of him that was Western in his Southwestern origin he kept to the end . . ." (p. 35). Elsewhere in *My Mark Twain*, however, he suggests that what is called "American humor" is in reality "of Southern origin" (p. 171).

Woodrow Wilson, soon found themselves modifying their political opinions although other Southern characteristics remained with them to the end. The influence of Mark Twain's years in the South was deep and lasting. It is, I think, no mere coincidence that his attitude toward women resembles that which I have noted in the writings of Edward Coote Pinkney, Richard Henry Wilde, Poe, Lanier, and Thomas Nelson Page. It is seen in his almost worshipful attitude toward his wife and in his romantic adoration of Joan of Arc. His *Personal Recollections of Joan of Arc*, says Albert Bigelow Paine, was the only one of his books that he considered good enough to dedicate to Olivia Clemens.

In 1835, when Mark Twain was born, the Southern and Northern states along the Mississippi River had more in common with one another than they had with any of the states on the Atlantic seaboard. In the quarter of a century that followed, however, the states of the Old Northwest aligned themselves with the Northeast while the slaveholding states from Missouri southward made common cause with the Southeast. Missouri was a slave state, and most of its professional and political leaders came from Virginia, Kentucky, and Tennessee. In the Missouri of Mark Twain's youth the social life was Southern rather than Western, but it had more in common with Mississippi and Arkansas than it had with Tidewater Virginia or Low-Country South Carolina. Missouri was also a border state, and northern Missouri, where Mark Twain lived, was almost surrounded by free states. The outbreak of the war found the state hopelessly divided in its allegiance. After a brief experience as a Confederate militiaman, Mark Twain finally decided to go West with his brother Orion, who, living in Iowa, had taken the Northern side.

Hannibal, Missouri, where Mark Twain grew up, was a Southern town but not exactly the stagnant, sleepy little town described in a famous chapter in *Life on the Mississippi*. The frontier had passed westward before he was born, and Southerners of the upper class had moved in. They not only held the chief offices, but they took the initiative in establishing schools and libraries. The river was a vital connecting link with the outside world, and it kept Hannibal from the isolation and provincialism of inland Southern towns. Socially, the town seems to have been dominated by upper-class Virginians, the class to which by birth and breeding the novelist's father belonged.

"In Missouri," wrote Mark Twain in *Pudd'nhead Wilson*, "a recognized superiority attached to any person who hailed from Old Virginia; and this superiority was exalted to supremacy when a person of such nativity could also prove descent from the First Families of that great commonwealth."

His description of "the recognized first citizen of Dawson's Landing" might almost pass for a description of his own father:

The chief citizen was York Leicester Driscoll, about forty years old, judge of the county court. He was very proud of his old Virginian ancestry, and in his hospitalities and his rather formal and stately manners he kept up its traditions. He was fine and just and generous. To be a gentleman without stain or blemish —was his only religion, and to it he was always faithful. He was respected, esteemed, and beloved by all the community.

Fortunately we have brief glimpses of the little town of Hannibal as seen through the eyes of a Virginian who was living in Hannibal in the years 1849–1852. In the Duke University Library there are some letters—not used by any of Mark Twain's biographers—from William M. Cooke, a lawyer of good Virginia family who had studied at the University of Virginia. He came to Hannibal from St. Louis in the spring of 1849 two years after the death of Mark Twain's father. In August of the preceding year he had written to his Virginia friend, John Rutherfoord: "If I were a rich man I would, as you know, prefer living a lazy, luxurious life in old Virginia where a man may sometimes find gentlemen, but as a poor man I vastly prefer to live here." During his stay in Hannibal Cooke wrote nine letters to Rutherfoord. The letters are largely concerned with national and Virginia politics, but they give us interesting sidelights on Hannibal. At first Cooke was pleased with his new location, but later he was to call Hannibal "a dull Western town where you would witness every day the same monstrous scarcity of [law] business. . . ." On August 2, 1849, he wrote a brief description of Hannibal, which he said had a population of about three thousand and was second only to St. Louis among Missouri towns.

Its chief mercantile business is beef & pork packing, chief law-business before the *justices of the peace* [Mark Twain's father had held such an office], and chief social occupation gossiping. The country around Hannibal is pretty, and the Circuit on which I practice pleasant and, I think, profitable. The society of Hannibal is, of course, very limited, but is about as good as is generally found in a village. We hope to make it a great place by connecting it with St Joseph on the Missouri river by means of a rail-road, which would then throw into our town all the products & travel of the Platte country which is the richest in the State.

In the course of time Cooke acquired a house which he thought as comfortable as any in the town. He was fond of grouse-shooting, but he would not play cards for either pleasure or money. In 1851 he was elected Judge of the Hannibal Court of Common Pleas, but he resented the "low & vulgar demagoguism" involved in political life in Missouri and, he feared, in Virginia as well. It was difficult, he had learned, to be at once a gentleman and a candidate for office. "The fact is," he wrote, "the West is no place for a gentleman of sensibility. Sensibility is not current here: men ring it on the counter & reject it as counterfeit." In another letter he wrote: "Indeed here all men are equal, and such a thing as a distinct class of ladies & gentlemen has no existence. The power is usually in the hands of the hog-killers, carpenters, stable-men, & negro-buyers: and to pander to the wishes or caprices of a negro-buyer! pah! my gorge rises at the very thought of it!"

As a Virginia gentleman of the class to which Cooke belonged, that unsuccessful lawyer, John Marshall Clemens, must have felt himself somewhat degraded when he opened a store. He was in no position to match the hospitalities of the Howards and the Driscolls. When Mark Twain's older brother Orion became a printer's apprentice—Sam was to become one a few years later—the youth regarded it as a step downward, for printing was a "trade." As the son of a gentleman and a prospective heir of land in Tennessee, he felt that he was entitled to a profession like his father's.

John Marshall Clemens, who died when Sam was twelve years old, was a Virginian of the slaveholding class. His father, Samuel Clemens, is described as "a man of culture and literary taste." That father died when John Clemens was seven. His mother moved with her children to Kentucky and married again. In 1823 John Clemens, now a young lawyer, married the attractive Jane Lampton, who belonged to a good Kentucky family. He was never a very successful lawyer, and he moved from place to place until he settled in the little town of Florida, Missouri, where Mark Twain was born in 1835. In 1839 John Clemens made his last move when he came to Hannibal. There he was active in community enterprises, including the establishment of a public library. His religious views—he is said to have been an agnostic, like his son—were probably a survival from the Deistic beliefs common among Virginia planters at the time of his birth. Not long before he died, he lost nearly everything he owned because, it is said, he had endorsed a note for a large amount of money for one Ira Stout, who defaulted and left John Clemens to pay. It was just such overgenerous willingness to endorse notes for one another that ruined scores of Virginians in Alabama and Mississippi when the flush times came to an end in 1837. John Marshall Clemens, however, to the last held on to his thousands of untilled acres in East Tennessee, confident that some day they would make his children rich.

Jane Lampton is described as beautiful, fond of dancing, an expert horsewoman, witty, possessing the Southern drawl and a manner of telling a story much like that of her famous son. She married John Clemens on the rebound after a lover's quarrel with a Kentucky doctor to whom she was engaged. Her life was a hard one, wandering from place to place with an ever-increasing family and always disappointed in the hope of finding the home to which she felt her social position entitled her. It is small wonder that she turned increasingly to the stern Presbyterian doctrines which had so strong a hold upon the ante-bellum South. Her sense of humor and her large human sympathies, however, never deserted her. In his later life Mark Twain was perhaps more of a skeptic than his father had been, but he never completely escaped from the conscientious scruples of his mother's religion. "Into his humor," writes Edgar M. Branch, "went the compassion of Jane Clemens, the clearsighted integrity of John Marshall Clemens, and the moral conviction and indignation of both."

The printer's shop—so Lincoln is supposed to have said—is "the poor man's college." Like Howells and Whitman and Harris, Mark Twain served his time as typesetter and finally emerged into literature through the gateway of journalism. Few of the best writers of his generation were college-bred, like the great New Englanders who had attended Harvard and Bowdoin. Mark Twain often insisted that he "didn't know anything about books," but there is plenty of evidence that he read widely if somewhat unsystematically. His sister Pamela and his brothers Orion and Henry were inveterate readers. He had read the Bible through by the time he was fifteen. Books and newspapers and magazines came to the printing office where he worked, and the newspapers of those days carried more literary materials than is customary now. There were five newspapers in Hannibal in the early fifties and they carried advertisements of no less than four bookstores.

One day on his way home from the printing office Mark Twain picked up a stray page torn from a book on Joan of Arc. Reading it aroused in him a sympathy for the persecuted and a hatred of tyranny and treachery. It also led him to the serious reading of history and biography. His reading during his years in the South did not differ markedly from what any young Southerner of his class might have read. His father is said to have read *The Song of Hiawatha*, but I find little evidence that Mark Twain in his earlier years was reading the classic New Englanders. Even when he was living in New England he seems to have cared as little for them, except Dr. Holmes, as they cared for him. Among the authors he is known to have read are Poe, Paine, Goldsmith, Swift, Shakespeare, Milton, Dickens, Cervantes, and Rabelais. His taste in fiction apparently led him to some of the eighteenth-century British novelists, whose pictures of life were not hampered by Victorian reticence and prudery. In mature life he had many literary aversions. He did not care for Scott, Cooper, Jane Austen, or Henry James. In his early years he read many of the sketches of the Southern humorists and some of the Northern as well, but the former were closer to the humorous stories which he heard told up and down the Mississippi River.

During the eight years beginning in 1853 Mark Twain saw much of American life, first as a wandering printer and later as a river pilot. He worked in New York, Philadelphia, Keokuk, Cincinnati, and St. Louis. The four years immediately preceding the outbreak of war were, he thought, the happiest of his life: he was a pilot on a Mississippi River steamboat. Mark Twain's Southern period is less important for the writing he did than it is for the accumulation of the rich and varied experiences essential to the future novelist. "So many writers, Conrad for instance," wrote Scott Fitzgerald, "have been aided by being brought up in a métier utterly unrelated to literature. It gives abundance of material and, more important, an attitude from which to view the world. So much writing nowadays suffers both from lack of an attitude and from sheer lack of any material, save what is accumulated in a purely social life." In a fragment of a letter written in 1891 Mark Twain noted that so far as "personal experience" counted, he was exceptionally well equipped for writing novels. He once remarked of his four years as a pilot: "In that brief, sharp schooling I got personally and familiarly acquainted with all the different types of human nature that are to be found in fiction, biography, or history." It was a man's world, however, and one may doubt whether in those years Mark Twain had the good fortune to know intimately many women of the better class. Certainly there are few of them in his books.

The outbreak of war brought an end to piloting, and soon Samuel Clemens went to Nevada, where the Civil War looked not so much like the greatest event in American history as an unfortunate interruption in the development of the Far West. It was not until later that Mark Twain understood the significance of this epoch in American history. In Chapter XVIII of *The Gilded Age* (1873) we read: "The eight years from 1860 to 1868 uprooted institutions that were centuries old, changed the politics of a people, transformed the social life of half the country, and wrought so profoundly upon the entire national character that the influence cannot be measured short of two or three generations." The passage appears in a chapter attributed to Mark Twain's collaborator, Charles Dudley Warner, but presumably it represented Mark's own thinking and experience. What the war meant to the Lower South he was to see for himself when in 1882 he returned for a journey down the Mississippi River.

In Nevada Mark Twain tried mining, hoping to make his fortune, returned to journalism and worked with other talented journalists and humorists, spent some time in California, where Bret Harte contributed something to his training as a writer, visited the Hawaiian Islands, returned as a humorous lecturer, and then as author of the great comic hit, "The Celebrated Jumping Frog of Calaveras County," came East as a popular lecturer and literary comedian.

Mark Twain had not escaped the Southern humorist tradition by going West. "The Jumping Frog" story, which he might have heard from Negro workers on the Louisiana levees, was written in the manner of the tall tales of the Old Southwest. The narrative technique which he employed had been developed by George W. Harris, Thomas Bangs Thorpe, and other Southern humorists. Mark Twain in a letter to his mother and sister referred to the story as a "villainous backwoods sketch," and he was no more proud of it than Bret Harte was of "The Heathen Chinee." Nevertheless, in this sketch, written out at the request of "Artemus Ward," he was beginning to find himself as a writer. There was nothing bookish or artificial about the language he employed, and there was no conscious effort to be literary. He was on his way to becoming a master of American colloquial English. In an illuminating essay, "How to Tell a Story," he was to write with some exaggeration: "The art of telling a humorous story—understand, I mean by word of mouth, not print—was created in America, and has remained at home." He was as yet, however, a talker rather than a writer; he was comparatively undisciplined; and he often failed to recognize the vast difference between his best writing and his worst. Always, partly as a result of his playing the part of the literary comedian so long, he was likely to yield to the temptation to burlesque or pull off a hoax rather than write a story that rings true.

Mark Twain came East as a Western humorist and found himself acceptable as a literary comedian. Had he posed as a Southerner, he would probably have found his Northern audiences as unresponsive as George W. Bagby had found his when he gave a humorous lecture in New York on the Virginia Negro. In 1870 he married Olivia Langdon, who belonged to a well-to-do family in Elmira, New York. Elmira society regarded him as a crude Western comedian, not acceptable in the best social circles. Jervis Langdon, Olivia's father, however, saw something better in him. After all, was he not a Southerner of good family rather than a crude specimen of the Wild West? Mark Twain still thought of himself as a humorist and a newspaperman, but Olivia Langdon saw in him a gentleman and a potential writer of something better than the "Jumping Frog" story or *Innocents*

Abroad. So also did William Dean Howells, who was to do far more for him as a writer than Bret Harte or Mrs. Fairbanks had done. His service to Mark Twain was similar to what the editors of *Scribner's Monthly* were doing for Cable, Harris, and Page, but it went beyond that. Howells praised his books and made bold to publish his writings in the *Atlantic Monthly* even though the great New Englanders made little of him either as a man or as an author. Howells invited him to speak at the Whittier birthday dinner of 1877, and Mark Twain, yielding to the temptation to burlesque, played the part of the Western humorist with disastrous results. His reputation as a humorist insured a large sale for his books, but it was something of a handicap when he turned to more serious writing, as he did in *The Prince and the Pauper* (1882). As his daughters grew up, they—and he— came to resent his reputation as merely that of "a maker of funny speeches" and a writer of humorous books.[47]

Before his marriage in 1870 Mark Twain had done comparatively little with the rich materials which his varied life had given him. He was slow to realize that his best asset was the Southern life he had known in his youth. If it occurred to him to write a book about those years, he probably thought that neither Mrs. Clemens, Howells, nor his Northern readers would welcome a romance dealing with any portion of the late Confederacy. As an artist Mark Twain was always, in the words of Dixon Wecter, "a kind of pocket miner, stumbling like fortune's darling upon native ore of incredible richness and exploiting it with effortless skill—but often gleefully mistaking fool's gold for the genuine article, or lavishing his strength upon historical diggings long since played out." Too frequently he forgot the wise words he wrote in "What Paul Bourget Thinks of Us." "Almost the whole capital of the novelist," he said, "is the slow accumulation of *un*conscious observation—absorption." The novelist must acquire his knowledge of a people by "years and years of intercourse with the life concerned; of living it, indeed; sharing personally in its shames and prides, its joys and griefs, its loves and hates, its prosperities and reverses, its shows and shabbinesses, its deep patriotisms, its whirlwinds of political passion, its adorations. . . ." It was thus that Mark Twain had absorbed the life of the Mississippi River country. "Bret Harte," he said, "got his California and Californians by unconscious absorption, and put both of them into his tales alive. But when he came from the Pacific to the Atlantic and tried to do Newport life from study—conscious observation—his failure was absolutely monumental." Mark Twain's European fictions are not monumental

---

[47] For Susy Clemens's attitude, see Grace King, *Memories of a Southern Woman of Letters* (1932), pp. 173–174.

failures, but we could easily spare most of them for another book like *The Adventures of Huckleberry Finn.*

A letter from Will Bowen, whom he addressed as "My First, Oldest & Dearest Friend," which he answered on February 6, 1870, just four days after his marriage to Olivia Clemens, brought back many recollections of their boyhood experiences in Hannibal. "Your letter has stirred me to the bottom," he wrote. "The fountains of my great deep are broken up & I have rained reminiscences for four & twenty hours. The old life has swept before me like a panorama; the old days have trooped by in their old glory again; the old faces have looked out of the mists of the past; old footsteps have sounded in my listening ears; old hands have clasped mine, old voices have greeted me, & the songs I loved ages & ages ago have come wailing down the centuries! Heavens what eternities have swung their hoary cycles about us since those days were new!" [48] In his letter Mark Twain recalled numerous experiences which he had shared with Bowen in Hannibal. Half a dozen of them were to reappear in *Tom Sawyer* or *Huckleberry Finn.* At this time, however, he regarded himself not as a novelist but as a newspaperman. In his first attempt at the novel, *The Gilded Age* (1873), which he wrote in collaboration with his Hartford neighbor, Charles Dudley Warner, he made some slight use of his father's Tennessee mountain land, and out of his cousin James Lampton, his brother Orion, and perhaps himself as well, he created the character of Colonel Sellers.

In the fall of 1874 when Howells asked him to write something for the *Atlantic Monthly,* he replied that he had nothing to write about. Shortly afterward, however, he unexpectedly found his theme. He was telling his friend Joe Twichell about his life as pilot on the Mississippi when Twichell suddenly exclaimed: "What a virgin subject to hurl into a magazine!" The subject proved acceptable to the editor of the *Atlantic,* which was just beginning to be hospitable to Southern writers, and Mark Twain wrote "Old Times on the Mississippi." [49] What he had written was the best thing he had yet done, but it was not enough to make a book, he thought, and he laid it aside.

The memories of his boyhood continued to haunt him, and in 1876 he

[48] *Mark Twain's Letters to Will Bowen* (Austin, Tex., 1941), [ed. Theodore Hornberger], p. 18. After Bowen had visited him in Hartford, Mark Twain wrote on Nov. 4, 1888: "I wish you could have stayed longer with us; I would have liked to bring up every creature we knew in those days,—even the dumb animals—it would be bathing in the fabled Fountain of Youth" (p. 26).

[49] Presumably neither Twichell nor Mark Twain had read George Ward Nichols' article, "Down the Mississippi," in *Harper's Magazine,* XLI, 835–845 (Nov., 1870), which gives some account of the difficulties of piloting a steamboat on the great river.

published *The Adventures of Tom Sawyer*. This, however, appeared not as a Southern local-color story but as a boys' book. Howells, however, in his review in the *Atlantic* for December, 1875, called attention to the Missouri background: ". . . the whole little town lives in the reader's sense, with its religiousness, its lawlessness, its droll social distinctions, its civilization qualified by its slaveholding, and its traditions of the wilder West which has passed away. The picture will be instructive to those who have fancied the whole Southwest a sort of vast Pike County, and have not conceived of a sober and serious and orderly contrast to the sort of life that has come to represent the Southwest in literature."

Mark Twain began *Huckleberry Finn* in 1876, but apparently he found no one to encourage him to go on with it. Nevertheless, as he watched the changing taste of the reading public, he could hardly have failed to note that Southern stories were becoming extraordinarily popular. The Northern magazines were full of them in 1882 when he returned to the Mississippi for materials to finish his *Life on the Mississippi* and *Huckleberry Finn*. He went down the Mississippi on a steamboat, refreshing his memories of Southern scenes, and at his request Joel Chandler Harris came from Atlanta to meet him and Cable in New Orleans.

The later chapters in *Life on the Mississippi* are on the level of Mark Twain's travel books; they are primarily good reporting rather than literature. They are interesting, however, for the writer's impressions of the Lower South, which he had not seen for more than twenty years. "I found," he writes, "the half-forgotten Southern intonations and elisions as pleasing to my ear as they had formerly been. A Southerner talks music. At least it is music to me, but then I was born in the South." Had he ever before told his readers that he was a Southerner by birth? Not until nine years later would he describe his brief and inglorious experience as a Confederate soldier.

After years of living in the West, in New England, and in Europe, however, Mark Twain was far from pleased with all that he saw in the Mississippi Valley. The South was unprogressive; Yankee business methods and New England thrift would improve it. He lost patience with the "wordy, windy, flowery 'eloquence,' romanticism, sentimentality" of much Southern journalistic writing. What the South needed was more writers of the newer sort like Cable and Harris. He wrote: "But when a Southerner of genius writes modern English, his book goes upon crutches no longer, but upon wings; and they carry it swiftly all about America and England—as witness the experience of Mr. Cable and 'Uncle Remus,' two of the very few Southern authors who do not write in the Southern style." As I have noted many pages earlier,[50] Mark Twain attributed most of what was bad in Southern life and writing to the influence of Sir Walter Scott, whose books he disliked. His explanation is too simple to have much truth in it. Mark Twain had been out of touch with Southern life so long that, like many Northern travelers and historians, he had come to look for some simple formula which would explain the many differences between the two sections. It is easier to pardon him than it is the too numerous writers who have taken his theory in all seriousness.

His visit to the South, his meeting in New Orleans with Cable and Harris, and his reading of their books all contributed to strengthening his interest in Southern scenes. In 1884, a year before he published *Huckleberry Finn*, he began giving platform readings with Cable in many parts of the country. On New Year's Day, 1885, he wrote to his wife from Paris, Kentucky: "Whenever we strike a Southern audience they laugh themselves all to pieces. They catch a point before you can get it out—& then, if you are not a muggins, you *don't* get it out; you leave it unsaid. It is a great delight to talk to such folks." It was the era of Southern themes, and he was capitalizing on it, as were some Northern writers whose knowledge of Southern life was infinitely less than his.

Huckleberry Finn is Mark Twain's masterpiece in humor, local color, and romance. Along with *The Scarlet Letter* and *Moby-Dick*, it is one of the three or four greatest American novels—although no one of the three, be it noted, is an orthodox novel. It is probably the greatest novel that deals with Southern life. In form it is a picaresque romance, but it is also a panorama of life on the Mississippi. It is a story of the Western South written by one who, fortunately, no longer shared certain Southern prepossessions. Nevertheless, in its use of local color and dialect and in a certain nostalgic tenderness toward the past it bears a close relation to the writings of his Southern contemporaries. In imagination Mark Twain left the world of New England convention and respectability for the freer life of a boy on a raft drifting down the great river far from Sunday and weekday schools in a world where no one put on a coat for dinner or worried about what the neighbors would say. By choosing the son of the town drunkard as his narrator he escaped the literary language that sometimes betrayed him and escaped likewise from the restrictions of the genteel tradition. Like Harris and Page, he was at his best when he put his story into the mouth of one who speaks in dialect.

Huck Finn, however, is no faithful ex-slave glorifying the old regime. His father is no more of an aristocrat than a mudcat, as he tells us, and Huck looks askance at the Southern gentry so anxious to preserve their human property. His attitude toward the runaway slave seems historically improbable, but Jim is one of the best Negro characters in fiction after Uncle Remus. Mark Twain, perhaps because he had lived so long in New England as a neighbor of Mrs. Stowe, saw the Old South much as Cable had pictured it in *The Grandissimes*. There is in his picture of slavery a little too much of the old Abolitionist legend of the Deep South. The darker aspects of life in the Old South are admirably summed up by Dixon Wecter:

The odyssey of Huck's voyage through the South reveals aspects of life darker than the occasional melodrama of *Tom Sawyer*. We are shown the sloth and sadism of poor whites, backwoods loafers with their plug tobacco and Barlow knives, who sic dogs on stray sows and "laugh at the fun and look grateful for the noise," or drench a stray cur with turpentine and set him afire. We remark the cowardice of lynching parties; the chicanery of patent medicine fakers, revivalists, and exploiters of rustic ribaldry; the senseless feudings of the gentry. In the background broods fear: not only a boy's apprehension of ghosts, African superstitions, and the terrors of the night, nor the adults' dread of black insurrection, but the endless implicated strands of robbery, floggings, drowning, and murder. Death by violence lurks at every bend of road or river.

This is not the Southern life we find in Page's stories of ante-bellum Virginia, where the rough edges of social life had been worn round and smooth. It is in some ways remarkably like the Alabama and Mississippi pictured in Simms's Border Romances and in the sketches of Johnson Jones Hooper and Joseph Glover Baldwin—a land of fools and rascals where disorder and violence were not uncommon. In its darker aspects Mark Twain's picture recalls not only Cable's Louisiana but also the Yoknapatawpha County of William Faulkner's Mississippi. The Grangerfords and Shepherdsons are Kentuckians of the planter class and, though so different from Kennedy's Frank Meriwether and Page's Dr. Cary, are rather memorable in their way. Mary Jane Wilks is one of Mark Twain's very few portraits of Southern women of the better class.

Huckleberry Finn represents not only the peak of its author's achievement but also the climax of the humorous tradition in which he worked. In this novel, says Edgar M. Branch, Mark Twain "brings together many lines of development and fulfills early promise. Into its making went oral narrative and Washoe burlesque, practice with native characters and their speech, formulas of the journalist and lecturer, viewpoints of the westerner, and experiences of the Hannibal boy and the river pilot. In this novel humor is deepened with pathos and matured into wisdom. Here romance and realism are held in delicate balance." How close the narrative technique of

Huckleberry Finn is to the tall tales of the Southwest is seen in the discarded episode which Mark Twain printed in Chapter III of *Life on the Mississippi*. In Chapter XX of *Huckleberry Finn* the King pretends to be converted and robs a camp meeting in a manner clearly reminiscent of one of the exploits of Simon Suggs. Even with the help of Howells, Mark Twain never mastered the art of constructing a novel. He was, like the old Southern humorists and his friend Harris, at his best in brief episodes. His theory of a narrative was that a tale should, so to speak, tell itself. The writer should "merely hold the pen and let the story . . . say, after its own fashion, what it desires to say." There should be "no hesitancies, no delays, no cogitations, no attempts at invention."

With so naïve a theory as this, Mark Twain could be as formless as Thomas Wolfe would have been without Maxwell Perkins to help him. In *Huckleberry Finn* he had fortunately two great characters whose experiences give the novel a kind of unity, for the novel is perhaps as much the story of Jim's effort to escape being sold down the river as it is of Huck's effort to escape at once his drunkard father and Miss Watson's attempts at making him genteel. Occasionally Mark Twain attributes to Huck ideas and words that are above his rearing and mentality. We accept the masterly exposition of Huck's struggles with his conscience as we accept one of Shakespeare's marvelous soliloquies knowing that kings and generals do not speak in blank verse.

There are of course serious defects in the book, considered as a novel. Jim's efforts to escape slavery seem rather ironic when at the end we learn that he has been free all the time. The closing chapters, beginning with Tom Sawyer's reappearance, are almost pure burlesque. What we remember about the book is its portrait gallery: Huck's father, Colonel Grangerford and his son Buck, the Duke and the King, Mary Jane Wilks, and above all the Negro Jim and Huck himself. Some of our twentieth-century novelists are masters of technical methods such as Mark Twain never was; but whatever be the explanation, they have created few memorable characters—and it is great characters that perhaps more than anything else keep old books like *Huckleberry Finn* alive.

In *Pudd'nhead Wilson* (1894) Mark Twain once more returned to the Southern scene. The book was, after two or three years of tinkering with it, finally published while its author was on the verge of bankruptcy. In an appendix, "Those Extraordinary Twins," he gives some account of his difficulties with the novel. It had turned from comedy to tragedy—"a most embarrassing circumstance." Worse still, he had finally discovered after many months that "it was not one story, but two stories tangled together."

He pulled one of the stories out, and yet *Pudd'nhead Wilson* in spite of some excellent scenes is not a good novel. Mark Twain was too anxious to make fictional use of the then novel device of finger-printing. The titular hero, David Wilson, passed for a fool because he made a joke that the town did not understand. Mark Twain had been away from Hannibal too long. The joke seems to me typically small-town; the village yokels would have yelled with delight when they heard it.

In the story two babies are exchanged in the cradle. Roxy, the slave nurse, almost white, who swaps them, has a horror of being sold down the river. The white son of Percy Driscoll, who is an F.F.V., is brought up as a slave while Roxy's own child with its one-thirty-secondth of Negro blood, is brought up as Driscoll's son and heir. It is a rather daring story of miscegenation, and Roxy is a convincing character. The author, however, is more concerned with the acts and emotions of her son, who for no obvious reason turns out to be a contemptible coward and thief. The story as I have summarized it has implications which the novelist should have foreseen; namely, that it is the taint of Negro blood that prevents Tom from growing up a brave and honorable gentleman. One can imagine the kind of novel that Thomas Dixon would have made out of this situation. Cable or Faulkner could have handled it better than Mark Twain.

Mark Twain's later writings have little to do with the South. "From recollections of his Hannibal boyhood," says Dixon Wecter, "he gravitated toward a new but distinctly artificial romanticism, 'the pageant and fairy tale' of life in medieval Europe." The revival of historical romance, then rapidly displacing the vogue of local color, was in part no doubt the reason for his writing the *Personal Recollections of Joan of Arc* (1896). He overrated *Joan of Arc* because of the enormous labor involved in making himself familiar with a remote period in French history. Like Cable, he never perhaps quite realized that a novelist's best material is the life he has lived before the age of twenty-five.

In the posthumous *The Mysterious Stranger* (1916), although the scene is ostensibly medieval Austria, the boys we meet are strangely like those of Tom Sawyer's gang in ante-bellum Missouri. It is a pessimistic book, but it is beautifully written. There have been many attempts to explain Mark Twain's pessimism. No doubt his failure in business and the loss of his wife and two children had much to do with it. Perhaps also there was in his make-up a certain inability, after his many years in the South and the West, fully to adjust himself to life in New England and New York. Arthur Hobson Quinn has noted that most of his finest characters are under eighteen years of age: Tom Sawyer, Huck Finn, Buck Grangerford, the

English Prince, Tom Canty, Joan of Arc, the boys in *The Mysterious Stranger*, and others. Olivia Clemens called her husband "Youth," and she knew him better than any one else. He was not born to become the American Jonathan Swift, the satirist of America's Gilded Age, as Van Wyck Brooks argued in *The Ordeal of Mark Twain*. He was a humorist and a romancer, and the books by which he is remembered are chronicles of his youth in the Old South.

VI

EPILOGUE
THE TWENTIETH CENTURY

1

The Passing of the New South, 1901–1920

WHILE THIS survey of Southern literary history ends properly in 1900, it may be useful to glance briefly at more recent developments. Many Northern and some Southern critics, it seems to me, still distribute their praise and blame amiss because they do not understand the historical factors which in some measure even yet condition life and literature in the South. The difficult but fascinating undertaking of writing a history of the Southern renaissance of the twentieth century I shall leave to other scholars.

The first two decades of the present century were in many respects a continuation of the New South. The Northern industrial belt was extended into the Southern piedmont as far as Birmingham, which was becoming a Southern Pittsburgh. There was great improvement in schools and colleges. The yellow fever, the hookworm disease, and malaria were coming under control. It was a time of material progress, and yet Southerners could not help noticing that, as in the years before the Civil War, the South did not fully share in the prosperity of the nation. They noted also that most of the Southern railroads, mills, and factories were owned or controlled by capitalists in the great cities of the Northeast. It was disturbing, too, to see many of the ablest young men going to the North or the West because of the greater opportunities offered there. Conservative Southerners were wondering if the South were not destined to lose all its distinctive characteristics in a drab national pattern such as was soon to be notably satirized in Sinclair Lewis's *Main Street* and *Babbitt*. Why should the South become a second Middle West? they asked. Was not one enough?

The South was still a Solid South in the political sense, but pressures from the outside tended strongly to make that section conform to the national pattern. Many young Southerners were enrolled in Northern universities and colleges, and there were Northern teachers in increasing numbers in Southern schools. Northerners in larger numbers were going to

Atlanta, Richmond, and Dallas; and parts of Florida were becoming more Northern than Southern. The powerful influences exerted by Northern magazines, newspapers, and books, by the motion picture and the radio tended to break down Southern resistance to change, especially among the urban population. Southern traits seemed to be fading away. Conservative Southern parents noted the decay of manners among their children. The youngsters were becoming just like the Yankees, they said, always asking the cost of everything and estimating its value in dollars and cents.

There was notable improvement in race relations. The number of lynchings decreased. (There have been none since 1951.) With the increasing migration of Negro workers to the North, the race problem was no longer exclusively Southern. Indeed, race riots were more common in the North than anywhere else. Northerners for the most part still felt that the South should be permitted, within its own boundaries, to handle the Negro problem without interference from the outside. Yet the Compromise established in the 1870's, though it still held, was becoming increasingly unstable. Some young Southerners were beginning to rebel against it, and there were indications that the North would not long abide by it. After 1920 in fact there was to develop what would look to conservative Southerners something like a new Abolitionist crusade against a backward and semibarbarous South.

Except for a few new writers, like O. Henry, Ellen Glasgow, and James Branch Cabell, it was a slack time in Southern literature. The older writers who survived were producing nothing of much importance and were rapidly going out of fashion. In 1912, for example, Mary Noailles Murfree, finding that publishers no longer wanted her later stories, sold to the Houghton Mifflin Company the rights to her fifteen books for only $1,159.81. Perhaps she might have found her later work acceptable if she had followed Walter Hines Page's advice to paint the Southern mountaineers as doomed by heredity and the lack of opportunity. The newer writers were beginning to attack or to laugh at Southern conventions and ideals. None of them, however, broke so completely with the past as the young writers who emerged in the 1920's.

2

O. Henry

AT THE TIME of his death William Sydney Porter (1862–1910) was the most popular short story writer in America. He achieved his success while living in New York as a chronicler of its "four million" inhabitants, and not many of his readers ever thought of him as a Southerner. Yet he was born and reared in North Carolina, and in his early manhood he served his apprenticeship on a Texas newspaper. It was not until after he was sent to a Federal prison in Ohio that he began to produce stories for the New York magazines. In all his work one feels a strong sympathy for the unfortunate, the people who have not got on, which is no doubt in part due to his own experience. There is local color in his stories; but, more than any of his predecessors, he was interested in contrasting sectional types, Northern and Southern, Eastern and Western.

At the time O. Henry began writing, the short story was more nearly stereotyped than it had ever before been. Magazine editors were more interested in technical skill than in reality. O. Henry wrote for the sophisticated reader who thought he knew all the possible turns a story might take, and he made it his business to surprise his unwary reader at every possible point. The surprise ending was not his invention, but he used it more often and more unscrupulously than Aldrich or Stockton had done. As a result, stories like "The Romance of a Busy Broker" pall upon a second reading—which is the best test of the quality of a story. The reader simply does not believe that a Wall Street broker can be so distraught by business that he forgets his marriage only yesterday to his stenographer and proposes to her all over again.

In O. Henry's Southern stories one feels a certain antipathy to "Southern chivalry" and aristocracy, but many of his characters are of the most conventional kind. "The Guardian of the Accolade" is the story of a faithful ex-slave who sees his old master, as he thinks, absconding on an early morning train with money stolen from the bank. Imploring the banker in the name of his dead wife, who had always looked upon him as her knight, "pure and fearless and without reproach," the old darky begs the banker to give him the satchel in his hand before he boards the train. Reluctantly the banker gives it up. What was in the satchel? Not stolen money but "two quarts of the finest old silk-velvet Bourbon . . . you ever wet your lips with"! In "Thimble, Thimble," a story definitely in the Stockton manner, an old Virginia darky is called upon while in New York to distinguish a Northern Carteret whom he has never seen from a Southern cousin whom he has not seen since his childhood. The difference between Southerner and Northerner turns out to be as trivial as a difference in neckties or perhaps a willingness to pay blackmail to an adventuress. "Best-Seller" is a clever variation of the intersectional love story. It is at once a defense of romance and the love story of a Pittsburgh plateglass salesman and a Virginia girl. Her father is the lineal descendant of belted earls and lives in a "mansion" of fifty rooms in some of which the ceiling is twenty-eight feet high! "A Black-jack Bargainer" is the story of a poor-white couple in the mountains who on becoming suddenly rich try to buy from Yancey Goree, the last of his clan, not only the family homestead but also the Goree feud with the Coltranes because that seems the only way the humble Garveys can get into the "quality." This is pure vaudeville, or else it shows an abysmal ignorance of the nature of feuds in the Southern Appalachians. There was not much indeed that O. Henry would not sacrifice for effect. He knew that Northern readers of John Fox, Jr., would accept his story as plausible if not authentic. And yet, incredible as it may seem, the late William Lyon Phelps found in this absurd story "profound ethical passion" and two Northern anthologists—Angus Burrell and Bennett Cerf—have included it in a collection of the finest American short stories!

Best perhaps of all O. Henry's stories—although the citizens of Nashville long resented it as an attack on their city—is "A Municipal Report." O. Henry took up as a challenge Frank Norris's dogmatic pronouncement: "Fancy a novel about Chicago or Buffalo, let us say, or Nashville, Tennessee! There are just three big cities in the United States that are 'story cities'—New York, of course, New Orleans, and, best of the lot, San Francisco." Caesar, the carriage driver, is a good portrait of the faithful ex-slave, but his mistress, Azalea Adair, the brilliant essayist and proud specimen of penniless gentility, is less convincing. Best of all is her husband, "Major" Wentworth Caswell, the professional Southerner, a type that O. Henry detested. Here for once O. Henry's technique suited his theme. Ordinarily he could not resist the temptation to burlesque any more than Mark Twain could.

3
Ellen Glasgow

ELLEN GLASGOW (1874–1945), who, for want of other explanation, sometimes thought she was born a radical, appeared on the scene in 1897 with a first novel that would have seemed more appropriate to the 1920's. For the protagonist of The Descendant, she chose a rebel, a poor-white and illegitimate to boot. "But," declared one of her elderly kinsmen, "it is incredible that a well-brought-up Southern girl should even know what a bastard is." Relatives of her own sex advised her, for Richmond had no great respect for local talent: "If you must write, do write of Southern ladies and gentlemen." In her girlhood a maiden aunt used to give her every Christmas a romance of the Confederacy. Of these books, Miss Glasgow remarks that they "one and all, followed faithfully a well-worn and standardized pattern. A gallant Northern invader (though never of the rank and file) must rescue the person and protect the virtue of a spirited yet clinging Southern belle and beauty." Even as a child Ellen Glasgow could not believe that war was like that. From the beginning of her career she attacked the "evasive idealism" which shut its eyes to actualities. "What the South needs," she often said, "is blood and irony."

In her collected prefaces, A Certain Measure (1943), from which I am quoting, she traced with sure skill her development as a novelist. "I had not in the beginning, and I have not now," she wrote, "the slightest interest in fiction as a trade. Only as a form of art has fiction ever concerned me." Fortunately, she was not entirely dependent upon the income from her books. She could resist the pleas of publishers and readers to write "an optimistic novel of the Far West" or to write "rather more like Joyce" or Thomas Nelson Page. By the time she was twenty-five or -six she had read Balzac, Flaubert, Maupassant, and "every celebrated novel in English." She had read so widely in scientific writings that it required, she says, "total immersion in the centuries of sound English prose to restore my natural ear for rhythm and my instinct for style." In later years she certainly read Henry James, but I do not think she was much influenced by other American writers. Perhaps The Voice of the People owes something to Howells' The Rise of Silas Lapham, and she may have found in the novels of Cable a precedent for her frank criticism of Southern life. Yet literary rebel though she was in her youth, Ellen Glasgow did not make the mistake of breaking completely with the Southern tradition. Perhaps some later Southern novelists would be wise to ponder the following passage in her intellectual autobiography:

The old South, genial, objective, and a little ridiculous—as the fashions of the past are always a little ridiculous to the present—has vanished from the world of fact to reappear in the permanent realm of fable. . . . What we are in danger of forgetting is that few possessions are more precious than a fable that can no longer be compared to a fact. The race that inherits a heroic legend must have accumulated an inexhaustible resource of joy, beauty, laughter, and tragic passion. To discard this rich inheritance in the pursuit of the standard utilitarian style is, for the Southern novelist, pure folly.

The Battle-Ground (1902) was the first of a series of novels which compose, "in the more freely interpretative form of fiction, a social history of Virginia from the decade before the Confederacy"; and the major theme of the series is "the rise of the middle class as the dominant force in Southern democracy." Although the novels of her earlier period are less expertly written than those of her later phase, no other state except perhaps the fabulous Mississippi of William Faulkner figures in a comparable series of noteworthy novels. In *The Battle-Ground* (1902), a story of the Civil War, she pictured "the last stand in Virginia of the aristocratic tradition." She dealt with the rise of the poorer whites and the decline of the old planter families in *The Voice of the People* (1900), *The Romance of a Plain Man* (1909), and *The Miller of Old Church* (1911). *The Deliverance* (1904) is at once a story of Reconstruction and of life on a tobacco farm. In *Virginia* (1913) and in *Life and Gabriella* (1916) she attacked the traditional upbringing of the Southern lady. Virginia's education, she said, was such as "to paralyze her reasoning faculties so completely that all danger of mental unsettling, or even movement, was eliminated from her future." In 1913 Mary Johnston, whose popular vogue far outshadowed Miss Glasgow's, published *Hagar*, another vigorous attack upon the Southern ideal of the "lady." By that time even the conservative Thomas Nelson Page had entered upon his final, national phase.

At the end of the First World War Miss Glasgow felt that she had completed her "social history." She had developed slowly. She now entered a new phase of her development. Her new manner and style show that she had studied to good purpose Henry James and other moderns. The first novel in her later manner, *Barren Ground* (1925), attracted wide attention. On the dust wrappers her publishers announced that "with *Barren Ground* realism at last crosses the Potomac"! Some reviewers, ignorant that her first novel had been published twenty-eight years before, saluted her as a promising young novelist. In later years she quoted with approval Stuart P. Sherman's remark: "Northern critics have never known how to take her." They insisted upon considering her as either a historical romancer or a local colorist, not seeing that the problems treated in her fiction were not merely local but also national or even worldwide. She must have felt puzzled when the Northern juries that awarded the Pulitzer prize for fiction passed over all the best of her earlier and later novels to award it to *In This Our Life* (1941), a novel which she was too ill to give the last final revision which she had given to all her earlier books.

Barren Ground and *Vein of Iron* (1935) are fundamentally tragic, but *The Romantic Comedians* (1926) and *They Stooped to Folly* (1929) are sophisticated and disillusioned comedies, which owe something to the influence of her friend and neighbor, James Branch Cabell. In these satires she attacked the vanity and egotism of the male animal with a skill rarely equaled since the appearance in 1879 of Ibsen's *A Doll's House* and Meredith's *The Egoist*. Through all her novels indeed runs the theme which Cabell has called "The Tragedy of Everywoman, As It Was Lately Enacted in the Commonwealth of Virginia." Cabell sees Miss Glasgow as "a witty and observant woman, a poet in grain, who was not at any moment in her writing quite devoid of malice, nor of an all-understanding lyric tenderness either; and who was not ever, through any tiniest half-moment, deficient in craftsmanship."

A blend of the tragic and the comic appears in *The Sheltered Life* (1932), a story of Richmond, beginning not long before the First World War broke in upon "the age of make-believe." The background is "a shallow and aimless society of happiness-hunters, who lived in a perpetual flight from reality, and grasped at any effort-saving illusion of passion or pleasure." Against such a background she placed one of her finest characters, old General Archbald, "a lover of wisdom, a humane and civilized soul, oppressed by the burden of tragic remembrance." ". . . into his lonely spirit," she wrote, "I have put much of my ultimate feeling about life. He represents the tragedy, wherever it appears, of the civilized man in a world that is not civilized." His arch-antagonist—and hers—is "inhumanity."

4

James Branch Cabell

ALTHOUGH JAMES BRANCH CABELL (1879–   ) published *The Eagle's Shadow* as early as 1904, it was the attempted suppression of *Jurgen* in 1919 that brought him to the attention of the youthful intelligentsia. Until the advent of the Great Depression, he enjoyed an enormous vogue among them. That vogue has passed, and it is clear that for a time he was much overrated. He is out of fashion now, but the few who care for carefully polished English prose have not been able to forget him. Cabell began writing when the historical romance was still the vogue. The series which he calls "The Biography of the Life of Manuel"—the scenes of which are laid in the imaginary medieval French province of Poictesme—are ostensibly historical romances like the French novels of Maurice Hewlett; but into them their author put so much of the modern temper of disillusionment and skepticism that one finds it difficult to believe in the reality of his fictions. Cabell apparently found it difficult to keep up the game of make-believe, as earlier romancers had done. Somewhat more credible are the stories that he laid in Lichfield, in which figure certain characteristics of his native Richmond-in-Virginia.

In his stories of Virginia, notably in *The Rivet in Grandfather's Neck*

(1915), Cabell directs much of his satire at the ways and ideals of the New South. He shatters the illusion of the Virginia aristocracy by showing how many of its gentlemen and ladies, though professing the traditional ideals, completely disregard them in their living. The "age of chivalry," whether in Virginia or in Poictesme—the age of gentle breeding and superior culture—turns out to be full of vanity, deceit, lust, and rapacity. Yet Cabell's attitude toward his fellow F.F.V.'s is an ambivalent one. It is as though he were saying to his readers: "Here we are with all our many faults; yet are we not still the fine flower of civilization?"

Whatever their setting, Cabell's romances could hardly have been written outside of the South. Ellen Glasgow in *A Certain Measure* has pointed to the Southern characteristics of his romances:

A long tradition and a thick deposit of hopes and fears had flowered again in the serene disenchantment of his philosophy. The austere perfection of his art, with its allegorical remoteness and that strangely hollow ring which echoes the deeper human tones of passion and pity, could have sprung only from a past that has softened and receded into the eternal outline of legend. Certainly it is an art that belongs by inheritance to the South, though it may appear to contain no element we define narrowly as Southern, except, perhaps, the gaiety and gallantry of its pessimism.

The stylistic qualities that Cabell has striven for—as he explains in *Beyond Life* (1919), one of the most substantial of his books—are "distinction and clarity, . . . beauty and symmetry, . . . tenderness and truth and urbanity." Readers have found in his novels less of "tenderness" and "truth" than of "distinction" and "urbanity." Some of them complain, too, that while Cabell writes beautifully, there is little substance in his books. They complain also of a certain preciosity, and they object to the cavalier manner in which in "The Biography of Manuel" he mingles such diverse elements as the legend of Troy, the Arthurian romances, pseudo-French history, and Russian folk tales.

Cabell is no admirer of the American classics, and he found his models in Congreve and other British masters of the lighter prose style. For him, as he has explained in *Ladies and Gentlemen* (1934), all of the earlier American literature that seems to count is a "sufficing amount of Poe; and a tiny fraction of Mark Twain." His view of the function of literature is very close to that of Poe—and, I may add, Mark Twain was an admirer of Cabell's early romances. Cabell's work owes little or nothing to the New England literary masters, and has not much in common with that of the better-known Northern novelists of his own time.

5
A Divided South, 1921–1953

In My Friendly Contemporaries (1932) Hamlin Garland recorded his impressions of the South in 1919. It was, he found, "an unkempt, empty land, a land of tiny cabins with outside chimneys, and ugly, unpainted houses set in disorderly lawns. . . ." He could see no beauty in the Southern landscape, and he concluded that the writers of the New South "had conspired to maintain the fiction of a 'Sunny South' dotted with stately mansions and odorous with magnolia blooms." In his notebook he wrote: "Now . . . it is the duty of the men and women who see this land with present-day training to picture it as it really is, an unlovely time of sorry transition."

"The Sahara of the Bozart," which H. L. Mencken first printed in the New York Evening Mail in November, 1917, and reprinted in his Second Series of Prejudices in 1920, provoked outbursts of denunciation from Southern Congressmen and newspaper editors, but it served also as a challenge to the "Young Intellectuals" of the Southern states. Mencken was not given to understatement. The entire South, he said,

for all its size and all its wealth and all the "progress" it babbles of . . . is almost as sterile, artistically, intellectually, culturally, as the Sahara Desert. There are single acres in Europe that house more first-rate men than all the states south of the Potomac. . . . If the whole of the late Confederacy were to be engulfed by a tidal wave tomorrow, the effect upon the civilized minority of men in the world would be but little greater than that of a flood on the Yang-tse-Kiang. It would be impossible in all history to match so complete a drying-up of a civilization.

Mencken was a Baltimorean, and his diagnosis of what was wrong with the South differed radically from the traditional Northern interpretation. Before 1850, he said, the South had had a civilization far superior to that established in New England by shopkeepers and theologians. In the Old South a "civilized minority" had understood the art of living and possessed "the vague thing we call culture." The later South had lost its "capacity for producing ideas" and it had taken on "the worst intolerance of ignorance and stupidity." Mencken would have agreed with Walter Hines Page that the South had far too little intellectual curiosity and was haunted by the "Ghost of the Confederate Dead, the Ghost of religious orthodoxy, the Ghost of Negro domination." Mencken saw the South as in the grip of "Baptist and Methodist barbarism" and "the philistinism of the new type of town-boomer." The real reason for the South's decadence was that it had "simply been drained of all its best blood by war and emigration." The poor-whites, who represented the worst blood of Europe, were in power. If those earlier Baltimoreans, Albert Taylor Bledsoe and William Hand Browne, could have been alive to read "The Sahara of the Bozart" in 1920, they might well have believed that their gloomiest predictions about the New South had come true.

Mencken had unwittingly released his blast against the "booboisie" of the Southern "Bible Belt" just as a literary renaissance was about to get under way. He had mentioned Cabell as "the single southern prose writer who can write," but throughout the 1920's he was hailing the emergence of one new Southern writer after another. In January, 1924, he and George Jean Nathan launched the *American Mercury*, and soon many a bright Southern collegian was reading it from one green cover to the other. At the end of the second year of the *Mercury* Mencken pointed to his discovery —proudly as though it were in part his own achievement—that in its first two years the South had furnished twenty-three contributors and fifty-five contributions as against New England's twenty-four contributors and forty-one contributions. Mencken diligently scanned the little literary magazines which were springing up all over the South—the *Reviewer* in Richmond, the *Southwest Review* in Dallas, the *Double Dealer* in New Orleans, and many more—and he solicited articles from contributors whose work he liked.[1]

In the 1920's the South had its rebellious "Young Intellectuals," its "Flaming Youth, Southern Style." Many of its young men and women during the First World War had seen Europe or other parts of the United States and did not want to return to the small towns or the farms where they had grown up. They read *Main Street* with a conviction that it was a true picture of the drab Southern small town, and when *Babbitt* appeared they proceeded to denounce boosters and "realtors" and Rotary Clubs. Some of them went to Greenwich Village or to Paris and wrote novels, mostly unpublished, about the tyranny of public opinion and the failure of American democracy. Naturally, they blamed the older generation for bringing on a war planned to "make the world safe for democracy." A Southern playwright, Laurence Stallings, collaborated with a Middle Westerner, Maxwell Anderson, to present the younger generation's conception of war in *What Price Glory?* (1924). Another Southerner, Joseph Wood Krutch, expressed in *The Modern Temper* (1929) their feeling of disillusionment and pessimism.

---

[1] For Mencken's interest in the *Reviewer*, see Emily Clark, *Innocence Abroad* (1931), chaps. 1 and vi, and Cabell, *Let Me Lie* (1947), Part Nine. See also Oscar Cargill, "Mencken and the South," *Ga. Rev.*, VI, 369–376 (Winter, 1952).

Sigmund Freud and James Joyce had taught the superlative importance of sexual complexes and repressions, and the youthful writers felt as though they had arrived at the ultimate wisdom of the initiated. Prudery and platitude were out, and there were dozens of Southern aspirants for the role of Dreiser, Lewis, and Hemingway. Belatedly, the South found its New Poets, too, and there were active and productive poetry societies, especially in Charleston, Dallas, and Nashville.

The younger Southern writers found a freedom of expression not known to their predecessors. They were sympathetic with the Negro writers of Harlem, and some of them published stories of Negro life more reminiscent of *Uncle Tom's Cabin* than of *Nights with Uncle Remus*. In 1903 John Spencer Bassett had almost lost his professorship at Trinity College (now Duke University) for writing in the *South Atlantic Quarterly*: "Now [Booker T.] Washington is a great and good man, a Christian statesman, and take him all in all the greatest man, save General Lee, born in the South in a hundred years. . . ." The campaign to get Bassett fired had been led by Josephus Daniels, editor of the Raleigh *News and Observer* and then regarded as a Southern liberal. In 1927–1928, however, student literary magazines at Duke and the University of North Carolina featured stories and poems by the new Negro writers and were not even threatened with censorship or suppression.

The revolt of the young Southerners, however, is not to be confused with that of the intelligentsia in the Middle West or in the great metropolitan areas. They were more than ever impatient with the traditional ideals of the Southern gentleman and lady. They glorified not the planter and the Southern belle but primitive types, drawn especially from the Negroes and the poor-whites. The writers of the New South, especially Thomas Nelson Page, they thought, had created a legend of the Old South which was both repellent and unhistorical. That legend was described by W. J. Cash in *The Mind of the South* (1941):

Perpetually suspended in the great haze of memory, it hung, as it were, poised, somewhere between earth and sky, colossal, shining, and incomparably lovely— a Cloud-Cuckoo Land wherein at last everybody who had ever laid claim to the title of planter would be metamorphosed with swift precision, beyond any lingering shade of doubt, into the breathing image of Marse Chan and Squire Effingham, and wherein life would move always in stately and noble measure through scenery out of Watteau.

The realism of some of the younger Southern writers went far beyond that of Howells or Ellen Glasgow. With some of them, it seems, the new realism, now called naturalism, entered a *cul de sac* from which there was no exit. Miss Glasgow expressed her opinion of the "hard-boiled" school in *A Certain Measure:*

One may admit that the Southern States have more than an equal share of degeneracy and deterioration; but the multitude of half-wits, and whole idiots, and nymphomaniacs, and paranoiacs, and rakehells in general, that populate the modern literary South could flourish nowhere but in the weird pages of melodrama. There is no harm in the fashion, one surmises, until it poses as realism. It may be magnificent, indeed, but it is not realism, and it is not peculiarly Southern.

How far the fashion in Southern fiction had changed since the time of the genteel writers of the New South was admirably suggested by Grant C. Knight when after reading a story by Faulkner he indicated how a "hard-boiled" Southern writer in 1935 might have handled the plot of James Lane Allen's *The Doctor's Christmas Eve,* a story not untouched by the realism of Howells. Allen's novel, as Knight outlines its plot, is "a story of domestic infelicity, of a physician in love with his best friend's wife, of that wife's neglect by her husband, of the things that have made the doctor what he is, of the meeting of the children of both families, of the death of the Birney boy and the drawing together of father and mother." This is how Faulkner might have treated the situation:

The scene would have been placed farther south, say in Mississippi or Georgia. We might first discover Dr. Birney, a decayed scion of a decaying aristocratic family, fleeing from bloodhounds that are pursuing him through a pine forest. Exhausted, he would stop at a negro's cabin, and while drinking from a gourd he would review his past life in such a way that we would understand why he had lost the right woman and married the wrong one. After he disappeared into the wood a mob would reach the cabin and explain that the fugitive had cut his wife's throat. Then again we would follow the doctor's thoughts while he runs terror-stricken from the shouts closing in upon him; by means of this review we would learn that he has seduced Mrs. Ousley because, being half black, she had always hated her husband, who was pure white. By this time Dr. Birney would have circled back to his house, which he would set on fire in order to destroy his two sleeping children. When the mob captures him he will be first hanged and then burned, while an idiot boy explains to a black prostitute how well the punishment fits the crime. The negress will then reveal that Dr. Birney is her grandson and the mob will caper with joy upon being told that it has lynched a part negro.[2]

---

[2] Grant C. Knight, *James Lane Allen and the Genteel Tradition* (1935), pp. 271–272. See also "A Scythe for Mother"—which its author calls "a fairly typical representation of the South in modern fiction"—in William T. Polk, *Southern Accent* (1953), pp. 15–17.

Once again the Northern novelist found it profitable to lay his scene in the South and to capitalize on the vogue for Southern stories. When Northern writers, like James Boyd and Hervey Allen, who had lived in the South, turned to Southern scenes, the result might be something noteworthy. Many, however, knew no more about the South than the Northern writers of the eighties and nineties who had found it profitable to write sentimental intersectional love stories. Their conception of the South was, in the words of Donald Davidson, that of "a region full of little else but lynchings, shootings, chain gangs, poor whites, Ku Kluxers, hookworm, pellagra, and a few decayed patricians whose chief intent is to deprive the uncontaminated, spiritual-singing Negro of his life and liberty." [3]

One of the worst specimens of Northern fiction dealing with Southern life is Howard Fast's *Freedom Road* (1944). The novel is dedicated "To the men and women, black and white, yellow and brown, who have laid down their lives in the struggle against fascism." Fast's thesis is that the Southern interpretation of Reconstruction was merely a rationalization of that section's determination to perpetuate racial discrimination. Lincoln's plans for the South were foolish. The really great statesman of the North was Thaddeus Stevens—the Pennsylvania Congressman who hated white Southerners and kept a Negro housekeeper supposed to be his mistress. If only Stevens' policy of bayonet rule had been continued indefinitely, something approaching a happy Utopian millennium would have dawned upon the Southern states. In fact, Fast maintains in "An Afterword" that during the eight-year period in which "the Negro had been given the right to exist in this nation as a free man," "he had created a fine, a just, and a truly democratic civilization." This is myth-making with a vengeance. The old Abolitionists might be pardoned for their ignorance of Southern history but not a historical novelist of the twentieth century with some pretensions to scholarship.

When Cable began expressing his views of the race question in the eighties, he found the South arrayed almost solidly against him. In the 1920's and 1930's, however, there was no longer a literary Solid South. The masses condemned Faulkner and Caldwell without taking the trouble to read their works, but the reaction of the intellectuals was mixed. A minority greeted them as heralds of a new literary freedom, yet many intelligent Southern readers were indignant. It seemed to them that Faulkner and Caldwell were in a sense betraying their own section in order to sell their books in the North.

The case of the Southern liberals who found themselves under attack from

[3] *The Attack on Leviathan* (1938), p. 156.

the Neo-Abolitionists of North and South was never better stated than in Louis B. Wright's article, "Myth-Makers and the South's Dilemma." The article appeared in the Autumn, 1945, number of the *Sewanee Review*, then edited by Allen Tate; and it may be doubted whether in that year its author could have found a Northern magazine editor willing to print it. "In the eyes of left-wing reformers," said Wright, "the Southern white finds himself damned if he does and damned if he doesn't." "When Southerners treat Negroes well, they are 'rationalizing their guilt complex,' or they want to 'rationalize an exaggerated ego' which makes them 'contemptibly patronizing' and anxious to retain feudal vestiges of patronage toward inferiors. If they try to explain the economic reasons why social progress has been slow, they are 'rationalizing the *status quo*.'" The new nationwide interest in the South, Wright notes, "finds its deepest satisfaction not in the fragrance of magnolias but in *fleurs du mal*, in the clowning bawdry of Erskine Caldwell and the exotic perversions of William Faulkner." Lillian Smith's *Strange Fruit* is "a sort of inverted pastoral romance." "But many an outlander reading the story," he suggests, "is certain that North Georgia is a region where every white boy lusts after irresistible Negro girls; where these eager youths engage in erotic dalliance until overtaken by Envy, Jealousy, Revenge and Hate (personified by libidinous Baptist preachers, anemic white girls, vengeful Negro men, and assorted specimens of poor whites)."

Why did Northern readers enjoy novels and plays which Southerners resented as distortions of the truth? Was there not something malicious in the pleasure which the Northern reader got out of the stories of Erskine Caldwell? A Texas friend of mine who went to see a performance of *Tobacco Road* in New York wondered what kept the play on the stage year after year. In the hope of finding some clew, he listened eagerly during the intermissions for comments from the spectators. He thought that perhaps he had found the secret of the play's popularity when he overheard a Northern young woman say to her husband or sweetheart: "And these Southerners think they are so much better than we are!"

If we ask why a Southerner would write stories of this kind, Wright suggests a plausible answer: "Southern authors, and would-be authors, discouraged by an accumulating pile of rejection slips, at last discerned that crinoline romanticism was out, but that a hangman's noose and a faggot would work a charm. Once having realized what the customers wanted, the writing profession, both North and South, got on with the job of production."

Lanterns on the Levee (1941), the autobiography of the poet-planter-lawyer William Alexander Percy, reveals the plight of the conservative

Southerner who had "witnessed a disintegration of that moral cohesion of the South which had given it its strength and its sons their singleness of purpose and simplicity."

The old Southern way of life in which I had been reared existed no more and its values were ignored or derided. Negroes used to be servants, now they were problems; manners used to be a branch of morals, now they were merely bad; poverty used to be worn with style and dignity, now it was a stigma of failure; politics used to be the study of men proud and jealous of America's honor, now it was a game played by self-seekers which no man need bother his head about; where there had been an accepted plan of living, there was no pattern whatsoever.

When the Southern Agrarians, whose headquarters were at Vanderbilt University in Nashville, published their symposium, *I'll Take My Stand*, in 1930, Northern critics were frankly puzzled. They could understand—for the Depression had arrived—an attack upon the evils of industrialism: overproduction, unemployment, and a glaring inequality in the distribution of wealth; but they found it incredible that intelligent men should advocate a return to the ideals of the Old South of slavery and semibarbarism. It was like Don Quixote charging the windmills or Captain Ahab with a six-inch knife seeking the fathoms-deep heart of the leviathan White Whale. The explanation involves a brief digression into history and economics.

After the First World War, Northern criticism of the South's treatment of the Negro became more open and more violent. The election in 1920 of a Republican President seemed to serve as a signal for denunciations in Congress and in the Northern press. The Georgia chain gangs, the Harlan mine troubles, the Scopes trial in Dayton, Tennessee, the rantings of Southern political demagogues, and the activities of the new Ku Klux Klan—for which the South received the blame although the Klan was equally strong in the Middle West—all supplied materials for critics of the South. With some feeling Donald Davidson remarked in *The Attack on Leviathan* (1938) that while "the major problem before the American people was how to adjust an overexpanded industrial machine to post-war conditions, it was again the Southern 'outrage' that kept the public amused while the way was being greased for Hoover prosperity and the great debacle of 1929." Enlightened Southerners found themselves increasingly embarrassed when they advocated any measures calculated to improve race relations. Northern criticism was one of the factors that enabled Southern political demagogues to keep themselves in power.

Under Franklin D. Roosevelt and Harry S. Truman, Democrats though they were, hostility to the South increased notably. The South was the nation's "No. 1 Economic Problem," and it must be "Americanized." Roosevelt and Truman discovered that the South was not politically important, especially since the Negroes in many Southern states were deserting the Republican party *en masse*. With the abolition in 1936 of the two-thirds rule by the Democratic National Convention, the South had lost its power to prevent the nomination of a hostile candidate. In 1944 it became clear that the Northern labor unions would probably veto the nomination of any Southern candidate no matter what his record. The "Dixiecrat" attempt to defeat Truman in 1948 was a complete failure. In the 1952 Democratic National Convention Northern left-wingers, in their desire to get control of the party, came perilously close to kicking out of the party the Democrats of Virginia and South Carolina, the states that claim as their own its two patron saints, Thomas Jefferson and Andrew Jackson.

Northern New Dealers and Fair Dealers denounced the poll tax, the segregation laws, unequal educational facilities for black and white, landowners who rented to sharecroppers, and many other things. The South was to be reformed by placing Federal laws upon the statute books as in the days of Thaddeus Stevens and Charles Sumner. The proposed laws might be excellent, but could they be enforced in states where only a minority was in favor of them? Southerners wondered if the desire to put FEPC laws on the statute books did not come primarily from a desire to punish the South. Only nine of the Northern states had passed laws to prevent employers from discriminating on racial grounds. Ignorant idealists, it seemed, men who knew nothing about the South, wanted to reform it overnight. Communists and fellow-travelers joined in denouncing the South as a backward, semi-barbarous region.[3a] On the stage, the screen, and the radio it became the fashion to ridicule the Southern accent. Southern women complained that their servants were becoming increasingly arrogant and unreliable. Sometimes they blamed it on the supposed "Eleanor Clubs," attributed to Mrs. Roosevelt. William Alexander Percy expressed the feeling of many Southern whites when he wrote in *Lanterns on the Levee* (1941): "The noblest of them [white Northern sentimentalists], such as Mrs. Roosevelt, accomplish their insidious evil quite unsuspectingly and with the highest motives. It will never occur to them that the results, however pitiful or savage, will have been of their making." No Northerner would believe Percy when he argued that "the improvement [in race relations], if improvement there is, is due solely to the white man," or take him seriously when he said: "A super-

---

[3a] Eugene Holmes wrote in "A Writer's Social Obligations": "Terrorism is so much the rule through the South as to permit one to say that this section of the country is already fascized" (*The Writer in a Changing World*, ed. Henry Hart, 1937, p. 174).

abundance of sympathy has always been expended on the Negro . . . but no sympathy whatever, so far as I am aware, has ever been expended on the white man living among Negroes. Yet he, too, is worthy not only of sympathy but of pity, and for many reasons." Northern critics of the South's treatment of the Negro had little to say about discriminatory treatment in the Northern cities. They seemed not to realize that there was race prejudice on both sides of the color line. They forgot the growing hatred of all whites in Asia and Africa. They did not see that many Negro newspapers almost invariably took the side of the Negro in every difficulty between whites and blacks. Indeed, so biased were many Negro papers that one Negro editor, Warren H. Brown, protested against their policies in the *Saturday Review of Literature* for December 19, 1942.

In *The Significance of Sections in American History* (1932) the eminent historian, Frederick J. Turner, pointed out that the various sections are not to be regarded as vestiges of earlier historical movements but as living functions of the nation. It was fatal, he suggested, not to take into consideration sectional differences in all national planning. Turner's earlier essays on the significance of the frontier had led to the rewriting of American history, but his later work went almost unnoticed except by students of American history and sociology. *I'll Take My Stand* attracted some attention in literary circles, but two much more impressive attacks upon Northern industrialism went comparatively unnoticed. These were Walter Prescott Webb's *Divided We Stand* (1937) and Donald Davidson's *The Attack on Leviathan* (1938).

In *Divided We Stand* Professor Webb, author of that historical classic, *The Great Plains* (1931), maintained that after the Civil War, which left industrialism without a check, the North had "extended its economic conquest" over the South and the West "until it owns not only its own section but a controlling interest in the South and the West." In spite of the fact that the South and the West contained a great part of the resources of the nation, capitalists in the Northeast, he estimated, had managed to acquire the ownership or control of from 80 to 95 per cent of the wealth of the entire country. Whether one looked at the nation's large corporations, its bank deposits, its railroads, its factories, or merely the number of persons in the high-income brackets, he said, backing his contention by statistics, the result was the same. The North owned the machinery and the patents. By means of a high tariff and discriminatory freight rates it had taken its toll from other sections. The comparatively poor South, in addition to pensioning its own soldiers had had to pay millions in pensions to Union veterans. Worse still, by means of its system of chain stores the North was now crowding the independent merchant to the wall whether he sold drugs, groceries, clothing, or auto supplies. A druggist in Austin, Texas, told Webb that out of some ten thousand items on his shelves, at least 9,900 came from Northern firms.

Webb conceded that there were many persons living in the Northern states who did not share in the wealth being drawn from the South and the West. Nevertheless, he pointed out, they profited in better schools, roads, and other things. Northern millionaires often gave generously of their money to charitable and educational institutions, but it was a rare event, Webb noted, when they gave to institutions situated in the regions from which their wealth had been drawn. In short, the situation as Webb described it in 1937 bore a striking resemblance to the "cotton triangle" and the tariff laws against which Southern economists and politicians had thundered a century earlier.[4] Nor could Webb see in 1937 that the New Deal had done much to alter the situation.

The contributors to *I'll Take My Stand* saw the South as led astray by Southern liberals, like Henry W. Grady and Walter Hines Page, who shared none of Henry Adams's doubts about the gospel of "Progress." Such men, the Agrarians contended, had led the South into a way of life alien to its native genius. During the Great Depression, when the stock of the big businessman had sunk to an all-time low, readers in the urban North might relish the Agrarian attack upon him from an unexpected quarter. It was difficult for Northern readers, however, to sympathize with the "Neo-Confederates" when they openly advocated an Agrarian society. This they defined as "one in which agriculture is the leading vocation, whether for wealth, for pleasure, or for prestige—a form of labor that is pursued with intelligence and leisure." Agriculture, they said, is "the best and most sensitive of vocations."

Some Southern readers, knowing what was the actual lot of the farmer in 1930, wondered whether any of the Agrarians had a firsthand knowledge of life on a cotton or tobacco farm. Among the contributors to *I'll Take My Stand* there were two or three able and well-trained historians, but the impression made on the reader by most of the contributors is that they did not know their Southern history. Their Old South was too much like the idealized picture in Page's *In Ole Virginia*. For the very small minority who owned great plantations and were able to cultivate the art of living, life in the Old South was attractive enough. But if one could not belong to the small leisure class, who would wish to return to the Old South of Ransy Sniffles, old-field schools, and the hookworm disease? What South-

[4] See also B. B. Kendrick, "The Colonial Status of the South," *Jour. So. Hist.*, VIII, 3–22 (Feb., 1942).

ern farmer would be willing to give up his McCormick reaper and his tractor and return to the backbreaking cradle and the bull-tongue plow? Many Southerners, much as they sympathized with the Agrarian indictment of industrialism, felt that perhaps the remedy was to be found in still further industrialization which would bring to the farmer rural electrification, good roads, telephones, and other modern conveniences. At any rate, it was too late to go back to the old way of life. If the South was to compete with its tobacco and its cotton in a world market, it must have the best of modern machinery.[5]

This is not the place to survey the achievements of the writers who have created the notable Southern renaissance of this century. Some day they will find their special historian. Meanwhile they have not gone without recognition from the historians who concern themselves with contemporary literature. I shall use my remaining space in an attempt to indicate the complicated relationship of Southern literature to our national literary tradition.

6

The South in American Literature

THE EARLIER historians of Southern literature ignored the writings of all but natives of their section and so, it seems to me, failed to appreciate the full significance of the place which the South holds in our national literature. Much of the best indeed that has been written about Southern life, especially in the Old South, came from the pens of outsiders. Northern and European visitors were frequently impressed by features of the social life which to the native Southerners seemed a mere matter of course.[6] It was a New Yorker, James Fenimore Cooper, who drew in *The Spy* the first notable portrait of a dashing Virginia cavalryman and so perhaps suggested to Kennedy, Caruthers, and Simms the richness of the Southern historical background.

[5] In their *Economic Resources and Policies of the South* (1951), p. 367, two able Southern economists, Calvin B. Hoover and B. U. Ratchford, conclude that while industrialization "is not an unmixed blessing," "there is a large net advantage on the side of industry and that industrialization provides the principal means for raising incomes in the South." "The income of Southerners," they point out, "would have to be increased by about 50 per cent to make it roughly equal to the income of non-southerners" (p. 364).

[6] The list of British writers who have been attracted to Virginia alone is a long one; and it includes Michael Drayton, Daniel Defoe, John Davis, G. P. R. James, Thackeray, Arthur Granville Bradley, John Masefield, John Buchan, and David Garnett.

The first important novels of Kentucky were written by James Kirke Paulding of New York and Robert Montgomery Bird of Pennsylvania. Among the many Northern writers who in the later nineteenth century made use of Southern materials, especially in fiction, are Constance Fenimore Woolson, Thomas Bailey Aldrich, Frank R. Stockton, Albion W. Tourgée, Bret Harte, Mary Wilkins Freeman, and Sarah Orne Jewett and in the twentieth century, Owen Wister, Joseph Hergesheimer, Hervey Allen, James Boyd, Kenneth Roberts, Vachel Lindsay, Elinor Wylie, and Willa Cather, who though born in Virginia grew up in Nebraska.

Most of those whom I have named wrote of the South with some knowledge and a certain degree of sympathy, but there were other Northern writers for whom the slaveholding South represented an ominous economic, political, and moral problem. For Emerson, Lowell, Mrs. Stowe, John W. De Forest, and others, the South was an obstacle to the development of industry, religion, and democracy; and they wanted to "Americanize" it. In their eyes the literature of the Old South was unacceptable because it had grown out of the iniquitous slavery regime.

Mrs. Stowe, Joseph Hergesheimer, and many another Northern writer have commented upon the extraordinary richness of Southern life as material for literature, and some of them have wondered why Southern writers have not made more of it. John Townsend Trowbridge, who spent four months in the devastated Southern states in 1865, wrote in My Own Story (1903): ". . . no other country or epoch ever furnished such abundant and rich materials for romantic or realistic fiction, humorous, tragic, pathetic, picturesque, full of great events and of the most amazing contrasts of characters and conditions, as appealed to the heart and imagination in the old slave states, at that period of social upheaval." The literature of the New South did not satisfy Trowbridge. He continued: "That the currents, counter-currents, and sombre abysses of that troubled time have floated some bright fiction, must be freely admitted. That they did not burst forth and overflow in tidal waves of power and passion, lifting a great and enduring literature, is the marvel."

The literature which deals with the incomparably rich materials of Southern life represents two widely divergent literary traditions, which even in the twentieth century are not fully reconciled.[7] There is the South of the Abolitionists, of Uncle Tom's Cabin, and The Biglow Papers: a semibarbarous land which must somehow be made to fit into the "national" pattern. And there is the rival Southern tradition, best expressed in Nights

[7] Parts of the discussion which follows are taken from an unfinished study, "The American Writer and the Literary Tradition."

with Uncle Remus and *In Ole Virginia*, that the slave plantation represented an almost idyllic existence, a land of chivalrous planters and loyal and contented slaves. Before the Civil War Northern readers rejected that conception as expressed in Grayson's *The Hireling and the Slave*, but in the eighties and nineties they delighted in Southern stories based largely upon the same conception of the plantation.

In the twentieth century some Northern and Southern writers have reverted in some degree to the unsympathetic attitude of the Abolitionists and have pictured the South as a backward and intolerant region, not fully Americanized and out of step with democracy and industrial progress. As a result, much Northern discussion of Southern problems suffers from ignorance and misunderstanding. The Northerner too frequently still looks for some simple formula which will explain the complexities and the contradictions of Southern life. There is of course no such formula.

The slaveholding South was until after 1830 in the main content to get its reading matter, apart from local newspapers, from England and the Northern states. But after the founding of Garrison's *Liberator* in 1831 and the rise of the New England "School" of writers, the South found itself unable to accept much of the new literature which emanated from the Northern states. It then began half consciously building up a regional literature, modeled upon English writers, which was also in part a literature of defense. The South was more or less consciously building up a rival literary tradition. Exasperated by the misrepresentations of the antislavery writers, the conservative South saw itself as the defender of the constitutional rights of the states and as the victim of a moral crusade conducted by an alliance of zealots, doctrinaires, and unscrupulous politicians determined to separate the Southern planters from their natural political allies, the Northern and Western farmers. The South also felt itself exploited, as in some degree it undoubtedly was, by the merchants and manufacturers of the North.

The literature of the Old South was intrinsically more important than the Northern literary historians were willing to admit. Not until the twentieth century did their successors realize how completely their point of view had been determined by the dominant New England literary tradition. That tradition, provincial though it seemed to Simms, Poe, Boker, and Henry James, was for a time accepted as a genuinely national literary tradition. Its success was due in large part to its impassioned idealism and its undoubted literary power. Emerson, Hawthorne, Thoreau, and Longfellow had no peers among writers in other sections except Poe, Melville, and Whitman; and these three writers were long unacceptable not only in New England but in other parts of America.[8] Its Puritan inheritance and its geographical position gave New England a unity of feeling which the Southern states did not have until after 1850. New England had a remarkably fine educational and cultural tradition. Most of its writers had attended Harvard College, and they lived in or near Boston. In this regional capital the author's social standing was much higher than it was in New York, Philadelphia, or Charleston; and in no other American city was there so keen an interest in culture or ideas. In the publishing house of Ticknor and Fields, which in 1859 took over the *Atlantic Monthly*, the New England writers had a publishing house which appreciated the high quality of their writings and knew how to market them efficiently.

The literature of New England was in large part written by ministers or ex-ministers or the sons of ministers, by teachers, lecturers, and reformers promoting one or another of the numerous causes obnoxious to the conservative South. That literature was not greatly concerned with art although it had a fine artist in Hawthorne and a great prose writer in Thoreau. The New England writers had little patience with criticism on artistic grounds. Poe constantly chided them for their ingrained didacticism, but his criticism made little impression upon them. Howells, who knew and loved them, wrote in his *Literary Friends and Acquaintance* (1900): "They or their fathers had broken away from orthodoxy in the great schism at the beginning of the century, but, as if their heterodoxy were conscience-stricken, they still helplessly pointed the moral in all they did; some pointed it more directly, some less directly; but they all pointed it."

The New England writers sought each in his own way to make righteousness and the will of God to prevail. To their Southern readers they seemed to be trying to make over on the Yankee pattern a nation which they knew very little about. The Abolitionists and Transcendentalists in fact were singularly blind to the dangers of the industrial revolution which was sweeping over their section. They were much more concerned about the sins of the distant South than they were about what was happening in their own factories and shipyards and in the Irish slums in the heart of Boston. The attempt to "Americanize" the South in the Reconstruction period was to prove disastrous.

Those other literary capitals, Philadelphia and New York, were slow to accept the New England hegemony and yield precedence to Boston. By virtue of their geographical position and their strong commercial ties with the South and the West, they were more national in their outlook and more

[8] For the failure of most New England writers to appreciate the writings of Poe, see pp. 542–549.

hospitable to Southern writers, who often went there to have their books published. In the thirties and forties, when Poe lived and Simms often visited in New York, they and other Southern writers were on intimate terms with some New York writers, editors, and publishers. But the rapid progress westward of the expanding industrial belt tended to unite the people of the North and to turn them against a rural civilization based upon slavery. As the controversy over slavery became acute, most of the New York writers, editors, and publishers took sides against the South. There were in fact many New Englanders who held important positions on the New York magazines and newspapers. Of the thirty-eight writers whom Poe discussed in "The Literati of New York City" exactly one half were natives of New England. For the next generation our literary tradition was to be a New York– New England tradition. The Southern writers, finding themselves no longer welcome in the great Northern cities, became more insistent that the South must build up its own literature.

Although Simms and Poe regarded the literature of New England as a purely sectional literature and Henry James deplored its provinciality, there were important national elements in it—more than our intellectual rebels of the 1920's who rejected it were willing to admit. (We know now that if New England had been like other sections of the country, Emerson, Hawthorne, and Thoreau might never have developed into the major figures they unquestionably are.) The literature of New England included controversial elements which were ultimately to win national acceptance. In the long dispute over slavery and the nature of the Union, New England, we may say, bet on the winning side. The antislavery faction, numerically small in the beginning, eventually won over to its cause the major part of the divided nation. The freeing of the slaves had the effect of justifying Channing, Whittier, Emerson, and Lowell for having taken the stand that human slavery was incompatible with democracy, Christianity, and industrial progress. The South paid the penalty for turning its back upon the liberalism of Jefferson, whose mantle in a sense fell not upon Jefferson Davis but upon that son of Virginia parents, Abraham Lincoln. In the 1850's New England found itself aligned with the states north of the Potomac and the Ohio and thrust into a position of cultural and literary if not of political leadership. A new sense of unity with the states west of the Hudson resulted. There was no more talk of secession in New England.

By 1870 New Englanders had written perhaps half of what is important in our earlier literature; and since Poe, Melville, and Whitman were not widely recognized as great writers, they seemed to have written much more of it. By 1870 also New England had created the canon of the Great American Writers. The beginnings of the process can be seen in the anthologies of Samuel Kettell and Rufus W. Griswold. It is evident also in the first version of Hawthorne's "The Hall of Fantasy" (1843), and it is clearly apparent in Lowell's A Fable for Critics (1848). Lowell mentioned no writer who lived south or west of New York, but he found no difficulty in making places for Bronson Alcott, Orestes Brownson, John Neal, Charles F. Briggs, Theodore Parker, Margaret Fuller, and Lydia Maria Child. Of most of these the Southern reviewers of A Fable had never heard except perhaps as·authors of antislavery propaganda; and they denounced Lowell's poem as a sectional product, which undoubtedly it was. Most of our influential early critics were New Englanders, and their critical opinions were often echoed in our earlier literary histories, which gave scant attention to writers from the South and the West. George W. Cable, who in effect turned Abolitionist after the Civil War, was the first writer of the New South who could without difficulty be fitted into the then dominant New York–New England literary tradition.

In the creation of the canon of the Great American Writers the Boston publishers, especially Ticknor and Fields and the Houghton Mifflin Company, played an important part.[9] On their lists they had more great books than all of the New York and Philadelphia publishers put together, and they played them up as such throughout the North, the West, and eventually the South as well. Howells, who as a young man read their books in Ohio, once remarked: "Ticknor and Fields . . . were literary publishers in a sense such as the business world has known nowhere else before or since." The tribute is probably deserved, but Howells was a poor prophet when he went on to say: "Their imprint was a warrant of quality to the reader, and of immortality to the author." Alas! the Ticknor and Fields imprint brought no immortality to many on its list, including those Southern poets Timrod and Hayne, who before the Civil War paid the house to bring out their poems.

In the 1870's the Houghton Mifflin Company initiated its notable American Men of Letters series of biographies, which it advertised as "Collectively, . . . a biographical history of American Literature." The authors included were much the same as those mentioned in Lowell's A Fable for Critics, and in earlier years the series might more appropriately have been called the New England Men of Letters series. Eventually it included Poe, Whitman, Simms, Lanier, and Bayard Taylor, but the West continued unrepresented. It was Cable who was first asked to write the life of Simms, and

⁹ This is pointed out in Howard Mumford Jones, The Theory of American Literature (1948), pp. 85–87, 112.

when he finally gave it up, the assignment was given to W. P. Trent. Obviously the publishers wanted the Simms biography written by a thoroughly reconstructed Southerner. The new American Men of Letters series, now being published by the William Sloane Associates, exhibits a greatly altered canon of Great American Writers.

Most of our early literary historians were New Englanders—all honor to them! One cannot accuse these hardworking scholars, investigating a neglected field, of any intentional discrimination against writers from other sections; but nonetheless it is obvious now that for them the literary history of America was primarily the story of the rise and decline of the New England "School." The historians made room for Irving and Cooper, but they could not fit Whitman, Melville, or Poe into the dominant literary tradition. Simms and his fellows of the Old South were hopelessly discredited.

Barrett Wendell's A Literary History of America (1900) is one of the most engagingly written of our literary histories, but its proportions are astonishing. In his 530 pages of text Wendell gave to the West a chapter of only 15 pages; to "Literature in the South" he gave 20. The remainder is devoted to New York, Pennsylvania, and New England—mostly New England.[10] It is clear that Wendell had read Trent's life of Simms and a few poems by Timrod and Lanier, but almost the only piece of Southern writing to arouse his enthusiasm was Dr. Ticknor's "Little Giffen." The accusation which Bernard DeVoto unjustly brought against Van Wyck Brooks is certainly applicable to Wendell: ". . . the inability to credit the reality of any portion of the country except New England . . . was central in the literary tradition which he accepted."

How strong the New York–New England tradition was in the eighties and nineties may be seen from a glance at the various ratings of American authors undertaken by the New York literary weekly, the Critic. On April 12, 1884, after polling its readers, the weekly published "Our Forty Immortals," a list of living Americans whom the Critic suggested as a nucleus for a possible American academy of letters. The first five places went to Holmes, Lowell, Whittier, Bancroft, and Howells. Henry James rated only thirteenth, and Whitman was twentieth, two notches below the forgotten Richard Henry Stoddard. Melville apparently got no votes. The only authors of Southern birth were Cable, who was twelfth, and Mark Twain, who won fourteenth place. In its issue of July 19, 1890, the Critic selected "Nine New 'Immortals' " to replace those who had died. Joel Chandler Harris came in as eighth. On August 21, 1890, the New York Nation analyzed the final list of

---

[10] For Wendell's changing opinion of Poe, see pp. 548–549.

forty and concluded that, whether one classified the writers according to the states in which they were born or in which they now lived: "New England and New York, it seems, still furnish the bulk of the recognized authors of the nation. . . ." Of the total number no less than twenty-five had been born in New England, seventeen in Massachusetts alone; and fourteen of the forty were graduates of Harvard.

Like the *Critic's* readers, the literary historians failed to realize that something like a revolution was taking place in American literature in the later nineteenth century. They failed to note that the center of literary production, like the center of population, had shifted to the west and south of New York City. By 1870 the greater New England writers had done their best work and were leaving only feeble heirs to carry on the New England tradition—a tradition now diluted and weakened by a heavy infusion of the sentimental and the genteel. Except for Sarah Orne Jewett and the still unknown Emily Dickinson, the really important writers living in New England—Howells, Henry James, and Mark Twain—were outsiders, whose literary aims were widely different from those of Emerson, Holmes, and Longfellow. The younger reformers, like Edward Bellamy, Henry George, and Howells, could not find in Transcendentalist thought a solution for the enigma of the intimate connection between industrial progress and poverty, riches and exploitation. Bellamy was a New Englander, but Howells and George had lived in the West, which was now more than ever determined to make a place for itself in American literature.

Meanwhile, although it pained Bostonians to admit it, the literary leadership was passing to New York. In that rapidly growing metropolis the literary outlook was different, even to editors and publishers who had grown up in New England. Whatever the editor's or publisher's personal preferences might be, he wanted a nationwide market for his wares. He saw in the West and the South a great increase in potential buyers of books and magazines. He noted also the emergence of new Western and Southern writers whose work was in demand. There was also, he saw, a shift in the taste of the reading public. What his readers liked best, he discovered, was not Transcendentalist essays, lectures, and poems but novels and local-color short stories. The new national literature was largely regional in nature, but it was as never before directed to a nationwide audience. With the emergence of the literary West and the New South our literature became national in a sense in which it had never been before the Civil War.

The West had long been jealous of the literary domination of New England. Edward Eggleston of Indiana wrote in the Preface to *The Hoosier Schoolmaster* (1871): "It used to be a matter of no little jealousy with us,

I remember, that the manners, customs, thoughts, and feelings of New England country people filled so large a place in our books, while our life, not less interesting, not less romantic, and certainly not less filled with humorous and grotesque material, had no place in literature. It was as though we were shut out of good society." Margaret Lynn, growing up on a Midwestern prairie, found the nature poetry of New England as remote as that of Tennyson from the landscape she knew and wanted portrayed in literature. The West, which knew that geographically it was the major part of the nation, resented the condescension of Easterners much as Lowell resented the condescension of European visitors. Of the Eastern attitude toward Nebraska while she was writing O Pioneers! (1913) Willa Cather wrote in 1931: "As everyone knows, Nebraska is distinctly déclassé as a literary background; its very name throws the delicately attuned critic into a clammy shiver of embarrassment. Kansas is almost as unpromising." "Colorado," she added, "is considered quite possible. Wyoming really has some class, like well-cut riding breeches. But a New York critic voiced a very general opinion when he said: 'I simply don't care a damn what happens in Nebraska, no matter who writes about it.' " No reputable critic would make such a statement now. For the past half century it has been Western more often than Eastern or Southern writers who have set the pace, especially in fiction. In the eyes of the Westerner both the New Englander and the Southerner were provincial types. He agreed with James Bryce that the West is the most American part of the United States; and he welcomed Frederick J. Turner's pronouncement in 1893: "The true point of view in the history of this nation is not the Atlantic coast, it is the Great West."

Rebellion against literary conventions and traditional ideals is a recurrent phenomenon in the history of all literatures; but our genteel critics and professors of English were not prepared for the revolt of unprecedented violence which broke out in the 1920's. The youthful intelligentsia seemed bent on throwing overboard our whole literary and cultural inheritance, and they had a special animus against New England. Longfellow was for them synonymous with all that was bad in our literary tradition. In America's Coming of Age (1915) Van Wyck Brooks briefly considered the New England poets and found them lacking in the elements of greatness. In his later phase Brooks wrote more soberly in 1934: "A decade or two ago, we were all engaged in a game that might have been called bearding the prophets, all too ready to say, 'Go up, thou bald-head,' in the presence of the Elishas of the moment. We had had too much of the old New England poets. We were tired of hearing Longfellow called 'the Just,' and inscribed our shards against him, even to the number of six thousand, as the inconstant Athenians used to do."

In the 1920's the reputations of most of the older New England writers had sunk to an all-time low. How low is apparent to one who glances at "The New Order of Critical Values," which appeared in *Vanity Fair* in April, 1922, or "Spring Elections on Mount Olympus," published in the *Bookman* one month later. In the *Bookman's* list, on a scale ranging from +25 to −25, Longfellow rated only +.6 while Whitman with +17.1 was near the top of the list.

Scholars and critics in academic circles were among the last to concede that the New England literary tradition was outmoded. In this era of revolt the attempt of the New England-born Stuart P. Sherman to revive the faded Puritan tradition seemed like an anachronism. In two essays in *The Genius of America* (1923), published while he was still a professor of English at the University of Illinois, he argued that the Puritan inheritance is the central element in our literary and cultural tradition. In "What is a Puritan?" he even maintained that "the Puritan is profoundly in sympathy with the modern spirit, is indeed the formative force in the modern spirit." To H. L. Mencken all this seemed reactionary, as undoubtedly it was. "Historically," wrote Mencken, "there is . . . nothing but folly and ignorance in all the current prattle about a restoration of the ancient American tradition. The ancient American tradition, in so far as it was vital and productive and civilized, was obviously a tradition of individualism and revolt, not of herd-morality and conformity." What the conservative academic critics were defending, he said, was not "a tradition that would take in Poe, Hawthorne, Emerson, Whitman and Mark Twain, but a tradition that would pass over all these men to embrace Cooper, Bryant, Donald G. Mitchell, N. P. Willis, J. G. Holland, Charles Dudley Warner, Mrs. Sigourney and the Sweet Singer of Michigan."

Sherman and other conservative critics noted with dismay the number of new writers with German, Jewish, Scandinavian, and other un-English names: Mencken, Dreiser, Sandburg, Untermeyer, Dos Passos, Adamic, etc. The descendants of millions of European immigrants, now coming into their cultural inheritance, had scant respect for the Puritan ideal or the New England literary tradition. These new writers were making our literature in some respects more truly national than it had ever been before. Mencken, who stoutly championed Dreiser and other new writers, was perhaps correct in saying: "The rancorous animosity that has pursued such men as Dreiser is certainly not wholly aesthetic, or even moral: it is, to a very large extent, racial."

The new American literature of the 1920's and 1930's, in spite of its brilliance and its power, disturbed conservative readers in the South as well as in New England and the West. The South had finally accepted the New York–New England literary tradition, with some reservations, as its own; and Southerners resented the attacks upon Longfellow almost as much as they would have resented similar criticism of Lanier.

In the two decades between the two World Wars it seemed to conservative American readers, especially outside the great cities, that many of our ablest writers had abandoned much of the best in our traditional literary ideals. The new writers seemed possessed by a mood of desperate unhappiness. The modern world as the novelists and poets painted it was a wasteland over which wandered men and women driven on by primitive urges but without either faith or hope. Their own country seemed to these writers a decadent land, without faith in its traditional ideals, fast drifting toward anarchy or some form of totalitarianism.

Viewed in the historical perspective, much of the literature of the twenties and thirties now seems a strange product to come out of a nation fast becoming the greatest of world powers. Was it any wonder that European dictators and Japanese imperialists thought the United States incapable of waging an effective war against them? No doubt the social satires and social criticism of Dreiser, Lewis, Farrell, and Dos Passos served sometimes to awaken their complacent countrymen and make them face the shortcomings of the society in which they lived, but the effect upon European and Asiatic readers has not been happy. They derive their notions of American life largely from our novels and our motion pictures; and if they now distrust our motives when we are trying to solve the world's problems, is it any wonder when we remember the books and the pictures we have sent them? There is no doubt that some of our ablest writers, Southern as well as Northern, unwittingly played into the hands of Nazi and Communist propagandists.[11] In an age when so many millions have suddenly discovered that there is an American literature, it is unfortunate that we cannot persuade

---

[11] Van Wyck Brooks, who is not a Southerner, writes: "Who can be happy that, in France, America is the country of Richard Wright's Native Son and Black Boy, in which Negroes are shot like blackbirds in trees or given knives, to fight one another, like gamecocks, for the amusement of Tennessee whites? Or the country of Erskine Caldwell's stories in which sheriffs go fishing when lynchings occur and 'nigger hunting' and 'possum hunting' are on the same level?" (The Writer in America, 1953, pp. 98–99).

A French scholar, Lucienne Escoube, in "Les Plantations et les Etats du Sud dans la littérature américaine," Mercure de France, CCCIII, 64–77 (May, 1948), urged French readers to acquaint themselves with the fiction of Kennedy, Simms, Stark Young, and Margaret Mitchell as a corrective to the distorted pictures given by Faulkner and Caldwell.

them to read the poems of Robert Frost or the novels of Willa Cather and Ellen Glasgow in which they might find an America that they could learn to like and respect.

By the beginning of the Second World War the force of the great literary rebellion seemed to have spent itself. The attack on Pearl Harbor, if not the outbreak of war in Europe in 1939, made many Americans feel that their writers had been, so to speak, selling their country short. Democracy, when one has to fight for it, becomes the most precious of possessions. Jefferson, Emerson, and Whitman revealed their true stature in those trying times. Meanwhile Van Wyck Brooks, now in his later phase, had discovered the real greatness of Emerson, and in *The Flowering of New England* (1936) he had brought to life the fading figures in our greatest single group of writers and shown that there was still vitality in the New England cultural tradition. In *On Literature Today* (1941) he maintained that the "mood of health, will, courage, faith in human nature" was "the dominant mood in the history of literature" in Europe as well as America. He protested against the notion, so prevalent in the twenties and thirties, that "life is a dark little pocket" or "the plaything in Theodore Dreiser's phrase, of 'idle rocking forces' or currents of material interest." In their later books Hemingway, Dos Passos, and Steinbeck seemed to be returning to something approximating the traditional American ideals. So also did William Faulkner, who when he received the Nobel Prize for Literature said in Stockholm:

. . . I decline to accept the end of man. . . . He is immortal, not because he alone among creatures has an inexhaustible voice, but because he has a soul, a spirit capable of compassion and sacrifice and endurance. The poet's, the writer's, duty is to write about these things. It is his privilege to help man endure by lifting his heart, by reminding him of the courage and honor and hope and pride and compassion and pity and sacrifice which have been the glory of the past. The poet's voice need not merely be the record of man, it can be one of the props, the pillars to help him endure and prevail.

It is, I think, significant that the words of this Southern writer met with such nationwide approval. They suggest that American literature has returned in some measure to its traditional ideals. Faulkner's words would have pleased Jefferson, Emerson, Whitman, Cable, and Lanier. They seem to have pleased even some of our literary expatriates who in the twenties flocked to the Left Bank of the Seine but later came back to this country to discover the worth of a literary tradition which they had once been willing completely to discard. Since the Second World War, however, the mood of most American writers is that of men and women who have been chastened by adversities. The somewhat complacent optimism of Jefferson, Emerson, and Whitman is a thing of the past.

Since the time of Sidney Lanier and Joel Chandler Harris the South has been as loyal to the Union as any other section of the nation, and it has in the main accepted the traditional ideals of American literature. Nevertheless, the Southern writer's lot has not been a very happy one. Always, if he wished to live by his pen, he has had to take his articles and books to the great Northern cities; and he has often found the Northern editors and publishers difficult to please. This necessity restrained him from the expression of a provincial or an unreconstructed point of view, but it was sometimes a real handicap. Often he could not become an adequate spokesman for the point of view of the society in which he lived. The Southern writer has found it difficult to follow the changing Northern conceptions of the South. So also have some Northern writers who lived in the South. Albion W. Tourgée, who spent several years in trying to reconstruct North Carolina, found so many Northern readers unwilling to accept the picture he drew in A Fool's Errand that he wrote in the Preface to A Royal Gentleman (1881): "The trouble is that the Northern man has made up a South for himself, and, without the least hesitation, criticises any departure from the original of his own imagination as untrue to life."

The Northern attitude toward the South resembles the English attitude toward Ireland. For the English, Ireland has always been a problem and the Irish a peculiarly unreasonable people, and yet the appeal of Irish humor, song, and sentiment is irresistible. In 1914 Ireland wanted no part in the War against Germany, but English soldiers went off to France singing "It's a Long, Long Way to Tipperary." The Northerner yells when the band plays "Dixie" and he loves the sweet sentimentality of "Swanee River" and "My Old Kentucky Home"; he responds to the humor of the Southern Negro; but he still regards the South as a problem, a section sadly in need of being reformed in the good old New England fashion. For him too often the South is still not quite a part of the United States, and he takes it for granted that most of its opinions are wrong-headed. Even Northern historians are still likely in their unguarded moments to speak of "the South and the nation." To the Southerner it would seem that the mind of the average Northerner holds the most contradictory notions of his section, and he never knows which will come out.

Northern ignorance of the South, as Cleanth Brooks has pointed out, often leads to a misunderstanding of the Southern writer's attitude toward his material: ". . . the Southern author who essays the fantastic may dis-

cover to his amusement or alarm that he is a savage realist mercilessly ex-
posing a land of Yahoos, or he may be quite as much surprised to discover
that his serious consideration of a topic is a willful exploitation of the unreal
and romantic." Brooks suggests that "it is quite as disastrous for the writer
to be swayed too much by what New York likes, as to be pridefully contemptuous of anything except what he feels will flatter the prejudices of his
own section." [12]

In the nineteenth century, as in the twentieth, the Southern writer always
had to remember that his chief market lay outside the South. Publishers
and magazine editors did not hesitate to remind him that certain Southern attitudes and opinions were not acceptable to Northern readers. The
North has seldom or never been willing to listen to serious Southern
criticism of its ideals and its way of life even though the characteristics
which disturbed the Southern critics were often the identical traits which
European critics have harped upon for the last century and a half.

Southern literature is still produced primarily for the Northern market,
and there is always the temptation for the Southern writer to distort his
picture of life to make it fit into a pattern acceptable to readers north of the
Mason-Dixon Line. (Some Western Regionalists and more than an occasional New Englander have found themselves laboring under a similar
handicap.) Even if the Southerner writes primarily for readers in his own
section, he must still conform to the pattern set in the North. If he does
not, his book is almost certain to remain unpublished. If it is published, he
must wait for the Northern journals to approve; otherwise, Southern readers
may never hear of it, and Southern booksellers will not stock it. The situation works to the advantage of a writer, like Cable or Erskine Caldwell,
whose conscience permits him to give his Northern readers what they want
and who does not care greatly for the approval of those who are in a position to judge the truth or falsity of his pictures of Southern life. The situation works to the disadvantage of writers like the Southern Agrarians, who
were not willing to distort the picture to suit the whims of Northern editors
and publishers.

What the Northern reader finds acceptable varies from decade to decade.
The mind of the average Northerner is likely on examination to reveal a
jumble of discordant notions about the South derived promiscuously from

---

[12] "What Deep South Literature Needs," *Sat. Rev. of Lit.*, XXV, 8–9, 29–30 (Sept.
19, 1942). For other discussions of the difficulties of the twentieth-century Southern
author, see Jonathan Daniels, "F. O. B. Dixie," *Sat. Rev. of Lit.*, XIV, 3–4 (Aug. 29,
1936); Arlin Turner, "The Southern Novel," *Southwest Rev.*, XXV, 205–212 (Jan.,
1940); and Allen Tate, "The Profession of Letters in the South," *Reactionary Essays
on Poetry and Ideas* (1936).

Mrs. Stowe, the Abolitionists, the Negro minstrel show, Republican party propaganda, New Deal liberalism, the Uncle Remus stories, Thomas Nelson Page, *Gone with the Wind*, *Tobacco Road*, and various other sources, literary and nonliterary. There is no predicting when this or that "myth" will come into favor. For the average Northerner is not interested in the complexities or the contradictions of Southern life and thought. Always he wants a formula which provides a simple and plausible explanation. In the eighties and nineties it was the faithful ex-slave, the chivalrous planter-soldier, the sweet and refined Southern lady, and the generous Union soldier, all seen in the magic of moonlight with the odor of roses and magnolias in the air. Nothing of the sort has been acceptable in recent years except perhaps for the momentary vogue of Stark Young's *So Red the Rose* (1934).[13]

Once again, as in the days of the old Abolitionists, it is the fashion to emphasize what is primitive and semibarbarous in Southern life. There are many Southerners who feel about Erskine Caldwell and Lillian Smith precisely as Hayne and Gayarré felt about Cable; namely, that they are distorting the life they portray in order to sell their books in the North. No doubt they are unjust to these writers, but it is not a healthy situation, and it helps to explain why for a century and a half some aspects of Southern life have not been adequately represented in the work of Southern writers. It helps to explain also why some who might perhaps have contributed notably to our literature published little or abandoned literature altogether.

The Regionalist writers of the South—and the West—vigorously attacked the Northern monopoly of publishing houses and critical organs which made it difficult for the Regionalist to find readers even in his own section. The United States, they pointed out, has no literary capital such

[13] The unprecedented popularity of Margaret Mitchell's *Gone with the Wind* (1936) may be explained in part by its successful mingling of new and old elements. It has something of the legend of the Old South as a land of romance and charm and something also of the later legend of the South as a land of violence. It is, in addition, an absorbing story told with rare skill, and it fitted into the disillusioned mood of the modern world, in Europe as well as in America. None of its leading characters seems to me typically Southern except perhaps Melanie. Rhett Butler belongs to melodrama, and Scarlett O'Hara, the daughter of a new-rich immigrant planter, is more nearly akin to Becky Sharp than to earlier heroines of Southern romances.

Miss Mitchell was pleased with the Southern speech of the actors in the motion picture, but she was annoyed "at the profusion of white columns on the Georgia plantation homes, put there by Hollywood as a concession to traditional notions about the South, despite the explicit statement in the book that Tara was a rambling old farmhouse, and the further fact that it was situated in a section of Georgia where columns were almost non-existent" (Virginius Dabney, *Below the Potomac*, 1942, p. 16).

as London has been for Great Britain and Paris for France or even such a capital as Boston was for New England in the mid-nineteenth century. New York, they said, is not a true capital; it is only a literary market. And yet, they charged, the New York publishers and magazine editors assumed that their city was the literary and cultural capital of the United States and so justified themselves in dictating to Americans in other regions what they should read and thus what writers in those regions should write.

The case of the Southern and Western Regionalists was forcefully presented by Donald Davidson in essays in *I'll Take My Stand* (1930), *Culture in the South* (1934), and in greater detail in *The Attack on Leviathan: Regionalism and Nationalism in the United States* (1938), an important and greatly neglected book. In his essay, "The Trends of Literature," in *Culture in the South* Davidson pointed out the dilemma of the Southern writer, impelled in one direction by the social and literary programs that "emanate from the metropolis, bearing in their train a host of powerful aesthetic ideas and literary modes. . . . His sense of loyalty to his own tradition, indeed his fidelity as an artist to his subject-matter, pulls him in an opposite direction. There is a tragic contradiction, which results in painful self-consciousness, in split personalities, in dubious retreats, in Hamlet hesitations. How could it be otherwise, if the artist is expected to produce a literature that is 'modern' and expressive of the South, while in the same breath he is urged to repudiate the southern past . . . ?"

The great Northern cities patronize art and literature, argued Davidson, but they produce little that is significant. What the urban writers do produce tends to be "dissociated from place, experimental, absolute, sophisticated; this is the art of the expatriates and cosmopolitans. Others are realists and propagandists; their art is the agent of the social conception out of which it grows." The more important writers, he pointed out, come not from the metropolitan areas but from the provinces, and they migrate to New York at peril to their artistic integrity. The provinces always produce their traditional spokesmen, only to see them transformed: ". . . its Mark Twains go to Boston, its Henry Jameses to England, where they learn to apologize; or the same thing may happen to them if they remain physically at home."

Davidson notes the varying reactions of the chief contemporary Southern writers to the dilemma they face. Cabell takes refuge in "romantic irony." Others trim their art to fit the demand for what north of the Potomac will look like Southern "realism." T. S. Stribling, Paul Green, and others give us "a new myth, which apotheosizes and exalts the rich primitiveness of the Negro—primitiveness being a quality denied to tired moderns and therefore precious in their eyes. . . ." Their work is "palpably tinged with latter-day abolitionism," and they write like spiritual companions of Harriet Beecher Stowe. With other writers in mind, Davidson asks, Why should a Southerner write like a Greenwich Villager? Why is it that so many Southerners cannot "write about indubitably Southern themes, even the Southern legends, places, heroes . . . ?" The dilemma, as Davidson points out, is such that "a poet cannot be 'Southern' without behaving like a fool; and if he tries not to be a fool, he will not be recognizably 'Southern.' "

Mr. Davidson, who is not only a shrewd critic but a competent scholar and an accomplished poet, has forcibly set forth the dilemma of the Southern writer; and it is a real one. And yet, although he does not emphasize the fact, it is in a slightly different form the old problem which confronted Simms, Timrod, Hayne, Lanier, and other writers who wished to write about Southern life without sacrificing their integrity and still make what they wrote acceptable in the Northern literary market. This rather anomalous situation, as I have remarked elsewhere, accounts in part for the literary sterility with which the South has been periodically charged for almost a century and a half.

Perhaps it is just as well that the South is still a conservative force in the national literature—whether one looks at it as a book market, perhaps none too important nowadays, or as a place where new writers are born and reared. American literature today stands in need of a conservative force to counteract the sudden changes dictated by literary fashion which often leave the writer powerless to keep pace with them. It needs something to keep our writers from getting out of touch with American provincial life and from sharing the delusion that the only important thing is to keep abreast of the newest literary modes imported from London or Paris. As one looks back upon the American literary scene in the twenties and notes how many of our writers, some of them of course Southerners, went all out for cynicism and disillusionment and then in the thirties plumped for Communism or something closely akin to it, it would seem that our literature stands in need of some force that would prevent a complete break with a worthy and still usable literary tradition. What the South has never been able to understand, says Davidson in *The Attack on Leviathan*, is "how the North, in its astonishing quest for perfection, can junk an entire system of ideas almost overnight, and start on another one which is newer but no better than the first." Joseph Wood Krutch wrote some years ago: "The real weakness of American criticism lies not in any lack of enthusiasm, suggestiveness, or even brilliance, but in the sporadic, unstable, irresponsible nature of its enthusiasms; in, that is to say, the obviously adolescent character of its repeated conviction that it is mature at last. American literature will not 'come of age' until the masterpieces upon which it bases its claims have not all been chosen from the publications of the last two years. . . ."

The South of today is a divided South, and its writers have not the unity of feeling that prevailed in the 1850's or the 1880's. Many of its writers would agree with the Agrarians only in part, and some of them—especially those who no longer live in the South—would not agree with them at all. From the national point of view, it is fortunate that the twentieth century has brought to the Southern writer, as to those of the North and the West, a new freedom of expression. He no longer feels compelled to subscribe to the conventional opinions of the region in which he lives. Certainly Thomas Wolfe, William Faulkner, Paul Green, and many others have portrayed aspects of Southern life with a freedom which few of their predecessors except Cable and Ellen Glasgow dared to claim. In perhaps no earlier period would either Southern or Northern readers have cared to read such books as Wolfe's *Look Homeward, Angel,* T. S. Stribling's *Birthright,* DuBose Heyward's *Porgy,* Julia Peterkin's *Black April,* or Elizabeth Madox Roberts' *The Time of Man.* In no earlier period would William Faulkner's cycle of Mississippi stories have found favor.

Nevertheless, Faulkner had to wait long before many persons in his own country were willing to acknowledge his merits. Indeed, widespread recognition came only after he had won the Nobel Prize for Literature in 1950. The failure to appreciate Faulkner's earlier novels was due in part to the difficulty which readers of conservative tastes have so often had with the work of an original literary genius. For Southern readers, however, there were special difficulties which stood in the way of their appreciating such books as *The Sound and Fury* and *As I Lay Dying.* Their literary tastes inclined them to romantic rather than to naturalistic fiction, and they were accustomed to seeing their own land and people through the eyes of Joel Chandler Harris and Thomas Nelson Page. And when Faulkner confessed that he had deliberately put into *Sanctuary* (1931) elements which he knew would shock Mississippians, they mistakenly concluded that he had libeled his own section either out of pure perversity or in order to sell his books in the North. In the twenties and thirties Southern readers were reluctant to admit that the South had its perverts and degenerates and that crime and violence were as much a part of life in the South as in Chicago and Detroit. Faulkner, moreover, seemed to go out of his way to express an unorthodox view of the Negro problem. When the telegraph brought the news that Faulkner had won the Nobel Prize, the editor of the Jackson *Daily News* wrote: "He is a propagandist of degradation and properly belongs to the privy school of literature."

If the editor of the Daily News had taken the trouble to read the address which Faulkner delivered when he received the Nobel Prize, he would have discovered a different Faulkner from the one he had condemned, I dare say, without reading his books. What troubles some of those who have read Faulkner's books, however, is that they contain so little of the spirit of the Nobel Prize Address. One can find something of the kind, nevertheless, if he persists in looking for it. At the end of the fine short story, "The Bear," the father, remembering the closing lines of the "Ode on a Grecian Urn," says to his young son: "He [Keats] was talking about truth. Truth doesn't change. Truth is one thing. It covers all things which touch the heart—honor and pride and pity and justice and courage and love. Do you see now?" More than a century earlier John Randolph of Roanoke, in explaining to his nephew the ideal of a gentleman, had written: "Lay down this as a principle, that *truth* is to the other virtues, what vital air is to the human system." Thomas Dabney of Virginia and Mississippi, certainly one of the finest gentlemen of the Old South, might have seen in Faulkner's words a fitting expression of his own ideal.

Intelligent Southerners of a younger generation have found in Faulkner's books evidence of the genuine love of the South which makes him content to live in Mississippi.[14] Donald Davidson and John Crowe Ransom—both contributors to *I'll Take My Stand*—have not found in Faulkner a rebel against traditional Southern ideals. There are notable passages in *Sartoris*, *The Unvanquished*, *The Knight's Gambit*, and even in *Sanctuary* and *Requiem for a Nun* which make it plain that Faulkner's sympathies are not with the Snopeses, who represent the unscrupulous poor-white stock, but with the Negroes and with declining planter families like the Sartorises.

Readers of books in the Southern states—always oversensitive to criticism of their region—would do well to accept the literature which deals with Southern life for whatever *literary* value it may have. Fidelity to actuality or to the South's conception of itself is not the only criterion. We do not read *The Scarlet Letter* to find out how seventeenth-century New England Puritans lived; if we did, we should come away with the very wrong im-

14 See, for example, Faulkner's article on Mississippi in *Holiday* for April, 1954. John K. Hutchens, after talking with Faulkner, wrote in the New York *Herald Tribune* for Oct. 31, 1948: "He [Faulkner] guesses the Dixiecrats will carry Mississippi this Tuesday, and 'I'd be a Dixiecrat myself if they hadn't hollered "Nigger." I'm a States' Rights Man. Hodding Carter's a good man, and he's right when he says the solution of the Negro problem belongs to the South.'"

pression that they were all stern fanatics and not in fact as diverse as human beings have been in all ages and all nations.

Southerners are by no means unique in finding reason for being displeased at the way their own writers have represented them. It was a long time before the descendants of the Dutch in Irving's New York could laugh at Diedrich Knickerbocker's comic history, although eventually the term "Knickerbocker" was applied to everything which New Yorkers felt to be distinctive about their city. Certain persons in Salem, Massachusetts, resented the way Hawthorne had portrayed them in *The House of the Seven Gables*. Californians thought themselves libeled by Bret Harte's stories of the mining camps; and "The Outcasts of Poker Flat" and "The Luck of Roaring Camp" were certainly not good advertising for the merchants of San Francisco. In California and Oklahoma there are persons who grow angry when one mentions *The Grapes of Wrath*. Cultivated Bostonians of today have found themselves held up to ridicule before plebeian Americans in Cleveland Amory's *The Proper Bostonians* and the satires of John P. Marquand—by writers who have "betrayed" the social class to which by birth they belong! The descendants of the great Boston merchants and shipowners must find it exceedingly painful to be pictured in popular novels and on the screen as mummies and stuffed shirts. Their own Dr. Holmes and even the Ohio-born Howells had pictured them in far more kindly fashion. In time perhaps the Creoles of Louisiana may learn to forgive Cable for "Madame Delphine" and *The Grandissimes*, and eventually Mississippians may point with pride to a recent winner of the Nobel Prize for Literature. It may take longer for Georgians to learn to laugh at the distorted picture they see in the mirror held up before them by Erskine Caldwell and Lillian Smith. Fortunately, Georgia has more writers of whom it may justly be proud than most other American states. The unfavorable reaction of an American region which finds itself figuring in realistic fiction has become almost a behavior pattern. Asheville's reaction to *Look Homeward, Angel* and Nashville's to "A Municipal Report" are typical.

It is idle for the South to expect always to find in serious fiction what will seem to Southerners an accurate picture of its life. Such a picture, to be recognized by the sitters as a true one, would have to be flattering; and the conscientious novelist is not willing to go so far as the professional photographer in pleasing those whom it is his business to portray. On February 26, 1930, Maxwell Perkins wrote to Erskine Caldwell: "The trouble is, very few people, even in the least provincial communities, seem to understand that the *motive* for fiction, or the impulse from which it arises, is a serious one. They think of fiction as having no value excepting that of amusing and passing the time; and so it is impossible for them to understand why it could not just as well be pleasant and pretty."

We must accept our writers for what they can do best. Perhaps holding the mirror up to nature—at least in the sense which the Shakespearean phrase suggests to the casual reader—is not a primary function of the serious writer. No author, not even Sophocles—praised in Matthew Arnold's famous phrase—ever "saw life steadily and saw it whole." The essence of art is selection. The writer must portray what he can see, what seems to him significant, what his technical endowment will permit him to write, and, as I have insisted, what will bring him an income from the literary market.

Each section of the United States is unfortunately something of a legend to the people of every other section. The Kentuckian's conception of Wyoming is misty and outmoded. The Rhode Islander's notion of Alabama is likewise vague and distorted. The outsider's notions of the South are colored by legend—by many legends. It is the land of Cavaliers and of poor-whites, of Jeeter Lesters and Kentucky colonels, of magnolia gardens and eroded hillsides, of tenant farmers and heroes of the Lost Cause, of George Washington and Jim Ferguson and Eugene Talmadge, of Thomas Jefferson and Simon Legree, of mountain feudists and Robert E. Lee. The various conceptions of the South—the many Souths of fact and legend—have embodied themselves in books which still nourish a twofold Southern legend: Uncle Tom's Cabin and In Ole Virginia, Tobacco Road and So Red the Rose, Sanctuary and Gone with the Wind, Nights with Uncle Remus and I'll Take My Stand, Weems's Life of Washington and Huckleberry Finn.

"Time," wrote Emerson in the essay on "History," "dissipates to shining ether the solid angularity of facts. No anchor, no cable, no fences avail to keep a fact a fact." The distorted fact becomes a symbol. "Who cares what the fact was," Emerson concluded, "when we have made a constellation of it to hang in heaven an immortal sign?" The South has furnished to the nation more than its proportionate number of American symbols. Their accuracy, or lack of it, is probably not the best gauge of their value. By such reasoning at least the Southerner might reconcile himself to the inevitable.

A literary historian, however, cannot conclude on such a note. For him the actual fact, which Emerson deprecated, is what he must build upon, and he is often hard beset to find it. As Carl Van Doren once suggested to me, the actual South of earlier periods is buried from view by as many legends as there were ruined cities which Schliemann found overlaying the remains of Homer's Troy.

There are many misconceptions about Southern literature, too. For the historian they have little value, symbolic or other. I have tried as best I could to tell the story without regard to them and with no desire either to glorify or to depreciate the South's literary achievement. If the conditions of life in the South had been more propitious, that achievement would have been greater. And yet the writings of Byrd, Jefferson, Simms, Poe, Lanier, Cable, Mark Twain, Ellen Glasgow, and William Faulkner are nothing any one need apologize for; they are an important part of the literature of the American people.

In this and in earlier sections I have had much to say—too much, some of my readers will think—about Southern dissatisfaction with the Northern treatment of Southern life. This I have done with no desire to perpetuate ill feeling between the sections but in an effort to explain the historical basis of the Southern attitude. Beyond question, the South has been too sensitive to criticism of its way of life. It has often been intolerant of ideas which may now be regarded as not merely Northern but American. Beyond question, Southern oversensitiveness and intolerance have been a handicap to the Southern writer. No nation or section can expect its writers merely to flatter its prejudices or conceal its shortcomings. Such an attitude debars the creative writer from exercising a legitimate function of his craft. Until the twentieth century the United States had few writers who dared to find fault with their country's ideals or way of life. And yet in the Northern states Cooper, Melville, and Thoreau never hesitated to tell their countrymen of their faults. The nineteenth-century South had few such critics except Cable and such minor figures as Conway and Helper, and it repudiated them.

The Southern states are now economically and socially an integral part of the nation such as they never were before. The rapid industrialization of the South in the twentieth century has made the urban South at least almost indistinguishable from the urban North and West, and sectional differences seem destined to eventual extinction. The Southern writer of today need not portray Southerners as a peculiar people whom the outsider cannot understand. No longer need he play up the superiority of everything Southern. Except for the vagaries of literary fashion, he has a freedom of expression that his nineteenth-century predecessors rarely dared to claim. New ideas and new literary modes reach him more promptly than they came to Simms or Timrod. There was much writing in the ante-bellum South, but only Poe made any real contribution to either literary theory or literary technique. In the freer intellectual climate of the twentieth century James Branch Cabell, Ellen Glasgow, John Crowe Ransom, Allen Tate,

Donald Davidson, Robert Penn Warren, William Faulkner, and others have made notable contributions to both literary theory and literary technique.

The Southern writers of the future will not, I trust, make the mistake, made by so many of our American writers, of repudiating the best in our national literary tradition. And they will not, I hope, make the mistake of breaking completely with the Southern past. "To discard this rich inheritance in the pursuit of a standard utilitarian style," as Ellen Glasgow said, "is, for the Southern novelist, pure folly."

BIBLIOGRAPHY

THE FIRST of the three divisions which follow is a bibliographical essay in which I have indicated the relative value of those books which the student of Southern literary history must consult most frequently. The second division gives important references to the following general topics: Authorship in the South; Cities and Towns; The Civil War; Education; Fiction; The Fine Arts; The Humorists; Intersectional Literary Relations; Libraries, Reading, and Literary Taste; Magazines; Newspapers; Poetry; Political and Economic Thought; Printing and Publishing; Religion; Scholarly Interests; Social Life; Theater and Drama; Travelers; and Women Writers. The third and last division consists of bibliographical materials, arranged alphabetically, for the more important writers—Northern as well as Southern—who are discussed in separate chapters in my text. There are excellent and readily available bibliographies for such major writers as Poe, Emerson, Mark Twain, and Lanier. For such writers I have limited my bibliographies to new or neglected materials not listed, for instance in the *Literary History of the United States*. For the numerous minor writers I have included all materials which I thought would be of use to the student.

The abbreviations used in the footnotes and the Bibliography will give the scholar no trouble, but perhaps the general reader should be given a clew to some of them. The following are typical examples:

> *Va. Quart. Rev.*—*Virginia Quarterly Review*
> *No. Am. Rev.*—*North American Review*
> *Jour. So. Hist.*—*Journal of Southern History*
> N.S.—*new series*

I have had occasion so many times to refer to the *Southern Literary Messenger*, the *Southern Quarterly Review*, the *South Atlantic Quarterly*, and the *William and Mary Quarterly* that I have given these as S.L.M., S.Q.R., S.A.Q., and W.M.Q. The comprehensive literary histories are likewise abbreviated.C.H.A.L. is *The Cambridge History of American Literature*; L.H.U.S. is the *Literary History of the United States*; and L.A.P. is *The Literature of the American People*.

I. GENERAL STUDIES

The most useful works for the student are two volumes in the American Writers Series: Edd Winfield Parks (ed.), *Southern Poets* (1936) and Gregory Paine (ed.), *Southern Prose Writers* (1947). Each volume includes a good critical and historical introduction and a useful annotated bibliography. Professor Parks in his *Segments of Southern Thought* (1938) has discussed in greater detail Hugh Swinton Legaré, William J. Grayson, George W. Harris, Richard Malcolm Johnston, and other writers. He expects soon to complete a study of Southern ante-bellum literary criticism. *The Literature of the South* (1952), edited by R. C. Beatty, F. C. Watkins, and T. D. Young, is the largest collection of Southern writings available to the student, but there are errors in some of the biographical sketches.

With few exceptions, books and articles about the literature of the South published before 1900, whatever their biographical value, are practically worthless as criticism. Many of them are the work of uncritical writers whose chief purpose seems to have been to show that the South had a literature and a culture which the North had persistently underrated. Such books as Louise Manly's *Southern Literature* (Richmond, 1895) and Mildred L. Rutherford's *The South in History and Literature* (Atlanta, 1907), both marred by many factual errors, prejudiced scholars against all sectional studies. An earlier work, James Wood Davidson's *The Living Writers of the South* (New York, 1869), is also uncritical and undiscriminating, but it contains information about numerous minor figures not readily available elsewhere. The great need was for good biographical and critical studies, but little was accomplished until the 1890's when a few Southern scholars, trained for the most part in Northern universities, began to investigate the field. For further details, see Clarence Gohdes, "On the Study of Southern Literature," W.M.Q., 2nd ser. XVI, 81–87 (Jan., 1936), and Guy A. Cardwell, "On Scholarship and Southern Literature," S.A.Q., XL, 60–72 (Jan., 1941).

The first notable study was William P. Trent's *William Gilmore Simms* (1892). Trent gave an admirable picture of Simms the man, but he showed a marked lack of sympathy with the main currents of Southern thought in Simms's time; and his critical estimates were often warped by his conviction that romances, to have enduring value, must be "ennobling." Trent's *Southern Writers* (1905) is still one of the better anthologies, and the biographical sketches are in general accurate and informative.

The promising work of a Southern scholar trained in Germany was cut short by the premature death of William Malone Baskervill (1850–1899) of Vanderbilt University. His "Southern Literature" (*PMLA*, VII, 89–100, 1892) is probably the earliest article on the subject to find a place in a scholarly journal. In 1897 he published his *Southern Writers*, Vol. I, which includes essays on Sidney Lanier, George W. Cable, Joel Chandler Harris, Mary Noailles Murfree, and Maurice Thompson. The Duke University Library has some of the letters which Baskervill received from Harris and other Southern authors. Baskervill's friends and former pupils published in 1903 a second volume of *Southern Writers* which includes essays on Richard Malcolm Johnston, Sherwood Bonner, Thomas Nelson Page, Mrs. Burton Harrison, and Grace King. S. A. Link's *Pioneers of Southern Literature* (2 vols.; Nashville, 1899, 1900) contains readable but rather thin essays on Simms, Hayne, Timrod, John Esten Cooke, Francis Orray Ticknor, and the War Poets of the South. Montrose J. Moses' *The Literature of the South* (1910) is valuable for a kindly critic's reaction to the works of such Southern writers as he was able to read. A specialist in American drama, Moses knew too little about Southern history, and he had available to him too few scholarly studies to supply much-needed factual information.

Two multiple-volume works of unequal value which the student must use with discretion are: *The South in the Building of the Nation* (12 vols.; Richmond, 1909–1913) and *A Library of Southern Literature* (17 vols.; Atlanta, 1908–1923). These works were planned to represent the best scholarship of the South, but in the early 1900's there were unfortunately not enough competent scholars to cover adequately the wide range of subjects and authors that had to be included. There were at that time some well-trained specialists in Southern history, but in Southern—or even American—literary history there were the merest handful. *The South in the Building of the Nation* is on the whole a creditable performance. Volumes VII and X contain some excellent materials on intellectual and cultural life in the South. The selections in *A Library of Southern Literature* are in the main well chosen—and there are many of them —but the biographical and critical introductions vary from competent to mediocre. The work was apparently undertaken because it seemed to sensitive Southerners that Northern anthologies, especially the Stedman-Hutchinson *Library of American Literature* (11 vols., New York, 1889–1890), had neglected the Southern writers. The general editors and many of the individual contributors labored under the delusion that one could treat adequately the life and literature of the South without relating them to the life and literature of the rest of the country. They were concerned less with ascertaining important facts and making judicial critical estimates than they were with combating the old Abolitionist notion of the cultural insignificance of the South. When the last supplementary volume appeared in 1923, it struck the youthful Paul Green as an anachronism. And so when he became editor of the *Reviewer*, he used it as a point of departure in his statement of editorial policy. In "A Plain Statement" in the January, 1925, number, he wrote: "Its six-hundred and forty-two pages but reiterate that loud ranting note of ineffectuality so long common among us."

Meanwhile Charles W. Kent at the University of Virginia, where C. Alphonso Smith joined him in 1910, had stimulated some of his graduate students to begin a systematic study of Southern writers; and William P. Trent, now at Columbia University, directed the attention of his students to neglected aspects of the subject. Most of the early dissertations on Southern topics seem inadequate now, but they were of considerable value in their time. Sidney E. Bradshaw's *On Southern Poetry Prior to 1860* (1900) contained valuable bibliographical information. E. R. Rogers' *Four Southern Magazines* (1902) covered in outline form *De Bow's Review*, the *Southern Literary Messenger*, and the two Charleston quarterlies, any one of which might have supplied materials for a larger and much more thorough monograph. James G. Johnson's *Southern Fiction Prior to 1860: An Attempt at a First-Hand Bibliography* (1909) called attention to a surprising number of Southern novels, but it contains some titles which later scholars have failed to identify. An early study of South Carolina writers, Ludwig Lewisohn's "Books We Have Made," is unfortunately available only to those who have access to a file of the Charleston *News and Courier*, July 5 to September 20, 1903. The Charleston Library Society has a set of Lewisohn's articles bound for convenient use.

The early literary historians who tried to fit Southern writing into the national pattern, as I pointed out in my concluding chapter, were almost all New England men. They were handicapped by the lack of adequate biographical and critical studies and by the difficulty of finding important books, manuscripts, and periodicals. Neither the life nor the literature of the South lends itself to easy generalization. In order to write intelligently about Southern literature, it was necessary to devote to it much more time and effort than was necessary in discussing the writers of New York and New England. Many of the early Northern historians, to judge from their cursory glances at the subject, seem to have proceeded on the assumption that the land of the slaveholders ranked so low in the scale of civilization that it could not possibly produce writers of importance.

For the seventeenth and eighteenth centuries the best general works are still Moses Coit Tyler's *A History of American Literature, 1607–1765* (1878) and *A Literary History of the American Revolution* (1897). Considering the difficulties under which he worked singlehanded, Tyler's achievement was remarkable. He took pains to find rare books and pamphlets, and he discussed nothing which he had not actually read. Naturally, he failed to find certain important materials, but his greatest error was in assuming that the Colonial newspapers were of almost no literary importance. How mistaken he was is evident in the work of one of Trent's students, Elizabeth C. Cook's *Literary Influences in Colonial Newspapers, 1704–1750* (1912). Tyler treated with discrimination and skill a few early Southern writers, but he showed himself lacking in appreciation for the greatest of them all, William Byrd. A preacher as well as a scholar, Tyler probably regarded Byrd as a frivolous person whose writings could have little significance. Like the other New England historians, he discussed the Puritan divines with much greater sympathy.

In his *A History of American Literature since 1870* (1915), an important pioneer work, Fred Lewis Pattee included excellent brief discussions of the more important writers of the New South. In *The Colonial Mind* (1927), the first volume of *Main Currents in American Thought*, Vernon L. Parrington gave comparatively little attention to Southern writers except Jefferson; but in *The Romantic Revolution in America* (1927) he included a section on "The Mind of the South" (pp. 3–179) which, though it omits important writers, surpasses all earlier literary studies of the Old South. Parrington's Jeffersonian leanings did not prevent him from giving sympathetic discussions to writers who had turned their backs upon Jeffersonian liberalism.

In *The World of Washington Irving* (1944) and *The Times of Melville and Whitman* (1947) Van Wyck Brooks brought to life certain Southern writers with a skill that other literary historians must envy. In the latter volume his treatment of the New South is particularly good. Brooks's various chapters on the South are reprinted in *A Chilmark Miscellany* (1948) and may be read there to better advantage than in his five-volume literary history.

The Cambridge History of American Literature (4 vols., 1917–1921), of which W. P. Trent was editor-in-chief, is uneven in its treatment of the South. It contains, however, excellent chapters by certain Southern scholars: John Spencer Bassett, Edwin Mims, C. Alphonso Smith, and one or two others. The bibliographies are in some instances still the best available. Two other comprehensive literary histories, each of them admirable in many ways, have been published in recent years. *The Literature of the American People* (1951), by Arthur H. Quinn, Kenneth B. Murdock, Clarence Gohdes, and George F. Whicher, contains an excellent account of the chief writers of the Old South by Quinn and able but all-too-brief discussions of other Southern writers by Murdock, Gohdes, and Whicher. The more ambitious *Literary History of the United States* (3 vols., 1948), edited by Robert E. Spiller and others, contains a bibliographical third volume which is better than anything else available to the student of American literature. There are, however, some omissions and inaccuracies which suggest that the compilers of the bibliography were not familiar with some of the books and articles which they listed. Certain Southern authors of importance, like Washington Allston and Charles Gayarré, are mentioned in the bibliography but not discussed in the text. The bibliography is exceptionally good for materials published between 1915 and 1946, but it omits important earlier materials not to be found in the twentieth-century check-lists known to all specialists. Some of the materials listed under Simms and Hayne are of far less importance to the student than Hayne's omitted three-part article on "Ante-Bellum Charleston," which appeared in the *Southern Bivouac* as long ago as 1885. There are suggestive and well-written chapters on Southern writers by Louis B. Wright, John D. Wade, Henry Nash Smith, and Arthur P. Hudson. Wade's chapter, however, contains many minor factual errors. The late F. O. Matthiessen's chapter on Poe, excellent though it is in other respects, makes little of the poet's Southern background. For the literary historian, the problem of finding space for the adequate discussion of minor writers is an acute problem—and the majority of Southern writers are minor. Nevertheless, it is disconcerting to find that in the *L.H.U.S.* the space actually given to the South is almost as disproportionate as that in Barrett Wendell's *Literary History of America*, published nearly half a century earlier.[1]

The writers of the New South have fared better in our literary histories than their ante-bellum predecessors. The historians, however, have neglected the post-bellum Southern magazines and ultraconservative writers like Albert Taylor Bledsoe and Charles Colcock Jones, Jr., who distrusted Henry W. Grady, Walter Hines Page, and other exponents of the New South. The historians have gen-erally treated the New South as though it differed little from other sections, and as a result they have made large and inexact generalizations about the later American literature. They have failed to see how greatly the writers of the New South were indebted to the humorists and writers of fiction who preceded them.

Comparatively little attention has been paid to the Southern poets, but there are notable exceptions. In *The Life and Works of Edward Coote Pinkney* (1926) Thomas Ollive Mabbott and Frank L. Pleadwell made a substantial contribution to scholarship. S. Foster Damon's *Thomas Holley Chivers* (1930) resurrected a forgotten poet. There are few scholarly editions of the works of major Ameri-can writers. The only one which approaches the ideal of a definitive edition is the Centennial edition of *The Works of Sidney Lanier* in 10 volumes, published in 1945 by the Johns Hopkins Press. It is worth noting that the general editor, Charles R. Anderson, and all the coeditors are either Southerners or Northern scholars long associated with universities in the South.

Southern writers of fiction have fared better in special studies than in the all-inclusive literary histories. Carl Van Doren's *The American Novel* (1921; revised ed., 1940), Arthur H. Quinn's *American Fiction* (1936), Fred Lewis Pattee's *The Development of the American Short Story* (1923), Alexander Cowie's *The Rise of the American Novel* (1948), and Ernest E. Leisy's *The American Historical Novel* (1949), all show evidence of careful study and give Southern fiction an important place in the national pattern. Southern orators

---

[1] I have pointed out in much greater detail some of the shortcomings of the *L.H.U.S.* in "The Old South in Literary Histories," *S.A.Q.*, XLVIII, 452–467 (July, 1949).

are also ably treated in W. N. Brigance (ed.), *A History and Criticism of American Public Address* (2 vols., 1943).

The indispensable *Dictionary of American Biography* (21 vols., 1928–1937) cannot, like the anthologies of Rufus W. Griswold, be charged with neglecting the Southern writers, for even many of the forgotten women writers of subliterary novels are included. It does omit, however, William J. Grayson, whom Parrington had already treated sympathetically, and James M. Legaré, one of the best poets of the Old South. Like most other reference books, the *D.A.B.* is more dependable for the major writers than for the many minor figures whom no scholar has carefully studied. In some instances the biographical sketches were written by specialists in history or economics, each competent in his particular field, who failed to recognize the literary importance of such writers as, for example, George Tucker, who was not only an economist but also a historian, a biographer, and an essayist. Since the appearance of the *D.A.B.*, the quality of reference works has notably improved. James D. Hart's *The Oxford Companion to American Literature* (revised ed., 1948) is one of the best. *The Biographical Directory of the American Congress, 1774–1927* (Washington, 1928) supplies brief and accurate sketches of those Southern writers who were members of Congress: Richard Henry Wilde, William J. Grayson, Hugh S. Legaré, and several others.

The once indispensable compilations of Rufus W. Griswold and the Duyckinck brothers have been superseded by the *D.A.B.*, but for a few writers of the Old South there is still no better source of information. All later accounts of Richard Dabney are based upon the sketch which Lucian Minor wrote for the Duyckincks' *A Cyclopaedia of American Literature* (New York, 1855), and all accounts of Washington Allston quote from the reminiscences which Irving wrote out for the *Cyclopaedia*. Both Griswold and the Duyckincks based many of their biographical sketches on letters written by the authors themselves or by persons who had known them. Fortunately, many of these letters are preserved in the Griswold Collection in the Boston Public Library and the Duyckinck Collection in the New York Public Library. Some of the letters which Griswold received were published in part by his son, W. M. Griswold, in *The Correspondence . . . of Rufus W. Griswold* (Cambridge, Mass., 1898), which employs a curious system of simplified spelling which would have greatly surprised the letter writers. Griswold edited three widely read anthologies: *The Poets and Poetry of America* (1842), *The Prose Writers of America* (1847), and *The Female Poets of America* (1849). He incorporated new materials in the numerous later editions of *The Poets and Poetry of America*. Griswold was repeatedly and with some justice charged with giving too much space to his native New England and too little to the South, but there is no mistaking his admiration for Richard Henry Wilde and Philip Pendleton Cooke, whom he regarded as a better poet than Poe. It is obvious now that Griswold was slow to appreciate the importance of Emerson and some other New England writers and that many whom he overrated belonged to New York and Pennsylvania rather than to New England. Before the Duyckincks published their *Cyclopaedia*, Evert Duyckinck took the precaution of consulting Simms, John Esten Cooke, and other Southerners, with the result that the *Cyclopaedia* seemed to most Southern reviewers eminently fair to that section. The *Cyclopaedia* contains some information of which little use has been made; it identifies, for example, the authors of a number of important articles published anonymously in the *Southern Quarterly Review*.

Except for Poe, Lanier, and political figures like Jefferson, Madison, and Calhoun, there are too few scholarly biographies of Southern writers. Among those that I have found most useful are W. P. Trent's *William Gilmore Simms* (1892), John O. Beaty's *John Esten Cooke: Virginian* (1922), John D. Wade's *Augustus Baldwin Longstreet* (1924), J. L. King's *Dr. George William Bagby* (1927), S. Foster Damon's *Thomas Holley Chivers: Friend of Poe* (1930), Richmond C. Beatty's *William Byrd of Westover* (1932), Linda Rhea's *Hugh Swinton Legaré* (1934), Philip Graham's *The Life and Poems of Mirabeau B. Lamar* (1938), Richard Beale Davis's *Francis Walker Gilmer* (1939) and his edition of *Chivers' Life of Poe* (1952), John D. Allen's *Philip Pendleton Cooke* (1942), Harvey Wish's *George Fitzhugh* (1943), Curtis Carroll Davis's *Chronicler of the Cavaliers: A Life of the Virginia Novelist Dr. William A. Caruthers* (1953), a Duke University dissertation, 1947, W. Stanley Hoole, *Alias Simon Suggs: The Life and Times of Johnson Jones Hooper* (1952); and the various books and articles on William Byrd by Louis B. Wright and Maude H. Woodfin. For the writers of the New South I am indebted to the biographies of Lanier by Edwin Mims (1905) and Aubrey H. Starke (1933), Grant C. Knight's *James Lane Allen and the Genteel Tradition* (1935), Harriet R. Holman's "The Literary Career of Thomas Nelson Page" (Duke Univ. dissertation, 1947), Edd W. Parks, *Charles Egbert Craddock* (1941), the biographies of Joel Chandler Harris by R. L. Wiggins (1918) and Julia Collier Harris (1918), Kjell Ekström's *George W. Cable* (1950), Arlin Turner's various articles on Cable, and the publications of the many scholars who have discussed the work of Mark Twain.

Southern history has been much more thoroughly worked than the closely related field of Southern literary history, and I am indebted to those historians who have written upon cultural and literary subjects—even though some of them show no great appreciation of literary values. Much that was written before 1910 is prejudiced or otherwise inadequate. The earlier Southern historians were on the defensive, trying to justify the position of their section in the long period of controversy culminating in the Civil War. The work of the German-born Hermann von Holst and the early Northern historians is often invalidated by their uncritical acceptance of the notion that the Civil War was the result of a gigantic Southern conspiracy. Nowadays, however, it is often difficult to distinguish by internal evidence a historical work written by a Northerner from one written by a Southern historian.

The twentieth century has produced a number of exceptionally able historians of the Old South. Among the more valuable works—all published since the First World War—are William E. Dodd's *The Cotton Kingdom* (1919), Ulrich B. Phillips' *Life and Labor in the Old South* (1929), Clement Eaton's *Freedom of Thought in the Old South* (1940), and Frank L. Owsley's *Plain Folk of the Old South* (1949). A ten-volume *History of the South*, under the general editorship of Wendell H. Stephenson and E. Merton Coulter, is being sponsored jointly by Louisiana State University and the University of Texas. The volumes which have thus far appeared are most of them historical works of the first order: Coulter's *The South during Reconstruction, 1865–1877* (1947) and *The Confederate States of America, 1861–1865* (1950), Charles S. Sydnor's *The Development of Southern Sectionalism, 1819–1848* (1948), Wesley F. Craven's *The Southern Colonies in the Seventeenth Century, 1607–1689* (1949), Avery O. Craven, *The Growth of Southern Nationalism, 1848–1861* (1953), and C. Vann Woodward's *Origins of the New South, 1877–1913* (1951). Each volume contains a useful "Critical Essay on Authorities." The treatment of literary culture in the South is disappointing. Some of the better one-volume histories of the South are: Clement Eaton, *A History of the Old South* (1949); Robert S. Cotterill, *The Old South* . . . (revised ed., 1939); William B. Hesseltine, *The South in American History* (1943), first published in 1936 as *A History of the South, 1607–1936*; and Francis B. Simkins, *A History of the South* (1953), which first appeared under the title *The South, Old and New: A History, 1820–1947* (1947). Although published nearly twenty years ago, *The South Looks at Its Past* (1935), by Benjamin B. Kendrick and Alex M. Arnett, provides a useful corrective to the traditional conception of the ante-bellum South.

Every Southern state has at least one historical journal which occasionally prints an article on some literary or cultural subject. The Virginia journals down to 1930 are indexed in Earl Gregg Swem's *The Virginia Historical Index* (2 vols., 1934, 1936). The *Journal of Southern History*, founded in 1935 as the organ of a very active Southern Historical Association, has published some important materials. A most useful reference work of its kind is Henry P. Beers's *Bibliographies in American History* (revised ed., 1942), which lists many local histories.

In general, it may be said that historians of the Old South have paid more attention to the states along the Atlantic seaboard than to those that lie west of the Appalachians; that more work has been done on political, social, and economic subjects than upon constitutional or cultural history; and, finally, that much more attention has been devoted to the fascinating life of the large-scale planters than to either the common people of the Old South or Southern towns and cities, where most Southern literature was written and where much of it first appeared in print. The Reconstruction period is the subject of many competent political studies, many of them inspired by the late W. A. Dunning of

Columbia University; but much less has been done with social, economic, and cultural life in the New South.

There is no single good comprehensive bibliography of the literature of the South. There are, however, usable brief bibliographies in Edd W. Parks (ed.), *Southern Poets* (1936) and Gregory Paine (ed.), *Southern Prose Writers* (1947). Some Southern writers are included in the bibliographies in *L.H.U.S.*, but many of these are not inclusive enough. The best guide to materials in the scholarly journals is Lewis Leary (comp.), *Articles on American Literature . . . 1920–1945* (1947), now being revised to cover the period from 1900 through 1950. For articles which have been published since 1950, see the quarterly check lists in *American Literature*. For dissertations on Southern writers, see Ernest E. Leisy and Jay B. Hubbell (eds.), "Doctoral Dissertations in American Literature," *Am. Lit.*, IV, 419–465 (Jan., 1933), and Lewis Leary (ed.), "Doctoral Dissertations in American Literature, 1933–1948," *Am. Lit.*, XX, 169–230 (May, 1948). See also the "Annual Bibliography" in *PMLA* and, in the same journal beginning with 1948, "Research in Progress in the Modern Languages and Literatures." The *South Atlantic Bulletin* prints each year a "Bibliography of Southern Literary Culture" and a list of M.A. and Ph.D. theses completed at Southeastern colleges and universities. It has also published articles describing notable collections in Southern libraries. See also L. R. Wilson and R. B. Downs, "Special Collections for the Study of History and Literature in the Southeast," *Papers* of Bibliog. Soc. of Am., XXVIII, 97–131 (1934).

Rare books can often be located by consulting Charles Evans, *American Bibliography* (12 vols., 1903–1934), which includes books printed up to 1820, and Joseph Sabin and others, *A Dictionary of Books Relating to America . . .* (29 vols., 1868–1936). The Library of Congress card catalogue and the union catalogues at the Library of Congress and the University of Pennsylvania are extremely useful to those looking for rare books. In searching for magazine materials, I have consulted those two useful card catalogues compiled with the assistance of the W.P.A.: the index to American magazines to 1850, started by Professor Oscar Cargill, at New York University, and the bibliography of American literature compiled at the University of Pennsylvania under the supervision of Dr. Edward H. O'Neill.

Manuscript materials, more difficult to locate than rare books and periodicals, are not so plentiful for the older Southern writers as one could wish. Southerners were less in the habit of preserving letters than their contemporaries in some of the Northern states. Fire, neglect, removal from one residence to another, and the destructive effect of the American Revolution and the Civil War account for the loss of many manuscripts. Some important materials are doubtless still in private hands. Others are to be found not in the Southern libraries where one might expect to find them but in the great Northern and Western libraries. It is a matter of chagrin to Virginia librarians that so much of the state's historical materials are to be found only in libraries in North Carolina, Wisconsin, and California.

A few Southern libraries, including those of Duke University and the University of North Carolina, have published catalogues of their more important manuscript collections. In the third section of my Bibliography I have given the location of some important manuscript materials for William Byrd, Thomas Holley Chivers, John Esten and Philip Pendleton Cooke, William J. Grayson, Paul Hamilton Hayne, John Pendleton Kennedy, William Munford, Thomas Nelson Page, Albert Pike, John R. Thompson, Henry Timrod, Beverley Tucker, Richard Henry Wilde, and William Wirt. Other manuscript materials may often be located by consulting the bibliographical works listed under the names of individual writers.

II. IMPORTANT TOPICS

Authorship in the South

For the twentieth century, see Jonathan Daniels, "F.O.B. Dixie," *Sat. Rev. of Lit.*, XIV, 3–4 (Aug. 29, 1936) and Allen Tate, "The Profession of Letters in the South," *Reactionary Essays on Poetry and Ideas* (1936). For earlier periods, see Edward Ingle, "Literary Aspirations," *Southern Sidelights* (1896), pp. 196–219; Thomas Nelson Page, "Authorship in the South before the War," *The Old South* (1912), pp. 67–109; W. M. Baskervill, "Southern Literature," *PMLA*, VII, 89–100 (1892); J. S. Bassett, "The Bottom of the Matter" and "The Problems of the Author in the South," *S.A.Q.*, I, 99–106, 201–208 (April, July, 1902); and [Walter Hines Page?], "Literature in the South," *Critic*, X, 322–324 (June 25, 1887). See also Lafcadio Hearn's articles, "Southern Novels," "A Southern Magazine," "Southern Literature," and "Southern Literature and 'Observer'" in his *Essays on American Literature* (Tokyo, 1929).

Among the best of the many still earlier discussions of the problem are "On the Low State of Polite Letters in Virginia," *Letters from Virginia, Translated from the French* (Baltimore, 1816), attributed to George Tucker; two articles by William Gilmore Simms: "Southern Literature: Its Conditions, Prospects and History . . . ," *Magnolia*, III, 1–6, 69–74 (Jan. and Feb., 1841) and "Literary Prospects of the South," *Russell's Mag.*, III, 193–206 (June, 1858); and Henry Timrod, "Literature in the South," *Russell's Mag.*, V, 385–395 (Aug., 1859), reprinted in Edd W. Parks (ed.), *The Essays of Henry Timrod* (1942), pp. 83–102. See also Timrod's editorials reprinted in Jay B. Hubbell (ed.), *The Last Years of Henry Timrod* (1941), pp. 132–145. The chapter on "Southern Literature" in Hinton Rowan Helper, *The Impending Crisis of the South* (1859) is an able statement of the Abolitionist explanation of the literary poverty of the South. Very different is the view of John H. Bocock, "Authorship at the South," *So. Presbyt. Rev.*, XX, 235–262 (April, 1869), reprinted in *New Eclectic*, V, 77–95 (July, 1869) and in *Selections from the Religious and Literary Writings of John H. Bocock* (Richmond, 1891). For a full discussion of the whole matter, with many additional references, see Jay B. Hubbell, "Literary Nationalism in the Old South," *American Studies in Honor of William Kenneth Boyd* (1940), ed. D. K. Jackson, pp. 175–220.

Cities and Towns

For the Colonial period two very useful studies are: Carl Bridenbaugh, *Cities in the Wilderness, 1625–1742* (1948) and T. J. Wertenbaker, *The Golden Age of Colonial Culture* (1942). There are brief accounts of towns and cities in the W.P.A. guides to the various states and cities; the New Orleans guide is one of the best. See also Mildred Cram, *Old Seaport Towns of the South* (1917) and Lyman P. Powell (ed.), *Historic Towns of the Southern States* (1900).

Other studies of some value are: Elihu S. Riley, *"The Ancient City": A History of Annapolis, in Maryland, 1649–1887* (Annapolis, 1887)—Clayton C. Hall (ed.), *Baltimore: Its History and Its People* (3 vols., 1912); J. C. French, "Poe's Literary Baltimore," *Md. Hist. Mag.*, XXXII, 101–112 (June, 1937); and J. E. Uhler, "The Delphian Club: A Contribution to the Literary History of Baltimore," *ibid.*, XX, 305–346 (Dec., 1925)—F. P. Bowes, *The Culture of Early Charleston* (1942); Jacob N. Cardozo, *Reminiscences of Charleston* (Charleston, 1866); Charles Fraser, *Reminiscences of Charleston* (Charleston, 1854); Paul Hamilton Hayne, "Ante-bellum Charleston," *So. Bivouac*, N.S. I, 193–202, 257–268, 327–336 (Sept., Oct., Nov., 1885); William Stanley Hoole, "Literary and Cultural Background of Charleston, 1830–1860" (Duke Univ. dissertation, 1934); Mrs. St. Julien Ravenel, *Charleston: The Place and the People* (1906); William Gilmore Simms, *Father Abbot, or, The Home Tourist* (Charleston, 1849) and "Charleston: The Palmetto City," *Harper's Mag.*, XV, 1–22 (June, 1857); and Samuel G. Stoney and Bayard Wooten, *Charleston: Azaleas and Old Bricks* (1937)—George W. Ranck, *History of Lexington, Kentucky* (Cincinnati, 1872)—Gerald M. Capers, *The Biography of a River Town: Memphis* (1939); Marshall Wingfield, *Literary Memphis: A Survey of Its Writers and Writings* (Memphis, 1942); and a better study, Margaret Chisman, "Literature and Drama in Memphis, Tennessee, to 1860" (a Duke Univ. master's thesis, 1942)—F. Garvin Davenport, *Cultural Life in Nashville, 1825–1860* (1941)—Edward Larocque Tinker, *Creole City: Its Past and Its People* (1953) and Grace King, *New Orleans: The Place and the People* (1895)— T. J. Wertenbaker, *Norfolk: Historic Southern Port* (1931)—Agnes Bondurant, *Poe's Richmond* (1942); Robert Beverley Munford, *Richmond Homes and Memories* (Richmond, 1936); and Mrs. Mary N. Stanard, *Richmond: Its People and Its Story* (1923)—Lyon G. Tyler, *Williamsburg: The Old Colonial Capital* (Richmond, 1907).

The Civil War

Standard historical works are James G. Randall, *The Civil War and Reconstruction* (1937) and E. Merton Coulter, *The Confederate States of America, 1861–1865* (1950), which contains an excellent bibliography. For a good popular account, see Robert Selph Henry, *The Story of the Confederacy* (revised ed., 1948). Other useful works are James Truslow Adams, *America's Tragedy* (1934); Gamaliel Bradford, *Confederate Portraits* (1914) and *Lee the American* (1912); D. L. Dumond (ed.), *Southern Editorials on Secession* (1931); John Beauchamp Jones, *A Rebel War Clerk's Diary* (1866, 1935); Frank L. Owsley, *State Rights in the Confederacy* (1925) and *King Cotton Diplomacy* (1931); Charles W. Ramsdell, *Behind the Lines in the Southern Confederacy* (1944); F. B. Simkins and J. W. Patton, *The Women of the Confederacy* (1936); and N. W. Stephenson, *The Day of the Confederacy* (1920). Douglas S. Freeman's *The South to Posterity: An Introduction to the Writings of Confederate History* (1939) is a useful guide to the vast mass of material written since the Civil War. Freeman's *R. E. Lee* (4 vols., 1934–1935) is one of the great American biographies, and his *Lee's Lieutenants* (3 vols., 1942–1944) is indispensable for the study of the war in Virginia. See also Thomas J. Pressly, *Americans Interpret Their Civil War* (1954) and James G. Randall, *Lincoln and the South* (1946).

Of the numerous anthologies of Confederate songs and ballads two of the best are William Gilmore Simms's *War Poetry of the South* (1866) and Francis F. Browne's *Bugle-Echoes: A Collection of the Poetry of the Civil War, Northern and Southern* (1886). In many collections the editors either failed to identify the authors of numerous songs or ascribed them to the wrong authors. There are many such errors in Claudius Meade Capps (ed.), *The Blue and the Gray: The Best Poems of the Civil War* (1943). Esther P. Ellinger, *The Southern Poetry of the Civil War* (1918), a University of Pennsylvania dissertation privately printed, has a good bibliography and a useful finding-list. Two useful brief studies are Brander Matthews, "The Songs of the War," *Century Mag.*, XXXIV, 619–629 (Aug., 1887), reprinted in his *Pen and Ink* (1902), and Edwin Mims, "Poets of the Civil War II: The South," *C.H.A.L.*, II, 288–312, 585–588. In *Songs of the Confederacy* (1951) Richard B. Harwell reprinted the words and music of thirty-eight of the best songs. See also his *Confederate Music* (1950) and *Cornerstones of Confederate Collecting* (1952; revised ed., 1953).

For folk songs of the war, see A. P. Hudson (ed.), *Folksongs of Mississippi* (1936), chap. x, "Songs of the Civil War"; William A. Owens (ed.), *Texas Folk Songs* (1950), pp. 271–279; A. M. Williams, "Folk-Songs of the Civil War," *Jour. Am. Folk-lore*, V, 265–283 (Oct.–Dec., 1892); and the editorial section "Salmagundi," *So. Bivouac*, N.S. I, 126–127, 190, 192 (July, Aug., 1885).

Education

The subject is discussed in a series of chapters in *The South in the Building of the Nation*, X, 184–427. T. C. Johnson, Jr., *Scientific Interests in the Old South* (1936) supplies a needed corrective to the tradition that little was taught in Southern schools except mathematics and the ancient classics. Two useful studies are Alma P. Foerster, "The State University in the Old South" (a Duke Univ. dissertation, 1939) and Albea Godbold, *The Church College of the Old*

South (1944), which treats only colleges in the South Atlantic states. See also D. G. Tewksbury, *The Founding of American Colleges and Universities before the Civil War* (1932); Charles F. Thwing, *History of Higher Education in America* (1906), which gives statistics for Southern students at Harvard, Yale, and Princeton; Donald R. Cone, "The Influence of Princeton on Higher Education in the South before 1825," W.M.Q., 3rd ser. II, 359–396 (Oct., 1945); and J. S. Ezell, "A Southern Education for Southrons," *Jour. So. Hist.*, XVII, 303–327 (Aug., 1951).

Some useful histories of particular institutions are: Herbert B. Adams, *The College of William and Mary* (1887); P. A. Bruce, *History of the University of Virginia, 1819–1919* (5 vols., 1920–1922); Kemp P. Battle, *History of the University of North Carolina* (2 vols., 1907, 1912); E. Merton Coulter, *College Life in the Old South* (1928; revised ed., 1951), a history of the University of Georgia; J. H. Easterby, *A History of the College of Charleston* (1935); and Nora C. Chaffin, *Trinity College, 1839–1892: The Beginnings of Duke University* (1950).

For academies, see E. Merton Coulter, "The Ante-bellum Academy Movement in Georgia," *Ga. Hist. Quart.*, V., 11–42 (Dec., 1921), John Gould Fletcher, "Education Past and Present," *I'll Take My Stand. By Twelve Southerners* (1930); Edgar W. Knight, *Public Education in the South* (1921); and James W. Mobley, "The Academy Movement in Louisiana," *La. Hist. Quart.*, XXX, 738–978 (July, 1947). For the most famous of Southern academies, see Ralph M. Lyon, "Moses Waddel and the Willington Academy," *N.C. Hist. Rev.*, VII, 284–299 (July, 1931); Margaret L. Coit, "Moses Waddel: A Light in the Wilderness," *Ga. Rev.*, V, 34–47 (Spring, 1951); Moses Waddel, "Memoir," ed. E. Merton Coulter, *Ga. Hist. Quart.*, VIII, 304–334 (Dec., 1924); John N. Waddel, *Memorials of Academic Life: Being an Historical Sketch of the Waddel Family* (Richmond, 1891); and Augustus Baldwin Longstreet, *Master William Mitten* (Macon, 1864).

For the public schools, old-field schools, etc., see Knight, *op. cit.*; Charles W. Dabney, *Universal Education in the South* (2 vols., 1936); and R. M. Johnston, "Early Educational Life in Middle Georgia," *Report* of the U.S. Commissioner for Education for the Year 1894–1895, II, 1699–1733, and *ibid.* for 1895–1896, I, 839–886. Edgar W. Knight (ed.), *A Documentary History of Education in the South before 1860* (5 vols., 1949–1953) contains a wealth of materials on many aspects of the subject.

Fiction

The chief Southern writers of fiction are treated, often too briefly, in the standard works already cited by Van Doren, Quinn, Cowie, Pattee, and Leisy. See also Lillie D. Loshe, *The Early American Novel* (1907; reissued, 1930) and Edwin Mims (ed.), *History of Southern Fiction*, Vol. VIII in *The South in the Building of the Nation.* Lyle H. Wright, *American Fiction, 1774–1850: A . . . Bibliography* (1939; revised ed., 1948) largely supersedes J. G. Johnson, *Southern Fiction Prior to 1860: An Attempt at a First-Hand Bibliography* (1909) and Oscar Wegelin, *Early American Fiction, 1774–1830* (3rd ed., 1929). For Thomas Atwood Digges's *Adventures of Alonso* (London, 1775), see Robert H. Elias, "The First American Novel," *Am. Lit.*, XII, 419–434 (Jan., 1941). See also Curtis Carroll Davis, "Virginia's Unknown Novelist: The Career of J. S. French, a Southern Colonel of Parts," *Va. Mag.*, LX, 551–581 (Oct., 1952).

For Southern life in fiction, see Ima H. Herron, *The Small Town in American Literature* (1939), chap. ix, " 'Southerntown' in Back Country and Tidewater"; Isabella D. Harris, "The Southern Mountaineer in Fiction, 1824–1910" (Duke Univ. dissertation, 1948); Carvel E. Collins, "Nineteenth-Century Fiction of the Southern Appalachians," *Bulletin of Bibliog.*, XVII, 186–190, 215–219 (Sept.–Dec., 1942; Jan.–April, 1943); Lawrence S. and Algernon D. Thompson (comps.), *The Kentucky Novel* (1953); Jay B. Hubbell, "Cavalier and Indentured Servant in Virginia Fiction," *S.A.Q.*, XXVI, 22–39 (Jan., 1927) and *Virginia Life in Fiction* (Dallas, 1922), a Columbia University dissertation privately printed in abstract form, with a bibliography; Albert Keiser, *The Indian in American Literature* (1933); C. P. Lee, "Decline and Death of the Southern Gentleman," *Southwest Rev.*, XXXVI, 164–170 (Summer, 1951); Shields McIlwaine, *The Southern Poor-White from Lubberland to Tobacco Road* (1939); James S. Purcell, Jr., "The Southern Poor White in Fiction" (Duke Univ. master's thesis, 1938); Lizzie C. McVoy, *A Bibliography of Fiction by Louisianians on Louisiana Subjects* (1935); Rebecca W. Smith, "Catalogue of the Chief Novels and Short Stories by American Authors Dealing with the Civil War and Its Effects," *Bulletin of Bibliog.*, XVI, 193–194 (Sept., 1935); XVII, 10–12, 33–35, 53–55, 72–75 (Sept., 1940; Jan.–April, 1941); John H. Nelson, *The Negro Character in American Literature* (1926); and Sterling Brown, *The Negro in American Fiction* (1937). Briefer studies of some value are Tremaine McDowell, "The Negro in the Southern Novel Prior to 1850," *Jour. Eng. and Ger. Philol.*, XXV, 455–473 (4th quarter, 1926); Charles Forster Smith, "Southern Dialect in Life and Literature," *So. Bivouac*, N.S. I, 343–351 (Nov., 1885); and Ellen Glasgow, "The Novel in the South," *Harper's*, CXLIII, 93–100 (Dec., 1928).

The Fine Arts

For the general cultural background, see F. P. Bowes, *The Culture of Early Charleston* (1942); T. J. Wertenbaker, *The Golden Age of Colonial Culture* (1942); Howard M. Jones, *America and French Culture, 1750–1848* (1927); F. Garvin Davenport, *Cultural Life in Nashville, 1825–1860* (1941); and many of the works cited under *Cities and Towns*. For the general American background, see Arthur H. Quinn, *L.A.P.*, chap. 28, "Literature and the Allied Arts."

There are chapters on painting, sculpture, architecture, and pottery in Vol. X of *The South in the Building of the Nation* and a chapter on music in Vol. VIII. *Culture in the South* (1934), ed. W. T. Couch, has chapters on the fine arts and handicrafts.

Painting in the South is discussed briefly in Virgil Barker, *American Painting: History and Interpretation* (1950) and James T. Flexner, *American Painting: First Flowers of Our Wilderness* (1947). See also Ben E. Looney, "Historical Sketch of Art in Louisiana," *La. Hist. Quart.*, XVIII, 382–396 (April, 1935); Isaac N. Cline, *Art and Artists in New Orleans during the Last Century* (New Orleans, 1922); and Jan T. Fortune and Jean Burton, *Elisabet Ney* (1943).

For architecture, in which the Southern achievement was perhaps most distinctive, see James C. Bonner, "Plantation Architecture of the Lower South on the Eve of the Civil War," *Jour. So. Hist.*, XI, 370–388 (Aug., 1945); Elizabeth Curtis, *Gateways and Doorways of Charleston, South Carolina* (1926); Helen M. P. Gallagher, *Robert Mills: Architect of the Washington Monument, 1781–1855* (1935); Talbot F. Hamlin, *Greek Revival Architecture in America* (1944); Fiske Kimball, *Thomas Jefferson, Architect* (1916); Lewis Mumford, *The South in Architecture* (1941); Alice H. R. Smith, *The Dwelling Houses of Charleston, South Carolina* (1917); J. Frazer Smith, *White Pillars: Early Life and Architecture of the Lower Mississippi Valley Country* (1941); Thomas T. Waterman and John A. Barrows, *Domestic Colonial Architecture of Tidewater Virginia* (1932); and Edward T. H. Shaffer, *Carolina Gardens* (1937).

For music, see Oscar G. T. Sonneck, *Early Opera in America* (1915) and *Early Concert-Life in America, 1731–1800* (Leipzig, 1907); John T. Howard, *Our American Music: Three Hundred Years of It* (revised ed., 1946); and the *Bio-Bibliographical Index of Musicians in the United States from Colonial Times* (Washington, 1941).

For Southern folk songs, see under *Poetry* and *Civil War*.

The Humorists

Standard works are: Walter Blair, *Native American Humor, 1800–1900* (1937); Bibliography, pp. 163–196, and *Tall Tale America* (1944); Thomas D. Clark, *The Rampaging Frontier* (1939); A. P. Hudson (ed.), *Humor of the Old Deep South* (1936); Franklin J. Meine (ed.), *Tall Tales of the Southwest* (1930); Jennette Tandy, *Crackerbox Philosophers in American Humor and Satire* (1925); James R. Masterson, *Tall Tales of Arkansaw* (1942); Constance Rourke, *American Humor: A Study of the National Character* (1931); Richard M. Dorson (ed.), *David Crockett: American Comic Legend* (1939); Mody C. Boatright, *Tall Tales from Texas* (1934); and Joseph Leach, *The Typical Texan: Biography of an American Myth* (1952).

For divergent views as to the sources and national quality of American humor, see Walter Blair's review of *American Humor* and Miss Rourke's reply in *Am. Lit.*, III, 340–343 (Nov., 1931) and IV, 207–210 (May, 1932); DeLancey Ferguson's two articles in *Am. Scholar*: "The Roots of American Humor," IV, 41–49 (Winter, 1935) and "American Humor: Roots or Flowers?" IV, 380–383 (Summer, 1935) and Miss Rourke's reply to Ferguson's earlier article, IV, 249–252 (Spring, 1935).

Older books which are still worth consulting are: William T. Porter (ed.), *The Big Bear of Arkansas* (1845) and *A Quarter Race in Kentucky* (1846); Henry Watterson (ed.), *Oddities in Southern Life and Character* (1882); and Oliver P. Baldwin (ed.), *Southern and South-Western Sketches* (Richmond, [1855]). Other materials of some value are: Walter Blair, "Burlesques in Nineteenth-Century American Humor," *Am. Lit.*, II, 236–247 (Nov., 1930) and "The Popularity of Nineteenth-Century American Humorists," *ibid.*, III, 175–194 (May, 1931); Will D. Howe, "Early Humorists," *C.H.A.L.*, II, 148–159; Bibliography, pp. 502–511; Eugene Current-Garcia, "Newspaper Humor in the Old South," *Ala. Rev.*, II, 102–121 (April, 1949); Jay B. Hubbell, "Charles Napoleon Bonaparte Evans: Creator of Jesse Holmes the Fool-Killer," *S.A.Q.*, XXXVI, 431–446 (Oct., 1937); and Louis J. Budd, "Gentlemanly Humorists of the Old South," *So. Folklore Quart.*, Dec., 1953.

Intersectional Literary Relations

This is a neglected field. Scholars have devoted far more attention to Anglo-American literary relations than to the relations of Northern and Eastern writers with those of the South and the West. The only general study is Max L. Griffin, "The Relations with the South of Six Major Northern Writers" (Univ. of N. C. dissertation, 1942), which deals with Irving, Cooper, Bryant, Longfellow, Lowell, and Whittier. Prof. Griffin has published some of his findings in "Whittier and Hayne: A Record of Friendship," *Am. Lit.*, XIX, 41–58 (March, 1947); "Cooper's Attitude toward the South," *Studies in Philol.*, XLVIII, 67–76 (Jan., 1951); "Bryant and the South," *Tulane Studies in Eng.*, I (1949), pp. 53–80, and "Lowell and the South," *ibid.*, II (1950), pp. 75–102. There are scattered materials in J. C. Derby, *Fifty Years among Authors, Books, and Publishers* (1884) and Paul H. Buck, *The Road to Reunion* (1937).

For the relations of Hayne, Simms, and Timrod with Northern writers, see Victor H. Hardendorff, "Paul Hamilton Hayne and the North" (Duke Univ. master's thesis, 1942); Jay B. Hubbell (ed.), *The Last Years of Henry Timrod* (1941), pp. 104–120, "Some New Letters of Constance Fenimore Woolson [to Hayne]," *New Eng. Quart.*, XIV, 715–735 (Dec., 1941), and "Five Letters from George Henry Boker to William Gilmore Simms," *Penn. Mag. of Hist. and Biog.*, LXIII, 66–71 (Jan., 1939); D. M. McKeithan (ed.), *A Collection of Hayne Letters* (1944), consult Index; Charles Duffy (ed.), *The Correspond-*

ence of Bayard Taylor and Paul Hamilton Hayne (1945); and E. G. Bernard, "Northern Bryant and Southern Hayne," *Colophon*, N.S. I, 536–540 (Spring, 1936).

For the important relations of Southern writers to Northern magazine editors, see L. Frank Tooker, *The Joys and Tribulations of an Editor* (1924); Robert Underwood Johnson, *Remembered Yesterdays* (1923); *The Letters of Richard Watson Gilder* (1916); and biographies of George W. Cable, Sidney Lanier, Joel Chandler Harris, James Lane Allen, Mary Noailles Murfree, Frances Hodgson Burnett, and others.

Other materials are: Richard Walser, "The North Carolina Sojourn of the First American Novelist [William Hill Brown]," *N. C. Hist. Rev.*, XXVIII, 138–155 (April, 1951); H. H. Hoeltje, "Emerson in Virginia," *New Eng. Quart.*, V, 753–768 (Oct., 1932); Killis Campbell, "The Kennedy Papers," 2nd article, *Sewanee Rev.*, XXI, 193–208 (April, 1917); W. M. Griswold (ed.), *Passages from the Correspondence . . . of Rufus W. Griswold* (Cambridge, Mass., 1898), which prints in part some letters from Southern writers: and Frank J. and Frank W. Klingberg (eds.), *The Correspondence between Henry Stephens Randall and Hugh Blair Grigsby, 1856–1861* (1952). *The Letters of William Gilmore Simms* in 5 vols., of which only Vols. I and II have yet appeared (1953) contains many letters addressed to James Lawson, Evert Duyckinck, and other Northern writers. Simms's many letters from Northern writers were almost all destroyed by fire.

Libraries, Reading, and Literary Taste

For the seventeenth and eighteenth centuries, see F. P. Bowes, *The Culture of Early Charleston* (1942); Hennig Cohen, *The South Carolina Gazette, 1732–1775* (1953), chap. 11; G. K. Smart, "Private Libraries in Colonial Virginia," *Am. Lit.*, X, 24–52 (May, 1938); Louis B. Wright, *The First Gentlemen of Virginia* (1940), "The 'Gentleman's Library' in Early Virginia," *Huntington Library Quart.*, I, 3–61 (Oct., 1937), and "Pious Reading in Colonial Virginia," *Jour. So. Hist.*, VI, 383–392 (Aug., 1940); W. S. Powell, "Books in the Virginia Colony before 1624," *W.M.Q.*, 3rd ser. V, 177–184 (April, 1948); J. M. Jennings, "Notes on the Original Library of the College of William and Mary in Virginia, 1693–1705," *Papers* Bibliog. Soc. of America, XL, 239–267 (3rd quart., 1947); Julia C. Spruill, "The Southern Lady's Library," *S.A.Q.*, XXXIV, 23–41 (Jan., 1935), reprinted in her *Women's Life and Work in the Southern Colonies* (1938); and J. T. Wheeler, "Reading Interests of the Professional Classes in Colonial Maryland, 1700–1776," *Md. Hist. Mag.*, XXXVI, 184–201 (June, 1941), "Reading Interests of Maryland Planters and Merchants, 1700–1776," *ibid.*, XXXVII, 26–41 (March, 1942), and "Reading and Other Recreations of Marylanders," *ibid.*, XXXVIII, 37–55, 167–180 (March, June, 1943); James S. Purcell, Jr., "Literary Culture in North Carolina before 1820" (Duke Univ.

dissertation, 1950); and James Napier, "Some Book Sales in Dumfries, Virginia, 1794–1796," *W.M.Q.*, 3rd ser. X, 441–445 (July, 1953).

For the nineteenth century, see W. D. Houlette, "Plantation and Parish Libraries of the Old South" (Univ. of Iowa dissertation, 1933); E. R. Lancaster (ed.), "Books Read in Virginia [and North Carolina] in Early Nineteenth Century, 1806–1823," *Va. Mag.*, XLVI, 56–59 (Jan., 1938); Grace W. Landrum, "Notes on the Reading of the Old South," *Am. Lit.*, III, 60–71 (March, 1931); H. S. Gulliver, "Thackeray in Georgia," *Ga. Rev.*, I, 35–43 (Spring, 1947); Mary P. Fletcher, "Arkansas Pioneers: What They Were Reading a Century Ago," *Ark. Hist. Quart.*, VIII, 211–214 (Autumn, 1949); R. P. McCutcheon, "Books and Booksellers in New Orleans, 1730–1830," *La. Hist. Quart.*, XX, 606–618 (July, 1937); F. Garvin Davenport, *Cultural Life in Nashville, 1825–1860* (1941), pp. 170–173; Elizabeth Norton, "The Old Library of Transylvania College," *Filson Club Hist. Quart.*, I, 123–133 (April, 1927); Walton R. Patrick, "Literature in the Louisiana Plantation Home Prior to 1861" (La. State Univ. dissertation, 1937), "A Circulating Library of Antebellum Louisiana," *La. Hist. Quart.*, XXIII, 3–12 (Jan., 1940), and "Reading Taste in Louisiana," *Studies for William A. Read* (1940), pp. 288–300; and J. F. McDermott, *Private Libraries in Creole Saint Louis* (1938).

For public and semipublic libraries, see R. P. McCutcheon, "Libraries in New Orleans, 1771–1833," *La. Hist. Quart.*, XX, 1–9 (Jan., 1937); J. F. McDermott, "Public Libraries in St. Louis, 1811–1839," *Library Quart.*, XIV, 9–27 (Jan., 1944) and "Everybody Sold Books in Early St. Louis," *Pubs.' Weekly*, CXXXII, 248–250 (July 24, 1937); B. E. Powell, "The Development of Libraries in Southern State Universities to 1920" (Univ. of Chicago dissertation, 1947); E. L. Pennington, "The Beginnings of the Library in Charles Town, South Carolina," Am. Antiq. Soc. *Proceedings*, n.s. XLIV, 159–187 (1934); Frances L. Spain, "Libraries of South Carolina: Their Origins and Early History, 1700–1830" [abstract of a Univ. of Chicago dissertation], *Library Quart.*, XVII, 28–42 (Jan., 1947); J. T. Wheeler, "Booksellers and Circulating Libraries in Colonial Maryland," *Md. Hist. Mag.*, XXXIV, 1–137 (June, 1939), "The Layman's Libraries and the Provincial Library," *ibid.*, XXXV, 60–73 (March, 1940), and "Thomas Bray and the Maryland Parochial Libraries," *ibid.*, XXXIV, 246–265 (Sept., 1939); S. B. Weeks, "Libraries and Literature in North Carolina in the Eighteenth Century," Am. Hist. Assn. *Report* for 1895.

On literary taste in the South, see Louis B. Wright, "The Classical Tradition in Colonial Virginia," *Papers* Bibliog. Soc. of Am., XXXIII, 85–97 (Sept., 1939) and "Richard Lee II: A Belated Elizabethan in Virginia," *Huntington Library Quart.*, II, 1–35 (Oct., 1938); R. B. Davis, "Literary Tastes in Virginia before Poe," *W.M.Q.*, 2nd ser. XIX, 55–68 (Jan., 1939); Constance Fenimore Woolson, "Literary Taste in the South," *Atlantic Monthly*, XLII, 245–247 (Aug., 1878); and Rhoda C. Ellison, "Early Alabama Interest in Southern Writers," *Ala. Rev.*, I, 101–110 (April, 1948).

As I have indicated earlier, many studies of literary influence pay little attention to the Southern states. Some which have value are: Merle Curti, "The Great Mr. Locke: America's Philosopher," *Huntington Library Bulletin*, No. 11, pp. 107–151 (April, 1937); Guy A. Cardwell, "The Influence of Addison and Steele on Charleston Periodicals, 1795–1860," *Studies in Philol.*, XXXV, 546–570 (July, 1938) and "Charleston Periodicals, 1795–1860: A Study in Literary Influences . . ." (Univ. of N. C. dissertation, 1936); and Paul M. Spurlin, *Montesquieu in America, 1760–1801* (1940) and "Rousseau in America, 1760–1809," *French-Am. Rev.*, I, 8–16 (Jan.–March, 1948).

For the influence of Sir Walter Scott, see Grace W. Landrum, "Sir Walter Scott and His Literary Rivals in the Old South," *Am. Lit.*, II, 256–276 (Nov., 1930); H. F. Bogner, "Sir Walter Scott in New Orleans, 1818–1832," *La. Hist. Quart.*, XXI, 420–517 (April, 1939); and G. Harrison Orians, "The Romance Ferment after *Waverley*," *Am. Lit.*, III, 408–431 (Jan., 1932) and "Walter Scott, Mark Twain, and the Civil War," *S.A.Q.*, XL, 342–359 (Oct., 1941).

Magazines

For general discussion, see Jay B. Hubbell, "Southern Magazines," *Culture in the South* (1934), ed. W. T. Couch, pp. 159–182, and Edwin Mims, "Southern Magazines," *The South in the Building of the Nation*, VII, 457–469. The first volume of F. L. Mott, *A History of American Magazines* (3 vols., 1930–1938) contains much valuable material, but there is little in Vols. II and III. E. R. Rogers, *Four Southern Magazines* (1902) treats too briefly *S.L.M.*, *De Bow's Rev.*, and the two Charleston quarterlies. See also Gertrude Gilmer, *Checklist of Southern Periodicals to 1861* (1934) and Gertrude Gilmer Odum, "Maryland Magazines—Ante-bellum," *Md. Hist. Mag.*, XXIX, 120–131 (June, 1934); Bertha-Monica Stearns, "Southern Magazines for Ladies, 1819–1860," *S.A.Q.*, XXXI, 70–87 (Jan., 1932); and H. S. Stroupe, "The Religious Press in the South Atlantic States, 1802–1865" (Duke Univ. dissertation, 1942).

Other materials are: Guy A. Cardwell, "Charleston Periodicals, 1795–1860" (Univ. of N. C. dissertation, 1936) and "The Influence of Addison and Steele on Charleston Periodicals, 1795–1860," *Studies in Philol.*, XXXV, 546–570 (July, 1938); W. S. Hoole, *A Check-List and Finding-List of Charleston Periodicals, 1732–1864* (1936), "The Gilmans and *The Southern Rose*," *N. C. Hist. Rev.*, XI, 116–128 (April, 1934), and "William Gilmore Simms's Career as Editor," *Ga. Hist. Quart.*, XIX, 47–54 (March, 1935); B. H. Flanders, *Early Georgia Magazines* (1944); Max L. Griffin, "A Bibliography of New Orleans Magazines," *La. Hist. Quart.*, XVIII, 493–556 (July, 1935); H. C. Nixon, "*De Bow's Review*," *Sewanee Rev.*, XXXIX, 54–61 (Jan.–March, 1931); O. C. Skipper, "J. D. B. De Bow, the Man," *Jour. So. Hist.*, X, 404–423 (Nov., 1944); G. C. Keidel, "Early Maryland Magazines," *Md. Hist. Mag.*, Vols. XXVIII–XXX; and Gilbert Chinard, "La Littérature française dans le sud des Etats-Unis, d'après le 'Southern Literary Messenger' (1834–1864)," *Revue de Littérature Comparée*, 8th year (Jan.–March, 1928). Earl G. Swem (comp.), *The Virginia Historical Index* (2 vols., 1934, 1936) is an indispensable guide to materials in the Virginia historical journals down to 1930. The W.P.A. Index to American Magazines (to 1850) at New York University has been useful in identifying articles by Southern writers in Northern magazines. For location of magazine files, see Winifred Gregory (comp.), *Union List of Serials in the Libraries of the United States and Canada* (1927; revised ed., 1943).

Much of the material published in ante-bellum Southern magazines is anonymous or pseudonymous. For *S.L.M.*, see David K. Jackson, *The Contributors and Contributions to The Southern Literary Messenger* (Charlottesville, Va., 1936) and *Poe and The Southern Literary Messenger* (Richmond, 1934). The Charleston Library Society has a manuscript list which identifies the authors of most articles in the *Southern Rev.* (1828–1832). The New York Public and the Duke Univ. libraries have files of *Russell's Mag.* (1857–1860) in which the names of contributors were identified, presumably by William A. Courtenay. A few of the attributions are clearly wrong. Some of the contributors to the *Southern Quarterly Rev.* (1842–1857) are identified in the Duyckincks' *Cyclopaedia of American Literature*. Still others can be found by consulting reviews in the Charleston newspapers and *The Letters of William Gilmore Simms* (5 vols., 1952–   ).

For the later nineteenth century, I am indebted to two Duke Univ. master's theses: Mrs. Laura N. Young, "Southern Literary Magazines, 1865–1887: With Special Reference to Literary Criticism" (1940) and Mary F. Covington, "The *Atlantic* and *Harper's* in Relation to Southern Literature, 1865–1900" (1938). I am also somewhat indebted to three of my graduate students whose dissertations are not yet (1953) completed: John C. Guilds, Jr., "Simms as a Magazine Editor, 1825–1845"; Ray M. Atchison, "Southern Literary Magazines, 1865–1887"; and Rayburn S. Moore, "Southern Writers and Northern Literary Magazines, 1865–1890."

Newspapers

There are several historical accounts of American newspapers, but the best is F. L. Mott, *American Journalism: A History* (1941). Indispensable in locating materials are Clarence S. Brigham (comp.), *History and Bibliography of American Newspapers, 1690–1820* (2 vols., 1947) and Winifred Gregory (comp.), *American Newspapers, 1821–1936: A Union List of Files Available in the United States and Canada* (1937). See also Lester J. Cappon, *Virginia Newspapers, 1821–1936: A Bibliography with Historical Introduction and Notes* (1936) and Katherine K. Weed and Richmond P. Bond (comps.), *Studies of British [and American] Newspapers . . . to 1800: A Bibliography* (1947). In the larger libraries many of the eighteenth-century newspapers are available in photostat or microfilm; see Brigham, *op. cit.*

The most valuable literary studies of Southern newspapers are Elizabeth C. Cook, *Literary Influences in Colonial Newspapers, 1704–1750* (1912); Rhoda C. Ellison, *Early Alabama Publications* (1947), which covers the period 1807–1870; and James S. Purcell, Jr., "Literary Culture in North Carolina before 1820" (Duke Univ. dissertation, 1950). See also Philip Davidson, *Propaganda and the American Revolution, 1763–1783* (1941)· M. C. Howard, "*The Maryland Gazette*, an American Imitator of the *Tatler* and the *Spectator*," *Md. Hist. Mag.*, XXIX, 295–298 (Dec., 1934); Hennig Cohen, *The South Carolina Gazette, 1732–1775* (1953); Herbert Ravenel Sass, *Outspoken: 150 Years of The [Charleston] News and Courier* (1953); R. M. Myers, "The Old Dominion Looks to London: A Study of the English Literary Influences upon *The Virginia Gazette*, 1736–1766," *Va. Mag.*, LIV, 195–217 (July, 1946); R. L. Rusk, *The Literature of the Middle Western Frontier* (2 vols., 1925), for early Kentucky newspapers; Edward Larocque Tinker, *Bibliography of the French Newspapers and Periodicals of Louisiana* (1933); Bell I. Wiley, "Camp Newspapers in the Confederacy," *N. C. Hist. Rev.*, XX, 327–335 (Oct., 1935); Lawrence C. Wroth, *The Colonial Printer* (revised ed., 1938) and *William Parks* (1926); and Clement Eaton, "Winifred and Joseph Gales, Liberals in the Old South," *Jour. So. Hist.*, X, 461–474 (Nov., 1944).

Poetry

Apart from Poe, Lanier, and Timrod, much more attention has been given to Southern fiction than to Southern poetry. The most useful single volume is Edd W. Parks (ed.), *Southern Poets: Representative Selections, with Introduction, Bibliography, and Notes* (1936). See also the essays, "Southern Poetry" and "Southern Poetic Theory," in Parks's *Segments of Southern Thought* (1938); H. N. Snyder, "Characteristics of Southern Poetry from the Beginning to 1865," *The South in the Building of the Nation*, VII, 1–24; Philip Graham (ed.), *Early Texas Verse, 1835–1850* (1936); C. W. Hubner (ed.), *Representative Southern Poets* (1906); A. C. Gordon, Jr., *Virginian Writers of Fugitive Verse* (1923); F. V. N. Painter, *Poets of the South* (1903) and *Poets of Virginia* (1907); R. G. Walser (ed.), *North Carolina Poetry* (revised ed., 1951); and H. W. Longfellow (ed.), *Poems of America: Southern States* (1882).

Many forgotten volumes of verse—most of which have no intrinsic value—are listed in Oscar Wegelin (comp.), *Early American Poetry* (2nd ed., 1930); S. E. Bradshaw, *On Southern Poetry Prior to 1860* (1900); and J. C. Stockbridge, *Index to American Poetry and Plays in the Collection of C. Fiske Harris* (revised ed., Providence, R. I., 1886).

The South is especially rich in folklore and in folk songs and ballads of many kinds. In the twentieth century private collectors and state folklore societies have published many of these songs and ballads. The most recent and the most complete is *The Frank C. Brown Collection of North Carolina Folklore* in five volumes, of which the first three were published in 1952. The first collection of its kind was *Slave Songs of the United States* (1867; reissued 1929), edited by W. F. Allen and two other Northern teachers. In the same year Thomas Wentworth Higginson published his "Negro Spirituals" in the *Atlantic Monthly*, XIX, 685–694 (June, 1867). For a Southern physician who recorded some Negro folk songs in 1838, see Jay B. Hubbell, "A Persimmon Beer Dance in Ante-Bellum Virginia," *S.L.M.*, N.S. V, 461–466 (Nov.–Dec., 1943).

Some of the more notable collections are: A. K. Davis, *Traditional Ballads of Virginia* (1929); A. P. Hudson, *Folksongs of Mississippi* (1936); G. P. Jackson, *White Spirituals in the Southern Uplands* (1933); John A. and Alan Lomax, *Cowboy Songs and Other Frontier Ballads* (1910; revised and enlarged ed., 1938); J. W. Johnson, *The Book of American Negro Spirituals* (1925); W. A. Owens, *Texas Folk Songs* (1950); Dorothy Scarborough, *A Song Catcher in Southern Mountains* (1937) and *On the Trail of Negro Folk-Songs* (1925); C. J. Sharp, *English Folk Songs from the Southern Appalachians* (1917, 1932), and N. I. White, *American Negro Folk-Songs* (1928).

See also under *Civil War.*

Political and Economic Thought

Certain aspects of Southern political and economic thought are discussed in Charles E. Merriam, *A History of American Political Theories* (1903); Joseph Dorfman, *The Economic Mind in American Civilization, 1606–1865* (2 vols., 1946); and Merle Curti, *The Growth of American Thought* (revised ed., 1951).

The chief articles written in defense of slavery are contained in William Harper and others, *The Pro-Slavery Argument* . . . (Charleston, 1852) and E. N. Elliott and others, *Cotton Is King, and Pro-Slavery Argument* . . . (Augusta, 1860). The fullest discussion is W. S. Jenkins, *Pro-Slavery Thought in the Old South* (1935). See also Wilfred Carsel, "The Slaveholders' Indictment of Northern Wage Slavery," *Jour. So. Hist.*, VI, 504–520 (Nov., 1940); C. S. Boucher, "In Re That Aggressive Slavocracy," *Miss. Valley Hist. Rev.*, VIII, 13–79 (June–Sept., 1921); Harvey Wish, "Aristotle, Plato, and the Mason-Dixon Line," *Jour. Hist. Ideas*, X, 254–266 (April, 1949); and H. G. and W. L. Duncan, "The Development of Sociology in the Old South," *Am. Jour. Sociology*, XXXIX, 649–656 (March, 1934).

Other materials of importance are: Jesse T. Carpenter, *The South as a Conscious Minority, 1789–1861* (1930); Avery Craven, *The Coming of the Civil War* (1942); Clement Eaton, *Freedom of Thought in the Old South* (1940); Basil L. Gildersleeve, "The Creed of the Old South," *Atlantic Monthly*, LXIX, 75–87 (Jan., 1892), reprinted separately in 1915; Fletcher Green, *Constitutional Development in the South Atlantic States, 1776–1860* (1930) and "Democracy in the Old South," *Jour. So. Hist.*, XII, 3–23 (Feb., 1946); Thomas P. Kettell, *Southern Wealth and Northern Profits* (New York, 1860); Lillian A. Kibler, *Benjamin F. Perry: South Carolina Unionist* (1946); Ulrich B. Phillips, *The Course of the South to Secession* (1939), "Economic and Political Essays in the Ante-bellum South" in *The South in the Building of the Nation*, VII, 173–199, and "The Literary Movement for Secession" in *Studies in Southern History and Politics Inscribed to W. A. Dunning* (1914); Joseph C. Robert, *The Road from Monticello: A Study of the Virginia Slavery Debate of 1832* (1941); and Herbert Wender, *Southern Commercial Conventions, 1837–1859* (1930).

Printing and Publishing

A standard work is Douglas C. McMurtrie, *A History of Printing in the United States*, Vol. II, *Middle & South Atlantic States* (1936), which contains valuable bibliographies and notes. There is little material on the nineteenth century. McMurtrie did not live to complete Vols. I, III, and IV. Even for the South Atlantic states, there are still materials of value in Isaiah Thomas, *The History of Printing in America* (2nd ed., 2 vols.; Albany, N. Y., 1874). Mc-Murtrie published, or stimulated others to publish, numerous check lists of early imprints of many states; see Charles F. Heartman, *McMurtrie Imprints: Bibliography of Separately Printed Writings by Douglas C. McMurtrie* (Hattiesburg, Miss., 1942). Rare books can often be located by consulting Charles Evans, *American Bibliography* (12 vols., 1903–1934), which attempts to list every American book printed up to 1820, and Joseph Sabin and others, *A Dictionary of Books Relating to America* (29 vols., 1868–1936). Orville A. Roorbach, *Bibliotheca Americana* (1852) and its supplements, 1855, 1858, 1861, give important lists of Southern and Northern publishers. See also the lists of printers and publishers, classified by states, in Charles Evans, *American Bibliography*. Later books of some value are Hellmut Lehmann-Haupt and others, *The Book in America* (1939, 1951); John T. Winterich, *Early American Books and Printing* (1935); and Lawrence C. Wroth, *William Parks* (1926) and *The Colonial Printer* (revised ed., 1938). H. W. Boynton, *Annals of American Bookselling, 1638–1850* (1935) is of no value so far as the Southern states are concerned. Rollo G. Silver's *The Baltimore Book Trade, 1800–1825* (1953) lists a large number of printers, publishers, and booksellers.

J. C. Derby, *Fifty Years among Authors, Books and Publishers* (1884) contains more information about the sale of books in the South than J. H. Harper, *The House of Harper* (1912) and other histories of metropolitan publishing houses. The best general study is Earl L. Bradsher's chapter and bibliography, "Book Publishers and Publishing," *C.H.A.L.*, IV, 533–553, 806–810. See also Bradsher's *Mathew Carey: Editor, Author, and Publisher* (1912) and "An Early

American Publisher and His Audience," *Sewanee Rev.*, XXI, 287–296 (July, 1913). Mrs. Emily E. F. Skeel (ed.), *Mason Locke Weems: His Works and Ways* (3 vols., 1929) contains many letters from Weems to Carey and throws much light upon what was read in the South Atlantic states in the first quarter of the nineteenth century. See also R. L. Brunhouse, "David Ramsay's Publication Problems, 1784–1808," *Papers Bibliog. Soc. Am.*, XXXIX, 51–67 (1945); W. S. Tryon, "The Publications of Ticknor and Fields in the South, 1840–1865," *Jour. So. Hist.*, XIV, 305–330 (Aug., 1948); and William Charvat, "The People's Patronage," *L.H.U.S.*, I, 513–525. For Confederate publishers and imprints, see J. L. King, *Dr. George William Bagby* (1927), chap. vii, and R. B. Harwell, *Confederate Belles-Lettres* (Hattiesburg, Miss., 1941), which contains a check list and a useful bibliography.

After 1820 the Northern publishers practically monopolized the reprinting of European books, but in the two preceding decades the Southern printers brought out some important titles.

Byron's *English Bards and Scotch Reviewers* was reprinted in Charleston in 1811. Scott's *The Lay of the Last Minstrel* was reprinted in Savannah in the same year and in Baltimore in 1812; and *The Field of Waterloo* in Lexington, Ky., in 1816. From Alexandria, Va., came American editions of William Godwin's *St. Leon* in 1802 and *Fleetwood* in 1805. Some books appeared under a dual imprint. For example, in 1820 Samuel Rogers' *The Pleasures of Memory, and Other Poems* and James Thomson's *The Seasons* were published in New York by R. & W. A. Bartow and in Richmond by W. A. Bartow. Mrs. Amelia Opic's *The Father and Daughter* was reprinted in Richmond in 1806 by S. Grantland. Thomas Campbell's *Poetical Works* was published in Baltimore in 1814. Three of Maria Edgeworth's books were reprinted in Georgetown, D.C.: *Tales of Fashionable Life* (1809), *The Modern Griselda* (1810), and *Letters for Literary Ladies* (1810). *The Absentee* was reprinted in Washington in 1812.

Eighteenth-century English authors were still being reprinted in the South. Burns's *Poetical Works* was reprinted at Alexandria in 1813 and again in Baltimore in 1815. Hannah More's *Practical Piety* was reprinted in Baltimore in 1812. Hugh Blair's *Sermons* in two volumes had been reprinted there for Mason Locke Weems in 1792–1793. Isaac Watts's *Poems* were reprinted in Lexington, Ky., in 1815, and his *Hymns and Spiritual Songs* in Paris, Ky., the following year. Goldsmith's *An Abridgment of the History of England* was reprinted in Alexandria in 1811 and his *Citizen of the World* in Baltimore in 1816. Bunyan's *The Holy War* appeared in Baltimore in 1812, and Johnson's *Dictionary* was reprinted there in 1814. His *Rasselas* had been reprinted in Frederick, Md., in 1810.

In her *Alexander Pope's Prestige in America, 1725–1835* (1949) Agnes Marie Sibley listed approximately 160 American editions of Pope's *An Essay on Man* which were published in the years 1747–1850. Four of these were printed in the South: two in Baltimore, 1804, 1812; one in Richmond, 1805; and one in Lexington, Kentucky, 1816. Of the six American editions of Pope's *Iliad* one was printed in Baltimore in 1812. Of the four American editions of his *Odyssey* one appeared in Georgetown, D.C., in 1813. His *Poetical Works* was republished in Baltimore in 1814. In 1836 William C. Bell published in Lexington, Kentucky, his own *An Analysis of Pope's Essay on Man*.

Thomas Holcroft's translation of Goethe's *Hermann und Dorothea* was reprinted in Richmond in 1805; Kotzebue's *Lovers' Vows* in Baltimore in 1808; Voltaire's *Charles XII of Sweden* in Frederick, Md., in 1808; Condorcet's *Historical View of the Progress of the Human Mind* in Baltimore in 1802; and Swedenborg's *A Treatise concerning Heaven and Hell* in Baltimore in 1812.

Many but by no means all of these reprints are to be found in the Huntington Library and the Library of Congress. A systematic search would doubtless add other titles.

Religion

The South in the Building of the Nation has a section on "The Religious Life of the South," X, 428–566. Allen Tate's suggestive essay, "Religion and the Old South," first published in *I'll Take My Stand* (1930), appeared in a lengthened version in his *Reactionary Essays on Poetry and Ideas* (1936), pp. 167–190. The best general accounts are found in W. W. Sweet, *The Story of Religion in America* (revised ed., 1939) and in greater detail in his *Religion in Colonial America* (1942), which contains a valuable bibliography. See also Sweet's three volumes in his Religion on the American Frontier series dealing with the Baptists, Methodists, and Presbyterians. Deism is discussed with almost no attention to the Southern states in G. Adolf Koch, *Republican Religion: The American Revolution and the Cult of Reason* (1933) and Herbert M. Morais, *Deism in Eighteenth Century America* (1934).

Other materials may be found in William H. Foote, *Sketches of Virginia* (First Series, Philadelphia, 1850; Second Series, 1855); Paul L. Garber, *James Henley Thornwell: Presbyterian Defender of the Old South* (1943); Wesley M. Gewehr, *The Great Awakening in Virginia, 1740–1790* (1930); Albea Godbold, *The Church College of the Old South* (1944); Clarence Gohdes, "Some Notes on the Unitarian Church in the Ante-bellum South . . . ," *American Studies in Honor of William Kenneth Boyd* (1940), pp. 327–366; Francis L. Hawks, *Contributions to the Ecclesiastical History of the United States* (2 vols., New York, 1836); William Meade, *Old Churches, Ministers, and Families of Virginia* (2 vols., 1857); Niels H. Sonne, *Liberal Kentucky, 1780–1828* (1939); John D. Wade, *Augustus Baldwin Longstreet* (1924); and Henry S. Stroupe, "The Religious Press in the South Atlantic States, 1802–1865" (Duke Univ. dissertation, 1942).

Scholarly Interests

The best general treatment of the subject is found in John Bell Henneman (ed.), *History of the Literary and Intellectual Life of the South*, which is Vol. VII of *The South in the Building of the Nation*. It contains among other materials Charles Forster Smith's "The South's Contributions to Classical Studies" and Colyer Meriwether's "Historical Studies in the South."

In the same volume appears Henneman's "English Studies in the South," which in a fuller form was printed in the *Sewanee Rev.*, II, 180–197 (Feb., 1894) and in his *Shakespearean and Other Papers* (Sewanee, Tenn., 1911). This volume also contains "Two Pioneers in the Historical Study of English: Thomas Jefferson and Louis Klipstein." A. A. Kern, "A Pioneer in Anglo-Saxon," *Sewanee Rev.*, XI, 337–344 (July, 1903) gives an account of Edward Dromgoole Sims. E. W. Parks in "Professor Richard Malcolm Johnston," *Ga. Hist. Quart.*, XXV, 1–15, (March, 1941) gives an account of Johnston's teaching of English at the University of Georgia. Henry Ruffner's "Essays on the Early Language and Literature of England" appeared in *S.L.M.*, XIII, 307–312, 373–380, 479–485 (May, June, Aug., 1847). Wilkins Tannehill, *Sketches of the History of Literature* (Nashville, 1827) is discussed in my text. William Archer Cocke, "Sketches of Southern Literature," *Magnolia Weekly* (Richmond), II, 22–23, 31, 36–37, 46, 54, 63, 70–71 (Oct. 17 to Nov. 28, 1863) is a prejudiced and inferior performance. Somewhat better are Simms's articles on earlier South Carolina writers which appeared under various titles in Vols. I and II (1869–1870) of the Charleston *XIX Century*. For some account of the first competent student of the literature of the New South, see John Bell Henneman, "The Late Professor [William Malone] Baskervill," *Sewanee Rev.*, VIII, 26–44 (Jan., 1900).

There are some materials on Southern scientists in W. M. and Mabel S. C. Smallwood, *Natural History and the American Mind* (1941) and T. C. Johnson, Jr., *Scientific Interests in the Old South* (1936). Southern economists are ably treated in Joseph Dorfman, *The Economic Mind in American Civilization, 1606–1865* (2 vols., 1946). Frank Freidel, *Francis Lieber: Nineteenth-Century Liberal* (1947) gives a detailed account of Lieber's writings in political science while teaching at the University of South Carolina.

Leslie W. Dunlap, *American Historical Societies, 1790–1860* (1944) gives a brief history of each of the Southern historical societies, with many references to source materials. See also Michael Kraus, *The Writing of American History* (1953); E. Merton Coulter, "What the South Has Done about Its History," *Jour. So. Hist.*, II, 3–28 (Feb., 1936); S. B. Weeks, "The North Carolina Historians," *Publications* of N. C. Hist. Commission, Bulletin No. 18 (1915), pp. 71–86; J. G. de Roulhac Hamilton, "The Preservation of North Carolina History," *N. C. Hist. Rev.*, IV, 3–21 (Jan., 1927); C. S. Sydnor, "Historical Activities in Mississippi in the Nineteenth Century," *Jour. So. Hist.*, III, 139–160

(May, 1937). Wendell H. Stephenson is preparing a book on the later Southern historians. See his "A Half Century of Southern Historical Scholarship," *Jour. So. Hist.*, XII, 313–344 (Aug., 1946), "William Garrott Brown: Literary Historian and Essayist," *ibid.*, XI, 3–32 (Feb., 1945), and "William P. Trent as a Historian of the South," *ibid.*, XV, 151–177 (May, 1949).

Other materials will be found in the historical accounts of Southern colleges and universities listed under *Education*.

Social Life

Virginia social life in the Colonial period is described in Robert Beverley, *The History and Present State of Virginia* (1705, 1722, 1947); Hugh Jones, *The Present State of Virginia* (1724); and *William Byrd's Natural History of Virginia* (1940), ed. R. C. Beatty and W. J. Mulloy. For the life of the great planters on the eve of the Revolution, see Douglas S. Freeman, *George Washington* (1948–   ), Vol. I., chaps. i and iv, and H. D. Farish (ed.), *Journal & Letters of Philip Vickers Fithian, 1773–1774* (1943). Other valuable studies are P. A. Bruce, *Social Life in Virginia in the Seventeenth Century* (1907); T. J. Wertenbaker, *The Planters of Colonial Virginia* (1922); Louis B. Wright, *The First Gentlemen of Virginia* (1940); and Julia C. Spruill, *Women's Life and Work in the Southern Colonies* (1938). See also Edmund S. Morgan, *Virginians at Home: Family Life in the Eighteenth Century* (1952).

For Virginia life in the nineteenth century, see J. P. Kennedy, *Swallow Barn* (1832, 1851, 1929); Thomas Nelson Page, *Social Life in Old Virginia* (1897); George Cary Eggleston, "The Old Régime in the Old Dominion," *Atlantic Monthly*, XXXVI, 603–616 (Nov., 1875); and Jay B. Hubbell, *Virginia Life in Fiction* (1922). The first part of G. P. R. James's *The Old Dominion* (1856) gives an attractive picture of Virginia life as seen by an English novelist who spent several years in the state. *Sketches from Old Virginia* (1897) by another English writer, Arthur Granville Bradley, who lived in Virginia for several years after the Civil War, supplies a useful check upon the Southern disposition to glorify the past.

The social life of the Lower South is described in William Gilmore Simms, *The Golden Christmas* (Charleston, 1852); D. R. Hundley, *Social Relations in Our Southern States* (New York, 1860); [J. H. Ingraham], *The South-West. By a Yankee* (New York, 1835); Richard Malcolm Johnston, "Middle Georgia Rural Life," *Century*, XLIII, 737–743 (March, 1892); and Susan Dabney Smedes, *Memorials of a Southern Planter* (1887), a life of her father, Thomas Dabney. Frederick Law Olmsted's three separate accounts of his travels through the South were reprinted in *The Cotton Kingdom* (1860). Two of the best modern studies are William E. Dodd, *The Cotton Kingdom* (1919) and U. B. Phillips, *Life and Labor in the Old South* (1929).

Other useful works by modern historians are: Rosser H. Taylor, *Ante-bellum*

South Carolina: A Social and Cultural History (1942) and "The Gentry of Ante-bellum South Carolina," *N. C. Hist. Rev.*, XVII, 114–131 (April, 1940); Minnie C. Boyd, *Alabama in the Fifties* (1931); F. Garvin Davenport, *Ante-bellum Kentucky: A Social History* (1943); Guion G. Johnson, *Ante-bellum North Carolina: A Social History* (1937) and *A Social History of the Sea Islands* (1930); and F. P. Gaines, *The Southern Plantation: A Study in the Development and Accuracy of a Tradition* (1924). Edwin H. Cady, *The Gentleman in America: A Literary Study in American Culture* (1949) does not pay much attention to the South.

For social life at summer resorts, see William Gilmore Simms, "Summer Travel in the South," *S.Q.R.*, N.S. II, 24–65 (Sept., 1850); Perceval Reniers, *The Springs of Virginia* (1941); and Lawrence F. Brewster, *Summer Migrations and Resorts of South Carolina Low-Country Planters* (1947).

Most of the studies listed above pay scant attention to the yeomen farmers, who are treated much more fully in Frank L. Owsley, *Plain Folk of the Old South* (1949). See also T. P. Abernethy, *From Frontier to Plantation in Tennessee* (1932) and Everett Dick, *The Dixie Frontier* (1948). For life in the Appalachians, see J. C. Campbell, *The Southern Highlander and His Homeland* (1921) and Isabella D. Harris, "The Southern Mountaineer in Fiction, 1824–1910" (Duke Univ. dissertation, 1948).

For the Southern poor-whites, see Paul H. Buck, "The Poor Whites of the South," *Am. Hist. Rev.*, XXXI, 41–55 (Oct., 1925); A. N. J. Den Hollander, "The Tradition of 'Poor Whites,'" *Culture in the South* (1934), ed. W. T. Couch, pp. 403–431; Shields McIlwaine, *The Southern Poor-White* (1939); James S. Purcell, Jr., "The Southern Poor White in Fiction" (Duke Univ. master's thesis, 1938), which has an excellent historical introduction.

For social life in Southern cities, see the works cited under *Cities and Towns* and Dixon Wecter, *The Saga of American Society* (1937), which supplies further bibliographical data.

Among the many studies of slavery are Ulrich B. Phillips, *American Negro Slavery* (1918); John Hope Franklin, *From Slavery to Freedom: A History of American Negroes* (1947); Charles S. Sydnor, *Slavery in Mississippi* (1933); Ralph B. Flanders, *Plantation Slavery in Georgia* (1933); and Rosser H. Taylor, *Slaveholding in North Carolina* (1926).

Theater and Drama

Extensive bibliographical materials and long lists of plays are given in Arthur H. Quinn, *A History of the American Drama from the Beginning to the Civil War* (revised ed., 1943), pp. 395–462, and *A History of the American Drama from the Civil War to the Present Day* (revised ed., 1936), pp. 305–402. There are some materials on the theater in the South in Glenn Hughes, *A History of the American Theatre, 1700–1950* (1951), Arthur Hornblow, *History of the*

Theatre in America from Its Beginnings to the Present Time (2 vols., 1919), and G. O. Seilhamer, *History of the American Theatre* (3 vols., 1888–1891).

Some useful studies are: Eola Willis, *The Charleston Stage in the XVIII Century* (1924); E. D. Seeber, "The French Theatre in Charleston in the Eighteenth Century," *S. C. Hist. and Geneal. Mag.*, XLII, 1–7 (Jan., 1941); William Stanley Hoole, *The Ante-bellum Charleston Theatre* (1946), "Charleston Theatres," *Southwest Rev.*, XXV, 193–204 (Jan., 1940), "Charleston Theatricals during the Tragic Decade," *Jour. So. Hist.*, XI, 538–547 (Nov., 1945), and "Two Famous Theatres of the Old South," *S.A.Q.*, XXXVI, 273–277 (July, 1937)—R. H. Land, "The First Williamsburg Theater," *W.M.Q.*, 3rd ser. V, 259–374 (July, 1948); Martin S. Shockley, "A History of the Theatre in Richmond, Virginia" (Univ. of N. C. dissertation, 1938), "American Plays in the Richmond Theatre, 1819–1838," *Studies in Philol.*, XXXVII, 100–119 (Jan., 1940), "The Richmond Theatre, 1780–1790," *Va. Mag.*, LX, 421–436 (July, 1952), "The Proprietors of Richmond New Theatre of 1819," *W.M.Q.*, 2nd ser. XIX, 302–306 (July, 1939), "Shakespeare's Plays in the Richmond Theatre, 1819–1838," *Shakespeare Assn. Bulletin*, XV, 88–94 (April, 1940), and "First American Performances of English Plays in Richmond before 1819," *Jour. So. Hist.*, XIII, 91–105 (Feb., 1947); E. A. Wyatt, "Three Petersburg Theatres," *W.M.Q.*, 2nd ser. XXI, 83–110 (April, 1941)—Donald J. Rulfs, "The Professional Theater in Wilmington, 1858–1870," *N. C. Hist. Rev.*, XXVIII, 119–136 (April, 1951) and "The Ante-bellum Professional Theater in Raleigh," *ibid.*, XXIX, 344–358 (July, 1952)—Nelle Smither, "A History of the English Theatre at New Orleans, 1806–1842," *La. Hist. Quart.*, XXVIII, 85–276, 361–572 (Jan., April, 1945) and John S. Kendall, *The Golden Age of the New Orleans Theater* (1952); R. P. McCutcheon, "The First English Plays in New Orleans," *Am. Lit.*, XI, 183–199 (May, 1939); and J. P. Roppolo, "Audiences in New Orleans Theatres, 1845–1861," *Tulane Studies in Eng.*, II (1950), 121–136—W. B. Gates, "The Theatre in Natchez," *Jour. Miss. Hist.*, III, 71–129 (April, 1941); J. M. Free, "The Ante-bellum Theatre of the Old Natchez Region," *ibid.*, V, 14–27 (Jan., 1943); W. B. Hamilton, "The Theater of the Old Southwest," *Am. Lit.*, XII, 471–485 (Jan., 1941)—W. R. Hogan, "The Theatre in the Republic of Texas," *Southwest Rev.*, XIX, 374–401 (July, 1934); E. G. Fletcher, "The Beginnings of the Professional Theatre in Texas," Univ. of Texas *Bulletin*, June 1, 1936, pp. 1–53—W. G. B. Carson, *The Theatre on the Frontier: The Early Years of the St. Louis Stage* (1932).

Travelers

The writings of the travelers are of especial value because they often commented on aspects of Southern life which the native writers seldom noticed. Virginia planter life on the eve of the Revolution is well described in the *Journal & Letters* (1943) of Philip Vickers Fithian, ed. H. D. Farish. Janet Schaw's *Journal of a Lady of Quality* (1921), ed. Prof. and Mrs. C. M. Andrews, gives a vivid but unsympathetic account of the North Carolina Revolutionists. South Carolina in 1773 is pictured in the *Memoir of the Life of Josiah Quincy Jun.* (Boston, 1825) and in "Journal of Josiah-Quincy, Junior, 1773," Mass. Hist. Soc. *Proceedings*, XLIX, 424–481 (1915–1916). Notable for its descriptions of Southern flora and fauna is William Bartram, *Travels through North and South Carolina, Georgia, East and West Florida* . . . (1791).

James Kirke Paulding, *Letters from the South* (2 vols., New York, 1817) gives a gossipy, sympathetic picture of Virginia in 1816. Slightly less kindly is the picture given in "Arthur Singleton, Esq." [Henry Cogswell Knight], *Letters from the South and West* (Boston, 1824) and Henry Barnard, "The South Atlantic States in 1833, as Seen by a New Englander," ed. Bernard C. Steiner, *Md. Hist. Mag.*, XIII, 267–386 (Dec., 1918). William Cullen Bryant's observations are recorded in "A Tour in the Old South," *Prose Writings* (1884), II, 23–50, and in *Letters of a Traveller* (1850). John W. De Forest, whose treatment of Southern life is discussed in my text, collected his magazine articles for *A Union Officer in the Reconstruction*, which was not published until 1948. Frederick Law Olmsted's three earlier volumes were reprinted in *The Cotton Kingdom* (1860). Of exceptional interest are John James Audubon's descriptions of the Western South as given in his *Delineations of American Scenery and Character* (1926), ed. F. H. Herrick, and *Audubon's America* (1940), ed. Donald C. Peattie. The Natchez region is well described in [Joseph Holt Ingraham], *The South-West. By a Yankee* (1835).

The Swedish novelist Fredrika Bremer left a record of her Southern impressions in *Homes of the New World*, trans. Mary Howitt (2 vols., New York, 1853). For French travelers, see Lee W. Ryan, *French Travelers in the Southeastern United States, 1775–1800* (1939); Frank Monaghan, "French Travellers in the United States, 1765–1931," *Bulletin* of N. Y. Public Library, Vol. XXXVI (March–Oct., 1932); Gilbert Chinard, "Chateaubriand en Amérique," *Modern Philol.*, IX, 129–149 (July, 1911). Alexis de Tocqueville's famous *Democracy in America* (2 vols., 1835, 1839) pays little attention to the Southern states. Some account of his Southern travel is given in George W. Pierson, *Tocqueville and Beaumont in America* (1938). Emerson's friend, Achille Murat, paints an attractive picture of Southern society in *Esquisse moral et politique des États-Unis* . . . (Paris, 1832), published in English as *America and the Americans* (New York, 1849). See also A. J. Hanna, *A Prince in Their Midst: The Adventurous Life of Achille Murat on the American Frontier* (1946).

For a bibliography of works by British travelers with selections from their writings, see Allan Nevins (ed.), *American Social History as Recorded by British Travellers* (1923), revised and republished as *America through British Eyes* (1948). See also Jane L. Mesick, *The English Traveller in America, 1780–1835*. Some of the more notable British travel books which describe the South are James Silk Buckingham, *The Slave States of America* (2 vols.; London, 1842); John Davis, *Travels of Four Years and a Half in the United States* (Bristol,

England, 1803), reprinted in New York in 1909; Philip H. Gosse [father of
Edmund Gosse], *Letters from Alabama*, (*U.S.*) *Chiefly Relating to Natural
History* (London, 1859); Fanny Kemble, *Journal of a Residence on a Georgia
Plantation* (New York, 1863), which needs to be corrected by her daughter
Frances Butler Leigh's *Ten Years on a Georgia Plantation since the War* (Lon-
don, 1883); and Sir Charles Lyell, *A Second Visit to the United States* . . .
(2 vols., London, 1849).

Charles Dickens, *American Notes* (1842) contains a chapter on slavery which
is based largely on Theodore Weld's compilation, *American Slavery as It Is*
(1839). See Louise H. Johnson, "The Source of the Chapter on Slavery in
Dickens's *American Notes*," *Am. Lit.*, XIV, 427–430 (Jan., 1943). William
Makepeace Thackeray's comments on Southern life are found in "A Mississippi
Bubble" in his *Roundabout Papers* (1863), in *The Virginians* (1857–1859),
and in numerous letters. See Jay B. Hubbell, "Thackeray and Virginia," *Va.
Quart. Rev.*, III, 76–86 (Jan., 1927); Gordon N. Ray (ed.), *The Letters and
Private Papers of William Makepeace Thackeray* (4 vols., 1945–1946); Eyre
Crowe, *With Thackeray in America* (London, 1893); and James G. Wilson
(ed.), *Thackeray in the United States* (1904).

Women Writers

For the general background, Fred Lewis Pattee, *The Feminine Fifties* (1940)
is excellent, but the only Southern writers whom he discusses are Mrs. E. D.
E. N. Southworth and Mrs. Caroline Lee Hentz. See also Herbert R. Brown,
The Sentimental Novel in America, 1789–1860 (1940) and Alexander Cowie,
The Rise of the American Novel (1948) and "The Vogue of the Domestic
Novel," *S.A.Q.*, XLI, 416–424 (Oct., 1942). A number of Southern women
writers are included in *D.A.B.*, and there are sketches of seventy-five in James
Wood Davidson, *The Living Writers of the South* (New York, 1869). Southern
magazines for women are discussed in F. L. Mott, *A History of American Magazines* and in Bertha-Monica Stearns, "Southern Magazines for Ladies, 1819–
1860," *S.A.Q.*, XXXI, 70–87 (Jan., 1932). For Southern women who wrote
of their experiences in the Civil War, see Douglas S. Freeman, *The South to
Posterity* (1939). For Louisa S. McCord, see Margaret F. Thorp, *Female Persuasion* (1949), chap. vi.

A considerable amount of information is contained in the following anthologies: "Mary Forrest" [Mrs. Julia D. Freeman], *Women of the South Distinguished in Literature* (New York, 1860); Rufus W. Griswold, *The Female
Poets of America* (Philadelphia, 1849); John S. Hart, *The Female Prose Writers
of America* (4th ed.; Philadelphia, 1864); Caroline May, *The American Female
Poets* (Philadelphia, 1848); and "Ida Raymond" [Mrs. Mary T. Tardy], *Southland Writers* (Philadelphia, 1870), reprinted as *Living Female Writers of the
South* (Philadelphia, 1872).

III. INDIVIDUAL WRITERS

Washington Allston

The only full-length biography is *Life and Letters of Washington Allston* (New York, 1892), by Jared B. Flagg. Flagg, the son of Allston's half-brother, had studied art with Allston. Some of the factual errors in Flagg's biography are pointed out in Edgar P. Richardson, *Washington Allston: A Study of the Romantic Artist in America* (1948). This valuable study is concerned primarily with Allston's paintings, but it contains a good brief discussion of Allston's writings and their relation to his painting. Richardson's Bibliography, pp. 220–228, is excellent. See also Anon., "Some Unpublished Correspondence of Washington Allston," *Scribner's Mag.*, XI, 68–83 (Jan., 1892) and G. D. Chase, "Some Washington Allston Correspondence," *New Eng. Quart.*, XVI, 628–634 (Dec., 1943).

The literary histories contain little discussion of Allston's writings. For reviews of *The Sylphs of the Seasons* (London and Boston, 1813), see "B" in *Analectic Mag.*, VI, 151–158 (Aug., 1815), and R. H. Dana, Sr., in *No. Am. Rev.*, V, 365–389 (Sept., 1817), reprinted in Dana's *Poems and Prose Writings* (New York, 1850), which includes also "The Death of Washington Allston."

For reviews of *Monaldi: A Tale* (Boston, 1841), see C. C. Felton in *No. Am. Rev.*, LIV, 397–419 (April, 1842); George W. Peck in *Am. Whig Rev.*, VII, 341–357 (April, 1848); W. G. Simms in *S.Q.R.*, IV, 363–414 (Oct., 1843); *S.L.M.*, VIII, 286–289 (April, 1842), written by some one living in Cheraw, S. C., who had known Allston.

For reviews of *Lectures on Art and Poems* (New York, 1850), see C. C. Felton in *No. Am. Rev.*, LXXI, 149–168 (July, 1850) and George W. Peck in *Am. Whig Rev.*, XII, 17–32 (July, 1850).

Further materials may be found in letters and biographies of artists and writers who knew Allston: Irving, Coleridge, Wordsworth, Southey, S. F. B. Morse, William Dunlap, C. R. Leslie, and others. For manuscript materials, see Richardson, *op. cit.*, p. 220.

For Allston as a painter, see Richardson, *op. cit.*; Virgil Barker, *American Painting* (1950), pp. 339–351; Washington Irving, "Washington Allston,"

Spanish Papers (1866), first published in the Duyckincks' *Cyclopaedia of American Literature* (1855); Martha Hale Shackford, *Wordsworth's Interest in Painters and Pictures* (Wellesley, Mass., 1945); Oliver Wendell Holmes, "Exhibition of Pictures Painted by Washington Allston," *No. Am. Rev.*, L, 358–381 (April, 1840); Sarah Clarke, "Our First Great Painter, and His Works," *Atlantic Monthly*, XV, 129–140 (Feb., 1865); James T. Soby, "Washington Allston, Eclectic," *Sat. Rev. of Lit.*, XXX, 28–29 (Aug. 23, 1947); Annie N. Meyer, "A Portrait of Coleridge by Washington Allston," *Critic*, XLVIII, 138–141 (Feb., 1906); Cuthbert Wright, "The Feast of Belshazzar," *New Eng. Quart.*, X, 620–634 (Dec., 1937); Margaret J. Preston, "Art in the South," *So. Rev.*, XXVI, 394–408 (July, 1879); Margaret Fuller, "A Record of Impressions Produced by the Exhibition of Mr. Allston's Pictures . . . ," *Literature and Art* (New York, 1852), Part II, pp. 108–121; William Dunlap, *A History of the Rise and Progress of the Arts of Design in the United States* (2 vols.; New York, 1834), II, 152–188; Elizabeth P. Peabody, *Last Evening with Allston, and Other Papers* (Boston, 1886), which in addition to the title essay contains "Life and Genius of Allston" and "Exhibition of Allston's Paintings in Boston in 1839"; and Mrs. Anna Jameson, *Memoirs and Essays* (London, 1846), pp. 159–205.

George William Bagby

The only biography is Joseph L. King, Jr., *Dr. George William Bagby: A Study of Virginian Literature, 1850–1880* (1927); Bibliography, pp. 189–193. See also La Salle C. Pickett, *Literary Hearthstones of Dixie* (1912), pp. 225–250. Many of Bagby's writings remain uncollected. The fullest collection is *Selections from the Miscellaneous Writings of Dr. George William Bagby* (2 vols.; Richmond, 1884, 1885). Later collections are: *The Old Virginia Gentleman and Other Sketches* (New York, 1911), ed. Thomas Nelson Page, and *The Old Virginia Gentleman and Other Sketches* (Richmond, 1938), ed. Ellen M. Bagby. In spite of the identical titles, the contents of the two volumes are not the same. For Bagby's publications in *S.L.M.*, see D. K. Jackson, *The Contributors and Contributions to The Southern Literary Messenger* (Charlottesville, Va., 1936).

Joseph Glover Baldwin

There is no published biography, but see J. H. Nelson's sketch in *D.A.B.* Other biographical and critical materials will be found in H. H. Bancroft, *History of California*, VII (1890), 221–222, 233–234; Walter Blair, *Native American Humor* (1937); William Braswell, "An Unpublished California Letter of Joseph Glover Baldwin," *Am. Lit.*, II, 292–294 (Nov., 1930); Reuben Davis, *Recollections of Mississippi and Mississippians* (1891), pp. 60–64; Rhoda C.

Ellison, *Early Alabama Publications* (1947), pp. 167–169; H. D. Farish, "An Overlooked Personality in Southern Life," *N. C. Hist. Rev.*, XII, 341–353 (Oct., 1935) [Samuel Hale was the original of Baldwin's "Samuel Hele, Esquire"]; William Garrett, *Reminiscences of Public Men in Alabama* (1872), pp. 388–389; Eugene Current-Garcia, "Joseph Glover Baldwin: Humorist or Moralist?" *Ala. Rev.*, V, 122–141 (April, 1952); S. A. Link, *Pioneers of Southern Literature*, II, 486–504; George F. Mellen, "Joseph G. Baldwin and the 'Flush Times,' " *Sewanee Rev.*, IX, 171–184 (April, 1901), more detailed than Mellen's sketch in *A Library of Southern Literature*, I, 175–181; Samuel B. Stewart, "Joseph Glover Baldwin" (unpublished Vanderbilt Univ. dissertation, 1942); Jennette Tandy, *Crackerbox Philosophers* (1925) pp. 80–83; T. B. Wetmore, "Joseph G. Baldwin," *Transactions* Ala. Hist. Soc., 1897–1898, II, 67–73.

Five of the sketches which Baldwin contributed to *S.L.M.* were not included in *The Flush Times,* and nine of the pieces published in the book had not been published in *S.L.M.* See J. F. McDermott, "Baldwin's 'Flush Times of Alabama and Mississippi'—A Bibliographical Note," *Papers* Bibliog. Soc. Am., XLV, 251–256 (3rd quarter, 1951). Two sketches which were not reprinted from *S.L.M.* are: "California Flush Times," XIX, 665–670 (Nov., 1853), and "Old Uncle John Rosser and the Billy Goat," XX, 120–123 (Feb., 1854).

Robert Beverley

The best accounts of Beverley are to be found in Louis B. Wright, *The First Gentlemen of Virginia* (1940), chap. x, "Robert Beverley II: Historian and Iconoclast"; "Beverley's History . . . of Virginia (1705), a Neglected Classic," *W.M.Q.*, 3rd ser. I, 49–64 (Jan., 1944), and the Introduction to Wright's edition of Beverley's *The History and Present State of Virginia* (1947), which reprints the text of the 1705 edition. See also M. C. Tyler, *A History of American Literature, 1607–1765* (1878), II, 264–267; Fairfax Harrison, "Robert Beverley, the Historian of Virginia," *Va. Mag.*, XXXVI, 333–344 (Oct., 1928); W. G. Stanard, "Major Robert Beverley and His Descendants," *ibid.*, II, 405–413 (April, 1895), III, 47–52, 169–176 (July, Oct., 1895); and Charles Campbell's Introduction to his edition of Beverley's *History of Virginia* (Richmond, 1855). Further references to Beverley are given in *The Virginia Historical Index* (2 vols., 1934, 1936), ed. Earl Gregg Swem.

Beverley probably wrote the pamphlet, *An Essay upon the Government of the English Plantations* . . . (London, 1701), reprinted in 1945 by the Huntington Library with an Introduction by Louis B. Wright and some memoranda by William Byrd. The pamphlet—which has been praised by Lawrence C. Wroth as not excelled by any other American political writing before 1750—is a reply to an earlier pamphlet by Charles Davenant, one of the many Englishmen who wrote about the colonies without firsthand knowledge.

Jonathan Boucher

Allen Johnson wrote the excellent sketch in *D.A.B.* See also James E. Pate, "Jonathan Boucher, an American Loyalist," *Md. Hist. Mag.*, XXV, 305–319 (Sept., 1930) and Robert G. Walker, "Jonathan Boucher: Champion of the Minority," *W.M.Q.*, 3rd ser. II, 3–14 (Jan., 1945).

Boucher's letters and autobiographical writings are the most important source of information. See especially his *The Reminiscences of an American Loyalist* (Boston, 1925); the brief autobiography, "Jonathan Boucher, 1738–1804, by Himself," ed. Marcella W. Thompson, *Blackwood's*, CCXXXI, 315–334 (March, 1932); and "Letters of Rev. Jonathan Boucher," *Md. Hist. Mag.*, VII, 1–26, 150–165, 286–304, 337–356 (March, June, Sept., and Dec., 1912); VIII, 34–50 (March, 1913). Some letters written by, and addressed to, Boucher appear in *Letters of Richard Radcliffe and John James* (Oxford, England, 1888), ed. Margaret Evans. See also E. C. Chorley (ed.), "Correspondence between the Right Reverend John Skinner, Jr., and the Reverend Jonathan Boucher, 1786," *Hist. Mag. Prot. Episc. Church*, X, 163–175 (June, 1941). For Boucher's correspondence with George Washington, see Moncure D. Conway, "George Washington and Rev. Jonathan Boucher," *Lippincott's*, XLIII, 722–733 (May, 1889) and W. C. Ford (ed.), *Letters of Jonathan Boucher to George Washington* (Brooklyn, 1898). According to Conway, Thackeray read the Washington-Boucher correspondence while writing *The Virginians*.

For criticism, see M. C. Tyler, *Literary History of the American Revolution*, I, 316–328, and V. L. Parrington, *Main Currents in American Thought*, I, 214–218. Of some interest to students of American English is Allen Walker Read, "Boucher's Linguistic Pastoral of Colonial Maryland," *Dialect Notes*, VI, 353–360 (Dec., 1933).

Daniel Bryan

There is no sketch of Bryan in any standard reference work. The best account is Elizabeth Binns, "Daniel Bryan: Poe's Poet of 'the Good Old Goldsmith School,'" *W.M.Q.*, 2nd ser. XXIII, 465–473 (Oct., 1943). For Poe's brief comment, see his *Works* (Va. ed.), XV, 218. See also John W. Wayland, *A History of Rockingham County, Virginia* (Dayton, Va., 1912), p. 136, and Mary G. Powell, *The History of Old Alexandria, Virginia* (Richmond, 1928), pp. 209, 302, 362. Bryan was Postmaster in Alexandria from 1820 to 1853. His maximum salary (in 1846) was $1,987.96 (Powell, *op. cit.*, pp. 209, 362). There is a brief discussion of Bryan's poems in F. V. N. Painter, *Poets of Virginia* (1907), pp. 57–59. See also C. William Miller, "Letters from Thomas White of Virginia to Scott and Dickens," *English Studies in Honor of James Southall Wilson* (1951), pp. 67–71. The Griswold Collection in the Boston Public Library contains a few letters by Bryan. In a letter to Griswold, he claimed as his the unsigned poem, "Strains of the Grotto: A Lyric Poem. Commemorative of Wyer's Cave," *S.L.M.*, III, 445–446 (July, 1837). "The Mother and Daughter Land" appeared in the *New-York Mirror*, VII, 185 (Dec. 19, 1829). Bryan's last publication seems to have been *A Tribute to the Memory of the Rev. George C. Cookman: Consisting of a Brief Discourse; and The Lost Ship, A Poem on the Fate of the Steamer President: Delivered in the Alexandria Lyceum, June 15, 1841* (Alexandria, 1841).

The Mountain Muse was reviewed in the *Analectic Mag.*, VI, 170–171 (Aug., 1815). Some copies of the book contain a list of subscribers. *The Appeal for Suffering Genius* was reviewed by Jared Sparks in *No. Am. Rev.*, XXIV, 212–214 (Jan., 1827), and by William Gilmore Simms (?) in *So. Lit. Gazette*, I, 308–314 (Feb. 4, 1829).

William Byrd

Few of Byrd's writings were published until Edmund Ruffin brought out *The Westover Manuscripts* (Petersburg, Va., 1841), almost a century after Byrd's death. Ruffin had first printed *The Westover Manuscripts*—with title page and separate pagination—as an appendix to Vol. IX of his *Farmers' Register*, beginning Oct. 31, 1841. The manuscripts had been placed at his disposal by the late George E. Harrison of "Brandon" (*Farmers' Register*, VII, 106–108, Feb. 28, 1839). The Petersburg *Republican* in 1822 had printed about one fourth of "The History of the Dividing Line," possibly more in numbers now lost (Maude H. Woodfin, in *W.M.Q.*, 3rd ser. I, 363–373, Oct., 1944). At least three extracts from "The History of the Dividing Line" appeared in the *Am. Turf Register* (Baltimore), V, 430–431, 480–481, 574–575 (April, May, July, 1834).

Somewhat better than Ruffin's edition was T. H. Wynne (ed.), *A History of the Dividing Line and Other Tracts* (2 vols.; Richmond, 1866). The best edition, though it lacks much of being complete, is John Spencer Bassett (ed.), *The Writings of "Colonel William Byrd of Westover in Virginia Esqr"* (1901). "The Secret History of the Line" was first published in William K. Boyd (ed.), *William Byrd's Histories of the Dividing Line* (Raleigh, N. C., 1929). For two pages of the manuscript that Boyd did not find, see Maude H. Woodfin, "The Missing Pages of William Byrd's Secret History of the Line," *W.M.Q.*, 3rd ser. II, 63–70 (Jan., 1945). The surveyors' notes were published in *The Colonial Records of North Carolina* (Raleigh), II (1886), 750–757, 799–815.

All printed versions of "The History of the Dividing Line" are based on the "Brandon" Manuscript, which is a copy of one in the possession of the American Philosophical Society in Philadelphia. The Society also has the manuscript of "The Secret History of the Line" except for the two missing pages, which are in Williamsburg. Jefferson secured the manuscript of "The Secret History" for the Society's library.

Not included in any edition of Byrd's writings are: *Description of the Dismal*

Swamp and a Proposal to Drain the Swamp (1922), ed. Earl G. Swem, published earlier in the *Columbian Mag.* for April, 1789, and in the *Farmers' Register*, IV, 521–524 (Jan. 1, 1837); *William Byrd Esqʳ Accounts as Solicitor General . . . Letters Writ to Facetia by Veramour* [Byrd], privately printed for Thomas F. Ryan about 1913 in an edition of 15 copies, with notes by R. T. N.; and *William Byrd's Natural History of Virginia* (1940), ed. Richmond C. Beatty and W. J. Mulloy. This is a reprint, with an English translation, of Byrd's "eine kurze Beschreibung von Virginia," which appeared in a booklet of two hundred pages published in 1737 at Berne by the Helvetische Societät under the title *Neu-gefundenes Eden. . . .* The Library of Congress has what may be a unique copy of this book. It was listed in *C.H.A.L.,* I (1917), 368, but apparently no scholar examined it for more than two decades. The booklet contains some account of Byrd, written by the Society's agent, Samuel Jenner, which unfortunately Beatty and Mulloy did not reprint. Two memoranda by Byrd are included in a pamphlet attributed to Robert Beverley in Louis B. Wright (ed.), *An Essay upon the Government of the English Plantations on the Continent of America* (*London, 1701*) . . . (San Marino, Calif.: The Huntington Library, 1945).

The only full-length biography is Richmond C. Beatty, *William Byrd of Westover* (1932), a Vanderbilt Univ. dissertation; Bibliography, pp. 225–229. See also T. J. Wertenbaker's sketch in *D.A.B.;* P. A. Bruce, *The Virginia Plutarch* (1929); Ella Lonn, *The Colonial Agents of the Southern Colonies* (1945), pp. 118–123, 213, 273–274, 375, etc.; Louis B. Wright, *The First Gentlemen of Virginia* (1940), chap. xi, "The Byrds' Progress from Trade to Genteel Elegance"; and the introductions to the works by Bassett and Boyd cited above.

Much light is thrown upon Byrd's life by *The Secret Diary of William Byrd of Westover, 1709–1712* (1941), ed. Louis B. Wright and Marion Tinling, and *Another Secret Diary of William Byrd of Westover, 1739–1741: With Letters & Literary Exercises, 1696–1726* (1942), ed. Maude H. Woodfin and Marion Tinling. The latter volume prints for the first time many new letters and some interesting "characters" and reprints poems by "Mr. Burrard" from *Tunbrigalia: or, Tunbridge Miscellanies for the Year 1719* (London, 1719), and Byrd's pamphlet, *A Discourse concerning the Plague, with some Preservatives against it* (London, 1721). A third portion of the secret diary, in the possession of the Virginia Historical Society and still unpublished, covers the period Dec. 13, 1717—May 19, 1721.

Many of Byrd's letters have been published—not always accurately or completely—in "Letters of William Byrd, 2d, of Westover, Va.," *Va. Mag.,* IX, 113–130, 225–251 (Oct., 1901; Jan., 1902) and "Letters of the Byrd Family," *ibid.,* XXXV, 221–245, 371–389 (July, Oct., 1927); XXXVI, 36–44, 113–123, 209–222, 353–362 (Jan., April, July, Oct., 1928); XXXVII, 28–33, 101–118, 242–252, 301–315 (Jan., April, July, Oct., 1929); XXXVIII, 51–63, 145–156, 347–360 (Jan., April, Oct., 1930); and XXXIX, 139–145, 221–229 (April, July, 1931). See also "Letters of Colonel William Byrd," *Am. Hist. Rev.,* I, 88–90

(Oct., 1895) and R. A. Brock (ed.), *The Official Letters of Alexander Spotswood* (2 vols.; Richmond, 1882, 1885). Other Byrd letters are found in W.M.Q., 2nd ser. I, 186–200 (July, 1921) and VI, 303–325 (Oct., 1926). Byrd's correspondence with the Orrerys appears in *The Orrery Papers* (2 vols., 1903), ed. The Countess of Cork and Orrery. Byrd's letters to John Custis are printed in George Washington Parke Custis, *Recollections and Private Memoirs of Washington* (New York, 1860), pp. 26–33. A few of Byrd's best letters are reprinted in Jay B. Hubbell (ed.), *American Life in Literature* (1936; revised ed., 1949).

Bassett's edition of the *Writings* gives a catalogue of Byrd's private library. The contents of the library are discussed in Carl L. Cannon, "William Byrd II of Westover," *Colophon*, N.S. III, 291–302 (Spring, 1938) and in his *American Book Collectors and Collecting* (1941), chap. ii; G. R. Lyle, "William Byrd, Book Collector," *Am. Book Collector*, V, 163–165, 208–211 (May–June, July, 1934); W. D. Houlette, "The Byrd Library," *Tyler's Quart. Hist. and Geneal. Mag.*, XVI, 100–109 (Oct., 1934); and Lyman C. Draper, "The Westover Library," *Va. Hist. Register*, IV, 87–90 (April, 1851).

Among the more important magazine materials are: Willie T. Weathers, "William Byrd: Satirist," W.M.Q., 3rd ser. IV, 27–41 (Jan., 1947); Constance Cary Harrison, "Colonel William Byrd of Westover, Virginia," *Century*, XLII, 163–178 (June, 1891); Maude H. Woodfin, "William Byrd and the Royal Society," *Va. Mag.*, XL, 23–34 (Jan., 1932) and "Thomas Jefferson and William Byrd's Manuscript Histories of the Dividing Line," W.M.Q., 3rd ser. I, 363–373 (Oct., 1944); Louis B. Wright, "William Byrd's Defense of Sir Edmund Andros," W.M.Q., 3rd ser. II, 47–62 (Jan., 1945); Louis B. Wright and Marion Tinling, "William Byrd of Westover, an American Pepys," S.A.Q., XXXIX, 259–274 (July, 1940); J. S. Wilson, "William Byrd and His Secret Diary," W.M.Q., 2nd ser. XXII, 165–174 (April, 1942); Lewis Leary, "A William Byrd Poem," W.M.Q., 3rd ser. IV, 356 (July, 1947). J. R. Masterson in "William Byrd in Lubberland," *Am. Lit.*, IX, 153–170 (May, 1937), points out that other early visitors to North Carolina supported Byrd's indictment of the border population. For other materials, see Earl G. Swem (ed.), *The Virginia Historical Index* (2 vols., 1934, 1936).

There is no adequate discussion of Byrd's literary importance, but see *L.H.U.S.*, I, 45–46, and III, 429–431 (Bibliography); *L.A.P.*, pp. 32–34; M. C. Tyler, *op. cit.*, II, 270–279; Beatty, *op. cit.*, *passim.*; and V. L. Parrington, *Main Currents in American Thought*, I, 138–140.

George W. Cable

The official biography, *George W. Cable: His Life and Letters* (1928), by his daughter Mrs. Lucy L. C. Biklé contains many letters and a Bibliography, pp. 303–306. More useful to the student for the period it covers is the work of a Swedish scholar, Kjell Ekström, *George Washington Cable: A Study of His*

Early Life and Work (Upsala and Cambridge, Mass., 1950); Bibliography, pp. 185–193. There is a bibliography in *L.H.U.S.*, III, 433–434. Arlin Turner, who is writing what promises to be the definitive biography, has published: "A Novelist Discovers a Novelist: The Correspendence of H. H. Boyesen and George W. Cable," *Western Humanities Rev.*, V, 343–372 (Autumn, 1951); "George W. Cable: Novelist and Reformer," *S.A.Q.*, XLVIII, 539–545 (Oct., 1949); "George Washington Cable's Literary Apprenticeship," *La. Hist. Quart.*, XXIV, 169–186 (Jan., 1941); "Whittier Calls on George W. Cable," *New Eng. Quart.*, XXII, 92–96 (March, 1949); and "George W. Cable's Beginnings as a Reformer," *Jour. So. Hist.*, XVII, 135–161 (May, 1951). For Cable's experiences on the lecture platform, see Guy A. Cardwell, *Twins of Genius* (1953), "George W. Cable Becomes a Professional Reader," *Am. Lit.*, XXIII, 467–470 (Jan., 1952), "The First Public Address of George W. Cable, Southern Liberal," *Washington Univ. Studies* (1951), pp. 67–76; and "Mark Twain's 'Row' with George Cable," *Mod. Lang. Quart.*, XIII, 363–371 (Dec., 1952); D. H. Bishop, "A Commencement in the Eighties: George W. Cable's First Public Address," *Southwest Rev.*, XVIII, 108–114 (Jan., 1933); and Fred W. Lorch, "Cable and His Reading Tour with Mark Twain in 1884–1885," *Am. Lit.*, XXIII, 471–486 (Jan., 1952).

Other materials of some value are: James Barrie, "A Note on Mr. Cable's 'The Grandissimes,'" *Bookman*, VII, 401–403 (July, 1898); W. M. Baskervill, *Southern Writers*, I (1897), 299–356; Philip Butcher, "George W. Cable: History and Politics," *Phylon*, IX, 137–145 (2nd Quart., 1948); J. O. Eidson, "G. W. Cable's Philosophy of Progress," *Southwest Rev.*, XXI, 211–216 (Jan., 1936); Kjell Ekström, "The Cable-Howells Correspondence," *Studia Neophilologica*, XXII, 48–61 (1950); Lafcadio Hearn, "The Scenes of Cable's Romances," *Century*, n.s. V, 40–47 (Nov., 1883); Grace King, *Memories of a Southern Woman of Letters* (1932), *passim*; F. L. Pattee, *A History of American Literature since 1870* (1915), pp. 246–253; A. H. Quinn, *American Fiction* (1936), pp. 345–351; Mattie Russell, "George Washington Cable Letters in the Duke University Library," *Library Notes*, No. 25, 1–13 (Jan., 1951); E. L. Tinker, "Cable and the Creoles," *Am. Lit.*, V, 313–326 (Jan., 1934); H. R. Warfel, "George W. Cable Amends a Mark Twain Plot," *Am. Lit.*, VI, 328–331 (Nov., 1934). In "Early New Orleans Society: A Reappraisal," *Jour. So. Hist.*, XVIII, 20–36 (Feb., 1952), Joseph G. Tregle, Jr., indirectly suggests that Cable's picture of the quadroon balls is highly romanticized. See also Rayburn S. Moore's forthcoming article in *Am. Lit.*, " 'Don Joaquin': A Forgotten Story by George W. Cable."

John C. Calhoun

The best and most detailed account is to be found in Charles M. Wiltse, *John C. Calhoun: Nationalist, 1782–1828* (1944); *John C. Calhoun: Nullifier, 1829–*

1839 (1949); and *John C. Calhoun: Sectionalist, 1840–1850* (1951), each of which contains a bibliography. See also Wiltse's "Calhoun and the Modern State," *Va. Quart. Rev.*, XIII, 396–408 (Summer, 1937). A good brief biography is Margaret L. Coit, *John C. Calhoun: American Portrait* (1950), which was awarded the Pulitzer Prize for Biography. See also her "Calhoun and the Downfall of States' Rights," *Va. Quart. Rev.*, XXVIII, 191–208 (Spring, 1952), and Harold Schultz, "A Century of Calhoun Biographies," *S.A.Q.*, L, 248–254 (April, 1951). Hermann von Holst, *John C. Calhoun* (1882) gives a biased interpretation. *The Life of John C. Calhoun* (New York, 1843) seems to have been written by R. M. T. Hunter with some assistance from Calhoun. Col. W. Pinckney Starke's biographical sketch appears in "Correspondence of John C. Calhoun," *Report* of Am. Hist. Assn. for . . . 1899, Vol. II (1900). *The Works of John C. Calhoun* (6 vols.; New York, 1851) contains many but not all of his speeches. See also John M. Anderson (ed.), *Calhoun: Basic Documents* (1952). There is a bibliography in *L.H.U.S.*, III, 435–436.

Other materials of value to the student are to be found in: V. L. Parrington, *Main Currents in American Thought*, II, 68–82; Gamaliel Bradford, *As God Made Them* (1929); R. H. Gabriel, *The Course of American Democratic Thought* (1940); Charles E. Merriam, *A History of American Political Theories* (1920), pp. 228–242, 267–284; and H. L. Curry's chapter on Calhoun in *A History and Criticism of American Public Address* (1943), ed. W. N. Brigance.

Charles Carroll of Carrollton

There are two biographies: Kate Mason Rowland, *The Life of Charles Carroll of Carrollton* (1898) and Joseph Gurn, *Charles Carroll of Carrollton* (1932). See also *Unpublished Letters of Charles Carroll* . . . (1902), ed. Thomas M. Field. For William C. Macready's account of Carroll in old age, see his *Reminiscences* (1875), I, 322. The articles by Dulany and Carroll in the *Md. Gazette* are reprinted in Kate Mason Rowland's biography and in Elihu S. Riley (ed.), *Correspondence of "First Citizen"—Charles Carroll of Carrollton, and "Antilon"—Daniel Dulany, Jr.*, 1773 . . . (Baltimore, 1902).

William Alexander Caruthers

The only important source of information about Caruthers is Curtis Carroll Davis's Duke Univ. dissertation, "Chronicler of the Cavaliers: The Career and Opinions of William Alexander Caruthers, M.D., 1802–1846" (1947), which with some new materials was published by the Dietz Press in 1953. Davis has also published "Chronicler of the Cavaliers: Some Letters to and from William Alexander Caruthers," *Va. Mag.*, LV, 213–232 (July, 1947); ". . . Three More Letters from and to William Alexander Caruthers," *ibid.*, LVII, 55–66 (Jan., 1949); "An Early Historical Novelist Goes to the Library: William A. Caruthers and His Reading," N. Y. Public Library *Bulletin*, LII, 4, 159–170 (April, 1948); "A Virginia Romancer and His Reading: Literary Allusions in the Work of William A. Caruthers," *Tyler's Quart. Hist. and Geneal. Mag.*, XXX, 21–33 (July, 1948); "The Virginia 'Knights' and Their Golden Horseshoes: Dr. William A. Caruthers and an American Tradition," *Mod. Lang. Quart.*, X, 490–507 (Dec., 1949); and "The First Climber of the Natural Bridge: A Minor American Epic," *Jour. So. Hist.*, XVI, 277–290 (Aug., 1950). Parrington's discussion of Caruthers' novels in *Main Currents in American Thought*, II, 41–46, is excellent.

Thomas Holley Chivers

The fullest source of information is S. Foster Damon, *Thomas Holley Chivers: Friend of Poe* (1930), which gives a brief bibliography of articles on Chivers, pp. 287–288. See also the bibliography in *L.H.U.S.*, III, 440–441. There are Chivers MSS in the Duke Univ. Library and the Huntington Library. Much of the material in the Huntington Library was published by George E. Woodberry in "The Poe-Chivers Papers," *Century Mag.*, LXV (N.S. XLIII), 435–447, 545–558 (Jan. and Feb., 1903), reprinted in part in Woodberry, *Edgar Allan Poe* (revised ed., 1909), II, 376–390. Much more accurate and complete and admirably edited is *Chivers' Life of Poe* (1952), ed. Richard Beale Davis.

The only one of Chivers' books which has been reprinted is *Virginalia* (Brooklyn: Eugene L. Schwaab, 1942). Portions of Chivers' prefaces to *Nacoochee, Memoralia,* and *Virginalia* are reprinted in Edd W. Parks (ed.), *Southern Poets* (1936). Some of the best of Chivers' poems were reprinted by the late Lewis Chase in *The Oglethorpe Book of Georgia Verse* (1930). Mrs. Chase has completed the biography of Chivers begun by Dr. Chase, but it has not yet been published.

Chivers' relations with Poe are discussed in Landon C. Bell, *Poe and Chivers* (Columbus, O., 1931) [takes issue with Damon on the question of Chivers' priority in the use of metrical devices, etc.]; Joel Benton, *In the Poe Circle* (1899); James A. Harrison, "Poe and Chivers," in Poe, *Works* (Virginia ed.), VII, 266–288; C. W. Hubner (ed.), *Representative Southern Poets* (1906), pp. 177–193; James Huneker, "A Precursor of Poe" in *The Pathos of Distance* (1913), pp. 285–290; Thomas Ollive Mabbott, "On Chivers' *Conrad and Eudora*" in his edition of *Poe's Politian* (1923); A. G. Newcomer, "The Poe-Chivers Tradition Reexamined," *Sewanee Rev.*, XII, 20–35 (Jan., 1904); Killis Campbell, "A Bit of Chiversian Mystification," Univ. of Texas *Studies in English*, No. X, 152–154 (1930).

Samuel Langhorne Clemens, "Mark Twain"

There is an excellent bibliography in *L.H.U.S.*, III, 442–450, which lists other books and articles containing bibliographical information. Mark Twain's debt to the Southern humorists is pointed out in Walter Blair, *Native American Humor* (1937), pp. 147–162; Edgar M. Branch, *The Literary Apprenticeship of Mark Twain* (1950); Franklin J. Meine (ed.), *Tall Tales of the Southwest* (1930); Bernard DeVoto, *Mark Twain's America* (1932); Minnie M. Brashear, *Mark Twain: Son of Missouri* (1934); and Edd W. Parks, "Mark Twain as Southerner," *Segments of Southern Thought* (1938). See also the late Dixon Wecter's *Sam Clemens of Hannibal* (1952) and his chapter on Mark Twain in *L.H.U.S.*, II, 917–939, and D. M. McKeithan, "Mark Twain's Letters of Thomas Jefferson Snodgrass," *Philol. Quart.*, XXXII, 353–365 (Oct., 1953).

Other materials of value for Southern aspects of Mark Twain's life and writings are: Theodore Hornberger (ed.), *Mark Twain's Letters to Will Bowen* (Austin, Tex., 1941); Ernest E. Leisy (ed.), *The Letters of Quintus Curtius Snodgrass* (Dallas, Tex., 1946) and "Mark Twain and Isaiah Sellers," *Am. Lit.*, XIII, 398–405 (Jan., 1942); Katherine Buxbaum, "Mark Twain and American Dialect," *Am. Speech*, II, 233–236 (Feb., 1927); Dudley R. Hutcherson, "Mark Twain as a Pilot," *Am. Lit.*, XII, 353–355 (Nov., 1940); George I. Bidewell, "Mark Twain's Florida Years," *Mo. Hist. Rev.*, XL, 159–173 (Jan., 1946); G. Harrison Orians, "Walter Scott, Mark Twain, and the Civil War," *S.A.Q.*, XL, 342–359 (Oct., 1941); and Guy A. Cardwell, *Twins of Genius* (1953) and "Mark Twain's 'Row' with George Cable," *Mod. Lang. Quart.*, XIII, 363–371 (Dec., 1952); and Fred W. Lorch, "Cable and His Reading Tour with Mark Twain in 1884–1885," *Am. Lit.*, XXIII, 471–486 (Jan., 1952).

Joseph Beckham Cobb

For information about Cobb, I am heavily indebted to George T. Buckley, "Joseph B. Cobb: Mississippi Essayist and Critic," *Am. Lit.*, X, 166–178 (May, 1938), which brings together the little that is known about his life. Cobb's *Mississippi Scenes* (1851) was reviewed briefly in *S.L.M.*, XVII, 584 (Sept., 1851) and *De Bow's Rev.*, X, 600 (May, 1851) and in somewhat more detail in *Lit. World*, VIII, 235–236 (March 22, 1851), which pointed out the similarity of the "Rambler Papers" to the earlier writing of Washington Irving.

Moncure Daniel Conway

Conway's *Autobiography* (2 vols., 1904) is an important source of information for both its author and the many prominent Americans and Englishmen whom he knew. Mary E. Burtis, *Moncure Conway, 1832–1907* (1952) gives the best available account of Conway's life and thought. See also W. B. Cairns's sketch in *D.A.B.*; J. S. Bassett, "An Exile from the South," *S.A.Q.*, IV, 82–90 (Jan., 1905); and Philip S. Campbell, "Moncure Daniel Conway" (Duke Univ. master's thesis, 1941). Conway's *Addresses and Reprints* (1909) lists over seventy books and pamphlets, but there is no bibliography of his numerous contributions to periodicals. For the Cincinnati *Dial*, see Clarence Gohdes, *The Periodicals of American Transcendentalism* (1931), chap. ix. Many of Conway's manuscripts are in the Columbia Univ. Library.

Ebenezer Cooke

The best account of Cooke is in James T. Pole, "Ebenezer Cook and *The Maryland Muse*," *Am. Lit.*, III, 296–302 (Nov., 1931); but see also M. C. Tyler, *A History of American Literature, 1607–1765* (1878), II, 255–260; W. B. Norris, "Some Recently-Found Poems on the Calverts," *Md. Hist. Mag.*, XXXII, 112–135 (June, 1937); and Anon., "An Unpublished Poem by the Author of The Sot Weed Factor," *ibid.*, XIV, 172–173 (June, 1919). *The Sot-Weed Factor* was reprinted in New York in 1865 with an Introduction by Brantz Mayer. It was reprinted also in Bernard Steiner (ed.), *Early Maryland Poetry* (1900) and in Loker Raley (ed.), *300 Years: The Poets and Poetry of Maryland* (1937). See also "*The Maryland Muse*. By Ebenezer Cooke. A Facsimile, with an Introduction," by Lawrence C. Wroth, Am. Antiq. Soc. *Proceedings*, N.S. XLIV, 267–335 (1934). *Sotweed Redevivus* may be found in Steiner, *op. cit.*

John Esten Cooke

The only biography is John O. Beaty, *John Esten Cooke, Virginian* (1922), a Columbia Univ. dissertation based largely on MS materials which at that time were in possession of Cooke's descendants. See also Beaty's sketch in *D.A.B.*; Chester R. Goolrick, Jr., "The Scrapbook of John Esten Cooke," *Va. Mag.*, LVIII, 516–518 (Oct., 1950); J. L. Armstrong in *A Library of Southern Literature*, III, 1031–1038; A. H. Quinn, *American Fiction* (1936), 126–131; S. A. Link, *Pioneers of Southern Literature*, I, 248–270; Carl Holliday, "John Esten Cooke as a Novelist," *Sewanee Rev.*, XIII, 216–220 (April, 1905); Carvel Collins, "John Esten Cooke and Local Color," *S.L.M.*, N.S. VI, 82–84 (Jan.–Feb., 1944); Jay B. Hubbell, "The War Diary of John Esten Cooke," *Jour. So. Hist.*, VII, 526–540 (Nov., 1941); Emma Bain Johnson, "John Esten Cooke and the Civil War" (Duke Univ. master's thesis, 1943); J. C. Derby, *Fifty Years among Authors, Books and Publishers* (1884), pp. 400–406; Margaret J. Preston, "A Virginian of the Virginians," *Critic*, N.S. VI, 181 (Oct. 16, 1886); Oscar Wegelin, "A Bibliography of the Separate Writings of John Esten Cooke," *Am. Collector*, I, 96–99 (Dec., 1925), republished in pamphlet form in 1925 and 1941. Some of Cooke's numerous contributions to periodicals are listed by Beaty, but there is no complete bibliography. There are Cooke MSS in the Duke University Library, the Library of Congress, and in the Boston Public Library (in the Griswold Papers). A recent study is Richard B. Harwell, "John Esten Cooke, Civil War Correspondent," *Jour. So. Hist.*, XIX, 501–516 (Nov., 1953).

Cooke is occasionally confused with his uncle, the doctor and theologian of the same name who lived in Kentucky. The name *Esten* is pronounced *East-en* with the accent on the first syllable.

Philip Pendleton Cooke

The two best accounts of Cooke's life and writings are John D. Allen, *Philip Pendleton Cooke* (1942), condensed from a Vanderbilt Univ. dissertation, and David K. Jackson, "Philip Pendleton Cooke: Virginia Gentleman, Lawyer, Hunter, and Poet," *American Studies in Honor of William Kenneth Boyd* (1940), pp. 282–326. Allen has an excellent Bibliography, pp. 106–120, which, however, fails to list Jackson's study. For uncollected materials, see Allen's Bibliography and Jackson, *The Contributors and Contributions to The Southern Literary Messenger* (1936). "The Ballad of Count Herman" is printed in W. J. Hogan, "An Unpublished Poem of Philip Pendleton Cooke," *Educational Forum*, I, 81–86 (Nov., 1936).

Other materials are: J. C. Metcalf's sketch in *D.A.B.*; Rufus W. Griswold, "Philip Pendleton Cooke," *International Monthly Mag.*, IV, 300–303 (Oct., 1951), reprinted in *S.L.M.*, XVII, 669–673 (Oct.–Nov., 1851); [John R. Thompson?], "Recollections of Philip Pendleton Cooke: The Author of 'Florence Vane,'" *S.L.M.*, XXVI, 419–432 (June, 1858); "The Kennedy Papers," ed. Killis Campbell, *Sewanee Rev.*, XXV, 351–352 (July, 1917); biographical sketch by John Esten Cooke in John S. Hart, *A Manual of American Literature* (1872); *Passages from the Correspondence . . . of Rufus W. Griswold* (1898), pp. 190–197.

Reviews of Cooke's *Froissart Ballads and Other Poems* (Philadelphia, 1847) appeared in *Knickerbocker*, XXIX, 366 (April, 1847); *Lit. World*, I, 173–175 (March 27, 1847); and *S.L.M.*, XIII, 437–441 (July, 1847). The last was written by Beverley Tucker.

The John Esten Cooke Papers in the Duke Univ. Library contain a number of P. P. Cooke's letters to his father and also J. E. Cooke's MS sketch of his brother. Among the J. E. Cooke MSS in the Library of Congress is a letter to Griswold, June 6, 1851, which comments on P. P. Cooke's reading, etc. P. P. Cooke's letters to Griswold, published in part in the *Correspondence*, are in the Boston Public Library.

Thomas Cooper

The best biography is Dumas Malone, *The Public Life of Thomas Cooper* (1926); Malone also wrote the sketch in *D.A.B.* See also Maurice Kelley, *Additional Chapters on Thomas Cooper* (1930), Univ. of Maine *Studies*, 2nd ser., no. 15; H. Milton Ellis, "Thomas Cooper: A Survey of His Life," *S.A.Q.*, XIX, 24–42 (Jan., 1920); and "Letters of Dr. Thomas Cooper, 1825–1832," *Am.*

Hist. Rev., VI, 725–736 (July, 1901). For "Memoranda of Table-Talk of Judge Cooper" as recorded by D. J. McCord, see the Duyckincks' *Cyclopaedia of American Literature* (1855), II, 332–333. Perhaps some reader may be interested in Cooper's confirmation of Macaulay's estimate of James Boswell: "Boswell was the greatest fool I ever knew. He was a real idiot."

For Cooper's thought, see Woodbridge Riley, *American Philosophy: The Early Schools* (1907), pp. 407–420; *Philosophy in America* (1939), ed. P. R. Anderson and Max H. Fisch, pp. 247 ff.; and Joseph Dorfman, *The Economic Mind in American Civilization* (1946), II, 527–539, 844–847. Cooper's *Lectures on the Elements of Political Economy* (1826) was reviewed, favorably on the whole, in *No. Am. Rev.*, XXV, 408–425 (Oct., 1827), and by George Tucker in *Am. Quart. Rev.*, I, 309–331 (June, 1827). One of Cooper's severest indictments of the clergy is found in *The Right of Free Discussion*, printed as an appendix to his *Lectures* (2nd ed.; Columbia, S. C., 1829).

Dumas Malone does not believe that Cooper wrote *Memoirs of a Nullifier. Written By Himself. By a Native of the South* (Columbia, S. C., 1832). The copy in the Huntington Library contains a note to the effect that Mr. A. S. Salley attributed the authorship to A. S. Johnston, of Columbia, S. C. This extravaganza, which contains satire on New England, was reviewed in *No. Am. Rev.*, XLIV, 242–245 (Jan., 1837). The pamphlet was reprinted in New York in 1860 "with a Historical Sketch of Nullification in 1832–33." Asa Greene is credited with the authorship of *A Yankee among the Nullifiers: An Auto-Biography. By Elnathan Elmwood, Esq.*, of which the New York Public Library has two editions, both published in New York in 1833. Christopher G. Memminger, the first Confederate Secretary of the Treasury, was the author of *The Book of Nullification. By a Spectator of the Past* (Charleston, 1830). This satire in biblical language is reprinted in H. D. Capers, *The Life and Times of C. G. Memminger* (Richmond, 1893).

John Cotton

The only extended account is Jay B. Hubbell, "John and Ann Cotton, of 'Queen's Creek,' Virginia," *Am. Lit.*, X, 179–201 (May, 1938). Lawrence C. Wroth expressed the opinion that "The Burwell Papers" was an expansion of Mrs. Cotton's briefer account; see his edition of "*The Maryland Muse . . . ,*" *Am. Antiq. Soc. Proceedings*, n.s. XLIV, 304–306 (1934). "C. H." is identified as Christopher Harris in Francis Burton Harrison, "Footnotes upon Some XVII Century Virginians," *Va. Mag.*, L, 289–299 (Oct., 1942). The best text of "The Burwell Papers" is in the *Proceedings* of Mass. Hist. Soc., IX, 299–342 (Aug., 1866). For Moses Coit Tyler's interest in Cotton, see C. E. Schorer, " 'One Cotton, of Acquia Creek, Husband of Ann Cotton,' " *Am. Lit.*, XXII, 342–345 (Nov., 1950).

For the numerous writings occasioned by Bacon's Rebellion, see Anon., "List of Manuscript Sources for Bacon's Rebellion Which Have Been Printed," Va. Mag., XIV, 296–301 (Jan., 1907) and Mary Newton Stanard, The Story of Bacon's Rebellion (1907), pp. 171–181. For a discussion of the literary quality of these materials, see Howard M. Jones, The Literature of Virginia in the Seventeenth Century (1946), pp. 40–46, and Bertha-Monica Stearns, "The Literary Treatment of Bacon's Rebellion in Virginia," Va. Mag., LII, 163–179 (July, 1944).

William Crafts

The fullest account of Crafts' life is Samuel Gilman's Memoir in A Selection, in Prose and Poetry, from the Miscellaneous Writings of the Late William Crafts (Charleston, 1828). See also George H. Genzmer's sketch in D.A.B. and Charles Fraser, Reminiscences of Charleston (Charleston, 1854), pp. 82–84. The only criticism of importance except that of Hugh S. Legaré is found in V. L. Parrington, Main Currents in American Thought, II, 112–114.

David Crockett

The best published biography is Constance Rourke, Davy Crockett (1934). See also her American Humor (1931) and "Davy Crockett: Forgotten Facts and Legends," Southwest Rev., XIX, 149–161 (Winter, 1934). James Atkins Shackford, "The Autobiography of David Crockett" (Vanderbilt Univ. dissertation, 1948) has an extensive bibliography. Shackford has published "David Crockett and North Carolina," N.C. Hist. Rev., XXVIII, 298–315 (July, 1951) and "The Author of David Crockett's Autobiography," Boston Pub. Library Quart., III, 294–303 (Oct., 1951). Shackford thinks that Crockett's collaborator was Thomas Chilton. In "The Authorship of David Crockett's 'Autobiography,'" Ga. Hist. Quart., VI, 265–268 (Sept., 1922) John D. Wade maintains that Augustin Smith Clayton had a large share in the books attributed to Crockett, particularly The Life of Martin Van Buren. A notice in So. Lit. Jour., II, 408 (July, 1836) refers to "Col. [J. S.] French, of Mississippi, author of the 'Life of David Crockett.'" In Fifty Years among Authors, Books and Publishers (1884), pp. 552–553, J. C. Derby states that Matthew St. Clair Clarke wrote the Narrative and Richard Penn Smith the Exploits and Adventures in Texas.

Other materials will be found in: A. P. Foster, "David Crockett," Tenn. Hist. Mag., IX, 166–177 (Oct., 1925); T. P. Abernethy, From Frontier to Plantation in Tennessee (1932); Walter Blair, Native American Humor (1937) and "Six Davy Crocketts," Southwest Rev., XXV, 443–462 (July, 1940); Jennette Tandy, Crackerbox Philosophers (1925); "Letters of Davy Crockett," Am. Hist. Mag., V, 41–47 (Jan., 1900); K. W. Porter, "Davy Crockett and John Horse: A Possible Origin of the Coonskin Story," Am. Lit., XV, 10–15 (March, 1943); and John E. Semmes, John H. B. Latrobe and His Times (1917), pp. 364–365.

For the Crockett legend, see the article by Blair cited *above;* V. L. O. Chittick, "Ring-Tailed Roarers," *Frontier,* XIII, 257–264 (May, 1933); Richard M. Dorson (ed.), *Davy Crockett: American Comic Legend* (1939) [selections from the Crockett almanacs] and "Davy Crockett and the Heroic Age," So. *Folklore Quart.,* VI, 95–102 (June, 1942); Charles W. Lomas, "Crockett's Almanacks and the Typical Texan," *Southwest Rev.,* XXXV, 88–95 (Spring, 1950); and James R. Masterson, *Tall Tales of Arkansaw* (1942), chap. iii, "Davy Crockett in Arkansaw."

Richard Dabney

Later biographical sketches are based almost entirely on that written by Lucian Minor for the Duyckincks' *Cyclopaedia of American Literature* (1855), II, 98–100. Minor's estimate of Dabney is colored by his strong temperance feelings. See also the sketch by A. C. Gordon, Jr., in *D.A.B.;* Earl L. Bradsher, "Richard Dabney," *Sewanee Rev.,* XXIII, 326–336 (July, 1915); [George Tucker], *Letters from Virginia, Translated from the French* (Baltimore, 1816), Letter X; and Paul Allen's review in the *Port Folio,* 4th ser. VI, 56–58 (July, 1815)—two of Dabney's poems were reprinted in this issue. Nine of Dabney's poems were included in William Roscoe's *Specimens of the American Poets* (London, 1822) with the comment that Dabney's poems were not well known in his own country and that his style partook of "all the characteristic faults of his countrymen's—carelessness, roughness, and occasional want of good taste." For the mistaken attribution to Dabney of Thomas Love Peacock's *Rhododaphne,* see *Va. Evangelical and Lit. Mag.,* II, 225–230 (May, 1819), and *S.L.M.,* IX, 329, 390–391, 638–639 (June, July, Oct., 1843).

Samuel Davies

The best accounts are found in W. W. Sweet, *Religion in Colonial America* (1942), pp. 296–301; W. M. Gewehr, *The Great Awakening in Virginia* (1930), chap. iv, pp. 68–105; W. H. Foote, *Sketches of Virginia* . . . (Philadelphia, 1850), pp. 157–307; and John Holt Rice, *Memoir of Samuel Davies* (Boston, 1832), which was first published in Rice's *Va. Evangelical and Lit. Mag.,* Vol. II (1819). Some of Davies' letters appeared in *ibid.,* II, 535–543 and VI, 567–569 (1823). See also J. E. Pomfret's sketch in *D.A.B.;* J. G. Hughes, Jr., "Samuel Davies," *John P. Branch Hist. Papers,* IV, 65–79 (June, 1914); W. W. Henry, *Patrick Henry* (1891), I, 12–16; M. C. Tyler, *A History of American Literature,* 1607–1765 (1878), II, 241–244; and L. F. Benson, "President Davies as a Hymn Writer," *Jour. Presbyterian Hist. Soc.,* II, 277–286 (Sept., 1904).

John Davis

The best source of information is Thelma Louise Kellogg, *The Life and Works of John Davis* (Orono, Maine, 1924), Univ. of Maine *Studies*, 2nd ser., No. 1. Miss Kellogg gives two dates for Davis's death: 1853 and 1854. See also Robert A. Law, "The Bard of Coosawhatchie," *Texas Rev.*, VII, 133–156 (Jan., 1922).

Daniel Dulany

Newton D. Mereness wrote the sketch in *D.A.B.* A fuller account is R. H. Spencer, "Hon. Daniel Dulany, 1722–1797," *Md. Hist. Mag.*, XIII, 143–160 (June, 1918). The best discussion of Dulany as a writer is in M. C. Tyler, *Literary History of the American Revolution* (1897), I, 101–111. Dulany's *Considerations* was first published in Annapolis in Oct., 1765, without his name. It was quickly reprinted in London and elsewhere with the place of publication usually given as "North America." It was reprinted in the *Md. Hist. Mag.* in 1911 and 1912. The pamphlet supplied material for one of William Pitt's great speeches (Tyler, *op. cit.*, I, 111). See also under *Charles Carroll*.

William Elliott

There are brief sketches of Elliott in *D.A.B.* (by John D. Wade); the Duyckincks' *Cyclopaedia of America Literature* (1880), I, 796–799; and *The Biographical Directory of the American Congress, 1774–1927* (1928); but much the best biographical sketch is Lewis Pinckney Jones, "William Elliott, South Carolina Nonconformist," *Jour. So. Hist.*, XVII, 361–381 (Aug., 1951). The New York Public Library has two rare pamphlets dealing with charges made by Thomas E. Miller that it was by corrupt methods that Elliott had defeated him as a candidate for the 51st Congress.

Carolina Sports by Land and Water (Charleston, 1846) was reprinted in New York in 1850 and 1859, in London by Richard Bentley in 1867 (the source of my quotations), and in Columbia, S. C., in 1918. Some of the sketches in *Carolina Sports* had appeared earlier in the *So. Lit. Journal*, N.S. II and III (1837–1838) and, according to Lewis Pinckney Jones, in the *American Turf Register*. Even after the publication of *Carolina Sports*, the Charleston newspapers continued to print fishing and hunting stories over Elliott's pen names, "Piscator" and "Venator." *Carolina Sports* was reviewed in *S.Q.R.*, XII, 67–90 (July, 1847) and by F. G. Cary in *No. Am. Rev.*, LXIII, 316–334 (Oct., 1846).

The Univ. of S. C. Library and the New York Public have copies of the rare *Fiesco: A Tragedy.* "By an American" (New York, 1850). Among Elliott's pamphlet publications are: *Address to the People of St. Helena Parish* (Charleston, 1832); *The Planter Vindicated* . . . (Charleston, 1842); and *The Letters of Agricola* (Greenville, S. C., 1852).

Elliott contributed to the *Southern Review* anonymous reviews of Scott's *Anne of Geierstein*, IV, 498–522 (Nov., 1829) and Gifford's edition of the works of Ben Jonson, VI, 91–116 (Aug., 1830). He wrote articles on agricultural topics for John D. Legaré's *Southern Agriculturist* in Feb. and April, 1828. He also contributed occasionally to *De Bow's Review*.

Ralph Waldo Emerson

Emerson's comments on the South are easily found by consulting the indexes to *The Complete Works* (Centenary ed., 12 vols., 1903–1904); the *Journals* (10 vols., 1909–1914); the *Letters* (6 vols., 1939), ed. R. L. Rusk; and Rusk, *Life* (1949). See also H. H. Hoeltje, "Emerson in Virginia," *New Eng. Quart.*, V, 753–768 (Oct., 1932); Marion Sadler, "Emerson and the South" (Duke Univ. master's thesis, 1935); Marjory M. Moody, "The Evolution of Emerson as an Abolitionist," *Am. Lit.*, XVII, 1–21 (March, 1945); and Moncure D. Conway, *Emerson at Home and Abroad* (1882).

Daniel Decatur Emmett

C. B. Galbreath, *Daniel Decatur Emmett* (Columbus, O., 1904); Carl Wittke, *Tambo and Bones* (1930), pp. 205–209; Hans Nathan, "The First Negro Minstrel Band and Its Origin," *So. Folklore Quart.*, XVI, 132–144 (June, 1952); Fannie L. G. Cole's sketch in *D.A.B.* In the *Confederate Veteran*, III, 266–269 (Sept., 1895), the editor, S. A. Cunningham, described a visit to Emmett and printed the words of the song from an autographed copy of the original manuscript.

George Fitzhugh

Harvey Wish's excellent biographical and critical study, *George Fitzhugh: Propagandist of the Old South* (1943) supersedes his earlier and briefer study, *George Fitzhugh: Conservative of the Old South* (1938). See also W. S. Jenkins, *Pro-Slavery Thought in the Old South* (1935).

Charles Gayarré

There is brief bibliography in *L.H.U.S.*, III, 529–530, but Gayarré's writings are not discussed in the text. The fullest accounts of Gayarré are E. L. Tinker, "Charles Gayarré," *Papers* Bibliog. Soc. of Am., XXVII, Part I, 24–64 (1933), with a ten-page Bibliography, and Charles R. Anderson, "Charles Gayarré and

Paul Hayne: The Last Literary Cavaliers," *American Studies in Honor of William Kenneth Boyd* (1940), pp. 221–281. The Duke Univ. Library has a brief MS autobiography very similar to the "Biographical Sketch of the Honorable Charles Gayarré," ed. H. P. Dart, *La. Hist. Quart.*, XII, 5–27 (Jan., 1929). The April, 1950, number of *La. Hist. Quart.* is devoted largely to Gayarré. Of especial interest is "Some Letters of Charles Etienne Gayarré [to Evert Duyckinck] on Literature and Politics," XXXIII, 223–254. See also Paul H. Hayne's two articles on Gayarré in *So. Bivouac*, N.S. II, 28–37, 108–113 (June, July, 1886); J. H. Nelson, "Charles Gayarré: Historian and Romancer," *Sewanee Rev.*, XXXIII, 427–438 (Oct., 1925); Michael Kraus, *A History of American History* (1937), pp. 260–262; and Grace King, *Memories of a Southern Woman of Letters* (1932), pp. 30–45.

Francis Walker Gilmer

There is a good detailed account in Richard Beale Davis, *Francis Walker Gilmer: Life and Learning in Jefferson's Virginia* (Richmond, 1939); Bibliography, pp. 391–398. See also Davis's *Correspondence of Thomas Jefferson and Francis Walker Gilmer, 1814–1826* (1946) and "A Postscript on Thomas Jefferson and His University Professors," *Jour. So. Hist.*, XII, 422–432 (Aug., 1946). For Gilmer's mission to Europe, see also W. P. Trent, *English Culture in Virginia* (Baltimore, 1889) and P. A. Bruce, *History of the University of Virginia*, I, 356–376. Prof. Davis has also published "Forgotten Scientists in Georgia and South Carolina," *Ga. Hist. Quart.*, XXVII, 271–284 (Sept., 1943) and "The Early American Lawyer and the Profession of Letters," *Huntington Library Quart.*, XII, 191–205 (Feb., 1949), which contains some new letters from Hugh S. Legaré to Gilmer.

William John Grayson

The best brief sketch is in *The Biographical Directory of the American Congress, 1774–1927* (Washington, 1928). Grayson's name is one of the most conspicuous of those not included in *D.A.B.* My chief source of information is Grayson's MS "Autobiography" in the Univ. of S. C. Library. It was transcribed and edited in an unpublished Univ. of S. C. dissertation (1933) by Robert D. Bass. Dr. Bass's Introduction supplements Grayson's own account of his life. The "Autobiography" has since been published in the *S. C. Hist. and Geneal. Mag.*, beginning in July, 1947, and ending in April, 1950. The only notable critical discussions of Grayson's writings are Parrington, *Main Currents in American Thought*, II, 103–108, and Thomas D. Jarrett, "The Literary Significance of William J. Grayson's *The Hireling and the Slave*," *Ga. Rev.*, V, 487–494 (Winter, 1951).

Grayson's chief separate publications are: *Letter to His Excellency White-*

marsh B. *Seabrook, Governor of the State of South Carolina* (Charleston, 1850); *The Hireling and the Slave, Chicora, and Other Poems* (Charleston, 1856); *The Letters of Curtius* (Charleston, 1857), reprinted from the Charleston *Courier; The Country* (Charleston, 1858); *Marion* (privately printed in Charleston in 1860), reprinted from *Russell's Mag.*, IV, 212–218, 313–321, 406–414, 505–509 (Dec., 1858; Jan., Feb., March, 1859); *Remarks on Mr. [John Lothrop] Motley's Letter in the London Times on the "State of the Country"* (Charleston, 1861); *James Louis Petigru: A Biographical Sketch* (New York, 1866); *Selected Poems by William J. Grayson*, ed. [his daughter] Mrs. William H. Armstrong (New York and Washington, 1907). There are uncollected articles in *S.Q.R.*, *De Bow's Rev.*, and *Russell's Mag.*

Dr. Alexander Hamilton

Much the best source of information is *Gentleman's Progress: The Itinerarium of Dr. Alexander Hamilton 1744* (1948), ed. Carl Bridenbaugh from the manuscript in the Huntington Library. In 1907 William Bixby in St. Louis printed for private distribution a small edition edited by A. B. Hart. The *Itinerarium* is briefly discussed by George P. Winship in *C.H.A.L.*, I, 11–13 and by Kenneth B. Murdock in *L.A.P.*, pp. 103–105.

George W. Harris

Donald Day has published three important articles based upon his Univ. of Chicago dissertation, "The Life and Works of George W. Harris" (1942): "The Life of George Washington Harris," *Tenn. Hist. Quart.*, VI, 3–38 (March, 1947); "The Political Satires of George W. Harris," *ibid.*, IV, 320–338 (Dec., 1945); and "The Humorous Works of George W. Harris," *Am. Lit.*, XIV, 391–406 (Jan., 1943). See also Walter Blair, *Native American Humor* (1937) and "Sut Lovingood," *Sat. Rev. of Lit.*, XV, 3–4, 16 (Nov. 7, 1936) and Jennette Tandy, *Crackerbox Philosophers* (1925), pp. 93–94. There is a highly eulogistic passing allusion in F. O. Matthiessen, *American Renaissance* (1941), p. xiii. Not included in *Sut Lovingood's Yarns* (New York, 1867) is *Sut Lovingood's Travels with Old Abe Lincoln* (Chicago: The Black Cat Press, 1937), ed. Edd W. Parks.

Joel Chandler Harris

The best biography is by his daughter-in-law, Julia Collier Harris, *The Life and Letters of Joel Chandler Harris* (1918); Bibliography, pp. 603–610. See also Mrs. Harris's "Joel Chandler Harris: The Poetic Mind," *Emory Univ. Quart.*, III, 21–29 (March, 1947). Mrs. Harris edited *Joel Chandler Harris: Editor and Essayist: Miscellaneous Literary, Political, and Social Writings*

(Chapel Hill, N. C., 1931). Robert L. Wiggins, *The Life of Joel Chandler Harris* . . . (Nashville, 1918) deals with Harris's early life and reprints writings not readily available elsewhere; Bibliography, pp. 429–444. See also the bibliography in *L.H.U.S.*, III, 540–542, for a list of Harris's separate publications. *Seven Tales of Uncle Remus by Joel Chandler Harris* (Atlanta: The Library, Emory University, 1948), ed. T. H. English, includes uncollected items, two of which had not previously been printed. Two important letters from Harris to W. M. Baskervill are printed in Jay B. Hubbell (ed.), "Letters of Uncle Remus," *Southwest Rev.*, XXIII, 216–223 (Jan., 1938).

Some of the more important critical studies are: W. M. Baskervill, *Southern Writers*, I (1902), 41–88; Arthur H. Quinn, *American Fiction* (1936), pp. 374–384; John D. Wade, "Profits and Losses in the Life of Joel Chandler Harris," *Am. Rev.*, I, 17–35 (April, 1933); Louise Dauner, "Myth and Humor in the Uncle Remus Tales," *Am. Lit.*, XX, 129–143 (May, 1948); T. H. English, "The Twice-Told Tale and Uncle Remus," *Ga. Rev.*, II, 447–460 (Winter, 1948) and "Joel Chandler Harris's Earliest Literary Project," *Emory Univ. Quart.*, II, 176–185 (Oct., 1946); Elsie C. Parsons, "Joel Chandler Harris and Negro Folklore," *Dial*, LXVI, 491–493 (May 17, 1919); John Stafford, "Patterns of Meaning in *Nights with Uncle Remus*," *Am. Lit.*, XVIII, 89–108 (May, 1946); and Ruth I. Cline, "The Tar-Baby Story," *Am. Lit.*, II, 72–78 (March, 1930).

Paul Hamilton Hayne

The only published biography is Kate Harbes Becker, *Paul Hamilton Hayne: His Life and Letters* (1951), which makes little use of the many unpublished letters of Hayne. Prof. James S. Purcell, Jr., of Davidson College, is engaged in the preparation of a biography and a collection of letters. Hayne's relations with Northern writers are discussed in Victor H. Hardendorff, "Paul Hamilton Hayne and the North" (Duke Univ. master's thesis, 1942). Hayne figures prominently in W. P. Trent, *William Gilmore Simms* (1892) and Jay B. Hubbell (ed.), *The Last Years of Henry Timrod* (1941). Many of Hayne's numerous letters have been printed. See particularly D. M. McKeithan (ed.), *A Collection of Hayne Letters* (Austin, Tex., 1944); Charles Duffy (ed.), *The Correspondence of Bayard Taylor and Paul Hamilton Hayne* (1945) and "A Southern Genteelist: Letters by Paul Hamilton Hayne to Julia C. R. Dorr," *S. C. Hist. and Geneal. Mag.*, LII, 65–73, 154–165, 207–217 (April, July, Oct., 1951); LIII, 19–30 (Jan., 1952). The relations between Lanier and Hayne are briefly but ably treated in Charles R. Anderson, "Poet of the Pine Barrens," *Ga. Rev.*, I, 280–293 (Fall, 1947), and Hayne's correspondence with Gayarré is given, more fully, in Anderson's "Charles Gayarré and Paul Hayne: The Last Literary Cavaliers," *American Studies in Honor of William Kenneth Boyd* (1940), ed. D. K. Jackson, pp. 221–281. There is a brief bibliography in *L.H.U.S.*, III, 554–556.

Many published letters are included in the miscellaneous materials which follow: E. G. Bernard, "Northern Bryant and Southern Hayne," *Colophon*, N.S. I, 536–540 (Spring, 1936); J. E. Bowen, "A Brief Correspondence with Paul Hamilton Hayne," *Lippincott's Mag.*, XLVI, 368–374 (Sept., 1890); J. T. Brown, Jr., "Paul Hamilton Hayne," *Sewanee Rev.*, XIV, 236–247 (April, 1906); Essie B. Cheesborough, "Recollections of Paul H. Hayne" [holograph MS in the Duke Univ. Library, based upon letters written to her by Hayne]; *Check List of the Paul Hamilton Hayne Library*, Duke Univ. *Bulletin*, No. 2, July, 1930 [does not include certain books acquired later]; R. A. Coleman, "Hayne Writes to Trowbridge," *Am. Lit.*, X, 483–486 (Jan., 1939); J. W. Davidson, *The Living Writers of the South* (New York, 1869), pp. 242–250; R. B. Davis, "An Unpublished Poem by Paul Hamilton Hayne," *Am. Lit.*, XVIII, 327–329 (Jan., 1947), "Paul Hamilton Hayne to Dr. Francis Peyre Porcher," *Studies in Philol.*, XLIV, 529–548 (July, 1947), and "The Southern Dilemma: Two Unpublished Letters of Paul Hamilton Hayne," *Jour. So. Hist.*, XVIII, 64–70 (Feb., 1951); F. B. Dedmond, "Paul Hamilton Hayne and the Poe Westminster Memorial," *Md. Hist. Mag.*, XLV, 149–151 (June, 1950), "Paul Hamilton Hayne's 'Poe': A Note on a Poem," *Ga. Hist. Quart.*, XXXVII, 52–53 (March, 1953), and "The Poems of Paul Hamilton Hayne to Frances Christine Fisher," *N. C. Hist. Rev.*, XXVIII, 408–413 (Oct., 1951); J. De-Lancey Ferguson, "A New Letter of Paul Hamilton Hayne," *Am. Lit.*, V, 368–370 (Jan., 1934); Max L. Griffin, "Whittier and Hayne: A Record of Friendship," *Am. Lit.*, XIX, 41–58 (March, 1947); R. B. Harwell, "A Confederate View of the Southern Poets," *Am. Lit.*, XXIV, 51–61 (March, 1952) [reprints Hayne's "The Southern Lyre" from *So. Illustrated News* for Nov. 22, 1862]; William Hamilton Hayne, "Paul H. Hayne's Methods of Composition," *Lippincott's Mag.*, L, 793–796 (Dec., 1892); A. L. Hench, "Three Letters to the Haynes from Richard Blackmore," *Am. Lit.*, IV, 199–207 (May, 1932); T. W. Higginson, "Paul Hamilton Hayne," *Chautauquan*, VII, 228–232 (Jan., 1887); W. S. Hoole, "Seven Unpublished Letters of Paul Hamilton Hayne," *Ga. Hist. Quart.*, XXII, 273–285 (Sept., 1938); Jay B. Hubbell, "Some New Letters of Constance Fenimore Woolson [to Hayne]," *New Eng. Quart.*, XIV, 715–735 (Dec., 1941) and "George Henry Boker, Paul Hamilton Hayne, and Charles Warren Stoddard: Some Unpublished Letters," *Am. Lit.*, V, 146–165 (May, 1933); C. W. Hubner (ed.), *Representative Southern Poets* (1906), pp. 55–82; Sidney Lanier, *Music and Poetry* (1898), pp. 197–211; S. A. Link, *Pioneers of Southern Literature*, I, 43–87; D. M. McKeithan, "Paul Hamilton Hayne and *The Southern Bivouac*," University of Texas *Studies in English*, No. XVII, 112–123 (1937), "Paul Hayne's Reputation in Augusta at the Time of His Death," *ibid.*, No. XVIII, 165–173 (1938), and "Paul Hamilton Hayne Writes to the Granddaughter of Patrick Henry," *Ga. Hist. Quart.*, XXXII, 22–28 (March, 1948); Edwin Mims in *Library of Southern Literature*, V, 2265–2271; La Salle C. Pickett, *Literary Hearthstones of Dixie* (1912), pp. 69–96; Margaret

J. Preston, "Paul Hamilton Hayne," *So. Bivouac*, N.S. II, 222–229 (Sept., 1886) and Introduction to Hayne's *Poems* (Boston, 1882); J. C. Routh, Jr., "Some Fugitive Poems of Paul Hamilton Hayne," *S.A.Q.*, IX, 327–333 (Oct., 1910); Harry Shaw, "Paul Hamilton Hayne to Richard Henry Stoddard," *Am. Lit.*, IV, 195–199 (May, 1932); Aubrey Starke, "Sidney Lanier and Paul Hamilton Hayne: Three Unpublished Letters," *Am. Lit.*, I, 32–39 (March, 1929)—see also Lanier, *Writings* (Centennial ed., 1945), Index; Maurice Thompson, "The Last Literary Cavalier," *Critic*, XXXVIII, 352–354 (April, 1901); and H. B. Rouse and F. C. Watkins, "Some Manuscript Poems by Paul Hamilton Hayne," *Emory Univ. Quart.*, VIII, 83–91 (June, 1952).

The Duke Univ. Library has Hayne's private library and a large collection of his manuscripts, including letters written by and addressed to him, diaries, and clippings. The Johns Hopkins Univ. Library has some forty-odd letters from Hayne to Lanier. There are many Hayne letters in other libraries and in the hands of collectors.

Hinton Rowan Helper

H. T. Lefler, *Hinton Rowan Helper: Advocate of a "White America"* (Charlottesville, Va., 1935); William Polk, "The Hated Helper," *S.A.Q.*, XXX, 177–189 (April, 1931); D. R. Barbee, "Hinton Rowan Helper," *Tyler's Hist. and Geneal. Mag.*, XV, 145–172 (Jan., 1934); "Savoyard" [E. W. Newman], *In the Pennyrile of Old Kentucky* (Washington, 1911), pp. 118–123; J. G. de Roulhac Hamilton's sketch in *D.A.B.*; Clement Eaton, *Freedom of Thought in the Old South* (1940); J. S. Bassett, *Anti-Slavery Leaders of North Carolina* (1889); S. B. Weeks, "Anti-Slavery Sentiment in the South: With Unpublished Letters from John Stuart Mill and Mrs. Stowe," *So. History Assn. Publications*, II, 87–130 (April, 1898); and U. B. Phillips, "Economic and Political Essays in the Ante-Bellum South," *South in the Building of the Nation*, VII, 173 ff.

Patrick Henry

The best biographies are those by his grandson, William Wirt Henry (1891, in 3 vols.), Moses Coit Tyler (1887), and George Morgan (1907; revised ed., 1929). None of these, however, makes use of the "Journal of a French Traveller in the Colonies," *Am. Hist. Rev.*, XXVI, 726–747 (July, 1921), quoted in my text. The best recent study of Henry's oratory is that by Louis Mallory in W. N. Brigance (ed.), *A History and Criticism of American Public Address* (1943), II, 580–602. Later investigators have corrected William Wirt's widely read *Sketches of the Life of Patrick Henry* (1817), which is discussed in my text. See also the able discussion of the "Give Me Liberty, or Give Me Death" speech in Douglas S. Freeman, *George Washington*, III (1951), 404 n. 56.

Johnson Jones Hooper

All earlier accounts of Hooper are superseded by W. Stanley Hoole, *Alias Simon Suggs: The Life and Times of Johnson Jones Hooper*, published by the University of Alabama Press in 1952; Bibliography, pp. 252–271. Hooper's work is briefly discussed in Jennette Tandy, *Crackerbox Philosophers* (1925) and Walter Blair, *Native American Humor* (1937).

Joseph Holt Ingraham

For Ingraham's life, see Dorothy Dondore's sketch in *D.A.B.* and Warren G. French, "A Sketch of the Life of Joseph Holt Ingraham," *Jour. Miss. Hist.*, XI, 155–171 (July, 1949). See also Alexander Cowie, *The Rise of the American Novel* (1948), pp. 288–292; F. L. Mott, *Golden Multitudes* (1947), pp. 94–95; James D. Hart, *The Popular Book* (1950), pp. 98–99, 118; and Don Seitz, "A Prince of Best Sellers," *Pubs.' Weekly*, CXIX, 940 (Feb. 21, 1931). Many of Ingraham's novels are listed in Lyle H. Wright, *American Fiction, 1774–1850: A . . . Bibliography* (revised ed., 1948).

James Iredell

The best account is the biography by his son-in-law, Griffith J. McRee, *Life and Correspondence of James Iredell* (2 vols., New York, 1857). The *D.A.B.* sketch was written by J. G. De R. Hamilton. Iredell's political activities are discussed in Nettie S. Herndon, "James Iredell" (unpublished Duke Univ. dissertation, 1944), which contains a full bibliography. There are Iredell MSS in the libraries of Duke Univ., the Univ. of North Carolina, and the N. C. Department of Archives and History. Iredell's *Answer to Mr. [George] Mason's Objections to the New Constitution . . .* was printed serially in 1788 in the *State Gazette* and in the *Norfolk and Portsmouth Journal*; and although no copy survives, it was advertised as "Just published" in pamphlet form. It was reprinted in P. L. Ford (ed.), *Pamphlets on the Constitution of the United States . . . , 1787–1788* (Brooklyn, 1888).

Washington Irving

There is a chapter on Irving and the South in Max L. Griffin, "The Relations with the South of Six Major Northern Writers" (Univ. of N. C. dissertation, 1942). See also Minnie C. Yarborough (ed.), *The Reminiscences of William C. Preston* (1933) and her "Rambles with Washington Irving . . . ," *S.A.Q.*, XXIX, 423–439 (Oct., 1930); M. B. Seigler, "Washington Irving to William C. Preston: An Unpublished Letter," *Am. Lit.*, XIX, 256–259 (Nov., 1947);

R. B. Davis, "Washington Irving and Joseph C. Cabell," *English Studies in Honor of James Southall Wilson* (1951), pp. 7–22; Susan S. Bennett, "The Cheves Family of South Caroline" [includes a letter from Irving about Langdon Cheves], *S. C. Hist. and Geneal. Mag.*, XXXV, 130–152 (Oct., 1934); and Stanley T. Williams and Leonard B. Beach (eds.), "Washington Irving's Letters to Mary Kennedy," *Am. Lit.*, VI, 44–65 (March, 1934). For other materials, consult Williams, *The Life of Washington Irving* (2 vols., 1935), see Index; and Williams and Mary E. Edge, *A Bibliography of the Writings of Washington Irving* (1936).

Thomas Jefferson

For Jefferson's early life, see Dumas Malone, *The Young Jefferson* (1948) and *Jefferson and the Rights of Man* (1951), which carry the story down to 1792. Three other volumes are to follow. Of numerous other biographical studies one of the best is Gilbert Chinard, *Thomas Jefferson: The Apostle of Americanism* (1929). George Tucker, who knew Jefferson in his last years, published in 1837 a two-volume life which still has some value. For other materials, see *L.H.U.S.*, III, 595–602.

Princeton University has begun publication of a complete edition of *The Papers of Thomas Jefferson* (1950–   ), under the general editorship of Julian P. Boyd, which is expected to run to fifty volumes or more. Meanwhile the best edition is *The Writings of Thomas Jefferson* (10 vols., 1892–1899), ed. P. L. Ford. A fuller edition, though the text is often untrustworthy, is the Memorial Ed. of *The Writings of Thomas Jefferson* (20 vols., 1903–1904), ed. A. A. Lipscomb and A. L. Bergh.

Useful volumes of selections are: *Life and Selected Writings of Thomas Jefferson* (Modern Library, 1944), ed. Adrienne Koch and William Peden; *Alexander Hamilton and Thomas Jefferson: Representative Selections* (American Writers Series, 1934), ed. F. C. Prescott; *The Best Letters of Thomas Jefferson* (1926), ed. J. G. de Roulhac Hamilton; and *Extracts from the Correspondence of John Adams and Thomas Jefferson* (1925), ed. Paul Wilstach, author of *Jefferson and Monticello* (revised ed., 1931).

Other works of value are R. B. Davis (ed.), *Correspondence of Thomas Jefferson and Francis Walker Gilmer* (1946); Adrienne Koch, *Jefferson and Madison: The Great Collaboration* (1950); *The Jefferson Cyclopedia* (1900), ed. J. P. Foley; E. Millicent Sowerby, *Catalogue of the Library of Thomas Jefferson*, Vol. I (1952); Charles A. Beard, *Economic Origins of Jeffersonian Democracy* (1915); W. G. Bean, "Anti-Jeffersonianism in the Ante-bellum South," *N. C. Hist. Rev.*, XII, 103–124 (April, 1935); Carl Becker, *The Declaration of Independence* (1922, 1942); Julian P. Boyd, *The Declaration of Independence: The Evolution of the Text as Shown in Facsimiles . . .* (1945); Helen D. Bullock (ed.), *My Head and My Heart: A Little History of Thomas Jefferson and*

Maria Cosway (1945), [but see Julian P. Boyd's review in N. Y. *Times Book Rev.*, Dec. 23, 1945]; Eleanor D. Berman, *Thomas Jefferson among the Arts* (1947); Gilbert Chinard (ed.), *The Commonplace Book of Thomas Jefferson* (1926) and *The Literary Bible of Thomas Jefferson* (1928); William D. Gould, "The Religious Opinions of Thomas Jefferson," *Miss. Valley Hist. Rev.*, XX, 191–208 (Sept., 1933); Edd W. Parks, "Jefferson as a Man of Letters," *Ga. Rev.*, VI, 450–459 (Winter, 1952); M. J. Herzberg, "Thomas Jefferson as a Man of Letters," *S.A.Q.*, XIII, 310–327 (Oct., 1914); R. J. Honeywell, *The Educational Work of Thomas Jefferson* (1931); Adrienne Koch, *The Philosophy of Thomas Jefferson* (1943); Karl Lehmann, *Thomas Jefferson: American Humanist* (1947); H. C. Montgomery, "Thomas Jefferson as a Philologist," *Am. Jour. Philol.*, LXV, 367–371 (Oct., 1944); Maude H. Woodfin, "Contemporary Opinion in Virginia of Thomas Jefferson," in *Essays in Honor of William E. Dodd* (1935), ed. Avery Craven, pp. 30–85; and V. L. Parrington, *Main Currents in American Thought*, I, 342–356.

Thomas Johnson

For the little that is known of Johnson's life, see John Wilson Townsend, *Kentuckians in History and Literature* (1907) and *Kentucky in American Letters, 1784–1912* (1913), in which some of Johnson's poems were reprinted. In 1949 the Bluegrass Bookshop of Lexington reprinted *The Kentucky Miscellany* (4th ed.; Lexington, 1821), in an edition of only fifty copies, under the title *O Rare Tom Johnson, Kentucky's First Poet.* . . . Townsend wrote the Introduction. See also R. L. Rusk, *The Literature of the Middle Western Frontier* (1925), I, 320–323.

Richard Malcolm Johnston

Johnston's *Autobiography* (1901) throws some light upon his literary career, but needs to be supplemented by Francis T. Long, "The Life of Richard Malcolm Johnston in Maryland, 1867–1898," *Md. Hist. Mag.*, XXXIV, 305–324 (Dec., 1939), XXXV, 270–286 (Sept., 1940), and XXXVI, 54–69 (March, 1941). Long also wrote the sketch in *D.A.B.* For Johnston's relations with Lanier, consult the Index to the Centennial ed. of *The Writings of Sidney Lanier*. For his Middle Georgia background, see Johnston's "Early Educational Life in Middle Georgia" in the *Report* of the U. S. Commissioner of Education for the Year 1894–1895, II, 1699–1733, and *ibid.* for 1895–1896, I, 839–886; "The Planter of the Old South," *So. History Assn. Publications*, I, 35–44 (Jan., 1897); and "Middle Georgia Rural Life," *Century*, XLIII, 737–742 (March, 1892). Lessie B. Brinson, *A Study of the Life and Works of Richard Malcolm Johnston* (Nashville, 1937) is an abstract of a Peabody College dissertation.

The literary historians have given little attention to Johnston's work. There is a brief discussion in F. L. Pattee, *A History of American Literature since 1890* (1915), pp. 299–301, with a list of his chief publications (p. 319). See also E. C. Stedman and S. B. Weeks, "Literary Estimate and Bibliography of Richard Malcolm Johnston," So. History Assn. *Publications*, II, 315–327 (Oct., 1898). W. A. Webb wrote the essay in *Southern Writers*, Vol. II (1903). See also Sophia Bledsoe Herrick, "Richard Malcolm Johnston," *Century*, XXXVI, 276–280 (June, 1888); Charles Forster Smith, "Richard Malcolm Johnston," *Quart. Rev. of M. E. Church South*, XXXIV (N.S. XI), 280–295 (Jan., 1892); and E. W. Parks, *Segments of Southern Thought* (1938), pp. 223–244.

The Duke Univ. Library has an undated pamphlet, tentatively dated 1862, entitled *Five Chapters of a History: A Georgia Court, Forty Years Ago*. The story is identical with that in Johnston's first book, *Georgia Sketches from the Recollections of an Old Man* (Augusta, 1864) entitled "Judge Mike and His Court; or, Five Chapters of a Georgia History."

John Pendleton Kennedy

The fullest account is found in Henry T. Tuckerman, *The Life of John Pendleton Kennedy*, which was included in Kennedy's *Collected Works* (10 vols., New York, 1871); but see also Edward Gwathmey, *John Pendleton Kennedy* (1931). Kennedy left many of his papers in the Peabody Institute Library in Baltimore with the stipulation that they were not to be opened until thirty years after his death. They include numerous letters and a diary which he kept for many years. For Kennedy's relations with other writers, see "The Kennedy Papers," ed. Killis Campbell, *Sewanee Rev.*, XXV, 1–19, 193–208, 348–360 (Jan., April, July, 1917). Kennedy's intimate friend, John H. B. Latrobe, wrote the sketch in *Appleton's Cyclopedia of American Biography*, III, 517. See also John E. Semmes, *John H. B. Latrobe and His Times* (Baltimore, 1917), pp. 430–436. For the reminiscences of another Baltimore friend, see James Wynne, "John P. Kennedy," *Harper's*, XXV, 335–340 (Aug., 1862).

For bibliographical details, see Merle Johnson, "American First Editions: John Pendleton Kennedy," *Pubs,' Weekly*, CXXII, 589 (Aug. 20, 1932); Jacob Blanck, *Merle's Johnson's American First Editions* (4th ed., 1942); *L.H.U.S.*, III, 604–605; and Kennedy's *Horse-Shoe Robinson* (1937), ed. E. E. Leisy, pp. xxix-xxxii. See also Lloyd W. Griffin, "The John Pendleton Kennedy Manuscripts," *Md. Hist. Mag.*, XLVIII, 327–336 (Dec., 1953).

The Blackwater Chronicle (New York, 1853), sometimes wrongly ascribed to J. P. Kennedy, was, according to Tuckerman, written by his brother Pendleton ("Pent") Kennedy. It has sometimes been mistakenly ascribed also to their cousin David Hunter Strother ("Porte Crayon"), who illustrated the book. Strother himself wrote a different account of this visit to the Blackwater region in Randolph County, now West Virginia: "The Virginian Canaan. By a Virginian," *Harper's Mag.*, VIII, 18–36 (Dec., 1853). In the article Strother refers to himself as "Porte Crayon" and to Pendleton Kennedy as "Mr. Penn, the author." The illustrations in *The Blackwater Chronicle* are not the same as those in Strother's article, which is the first of a series of illustrated sketches of the South. The best-known of these were collected in his *Virginia Illustrated* (New York, 1857). In this book and in "The Virginian Canaan" Strother refers to J. P. Kennedy as "X. M. C.," i.e., Ex-Member of Congress.

Some of the better reviews of Kennedy's books are: *Swallow Barn*: A. H. Everett in *No. Am. Rev.*, XXXVI, 519–544 (April, 1833)—*Horse-Shoe Robinson*: W. G. Simms in *S.Q.R.*, N.S. VI, 203–220 (July, 1852); *Am. Quart. Rev.*, XVIII, 240–242 (Sept., 1835)—*Rob of the Bowl*: Burton's *Gentleman's Mag.*, IV, 64–66 (Jan., 1939)—*Memoirs of the Life of William Wirt*: Francis Bowen in *No. Am. Rev.*, LXX, 255–259 (Jan., 1850). See also "Kennedy's Novels" (including *Quodlibet*) in *New-York Rev.*, X, 144–152 (Jan., 1842).

Critical materials are found in V. L. Parrington, *Main Currents in American Thought*, II, 46–56; the introductions to *Swallow Barn* (1929), ed. Jay B. Hubbell, and *Horse-Shoe Robinson* (1937), ed. E. E. Leisy; Leisy's *The American Historical Novel* (1949); J. E. Uhler, "Kennedy's Novels and His Posthumous Works," *Am. Lit.*, III, 471–479 (Jan., 1932); M. J. Moses, *The Literature of the South* (1910), pp. 247–252; Emanuel Spencer, "The Successful Novel of Fifty-Six Years Ago: 'Horse-Shoe Robinson,'" *Mag. of Am. Hist.*, XXIX, 42–49 (Jan., 1893); and Poe's review of *Horse-Shoe Robinson*, reprinted in *Works* (Va. ed.), VIII, 4–11. See also J. E. Cooke, "The Author of Swallow Barn," *Appletons' Jour.*, X, 205–206 (Aug., 1873); Jay B. Hubbell, "Thackeray and Virginia," *Va. Quart. Rev.*, III, 76–86 (Jan., 1927); J. R. Moore, "Kennedy's *Horse-Shoe Robinson*: Fact or Fiction?" *Am. Lit.*, IV, 160–166 (May, 1932); and for the actual James Robinson, Rhoda C. Ellison, "Early Alabama Interest in Southern Writers," *Ala. Rev.*, I, 101–110 (April, 1948).

Francis Scott Key

The best biography is E. S. Delaplaine, *Francis Scott Key: Life and Times* (1937); Bibliography, pp. 481–488; but see also Victor Weybright, *The Story of Francis Scott Key* (1935); Clarence [Lawrence?] C. Wroth, "Francis Scott Key as a Churchman," *Md. Hist. Mag.*, IV, 154–170 (June, 1909); Allan Westcott's sketch in *D.A.B.*; T. C. McCorvey, *The Mission of Francis Scott Key to Alabama in 1833* (1904), also in Ala. Hist. Soc. *Transactions*, IV, 141–165 (1904); McHenry Howard, "Date of Francis Scott Key's Birth," *Md. Hist. Mag.*, II, 137–140 (June, 1907); and M. E. Lippencott, "O'er the Land of the Free," *N. Y. Hist. Soc. Quart.*, XXV, 28–36 (Jan., 1941).

Joseph Brown Ladd

The best sources of information are Lewis Leary's two articles: "A Forgotten Charleston Poet: Joseph Brown Ladd," *Americana*, XXXVI, 571–588 (Oct.,

1942) and "The Writings of Joseph Brown Ladd," *Bulletin of Bibliog.*, XVIII, 131–133 (Jan.–April, 1945). See also Granville Hicks's sketch in *D.A.B.* and the biographical sketch by W. B. Chittenden in *The Literary Remains of Joseph Brown Ladd, M.D.* (New York, 1832), edited by the poet's sister, Mrs. Elizabeth Haskins. On Feb. 16 and 27, 1830, Simms's *City Gazette and Commercial Advertiser* carried announcements of Ladd's collected writings and gave some biographical details.

Mirabeau B. Lamar

The best sources of information are Herbert P. Gambrell, *Mirabeau Bonaparte Lamar* (Dallas, Tex., 1934) and Philip Graham, *The Life and Poems of Mirabeau B. Lamar* (Chapel Hill, N. C., 1938); Bibliography, pp. 317–321. See also Graham's "Mirabeau Lamar's First Trip to Texas," *Southwest Rev.*, XXI, 369–389 (July, 1936); R. G. Caldwell's sketch in *D.A.B.*; and Francis Copcutt, "A Sketch of the Life of Mirabeau B. Lamar," *Knickerbocker*, XXV, 377–387 (May, 1845).

Sidney Lanier

There are two good biographies: Edwin Mims, *Sidney Lanier* (1905) in the American Men of Letters series and Aubrey Starke, *Sidney Lanier: A Biographical and Critical Study* (1933); Bibliography, pp. 455–473. Both these biographies were published before the appearance in 1945 of the Centennial ed. of Lanier's *Works* in 10 vols., under the general editorship of Charles R. Anderson, which includes many hitherto unpublished letters and other new materials. Vol. VI includes an extensive Bibliography compiled by Philip Graham and Frieda C. Thies (pp. 379–412). See also *L.H.U.S.*, III, 605–608. Some materials not listed in the above are: Charles R. Anderson, "Two Letters from Lanier to Holmes," *Am. Lit.*, XVIII, 321–326 (Jan., 1947); "Lanier and Science: Addenda," *Mod. Lang. Notes*, LXVI, 395–398 (June, 1951); and "Poet of the Pine Barrens" [the Hayne-Lanier correspondence], *Ga. Rev.*, I, 280–293 (Fall, 1947); Nathalia Wright, "The East Tennessee Background of Sidney Lanier's *Tiger-Lilies*," *Am. Lit.*, XIX, 127–138 (May, 1947); Lewis Leary, "The Forlorn Hope of Sidney Lanier," *S.A.Q.*, XLVI, 263–271 (April, 1947); John G. Fletcher, "Sidney Lanier," *Univ. Kansas City Rev.*, XVI, 97–102 (Winter, 1949); Allen P. Tankersley, *College Life at Old Oglethorpe* (Athens, Ga., 1951); Count D. Gibson, "The Wonderful Marshes of Glynn," *Emory Univ. Quart.*, III, 116–121 (June, 1947); and Mose Daniels, *The Marshes of Glynn* [by] *Sidney Lanier: A Photographic Interpretation* (1949).

John Lawson

Apart from what can be inferred from his book, not much is known about Lawson's life. See W. K. Boyd's sketch in *D.A.B.*; Kenneth B. Murdock in *L.A.P.*, pp. 28–30; S. B. Weeks, "Libraries and Literature in North Carolina in the Eighteenth Century" in *Annual Report* of Am. Hist. Assn. for 1895 (1896), pp. 224–232; and Vincent H. Todd (ed.), *Christoph Von Graffenried's Account of the Founding of New Bern* (Raleigh, 1920); and M. C. Tyler, *A History of American Literature, 1607–1765* (1878), II, 282–289.

Arthur Lee

Edmund C. Burnett wrote the sketch in *D.A.B.* Richard H. Lee, son of Lee's brother Richard Henry, is the author of *Life of Arthur Lee* (Boston, 1829). See also Burton J. Hendrick, *The Lees of Virginia* (1935). Some Loyalist Virginian refugee and not Arthur Lee is clearly the author of a book sometimes attributed to him: *The American Wanderer through Various Parts of Europe, in a Series of Letters to a Lady. . . . By a Virginian* (London, 1783). Lee, however, was apparently the author of the letter "To the King," which appears as a preface to the London, 1774, edition of Jefferson's *A Summary View of the Rights of British America.* See T. P. Abernethy's Introduction to the New York, 1943, edition. In 1769 William Rind printed in one volume Lee's *The Monitor* and John Dickinson's *Letters from a Farmer in Pennsylvania. The Monitor* had been reprinted in the N. Y. *Journal of Commerce* in April, 1768, and in the *S.-C. Gazette* in June of the same year (Philip Davidson, *Propaganda and the American Revolution*, 1941, p. 244). See also T. P. Abernethy, "The Origin of the Franklin-Lee Imbroglio," *N. C. Hist. Rev.*, XV, 41–52 (Jan., 1938).

Richard Henry Lee

Lee's son, Richard H. Lee, published a *Memoir of the Life of Richard Henry Lee . . .* (2 vols.; Philadelphia, 1825). A more recent account is found in Burton J. Hendrick, *The Lees of Virginia* (1935). *The Letters of Richard Henry Lee* (1914) was edited by J. C. Ballagh. For a fuller account of the Wakefield school which Lee attended, see *The Victoria History of the County of Yorkshire* (London, n.d.). For Lee's grandfather, see Louis B. Wright, "Richard Lee II, a Belated Elizabethan in Virginia," *Huntington Library Quart.*, II, 1–35 (Oct., 1938), and *The First Gentlemen of Virginia* (1940), pp. 212–234. Only the first of Lee's two pamphlets on the Federal Constitution was reprinted in *Pamphlets on the Constitution of the United States* (Brooklyn, 1888), ed. P. L. Ford.

Hugh Swinton Legaré

The fullest account of Legaré's life and work (the name is pronounced *Le-gree*) is in Linda Rhea, *Hugh Swinton Legaré: A Charleston Intellectual* (1934). The sketch in *D.A.B.* is by J. G. de Roulhac Hamilton. There are important references to Legaré in *Life, Letters, and Journals of George Ticknor* (2 vols., 1876), ed. George S. Hillard. See also Paul H. Hayne, *Lives of Robert Young Hayne and Hugh Swinton Legaré* (1878); B. J. Ramage, "Hugh Swinton Legaré," *Sewanee Rev.*, X, 43–55, 167–180 (Jan., April, 1902); and William C. Preston, *Eulogy on Hugh Swinton Legaré: Delivered at the Request of the City of Charleston* (Charleston, 1843).

Not all of Legaré's contributions to the *Southern Rev.* are included in the *Writings of Hugh Swinton Legaré* . . . (2 vols., Charleston, Philadelphia, and New York, 1845, 1846), edited by his sister Mary Legaré Bullen. Vol. I contains a Memoir written by Edward W. Johnston, an older brother of General Joseph E. Johnston (*W.M.Q.*, 2nd ser. IX, 328–329, Oct., 1929). See also "Il Secretario" [Edward W. Johnston], "Life and Labors, Literary, Professional and Public, of Legare," *Am. Whig Rev.*, II, 416–430 (Oct., 1845). The *Writings* was reviewed by George Frederick Homes in *S.Q.R.*, IX, 321–361 (April, 1846) and George Ripley in *Harbinger*, II, 332–333 (May 2, 1846).

The Charleston Library Society has a manuscript list of articles in the *Southern Rev.* (with the exception of the fourth number) which gives the names of most of the authors. The chief source of this information is a list furnished by Peter J. Shand (Columbia *State*, Nov. 30, 1924), who had access to a file supposed to have been marked by Stephen Elliott, Jr. This is my chief basis for ascribing to Legaré the articles, not in the *Writings*, mentioned in my text: Pollok's *The Course of Time*, II, 454–470 (Nov., 1828); Robert Montgomery, II, 290–302 (Aug., 1828); Bulwer-Lytton, III, 467–495 (May, 1829); VII, 192–213 (May, 1831); "Sir Philip Sidney's Miscellanies," V, 295–318 (May, 1830); "Jeremy Bentham and the Utilitarians," VII, 261–296 (Aug., 1831); Scott's *The Fair Maid of Perth*, II, 216–263 (Aug., 1828); "Early Spanish Ballads," V, 62–99 (Feb., 1830); James Gates Percival, I, 442–457 (May, 1828); Irving's *Life of Columbus*, II, 1–31 (Aug., 1828); Fenimore Cooper's *The Wept of Wish-ton-Wish*, V, 207–226 (Feb., 1830); Cooper's *The Bravo*, VIII, 382–399 (Feb., 1832); *Poems* of William Cullen Bryant, VIII, 443–462 (Feb., 1832).

The best criticism is that of V. L. Parrington in *Main Currents in American Thought*, II, 114–124. Other materials are: Richard Beale Davis, "The Early American Lawyer and the Profession of Letters," *Huntington Library Quart.*, XII, 191–205 (Feb., 1949), which contains some letters addressed to Francis Walker Gilmer; Edd W. Parks, "Legaré and Grayson: Types of Classical Influences on Criticism in the Old South," *Segments of Southern Thought* (1938), pp. 156–171; E. H. Eby, "American Romantic Criticism, 1815–1860" (Univ. of Wash. dissertation, 1927); W. C. Rives, "H. S. Legaré, Late Attorney General of the United States," *S.L.M.*, IX, 570–574 (Sept., 1843); "Life and Career of Hugh S. Legare. By a New Contributor," *Scott's Monthly Mag.* (Atlanta), II, 496–505 (June, 1866).

Legaré's letter of October 10, 1841, from which I have quoted, was published in the Charleston *Self Instructor*, I, 77–80 (Jan., 1854) and is given in full in Guy A. Cardwell, "Charleston Periodicals, 1795–1860" (Univ. of N. C. dissertation, 1936), pp. 38–39. The letter does not appear in Legaré's *Writings*. Legaré's letter to Jesse Burton Harrison, Nov. 3, 1828, from which I have quoted, is printed in *Aris Sonis Focisque* (privately printed, 1910), ed. Fairfax Harrison, pp. 99–100, which also contains Harrison's "English Civilization," which first appeared in the *So. Rev.* for Feb., 1832. The Library of Congress has two copies of a catalogue of Legaré's private library (Washington, 1843, 1848).

James M. Legaré

Our chief sources of information about Legaré's life and writings are three articles—all in the *N. C. Hist. Rev.*—by Curtis Carroll Davis, who hopes some time to bring out a complete edition of Legaré's poems: "Poet, Painter, and Inventor: Some Letters by James Mathewes Legaré," XXI, 215–231 (July, 1944); "A Letter from the Muses: The Publication and Critical Reception of James M. Legaré's '*Orta-Undis, and Other Poems*' (1848)," XXVI, 417–438 (Oct., 1949); and "Fops, Frenchmen, Hidalgos, and Aztecs: . . . the Prose Fiction of J. M. Legaré of South Carolina (1823–59)," XXX, 524–560 (Oct., 1953). See also Davis's "The Several-Sided James Mathewes Legaré: Poet," *Transactions* Huguenot Soc., S. C., No. 57 (1952), pp. 5–12. There is a notice of Legaré's death in *Russell's Mag.*, V, 370–372 (July, 1859). See also E. A. and G. L. Duyckinck, *A Cyclopaedia of American Literature* (1855), II, 720, and R. W. Griswold, *The Poets and Poetry of America* (1872), pp. 577–578. Five of Legaré's poems are reprinted in E. W. Parks (ed.), *Southern Poets* (1936), pp. 93–99. Ludwig Lewisohn has high praise for Legaré's poems both in *A Library of Southern Literature* and in the Charleston *News and Courier* for Aug. 16, 1903.

Orta-Undis, and Other Poems (Boston, 1848) was reviewed in *Lit. World*, III, 283 (May 13, 1848); *Holden's Dollar Mag.*, I, 375–376 (June, 1848); *S.L.M.*, XIV, 388–389 (June, 1848); *So. Lit. Gazette*, I, 127 (Aug. 26, 148); *Christian Examiner*, XLV, 306 (Sept., 1848); *De Bow's Rev.*, VI, 159 (Aug., 1848); and by Simms in *S.Q.R.*, XVI, 224–232 (Oct., 1849).

For Legaré's contributions to the *S.L.M.*, mostly uncollected, see D. K. Jackson, *The Contributors and Contributions to The Southern Literary Messenger* (Charlottesville, Va., 1936). Legaré's prose writings are discussed in Davis's third article. Some of his uncollected poems are: *Knickerbocker*: "Thanatokallos,"

XXXIV, 204–206 (Sept., 1849) and "Janette," XXXV, 245–246 (March, 1850)—*Lit. World:* "To the 'Sweetest Rose of Georgia,' " III, 266 (May 6, 1848); "Maize in Tassel," III, 287 (May 13, 1848); "To Jasmines in December," IV, 456 (May 26, 1849); and "A Laurel Blossom," V, 50 (July 21, 1849) —*So. Lit. Gazette:* "The Rustic Seat," I, 41 (June, 1848); "A Song for 'The Rose,' " I, 137 (Sept. 9, 1848); and "The Trouvere's Rose," I, 281 (Jan. 20, 1849).

The only known portrait of Legaré appeared with his story, "The Loves of Mary Jones," in *The Knickerbocker Gallery* (New York, 1855), pp. 347–371.

Richard Lewis

The best account of Lewis is in C. Lennart Carlson, "Richard Lewis and the Reception of His Work in England," *Am. Lit.*, IX, 301–316 (Nov., 1937). See also Bernard Steiner, *Early Maryland Poetry* (1900); W. B. Norris, "Some Recently-Found Poems on the Calverts," *Md. Hist. Mag.*, XXXII, 112–135 (June, 1937). Lewis's "Description of Spring" was reprinted in *American Poetry* (1918), ed. Percy H. Boynton, who has high praise for the poem.

Augustus Baldwin Longstreet

John D. Wade, *Augustus Baldwin Longstreet: A Study of the Development of Culture in the South* (1924) is one of the better biographies of Southern writers; Bibliography, pp. 373–383. See also Wade's sketch in *D.A.B.* and his chapter on Longstreet in *Southern Pioneers in Social Interpretation* (1925), ed. H. W. Odum. Bishop O. P. Fitzgerald, *Judge Longstreet: A Life Sketch* (Nashville, 1891) is a poor biography, but it contains a few important letters and speeches. There are biographical sketches in J. W. Davidson, *The Living Writers of the South* (1869), pp. 337–342; F. B. Dexter, *Biographical Sketches of the Graduates of Yale College*, VI (1912), 580–583; and John W. Johnson in Miss. Hist. Soc. *Publications*, XII, 122–135 (1912). See also "An Unreprinted *Georgia Scene* ['Dropping to Sleep']," *Emory University Quart.*, II, 100–101 (June, 1946).

For criticism of *Georgia Scenes*, see Wade, *Longstreet*, chaps. vi and vii; Poe, *Works* (Va. ed.), VIII, 257–265; S. A. Link, *Pioneers of Southern Literature*, II, 471–485; and V. L. Parrington, *Main Currents in American Thought*, II, 166–172. For Longstreet's place in American humor, see Walter Blair, *Native American Humor* (1937) and Jennette Tandy, *Crackerbox Philosophers* (1925).

For the influence of Oliver Hillhouse Prince's "The Militia Company Drill" (included in *Georgia Scenes*) upon Thomas Hardy's *The Trumpet Major*, chap. xxiii, see Wade, *Longstreet*, pp. 179–180; C. J. Weber, "A Connecticut Yankee in King Alfred's Country," *Colophon*, n.s. I, 525–535 (Spring, 1936); and the *Critic*, II, 25–26, 55 (Jan. 28, Feb. 25, 1882). Prince's sketch first appeared in the Washington, Ga., *Monitor* on June 6, 1807 (*Ga. Hist. Quart.*, XXX, 270 n., Dec., 1946).

James Russell Lowell

The latest biographies, both by Southern scholars, are Richmond C. Beatty, *James Russell Lowell* (1942) and Leon Howard, *Victorian Knight Errant* (1952), which treats only Lowell's early life and work. I am indebted to Max L. Griffin's careful study, "Lowell and the South," *Tulane Studies in Eng.*, II (1950), 75–102. Griffin has underestimated Lowell's hostility to the South. Many of Lowell's comments on the South are found in his *Political Essays* (1888), most of which first appeared in the *No. Am. Rev.* See also *The Anti-Slavery Papers of James Russell Lowell* (2 vols., 1902), not included in his collected writings. "Mr. Worsley's Nightmare," *Nation*, II, 426–428 (April 5, 1866) does not appear in Lowell's collected poems, presumably because he came to disapprove of his attack on General Lee. It is reprinted in Thelma M. Smith (ed.), *Uncollected Poems of James Russell Lowell* (1950), pp. 144–151. Lowell's sketch of his Virginia friend, John Francis Heath, appears in his *Prose Works*, VII, 45 n. For other bibliographical materials, see *L.H.U.S.*, III, 628–634.

James Madison

Irving Brant has published three volumes of what promises to be the standard biography: *James Madison: The Virginia Revolutionist* (1941), *James Madison: The Nationalist* (1948), and *James Madison: Secretary of State* (1953), covering the years 1751–1809. See also Adrienne Koch, *Jefferson and Madison: The Great Collaboration* (1950). There is a good earlier biography (1902) by Gaillard Hunt, who edited *The Writings of James Madison* . . . (9 vols., 1900–1910). See also Douglass Adair (ed.), "James Madison's Autobiography," *W.M.Q.*, 3rd ser. II, 191–209 (April, 1945). Brief accounts of Madison at "Montpelier" are found in *Literary Life of James K. Paulding* (1867), ed. William I. Paulding, pp. 73–75, and Harriet Martineau, *Retrospect of Western Travel* (1838), pp. 190–198.

For Madison as a writer, see Louis C. Schaedler, "James Madison, Literary Craftsman," *W.M.Q.*, 3rd ser. III, 515–533 (Oct., 1946); W. E. Moore, "James Madison, the Speaker," *Quart. Jour. Speech*, XXXI, 155–162 (April, 1945); and Saul K. Padover (ed.), *The Complete Madison: His Basic Writings* (1953).

For Madison's part in the writing of *The Federalist*, see Douglass Adair, "The Authorship of the Disputed Federalist Papers," *W.M.Q.*, 3rd ser. I, 97–122, 235–264 (April, July, 1944) and two articles by Edward G. Bourne in his *Essays in Historical Criticism* (1901).

"Jonathan Bull and Mary Bull" was first published in *S.L.M.*, I, 342–345 (March, 1835). It was reprinted in *De Bow's Rev.*, XXI, 369–374 (Oct., 1856).

John Marshall

The standard biography is Albert J. Beveridge, *The Life of John Marshall* (4 vols., 1916–1919). Not available to Beveridge was *An Autobiographical Sketch by John Marshall* . . . (Ann Arbor, Mich., 1937), ed. John Stokes Adams, which contains some new information about Marshall's education. The sketch was written for Justice Joseph Story. There is a good brief discussion of Marshall's *Life of Washington* in Michael Kraus, *The Writing of American History* (1953), pp. 84–86. See also William A. Bryan, *George Washington in American Literature, 1775–1865* (1952), pp. 89–93. The sketch of Marshall in Letter V of William Wirt's *The Letters of the British Spy* (1803) has sometimes been mistaken for a sketch of Jefferson.

George Mason

The best source of information is Kate Mason Rowland, *The Life of George Mason* (2 vols., 1892). See also H. J. Eckenrode, *The Revolution in Virginia* (1916), Index. *The Objections of the Hon. George Mason, to the Proposed Foederal Constitution* (1788) was reprinted in *Pamphlets on the Constitution of the United States* (Brooklyn, 1888), ed. P. L. Ford.

William Maxwell

Besides J. D. Eggleston's sketch in *D.A.B.*, there are brief accounts of Maxwell in the *Va. Historical Reporter*, II, 5–6, and in F. B. Dexter, *Biographical Sketches of the Graduates of Yale College*, V (1911), 520–522. The New York Public Library has the Reverend W. H. T. Squires' fourteen-page *A Virginian of Ante-bellum Days*, apparently reprinted from the *Union Seminary Mag.* of Richmond. Maxwell's poems are discussed in a book probably written by Hugh Blair Grigsby, *Letters by a South-Carolinian* (Norfolk, 1827), Letter V, "Mr. Maxwell." Maxwell's portrait is found in A. J. Morrison, *The College of Hampden-Sidney* . . . (Richmond, 1912), opposite p. 122. See also *Forty Years' Familiar Letters of James W. Alexander, D.D.* (New York, 1860), I, 103–104.

Neither Griswold nor the Duyckinck brothers included any of Maxwell's poems in their collections, but Samuel Kettell gave four pages to them in his *Specimens of American Poetry* (1829), II, 155–159, and William Roscoe reprinted nine in his *Specimens of the American Poets* (London, 1822), pp. 173–187.

Maxwell's eulogy on John Marshall, delivered before the Virginia Historical Society, was published in *S.L.M.*, II, 260–261 (March, 1836). There are two uncollected poems in the same magazine: "Sacred Song," II, 554 (Aug., 1836) and "Lines on the Death of Wolfe," III, 6 (Jan., 1837). "To My Heart" appeared in the *New-York Mirror*, VI, 23 (July 26, 1828).

The Yale University Library contains no correspondence between Maxwell and Dwight, but it contains some manuscript materials dealing chiefly with his life as a student at Yale.

Alexander Beaufort Meek

The fullest account is in Herman C. Nixon, *Alexander Beaufort Meek: Poet, Orator, Journalist, Historian, Statesman* (Auburn, Ala., 1910); pp. 30–53 contain some uncollected poems. There are a few letters from Meek to Simms in C. H. Ross, "Alexander Beaufort Meek," *Sewanee Rev.*, IV, 411–427 (Aug., 1896). Peter J. Hamilton wrote the sketch in A *Library of Southern Literature*, VIII, 3599 ff. There is an interesting account of Meek in William Russell Smith, *Reminiscences of a Long Life* . . . (Washington, D. C., 1889), especially I, 315–344. See also William Garrett, *Reminiscences* . . . (1872), pp. 711–713; M. G. Figh, "Alexander Beaufort Meek: Pioneer Man of Letters," *Ala. Hist. Rev.*, II, 127–151 (Summer, 1940); Rhoda C. Ellison, *Early Alabama Publications* (1947), especially pp. 152–153; and Henry S. Canby, "Mr. Meek on America," *Sat. Rev. of Lit.*, VII, 661, 664 (April 16, 1932). The Duke Univ. Library contains a few Meek MSS and a file of Meek's magazine, the *Southron*. In "The Autobiography of a Monomaniac . . . ," *Holden's Dollar Mag.*, III, 278–279 (May, 1849), John Tomlin printed a letter from Meek in which the poet listed the magazines to which he had contributed.

Robert Munford

Biographical materials on Munford are scanty, partly because his home at "Richland" was burned early in the nineteenth century. See the "Diary of William Beverley of 'Blandfield' during a Visit to England, 1750," *Va. Mag.*, XXXVI, 27–35, 161–169 (Jan., April, 1928); "Some Letters of William Beverley," *W.M.Q.*, 1st ser. III, 223–239 (April, 1895); Beverley B. Munford, *Random Recollections* (privately printed, 1905), pp. 217–220; Philip Slaughter, A *History of Bristol Parish*, Va. (2nd ed., Richmond, 1879), pp. 194–195; *The Bland Papers* (Petersburg, Va., 1840), ed. Charles Campbell, pp. 9–10, 13–14; and A. H. Quinn, A *History of the American Drama* . . . to the Civil War (1923), pp. 54–56. For a fuller account of the Wakefield school which Munford attended, see *The Victoria History of the County of Yorkshire* (London, n.d.).

In 1798, fourteen years after his father's death, William Munford had his father's works published in Petersburg, Va., under the title *A Collection of Plays and Poems, by the Late Col. Robert Munford, of Mecklenburg, in the State of Virginia*. Among the few libraries known to possess copies are the Virginia State Library, the Boston Public, the Brown Univ. Library, the Library Company of Philadelphia, and the Library of Congress. There is a copy also in the possession of Mr. and Mrs. George P. Coleman in Williamsburg. One of the two poems entitled "Letters from the Devil" had appeared over the pseudonym "Diabolus" in the *Virginia Gazette* in Aug., 1779, as "The D——l to M—— M——, of Meck——g."

Additional materials are given in Munford's *The Candidates; or, The Humours of a Virginia Election* (Williamsburg, Va., 1948), ed. Jay B. Hubbell and Douglass Adair, reprinted from *W.M.Q.*, 3rd ser. V, 217–257 (April, 1948), and in "Robert Munford's *The Patriots*," ed. Courtlandt Canby, *W.M.Q.*, 3rd ser. VI, 437–502 (July, 1949).

William Munford

The fullest account of Munford's life and work is given in Ralph E. Purcell, "William Munford: A Biographical and Critical Study" (Duke Univ. master's thesis, 1941), which is based largely upon MS materials in the Duke University Library. See also Theodore Cox's sketch in *D.A.B.*; R. B. Davis, "Homer in Homespun—A Southern Iliad," *S.L.M.*, N.S. I, 647–651 (Oct., 1939); George Wythe Munford, *The Two Parsons* (Richmond, 1884); and Anon., "Obituary," *Va. Evangelical and Lit. Mag.*, VIII, 455–456 (1825).

There is some biographical material in the first two of the following reviews of Munford's *Iliad*: [Beverley Tucker], "Munford's Homer," *S.L.M.*, XII, 445–452 (July, 1846); "H" [George Frederick Holmes], "Munford's Homer," *S.Q.R.*, X, 1–45 (July, 1846); [C. C. Felton], "Munford's Homer's Iliad," *No. Am. Rev.*, LXIII, 149–165 (July, 1846); [Charles A. Bristed], "Translators of Homer," *Am. Whig Rev.*, IV, 350–372 (Oct., 1846); [Nathaniel L. Frothingham], "Munford's Iliad," *Christian Examiner*, XLI, 205–213 (Sept., 1846); and [Charles Fenno Hoffman], "Homer's Iliad," *Lit. World*, I, 459–461, 485–487, 507–510 (June 19 and 26, July 3, 1847).

Theodore O'Hara

The best accounts of O'Hara are George H. Genzmer's sketch in *D.A.B.* and Major Edgar Erskine Hume, *Colonel Theodore O'Hara: Author of The Bivouac of the Dead* (Charlottesville, Va., 1936). See also Robert Burns Wilson, "Theodore O'Hara," *Century*, XL, 106–110 (May, 1890); Sidney Herbert, "Colonel Theodore O'Hara . . . ," *Ky. State Hist. Soc. Register*, XXXIX, 230–236 (July, 1941); and George W. Ranck, *O'Hara and His Elegies* (Baltimore, 1875), republished as *The Bivouac of the Dead and Its Author* (New York, 1898).

952

For discussions of the comparative merits of the two versions of "The Bivouac of the Dead," see three articles in the *So. Bivouac*, N.S. II: Daniel E. O'Sullivan, "Theodore O'Hara," 489–494 (Jan., 1887); Susan B. Dixon, "The Bivouac of the Dead," 641–643 (March, 1887); and an untitled note by J. M. Wright, 644–645 (March, 1887). Both versions of the poem are given in W. P. Trent (ed.), *Southern Writers* (1905).

Thomas Nelson Page

Page's brother Rosewell Page wrote *Thomas Nelson Page: A Memoir of a Virginia Gentleman* (1923), which is not very informative. Much more valuable than any other study of Page is Harriet R. Holman, "The Literary Career of Thomas Nelson Page, 1884–1910" (Duke Univ. dissertation, 1947); Bibliography, pp. 243–275. Dr. Holman's study is based largely on the Page MSS in the Duke Univ. Library. For published bibliographical materials, see *L.H.U.S.*, III, 673–674; Jacob Blanck, *Merle Johnson's American First Editions* (4th ed., 1942); and Lester J. Cappon, *Bibliography of Virginia History since 1865* (1930), pp. 764–771. The Plantation edition of *The Novels, Stories, Sketches and Poems of Thomas Nelson Page* in 18 vols. was published in New York by Charles Scribner's Sons in 1906–1912.

The best criticism of Page's writings, apart from Dr. Holman's dissertation, is found in Edwin Mims, "Thomas Nelson Page" in *Southern Writers*, II (1903), 120–151 and "Thomas Nelson Page," *Atlantic Monthly*, C, 109–115 (July, 1907), and Arthur H. Quinn, "Passing of a Literary Era," *Sat. Rev. of Lit.*, I, 609–610 (March 21, 1925) and *American Fiction* (1936), pp. 357–362.

Other materials of varying value are: W. M. E. Rachal (ed.), "Some Letters of Thomas Nelson Page," *Va. Mag.*, LXI, 179–185 (April, 1953); Charles W. Coleman, Jr., "The Recent Movement in Southern Literature," *Harper's*, LXXIV, 837–855 (May, 1887); H. B. Fuller, "Thomas Nelson Page," *Freeman*, VII, 450–452 (July 18, 1923); F. P. Gaines, *The Southern Plantation* (1924); A. C. Gordon, "Thomas Nelson Page: An Appreciation," *Scribner's Mag.*, LXXIII, 75–80 (Jan., 1923), reprinted in Gordon's *Virginian Portraits* (Staunton, Va., 1924); Mrs. L. H. (Corra) Harris, "The Waning Influence of Thomas Nelson Page," *Current Opinion*, XLIII, 171–172 (Aug., 1907), reprinted from the N. Y. *Evening Post*; Charles W. Kent, "Thomas Nelson Page," *S.A.Q.*, VI, 263–271 (July, 1907); F. L. Pattee, *A History of American Literature since 1870* (1915), pp. 265–270; Ronald Tree, "Thomas Nelson Page," *Forum*, LXIX, 1137–1142 (Jan., 1923); and H. A. Toulmin, *Social Historians* (1911), pp. 1–32.

John Williamson Palmer

Allan Westcott wrote the sketch in *D.A.B.* Palmer's account of the writing of "Stonewall Jackson's Way" is given in *The Photographic History of the*

Civil War, IX, 86, 88. See also Francis F. Browne, Bugle-Echoes (1886), p. 28, and F. L. Mott, A History of American Magazines, II, 121.

Albert Pike

The only published biographies are by Fred W. Allsopp: The Life Story of Albert Pike (Little Rock, 1920) and Albert Pike: A Biography (Little Rock, 1928). See also Susan B. Riley, The Life and Works of Albert Pike to 1860 (Nashville, 1934), abstract of a dissertation written at George Peabody College, and "Albert Pike in Tennessee," Tenn. Hist. Quart., IX, 291–305 (Dec., 1950). There is a brief account of Pike in Henry S. Foote, The Bench and Bar of the Southwest (St. Louis, 1876), pp. 187–191. For Pike's travels in the Southwest, see David Donoghue, "Explorations of Albert Pike in Texas," Southwestern Hist. Quart., XXXIX, 135–138 (Oct., 1935), and Walter Lee Brown, "Albert Pike's First Experiences in Arkansas," Ark. Hist. Quart., X, 67–84 (Spring, 1951). For Pike's relations with the Indians, consult the indexes to Annie Heloise Abel's three volumes: The American Indian as Slaveholder and Secessionist (1915), The American Indian as Participant in the Civil War (1919), and The American Indian under Reconstruction (1925). See also Virgil L. Baker, "Albert Pike: Citizen Speechmaker of Arkansas," Ark. Hist. Quart., X, 138–156 (Summer, 1951), reprinted from So. Speech Jour. for March, 1951, James R. Masterson, Tall Tales of Arkansas (1942), pp. 281–287, and Eugene Nolte, "The Plagiarism of an Albert Pike Poem ['Every Year']," Ark. Hist. Quart., XII, 1–7 (Spring, 1953).

The sketch in R. W. Griswold, The Poets and Poetry of America is based on a letter from Pike, now in the Griswold Collection (Boston Public Library). Pike contributed much material, including an autobiographical sketch, to John Hallum, Biographical and Pictorial History of Arkansas, I (Albany, 1887), 215–221. The library in the Scottish Rite Masonic Temple in Washington contains a copy of Hallum's book with corrections in Pike's handwriting. In 1886 Pike dictated at greater length his reminiscences (MS in the Temple library); most of these were published in the New Age Mag., Vols. XXXVII and XXXVIII (1929–1930).

William L. Boyden, Librarian of the Supreme Council 33°, published a Bibliography of the Writings of Albert Pike (Washington, 1921), based chiefly upon materials in the library. See also Susan B. Riley, The Life and Works of Albert Pike to 1860. The Scottish Rite library has a typewritten copy of Miss Riley's "Poems by Albert Pike Not Found in His Collected Works Compiled from Magazines, Newspapers, Manuscripts, and Miscellaneous Sources." Miss Riley gives the texts of sixty-one poems not mentioned in Boyden's fairly inclusive Bibliography.

Manuscripts in the Scottish Rite Temple library include "Vocabularies of Indian Languages," collected in 1857 and 1861, and five volumes of "Essays."

The twenty-eight essays, written with a goosequill pen, were addressed to the sculptress Vinnie Ream (later Mrs. Hoxie). "Of Self-Education," "Of Wrecks and Waifs in Poetry," and "Of My Books and Studies" throw light upon Pike's literary tastes and scholarly interests as well as his philosophy of life. They were apparently written in Washington before 1880.

The only book that Pike himself formally published is *Prose Sketches and Poems, Written in the Western Country* (Boston, 1834). He did, however, reprint many of his poems, with some revision, for private distribution in *Nugae* (Philadelphia, 1854) and *Hymns to the Gods and Other Poems* ([New York], 1873). One of the 150 copies of *Nugae* was reviewed in *Knickerbocker Mag.*, XLIV, 81–84 (July, 1854). Since Pike's death his poems have been republished in Little Rock by Fred W. Allsopp in three volumes edited by Pike's daughter, Mrs. Lilian Pike Roome: *Gen. Albert Pike's Poems* (1900), *Hymns to the Gods and Other Poems* (1916), and *Lyrics and Love Songs* (1916). Pike's *Lectures of the Arya* (Louisville, 1930) was published by the Scottish Rite Supreme Council. His "Anecdotes of the Arkansas Bar," which first appeared in the *Spirit of the Times*, was republished in W. T. Porter (ed.), *The Big Bear of Arkansas* (1845), pp. 158–163. "The Walking Gentleman" essays were published in *Knickerbocker*, XXV, 209–215 (March, 1845); XXVII, 140–144, 230–237, 398–404 (Feb., March, April, 1846). The Index identifies these as Pike's. For these essays he drew upon a series of eleven essays published under the same title in the *Arkansas Advocate*, in 1834. The Library of Congress has many early numbers of the *Advocate*.

Edward Coote Pinkney

The standard work is *The Life and Works of Edward Coote Pinkney: A Memoir and Complete Text of His Poems and Literary Prose* . . . (1926), ed. Thomas Ollive Mabbott and Frank Lester Pleadwell. See also C. H. Ross, "Edward Coate Pinkney," *Sewanee Rev.*, IV, 287–298 (May, 1896); W. F. Melton, "Edward Coote Pinkney," *S.A.Q.*, XI, 328–336 (Oct., 1912), which first established the correct spelling of the poet's middle name; J. P. Simmons, "Edward Coote Pinkney—American Cavalier Poet," *ibid.*, XXVIII, 406–418 (Oct., 1929); and F. W. P. Greenwood's review of Pinkney's *Poems* in *No. Am. Rev.*, XXI, 369–376 (Oct., 1825). The sketch of Pinkney in Griswold's *The Poets and Poetry of America* (1842) was probably written by Poe's friend Frederick William Thomas (J. L. Neu, "Rufus Wilmot Griswold," Univ. of Tex. *Studies in English*, No. 5, 1925, p. 118). F. L. Mott in *A History of American Magazines*, Vol. I, between pp. 408 and 409, reproduces from the *New-York Mirror* of Jan. 26, 1828, portraits of nine American poets, of whom Pinkney was one.

John Neal's description of William Pinkney appears in *Randolph, A Novel* (n.p., 1823), II, 235–244. William Wirt regarded it as an accurate portrait, but it seems to me so offensive that I do not wonder that young Pinkney resented it. In Neal's *Wandering Recollections of a Somewhat Busy Life* (1869), p. 238, Neal states that he used the challenge to a duel in his next novel, *Errata* (1823).

Edgar Allan Poe

There are good working bibliographies of Poe in *L.H.U.S.*, III, 689–696; Margaret Alterton and Hardin Craig (eds.), *Edgar Allan Poe: Representative Selections* (1935), pp. cxix–cxxxiii; Arthur H. Quinn, *Edgar Allan Poe: A Critical Biography* (1941), pp. 763–770; and Quinn and E. H. O'Neill (eds.), *The Complete Poems and Stories of Edgar Allan Poe, with Selections from His Critical Writings* (1946), II, 1089–1092. The best edition is *The Complete Works of Edgar Allan Poe* (17 vols., 1903), ed. James A. Harrison; but it has long been out of print and it omits writings, chiefly reviews, known to be Poe's and includes some reviews now known to have been written by other hands. See William Doyle Hull, "A Canon of the Critical Works of Edgar Allan Poe" (Univ. of Va. dissertation, 1941).

For Poe's Southern background, see Agnes Bondurant, *Poe's Richmond* (1942), a Duke master's thesis which occasioned the essay on "Mr. Ritchie's Richmond" in James Branch Cabell's *Let Me Lie* (1947); Charles W. Kent, "Poe's Student Days at the University of Virginia," *Bookman*, XIII, 430–440 (July, 1901); E. A. Alderman, "Edgar Allan Poe and the University of Virginia," *Va. Quart. Rev.*, I, 78–84 (April, 1925); and P. A. Bruce, "Background of Poe's University Life," *S.A.Q.*, X, 212–226 (July, 1911) and *History of the University of Virginia* (5 vols., 1920–1922), see Index; J. C. French, "Poe's Literary Baltimore," *Md. Hist. Mag.*, XXXIII, 101–112 (June, 1937) and "Poe and the Baltimore *Saturday Visiter*," *Mod. Lang. Notes*, XXXIII, 257–267 (May, 1918); J. S. Wilson, "The Young Man Poe," *Va. Quart. Rev.*, II, 238–253 (April, 1926); Killis Campbell, "Poe's Treatment of the Negro and of Negro Dialect," Univ. of Tex. *Studies in English*, No. XVI, 107–114 (1936), "Poe's Reading," *ibid.*, No. V, 166–196 (1925) and No. VII, 175–180 (1927); Jay B. Hubbell, "Poe's Mother With a Note on John Allan," *W.M.Q.*, 2nd ser. XXI, 250–254 (July, 1941) and " 'O Tempora! O, Mores!' A Juvenile Poem by Edgar Allan Poe," Univ. of Colo. *Studies*, ser. B, II, 314–321 (Oct., 1945); W. S. Hoole, "Poe in Charleston, S. C.," *Am. Lit.*, VI, 78–80 (March, 1934); David K. Jackson, *Poe and the Southern Literary Messenger* (Richmond, 1934), originally a Duke Univ. master's thesis; Sidney P. Moss, "Poe and the *Norman Leslie* Incident," *Am. Lit.*, XXV, 293–306 (Nov., 1953); John Hill Hewitt, *Recollections of Poe* (Emory Univ. Library, 1949), ed. R. B. Harwell; and R. B. Davis, "Poe and William Wirt," *Am. Lit.*, X, 331–339 (Nov., 1939) [the "Letter from Mr. Wirt to a Law Student," *S.L.M.*, I, 33–36 (Oct., 1834), which Miss Alterton thought was addressed to Poe, was actually written to H. W. Miller of the Univ. of N. C.].

Some important recent works are Carroll D. Laverty, "Science and Pseudo-Science in the Writings of Edgar Allan Poe" (Duke Univ. dissertation, 1951); J. B. Reece, "Poe and the New York Literati" (Duke Univ. dissertation, 1954); Albert J. Lubell, "Edgar Allan Poe, Critic and Reviewer" (New York Univ. dissertation, 1950); Allan G. Halline, "Moral and Religious Concepts in Poe," Bucknell Univ. Studies, II (1950), 126-150; Nelson F. Adkins, " 'Chapter on American Cribbage': Poe and Plagiarism," Papers Bibliog. Soc. Am., XLII, 169-210 (3rd quart., 1948); and N. B. Fagin, The Histrionic Mr. Poe (1949), which labors its thesis very hard. A better appraisal of Poe is found in Haldeen Braddy, Glorious Incense: The Fulfillment of Edgar Allan Poe (1953), which has a good selective bibliography. I am preparing the chapter on Poe for a bibliographical guide to eight major American writers, sponsored by the American Literature Group of the Modern Language Association.

Margaret Junkin Preston

The fullest source of information is The Life and Letters of Margaret Junkin Preston (1903), by her stepdaughter Elizabeth Preston Allan. James A. Harrison's "Margaret J. Preston: An Appreciation" is given in an Appendix. See also Janie M. Baskervill's essay in Southern Writers: Second Series (1903), pp. 23–42; La Salle Corbell Pickett, Literary Hearthstones of Dixie (1912), pp. 253–279; Charles W. Hubner (ed.), Representative Southern Poets (1906), pp. 148–165; and Marshall W. Fishwick, "Margaret Junkin Preston: Virginia Poetess," Commonwealth, XVIII, 13–14 (July, 1951). The Hayne MSS in the Duke Univ. Library contain most of the many letters which passed between Mrs. Preston and Paul Hamilton Hayne.

James Ryder Randall

John C. French wrote the sketch in D.A.B. The first collection of Randall's poems appeared in the year he died: Maryland, My Maryland and Other Poems (Baltimore, 1908). For Randall's various accounts of the writing of the famous song, see Brander Matthews, "The Songs of the War," Century, XXXIV, 619–629 (Aug., 1887), reprinted in his Pen and Ink (1902); Francis F. Browne (ed.), Bugle-Echoes (1886), p. 24; J. C. Derby, Fifty Years among Authors, Books and Publishers (1884), pp. 662–665; Matthew Page Andrews' Introduction to The Poems of James Ryder Randall (New York, 1910); Andrews' The Women of the South in War Times (Baltimore, 1920), pp. 66–69; and his sketch of Randall in The Library of Southern Literature. See also Mrs. Burton Harrison, Recollections Grave and Gay (1911), pp. 57–60 and J. E. Uhler, "James Ryder Randall in Louisiana," La. Hist. Quart., XXI, 532–546 (April, 1938).

Innes Randolph

There is a brief biographical sketch in the Preface to Randolph's *Poems* (Baltimore, 1898), presumably written by his son Harold, in whose name the book was copyrighted. For Randolph's relations with Lanier, see Lanier, *Writings* (Centennial ed.), especially Vols. VII and IX; consult Index. Thomas Cooper De Leon gives some account of Randolph in his *Four Years in Rebel Capitals* (1890), p. 311, and *Belles, Beaux and Brains of the 60's* (1907, 1909). De Leon praised highly Randolph's narrative poem, "Torchwork: A Tale of the Shenandoah," which appeared in De Leon's Baltimore magazine, the *Cosmopolite*, I, 40–46 (Jan., 1866). The Harvard, New York Public, and Brown University libraries have copies of *The Grasshopper; A Tragic Cantata*, by Innes Randolph, illustrated by A. I. Volck . . . (Baltimore, 1878). The *So. Opinion* of Richmond, Sept. 19, 1868, printed an anonymous imitation of "The Good Old Rebel" under the title "I'm a Gay Old Carpet-Bagger. Comic Song for the Present Times in Richmond."

John Randolph of Roanoke

The standard biography is W. C. Bruce, *John Randolph of Roanoke* (2 vols., 1922). There is an excellent brief sketch by William E. Stokes, Jr., in his and Francis L. Berkeley, Jr.'s *The Papers of Randolph of Roanoke: A Preliminary Checklist* . . . (Charlottesville, Va., 1950), pp. 9–19. Of some value is H. A. Garland, *The Life of John Randolph of Roanoke* (2 vols., 1850), reviewed very unfavorably by Beverley Tucker in *S.Q.R.*, n.s. IV, 41–61 (July, 1851). See also Hugh Blair Grigsby, "The Randolph Library," *S.L.M.*, XX, 76–79 (Feb., 1854) and Anon., "Letters of John Randolph, of Roanoke, to General Thomas Marsh Forman," *Va. Mag.*, XLIX, 201–216 (July, 1941). For Randolph's relations with Key, see E. S. Delaplaine, *Francis Scott Key: Life and Times* (1937). For his friendship with Gilmer, see Richard Beale Davis, *Francis Walker Gilmer* (1939), Part III, chap. iii.

The best and most recent study of Randolph's ideas is Russell Kirk, *Randolph of Roanoke: A Study in Conservative Thought* (1951), which has a good Select Bibliography, pp. 177–183. For descriptions of Randolph, see Francis W. Gilmer, *Sketches, Essays, and Translations* (2nd ed.; Baltimore, 1828); Frederick W. Thomas, *John Randolph, of Roanoke, and Other Sketches of Character* . . . (1853); W. I. Paulding, *Literary Life of James K. Paulding* (1867), pp. 237–243; Thomas H. Benton, *Thirty Years' View* (1854), I, 473–475; and Claude G. Bowers, *Jefferson in Power* (1936), chap v. An earlier study is Joseph G. Baldwin, *Party Leaders* (1855), pp. 135–276. See also Mary H. Coleman, "Whittier on John Randolph of Roanoke," *New Eng. Quart.*, VIII, 551–555 (Dec., 1935).

958   BIBLIOGRAPHY

Abram Joseph Ryan

Richard J. Purcell wrote the sketch in the *D.A.B.* See also the Memoir by
John Moran in the 12th ed. of Ryan's *Poems* (Baltimore, 1888) and the account
by Hannis Taylor in *The Library of Southern Literature*. Ryan's *Poems: Patriotic,
Religious, Miscellaneous* first appeared in 1880. Some new poems were added
in the 11th and later eds. See also Kate White, "Father Ryan—The Poet-Priest
of the South," *S.A.Q.*, XVIII, 69–74 (Jan., 1919); Young E. Allison, "How
Father Ryan Died," *So. Bivouac*, N.S. II, 167–177 (Aug., 1886); and J. H.
Hewlett, "An Unknown Poem by Father Ryan," *Mod. Lang. Notes*, XLIV,
259–261 (April, 1929).

Janet Schaw

The only important source of information is the *Journal of a Lady of Quality;
Being the Narrative of a Journey from* SCOTLAND *to the West Indies, North
Carolina, and Portugal, in the years* 1774 *to* 1776, edited by Evangeline W.
Andrews and Charles M. Andrews. The book was published by the Yale Uni-
versity Press in 1921 and in revised editions including new materials in 1934
and 1939.

John Shaw

The chief source of information is the memoir—attributed to John E. Hall—
in *Poems by the Late Doctor John Shaw, to which is prefixed a Biographical
Sketch of the Author* (Philadelphia and Baltimore, 1810). See also George H.
Genzmer's sketch in *D.A.B.* Dr. Shaw contributed to the *Port Folio*, often using
the pen name "Ithacus." For unsigned contributions, see R. C. Randall, "Authors
of the *Port Folio* Revealed by the Hall Files," *Am. Lit.*, XI, 408 (Jan., 1940).

William Gilmore Simms

W. P. Trent, *William Gilmore Simms* (1892) gives an admirable portrait
of the man, but sounder critical appraisals are to be found in V. L. Parrington,
Main Currents in American Thought, II, 125–136, and Hampton M. Jarrell,
"William Gilmore Simms: Realistic Romancer" (Duke Univ. dissertation,
1932). Much new biographical material is being made available in *The Letters
of William Gilmore Simms* (5 vols., 1952–   ), ed. Mary C. Simms Oliphant,
Alfred T. Odell, and T. C. Duncan Eaves, of which only Vols. I and II have
yet (1953) appeared. Prof. Odell published in the Furman Univ. *Bulletin* two
groups of Simms's letters: "Letters . . . to James H. Hammond," XXVI, 3–15
(May, 1943) and "William Gilmore Simms in the Post-War Years [letters to
Evert Duyckinck]," XXIX, 5–20 (May, 1946).

Bibliographical materials are given in *L.H.U.S.*, III, 720–723; Trent, *Simms*, pp. 333–342; *The Yemassee* (1937), ed. Alexander Cowie; and *Catalogue of the* [A. S.] *Salley Collection of the Works of Wm. Gilmore Simms* (Columbia, S. C., 1943). The *Catalogue* practically supersedes not only Salley's earlier bibliographies in So. History Assn. *Publications*, I, 269–295 (Oct., 1897); XI, 343–344 (Sept.–Nov., 1907) but also Oscar Wegelin's bibliography of Simms's separate publications in *Am. Book Collector*, Vol. III (1933), revised and published in book form at Hattiesburg, Miss., in 1941.

William Cullen Bryant wrote the chapter on "Woodlands" in *Homes of American Authors* (New York, 1853), which was reprinted by Elbert Hubbard, in *Little Journeys to the Homes of American Authors* (New York, 1896). See also Max L. Griffin, "Bryant and the South," *Tulane Studies in Eng.*, I (1949), 53–80. Carl Van Doren's sketch in *D.A.B.* is excellent. Other materials are to be found in: J. W. Davidson, *The Living Writers of the South* (1869), pp. 508–526; John Erskine, *Leading American Novelists* (1910), pp. 131–177; Paul H. Hayne, "Ante-bellum Charleston," *So. Bivouac*, N.S. I, 257–268 (Oct., 1885); J. W. Higham, "The Changing Loyalties of William Gilmore Simms," *Jour. So. Hist.*, IX, 210–223 (May, 1943); C. Hugh Holman, "The Influence of Scott and Cooper on Simms," *Am. Lit.*, XXIII, 203–218 (May, 1951), "William Gilmore Simms' Picture of the Revolution as a Civil Conflict," *Jour. So. Hist.*, XV, 441–462 (Nov., 1949), and "Simms and the British Dramatists," *PMLA*, LXV, 346–359 (June, 1950); W. S. Hoole, "A Note on Simms's Visits to the Southwest," *Am. Lit.*, VI, 334–336 (Nov., 1934), "William Gilmore Simms's Career as Editor," *Ga. Hist. Quart.*, XIX, 47–54 (March, 1935), and "Simms' *Michael Bonham*: A 'Forgotten' Drama of the Texas Revolution," *Southwestern Hist. Quart.*, XLVI, 225–261 (Jan., 1942); Jay B. Hubbell (ed.), *The Last Years of Henry Timrod* (1941), see Index, and "Five Letters from George Henry Boker to William Gilmore Simms," *Penn. Mag. Hist. and Biog.*, LXIII, 66–71 (Jan., 1939); Hampton M. Jarrell, "Falstaff and Simms's Porgy," *Am. Lit.*, III, 204–212 (May, 1931), "Simms's Visits to the Southwest," *ibid.*, V, 29–35 (March, 1933) [but see Hoole, *above*], and "William Gilmore Simms— Almost a Historian," *S. C. Hist. Assn. Proceedings* (1947), pp. 3–8; Albert Keiser, *The Indian in American Literature* (1933), pp. 154–174; R. I. McDavid, "*Ivanhoe* and Simms' *Vasconselos*," *Mod. Lang. Notes*, LVI, 294–297 (April, 1941); J. Allen Morris, "The Stories of William Gilmore Simms," *Am. Lit.*, XIV, 20–35 (March, 1942) and "Gullah in the Stories and Novels of William Gilmore Simms," *Am. Speech*, XXII, 46–53 (Feb., 1947); D. M. McKeithan, *A Collection of Hayne Letters* (1944), see Index; La Salle C. Pickett, *Literary Hearthstones of Dixie* (1912), pp. 125–148; A. H. Quinn, *American Fiction* (1936), pp. 114–123; J. A. Russell, "The Southwestern Border Indian in the Writings of William Gilmore Simms," *Education*, LI, 144–157 (Nov., 1930); F. W. Simpson, "William Gilmore Simms and the 'Southern Quarterly Review'" (Furman Univ. master's thesis, 1946); Randall Stewart (ed.), "Hawthorne's Contributions to the Salem Advertiser" [Simms's *Views and Reviews*], *Am. Lit.*, V, 331–332 (Jan., 1934); Edward Stone, "'Caleb Williams' and 'Martin Faber': A Contrast," *Mod. Lang. Notes*, LXII, 480–483 (Nov., 1947), a refutation of the thesis of F. H. Deen, "The Genesis of *Martin Faber* in *Caleb Williams*," *ibid.*, LIX, 315–317 (May, 1944); Carl Van Doren, *The American Novel* (revised ed., 1940), pp. 50–55; John Welsh, "The Mind of William Gilmore Simms: His Social and Political Thought" (Vanderbilt Univ. dissertation, 1951); Alfred Van R. Westfall, *American Shakespearean Criticism* (1939), pp. 137–141; Edd W. Parks, "Simms's Edition of the Shakespeare Apocrypha," *Studies in Shakespeare* (1952), pp. 30–39; Grace W. Whaley, "A Note on Simms's Novels," *Am. Lit.*, II, 173–174 (May, 1930); James G. Wilson, "Recollections of American Authors: William Gilmore Simms," *Book News Monthly*, XXX, 711–715 (June, 1912). See also Stanley T. Williams, "Spanish Influences on the Fiction of William Gilmore Simms," *Hispanic Rev.*, XXI, 221–228 (July, 1953) and J. Wesley Thomas's forthcoming article in *Am. Lit.*, "The German Sources of William Gilmore Simms."

Certain titles have been wrongly ascribed to Simms. He apparently had nothing to do with *Transatlantic Tales, Sketches, and Legends. By Various American Authors. Collected and arranged by Gilmore Simms, Esq. . . .* (London, 1842). See *Letters*, I, 346 n. *Poems of a Collegian* (1833) is by Thomas Semmes. "Sidney's" *Letters to William E. Channing* (Charleston, 1837) was written by Daniel K. Whitaker, who inscribed the Library of Congress copy: "To Prof. Geo. Bush with the respects of the author D. K. Whitaker." *Osceola; or, Fact and Fiction: A Tale of the Seminole War* (1838) is clearly not Simms's work; it has also been attributed to James Birchett Ransom and to Seymour R. Duke, in whose name it is copyrighted. *The Code of Honor: or, The Thirty-Nine Articles. . . . By a Southron* (New York and Baltimore, 1847), a handbook for duelists which claims to be written by one with considerable experience in dueling, is written in a style very different from Simms's.

Another item wrongly attributed to Simms is found in *A Pilgrimage to Salem in 1838. By a Southern Admirer of Nathaniel Hawthorne. Reprinted from "The Southern Rose"* (*Charleston, S. C.*) *of March 2 and 16, 1839, with a* Foreword *by Victor Hugo Paltsits*, Another View *by John Robinson, and* A Rejoinder *by Mr. Paltsits* (Salem, 1916). The article was actually written by Dr. Samuel Gilman, whose wife Caroline edited the *Southern Rose*. He reprinted it under the title "A Day of Disappointment in Salem" in his *Contributions to Literature* (Boston, 1856), pp. 474–496.

Except for his short stories, which are listed in J. Allen Morris's article, cited above, there is no bibliography of Simms's numerous contributions to magazines and newspapers, and most of the poems he printed after 1853 have not been republished in book form. Among his uncollected prose writings is an account of South Carolina writers published in the Charleston *XIX Century*, Vols. I and II (1869–1870), under varying titles: "Our Early Authors," etc. There are Simms MSS, chiefly letters, in the Univ. of S. C. Library; in the Hayne Collection in the Duke Univ. Library; in the Ferris Collection at Columbia Univ. (which does not contain all the MSS which were in it when Trent was preparing his life of Simms); the Griswold Collection in the Boston Public Library; in the John R. Thompson Collection at the Univ. of Virginia; the Bryant and Duyckinck collections in the New York Public Library; the Library of Congress; etc. Most of Simms's many letters from other writers were burned during the Civil War. He sold his collection of Revolutionary historical materials to the Long Island Historical Society. The Duke Univ. Library has twenty-two books which were once in Simms's library of more than ten thousand volumes.

Charles Henry Smith, "Bill Arp"

J. M. Steadman wrote the sketch in *D.A.B.* There is some biographical material by his grandson in Anon., " 'Bill Arp'—Humorist," *Tyler's Hist. and Geneal. Mag.*, XXXI, 25–33 (July, 1949); in D. W. Newsom, "Bill Arp" in *Trinity Coll. Hist. Soc. Publications* (Durham, N. C., 1910); and James E. Ginther, "Charles Henry Smith, Alias 'Bill Arp.' " *Ga. Rev.*, IV, 313–322 (Winter, 1950). For critical materials, see Jennette Tandy, *Crackerbox Philosophers* (1925); Walter Blair, *Native American Humor* (1937); and Salem Dutcher, "Bill Arp and Artemus Ward," *Scott's Monthly Mag.* (Atlanta), II, 472–478 (June, 1866). I am indebted to a Duke Univ. master's thesis by Louella Landrum: "Charles Henry Smith (Bill Arp): Georgia Humorist" (1938).

Captain John Smith

The best edition of Smith's writings is *Travels and Works of Captain John Smith . . .* , 2 vols. (1884), ed. Edward Arber, reprinted in 1910 with an Introduction and some corrections by A. G. Bradley. For Smith's various writings, see *L.H.U.S.*, III, 725–727, and Joseph Sabin and others, *Dictionary of Books Relating to America*, XX, 218–265 (collation and description by Wilberforce Eames). Of historical interest is the edition of *The True Travels* (Richmond, 1819), ed. John Holt Rice with the assistance of Francis W. Gilmer. A much better edition is that of John Gould Fletcher and Lawrence C. Wroth, published in 1930. Perhaps the best biography is John Gould Fletcher, *John Smith —Also Pocahontas* (1928). Good brief accounts are James Truslow Adams' sketch in *D.A.B.* and Samuel E. Morison's in *Builders of the Bay Colony* (1930), pp. 3–20.

The best discussion of Smith as a writer is found in Howard Mumford Jones, *The Literature of Virginia in the Seventeenth Century* (1946), pp. 16–23, but see also Moses Coit Tyler, *A History of American Literature, 1607–1765* (1878), I, 18–38.

On the question of Smith's reliability as a historian, see Jarvis M. Morse, "John Smith and His Critics: A Chapter in Colonial Historiography," *Jour. So. Hist.*, I, 123–137 (May, 1935); Henry Adams, "Captain John Smith," *No. Am. Rev.*, CIV, 1–30 (Jan., 1867); Lawrence C. Wroth's bibliographical note in *The True Travels* (1930), pp. 76–79; and Lewis L. Kropf's discussion of *The True Travels* in *Am. Hist. Rev.*, III, 737–738 (July, 1898) and in *Notes and Queries*, 7th ser. IX, 1–2, 41–43, 102–104, 161–162, 223–224 (1890). Many of the poems, novels, and plays dealing with the Smith-Pocahontas story are listed in the bibliography of Jay B. Hubbell, *Virginia Life in Fiction* (Dallas, 1922), abstract of a Columbia Univ. dissertation.

Harriet Beecher Stowe

The best and latest biography is Forrest Wilson, *Crusader in Crinoline: The Life of Harriet Beecher Stowe* (1941), but see also Annie Fields, *Life and Letters of Harriet Beecher Stowe* (1897). Charles H. Foster, *The Rungless Ladder: Harriet Beecher Stowe and New England Puritanism* (to be published by the Duke University Press in 1954) is an important critical study. For *Uncle Tom's Cabin*, see John H. Nelson, *The Negro Character in American Literature* (1926), pp. 73–81; Herbert R. Brown, *The Sentimental Novel in America* (1940), Book II, chap. iii, "Uncle Tom's and Other Cabins"; Alexander Cowie, *The Rise of the American Novel* (1948), pp. 447–463; Tremaine McDowell, "The Use of Negro Dialect by Harriet Beecher Stowe," *Am. Speech*, VI, 322–326 (June, 1931); James Lane Allen, "Mrs. Stowe's 'Uncle Tom' at Home in Kentucky," *Century*, XXXIV, 852–867 (Oct., 1887); Frances Hodgson Burnett, *The One I Knew Best of All* (1893), pp. 237–238; Julia Collier Harris (ed.), *Joel Chandler Harris: Editor and Essayist* (1931), pp. 115 ff.; Jennette R. Tandy, "Pro-Slavery Propaganda in American Fiction in the Fifties," *S.A.Q.*, XXI, 41–50, 170–178 (Jan., April, 1922); and Margaret A. Browne, "Southern Reactions to 'Uncle Tom's Cabin'" (Duke Univ. master's thesis, 1941), Louisa S. McCord's review of *Uncle Tom's Cabin* appeared in the *So. Quart. Rev.*, N.S. VII, 81–120 (Jan., 1853). There is a bibliography in *L.H.U.S.*, III, 736–738.

William Strachey

Much of my information about Strachey comes from Charles Richard Sanders, "William Strachey, the Virginia Colony, and Shakespeare," *Va. Mag.*, LVII, 115–132 (April, 1949), which gives a somewhat fuller account than appears in his *The Strachey Family* (1953). See also A. C. Gordon, Jr.'s, sketch in *D.A.B.*; Howard Mumford Jones, *The Literature of Virginia in the Seventeenth Century* (1946), pp. 5, 24–26; M. C. Tyler, *A History of American Literature*, 1607–1765 (1878), I, 41–45; and Alexander Brown, *The Genesis of the United States* (1897), II, 562–568.

For Strachey's possible influence on Shakespeare's *The Tempest*, see Sanders, *op. cit.*; G. L. Kittredge (ed.), *The Tempest* (1939), pp. xiv–xv; R. R. Cawley, "Shakespeare's Use of the Voyagers in *The Tempest*," *PMLA*, XLI, 688–726 (Sept., 1926); J. D. Rea, "A Source for the Storm in *The Tempest*," *Mod. Philol.*, XVII, 279–286 (Sept., 1919); and C. M. Gayley, *Shakespeare and the Founders of Liberty in America* (1917), pp. 53–69.

Wilkins Tannehill

Tannehill is mentioned in the Duyckincks' *Cyclopaedia of American Literature* (1855), II, 665, in connection with his nephew, Charles Wilkins Webber [for Webber, see Henry Nash Smith, *Virgin Land*, 1950, pp. 72–77]; *A Library of Southern Literature*, XV, 425; *History of Nashville, Tennessee* (1890), by several hands; W. W. Clayton, *History of Davidson County, Tennessee* (1880), pp. 232, 233; W. T. Hale and D. L. Merritt, *A History of Tennessee* (1913), II, 445–448; and in the *Tenn. Hist. Quart.*, III, 197–200 (Sept., 1944). Tannehill's name does not appear in the index to F. Garvin Davenport, *Cultural Life in Nashville, on the Eve of the Civil War* (1941). See also Clarence Gohdes, "Some Notes on the Unitarian Church in the Ante-bellum South," *American Studies in Honor of William Kenneth Boyd* (1940), p. 330.

Tannehill's *Sketches* was reviewed in the *Critic*, I, 380–382 (April 18, 1829); *Quart. Jour. and Rev.*, I, 302–319 (Oct., 1846); and *Hesperian*, II, 172 (Dec., 1838), which also published Tannehill's "Literature of the Moors of Spain," II, 102–108 (Dec., 1838). For the passage in my text quoted from the *Western Monthly Mag.* for Sept., 1834, see II, 497.

Tannehill is said to have published in Nashville in 1846 *Sketches of the History of Roman Literature*, which I have been unable to find. According to Clayton, *op. cit.*, p. 233: "He wrote a second edition of his 'History of Literature.' The manuscript (two volumes, folio) was delivered to the State Historical Society after his death." The Lawson McGhee Library in Knoxville has a copy of a juvenile book ascribed to Tannehill: *Tales of the Revolution. By a Young Gentleman of Nashville* (Nashville, 1833).

John Taylor of Caroline

The only book-length biography is that of Henry H. Simms (1932). See also Avery Craven's sketch in *D.A.B.* and "The Agricultural Reformers of the Antebellum South," *Am. Hist. Review*, XXXIII, 302–314 (Jan., 1928); William D. Grampp, "John Taylor: Economist of Southern Agrarianism," *So. Economic Jour.*, XI, 255–268 (Jan., 1945). Important studies of Taylor's thought are B. F. Wright, "The Philosopher of Jeffersonian Democracy," *Polit. Sci. Rev.*, XXII, 870–892 (Nov., 1928); Eugene T. Mudge, *The Social Philosophy of John Taylor of Caroline* (1939); Charles A. Beard, *Economic Origins of Jeffer-*

sonian Democracy (1915), chap. xii; William E. Dodd, "John Taylor, of Caroline, Prophet of Secession," *Branch Hist. Papers*, II, 214–252 (June, 1908); A. N. Lytle, "John Taylor and the Political Economy of Agriculture," *Am. Rev.*, III, 432–447, 630–643 (Sept., Oct., 1934) and IV, 84–99 (Nov., 1934); and Bernard Drell, "John Taylor of Caroline and the Preservation of an Old Social Order," *Va. Mag.*, XLVI, 285–298 (Oct., 1938). There is an important chapter in V. L. Parrington, *Main Currents in American Thought*, II, 14–19. In 1950 the Yale University Press published a new edition of Taylor's *An Inquiry into the Principles and Policy of the Government of the United States*, with an Introduction by Roy F. Nichols.

John R. Thompson

The fullest accounts of Thompson's life are found in the biographical introduction to *Poems of John R. Thompson* (1920), ed. J. S. Patton and a Univ. of Va. dissertation by J. Roddey Miller, Jr. (1930). Among the Thompson MSS in the Univ. of Va. Library is the manuscript of *Across the Atlantic*, of which the entire edition was destroyed by fire. An instalment of Thompson's European diary was published by R. H. Stoddard in *Lippincott's*, XLII, 697–708 (Nov., 1888). James Grant Wilson published four instalments of "John R. Thompson and His London Diary, 1864–5" in the *Criterion* (photostats in the Thompson MSS). Among the Thompson MSS are copies of letters made for John S. Patton from materials in other collections. There is a good brief account of Thompson's last years in Allan Nevins, *The Evening Post* (1922), pp. 407–441. See also Jay B. Hubbell (ed.), *The Last Years of Henry Timrod* (1941), pp. 70–74; David K. Jackson (ed.), "Some Unpublished Letters of John R. Thompson and Augustin Louis Taveau," W.M.Q., 3rd ser. XVI, 206–221 (April, 1936); and Mrs. Burton Harrison, *Recollections Grave and Gay* (1916), pp. 119–124.

William Tappan Thompson

The best account of Thompson is Henry Prentice Miller, "The Background and Significance of *Major Jones's Courtship*," *Ga. Hist. Quart.*, XXX, 267–296 (Dec., 1946), based upon his Univ. of Chicago dissertation, "The Life and Works of William Tappan Thompson" (1942). In "The Authorship of *The Slaveholder Abroad*," *Jour. So. Hist.*, X, 92–94 (Feb., 1944), Miller points out that not Thompson but Ebenezer Starves was the author. See also Walter Blair, *Native American Humor* (1937); Jennette Tandy, *Crackerbox Philosophers* (1925); Bertram H. Flanders, *Early Georgia Magazines* (1944); C. P. Lamar in *A Library of Southern Literature*, XII, 5283–5286; S. A. Link, *Pioneers of Southern Literature*, II, 525–533; and Maurice Thompson, "An Old Southern Humorist," *Independent*, L, 1103–1105 (Oct. 20, 1898).

Francis Orray Ticknor

Ticknor's middle name—*Orray* and not *Orrery*—is frequently misspelled. The best published account of Ticknor's life and work is Sarah Cheney, "Francis Orray Ticknor," *Ga. Hist. Quart.*, XXII, 138–159 (June, 1938), a condensation of her Duke Univ. master's thesis. There are two editions of Ticknor's poems, both published after his death: *The Poems of Frank O. Ticknor, M.D.* (Philadelphia, 1879), ed. K. M. R. [Kate Mason Rowland], with an Introductory Notice of the Author by Paul H. Hayne, and *The Poems of Francis Orray Ticknor* (New York, 1911), ed. Michelle Cutliff Ticknor. The second edition, though not complete, includes more poems than the first. Ticknor's letters to Hayne are in the Duke Univ. Library.

Henry Timrod

There is no adequate biography, but see Henry T. Thompson, *Henry Timrod: Laureate of the Confederacy* (Columbia, S. C., 1928); Virginia P. Clare, *Harp of the South* (Oglethorpe Univ. Press, 1936); G. A. Wauchope, *Henry Timrod: Man and Poet* (Univ. of S. C. *Bulletin*, April, 1915); and the biographical sketches prefixed to the two collections of Timrod's poems: *The Poems of Henry Timrod* (New York, 1873), ed. Paul Hamilton Hayne, and *The Poems of Henry Timrod* (Boston, 1899; Richmond, 1901), sponsored by The Timrod Memorial Association. There is a brief bibliography in *L.H.U.S.*, III, 747–748.

The Uncollected Poems of Henry Timrod (Univ. of Ga. Press, 1942), ed. Guy A. Cardwell, Jr., is made up chiefly of early poems. Timrod's critical prose is reprinted in *The Essays of Henry Timrod* (Univ. of Ga. Press, 1942), ed. Edd W. Parks. *The Last Years of Henry Timrod* (Duke Univ. Press, 1941), ed. Jay B. Hubbell, contains some uncollected poems and editorials, some letters of Timrod, and letters about him by Simms, Whittier, John R. Thompson, and others, drawn chiefly from the Paul Hamilton Hayne MSS in the Duke Univ. Library. Prof. T. C. Duncan Eaves has discovered evidence that Timrod's letter to Hayne, dated March 7, 1866 (p. 51), was actually written one year later.

Other materials of varying importance are to be found in W. P. Trent, *William Gilmore Simms* (1892); D. M. McKeithan (ed.), *A Collection of Hayne Letters* (1944), see Index; John Dickson Bruns, "A Lecture on Timrod," Charleston *Sunday News*, April 30, 1899; Guy A. Cardwell, Jr., "The Date of Henry Timrod's Birth," *Am. Lit.*, VII, 207–208 (May, 1935); William Fidler, "Henry Timrod: Poet of the Confederacy," *S.L.M.*, n.s. II, 527–532 (Oct., 1940), "Unpublished Letters of Henry Timrod [to Rachel Lyons]," *ibid.*, II, 532–535, 605–611, 645–651 (Oct., Nov., Dec., 1940), and "Seven Unpublished Letters of Henry Timrod," *Ala. Rev.*, II, 139–149 (April, 1949); T. O. Mabbott, "Some Letters of Henry Timrod," *Am. Collector*, III, 191–195 (Feb., 1927); Walter

Hines Page, "Henry Timrod," *South-Atlantic* (Wilmington, N. C.), I, 359–367 (March, 1878); Burton J. Hendrick, *The Earlier Life and Letters of Walter Hines Page* (1928), pp. 325–328; Edd W. Parks, "Timrod's College Days," *Am. Lit.*, VIII, 294–296 (Nov., 1936) and "Timrod's Concept of Dreams," *S.A.Q.*, XLVIII, 584–588 (Oct., 1949); Lewis Patton, "An Unpublished Poem by Henry Timrod," *Am. Lit.*, X, 222–223 (May, 1938); Henry E. Shepherd and A. S. Salley, Jr., "Henry Timrod: Literary Estimate and Bibliography," So. History Assn. *Publications*, III, 274–280 (Oct., 1899); M. B. Seigler, "Henry Timrod and Sophie Sosnowski," *Ga. Hist. Quart.*, XXXI, 172–180 (Sept., 1947); Rupert Taylor, "Henry Timrod's Ancestress, Hannah Caesar," *Am. Lit.*, IX, 419–430 (Jan., 1938); L. Frank Tooker, "Henry Timrod, the Poet," *Century*, XXXIII, 932–934 (April, 1898); and G. P. Voigt, "Timrod's Essays in Literary Criticism," *Am. Lit.*, VI, 163–167 (May, 1934), "New Light on Timrod's 'Memorial Ode,' " *ibid.*, IV, 395–396 (Jan., 1933), and "Timrod in the Light of Newly Revealed Letters," *S.A.Q.*, XXXVII, 263–269 (July, 1938). Lizette Woodworth Reese's sonnet, "Timrod," appeared in *Atlantic Monthly*, LXXXV, 138 (Jan., 1900).

A brief sketch of William Henry Timrod and five of his poems are found in *The Poems of Henry Timrod* (New York, 1873), ed. Paul Hamilton Hayne. See also Guy A. Cardwell, Jr., "William Henry Timrod, the Charleston Volunteers, and the Defense of St. Augustine," *N. C. Hist. Rev.*, XVIII, 27–37 (Jan., 1941); William Gilmore Simms, "Early Writers of South Carolina," *XIX Century* (Charleston), II, 695–697 (Feb., 1870); and Jay B. Hubbell, *The Last Years of Henry Timrod* (1941), pp. 165–178. The Charleston Library Society has a copy of the rare volume, *Poems, on Various Subjects* (Charleston, 1814). Two portions of what seems an otherwise lost poetic drama are found in *So. Lit. Jour.*, I, 270–273 (Dec., 1835) and *So. Rose*, V, 200 (Aug., 1837).

(Nathaniel) Beverley Tucker

Carl Bridenbaugh wrote the sketch in *D.A.B.* and the introduction to the "Americana Deserta" series edition of Tucker's *The Partisan Leader* (1933). See also Mary Haldane Coleman, *St. George Tucker* (Richmond, 1938) and *Virginia Silhouettes* (Richmond, 1934); John D. Allen, *Philip Pendleton Cooke* (1942); J. F. McDermott, "Nathaniel Beverley Tucker in Missouri," *W.M.Q.*, 2nd ser. XX, 504–507 (Oct., 1940); Maude H. Woodfin, "Nathaniel Beverley Tucker: His Writings and Political Theories; with a Sketch of His Life," *Richmond College Historical Papers*, II, 9–42 (June, 1917); E. A. and G. L. Duyckinck, *A Cyclopaedia of American Literature* (1855), I, 665–666 [contains a letter from Simms]; "Correspondence of Judge Tucker" [letters to Tucker], *W.M.Q.*, 1st ser. XII, 84–96, 142–155 (Oct., 1903, and Jan., 1904). For Tucker's correspondence with Simms, see *The Letters of William Gilmore Simms* (5 Vols., 1952–   ) and W. P. Trent, *William Gilmore Simms* (1892).

The best source of information that I have found is Noma Lee Goodwin, "The Published Works of Nathaniel Beverley Tucker" (Duke Univ. master's thesis, 1947). Miss Goodwin examined the Tucker Papers in the Library of Congress and the Tucker-Coleman Papers in the Research Department, Colonial Williamsburg, Inc. Her bibliography of Tucker's writings includes among items in *S.L.M.* not previously attributed to Tucker two reviews of Dickens, III, 323–325 and 525–532 (May and Sept., 1837) and a review of P. P. Cooke's *Froissart Ballads*, XIII, 437–441 (July, 1847). The review of Manzoni's *I Promessi Sposi*, which appeared in *S.L.M.*, I, 520–522 (May, 1835) and which is reprinted in the Virginia ed. of Poe's *Works*, VIII, 12–19, is almost certainly Tucker's and not Poe's. The reviewer's estimates of Bulwer-Lytton and Lady Blessington and the slurs at women in public life are far more characteristic of Tucker than of Poe.

For Tucker's relations with Poe, see J. S. Wilson (ed.), "Unpublished Letters of Edgar Allan Poe," *Century*, CVII, 652–656 (March, 1924), and biographies of Poe by A. H. Quinn, J. A. Harrison, and Hervey Allen.

George Tucker

There is no biography of Tucker. Broadus Mitchell's sketch in *D.A.B.* makes too little of his literary work. R. L. Harrison wrote the sketch in *A Library of Southern Literature*. Of some biographical value are Robley Dunglison, *An Obituary Notice of Professor George Tucker*, reprinted from Am. Philos. Soc. *Proceedings*, IX, 64–70; P. A. Bruce, *History of the University of Virginia*, see Index; and Douglass Sherley, "Our University. II, George Tucker . . . ," *Va. Univ. Mag.*, XIX, 539–574 (June, 1880). Bruce seems to have read an unpublished autobiographical sketch, parts of which were read to Sherley by one of Tucker's daughters. See also two articles in the Univ. of Va. *Alumni Bulletin:* H. P. Johnson, "The First Chairman of Our Faculty as an Essayist," IX, 520–524 (Oct., 1916), and T. R. Snavely, "George Tucker as an Economist," XVI, 109–130 (April, 1923). In her *Retrospect of Western Travel* (1838), pp. 202–208, Harriet Martineau expressed her delight in Tucker's "lively, sensible, and earnest conversation." She lists the textbooks which he was using in 1835.

Tucker's *Essays on Various Subjects of Taste, Morals, and National Policy* (Georgetown, D. C., 1822) was reviewed by Edward Everett in *No. Am. Rev.*, XVI, 45–58 (Jan., 1823). Some discussion of Tucker's literary writings is found in Leonard C. Helderman's two articles: "A Social Scientist of the Old South," *Jour. So. Hist.*, II, 148–174 (May, 1936), and "A Satirist in Old Virginia," *Am. Scholar*, VI, 481–497 (Autumn, 1937). Tucker's part in *The Rainbow* is discussed in Jay B. Hubbell, "William Wirt and the Familiar Essay in Virginia," *W.M.Q.*, 2nd ser. XXIII, 136–152 (April, 1943). See also J. W. Wayland, "The Virginia Literary Museum," *Publications* of So. History Assn., VI, 1–14 (Jan., 1902). The *Museum* published a series of articles entitled "Americanisms," probably by Tucker, which were reprinted in *The Beginnings of American English* (1931), ed. M. M. Mathews, chap. ix.

For Tucker's economic writings, see J. J. Spengler, "Population Doctrines in the United States," *Jour. Polit. Ec.*, XLI, 435–437, 648–654 (Aug. and Oct., 1933); J. R. Turner, *The Ricardian Rent Theory in Early American Economics* (1921), chap. v, "George Tucker"; and Joseph Dorfman, *The Economic Mind in American Civilization* (1946), II, 539–551. See also Michael Kraus, *A History of American History* (1937), pp. 257–260, and Merle Curti, *The Growth of American Thought* (1951), pp. 441–442.

The earliest of Tucker's publications that I have seen is his *Letter to a Member of the General Assembly of Virginia, on the subject of the Late Conspiracy of the Slaves; with a Proposal for Their Colonization* (Baltimore, 1801); copy in possession of the Charleston Library Society. This seems to be a second edition of a pamphlet first published in Richmond. Tucker published in Richmond newspapers over the pseudonym "Hickory Cornhill" some widely read verses attacking the game of loo, then extremely popular in Richmond (Samuel Mordecai, *Richmond in By-Gone Days*, Richmond, 1856, pp. 194–197). Among the writings that I have not discussed are Tucker's *Memoir of . . . John P. Emmet, M.D.* (Philadelphia, 1845) and *America and the West Indies, Geographically Described* (London, 1841, 1845), by George Long, George Richardson Porter, and George Tucker. In the Preface it is stated that Tucker wrote chap. xi, "United States of North America," pp. 198–352. P. A. Bruce, *op. cit.*, II, 23, mentions as Tucker's last production some unpublished verses entitled "Pleasures Left to Old Age." There are many uncollected magazine articles, chiefly on economic subjects.

Nathaniel and St. George Tucker

Lewis Leary's brief monograph, *The Literary Career of Nathaniel Tucker, 1750–1807* (Durham, N. C., 1951) is based chiefly upon the Tucker-Coleman MSS on deposit at Colonial Williamsburg, Inc. See also Leary's "Introducing Nathaniel Tucker," *Bermuda Hist. Quart.*, IV, 132–136 (July–Sept., 1947) and "The Published Writings of Nathaniel Tucker, 1750–1807," *Bulletin of Bibliog.*, XX, 5–6 (Jan.–April, 1950). *The Bermudian* was reprinted in *Am. Museum*, VI, 254–260 (Sept., 1789).

The only biography of the younger Tucker is Mary Haldane Coleman, *St. George Tucker: Citizen of No Mean City* (Richmond, 1938), which gives little information about Tucker's writings. Mrs. Coleman edited *Virginia Silhouettes: Contemporary Letters concerning Negro Slavery in the State of Virginia* (Richmond, 1934), which includes letters by Tucker and his son Beverley. In this volume Mrs. Coleman republished, from a copy corrected by the author, *Tucker's A Dissertation on Slavery . . .* (Philadelphia, 1796).

Additional materials are: A. M. Dobie's sketch in *D.A.B.*; Charles W. Coleman, "St. Mémin Portraits: St. George Tucker," *Mag. of Am. Hist.*, VII, 217–221 (Sept., 1881); Mrs. George P. Coleman (ed.), "Randolph and Tucker Letters," *Va. Mag.*, XLII, 129–131, 211–221 (Jan., April, 1934); XLIII, 41–46 (Jan., 1935) [the second instalment includes a long autobiographical sketch]; J. Randolph Tucker, "The Judges Tucker of the Court of Appeals of Virginia," *Va. Law Register*, I, 789–812 (March, 1896); S. S. Patteson, "The Supreme Court of Appeals of Virginia, Part I," *Green Bag*, V, 320–322 (July, 1893); Sallie E. Marshall Hardy, "Some Virginia Lawyers of the Past and Present," *Green Bag*, X, 57–58 (Feb., 1898); H. St. George Tucker, "Patrick Henry and St. George Tucker," *Univ. of Penn. Law Rev.*, LXVII, 69–74 (Jan., 1919); and R. M. Hughes, "Belles of Williamsburg," *W.M.Q.*, 1st ser. X, 172 (April, 1930).

George Washington

The best edition of Washington's *Writings* is that edited by John C. Fitzpatrick (41 vols., 1931–1944). Saxe Commins has included the best materials in his one-volume *Basic Writings of George Washington* (1948). The late Douglas S. Freeman published five volumes of what promised to be a definitive biography. A sixth is to be published in 1954. See also James H. Penniman, *George Washington as Man of Letters* (1918); Paul L. Ford, *Washington and the Theatre* (1899); and Stuart P. Sherman, "George Washington as a Diarist," *Critical Woodcuts* (1926), pp. 296–310.

For Washington's literary role, see William A. Bryan, *George Washington in American Literature, 1775–1865* (1952); Burton E. Stevenson (ed.), *Great Americans as Seen by the Poets* (1933); and Dixon Wecter, *The Hero in America* (1941). Bryan's article, "George Washington, Symbolic Guardian of the Republic," *W.M.Q.*, 3rd ser. VII, 53–63 (Jan., 1950), points out how differently, in the years immediately preceding the Civil War, North and South interpreted the life and political opinions of Washington.

Mason Locke Weems

Lawrence C. Wroth, *Parson Weems* (1911) is a good brief biography. The factual matter in Harold Kellock, *Parson Weems of the Cherry-Tree* (1928) is nearly all taken from Wroth; see Verner W. Crane's review in *Am. Lit.*, I, 330–331 (Nov., 1929). See also Mrs. Emily E. F. Skeel's sketch in *D.A.B.* and her important *Mason Locke Weems: His Works and Ways* (3 vols., 1929). Vol. I is a biography begun by her brother, Paul Leicester Ford; Vols. II and III are a collection of Weems's letters, chiefly to Mathew Carey. In 1929 Mrs. Skeel republished under the title *Three Discourses* three of Weems's most interesting pamphlets: *Hymen's Recruiting Sergeant, God's Revenge against Adultery*, and *The Drunkard's Looking Glass*. See also Mrs. Roswell Skeel, Jr., "Mason Locke Weems: A Postscript," *New Colophon*, III, 243–249 (1950).

There are some Weems letters in William Gilmore Simms's excellent essay, "Weems, the Biographer and Historian," *Views and Reviews, Second Series* (New York, 1845), pp. 123–141. For Weems's *Life of Washington*, see William A. Bryan, *George Washington in American Literature, 1775–1865* (1952), especially pp. 92–96, and two articles by Bryan: "Three Unpublished Letters of Parson Weems," *W.M.Q.*, 2nd ser. XXIII, 272–277 (July, 1943) and "The Genesis of Weems' 'Life of Washington,'" *Americana*, XXXVI, 147–165 (April, 1942). Other materials will be found in: C. A. Ingrahim, "Mason Locke Weems: A Great American Author and Distributor of Books," *Americana*, XXV, 469–485 (Oct., 1931); A. Edward Newton, "Parson Weems's Washington Once More," *Colophon*, N.S. I, 367–370 (Winter, 1936); and James S. Purcell, Jr., "A Book Pedlar's Progress in North Carolina," *N. C. Hist. Rev.*, XXIX, 8–23 (Jan., 1952).

Williams Charles Wells

R. H. Shryock wrote the sketch in *D.A.B.* See also "Memoir of William Charles Wells, M.D.," *Gentleman's Mag.*, LXXXVII, 467–471 (Nov., 1817) and Elisha Bartlett, *A Brief Sketch of the Life, Character, and Writings of William Charles Wells . . .* (Louisville, Ky., 1849). Louise Susannah (Wells) Aikman, *The Journal of a Voyage from Charleston, S. C., to London Undertaken during the American Revolution* (New York: The New York Historical Society, 1906) gives some information about the various members of the Wells family. Her sister's two novels are briefly discussed in Lillie D. Loshe, *The Early American Novel* (1905). For the newspapers conducted by the various members of the Wells family, see Clarence S. Brigham, *History and Bibliography of American Newspapers* (2 vols.; Worcester, Mass., 1947) and Isaiah Thomas, *The History of Printing in America* (Albany, N. Y., 1874), I, 340–351; II, 169–173. Thomas once worked for Robert Wells.

Richard Henry Wilde

The best account of Wilde's life is found in Aubrey H. Starke, "Richard Henry Wilde: Some Notes and a Check-List," *Am. Book Collector*, IV, 226–232, 285–288 (Nov. and Dec., 1933); V, 7–10 (Jan., 1934). See also Starke's "The Dedication of Richard Henry Wilde's *Hesperia*," *ibid.*, VI, 204–209 (May–June, 1935) and "Richard Henry Wilde in New Orleans and the Establishment of the University of Louisiana," *La. Hist. Quart.*, XVII, 605–624 (Oct., 1934). *The Biographical Directory of the American Congress* (1928) gives an accurate summary of Wilde's political career. The poet's son, John P. Wilde, furnished biographical data for the Duyckincks' *Cyclopaedia of American Literature* (1855) and for Stephen F. Miller, *The Bench and Bar of Georgia* (Philadelphia, 1858), II, 342–368. See also Charles C. Jones, Jr., *The Life,*

Literary Labors and Neglected Grave of Richard Henry Wilde (1885). The Duke Univ. Library has Jones's own copy of this booklet with letters about Wilde from Whittier and others bound in. Sir Charles Lyell gave a brief account of Wilde in *A Second Visit to the United States of North America* (2nd ed., London, 1850), II, 121–129, 165. For Wilde as a speaker, see Henry Tudor, *Narrative of a Tour in North America* (London, 1834), II, 447–448. There is a brief account of Mrs. White-Beatty in A. J. Hanna, *A Prince in Their Midst: The Adventurous Life of Achille Murat* (1946), pp. 219–220. Wilde's death occasioned poems by A. B. Meek, "The Death of Richard Henry Wilde," *Songs and Poems of the South* (New York, 1857), pp. 107–109, and J. T. [John Tomlin], "Lines on the Death of the Hon. Richard Henry Wilde," *Holden's Dollar Mag.*, I, 138 (March, 1848).

For Wilde's Italian studies, see T. W. Koch, *Dante in America* (1896), pp. 23–36; C. B. Beall, "Un Tassista americano di cent'anni fa, R. H. Wilde," *Bergamum*, XVII, 91–99 (July, 1939); James K. Paulding, "Secret History of Tasso," *Knickerbocker*, VIII, 447–454 (Oct., 1836); and Washington Irving, "American Researches in Italy: Life of Tasso: Recovery of a Lost Portrait of Dante," *ibid.*, XVI, 319–322 (Oct., 1841). A major portion of Wilde's "Powers the Sculptor," *Knickerbocker*, XVIII, 523–529 (Dec., 1841), is a translation of A. M. Migliarini's article on Powers in the Rome *Giornale Arcadico*. Wilde published three of his translations from Italian lyric poets: "Dante's Canzone iv," *Orion*, 24–25 (March, 1842); "Odi D'un Nom' Che Muore," *Magnolia*, N.S. II, 117 (Feb., 1843); and "O Se Tu Fosti Meco," *Graham's Mag.*, XXII, 235 (April, 1843).

In *The Poets and Poetry of Europe* (Philadelphia, 1845) Longfellow reprinted eighteen of Wilde's translations from Tasso. In his journal for Oct. 2, 1845, Longfellow wrote: "Richard Henry Wilde, from New Orleans, called, with his white floating locks" (*Life*, II, 22). The *Conjectures* was reviewed in the *Dial*, II, 399–407 (Jan., 1842) by Margaret Fuller; *Knickerbocker*, XIX, 78–82 (Jan., 1842); and *No. Am. Rev.*, LIV, 501–504 (April, 1842), which commented upon the "air of elegant scholarship and refined literary taste [which] pervades these volumes" and noted that the poetic translations were of "very remarkable merit." The book is briefly discussed with some praise in Robert Browning's essay on Chatterton in *Foreign Quart. Rev.*, XXIX, 465–483 (July, 1842). See also Louise Greer, "Richard Henry Wilde to Elizabeth Barrett Barrett: An Unpublished Sonnet," *English Studies in Honor of James Southall Wilson* (1951), pp. 73–79.

For Wilde's most famous poem, see the first article cited under Starke, above; Jones, *op. cit.*; J. W. Davidson, "The Authorship of 'My Life Is Like the Summer Rose,'" *S.L.M.*, XXIII, 249–253 (Oct., 1856); Anthony Barclay, *Wilde's Summer Rose; or The Lament of the Captive* . . . (Savannah: Georgia Historical Society, 1871), reprinted from *New-York Mirror* for Feb. 28, 1835. There are at least seven musical settings of the poem, including one by Sidney Lanier.

The Library of Congress has manuscripts of many of Wilde's unpublished poems, his translations from the Italian lyric poets, and "The Life and Times of Dante with Sketches of the State of Florence and His Friends and Enemies." There are a few MSS in the Duke Univ. Library. His letters to Rufus W. Griswold are in the Boston Public Library.

Starke lists five published speeches which Wilde delivered in the House of Representatives. Griswold printed a portion of one of them in *The Prose Writers of America* (1847).

Augusta Jane Evans Wilson

William Perry Fidler, *Augusta Evans Wilson, 1835–1909: A Biography* (1951) is a well-documented account of her life and work, but it contains no bibliography. See also Fidler, "Augusta Evans Wilson as Confederate Propagandist," *Ala. Rev.*, II, 32–44 (Jan., 1949); T. C. De Leon, "Biographical Reminiscences . . ." in the 1913 ed. of her *Devota*, first published in 1907; W. W. Brewton, "St. Elmo and St. Twelmo," *Sat. Rev. of Lit.*, V, 1123–1124 (June 22, 1929); E. E. Calkins, "St. Elmo: or, Named for a Best Seller," *ibid.*, XXI, 3–4, 14, 16–17 (Dec. 16, 1939); [A. B. Maurice], "St. Elmo and Its Author," *Bookman*, XVI, 12–14 (Sept., 1902); F. L. Mott, *Golden Multitudes* (1947), pp. 126–127; La Salle Corbell Pickett, *Literary Hearthstones of Dixie* (1912), pp. 283–305; and J. C. Derby, *Fifty Years among Authors, Books and Publishers* (1884), pp. 389–399. For the discussions of *St. Elmo* and *Vashti* quoted in the text, see *Scott's Mag.*, III, 218–222 (March, 1867); *De Bow's Rev.*, N.S. III, 268–273 (March, 1867); and *Home Monthly*, VIII, 59–60 (Jan., 1870), 193–199 (April, 1870), and 277–282 (May, 1870). *Vashti* was reviewed very unfavorably in the *Cosmopolitan Monthly* (Atlanta), N.S. I, 71–72 [Jan., 1870].

William Wirt

The only biography is John P. Kennedy, *Memoirs of the Life of William Wirt* (2 vols.; Philadelphia, 1849; revised ed., 1850). This book, undertaken at the request of Wirt's family after Washington Irving and others had declined to write it, includes many letters and gives a detailed account of Wirt's political activities, but it somewhat neglects his literary work and it slights the years before his second marriage (see Warden, *Chase*, cited below, pp. 231, 234–235). Many of the letters are given only in part and some of them not very accurately. Kennedy's friend Peter Hoffman Cruse wrote the "Biographical Sketch of William Wirt" prefixed to the 10th edition (often reprinted) of *The Letters of the British Spy* (New York, 1832). There is a good brief description of Wirt in John E. Semmes, *John H. B. Latrobe and His Times, 1803–1891* (Baltimore, 1917), pp. 201–202. There is a fuller description in John Neal's novel *Randolph*

(1823), II, 229–234, of which Wirt remarked: ". . . both his censure and his praise are much overwrought."

There was a London edition of *The Letters of the British Spy* in 1812, which I have not seen. The *Analectic Mag.*, I, 146 (Feb., 1813) copied from the *British Critic* a paragraph in which the book is described as "a creditable example of the progress of the Americans in elegant literature. . . ." The *Port Folio* in Nov. and Dec., 1804, and Jan., 1805, published six instalments of "The British Spy in Boston," which Wirt thought were written by Robert Walsh. They include portraits of such well-known Bostonians as Fisher Ames, Harrison Gray Otis, and Theophilus Parsons. John E. Hall, the publisher of the *Port Folio*, apparently wrote some "Old Bachelor" numbers for an unidentified Baltimore newspaper ("MS. Letter of Wm. Wirt," *S.L.M.*, XV, 698, Nov., 1849).

For some account of James Waddell, see William Meade, *Old Churches, Ministers and Families of Virginia* (1857), II, 87–88, 129–130, and R. W. Bailey, " 'The Blind Preacher' and 'The British Spy,' " *S.L.M.*, X, 679–680 (Nov., 1844).

For reviews, generally favorable, of Wirt's *Sketches of the Life and Character of Patrick Henry* (Philadelphia, 1817), see Jared Sparks in *No. Am. Rev.*, VI, 293–324 (March, 1818); *Analectic Mag.*, X, 441–470 (Dec., 1817); "P" in *Am. Monthly Mag.*, II, 412–427 (April, 1818); *Port Folio*, 5th ser. IV, 520–523 (Dec., 1817); and *Va. Evangelical and Lit. Mag.*, I, 27–36, 74–80, 124–128 (Jan., Feb., March, 1818). The "Give Me Liberty, or Give Me Death" speech was first printed in the *Port Folio*, 5th ser. II, 460–468 (Dec., 1816).

Other materials are: Frank P. Cauble, "William Wirt and His Friends: A Study in Southern Culture" (Univ. of N. C. dissertation, 1933); Ninian W. Edwards, *History of Illinois, from 1778 to 1833; and Life and Times of Ninian Edwards* (Springfield, Ill., 1870) [Wirt's letters to the Edwardses are given on pp. 404–476]; Robert B. Warden, *An Account of the Private Life and Public Services of Salmon Portland Chase* (Cincinnati, 1874); Frederick W. Thomas, *John Randolph, of Roanoke, and Other Sketches of Character, Including William Wirt* (Philadelphia, 1853); Richard Beale Davis, *Francis Walker Gilmer* (1939) and "Poe and William Wirt," *Am. Lit.*, XVI, 212–220 (Nov., 1944); Jay B. Hubbell, "William Wirt and the Familiar Essay in Virginia," *W.M.Q.*, 2nd ser. XXIII, 136–152 (April, 1943) [No. VIII in the first series of *The Rainbow*, not identified in this article, was written by George Hay and is entitled "Truth and Eloquence: An Allegory."]; V. L. Parrington, *Main Currents in American Thought*, II, 30–35; and John Neal, *Randolph* (n.p., 1823), II, 156, 229–234, and Neal's *American Writers* (1937), ed. F. L. Pattee, pp. 183–184.

Of Wirt's numerous letters to Dabney Carr, the earlier are in the Va. State Library; the later, in the Univ. of N. C. Library. Most of the letters to Francis W. Gilmer are in the Univ. of Va. Library. The Library of Congress has some Wirt letter books, and there is some material in the St. George Tucker MSS in

Williamsburg and more in the Maryland Historical Society's collection in Balti-more. The Goldsborough-Wirt Papers in the Univ. of N. C. Library contain Wirt's "Reminiscences," which cover only the years before he entered Hunt's school in 1787.

Some of Wirt's writings have never been printed. There are a few specimens of his light verse in the St. George Tucker papers in Williamsburg. Warden, *op. cit.*, p. 125, mentions "Agnes Wirt; a Story," written by Wirt after the death of a daughter. An obituary notice in the *Western Monthly Mag.* (Cin-cinnati), II, 221–222 (April, 1834) mentions a farce entitled "The County Court Lawyer." Warden, *op. cit.*, p. 797, gives a portion of Chase's diary in which passages are quoted from the play. This may or may not be the play of which Wirt wrote to Dabney Carr, March 31, 1813: ". . . I have a sentimental drama (*la comedie larmoyante*) nearly finished. . . ."

For Elizabeth Gamble Wirt's *Flora's Dictionary* (Baltimore, 1829), see Sarah P. Stetson, "Mrs. Wirt and the Language of the Flowers," *Va. Mag.*, LVII, 376–389 (Oct., 1949).

Constance Fenimore Woolson

John D. Kern, *Constance Fenimore Woolson: Literary Pioneer* (1934) gives a good general account of her life and writings; Bibliography, pp. 180–194. There is much biographical material in Clare Benedict (ed.), *Five Generations* (3 vols.; London, 1929–1932), especially *Constance Fenimore Woolson* (1930, 1932). Portions of her fifteen letters to Paul Hamilton Hayne are printed in Jay B. Hubbell (ed.), "Some New Letters of Constance Fenimore Woolson," *New Eng. Quart.*, XIV, 715–735 (Dec., 1941). The best discussions of Miss Wool-son's Southern stories are to be found in Van Wyck Brooks, *The Times of Melville and Whitman* (1947), pp. 341–350; Arthur H. Quinn, *American Fic-tion* (1936), pp. 332–342; F. L. Pattee, "Constance Fenimore Woolson and the South," *S.A.Q.*, XXXVIII, 130–141 (April, 1939); and L. N. Richardson, "Constance Fenimore Woolson, 'Novelist Laureate' of America," *S.A.Q.*, XXXIX, 18–36 (Jan., 1940). Miss Woolson's "Literary Taste in the South" was published in The Contributors' Club of the *Atlantic Monthly*, XLII, 245–247 (Aug., 1878).

John Joachim Zubly

The sketch in *D.A.B.* is by Marjorie Daniel, who wrote a more detailed ac-count in "John Joachim Zubly—Georgia Pamphleteer of the Revolution," *Ga. Hist. Quart.*, XIX, 1–16 (March, 1935), which includes a list of Zubly's publi-cations. See also Eunice R. Perkins, "John Joachim Zubly, Georgia's Conscien-tious Objector," *Ga. Hist. Quart.*, XV, 313–323 (Dec., 1931); Charles C. Jones, Jr., *Biographical Sketches of the Delegates from Georgia to the Continental Congress* (Boston, 1891); and M. C. Tyler, *Literary History of the American Revolution* (1897), I, 483–486.

Index

[*The name of each writer who is treated in a separate chapter is printed in capitals; and the page numbers in italics which immediately follow his name refer to this chapter. Less important references are printed in roman type. Pages 882-974 refer to the Bibliography.*]

DATE DUE

MAY 23 '66				
DEC 5 '66				
JAN 3 '67				
JAN 4 '67				
JAN 13 '67				
MAR 21 '67				